Weiss Ratings' Guide to Banks

Weiss Ratings' Guide to Banks

A Quarterly Compilation of Financial Institutions Ratings and Analyses

Spring 2015

GREY HOUSE PUBLISHING

Weiss Ratings
4400 Northcorp Parkway
Palm Beach Gardens, FL 33410
561-627-3300

Published by Grey House Publishing, Inc., located at 4919 Route 22, Amenia, NY 12501; telephone 518-789-8700. Grey House Publishing neither guarantees the accuracy of the data contained herein nor assumes any responsibility for errors, omissions or discrepancies. Grey House Publishing accepts no payment for listing; inclusion in the publication of any organization, agency, institution, publication, service or individual does not imply endorsement of the publisher.

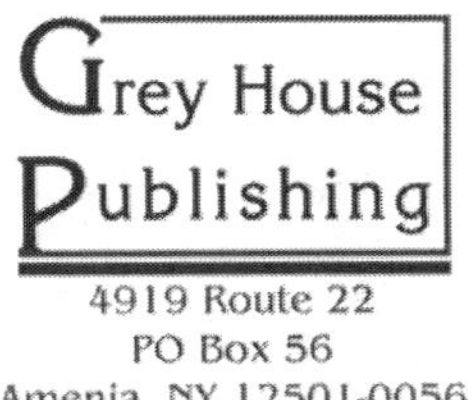

Edition No. 97, Spring 2015

ISBN: 978-1-61925-577-7
ISSN: 2158-5962

Contents

Terms and Conditions

This Document is prepared strictly for the confidential use of our customer(s). It has been provided to you at your specific request. It is not directed to, or intended for distribution to or use by, any person or entity who is a citizen or resident of or located in any locality, state, country or other jurisdiction where such distribution, publication, availability or use would be contrary to law or regulation or which would subject Weiss Ratings or its affiliates to any registration or licensing requirement within such jurisdiction.

No part of the analysts' compensation was, is, or will be, directly or indirectly, related to the specific recommendations or views expressed in this research report.

This Document is not intended for the direct or indirect solicitation of business. Weiss Ratings, LLC and its affiliates disclaims any and all liability to any person or entity for any loss or damage caused, in whole or in part, by any error (negligent or otherwise) or other circumstances involved in, resulting from or relating to the procurement, compilation, analysis, interpretation, editing, transcribing, publishing and/or dissemination or transmittal of any information contained herein.

Weiss Ratings has not taken any steps to ensure that the securities or investment vehicle referred to in this report are suitable for any particular investor. The investment or services contained or referred to in this report may not be suitable for you and it is recommended that you consult an independent investment advisor if you are in doubt about such investments or investment services. Nothing in this report constitutes investment, legal, accounting or tax advice or a representation that any investment or strategy is suitable or appropriate to your individual circumstances or otherwise constitutes a personal recommendation to you.

The ratings and other opinions contained in this Document must be construed solely as statements of opinion from Weiss Ratings, LLC., and not statements of fact. Each rating or opinion must be weighed solely as a factor in your choice of an institution and should not be construed as a recommendation to buy, sell or otherwise act with respect to the particular product or company involved.

Past performance should not be taken as an indication or guarantee of future performance, and no representation or warranty, expressed or implied, is made regarding future performance. Information, opinions and estimates contained in this report reflect a judgment at its original date of publication and are subject to change without notice. Weiss Ratings offers a notification service for rating changes on companies you specify. For more information visit WeissRatings.com or call 1-877-934-7778. The price, value and income from any of the securities or financial instruments mentioned in this report can fall as well as rise.

Date of Data Analyzed: September 30, 2014

Data Source: Call Report data provided by SNL Financial.

Welcome to Weiss Ratings
Guide to Banks

Most people automatically assume their bank will survive, year after year. However, prudent consumers and professionals realize that in this world of shifting risks, the solvency of financial institutions can't be taken for granted. After all, your bank's failure could have a heavy impact on you in terms of lost time, lost money (in cases of deposits exceeding the federal insurance limit), tied-up deposits, lost credit lines, and the possibility of being shifted to another institution under not-so-friendly terms.

If you are looking for accurate, unbiased ratings and data to help you choose a commercial bank, savings bank, or savings and loan for yourself, your family, your company or your clients, Weiss Ratings' Guide to Banks gives you precisely what you need.

Weiss Ratings' Mission Statement

Weiss Ratings' mission is to empower consumers, professionals, and institutions with high quality advisory information for selecting or monitoring a financial services company or financial investment.

In doing so, Weiss Ratings will adhere to the highest ethical standards by maintaining our independent, unbiased outlook and approach to advising our customers.

Why rely on Weiss Ratings?

Weiss Ratings provides fair, objective ratings to help professionals and consumers alike make educated financial decisions.

At Weiss Ratings, integrity is number one. Weiss Ratings never takes a penny from rated companies for issuing its ratings. And, we publish Weiss Financial Strength Ratings without regard for institutions' preferences. Our analysts review and update Weiss ratings each and every quarter, so you can be sure that the information you receive is accurate and current – providing you with advance warning of financial vulnerability early enough to do something about it.

Other rating agencies focus primarily on a company's current financial solvency and consider only mild economic adversity. Weiss Ratings also considers these issues, but in addition, our analysis covers a company's ability to deal with severe economic adversity in terms of a sharp decline in the value of its investments and a drop in the collectibility of its loans.

Our use of more rigorous standards stems from the viewpoint that a financial institution's obligations to its customers should not depend on favorable business conditions. A bank must be able to honor its loan and deposit commitments in bad times as well as good.

Weiss's rating scale, from A to F, is easy to understand. Only a few outstanding companies receive an A (Excellent) rating, although there are many to choose from within the B (Good) category. A large group falls into the broad average range which receives C (Fair) ratings. Companies that demonstrate marked vulnerabilities receive either D (Weak) or E (Very Weak) ratings. So, there's no numbering system, star counting, or color-coding to keep track of.

How to Use This Guide

The purpose of the *Guide to Banks* is to provide consumers, businesses, financial institutions, and municipalities with a reliable source of banking industry ratings and analysis on a timely basis. We realize that the financial safety of a bank is an important factor to consider when establishing a relationship. The ratings and analysis in this Guide can make that evaluation easier when you are considering:

- A checking, merchant banking, or other transaction account
- An investment in a certificate of deposit or savings account
- A line of credit or commercial loan
- Counterparty risk

The rating for a particular company indicates our opinion regarding that company's ability to meet its obligations – not only under current economic conditions, but also during a declining economy or in an environment of increased liquidity demands.

To use this Guide most effectively, we recommend you follow the steps outlined below:

Step 1 To ensure you evaluate the correct company, verify the company's exact name as it was given to you. It is also helpful to ascertain the city and state of the company's main office or headquarters since no two banks with the same name can be headquartered in the same city. Many companies have similar names but are not related to one another, so you will want to make sure the company you look up is really the one you are interested in evaluating.

Step 2 Turn to Section I, the Index of Banks, and locate the company you are evaluating. This section contains all federally-insured commercial banks and savings banks. It is sorted alphabetically by the name of the company and shows the main office city and state following the name for additional verification.
If you have trouble finding a particular institution or determining which is the right one, consider these possible reasons:

- You may have an incorrect or incomplete institution name. There are often several institutions with the same or very similar names. So, make sure you have the exact name and proper spelling, as well as the city in which it is headquartered.
- You may be looking for a *bank holding company*. If so, try to find the exact name of the main bank in the group and look it up under that name.

Step 3 Once you have located your specific company, the first column after the state shows its current Weiss Financial Strength Rating. Turn to *About Weiss Financial Strength Ratings* for information about what this rating means. If the rating has changed since the last edition of this Guide, a downgrade will be indicated with a down triangle ▼ to the left of the company name; an upgrade will be indicated with an up triangle ▲.

Step 4 Following the current Weiss Financial Strength Rating are two prior ratings for the company based on year-end data from the two previous years. Use this to discern the longer-term direction of the company's overall financial condition.

Step 5 The remainder of Section I; provides insight into the areas our analysts reviewed as the basis for assigning the company's rating. These areas include size, capital adequacy, asset quality, profitability, liquidity, and stability. An index within each of these categories represents a composite evaluation of that particular facet of the company's financial condition. Refer to the Critical Ranges In Our Indexes table for an interpretation of which index values are considered strong, good, fair, or weak. In most cases, lower-rated companies will have a low index value in one or more of the indexes shown. Bear in mind, however, that Weiss Financial Strength Rating is the result of a complex qualitative and quantitative analysis which cannot be reproduced using only the data provided here.

Step 6 If the company you are evaluating is not highly rated and you want to find a bank with a higher rating, turn to the page in Section II that has your state's name at the top. This section contains Weiss Recommended Companies (rating of A+, A, A- or B+) that have a branch office in your state. If the main office telephone number provided is not a local telephone call or to determine if a branch of the bank is near you, consult your local telephone Yellow Pages Directory under "Banks," "Savings Banks," or "Savings and Loan Associations." Here you will find a complete list of the institution's branch locations along with their telephone numbers.

Step 7 Once you've identified a Weiss Recommended Company in your local area, you can then refer back to Section I to analyze it.

Step 8 In order to use Weiss Financial Strength Ratings most effectively, we strongly recommend you consult the *Important Warnings and Cautions* listed. These are more than just "standard disclaimers." They are very important factors you should be aware of before using this Guide. If you have any questions regarding the precise meaning of specific terms used in the Guide, refer to the Glossary.

Step 9 Make sure you stay up to date with the latest information available since the publication of this Guide. For information on how to set up a rating change notification service, acquire follow-up reports, check ratings online or receive a more in-depth analysis of an individual company, call 1-877-934-7778 or visit www.weissratings.com.

About Weiss Financial Strength Ratings

Weiss Financial Strength Ratings represent a completely independent, unbiased opinion of an institution's financial safety – now, and in the future. The ratings are derived, for the most part, from quarterly financial statements filed with federal regulators. Although we seek to maintain an open line of communication with the companies being rated, we do not grant them the right to influence the ratings or stop their publication.

Weiss Financial Strength Ratings are assigned by our analysts based on a complex analysis of hundreds of factors that are synthesized into five indexes: capitalization, asset quality, profitability, liquidity and stability. These indexes are then used to arrive at a letter grade rating. A good rating requires consistency across all indexes. A weak score on any one index can result in a low rating, as insolvency can be caused by any one of a number of factors, such as inadequate capital, poor underwriting practices, operating losses, or the failure of an affiliated company.

The primary components of Weiss Financial Strength Rating are as follows:

- **Capitalization Index** gauges capital adequacy in terms of each institution's cushion to absorb future operating losses under various potential business and economic scenarios as they may impact the company's net interest margin, securities' values, and the collectibility of its loans.
- **Asset Quality Index** measures the quality of the institution's past underwriting and investment practices, as well as its loss reserve coverage.
- **Profitability Index** measures the soundness of the company's operations and the contribution of profits to the company's financial strength. The profitability index is a composite of five sub-factors: 1) gain or loss on operations; 2) rates of return on assets and equity; 3) management of net interest margin; 4) generation of noninterest-based revenues; and 5) overhead expense management.
- **Liquidity Index** values a company's ability to raise the necessary cash to satisfy creditors and honor depositor withdrawals.
- **Stability Index** integrates a number of sub-factors that affect consistency (or lack thereof) in maintaining financial strength over time. Sub-factors include 1) risk diversification in terms of company size and loan diversification; 2) deterioration of operations as reported in critical asset, liability, income and expense items, such as an increase in loan delinquency rates or a sharp increase in loan originations; 3) years in operation; 4) former problem areas where, despite recent improvement, the company has yet to establish a record of stable performance over a suitable period of time; and 5) relationships with holding companies and affiliates.

Each of these indexes is measured according to the following range of values.

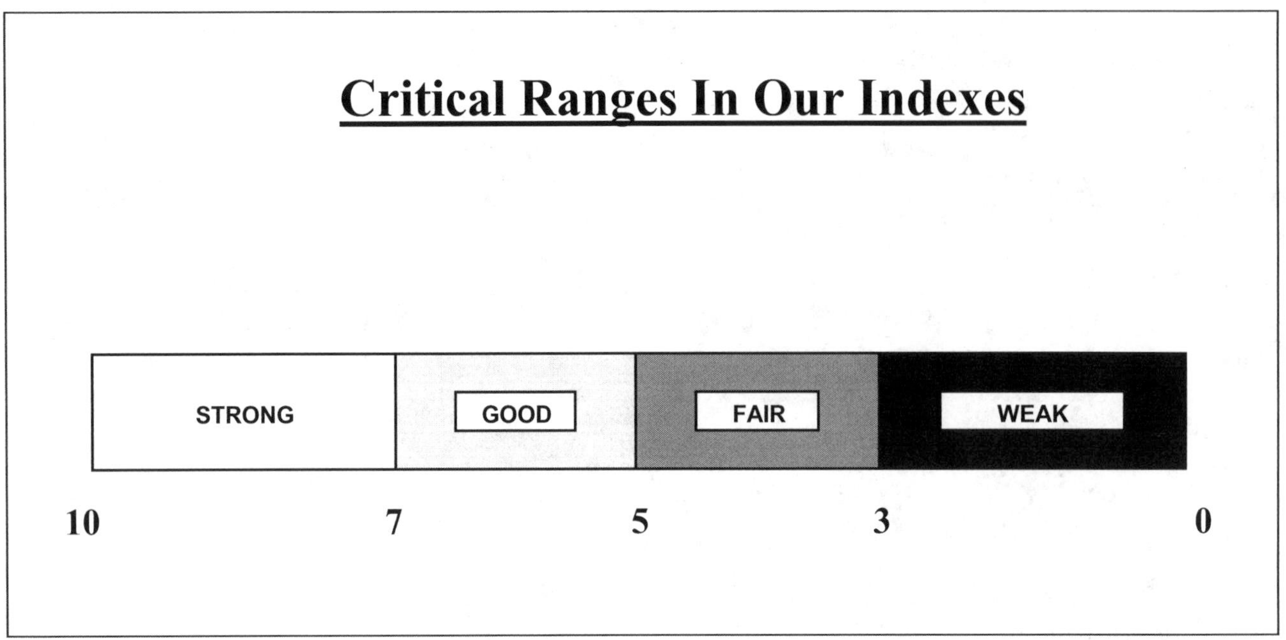

Finally, the indexes are combined to form a composite company rating which is then verified by one of our analysts. The resulting distribution of ratings assigned to all banks looks like this:

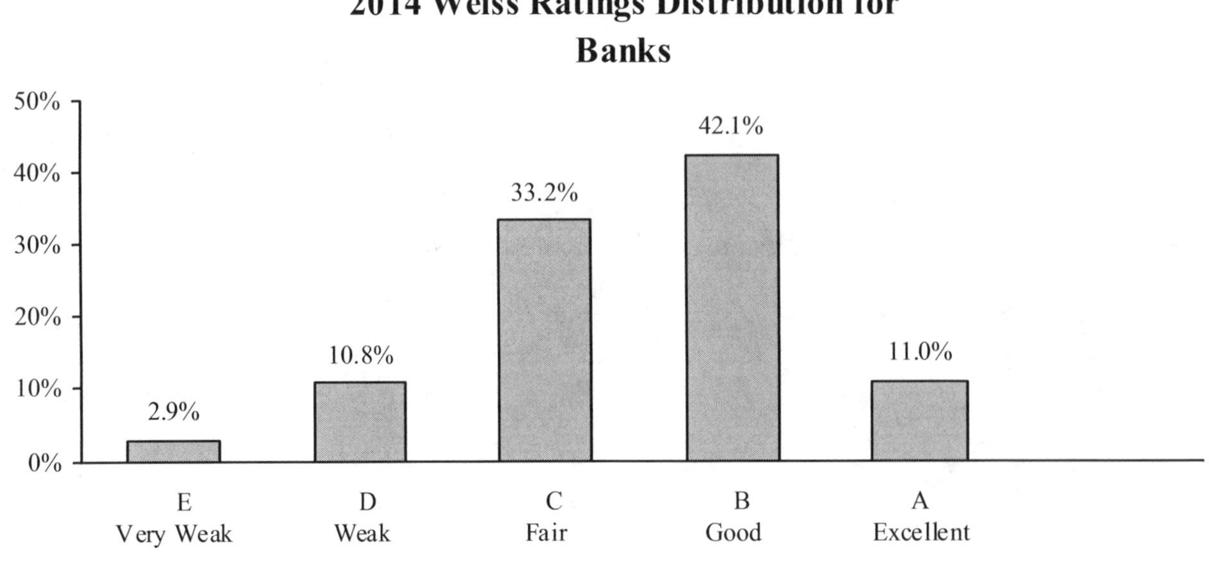

What Our Ratings Mean

A **Excellent.** The institution offers excellent financial security. It has maintained a conservative stance in its business operations as evidenced by its strong equity base, top-notch asset quality, steady earnings, and high liquidity. While the financial position of any institution is subject to change, we believe that this institution has the resources necessary to deal with *severe* economic conditions.

B **Good.** The institution offers good financial security and has the resources to deal with a variety of adverse economic conditions. It comfortably exceeds the minimum levels for all of our rating criteria and is likely to remain healthy for the near future. Nevertheless, in the event of a *severe* recession or major financial crisis, we feel that this assessment should be reviewed to make sure that the institution is still maintaining adequate financial strength.

C **Fair.** The institution offers fair financial security, is currently stable, and will likely remain relatively healthy as long as the economic environment avoids the extremes of inflation or deflation. In a prolonged period of adverse economic or financial conditions, however, we feel this institution may encounter difficulties in maintaining its financial stability.

D **Weak.** The institution currently demonstrates what we consider to be significant weaknesses which could negatively impact depositors or creditors. In an unfavorable economic environment, these weaknesses could be magnified.

E **Very Weak.** The institution currently demonstrates what we consider to be significant weaknesses and has also failed some of the basic tests that we use to identify fiscal stability. Therefore, even in a favorable economic environment, it is our opinion that depositors or creditors could incur significant risks.

F **Failed.** The institution has been placed under the custodianship of regulatory authorities. This implies that it will be either liquidated or taken over by another financial institution.

\+ **The plus sign** is an indication that the institution is at the upper end of the letter grade rating.

\- **The minus sign** is an indication that the institution is at the lower end of the letter grade rating.

U **Unrated Institutions.** The institution is unrated due to insufficient data at the time its rating was updated.

Peer Comparison of Bank Financial Strength Ratings

Weiss Ratings	Veribanc	Bauer Financial	IDC Financial	Bankrate.com	Lace Financial
A+, A, A-	Green, Three Stars w/ Blue Ribbon recognition	5 stars, 4 stars	201-300	1, Five stars	A+, A
B+, B, B-	Green, Three Stars w/out Blue Ribbon recognition	3 ½ stars	166-200	2, Four stars	B+
C+, C, C-	Green Two Stars, Yellow Two Stars	3 stars	126-165	3, Three stars	B, C+
D+, D, D-	Green one star, Yellow one star, Green no stars	2 stars	76-125	4, Two stars	C, D
E+, E, E-	Yellow no stars, Red no stars	1 star	1-75	5, One star	E

Important Warnings and Cautions

1. **A rating alone cannot tell the whole story.** Please read the explanatory information contained here, in the section introductions and in the appendix. It is provided in order to give you an understanding of our rating philosophy as well as to paint a more complete picture of how we arrive at our opinion of a company's strengths and weaknesses. In addition, please remember that our financial strength rating is not an end-all measure of an institution's safety. Rather, it should be used as a "flag" of possible troubles, suggesting a need for further research.

2. **Financial strength ratings shown in this directory were current as of the publication date.** In the meantime, the rating may have been updated based on more recent data. Weiss Ratings offers a notification service for ratings changes on companies that you specifiy. For more information call 1-877-934-7778 or visit www.weissratings.com.

3. **When deciding to do business with a financial institution, your decision should be based on a wide variety of factors in addition to Weiss Financial Strength Rating**. These include the institution's pricing of its deposit instruments and loans, the fees you will be charged, the degree to which it can help you meet your long-term planning needs, how these costs/benefits may change over the years, and what other choices are available to you given your current location and financial circumstances.

4. **Weiss Financial Strength Ratings represent our opinion of a company's insolvency risk.** As such, a high rating means we feel that the company has less chance of running into financial difficulties. A high rating is not a guarantee of solvency nor is a low rating a prediction of insolvency. Weiss Financial Strength Ratings are not deemed to be a recommendation concerning the purchase or sale of the securities of any bank that is publicly owned.

5. **All firms that have the same Weiss Financial Strength Rating should be considered to be essentially equal in safety.** This is true regardless of any differences in the underlying numbers which might appear to indicate greater strengths. Weiss Financial Strength Rating already takes into account a number of lesser factors which, due to space limitations, cannot be included in this publication.

6. **A good rating requires consistency.** If a company is excellent on four indicators and fair on one, the company may receive a fair rating. This requirement is necessary due to the fact that fiscal problems can arise from any *one* of several causes including poor underwriting, inadequate capital resources, or operating losses.

7. **Our rating standards are more conservative than those used by other agencies.** We believe that no one can predict with certainty the economic environment of the near or long-term future. Rather, we assume that various scenarios – from the extremes of double-digit inflation to a severe recession – are within the range of reasonable possibilities over the next one or two decades. To achieve a top rating according to our standards, a company must be adequately prepared for the worst-case reasonable scenario, without impairing its current operations.

8. **We are an independent rating agency and do not depend on the cooperation of the companies we rate**. Our data are derived, for the most part, from quarterly financial statements filed with federal regulators. Although we seek to maintain an open line of communication with the companies being rated, we do not grant them the right to influence the ratings or stop their publication. This policy stems from the fact that this Guide is designed for the protection of our customers.

9. **Inaccuracies in the data issued by the federal regulators could negatively impact the quality of a company's Financial Strength Rating.** While we attempt to find and correct as many data errors as possible, some data errors inevitably slip through. We have no method of intercepting fraudulent or falsified data and must take for granted that all information is reported honestly to the federal regulatory agencies.

10. **Institutions that operate exclusively or primarily as a trust company may have skewed financial information.** Due to the nature of their business, these companies often record high profit levels compared to other more "traditional" banks. Trust companies can usually be recognized by the initials "TC" or "& TC" in their names.

11. **This Guide does not cover nonbank affiliates of banking companies.** Although some nonbank companies may be affiliated with the banks cited in this Guide, the firms are separate corporations whose financial strength is only partially dependent on the strength of their affiliates.

12. **There are many companies with the same or similar sounding names, despite no affiliation whatsoever.** Therefore, it is important that you have the exact name, city, and state of the institution's headquarters before you begin to research the company in this Guide.

13. **Affiliated companies do not automatically receive the same rating.** We recognize that a troubled institution may expect financial support from its parent or affiliates. Weiss Financial Strength Ratings reflect our opinion of the measure of support that may become available to a subsidiary bank, if the subsidiary were to experience serious financial difficulties. In the case of a strong parent and a weaker subsidiary, the affiliate relationship will generally result in a higher rating for the subsidiary than it would have on a stand-alone basis. Seldom, however, would the rating be brought up to the level of the parent.

    This treatment is appropriate because we do not assume the parent would have either the resources or the will to "bail out" a troubled subsidiary during a severe economic crisis. Even when there is a binding legal obligation for a parent corporation to honor the obligations of its subsidiary banks, the possibility exists that the subsidiary could be sold and lose its parental support. Therefore, it is quite common for one affiliate to have a higher rating than another. This is another reason why it is especially important that you have the precise name of the company you are evaluating.

14. **This publication does not include foreign banking companies, or their U.S. branches.** Therefore, our evaluation of foreign banking companies is limited to those U.S. chartered domestic banks owned by foreign banking companies. In most cases, the U.S. operations of a foreign banking company are relatively small in relation to the overall size of the company, so you may want to consult other sources as well. In any case, do not be confused by a domestic bank with a name which is the same as – or similar to – that of a foreign banking company. Even if there is an affiliation between the two, we have evaluated the U.S. institution based on its own merits.

Section I

Index of Banks

An analysis of all rated

U.S. Commercial Banks and Savings Banks

Institutions are listed in alphabetical order.

Section I Contents

This section contains Weiss Financial Strength Ratings, key rating factors, and summary financial data for all U.S. federally-insured commercial banks and savings banks. Companies are sorted in alphabetical order, first by company name, then by city and state.

<u>*Left Pages*</u>

1. **Institution Name**	The name under which the institution was chartered. If you cannot find the institution you are interested in, or if you have any doubts regarding the precise name, verify the information with the bank itself before proceeding. Also, determine the city and state in which the institution is headquartered for confirmation. (See columns 2 and 3.)
2. **City**	The city in which the institution's headquarters or main office is located. With the adoption of intrastate and interstate branching laws, many institutions operating in your area may actually be headquartered elsewhere. So, don't be surprised if the location cited is not in your particular city. Also use this column to confirm that you have located the correct institution. It is possible for two unrelated companies to have the same name if they are headquartered in different cities.
3. **State**	The state in which the institution's headquarters or main office is located. With the adoption of interstate branching laws, some institutions operating in your area may actually be headquartered in another state.
4. **Financial Strength Rating**	Weiss rating assigned to the institution at the time of publication. Our ratings are designed to distinguish levels of insolvency risk and are measured on a scale from A to F based upon a wide range of factors. See *About Weiss Financial Strength Ratings* for specific descriptions of each letter grade. Highly rated companies are, in our opinion, less likely to experience financial difficulties than lower rated firms. See *About Weiss Financial Strength Ratings* for more information. Also, please be sure to consider the warnings beginning regarding the ratings' limitations and the underlying assumptions.
5. **Prior Year Financial Strength Rating**	Weiss rating assigned to the institution based on data from December 31 of the previous year. Compare this rating to the company's current rating to identify any recent changes.
6. **Financial Strength Rating Two Years Prior**	Weiss rating assigned to the institution based on data from December 31 two years ago. Compare this rating to the ratings in the prior columns to identify longer term trends in the company's financial condition.

7. Total Assets

The total of all assets listed on the institution's balance sheet, in millions of dollars. This figure primarily consists of loans, investments (such as municipal and treasury bonds), and fixed assets (such as buildings and other real estate).

Overall size is an important factor which affects the company's ability to diversify risk and avoid vulnerability to a single borrower, industry, or geographic area. Larger institutions are usually, although not always, more diversified and thus less susceptible to a downturn in a particular area. Nevertheless, do not be misled by the general public perception that "bigger is better." Larger institutions are known for their inability to quickly adapt to changes in the marketplace and typically underperform their smaller brethren.

8. One Year Asset Growth

The percentage change in total assets over the previous 12 months. Moderate growth is generally a positive since it can reflect the maintenance or expansion of the company's market share, leading to the generation of additional revenues. Excessive growth, however, is generally a sign of trouble as it can indicate a loosening of underwriting practices in order to attract new business.

9. Commercial Loans/ Total Assets

The percentage of the institution's asset base invested in loans to businesses. Commercial loans are the traditional bread and butter of commercial banks, although many have increased their business lending in recent years.

10. Consumer Loans/ Total Assets

The percentage of the institution's asset base invested in loans to consumers, primarily credit cards. Consumer lending has grown rapidly in recent years due to the high interest rates and fees institutions are able to charge. On the down side, consumer loans usually experience higher delinquency and default rates than other loans, negatively impacting earnings down the road.

11. Home Mortgage Loans/ Total Assets

The percentage of the institution's asset base invested in residential mortgage loans to consumers, excluding home equity loans. Savings banks have traditionally dominated mortgage lending.

This type of loan typically experiences lower default rates. However, the length of the loan's term can be a subject for concern during periods of rising interest rates.

12. Securities/ Total Assets

The percentage of the institution's asset base invested in securities, including U.S. Treasury securities, mortgage-backed securities, and municipal bonds. This does not include securities the institution may be holding on behalf of individual customers.

Although securities are similar to loans in that they represent obligations to pay a debt at some point in the future, they are a more liquid investment than loans and usually present less risk of default. In addition, mortgage-backed securities can present less credit risk than holding mortgage loans themselves due to the diversification of the underlying mortgages.

13. Capitalization Index

An index that measures the adequacy of the institution's capital resources to deal with potentially adverse business and economic situations that could arise. It is based on an evaluation of the company's degree of leverage compared to total assets as well as risk-adjusted assets. See the Critical Ranges In Our Indexes for a description of the different critical levels presented in this index.

14. Leverage Ratio

A regulatory ratio defined by the federal banking regulators as core (tier 1) capital divided by tangible assets. This ratio answers the question: How much does the institution have in stockholders' equity for every dollar of assets? Thus, the Leverage Ratio represents the amount of actual "capital cushion" the institution has to fall back on in times of trouble. We feel that this is the single most important ratio in determining financial strength because it provides the best measure of an institution's ability to withstand losses.

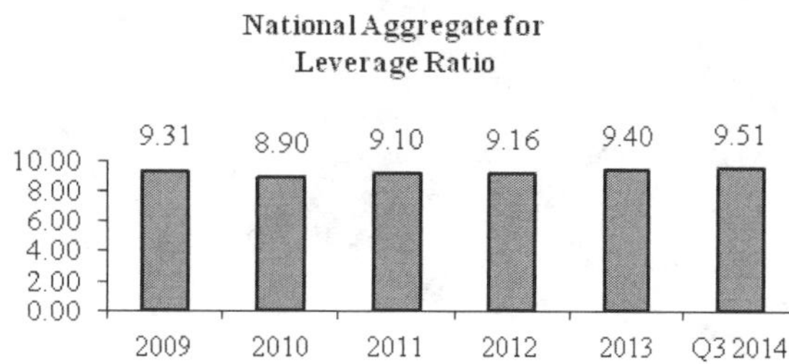

15. Risk-Based Capital Ratio

A regulatory ratio defined by the federal banking regulators as total (tier 1 + tier 2) capital divided by risk-weighted assets. This ratio addresses the issue that not all assets present the same level of credit risk to an institution. As such, all assets and certain off-balance sheet commitments are assigned to risk categories based on the level of credit risk they pose and then weighted accordingly to arrive at risk-weighted assets.

For instance, assets with virtually no risk, such as cash and U.S. Treasury securities, are risk-weighted at 0% and therefore, not included in the calculation. Assets with low risk, for example, high quality mortgage-backed securities and state and municipal bonds, are partially weighted at 20%.

Those assets possessing moderate risk, such as residential mortgages and state and local revenue bonds are partially weighted at 50%. And finally, assets considered to possess "normal" or "high" risk, including certain off-balance sheet commitments such as unfunded loans, are risk-weighted at 100%. The summation of these categories of risk-weighted assets results in the figure used in the denominator of this ratio.

Please be aware that not all banks and savings banks are required to report risk-weighted assets as defined by the federal regulators. Consequently, we have estimated this figure when necessary based on estimates used by the regulators themselves.

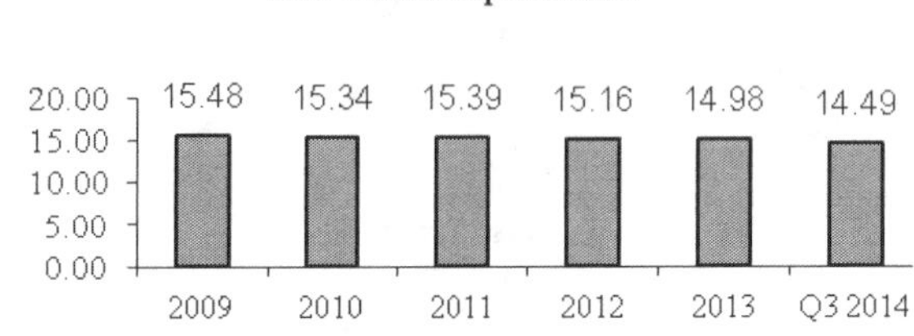

Right Pages

1. Asset Quality Index

An index that measures the quality of the institution's past underwriting and investment practices, as well as its loss reserve coverage. See the Critical Ranges In Our Indexes for a description of the different critical levels presented in this index.

2. Adjusted Nonperforming Loans/ Total Loans

The percentage of the institution's loan portfolio which is either past due on its payments by 90 days or more, or no longer accruing interest due to doubtful collectability plus a portion of all restructured loans, less government guaranteed GNMA loans and those loans protected by the FDIC. This ratio is affected primarily by the quality of the institution's underwriting practices and the prosperity of the local economies where it is doing business. While only a portion of these loans will actually end up in default, a high ratio here will have several negative consequences including increased loan loss provisions, increased loan collection expenses, and decreased interest revenues.

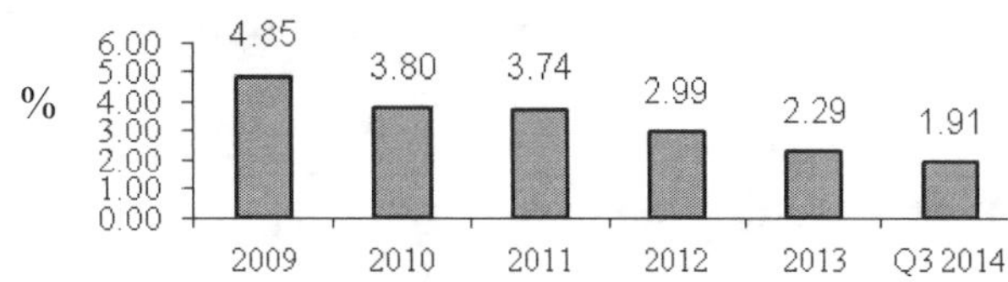

[1]Nonperforming loans were adjusted in 2011 to include a portion of all restructured loans, less government guaranteed GNMA loans and those loans protected by the FDIC.

3. Adjusted Nonperforming Loans/ Capital

The percentage of past due 90 days and nonaccruing loans plus a portion of all restructured loans, less government guaranteed GNMA loans and those loans protected by the FDIC to the company's core (tier 1) capital plus reserve for loan losses. This ratio answers the question: If all of the bank's significantly past due and nonaccruing loans were to go into default, how much would that eat into capital? A large percentage of nonperforming loans signal imprudent lending practices which are a direct threat to the equity of the institution.

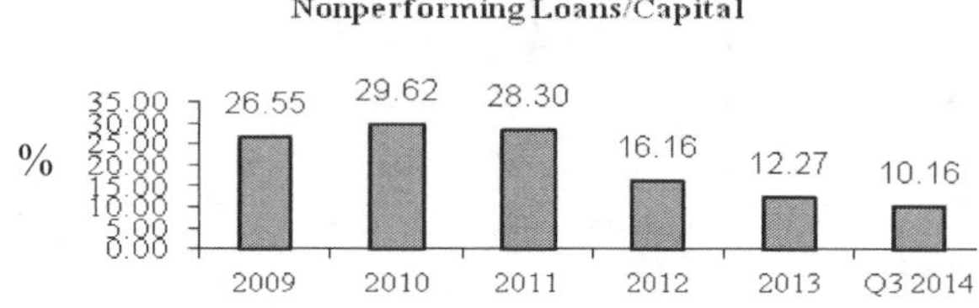

[1] Nonperforming loans were adjusted in 2011 to include a portion of all restructured loans, less government guaranteed GNMA loans and those loans protected by the FDIC.

4. Net Charge-offs/ Average Loans

The ratio of foreclosed loans written off the institution's books since the beginning of the year (less previous write-offs that were recovered) as a percentage of average loans for the year. This ratio answers the question: What percentage of the bank's past loans have actually become uncollectible? Past loan charge-off experience is often a very good indication of what can be expected in the future, and high loan charge-off levels are usually an indication of poor underwriting practices.

5. Profitability Index

An index that measures the soundness of the institution's operations and the contribution of profits to the company's financial strength. It is based on five sub-factors: 1) gain or loss on operations; 2) rates of return on assets and equity; 3) management of net interest margin; 4) generation of noninterest-based revenues; and 5) overhead expense management. See the Critical Ranges In Our Indexes for a description of the different critical levels presented in this index.

6. Net Income

The year-to-date net profit or loss recorded by the institution, in millions of dollars. This figure includes the company's operating profit (income from lending, investing, and fees less interest and overhead expenses) as well as nonoperating items such as capital gains on the sale of securities, income taxes, and extraordinary items.

7. Return on Assets

The ratio of net income for the year (year-to-date quarterly figures are converted to a 12-month equivalent) as a percentage of average assets for the year. This ratio, known as ROA, is the most commonly used benchmark for bank profitability since it measures the company's return on investment in a format that is easily comparable with other companies.

Historically speaking, a ratio of 1.0% or greater has been considered good performance. However, this ratio will fluctuate with the prevailing economic times. Also, larger banks tend to have a lower ratio.

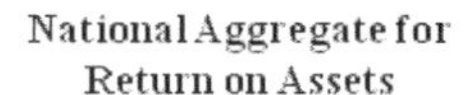

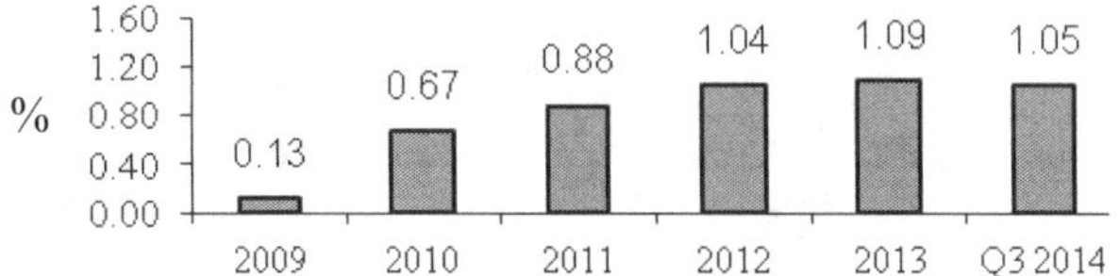

8. Return on Equity

The ratio of net income for the year (year-to-date quarterly figures are converted to a 12-month equivalent) as a percentage of average equity for the year. This ratio, known as ROE, is commonly used by a company's shareholders as a measure of their return on investment. It is not always a good measure of profitability, however, because inadequate equity levels at some institutions can result in unjustly high ROE's.

9. Net Interest Spread

The difference between the institution's interest income and interest expense for the year (year-to-date quarterly figures are converted to a 12-month equivalent) as a percentage of its average revenue-generating assets. Since the margin between interest earned and interest paid is generally where the company generates the majority of its income, this figure provides insight into the company's ability to effectively manage interest spreads.

A low Net Interest Spread can be the result of poor loan and deposit pricing, high levels of non-accruing loans, or poor asset/liability management.

10. Overhead Efficiency Ratio

Total overhead expenses as a percentage of total revenues net of interest expense. This is a common measure for evaluating an institution's ability to operate efficiently while keeping a handle on overhead expenses like salaries, rent, and other office expenses. A high ratio suggests that the company's overhead expenses are too high in relation to the amount of revenue they are generating and/or supporting. Conversely, a low ratio means good management of overhead expenses which usually results in a strong Return on Assets as well.

11. Liquidity Index

An index that measures the institution's ability to raise the necessary cash to satisfy creditors and honor depositor withdrawals. It is based on an evaluation of the company's short-term liquidity position, including its existing reliance on less stable deposit sources. See the Critical Ranges In Our Indexes for a description of the different critical levels presented in this index.

12. Liquidity Ratio

The ratio of short-term liquid assets to deposits and short-term borrowings. This ratio answers the question: How many cents can the institution easily raise in cash to cover each dollar on deposit plus pay off its short-term debts? Due to the nature of the business, it is rare (and not expected) for an established bank to achieve 100% on this ratio. Nevertheless, it serves as a good measure of an institution's liquidity in relation to the rest of the banking industry.

National Aggregate for
Liquidity Ratio

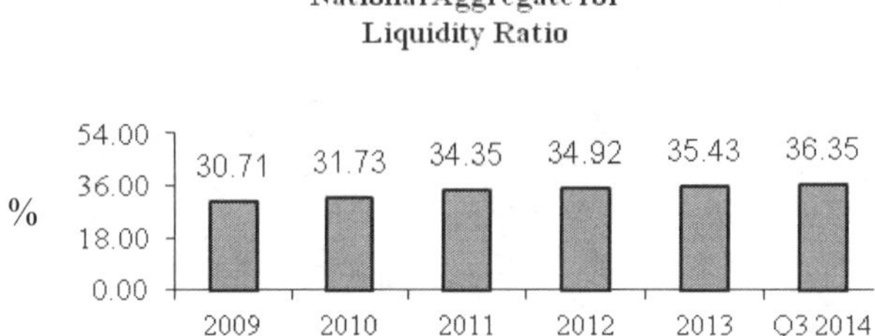

13. Hot Money Ratio

The percentage of the institution's deposit base that is being funded by jumbo CDs and brokered deposits. Jumbo CDs (high-yield certificates of deposit with principal amounts of at least $100,000) and brokered deposits (pooled funds sold by brokers seeking the highest interest rate available) are generally considered less stable (and more costly) and thus less desirable as a source of funds.

National Aggregate for
Hot Money Ratio

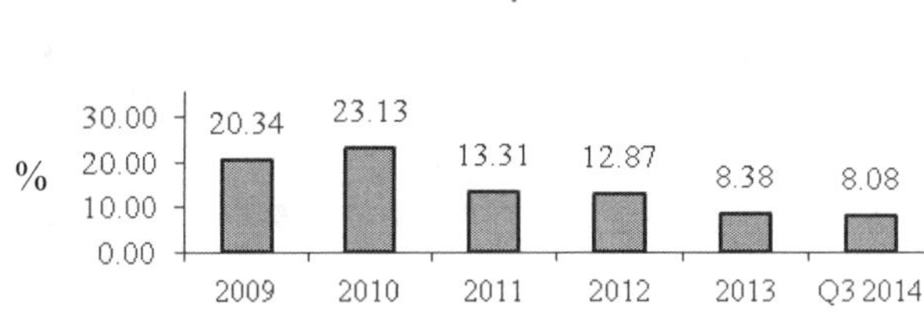

14. Stability Index

An index that integrates a number of factors such as 1) risk diversification in terms of company size and loan diversification; 2) deterioration of operations as reported in critical asset, liability, income and expense items, such as an increase in loan delinquency rates or a sharp increase in loan originations; 3) years in operation; 4) former problem areas where, despite recent improvement, the company has yet to establish a record of stable performance over a suitable period of time; and 5) relationships with holding companies and affiliates. See the Critical Ranges In Our Indexes for a description of the different critical levels presented in this index.

Name	City	State	Rating	2013 Rating	2012 Rating	Total Assets ($Mil)	One Year Asset Growth	Asset Mix (As a % of Total Assets) Comm-ercial Loans	Cons-umer Loans	Mort-gage Loans	Secur-ities	Capital-ization Index	Lever-age Ratio	Risk-Based Capital Ratio
▲ 1880 BANK	Cambridge	MD	**C-**	D-	D-	190.5	-2.13	4.8	0.6	19.5	15.7	**10.0**	11.3	20.0
1919 INVESTMENT COUNSEL & TR	Baltimore	MD	**U**	U	B	79.7	7.70	0.0	0.0	0.0	12.2	**10.0**	87.9	108.1
1ST ADVANTAGE BANK	Saint Peters	MO	**D-**	E+	E-	76.8	4.68	11.5	0.3	9.0	3.6	**5.1**	8.9	11.1
▲ 1ST BANK	Broadus	MT	**A-**	A-	B+	58.0	-61.86	7.6	1.7	1.4	0.0	**10.0**	14.0	66.9
1ST BANK & TRUST	Broken Bow	OK	**A+**	A+	A	128.4	7.23	4.2	13.0	17.2	35.3	**10.0**	11.4	20.8
▲ 1ST BANK NA	Texarkana	TX	**B-**	C	C	310.3	6.58	10.8	3.0	20.0	9.4	**9.4**	10.6	14.7
1ST BANK OF SEA ISLE CITY	Sea Isle City	NJ	**C+**	B-	C+	249.3	3.55	0.3	0.3	43.4	3.6	**7.3**	9.2	17.3
1ST BANK YUMA	Yuma	AZ	**B-**	B-	B-	212.9	12.00	9.8	0.9	4.7	17.2	**7.9**	9.6	14.1
1ST CAMERON STATE BK	Cameron	MO	**C-**	C-	C	51.7	-3.40	0.5	1.5	41.1	18.2	**7.2**	9.2	19.8
1ST CAPITAL BANK	Monterey	CA	**B-**	B-	B-	443.6	20.51	11.8	0.1	20.7	22.9	**7.0**	9.0	14.8
1ST CENTURY BANK NA	Los Angeles	CA	**C+**	B-	C	584.0	9.70	9.4	0.5	18.5	12.2	**7.9**	9.6	13.3
1ST COLONIAL COMMUNITY BANK	Cherry Hill	NJ	**C-**	C-	D+	352.5	11.82	5.3	0.7	28.1	32.1	**5.2**	7.2	13.2
1ST COMMUNITY BANK	Sherrard	IL	**C-**	C-	C-	69.8	-0.11	10.3	2.5	20.2	25.8	**6.3**	8.3	12.9
1ST CONSTITUTION BANK	Cranbury	NJ	**C**	B-	B-	954.3	20.77	24.2	0.1	6.7	26.7	**6.4**	9.1	12.0
▲ 1ST ENTERPRISE BANK	Los Angeles	CA	**B**	B-	C+	800.7	9.49	25.2	0.6	4.6	20.9	**5.5**	9.5	11.4
1ST EQUITY BANK	Skokie	IL	**C+**	C	C	97.9	-8.25	10.8	0.1	19.0	0.0	**10.0**	14.9	24.8
1ST EQUITY BANK NORTHWEST	Buffalo Grove	IL	**D**	C-	C-	40.0	-10.13	3.4	0.4	25.2	0.0	**10.0**	21.0	29.2
1ST FINANCIAL BANK USA	Dakota Dunes	SD	**C+**	B-	B+	684.5	-1.60	0.3	71.8	0.0	8.3	**10.0**	17.5	22.3
1ST MANATEE BANK	Parrish	FL	**B+**	B	C+	107.8	4.31	31.0	0.3	17.4	13.3	**9.4**	10.6	14.8
1ST NATIONAL BK	Lebanon	OH	**B**	B-	C-	129.0	8.10	1.4	0.9	28.5	13.0	**10.0**	11.2	16.7
1ST NATIONAL BK OF SOUTH FL	Homestead	FL	**C-**	C-	D+	308.4	0.41	0.8	0.4	21.9	26.0	**8.0**	9.7	16.1
1ST NATIONAL COMMUNITY BANK	East Liverpool	OH	**C+**	C+	C+	134.2	-4.09	8.3	6.2	13.6	33.9	**7.8**	9.5	17.8
1ST SECURITY BANK OF WA	Mountlake Terrace	WA	**B+**	B	C+	471.6	19.08	11.3	29.6	13.7	10.5	**9.9**	11.8	14.9
▲ 1ST SOURCE BANK	South Bend	IN	**A-**	A-	B	4807.9	3.62	40.8	2.3	8.2	16.8	**10.0**	11.4	15.1
▼ 1ST STATE BK	Saginaw	MI	**C+**	B	B-	196.1	5.91	28.3	0.9	8.2	8.1	**7.9**	10.0	13.3
1ST STATE BK OF MASON CITY	Mason City	IL	**B**	B	B-	28.9	-0.02	1.7	12.3	15.2	36.7	**10.0**	11.7	27.0
1ST SUMMIT BANK	Johnstown	PA	**B**	B	B	892.2	4.03	6.3	3.2	21.9	46.7	**6.3**	8.3	16.5
1ST TRUST BANK INC	Hazard	KY	**C**	C+	C	179.4	15.22	34.0	2.5	11.2	2.1	**4.1**	8.0	10.6
1ST UNITED BANK	Faribault	MN	**B-**	B	C	145.7	2.19	10.1	1.8	10.2	30.4	**6.7**	8.7	12.7
▲ 21ST CENTURY BANK	Loretto	MN	**B-**	C-	C-	356.2	-6.91	14.8	0.2	8.6	15.6	**10.0**	13.0	19.2
5 STAR BANK	Colorado Springs	CO	**B**	B-	B	167.5	-1.87	5.1	0.1	6.9	24.2	**10.0**	22.0	30.2
A J SMITH FSB	Midlothian	IL	**C+**	C-	D+	215.9	-3.83	0.0	0.1	44.7	26.8	**10.0**	13.6	31.6
▲ AB&T NATIONAL BK	Albany	GA	**C**	D+	D-	132.2	0.94	15.6	3.4	16.8	9.9	**7.4**	9.6	12.8
ABACUS FSB	New York	NY	**D**	C-	C-	251.4	-0.67	0.0	0.1	25.9	14.9	**10.0**	14.6	27.6
ABBEVILLE B&L ST CHARTERED	Abbeville	LA	**B-**	B-	B+	59.9	9.00	0.0	0.2	46.5	1.0	**10.0**	24.0	33.1
▲ ABBEVILLE FIRST BANK	Abbeville	SC	**C+**	C-	D	66.5	-2.07	0.2	0.8	42.8	35.3	**8.6**	10.0	21.5
ABBYBANK	Abbotsford	WI	**B-**	B-	C+	327.6	-3.36	3.2	0.6	16.3	8.9	**8.0**	9.6	14.2
▼ ABC BANK	Chicago	IL	**D-**	D	C-	333.3	0.96	2.2	0.5	10.8	22.3	**9.9**	10.9	15.5
ABINGTON BANK	Abington	MA	**C+**	C+	C+	120.6	3.20	1.1	0.1	44.6	15.2	**6.8**	8.8	14.1
▲ ACADEMY BANK NA	Colorado Springs	CO	**A-**	B	B-	313.2	7.17	9.0	0.6	4.9	32.4	**10.0**	22.3	48.1
ACADIA TRUST NA	Portland	ME	**U**	U	U	10.1	-14.03	0.0	0.0	0.0	0.0	**10.0**	90.9	289.6
ACB BANK	Cherokee	OK	**B-**	B-	C+	89.7	12.95	9.5	4.8	9.7	18.5	**6.7**	8.8	12.3
▲ ACCESS BANK	Omaha	NE	**B-**	C+	B-	221.8	14.72	29.5	1.4	8.6	13.1	**6.3**	9.0	12.0
ACCESS NATIONAL BK	Reston	VA	**A-**	A-	B+	1014.5	19.91	18.4	0.7	19.8	14.0	**6.8**	9.2	12.3
ACCESSBANK TEXAS	Denton	TX	**C+**	C+	C-	134.2	3.00	19.1	0.4	12.6	17.3	**10.0**	12.1	18.5
▲ ACKLEY STATE BK	Ackley	IA	**B**	B-	C+	144.3	-1.04	11.2	1.6	8.5	23.0	**7.1**	10.4	12.6
ACNB BANK	Gettysburg	PA	**B**	B	B-	1055.3	3.42	3.5	1.5	33.5	18.5	**6.9**	8.9	14.1
ADAMS BANK & TRUST	Ogallala	NE	**B**	B	B-	628.9	4.94	11.5	2.1	11.8	8.9	**9.7**	11.9	14.8
ADAMS COMMUNITY BANK	Adams	MA	**C+**	C+	C	392.0	1.14	2.7	2.3	61.9	6.8	**10.0**	11.7	19.2
ADAMS COUNTY BANK	Kenesaw	NE	**B-**	B-	B-	160.1	-2.85	4.4	1.2	5.2	30.1	**5.7**	7.7	12.1
ADAMS COUNTY BUILDING & LOAN	West Union	OH	**C-**	C	C	24.5	-4.52	0.0	0.5	37.1	23.7	**10.0**	16.6	36.3
▲ ADAMS DAIRY BANK	Blue Springs	MO	**B-**	B-	B-	93.6	22.48	2.4	0.4	27.8	19.3	**8.2**	9.8	17.4
ADAMS STATE BK	Adams	NE	**B+**	B+	B+	47.4	0.62	3.7	4.7	14.5	28.3	**10.0**	18.2	26.8
ADIRONDACK BANK	Utica	NY	**C**	C+	C	676.7	9.55	14.0	1.7	21.0	30.4	**5.4**	7.4	15.0
ADIRONDACK TRUST CO	Saratoga Springs	NY	**B-**	B-	B-	1008.9	-0.93	6.3	9.2	13.1	25.1	**8.1**	9.7	16.3
▼ ADMIRALS BANK	Boston	MA	**D+**	D+	D-	510.6	-16.49	1.6	4.7	36.8	0.2	**9.4**	10.6	14.9
ADRIAN BANK	Adrian	MO	**B**	B-	C-	130.6	2.16	8.9	4.8	11.3	24.9	**8.1**	9.7	14.9
ADRIAN STATE BK	Adrian	MN	**C**	C	C	41.9	-0.26	7.1	1.2	3.4	26.1	**6.7**	8.7	14.1
▲ ADVANTAGE BANK	Loveland	CO	**E**	E-	E-	264.1	3.17	12.7	0.2	14.4	4.7	**0.0**	2.4	3.3
ADVANTAGE BANK	Oklahoma City	OK	**B**	A-	B+	58.7	-1.45	5.6	4.6	17.9	33.3	**10.0**	11.4	19.3

Asset Quality Index	Adjusted Non-Performing Loans as a % of Total Loans	Adjusted Non-Performing Loans as a % of Capital	Net Charge-Offs Avg Loans	Profitability Index	Net Income ($Mil)	Return on Assets (R.O.A.)	Return on Equity (R.O.E.)	Net Interest Spread	Overhead Efficiency Ratio	Liquidity Index	Liquidity Ratio	Hot Money Ratio	Stability Index
2.9	4.33	22.3	0.48	**2.1**	1.0	0.67	6.16	3.27	80.3	**2.2**	20.3	18.5	**4.0**
6.6	na	0.0	na	**10.0**	3.2	5.33	6.05	3.38	84.3	**3.8**	125.0	100.0	**6.8**
0.0	8.41	70.9	0.79	**1.5**	0.1	0.18	1.99	3.87	92.6	**1.2**	6.5	26.4	**2.0**
8.6	0.00	0.0	0.08	**8.3**	5.6	4.91	45.33	2.95	37.4	**6.7**	78.2	6.4	**7.2**
8.3	0.15	0.6	0.05	**9.7**	2.3	2.40	21.16	4.42	49.8	**5.1**	39.7	9.2	**8.3**
5.3	0.57	4.0	0.18	**4.7**	2.7	1.18	11.52	4.44	73.3	**1.4**	5.2	22.6	**5.5**
6.0	0.77	5.4	0.19	**3.2**	0.6	0.31	3.28	3.52	80.8	**3.6**	24.5	12.2	**4.6**
3.9	0.67	4.5	0.09	**4.4**	1.1	0.68	6.76	4.63	77.9	**3.4**	22.8	12.7	**6.2**
8.9	0.36	2.1	0.06	**2.2**	0.1	0.21	2.35	2.99	90.5	**3.3**	32.2	15.8	**3.0**
6.4	0.49	3.5	-0.02	**3.3**	1.3	0.42	4.56	3.07	73.2	**4.4**	18.1	6.6	**5.4**
8.5	0.16	1.1	-0.08	**3.0**	1.9	0.45	4.60	3.30	83.2	**4.2**	20.4	8.3	**4.7**
4.8	1.83	13.8	0.36	**2.6**	0.8	0.32	4.43	3.09	78.4	**3.7**	3.2	8.8	**2.4**
5.3	0.69	5.1	0.03	**3.2**	0.3	0.57	7.56	3.02	77.7	**1.0**	25.3	37.8	**4.3**
4.3	1.77	11.8	1.27	**3.0**	2.5	0.36	3.50	3.86	71.9	**3.4**	21.7	12.7	**5.9**
7.3	0.04	0.3	0.33	**4.9**	4.9	0.86	9.14	3.57	66.6	**5.2**	21.9	1.3	**5.8**
2.7	6.03	24.4	-0.31	**4.4**	0.8	1.10	7.30	2.68	60.5	**1.9**	38.2	34.7	**6.3**
0.0	15.86	58.6	0.18	**0.4**	-0.1	-0.29	-1.42	2.74	111.0	**1.1**	26.6	36.3	**5.0**
2.4	2.94	10.5	3.59	**6.8**	4.9	0.96	5.42	17.93	73.8	**0.6**	22.7	75.0	**7.9**
8.4	0.02	0.2	0.23	**4.8**	0.4	0.48	4.51	4.30	89.1	**1.4**	17.3	26.7	**5.8**
4.1	2.50	15.0	0.28	**4.4**	0.8	0.91	7.96	3.90	81.3	**1.5**	10.2	23.7	**5.7**
3.3	3.10	17.7	0.00	**2.6**	1.0	0.45	4.92	3.32	86.2	**3.8**	27.4	11.8	**3.6**
4.5	1.95	9.7	0.10	**3.8**	0.7	0.73	7.69	3.75	83.3	**5.1**	27.4	4.1	**4.9**
5.9	0.21	1.3	0.25	**5.5**	3.0	0.93	7.76	5.10	72.9	**0.9**	13.9	33.0	**5.3**
5.5	0.82	4.8	0.02	**7.6**	46.4	1.29	9.96	3.72	59.8	**3.0**	16.5	14.4	**9.8**
3.1	2.32	15.4	0.15	**4.1**	0.9	0.62	6.22	3.74	71.8	**2.0**	14.1	18.8	**5.9**
7.9	0.94	3.2	-0.03	**4.2**	0.2	1.06	9.75	2.67	61.8	**4.9**	63.6	14.2	**5.5**
7.9	0.43	2.4	0.16	**5.4**	7.3	1.12	13.92	3.35	56.3	**3.8**	35.7	14.7	**5.4**
2.7	1.95	19.2	0.32	**4.0**	0.7	0.60	7.15	3.86	70.8	**0.6**	12.9	52.5	**3.7**
3.6	2.51	16.6	0.02	**6.2**	1.7	1.56	17.36	4.20	69.1	**5.9**	37.4	2.6	**6.4**
3.3	2.76	15.2	0.63	**4.8**	2.2	0.81	6.54	3.61	54.1	**1.7**	18.6	22.4	**5.2**
5.6	1.34	4.1	0.61	**5.0**	2.0	1.52	7.01	3.85	69.4	**3.9**	36.4	14.3	**6.8**
6.0	3.09	11.7	0.97	**2.8**	2.0	1.24	9.26	2.29	76.5	**4.2**	40.9	14.5	**5.6**
4.5	0.74	5.8	0.03	**3.1**	1.0	1.03	11.13	3.79	87.5	**3.7**	10.7	10.2	**3.3**
6.6	1.00	3.6	0.01	**0.0**	-1.8	-0.94	-6.13	2.90	153.7	**2.6**	46.0	30.2	**7.1**
3.0	4.22	14.7	0.00	**6.9**	0.4	0.96	3.91	3.86	76.8	**1.6**	12.8	22.6	**9.6**
4.3	3.45	17.0	0.05	**4.2**	0.7	1.34	13.11	4.04	76.1	**2.4**	41.9	29.5	**3.5**
4.3	1.57	10.7	0.13	**4.5**	1.9	0.75	7.88	3.40	65.7	**2.4**	21.3	17.7	**6.0**
0.0	8.57	49.7	0.57	**3.6**	1.7	0.69	6.62	4.12	71.2	**0.9**	21.2	35.1	**5.2**
3.0	3.66	29.2	-0.02	**3.1**	0.4	0.46	5.50	3.40	81.9	**4.3**	22.4	7.7	**4.5**
7.5	2.15	3.5	1.59	**10.0**	5.2	2.21	10.23	2.39	69.0	**6.0**	65.8	10.7	**9.2**
6.5	na	0.0	na	**7.0**	0.5	7.22	7.71	0.50	78.7	**4.0**	563.3	101.0	**7.0**
4.8	1.37	10.2	-0.04	**9.5**	1.4	2.17	25.17	4.99	54.0	**1.8**	6.2	18.9	**4.2**
7.9	0.05	0.4	0.01	**4.4**	1.2	0.76	8.75	4.05	69.8	**1.4**	18.0	27.2	**5.5**
8.3	0.16	1.2	-0.02	**9.5**	11.3	1.60	17.04	3.82	56.2	**1.5**	14.2	25.2	**8.4**
8.4	0.27	1.5	-0.07	**3.0**	0.7	0.68	5.55	3.81	89.2	**1.8**	29.9	28.6	**4.8**
5.7	0.51	3.0	0.32	**5.2**	1.4	1.22	10.96	3.65	71.4	**3.8**	29.0	12.3	**6.4**
5.3	1.58	11.1	0.15	**4.8**	7.0	0.91	10.19	3.60	67.8	**3.9**	9.4	8.7	**7.5**
4.8	0.74	4.9	-0.02	**6.6**	5.7	1.25	10.66	4.64	63.3	**2.3**	9.6	17.1	**7.3**
5.2	1.90	13.0	0.17	**2.6**	0.9	0.32	2.58	3.52	86.2	**2.6**	10.8	15.8	**6.3**
7.0	0.31	2.2	0.00	**6.0**	1.8	1.49	21.32	3.15	43.7	**1.4**	13.7	25.9	**4.2**
4.1	6.02	18.1	0.00	**2.0**	0.0	0.17	1.01	3.75	97.1	**2.7**	53.8	26.4	**5.9**
4.8	2.05	12.8	0.00	**5.0**	0.6	0.85	8.80	3.88	67.0	**1.3**	26.0	31.8	**4.8**
8.5	0.02	0.1	-0.03	**7.0**	0.6	1.68	9.95	3.63	53.3	**3.7**	37.2	15.8	**7.9**
4.9	1.03	8.4	0.18	**3.2**	2.6	0.51	6.83	3.39	81.9	**2.6**	6.7	15.4	**4.4**
5.4	1.01	5.9	0.02	**4.1**	5.7	0.76	6.82	3.01	76.4	**4.2**	16.1	8.3	**7.9**
2.3	2.99	19.7	0.46	**1.4**	-2.1	-0.50	-4.80	6.12	109.2	**0.9**	24.3	43.4	**4.5**
5.1	0.73	4.8	0.29	**8.0**	2.0	1.99	21.25	4.21	52.1	**3.1**	23.6	14.5	**6.3**
5.0	1.35	8.5	-0.04	**4.9**	0.4	1.27	14.39	3.39	62.8	**3.7**	20.2	11.1	**4.3**
4.1	0.00	0.0	0.00	**3.8**	1.1	1.89	75.10	5.62	53.9	**0.8**	18.2	41.6	**0.2**
6.8	1.32	6.4	0.17	**3.9**	0.3	0.66	5.78	4.91	85.1	**5.9**	39.3	3.8	**6.8**

Name	City	State	Rating	2013 Rating	2012 Rating	Total Assets ($Mil)	One Year Asset Growth	Asset Mix (As a % of Total Assets) Comm-ercial Loans	Cons-umer Loans	Mort-gage Loans	Secur-ities	Capital-ization Index	Lever-age Ratio	Risk-Based Capital Ratio
ADVANTAGE COMMUNITY BANK	Dorchester	WI	B+	B+	B+	130.0	2.88	11.1	2.9	17.4	13.9	9.8	10.9	15.8
AFFILIATED BANK	Arlington	TX	B-	B	B	457.6	9.51	4.3	2.1	31.8	0.8	9.2	10.8	14.3
AFFINITY BANK	Atlanta	GA	E-	E-	E-	261.2	-4.99	25.5	0.2	1.7	5.8	0.4	4.6	6.8
AIG FSB	Wilmington	DE	U	C-	B-	18.4	-97.69	0.0	0.0	0.0	75.0	10.0	83.3	365.9
AIMBANK	Littlefield	TX	B	B	B-	520.3	19.76	27.2	2.1	12.8	12.0	4.8	8.3	10.9
ALAMERICA BANK	Birmingham	AL	D	D	D	41.0	11.52	5.8	1.1	5.6	5.7	10.0	16.0	18.8
ALAMOSA STATE BK	Alamosa	CO	A-	A-	A-	206.6	10.40	5.3	4.5	10.8	26.1	7.1	9.0	17.2
ALBANY BANK & TRUST CO NA	Chicago	IL	C+	C	C	530.4	-0.81	5.3	0.3	3.7	19.1	10.0	14.7	25.1
ALBINA COMMUNITY BANK	Portland	OR	E+	E	E-	139.6	12.67	18.7	0.7	3.4	23.0	9.2	10.5	16.2
ALDEN STATE BK	Alden	NY	B	B+	B+	264.7	5.69	4.4	1.9	48.4	22.5	10.0	12.7	21.3
ALDEN STATE BK	Sterling	KS	D+	D+	C-	21.9	5.56	9.0	5.3	18.2	18.7	8.3	9.8	21.4
▲ ALDEN STATE BK	Alden	MI	B	C	C-	186.1	4.89	4.6	2.8	27.2	14.7	10.0	11.3	18.1
ALERUS FINANCIAL NA	Grand Forks	ND	A	A	A-	1490.7	16.12	23.3	5.1	14.5	13.9	7.7	10.1	13.1
ALGONQUIN STATE BK NA	Algonquin	IL	D	D+	C-	132.2	-4.67	2.3	0.6	14.6	58.5	10.0	11.7	31.4
ALL AMERICA BANK	Oklahoma City	OK	B-	B-	C	122.9	-4.17	2.0	0.3	6.5	42.8	7.7	9.5	13.9
ALLEGHENY VALLEY BK PITTSBURGH	Pittsburgh	PA	B-	C+	C+	413.5	4.51	5.8	0.3	27.2	24.2	7.1	9.1	13.5
ALLEGIANCE BANK TEXAS	Houston	TX	B	B-	C+	1239.3	40.46	16.9	0.8	9.7	7.2	7.0	9.4	12.5
ALLIANCE BANK	Sulphur Springs	TX	B-	B-	C+	626.4	8.22	7.7	1.6	7.3	46.7	7.3	9.2	18.9
ALLIANCE BANK	Broomall	PA	B-	C+	C+	423.2	-2.80	2.9	0.9	27.8	12.1	10.0	14.1	23.0
ALLIANCE BANK	Francesville	IN	B+	B	B-	310.1	-2.21	8.0	0.6	6.4	39.9	7.4	9.3	15.8
ALLIANCE BANK	Topeka	KS	C+	C+	C+	92.3	3.14	11.9	2.2	16.2	16.2	9.0	10.3	17.5
ALLIANCE BANK	Mondovi	WI	B-	B-	B-	157.6	4.48	5.5	3.6	13.5	38.2	7.7	9.4	16.4
ALLIANCE BANK	Cape Girardeau	MO	B+	B+	B-	168.3	8.07	3.8	3.3	16.0	13.4	6.1	11.4	11.8
▲ ALLIANCE BANK	Saint Paul	MN	C+	D+	D	557.4	-5.41	14.5	1.4	6.9	14.1	10.0	12.4	15.9
ALLIANCE BANK & TRUST CO	Gastonia	NC	E-	E-	E+	163.2	-0.09	5.2	0.2	21.0	15.8	0.0	3.1	5.4
ALLIANCE BANK CENTRAL TEXAS	Waco	TX	D+	D+	D	188.9	1.00	3.2	2.5	30.9	33.7	8.6	10.1	19.9
▼ ALLIANCE BANKING CO	Winchester	KY	C-	C	C-	61.5	2.35	6.0	1.9	43.9	1.1	8.0	9.7	14.9
▲ ALLIANT BANK	Madison	MO	C+	C	C-	141.7	22.10	4.7	1.5	22.4	7.1	7.9	9.6	14.1
ALLIED BANK	Mulberry	AR	E+	D-	D-	119.6	-17.05	17.7	3.0	14.9	7.4	4.8	6.8	11.7
ALLIED FIRST BANK SB	Oswego	IL	E-	E-	E-	118.1	-2.07	8.9	3.1	29.8	13.3	1.1	4.3	8.1
ALLNATIONS BANK	Calumet	OK	C+	C	C+	49.3	8.75	14.3	10.0	2.2	40.4	7.0	9.0	18.9
ALLY BANK	Midvale	UT	A-	B+	B+	100770.8	9.39	32.7	27.5	5.8	10.9	10.0	15.7	18.0
ALMA BANK	Astoria	NY	B+	B	B	970.0	0.69	16.3	0.1	2.6	9.9	10.0	12.2	16.6
▲ ALMA EXCHANGE BANK & TRUST	Alma	GA	D+	D	D	84.9	0.75	6.1	3.5	7.6	13.1	7.0	9.0	14.3
ALMENA STATE BK	Almena	KS	C	C	C-	34.2	13.03	12.9	7.6	11.2	3.1	3.3	8.0	10.1
ALOSTAR BANK OF COMMERCE	Birmingham	AL	C	C-	C-	917.9	19.08	59.7	0.0	0.8	18.8	10.0	18.8	24.7
ALPINE BANK	Glenwood Springs	CO	B+	B	C+	2481.0	6.73	3.1	1.0	17.7	22.6	7.3	9.2	13.6
ALPINE BANK & TRUST CO	Rockford	IL	B	B-	C+	1183.5	5.22	9.3	5.1	8.1	37.6	6.6	8.6	14.6
▲ ALPINE CAPITAL BANK	New York	NY	B	B-	B-	231.0	-4.93	5.3	3.5	7.7	15.2	10.0	14.8	19.7
ALTA VISTA STATE BK	Alta Vista	KS	C+	C+	C+	20.0	5.72	2.7	1.3	10.8	55.4	10.0	13.1	31.3
ALTAMAHA BANK & TRUST CO	Vidalia	GA	B-	C+	C	146.1	-4.45	8.7	5.7	20.4	12.9	9.3	10.6	14.9
ALTAPACIFIC BANK	Santa Rosa	CA	B+	B	B+	350.4	46.92	3.8	0.8	2.1	25.3	10.0	13.6	16.5
▲ ALTERRA BANK	Leawood	KS	C+	C	C-	238.2	18.79	29.8	0.1	5.2	1.4	5.1	8.4	11.1
▲ ALTON BANK	Alton	MO	B-	C+	C+	64.1	9.15	3.3	6.7	17.9	42.3	10.0	11.3	21.3
ALTOONA FIRST SB	Altoona	PA	B-	C+	B	210.0	0.42	3.0	3.6	32.1	6.9	10.0	12.4	21.6
ALTURA STATE BK	Altura	MN	A-	A-	A-	48.7	1.02	4.6	1.8	10.5	16.5	10.0	15.0	23.4
ALVA STATE BK & TRUST CO	Alva	OK	A-	A-	A-	287.3	20.29	7.5	2.5	3.4	29.5	10.0	14.1	20.1
AMALGAMATED BANK	New York	NY	D	D	D	3632.9	-3.84	12.1	0.1	11.8	38.7	6.5	8.6	13.8
▲ AMALGAMATED BANK OF CHICAGO	Chicago	IL	D+	D	D-	748.5	-2.06	5.1	7.1	2.5	24.4	5.5	7.5	13.4
AMARILLO NATIONAL BK	Amarillo	TX	A-	B+	A-	3652.9	4.95	25.3	16.4	6.0	8.1	8.3	11.0	13.6
AMBANK	Silver City	NM	B	B-	B-	123.2	-0.51	12.1	3.2	15.1	40.5	8.3	9.9	20.4
AMBLER SB	Blue Bell	PA	B-	B	B-	320.3	0.70	0.0	0.1	49.7	30.1	9.3	10.5	22.4
AMBOY BANK	Old Bridge	NJ	B	B-	C-	2152.3	-0.27	1.6	0.0	18.7	22.7	10.0	13.7	16.2
AMEGY BANK NA	Houston	TX	B	B	B-	13575.5	1.80	35.5	1.2	10.2	2.2	9.2	12.0	14.4
AMERASIA BANK	Flushing	NY	B+	B+	B+	398.8	1.84	4.7	0.2	16.2	1.8	9.0	11.2	14.1
AMERIANA BANK	New Castle	IN	C+	C	C-	470.7	7.79	6.2	0.4	28.5	12.1	7.6	9.4	15.5
AMERICA CALIFORNIA BANK	San Francisco	CA	C+	C	D+	142.4	3.37	3.2	0.0	9.7	0.2	10.0	11.8	19.6
AMERICAN BANK	Fond Du Lac	WI	A	A	A	276.9	9.27	14.4	0.3	10.1	23.3	10.0	18.3	31.0
▲ AMERICAN BANK	Bozeman	MT	C-	D	D-	321.4	4.07	15.2	0.4	13.3	7.7	8.3	9.8	18.7
AMERICAN BANK	Allentown	PA	B+	B+	B+	514.8	0.54	10.1	0.1	11.4	18.2	8.2	9.9	13.5

Asset Quality Index	Adjusted Non-Performing Loans as a % of Total Loans	Adjusted Non-Performing Loans as a % of Capital	Net Charge-Offs / Avg Loans	Profitability Index	Net Income ($Mil)	Return on Assets (R.O.A.)	Return on Equity (R.O.E.)	Net Interest Spread	Overhead Efficiency Ratio	Liquidity Index	Liquidity Ratio	Hot Money Ratio	Stability Index
7.7	0.33	2.0	0.13	5.5	0.9	0.94	8.60	3.36	60.8	4.2	28.6	10.0	6.4
3.8	1.13	8.5	0.02	9.1	4.7	1.53	13.08	5.34	69.7	0.6	7.2	46.8	6.0
0.0	4.57	56.9	0.09	1.9	0.6	0.30	7.04	2.67	88.4	0.8	17.3	42.5	0.6
10.0	na	0.0	na	4.2	0.9	2.22	1.86	0.56	85.3	5.0	538.8	100.0	4.7
7.5	0.20	1.8	-0.04	6.3	5.8	1.58	18.99	3.99	62.1	1.2	2.8	25.0	6.5
1.3	8.22	31.1	0.14	0.0	-1.0	-3.37	-20.26	4.72	125.5	0.7	18.4	61.9	4.1
8.7	0.11	0.6	0.01	7.0	2.5	1.71	18.91	3.41	52.0	3.4	32.4	15.6	6.3
4.5	1.64	6.3	1.34	3.1	1.5	0.37	2.48	2.91	68.8	2.3	36.7	26.8	7.4
2.3	4.31	24.1	-0.06	2.4	0.4	0.35	3.34	3.57	92.5	4.5	29.7	8.5	2.5
4.5	3.42	18.0	0.10	5.3	1.8	0.93	7.35	3.93	59.7	3.4	19.0	12.3	7.3
8.8	0.00	0.0	0.01	1.7	0.0	0.18	1.78	3.18	94.0	5.0	54.4	10.7	4.5
4.4	3.28	17.6	0.20	6.4	1.6	1.22	10.99	4.62	56.2	5.1	35.9	7.7	5.3
8.0	0.27	1.8	-0.01	9.3	16.3	1.56	14.13	3.90	75.9	3.9	7.2	8.8	8.9
3.3	8.74	22.1	2.51	0.0	-0.3	-0.29	-2.61	3.20	103.2	5.8	53.4	9.3	4.0
5.5	1.08	5.1	0.59	4.3	0.8	0.88	9.63	3.50	77.8	5.6	41.9	7.0	5.7
4.2	1.55	10.9	0.08	4.2	2.4	0.80	7.22	3.64	72.7	4.2	23.4	8.5	6.2
6.6	0.28	2.2	0.08	4.7	7.2	0.81	8.07	4.29	65.3	1.6	22.4	28.8	7.5
7.1	0.51	2.3	0.04	4.5	5.4	1.17	12.68	3.25	73.4	4.7	33.7	9.3	5.9
6.3	1.39	6.6	0.08	3.7	1.9	0.60	4.23	3.71	73.5	2.7	24.9	16.6	6.5
7.0	0.27	1.4	0.06	6.4	3.7	1.57	16.45	3.74	62.8	5.0	39.2	9.4	6.6
4.9	1.35	7.6	0.14	3.8	0.4	0.55	5.34	3.56	72.8	3.1	31.8	16.6	5.2
4.4	2.47	13.0	0.07	3.5	0.9	0.73	8.61	3.24	77.5	4.8	42.8	11.5	5.6
7.4	0.27	1.7	0.23	6.6	1.3	1.10	9.67	4.25	61.0	3.6	12.2	11.0	6.8
2.8	3.03	16.7	-0.07	5.9	6.6	1.58	12.81	4.15	67.0	2.4	16.1	17.0	5.9
0.3	5.20	81.6	0.58	0.0	-1.2	-0.95	-28.55	3.04	128.0	0.8	17.9	39.4	2.4
5.8	0.61	3.2	0.40	1.5	0.4	0.25	2.47	3.47	93.2	2.6	40.0	25.8	4.1
5.0	1.30	9.7	0.11	1.8	0.0	0.04	0.40	3.81	96.3	0.9	13.7	33.3	3.9
5.0	0.27	2.0	0.09	5.5	1.0	0.97	9.47	4.75	80.1	1.0	14.5	32.1	6.3
0.3	8.11	53.8	-0.18	0.0	-0.8	-0.84	-12.62	3.18	125.7	1.1	26.5	37.8	2.2
0.3	5.59	63.0	1.06	0.0	-0.4	-0.43	-8.05	3.32	103.7	0.9	25.0	43.5	0.8
4.1	2.30	9.6	-0.08	4.0	0.2	0.64	6.03	3.51	71.7	5.8	51.0	7.5	6.3
5.6	0.88	3.8	0.19	6.3	847.9	1.13	7.34	2.42	62.6	0.8	14.9	40.5	8.3
4.9	1.11	6.5	-0.01	4.9	5.1	0.71	6.08	3.89	72.3	1.2	22.9	32.1	7.5
1.2	8.31	48.7	0.45	1.1	0.0	0.05	0.53	3.64	93.5	3.2	24.1	13.7	3.0
7.4	0.12	1.3	0.00	8.9	0.4	1.79	23.69	5.73	70.2	0.7	4.1	32.8	5.6
5.5	2.86	9.5	1.48	2.4	2.5	0.38	1.98	3.98	82.4	1.0	24.9	37.1	4.8
5.4	1.87	11.4	-0.03	5.8	19.6	1.09	10.68	4.40	70.5	4.5	21.9	7.7	8.1
5.9	1.10	6.1	0.05	5.7	12.8	1.48	16.17	3.16	72.6	4.5	32.6	13.0	6.9
6.9	1.20	4.2	0.00	4.0	1.7	0.94	6.39	2.80	66.4	4.1	44.2	15.5	8.1
7.1	2.73	7.8	-0.32	4.1	0.2	1.01	7.97	3.32	73.3	2.3	42.8	25.8	5.0
4.3	1.24	8.2	0.58	5.3	1.4	1.23	12.60	5.14	70.4	1.9	18.0	20.0	5.1
4.9	2.10	9.4	-0.02	5.9	2.1	0.88	5.62	5.13	69.1	3.0	23.2	14.9	7.0
4.0	1.10	9.6	0.34	5.4	1.6	0.96	10.29	4.22	66.5	0.7	17.2	51.9	4.3
5.3	2.13	8.9	0.22	6.5	0.7	1.56	14.00	4.04	62.4	3.5	37.0	16.6	7.3
7.8	0.75	3.8	0.16	3.2	0.7	0.47	3.87	3.20	78.0	2.6	35.4	21.2	5.9
8.7	0.47	1.8	0.00	7.9	0.7	1.83	12.12	3.68	49.2	4.5	40.5	12.8	9.3
6.0	1.27	5.3	-0.55	7.5	3.1	1.58	13.20	3.43	45.7	2.9	42.4	22.8	8.7
2.7	4.50	25.5	0.16	0.8	-3.0	-0.11	-1.23	2.48	98.4	3.1	15.6	14.1	4.2
1.5	6.45	37.8	0.47	3.3	2.8	0.47	7.03	2.95	82.3	5.1	27.1	3.5	2.1
5.5	0.79	5.3	0.24	8.8	59.5	2.09	19.94	3.40	49.3	2.5	11.3	16.2	9.9
3.0	1.99	8.3	0.25	3.5	0.7	0.69	5.16	4.18	82.0	3.7	30.5	13.2	7.5
7.5	0.73	4.0	0.16	3.5	2.0	0.82	8.06	3.35	72.3	2.7	35.6	20.8	5.7
5.0	3.99	16.3	-0.14	4.4	15.4	0.95	8.55	3.26	66.3	2.7	16.7	15.8	8.1
5.1	0.76	4.3	0.21	5.2	84.9	0.83	5.06	3.13	66.1	5.3	22.1	2.6	7.6
5.9	0.31	2.4	0.01	9.7	4.3	1.51	13.96	5.11	38.4	0.6	8.5	45.9	7.4
3.5	2.23	15.0	0.13	3.9	2.3	0.65	6.77	3.58	76.8	3.4	19.3	12.2	5.3
5.5	0.16	0.8	0.25	3.2	0.5	0.47	3.80	3.26	76.1	2.7	34.5	19.8	5.4
8.6	0.43	1.2	-0.93	6.3	2.1	1.02	5.80	3.41	56.5	5.4	45.2	8.9	9.3
2.9	2.19	14.0	0.04	6.1	4.6	1.91	18.65	3.66	74.2	4.2	16.2	7.4	3.7
7.0	0.34	2.2	0.00	5.1	3.6	0.93	9.18	2.76	51.3	3.9	19.0	9.8	7.1

Name	City	State	Rating	2013 Rating	2012 Rating	Total Assets ($Mil)	One Year Asset Growth	Asset Mix (As a % of Total Assets) Comm-ercial Loans	Cons-umer Loans	Mort-gage Loans	Secur-ities	Capital-ization Index	Lever-age Ratio	Risk-Based Capital Ratio
▲ AMERICAN BANK	Wagoner	OK	**C+**	C	B-	30.2	0.14	1.3	6.3	4.5	50.0	**10.0**	20.4	59.8
▲ AMERICAN BANK	Bethesda	MD	**C+**	C	C-	438.0	1.67	4.7	0.7	25.9	1.0	**10.0**	11.1	34.7
AMERICAN BANK & TRUST	Wessington Springs	SD	**A-**	A-	B+	597.2	44.61	10.6	2.7	1.5	24.2	**8.4**	10.1	13.7
AMERICAN BANK & TRUST CO	Opelousas	LA	**B+**	B	B	163.5	4.66	8.8	4.2	21.6	34.3	**9.4**	10.6	19.8
AMERICAN BANK & TRUST CO	Tulsa	OK	**C**	C	C	193.1	-0.91	19.8	0.5	3.3	42.8	**7.8**	9.5	17.8
AMERICAN BANK & TRUST CO INC	Covington	LA	**C**	C	C-	118.5	8.40	5.2	2.7	15.0	13.9	**7.3**	9.2	16.7
AMERICAN BANK & TRUST CO INC	Bowling Green	KY	**B+**	B	B	255.5	-1.32	5.9	2.4	39.2	6.4	**7.5**	9.4	13.9
AMERICAN BANK & TRUST CO NA	Davenport	IA	**D+**	D-	D-	357.4	-0.91	8.9	0.7	19.9	35.0	**10.0**	11.0	18.8
AMERICAN BANK & TRUST CUMBERLD	Livingston	TN	**B-**	B-	C	182.6	23.23	11.9	8.0	30.3	7.0	**6.2**	8.6	11.9
AMERICAN BANK & TRUST WI	Cuba City	WI	**C**	C+	C	142.6	4.27	13.1	2.6	7.5	11.6	**9.5**	10.6	15.1
AMERICAN BANK CENTER	Dickinson	ND	**B+**	B+	B	1218.5	20.46	5.1	9.9	5.2	38.6	**6.0**	8.0	13.5
AMERICAN BANK NA	Le Mars	IA	**B**	B	B-	261.2	-1.25	10.0	1.3	5.3	3.8	**7.7**	10.5	13.1
AMERICAN BANK NA	Corpus Christi	TX	**B**	B	B+	1293.1	7.03	19.4	0.6	5.8	26.4	**5.9**	7.9	13.8
AMERICAN BANK NA	Dallas	TX	**D+**	D+	D+	61.5	15.36	3.2	27.4	1.4	56.5	**6.1**	8.1	16.1
AMERICAN BANK NA	Waco	TX	**C+**	C+	B-	409.9	6.42	9.2	1.8	15.8	29.9	**7.5**	9.3	17.6
AMERICAN BANK OF BAXTER SPRING	Baxter Springs	KS	**D-**	D-	D-	95.6	-3.80	3.8	1.6	8.6	29.2	**6.9**	8.9	20.0
AMERICAN BANK OF COMMERCE	Wolfforth	TX	**B-**	B-	B-	712.7	4.06	10.4	0.7	6.6	30.5	**7.8**	9.5	14.0
AMERICAN BANK OF COMMERCE	Provo	UT	**B**	B	C	80.8	22.62	4.5	0.9	4.7	0.0	**10.0**	12.6	18.5
AMERICAN BANK OF HUNTSVILLE	Huntsville	AL	**D-**	D-	D-	129.8	-15.62	6.6	1.6	29.3	2.0	**6.4**	8.4	12.4
▼ AMERICAN BANK OF MISSOURI	Wellsville	MO	**B-**	B-	C	137.0	13.84	2.9	0.2	39.2	6.7	**9.6**	10.7	16.7
AMERICAN BANK OF OKLAHOMA	Collinsville	OK	**C-**	C-	C	205.2	29.03	19.0	19.0	17.8	0.2	**4.6**	9.2	10.8
AMERICAN BANK OF ST PAUL	Saint Paul	MN	**D**	E+	E-	301.8	-7.82	5.0	0.2	5.7	30.4	**6.7**	8.7	15.2
AMERICAN BANK OF TEXAS	Sherman	TX	**B**	B	B	2190.5	6.67	7.0	1.1	4.3	20.0	**10.0**	13.0	18.0
▲ AMERICAN BANK OF THE NORTH	Nashwauk	MN	**E+**	E	E-	546.2	-0.20	12.9	2.4	22.6	12.4	**2.5**	6.2	9.5
AMERICAN BUSINESS BANK	Los Angeles	CA	**B-**	B-	B-	1477.6	8.93	13.7	0.3	0.2	50.2	**6.1**	8.1	16.8
AMERICAN CHARTERED BANK	Schaumburg	IL	**B-**	C	C	2551.5	3.98	23.2	0.0	10.1	19.3	**6.5**	8.6	12.4
AMERICAN CITY BANK	Tullahoma	TN	**C+**	C+	C+	253.3	-4.20	20.5	5.8	22.7	8.4	**10.0**	15.2	18.6
AMERICAN COMMUNITY BANK	Glen Cove	NY	**C**	D+	C	153.6	-13.47	4.5	0.0	4.7	17.5	**10.0**	14.6	17.9
AMERICAN COMMUNITY BANK & TR	Woodstock	IL	**B**	B-	C+	477.2	-0.15	6.6	0.1	10.9	10.7	**10.0**	14.4	21.4
▲ AMERICAN CONTINENTAL BANK	City of Industry	CA	**B**	B-	C	193.7	14.83	4.2	0.0	8.1	11.2	**10.0**	12.9	20.4
AMERICAN EAGLE BANK	South Elgin	IL	**D**	D	D-	173.1	0.65	1.8	48.8	8.1	6.1	**3.4**	8.2	10.2
AMERICAN EAGLE BANK OF CHICAGO	Chicago	IL	**D**	D-	D-	75.9	4.79	2.1	41.3	5.5	0.0	**7.3**	10.3	12.8
AMERICAN ENTERPRISE BANK	Buffalo Grove	IL	**D-**	D-	D-	236.2	5.70	15.3	0.0	2.5	9.7	**6.5**	8.6	12.2
AMERICAN ENTERPRISE BANK OF FL	Jacksonville	FL	**D**	D	D-	197.1	0.32	18.2	4.2	11.2	10.2	**6.2**	8.2	12.7
AMERICAN EXCHANGE BANK	Henryetta	OK	**B**	B	B-	61.5	-3.57	5.1	10.3	28.2	19.3	**10.0**	11.0	16.9
AMERICAN EXCHANGE BANK	Elmwood	NE	**B-**	B-	B	41.8	2.90	12.5	2.2	7.3	32.1	**10.0**	11.9	16.1
AMERICAN EXCHANGE BANK LINDSAY	Lindsay	OK	**B+**	A-	B+	58.1	16.93	9.0	1.7	8.3	53.3	**9.4**	10.6	22.9
▲ AMERICAN EXP CENTURION BK	Salt Lake City	UT	**B+**	B+	B+	31974.5	-3.64	0.2	61.9	0.0	2.0	**10.0**	18.8	21.4
▲ AMERICAN EXPRESS BANK FSB	Salt Lake City	UT	**B+**	B+	B+	43047.9	11.78	44.7	42.1	0.0	1.2	**10.0**	15.9	17.1
AMERICAN FEDERAL BANK	Fargo	ND	**B-**	B-	B-	482.0	3.39	4.9	1.4	14.3	6.8	**6.6**	8.6	12.7
AMERICAN FIRST NATIONAL BK	Houston	TX	**B**	C+	C+	1062.0	14.94	8.8	0.4	3.7	3.8	**10.0**	13.3	16.7
▼ AMERICAN FOUNDERS BANK INC	Lexington	KY	**E-**	E	E+	282.5	-2.01	13.9	0.7	18.4	15.3	**2.9**	6.5	10.0
AMERICAN GATEWAY BANK	Port Allen	LA	**C+**	C	C-	362.2	-3.32	3.1	0.7	7.4	31.9	**10.0**	11.6	22.6
▲ AMERICAN HEARTLAND BANK & TR	Sugar Grove	IL	**D**	D-	D-	131.4	19.33	16.9	0.1	15.2	5.9	**8.7**	10.9	13.9
AMERICAN HERITAGE BANK	Sapulpa	OK	**B-**	B-	B-	1019.0	2.24	5.5	4.0	13.5	57.1	**6.5**	8.5	21.9
AMERICAN HERITAGE BANK	Clovis	NM	**C**	C	C+	81.1	12.43	10.7	0.9	6.8	25.7	**8.5**	10.0	14.5
AMERICAN HERITAGE NATIONAL BK	Long Prairie	MN	**A-**	A-	A-	228.8	3.81	12.5	0.4	6.7	3.3	**10.0**	12.1	17.1
AMERICAN INTERSTATE BK	Elkhorn	NE	**A**	A	A-	108.2	1.32	9.2	1.1	22.2	8.6	**10.0**	11.8	16.5
▲ AMERICAN INVESTORS BANK & MTG	Eden Prairie	MN	**C**	C-	D+	92.5	-8.88	0.1	1.4	22.2	46.4	**6.2**	8.2	15.5
AMERICAN LOAN & SAVINGS ASSN	Hannibal	MO	**D**	D	C-	5.1	-10.16	0.0	0.1	62.4	0.0	**10.0**	12.5	32.2
AMERICAN METRO BANK	Chicago	IL	**E**	E-	E-	61.7	-12.52	5.5	0.1	20.9	0.0	**6.6**	8.7	13.5
▲ AMERICAN MIDWEST BANK	Sycamore	IL	**C+**	C-	C-	468.6	2.53	10.8	4.9	15.3	13.2	**9.7**	10.8	15.4
AMERICAN MOMENTUM BANK	College Station	TX	**C+**	C	C-	1041.8	11.14	7.1	0.2	9.1	7.4	**10.0**	17.0	18.5
▲ AMERICAN NATIONAL BK	Oakland Park	FL	**B-**	C+	C-	281.4	19.69	4.5	0.1	1.4	9.3	**10.0**	12.1	17.1
AMERICAN NATIONAL BK	Ardmore	OK	**A-**	A-	B+	347.9	8.27	8.3	5.7	15.1	42.1	**7.7**	9.4	16.5
AMERICAN NATIONAL BK	Omaha	NE	**B+**	B+	B+	2164.8	2.88	11.3	21.1	7.8	21.0	**7.3**	9.4	12.7
AMERICAN NATIONAL BK & TRUST	Wichita Falls	TX	**B**	B	B-	433.7	3.68	4.7	4.0	11.7	20.3	**10.0**	11.7	18.6
AMERICAN NATIONAL BK & TRUST	Danville	VA	**A**	A	B+	1317.2	-0.38	9.1	0.4	13.4	24.9	**10.0**	11.8	17.6
AMERICAN NATIONAL BK OF MN	Brainerd	MN	**C-**	C+	D+	248.0	-1.13	2.9	1.7	23.8	10.0	**10.0**	12.4	17.8
▲ AMERICAN NATIONAL BK OF SIDNEY	Sidney	NE	**C**	C	C	86.6	2.16	7.1	10.3	4.1	37.8	**8.3**	9.9	22.0

Asset Quality Index	Adjusted Non-Performing Loans as a % of Total Loans	Adjusted Non-Performing Loans as a % of Capital	Net Charge-Offs Avg Loans	Profitability Index	Net Income ($Mil)	Return on Assets (R.O.A.)	Return on Equity (R.O.E.)	Net Interest Spread	Overhead Efficiency Ratio	Liquidity Index	Liquidity Ratio	Hot Money Ratio	Stability Index
8.6	0.00	0.0	0.00	2.7	0.1	0.55	2.78	3.32	83.4	6.8	91.9	8.2	5.7
5.2	3.72	13.4	0.55	3.2	1.0	0.32	2.80	2.04	91.0	6.1	60.4	9.5	4.5
7.5	0.17	1.1	0.00	7.0	6.3	1.60	15.61	4.18	59.9	3.1	12.1	13.4	8.5
7.8	0.39	1.9	0.01	5.9	1.8	1.48	14.71	4.05	63.1	4.7	32.3	8.5	6.6
4.3	3.11	12.7	0.03	2.7	0.4	0.27	2.90	2.65	85.4	4.0	50.3	17.6	5.8
5.1	1.00	5.4	-0.09	3.1	0.3	0.36	3.83	3.79	90.9	4.6	45.5	13.3	4.3
5.3	0.97	7.9	0.15	6.8	3.0	1.55	16.79	4.19	63.2	1.6	12.6	23.0	6.4
1.8	6.08	28.0	0.16	3.1	2.6	0.96	9.78	3.61	94.4	4.2	23.5	8.7	3.8
5.0	0.46	4.2	0.06	6.7	1.9	1.49	17.81	4.39	62.4	0.7	11.7	44.3	4.5
3.5	2.00	13.2	0.45	4.0	0.6	0.55	4.43	3.53	71.3	3.8	20.8	10.6	6.9
6.3	0.72	4.7	-0.02	6.6	10.1	1.15	13.52	3.81	64.6	4.9	15.6	3.3	8.2
5.5	0.56	4.2	0.26	6.4	2.7	1.37	12.78	3.39	53.2	2.7	9.8	15.2	7.5
8.4	0.24	1.6	0.04	4.8	10.6	1.14	13.83	3.73	69.5	6.7	40.5	2.5	7.7
6.9	0.45	1.7	2.03	3.5	0.2	0.48	6.50	4.77	61.5	3.0	69.6	36.9	1.3
4.4	2.03	11.1	0.09	3.9	2.5	0.84	9.04	3.07	74.2	1.4	22.3	27.7	5.7
0.3	17.91	70.2	5.75	0.0	-1.5	-1.90	-21.38	2.03	134.6	3.5	26.3	12.9	3.9
5.7	0.82	4.9	-0.02	4.1	3.5	0.67	6.93	3.66	74.5	2.7	27.4	17.3	5.5
3.6	2.52	12.5	0.16	5.1	0.5	0.82	6.78	3.93	72.4	4.5	39.0	12.1	5.5
1.9	3.06	25.5	-0.03	0.3	-0.3	-0.25	-3.03	3.94	106.7	0.7	8.8	35.5	2.5
3.6	1.89	13.2	-0.02	5.6	1.0	0.97	7.31	4.09	68.8	1.7	4.5	19.3	6.0
2.2	1.63	14.9	0.01	4.9	1.2	0.89	10.10	5.04	76.3	0.6	8.8	43.2	4.1
3.4	3.48	15.3	-1.00	5.3	2.9	1.27	16.81	2.94	87.5	5.5	39.8	6.9	3.0
4.0	1.86	8.6	0.01	6.8	19.4	1.22	8.69	3.73	55.1	4.9	31.2	10.9	9.6
0.3	7.12	71.9	0.95	3.2	3.2	0.78	13.06	3.77	81.3	3.8	6.7	8.7	2.9
9.0	0.20	1.0	-0.14	4.2	8.7	0.81	10.86	3.27	61.0	6.3	43.7	5.6	6.6
4.8	1.39	10.5	0.61	4.5	12.8	0.68	8.24	3.66	61.5	5.1	22.4	4.2	5.0
2.5	2.20	11.6	0.41	9.7	4.5	2.34	13.67	5.17	49.0	1.0	7.3	30.5	7.5
2.0	3.64	15.8	0.25	3.7	0.6	0.46	3.35	4.54	82.6	2.2	22.9	18.8	7.4
6.5	1.41	5.9	0.48	4.2	2.6	0.75	5.34	3.27	60.0	2.5	32.9	20.6	6.4
4.4	1.70	7.9	0.00	4.9	1.2	0.86	6.45	3.39	60.2	1.9	39.3	39.1	6.4
1.2	1.49	14.1	0.30	8.1	1.6	1.27	15.51	4.72	53.5	0.5	5.7	49.3	3.8
0.6	3.58	24.7	0.33	2.9	0.2	0.36	3.36	3.96	78.3	0.5	12.2	60.6	4.0
1.3	6.06	37.0	0.03	0.0	-1.8	-1.00	-11.38	3.20	122.7	1.8	21.3	21.9	3.1
1.4	4.37	32.0	0.34	1.2	0.0	0.03	0.31	3.44	99.2	1.4	23.2	27.8	3.9
5.3	1.29	7.3	1.09	4.8	0.5	1.12	10.10	5.06	77.3	4.1	31.4	11.8	5.6
8.4	0.37	1.8	0.96	3.7	0.3	0.77	6.75	3.83	68.8	3.4	28.4	14.1	5.2
8.8	1.33	2.6	-0.07	6.2	0.5	1.11	10.07	3.94	67.4	6.2	71.3	8.8	6.8
4.6	1.05	3.2	2.84	10.0	1407.7	5.72	29.59	5.03	47.8	2.4	44.5	75.6	8.8
5.6	0.66	3.4	1.69	10.0	1566.3	5.15	30.83	6.14	60.5	4.3	15.2	7.0	9.1
7.1	0.32	3.0	-0.04	4.5	3.3	0.96	10.88	4.06	75.6	2.0	6.8	18.1	5.6
3.9	1.54	9.1	-0.01	7.6	9.3	1.23	9.10	4.41	55.9	0.9	14.9	36.5	10.0
1.9	3.02	29.0	0.50	0.7	-0.7	-0.36	-8.30	3.49	106.3	1.9	19.1	20.0	0.1
4.8	3.81	14.6	0.25	2.8	1.5	0.53	4.57	3.35	85.9	2.7	29.8	17.9	4.8
1.0	2.66	17.7	1.27	3.1	0.5	0.52	4.62	3.93	68.7	0.7	13.7	42.6	4.6
9.0	0.42	1.7	0.28	4.0	7.4	0.96	11.16	3.18	72.6	3.7	26.6	15.0	7.7
3.1	2.77	16.1	0.20	4.7	0.5	0.84	8.48	4.05	67.9	2.3	33.0	22.7	5.5
6.5	0.36	2.2	0.01	7.4	2.0	1.16	9.97	3.79	52.7	4.2	15.3	7.6	7.4
8.5	0.02	0.2	-0.02	8.8	1.6	2.04	18.40	3.73	46.1	2.9	13.4	14.2	8.1
6.4	1.09	6.4	0.78	3.7	0.4	0.53	7.30	3.09	57.6	3.2	45.2	20.2	2.8
7.8	0.25	1.4	1.89	0.0	-0.1	-3.12	-23.28	3.84	225.5	2.1	33.0	20.4	6.0
0.0	26.66	171.0	-0.11	0.0	-1.3	-2.58	-31.73	2.96	183.6	0.8	21.7	51.9	1.3
3.8	0.84	5.5	0.49	3.7	2.4	0.67	5.66	4.29	79.1	3.5	12.2	11.4	5.9
3.1	2.48	11.9	0.00	6.8	7.5	1.00	5.71	5.08	65.3	2.2	9.4	17.5	8.6
3.5	2.31	12.2	0.00	4.1	1.4	0.74	6.03	3.56	67.0	5.0	36.6	8.7	6.4
7.9	0.42	2.1	0.01	6.1	3.9	1.52	15.55	3.87	61.9	2.0	39.5	36.4	6.8
5.1	0.76	5.5	0.03	7.0	25.6	1.59	15.66	3.91	61.4	4.1	9.9	7.3	8.9
4.0	2.80	13.7	-0.01	4.8	2.8	0.87	6.84	3.34	77.1	3.5	15.6	11.3	7.5
7.0	0.61	3.1	0.02	6.1	10.4	1.07	7.15	3.77	64.0	2.1	21.4	21.1	9.9
3.4	4.16	21.1	-0.08	1.2	-0.7	-0.38	-3.00	4.63	113.5	1.8	20.0	21.1	6.1
8.4	0.05	0.2	0.01	2.8	0.4	0.53	5.53	2.66	79.6	5.1	37.0	8.2	5.3

Name	City	State	Rating	2013 Rating	2012 Rating	Total Assets ($Mil)	One Year Asset Growth	Asset Mix (As a % of Total Assets): Commercial Loans	Consumer Loans	Mortgage Loans	Securities	Capitalization Index	Leverage Ratio	Risk-Based Capital Ratio
AMERICAN NATIONAL BK OF TEXAS	Terrell	TX	**B**	B-	B	2487.3	10.25	5.9	1.6	13.8	26.0	**6.5**	8.5	13.8
AMERICAN NB OF BEAVER DAM	Beaver Dam	WI	**C**	C	C	114.5	1.31	5.7	1.4	26.1	25.3	**9.2**	10.5	15.7
AMERICAN NB OF MT PLEASANT	Mount Pleasant	TX	**B+**	B+	B-	92.0	4.03	9.8	9.2	20.3	28.0	**10.0**	11.6	22.5
AMERICAN NB-FOX CITIES	Appleton	WI	**B-**	B-	C+	243.5	0.44	17.5	0.5	4.9	21.1	**10.0**	11.7	16.6
AMERICAN PATRIOT BANK	Greeneville	TN	**E-**	E-	E-	71.3	-5.29	7.5	1.3	23.0	3.5	**0.0**	2.0	4.0
▲ AMERICAN PLUS BANK NA	Arcadia	CA	**A**	A-	B	292.9	2.68	1.6	0.0	23.6	1.6	**10.0**	15.4	19.0
AMERICAN PRIDE BANK	Macon	GA	**B**	B+	C+	117.7	2.09	1.5	0.3	7.0	20.2	**10.0**	23.3	32.3
AMERICAN RIVER BANK	Rancho Cordova	CA	**B**	B-	C+	615.9	2.21	3.9	0.1	2.6	45.1	**10.0**	11.8	23.0
AMERICAN RIVIERA BANK	Santa Barbara	CA	**B+**	B+	B+	219.6	26.68	9.6	0.6	21.2	3.3	**10.0**	11.5	16.9
AMERICAN SAVINGS BANK	Middletown	OH	**C+**	C+	B-	38.0	-3.04	4.6	0.8	51.4	2.5	**10.0**	18.3	31.1
AMERICAN SAVINGS BANK FSB	Portsmouth	OH	**C**	C-	D	251.0	-2.75	3.2	1.7	45.7	14.0	**7.4**	9.3	15.2
AMERICAN SAVINGS BANK FSB	Honolulu	HI	**B**	B	C+	5442.3	5.48	13.2	2.0	40.4	9.8	**7.1**	9.1	12.6
AMERICAN SAVINGS FSB	Munster	IN	**B-**	C+	C-	185.1	4.34	6.0	0.8	39.2	4.3	**8.9**	10.2	15.0
AMERICAN SB	Tripoli	IA	**A**	A	A-	51.8	-0.18	11.1	2.4	10.2	53.1	**10.0**	17.1	27.8
AMERICAN STATE BK	Sioux Center	IA	**B-**	B-	B	700.5	12.94	15.7	1.4	3.2	0.7	**7.8**	11.3	13.2
AMERICAN STATE BK	Osceola	IA	**B**	B	B-	165.8	9.82	9.6	4.4	14.2	19.6	**7.3**	9.2	13.3
AMERICAN STATE BK	Oldham	SD	**C-**	C-	C	28.3	-5.85	6.4	1.0	2.2	35.0	**7.8**	9.5	30.7
AMERICAN STATE BK	Arp	TX	**B-**	B-	B	271.7	2.10	10.0	4.0	19.1	22.2	**10.0**	11.7	18.4
▲ AMERICAN STATE BK & TRUST CO	Great Bend	KS	**C+**	C	C+	353.5	23.82	8.0	2.0	2.0	45.3	**8.0**	9.7	14.5
AMERICAN STATE BK & TRUST CO	Williston	ND	**A-**	A-	B+	604.9	11.77	6.5	3.9	7.3	53.1	**6.0**	8.0	16.1
▲ AMERICAN STATE BK OF GRYGLA	Grygla	MN	**B**	B	B-	49.1	102.39	4.5	5.1	15.6	21.6	**10.0**	13.3	17.8
AMERICAN TRUST & SB	Dubuque	IA	**C+**	C+	C	970.6	7.77	15.6	2.3	6.0	9.6	**7.6**	10.7	13.0
AMERICAN TRUST & SB	Lowden	IA	**B-**	B-	B-	39.3	8.27	2.4	2.3	0.7	50.0	**10.0**	15.0	17.3
AMERICAN TRUST BANK	Kirksville	MO	**C+**	C+	C-	60.7	5.52	3.0	0.9	25.9	1.0	**8.5**	10.0	15.6
▲ AMERICAN TRUST BANK OF EAST TN	Knoxville	TN	**B-**	C-	D+	139.0	3.86	11.9	1.0	19.2	8.7	**10.0**	12.0	17.1
AMERICAN UNION S&LA SB	Chicago	IL	**D+**	C	B-	6.8	-0.53	0.0	0.3	33.0	48.6	**10.0**	11.8	40.6
AMERICANA COMMUNITY BANK	Sleepy Eye	MN	**E-**	E	E-	114.9	-6.46	4.7	0.9	8.9	20.3	**2.8**	5.3	9.8
AMERICANWEST BANK	Spokane	WA	**B-**	C+	B-	4086.6	11.23	7.9	0.4	8.7	25.9	**7.8**	9.5	13.8
▲ AMERICAS COMMUNITY BANK	Blue Springs	MO	**B**	C	D+	25.9	-2.34	13.1	0.3	24.2	9.7	**10.0**	12.9	19.0
AMERICAS UNITED BANK	Glendale	CA	**B-**	B	B-	159.7	32.23	8.6	0.0	0.1	9.1	**10.0**	13.1	19.7
▲ AMERIFIRST BANK	Union Springs	AL	**D**	D-	D	147.2	2.47	8.0	2.7	17.5	29.8	**8.5**	10.0	15.6
AMERIPRISE NATIONAL TRUST BANK	Minneapolis	MN	**U**	U	C	39.8	-23.74	0.0	0.0	0.0	27.3	**10.0**	89.1	382.1
AMERIS BANK	Moultrie	GA	**B-**	B	C	3995.3	41.75	5.2	1.0	20.8	13.3	**8.0**	9.7	14.5
▼ AMERISERV FINANCIAL BANK	Johnstown	PA	**C+**	B-	B-	1043.6	3.28	11.3	1.7	19.1	13.0	**6.8**	9.4	12.4
AMERISTATE BK	Atoka	OK	**B+**	B+	B	207.9	7.54	7.8	7.4	17.2	3.7	**6.9**	8.9	13.9
AMFIRST BANK NA	McCook	NE	**B-**	C+	C-	250.3	2.72	9.0	6.0	6.7	15.2	**8.1**	9.7	14.1
AMG NATIONAL TRUST BANK	Englewood	CO	**A-**	A-	A-	300.2	49.47	4.2	4.3	4.9	43.6	**6.7**	8.7	13.4
AMISTAD BANK	Del Rio	TX	**B-**	B-	A-	26.7	-4.37	3.2	2.6	9.8	8.0	**10.0**	13.5	16.6
▼ AMORY FS&LA	Amory	MS	**C-**	C	C	95.6	-4.64	0.0	0.6	71.5	14.1	**9.3**	10.5	23.8
ANADARKO BANK & TRUST CO	Anadarko	OK	**C+**	B-	C	83.2	19.15	6.1	0.5	9.1	14.2	**8.5**	10.0	14.0
ANAHUAC NATIONAL BK	Anahuac	TX	**B**	B	B-	100.5	8.64	6.3	8.8	18.0	31.9	**7.5**	9.3	16.1
▲ ANB BANK	Denver	CO	**C+**	C	C	2160.8	2.83	6.0	0.3	6.9	46.0	**6.9**	8.9	14.9
ANCHOR BANK	Aberdeen	WA	**C**	D+	D+	385.8	-4.37	4.3	1.8	18.7	11.6	**10.0**	13.8	18.3
ANCHOR BANK NA	Saint Paul	MN	**B+**	B+	B-	1444.8	0.41	21.6	0.4	6.1	19.3	**7.3**	9.5	12.8
ANCHOR COMMERCIAL BANK	Juno Beach	FL	**E**	E-	E-	102.5	3.13	10.2	2.6	11.4	24.2	**6.9**	8.9	15.6
▲ ANCHOR D BANK	Texhoma	OK	**A-**	B	B+	185.0	1.58	5.0	7.2	5.6	30.5	**8.5**	10.0	15.5
▲ ANCHOR STATE BK	Anchor	IL	**D**	D-	D	15.3	1.49	2.1	1.1	4.7	25.8	**7.5**	9.3	22.9
ANCHORBANK FSB	Madison	WI	**E+**	E+	E-	2104.9	-3.93	0.7	6.1	31.5	13.9	**8.6**	10.1	18.0
▼ ANDALUSIA COMMUNITY BANK	Andalusia	IL	**D+**	C-	C-	42.6	-7.25	6.5	6.6	33.4	24.5	**10.0**	14.1	26.6
ANDERSON BROTHERS BANK	Mullins	SC	**D-**	D-	E+	486.6	4.71	6.1	27.8	15.8	7.4	**6.6**	8.8	12.2
ANDERSON STATE BK	Oneida	IL	**C+**	C+	C	82.0	-3.74	3.0	3.8	5.7	41.3	**10.0**	13.8	27.1
ANDES STATE BK	Lake Andes	SD	**C-**	C-	C-	23.8	15.86	7.6	4.6	6.2	27.5	**8.6**	10.0	19.1
ANDOVER BANK	Andover	OH	**A-**	A-	B+	346.1	4.30	3.3	1.0	25.2	50.5	**9.0**	10.3	23.5
ANDOVER STATE BK	Andover	KS	**C**	C	C-	72.2	6.29	11.0	1.1	28.3	2.2	**6.6**	8.8	12.2
ANDREW JOHNSON BANK	Greeneville	TN	**B**	B-	B-	300.3	4.23	6.3	2.2	35.1	9.2	**8.3**	9.8	15.1
ANDROSCOGGIN SB	Lewiston	ME	**B-**	C+	C	799.3	5.40	11.3	0.2	26.0	10.9	**8.9**	10.9	14.1
ANGELINA SAVINGS BANK SSB	Lufkin	TX	**B-**	B-	B-	59.6	4.36	7.6	15.2	22.6	0.7	**7.0**	9.0	20.5
ANN ARBOR STATE BK	Ann Arbor	MI	**A-**	B+	B+	232.7	9.99	15.5	0.2	7.3	30.9	**9.7**	10.8	16.5
ANNA STATE BK	Anna	IL	**B+**	B+	B+	72.9	8.12	2.0	2.8	25.0	44.1	**10.0**	15.4	32.1
ANNA-JONESBORO NATIONAL BK	Anna	IL	**B-**	B-	B	228.6	-0.14	3.8	6.1	26.8	44.0	**10.0**	12.7	26.8

Arrows denote recent upgrades ▲ or downgrades ▼

Asset Quality Index	Adjusted Non-Performing Loans as a % of Total Loans	Adjusted Non-Performing Loans as a % of Capital	Net Charge-Offs / Avg Loans	Profitability Index	Net Income ($Mil)	Return on Assets (R.O.A.)	Return on Equity (R.O.E.)	Net Interest Spread	Overhead Efficiency Ratio	Liquidity Index	Liquidity Ratio	Hot Money Ratio	Stability Index
7.4	0.32	2.3	0.00	4.6	14.7	0.82	8.63	3.60	75.9	3.9	8.8	8.8	7.1
4.5	2.27	14.1	0.25	3.2	0.5	0.62	5.96	3.89	83.2	4.9	29.5	5.9	4.7
7.9	0.41	1.9	0.34	6.1	1.0	1.48	13.09	4.34	65.5	2.3	20.7	18.1	6.1
3.7	2.39	12.2	0.24	7.7	3.4	1.79	15.40	3.32	50.3	0.9	24.2	50.6	8.4
0.3	12.23	192.9	-0.08	0.0	-0.7	-1.26	-58.41	3.72	146.1	2.0	16.8	19.3	0.0
7.7	0.00	0.0	0.00	9.4	3.3	1.51	10.15	3.79	43.0	0.8	15.0	37.1	7.6
6.6	1.54	4.4	0.00	4.5	0.6	0.69	3.02	4.68	77.4	0.8	17.8	36.6	6.0
4.8	3.53	12.0	-0.16	4.4	3.4	0.77	5.24	3.59	68.3	4.9	50.1	12.8	7.1
8.7	0.16	0.9	-0.14	4.5	1.0	0.68	5.36	4.38	74.4	4.4	27.1	8.2	6.4
6.4	2.65	10.1	0.00	2.2	0.0	0.04	0.21	4.75	99.9	3.7	19.0	11.0	5.8
3.2	1.90	14.9	0.15	3.4	1.0	0.51	5.13	3.61	82.4	1.9	17.4	19.5	5.2
5.1	1.04	8.5	0.01	5.8	39.5	0.98	9.92	3.73	66.7	4.8	8.6	2.5	8.6
4.3	1.75	12.2	-0.07	4.4	0.9	0.67	6.44	3.99	72.5	2.5	14.2	16.2	5.0
9.0	0.01	0.0	0.00	7.9	0.7	1.83	10.65	3.79	47.5	5.3	66.8	12.9	9.1
3.5	0.97	6.9	0.00	9.5	10.2	2.03	17.51	3.62	46.5	3.3	9.2	11.7	7.8
5.4	0.57	4.0	0.02	6.6	1.8	1.49	17.83	4.23	63.5	1.3	11.3	26.6	6.8
9.6	0.53	1.1	0.00	1.7	0.1	0.23	2.51	2.40	96.1	6.9	76.3	4.8	4.8
6.6	0.20	1.0	0.05	2.9	0.9	0.43	3.23	3.84	84.3	0.7	12.2	39.5	4.9
5.3	0.15	0.7	0.00	6.1	3.1	1.32	13.43	4.01	59.8	4.2	25.8	9.4	6.3
6.1	1.18	5.7	0.04	9.3	9.6	2.13	26.64	3.65	45.5	6.0	46.6	5.5	6.5
8.4	0.01	0.1	-0.01	4.8	0.2	1.05	10.31	3.96	77.6	5.1	42.3	10.1	5.9
4.1	1.33	9.1	0.15	4.1	5.0	0.71	6.52	3.46	78.6	4.2	12.4	7.3	6.4
9.6	0.03	0.0	-2.22	3.1	0.2	0.64	3.86	3.19	79.0	6.1	78.9	10.6	4.9
6.1	0.72	5.0	0.04	5.0	0.4	0.87	8.95	3.58	61.0	1.5	24.1	27.7	4.5
4.5	1.16	7.1	2.20	7.5	1.8	1.77	15.55	4.25	67.6	1.3	16.4	27.9	5.6
9.8	0.00	0.0	0.00	0.6	0.0	-0.27	-2.28	3.57	108.1	5.5	72.6	11.1	6.1
1.7	4.58	38.8	-0.09	2.1	0.1	0.07	1.98	3.56	100.6	5.2	32.5	5.1	0.3
6.7	0.53	3.5	-0.09	4.5	23.5	0.79	5.82	4.23	73.5	3.8	17.1	10.4	6.7
7.4	0.00	0.0	0.00	7.2	0.5	2.26	18.03	4.03	58.7	0.8	19.5	43.9	5.4
7.4	0.35	1.7	-0.05	3.5	0.4	0.39	2.44	3.38	80.1	1.9	35.8	31.8	5.8
4.6	1.44	8.1	0.23	0.8	0.1	0.11	1.14	3.48	93.5	2.0	25.5	21.2	3.3
10.0	na	0.0	na	4.0	0.0	-0.05	-0.06	2.43	85.8	10.0	747.7	0.0	5.6
3.8	2.32	17.1	0.21	6.2	31.2	1.14	10.69	4.91	69.7	3.3	10.5	12.3	6.2
7.5	0.38	2.9	0.09	3.2	2.9	0.38	3.86	3.69	86.0	3.1	3.7	12.5	7.2
5.8	0.47	3.4	0.72	8.5	3.1	1.98	22.08	4.50	64.1	1.5	19.9	25.3	6.2
5.7	0.32	2.1	0.21	4.2	1.6	0.86	8.66	4.40	74.6	1.7	15.1	21.1	5.3
8.8	0.00	0.0	0.00	9.3	3.3	1.65	19.53	1.95	75.7	5.3	18.5	0.2	5.4
7.8	1.02	4.4	0.00	4.4	0.1	0.67	5.28	4.63	82.5	5.5	33.8	4.0	5.9
4.6	1.92	12.7	0.62	2.1	0.1	0.16	1.57	3.22	84.8	1.1	27.9	49.4	5.6
7.6	0.12	0.7	-0.05	3.8	0.5	0.80	7.88	4.13	82.7	1.8	23.2	21.8	4.9
7.0	0.43	2.5	-0.05	5.6	1.0	1.37	15.10	4.70	71.1	2.4	32.4	20.7	6.6
9.0	0.33	1.5	-0.09	3.7	14.9	0.94	10.61	2.99	74.2	5.6	28.4	5.0	6.4
3.1	2.57	12.5	0.13	1.9	1.0	0.35	2.61	3.96	92.7	1.7	13.6	21.5	4.5
6.4	0.61	4.3	0.07	7.2	13.7	1.28	13.46	3.98	59.1	4.7	10.7	3.8	6.8
0.3	15.57	92.9	0.41	2.9	1.7	2.11	21.64	3.44	94.2	2.0	35.0	29.7	2.3
8.2	0.02	0.1	0.00	6.6	2.5	1.84	18.68	4.21	61.6	1.2	28.9	47.2	6.6
4.6	3.58	12.1	0.00	1.8	0.0	0.22	2.68	2.60	91.2	5.5	58.1	8.7	3.0
1.3	5.40	32.6	1.43	2.4	9.9	0.63	6.51	3.61	89.0	4.9	18.3	3.9	5.1
5.4	2.86	10.7	0.04	0.4	0.0	-0.10	-0.69	4.27	107.7	5.1	45.5	10.4	5.8
0.4	3.45	26.6	1.49	7.6	5.2	1.45	17.04	7.87	65.3	0.9	13.0	32.7	3.3
9.0	0.47	1.1	0.52	2.6	0.2	0.38	2.85	2.41	81.4	4.6	69.0	17.0	6.7
8.8	0.18	0.8	0.00	2.9	0.1	0.45	4.51	3.04	81.5	1.5	36.8	32.5	2.3
6.8	1.17	4.5	0.16	5.6	3.1	1.22	11.72	3.81	66.7	5.3	46.5	10.2	6.7
4.5	1.16	10.1	0.03	3.3	0.2	0.38	4.32	4.12	86.1	2.9	7.4	13.8	4.0
4.9	1.18	8.7	0.12	6.6	2.4	1.09	11.28	4.96	64.2	3.7	14.1	10.2	5.6
4.3	1.52	10.7	0.18	4.3	4.5	0.77	6.71	3.55	68.8	1.5	12.5	23.3	6.7
6.3	0.39	2.3	0.06	3.9	0.3	0.61	6.47	3.75	78.8	5.4	47.4	9.0	4.8
8.9	0.13	0.7	0.00	6.9	2.2	1.37	12.82	3.91	57.4	3.3	40.5	18.7	5.9
8.2	1.31	4.0	0.03	5.0	0.5	0.94	6.22	3.56	63.5	3.8	41.4	16.0	7.8
3.3	5.03	19.4	0.70	5.3	1.8	1.03	8.24	4.00	59.2	2.2	30.3	22.0	6.5

Name	City	State	Rating	2013 Rating	2012 Rating	Total Assets ($Mil)	One Year Asset Growth	Asset Mix (As a % of Total Assets) Comm-ercial Loans	Cons-umer Loans	Mort-gage Loans	Secur-ities	Capital-ization Index	Lever-age Ratio	Risk-Based Capital Ratio
ANNANDALE STATE BK	Annandale	MN	**B-**	B-	B-	131.4	-1.09	4.3	1.3	20.6	39.4	**10.0**	12.1	16.2
ANSTAFF BANK NA	Green Forest	AR	**B+**	B+	B	412.6	4.05	5.4	2.4	10.6	30.9	**9.6**	10.7	17.9
ANTHEM BANK & TRUST	Plaquemine	LA	**D**	D+	C-	133.0	16.32	6.5	1.4	14.5	36.1	**8.0**	9.7	17.0
ANTWERP EXCHANGE BANK CO	Antwerp	OH	**B-**	B-	B-	94.0	2.20	7.5	3.3	25.1	22.5	**7.9**	9.6	14.9
ANZ GUAM INC	Hagatna	GU	**C+**	B-	C	320.9	-3.36	12.1	2.6	14.8	0.0	**10.0**	14.3	41.5
APOLLO BANK	Miami	FL	**C-**	C-	C-	474.6	84.85	6.1	0.2	14.8	20.3	**7.5**	9.4	13.0
APOLLO TRUST CO	Apollo	PA	**B**	B	B-	150.6	-2.39	5.6	1.4	15.6	62.2	**10.0**	11.1	24.9
APPLE BANK FOR SAVINGS	New York	NY	**C+**	C+	C+	11688.2	-1.68	47.0	0.2	2.6	7.9	**4.1**	6.1	15.5
▼ APPLE CREEK BANKING CO	Apple Creek	OH	**C+**	B-	C+	130.3	21.10	4.0	0.6	22.7	17.1	**5.3**	7.3	12.5
APPLE RIVER STATE BK	Apple River	IL	**B-**	B-	C+	278.1	2.24	15.5	4.0	11.6	32.9	**7.7**	9.5	15.3
▼ APPLIED BANK	Newark	DE	**A**	A+	A+	282.7	53.16	0.3	0.0	3.3	0.0	**6.0**	8.0	41.6
▲ AQUESTA BANK	Cornelius	NC	**B-**	C+	C-	251.0	11.17	10.0	0.1	6.4	27.1	**6.2**	9.4	11.9
▲ ARBOR BANK	Nebraska City	NE	**C+**	C	C	243.1	7.38	7.2	2.0	12.8	23.5	**6.0**	8.0	11.8
ARCOLA FIRST BANK	Arcola	IL	**B+**	B+	A-	118.8	4.16	0.6	0.2	4.4	79.1	**9.6**	10.8	29.5
ARGENT TRUST CO NA	Ruston	LA	**U**	U	U	7.1	10.21	0.0	0.0	0.0	1.4	**10.0**	89.1	123.5
ARGENTINE FEDERAL SAVINGS	Kansas City	KS	**C**	C	C+	51.6	-6.68	0.0	0.4	67.8	11.7	**10.0**	13.6	27.7
ARIZONA BANK & TRUST	Phoenix	AZ	**B-**	B-	C+	471.7	13.61	14.5	1.7	21.7	17.3	**8.6**	10.1	14.6
ARKANSAS COUNTY BANK	De Witt	AR	**B**	B-	B-	180.9	3.02	5.4	3.6	13.8	30.5	**8.8**	10.2	16.8
ARLINGTON BANK	Upper Arlington	OH	**A-**	B+	C	268.8	3.76	1.8	0.5	42.7	7.4	**10.0**	11.7	18.5
ARLINGTON STATE BK	Arlington	MN	**B-**	B-	C+	56.1	1.53	2.7	1.6	4.6	41.3	**8.7**	10.1	21.6
▲ ARMED FORCES BANK NA	Fort Leavenworth	KS	**B**	C+	D+	1582.1	0.34	15.3	0.6	6.2	38.3	**10.0**	25.8	47.8
▲ ARMED FORCES BANK OF CA NA	San Diego	CA	**A**	B	B	16.6	-11.17	14.4	1.1	21.1	22.8	**10.0**	32.9	72.8
ARMSTRONG BANK	Muskogee	OK	**B+**	B+	B	652.8	4.27	5.8	7.7	19.1	18.4	**10.0**	12.9	18.7
ARMSTRONG COUNTY BLDG & LOAN	Ford City	PA	**C+**	C+	C	90.5	1.54	0.0	1.2	51.8	35.3	**10.0**	13.6	24.9
AROOSTOOK COUNTY FS&LA	Caribou	ME	**B-**	C+	B-	97.0	-1.05	4.5	2.5	65.0	14.5	**10.0**	11.8	22.2
▲ ARROWHEAD BANK	Llano	TX	**C+**	C	C+	147.7	9.45	5.1	4.1	11.7	21.4	**8.5**	10.0	17.6
ARTHUR STATE BK	Union	SC	**E-**	E-	E-	512.7	-0.57	5.8	1.6	23.3	13.4	**1.3**	5.7	8.3
ARTISANS BANK	Wilmington	DE	**E-**	E-	E+	478.1	1.59	5.0	0.2	15.0	24.7	**2.8**	6.3	9.8
ARUNDEL FSB	Glen Burnie	MD	**B-**	B-	B-	464.6	-1.42	0.0	0.0	51.6	41.1	**10.0**	13.1	33.0
ARVEST BANK	Fayetteville	AR	**C**	C-	D+	14954.7	7.10	8.5	5.8	16.2	27.8	**7.6**	9.4	16.5
ASHEVILLE SB SSB	Asheville	NC	**C**	C-	C	748.0	1.24	2.0	4.6	21.9	20.0	**10.0**	12.3	21.0
ASHTON STATE BK	Ashton	IA	**B+**	B+	B+	48.3	5.17	6.5	3.4	13.7	34.2	**9.8**	10.9	15.7
▼ ASHTON STATE BK	Ashton	NE	**D+**	D+	C-	22.8	-0.57	2.1	1.6	0.5	7.3	**6.6**	8.6	14.7
▲ ASIA BANK NA	Flushing	NY	**B+**	B-	C+	492.0	4.24	0.4	0.1	7.5	0.5	**10.0**	14.6	19.0
ASIAN BANK	Philadelphia	PA	**D**	D	E+	104.0	23.85	0.8	0.1	9.8	7.6	**7.4**	9.3	12.9
ASIAN PACIFIC NATIONAL BK	San Gabriel	CA	**B**	B-	B+	55.5	3.19	0.1	0.1	0.3	39.4	**10.0**	16.3	28.4
ASSOCIATED BANK NA	Green Bay	WI	**B-**	B-	C+	25498.2	9.03	20.4	1.8	20.5	21.9	**7.3**	9.2	13.8
ASSOCIATED TRUST CO NA	Green Bay	WI	**U**	U	U	35.7	33.07	0.0	0.0	0.0	2.8	**10.0**	89.2	167.0
ASTORIA BANK	Lake Success	NY	**C+**	C+	C	15376.2	-3.63	0.4	0.1	46.4	15.6	**9.3**	10.6	19.2
ASTRA BANK	Scandia	KS	**B**	B	B-	272.8	4.85	6.9	1.7	8.6	29.2	**6.2**	9.1	11.9
ATASCOSA NATIONAL BK	Pleasanton	TX	**C-**	C+	C	97.2	6.74	2.3	1.3	1.6	26.3	**5.3**	7.3	23.9
ATHENS FEDERAL COMMUNITY BANK	Athens	TN	**B**	B-	B	301.7	2.09	5.3	4.0	30.9	9.7	**10.0**	11.3	16.8
ATHENS STATE BK	Athens	IL	**B-**	B	B+	131.0	0.25	2.8	7.3	25.5	26.6	**7.6**	9.4	18.2
ATHOL SB	Athol	MA	**B-**	B-	B-	340.3	-1.12	1.2	4.0	43.0	34.7	**10.0**	13.9	28.1
ATKINS SB & TRUST	Atkins	IA	**B+**	B	B-	78.0	7.41	7.8	3.9	9.2	41.3	**9.8**	10.8	15.7
ATLANTA NATIONAL BK	Atlanta	IL	**C+**	C+	B-	61.2	-2.37	2.5	4.2	7.1	68.7	**10.0**	11.4	28.9
ATLANTIC CAPITAL BANK	Atlanta	GA	**C+**	C+	C+	1298.6	15.84	28.9	0.7	0.1	11.9	**6.1**	10.8	11.8
ATLANTIC COAST BANK	Jacksonville	FL	**E**	E-	E-	715.3	-0.07	3.6	7.4	34.1	25.8	**8.8**	10.2	17.8
ATLANTIC COMMUNITY BANK	Bluffton	SC	**D+**	D	D-	77.5	0.79	3.8	0.6	25.8	1.1	**6.9**	8.9	13.3
ATLANTIC COMMUNITY BANKERS BK	Camp Hill	PA	**B**	C+	C	534.3	-4.18	1.5	0.0	0.6	12.1	**10.0**	12.7	27.4
▲ ATLANTIC NATIONAL BK	Brunswick	GA	**B-**	C	D	142.5	-0.63	7.9	1.3	41.7	4.9	**9.8**	10.9	18.4
ATLANTIC STEWARDSHIP BANK	Midland Park	NJ	**C**	C-	D+	671.4	-2.36	3.6	0.1	15.4	28.6	**7.2**	9.1	14.3
ATLANTIC TRUST COMPANY NA	Atlanta	GA	**U**	U	B+	182.3	-4.71	0.0	0.0	0.0	0.0	**10.0**	69.4	104.0
AUBURN BANKING CO	Auburn	KY	**B-**	B-	C+	73.0	1.73	7.1	5.1	26.9	25.3	**6.7**	8.7	15.1
AUBURN SAVINGS BANK FSB	Auburn	ME	**D-**	D-	D	73.0	2.20	3.3	0.5	61.7	4.9	**6.0**	8.0	13.2
AUBURN STATE BK	Auburn	NE	**A-**	A-	A-	98.3	1.90	5.2	2.7	15.8	29.9	**10.0**	19.1	30.5
AUBURNBANK	Auburn	AL	**B**	B-	B-	782.0	4.95	6.5	1.5	13.2	33.9	**8.7**	10.1	18.2
AUDUBON SB	Audubon	NJ	**D-**	D-	D	183.0	-3.44	1.3	0.0	30.5	25.1	**4.0**	6.2	10.5
AUDUBON STATE BK	Audubon	IA	**B**	B	B	102.2	6.32	7.7	3.6	9.1	16.0	**6.2**	8.2	12.5
AUSTIN BANK TEXAS NA	Jacksonville	TX	**A**	A	A	1504.6	4.88	11.3	6.8	24.1	14.5	**10.0**	11.2	17.2

Arrows denote recent upgrades ▲ or downgrades ▼

Asset Quality Index	Adjusted Non-Performing Loans as a % of Total Loans	Adjusted Non-Performing Loans as a % of Capital	Net Charge-Offs Avg Loans	Profitability Index	Net Income ($Mil)	Return on Assets (R.O.A.)	Return on Equity (R.O.E.)	Net Interest Spread	Overhead Efficiency Ratio	Liquidity Index	Liquidity Ratio	Hot Money Ratio	Stability Index
5.2	4.54	17.7	0.01	**3.7**	0.8	0.82	6.94	3.49	77.0	**5.2**	36.2	7.1	**6.4**
4.8	2.20	10.7	0.06	**5.8**	4.0	1.30	12.06	3.66	65.0	**2.6**	29.4	18.6	**7.7**
3.4	3.28	17.6	0.09	**0.7**	-0.1	-0.15	-1.43	3.29	105.3	**2.2**	25.7	19.2	**5.1**
6.5	0.57	3.9	0.29	**3.9**	0.5	0.72	7.27	3.80	74.9	**4.3**	19.2	6.9	**5.6**
5.7	2.67	7.8	0.46	**2.5**	0.7	0.30	2.07	2.99	87.5	**6.2**	60.9	9.0	**6.0**
3.1	1.86	12.7	-0.01	**0.7**	-0.9	-1.23	-17.81	13.08	112.0	**2.4**	28.9	19.1	**3.6**
9.7	0.11	0.3	0.03	**4.4**	1.0	0.85	8.03	3.78	75.8	**6.0**	58.7	9.7	**6.9**
7.5	0.07	1.0	0.00	**3.7**	42.4	0.49	5.90	1.67	53.7	**1.8**	18.9	22.7	**6.2**
7.2	0.35	2.9	0.00	**3.9**	0.5	0.61	8.12	4.13	78.8	**5.4**	34.2	4.4	**3.2**
4.9	1.22	7.1	-0.06	**4.9**	2.5	1.20	13.21	3.56	64.4	**2.3**	21.8	18.2	**4.6**
9.4	0.00	0.0	0.01	**5.7**	3.1	0.86	9.55	1.44	59.2	**7.8**	73.8	0.4	**9.3**
6.1	0.53	3.2	0.02	**4.4**	1.3	0.73	7.91	3.98	74.1	**1.8**	27.0	24.5	**4.3**
4.4	1.54	12.2	-0.01	**3.3**	1.2	0.66	8.23	3.40	79.3	**3.1**	7.0	12.6	**3.7**
10.0	0.00	0.0	0.00	**5.3**	1.2	1.33	11.57	3.37	57.0	**6.3**	79.5	10.9	**8.0**
10.0	na	0.0	na	**9.5**	0.4	7.04	7.78	0.76	89.4	**4.0**	273.9	101.0	**5.4**
8.9	0.31	1.6	0.14	**2.2**	0.1	0.13	1.03	3.97	94.1	**3.0**	21.7	14.8	**6.1**
4.8	0.78	5.3	0.12	**4.9**	2.6	0.75	7.06	4.31	82.2	**2.8**	22.1	15.6	**5.3**
4.9	1.00	5.8	0.22	**5.4**	1.7	1.26	12.83	4.01	64.1	**1.9**	19.5	19.8	**6.6**
6.0	1.24	7.8	0.05	**7.1**	2.3	1.14	10.00	3.95	63.9	**1.8**	19.6	21.4	**6.7**
9.2	0.04	0.1	-0.02	**4.2**	0.4	1.01	9.53	3.48	68.3	**5.3**	59.5	11.6	**5.1**
8.0	1.94	3.1	-0.42	**8.5**	26.8	2.18	7.98	2.81	63.9	**5.7**	43.5	9.9	**9.3**
9.5	0.00	0.0	0.42	**1.0**	0.0	-0.27	-0.85	2.33	100.5	**7.2**	70.5	0.0	**8.5**
5.3	1.49	7.7	0.19	**9.6**	12.3	2.55	18.63	5.37	59.1	**1.7**	25.6	24.7	**9.1**
9.1	0.64	2.8	0.00	**2.6**	0.3	0.41	2.98	1.65	69.3	**2.0**	38.5	32.8	**6.6**
6.7	1.42	8.7	0.36	**3.5**	0.3	0.43	3.67	3.55	73.9	**3.3**	24.5	13.6	**5.8**
8.6	0.04	0.2	0.10	**3.5**	0.7	0.61	6.07	3.24	73.8	**5.5**	40.2	7.0	**5.1**
2.1	3.09	30.4	0.59	**2.2**	1.1	0.28	4.98	3.61	90.8	**3.5**	20.9	12.0	**0.3**
2.1	3.30	28.6	-0.06	**1.9**	1.5	0.40	7.03	3.22	90.4	**2.8**	25.6	16.4	**0.3**
9.3	0.73	3.1	0.10	**3.0**	1.1	0.32	2.49	2.64	77.2	**3.1**	48.8	25.7	**6.8**
3.1	2.32	13.0	0.16	**4.5**	85.8	0.78	7.15	3.03	78.8	**5.9**	33.0	5.3	**8.3**
7.0	1.15	5.8	0.07	**2.4**	2.1	0.37	3.09	2.91	91.3	**4.1**	33.3	12.3	**5.6**
5.0	3.16	16.8	0.15	**7.3**	0.6	1.61	15.05	3.58	47.1	**3.4**	37.0	16.8	**7.7**
4.7	1.94	10.2	0.04	**2.0**	0.0	0.11	1.27	3.52	61.7	**2.2**	43.4	26.7	**3.9**
5.9	0.70	3.8	0.08	**8.2**	4.2	1.15	8.07	4.31	50.3	**1.2**	16.8	28.9	**8.5**
1.3	3.21	25.1	-0.04	**2.2**	0.2	0.33	3.57	3.71	81.4	**1.3**	22.0	29.8	**2.5**
7.8	0.00	0.0	0.00	**3.7**	0.3	0.80	4.97	3.37	74.5	**1.5**	35.2	58.1	**7.9**
4.4	1.28	8.8	0.08	**4.6**	151.0	0.82	6.82	3.20	68.4	**5.0**	11.8	2.2	**9.3**
10.0	na	0.0	na	**8.0**	5.3	22.16	26.12	0.58	75.4	**4.0**	377.6	101.0	**6.3**
4.4	1.40	9.7	0.20	**3.6**	81.3	0.69	6.22	2.46	67.6	**3.8**	8.4	9.4	**7.6**
6.9	0.35	2.1	-0.01	**5.6**	2.5	1.28	13.71	4.06	66.1	**4.0**	23.6	9.6	**5.7**
10.0	0.00	0.0	0.00	**1.9**	0.2	0.27	3.56	1.38	86.8	**7.2**	92.4	5.8	**3.5**
4.4	2.15	13.8	0.32	**6.1**	2.2	0.98	8.78	4.53	72.4	**2.2**	7.8	17.2	**7.1**
5.0	1.41	7.9	0.17	**4.1**	0.9	0.89	9.50	3.47	73.8	**4.3**	41.9	14.0	**6.1**
9.4	0.35	1.4	0.14	**3.0**	1.2	0.46	3.21	2.95	85.0	**4.3**	45.0	14.8	**7.2**
8.6	0.03	0.2	-0.04	**7.1**	1.0	1.70	16.89	3.46	38.5	**3.5**	49.6	19.0	**5.8**
9.3	0.78	1.7	0.04	**3.3**	0.3	0.66	5.98	2.75	75.9	**6.0**	71.5	10.2	**6.3**
7.4	0.33	2.3	0.00	**3.8**	5.5	0.62	5.59	2.85	68.7	**2.6**	19.6	17.0	**7.5**
2.8	3.47	20.1	0.24	**0.8**	0.9	0.16	1.69	2.60	88.2	**2.2**	14.8	17.9	**2.2**
2.5	2.91	22.5	0.99	**2.6**	1.0	1.80	17.71	4.20	90.7	**1.4**	23.2	28.3	**3.0**
6.2	3.32	8.7	0.28	**4.5**	3.2	0.90	7.44	1.95	73.1	**3.7**	62.0	25.9	**6.5**
4.7	1.08	6.7	-0.12	**4.4**	1.2	1.13	10.84	3.29	80.6	**2.1**	18.8	18.9	**4.5**
4.3	1.04	6.5	0.02	**2.9**	2.2	0.44	4.72	3.51	81.8	**3.2**	28.6	15.4	**4.8**
6.5	na	0.0	na	**9.5**	5.2	4.69	5.29	0.47	87.0	**4.1**	119.7	64.9	**7.0**
4.7	1.78	12.7	0.04	**7.6**	1.0	1.78	25.31	4.06	58.3	**2.2**	13.3	17.6	**6.1**
2.8	2.48	23.4	1.18	**0.3**	-0.3	-0.60	-7.26	3.77	91.6	**1.2**	6.1	26.2	**3.0**
8.8	0.59	1.8	-0.05	**6.0**	0.9	1.20	6.45	3.53	53.6	**4.0**	30.9	11.8	**8.1**
6.1	0.73	3.5	0.14	**5.0**	5.7	0.99	10.10	3.17	58.5	**2.3**	32.5	22.7	**5.4**
4.8	1.65	15.4	0.20	**0.0**	-0.2	-0.15	-2.53	2.75	124.6	**3.5**	6.7	10.6	**2.1**
5.2	0.66	5.1	0.00	**7.6**	1.3	1.63	18.96	3.55	62.5	**2.1**	20.3	18.9	**6.8**
7.2	0.43	2.6	0.36	**7.4**	12.7	1.15	9.81	4.21	61.5	**3.4**	16.1	12.6	**9.6**

Name	City	State	Rating	2013 Rating	2012 Rating	Total Assets ($Mil)	One Year Asset Growth	Asset Mix (As a % of Total Assets) Commercial Loans	Consumer Loans	Mortgage Loans	Securities	Capitalization Index	Leverage Ratio	Risk-Based Capital Ratio
▲ AUSTIN CAPITAL BANK SSB	Austin	TX	**B**	C	C-	70.2	25.17	5.5	0.0	30.4	3.4	**9.1**	10.4	15.6
AUSTIN COUNTY STATE BK	Bellville	TX	**B**	B	B-	117.6	21.94	17.0	3.0	26.7	15.6	**7.5**	9.3	14.3
▼ AUTO CLUB TRUST FSB	Dearborn	MI	**D**	C-	B-	75.7	13.33	0.0	6.2	35.1	51.7	**10.0**	51.2	109.9
AVB BANK	Broken Arrow	OK	**C+**	C+	B-	265.3	8.87	18.9	0.6	6.9	20.3	**10.0**	13.7	17.7
▲ AVENUE BANK	Nashville	TN	**C+**	C+	C-	973.4	15.79	18.7	0.4	8.1	22.0	**7.0**	9.2	12.5
AVIDBANK	Palo Alto	CA	**B-**	B-	B-	484.4	0.25	23.2	0.5	0.9	16.3	**7.2**	10.2	12.7
AVIDIA BANK	Hudson	MA	**C+**	C+	C-	1171.5	3.39	12.0	0.6	28.1	19.1	**5.9**	7.9	11.7
AVON CO-OP BANK	Avon	MA	**C-**	C	C	81.7	8.12	0.2	1.5	68.4	16.3	**9.6**	10.7	22.2
AVON STATE BK	Avon	MN	**B-**	B	B-	107.3	0.95	2.8	2.8	26.7	47.4	**10.0**	12.6	30.3
AXIOM BANK	Maitland	FL	**B**	B-	C	696.3	16.29	0.7	0.0	65.4	4.5	**10.0**	12.9	25.4
B & L BANK	Lexington	MO	**C**	C-	D+	122.8	-5.65	2.3	1.7	33.8	32.0	**10.0**	11.6	22.7
BAC FLORIDA BANK	Coral Gables	FL	**C-**	D+	D	1536.0	12.41	6.6	0.4	56.1	3.9	**6.4**	8.4	18.8
▲ BADGER BANK	Fort Atkinson	WI	**A-**	B	B-	117.1	2.14	3.9	3.8	30.0	21.3	**10.0**	11.1	19.1
BAILEYVILLE STATE BK	Seneca	KS	**C-**	D+	D+	40.6	5.23	10.3	2.3	13.9	36.0	**7.0**	9.0	15.3
BAKER-BOYER NATIONAL BK	Walla Walla	WA	**B**	B+	B	554.2	3.72	9.5	1.6	12.2	37.5	**6.5**	8.5	14.6
BALBOA THRIFT & LOAN ASSN	Chula Vista	CA	**B-**	C+	C+	206.1	1.03	0.1	80.1	0.9	0.0	**10.0**	16.7	18.8
BALDWIN STATE BK	Baldwin City	KS	**C**	C	C-	71.5	-5.23	4.5	5.9	15.4	46.5	**8.0**	9.7	24.1
BALLINGER NATIONAL BK	Ballinger	TX	**C+**	C+	B-	44.8	0.41	4.9	4.5	10.5	46.2	**8.9**	10.2	23.6
BALLSTON SPA NATIONAL BK	Ballston Spa	NY	**C+**	C	D+	415.4	-0.43	4.5	5.7	30.5	17.4	**7.4**	9.2	15.0
BALLY SB	Bally	PA	**C-**	C-	C-	51.1	0.15	0.1	0.0	40.9	20.0	**6.0**	8.0	25.0
BALTIC STATE BK	Baltic	OH	**C**	B	B-	44.4	-0.45	5.4	5.4	50.9	16.3	**9.8**	10.9	17.7
▲ BANAMEX USA	Los Angeles	CA	**B-**	C+	B-	1151.0	-10.94	13.2	5.5	0.1	27.0	**10.0**	13.5	38.6
▲ BANC OF CALIFORNIA NA	Irvine	CA	**B**	B-	C+	4537.4	71.40	7.6	0.6	51.2	6.8	**8.2**	9.8	15.8
BANCCENTRAL NA	Alva	OK	**C+**	B-	C	492.0	54.57	10.2	1.0	2.5	58.8	**4.9**	6.9	14.1
BANCFIRST	Oklahoma City	OK	**B**	B	B	6386.7	8.12	12.1	4.2	11.6	8.2	**6.2**	8.2	13.5
BANCO DO BRASIL AMERICAS	Miami	FL	**C-**	D	C-	232.5	108.66	3.7	1.6	23.0	19.7	**10.0**	14.0	38.9
BANCO POPULAR DE PUERTO RICO	San Juan	PR	**D+**	D+	D+	26483.0	-0.74	6.5	12.5	24.4	15.1	**9.0**	10.3	16.4
▼ BANCO POPULAR NORTH AMERICA	New York	NY	**D+**	C	C-	7133.4	-19.05	2.7	1.3	17.1	25.0	**10.0**	15.6	27.3
▼ BANCO SANTANDER PUERTO RICO	San Juan	PR	**D+**	C-	C-	5890.8	-12.12	24.9	8.6	24.3	2.9	**10.0**	14.2	24.6
BANCORP BANK	Wilmington	DE	**C-**	C	C	4278.8	7.65	8.1	9.4	5.0	35.9	**5.5**	7.5	12.2
BANCORPSOUTH BANK	Tupelo	MS	**B**	B-	C	13063.9	1.08	11.8	2.1	17.9	16.9	**8.7**	10.2	14.0
▲ BANCROFT STATE BK	Bancroft	WI	**C-**	D	D+	69.4	1.39	7.2	3.7	24.0	18.5	**7.2**	9.1	15.1
BANDERA BANK	Bandera	TX	**B**	B	B+	50.4	3.58	4.7	5.1	33.1	7.4	**10.0**	12.0	26.8
BANESCO USA	Coral Gables	FL	**C-**	C	D+	885.2	9.76	11.1	0.0	9.9	25.0	**8.1**	9.7	14.9
BANGOR SB	Bangor	ME	**B-**	B-	B-	3045.2	0.24	7.1	0.7	24.3	24.1	**8.6**	10.1	15.6
BANK & TRUST CO	Litchfield	IL	**B-**	B-	C+	265.3	-1.14	7.0	6.7	17.7	25.8	**8.6**	10.1	15.4
BANK & TRUST SSB	Del Rio	TX	**B+**	B+	B+	426.8	2.47	6.1	2.0	29.5	34.9	**6.6**	8.6	18.0
BANK @LANTEC	Virginia Beach	VA	**C-**	C	C-	109.9	14.72	1.2	0.8	44.9	9.4	**9.3**	10.5	16.2
BANK 1ST	West Union	IA	**B**	B+	B	122.6	3.23	4.8	2.5	14.0	32.4	**8.4**	10.0	17.4
▲ BANK 2	Oklahoma City	OK	**A-**	B	B	114.3	5.07	3.9	1.2	20.1	21.7	**10.0**	12.5	20.2
BANK 21	Carrollton	MO	**C+**	C	C	89.0	49.05	14.4	1.8	28.2	17.9	**6.1**	8.1	12.7
BANK 7	Oklahoma City	OK	**B+**	B-	C	447.6	34.50	38.5	1.6	6.9	0.4	**6.3**	9.2	12.0
BANK CBO	Oregon	MO	**D+**	D+	C	58.9	20.75	4.7	0.8	14.7	35.1	**7.4**	9.3	15.9
▼ BANK FEDERATED ST MICRONESIA	Pohnpei	FM	**B**	B+	A-	122.7	9.70	9.5	10.3	2.1	19.1	**10.0**	16.0	41.2
BANK FIRST NATIONAL	Manitowoc	WI	**B+**	B+	B	1092.4	5.49	18.7	2.1	18.0	9.9	**6.0**	8.7	11.8
BANK FORWARD	Hannaford	ND	**C+**	C-	D	486.8	-0.51	8.0	2.5	12.8	8.5	**5.4**	8.8	11.3
BANK INDEPENDENT	Sheffield	AL	**B+**	B+	B	1140.6	4.73	18.7	2.1	20.0	4.2	**8.3**	11.4	13.6
BANK IOWA	West Des Moines	IA	**B-**	B-	B	1113.7	0.08	8.1	1.3	9.7	27.0	**7.2**	9.1	14.0
BANK LEUMI USA	New York	NY	**C**	C	C	5111.0	-1.27	35.2	0.0	0.6	15.8	**8.8**	10.2	14.9
BANK MIDWEST	Spirit Lake	IA	**B**	B+	B	695.3	0.15	15.6	1.2	7.2	14.6	**7.6**	9.8	13.0
BANK MUTUAL	Brown Deer	WI	**B-**	C	C-	2326.3	-0.23	8.8	1.0	25.8	21.6	**10.0**	11.4	18.3
BANK NA	McAlester	OK	**B**	B+	B+	401.5	1.63	4.4	3.4	15.2	30.8	**6.8**	8.8	16.4
BANK NORTHWEST	Hamilton	MO	**B**	B	B+	105.3	6.72	16.7	2.4	13.9	12.2	**6.5**	8.9	12.2
BANK OF ABBEVILLE & TRUST CO	Abbeville	LA	**B-**	B-	B	175.2	2.65	4.7	2.7	9.4	58.7	**10.0**	15.9	38.0
BANK OF ADVANCE	Advance	MO	**A**	A	A	306.1	4.83	6.5	7.7	29.6	19.0	**10.0**	15.6	22.8
▲ BANK OF AGRICULTURE & COMMERCE	Stockton	CA	**C**	C-	D	491.5	-2.14	7.9	1.8	6.7	29.0	**8.1**	9.8	15.0
BANK OF AKRON	Akron	NY	**B**	B	B-	266.3	6.32	10.3	1.1	13.5	19.1	**7.5**	9.5	13.0
BANK OF ALAPAHA	Alapaha	GA	**B**	B+	B-	134.8	5.91	18.3	7.2	13.0	17.4	**8.5**	11.4	13.8
BANK OF ALMA	Alma	WI	**A-**	B+	B-	196.2	-0.57	3.6	1.0	10.3	49.1	**10.0**	37.5	66.7
▲ BANK OF AMERICA CALIFORNIA NA	San Francisco	CA	**C**	C-	C+	25336.0	-0.95	0.0	0.0	72.2	0.0	**8.0**	9.7	24.7

Asset Quality Index	Adjusted Non-Performing Loans as a % of Total Loans	Adjusted Non-Performing Loans as a % of Capital	Net Charge-Offs / Avg Loans	Profitability Index	Net Income ($Mil)	Return on Assets (R.O.A.)	Return on Equity (R.O.E.)	Net Interest Spread	Overhead Efficiency Ratio	Liquidity Index	Liquidity Ratio	Hot Money Ratio	Stability Index
8.4	0.00	0.0	-0.01	5.1	0.9	1.98	17.94	4.00	75.2	1.2	18.1	30.5	5.8
7.4	0.19	1.3	0.00	5.9	1.1	1.38	14.98	4.52	61.7	1.4	24.9	28.4	5.8
9.6	0.00	0.0	0.00	0.0	-5.4	-10.19	-17.27	2.34	377.6	4.6	87.4	19.1	5.8
4.8	2.82	13.0	-0.66	3.2	0.9	0.45	3.19	4.08	79.7	1.2	6.6	27.0	6.4
7.1	0.36	2.5	0.00	3.4	4.3	0.62	6.69	3.32	71.2	1.7	29.4	29.3	5.0
4.5	2.17	11.9	-0.02	3.8	1.8	0.49	4.85	3.60	77.0	5.0	36.8	8.4	5.1
4.2	1.81	16.4	0.09	3.8	5.7	0.67	7.60	3.49	73.4	1.7	12.0	21.5	6.6
5.6	1.68	11.9	0.02	2.0	0.2	0.34	3.06	2.99	90.0	1.5	21.6	27.0	6.3
6.2	2.71	8.8	0.39	3.4	0.6	0.75	6.83	2.96	71.9	6.2	61.9	9.3	5.7
5.1	3.49	18.5	0.14	4.1	3.1	0.63	4.61	3.68	71.5	1.1	24.0	33.4	7.5
4.4	3.91	16.9	0.06	2.5	0.4	0.39	3.31	3.01	88.2	4.2	36.5	12.9	5.5
2.6	3.39	28.3	0.09	3.8	7.7	0.69	8.18	2.76	67.4	0.8	16.8	45.4	5.8
7.8	0.44	2.4	0.12	6.4	1.0	1.10	9.66	4.17	64.6	4.6	29.2	8.3	5.4
7.0	0.53	3.3	-0.02	3.2	0.2	0.62	7.24	3.40	77.9	4.1	35.8	13.0	3.0
6.1	1.11	6.1	0.25	5.1	4.0	0.95	11.34	3.31	75.1	5.7	37.9	4.7	6.6
3.3	1.15	5.9	1.18	9.0	1.8	1.20	7.38	8.72	62.7	0.5	8.3	52.6	8.4
5.1	1.58	6.4	0.49	3.1	0.4	0.69	7.12	2.75	79.1	5.4	39.9	7.3	4.4
3.3	4.61	16.3	0.07	3.8	0.3	0.92	9.13	3.55	81.2	4.4	61.9	16.8	6.0
3.5	2.24	15.1	0.09	3.7	2.1	0.69	7.85	3.47	75.2	4.8	15.4	3.6	4.8
3.3	4.63	25.7	0.94	4.2	0.3	0.83	10.42	2.12	45.7	4.0	54.4	17.4	4.0
8.9	0.11	0.7	0.09	3.2	0.1	0.34	3.09	4.61	92.3	3.7	24.3	11.5	6.4
9.2	0.62	1.3	1.43	0.0	-77.1	-8.65	-49.56	2.11	578.4	6.1	71.1	12.1	6.5
4.8	1.33	11.3	0.01	4.7	30.1	0.99	9.68	3.96	82.5	3.1	12.0	13.4	6.9
7.9	0.57	2.6	0.00	3.3	2.8	0.92	10.15	3.68	84.6	3.3	49.5	22.6	5.6
6.6	0.70	4.7	0.03	5.2	47.5	1.00	11.47	3.07	65.4	5.8	33.1	6.1	8.0
7.6	0.00	0.0	0.02	5.5	4.8	3.10	15.26	2.60	73.9	5.9	60.9	10.5	4.7
0.9	6.47	36.9	1.37	3.8	167.0	0.83	6.79	5.58	61.2	2.2	12.4	18.0	7.0
5.2	1.04	4.0	1.32	1.0	-80.8	-1.28	-7.00	3.22	135.3	3.3	13.3	12.5	5.5
0.9	6.01	29.7	1.07	4.3	33.4	0.72	5.15	4.16	58.4	4.0	20.4	10.0	6.5
4.8	1.56	10.2	0.07	2.4	-16.4	0.26	3.78	1.57	88.6	7.5	50.7	0.2	4.6
5.9	0.54	3.7	0.13	5.1	91.0	0.94	7.77	3.59	73.9	3.8	7.4	9.2	8.1
4.5	1.69	11.1	-0.23	2.6	0.2	0.38	4.38	3.70	86.9	3.6	30.0	13.6	2.8
5.7	2.55	11.9	0.19	4.8	0.4	1.09	9.06	3.98	73.3	3.7	40.1	16.6	7.4
4.7	1.57	10.0	0.06	1.9	0.4	0.07	0.73	4.22	94.8	2.7	34.1	19.3	4.5
6.7	0.74	4.7	0.15	3.8	15.7	0.69	6.54	3.44	73.9	3.4	5.5	11.4	8.2
5.6	0.50	3.0	-0.17	4.1	1.3	0.67	6.56	3.90	74.4	2.5	25.3	17.4	5.6
8.8	0.16	1.0	-0.02	5.5	4.1	1.31	13.28	3.73	70.5	3.1	24.5	14.5	6.6
5.2	1.23	8.9	0.04	1.9	0.1	0.13	1.11	3.48	94.1	3.7	15.4	10.5	5.5
8.7	0.07	0.4	0.01	4.4	0.9	0.95	9.84	3.56	70.8	4.7	42.0	12.2	6.7
5.9	0.76	3.5	0.00	5.3	0.8	0.74	5.71	4.23	82.3	0.9	24.6	41.7	7.4
8.5	0.00	0.0	-0.05	4.6	0.7	1.05	11.97	3.74	73.4	3.4	20.0	12.5	3.1
4.9	0.73	5.9	0.07	10.0	7.9	2.41	26.49	5.49	47.7	0.8	17.7	36.8	7.0
9.0	0.00	0.0	0.38	5.3	0.4	0.98	12.80	3.86	58.0	1.5	12.1	23.6	1.7
3.8	9.30	18.6	0.12	5.0	0.9	1.03	6.52	4.41	72.9	5.1	74.1	16.3	8.8
7.1	0.42	3.5	0.12	6.8	9.6	1.20	12.40	3.72	52.0	3.7	7.0	9.8	8.4
3.4	1.24	10.6	0.07	4.7	3.8	1.05	10.66	3.93	82.0	3.3	2.8	11.5	5.0
4.7	1.23	8.7	0.30	6.0	8.6	1.04	8.34	5.95	74.4	3.4	6.4	11.1	9.4
6.3	1.00	6.4	0.03	4.3	8.3	0.99	11.40	3.45	65.6	5.2	30.3	8.6	7.2
3.5	3.02	19.1	0.33	2.4	8.2	0.21	1.97	2.86	79.4	1.4	25.1	49.4	7.2
5.2	1.08	7.6	0.02	6.3	7.6	1.47	13.43	4.43	68.6	3.7	8.3	9.8	8.0
7.1	0.68	3.9	0.13	3.8	11.3	0.65	5.54	3.26	72.6	4.4	21.6	8.2	6.9
4.7	1.78	9.5	0.07	6.2	4.6	1.50	17.63	3.79	65.1	4.5	49.7	14.9	5.3
5.2	0.48	3.9	0.23	9.1	1.7	2.16	25.20	4.62	52.8	2.7	11.2	15.2	6.8
8.2	2.26	3.8	-0.06	3.4	0.9	0.65	4.42	3.31	78.4	3.8	67.0	24.9	7.1
6.1	1.39	6.3	0.10	10.0	5.9	2.58	17.30	4.93	47.6	2.4	10.6	16.5	9.5
3.5	1.74	10.1	0.29	3.3	2.7	0.72	7.88	3.99	80.5	5.1	33.2	6.7	5.2
5.3	1.02	7.0	0.01	4.5	1.5	0.78	7.73	4.28	71.9	2.8	13.3	14.9	6.9
5.9	0.62	3.4	0.24	5.2	0.9	0.92	8.35	3.86	61.9	1.5	19.6	25.2	6.1
5.5	7.23	8.9	0.17	9.5	3.2	2.17	5.95	4.19	21.5	7.2	78.0	5.3	8.8
2.8	4.90	33.3	0.17	9.8	385.0	1.85	22.03	3.11	16.8	6.0	26.8	1.0	7.3

Name	City	State	Rating	2013 Rating	2012 Rating	Total Assets ($Mil)	One Year Asset Growth	Asset Mix (As a % of Total Assets) Commercial Loans	Consumer Loans	Mortgage Loans	Securities	Capitalization Index	Leverage Ratio	Risk-Based Capital Ratio
▲ BANK OF AMERICA NA	Charlotte	NC	**C**	C-	C	1524575.0	5.96	13.2	4.9	14.2	21.0	**7.0**	9.0	13.9
▼ BANK OF AMERICAN FORK	American Fork	UT	**B**	B	C+	1077.2	4.59	10.0	0.8	5.3	26.1	**10.0**	11.6	16.6
BANK OF ANGUILLA	Anguilla	MS	**B**	B-	B	128.8	4.92	7.0	6.3	5.5	25.7	**10.0**	11.1	15.6
▲ BANK OF ANN ARBOR	Ann Arbor	MI	**B**	B-	C+	1071.3	12.97	13.0	1.0	9.2	14.1	**5.4**	7.4	12.2
▼ BANK OF ASH GROVE	Ash Grove	MO	**B-**	B+	A-	71.0	-2.02	13.2	0.9	15.7	28.9	**6.5**	8.5	12.9
BANK OF AUGUSTA	Augusta	AR	**B**	B	B-	79.1	7.20	10.3	3.8	14.7	28.0	**9.6**	10.7	17.1
BANK OF BAKER	Baker	MT	**A-**	A-	B+	157.1	16.44	12.5	1.9	6.2	21.1	**6.3**	8.4	14.3
BANK OF BARTLETT	Bartlett	TN	**D-**	D-	D-	350.7	0.06	3.8	1.6	12.1	30.6	**3.3**	5.7	10.1
BANK OF BEARDEN	Bearden	AR	**B**	B+	B+	42.9	3.26	13.9	8.1	14.3	25.5	**10.0**	13.9	25.8
BANK OF BEAVER CITY	Beaver	OK	**B-**	B-	C+	143.9	0.35	10.8	2.9	14.9	37.3	**6.5**	8.6	14.8
BANK OF BELLE GLADE	Belle Glade	FL	**C**	C	C-	82.7	-4.41	3.7	1.0	13.4	45.6	**7.0**	9.0	27.7
BANK OF BELLEVILLE	Belleville	IL	**B-**	B-	C+	114.1	7.58	13.9	0.7	14.5	15.9	**6.6**	8.6	12.9
BANK OF BENNINGTON	Bennington	NE	**C**	C-	B-	76.6	5.63	20.2	2.3	13.9	8.5	**10.0**	13.1	15.2
BANK OF BENNINGTON	Bennington	VT	**C+**	C+	C+	365.7	6.61	2.2	0.3	56.9	11.3	**7.7**	9.4	17.0
▲ BANK OF BENOIT	Benoit	MS	**C-**	D+	D	18.1	3.95	5.2	10.8	3.5	35.2	**10.0**	11.2	30.9
BANK OF BILLINGS	Billings	MO	**C**	C	C+	53.0	-1.46	6.4	4.2	31.3	10.2	**8.0**	9.6	15.2
BANK OF BIRD-IN-HAND	Bird in Hand	PA	**D**			64.2	-9999	1.6	0.1	17.4	0.0	**10.0**	24.3	32.5
BANK OF BIRMINGHAM	Birmingham	MI	**C**	C	C+	204.5	12.31	11.8	1.1	7.2	2.8	**4.2**	8.5	10.6
▲ BANK OF BLUE VALLEY	Overland Park	KS	**C**	D+	D	631.0	-0.19	20.0	1.2	6.3	15.4	**9.3**	11.4	14.4
BANK OF BLUFFS	Bluffs	IL	**B-**	B-	B	60.4	7.51	4.3	6.3	14.9	43.1	**10.0**	14.3	24.8
BANK OF BOLIVAR	Bolivar	MO	**C+**	B-	C	217.1	5.69	5.0	2.6	22.7	15.0	**8.7**	10.2	14.6
BANK OF BOLIVAR COUNTY	Shelby	MS	**D+**	D+	C+	15.9	-5.31	6.3	2.2	1.1	61.1	**10.0**	11.3	37.5
BANK OF BOTETOURT	Buchanan	VA	**C+**	C-	D	313.4	1.78	5.3	4.1	24.2	7.4	**7.8**	9.5	14.0
BANK OF BOURBONNAIS	Bourbonnais	IL	**B**	B	B-	90.9	5.86	3.1	2.9	8.4	16.7	**6.9**	8.9	16.9
BANK OF BOZEMAN	Bozeman	MT	**D+**	D	D-	64.1	1.24	11.5	1.3	15.9	6.7	**8.8**	10.2	14.6
BANK OF BRENHAM NA	Brenham	TX	**B+**	B+	B	123.1	23.43	5.1	2.4	17.3	49.5	**6.9**	9.0	23.9
▼ BANK OF BREWTON	Brewton	AL	**C**	B-	B+	51.9	-5.55	9.9	4.9	2.1	61.3	**10.0**	18.3	36.2
BANK OF BRIDGER NA	Bridger	MT	**B**	B	B-	364.7	8.64	6.2	3.4	8.5	45.0	**6.8**	8.8	16.7
BANK OF BRODHEAD	Brodhead	WI	**B+**	B+	B+	139.4	1.20	5.4	1.7	9.1	43.9	**10.0**	13.6	24.9
BANK OF BROOKFIELD-PURDIN NA	Brookfield	MO	**B-**	B-	B-	88.1	4.76	1.4	1.7	7.0	52.8	**10.0**	11.0	27.8
BANK OF BROOKHAVEN	Brookhaven	MS	**B+**	B+	B	139.3	3.70	7.8	3.3	10.5	39.1	**10.0**	11.3	18.9
BANK OF BUFFALO	Buffalo	KY	**A-**	B	B+	73.1	1.52	2.0	6.7	26.4	40.8	**10.0**	11.1	18.3
BANK OF BURLINGTON	Burlington	CO	**C+**	C+	B-	88.0	24.42	4.0	0.5	0.1	52.8	**5.5**	7.5	26.2
BANK OF CADIZ & TRUST CO	Cadiz	KY	**B-**	C+	C	106.4	3.97	4.2	4.1	29.7	27.6	**6.4**	8.4	16.3
BANK OF CAIRO & MOBERLY	Moberly	MO	**A**	A	A	97.4	0.05	10.3	3.0	23.9	22.6	**10.0**	17.2	25.9
BANK OF CALHOUN COUNTY	Hardin	IL	**C-**	C-	C-	69.4	3.76	1.4	2.0	25.6	41.6	**5.9**	7.9	16.8
▲ BANK OF CAMDEN	Camden	TN	**C+**	C+	B-	335.6	22.25	1.5	2.4	42.3	8.2	**10.0**	13.1	19.9
▲ BANK OF CAMILLA	Camilla	GA	**C**	C-	D+	94.7	-8.78	4.5	2.1	14.2	28.5	**10.0**	14.4	24.4
BANK OF CANEYVILLE	Caneyville	KY	**C+**	C+	C+	49.9	1.51	1.5	1.7	14.5	58.2	**6.7**	8.7	20.1
BANK OF CANTON	Canton	MA	**C**	C	C-	640.4	3.66	2.8	0.3	46.9	11.7	**6.8**	8.9	15.3
BANK OF CAPE COD	Hyannis	MA	**C**	C	C-	243.8	16.81	12.7	0.0	4.5	6.7	**7.4**	10.1	12.8
BANK OF CARBONDALE	Carbondale	IL	**B-**	B	C+	235.3	6.69	7.6	2.7	14.2	25.9	**10.0**	11.7	18.1
BANK OF CASHTON	Cashton	WI	**C+**	C	C+	77.8	8.97	14.9	1.6	10.8	31.9	**7.7**	9.5	16.4
BANK OF CASTILE	Castile	NY	**B**	B	B-	1130.9	4.38	13.5	0.8	15.4	26.4	**5.8**	7.8	11.8
▲ BANK OF CATTARAUGUS	Cattaraugus	NY	**C-**	D+	C-	18.6	7.01	2.7	6.6	24.6	28.3	**7.2**	9.1	17.5
BANK OF CAVE CITY	Cave City	AR	**B-**	B-	B-	96.9	2.12	2.5	4.3	25.9	24.0	**8.6**	10.1	16.3
BANK OF CENTRAL FLORIDA	Lakeland	FL	**B-**	B-	B-	341.6	6.87	18.5	1.4	15.2	18.5	**9.3**	10.6	14.9
BANK OF CHARLES TOWN	Charles Town	WV	**C-**	C-	D+	309.4	5.40	3.1	2.5	35.3	10.2	**8.4**	9.9	14.4
BANK OF CHARLOTTE COUNTY	Phenix	VA	**A-**	A-	A-	127.8	3.35	6.1	3.8	39.3	15.9	**10.0**	13.3	19.7
BANK OF CHEROKEE COUNTY	Hulbert	OK	**C+**	C+	C+	102.7	-0.58	3.8	7.5	22.5	20.1	**6.0**	8.0	13.7
BANK OF CHESTNUT	Chestnut	IL	**D+**	D+	D	16.3	-4.36	4.1	10.4	29.1	30.0	**8.9**	10.3	17.4
BANK OF CLARENDON	Manning	SC	**A-**	A-	A-	212.9	4.09	6.8	3.1	14.4	25.3	**10.0**	14.5	23.9
BANK OF CLARKE COUNTY	Berryville	VA	**A-**	A-	B	602.0	3.67	4.9	2.2	31.3	15.9	**10.0**	12.2	17.7
BANK OF CLARKS	Clarks	NE	**D+**	D+	C-	36.5	-1.81	6.8	12.0	4.4	10.6	**8.7**	10.2	14.9
BANK OF CLARKSON	Clarkson	KY	**A-**	A-	A-	117.8	-1.57	0.7	4.0	28.0	40.6	**9.8**	10.9	23.6
BANK OF CLEVELAND	Cleveland	TN	**B**	B	B-	221.7	-0.29	2.4	0.7	18.1	0.0	**10.0**	17.0	23.1
BANK OF CLOVIS	Clovis	NM	**B**	B	B	203.4	15.65	11.4	3.1	5.5	32.6	**10.0**	11.0	25.4
BANK OF COLORADO	Fort Collins	CO	**B+**	B+	B	2675.4	6.77	3.7	1.1	11.0	28.1	**7.1**	9.0	13.8
BANK OF COLUMBIA	Columbia	KY	**D**	D	D	125.6	-0.69	10.6	4.5	17.2	23.4	**9.3**	10.5	15.6
BANK OF COMMERCE	Greenwood	MS	**B**	B	B	337.1	13.72	5.8	4.3	20.9	19.3	**6.1**	8.2	12.6

Asset Quality Index	Adjusted Non-Performing Loans as a % of Total Loans	Adjusted Non-Performing Loans as a % of Capital	Net Charge-Offs Avg Loans	Profitability Index	Net Income ($Mil)	Return on Assets (R.O.A.)	Return on Equity (R.O.E.)	Net Interest Spread	Overhead Efficiency Ratio	Liquidity Index	Liquidity Ratio	Hot Money Ratio	Stability Index
3.0	2.64	14.6	0.18	**4.5**	9545.0	0.88	7.03	2.44	70.9	**6.5**	41.8	3.7	**9.5**
4.5	1.42	7.5	0.16	**7.5**	10.1	1.29	11.27	4.42	61.0	**5.5**	32.2	7.3	**8.3**
5.0	1.44	6.7	0.80	**4.2**	0.7	0.78	7.42	4.41	76.5	**1.2**	15.8	29.6	**5.6**
8.0	0.33	2.5	-0.02	**6.2**	8.9	1.21	16.60	3.81	58.3	**4.9**	29.6	10.0	**5.4**
5.4	0.93	6.2	0.00	**3.5**	0.2	0.83	6.16	2.82	72.4	**2.6**	29.6	18.8	**6.4**
5.6	0.90	4.9	0.18	**5.6**	0.6	1.04	10.48	4.93	68.4	**1.8**	28.1	26.5	**6.2**
7.3	0.65	4.0	-0.03	**9.1**	2.2	1.94	22.84	4.25	45.8	**4.9**	23.4	3.6	**6.6**
3.3	2.66	21.7	0.23	**1.2**	-0.1	-0.04	-0.56	3.04	100.4	**4.5**	28.2	8.0	**1.7**
6.5	1.86	6.0	0.01	**4.1**	0.3	0.93	6.86	3.21	68.8	**4.2**	43.9	14.7	**7.7**
5.5	1.24	7.2	-0.02	**5.2**	1.4	1.28	16.02	4.02	68.4	**2.4**	33.4	22.3	**5.3**
7.9	0.73	2.3	0.55	**2.6**	0.2	0.30	3.63	2.24	81.5	**6.9**	57.7	1.2	**4.3**
8.6	0.09	0.7	0.00	**4.2**	0.6	0.68	8.25	3.54	71.1	**1.4**	20.3	27.4	**4.9**
4.5	1.35	7.2	-0.06	**4.9**	0.4	0.73	7.24	3.94	79.1	**4.7**	16.8	4.6	**5.5**
5.6	1.05	8.1	0.07	**3.6**	1.8	0.70	7.36	3.13	74.3	**1.7**	15.0	21.0	**5.5**
5.9	2.55	6.2	0.38	**2.5**	0.1	0.38	3.63	3.74	84.5	**2.8**	72.6	34.2	**3.3**
2.4	1.70	11.9	0.38	**1.6**	0.0	0.10	0.71	4.00	92.5	**4.1**	14.9	8.3	**5.3**
8.8	0.00	0.0	0.00	**0.0**	-1.1	-2.82	-9.30	1.20	211.1	**3.7**	33.8	14.6	**2.0**
4.2	0.60	5.3	0.00	**4.9**	1.3	0.85	10.03	3.74	68.1	**0.7**	13.3	40.3	**4.7**
4.9	0.94	5.4	0.97	**3.7**	10.1	2.21	20.33	3.52	89.3	**3.4**	18.9	12.4	**5.5**
6.9	1.99	7.3	0.02	**3.3**	0.3	0.73	5.61	3.17	77.7	**2.7**	37.0	21.3	**7.0**
6.4	0.49	3.4	0.30	**3.7**	1.0	0.65	6.46	3.90	80.8	**2.0**	14.4	19.0	**5.5**
9.6	0.00	0.0	0.00	**1.1**	0.0	0.13	1.46	3.08	102.2	**4.4**	47.6	12.3	**3.8**
3.2	2.34	17.4	0.13	**4.2**	1.8	0.75	8.02	3.84	73.5	**1.8**	18.4	20.7	**4.4**
8.4	0.00	0.0	0.48	**2.9**	0.2	0.29	3.24	2.25	77.5	**2.2**	42.0	33.0	**5.5**
6.0	0.56	3.2	-0.02	**1.8**	0.1	0.10	0.97	3.76	97.6	**1.1**	27.3	36.9	**3.3**
5.2	1.47	5.3	0.06	**3.6**	0.4	0.82	6.51	3.12	68.4	**4.7**	63.5	17.0	**7.6**
5.8	5.50	8.1	-0.03	**2.0**	-0.1	-0.14	-0.84	3.76	105.4	**5.9**	48.7	5.7	**6.6**
7.0	0.42	2.1	0.10	**4.9**	2.6	0.96	10.51	3.60	59.0	**2.6**	34.5	20.2	**5.5**
9.2	0.33	1.2	0.20	**5.1**	1.0	0.93	6.95	3.80	62.1	**3.1**	49.3	25.2	**7.7**
9.5	0.24	0.6	-0.01	**3.4**	0.5	0.76	6.90	2.59	73.0	**6.2**	62.0	7.1	**7.0**
8.8	0.21	0.9	0.05	**5.1**	1.0	0.98	8.71	3.70	65.9	**4.6**	34.8	10.1	**6.6**
6.2	1.37	6.4	0.29	**9.8**	1.4	2.64	23.04	4.39	36.8	**2.2**	45.7	39.7	**7.2**
10.0	0.00	0.0	0.00	**3.4**	0.5	0.72	9.43	2.10	63.3	**7.0**	88.5	6.4	**3.7**
8.5	0.16	1.1	0.00	**4.0**	1.0	1.25	15.83	3.68	80.2	**2.4**	28.0	19.0	**4.4**
6.8	1.55	5.1	0.00	**7.4**	1.0	1.37	8.37	4.10	56.5	**5.5**	39.5	6.6	**9.2**
7.6	0.49	2.7	-0.04	**2.5**	0.1	0.25	2.68	2.64	87.9	**3.4**	34.9	16.5	**3.7**
2.5	4.08	22.5	0.35	**10.0**	6.3	2.59	17.26	7.78	41.9	**0.6**	7.9	46.6	**7.5**
2.2	9.03	27.1	1.99	**2.6**	0.3	0.38	2.70	4.01	79.3	**2.1**	40.6	33.6	**5.6**
7.1	0.58	2.2	0.02	**3.8**	0.4	1.13	13.22	2.65	67.9	**5.2**	68.6	13.6	**4.0**
4.3	1.79	14.8	0.00	**3.1**	1.9	0.40	4.65	3.61	87.0	**3.8**	10.7	9.3	**4.7**
6.3	0.16	1.1	0.13	**2.5**	0.4	0.25	2.31	3.42	83.5	**0.7**	10.9	36.0	**5.6**
3.2	4.43	21.5	0.13	**5.4**	1.6	0.97	8.50	3.44	57.8	**4.3**	18.7	7.4	**6.8**
3.8	2.14	11.4	0.04	**6.7**	1.0	1.71	17.87	3.64	56.8	**5.0**	46.0	11.1	**6.6**
8.3	0.28	2.4	-0.02	**6.3**	9.3	1.11	14.78	3.56	55.7	**2.5**	11.4	16.2	**6.8**
8.8	0.25	1.2	0.00	**3.6**	0.1	0.52	6.25	4.83	86.1	**5.2**	26.1	1.5	**3.3**
4.1	1.89	10.5	0.15	**5.1**	0.9	1.25	13.00	4.06	71.1	**1.6**	19.0	24.6	**5.8**
7.5	0.25	1.6	0.00	**4.2**	1.9	0.74	7.16	3.49	65.6	**4.3**	25.1	8.0	**5.9**
1.9	4.78	34.9	0.15	**4.3**	1.6	0.71	7.32	3.87	73.1	**3.2**	10.4	12.5	**4.7**
5.6	1.55	8.2	0.17	**5.8**	1.1	1.11	8.29	4.62	63.1	**3.8**	14.0	10.0	**7.7**
4.6	1.19	8.6	0.49	**4.0**	0.4	0.57	8.14	4.37	80.2	**1.5**	16.8	24.6	**4.1**
1.7	5.03	29.6	-0.01	**4.1**	0.1	0.76	7.72	4.15	75.2	**2.5**	29.0	17.3	**3.9**
8.3	0.66	2.7	0.01	**5.7**	1.7	1.04	7.51	3.83	65.1	**2.9**	21.9	15.3	**8.1**
5.1	2.29	13.6	-0.03	**6.2**	4.8	1.08	8.85	4.26	69.0	**4.1**	20.3	9.0	**7.2**
0.1	3.42	21.2	0.71	**3.8**	0.2	0.58	6.05	4.06	77.6	**4.7**	25.7	5.6	**5.3**
6.1	1.24	5.3	0.13	**5.8**	1.0	1.11	11.21	3.59	60.5	**5.0**	53.1	13.4	**7.4**
4.6	1.68	7.2	0.39	**9.8**	2.6	1.60	9.41	5.23	54.0	**4.4**	18.9	6.6	**8.6**
7.5	1.26	5.2	0.04	**4.9**	1.4	1.01	8.97	3.81	63.4	**2.6**	37.4	23.7	**6.1**
6.4	0.64	4.2	0.02	**6.6**	29.7	1.57	15.61	3.48	58.4	**3.8**	17.4	10.7	**8.4**
1.3	4.89	29.0	0.39	**3.7**	0.9	0.92	9.72	4.12	72.6	**3.0**	28.2	15.9	**4.3**
6.3	0.59	4.6	0.11	**8.3**	3.5	1.45	18.00	4.29	41.2	**0.9**	9.5	32.1	**5.6**

Name	City	State	Rating	2013 Rating	2012 Rating	Total Assets ($Mil)	One Year Asset Growth	Asset Mix (As a % of Total Assets) Comm-ercial Loans	Cons-umer Loans	Mort-gage Loans	Secur-ities	Capital-ization Index	Lever-age Ratio	Risk-Based Capital Ratio
BANK OF COMMERCE	Chanute	KS	**B-**	B-	B-	173.6	-0.65	7.8	3.7	15.1	39.2	**6.1**	8.1	18.7
BANK OF COMMERCE	Sarasota	FL	**E-**	E-	E-	211.0	-3.82	3.9	0.5	6.4	21.4	**0.0**	3.1	7.4
BANK OF COMMERCE	White Castle	LA	**C+**	C+	B-	59.0	11.20	12.0	2.5	13.2	21.6	**10.0**	12.9	18.8
BANK OF COMMERCE	McLean	TX	**B+**	B+	B+	34.1	9.82	37.9	0.4	4.6	12.9	**10.0**	12.4	20.1
BANK OF COMMERCE	Chelsea	OK	**B**	B	B-	152.0	4.73	6.9	6.3	12.6	17.8	**10.0**	11.4	21.2
BANK OF COMMERCE	Chouteau	OK	**C+**	C+	C+	35.9	-0.72	3.7	5.2	22.9	14.6	**6.8**	8.8	17.0
BANK OF COMMERCE	Rawlins	WY	**B**	B-	C+	121.9	-1.49	8.8	2.9	11.3	49.3	**10.0**	11.2	24.2
BANK OF COMMERCE	Duncan	OK	**B**	C+	C	183.1	10.44	21.6	3.2	5.6	16.4	**8.0**	10.4	13.3
▲ BANK OF COMMERCE	Yukon	OK	**B-**	C+	B-	187.3	3.66	13.4	1.3	9.8	18.0	**9.9**	10.9	15.1
BANK OF COMMERCE	Stilwell	OK	**B**	B-	B	95.1	-2.43	22.2	5.1	10.0	26.1	**9.8**	10.8	18.9
BANK OF COMMERCE	Ammon	ID	**A-**	A-	B	960.0	2.27	11.5	1.5	2.1	20.7	**10.0**	15.6	25.1
BANK OF COMMERCE & TRUST CO	Crowley	LA	**B-**	B-	B-	337.0	-0.33	3.5	2.4	6.8	69.9	**10.0**	11.3	30.5
▲ BANK OF COMMERCE & TRUST CO	Wellington	KS	**B-**	C	C-	56.0	-1.82	9.6	4.7	15.5	47.4	**7.8**	9.5	21.8
▼ BANK OF CORAL GABLES	Coral Gables	FL	**E**	E	E	103.2	-0.78	6.9	0.1	19.7	27.9	**4.3**	6.3	12.9
BANK OF CORDELL	Cordell	OK	**C**	C	C	39.2	6.99	24.4	1.5	35.8	3.0	**6.3**	8.3	14.2
BANK OF COUSHATTA	Coushatta	LA	**C+**	C	C-	202.9	3.57	2.0	4.5	11.0	67.9	**6.4**	8.5	19.4
BANK OF CROCKER	Waynesville	MO	**C-**	C-	C-	126.0	-6.97	3.6	3.4	21.0	28.1	**9.5**	10.6	19.1
BANK OF CROCKETT	Bells	TN	**B**	B	B	136.3	-0.43	4.4	2.2	2.8	61.0	**10.0**	11.0	24.5
BANK OF CUSHING	Cushing	OK	**A-**	A-	A	120.9	4.80	11.9	6.4	3.2	53.4	**10.0**	11.0	17.2
BANK OF DADE	Trenton	GA	**A-**	A-	B	92.8	1.91	0.4	4.4	20.0	49.6	**10.0**	11.9	27.7
BANK OF DAWSON	Dawson	GA	**B+**	B+	B+	113.8	-3.83	3.3	3.6	16.8	33.1	**10.0**	16.9	29.5
BANK OF DEERFIELD	Deerfield	WI	**A-**	A-	B+	119.0	7.22	6.6	1.2	40.8	3.5	**10.0**	13.7	16.2
▲ BANK OF DELIGHT	Delight	AR	**A-**	B+	A-	80.5	1.18	18.5	7.8	13.6	22.6	**10.0**	22.3	32.5
BANK OF DELMARVA	Salisbury	MD	**D**	D-	D-	441.6	3.95	7.3	0.5	19.3	7.9	**7.2**	9.3	12.6
BANK OF DENTON	Denton	KS	**C+**	C+	B-	17.9	6.00	1.5	8.8	19.1	42.9	**10.0**	16.5	36.8
BANK OF DENVER	Denver	CO	**B-**	B	B	221.1	6.92	1.0	5.7	3.6	27.3	**6.8**	8.8	16.1
BANK OF DESOTO NA	Desoto	TX	**C+**	C+	B	187.6	3.63	4.9	15.8	13.2	2.0	**8.6**	10.1	18.0
BANK OF DICKSON	Dickson	TN	**B+**	B+	B+	220.8	1.71	3.8	2.1	32.7	38.8	**10.0**	12.1	24.0
BANK OF DIXON COUNTY	Ponca	NE	**B-**	C+	B-	84.3	5.42	9.1	5.8	10.0	26.5	**8.3**	9.8	17.8
BANK OF DONIPHAN	Doniphan	NE	**B-**	B	B-	98.2	5.10	8.4	7.9	13.4	14.8	**5.7**	8.8	11.6
BANK OF DUDLEY	Dublin	GA	**B**	B-	C	187.7	5.29	8.1	4.6	20.0	17.0	**10.0**	11.2	18.9
▲ BANK OF EARLY	Blakely	GA	**B-**	C+	C-	93.5	4.99	7.7	3.4	11.9	4.7	**10.0**	11.9	15.2
▼ BANK OF EASTERN OREGON	Heppner	OR	**C-**	C+	C	310.5	5.38	9.7	0.9	4.5	5.7	**7.4**	9.9	12.8
BANK OF EASTMAN	Eastman	GA	**E**	E-	E-	190.1	-2.76	11.9	4.2	21.8	8.9	**4.3**	6.3	11.2
▲ BANK OF EASTON	North Easton	MA	**B-**	C	C+	120.9	0.81	0.0	0.8	43.5	28.5	**10.0**	11.0	24.4
BANK OF EDISON	Edison	GA	**C+**	C+	C	39.3	-5.32	3.0	6.5	12.0	47.1	**8.7**	10.2	22.7
BANK OF EDMONSON COUNTY	Brownsville	KY	**A-**	A-	B	199.5	0.66	2.7	3.9	29.6	22.1	**10.0**	12.0	19.6
BANK OF EDWARDSVILLE	Edwardsville	IL	**B-**	B-	C	1675.5	-0.26	4.0	1.1	10.5	46.3	**7.8**	9.6	18.4
BANK OF ELGIN	Elgin	NE	**B-**	B-	C+	57.9	5.70	1.9	1.4	1.4	8.9	**7.4**	9.3	12.8
▲ BANK OF ELK RIVER	Elk River	MN	**D+**	E+	E-	359.1	-0.68	13.4	1.8	10.0	21.1	**6.3**	8.3	13.2
BANK OF ENGLAND	England	AR	**B**	B	C+	306.2	25.01	9.4	1.5	51.4	7.9	**10.0**	11.8	18.7
BANK OF ERATH	Erath	LA	**B+**	B+	A-	98.1	4.69	24.7	3.2	15.1	25.6	**10.0**	13.2	18.9
BANK OF ESTES PARK	Estes Park	CO	**C**	C	B	121.7	7.68	2.1	0.4	8.6	38.8	**8.0**	9.7	20.1
BANK OF EUFAULA	Eufaula	OK	**B-**	C+	C	97.4	5.19	11.5	7.2	16.7	40.7	**10.0**	13.4	28.3
BANK OF EVERGREEN	Evergreen	AL	**C+**	C	C-	54.6	4.20	13.5	5.3	24.0	27.2	**8.7**	10.1	16.9
BANK OF FAIRFIELD	Fairfield	WA	**C+**	C	D	149.2	-2.55	3.9	1.9	6.6	8.0	**7.8**	9.6	14.0
BANK OF FAIRPORT	Maysville	MO	**E**	E	D-	26.6	-0.01	2.3	1.6	10.4	50.2	**4.8**	6.8	13.5
BANK OF FARMINGTON	Farmington	IL	**A-**	B	B	137.4	5.12	5.1	5.6	17.9	27.1	**10.0**	11.4	17.2
BANK OF FAYETTE COUNTY	Piperton	TN	**C-**	D+	D+	330.6	2.43	3.2	7.9	31.0	10.8	**8.2**	9.8	14.0
BANK OF FAYETTEVILLE	Fayetteville	AR	**B**	B	C+	337.3	2.03	10.1	1.2	8.9	19.5	**10.0**	11.5	16.0
BANK OF FEATHER RIVER	Yuba City	CA	**B**	B	B	73.8	18.69	9.5	0.3	6.0	0.0	**10.0**	12.7	17.6
BANK OF FINCASTLE	Fincastle	VA	**C+**	B-	B	223.7	10.19	7.7	1.4	12.9	16.8	**10.0**	12.4	16.5
BANK OF FLOYD	Floyd	VA	**D**	D-	D	268.1	-0.37	15.6	0.3	11.0	31.3	**5.4**	7.4	12.2
BANK OF FOREST	Forest	MS	**B**	B	B	147.8	2.22	4.6	4.9	9.7	37.5	**10.0**	14.1	24.3
▲ BANK OF FRANKEWING	Frankewing	TN	**C-**	C-	C-	208.3	-2.15	4.8	4.3	20.5	20.3	**10.0**	11.1	17.7
BANK OF FRANKLIN	Meadville	MS	**B-**	B-	C	128.9	6.73	5.4	5.2	18.7	29.2	**8.0**	9.7	15.5
BANK OF FRANKLIN COUNTY	Washington	MO	**C-**	D+	D	206.8	-3.70	8.1	1.1	25.5	14.3	**7.6**	9.4	13.0
BANK OF GALESVILLE	Galesville	WI	**B**	B+	B	89.9	1.08	6.4	3.6	19.4	14.7	**10.0**	16.0	19.5
BANK OF GENEVA	Geneva	IN	**A-**	A	A	215.3	12.86	5.0	1.6	24.7	8.3	**9.5**	10.9	14.6
▲ BANK OF GEORGE	Las Vegas	NV	**C-**	D+	D-	124.3	8.45	14.8	0.2	0.3	7.8	**9.5**	10.6	20.6

Asset Quality Index	Adjusted Non-Performing Loans as a % of Total Loans	Adjusted Non-Performing Loans as a % of Capital	Net Charge-Offs / Avg Loans	Profitability Index	Net Income ($Mil)	Return on Assets (R.O.A.)	Return on Equity (R.O.E.)	Net Interest Spread	Overhead Efficiency Ratio	Liquidity Index	Liquidity Ratio	Hot Money Ratio	Stability Index
7.1	0.54	2.8	0.00	3.5	0.9	0.69	8.33	2.76	76.7	4.1	25.0	9.6	5.3
0.0	3.77	58.4	0.01	0.4	-0.3	-0.18	-9.54	3.09	106.1	2.4	21.3	17.8	0.2
8.7	0.31	1.4	0.00	2.9	0.2	0.51	4.16	3.33	85.0	3.8	17.1	10.3	5.9
8.6	0.38	1.6	0.25	6.0	0.3	1.33	10.11	3.08	61.0	2.5	34.9	22.2	7.6
7.0	0.78	3.5	0.25	4.8	1.3	1.16	10.70	4.26	70.9	1.8	28.6	26.7	5.5
7.7	0.40	2.3	-0.12	4.9	0.3	0.99	11.37	4.52	81.2	4.0	29.0	11.1	4.7
6.7	1.11	3.6	-0.01	4.5	0.8	0.88	8.04	3.69	67.8	1.8	28.8	26.3	5.9
3.9	1.64	10.8	0.14	9.2	2.9	2.18	20.29	4.61	52.3	1.0	16.4	32.2	7.7
5.4	0.76	4.6	0.25	7.7	1.8	1.29	12.23	4.27	60.8	3.5	28.7	13.9	6.1
3.7	2.06	12.2	0.44	5.2	0.9	1.22	11.58	4.37	68.3	1.6	13.5	22.4	6.4
6.2	1.60	5.5	0.21	6.8	9.2	1.30	8.49	3.74	50.8	4.1	48.8	16.9	7.8
8.8	0.99	2.1	-0.06	3.6	1.6	0.61	6.64	2.37	65.2	3.4	48.8	20.2	5.5
8.9	0.24	1.0	0.01	5.2	0.7	1.51	17.47	3.43	63.8	3.6	43.5	17.5	4.0
1.7	5.16	35.3	-0.44	0.0	-0.4	-0.54	-8.63	2.73	118.0	2.4	47.3	35.9	2.2
8.5	0.00	0.0	0.13	5.2	0.3	1.19	14.09	3.68	69.4	0.9	7.2	30.9	3.2
4.1	4.98	13.3	0.97	5.0	2.1	1.36	14.71	3.26	56.4	3.4	50.7	22.5	3.9
5.8	1.78	8.9	0.28	1.8	0.3	0.28	2.81	3.79	86.4	1.6	17.3	24.3	3.2
7.6	0.63	1.6	1.52	5.0	1.2	1.13	9.91	3.65	60.5	3.5	53.4	21.8	7.1
5.8	0.84	2.8	-0.27	9.2	1.4	1.55	13.89	5.07	59.7	4.5	64.7	18.0	8.8
7.2	1.90	6.6	-0.22	5.3	0.9	1.31	13.00	3.83	68.6	5.0	45.7	10.9	5.9
5.7	2.86	9.5	0.46	5.1	0.9	0.97	6.28	4.17	60.7	1.8	28.4	25.8	7.0
5.8	1.34	7.8	0.00	9.3	1.8	2.11	15.84	4.55	56.0	0.6	9.0	47.8	9.2
6.8	1.03	2.9	-0.03	6.8	1.0	1.66	7.49	4.00	54.4	2.0	30.8	25.2	8.2
0.8	3.82	29.2	0.48	3.2	2.9	0.92	9.24	4.05	69.4	1.8	11.3	19.8	3.5
7.7	0.66	1.6	0.06	3.5	0.1	0.76	4.57	3.27	71.8	6.1	60.0	5.1	6.2
7.4	0.03	0.2	0.24	4.1	1.1	0.68	7.72	3.48	71.3	4.0	21.9	9.5	5.2
3.0	2.07	11.0	0.23	9.6	3.0	2.16	21.32	7.23	59.8	2.4	43.6	31.4	7.7
6.9	1.14	5.2	0.08	4.2	1.3	0.81	6.49	3.44	70.3	3.0	36.1	18.7	7.6
4.4	1.49	8.3	0.77	3.9	0.4	0.65	6.72	3.49	64.0	3.0	25.2	15.0	4.9
6.0	0.52	4.3	0.28	3.6	0.4	0.58	5.72	4.24	80.5	4.0	17.7	8.9	6.4
4.4	2.90	16.4	0.05	4.6	1.2	0.87	8.00	4.08	72.7	2.8	17.7	15.4	5.5
5.0	1.09	7.4	0.05	5.0	0.8	1.10	9.38	4.71	75.4	1.2	6.8	25.9	6.0
1.8	3.57	27.1	0.50	5.7	2.1	0.92	9.25	5.25	69.3	4.0	10.7	7.9	5.2
0.3	10.66	88.9	0.98	5.3	2.8	1.96	35.26	3.76	65.2	1.5	23.4	26.3	1.1
10.0	0.42	2.1	0.00	3.9	0.6	0.66	6.07	2.78	67.6	3.9	43.2	16.4	6.0
5.8	1.16	5.0	0.21	3.3	0.2	0.67	7.42	3.86	83.4	2.8	35.5	19.5	4.8
6.7	0.97	5.5	0.03	6.1	2.3	1.52	12.87	4.00	60.4	0.8	17.1	37.6	7.0
6.3	2.18	8.4	0.40	4.0	10.3	0.84	9.10	2.67	68.7	3.5	22.6	14.0	7.2
4.5	0.65	4.9	-0.08	6.8	0.7	1.62	16.56	3.67	53.3	4.3	19.3	7.6	5.8
2.1	4.05	27.3	0.65	5.7	2.9	1.11	11.98	4.14	68.4	3.7	29.3	13.1	3.6
4.7	1.92	12.8	-0.01	9.6	3.5	1.70	13.74	3.97	88.6	0.6	6.0	38.6	7.9
8.6	0.04	0.2	0.06	4.2	0.5	0.72	5.52	4.19	77.4	3.4	30.2	14.9	7.6
9.3	0.00	0.0	0.00	2.9	0.4	0.46	5.00	2.86	85.6	7.0	58.1	2.9	5.5
5.1	3.40	9.8	0.67	3.6	0.6	0.75	5.64	3.82	67.8	3.0	35.8	18.7	6.6
3.6	2.58	15.1	0.46	5.8	0.4	1.09	11.20	4.51	58.9	1.6	29.3	30.1	4.1
5.5	0.39	2.6	0.03	3.7	0.6	0.55	5.65	4.20	82.3	3.6	22.7	11.6	5.0
3.1	4.97	20.2	1.41	1.1	0.1	0.30	5.55	2.97	94.6	4.3	38.3	13.0	0.3
5.8	1.68	9.3	0.22	6.7	1.4	1.36	12.32	3.85	52.4	1.7	21.2	23.2	6.9
2.5	2.12	15.7	0.24	5.4	2.2	0.91	9.51	4.61	65.8	1.3	3.2	23.5	5.3
5.1	1.98	11.0	0.19	4.4	1.9	0.76	6.13	3.73	71.0	4.2	22.2	8.6	5.6
4.9	1.36	8.2	0.16	7.5	0.6	1.16	8.72	5.09	65.5	1.0	20.2	33.2	7.6
1.6	5.75	29.8	0.08	3.9	1.1	0.71	5.70	3.30	72.8	3.1	21.5	14.4	6.7
3.9	1.94	14.1	-0.96	2.0	1.1	0.54	8.30	3.08	108.6	1.5	18.2	26.0	1.6
6.6	1.85	6.0	0.02	4.0	1.0	0.92	6.57	3.67	77.9	3.1	43.7	21.6	7.3
1.7	6.17	31.8	0.33	5.4	1.5	0.93	9.01	4.12	67.9	1.7	30.6	29.8	5.6
5.0	1.18	6.6	0.13	4.8	0.8	0.83	9.05	4.24	73.7	2.4	27.9	18.8	4.4
2.2	3.24	22.6	0.46	2.7	0.5	0.33	3.31	3.53	81.3	3.4	18.4	12.4	4.4
3.9	3.33	15.2	0.00	7.2	1.0	1.46	8.88	4.62	65.9	3.2	11.0	12.8	9.1
6.5	0.11	0.8	0.03	8.8	3.3	2.13	20.43	4.54	51.4	3.9	3.9	7.9	7.9
5.5	0.00	0.0	0.25	2.2	0.3	0.35	3.31	3.27	90.4	6.5	48.0	2.7	4.2

Name	City	State	Rating	2013 Rating	2012 Rating	Total Assets ($Mil)	One Year Asset Growth	Asset Mix (As a % of Total Assets) Commercial Loans	Consumer Loans	Mortgage Loans	Securities	Capitalization Index	Leverage Ratio	Risk-Based Capital Ratio
BANK OF GEORGETOWN	Washington	DC	**B**	B	B-	1049.8	17.88	4.8	0.1	10.0	22.4	**8.9**	10.8	14.1
BANK OF GEORGIA	Peachtree City	GA	**E-**	E-	E-	319.2	-3.17	3.1	0.7	9.1	19.6	**0.0**	3.4	6.0
BANK OF GIBSON CITY	Gibson City	IL	**C+**	C	C-	78.7	5.13	5.8	4.4	7.9	25.1	**6.2**	8.2	15.5
BANK OF GLEASON	Gleason	TN	**B+**	B+	B	121.1	0.01	2.5	5.9	10.4	62.4	**10.0**	18.0	39.3
BANK OF GLEN BURNIE	Glen Burnie	MD	**C+**	C	C	403.0	6.58	0.7	20.7	26.1	21.5	**6.3**	8.3	13.6
BANK OF GLEN ULLIN	Glen Ullin	ND	**B-**	B-	B-	53.4	4.56	5.8	1.8	0.1	2.2	**5.4**	8.8	11.3
BANK OF GRAIN VALLEY	Kansas City	MO	**A-**	A-	A	82.6	-4.56	9.4	0.9	6.3	32.1	**10.0**	21.3	39.0
▲ BANK OF GRANDIN	Grandin	MO	**B**	B-	B-	161.5	-1.31	8.4	5.9	11.6	46.8	**10.0**	14.3	23.0
▲ BANK OF GRAVETT	Gravette	AR	**B**	C+	C+	117.3	-5.86	2.6	4.4	22.9	23.9	**10.0**	15.6	28.4
BANK OF GREELEY	Greeley	KS	**B+**	B+	B+	37.2	4.55	4.1	3.8	14.5	20.4	**10.0**	12.2	23.0
BANK OF GREELEYVILLE	Greeleyville	SC	**D**	D	D+	78.4	-1.18	12.4	12.9	12.3	18.1	**7.8**	9.6	14.8
BANK OF GREENE COUNTY	Catskill	NY	**B+**	B+	B-	699.3	7.36	3.2	0.6	38.4	35.7	**6.8**	8.8	18.5
BANK OF GROVE	Grove	OK	**C**	C+	C+	138.2	10.59	3.9	3.1	37.2	12.4	**5.2**	7.2	11.1
BANK OF GUAM	Hagatna	GU	**C+**	C+	C+	1546.5	9.24	6.8	11.1	10.6	22.0	**4.8**	6.8	11.5
BANK OF GUEYDAN	Gueydan	LA	**C+**	B-	B-	85.9	3.62	3.6	6.8	2.3	63.9	**10.0**	18.2	44.6
BANK OF HALLS	Halls	TN	**B-**	B-	B	69.4	4.71	6.1	1.9	9.4	47.8	**10.0**	11.3	20.2
BANK OF HAMILTON	Hamilton	ND	**C+**	C+	C+	19.2	1.23	2.8	4.7	0.7	22.9	**10.0**	13.8	35.4
BANK OF HAMPTON ROADS	Virginia Beach	VA	**C**	D+	D-	1690.4	2.24	10.4	2.8	10.0	18.3	**8.6**	10.0	14.1
▲ BANK OF HANCOCK COUNTY	Sparta	GA	**B+**	B-	B-	83.7	-3.39	3.0	6.1	19.6	51.1	**10.0**	22.0	42.1
BANK OF HARLAN	Harlan	KY	**B-**	B-	C	123.8	2.15	8.0	1.7	24.2	38.9	**10.0**	11.5	17.5
BANK OF HARTINGTON	Hartington	NE	**C+**	C+	B-	68.5	5.08	15.2	2.9	6.4	22.1	**5.9**	7.9	11.7
BANK OF HAWAII	Honolulu	HI	**B**	B	B-	14551.1	4.72	5.0	3.9	16.9	46.7	**4.7**	6.7	15.6
BANK OF HAYS	Hays	KS	**B-**	B-	B-	260.3	11.01	12.7	1.9	8.5	41.9	**6.0**	8.0	15.2
BANK OF HAZELTON	Hazelton	ND	**C+**	C	C	43.6	-6.17	2.7	1.0	0.5	26.5	**7.4**	9.2	16.0
▲ BANK OF HAZLEHURST	Hazlehurst	GA	**D**	D-	D	111.7	2.29	21.4	5.6	6.3	21.1	**8.4**	9.9	16.9
BANK OF HEMET	Riverside	CA	**A**	A-	B	491.0	5.67	1.6	0.2	0.6	8.2	**10.0**	11.7	15.6
BANK OF HERRIN	Herrin	IL	**B-**	B-	C+	238.6	-0.38	8.6	2.7	15.4	34.8	**8.0**	9.7	16.0
BANK OF HILLSBORO	Hillsboro	MO	**B**	B	B	60.6	5.94	2.5	0.9	11.1	34.4	**9.0**	10.3	15.6
BANK OF HINDMAN	Hindman	KY	**B**	B	B-	169.5	2.73	6.0	1.6	8.1	60.0	**10.0**	11.1	21.5
BANK OF HOLLAND	Holland	NY	**C+**	C+	C+	91.7	0.66	1.0	1.8	45.6	24.1	**7.1**	9.0	17.0
BANK OF HOLLAND	Holland	MI	**B-**	C+	C	805.7	15.90	26.5	0.2	9.2	9.9	**6.4**	9.2	12.1
BANK OF HOLLY SPRINGS	Holly Springs	MS	**C+**	C+	C+	207.0	0.07	4.8	10.8	22.4	19.3	**10.0**	13.6	24.8
BANK OF HOLYROOD	Holyrood	KS	**B**	B	B	64.0	5.60	11.6	8.4	18.7	17.8	**9.6**	10.7	19.8
BANK OF HOUSTON	Houston	MO	**D-**	D+	D+	42.8	-1.40	4.2	1.3	8.2	35.0	**8.0**	9.7	18.5
BANK OF HYDRO	Hydro	OK	**B+**	B+	B	134.1	9.65	4.5	3.2	29.4	0.5	**5.4**	7.8	11.3
BANK OF IBERIA	Iberia	MO	**D+**	C-	C-	56.4	-0.65	4.2	10.4	36.8	7.8	**6.7**	8.7	13.4
BANK OF IDAHO	Idaho Falls	ID	**C+**	C	D	246.8	2.63	14.9	3.2	7.3	20.9	**7.5**	9.4	13.7
▲ BANK OF JACKSON	Jackson	TN	**B-**	C+	B-	151.1	6.40	5.2	1.3	15.4	53.1	**8.3**	9.9	20.7
▲ BANK OF JACKSON HOLE	Jackson	WY	**C+**	C-	D+	569.7	3.64	4.4	0.3	17.6	17.4	**9.9**	11.0	16.3
BANK OF JAMESTOWN	Jamestown	KY	**C+**	B-	C+	167.5	-0.48	2.5	2.9	10.7	51.1	**9.8**	10.9	17.7
BANK OF JENA	Jena	LA	**C-**	D+	D+	71.8	-1.19	3.1	5.7	12.7	43.1	**6.4**	8.4	17.4
BANK OF JONES COUNTY	Laurel	MS	**A-**	B+	A-	224.6	-1.48	5.6	2.9	10.4	61.0	**10.0**	12.1	30.5
BANK OF KAMPSVILLE	Kampsville	IL	**B+**	B+	A-	106.4	0.31	3.4	7.2	17.0	37.5	**10.0**	14.6	27.0
▲ BANK OF KAUKAUNA	Kaukauna	WI	**D**	D-	D-	90.5	0.20	16.2	1.1	15.7	6.5	**8.6**	10.0	14.2
BANK OF KENTUCKY INC	Crestview Hills	KY	**B**	B	B-	1825.5	1.35	13.9	0.8	6.8	21.3	**8.5**	10.4	13.8
BANK OF KEYSTONE	Keystone	NE	**B+**	B+	C+	63.8	6.82	8.0	3.9	1.8	11.5	**10.0**	11.7	15.3
BANK OF KILMICHAEL	Kilmichael	MS	**B-**	B-	B-	137.6	3.83	19.2	5.6	11.8	28.3	**6.6**	8.6	15.6
BANK OF KIRKSVILLE	Kirksville	MO	**C+**	C+	B-	506.1	-2.33	11.4	0.8	13.8	49.0	**8.3**	9.9	26.4
▲ BANK OF KREMLIN	Kremlin	OK	**B-**	C	C-	249.8	8.78	6.3	3.9	5.8	10.4	**9.7**	10.8	16.1
BANK OF LA FAYETTE GEORGIA	Lafayette	GA	**B**	B-	B-	230.2	1.19	0.9	4.9	23.4	54.8	**10.0**	13.2	33.1
▼ BANK OF LABOR	Kansas City	KS	**D+**	C-	C-	531.1	2.51	9.2	0.5	4.5	49.7	**8.9**	10.2	17.3
▲ BANK OF LAKE MILLS	Lake Mills	WI	**C+**	C-	C-	200.8	7.92	2.5	7.3	34.5	12.1	**9.0**	10.3	14.7
BANK OF LAKE VILLAGE	Lake Village	AR	**A-**	A-	B+	60.4	0.63	8.3	1.7	3.2	23.6	**9.9**	11.0	18.3
BANK OF LANCASTER	Kilmarnock	VA	**C**	C	D+	346.1	3.60	5.0	1.5	38.1	9.8	**7.4**	9.3	13.7
BANK OF LANDISBURG	Landisburg	PA	**B+**	B+	B+	257.8	-0.61	0.8	1.2	44.3	30.4	**10.0**	17.5	32.5
BANK OF LAVERNE	Laverne	OK	**B+**	B+	B+	64.6	5.61	5.9	8.3	1.4	40.5	**10.0**	15.1	29.3
BANK OF LAWRENCE COUNTY	Bridgeport	IL	**C+**	B-	B-	53.1	16.24	4.1	2.5	10.0	31.9	**9.1**	10.4	38.4
BANK OF LEES SUMMIT	Lees Summit	MO	**B-**	B-	C+	287.8	-0.19	4.6	0.3	5.9	34.0	**10.0**	12.3	25.3
BANK OF LEWELLEN	Lewellen	NE	**B**	B-	B	23.7	-0.57	4.5	2.4	0.1	22.4	**10.0**	25.4	48.5
BANK OF LEXINGTON INC	Lexington	KY	**B**	B	B	237.3	13.01	1.3	0.5	42.5	7.2	**8.0**	9.7	15.1

Asset Quality Index	Adjusted Non-Performing Loans as a % of Total Loans	Adjusted Non-Performing Loans as a % of Capital	Net Charge-Offs Avg Loans	Profitability Index	Net Income ($Mil)	Return on Assets (R.O.A.)	Return on Equity (R.O.E.)	Net Interest Spread	Overhead Efficiency Ratio	Liquidity Index	Liquidity Ratio	Hot Money Ratio	Stability Index
6.8	0.25	1.5	0.04	4.2	5.3	0.71	6.48	3.48	64.3	1.6	13.0	23.9	7.5
0.3	9.15	107.9	4.25	0.0	-1.1	-0.46	-9.62	3.41	66.8	2.4	22.3	18.0	0.1
2.5	2.22	14.7	0.01	4.9	0.5	0.88	7.38	3.10	56.6	3.9	24.9	10.2	5.5
7.7	0.85	1.4	0.25	5.1	1.0	1.14	6.23	4.09	54.9	4.1	80.2	25.5	7.3
3.7	0.89	7.0	0.35	2.8	1.5	0.50	5.96	3.44	85.2	3.0	28.7	16.3	4.7
4.0	0.55	5.7	0.25	10.0	0.9	2.38	22.35	5.06	45.7	0.6	2.3	33.6	7.4
9.0	0.09	0.2	0.00	5.6	0.9	1.35	6.50	3.48	61.3	5.2	52.8	11.0	9.2
4.0	4.67	14.5	0.30	8.3	2.3	1.92	13.82	4.08	46.3	2.7	44.1	27.3	8.6
5.8	2.32	8.6	0.14	4.1	0.9	0.95	6.65	4.13	77.8	2.5	30.3	19.1	5.2
8.1	0.06	0.3	0.06	4.4	0.3	1.06	8.95	3.13	67.6	5.1	43.0	9.8	6.6
1.0	4.11	25.9	0.47	3.0	0.0	0.04	0.42	4.80	80.7	2.2	27.7	20.1	5.1
5.5	1.57	9.5	0.18	5.5	4.9	0.97	11.34	3.57	61.9	4.8	9.4	2.8	6.3
5.2	0.82	7.9	0.44	4.9	1.1	1.12	15.81	4.02	66.1	1.2	21.4	31.3	2.4
3.6	2.24	19.1	0.43	4.3	7.0	0.66	9.71	4.64	80.3	2.8	25.2	18.4	4.8
9.1	1.44	1.7	0.32	2.5	0.2	0.29	1.58	2.25	86.8	3.8	85.5	29.3	6.8
5.2	4.20	14.6	0.10	6.4	0.7	1.31	11.06	4.10	57.2	2.2	38.5	30.1	6.8
9.4	0.09	0.1	1.00	2.2	0.0	0.26	1.99	1.61	82.1	6.8	90.2	6.7	5.2
3.2	3.11	18.4	0.71	3.2	10.4	0.87	8.17	3.34	80.8	2.2	24.0	23.1	5.3
7.4	2.18	4.1	0.28	5.1	0.7	1.13	5.27	4.24	66.2	4.4	53.2	15.3	7.0
5.3	3.07	11.5	0.08	3.1	0.4	0.40	3.40	3.79	85.1	2.7	45.4	28.6	5.6
8.3	0.00	0.0	0.00	5.3	0.7	1.41	17.97	4.15	71.5	4.2	11.3	7.2	5.2
6.9	0.92	5.7	0.00	6.1	118.2	1.11	16.40	2.95	59.4	5.3	35.0	9.5	5.7
7.5	0.49	3.1	0.01	4.9	1.8	0.96	11.99	3.23	54.4	4.2	39.5	13.7	4.5
8.8	0.00	0.0	-0.33	5.1	0.4	1.26	14.26	3.60	62.9	4.3	47.2	14.9	3.5
0.7	4.39	23.7	0.59	5.0	1.1	1.34	11.24	3.67	64.8	2.5	23.7	17.1	6.1
6.9	0.26	1.5	0.01	9.8	9.3	2.58	21.70	4.50	48.0	4.6	16.0	5.1	8.7
4.2	2.12	11.5	0.47	4.4	1.8	0.99	11.49	3.84	70.2	4.5	25.9	7.1	5.2
4.2	1.78	10.0	-0.08	4.6	0.4	1.01	9.28	4.31	70.3	3.8	30.8	13.0	6.4
4.8	4.01	10.5	0.08	3.6	1.1	0.84	5.91	3.02	69.9	2.9	58.8	40.1	7.0
5.2	1.68	11.2	0.03	3.8	0.5	0.71	8.29	4.23	78.4	4.2	27.5	10.0	4.8
4.5	0.71	5.6	-0.01	6.7	6.9	1.23	13.86	3.61	51.3	0.6	9.5	46.0	6.4
2.7	4.76	20.6	0.17	7.7	2.8	1.78	13.20	4.75	65.1	1.0	25.0	35.0	8.8
5.4	0.80	4.0	0.21	6.2	0.7	1.45	13.87	3.25	44.4	3.9	41.2	15.6	6.1
1.5	11.63	46.3	1.52	0.0	-0.5	-1.41	-13.98	3.05	125.1	5.1	46.3	10.7	4.1
7.9	0.01	0.1	-0.04	9.8	2.4	2.49	30.79	4.06	41.8	1.5	9.9	23.2	6.7
3.5	1.64	13.4	0.25	2.6	0.1	0.26	2.97	5.20	87.7	1.7	18.1	21.7	2.9
4.3	1.26	8.7	0.24	4.2	1.9	1.03	11.05	4.62	84.2	4.8	16.9	3.5	3.7
5.7	1.95	7.3	0.32	2.8	0.6	0.50	4.93	3.36	75.9	3.4	50.3	21.6	5.7
3.3	2.79	15.9	-0.06	6.0	5.0	1.19	11.17	3.72	54.4	4.3	30.9	10.6	6.0
5.1	3.76	13.8	0.61	3.8	0.8	0.63	6.26	3.89	70.3	2.9	37.1	19.5	5.2
2.5	3.95	19.3	0.12	3.9	0.5	0.82	10.05	4.00	81.4	5.4	41.5	7.5	4.1
9.5	0.01	0.0	0.61	5.2	2.0	1.14	9.89	2.83	45.7	4.1	72.7	23.0	7.2
8.5	0.34	1.2	-0.08	4.3	0.6	0.78	5.40	3.23	66.7	3.8	42.7	16.9	8.2
1.1	5.32	35.4	1.05	3.0	0.3	0.46	4.75	3.93	72.6	1.9	20.0	20.5	4.2
5.2	1.13	7.1	0.27	5.8	15.3	1.11	9.85	3.40	60.5	4.0	3.7	7.5	8.4
7.0	0.00	0.0	-0.01	6.6	0.8	1.60	14.40	3.97	57.5	3.9	13.4	9.0	7.0
6.1	0.37	2.2	-0.08	5.7	1.4	1.36	15.88	4.06	65.8	2.1	35.3	28.0	5.2
8.0	0.60	2.4	0.01	3.4	1.8	0.44	5.01	1.70	56.5	3.2	30.5	15.9	6.2
4.8	0.54	3.2	0.17	8.0	3.8	2.04	18.97	4.09	52.5	2.7	20.5	16.0	7.3
5.1	3.87	10.9	1.01	4.1	1.4	0.76	6.49	3.30	68.0	2.8	22.3	15.8	6.9
5.2	4.16	13.1	0.55	1.6	1.6	0.42	4.00	3.30	91.4	5.0	45.1	11.2	4.5
3.4	1.67	12.1	0.15	6.0	2.2	1.53	14.99	3.90	60.7	3.0	16.1	14.2	4.8
6.8	0.35	1.9	-0.08	4.4	0.3	0.69	6.44	4.18	70.3	2.9	22.5	15.2	5.9
5.0	0.83	6.5	0.12	2.9	1.1	0.45	4.68	4.02	82.5	2.4	11.4	16.6	4.2
5.6	4.12	14.3	0.02	5.0	2.0	1.04	6.02	3.28	58.1	2.6	23.6	17.0	8.2
8.4	0.33	0.8	0.03	5.0	0.5	1.11	7.34	4.10	64.9	3.7	50.4	18.5	7.0
8.9	0.00	0.0	0.30	3.1	0.2	0.48	4.47	2.12	76.0	6.0	73.9	10.7	4.7
6.8	0.36	1.0	0.04	4.0	1.7	0.80	4.22	3.28	67.4	6.4	59.2	7.4	7.1
8.6	0.00	0.0	-0.01	5.6	0.2	1.22	4.98	3.91	62.2	4.3	51.0	13.6	7.2
7.4	0.18	1.4	0.09	4.8	1.4	0.83	8.61	3.86	68.0	0.8	19.8	46.7	5.2

Name	City	State	Rating	2013 Rating	2012 Rating	Total Assets ($Mil)	One Year Asset Growth	Asset Mix (As a % of Total Assets): Comm-ercial Loans	Cons-umer Loans	Mort-gage Loans	Secur-ities	Capital-ization Index	Lever-age Ratio	Risk-Based Capital Ratio
▲ BANK OF LINCOLN COUNTY	Fayetteville	TN	**C+**	C-	C	129.7	-0.38	9.6	2.1	14.5	10.6	**10.0**	12.9	17.5
BANK OF LINDSAY	Lindsay	NE	**C-**	D+	C-	40.2	1.93	10.5	3.7	0.4	4.4	**3.8**	7.9	10.4
BANK OF LITTLE ROCK	Little Rock	AR	**C+**	C+	C	213.0	9.26	16.7	2.5	10.5	33.4	**9.0**	10.3	16.9
BANK OF LOCUST GROVE	Locust Grove	OK	**C**	C	B-	31.3	7.11	11.0	27.0	7.8	9.5	**8.6**	10.0	16.0
BANK OF LOUISIANA	Louisiana	MO	**C-**	D+	D+	52.3	1.90	4.5	1.5	15.9	32.7	**9.0**	10.4	18.8
▼ BANK OF LOUISIANA	New Orleans	LA	**D**	D+	C-	79.1	-6.41	1.0	8.5	32.5	1.1	**10.0**	14.0	22.9
BANK OF LUMBER CITY	Lumber City	GA	**C-**	C-	D	20.4	2.54	9.5	15.1	13.2	26.8	**10.0**	17.0	26.3
BANK OF LUXEMBURG	Luxemburg	WI	**C+**	B-	B	264.3	1.83	14.3	2.1	18.3	21.4	**9.1**	10.4	14.8
BANK OF MACKS CREEK	Macks Creek	MO	**E-**	E-	E-	19.7	-2.50	2.2	3.5	29.4	16.5	**3.8**	5.8	11.5
BANK OF MADISON	Madison	GA	**B**	B-	C	191.5	-5.79	3.8	1.1	15.8	27.3	**10.0**	15.6	25.3
BANK OF MAGNOLIA CO	Magnolia	OH	**B-**	B-	C+	78.1	4.05	5.1	2.8	24.1	43.0	**9.7**	10.8	20.3
▲ BANK OF MAINE	Portland	ME	**C-**	D+	D	790.2	-2.11	16.1	1.1	31.3	10.9	**8.2**	9.8	14.4
BANK OF MANHATTAN NA	El Segundo	CA	**D+**	C-	C-	496.1	3.92	13.1	5.0	16.8	5.6	**7.6**	9.9	13.0
BANK OF MAPLE PLAIN	Maple Plain	MN	**B**	B	B	74.6	-2.93	6.2	1.8	22.4	30.9	**10.0**	12.8	27.0
BANK OF MARIN	Novato	CA	**B-**	C+	B-	1802.3	21.49	7.0	1.2	5.2	18.5	**7.9**	10.0	13.3
▲ BANK OF MARINGOUIN	Maringouin	LA	**B-**	B-	B	50.2	1.15	6.3	5.0	12.5	30.4	**7.7**	9.5	21.1
▲ BANK OF MARION	Marion	VA	**B**	B-	C+	358.5	4.91	2.0	3.2	25.6	28.0	**10.0**	11.1	21.3
▼ BANK OF MAUMEE	Maumee	OH	**E+**	E	E-	32.0	13.51	16.1	2.8	2.6	0.0	**5.9**	7.9	14.5
BANK OF MAUSTON	Mauston	WI	**C**	B-	C+	268.1	3.63	3.4	2.3	14.2	39.8	**9.6**	10.8	15.5
BANK OF MAYSVILLE	Maysville	KY	**B**	B+	B+	113.9	-2.04	0.3	1.4	34.3	33.9	**10.0**	17.1	32.5
▲ BANK OF MCCRORY	McCrory	AR	**C+**	C+	C+	94.4	12.50	3.3	2.7	4.0	47.8	**7.8**	9.5	17.7
BANK OF MCKENNEY	McKenney	VA	**B-**	B	C+	217.6	-0.03	5.8	1.1	22.2	13.3	**9.2**	10.8	14.4
▲ BANK OF MEAD	Mead	NE	**B-**	C+	C+	28.1	1.65	6.2	4.3	13.7	37.6	**7.9**	9.6	20.3
BANK OF MICHIGAN	Farmington Hills	MI	**D**	D	D-	105.9	8.39	7.5	0.2	8.0	7.2	**7.2**	9.2	13.9
BANK OF MILAN	Milan	TN	**B-**	B	B-	61.8	-0.30	10.2	2.0	21.6	39.9	**7.4**	9.3	16.7
▲ BANK OF MILLBROOK	Millbrook	NY	**B-**	C+	B-	211.9	-0.15	2.3	2.5	26.0	38.8	**10.0**	11.1	24.1
BANK OF MILTON	Milton	WI	**C+**	C+	C+	97.2	-1.90	8.3	2.2	19.5	18.9	**5.0**	8.5	11.0
BANK OF MINDEN	Mindenmines	MO	**B-**	B	B+	29.5	2.70	10.9	2.0	15.4	13.8	**10.0**	14.2	25.8
BANK OF MINGO	Williamson	WV	**C**	C+	C+	98.7	-8.02	6.2	5.0	21.6	40.5	**10.0**	12.1	26.8
BANK OF MISSOURI	Perryville	MO	**A-**	A-	B	1051.0	1.67	8.7	2.3	19.3	19.1	**9.4**	11.0	14.5
BANK OF MODESTO	Modesto	IL	**C+**	C+	C+	45.4	1.26	6.4	3.4	5.6	32.6	**8.0**	9.7	15.6
BANK OF MONROE	Union	WV	**B+**	B	B+	122.7	-1.18	2.2	4.5	26.1	34.1	**10.0**	14.7	29.8
▲ BANK OF MONTANA	Missoula	MT	**A-**	B+	B	46.8	-5.50	12.7	1.7	20.1	0.0	**10.0**	12.2	17.7
BANK OF MONTGOMERY	Montgomery	IL	**D+**	D	C-	39.6	1.17	7.8	1.3	15.6	35.2	**7.2**	9.1	20.6
BANK OF MONTGOMERY	Montgomery	LA	**A-**	A-	A-	209.4	13.83	6.1	7.8	26.7	8.8	**8.2**	9.8	13.8
BANK OF MONTICELLO	Monticello	GA	**E-**	E-	E-	97.8	6.06	5.3	7.0	31.5	15.5	**4.2**	6.2	12.2
BANK OF MONTICELLO	Monticello	MO	**C**	C	B-	103.3	10.89	5.9	3.8	15.3	20.8	**5.8**	10.7	11.6
BANK OF MORTON	Morton	MS	**B+**	A-	A-	66.8	7.24	1.6	8.1	33.0	21.2	**10.0**	13.0	21.3
BANK OF MOUNDVILLE	Moundville	AL	**D+**	C	C	94.8	-17.24	4.8	2.3	3.0	66.8	**6.6**	8.6	20.6
BANK OF MOUNT HOPE INC	Mount Hope	WV	**B+**	B+	B+	126.2	1.99	12.4	8.0	16.4	43.3	**10.0**	11.6	28.9
BANK OF NAPA NA	Napa	CA	**B**	B	B	172.3	9.21	7.8	0.2	2.5	28.4	**10.0**	13.5	20.7
BANK OF NEBRASKA	La Vista	NE	**B**	B	C+	131.5	-1.18	11.7	0.5	16.8	0.2	**8.5**	10.0	14.0
BANK OF NEW CAMBRIA	New Cambria	MO	**C+**	C+	C-	33.8	8.06	1.6	1.8	6.9	28.5	**8.9**	10.3	17.7
BANK OF NEW CASTLE	New Castle	DE	**C**	C	B-	17.4	0.18	0.0	0.0	0.0	5.2	**10.0**	97.0	482.2
BANK OF NEW ENGLAND	Salem	NH	**C+**	C+	B-	623.7	13.79	6.0	0.1	0.8	0.2	**8.2**	12.7	13.5
BANK OF NEW GLARUS	New Glarus	WI	**B-**	C+	C	226.3	6.65	12.4	2.6	19.0	14.5	**8.0**	9.7	13.7
BANK OF NEW HAMPSHIRE	Laconia	NH	**C+**	C+	C+	1219.0	4.17	5.2	1.9	28.9	21.6	**8.1**	9.8	15.3
BANK OF NEW JERSEY	Fort Lee	NJ	**C+**	C+	B-	701.1	19.64	9.7	0.2	13.2	10.7	**5.3**	8.9	11.2
BANK OF NEW MADRID	New Madrid	MO	**B-**	B-	B	90.6	2.75	3.5	2.7	13.0	43.3	**8.0**	9.6	13.3
▼ BANK OF NEW MEXICO	Grants	NM	**B-**	B	B	161.4	26.66	3.9	1.3	3.1	56.3	**6.1**	8.1	14.9
BANK OF NEW ORLEANS	Metairie	LA	**B**	B	B	320.9	1.07	0.1	0.2	51.0	14.3	**10.0**	13.3	23.1
▲ BANK OF NEW YORK MELLON	New York	NY	**C+**	C+	C+	304867.0	4.59	0.7	0.0	0.8	36.6	**3.4**	5.4	13.5
▲ BANK OF NEWINGTON	Newington	GA	**D-**	E	E-	83.0	5.61	9.2	2.7	22.9	0.0	**5.1**	7.4	11.1
BANK OF NEWMAN GROVE	Newman Grove	NE	**C**	C	C	38.1	4.37	0.2	8.4	0.0	38.9	**6.9**	8.9	13.9
BANK OF NORTH CAROLINA	High Point	NC	**C+**	C+	C-	3733.2	25.83	4.6	0.4	13.3	13.2	**6.1**	8.7	11.9
BANK OF NORTHERN MICHIGAN	Petoskey	MI	**C+**	C+	C	412.1	5.43	17.2	0.6	10.1	15.0	**6.6**	8.6	12.9
BANK OF NY MELLON TRUST NA	Los Angeles	CA	**U**	U	B+	1931.1	-0.24	0.0	0.0	0.0	33.4	**10.0**	77.4	632.6
▲ BANK OF OAK RIDGE	Oak Ridge	NC	**C**	C-	D-	358.0	2.10	7.8	0.4	25.9	14.2	**7.3**	9.2	13.4
▲ BANK OF OAK RIDGE	Oak Ridge	LA	**B-**	C	C	51.2	-2.53	1.2	3.9	0.0	69.3	**9.7**	10.8	34.8
BANK OF OAKFIELD	Oakfield	WI	**B**	B	B	82.1	-1.48	7.0	1.0	14.9	17.3	**9.8**	10.9	16.3

Asset Quality Index	Adjusted Non-Performing Loans as a % of Total Loans	Adjusted Non-Performing Loans as a % of Capital	Net Charge-Offs Avg Loans	Profitability Index	Net Income ($Mil)	Return on Assets (R.O.A.)	Return on Equity (R.O.E.)	Net Interest Spread	Overhead Efficiency Ratio	Liquidity Index	Liquidity Ratio	Hot Money Ratio	Stability Index
3.3	3.14	15.2	0.46	**5.5**	0.9	0.91	7.08	4.95	62.1	**1.3**	22.0	29.4	**5.3**
6.8	0.00	0.0	0.00	**5.7**	0.3	0.91	11.73	4.09	70.9	**1.0**	12.9	30.8	**3.7**
3.5	2.84	13.0	1.11	**4.8**	1.4	0.92	9.01	4.42	79.1	**5.8**	43.5	5.9	**5.3**
5.5	0.64	3.2	0.22	**9.1**	0.3	1.41	14.27	5.22	62.7	**4.8**	30.4	7.0	**4.3**
2.0	6.06	29.0	0.08	**4.6**	0.5	1.12	11.33	3.75	77.8	**3.6**	30.3	13.8	**4.9**
1.2	9.20	36.1	0.14	**0.0**	-0.4	-0.72	-5.05	6.64	115.6	**5.0**	25.6	3.5	**5.2**
6.2	0.57	1.7	0.03	**2.4**	0.1	0.30	1.77	6.01	88.5	**2.7**	42.3	19.6	**4.3**
3.1	2.70	16.8	0.38	**4.2**	1.4	0.69	6.67	4.48	77.4	**3.9**	25.6	10.7	**5.7**
1.7	4.89	37.4	0.89	**0.1**	-0.1	-0.65	-10.69	4.06	115.9	**2.4**	25.4	17.4	**0.0**
4.5	4.40	16.7	0.22	**4.8**	1.5	0.98	7.03	4.13	66.6	**3.0**	22.4	14.9	**6.2**
6.3	1.63	6.4	0.76	**3.8**	0.4	0.74	6.51	3.51	76.8	**6.1**	44.5	3.8	**6.5**
4.0	1.83	13.6	0.33	**2.2**	1.5	0.25	2.01	3.69	87.5	**3.2**	13.1	12.7	**5.9**
5.1	0.46	3.4	0.07	**0.8**	-2.7	-0.73	-6.38	4.10	107.5	**3.1**	12.3	13.4	**5.1**
5.4	2.68	8.4	-0.01	**4.6**	0.7	1.18	9.11	3.31	60.3	**5.3**	44.9	9.2	**7.2**
4.1	1.34	9.1	-0.01	**7.1**	15.7	1.14	11.18	4.20	57.9	**4.5**	19.2	6.7	**8.5**
4.8	2.24	8.7	0.15	**2.4**	-0.1	-0.28	-2.68	3.19	85.4	**5.2**	37.6	7.7	**5.6**
5.1	2.92	13.7	0.20	**4.5**	2.5	0.94	8.58	3.54	67.8	**3.3**	28.3	14.6	**5.8**
2.1	4.21	24.0	2.14	**0.0**	-0.9	-3.61	-38.14	3.31	189.0	**4.3**	45.2	14.5	**2.1**
2.7	4.19	19.4	0.22	**8.1**	3.6	1.83	17.23	3.82	47.2	**2.3**	33.3	24.2	**7.6**
7.7	0.89	2.9	0.02	**4.3**	0.7	0.81	4.49	3.62	70.0	**2.9**	22.7	15.4	**8.1**
6.6	1.11	4.6	0.19	**4.4**	0.6	0.94	9.89	2.80	58.6	**5.5**	55.0	9.9	**4.3**
5.0	1.62	10.0	0.21	**4.6**	1.3	0.81	7.79	4.64	75.8	**2.8**	21.1	15.7	**5.7**
7.9	0.08	0.4	-0.12	**4.4**	0.2	0.90	9.87	3.34	63.7	**4.3**	41.8	13.6	**5.4**
1.3	2.75	19.4	0.08	**5.7**	0.8	1.03	11.56	4.27	73.9	**1.4**	24.1	29.4	**4.5**
8.0	0.43	2.1	-0.01	**4.4**	0.4	0.94	11.10	3.92	78.8	**4.9**	45.1	11.1	**5.4**
7.3	0.62	2.5	0.02	**3.6**	1.1	0.72	6.70	3.14	72.5	**5.8**	38.6	4.3	**6.3**
4.3	1.07	8.0	0.01	**5.1**	0.8	1.01	12.02	4.29	69.9	**3.1**	27.9	15.5	**6.2**
8.2	0.07	0.3	-0.12	**3.6**	0.1	0.53	3.90	3.71	81.3	**3.4**	52.3	19.8	**7.7**
2.4	8.77	27.3	5.90	**0.4**	-1.3	-1.69	-13.45	3.88	115.1	**3.3**	55.8	23.1	**4.9**
6.5	0.84	5.1	0.38	**5.4**	8.3	1.04	9.65	4.24	69.9	**2.2**	6.2	17.4	**8.9**
8.4	0.02	0.1	0.00	**3.6**	0.2	0.47	4.89	3.08	73.5	**4.7**	32.8	9.0	**5.0**
8.4	0.78	2.6	0.05	**4.8**	0.8	0.84	6.06	3.97	69.5	**3.3**	41.8	19.2	**7.3**
8.5	0.00	0.0	0.00	**8.9**	0.9	2.39	19.38	4.21	57.4	**1.0**	15.8	32.6	**7.4**
5.0	3.84	12.8	-0.17	**2.0**	0.2	0.55	6.11	2.82	89.3	**5.9**	63.8	9.4	**2.4**
5.6	0.89	6.9	0.23	**8.6**	3.0	1.94	20.34	5.01	63.1	**1.0**	8.6	30.3	**6.8**
1.3	3.59	30.0	0.45	**4.0**	0.8	1.10	19.50	3.95	70.0	**1.9**	23.5	20.8	**1.4**
2.5	3.12	18.4	0.07	**5.1**	0.9	1.20	11.98	3.63	66.4	**2.0**	17.8	19.3	**6.7**
5.3	1.69	8.3	0.14	**10.0**	1.2	2.50	19.66	5.07	55.0	**1.8**	27.0	25.1	**8.5**
7.7	0.65	1.6	0.14	**1.3**	-0.1	-0.10	-1.39	2.90	103.4	**2.2**	37.9	30.5	**3.0**
8.6	0.12	0.5	0.02	**4.1**	0.7	0.74	6.29	3.11	72.4	**3.7**	40.0	16.4	**7.3**
8.5	0.51	2.2	-0.08	**4.5**	0.9	0.74	5.55	3.79	67.4	**3.4**	40.3	17.9	**7.3**
4.1	0.89	6.4	-0.27	**5.7**	1.2	1.23	12.45	3.87	81.4	**2.9**	20.1	15.2	**6.8**
9.0	0.18	0.8	-0.06	**3.2**	0.1	0.49	4.78	3.60	84.3	**5.4**	47.8	9.3	**4.8**
7.6	0.00	0.0	0.00	**2.0**	0.0	0.15	0.15	0.39	30.6	**5.0**	327.1	100.0	**7.2**
3.4	1.06	7.1	-0.04	**7.7**	5.3	1.18	9.26	4.23	51.8	**0.9**	9.1	32.3	**8.0**
4.1	1.41	10.0	0.27	**5.0**	1.4	0.88	8.26	4.02	70.9	**3.2**	18.4	13.3	**6.4**
5.7	1.09	7.5	0.15	**3.2**	4.7	0.53	4.73	3.69	84.1	**4.0**	14.3	9.1	**7.9**
3.7	0.92	8.2	0.10	**4.1**	3.2	0.66	7.43	3.32	58.0	**0.7**	13.2	45.8	**6.1**
8.9	0.08	0.3	0.08	**4.1**	0.7	0.90	9.79	4.41	77.4	**1.7**	13.7	20.7	**4.9**
6.3	1.16	4.1	0.02	**2.9**	0.3	0.31	2.84	3.48	90.7	**4.7**	58.3	16.2	**6.2**
9.1	0.35	2.1	0.03	**4.7**	2.0	0.84	5.64	3.15	64.1	**1.2**	1.5	25.6	**8.1**
8.5	1.42	3.1	0.03	**4.0**	1646.0	0.78	10.89	0.97	72.3	**3.7**	60.2	28.9	**4.8**
0.9	5.03	46.9	0.81	**5.6**	0.9	1.59	22.41	4.56	70.5	**1.3**	10.4	26.6	**2.3**
7.1	0.00	0.0	-0.01	**2.6**	0.1	0.41	4.92	2.79	86.1	**4.0**	31.0	12.0	**4.5**
4.3	0.90	7.2	0.37	**4.5**	22.7	0.88	8.54	4.62	69.1	**1.1**	10.3	29.9	**6.2**
3.7	1.97	14.3	-0.05	**4.0**	2.1	0.76	8.87	3.22	69.8	**0.8**	15.8	35.6	**5.7**
6.5	na	0.0	na	**9.5**	60.0	4.14	4.74	0.78	67.6	**10.0**	319.5	0.0	**6.3**
3.6	1.71	12.7	0.89	**2.9**	1.6	0.60	6.44	4.05	74.4	**0.9**	18.4	35.4	**4.1**
9.8	0.02	0.0	-0.06	**4.1**	0.4	1.03	10.42	2.32	47.8	**3.6**	86.5	31.6	**5.4**
5.8	1.07	6.2	0.11	**5.2**	0.6	0.92	8.69	4.46	64.9	**2.0**	27.4	22.2	**5.0**

Name	City	State	Rating	2013 Rating	2012 Rating	Total Assets ($Mil)	One Year Asset Growth	Comm-ercial Loans	Cons-umer Loans	Mort-gage Loans	Secur-ities	Capital-ization Index	Lever-age Ratio	Risk-Based Capital Ratio
								Asset Mix (As a % of Total Assets)						
BANK OF OCEAN CITY	Ocean City	MD	**A-**	A-	A-	256.3	7.55	2.1	0.9	13.4	18.4	**8.8**	10.2	19.9
BANK OF ODESSA	Odessa	MO	**B**	B-	C+	236.3	1.73	4.0	2.7	24.3	26.3	**10.0**	20.9	46.5
▲ BANK OF OFALLON	OFallon	IL	**B+**	B	B+	305.2	5.37	5.9	2.0	37.4	29.1	**10.0**	13.2	26.7
BANK OF OHIO COUNTY INC	Beaver Dam	KY	**A**	A	A	90.9	1.92	6.9	1.0	11.0	39.2	**10.0**	21.6	35.6
BANK OF OKOLONA	Okolona	MS	**B**	B-	B-	145.0	0.78	21.7	6.8	16.0	22.5	**10.0**	11.4	16.9
▲ BANK OF OLD MONROE	Old Monroe	MO	**A**	B+	A-	307.3	1.78	3.9	0.9	10.6	39.3	**10.0**	12.7	20.5
BANK OF ONTARIO	Ontario	WI	**C+**	C-	C+	35.6	0.53	5.1	7.1	38.5	7.2	**10.0**	12.1	23.9
BANK OF ORCHARD	Orchard	NE	**B**	B-	B-	24.3	-0.25	9.1	5.2	0.7	26.8	**10.0**	13.3	26.0
BANK OF ORRICK	Orrick	MO	**D-**	D	D	33.9	3.56	3.1	2.7	14.9	31.3	**6.2**	8.2	15.5
BANK OF OSWEGO	Lake Oswego	OR	**D-**	D	D+	100.5	-14.81	13.2	3.2	9.0	17.3	**6.5**	8.5	17.5
BANK OF PALMER	Palmer	KS	**C**	C	C-	41.5	-1.46	2.7	3.5	10.9	44.6	**6.9**	9.0	16.8
BANK OF PENSACOLA	Pensacola	FL	**D+**	D+	C-	65.4	7.67	1.6	2.7	5.5	51.4	**10.0**	19.1	65.1
▼ BANK OF PERRY	Perry	GA	**E**	D-	E	116.4	6.47	10.7	2.0	17.1	12.4	**3.5**	7.0	10.3
▲ BANK OF PERRY COUNTY	Lobelville	TN	**C**	C-	C+	146.4	-2.56	7.9	14.7	38.8	4.4	**8.3**	9.9	15.1
BANK OF PINE HILL	Pine Hill	AL	**D+**	C-	C-	25.7	4.19	0.8	2.6	9.1	68.5	**10.0**	12.9	31.8
BANK OF PONTIAC	Pontiac	IL	**A-**	A-	A-	483.4	1.77	8.5	3.6	25.3	24.5	**10.0**	12.7	22.4
▲ BANK OF POYNETTE	Poynette	WI	**B-**	C+	C-	99.9	3.33	5.2	0.4	14.8	16.5	**8.1**	9.8	16.4
BANK OF PRAGUE	Prague	NE	**B**	B	B+	22.3	-0.13	13.5	9.2	3.1	23.3	**10.0**	16.5	22.0
BANK OF PRAIRIE DU SAC	Prairie Du Sac	WI	**A**	A-	A-	345.8	6.01	12.1	1.0	5.7	37.5	**10.0**	15.4	22.3
BANK OF PRAIRIE VILLAGE	Prairie Village	KS	**B**	B	B-	104.3	0.11	11.9	2.0	24.9	34.9	**7.0**	9.0	15.4
BANK OF PRESCOTT	Prescott	AR	**A-**	A-	B+	81.0	4.03	16.2	5.1	12.3	44.5	**10.0**	13.3	20.4
BANK OF PRINCETON	Princeton	NJ	**C+**	C+	C-	935.9	9.72	7.7	0.0	9.4	19.2	**5.3**	8.2	11.3
BANK OF PROTECTION	Protection	KS	**B**	B	B-	63.3	10.29	3.3	3.4	6.4	33.1	**9.6**	10.8	18.4
BANK OF PUTNAM COUNTY	Cookeville	TN	**B-**	B-	B-	382.0	0.02	3.0	3.7	25.7	36.2	**6.2**	8.2	24.4
BANK OF QUINCY	Quincy	IL	**B**	B	B+	143.0	13.32	13.9	3.4	15.2	6.7	**8.7**	10.9	13.9
BANK OF RANTOUL	Rantoul	IL	**A-**	B+	A-	222.9	-0.73	13.7	0.5	3.6	46.7	**7.5**	9.4	17.3
BANK OF RICHMONDVILLE	Cobleskill	NY	**B-**	B-	B	135.2	3.11	4.3	1.7	42.4	25.3	**10.0**	11.8	23.4
▲ BANK OF RINGGOLD	Ringgold	LA	**C+**	C-	C+	64.4	-4.27	1.7	2.6	11.9	49.9	**10.0**	15.3	47.7
BANK OF RIO VISTA	Rio Vista	CA	**C+**	C	C-	189.1	5.75	3.3	0.2	0.3	56.2	**10.0**	11.6	23.4
BANK OF RIPLEY	Ripley	TN	**C+**	B-	B	197.4	-5.65	1.6	6.6	12.1	49.8	**10.0**	13.8	26.3
▲ BANK OF RISON	Rison	AR	**C**	D+	C	30.9	29.20	11.5	6.6	9.8	11.0	**10.0**	13.9	21.8
BANK OF RIVER OAKS	Houston	TX	**B**	A-	B+	434.3	32.94	30.3	2.2	5.9	17.1	**8.0**	9.7	13.4
BANK OF ROMNEY	Romney	WV	**C+**	C+	C	258.1	4.99	3.7	5.5	40.2	25.3	**10.0**	11.5	19.7
BANK OF RUSTON	Ruston	LA	**B**	B	B	161.5	22.21	11.4	2.9	31.9	3.4	**9.4**	11.4	14.5
BANK OF SACRAMENTO	Sacramento	CA	**C+**	C+	C+	480.5	4.72	9.6	0.5	1.2	34.1	**8.9**	10.2	15.0
▲ BANK OF SALEM	Salem	AR	**B**	B-	C+	128.3	0.02	11.0	5.2	28.9	3.0	**10.0**	11.8	17.2
BANK OF SALEM	Salem	MO	**C+**	B-	C+	87.4	-4.94	3.2	3.2	30.2	34.3	**8.6**	10.0	19.9
BANK OF SAN ANTONIO	San Antonio	TX	**B**	B	B-	456.4	8.48	27.1	1.2	9.6	13.2	**7.1**	9.3	12.6
BANK OF SAN FRANCISCO	San Francisco	CA	**B**	B	B	161.2	14.85	38.6	0.6	11.9	0.0	**7.9**	10.0	13.2
BANK OF SAN JACINTO COUNTY	Coldspring	TX	**B**	B	B+	35.3	0.19	4.1	4.9	40.5	8.3	**10.0**	13.2	36.2
BANK OF SANTA BARBARA	Santa Barbara	CA	**D+**	C-	C-	170.2	9.54	15.8	0.5	3.3	1.8	**5.5**	8.3	11.4
BANK OF SANTA CLARITA	Santa Clarita	CA	**C**	C	C-	280.0	16.48	6.7	4.8	1.4	10.7	**6.9**	8.9	13.9
BANK OF SOPERTON	Soperton	GA	**C-**	D	E	37.6	10.29	14.1	6.0	23.1	13.9	**7.4**	9.3	15.1
BANK OF SOUTH CAROLINA	Charleston	SC	**B+**	B	B	376.4	12.69	12.9	1.4	12.0	28.4	**7.7**	9.5	14.8
BANK OF SOUTH TEXAS	Laredo	TX	**C-**	D	D-	85.7	12.66	5.7	1.9	29.6	12.5	**8.1**	9.7	14.5
BANK OF SOUTHERN CALIFORNIA NA	San Diego	CA	**C+**	C+	C	235.8	23.98	16.7	1.7	13.5	0.8	**9.5**	10.6	14.7
BANK OF SOUTHSIDE VIRGINIA	Carson	VA	**A**	A	A-	539.6	-0.10	2.6	16.2	10.3	20.1	**10.0**	16.0	30.9
BANK OF SPRINGFIELD	Springfield	IL	**C**	C	C-	828.5	13.83	14.8	1.5	10.1	10.9	**4.0**	8.3	10.5
BANK OF ST CROIX	Christiansted	VI	**D+**	C-	C	134.6	15.72	1.6	0.2	24.9	48.8	**7.8**	9.5	27.0
BANK OF ST ELIZABETH	Saint Elizabeth	MO	**A-**	B	B+	110.3	7.98	1.5	5.2	50.5	0.0	**7.7**	9.5	16.4
BANK OF ST FRANCISVILLE	Saint Francisville	LA	**B**	B-	C+	106.7	2.22	4.9	5.5	24.7	21.0	**8.8**	10.2	16.4
BANK OF STAPLETON	Stapleton	NE	**C-**	C-	D+	27.8	15.86	22.2	11.5	3.2	0.0	**5.2**	11.6	11.2
▲ BANK OF STAR CITY	Star City	AR	**B+**	B	B	93.3	-3.97	10.2	2.5	14.6	31.1	**10.0**	14.4	22.7
BANK OF STAR VALLEY	Afton	WY	**B**	B	B-	129.0	5.57	9.3	6.9	16.5	22.2	**10.0**	11.7	16.6
▲ BANK OF STEINAUER	Steinauer	NE	**D+**	C-	C	11.9	2.17	6.7	9.6	27.3	7.3	**6.6**	8.6	13.9
▲ BANK OF STOCKTON	Stockton	CA	**B+**	B-	B-	2292.7	7.82	7.7	9.2	6.8	33.8	**9.1**	10.4	16.2
BANK OF STRONGHURST	Stronghurst	IL	**C+**	C+	B-	78.2	-0.98	1.4	1.2	7.5	69.0	**10.0**	15.0	45.3
BANK OF SULLIVAN	Sullivan	MO	**C**	C-	C+	373.0	12.08	8.4	2.3	31.8	7.0	**5.3**	9.0	11.2
BANK OF SUN PRAIRIE	Sun Prairie	WI	**B**	B	C+	286.8	-2.70	5.7	1.3	10.6	6.4	**10.0**	15.4	19.5
BANK OF SUNSET & TRUST CO	Sunset	LA	**B+**	B+	B	123.1	-1.43	12.4	1.0	15.4	32.8	**7.7**	9.5	16.8

Asset Quality Index	Adjusted Non-Performing Loans as a % of Total Loans	Adjusted Non-Performing Loans as a % of Capital	Net Charge-Offs / Avg Loans	Profitability Index	Net Income ($Mil)	Return on Assets (R.O.A.)	Return on Equity (R.O.E.)	Net Interest Spread	Overhead Efficiency Ratio	Liquidity Index	Liquidity Ratio	Hot Money Ratio	Stability Index
8.1	0.46	2.3	-0.01	**5.8**	1.7	0.94	8.49	3.57	58.9	**5.1**	45.1	10.8	**6.0**
6.7	2.53	6.1	0.16	**5.5**	2.0	1.11	5.35	3.12	46.5	**5.0**	41.7	10.5	**6.7**
6.9	1.09	5.1	0.06	**5.0**	2.9	1.28	9.64	2.69	48.4	**2.2**	6.3	16.9	**7.7**
7.9	1.65	3.2	0.73	**8.8**	1.3	1.86	8.85	4.34	53.7	**5.6**	48.7	7.9	**9.1**
4.3	2.44	13.9	0.10	**8.2**	2.3	2.08	17.99	5.15	56.9	**1.0**	18.2	33.8	**7.0**
9.1	0.15	0.5	0.05	**6.9**	3.4	1.43	12.28	3.85	49.7	**2.8**	41.3	23.7	**6.7**
3.1	3.89	18.2	0.17	**5.1**	0.2	0.89	7.70	4.65	74.5	**2.5**	36.1	24.0	**6.9**
8.3	0.05	0.1	-0.01	**5.8**	0.3	1.28	10.42	3.11	51.5	**2.5**	43.2	22.8	**6.6**
3.8	1.59	9.2	1.80	**0.4**	-0.1	-0.40	-4.33	4.12	99.8	**4.9**	31.3	7.1	**3.0**
2.7	4.43	17.2	-1.13	**0.0**	-0.5	-0.60	-6.34	3.74	115.9	**6.8**	59.3	4.7	**2.9**
6.0	1.52	8.2	0.06	**3.9**	0.2	0.68	7.97	3.59	65.6	**4.6**	47.9	13.3	**4.6**
9.9	0.00	0.0	0.09	**0.0**	-0.3	-0.70	-3.51	2.14	134.3	**6.3**	83.7	10.1	**4.7**
0.0	15.62	150.3	1.61	**1.4**	-0.3	-0.34	-5.04	4.06	86.3	**2.2**	8.0	17.2	**1.5**
2.8	1.85	13.6	0.17	**8.6**	2.0	1.81	18.50	4.86	54.5	**1.0**	9.2	30.2	**7.0**
3.7	15.28	25.0	-0.02	**1.2**	0.1	0.25	2.06	2.65	103.9	**4.0**	75.5	21.9	**6.0**
6.0	1.56	7.4	0.27	**6.6**	4.0	1.10	8.75	3.79	53.0	**3.6**	24.4	11.9	**6.4**
3.7	2.27	13.6	0.44	**4.3**	0.6	0.81	8.71	3.30	70.2	**4.6**	35.2	10.3	**5.5**
7.8	0.02	0.1	0.04	**7.6**	0.3	1.74	10.87	3.98	65.6	**4.5**	27.3	6.3	**6.3**
7.2	0.62	2.2	-0.67	**9.4**	4.5	1.73	11.41	4.21	39.5	**5.4**	46.4	9.8	**8.8**
6.8	0.98	6.0	0.40	**4.6**	0.9	1.16	13.27	3.47	57.5	**2.3**	39.2	29.2	**4.9**
8.1	0.65	2.3	0.11	**6.1**	0.8	1.29	9.88	4.50	63.0	**2.4**	33.2	22.2	**7.3**
3.1	1.64	13.6	0.00	**5.0**	6.4	0.95	12.12	3.91	64.8	**1.7**	12.5	21.4	**5.1**
8.2	0.01	0.1	0.42	**5.2**	0.6	1.23	11.99	4.06	63.8	**1.8**	21.1	21.2	**5.8**
9.3	0.10	0.5	0.14	**4.6**	2.8	0.98	12.16	2.59	71.0	**4.1**	52.0	17.4	**5.5**
4.3	1.27	9.0	-0.06	**6.1**	1.4	1.33	12.16	4.02	66.9	**3.0**	12.2	13.6	**7.6**
7.4	0.07	0.3	1.16	**9.6**	3.8	2.25	22.67	4.27	38.9	**2.3**	11.7	17.2	**7.4**
5.7	2.20	11.3	0.20	**3.3**	0.5	0.50	4.39	4.03	80.5	**3.9**	14.2	9.2	**6.7**
9.7	1.49	2.1	-0.03	**2.8**	0.2	0.37	2.49	2.25	80.8	**5.0**	73.3	15.3	**6.7**
4.2	5.75	15.8	-0.25	**3.2**	0.8	0.58	4.59	3.15	82.0	**5.9**	54.2	8.7	**5.4**
5.9	3.69	10.3	0.08	**3.1**	1.0	0.65	4.53	4.18	87.4	**3.0**	42.5	21.4	**6.1**
2.9	3.75	14.8	0.72	**4.5**	0.3	1.31	8.13	6.27	58.8	**2.5**	35.0	22.7	**5.1**
8.3	0.05	0.3	0.18	**4.8**	2.4	0.77	7.99	3.70	69.3	**2.7**	28.3	17.6	**5.6**
2.6	5.15	27.5	0.39	**3.9**	1.2	0.63	6.07	4.02	73.5	**1.6**	22.9	25.7	**5.9**
7.2	0.53	3.8	0.00	**4.6**	0.9	0.81	6.96	4.51	72.8	**0.7**	10.9	35.1	**6.8**
6.3	0.45	2.4	-0.07	**4.0**	2.4	0.68	7.14	3.63	73.5	**2.1**	32.5	25.7	**5.0**
5.1	1.18	6.6	0.34	**7.9**	1.1	1.16	9.72	4.97	56.8	**1.3**	13.5	26.5	**6.9**
8.7	0.35	1.8	0.04	**2.8**	0.3	0.36	3.77	3.29	85.3	**2.7**	22.3	16.4	**5.9**
7.5	0.01	0.1	0.00	**5.1**	2.9	0.89	8.39	3.71	69.2	**4.4**	26.2	8.2	**6.7**
7.9	0.18	1.4	0.01	**4.6**	0.7	0.64	6.37	4.21	75.4	**2.5**	15.5	16.5	**5.6**
7.5	0.60	2.3	0.19	**4.6**	0.2	0.85	6.47	5.11	82.6	**5.9**	51.5	6.5	**6.7**
3.2	1.24	9.1	-0.18	**1.1**	-0.3	-0.28	-2.78	4.45	98.6	**3.9**	29.2	11.7	**3.4**
5.1	0.52	3.3	-0.01	**3.0**	0.9	0.44	5.32	2.99	75.0	**1.6**	25.3	26.5	**4.7**
4.3	1.29	8.8	-0.02	**5.3**	0.4	1.50	18.11	5.15	73.5	**2.6**	21.9	16.7	**1.9**
6.3	0.45	2.8	-0.02	**7.1**	3.4	1.28	12.71	4.31	60.4	**3.0**	23.8	15.1	**5.9**
2.2	2.14	15.3	-0.11	**3.7**	0.4	0.61	4.33	5.66	86.0	**1.7**	23.6	23.8	**5.8**
4.8	0.90	6.5	-0.24	**4.0**	1.5	0.92	8.00	4.26	85.2	**3.1**	15.3	13.5	**6.1**
7.6	0.99	2.6	0.17	**7.5**	6.5	1.59	9.97	3.88	58.5	**5.9**	54.6	9.0	**9.5**
3.3	1.77	16.1	0.02	**3.2**	2.7	0.46	5.51	3.49	81.3	**3.7**	6.1	9.8	**4.7**
3.7	6.51	23.9	0.03	**1.0**	0.2	0.21	1.95	3.01	104.8	**6.4**	60.6	7.5	**4.9**
6.1	0.02	0.2	-0.10	**9.5**	1.8	2.28	19.55	4.67	53.5	**3.9**	19.3	9.8	**8.4**
5.0	1.24	7.4	0.27	**4.8**	0.8	1.00	10.15	5.20	76.8	**2.0**	18.6	19.2	**5.7**
5.0	0.34	2.6	0.13	**8.2**	0.4	2.04	17.85	6.37	66.0	**2.2**	9.7	17.3	**3.7**
6.7	1.44	5.4	0.03	**5.2**	0.8	1.19	8.88	4.78	66.1	**3.8**	35.6	14.7	**7.0**
4.9	2.08	11.2	-0.02	**7.0**	1.6	1.73	15.31	4.28	61.0	**2.3**	23.6	18.4	**6.8**
8.2	0.00	0.0	0.97	**3.5**	0.1	0.70	8.93	3.84	76.3	**4.3**	24.3	7.1	**3.4**
5.3	1.21	6.0	0.20	**5.6**	16.5	1.04	7.05	3.82	63.4	**5.3**	38.4	10.5	**8.4**
9.8	0.00	0.0	0.07	**2.2**	-0.3	-0.50	-3.87	2.54	79.3	**5.0**	70.6	15.3	**7.0**
2.7	1.96	16.2	0.29	**5.6**	2.5	0.93	10.03	4.10	65.4	**1.5**	2.6	21.3	**5.0**
4.8	1.65	7.2	0.04	**5.4**	2.1	0.96	6.38	3.76	68.7	**3.6**	20.0	11.4	**6.5**
7.8	0.08	0.5	0.55	**4.8**	0.9	0.96	10.35	3.95	67.5	**1.7**	8.7	20.0	**6.1**

	Name	City	State	Rating	2013 Rating	2012 Rating	Total Assets ($Mil)	One Year Asset Growth	Comm-ercial Loans	Cons-umer Loans	Mort-gage Loans	Secur-ities	Capital-ization Index	Lever-age Ratio	Risk-Based Capital Ratio
									Asset Mix (As a % of Total Assets)						
	BANK OF TAMPA	Tampa	FL	**C+**	C+	C	1326.9	-1.01	15.9	2.1	5.4	29.8	**6.3**	8.4	13.3
▲	BANK OF TENNESSEE	Kingsport	TN	**B**	B-	C+	916.7	1.18	5.2	1.5	24.6	22.8	**7.2**	9.1	14.3
	BANK OF TERRELL	Dawson	GA	**B-**	B-	C+	140.5	-0.64	5.3	3.2	31.2	9.7	**9.8**	10.9	16.4
	BANK OF TESCOTT	Tescott	KS	**A**	A	A-	318.8	0.51	3.6	2.9	27.9	15.5	**10.0**	12.0	16.0
	BANK OF TEXAS	Midland	TX	**A-**	B+	B-	245.7	13.13	21.7	0.2	3.8	1.7	**10.0**	11.6	16.9
	BANK OF THE BLUEGRASS & TRUST	Lexington	KY	**B-**	C+	C	212.6	-3.29	1.6	1.7	21.0	24.7	**10.0**	13.7	22.5
	BANK OF THE CAROLINAS	Mocksville	NC	**E-**	E-	E-	396.4	-7.34	5.9	0.8	22.9	10.3	**9.7**	10.8	15.7
	BANK OF THE CASCADES	Bend	OR	**D+**	C	C-	2334.2	66.17	14.9	1.6	5.9	19.1	**4.5**	7.3	10.7
	BANK OF THE FLINT HILLS	Wamego	KS	**B**	B	B-	157.3	4.36	9.1	1.1	14.6	22.6	**9.2**	10.5	16.4
	BANK OF THE JAMES	Lynchburg	VA	**B-**	C+	C	451.9	3.75	9.5	1.2	23.6	8.1	**7.7**	9.4	13.3
	BANK OF THE MOUNTAINS INC	West Liberty	KY	**C+**	C	C	65.3	2.03	5.2	12.8	29.4	11.9	**9.4**	10.6	16.6
▲	BANK OF THE ORIENT	San Francisco	CA	**C-**	D	D	471.0	1.04	2.4	0.0	5.9	8.6	**10.0**	11.2	19.1
	BANK OF THE OZARKS	Little Rock	AR	**B**	B+	B+	6573.6	39.80	6.0	0.7	8.6	12.8	**7.0**	12.4	12.5
	BANK OF THE PACIFIC	Aberdeen	WA	**B-**	C+	C	748.6	4.64	11.6	4.6	10.0	12.2	**8.4**	9.9	13.9
	BANK OF THE PANHANDLE	Guymon	OK	**A**	A	A-	138.3	0.41	7.3	1.7	7.1	34.1	**10.0**	12.1	19.2
▲	BANK OF THE PRAIRIE	Olathe	KS	**C**	D+	D	82.5	5.43	16.1	0.5	23.6	9.8	**6.7**	8.7	12.8
	BANK OF THE ROCKIES NA	White Sulphur Spri	MT	**D+**	D	D-	125.6	5.43	5.8	1.6	11.2	22.2	**8.7**	10.2	15.4
	BANK OF THE SIERRA	Porterville	CA	**B-**	C	C-	1486.1	7.67	6.9	1.3	7.7	31.3	**10.0**	13.4	19.7
▼	BANK OF THE SOUTH	Pensacola	FL	**D+**	C-	B	71.4	1.53	0.2	0.6	3.1	67.0	**10.0**	20.4	79.9
	BANK OF THE SOUTHWEST	Roswell	NM	**B-**	B	B	170.6	8.83	26.9	2.9	10.9	0.2	**6.5**	8.5	15.0
	BANK OF THE VALLEY	Bellwood	NE	**B**	B-	B	148.4	16.07	5.2	2.0	3.4	14.4	**6.4**	9.7	12.1
	BANK OF THE WEST	Thomas	OK	**A**	A	A-	138.4	8.08	12.1	0.6	12.8	0.0	**9.1**	11.0	14.3
	BANK OF THE WEST	Grapevine	TX	**B-**	B-	B-	414.5	8.34	8.5	1.0	6.2	10.5	**6.6**	8.7	14.5
	BANK OF THE WEST	San Francisco	CA	**B**	B	B-	68874.3	5.82	11.1	19.7	10.1	13.7	**9.9**	12.0	14.9
▼	BANK OF THE WICHITAS	Snyder	OK	**B**	B+	B-	120.7	-2.72	4.8	3.3	8.6	35.2	**6.0**	8.0	12.1
	BANK OF TIOGA	Tioga	ND	**B**	B	B	154.0	17.94	10.0	2.8	4.2	27.0	**6.0**	8.0	19.8
	BANK OF TRAVELERS REST	Travelers Rest	SC	**B-**	B-	C	520.7	3.06	6.5	4.9	12.3	26.3	**7.8**	9.5	15.4
	BANK OF TURTLE LAKE	Turtle Lake	ND	**B**	B	B	47.2	10.59	5.6	5.2	1.6	20.8	**7.2**	9.1	13.1
	BANK OF URBANA	Urbana	MO	**B+**	B+	B+	176.0	4.93	3.4	2.7	16.0	49.2	**10.0**	14.2	31.1
	BANK OF UTAH	Ogden	UT	**A**	A	A-	873.0	8.20	5.7	0.3	2.9	13.5	**10.0**	13.4	18.1
▼	BANK OF UTICA	Utica	NY	**A**	A+	A+	1002.3	7.98	2.7	0.5	0.3	93.7	**10.0**	14.7	19.7
	BANK OF VERNON	Vernon	AL	**C-**	D+	D	140.6	-3.38	13.9	2.9	13.5	13.8	**10.0**	14.8	20.9
▲	BANK OF VERSAILLES	Versailles	MO	**C-**	D	D-	211.9	-4.34	0.6	0.6	54.7	5.6	**10.0**	11.0	18.5
	BANK OF VICI	Vici	OK	**C**	C	C-	44.9	0.53	13.1	14.5	4.0	25.0	**7.6**	9.4	19.6
▲	BANK OF VIRGINIA	Midlothian	VA	**D**	E+	D-	301.0	28.83	8.4	22.6	2.8	25.2	**6.7**	8.7	16.2
	BANK OF WALKER COUNTY	Jasper	AL	**B**	B	B-	71.9	-2.71	10.8	6.9	21.5	23.0	**10.0**	14.6	23.7
	BANK OF WALNUT GROVE	Walnut Grove	MS	**B+**	B+	A-	54.6	5.26	2.9	12.8	21.9	9.4	**10.0**	14.7	30.2
	BANK OF WALTERBORO	Walterboro	SC	**C+**	C	C	161.5	4.16	3.1	2.3	16.3	16.3	**10.0**	12.0	21.9
	BANK OF WASHINGTON	Washington	MO	**D-**	D	D-	648.8	-12.66	20.3	0.8	14.1	7.5	**8.7**	10.7	13.9
▲	BANK OF WASHINGTON	Lynnwood	WA	**C+**	D+	D	146.9	24.70	4.4	2.5	16.0	12.1	**10.0**	11.3	15.3
	BANK OF WAYNESBORO	Waynesboro	TN	**B**	B	B+	144.4	0.98	5.9	7.2	27.5	18.0	**10.0**	13.3	21.4
	BANK OF WEDOWEE	Wedowee	AL	**D+**	D+	C	114.0	1.51	6.0	4.4	17.3	48.2	**8.8**	10.2	21.8
	BANK OF WESTERN OKLAHOMA	Elk City	OK	**C+**	C+	C+	231.5	2.60	9.0	1.4	17.2	8.5	**5.0**	7.6	11.0
	BANK OF WESTON	Weston	MO	**C+**	B-	C	112.3	-2.81	8.5	0.8	19.0	16.3	**7.0**	9.0	12.9
	BANK OF WHITEWATER	Whitewater	KS	**D+**	D+	C-	20.1	-4.69	11.8	13.4	12.6	21.1	**6.7**	8.7	17.2
	BANK OF WHITTIER NA	Whittier	CA	**B-**	B	B-	56.0	-7.51	4.0	0.6	11.9	0.1	**10.0**	15.9	19.0
	BANK OF WIGGINS	Wiggins	MS	**B+**	B+	B+	185.9	-0.53	14.3	9.2	19.7	26.3	**10.0**	14.7	27.4
	BANK OF WINNFIELD & TRUST CO	Winnfield	LA	**B**	B	B+	136.7	-0.97	10.1	4.8	14.6	31.6	**10.0**	12.1	24.2
	BANK OF WINONA	Winona	MS	**B-**	B-	C+	111.9	2.73	1.5	3.2	15.2	45.9	**8.6**	10.1	21.8
▲	BANK OF WISCONSIN DELLS	Wisconsin Dells	WI	**B-**	C+	C-	409.2	1.62	8.4	0.5	9.3	13.6	**10.0**	11.5	15.2
	BANK OF WOLCOTT	Wolcott	IN	**B-**	B-	B-	140.0	5.85	7.1	1.5	19.2	26.8	**7.9**	9.6	14.8
	BANK OF WRIGHTSVILLE	Wrightsville	GA	**D-**	D-	D-	52.5	1.94	4.1	4.6	14.1	32.5	**6.3**	8.3	17.8
▼	BANK OF WYANDOTTE	Wyandotte	OK	**D+**	C-	C	14.1	16.75	7.9	9.5	11.4	30.0	**6.2**	8.2	13.8
	BANK OF YATES CITY	Yates City	IL	**C**	C+	C	64.4	1.35	6.5	17.7	20.5	30.9	**8.7**	10.1	15.8
	BANK OF YAZOO CITY	Yazoo City	MS	**B-**	B-	B-	228.2	2.34	5.7	2.7	17.9	37.6	**8.4**	9.9	16.8
	BANK OF YORK	York	AL	**C+**	C+	B-	106.0	22.97	4.2	3.0	6.6	57.8	**7.8**	9.6	19.8
	BANK OF YORK	York	SC	**B**	B	B	192.6	3.38	2.8	4.1	12.9	23.1	**10.0**	13.6	29.4
	BANK OF ZACHARY	Zachary	LA	**B**	B	B-	197.3	-0.21	2.5	2.2	23.3	45.1	**7.9**	9.6	21.5
	BANK OF ZUMBROTA	Zumbrota	MN	**C+**	B-	B-	148.2	2.14	12.1	3.5	13.1	22.2	**9.2**	11.6	14.3
	BANK PLUS	Estherville	IA	**C-**	C	C	123.9	1.56	5.3	2.1	9.9	14.8	**4.1**	8.3	10.6

Arrows denote recent upgrades ▲ or downgrades ▼

Asset Quality Index	Adjusted Non-Performing Loans as a % of Total Loans	Adjusted Non-Performing Loans as a % of Capital	Net Charge-Offs / Avg Loans	Profitability Index	Net Income ($Mil)	Return on Assets (R.O.A.)	Return on Equity (R.O.E.)	Net Interest Spread	Overhead Efficiency Ratio	Liquidity Index	Liquidity Ratio	Hot Money Ratio	Stability Index
4.7	2.28	13.9	-0.18	**3.9**	6.9	0.71	8.96	3.33	70.3	**6.7**	41.3	2.7	**6.0**
4.7	1.60	10.9	0.28	**4.7**	7.3	1.07	11.98	3.85	73.0	**4.2**	9.8	6.9	**5.5**
3.8	2.26	14.8	0.36	**5.9**	1.6	1.47	13.88	4.53	62.5	**0.8**	15.7	37.3	**5.7**
6.9	0.61	3.6	0.02	**8.9**	4.9	2.05	17.28	4.33	44.8	**2.2**	6.5	17.2	**8.5**
8.3	0.00	0.0	0.00	**5.5**	2.6	1.40	12.41	2.70	43.9	**1.0**	28.4	65.7	**6.5**
5.7	1.12	5.4	0.21	**6.7**	2.1	1.29	9.34	4.17	62.5	**3.4**	30.4	14.7	**6.7**
3.3	2.64	15.0	0.03	**0.0**	-5.6	-1.75	-44.16	2.93	152.0	**1.5**	23.8	27.8	**0.4**
4.0	1.59	12.9	-0.05	**1.9**	1.0	0.07	0.52	3.87	99.9	**4.7**	20.7	5.9	**6.2**
5.8	1.12	6.3	-0.02	**4.6**	1.1	0.98	8.92	3.80	72.2	**1.8**	15.4	20.2	**5.9**
5.1	0.94	7.5	0.14	**4.4**	2.8	0.85	9.56	4.06	72.4	**3.6**	10.7	10.6	**4.3**
4.1	1.52	8.9	0.40	**4.4**	0.3	0.66	6.25	5.57	82.1	**1.6**	17.6	23.9	**5.7**
3.5	2.42	12.4	-0.47	**1.4**	-1.1	-0.32	-2.79	3.57	117.6	**2.4**	32.8	21.3	**4.9**
4.7	1.08	6.4	0.13	**10.0**	88.5	2.10	15.00	5.54	44.6	**2.9**	5.2	13.4	**9.9**
4.1	1.09	7.7	0.08	**4.4**	4.5	0.83	7.27	4.28	77.6	**3.3**	7.8	11.6	**6.8**
8.6	0.00	0.0	0.00	**6.3**	1.6	1.56	12.26	3.94	64.8	**3.6**	34.7	15.5	**8.9**
4.5	0.56	4.3	0.06	**3.4**	0.3	0.41	4.02	4.59	85.0	**0.9**	10.2	31.8	**3.8**
1.5	4.97	28.0	0.03	**3.8**	0.7	0.72	6.45	4.58	91.8	**4.2**	26.3	9.3	**5.2**
4.0	3.16	13.5	0.16	**5.6**	12.1	1.11	7.71	4.04	65.9	**3.3**	28.5	17.6	**8.7**
10.0	0.98	1.1	0.00	**0.8**	-0.1	-0.14	-0.67	2.70	109.0	**7.5**	93.4	4.1	**5.1**
4.2	1.32	10.2	0.12	**4.8**	1.2	0.98	11.36	5.33	81.1	**5.2**	28.8	3.9	**5.3**
6.9	0.15	1.2	0.00	**5.5**	1.0	0.97	10.56	3.94	58.8	**0.9**	6.6	31.7	**5.8**
7.1	0.05	0.4	0.01	**9.9**	2.5	2.43	21.84	5.19	52.0	**1.0**	8.4	30.2	**8.7**
5.2	0.95	6.1	0.06	**4.8**	3.2	1.10	12.55	4.06	74.7	**5.1**	34.0	6.9	**5.3**
3.8	1.33	7.9	0.15	**4.7**	396.0	0.78	4.51	3.24	63.6	**2.9**	12.6	14.7	**8.6**
9.1	0.15	1.0	0.24	**4.3**	0.6	0.66	7.91	4.00	81.9	**3.9**	18.1	9.6	**7.4**
8.6	0.30	1.2	0.00	**6.4**	1.8	1.64	20.03	2.95	37.4	**6.4**	56.8	6.1	**4.7**
4.2	2.18	13.0	0.27	**5.0**	4.6	1.19	12.51	3.86	68.7	**2.3**	31.9	22.4	**5.8**
0.1	4.68	31.7	0.03	**5.3**	0.3	0.94	10.82	3.44	57.5	**1.8**	23.3	22.7	**5.0**
6.9	2.15	6.1	0.53	**4.7**	1.1	0.87	6.16	3.83	68.4	**5.8**	49.9	7.8	**7.7**
6.7	0.42	2.1	-0.05	**9.0**	9.5	1.52	11.03	3.92	63.0	**4.6**	23.8	5.9	**8.6**
9.0	8.66	3.4	-0.05	**5.6**	7.2	0.97	5.60	2.15	32.5	**5.8**	94.7	16.3	**9.0**
1.7	6.63	28.7	0.76	**4.2**	0.7	0.60	4.12	4.38	66.4	**1.6**	21.4	24.7	**5.6**
3.1	3.11	18.5	0.09	**5.1**	2.7	1.63	16.19	3.52	85.5	**2.3**	12.8	17.1	**4.9**
4.6	1.89	7.2	0.09	**3.5**	0.3	0.76	7.88	3.17	78.6	**2.8**	57.2	31.3	**4.3**
2.6	1.61	12.2	0.26	**1.1**	0.1	0.05	0.72	3.14	97.4	**1.1**	26.9	39.5	**2.0**
5.2	1.98	8.3	0.37	**4.1**	0.4	0.65	4.55	4.07	74.5	**1.4**	30.4	34.4	**6.2**
8.1	0.00	0.0	0.08	**4.9**	0.4	1.10	7.60	4.15	71.9	**2.8**	50.3	28.8	**7.8**
3.8	3.99	16.2	0.71	**2.9**	0.5	0.46	3.88	3.38	81.3	**2.4**	39.7	28.4	**5.2**
0.3	11.07	65.0	1.40	**1.4**	0.2	0.05	0.47	3.67	75.4	**4.2**	13.5	7.2	**5.0**
3.8	1.77	10.0	-0.10	**3.1**	1.0	0.94	8.18	3.65	80.1	**1.5**	18.9	25.0	**4.1**
3.9	3.51	15.7	0.11	**7.5**	1.4	1.26	9.68	4.37	57.8	**2.4**	26.4	18.3	**7.5**
3.0	5.49	20.5	-0.13	**1.9**	0.3	0.31	2.67	2.89	88.5	**4.6**	51.3	14.8	**5.1**
4.6	0.72	7.2	0.00	**6.3**	2.6	1.52	18.18	4.52	66.4	**2.2**	12.5	17.7	**5.5**
5.2	2.32	17.4	0.84	**3.2**	0.6	0.66	7.80	4.19	75.7	**3.5**	11.7	11.3	**5.1**
4.2	1.98	10.4	0.82	**4.6**	0.2	1.00	11.92	4.06	68.2	**4.5**	28.5	6.3	**3.0**
8.1	0.84	2.1	-1.06	**3.1**	0.1	0.33	2.07	2.12	87.9	**2.7**	62.5	41.7	**6.3**
6.4	1.07	4.3	0.12	**5.1**	1.4	0.98	6.95	4.06	67.7	**2.2**	30.0	22.4	**7.4**
3.6	5.69	20.2	0.04	**4.0**	0.9	0.86	7.32	3.39	74.7	**3.4**	36.8	17.1	**7.4**
4.3	5.03	16.6	0.14	**4.8**	1.0	1.21	12.83	3.99	64.8	**4.2**	55.9	18.0	**5.6**
4.3	1.08	6.3	0.33	**7.4**	3.9	1.28	11.16	4.13	44.8	**1.6**	15.7	22.5	**6.3**
4.4	1.99	12.6	0.35	**6.9**	1.7	1.64	18.45	3.80	54.9	**2.2**	32.7	25.4	**6.3**
3.6	3.31	16.2	0.23	**0.6**	0.0	0.02	0.39	3.17	99.3	**3.5**	51.4	19.4	**1.4**
4.3	2.63	13.7	0.32	**5.4**	0.1	1.01	11.50	5.68	81.4	**4.8**	35.0	6.4	**3.0**
4.1	1.66	10.0	0.06	**3.0**	0.2	0.50	4.91	3.87	85.7	**4.4**	33.2	10.5	**5.0**
7.3	0.40	1.9	0.09	**4.2**	1.4	0.82	9.00	3.74	72.4	**2.7**	30.2	18.2	**5.1**
8.3	0.27	0.9	-0.03	**3.3**	0.4	0.60	5.79	2.85	80.0	**2.3**	38.3	28.3	**5.8**
7.0	1.41	4.6	0.08	**3.9**	1.1	0.77	5.77	3.32	70.9	**4.3**	45.9	15.2	**6.9**
5.7	1.26	6.0	0.09	**4.4**	1.3	0.89	9.35	3.98	73.0	**3.7**	34.0	14.5	**5.7**
2.8	2.79	16.7	0.00	**5.1**	1.3	1.15	9.71	3.68	69.5	**1.4**	14.9	25.2	**6.5**
2.2	1.62	14.3	0.38	**4.9**	1.1	1.14	12.10	4.33	68.2	**1.7**	10.2	20.0	**5.5**

Name	City	State	Rating	2013 Rating	2012 Rating	Total Assets ($Mil)	One Year Asset Growth	Asset Mix (As a % of Total Assets) Commercial Loans	Consumer Loans	Mortgage Loans	Securities	Capitalization Index	Leverage Ratio	Risk-Based Capital Ratio
BANK REALE	Pasco	WA	**E-**	E	D-	38.7	-10.22	12.8	1.7	1.3	0.0	**2.9**	6.5	9.9
▲ BANK RHODE ISLAND	Providence	RI	**B**	C+	C+	1869.0	5.57	16.4	0.1	12.5	12.9	**6.1**	8.5	11.8
▲ BANK SNB	Stillwater	OK	**B**	B-	C+	1886.2	13.48	16.4	1.2	3.6	19.5	**10.0**	14.7	18.8
BANK STAR	Pacific	MO	**B-**	B-	C+	71.2	4.33	4.3	1.5	21.0	14.0	**7.9**	9.6	14.0
BANK STAR OF THE BOOTHEEL	Steele	MO	**B-**	B-	C+	109.2	1.92	3.3	6.2	24.8	15.9	**6.5**	8.5	13.2
▲ BANK STAR ONE	Fulton	MO	**B-**	C+	C+	86.1	-5.23	3.5	1.5	37.5	11.5	**10.0**	11.4	17.9
BANK TEXAS NA	Quitman	TX	**C+**	C+	B-	593.3	79.98	23.0	1.6	21.4	19.2	**9.9**	11.5	15.0
▲ BANK VI	Salina	KS	**C+**	D+	C-	64.3	-1.33	15.4	1.2	37.2	2.3	**9.0**	10.3	15.9
▲ BANK34	Alamogordo	NM	**D+**	D+	C	254.5	47.09	2.3	0.3	23.6	21.2	**10.0**	12.0	18.0
BANKCDA	Coeur dAlene	ID	**C-**	C	C	94.9	-1.49	13.9	0.6	7.0	23.6	**7.9**	9.6	14.6
BANKCHAMPAIGN NA	Champaign	IL	**B-**	B-	C+	193.9	0.57	13.1	0.2	20.7	18.1	**6.1**	8.1	12.6
BANKCHEROKEE	Saint Paul	MN	**D**	E+	E-	258.2	-1.61	22.3	0.4	7.4	25.5	**4.1**	6.1	13.0
BANKERS BANK	Madison	WI	**A-**	A-	C+	380.6	-9.45	0.6	0.8	0.6	5.5	**10.0**	15.1	42.7
▼ BANKERS BANK	Oklahoma City	OK	**B-**	B+	A-	231.4	2.91	3.8	0.9	1.5	0.2	**10.0**	13.8	21.5
BANKERS BANK NORTHEAST	Glastonbury	CT	**C+**	C+	B-	129.6	-0.47	0.2	1.9	0.8	45.3	**10.0**	11.8	35.6
▲ BANKERS BANK OF KANSAS	Wichita	KS	**C+**	C-	C	151.7	-7.44	8.1	10.7	1.1	5.4	**10.0**	13.5	19.6
BANKERS BANK OF KENTUCKY INC	Frankfort	KY	**B**	B+	B+	71.1	-1.42	2.5	0.0	0.9	0.0	**10.0**	17.7	45.8
▲ BANKERS BANK OF THE WEST	Denver	CO	**A-**	B	C	342.4	1.09	6.0	0.1	0.4	13.7	**10.0**	12.4	21.2
BANKERS TRUST CO	Cedar Rapids	IA	**B**	B	B-	439.0	-1.86	18.6	1.1	12.5	8.3	**7.9**	10.1	13.2
BANKERS TRUST CO	Des Moines	IA	**B**	B	B-	3007.7	1.73	17.9	0.3	9.1	14.7	**5.2**	8.7	11.2
▲ BANKFINANCIAL FSB	Olympia Fields	IL	**C-**	D	D-	1420.8	-1.46	17.9	0.2	9.6	2.6	**9.9**	11.0	15.5
BANKFIRST	Norfolk	NE	**A**	A	A-	308.3	4.35	11.7	4.4	6.9	29.7	**10.0**	13.2	18.6
▼ BANKFIRST FINANCIAL SERVICES	Columbus	MS	**C+**	B-	B-	713.6	-0.74	12.9	1.6	14.5	11.6	**7.5**	9.5	12.9
▼ BANKFIVE	Fall River	MA	**C**	C+	C+	753.1	0.50	8.0	0.8	23.9	15.8	**8.2**	9.8	14.4
BANKGLOUCESTER	Gloucester	MA	**D+**	D	D-	194.9	2.08	3.2	0.4	38.6	11.0	**6.8**	8.8	13.4
BANKIOWA OF CEDAR RAPIDS	Cedar Rapids	IA	**B**	B+	B	522.6	6.59	11.8	2.2	15.6	16.8	**8.6**	10.2	13.8
▲ BANKLIBERTY	Liberty	MO	**B+**	B-	C-	468.8	2.90	13.4	1.8	14.8	5.0	**10.0**	13.4	18.5
BANKNEWPORT	Newport	RI	**C+**	C+	C+	1276.2	6.33	4.6	0.4	40.7	15.0	**7.6**	9.4	13.3
BANKORION	Orion	IL	**B-**	C	C	403.0	-3.50	6.7	2.6	9.0	38.6	**7.0**	9.0	15.9
▼ BANKPACIFIC LTD	Hagatna	GU	**C+**	B-	B-	124.6	5.14	8.1	14.5	49.4	1.9	**10.0**	12.1	19.1
BANKPLUS	Belzoni	MS	**B**	B	B-	2422.3	1.19	7.4	2.1	14.7	33.5	**7.9**	9.6	15.8
BANKSOUTH	Dothan	AL	**A-**	A-	B-	168.2	-4.16	9.0	1.5	38.1	8.8	**10.0**	20.4	28.1
BANKSOUTH	Greensboro	GA	**B**	C+	C	375.2	2.11	1.1	1.4	40.2	6.1	**9.3**	10.5	16.0
▲ BANKSTAR FINANCIAL	Elkton	SD	**B-**	C	C	122.2	80.23	10.1	5.3	20.0	11.4	**7.4**	9.5	12.9
BANKTENNESSEE	Collierville	TN	**C+**	C+	C	259.4	5.75	13.6	2.6	17.8	6.9	**5.8**	9.6	11.6
▼ BANKTRUST FINANCIAL CORP	Henderson	KY	**C+**	C+	C-	136.3	1.74	9.4	1.8	37.4	16.6	**8.0**	9.6	14.6
BANKUNITED NA	Miami Lakes	FL	**A-**	A-	A-	17531.2	23.88	13.7	0.1	19.1	23.8	**7.8**	9.5	15.5
BANKVISTA	Sartell	MN	**C-**	C+	C	133.6	20.28	21.0	1.0	16.8	0.0	**7.4**	9.4	12.8
▲ BANKWELL BANK	New Canaan	CT	**B**	C+	C-	887.3	30.43	10.9	0.0	20.8	8.9	**10.0**	11.9	15.3
BANKWEST	Rockford	MN	**C**	C-	D+	115.9	6.27	10.7	1.5	15.4	9.9	**7.5**	9.3	14.4
BANKWEST INC	Pierre	SD	**C+**	B-	B-	879.2	5.95	10.0	9.4	4.6	14.4	**7.4**	9.6	12.9
▲ BANKWEST OF KANSAS	Goodland	KS	**B+**	B	B-	93.6	-4.28	4.5	1.5	2.5	23.2	**10.0**	12.6	17.6
BANNER BANK	Walla Walla	WA	**A-**	A-	B-	4516.4	11.43	14.4	2.3	11.7	12.2	**10.0**	12.1	15.3
BANNER BANKS	Birnamwood	WI	**B-**	B-	B	95.7	5.01	2.9	0.6	6.9	34.2	**10.0**	12.4	25.9
BANNER CAPITAL BANK	Harrisburg	NE	**A-**	A-	A-	116.1	5.39	10.2	2.4	1.9	15.9	**9.1**	11.2	14.3
BANTERRA BANK	Eldorado	IL	**B-**	B-	C+	1167.0	2.61	14.4	18.3	8.3	20.8	**7.8**	9.7	13.2
BAR HARBOR BANK & TRUST	Bar Harbor	ME	**B+**	B+	B	1438.1	4.32	3.6	0.8	30.0	32.5	**7.4**	9.3	17.4
BAR HARBOR S&LA	Bar Harbor	ME	**C+**	C+	C+	87.5	8.70	0.0	0.2	68.5	7.6	**6.3**	8.3	17.3
▲ BARABOO NATIONAL BK	Baraboo	WI	**D+**	E+	D-	441.5	-32.42	8.4	2.8	14.6	7.0	**10.0**	11.5	16.8
BARCLAYS BANK DELAWARE	Wilmington	DE	**C**	C+	C+	24157.1	14.90	0.7	80.3	0.7	0.2	**9.5**	11.0	14.6
BARCLAYS WEALTH TRUSTEES (US)	Wilmington	DE	**U**	U	U	13.2	13.15	0.0	0.0	0.0	0.0	**10.0**	95.0	430.3
▲ BARRE SB	Barre	MA	**D+**	D	D	152.7	1.26	3.3	1.5	48.2	15.0	**6.8**	8.8	14.6
▲ BARRINGTON BANK & TRUST CO NA	Barrington	IL	**B-**	C+	C+	1662.8	15.91	25.9	16.8	24.7	6.9	**5.3**	8.4	11.2
BARWICK BANKING CO	Barwick	GA	**D-**	E+	D-	11.5	3.24	2.0	1.4	2.9	42.9	**5.4**	7.4	35.6
BASILE STATE BK	Basile	LA	**C+**	C+	C+	57.7	1.81	7.1	12.4	40.0	6.0	**8.0**	9.7	16.1
BATH SAVINGS INSTITUTION	Bath	ME	**B-**	B	B	744.1	6.04	5.9	1.0	30.4	22.9	**9.8**	10.9	18.9
BATH STATE BK	Bath	IN	**C**	C+	C	147.3	-3.34	3.9	1.2	18.3	20.4	**7.7**	9.5	16.5
BATTLE CREEK STATE BK	Battle Creek	NE	**C+**	C+	C+	29.3	16.02	38.9	0.7	3.5	12.1	**10.0**	13.3	17.5
BAXTER STATE BK	Baxter Springs	KS	**B**	B-	B-	27.4	2.87	10.4	9.7	25.0	23.2	**10.0**	19.9	33.4
BAY BANK	Green Bay	WI	**D**	D-	D+	83.1	-1.15	8.3	3.8	15.5	17.8	**9.5**	10.7	17.0

Asset Quality Index	Adjusted Non-Performing Loans as a % of Total Loans	Adjusted Non-Performing Loans as a % of Capital	Net Charge-Offs Avg Loans	Profitability Index	Net Income ($Mil)	Return on Assets (R.O.A.)	Return on Equity (R.O.E.)	Net Interest Spread	Overhead Efficiency Ratio	Liquidity Index	Liquidity Ratio	Hot Money Ratio	Stability Index
0.8	5.83	45.4	0.58	**0.0**	-0.5	-1.78	-27.46	4.25	100.4	**1.3**	27.7	33.1	**1.5**
3.6	0.97	8.5	0.07	**4.7**	10.8	0.78	5.88	3.92	64.7	**3.6**	4.1	10.0	**7.5**
4.0	1.78	8.0	0.15	**6.8**	16.3	1.13	8.11	3.57	66.9	**2.0**	15.8	19.6	**7.8**
6.4	0.51	3.7	0.08	**4.9**	0.5	0.90	9.91	4.37	76.4	**4.7**	13.3	3.5	**4.7**
5.6	0.54	4.6	0.23	**6.4**	0.8	1.09	12.84	4.47	71.4	**0.9**	13.0	32.2	**5.1**
7.0	0.72	4.4	0.27	**6.5**	0.8	1.20	11.17	4.69	81.0	**4.2**	16.2	7.2	**5.2**
7.0	0.04	0.3	0.00	**2.8**	1.6	0.42	3.31	3.38	71.8	**0.7**	11.1	41.6	**6.3**
8.0	0.15	1.0	0.17	**3.6**	0.4	0.84	8.40	3.45	78.3	**4.2**	15.8	7.6	**3.4**
7.8	1.07	5.7	0.08	**4.9**	2.2	1.69	12.70	3.89	78.2	**1.8**	26.8	25.1	**5.4**
3.6	2.86	15.7	0.07	**2.0**	0.2	0.20	2.01	3.64	93.9	**4.3**	27.9	9.3	**5.0**
5.6	0.60	4.9	0.00	**5.3**	1.8	1.23	15.29	4.06	71.7	**1.3**	17.1	28.3	**5.6**
3.4	2.26	18.9	0.10	**2.8**	1.1	0.59	10.48	3.05	84.9	**4.9**	36.1	8.8	**1.0**
6.4	6.49	7.0	2.79	**5.0**	2.8	0.87	6.16	1.04	86.7	**7.1**	82.3	6.3	**6.6**
8.8	0.23	0.9	-0.05	**2.7**	0.2	0.10	0.70	2.96	97.4	**3.2**	47.9	23.4	**7.2**
7.3	2.70	5.0	0.02	**2.1**	0.2	0.15	1.27	1.60	97.7	**5.7**	31.1	1.3	**5.5**
3.2	3.49	13.6	1.02	**4.7**	0.9	0.74	5.86	3.01	84.9	**1.8**	37.7	39.6	**6.8**
8.9	0.00	0.0	0.02	**3.8**	0.2	0.43	2.30	3.62	98.8	**7.8**	82.3	0.0	**6.8**
7.8	1.20	4.6	0.16	**5.4**	2.9	1.16	9.22	2.50	78.8	**2.7**	50.9	32.3	**5.3**
6.2	0.05	0.3	-0.26	**4.8**	2.9	0.89	8.93	3.24	60.3	**0.7**	5.7	33.4	**6.7**
7.5	0.35	2.7	0.05	**5.1**	21.3	0.96	11.31	3.13	62.6	**4.0**	9.9	8.2	**6.9**
3.8	1.44	9.8	0.13	**2.6**	6.6	0.61	5.75	3.38	82.9	**4.5**	15.9	6.3	**5.3**
7.6	0.19	0.9	0.04	**6.8**	3.0	1.35	9.14	3.63	55.5	**4.6**	33.0	9.6	**8.2**
2.1	2.79	21.2	0.31	**4.9**	4.6	0.86	8.70	3.96	66.7	**2.4**	9.3	16.5	**5.6**
4.8	1.25	8.3	0.54	**2.5**	1.3	0.23	2.30	3.54	81.6	**1.9**	18.1	19.9	**6.1**
1.7	4.43	37.7	0.09	**3.2**	0.6	0.39	4.38	3.70	82.2	**1.8**	15.4	19.8	**5.0**
5.9	0.55	3.9	0.00	**5.3**	4.6	1.22	11.12	3.59	68.1	**3.4**	6.4	11.4	**7.5**
5.2	1.73	8.5	0.23	**5.5**	3.5	0.94	7.16	4.45	67.3	**3.6**	15.3	10.9	**7.1**
6.7	0.77	6.1	0.07	**3.0**	3.4	0.36	3.65	3.09	84.1	**3.8**	17.6	10.9	**7.6**
4.2	1.88	10.3	-0.01	**4.7**	3.0	0.97	9.46	3.63	60.5	**3.0**	19.0	14.2	**6.1**
2.1	3.62	24.2	0.07	**4.0**	0.4	0.48	3.85	5.49	89.6	**4.3**	9.9	6.0	**6.8**
5.3	2.31	12.3	0.41	**4.7**	16.0	0.88	9.45	3.56	74.5	**3.8**	18.7	11.0	**7.3**
8.7	0.28	1.1	0.54	**6.0**	1.8	1.37	6.97	3.99	65.0	**2.8**	8.0	14.6	**7.3**
4.7	1.57	11.0	0.27	**9.2**	5.6	2.06	19.40	4.85	82.9	**3.3**	10.2	12.1	**7.6**
4.3	0.66	5.4	0.02	**4.4**	0.9	0.96	9.59	4.29	74.4	**2.3**	9.0	17.1	**5.0**
3.2	0.93	7.0	0.58	**4.2**	1.7	0.92	8.37	4.50	71.3	**2.5**	5.7	15.5	**5.9**
2.7	2.57	19.6	0.10	**6.9**	1.1	1.15	9.71	4.67	69.2	**1.1**	6.3	27.7	**5.7**
8.5	0.30	2.0	0.16	**8.9**	162.1	1.35	12.72	4.84	55.1	**2.2**	23.3	21.5	**7.0**
2.3	1.76	14.5	0.03	**7.5**	1.0	1.08	11.23	4.36	61.3	**0.9**	10.8	32.2	**5.1**
5.0	0.86	5.6	-0.06	**4.8**	4.9	0.80	8.00	3.78	65.5	**1.4**	13.9	25.0	**6.3**
2.8	2.80	18.5	0.48	**4.7**	1.0	1.12	12.35	4.50	75.3	**5.0**	28.0	4.6	**4.0**
3.9	1.39	10.0	0.19	**8.4**	12.1	1.89	19.84	4.76	61.1	**1.3**	11.2	25.9	**6.6**
7.4	0.00	0.0	-0.01	**5.3**	0.9	1.17	9.23	4.53	71.2	**3.6**	22.2	11.5	**7.0**
6.1	0.79	4.6	-0.02	**7.7**	45.1	1.38	10.81	4.22	61.3	**3.4**	12.3	12.1	**8.0**
5.7	3.20	10.4	0.01	**3.1**	0.4	0.51	4.03	2.79	81.0	**5.7**	58.0	9.2	**6.6**
6.8	0.14	0.9	0.03	**6.7**	1.3	1.52	13.31	4.19	59.9	**1.4**	14.7	25.7	**7.3**
4.0	1.30	8.8	-0.01	**6.5**	13.5	1.53	15.75	3.91	62.9	**3.0**	13.1	14.0	**9.2**
6.9	0.73	4.6	0.19	**5.7**	12.4	1.17	12.25	3.40	52.6	**0.7**	6.4	35.0	**8.6**
5.8	1.14	10.1	0.00	**4.6**	0.5	0.85	10.32	2.61	48.5	**0.9**	20.1	37.1	**4.6**
1.3	8.94	46.5	0.48	**4.6**	7.5	1.89	21.29	3.15	68.9	**3.1**	22.1	14.0	**3.4**
2.6	1.32	8.5	2.59	**6.2**	122.1	0.76	5.77	7.69	55.6	**0.9**	16.9	43.5	**8.9**
10.0	na	0.0	na	**0.0**	-0.8	-8.57	-9.97	0.29	132.6	**4.0**	564.2	101.0	**5.6**
4.0	0.97	7.6	1.54	**1.6**	0.4	0.36	3.89	3.12	83.8	**3.9**	18.5	9.6	**4.0**
3.9	0.57	5.6	0.49	**7.1**	11.7	1.03	10.25	3.33	78.2	**3.2**	8.5	12.5	**6.3**
9.8	0.04	0.1	0.00	**0.3**	0.0	-0.45	-6.16	1.66	124.4	**5.4**	81.8	13.3	**1.4**
3.2	1.27	9.5	-0.09	**8.9**	0.9	1.96	21.30	5.18	63.1	**1.4**	13.5	26.0	**7.0**
5.6	0.88	5.1	0.14	**4.2**	4.2	0.78	6.70	3.22	72.0	**1.7**	16.7	21.3	**7.5**
2.9	2.76	17.6	0.01	**4.6**	1.2	1.09	10.87	3.81	72.8	**2.0**	27.7	22.6	**5.1**
7.2	0.00	0.0	0.00	**3.5**	0.1	0.42	3.65	3.54	85.6	**1.6**	21.7	24.4	**4.6**
6.5	1.78	4.9	-0.01	**6.7**	0.4	1.76	8.13	5.42	70.5	**5.0**	23.8	3.0	**6.4**
1.2	10.95	46.1	0.95	**3.4**	0.5	0.90	7.17	4.29	73.1	**1.7**	24.6	23.8	**5.3**

Name	City	State	Rating	2013 Rating	2012 Rating	Total Assets ($Mil)	One Year Asset Growth	Comm-ercial Loans	Cons-umer Loans	Mort-gage Loans	Secur-ities	Capital-ization Index	Lever-age Ratio	Risk-Based Capital Ratio
								Asset Mix (As a % of Total Assets)						
BAY BANK FSB	Lutherville	MD	C+	C+	B-	479.6	9.01	5.6	0.2	31.7	7.5	10.0	12.5	16.1
BAY CITIES BANK	Tampa	FL	C	C-	D+	542.9	11.12	10.6	3.8	7.4	13.3	10.0	11.3	16.2
BAY COMMERCIAL BANK	Walnut Creek	CA	B+	A-	A-	503.6	53.91	14.6	0.1	3.7	3.7	9.5	10.7	15.3
BAY PORT STATE BK	Bay Port	MI	D+	C-	C-	87.5	4.24	6.8	2.7	22.9	0.2	5.4	7.5	11.3
BAY STATE SB	Worcester	MA	C	C-	C-	324.1	13.18	2.2	2.2	46.5	9.5	7.5	9.4	14.0
BAY-VANGUARD FSB	Sparrows Point	MD	D+	D+	C-	173.8	-4.19	0.8	8.0	49.9	8.0	8.9	10.2	18.4
BAYBANK	Gladstone	MI	B	B	B-	82.9	-1.75	15.8	4.8	18.9	35.3	10.0	11.4	18.6
BAYCOAST BANK	Swansea	MA	C-	C-	C	1060.4	6.25	9.1	1.9	33.1	15.5	5.8	8.3	11.6
▲ BAYLAKE BANK	Sturgeon Bay	WI	B+	B	C	982.3	-0.05	12.9	0.6	11.1	22.7	10.0	11.1	16.3
BAYTREE NATIONAL BK & TRUST CO	Lake Forest	IL	E-	E-	E-	92.3	-32.53	4.5	0.3	12.0	6.5	0.0	3.3	5.3
BBCN BANK	Los Angeles	CA	C+	B-	B-	6923.3	9.59	14.4	0.5	0.8	10.3	9.7	11.6	14.7
▲ BCB COMMUNITY BANK	Bayonne	NJ	D+	D+	D+	1228.3	3.86	1.2	0.1	30.1	0.8	6.3	8.3	12.5
BCBANK INC	Philippi	WV	B-	C	C	112.9	7.18	6.8	4.0	17.2	20.3	10.0	11.2	16.4
BEACH COMMUNITY BANK	Fort Walton Beach	FL	E-	E-	E-	558.9	-2.84	5.6	0.2	15.1	7.6	0.1	3.9	6.3
BEACON BANK	Shorewood	MN	B-	B-	C	329.3	-2.16	17.6	1.9	6.7	33.7	8.9	10.3	15.5
BEAL BANK SSB	Plano	TX	C	C-	C	2180.5	-17.35	8.9	0.7	54.3	4.7	10.0	44.1	67.7
BEAL BANK USA	Las Vegas	NV	B-	C+	B-	5626.5	-11.24	34.1	0.0	9.0	29.4	10.0	36.7	41.1
▲ BEARDSTOWN SAVINGS SB	Beardstown	IL	C+	C	C-	44.7	2.38	0.9	5.1	50.8	26.1	10.0	11.5	23.1
BEARTOOTH BANK	Billings	MT	B-	B-	C	37.7	2.10	12.5	1.6	10.0	0.3	10.0	14.7	18.2
BEAUREGARD FSB	DeRidder	LA	A-	A-	A-	56.4	3.53	1.9	7.4	37.1	25.4	10.0	18.2	37.1
BEDFORD FSB	Bedford	IN	C	C	C-	118.5	0.01	3.2	3.0	62.8	0.2	7.5	9.3	15.4
BEDFORD LOAN & DEPOSIT BANK	Bedford	KY	B-	B	B	86.5	0.48	0.4	4.7	36.2	37.8	10.0	13.1	26.2
▼ BELGRADE STATE BK	Belgrade	MO	C	B-	C	224.1	8.83	10.1	4.0	28.3	16.1	7.9	9.6	15.4
BELL STATE BK & TRUST	Fargo	ND	B+	B+	B	3146.1	11.55	13.5	2.4	13.2	1.6	5.3	9.4	11.2
BELLEVUE STATE BK	Bellevue	IA	B-	B	B	87.6	1.46	13.3	5.2	15.7	11.3	6.4	13.0	12.0
▲ BELMONT BANK & TRUST CO	Chicago	IL	C+	C-	D+	269.0	14.87	7.7	0.3	11.2	22.5	8.8	10.2	15.3
BELMONT FS&LA	Belmont	NC	B-	B-	B-	98.4	-6.91	0.0	0.1	52.4	19.2	10.0	17.2	43.0
BELMONT SB	Bellaire	OH	C+	C+	C+	634.9	15.76	0.0	3.7	9.6	84.6	6.4	8.4	35.2
BELMONT SB	Belmont	MA	C-	C-	C-	1335.2	30.57	0.5	9.4	32.9	10.8	6.9	10.0	12.4
BELPRE SB	Belpre	OH	B-	B-	B-	53.6	3.16	0.0	26.5	53.3	3.1	10.0	15.8	24.0
BELT VALLEY BANK	Belt	MT	B-	B-	C-	58.4	-2.07	4.1	5.0	21.8	24.8	10.0	12.9	20.6
BEN FRANKLIN BANK OF ILLINOIS	Arlington Heights	IL	D-	D-	D-	87.2	-10.53	1.1	2.0	36.3	5.4	7.2	9.1	15.6
BENCHMARK BANK	Gahanna	OH	E+	E	E	123.7	7.63	2.3	0.0	35.5	5.6	4.8	7.2	10.9
BENCHMARK BANK	Plano	TX	B-	B-	A-	426.7	6.84	10.1	2.1	24.9	0.7	7.8	9.5	13.8
BENCHMARK COMMUNITY BANK	Kenbridge	VA	A	A-	B	477.3	4.84	6.0	3.6	42.5	8.1	10.0	11.3	17.6
BENDENA STATE BK	Bendena	KS	C+	C+	C	55.6	6.23	5.2	3.9	13.7	24.7	5.3	7.6	11.2
▲ BENEFICIAL MUTUAL SB	Philadelphia	PA	C	C-	D+	4353.7	-6.98	4.4	9.5	20.4	32.6	10.0	11.2	22.7
▲ BENEFICIAL STATE BANK	Oakland	CA	C-	D	D-	368.4	20.13	17.7	1.1	4.3	12.5	9.7	10.8	16.5
▼ BENEFIT BANK	Fort Smith	AR	D+	C-	D	187.5	-1.53	6.1	1.4	41.1	4.2	9.7	10.8	15.9
▲ BENNINGTON STATE BK	Salina	KS	A-	B	B	514.3	10.58	16.8	2.6	12.8	20.1	10.0	11.1	15.3
BENTON COUNTY STATE BK	Blairstown	IA	B+	B	B	42.4	5.77	10.6	0.2	8.7	14.3	10.0	13.3	15.9
▲ BENTON STATE BK	Benton	WI	D+	D+	D	61.4	5.20	9.0	8.1	30.2	5.0	5.4	7.7	11.3
▼ BERKSHIRE BANK	New York	NY	B	B+	A-	759.9	-1.25	1.3	0.0	9.7	48.4	10.0	16.0	36.8
BERKSHIRE BANK	Pittsfield	MA	C+	B-	C+	6336.0	16.67	11.4	5.8	25.0	17.4	5.0	7.3	11.0
BESSEMER TRUST CO	Woodbridge	NJ	A-	B+	B	631.7	-13.72	10.2	38.4	0.0	48.2	7.4	9.3	15.2
BESSEMER TRUST CO NA	New York	NY	B+	A-	B+	1708.1	-1.11	4.7	11.9	0.0	23.8	5.6	7.6	28.5
BESSEMER TRUST CO OF CA NA	San Francisco	CA	U	U	U	6.5	8.05	0.0	0.0	0.0	39.4	10.0	98.5	511.8
BESSEMER TRUST CO OF DE NA	Wilmington	DE	U	U	U	16.4	4.49	0.0	0.0	0.0	36.0	10.0	91.6	333.5
BETTER BANKS	Peoria	IL	C	C+	B-	287.6	14.48	4.1	8.4	22.7	39.7	5.8	7.8	17.0
▼ BEVERLY BANK	Beverly	MA	C	C+	B-	343.3	7.23	6.2	0.2	37.5	5.0	6.0	8.0	12.4
▲ BEVERLY BANK & TRUST CO NA	Chicago	IL	B-	C+	C	778.6	4.75	21.3	7.3	3.7	11.3	6.4	8.9	12.0
BIDDEFORD SB	Biddeford	ME	C	C	D+	382.4	6.94	5.3	0.7	41.7	13.3	8.7	10.2	13.9
BIG BEND BANKS NA	Marfa	TX	B	B+	A-	111.4	6.61	1.8	6.5	5.0	67.4	10.0	12.1	35.4
BIG HORN FSB	Greybull	WY	C+	C+	C	227.2	1.54	10.7	3.9	13.2	23.7	7.0	9.0	19.7
▲ BIPPUS STATE BK	Huntington	IN	B	B-	B	121.3	-0.59	15.9	3.4	10.6	16.1	9.4	11.2	14.5
BISCAYNE BANK	Coconut Grove	FL	C+	C+	C-	445.9	29.40	3.9	0.7	46.9	0.9	6.7	8.7	12.9
▲ BISON STATE BK	Bison	KS	D+	D+	C	9.5	-6.81	1.2	5.7	9.1	63.7	8.4	9.9	26.5
BITTERROOT VALLEY BANK	Lolo	MT	B-	C+	C	353.6	2.26	10.4	2.5	21.5	11.7	8.3	9.8	14.9
BK & TRUST BRYAN/COLLEGE STATN	Bryan	TX	B	B-	B-	417.9	16.64	6.4	1.0	19.3	13.2	8.0	9.6	15.3
BLACK HILLS COMMUNITY BANK NA	Rapid City	SD	B	A-	B+	153.1	11.32	16.5	0.7	8.9	5.8	10.0	12.8	15.4

Asset Quality Index	Adjusted Non-Performing Loans as a % of Total Loans	Adjusted Non-Performing Loans as a % of Capital	Net Charge-Offs / Avg Loans	Profitability Index	Net Income ($Mil)	Return on Assets (R.O.A.)	Return on Equity (R.O.E.)	Net Interest Spread	Overhead Efficiency Ratio	Liquidity Index	Liquidity Ratio	Hot Money Ratio	Stability Index
2.3	4.46	29.6	0.11	**3.6**	1.9	0.56	4.22	5.29	88.0	**1.8**	7.9	19.3	**4.3**
1.7	3.65	21.0	-0.01	**3.9**	3.2	0.79	6.53	3.94	76.6	**1.7**	28.1	27.9	**5.1**
7.7	0.32	2.0	0.51	**5.7**	3.9	1.18	9.64	3.97	62.5	**1.8**	32.1	29.6	**7.6**
4.0	1.14	12.3	0.11	**2.9**	0.2	0.31	4.14	4.20	86.7	**1.2**	7.9	26.2	**3.6**
3.7	2.13	17.7	0.28	**2.9**	0.9	0.40	4.09	3.75	82.1	**3.0**	12.5	13.9	**4.6**
1.8	3.88	26.6	0.24	**3.5**	0.6	0.41	3.83	4.27	72.4	**2.8**	18.1	15.2	**5.2**
4.7	3.26	14.7	0.08	**4.1**	0.5	0.75	6.45	4.15	74.5	**3.9**	43.7	16.0	**6.4**
5.1	1.17	10.2	0.07	**1.8**	3.2	0.41	4.53	3.40	96.9	**3.1**	19.3	14.3	**6.7**
5.4	1.54	8.4	0.13	**5.2**	7.4	1.01	8.33	3.74	65.2	**4.4**	17.8	6.4	**7.1**
0.3	4.61	71.1	3.72	**0.0**	-2.3	-2.96	-72.97	5.19	115.9	**1.5**	9.2	22.1	**0.0**
3.5	1.54	9.9	0.24	**9.2**	68.5	1.36	10.54	4.24	46.9	**1.0**	13.1	32.2	**8.2**
1.8	2.31	22.2	0.13	**3.2**	6.1	0.66	7.78	4.24	75.9	**1.1**	2.2	27.4	**6.9**
5.9	1.51	7.8	-0.04	**3.9**	0.5	0.62	5.86	3.77	78.1	**3.9**	23.2	10.0	**4.6**
0.0	26.48	332.4	1.12	**0.0**	-5.5	-1.28	-26.78	2.61	107.2	**1.0**	11.5	30.7	**0.8**
4.3	2.22	12.1	0.30	**4.5**	2.6	1.06	10.58	3.85	71.6	**4.2**	25.6	9.0	**6.0**
1.7	11.85	20.4	0.35	**10.0**	88.0	4.84	11.37	6.60	47.3	**0.7**	16.7	64.1	**8.1**
4.1	7.78	13.0	0.54	**10.0**	388.0	9.00	23.45	9.29	14.9	**1.4**	28.3	88.9	**8.1**
5.0	3.21	16.4	0.23	**4.1**	0.5	1.31	12.39	4.08	78.9	**3.1**	34.5	17.6	**4.4**
3.7	5.38	21.7	-0.49	**3.3**	0.2	0.62	4.26	3.90	82.5	**2.0**	26.0	20.4	**4.8**
5.9	2.12	6.6	0.43	**9.3**	0.9	1.99	11.25	4.59	57.2	**2.6**	35.7	21.1	**9.4**
3.0	2.48	21.0	0.28	**2.9**	0.3	0.33	3.66	3.99	88.2	**1.9**	7.9	19.0	**4.7**
5.0	2.81	10.8	0.60	**2.7**	0.3	0.45	3.61	3.89	86.9	**2.7**	38.1	22.1	**6.8**
2.7	2.96	20.1	0.61	**4.5**	1.3	0.81	8.68	4.24	72.8	**1.4**	18.8	26.7	**5.4**
6.2	0.45	4.1	0.02	**6.5**	23.0	1.02	10.62	4.11	73.4	**3.7**	6.3	9.8	**7.9**
4.0	1.93	10.9	-0.01	**8.8**	1.3	1.95	15.51	4.08	49.2	**4.2**	20.4	8.3	**8.4**
3.4	1.54	9.8	0.38	**6.7**	2.3	1.21	12.25	4.23	49.2	**0.9**	19.7	39.5	**5.7**
7.3	1.85	6.2	0.00	**3.4**	0.5	0.60	3.61	3.05	72.5	**2.1**	44.8	39.2	**7.4**
6.6	3.16	5.1	1.47	**5.2**	4.6	1.01	12.11	2.91	38.9	**2.7**	50.3	31.5	**3.9**
6.4	0.48	3.9	0.09	**2.5**	2.9	0.33	3.42	2.67	77.5	**2.6**	9.8	15.6	**6.9**
3.9	2.03	10.6	0.28	**3.0**	0.1	0.23	1.47	4.55	83.8	**1.6**	12.8	21.6	**6.7**
3.5	3.28	15.5	0.73	**5.3**	0.5	0.99	8.71	3.87	67.1	**3.1**	28.0	15.3	**5.3**
2.2	4.72	32.1	0.01	**0.0**	-0.9	-1.24	-13.61	3.16	143.0	**2.8**	24.5	15.8	**2.3**
0.3	6.42	61.9	0.35	**0.0**	-0.9	-1.03	-13.88	4.04	111.6	**1.2**	14.0	29.3	**2.5**
5.7	0.45	3.3	-0.02	**4.2**	2.3	0.72	7.35	4.07	92.4	**3.4**	18.8	12.3	**6.7**
8.0	0.43	2.8	0.05	**7.9**	4.7	1.32	11.87	4.53	63.0	**3.1**	15.9	13.8	**7.1**
7.6	0.27	2.3	0.08	**5.1**	0.5	1.22	16.69	3.58	61.2	**3.9**	7.5	8.2	**4.1**
5.6	0.63	2.9	0.24	**2.8**	14.0	0.42	3.08	2.90	83.4	**5.8**	39.5	8.1	**7.2**
2.8	2.54	14.7	-0.16	**3.0**	1.8	0.70	6.43	3.71	78.7	**1.2**	28.0	36.2	**4.7**
1.2	4.19	29.9	0.10	**3.8**	1.2	0.82	7.69	3.66	82.0	**1.2**	8.8	27.3	**5.2**
6.9	0.51	3.1	0.14	**8.4**	7.8	2.09	18.87	3.71	44.3	**3.4**	17.7	12.1	**8.4**
7.4	0.01	0.1	0.00	**7.1**	0.4	1.34	10.36	4.16	53.2	**2.4**	18.5	17.3	**7.0**
3.2	1.74	17.3	0.02	**3.9**	0.3	0.71	9.44	4.55	79.8	**0.6**	5.9	39.1	**4.4**
8.1	1.74	4.1	0.00	**3.9**	2.8	0.48	3.02	2.84	75.3	**3.6**	65.2	27.3	**8.5**
4.5	0.73	7.1	0.29	**3.4**	23.5	0.52	4.57	3.36	73.2	**1.9**	12.2	19.7	**8.3**
7.1	0.00	0.0	0.00	**9.8**	14.8	3.04	34.03	1.53	72.1	**5.1**	3.4	0.0	**7.1**
7.6	0.00	0.0	0.00	**9.5**	32.6	2.44	22.69	0.58	87.1	**7.7**	57.3	0.0	**8.9**
10.0	na	0.0	na	**8.5**	0.4	7.29	7.34	1.17	73.7	**4.0**	19719.4	101.0	**7.0**
10.0	na	0.0	na	**10.0**	3.6	31.53	35.12	0.59	73.2	**4.0**	1268.6	101.0	**7.0**
7.4	0.44	2.9	0.01	**2.3**	0.4	0.22	2.90	2.08	92.6	**4.3**	29.7	9.8	**3.8**
6.9	0.53	5.2	0.00	**2.5**	0.4	0.15	1.85	3.53	90.3	**3.0**	11.4	13.8	**4.6**
3.9	1.12	9.0	0.11	**5.4**	5.0	0.85	8.40	3.96	61.5	**1.8**	17.0	20.4	**5.7**
6.0	0.67	5.1	-0.40	**3.2**	2.0	0.73	7.17	3.41	88.0	**2.8**	14.5	14.8	**5.5**
9.2	0.80	1.3	-0.08	**4.0**	0.9	1.13	8.12	3.45	73.6	**6.3**	74.9	10.4	**8.5**
5.9	0.98	4.4	0.16	**3.0**	0.6	0.35	3.65	3.25	81.5	**5.3**	44.4	9.2	**5.2**
5.0	0.63	4.1	0.00	**6.3**	1.4	1.53	14.29	4.14	67.2	**4.1**	13.1	7.6	**5.9**
7.7	0.02	0.2	0.00	**8.3**	3.8	1.32	15.05	4.05	41.4	**1.1**	12.0	29.6	**3.3**
7.8	0.79	2.1	-0.29	**1.7**	0.0	0.15	1.82	2.94	95.1	**5.9**	58.1	6.0	**4.7**
4.0	1.98	13.4	-0.21	**6.4**	4.5	1.71	17.08	4.37	60.0	**4.9**	23.5	3.5	**6.1**
8.6	0.12	0.8	-0.17	**5.9**	3.4	1.15	11.61	4.28	58.3	**4.2**	23.9	8.8	**5.0**
6.7	0.55	3.2	-0.01	**3.8**	0.7	0.68	5.29	3.84	79.8	**0.8**	19.1	38.9	**7.9**

Name	City	State	Rating	2013 Rating	2012 Rating	Total Assets ($Mil)	One Year Asset Growth	Asset Mix (As a % of Total Assets) Commercial Loans	Consumer Loans	Mortgage Loans	Securities	Capitalization Index	Leverage Ratio	Risk-Based Capital Ratio
BLACK MOUNTAIN SB SSB	Black Mountain	NC	**B-**	B-	B+	37.4	5.08	0.0	0.2	59.9	0.0	**10.0**	12.3	29.9
▼ BLACK RIVER COUNTRY BANK	Black River Falls	WI	**B-**	B+	A-	68.1	0.43	4.5	4.3	38.1	7.5	**10.0**	14.4	23.9
BLACKHAWK BANK	Beloit	WI	**C-**	C-	D+	598.1	2.01	20.8	1.2	13.5	24.1	**7.0**	9.0	13.3
BLACKHAWK BANK & TRUST	Milan	IL	**A-**	B+	B	1109.2	2.75	8.9	1.1	8.6	56.3	**9.2**	10.4	20.2
BLACKRIDGEBANK	Fargo	ND	**D**	D	D	371.4	1.72	12.5	2.6	21.7	8.9	**7.2**	9.2	12.7
BLACKROCK INSTITUTIONAL TRUST	San Francisco	CA	**U**	U	U	4643.3	1.57	0.0	0.0	0.0	8.0	**10.0**	71.3	141.5
BLANCO NATIONAL BK	Blanco	TX	**B-**	B	C+	162.4	7.21	3.0	4.7	17.2	28.6	**8.4**	10.0	15.3
▲ BLC COMMUNITY BANK	Little Chute	WI	**B-**	C	C	179.2	0.10	6.9	0.8	15.8	14.8	**10.0**	15.8	21.7
BLENCOE STATE BK	Onawa	IA	**C+**	C+	B-	45.4	15.21	2.7	3.8	11.8	28.3	**7.4**	9.3	16.5
BLISSFIELD STATE BK	Blissfield	MI	**B-**	B	B-	92.5	2.29	4.2	2.0	22.0	38.2	**9.8**	10.9	20.9
▼ BLOOMBURG STATE BK	Bloomburg	TX	**C-**	C	C+	15.4	14.80	14.9	10.1	18.5	4.9	**8.7**	10.1	19.5
BLOOMFIELD STATE BK	Bloomfield	IN	**C-**	C-	D	377.6	-5.19	5.2	1.2	18.9	23.4	**10.0**	11.0	17.7
▲ BLOOMSDALE BANK	Bloomsdale	MO	**A-**	B	B	197.7	-0.68	2.8	1.8	21.0	35.4	**7.1**	9.1	16.0
BLUE GRASS FS&LA	Paris	KY	**C-**	C	C+	40.4	-1.38	0.9	4.7	66.4	10.0	**10.0**	27.0	51.3
▼ BLUE GRASS SB	Blue Grass	IA	**B-**	B	B-	180.0	-1.32	7.2	0.9	5.3	50.5	**10.0**	14.3	27.9
▲ BLUE GRASS VALLEY BANK	Blue Grass	VA	**C**	C-	C	37.9	-0.91	7.0	5.3	38.1	8.4	**10.0**	11.6	17.5
BLUE HILLS BANK	Hyde Park	MA	**C-**	C	B-	1683.9	39.14	8.2	1.9	28.2	25.2	**10.0**	15.8	23.3
BLUE RIDGE BANK	Walhalla	SC	**B**	B	B-	101.5	1.79	1.3	2.3	46.7	29.1	**9.5**	10.6	19.5
▼ BLUE RIDGE BANK & TRUST CO	Independence	MO	**C-**	D+	D	482.0	5.08	6.9	11.1	9.3	19.2	**6.8**	8.8	15.0
BLUE RIDGE BANK INC	Luray	VA	**B-**	B-	B-	228.3	8.05	6.5	1.5	29.4	16.0	**6.6**	8.7	14.0
▲ BLUEGRASS COMMUNITY BANK	Danville	KY	**B-**	C+	C-	63.9	8.53	8.1	2.3	30.3	17.1	**10.0**	11.2	18.0
BLUEHARBOR BANK	Mooresville	NC	**B**	B	C+	136.9	6.40	9.5	1.6	8.3	10.0	**10.0**	14.6	18.2
BLUERIDGE BANK	Frederick	MD	**C-**	C-	D+	188.9	7.71	12.6	0.7	13.8	11.9	**4.2**	8.0	10.6
BMO HARRIS BANK NA	Chicago	IL	**B-**	C+	C+	98480.6	8.42	15.1	8.0	8.8	15.8	**10.0**	11.7	16.6
BMO HARRIS CENTRAL NA	Chicago	IL	**U**	U	B+	7.6	0.62	0.0	0.0	0.0	0.0	**10.0**	86.7	443.6
BMW BANK OF NORTH AMERICA	Salt Lake City	UT	**B+**	B+	B	9977.8	0.62	0.0	73.1	0.0	25.2	**7.5**	11.9	12.9
BNA BANK	New Albany	MS	**A-**	A-	A-	426.3	0.13	1.4	4.9	19.0	37.7	**10.0**	12.9	23.5
BNB HANA BANK NA	Fort Lee	NJ	**D**	D	D	288.4	-12.26	1.2	0.0	1.6	18.3	**10.0**	13.8	19.6
BNC NATIONAL BK	Glendale	AZ	**B+**	B	B-	899.1	8.51	8.4	2.0	6.1	50.7	**8.7**	10.1	21.6
▲ BNY MELLON NA	Pittsburgh	PA	**B**	B	C+	16811.3	5.41	1.3	9.4	24.3	13.0	**5.9**	8.4	11.7
▲ BNY MELLON TRUST OF DELAWARE	Wilmington	DE	**B-**	B-	B-	140.1	7.93	0.0	0.0	37.3	0.0	**10.0**	59.0	94.6
BODCAW BANK	Stamps	AR	**B+**	B	B-	74.9	-2.08	6.2	5.4	7.0	55.3	**10.0**	11.0	22.0
BOELUS STATE BK	Boelus	NE	**C+**	C+	C+	14.7	-1.74	2.0	6.2	1.7	5.6	**10.0**	13.7	25.3
BOFI FEDERAL BANK	San Diego	CA	**A-**	B+	B	4820.5	46.88	5.0	0.4	54.6	9.3	**6.7**	8.7	15.5
BOGOTA SB	Bogota	NJ	**B+**	B+	B+	527.8	6.72	0.0	0.1	63.4	14.8	**9.6**	10.7	19.8
BOILING SPRINGS SB	Rutherford	NJ	**B-**	B-	C	1430.8	3.34	0.0	0.0	47.1	13.4	**10.0**	13.3	21.4
BOKF NA	Tulsa	OK	**B+**	B+	B	28881.5	7.32	19.7	1.4	7.7	34.5	**6.0**	8.0	12.1
BONANZA VALLEY STATE BK	Brooten	MN	**C-**	D+	D	60.5	12.45	12.9	3.3	25.6	15.4	**6.2**	8.2	11.9
BONDUEL STATE BK	Bonduel	WI	**A-**	A-	A-	53.2	1.81	10.4	2.3	5.9	48.1	**10.0**	22.4	54.5
BOONE BANK & TRUST CO	Boone	IA	**A-**	A-	A-	140.6	4.36	6.0	0.4	7.0	44.6	**8.9**	10.2	15.9
BOONE COUNTY NB OF COLUMBIA	Columbia	MO	**B**	B	B	1475.5	1.77	5.0	5.8	12.0	28.9	**5.5**	7.5	11.7
BOONVILLE FSB	Boonville	IN	**C-**	C	C	44.4	12.54	2.4	5.6	53.4	6.7	**9.2**	10.4	21.8
BORDER STATE BK	Greenbush	MN	**C+**	C-	D	369.5	6.60	12.2	6.0	11.5	15.3	**7.3**	10.0	12.8
BOSTON PRIVATE BANK & TRUST CO	Boston	MA	**B+**	B+	B-	6506.8	6.84	6.5	2.0	33.3	12.9	**7.5**	9.3	14.1
BOSTON TRUST & INVESTMENT MGMT	Boston	MA	**A-**	A-	A-	48.4	3.18	0.1	0.0	0.0	4.6	**10.0**	45.6	66.4
BOULEVARD BANK	Saint Louis	MO	**B-**	B-	C+	699.3	160.14	4.0	31.7	6.7	34.9	**5.5**	7.5	16.5
BOUNDARY WATERS BANK	Ely	MN	**E-**	E-	E-	113.3	0.64	2.6	0.8	22.5	11.9	**0.4**	5.0	6.9
BRADFORD NB OF GREENVILLE	Greenville	IL	**B**	B	B	264.4	7.48	3.3	1.3	17.3	40.1	**7.7**	9.4	17.3
BRADY NATIONAL BK	Brady	TX	**B-**	B-	B-	102.7	8.60	4.1	3.9	12.6	42.1	**7.4**	9.3	19.2
BRAINERD S&LA A FEDERAL ASSN	Brainerd	MN	**D**	D	D	65.0	3.81	0.1	1.3	44.7	18.8	**6.3**	8.3	14.4
BRAINTREE CO-OP BANK	Braintree	MA	**C-**	C-	C-	248.3	-0.37	2.6	0.6	45.4	27.3	**5.8**	7.8	15.9
▲ BRANCH BANKING & TRUST CO	Winston-Salem	NC	**B-**	C+	C	182901.2	4.15	10.1	8.3	19.4	22.8	**7.3**	9.2	13.6
BRAND BANK	Lawrenceville	GA	**D**	D-	E+	1829.1	7.44	24.8	3.7	14.1	7.4	**6.5**	9.3	12.2
BRANNEN BANK	Inverness	FL	**C+**	C+	C	421.8	5.17	0.2	1.1	37.2	36.9	**5.4**	7.4	20.4
BRANSON BANK	Branson	MO	**D+**	C-	C	170.8	0.95	3.8	1.5	22.4	4.4	**9.5**	10.7	14.6
BRANTLEY BANK & TRUST CO	Brantley	AL	**B+**	B+	B	66.0	1.73	5.7	7.0	5.5	51.6	**10.0**	15.1	29.7
▲ BRATTLEBORO S&LA	Brattleboro	VT	**C-**	C-	C-	179.8	2.47	4.6	1.9	48.0	0.9	**6.3**	8.3	12.3
BRAZOS NATIONAL BK	Richwood	TX	**B**	B+	B+	22.8	-16.68	1.9	4.0	62.8	0.0	**10.0**	17.1	36.7
BREDA SB	Breda	IA	**A-**	A-	B+	49.0	4.34	7.3	1.6	8.8	51.8	**10.0**	15.4	27.7
▼ BREMEN BANK & TRUST CO	Hazelwood	MO	**D**	D+	D	203.5	-3.04	16.3	0.3	6.8	29.4	**3.3**	5.9	10.2

Asset Quality Index	Adjusted Non-Performing Loans as a % of Total Loans	Adjusted Non-Performing Loans as a % of Capital	Net Charge-Offs Avg Loans	Profitability Index	Net Income ($Mil)	Return on Assets (R.O.A.)	Return on Equity (R.O.E.)	Net Interest Spread	Overhead Efficiency Ratio	Liquidity Index	Liquidity Ratio	Hot Money Ratio	Stability Index
10.0	0.00	0.0	0.00	**3.0**	0.1	0.37	2.97	2.99	82.2	**1.9**	39.3	42.2	**6.7**
3.0	4.66	23.0	0.00	**5.7**	0.6	1.25	8.97	3.87	65.3	**3.7**	21.7	11.4	**8.3**
2.4	2.72	18.7	0.80	**2.6**	1.8	0.40	3.97	3.83	83.1	**3.7**	9.6	10.0	**5.5**
7.5	0.90	3.2	0.13	**6.6**	9.6	1.18	11.79	3.65	49.5	**3.4**	19.2	12.9	**7.4**
1.0	2.81	22.6	0.08	**5.4**	2.4	0.87	6.61	4.50	68.3	**3.4**	14.7	11.9	**6.4**
6.5	na	0.0	na	**10.0**	281.5	8.11	10.93	1.50	70.4	**4.0**	43.6	101.0	**7.0**
6.3	0.45	2.6	0.06	**4.4**	1.1	0.89	9.10	4.87	79.0	**3.5**	30.3	14.1	**5.9**
4.8	1.21	5.2	-0.01	**7.9**	2.5	1.91	12.26	3.90	51.1	**1.6**	25.8	26.6	**8.4**
5.8	0.92	4.6	0.10	**4.0**	0.2	0.67	7.61	3.41	68.3	**5.4**	31.6	3.9	**4.3**
5.8	1.36	6.0	0.00	**4.0**	0.7	0.93	9.00	3.44	73.5	**5.0**	52.5	12.2	**6.1**
8.3	0.00	0.0	-0.12	**1.9**	0.0	-0.02	-0.18	3.19	100.3	**3.3**	46.7	17.6	**3.6**
4.2	2.71	15.1	0.65	**3.3**	1.8	0.64	5.56	4.11	82.4	**2.9**	29.3	17.0	**4.9**
6.1	0.50	2.9	0.26	**9.4**	3.3	2.26	23.22	4.26	48.4	**1.3**	29.0	34.5	**7.9**
4.5	6.22	17.0	0.37	**1.4**	0.0	-0.08	-0.32	3.92	90.8	**1.4**	28.3	31.7	**6.1**
6.2	2.67	7.8	2.59	**3.0**	0.6	0.43	2.96	2.75	40.4	**3.5**	53.0	22.7	**6.9**
2.2	4.68	27.0	-0.05	**4.4**	0.2	0.75	6.61	4.47	72.7	**3.0**	20.1	14.7	**6.0**
8.8	0.39	1.6	0.01	**1.3**	2.9	0.24	2.29	2.62	85.8	**3.8**	31.7	16.5	**8.7**
5.5	1.97	10.6	0.26	**4.9**	0.6	0.74	6.90	4.86	70.4	**3.0**	36.3	19.0	**6.0**
2.1	3.28	19.4	0.39	**3.4**	2.5	0.70	7.82	3.35	75.6	**3.9**	28.0	11.4	**3.7**
8.5	0.19	1.6	0.01	**4.9**	1.6	0.94	11.11	3.56	64.9	**1.1**	18.6	30.9	**4.5**
6.8	1.07	6.5	0.00	**3.4**	0.4	0.91	8.24	3.57	77.8	**1.3**	26.5	31.6	**6.3**
5.6	0.57	3.0	0.09	**4.8**	0.9	0.88	5.76	4.12	64.4	**3.1**	14.7	13.4	**6.5**
5.3	0.21	2.0	0.01	**2.3**	0.3	0.21	2.41	3.38	89.2	**1.4**	16.5	25.8	**4.2**
3.7	2.10	10.3	0.39	**3.1**	323.0	0.47	2.88	2.90	74.8	**5.4**	36.3	9.3	**8.5**
10.0	na	0.0	na	**3.7**	0.0	0.51	0.59	na	-354.6	**10.0**	733.5	0.0	**6.8**
5.6	0.17	1.0	0.29	**8.8**	101.4	1.36	11.87	2.85	27.2	**1.3**	27.6	91.4	**9.4**
5.3	2.88	11.1	0.17	**6.5**	4.4	1.36	10.95	3.92	52.7	**2.5**	31.4	19.8	**7.5**
3.2	3.85	14.9	3.01	**0.0**	-4.8	-2.12	-12.05	2.44	203.3	**2.1**	42.4	35.1	**4.7**
6.4	0.72	2.7	0.14	**6.4**	7.3	1.10	10.87	3.34	72.0	**4.0**	51.2	17.7	**5.7**
6.7	0.18	1.4	0.01	**6.4**	137.9	1.10	6.34	1.52	66.8	**1.0**	21.1	45.2	**7.9**
4.3	6.38	6.1	-0.21	**9.8**	1.9	1.90	3.23	3.82	53.9	**5.9**	31.4	0.0	**8.0**
7.8	1.17	3.5	0.01	**5.7**	0.8	1.35	13.20	3.90	53.3	**3.3**	68.5	30.0	**6.0**
8.4	0.00	0.0	0.00	**3.4**	0.1	0.57	4.27	2.44	70.6	**5.1**	51.8	9.5	**6.5**
6.9	0.62	5.7	0.04	**9.6**	51.1	1.65	19.06	4.21	31.0	**1.6**	13.9	23.8	**7.7**
6.6	0.75	5.5	0.01	**5.0**	3.1	0.81	7.68	2.72	49.1	**0.6**	10.4	43.4	**7.3**
4.6	2.57	14.7	0.10	**3.3**	4.9	0.47	3.45	3.33	73.7	**1.6**	11.3	22.4	**8.0**
6.3	0.72	4.3	-0.05	**6.5**	225.2	1.10	12.27	2.70	62.5	**5.0**	28.1	8.7	**7.9**
4.5	0.89	7.8	0.21	**4.1**	0.5	1.02	12.34	3.74	74.0	**1.0**	4.9	29.6	**4.3**
8.4	3.10	4.1	-0.01	**5.9**	0.5	1.25	5.66	3.85	54.2	**6.4**	83.2	9.4	**7.9**
9.0	0.11	0.4	0.00	**6.6**	1.3	1.32	12.90	3.77	54.8	**3.3**	42.2	19.2	**7.9**
7.6	0.57	3.9	-0.22	**7.3**	14.7	1.35	15.73	3.29	58.4	**5.1**	24.6	5.5	**7.2**
8.1	0.26	1.6	-0.04	**2.1**	0.1	0.20	1.80	3.29	93.0	**2.3**	31.9	22.5	**4.5**
3.7	1.30	9.1	-0.10	**4.7**	3.2	1.20	11.61	4.12	71.6	**2.0**	15.4	18.9	**4.3**
5.8	0.89	6.8	-0.20	**5.8**	51.1	1.08	11.55	3.14	59.1	**3.6**	14.5	11.5	**7.6**
6.5	0.00	0.0	0.00	**10.0**	15.1	45.93	54.01	4.52	53.7	**2.9**	85.0	100.0	**10.0**
5.3	0.40	2.2	0.14	**5.5**	5.4	1.50	13.33	3.27	51.0	**7.5**	61.0	0.2	**5.4**
1.0	1.66	25.9	-0.02	**3.4**	0.6	0.68	12.72	4.84	81.0	**0.7**	12.6	46.6	**0.3**
5.5	1.26	6.6	0.02	**5.1**	2.4	1.27	12.72	3.63	65.7	**3.8**	25.0	11.2	**6.4**
9.0	0.12	0.5	-0.03	**3.6**	0.6	0.74	9.48	2.99	79.4	**3.2**	35.3	17.5	**5.6**
2.6	3.54	27.3	0.32	**1.0**	0.0	0.04	0.48	3.19	105.6	**1.0**	24.7	34.7	**3.5**
4.1	2.16	16.2	0.05	**1.7**	0.4	0.21	2.79	3.09	92.1	**4.1**	35.0	13.0	**3.7**
4.0	1.07	7.2	0.31	**5.7**	1421.3	1.12	9.13	3.23	67.0	**4.0**	19.1	10.1	**8.9**
0.6	5.51	44.4	0.44	**2.6**	6.4	0.47	4.54	3.91	80.3	**1.2**	6.1	26.8	**5.8**
4.0	2.71	16.4	0.32	**3.4**	2.4	0.76	10.08	3.23	80.2	**4.9**	51.2	13.1	**4.6**
1.4	2.87	19.3	0.13	**5.2**	1.2	0.97	9.26	4.28	68.0	**1.3**	10.1	25.8	**5.5**
6.2	2.95	7.0	1.35	**6.1**	0.6	1.20	8.00	4.78	60.8	**4.1**	61.6	18.2	**6.6**
2.6	1.84	18.4	0.39	**2.0**	0.3	0.24	2.85	3.48	89.7	**3.9**	4.2	7.8	**3.4**
7.5	0.06	0.3	0.00	**6.2**	0.2	1.26	6.11	5.12	94.0	**3.2**	20.1	13.4	**5.7**
9.4	0.00	0.0	-0.01	**7.7**	0.6	1.61	10.58	4.75	56.7	**6.1**	61.4	7.3	**8.0**
1.4	4.25	31.7	0.99	**0.0**	-8.7	-5.52	-57.49	2.79	286.4	**1.9**	26.6	23.4	**3.6**

Name	City	State	Rating	2013 Rating	2012 Rating	Total Assets ($Mil)	One Year Asset Growth	Asset Mix (As a % of Total Assets) Comm-ercial Loans	Cons-umer Loans	Mort-gage Loans	Secur-ities	Capital-ization Index	Lever-age Ratio	Risk-Based Capital Ratio
BREMER BANK NA	Saint Paul	MN	**B-**	B-	B-	3563.8	23.66	11.3	1.4	4.0	16.5	**5.9**	8.2	11.7
BREMER TRUST NA	Saint Cloud	MN	**U**	U	U	10.3	13.26	0.0	0.0	0.0	2.9	**10.0**	90.5	175.1
BRENHAM NATIONAL BK	Brenham	TX	**C+**	C+	C+	282.3	4.45	6.0	1.2	7.2	46.6	**7.6**	9.4	18.6
BRENTWOOD BANK	Bethel Park	PA	**B-**	B-	B-	511.0	2.75	3.8	0.1	32.1	23.4	**8.6**	10.7	13.9
BRICKYARD BANK	Lincolnwood	IL	**D-**	D-	D-	118.4	-7.90	5.8	0.4	11.4	10.9	**6.4**	8.5	17.8
BRIDGE BANK NA	San Jose	CA	**B+**	B	C+	1756.6	19.09	49.1	0.0	0.5	18.2	**7.3**	10.2	12.7
▲ BRIDGE CITY STATE BK	Bridge City	TX	**B-**	C+	C	171.4	16.16	5.5	1.6	11.8	52.0	**6.8**	8.8	20.3
BRIDGE COMMUNITY BANK	Mount Vernon	IA	**B**	B	B-	80.2	6.60	10.5	7.1	17.7	20.9	**8.8**	10.2	15.1
BRIDGEHAMPTON NATIONAL BK	Bridgehampton	NY	**B-**	B	B	2217.7	30.36	10.4	0.4	6.0	37.1	**6.5**	8.5	13.0
▲ BRIDGEVIEW BANK GROUP	Bridgeview	IL	**D**	D-	E+	1075.4	3.19	9.3	0.1	13.4	13.9	**3.3**	6.7	10.2
BRIDGEWATER BANK	Bloomington	MN	**C+**	C	D	662.2	22.55	8.5	0.3	16.0	9.2	**6.7**	9.2	12.3
BRIDGEWATER SB	Raynham	MA	**C**	C	C	483.4	3.51	12.2	3.5	25.0	21.1	**7.1**	9.1	16.1
BRIGHTON BANK	Brighton	TN	**E-**	E-	E-	53.2	-8.16	14.1	2.8	13.7	11.0	**0.9**	5.7	7.9
▲ BRIGHTON BANK	Salt Lake City	UT	**A-**	B+	B	189.0	3.17	2.4	0.3	1.8	27.3	**10.0**	11.9	24.2
BRIMFIELD BANK	Brimfield	IL	**D+**	D	C	46.5	0.69	10.6	1.8	34.3	24.5	**8.7**	10.2	18.4
BRISTOL COUNTY SB	Taunton	MA	**B-**	B-	B-	1578.0	6.39	6.3	14.1	28.7	18.0	**10.0**	12.7	18.2
BROADWAY FEDERAL BANK FSB	Los Angeles	CA	**D-**	D-	D-	337.8	-2.24	0.2	0.0	12.4	5.3	**9.8**	10.8	16.9
BROADWAY NATIONAL BK	San Antonio	TX	**B**	B	B	3107.8	7.76	6.7	3.2	6.6	48.9	**8.5**	10.0	17.3
▲ BROOKLINE BANK	Brookline	MA	**B**	B-	C+	3562.9	11.22	18.5	10.2	11.1	6.2	**5.9**	9.4	11.7
BROOKVILLE BUILDING & SAVINGS	Brookville	OH	**C+**	C+	B-	43.5	-1.39	1.6	0.5	50.6	19.3	**10.0**	16.9	36.6
BROOKVILLE NATIONAL BK	Brookville	OH	**C-**	C-	C	108.8	1.34	4.8	3.1	12.6	51.7	**6.8**	8.8	24.2
BROWN BROTHERS HARRIMAN TC NA	New York	NY	**U**	U	U	13.4	10.62	0.0	0.0	0.0	60.4	**10.0**	67.9	157.1
BROWN BROTHERS HARRIMAN TRUST	Wilmington	DE	**U**	U	U	8.1	-2.13	0.0	0.0	0.0	72.5	**10.0**	81.9	244.4
BROWN COUNTY STATE BK	Mount Sterling	IL	**B+**	B+	A-	92.2	2.69	5.3	6.4	21.0	17.4	**7.4**	9.3	14.9
BRUNING STATE BK	Bruning	NE	**B**	B	B	330.8	8.36	4.8	0.7	2.1	38.7	**7.4**	9.3	14.7
BRUNSWICK BANK & TRUST CO	New Brunswick	NJ	**C**	C	D+	164.3	10.66	1.0	0.5	11.1	3.7	**10.0**	14.1	26.9
BRUNSWICK STATE BK	Brunswick	NE	**B**	B-	B	93.3	5.10	10.6	6.3	0.4	7.0	**6.3**	10.2	12.0
BRUSH COUNTRY BANK	Freer	TX	**C+**	C+	C+	46.4	-0.64	16.6	27.9	5.8	18.6	**6.0**	8.1	13.2
BRYANT BANK	Tuscaloosa	AL	**B-**	C+	C+	1236.2	6.29	11.1	1.1	9.0	29.0	**7.6**	9.4	14.6
BRYANT STATE BK	Bryant	SD	**B**	B	B	27.8	0.18	5.5	9.0	1.9	21.0	**10.0**	12.1	18.0
BRYN MAWR TRUST CO	Bryn Mawr	PA	**B+**	B+	B	2105.8	3.21	6.5	0.8	21.3	12.6	**7.1**	9.4	12.5
BTC BANK	Bethany	MO	**B**	B	B-	368.1	3.10	7.8	1.9	13.9	26.7	**10.0**	12.0	17.2
BUCKEYE COMMUNITY BANK	Lorain	OH	**C+**	C	C-	155.4	3.69	26.5	0.4	8.4	16.3	**8.9**	10.2	14.6
BUCKEYE STATE BANK	De Graff	OH	**D**	D+	C	36.8	26.46	6.5	3.8	10.4	53.2	**10.0**	13.0	29.8
BUCKHOLTS STATE BK	Buckholts	TX	**A-**	A-	A	71.7	11.24	8.5	5.1	7.9	53.3	**10.0**	13.9	35.8
BUCKLEY STATE BK	Buckley	IL	**B-**	B-	B-	45.4	-3.82	8.8	1.8	1.0	24.7	**10.0**	11.3	17.8
BUCKS COUNTY BANK	Doylestown	PA	**D+**	D+	D	187.3	5.48	13.8	0.0	10.9	4.7	**8.4**	10.3	13.7
BUENA VISTA NATIONAL BK	Chester	IL	**B**	B	B	207.9	-1.94	3.6	6.6	20.1	37.2	**8.3**	9.9	17.4
▲ BUFFALO FEDERAL BANK	Buffalo	WY	**C-**	C-	D+	111.5	-11.60	6.8	3.8	16.4	23.7	**9.6**	10.8	19.6
BUFFALO PRAIRIE STATE BK	Buffalo Prairie	IL	**B**	B	B	71.4	2.90	3.9	1.3	0.6	61.8	**10.0**	14.2	34.3
▲ BUILDERS BANK	Chicago	IL	**D+**	D-	E+	205.5	-23.99	0.0	0.0	5.3	26.4	**7.9**	9.6	16.1
BURKE & HERBERT BK & TRUST CO	Alexandria	VA	**A**	A-	A-	2615.6	-0.01	1.7	0.2	10.6	43.3	**10.0**	11.5	16.5
BURLING BANK	Chicago	IL	**D+**	D+	C-	116.3	5.39	7.3	0.6	17.7	39.2	**8.3**	9.9	19.6
BURTON STATE BK	Burton	TX	**B-**	B-	B-	59.3	10.03	1.3	4.8	10.8	9.7	**9.3**	10.5	30.0
BUSEY BANK	Champaign	IL	**B**	B-	B-	3460.0	-0.08	10.2	0.3	11.9	22.8	**10.0**	11.8	17.1
BUSINESS BANK	Appleton	WI	**D+**	D	D+	248.7	-0.40	9.6	0.0	4.2	22.7	**10.0**	13.0	20.4
▲ BUSINESS BANK	Burlington	WA	**E**	E-	E-	132.7	14.53	9.5	3.0	18.2	4.5	**8.0**	10.2	13.4
▲ BUSINESS BANK OF SAINT LOUIS	Clayton	MO	**B-**	C	C	543.2	5.19	19.5	0.1	5.4	9.8	**10.0**	12.3	15.0
BUSINESS BANK OF TEXAS NA	Austin	TX	**C-**	D+	C-	113.7	28.48	20.4	0.2	3.6	35.0	**10.0**	11.6	20.3
BUSINESS FIRST BANK	Baton Rouge	LA	**C+**	C+	C	696.2	1.96	27.2	0.8	5.1	10.9	**8.1**	10.8	13.5
BUTTE STATE BK	Butte	NE	**B-**	C+	C	43.5	0.74	12.3	3.2	2.1	26.9	**9.7**	10.8	18.5
BYRON BANK	Byron	IL	**B-**	C+	C-	237.8	5.79	4.3	1.9	14.1	36.4	**7.8**	9.5	17.7
BYRON STATE BK	Byron	NE	**C+**	C+	C+	44.6	0.34	10.4	5.3	4.3	8.9	**9.4**	11.0	14.5
▼ C US BANK	Cresco	IA	**B+**	A-	A-	441.4	8.03	10.5	3.7	11.3	23.9	**6.4**	10.9	12.1
C&G SB	Altoona	PA	**C+**	C+	B-	123.2	-4.71	0.3	6.3	67.5	14.8	**10.0**	15.1	29.0
▲ C1 BANK	Saint Petersburg	FL	**C**	D+	D+	1548.1	20.15	5.3	3.1	12.9	0.0	**10.0**	12.3	15.4
CABOOL STATE BK	Cabool	MO	**C**	C-	C-	64.0	0.37	4.5	2.0	11.8	21.2	**10.0**	14.2	23.6
CACHE BANK & TRUST	Greeley	CO	**D**	D	C-	155.7	-3.12	6.1	1.4	7.3	55.7	**6.5**	8.5	19.3
▼ CACHE VALLEY BANK	Logan	UT	**C+**	B	B+	810.3	18.70	10.8	0.9	5.9	1.5	**7.7**	10.5	13.1
▲ CADENCE BANK NA	Birmingham	AL	**B-**	C+	C-	7266.3	17.02	44.6	1.3	13.3	8.1	**7.6**	11.0	13.0

Asset Quality Index	Adjusted Non-Performing Loans as a % of Total Loans	Adjusted Non-Performing Loans as a % of Capital	Net Charge-Offs Avg Loans	Profitability Index	Net Income ($Mil)	Return on Assets (R.O.A.)	Return on Equity (R.O.E.)	Net Interest Spread	Overhead Efficiency Ratio	Liquidity Index	Liquidity Ratio	Hot Money Ratio	Stability Index
4.4	1.48	10.7	0.15	5.5	23.0	1.07	10.80	3.77	60.6	5.8	38.4	7.6	6.2
10.0	na	0.0	na	10.0	3.2	47.32	52.74	0.22	61.4	4.0	332.7	101.0	6.3
6.4	0.61	2.8	-0.19	3.7	1.9	0.91	9.66	3.49	75.0	5.8	53.4	9.2	5.2
8.5	0.30	1.9	0.02	4.3	3.0	0.80	8.09	3.06	65.2	3.3	13.0	12.3	5.6
2.0	6.32	29.4	3.11	0.0	-1.5	-1.59	-18.78	2.56	160.6	2.1	42.3	38.0	3.0
5.6	0.91	5.8	0.30	7.4	13.7	1.14	10.96	5.07	61.7	6.3	31.5	1.9	8.4
5.1	3.26	12.8	0.07	3.6	0.8	0.63	7.68	3.31	70.8	6.5	62.3	6.9	4.8
6.8	0.70	4.5	-0.07	5.1	0.6	1.01	10.40	3.73	68.8	2.9	19.6	14.9	5.9
8.3	0.33	2.1	0.08	4.2	10.4	0.66	8.14	3.47	68.0	5.0	23.5	5.4	6.8
1.6	4.32	39.2	0.50	3.1	34.6	4.46	54.61	3.83	93.3	3.1	14.9	13.9	4.5
3.7	0.74	5.9	0.13	9.9	8.0	1.65	19.24	4.55	35.9	0.8	16.4	38.7	5.2
7.2	0.15	1.1	0.08	2.7	1.2	0.32	3.19	3.46	86.0	3.8	24.8	10.7	5.3
0.3	4.72	57.4	1.13	1.4	0.1	0.25	4.55	4.08	96.2	1.5	11.4	23.5	0.0
5.3	4.47	14.9	-0.02	6.7	2.2	1.60	13.18	4.02	64.5	7.3	56.1	0.1	7.8
5.6	1.10	6.6	-0.17	1.4	0.1	0.23	2.27	3.30	98.0	2.4	17.3	17.1	3.6
4.5	1.46	8.8	0.02	3.4	7.9	0.75	5.14	3.16	80.6	3.7	22.6	12.8	9.4
0.3	5.96	38.0	-0.72	4.0	2.6	1.02	9.57	3.62	99.7	0.7	12.6	46.2	1.6
6.1	1.17	5.0	0.10	4.2	21.4	0.97	8.90	3.28	73.6	6.8	46.0	3.3	9.0
7.2	0.27	2.3	0.06	6.2	23.4	0.99	10.87	3.54	53.5	3.2	5.5	12.2	7.7
9.0	0.08	0.3	0.00	2.6	0.1	0.40	2.50	3.45	82.9	4.5	42.6	12.9	6.7
9.4	0.12	0.4	0.00	2.4	0.3	0.30	3.48	2.34	81.5	6.6	60.4	6.1	4.6
10.0	na	0.0	na	10.0	1.4	14.60	22.36	0.25	83.5	4.0	198.5	101.0	6.5
10.0	na	0.0	na	10.0	0.6	9.51	11.91	0.22	85.6	4.0	417.1	101.0	5.8
6.2	0.26	1.7	0.14	6.5	1.0	1.42	13.27	3.60	58.7	2.2	7.2	17.1	8.4
8.9	0.02	0.1	0.00	4.3	1.9	0.77	8.69	2.96	64.8	3.8	14.8	10.0	5.8
4.0	5.02	17.1	-0.03	1.7	0.1	0.06	0.38	3.53	97.9	3.9	46.4	17.1	5.5
5.8	0.20	1.6	0.04	9.7	1.6	2.34	24.19	3.78	45.9	0.7	9.9	36.3	6.9
6.8	0.00	0.0	0.04	8.1	0.6	1.92	20.73	4.45	60.2	3.3	34.5	16.5	5.7
7.4	0.54	3.2	-0.04	4.4	9.9	1.08	11.90	3.39	65.8	1.7	17.0	23.3	6.4
7.9	0.30	1.4	0.07	4.9	0.2	1.07	9.09	3.61	74.1	4.7	38.9	11.0	7.5
5.8	0.71	5.6	0.09	7.4	20.1	1.29	12.12	4.02	63.9	4.3	13.2	6.7	7.9
4.9	1.83	10.0	0.06	8.2	3.7	1.36	11.41	4.04	46.8	0.9	12.1	32.1	7.4
3.8	1.80	12.1	0.20	4.2	0.8	0.72	7.20	3.67	69.0	1.5	12.5	23.5	4.9
6.2	1.90	5.0	0.36	0.0	-0.6	-2.40	-14.53	3.33	176.2	4.7	43.3	12.0	3.9
8.9	0.10	0.2	0.01	6.4	0.8	1.59	11.18	3.46	58.6	5.0	67.6	14.6	8.1
8.6	0.00	0.0	-0.11	4.1	0.3	0.74	6.96	2.55	59.4	5.3	42.8	8.6	5.6
1.0	2.96	21.5	0.36	2.1	0.3	0.20	1.83	3.76	85.8	0.8	12.9	34.4	5.0
5.0	1.37	6.2	0.08	5.3	1.5	0.97	8.67	4.16	68.4	4.1	29.6	10.9	7.1
2.7	4.72	21.4	-0.08	2.7	0.3	0.31	2.89	4.22	94.7	3.9	35.8	13.9	5.2
7.1	6.13	8.3	1.36	3.8	0.3	0.55	3.97	2.48	43.3	4.1	92.0	27.0	7.0
2.6	2.28	11.4	0.00	5.2	3.0	1.82	22.42	3.78	84.3	0.3	1.4	63.6	2.1
6.6	1.87	7.7	0.02	7.2	24.3	1.26	10.72	3.96	57.7	5.2	37.9	10.9	10.0
2.4	5.44	27.5	0.00	1.3	0.1	0.17	1.98	2.79	90.6	4.1	46.0	16.0	4.4
9.0	0.61	1.5	-0.01	3.6	0.4	0.81	6.84	2.10	61.7	4.8	76.7	16.9	6.3
7.1	0.60	3.2	0.15	4.9	23.9	0.92	7.70	3.20	64.1	4.6	14.3	5.1	6.9
0.6	7.51	30.8	1.06	2.6	0.8	0.40	3.18	2.70	66.5	1.0	24.6	37.9	5.5
2.2	2.82	20.8	0.21	2.0	0.3	0.30	4.44	3.87	93.2	4.6	17.7	4.9	2.7
4.4	0.88	5.1	-0.14	4.7	3.1	0.80	6.52	3.30	68.7	1.2	20.2	29.9	6.6
8.9	0.00	0.0	0.00	1.8	0.3	0.39	3.33	3.38	82.1	1.6	34.9	40.6	6.1
5.5	0.51	3.4	0.02	3.9	3.5	0.67	6.48	3.61	71.4	1.1	16.9	31.3	6.0
5.1	1.71	8.3	0.00	4.8	0.4	1.11	10.31	3.80	70.4	2.2	37.6	29.2	4.8
5.0	2.07	10.3	0.07	4.3	1.8	1.11	10.33	3.42	72.7	1.7	19.0	22.6	5.4
4.0	0.73	4.7	0.09	7.5	0.5	1.54	15.11	3.37	37.0	1.7	24.8	25.1	5.8
5.4	0.54	3.3	0.74	6.8	4.7	1.49	12.81	3.68	54.2	3.1	23.4	14.5	8.4
6.6	1.18	5.7	0.02	3.1	0.5	0.50	3.42	3.30	79.1	4.3	20.5	7.4	7.6
2.5	1.86	11.2	0.35	4.2	5.4	0.50	5.00	4.28	70.8	2.5	20.8	18.1	6.2
3.1	5.15	19.6	0.16	2.0	0.1	0.26	1.81	3.85	92.7	5.1	37.7	8.6	5.1
7.5	0.31	1.2	0.09	1.2	0.2	0.12	1.56	2.93	93.7	3.6	53.6	21.2	2.8
3.2	1.59	10.3	0.13	8.1	6.3	1.10	10.16	4.65	62.9	2.6	20.0	16.7	8.8
4.4	0.72	5.1	0.12	3.9	34.3	0.66	4.17	4.29	73.5	2.4	8.7	16.5	6.2

Name	City	State	Rating	2013 Rating	2012 Rating	Total Assets ($Mil)	One Year Asset Growth	Asset Mix (As a % of Total Assets): Comm-ercial Loans	Cons-umer Loans	Mort-gage Loans	Secur-ities	Capital-ization Index	Lever-age Ratio	Risk-Based Capital Ratio
CALDWELL BANK & TRUST CO	Columbia	LA	**C+**	C+	C	151.1	44.71	6.7	9.6	28.7	6.0	**5.7**	9.6	11.6
CALHOUN COUNTY BANK INC	Grantsville	WV	**B-**	C+	C	129.8	3.56	6.2	8.3	40.8	13.8	**8.1**	9.7	17.4
CALIFORNIA BANK & TRUST	San Diego	CA	**B**	B	B-	11147.6	3.44	15.8	0.3	13.5	2.4	**9.2**	10.8	14.3
CALIFORNIA BANK OF COMMERCE	Lafayette	CA	**B**	B-	C+	428.6	14.15	38.8	0.1	1.4	9.2	**10.0**	14.1	15.8
CALIFORNIA BUSINESS BANK	Los Angeles	CA	**E**	E	E-	82.5	80.92	9.7	0.0	3.5	0.0	**10.0**	15.9	28.3
CALIFORNIA FIRST NATIONAL BK	Irvine	CA	**A**	A	A	540.4	16.35	27.7	0.0	0.0	8.0	**10.0**	19.8	20.1
CALIFORNIA PACIFIC BANK	San Francisco	CA	**A-**	B+	A-	101.5	-8.37	27.0	0.0	3.3	0.8	**10.0**	26.4	39.2
CALIFORNIA REPUBLIC BANK	Irvine	CA	**B+**	B	B	983.3	23.10	12.1	22.5	6.4	11.5	**5.6**	7.6	12.2
CALIFORNIA UNITED BANK	Encino	CA	**B-**	B-	C-	1450.8	7.93	20.5	0.3	1.4	9.6	**6.4**	9.4	12.0
▲ CALLAWAY BANK	Fulton	MO	**C+**	C	C	307.1	2.61	8.5	1.7	21.3	21.8	**7.9**	9.6	15.2
CALUMET COUNTY BANK	Brillion	WI	**C-**	C	C-	90.3	2.01	16.8	1.0	11.9	17.0	**9.5**	10.6	16.8
▲ CALUSA BANK	Punta Gorda	FL	**C**	C+	C-	166.8	12.51	3.8	0.3	37.6	18.4	**7.9**	9.6	15.1
CALVIN B TAYLOR BANKING CO	Berlin	MD	**A-**	A	A-	471.0	1.83	2.5	0.4	17.9	28.3	**10.0**	16.3	37.3
CAMBRIDGE APPLETON TRUST NA	Boston	MA	**U**	U	U	4.3	-3.03	0.0	0.0	0.0	0.0	**10.0**	64.8	307.5
CAMBRIDGE SB	Cambridge	MA	**C+**	C+	B-	2746.0	9.00	4.4	0.1	22.6	17.8	**8.2**	9.8	13.9
▲ CAMBRIDGE STATE BK	Cambridge	WI	**B-**	C+	C-	66.4	-9.79	3.2	0.9	24.2	13.3	**10.0**	14.8	26.3
▲ CAMBRIDGE STATE BK	Cambridge	MN	**C+**	C-	C	66.2	-3.45	9.0	0.8	19.4	19.1	**10.0**	12.9	21.7
CAMBRIDGE TRUST CO	Cambridge	MA	**B+**	B+	B+	1558.9	7.52	2.8	1.6	32.8	28.6	**5.6**	7.6	13.0
CAMDEN NATIONAL BK	Camden	ME	**B+**	B+	B	2718.1	5.90	6.6	0.7	25.7	28.8	**6.3**	8.3	13.9
CAMP GROVE STATE BK	Camp Grove	IL	**C-**	C-	C+	20.9	8.42	1.7	5.2	1.9	31.5	**10.0**	13.1	29.5
CAMPBELL & FETTER BANK	Kendallville	IN	**B-**	B-	B-	311.6	13.31	4.1	5.7	29.2	50.9	**8.3**	9.8	23.6
CAMPBELL COUNTY BANK	Herreid	SD	**A**	A	A	116.3	11.09	5.7	0.4	0.0	37.4	**10.0**	13.0	20.7
▼ CAMPUS STATE BK	Campus	IL	**D+**	D+	C-	24.5	5.09	0.0	8.2	21.2	28.7	**6.6**	8.6	17.5
CANANDAIGUA NATIONAL BK & TR	Canandaigua	NY	**B-**	B-	B-	2100.8	9.23	11.5	18.6	17.9	13.8	**5.5**	8.6	11.4
CANANDAIGUA NATIONAL TRUST CO	Sarasota	FL	**U**	U	U	3.7	-1.66	0.0	0.0	0.0	13.4	**10.0**	98.8	443.1
CANON NATIONAL BK	Canon City	CO	**B-**	B-	C-	255.0	8.98	5.9	0.3	10.3	30.4	**8.3**	9.9	16.2
CANTON CO-OP BANK	Canton	MA	**B-**	B-	B-	99.6	-1.16	0.0	0.1	30.4	36.7	**10.0**	16.1	34.7
CANTON STATE BK	Canton	MO	**D-**	D-	D+	34.7	-2.06	2.4	1.3	15.2	43.5	**6.0**	8.0	14.9
CANYON COMMUNITY BANK NA	Tucson	AZ	**D-**	D-	D-	70.0	-10.75	4.0	0.2	1.4	6.4	**4.3**	6.3	11.4
CAPAHA BANK SB	Cape Girardeau	MO	**B-**	C+	C	201.3	9.32	5.0	0.8	13.5	5.3	**6.3**	9.6	12.0
CAPE ANN SB	Gloucester	MA	**B-**	B-	B-	476.8	3.48	1.7	0.3	43.1	27.9	**10.0**	20.6	46.4
▲ CAPE BANK	Linwood	NJ	**B-**	C+	C-	1081.5	0.68	5.9	0.1	26.1	16.4	**7.9**	9.6	14.3
CAPE COD FIVE CENTS SB	Orleans	MA	**C+**	C+	B-	2653.6	9.98	5.0	0.3	54.1	12.7	**7.2**	9.2	15.1
CAPITAL BANK	Fort Oglethorpe	GA	**C+**	C+	C-	113.8	-1.05	3.4	0.5	23.0	14.8	**7.2**	9.2	13.9
▼ CAPITAL BANK	Little Rock	AR	**C-**	D+	C	155.0	0.37	8.0	1.7	5.1	58.1	**6.7**	8.7	17.9
CAPITAL BANK	Saint Paul	MN	**A-**	B+	B+	36.3	0.84	10.9	0.6	1.4	25.5	**9.5**	10.6	17.7
CAPITAL BANK	Houston	TX	**B**	B	B	315.4	8.34	9.1	2.1	7.9	9.3	**6.3**	9.0	12.0
CAPITAL BANK	San Juan Capistran	CA	**B+**	B+	B	241.4	39.07	8.6	0.1	11.1	1.4	**9.3**	10.6	14.4
CAPITAL BANK & TRUST CO FSB	Irvine	CA	**U**	U	A+	69.4	-0.49	0.0	0.0	0.0	71.0	**10.0**	68.7	185.3
▲ CAPITAL BANK NA	Rockville	MD	**C**	D+	C-	543.3	15.03	10.6	1.9	22.5	6.4	**8.1**	9.7	14.4
CAPITAL BANK NA	Coral Gables	FL	**C**	C-	C-	6690.1	1.25	14.3	3.6	14.1	15.5	**10.0**	13.4	18.2
CAPITAL BANK OF NEW JERSEY	Vineland	NJ	**B+**	B	B-	356.0	13.20	11.8	0.3	6.6	27.2	**7.2**	9.2	13.8
CAPITAL BANK OF TEXAS	Carrizo Springs	TX	**B-**	B-	B-	63.7	11.69	5.8	1.6	10.6	22.3	**10.0**	12.4	31.4
CAPITAL BANK SSB	El Paso	TX	**D**	D	C-	258.7	32.38	13.9	1.3	7.6	0.9	**10.0**	12.6	17.2
CAPITAL CITY BANK	Tallahassee	FL	**C-**	D+	C-	2481.1	-0.54	4.6	8.2	11.7	19.6	**9.5**	10.7	17.7
CAPITAL CITY BANK	Topeka	KS	**C+**	C	C	408.0	-3.44	12.6	1.6	13.8	31.1	**6.0**	8.0	12.8
CAPITAL COMMUNITY BANK	Provo	UT	**C+**	C-	C	165.9	16.20	8.7	8.5	4.9	1.0	**9.1**	11.7	14.2
CAPITAL ONE BANK (USA) NA	Glen Allen	VA	**C**	C	C	87398.1	11.50	5.6	68.9	0.0	19.3	**8.3**	9.9	15.2
CAPITAL ONE NA	McLean	VA	**C**	C+	C+	247492.3	5.42	6.7	21.0	12.2	18.1	**7.2**	9.1	13.9
▲ CAPITAL PACIFIC BANK	Portland	OR	**B-**	C	C	255.6	10.96	13.0	0.0	2.2	10.7	**8.2**	10.1	13.5
CAPITALMARK BANK & TRUST	Chattanooga	TN	**B-**	B-	B-	910.5	14.04	19.6	1.4	7.4	20.1	**7.6**	10.4	13.0
▼ CAPITOL BANK	Madison	WI	**B**	B	C+	277.2	0.66	6.7	0.6	9.3	25.2	**9.4**	10.6	15.0
CAPITOL CITY BANK & TRUST CO	Atlanta	GA	**E-**	E-	E-	275.9	-5.27	1.8	0.7	6.2	13.1	**0.0**	2.3	3.9
CAPITOL FSB	Topeka	KS	**B**	B	B+	9880.6	7.30	0.0	0.0	60.7	24.4	**10.0**	13.2	33.2
CAPITOL NATIONAL BK	Lansing	MI	**D-**	D	D-	119.1	1.51	9.0	0.5	9.1	3.4	**6.5**	8.5	16.0
CAPON VALLEY BANK	Wardensville	WV	**C**	C-	D+	148.6	0.63	1.9	8.4	36.5	10.5	**9.0**	10.3	15.8
CAPSTAR BANK	Nashville	TN	**C+**	B-	C+	1078.3	2.80	31.0	0.8	3.2	23.5	**4.4**	8.6	10.7
CAPSTONE BANK	Tuscaloosa	AL	**B-**	B	B-	425.9	5.00	19.6	2.0	11.5	7.7	**7.9**	10.4	13.3
CARDINAL BANK	McLean	VA	**B+**	A-	A-	3280.0	17.38	7.5	0.2	22.6	10.2	**6.3**	10.8	12.0
CARLSBAD NATIONAL BK	Carlsbad	NM	**A-**	A-	A	300.8	14.33	8.5	2.5	15.3	48.7	**6.9**	8.9	21.7

Asset Quality Index	Adjusted Non-Performing Loans as a % of Total Loans	Adjusted Non-Performing Loans as a % of Capital	Net Charge-Offs / Avg Loans	Profitability Index	Net Income ($Mil)	Return on Assets (R.O.A.)	Return on Equity (R.O.E.)	Net Interest Spread	Overhead Efficiency Ratio	Liquidity Index	Liquidity Ratio	Hot Money Ratio	Stability Index
3.5	1.57	13.9	0.13	**8.2**	2.1	2.14	22.98	6.25	62.7	**0.5**	6.8	46.5	**5.6**
4.3	1.87	12.6	0.12	**4.4**	0.7	0.72	7.79	4.61	76.0	**1.7**	22.5	23.7	**5.1**
4.3	1.35	9.1	0.03	**7.1**	79.0	0.95	6.88	4.12	67.4	**5.0**	18.5	3.0	**8.5**
7.3	0.47	2.3	-0.16	**4.9**	2.4	0.85	6.67	4.08	69.4	**2.7**	25.0	16.4	**6.6**
4.6	0.87	4.0	-0.81	**0.0**	-1.9	-3.69	-20.07	3.59	195.6	**0.6**	18.3	64.6	**3.5**
8.7	0.00	0.0	0.00	**6.0**	3.4	0.91	4.38	3.64	57.8	**0.5**	9.8	62.8	**9.3**
7.9	1.59	2.9	-0.45	**5.7**	0.6	0.86	3.24	3.93	67.8	**2.8**	58.1	44.3	**6.7**
7.3	0.05	0.4	0.12	**8.6**	9.6	1.49	19.41	4.79	67.2	**5.5**	26.2	0.4	**6.0**
7.0	0.36	2.4	-0.02	**4.5**	8.2	0.77	7.45	3.81	66.0	**5.3**	23.5	3.9	**7.2**
3.7	2.33	14.8	1.11	**4.6**	2.2	0.95	10.01	3.66	65.4	**4.3**	14.3	6.7	**5.1**
1.9	5.09	29.7	0.44	**2.5**	0.2	0.29	2.66	4.15	82.2	**3.3**	27.6	14.2	**5.2**
3.0	3.06	20.4	0.02	**2.7**	0.3	0.25	2.41	3.79	90.1	**3.8**	25.0	10.9	**4.2**
7.0	2.37	6.7	0.10	**5.7**	3.4	1.01	6.03	3.27	53.8	**6.2**	54.0	6.9	**8.0**
10.0	na	0.0	na	**10.0**	0.3	8.42	14.21	na	82.2	**4.0**	342.8	101.0	**5.0**
7.1	0.57	4.1	0.05	**3.4**	11.2	0.57	5.73	3.04	74.9	**3.8**	18.4	10.7	**7.6**
4.3	4.27	14.3	0.01	**3.0**	0.3	0.47	2.89	2.55	137.3	**3.8**	16.5	10.3	**5.4**
6.8	0.75	3.2	0.46	**3.0**	0.3	0.63	5.03	3.88	90.4	**6.4**	40.3	0.6	**5.0**
9.3	0.16	1.3	-0.01	**5.2**	11.1	0.98	13.26	3.40	69.4	**5.8**	32.2	5.3	**7.0**
5.5	1.09	7.8	0.13	**5.5**	19.5	0.98	10.19	3.22	58.7	**3.9**	14.5	9.6	**8.5**
2.6	8.61	24.1	0.00	**1.9**	0.1	0.46	3.47	3.01	93.6	**2.9**	58.4	25.3	**5.4**
8.4	0.29	1.3	0.00	**3.9**	1.7	0.77	8.26	3.02	68.8	**5.2**	46.8	10.6	**5.5**
8.5	0.00	0.0	0.00	**8.4**	1.9	2.17	16.98	3.96	46.7	**0.8**	16.9	38.4	**8.6**
7.3	0.52	3.0	0.00	**3.3**	0.1	0.63	7.53	2.53	77.3	**2.5**	41.1	21.5	**3.0**
4.0	1.04	9.1	0.17	**6.5**	16.2	1.08	12.62	3.77	64.7	**3.9**	5.6	8.0	**8.1**
10.0	na	0.0	na	**0.0**	-0.1	-2.80	-2.83	0.32	122.3	**4.0**	10806.5	101.0	**6.7**
7.5	0.24	1.3	0.07	**4.4**	1.5	0.80	7.65	4.19	75.5	**3.9**	24.7	10.3	**5.8**
7.8	1.58	4.7	0.23	**2.9**	0.3	0.37	2.41	2.70	85.5	**4.6**	54.2	14.5	**7.4**
2.5	5.09	30.6	0.12	**2.8**	0.2	0.58	6.91	3.26	81.6	**4.7**	37.6	10.7	**2.3**
1.7	7.03	44.3	1.57	**0.0**	-1.4	-2.43	-34.34	3.03	164.8	**6.0**	38.8	2.7	**2.1**
4.6	0.61	4.6	0.18	**4.9**	1.1	0.79	8.20	3.82	77.3	**2.0**	14.7	18.9	**5.0**
7.0	2.79	8.5	0.00	**3.4**	2.0	0.63	2.36	2.70	68.0	**3.0**	48.1	26.5	**7.8**
5.1	1.23	8.7	0.34	**4.1**	6.5	0.80	6.61	3.69	65.0	**2.2**	12.7	18.0	**7.7**
6.4	0.80	6.8	0.05	**3.4**	8.9	0.46	4.97	2.86	78.1	**3.6**	12.7	11.0	**7.3**
4.8	1.01	7.1	0.03	**3.2**	0.4	0.51	5.57	4.24	88.4	**4.2**	22.3	8.0	**3.7**
2.5	7.84	26.4	4.83	**0.3**	-1.0	-0.87	-9.41	2.68	70.0	**1.4**	34.1	67.6	**4.0**
9.0	0.00	0.0	-0.44	**3.9**	0.3	1.07	8.95	4.09	71.9	**5.9**	59.6	8.2	**5.4**
7.2	0.00	0.0	0.00	**5.5**	2.2	0.94	10.50	4.63	68.3	**2.0**	15.5	19.3	**5.6**
7.4	0.00	0.0	0.00	**9.3**	2.3	1.49	14.01	5.16	55.2	**1.3**	30.2	38.6	**4.7**
10.0	na	0.0	na	**10.0**	12.7	21.23	41.90	2.57	64.9	**10.0**	224.1	0.0	**7.0**
2.9	1.43	11.7	0.10	**9.0**	5.1	1.28	14.39	5.71	69.9	**1.2**	4.7	25.7	**6.5**
2.4	3.22	17.1	0.13	**4.9**	43.3	0.88	5.18	4.38	67.8	**2.8**	15.8	15.3	**5.7**
7.1	0.48	2.8	0.04	**5.8**	2.7	1.04	11.32	4.09	58.8	**5.2**	37.4	7.7	**5.4**
8.7	0.00	0.0	0.00	**3.9**	0.3	0.71	5.85	2.94	72.5	**5.1**	36.0	7.9	**6.9**
5.4	0.98	5.7	0.04	**0.0**	-2.4	-1.23	-9.54	3.44	128.0	**1.6**	22.3	25.6	**5.2**
3.0	3.17	16.2	0.50	**2.5**	8.0	0.42	3.20	3.40	89.2	**5.7**	26.3	2.6	**7.4**
5.7	0.71	4.8	0.07	**3.5**	1.9	0.60	7.79	3.14	77.8	**3.2**	17.3	13.4	**3.7**
4.0	0.70	4.7	-0.04	**5.9**	1.2	1.02	8.88	5.02	69.4	**0.8**	20.1	41.8	**5.2**
2.1	1.84	10.9	3.57	**10.0**	2371.0	3.81	37.20	11.97	45.5	**0.7**	13.5	54.8	**7.8**
3.6	1.45	8.8	0.84	**4.4**	1158.5	0.66	4.61	3.99	71.9	**6.5**	33.9	1.4	**7.0**
4.1	0.60	4.3	0.15	**5.2**	1.8	0.98	9.51	3.94	64.9	**2.4**	17.1	17.2	**5.3**
4.6	1.32	8.9	0.38	**4.3**	4.8	0.74	7.23	3.79	59.6	**1.6**	12.4	21.8	**6.0**
3.9	1.88	10.2	-0.03	**6.0**	2.1	0.99	9.58	3.34	55.8	**2.8**	28.7	17.1	**5.9**
0.0	14.63	280.3	1.84	**0.0**	-1.2	-0.58	-31.89	3.23	113.3	**0.6**	14.7	55.7	**0.0**
9.8	0.43	2.1	0.01	**4.5**	59.7	0.83	6.03	2.03	42.8	**2.5**	25.4	21.1	**9.4**
0.3	9.71	60.5	-0.02	**0.1**	-0.6	-0.60	-6.83	3.31	116.0	**4.7**	36.4	10.4	**2.9**
2.7	2.48	16.2	0.50	**3.8**	0.7	0.64	6.39	4.45	80.3	**1.9**	17.2	19.9	**4.9**
5.4	1.39	10.4	0.11	**3.6**	4.3	0.55	5.76	3.24	75.3	**1.8**	13.2	20.2	**7.0**
2.5	2.88	20.8	0.08	**4.8**	2.6	0.82	7.07	4.22	65.6	**1.5**	7.5	22.6	**6.2**
7.5	0.24	1.8	0.04	**6.6**	25.4	1.08	9.67	3.71	62.7	**1.2**	2.1	25.5	**9.1**
9.2	0.08	0.4	0.02	**6.1**	3.0	1.42	16.85	3.08	64.0	**6.0**	51.4	7.3	**6.0**

Name	City	State	Rating	2013 Rating	2012 Rating	Total Assets ($Mil)	One Year Asset Growth	Asset Mix (As a % of Total Assets) Commercial Loans	Consumer Loans	Mortgage Loans	Securities	Capitalization Index	Leverage Ratio	Risk-Based Capital Ratio
CARMINE STATE BK	Carmine	TX	**B+**	B+	B+	69.8	15.90	3.4	8.6	7.7	37.2	**10.0**	12.2	32.6
▲ CAROLINA ALLIANCE BANK	Spartanburg	SC	**B+**	B-	B-	416.4	70.35	10.9	0.8	8.9	14.9	**10.0**	11.7	15.2
CAROLINA BANK	Greensboro	NC	**C-**	D+	D+	668.7	0.18	8.7	0.2	14.1	10.8	**7.1**	9.0	13.6
CAROLINA BANK & TRUST CO	Darlington	SC	**B-**	B-	C-	391.9	1.38	6.9	1.8	16.9	10.7	**10.0**	11.7	17.6
CAROLINA PREMIER BANK	Charlotte	NC	**C**	C	D+	253.4	7.57	11.6	0.1	16.6	13.1	**6.2**	8.3	11.9
▲ CAROLINA TRUST BANK	Lincolnton	NC	**C-**	D-	D-	270.3	0.63	11.4	1.4	16.0	9.2	**6.1**	9.1	11.8
CARROLL BANK & TRUST	Huntingdon	TN	**B-**	B-	B-	262.8	3.80	4.9	7.0	26.8	17.2	**8.9**	10.3	15.4
CARROLL COMMUNITY BANK	Sykesville	MD	**C-**	D+	D	112.9	5.23	1.7	0.4	40.0	10.2	**7.4**	9.3	14.8
CARROLL COUNTY S&LA	Carrollton	MO	**C+**	C+	C+	22.4	-3.84	0.0	0.8	38.3	42.9	**10.0**	14.3	43.8
CARROLL COUNTY STATE BK	Carroll	IA	**B+**	B	B-	368.8	2.05	9.1	0.7	9.4	26.3	**9.1**	10.4	14.8
CARROLL COUNTY TC CARROLLTON	Carrollton	MO	**B**	B	B	148.3	3.81	3.5	1.6	6.8	48.0	**7.6**	10.8	13.0
CARROLLTON BANK	Carrollton	IL	**B**	B	B-	1150.3	1.57	23.4	0.9	10.8	15.4	**5.1**	7.9	11.1
CARROLLTON FEDERAL BANK	Carrollton	KY	**B-**	B-	C+	34.4	-5.98	0.0	3.7	47.8	11.6	**10.0**	13.2	24.6
CARSON BANK	Mulvane	KS	**C-**	C-	D+	101.0	1.03	7.3	2.6	19.5	31.6	**6.4**	8.4	15.9
CARSON NATIONAL BK OF AUBURN	Auburn	NE	**B-**	B-	B-	70.9	-2.21	2.6	1.2	6.4	56.6	**10.0**	12.5	25.1
CARTER BANK & TRUST	Martinsville	VA	**C+**	C+	C+	4678.8	1.07	3.5	0.7	3.3	39.8	**5.1**	7.1	12.1
CARTHAGE FS&LA	Carthage	NY	**B**	B	B	181.6	5.49	0.0	2.4	69.8	6.0	**9.8**	10.9	24.6
▲ CARVER FSB	New York	NY	**D**	D+	D-	647.0	1.74	6.4	0.1	18.6	15.1	**9.1**	10.4	19.2
CARVER STATE BK	Savannah	GA	**D+**	D	D	43.3	6.06	8.5	4.0	25.1	12.9	**9.0**	10.4	16.2
▼ CASEY COUNTY BANK	Liberty	KY	**C**	C+	B	161.9	-1.25	4.8	8.7	27.6	17.2	**10.0**	13.2	18.9
CASEY STATE BK	Casey	IL	**C+**	C	C	255.3	4.08	16.9	3.2	13.4	30.3	**9.7**	10.8	16.1
CASHMERE VALLEY BANK	Cashmere	WA	**B+**	B+	B	1318.6	3.56	4.7	9.8	8.2	37.4	**7.9**	9.6	17.3
CASS COMMERCIAL BANK	Saint Louis	MO	**A**	A	B	690.7	4.16	24.6	0.0	2.8	0.0	**10.0**	12.2	15.8
▲ CASS COUNTY BANK INC	Plattsmouth	NE	**B-**	C+	C	61.1	19.90	9.4	1.7	24.2	6.0	**9.7**	12.1	14.7
CASTLE ROCK BANK	Castle Rock	CO	**B+**	B	B-	126.5	8.93	2.5	0.6	14.6	30.0	**8.7**	10.1	19.9
CASTLE ROCK BANK	Castle Rock	MN	**A-**	A-	A-	171.3	1.96	11.8	4.0	11.5	50.8	**10.0**	13.6	27.3
CASTROVILLE STATE BK	Castroville	TX	**B-**	B-	B	124.3	-2.09	2.8	3.1	19.5	50.0	**7.5**	9.3	22.6
CATAHOULA-LASALLE BANK	Jonesville	LA	**C+**	B-	B	118.1	-1.11	15.8	7.0	5.1	27.9	**9.1**	10.4	19.9
CATHAY BANK	Los Angeles	CA	**B**	B	B-	11577.2	7.13	20.9	0.0	14.6	11.4	**10.0**	12.4	15.7
CATSKILL HUDSON BANK	Kingston	NY	**D+**	C	C-	446.9	5.03	13.5	0.3	2.6	41.3	**6.0**	8.0	13.9
CATTARAUGUS COUNTY BANK	Little Valley	NY	**C+**	C+	C+	189.5	2.58	10.5	1.5	18.3	23.6	**6.2**	8.2	12.9
▲ CATTLE NATIONAL BK & TRUST CO	Seward	NE	**A-**	B+	C+	224.6	6.09	2.6	0.8	17.4	20.7	**10.0**	11.9	17.5
CAYUGA LAKE NATIONAL BK	Union Springs	NY	**B+**	B+	A-	140.5	5.73	2.6	3.1	34.2	33.9	**7.0**	9.0	19.9
CB&S BANK	Russellville	AL	**C+**	C+	C	1448.6	-3.26	4.7	1.8	9.4	49.9	**8.9**	10.2	19.7
CBANK	Cincinnati	OH	**B**	B+	B+	103.6	24.14	25.5	0.8	9.1	5.0	**10.0**	16.4	20.6
CBC BANK	Bowling Green	MO	**D**	D	C	32.7	-4.46	4.6	1.3	12.3	43.2	**7.2**	9.2	19.5
CBC NATIONAL BK	Fernandina Beach	FL	**B-**	C+	D+	444.8	19.41	2.6	0.3	29.2	6.0	**8.2**	9.8	21.3
CBW BANK	Weir	KS	**B+**	B	C+	12.9	-0.40	3.2	1.0	4.5	16.7	**10.0**	16.1	29.4
CCB COMMUNITY BANK	Andalusia	AL	**B**	B	B-	430.1	2.67	9.3	2.4	18.0	7.2	**8.4**	10.5	13.7
CECIL BANK	Elkton	MD	**E-**	E-	E	340.4	-9.57	2.2	0.3	19.4	23.6	**1.9**	5.1	8.9
CECILIAN BANK	Cecilia	KY	**B-**	C+	C+	584.2	4.38	3.8	2.4	18.8	32.4	**6.9**	8.9	14.7
CEDAR HILL NATIONAL BK	Charlotte	NC	**U**	U	A	12.5	3.96	0.0	0.0	0.0	63.3	**10.0**	75.3	138.2
CEDAR RAPIDS BANK & TRUST CO	Cedar Rapids	IA	**B-**	B-	C+	822.4	26.13	16.8	1.0	6.8	24.2	**6.0**	8.0	11.9
CEDAR RAPIDS STATE BK	Cedar Rapids	NE	**D**	D+	C-	38.0	5.10	12.5	2.7	0.9	10.9	**3.5**	7.9	10.3
▲ CEDAR SECURITY BANK	Fordyce	NE	**C**	C+	B-	50.6	1.90	18.0	4.8	12.8	3.5	**9.6**	12.8	14.7
CEDAR VALLEY BANK & TRUST	La Porte City	IA	**C+**	C	C-	56.5	-5.52	9.2	2.5	6.8	52.4	**6.3**	8.3	17.0
CEDARSTONE BANK	Lebanon	TN	**C**	C	C-	168.9	-1.45	8.4	3.4	19.3	27.1	**6.8**	8.9	14.6
CELTIC BANK	Salt Lake City	UT	**C+**	C	C+	328.6	19.82	29.1	2.5	4.0	2.1	**10.0**	14.9	18.7
CENBANK	Buffalo Lake	MN	**B**	B	B	61.2	0.58	5.3	4.8	4.1	43.8	**6.1**	8.1	14.1
▲ CENDERA BANK NA	Bells	TX	**C+**	C-	C-	62.8	19.00	4.5	1.5	42.3	7.9	**10.0**	11.5	19.1
CENLAR FSB	Ewing	NJ	**B+**	B+	B	859.3	16.37	0.0	0.3	17.4	70.3	**6.6**	8.6	28.0
CENTENNIAL BANK	Lubbock	TX	**B-**	B-	B	738.5	2.00	11.3	2.3	9.4	24.9	**7.5**	9.3	13.2
CENTENNIAL BANK	Centennial	CO	**C-**	C-	D-	506.3	14.85	14.2	0.3	17.2	10.5	**6.4**	9.2	12.1
CENTENNIAL BANK	Conway	AR	**B-**	B-	C+	7187.8	73.09	7.7	0.8	13.2	19.0	**6.8**	9.4	12.4
CENTER NATIONAL BK	Litchfield	MN	**B+**	B+	B+	187.6	2.13	10.6	5.1	6.1	52.6	**9.0**	10.3	18.8
CENTER POINT BANK & TRUST CO	Center Point	IA	**B-**	B-	B-	31.6	-2.83	11.6	4.4	29.7	23.9	**6.6**	8.6	14.1
CENTERA BANK	Sublette	KS	**B**	B	B	252.9	3.36	6.6	1.5	7.9	42.1	**6.3**	8.4	14.8
▲ CENTERBANK	Milford	OH	**C**	C-	D+	123.8	5.02	16.8	0.6	19.0	7.8	**7.5**	9.8	12.9
CENTERPOINTE COMMUNITY BANK	Hood River	OR	**C+**	B-	B-	133.0	24.70	9.4	0.1	2.8	25.9	**5.8**	7.8	13.2
CENTERSTATE BK OF FLORIDA NA	Winter Haven	FL	**C+**	B-	C+	3628.0	55.69	6.9	1.6	15.6	14.9	**6.7**	8.7	13.7

Asset Quality Index	Adjusted Non-Performing Loans as a % of Total Loans	Adjusted Non-Performing Loans as a % of Capital	Net Charge-Offs Avg Loans	Profitability Index	Net Income ($Mil)	Return on Assets (R.O.A.)	Return on Equity (R.O.E.)	Net Interest Spread	Overhead Efficiency Ratio	Liquidity Index	Liquidity Ratio	Hot Money Ratio	Stability Index
8.7	0.19	0.4	-0.01	4.3	0.6	1.10	8.91	3.45	67.3	3.2	80.5	37.8	7.1
6.0	1.01	6.3	0.34	7.6	5.7	2.14	18.17	4.01	54.0	1.6	12.2	21.9	5.6
2.1	2.97	22.9	0.67	3.6	2.2	0.44	4.84	3.78	83.6	2.4	14.1	17.1	4.9
3.5	3.33	17.8	0.02	4.3	2.1	0.72	6.32	4.09	73.5	3.6	21.7	11.4	6.0
5.2	1.12	9.3	-0.02	3.0	0.9	0.46	5.06	4.28	85.4	1.7	21.7	23.4	4.3
3.2	1.81	14.4	-0.11	3.3	2.0	0.97	11.12	4.39	78.2	0.8	13.6	34.7	2.9
4.2	1.58	10.3	0.22	4.1	1.4	0.71	6.76	4.49	76.5	1.4	9.9	25.1	5.4
5.6	0.60	5.0	-0.02	2.7	0.3	0.33	3.70	3.67	85.6	1.7	16.7	21.2	4.0
9.4	1.24	3.6	0.00	2.4	0.0	0.20	1.43	1.82	79.1	3.4	62.9	20.8	5.9
5.7	0.59	3.4	0.13	4.7	2.6	0.95	9.25	4.10	69.5	2.2	30.4	22.3	6.4
6.0	1.77	6.5	-0.01	4.6	1.5	1.31	13.81	3.22	67.2	3.0	40.3	20.0	7.5
8.3	0.10	0.8	-0.03	4.9	10.6	1.24	16.05	3.08	61.7	2.4	15.5	17.6	7.4
5.9	2.21	11.1	0.14	2.8	0.1	0.29	2.30	3.75	89.7	1.9	19.9	20.1	5.9
5.2	1.25	7.6	0.12	2.2	0.3	0.34	4.32	3.11	90.5	3.3	18.9	13.0	3.1
9.4	0.00	0.0	0.21	3.3	0.3	0.64	5.23	2.48	69.6	3.6	34.8	15.1	6.2
4.6	2.10	13.5	0.01	3.7	23.9	0.68	8.31	2.62	60.6	3.1	40.6	26.9	6.6
8.2	0.35	2.6	0.02	4.7	1.0	0.77	7.09	3.41	64.1	1.5	13.0	24.2	6.1
2.7	3.09	17.2	0.21	0.8	-0.4	-0.10	-0.94	3.31	108.4	1.8	31.1	28.5	4.7
2.0	4.46	24.8	0.16	2.3	0.1	0.28	2.90	5.78	93.7	0.8	19.9	42.0	2.3
1.9	4.90	25.7	0.44	4.7	1.0	0.80	6.08	4.43	67.3	2.7	8.0	14.8	7.4
3.7	2.15	12.0	0.48	6.2	2.5	1.36	12.91	3.77	57.4	2.9	21.3	15.0	7.0
6.6	0.73	3.9	0.16	5.6	11.9	1.23	12.02	3.45	55.5	4.7	30.2	11.5	7.8
7.2	0.04	0.3	-0.04	7.2	5.5	1.09	9.37	3.33	48.8	3.3	23.6	13.3	7.7
4.0	0.76	5.3	-0.06	3.6	0.2	0.65	5.09	4.28	77.8	2.0	9.2	18.3	5.2
6.8	1.09	4.3	-0.06	5.4	1.2	1.31	13.42	3.75	64.1	2.9	45.6	25.2	6.1
6.2	2.92	8.9	-0.25	6.0	1.9	1.48	11.12	3.30	46.4	4.3	55.9	17.7	7.9
9.3	0.00	0.0	-0.04	4.3	0.8	0.85	9.30	3.21	66.2	1.9	34.2	30.1	5.2
4.8	1.70	7.8	0.11	3.8	0.8	0.86	8.73	3.33	73.9	3.6	45.7	18.5	5.6
4.7	1.42	8.3	-0.07	7.0	98.8	1.20	8.30	3.37	47.0	0.8	14.3	41.1	8.8
1.4	6.77	39.0	1.90	1.4	0.7	0.22	2.94	3.58	79.9	2.7	18.7	15.7	2.8
5.0	1.15	8.4	0.21	3.4	0.7	0.49	5.57	4.14	85.2	5.0	10.1	1.5	4.9
6.1	0.85	4.9	0.00	5.8	2.2	1.36	11.67	3.94	63.3	2.8	7.2	14.4	7.5
9.7	0.00	0.0	0.05	5.5	1.1	1.05	12.75	3.78	62.9	2.5	32.6	20.3	5.3
3.2	6.42	23.3	0.38	4.0	11.2	1.00	10.25	3.70	80.3	5.7	44.6	10.1	7.8
7.2	0.00	0.0	0.00	3.9	0.6	0.81	4.84	3.40	76.3	0.8	18.1	40.9	7.4
9.4	0.00	0.0	-0.09	1.0	0.0	-0.03	-0.32	2.80	109.0	6.0	47.9	4.8	3.6
4.9	1.90	11.7	0.23	4.4	2.4	0.78	7.46	4.08	87.8	0.9	4.3	30.5	3.7
9.7	1.36	1.3	-0.05	9.2	0.8	7.59	56.58	2.11	43.6	7.0	93.5	5.5	6.4
4.9	1.06	7.9	0.01	8.7	5.9	1.86	17.78	4.94	55.1	1.2	11.0	27.5	6.7
0.3	17.63	138.3	2.31	0.0	-4.5	-1.72	-31.49	2.81	152.5	0.9	14.9	32.8	1.8
4.6	1.69	10.0	1.22	4.9	3.7	0.86	9.55	3.55	65.7	2.3	29.5	19.8	5.7
10.0	na	0.0	na	9.5	0.3	3.71	4.86	1.12	78.5	10.0	290.9	0.0	8.0
4.6	1.31	9.5	0.17	4.5	5.9	0.96	11.17	3.43	66.7	1.1	16.2	31.1	5.7
6.4	0.06	0.6	0.06	4.9	0.3	1.07	13.50	4.03	65.3	1.0	4.2	29.0	3.0
2.9	1.55	9.8	0.04	8.3	0.6	1.52	12.43	4.28	50.7	2.0	9.6	18.6	6.9
8.6	0.42	1.9	-0.01	4.3	0.4	0.97	12.77	3.59	69.9	5.1	33.8	6.5	3.3
5.9	1.56	10.4	0.20	3.1	0.7	0.53	6.01	3.78	80.5	1.2	25.9	33.5	4.1
3.0	1.63	7.8	0.52	10.0	7.4	3.40	22.65	6.78	54.0	0.3	8.4	77.1	8.2
5.9	1.34	8.2	0.01	3.8	0.4	0.87	11.33	3.13	71.0	3.9	18.1	9.4	4.6
9.1	0.00	0.0	0.00	3.2	0.3	0.67	5.72	5.03	83.9	0.9	19.0	38.6	6.5
7.8	1.29	2.6	0.43	8.6	13.9	2.08	27.75	1.98	88.7	6.7	63.4	5.8	4.8
5.0	0.89	6.1	0.01	4.5	5.3	1.00	10.60	4.44	76.6	3.8	17.7	10.5	5.9
4.3	1.18	9.8	0.14	1.7	0.5	0.14	1.36	3.97	84.9	1.2	12.8	28.5	4.4
4.2	1.15	8.2	0.21	10.0	85.9	1.68	12.48	5.42	43.4	3.0	6.6	13.4	9.1
7.4	0.97	3.5	0.01	5.4	2.0	1.38	13.54	3.49	59.4	4.0	27.4	10.6	6.1
2.2	4.25	26.7	0.08	2.5	0.1	0.56	6.77	3.98	76.0	3.7	22.6	11.1	3.6
4.5	1.48	8.4	0.45	5.1	2.3	1.19	13.60	3.53	62.2	3.9	24.9	10.6	6.3
2.9	1.79	13.9	0.12	5.5	0.9	1.00	10.20	4.31	65.9	0.9	13.4	32.7	5.5
8.8	0.00	0.0	-0.01	3.5	0.4	0.41	4.95	3.67	79.9	6.1	43.8	3.7	4.0
3.7	2.18	15.7	0.08	2.8	7.8	0.31	2.85	4.46	88.7	4.2	19.2	8.4	7.0

Name	City	State	Rating	2013 Rating	2012 Rating	Total Assets ($Mil)	One Year Asset Growth	Asset Mix (As a % of Total Assets) Commercial Loans	Consumer Loans	Mortgage Loans	Securities	Capitalization Index	Leverage Ratio	Risk-Based Capital Ratio
CENTIER BANK	Merrillville	IN	B	B-	C	2577.5	13.23	3.5	0.3	19.1	7.0	10.0	11.5	15.0
CENTINEL BANK OF TAOS	Taos	NM	B	B	B+	190.5	2.22	2.0	1.2	21.3	46.3	7.2	9.1	22.1
CENTRAL BANK	Houston	TX	B	B-	B-	491.7	6.00	10.5	0.3	26.6	21.8	6.7	8.7	13.2
▼ CENTRAL BANK	Tampa	FL	C-	C	C+	89.6	25.06	4.2	0.0	6.1	15.5	9.7	12.5	14.7
CENTRAL BANK	Golden Valley	MN	B+	B	B-	1171.0	1.23	8.6	1.1	14.8	14.5	6.6	8.6	14.4
CENTRAL BANK	Storm Lake	IA	C+	C+	B-	638.5	26.11	20.7	1.9	14.9	4.5	7.0	10.3	12.5
CENTRAL BANK	Little Rock	AR	B+	B+	C+	98.5	3.34	5.6	0.3	12.8	32.7	10.0	16.3	27.8
CENTRAL BANK	Lebanon	MO	A-	B+	B+	256.7	-1.87	5.2	2.2	22.9	19.6	9.8	11.6	14.9
▲ CENTRAL BANK	Savannah	TN	E+	E	E-	107.5	-14.07	3.6	5.6	43.3	10.9	4.5	6.5	11.7
CENTRAL BANK	Provo	UT	A-	A-	B	794.6	8.81	4.3	1.2	4.1	33.2	10.0	15.9	24.5
CENTRAL BANK & TRUST	Lander	WY	B	B	B	152.7	-4.79	10.6	3.1	17.5	31.7	7.2	9.1	15.9
▲ CENTRAL BANK & TRUST CO	Hutchinson	KS	B	B-	C+	258.3	0.80	9.9	1.0	12.4	20.3	6.5	8.5	12.1
CENTRAL BANK & TRUST CO	Lexington	KY	C	D+	D	1924.0	-2.06	10.5	3.6	16.8	10.9	7.6	9.8	13.0
▼ CENTRAL BANK ILLINOIS	Geneseo	IL	B-	B	B	497.8	9.25	5.8	0.9	8.7	34.2	9.4	10.6	15.0
CENTRAL BANK OF AUDRAIN COUNTY	Mexico	MO	B	B	B-	144.2	-5.54	3.8	3.3	21.1	27.9	6.8	8.8	14.0
CENTRAL BANK OF KANSAS CITY	Kansas City	MO	C+	C+	C+	134.8	-6.23	9.6	0.1	4.0	1.5	10.0	16.1	22.4
CENTRAL BK LAKE OF THE OZARKS	Osage Beach	MO	B	B-	C+	586.0	5.90	3.6	4.4	15.5	20.0	6.4	8.4	14.7
CENTRAL BK OF JEFFERSON COUNTY	Louisville	KY	C-	D+	D	189.9	-7.47	7.9	1.2	19.3	8.5	7.3	9.2	12.7
CENTRAL FS&LA	Cicero	IL	D+	D-	D-	167.3	-2.84	0.0	0.1	35.5	19.7	8.2	9.8	24.6
CENTRAL FS&LA OF CHICAGO	Chicago	IL	C+	C+	C	98.1	4.01	0.0	0.0	29.0	7.5	10.0	23.1	34.0
CENTRAL FS&LA OF ROLLA	Rolla	MO	C+	C+	C+	65.1	-2.28	2.9	0.7	47.9	0.1	10.0	20.8	34.2
CENTRAL NATIONAL BK	Junction City	KS	B	B	B	831.0	1.61	3.3	1.8	10.5	40.2	10.0	11.4	21.6
CENTRAL NATIONAL BK	Waco	TX	B+	B	B	732.8	5.96	18.2	1.5	26.6	10.8	6.5	8.5	13.6
▼ CENTRAL NATIONAL BK & TRUST CO	Enid	OK	C+	B-	C-	604.0	4.37	16.4	5.0	8.7	14.1	6.8	8.8	14.1
CENTRAL NATIONAL BK & TRUST CO	Attica	IN	C+	C+	C+	60.9	-6.90	0.4	1.9	11.7	62.5	10.0	19.2	50.5
▲ CENTRAL NATIONAL BK OF POTEAU	Poteau	OK	A-	B+	B	224.6	0.15	4.7	4.0	13.2	44.6	7.8	9.5	22.1
CENTRAL PACIFIC BANK	Honolulu	HI	B+	B+	B-	4724.9	0.30	9.4	7.9	22.2	30.1	10.0	11.3	17.6
CENTRAL SB	Sault Sainte Marie	MI	C-	D+	C	252.1	-1.54	6.7	2.8	16.8	31.2	10.0	11.5	20.3
CENTRAL STATE BK	Pleasant Hill	IL	B-	B-	B-	118.0	2.29	11.8	10.8	28.5	3.9	10.0	14.9	18.8
CENTRAL STATE BK	State Center	IA	A-	B+	B-	213.9	5.78	19.9	0.3	2.4	43.2	10.0	12.6	16.7
CENTRAL STATE BK	Beulah	MI	B-	B-	B	74.9	-1.46	2.4	0.9	16.6	20.7	10.0	12.4	24.7
▲ CENTRAL STATE BK	Muscatine	IA	B+	B	C-	441.8	2.78	6.8	1.7	16.4	24.3	9.2	10.5	15.5
CENTRAL STATE BK	Elkader	IA	B+	B+	B	207.9	0.94	9.6	1.8	14.5	16.6	10.0	11.1	15.8
CENTRAL STATE BK	Calera	AL	A-	A-	A-	193.6	7.51	5.2	3.1	18.0	19.7	10.0	12.4	19.1
CENTRAL TRUST BANK	Jefferson City	MO	B-	B-	B-	2583.2	11.65	4.1	4.3	7.7	37.8	4.9	7.0	20.1
CENTRAL VALLEY COMMUNITY BANK	Fresno	CA	B	B-	C	1163.4	6.62	7.4	0.8	1.7	41.4	7.0	9.0	15.9
▼ CENTREBANK	Veedersburg	IN	C+	C+	C-	66.6	4.75	15.6	4.3	24.4	3.4	9.5	10.7	15.8
CENTREVILLE SB	West Warwick	RI	C+	C+	B-	988.4	2.04	0.2	1.2	36.8	51.7	10.0	22.7	51.4
▲ CENTRIC BANK	Harrisburg	PA	C	C-	C	316.7	3.53	10.3	0.2	12.8	9.2	6.1	8.2	12.1
▲ CENTRUE BANK	Streator	IL	D+	D	E	851.5	-3.49	6.2	0.3	8.4	15.9	5.8	7.8	12.3
CENTRUST BANK NA	Northbrook	IL	D-	D-	D-	64.4	1.37	19.5	0.1	7.0	13.2	7.1	9.1	12.5
CENTURY BANK	Shenandoah	IA	B	B	B-	83.9	-4.05	6.4	2.2	3.8	35.4	7.8	9.6	14.1
▲ CENTURY BANK	Lucedale	MS	B	B-	B-	254.8	0.80	4.1	12.5	14.3	21.5	10.0	11.0	15.9
CENTURY BANK	Santa Fe	NM	C+	C+	C	594.4	-0.66	18.0	0.4	6.0	32.6	8.1	9.7	14.8
CENTURY BANK & TRUST	Milledgeville	GA	C+	C	C-	227.4	2.99	7.1	1.6	17.6	22.4	9.4	10.6	17.1
CENTURY BANK & TRUST	Coldwater	MI	B	B	B-	275.7	4.55	11.8	2.1	15.9	22.1	10.0	12.0	18.0
CENTURY BANK & TRUST CO	Medford	MA	C+	C+	C+	3589.9	7.04	1.8	0.2	8.7	54.4	4.3	6.3	14.1
CENTURY BANK OF FLORIDA	Tampa	FL	D-	E+	D-	70.6	-2.40	14.3	1.0	20.4	7.0	6.2	8.2	12.9
CENTURY BANK OF GEORGIA	Cartersville	GA	B	B	B-	157.1	-0.19	5.1	0.8	12.0	5.7	10.0	12.6	22.9
CENTURY BANK OF KENTUCKY INC	Lawrenceburg	KY	C-	D+	D+	105.9	4.21	2.7	1.4	33.8	15.2	9.6	10.7	16.6
▲ CENTURY BANK OF THE OZARKS	Gainesville	MO	B+	B	B-	167.7	1.11	4.7	4.0	23.6	10.4	7.6	9.4	14.3
CENTURY S&LA	Trinidad	CO	C	C	C	100.1	-4.62	0.8	1.0	19.1	58.2	10.0	12.2	41.7
CENTURY SB	Vineland	NJ	C+	C+	C+	435.7	2.46	3.3	0.1	15.2	61.3	10.0	13.3	33.4
CERESCOBANK	Ceresco	NE	B+	B+	B+	44.7	0.00	8.8	5.1	20.7	24.9	10.0	15.0	20.3
▼ CERTUSBANK NA	Easley	SC	D	C-	B	1549.3	-10.87	16.8	0.4	9.7	12.5	2.9	6.4	9.9
▲ CFBANK	Fairlawn	OH	D	D-	D	305.0	24.34	15.8	0.8	16.5	2.7	9.2	11.1	14.3
▲ CFG COMMUNITY BANK	Baltimore	MD	B	B-	C	568.0	8.84	22.4	0.5	5.0	11.0	10.0	12.4	16.7
CHAIN BRIDGE BANK NA	McLean	VA	C+	B-	B-	370.3	20.95	3.2	0.6	22.9	50.4	6.0	8.0	15.2
▲ CHAMBERS BANK	Danville	AR	C-	D+	D	773.0	1.94	9.3	1.1	16.1	6.8	10.0	11.1	15.1
CHAMBERS STATE BK	Chambers	NE	B+	B+	A-	39.7	-2.84	7.9	2.6	0.8	0.9	10.0	25.7	36.5

Asset Quality Index	Adjusted Non-Performing Loans as a % of Total Loans	Adjusted Non-Performing Loans as a % of Capital	Net Charge-Offs Avg Loans	Profitability Index	Net Income ($Mil)	Return on Assets (R.O.A.)	Return on Equity (R.O.E.)	Net Interest Spread	Overhead Efficiency Ratio	Liquidity Index	Liquidity Ratio	Hot Money Ratio	Stability Index
4.8	1.08	7.5	0.10	**7.4**	23.0	1.25	11.50	3.90	60.8	**4.0**	13.1	9.0	**7.5**
7.8	1.28	5.4	0.00	**5.1**	1.9	1.29	14.59	3.37	66.7	**5.2**	48.0	10.8	**6.5**
8.0	0.08	0.6	-0.57	**6.8**	6.0	1.66	18.90	5.32	71.4	**1.5**	10.0	22.4	**5.6**
5.5	0.50	2.9	0.03	**1.7**	0.0	0.07	0.48	3.89	99.2	**1.1**	18.8	32.0	**5.1**
5.7	1.08	8.2	0.60	**6.2**	12.4	1.43	17.22	4.66	71.4	**3.6**	13.1	10.9	**7.8**
3.9	1.62	12.5	0.08	**8.2**	7.7	1.59	16.06	5.32	58.3	**1.6**	8.8	21.4	**5.8**
5.6	2.87	9.8	3.03	**5.5**	0.7	0.97	6.26	3.62	67.2	**1.0**	26.2	44.9	**5.9**
7.1	0.69	4.0	0.02	**5.9**	2.6	1.39	12.36	3.91	68.6	**2.8**	11.2	14.5	**6.5**
0.3	7.05	51.7	1.72	**1.7**	0.3	0.39	6.39	4.38	81.3	**1.1**	23.5	33.4	**1.8**
5.5	3.09	9.8	0.02	**9.0**	9.2	1.61	10.08	4.69	54.4	**3.7**	35.4	14.9	**7.9**
7.0	0.41	2.6	0.02	**6.9**	1.9	1.60	18.57	3.66	63.3	**4.1**	6.1	6.8	**6.3**
7.4	0.12	0.8	-0.48	**7.8**	3.8	1.96	23.94	3.94	58.2	**1.5**	16.1	24.5	**5.6**
3.0	2.34	17.1	0.23	**4.2**	12.1	0.85	8.19	4.01	77.2	**2.7**	10.7	15.2	**6.4**
3.8	2.76	13.3	-0.16	**7.6**	5.5	1.51	13.26	4.18	52.3	**4.2**	31.5	11.3	**7.1**
4.7	1.68	10.7	0.09	**6.8**	1.3	1.18	13.38	3.59	58.1	**4.5**	12.8	5.0	**6.6**
2.7	2.78	11.8	0.17	**6.1**	1.7	1.56	9.50	4.45	78.3	**1.9**	22.9	20.8	**6.6**
5.0	1.05	6.2	0.20	**7.8**	5.5	1.31	14.90	3.98	58.1	**2.7**	26.8	17.1	**6.5**
2.2	2.41	17.9	0.28	**2.1**	0.3	0.20	1.70	3.18	90.5	**1.4**	19.5	26.7	**5.4**
1.7	8.23	37.1	0.24	**1.6**	0.5	0.35	3.72	3.02	89.7	**3.4**	50.4	21.3	**4.4**
6.5	1.40	4.5	-0.04	**2.6**	0.2	0.20	0.89	3.68	90.7	**1.1**	23.6	32.6	**6.4**
6.4	1.98	7.5	0.01	**2.1**	0.1	0.12	0.55	3.13	88.4	**1.9**	22.1	20.9	**6.6**
8.4	0.06	0.2	-0.30	**4.6**	6.3	0.99	8.43	3.41	77.1	**4.9**	29.2	5.9	**7.0**
7.2	0.07	0.5	0.08	**6.9**	8.8	1.67	20.14	3.53	49.3	**1.9**	23.7	21.1	**6.8**
2.4	3.49	25.4	0.25	**4.7**	5.2	1.14	13.19	3.89	74.2	**4.0**	25.6	10.0	**5.3**
9.9	0.50	0.5	0.99	**2.9**	0.2	0.39	2.19	2.14	81.8	**7.1**	83.9	5.1	**6.1**
7.7	0.39	1.9	0.09	**7.1**	3.0	1.74	19.37	3.97	61.8	**2.1**	27.3	20.1	**6.8**
5.2	1.97	9.4	0.00	**4.9**	29.0	0.82	6.20	3.41	68.5	**2.1**	15.1	18.9	**7.3**
1.6	8.51	35.7	0.60	**3.9**	1.3	0.70	6.15	3.56	76.8	**2.9**	44.0	24.1	**6.3**
3.5	2.78	15.5	0.44	**10.0**	2.2	2.38	16.41	4.99	46.8	**1.3**	8.0	24.8	**8.8**
6.5	1.49	6.0	-0.03	**6.7**	2.4	1.63	14.18	3.31	49.3	**2.2**	46.2	44.0	**7.5**
4.8	3.56	12.9	0.02	**2.5**	0.2	0.27	2.19	2.92	89.9	**4.6**	57.2	15.1	**5.4**
5.8	0.76	4.5	0.09	**5.0**	3.5	1.10	10.07	3.71	65.1	**4.1**	31.9	11.6	**6.1**
7.4	0.44	2.7	0.03	**5.0**	1.7	1.09	9.53	3.72	68.6	**2.8**	25.4	16.2	**7.0**
7.9	0.70	3.4	0.13	**5.7**	1.9	1.34	11.16	4.56	69.0	**1.4**	13.7	25.9	**7.3**
6.2	1.86	7.9	0.13	**5.2**	15.4	0.88	10.06	2.17	68.6	**6.2**	37.9	4.6	**6.5**
5.3	1.20	6.1	0.33	**4.7**	8.0	0.93	8.03	4.14	73.5	**5.4**	42.0	11.1	**8.9**
3.4	2.30	14.4	0.16	**5.1**	0.4	0.86	8.26	5.10	72.2	**2.7**	24.2	16.4	**5.1**
9.9	0.65	1.3	0.05	**3.3**	7.0	1.00	3.91	2.70	75.0	**4.6**	69.8	18.3	**8.2**
5.4	0.52	4.5	0.06	**2.8**	1.0	0.42	5.21	3.44	79.3	**1.8**	10.9	19.7	**3.1**
1.5	4.07	29.2	0.24	**1.4**	1.9	0.28	3.60	3.33	87.6	**3.2**	7.4	12.3	**3.5**
0.3	10.20	64.7	2.94	**0.0**	-1.7	-3.53	-36.61	3.37	179.8	**0.6**	12.3	48.4	**2.9**
8.1	0.00	0.0	-0.01	**5.1**	0.6	1.00	11.14	3.47	61.5	**4.4**	33.3	10.9	**5.4**
4.8	0.84	4.5	0.22	**4.9**	1.5	0.80	7.58	4.85	77.7	**2.6**	18.8	16.1	**5.8**
5.2	1.37	7.4	0.15	**3.6**	3.4	0.78	8.02	4.36	80.8	**2.0**	21.2	19.8	**6.2**
3.6	2.52	14.7	0.09	**5.7**	1.8	1.10	10.96	4.27	67.3	**3.8**	19.7	10.6	**5.8**
4.3	3.49	16.5	0.36	**4.8**	1.8	0.89	8.17	3.57	73.3	**4.8**	33.4	8.6	**5.8**
8.7	0.58	3.2	0.01	**3.3**	17.5	0.65	11.42	2.30	67.2	**4.0**	13.5	9.2	**3.9**
1.5	7.15	49.1	1.50	**1.9**	0.2	0.30	3.74	3.74	92.1	**3.1**	23.4	14.3	**2.6**
4.6	3.72	14.6	0.11	**5.7**	1.2	1.01	8.19	3.93	67.9	**3.5**	40.1	17.7	**6.3**
2.0	4.90	31.1	0.27	**5.3**	1.1	1.30	13.13	3.97	70.7	**2.1**	10.6	18.3	**5.2**
5.4	0.88	6.0	0.09	**9.0**	2.5	2.00	20.76	4.75	59.0	**3.2**	12.2	12.8	**7.6**
5.9	5.21	12.2	0.49	**2.0**	0.1	0.17	1.41	2.66	83.2	**2.6**	55.2	53.7	**4.0**
8.2	1.81	3.8	0.52	**2.8**	1.5	0.46	3.79	2.74	75.5	**5.9**	63.7	11.1	**6.9**
8.4	0.55	2.1	-0.35	**7.0**	0.5	1.43	9.61	3.99	51.2	**4.1**	29.3	10.8	**6.7**
2.5	2.99	22.6	1.65	**0.0**	-39.0	-3.30	-40.70	4.69	153.1	**1.5**	19.8	27.1	**1.5**
1.9	2.03	13.1	-0.19	**1.2**	0.6	0.27	2.62	3.24	89.6	**0.7**	12.7	48.0	**3.5**
4.9	0.56	3.3	0.14	**9.1**	8.1	2.03	15.37	5.03	64.2	**1.0**	17.8	33.6	**8.4**
9.7	0.00	0.0	-0.04	**3.4**	1.5	0.55	6.53	2.95	75.3	**6.1**	54.3	7.2	**4.7**
1.6	5.67	31.4	0.09	**4.5**	4.1	0.71	6.23	4.03	77.5	**0.9**	18.4	34.2	**5.4**
7.1	0.57	1.4	0.00	**7.2**	0.5	1.71	6.92	3.17	44.5	**3.7**	45.0	17.3	**7.0**

Name	City	State	Rating	2013 Rating	2012 Rating	Total Assets ($Mil)	One Year Asset Growth	Asset Mix (As a % of Total Assets) Commercial Loans	Consumer Loans	Mortgage Loans	Securities	Capitalization Index	Leverage Ratio	Risk-Based Capital Ratio
CHAMPION BANK	Parker	CO	**D-**	D-	D-	61.7	-5.02	1.5	0.1	19.3	1.6	**8.6**	10.1	15.0
CHAMPLAIN NATIONAL BK	Willsboro	NY	**B-**	B-	B-	267.5	5.24	7.7	1.3	16.8	30.2	**6.8**	8.9	14.9
▼ CHAPPELL HILL BANK	Chappell Hill	TX	**D-**	C-	C+	24.1	-2.12	3.0	3.7	14.5	3.0	**10.0**	11.0	26.0
CHARLEROI FSB	Charleroi	PA	**C+**	C	B-	540.5	-3.08	1.8	1.8	40.7	37.6	**10.0**	13.0	28.6
CHARLES RIVER BANK	Medway	MA	**C-**	C-	C+	216.8	0.68	3.0	0.4	40.1	26.8	**6.2**	8.2	15.5
CHARLES SCHWAB BANK	Reno	NV	**B**	B	B+	105585.0	7.89	0.0	1.8	7.6	80.1	**5.1**	7.1	21.8
▼ CHARLEVOIX STATE BK	Charlevoix	MI	**C-**	C	D+	170.3	1.04	4.7	2.7	14.4	15.1	**6.5**	8.6	14.3
CHARLOTTE STATE BK & TRUST	Port Charlotte	FL	**D+**	D+	D+	278.3	4.31	0.2	0.1	14.6	34.7	**7.7**	9.4	16.8
▼ CHARTER BANK	Biloxi	MS	**C**	C+	C	113.8	1.30	13.6	1.2	20.0	20.0	**10.0**	11.8	16.2
CHARTER BANK	Corpus Christi	TX	**B**	B	B-	254.6	15.35	17.1	1.8	5.0	40.3	**4.3**	6.4	12.1
CHARTER BANK	Johnston	IA	**B+**	B+	B+	136.3	0.32	5.0	2.2	16.8	39.9	**9.4**	10.6	18.6
CHARTER BANK EAU CLAIRE	Eau Claire	WI	**A-**	A-	B	583.9	3.58	12.5	0.6	19.8	29.4	**10.0**	13.1	18.6
CHARTER WEST NATIONAL BK	West Point	NE	**B**	B	B-	200.4	4.97	10.9	3.4	10.7	14.9	**7.9**	9.8	13.2
CHARTERBANK	West Point	GA	**B**	B-	C+	1010.0	-7.65	2.5	0.5	18.5	18.7	**10.0**	17.7	27.9
▲ CHASE BANK USA NA	New York	NY	**C-**	C-	C-	142620.8	16.49	4.0	63.4	0.0	0.0	**6.3**	11.3	12.0
CHASEWOOD BANK	Houston	TX	**D+**	D+	C	104.2	-1.16	8.1	0.5	7.3	47.8	**6.5**	8.5	17.5
CHATTAHOOCHEE BANK OF GEORGIA	Gainesville	GA	**C+**	C	C	116.1	14.01	14.5	0.8	2.4	11.0	**10.0**	17.5	20.2
CHEAHA BANK	Oxford	AL	**A-**	B+	B-	186.4	1.64	3.9	5.7	21.3	35.4	**9.8**	10.9	18.3
CHELSEA BANK	Chelsea	MA	**C-**	C	C-	58.6	1.71	0.1	0.8	45.5	13.2	**8.3**	9.8	19.1
CHELSEA GROTON BANK	Norwich	CT	**C+**	C+	C+	937.9	1.57	3.6	0.8	44.2	25.4	**10.0**	14.3	22.5
CHELSEA SB	Belle Plaine	IA	**A-**	A-	B+	125.6	6.43	6.6	2.0	10.3	61.4	**10.0**	14.9	32.9
CHELSEA STATE BK	Chelsea	MI	**C+**	B-	C+	251.1	3.28	12.4	0.5	8.6	23.1	**9.7**	10.8	18.1
CHELTEN HILLS SB	Abington	PA	**D-**	D+	D-	34.3	-6.00	0.0	0.0	76.8	0.0	**8.4**	9.9	20.5
CHEMICAL BANK	Midland	MI	**C+**	C+	C	6588.7	5.42	12.4	11.9	21.9	13.5	**6.5**	8.8	12.2
CHEMUNG CANAL TRUST CO	Elmira	NY	**C+**	C+	C	1520.4	13.51	10.1	14.3	17.0	19.3	**4.7**	7.4	10.9
CHEROKEE STATE BK	Cherokee	IA	**A**	A	A	191.7	4.38	5.6	1.5	4.4	38.8	**10.0**	11.8	17.6
CHESAPEAKE BANK	Kilmarnock	VA	**C+**	C+	B-	654.1	0.11	15.7	1.6	10.1	29.5	**9.3**	10.5	14.6
▲ CHESAPEAKE BANK & TRUST CO	Chestertown	MD	**B-**	C	C	104.1	5.17	6.7	1.1	26.1	24.3	**10.0**	11.1	16.3
▲ CHESAPEAKE BANK OF MARYLAND	Baltimore	MD	**D+**	D-	D+	172.3	-6.03	0.7	0.5	38.3	9.2	**9.7**	10.8	17.5
▲ CHESTER COUNTY BANK	Henderson	TN	**B-**	C+	C+	68.5	-0.22	2.8	6.4	17.6	34.5	**7.8**	9.5	22.4
CHESTER NATIONAL BK	Chester	IL	**B-**	B-	B+	87.6	12.45	1.3	1.9	32.3	24.6	**9.2**	10.4	23.1
CHESTERFIELD STATE BK	Chesterfield	IL	**D**	D	C-	21.3	3.38	7.3	14.4	31.2	1.2	**6.8**	8.8	13.6
CHETOPA STATE BK & TRUST CO	Chetopa	KS	**B**	B	B-	30.8	7.17	4.8	3.5	15.9	25.3	**7.1**	9.1	16.4
CHEVIOT SAVINGS BANK	Cheviot	OH	**C+**	C+	B-	573.7	-2.63	1.2	0.2	37.0	28.8	**10.0**	14.1	25.6
▼ CHEYENNE STATE BK	Cheyenne	WY	**B-**	B	B-	39.1	11.23	7.3	4.1	17.3	11.2	**10.0**	15.0	20.9
CHICAGO TRUST CO NA	Lake Forest	IL	**U**	U	U	14.6	18.84	0.0	0.0	0.0	0.7	**10.0**	93.2	211.4
▼ CHICOPEE SB	Chicopee	MA	**C-**	C+	C	623.7	3.25	12.6	0.4	22.6	5.6	**10.0**	13.2	16.4
CHILLICOTHE STATE BK	Chillicothe	MO	**B**	B	C+	122.7	-4.30	4.8	4.0	26.4	36.2	**7.0**	9.0	18.7
▲ CHINATOWN FSB	New York	NY	**B-**	C-	C+	146.1	-5.96	0.0	0.6	18.2	1.7	**10.0**	19.5	31.1
▲ CHINO COMMERCIAL BANK NA	Chino	CA	**B+**	B-	C-	126.6	10.29	2.3	0.3	11.9	10.8	**9.1**	10.4	17.4
CHIPPEWA VALLEY BANK	Winter	WI	**C**	C	C-	299.2	8.34	5.9	0.5	22.2	9.3	**6.6**	8.6	12.9
CHISHOLM TRAIL STATE BK	Park City	KS	**C**	C	C-	75.7	0.94	1.3	3.2	21.9	25.7	**6.5**	8.5	18.9
CHOICE BANK	Oshkosh	WI	**B**	B	B-	222.6	11.78	13.8	0.3	26.1	9.0	**8.9**	10.3	15.5
CHOICE FINANCIAL GROUP	Fargo	ND	**B**	B-	C-	902.2	36.55	11.7	1.6	6.2	9.4	**6.5**	10.1	12.2
CHOICEONE BANK	Sparta	MI	**B-**	B-	C+	532.7	6.93	16.4	3.9	17.7	26.3	**7.4**	9.2	13.9
CIBM BANK	Champaign	IL	**C**	C-	C	499.6	13.54	12.3	0.4	17.7	18.5	**10.0**	12.2	15.0
CIERA BANK	Graham	TX	**B**	B	C+	483.7	87.13	10.6	4.5	12.3	18.7	**10.0**	11.3	15.8
CINCINNATI FS&LA	Cincinnati	OH	**C+**	C+	C	132.5	17.14	0.2	0.0	56.9	2.7	**6.9**	8.9	13.8
CINCINNATUS SAVINGS & LOAN CO	Cincinnati	OH	**C**	B-	C	83.0	-4.59	6.2	0.8	52.7	0.3	**10.0**	23.5	39.2
CISSNA PARK STATE BK	Cissna Park	IL	**C+**	C	C+	60.4	0.39	7.4	0.9	4.1	35.1	**6.0**	8.0	15.8
▼ CIT BANK	Salt Lake City	UT	**B**	B+	B+	20328.3	38.61	40.3	0.0	0.0	2.2	**9.1**	13.2	14.3
▲ CITIBANK NA	Sioux Falls	SD	**B-**	B-	C+	1377620.0	1.86	10.4	11.4	6.7	21.1	**7.7**	9.5	14.5
CITICORP TRUST DELAWARE NA	Greenville	DE	**U**	U	U	58.9	3.74	0.0	0.0	0.0	0.4	**10.0**	102.	467.9
CITIZENS & FARMERS BANK	West Point	VA	**B**	B-	B-	1312.3	34.22	2.7	22.5	19.9	16.8	**7.6**	9.4	15.2
CITIZENS & NORTHERN BANK	Wellsboro	PA	**A-**	A-	A	1242.9	1.89	4.1	0.8	25.2	40.0	**10.0**	12.0	24.0
CITIZENS 1ST BANK	Tyler	TX	**A**	A	A+	730.4	-2.27	3.3	1.3	11.0	60.8	**10.0**	19.7	47.3
CITIZENS ALLIANCE BANK	Clara City	MN	**B-**	B-	C+	520.2	10.13	20.0	1.8	9.0	16.9	**6.2**	9.1	11.9
CITIZENS B&TC GRAINGER COUNTY	Rutledge	TN	**B+**	A-	A-	193.8	4.25	1.9	2.9	10.1	56.3	**10.0**	17.1	37.2
CITIZENS B&TC OF JACKSON	Jackson	KY	**C**	C	C	139.9	9.79	7.3	7.8	20.6	6.6	**6.6**	9.1	12.2
CITIZENS BANK	Morehead	KY	**B-**	B-	C+	122.7	1.89	1.2	3.5	40.8	14.1	**6.3**	8.3	15.1

Asset Quality Index	Adjusted Non-Performing Loans as a % of Total Loans	Adjusted Non-Performing Loans as a % of Capital	Net Charge-Offs Avg Loans	Profitability Index	Net Income ($Mil)	Return on Assets (R.O.A.)	Return on Equity (R.O.E.)	Net Interest Spread	Overhead Efficiency Ratio	Liquidity Index	Liquidity Ratio	Hot Money Ratio	Stability Index
0.0	11.62	65.3	-0.09	0.7	-0.1	-0.13	-1.36	3.66	102.5	0.7	20.2	55.0	3.8
8.4	0.29	1.7	0.03	4.0	1.3	0.66	7.77	4.28	77.0	3.8	14.0	9.9	4.8
8.6	0.00	0.0	0.00	0.0	-0.1	-0.48	-4.26	2.23	120.4	4.7	60.8	13.3	5.3
9.4	0.20	0.8	0.00	2.8	2.0	0.49	3.90	2.20	74.3	2.7	44.8	28.0	7.1
5.8	0.92	7.0	0.00	2.3	0.5	0.30	3.70	3.08	95.2	3.0	29.4	16.7	4.8
9.9	0.36	0.6	0.01	5.2	696.0	0.90	12.82	1.67	20.7	8.4	91.3	0.7	5.6
2.3	3.77	24.1	-0.02	5.2	1.4	1.23	14.20	3.96	75.7	5.9	43.7	5.2	4.6
1.7	7.46	37.9	0.09	5.5	2.9	1.40	15.98	3.49	65.9	6.3	45.3	3.1	4.6
2.4	4.89	26.2	0.44	1.9	0.0	0.03	0.26	4.22	86.6	0.7	13.3	43.3	6.1
7.5	0.26	1.9	-0.17	10.0	6.2	3.39	42.63	7.34	52.4	5.7	50.6	8.9	6.2
9.0	0.21	1.0	0.01	5.5	1.1	1.04	9.83	3.37	57.8	4.5	50.6	15.3	6.8
6.2	1.18	5.4	-0.07	9.9	12.9	3.03	22.08	4.74	35.0	2.8	35.4	19.4	9.1
4.7	0.77	5.2	0.14	6.3	1.9	1.30	13.25	4.08	77.8	1.7	11.0	20.6	7.7
6.9	1.71	5.7	0.10	3.8	5.4	0.69	3.58	3.21	78.8	3.1	17.9	14.4	7.6
2.3	1.52	8.6	2.85	9.7	1528.7	1.57	7.79	8.51	53.4	1.4	26.5	68.7	7.7
7.3	0.00	0.0	0.00	1.5	0.1	0.13	1.72	3.03	94.5	2.8	58.7	50.5	4.0
7.4	0.00	0.0	0.00	2.5	0.3	0.36	2.00	3.39	87.0	1.9	22.8	20.8	6.5
8.8	0.09	0.4	0.12	8.6	2.3	1.68	16.33	5.10	52.8	0.9	21.2	35.4	6.1
2.4	3.82	25.1	0.00	2.1	0.1	0.16	1.67	3.38	95.1	3.8	18.2	10.5	4.7
6.8	1.81	8.1	0.11	2.9	3.8	0.54	3.67	3.20	82.3	4.1	30.6	11.1	7.8
7.5	1.04	2.2	0.26	6.0	1.4	1.46	10.81	3.59	55.1	6.5	75.4	9.2	9.0
3.5	3.19	15.0	0.39	5.5	2.5	1.28	11.61	3.94	67.0	5.4	39.5	7.3	6.7
0.3	9.10	67.3	0.00	3.8	0.2	0.91	9.71	3.64	67.6	0.8	19.1	42.4	3.2
3.3	1.76	14.2	0.18	5.7	49.4	1.05	10.29	3.56	62.7	3.9	12.4	9.3	8.4
3.2	1.53	14.0	0.25	4.0	6.2	0.56	6.13	3.55	78.4	4.3	7.2	5.6	7.1
8.6	0.24	1.1	-0.04	8.9	2.3	1.63	14.39	4.13	44.1	2.9	39.3	21.0	7.7
3.1	2.84	15.4	0.04	5.4	4.3	0.89	7.71	4.71	75.2	1.8	20.9	22.2	7.5
4.7	1.98	12.2	0.24	6.8	1.1	1.59	14.84	3.74	60.6	2.5	8.8	15.7	6.7
5.4	1.36	8.4	0.12	1.3	0.4	0.29	2.51	3.22	92.1	2.1	27.3	21.5	4.5
6.1	1.54	6.3	0.19	4.7	0.5	0.95	10.39	3.97	72.4	2.8	54.0	29.3	5.1
9.7	0.03	0.1	0.01	3.5	0.5	0.74	6.76	2.90	75.8	4.9	53.8	12.6	5.7
1.2	3.82	31.8	0.02	7.2	0.3	1.81	22.26	3.72	49.2	1.6	20.6	23.9	4.4
8.7	0.00	0.0	0.04	5.1	0.3	1.17	12.75	3.33	65.2	1.7	20.2	23.7	5.7
5.2	2.35	9.7	0.12	3.1	1.8	0.41	2.80	2.90	73.8	3.8	37.3	15.1	7.3
3.3	5.17	24.1	0.08	4.4	0.2	0.54	3.61	4.72	81.7	1.5	17.5	25.2	6.6
6.5	na	0.0	na	9.5	1.6	15.36	16.53	0.56	70.1	4.0	872.2	101.0	5.7
4.3	2.31	14.1	1.29	1.2	-0.8	-0.19	-1.41	3.57	83.1	2.5	14.6	16.2	7.8
5.0	2.03	11.2	0.24	5.8	1.4	1.41	16.35	3.15	57.9	5.2	33.0	5.8	6.6
4.3	3.18	9.9	-0.39	6.9	1.1	0.95	5.03	4.91	71.3	5.2	42.6	9.5	7.2
5.5	1.27	6.4	-0.32	6.2	1.0	1.05	10.12	3.80	66.6	5.3	37.1	6.5	5.8
3.3	2.01	16.2	0.42	5.1	2.7	1.32	14.48	4.48	68.4	4.2	18.1	7.8	4.8
7.6	0.47	2.4	0.06	3.0	0.3	0.59	6.99	3.16	87.2	6.1	49.3	4.9	4.6
6.0	0.59	4.0	-0.03	6.0	1.6	1.00	9.99	3.66	54.1	0.7	13.9	41.9	4.6
5.2	0.79	6.4	-0.42	10.0	16.9	2.87	29.77	4.70	49.0	1.4	9.7	23.8	6.5
3.6	1.74	11.3	0.07	5.4	4.2	1.07	9.03	3.97	69.3	3.4	26.2	13.4	6.8
5.0	2.06	11.8	0.09	2.3	1.0	0.28	2.32	3.53	89.9	3.6	10.2	10.6	4.4
4.3	1.56	8.8	0.03	9.1	7.1	1.93	15.20	4.77	55.3	1.9	18.8	19.8	8.5
5.1	1.50	13.2	0.21	2.8	0.3	0.34	3.51	2.98	82.9	0.8	10.1	34.0	4.6
5.5	2.92	9.7	0.39	1.7	0.1	0.07	0.31	4.04	90.7	1.8	16.4	20.3	5.8
8.9	0.00	0.0	0.00	3.5	0.4	0.79	9.71	2.44	68.6	5.1	46.3	10.5	4.5
7.6	0.59	3.1	0.32	4.2	90.8	0.69	4.58	2.83	61.3	0.8	18.6	62.4	8.4
5.0	2.18	9.3	1.20	5.0	9205.0	0.90	8.35	3.25	61.0	4.2	40.1	16.4	8.8
10.0	na	0.0	na	9.5	1.5	3.70	3.66	0.29	44.2	4.0	1663.2	101.0	7.0
4.7	1.22	6.7	1.59	7.5	11.1	1.12	11.01	6.62	63.7	3.1	22.4	15.5	9.0
5.3	2.59	10.5	0.33	7.5	12.4	1.35	9.80	3.81	61.1	4.0	7.1	7.9	10.0
8.9	1.15	1.9	0.05	8.0	11.8	2.13	10.96	3.38	30.4	3.2	52.7	26.1	10.0
3.7	1.41	10.3	0.01	7.2	6.8	1.77	18.24	4.17	54.1	1.6	8.9	20.7	6.3
4.8	9.81	19.0	1.28	4.4	1.2	0.81	4.78	3.92	69.6	4.5	53.7	15.8	8.4
2.8	2.03	16.3	0.18	4.3	0.8	0.81	7.55	4.53	80.6	0.7	12.1	36.2	5.5
4.3	1.03	8.3	0.28	4.0	0.8	0.84	8.41	4.18	79.1	3.9	16.8	9.9	5.3

Name	City	State	Rating	2013 Rating	2012 Rating	Total Assets ($Mil)	One Year Asset Growth	Asset Mix (As a % of Total Assets) Comm-ercial Loans	Cons-umer Loans	Mort-gage Loans	Secur-ities	Capital-ization Index	Lever-age Ratio	Risk-Based Capital Ratio
▲ CITIZENS BANK	Mount Vernon	KY	**C+**	C-	C-	139.4	-1.99	1.7	4.9	38.1	11.6	**9.2**	10.4	17.1
CITIZENS BANK	Olanta	SC	**B-**	B-	B-	381.6	-0.59	7.6	6.1	21.2	15.5	**7.4**	9.2	16.7
CITIZENS BANK	New Tazewell	TN	**C-**	D+	D-	151.3	3.65	9.3	3.5	27.5	10.9	**6.5**	8.5	12.4
CITIZENS BANK	Carthage	TN	**A+**	A+	A	526.5	2.39	3.7	3.2	13.1	58.1	**10.0**	16.7	28.5
CITIZENS BANK	Elizabethton	TN	**B+**	A-	B+	653.3	2.73	27.2	1.6	5.4	31.1	**10.0**	13.4	28.8
CITIZENS BANK	Hartsville	TN	**B-**	B-	C+	175.7	10.24	4.7	3.7	25.1	17.2	**7.4**	9.3	13.6
▲ CITIZENS BANK	Nashville	GA	**C**	D+	D+	252.6	-4.38	6.1	3.9	29.9	15.7	**10.0**	11.0	19.0
CITIZENS BANK	Columbia	MS	**B**	B	B-	381.2	2.66	7.8	7.9	23.3	13.4	**9.6**	10.7	16.6
CITIZENS BANK	Cairo	GA	**D**	D+	D	38.4	2.19	10.5	3.7	16.2	21.4	**10.0**	11.3	24.7
CITIZENS BANK	Enterprise	AL	**C+**	C+	C	105.0	12.20	10.0	1.7	9.3	36.8	**8.8**	10.2	20.0
CITIZENS BANK	Greensboro	AL	**A-**	A-	A-	98.1	0.77	6.5	6.3	9.1	41.1	**10.0**	12.4	23.2
CITIZENS BANK	Mooresville	IN	**C+**	C+	C	384.7	1.78	3.2	33.3	7.9	26.3	**8.2**	9.8	13.6
CITIZENS BANK	Amsterdam	MO	**C**	C	C	57.3	5.39	16.4	4.4	38.1	1.1	**3.8**	7.2	10.4
▼ CITIZENS BANK	Mukwonago	WI	**B-**	C+	C-	663.3	-1.01	18.3	0.7	11.4	17.6	**10.0**	12.5	21.3
CITIZENS BANK	Sac City	IA	**C+**	C+	C+	56.6	14.99	5.2	1.9	7.3	43.8	**6.0**	8.0	14.0
▲ CITIZENS BANK	Batesville	AR	**B**	B-	C	535.1	-1.68	4.5	2.2	20.0	38.0	**10.0**	11.1	21.0
▼ CITIZENS BANK	Hartford	KY	**C-**	B-	C+	26.3	-0.76	0.9	10.5	29.6	31.0	**10.0**	17.3	39.9
CITIZENS BANK	New Haven	MO	**C+**	C	D+	166.7	-0.90	7.2	1.6	22.6	14.8	**10.0**	12.9	19.1
CITIZENS BANK	Hickman	KY	**A-**	A-	B	114.0	-0.05	4.8	3.2	15.1	24.6	**10.0**	12.6	19.2
▲ CITIZENS BANK	Byhalia	MS	**B-**	C+	C+	69.8	-3.54	3.7	8.8	21.6	35.4	**10.0**	11.2	21.8
CITIZENS BANK	Kilgore	TX	**C+**	C	C+	394.3	8.51	19.6	1.0	5.2	14.8	**7.8**	9.5	17.4
CITIZENS BANK	Amarillo	TX	**B+**	B+	B+	136.9	6.13	4.0	0.5	3.8	9.2	**6.0**	9.1	11.8
CITIZENS BANK	Farmington	NM	**A-**	A-	A-	730.6	4.09	6.6	1.6	10.4	61.6	**7.1**	9.1	24.0
CITIZENS BANK	Corvallis	OR	**B+**	A-	A-	569.1	9.47	8.5	0.7	5.9	16.6	**10.0**	11.4	17.3
CITIZENS BANK & TRUST	Rock Port	MO	**B**	B	C+	87.1	6.14	10.8	3.5	8.6	46.9	**9.5**	10.6	23.4
▲ CITIZENS BANK & TRUST	Lake Wales	FL	**C**	D+	D	450.0	9.88	4.4	2.6	18.0	27.6	**7.2**	9.2	15.3
CITIZENS BANK & TRUST	Guntersville	AL	**C+**	B	B-	343.1	10.42	11.6	3.3	13.2	23.7	**8.1**	9.8	13.6
CITIZENS BANK & TRUST ARDMORE	Ardmore	OK	**B-**	B-	B	199.1	5.21	7.7	4.2	18.0	40.3	**7.9**	9.6	17.9
CITIZENS BANK & TRUST CO	Saint Paul	NE	**B+**	B+	B+	146.0	5.46	8.4	3.6	5.5	18.2	**7.1**	10.4	12.6
CITIZENS BANK & TRUST CO	Vivian	LA	**C-**	C-	C-	146.6	1.65	6.7	7.8	30.0	28.1	**9.2**	10.5	18.8
CITIZENS BANK & TRUST CO	Plaquemine	LA	**B**	B-	B-	233.4	1.81	4.9	1.2	21.1	11.6	**10.0**	11.7	17.5
▲ CITIZENS BANK & TRUST CO	Covington	LA	**C**	D+	C-	112.7	-0.28	3.7	1.2	20.5	16.6	**9.2**	10.5	17.4
CITIZENS BANK & TRUST CO	Eastman	GA	**D-**	D-	D-	125.4	-2.81	4.7	2.6	18.3	33.3	**4.6**	6.6	12.4
CITIZENS BANK & TRUST CO	Blackstone	VA	**A-**	A-	A-	336.6	0.00	3.1	2.1	25.4	29.6	**10.0**	12.4	22.6
▲ CITIZENS BANK & TRUST CO	Kansas City	MO	**C**	D+	D	888.5	2.59	13.4	0.8	17.0	24.7	**7.7**	9.4	14.6
▼ CITIZENS BANK & TRUST CO	Hutchinson	MN	**C**	C	C	202.2	5.74	12.2	1.4	20.0	33.6	**6.6**	8.6	15.1
CITIZENS BANK & TRUST CO	Big Timber	MT	**D+**	D+	C-	103.8	0.92	4.7	2.6	5.7	33.3	**7.9**	9.6	16.9
CITIZENS BANK & TRUST CO	Marks	MS	**C-**	C	D+	123.6	1.27	10.6	4.4	13.5	20.2	**6.2**	10.1	11.9
CITIZENS BANK & TRUST CO	Atwood	TN	**D+**	D+	D+	25.5	-2.33	0.3	14.2	20.5	40.4	**7.0**	9.0	21.2
CITIZENS BANK & TRUST CO	Campbellsville	KY	**B**	B+	A	176.2	-2.29	9.7	2.8	21.2	30.1	**10.0**	17.5	29.4
CITIZENS BANK & TRUST CO	Van Buren	AR	**A-**	B+	B-	360.6	2.96	12.0	5.6	19.2	33.9	**10.0**	11.7	20.4
CITIZENS BANK & TRUST INC	Trenton	GA	**B-**	B-	C	93.0	2.16	3.9	14.1	34.8	22.1	**9.9**	11.0	16.5
CITIZENS BANK CO	Beverly	OH	**A-**	A-	B+	177.0	67.87	4.3	2.7	19.6	45.6	**10.0**	11.9	23.8
CITIZENS BANK INC	Robertsdale	AL	**C**	C-	C	97.5	-7.87	3.8	2.6	20.6	19.1	**10.0**	11.1	17.5
CITIZENS BANK MINNESOTA	New Ulm	MN	**B+**	B+	B+	341.1	3.07	6.8	1.5	18.9	27.0	**9.2**	10.5	14.8
CITIZENS BANK NA	Providence	RI	**C**	C-	C+	101843.2	3.62	18.5	15.0	12.5	13.8	**10.0**	11.2	15.0
CITIZENS BANK NA	Abilene	TX	**B**	B	C+	112.7	8.43	14.5	6.3	10.8	18.4	**6.4**	8.4	12.5
CITIZENS BANK OF ADA	Ada	OK	**C+**	C+	C+	211.0	6.85	19.2	3.5	18.5	22.4	**6.6**	8.6	13.0
CITIZENS BANK OF AMERICUS	Americus	GA	**C+**	C+	C-	231.5	-4.81	9.7	1.9	11.0	15.0	**8.1**	9.8	15.8
CITIZENS BANK OF ASHVILLE OHIO	Ashville	OH	**C-**	D+	D-	104.2	3.87	5.5	1.1	26.9	23.8	**6.2**	8.2	15.3
CITIZENS BANK OF BLOUNT COUNTY	Maryville	TN	**C**	B-	C	319.5	-0.75	1.6	0.4	5.0	32.6	**10.0**	16.3	27.1
CITIZENS BANK OF CAPE VINCENT	Cape Vincent	NY	**C+**	C+	C+	55.8	-2.21	1.0	4.7	40.3	34.1	**9.0**	10.3	24.3
CITIZENS BANK OF CHARLESTON	Charleston	MO	**A-**	A-	B+	123.6	4.06	9.8	5.7	7.2	16.6	**10.0**	15.2	20.5
CITIZENS BANK OF CHATSWORTH	Chatsworth	IL	**E-**	E-	D-	36.8	-12.56	8.1	2.5	8.7	19.9	**5.2**	7.6	11.2
CITIZENS BANK OF CLOVIS	Clovis	NM	**B-**	B+	B-	330.5	-2.31	3.8	0.9	4.5	49.4	**8.7**	10.1	24.5
▼ CITIZENS BANK OF COCHRAN	Cochran	GA	**D+**	D+	D	74.2	10.38	5.3	4.2	15.5	37.0	**8.0**	9.6	16.9
CITIZENS BANK OF EDINA	Edina	MO	**A-**	A-	B+	67.6	3.54	11.5	3.3	6.7	7.6	**8.6**	10.8	13.8
▲ CITIZENS BANK OF EDINBURG	Edinburg	IL	**C**	C-	C	23.1	1.72	1.8	3.3	15.5	33.7	**7.6**	9.4	19.6
CITIZENS BANK OF EDMOND	Edmond	OK	**C**	C	C-	249.3	-1.52	6.5	0.8	15.3	17.0	**9.8**	10.9	16.0
CITIZENS BANK OF ELDON	Eldon	MO	**B**	B	B+	128.3	6.12	4.0	6.7	21.0	24.4	**10.0**	14.1	22.1

Asset Quality Index	Adjusted Non-Performing Loans as a % of Total Loans	Adjusted Non-Performing Loans as a % of Capital	Net Charge-Offs / Avg Loans	Profitability Index	Net Income ($Mil)	Return on Assets (R.O.A.)	Return on Equity (R.O.E.)	Net Interest Spread	Overhead Efficiency Ratio	Liquidity Index	Liquidity Ratio	Hot Money Ratio	Stability Index
3.4	1.76	11.7	0.40	**4.2**	0.9	0.88	8.77	4.35	76.9	**1.3**	15.3	28.1	**5.6**
4.8	1.10	6.4	0.16	**4.2**	2.0	0.67	7.02	3.82	75.2	**3.6**	31.3	14.1	**5.7**
2.3	2.42	20.8	0.15	**3.0**	0.6	0.53	6.71	5.04	85.8	**2.3**	12.4	17.4	**3.4**
8.2	2.05	4.4	0.17	**9.9**	9.1	2.31	14.67	4.89	31.8	**3.3**	66.5	32.5	**9.4**
4.9	2.48	11.5	0.10	**7.4**	7.7	1.63	11.44	4.31	59.7	**3.4**	23.7	12.6	**8.7**
4.6	1.22	8.9	0.14	**6.9**	1.4	1.12	12.49	4.76	57.9	**0.8**	9.0	33.5	**4.6**
3.0	3.96	20.9	0.58	**2.8**	0.9	0.44	4.07	3.80	77.0	**1.0**	23.2	35.7	**4.7**
4.4	1.43	8.9	0.05	**7.3**	4.8	1.73	18.57	4.78	64.0	**1.7**	18.5	22.4	**7.0**
4.6	2.12	8.0	1.02	**0.6**	-0.1	-0.17	-1.46	3.00	105.2	**3.3**	45.2	19.5	**4.0**
7.8	0.34	1.5	0.02	**2.9**	0.3	0.39	3.53	3.35	82.0	**3.5**	36.5	16.4	**5.4**
7.6	0.39	1.4	0.03	**7.3**	1.1	1.51	12.45	3.65	43.1	**2.5**	44.9	29.8	**7.1**
3.6	0.80	5.2	0.07	**3.2**	1.4	0.47	4.88	3.44	82.9	**4.0**	13.7	8.2	**4.9**
4.8	0.48	5.2	0.12	**6.5**	0.6	1.49	20.47	5.40	73.4	**4.3**	6.7	5.6	**4.6**
2.4	5.33	26.2	0.10	**3.6**	2.9	0.58	4.90	3.26	53.6	**3.3**	17.9	12.9	**6.4**
7.0	1.00	5.8	0.00	**4.5**	0.4	0.97	11.90	3.21	68.4	**2.3**	31.8	22.3	**4.6**
5.6	1.76	7.9	0.38	**4.5**	3.4	0.85	8.00	4.03	69.9	**1.9**	24.0	20.7	**6.3**
5.3	2.99	7.4	0.86	**1.3**	-0.1	-0.58	-3.32	3.89	94.2	**6.0**	60.6	8.0	**6.4**
3.3	4.58	21.4	-0.11	**3.3**	0.6	0.50	4.02	3.90	83.0	**4.4**	21.8	7.2	**6.2**
6.1	1.57	7.9	1.04	**5.6**	1.0	1.26	10.56	4.33	61.8	**1.0**	10.1	30.0	**6.9**
8.4	0.33	1.3	0.20	**4.2**	0.5	0.85	7.81	3.91	75.8	**3.5**	47.0	18.6	**5.5**
3.8	2.29	10.5	-0.17	**4.2**	2.0	0.67	7.30	3.26	70.8	**5.3**	41.7	8.9	**4.8**
6.2	0.00	0.0	0.01	**5.9**	1.5	1.44	15.52	4.04	62.5	**3.3**	19.4	13.0	**6.5**
9.1	0.16	0.5	0.05	**6.7**	8.8	1.62	19.14	3.21	55.5	**4.9**	63.0	15.7	**7.6**
7.4	0.89	4.3	0.01	**4.9**	3.1	0.76	6.66	3.78	69.1	**5.4**	32.6	3.8	**7.5**
7.1	0.65	2.3	0.05	**4.8**	0.8	1.17	10.96	3.11	67.4	**4.5**	36.3	11.2	**7.0**
2.8	2.58	16.2	0.08	**3.8**	2.9	0.87	9.85	3.91	80.9	**4.6**	21.0	5.3	**3.5**
2.7	2.89	17.9	0.26	**4.6**	1.9	0.76	7.65	4.51	65.5	**1.7**	15.7	21.5	**5.0**
9.0	0.06	0.3	-0.03	**4.2**	1.5	1.03	11.30	3.37	74.2	**4.0**	36.7	14.0	**6.3**
5.5	0.43	3.1	0.15	**8.1**	1.6	1.46	14.46	4.53	50.4	**2.6**	4.8	14.8	**7.0**
1.7	5.00	27.7	0.31	**5.9**	1.4	1.27	11.32	4.85	79.8	**3.4**	32.3	15.6	**7.1**
4.3	2.82	14.9	0.20	**4.9**	1.5	0.85	7.40	4.12	67.6	**3.7**	16.4	10.8	**6.6**
2.8	3.11	17.6	0.74	**3.6**	0.5	0.58	5.55	3.96	78.0	**4.0**	27.2	10.5	**5.4**
3.0	2.82	19.2	0.96	**1.3**	0.0	0.01	0.10	3.65	96.8	**3.7**	32.6	14.3	**0.6**
6.2	1.66	7.0	0.04	**6.1**	3.0	1.17	9.63	3.97	62.0	**3.9**	33.6	13.5	**7.0**
3.3	1.75	10.7	-0.10	**2.7**	3.3	0.48	4.75	3.38	84.8	**1.5**	6.6	21.5	**5.0**
2.1	4.10	26.4	0.18	**6.2**	2.3	1.51	18.06	3.59	55.4	**5.2**	24.9	2.1	**5.5**
2.0	4.83	22.8	0.13	**4.3**	0.5	0.67	6.03	3.64	72.5	**3.3**	41.4	18.8	**6.2**
2.2	3.05	19.3	0.29	**3.4**	0.8	0.76	8.01	3.66	77.7	**1.8**	15.1	20.5	**5.3**
3.9	3.15	13.5	-0.05	**2.7**	0.1	0.39	4.90	2.84	83.2	**1.4**	31.9	36.8	**3.2**
8.3	0.56	1.9	0.16	**6.1**	1.6	1.21	7.34	4.25	64.1	**3.4**	28.8	14.2	**7.5**
6.7	0.91	4.1	-0.35	**8.4**	4.2	1.54	13.40	4.43	50.2	**1.5**	21.7	26.7	**7.6**
4.2	1.54	8.1	0.15	**4.5**	0.4	0.59	5.55	5.15	76.5	**3.0**	24.0	15.0	**5.8**
9.0	0.72	2.7	0.00	**5.7**	1.3	1.02	8.69	4.09	64.1	**5.6**	45.3	7.7	**7.0**
5.8	1.74	9.6	0.08	**2.3**	0.2	0.20	1.88	4.19	91.4	**3.4**	19.2	12.7	**3.9**
8.0	0.27	1.6	-0.02	**5.0**	2.3	0.93	8.32	3.32	66.4	**3.7**	16.6	10.5	**6.3**
3.3	1.69	10.9	0.40	**3.4**	635.8	0.87	5.40	2.98	63.7	**4.2**	10.9	7.3	**6.7**
4.9	0.47	3.3	0.00	**7.9**	1.6	1.86	15.92	4.16	54.0	**1.6**	19.6	24.6	**9.4**
6.2	0.38	2.6	0.17	**3.7**	1.2	0.77	9.08	3.88	82.6	**3.7**	17.6	10.6	**5.1**
5.6	0.82	4.8	0.54	**4.6**	1.8	1.02	10.82	3.67	58.5	**2.5**	22.3	17.1	**3.6**
6.0	0.85	5.5	0.02	**2.6**	0.2	0.23	2.74	3.66	85.4	**3.9**	19.6	9.6	**3.9**
7.9	0.41	1.3	2.31	**2.0**	0.7	0.30	1.85	3.42	67.6	**3.1**	47.0	24.2	**6.0**
5.0	2.32	11.1	0.03	**3.6**	0.3	0.62	6.55	4.05	71.1	**4.3**	17.4	6.7	**5.4**
5.2	1.91	8.3	0.05	**9.0**	1.4	1.49	10.49	3.95	45.9	**2.2**	20.1	18.4	**8.3**
2.0	3.14	24.4	0.04	**0.0**	-0.1	-0.34	-4.81	3.39	111.6	**4.0**	14.4	8.5	**1.7**
9.2	0.02	0.1	0.00	**4.0**	2.3	0.94	10.73	2.52	64.8	**2.5**	37.7	24.5	**7.1**
1.3	9.75	44.4	1.63	**1.3**	-1.0	-1.73	-15.97	3.48	244.0	**1.9**	28.8	25.0	**4.0**
5.5	0.63	4.6	0.49	**9.7**	0.8	1.54	14.33	4.52	40.2	**3.1**	5.0	12.5	**6.5**
9.1	0.00	0.0	-0.02	**3.6**	0.1	0.66	7.30	3.08	69.8	**4.9**	44.9	9.2	**4.1**
3.0	2.23	13.3	-0.07	**5.3**	2.4	1.28	13.69	4.31	72.3	**4.1**	19.8	8.4	**4.3**
5.9	1.68	7.7	0.09	**4.7**	0.8	0.85	6.01	3.67	67.9	**4.2**	31.0	10.9	**7.8**

Name	City	State	Rating	2013 Rating	2012 Rating	Total Assets ($Mil)	One Year Asset Growth	Asset Mix (As a % of Total Assets) Commercial Loans	Consumer Loans	Mortgage Loans	Securities	Capitalization Index	Leverage Ratio	Risk-Based Capital Ratio
▲ CITIZENS BANK OF FAYETTE	Fayette	AL	**B**	B-	B-	196.2	1.62	11.4	4.9	5.1	56.2	**10.0**	18.0	35.2
▲ CITIZENS BANK OF FLORIDA	Oviedo	FL	**C-**	D-	D-	232.1	1.70	4.2	0.6	7.1	25.8	**6.7**	8.7	13.9
CITIZENS BANK OF KANSAS	Kingman	KS	**B-**	B-	B-	232.6	5.16	10.5	1.2	7.4	49.4	**7.6**	9.4	14.5
CITIZENS BANK OF LAFAYETTE	Lafayette	TN	**B-**	B-	C	658.4	38.29	2.5	5.9	15.9	42.6	**8.3**	9.8	19.5
CITIZENS BANK OF LAS CRUCES	Las Cruces	NM	**A-**	A-	A-	455.5	9.10	4.0	1.5	9.1	40.2	**7.4**	9.3	16.3
▲ CITIZENS BANK OF LOGAN	Logan	OH	**D**	E	E-	198.1	-5.65	7.9	6.5	31.6	18.7	**5.4**	7.4	13.0
▲ CITIZENS BANK OF NEWBURG	Rolla	MO	**C-**	C	D+	164.5	-1.28	6.3	3.7	22.0	21.3	**9.1**	10.4	15.9
▲ CITIZENS BANK OF NORTHERN KY	Newport	KY	**C+**	C+	C	238.8	-4.54	5.0	1.0	16.3	25.3	**8.1**	9.7	15.6
CITIZENS BANK OF OKLAHOMA	Pawhuska	OK	**B+**	A-	B-	194.1	15.68	31.1	1.3	7.4	3.4	**9.3**	11.2	14.4
▲ CITIZENS BANK OF PAGOSA SPRING	Pagosa Springs	CO	**C+**	C	C	73.4	2.52	3.3	0.3	10.1	41.6	**9.5**	10.7	18.0
CITIZENS BANK OF PENNSYLVANIA	Philadelphia	PA	**C+**	C	B-	31955.8	-1.70	17.1	4.7	11.2	31.0	**7.8**	9.5	16.9
CITIZENS BANK OF PHILADELPHIA	Philadelphia	MS	**C+**	C+	C+	889.5	2.09	4.6	2.8	10.2	46.2	**8.2**	9.8	17.6
CITIZENS BANK OF ROGERSVILLE	Rogersville	MO	**C**	C-	D+	70.2	9.55	11.0	4.1	17.1	26.9	**6.4**	8.4	13.2
CITIZENS BANK OF SWAINSBORO	Swainsboro	GA	**C+**	C+	C-	148.4	0.48	8.7	7.4	26.3	15.6	**9.1**	10.4	17.0
▲ CITIZENS BANK OF VALLEY HEAD	Valley Head	AL	**C-**	D	D+	25.5	-3.68	6.2	12.9	38.8	13.1	**10.0**	11.0	19.9
CITIZENS BANK OF WEST VIRGINIA	Elkins	WV	**B-**	C	D	214.6	3.78	5.4	10.2	35.3	13.4	**9.7**	10.8	18.4
CITIZENS BANK OF WESTON INC	Weston	WV	**B+**	A-	A-	187.6	3.19	16.4	3.7	20.1	25.3	**9.6**	10.8	18.3
CITIZENS BANK OF WINFIELD	Winfield	AL	**A**	A	B+	204.8	6.77	2.3	6.3	4.6	67.9	**10.0**	21.4	46.8
CITIZENS BANK VILLE PLATTE LA	Ville Platte	LA	**B**	B	B	240.3	0.48	5.7	5.0	25.6	32.1	**10.0**	13.0	29.8
▲ CITIZENS BANKING CO	Sandusky	OH	**C+**	C-	D+	1178.2	3.02	7.7	1.2	14.0	17.0	**6.6**	8.6	12.8
CITIZENS BK OF CUMBERLAND CTY	Burkesville	KY	**B**	B	C+	69.4	-0.12	6.7	12.1	26.6	10.9	**10.0**	12.3	18.8
CITIZENS BK OF FORSYTH COUNTY	Cumming	GA	**C+**	C	D+	235.1	7.23	4.9	1.8	14.5	29.2	**8.4**	9.9	15.0
CITIZENS BK OF MORGANTOWN INC	Morgantown	WV	**B**	B	B-	35.3	0.81	1.7	2.9	43.6	34.4	**10.0**	17.4	35.5
CITIZENS BK OF WASHINGTON CTY	Sandersville	GA	**C+**	C+	C-	215.7	-5.80	9.0	5.4	29.5	18.7	**9.2**	10.5	17.7
CITIZENS BUILDING & LOAN ASSN	Greer	SC	**B**	B	C+	118.9	-2.02	0.0	0.3	45.9	23.2	**10.0**	20.8	40.8
CITIZENS BUSINESS BANK	Ontario	CA	**A-**	A-	B+	7417.0	13.17	4.1	0.2	4.0	42.6	**9.4**	10.6	18.4
CITIZENS COMMERCE NATIONAL BK	Versailles	KY	**E-**	E-	E-	214.1	5.31	3.4	1.3	18.4	31.6	**3.2**	5.2	10.2
▲ CITIZENS COMMUNITY BANK	South Hill	VA	**C**	D+	C	166.3	3.37	7.4	2.5	26.9	11.0	**10.0**	12.7	17.5
▼ CITIZENS COMMUNITY BANK	Winchester	TN	**B**	B+	B-	194.6	8.20	14.0	4.4	16.5	18.3	**8.9**	11.5	14.1
CITIZENS COMMUNITY BANK	Hahira	GA	**B+**	B	C+	124.8	1.27	6.4	4.8	23.7	25.3	**9.3**	10.5	18.0
CITIZENS COMMUNITY BANK	Mascoutah	IL	**B**	B	C+	303.4	-0.07	6.8	1.7	17.1	29.7	**9.3**	10.5	17.1
CITIZENS COMMUNITY BANK	Pilot Grove	MO	**B-**	B-	C+	109.1	-2.30	4.6	2.4	18.4	19.1	**8.7**	10.2	15.3
CITIZENS COMMUNITY FEDERAL NA	Altoona	WI	**C**	C	C-	569.8	2.73	0.8	35.6	41.4	12.5	**8.5**	10.0	16.1
CITIZENS DEPOSIT BANK & TRUST	Vanceburg	KY	**B-**	C+	C	372.9	1.93	3.7	2.5	21.7	26.5	**8.0**	9.7	16.8
CITIZENS DEPOSIT BK ARLINGTON	Arlington	KY	**A**	A	A	175.4	4.16	10.2	5.1	17.7	36.0	**10.0**	13.8	23.0
CITIZENS EXCHANGE BANK	Fairmount	IN	**C**	C	C	60.1	0.37	3.5	4.5	22.9	27.5	**10.0**	11.7	27.2
▼ CITIZENS FIRST BANK	Clinton	IA	**C+**	B-	B-	165.4	3.51	28.9	2.8	11.3	10.5	**4.7**	9.8	10.8
CITIZENS FIRST BANK	The Villages	FL	**B**	B	B-	1642.2	3.22	0.3	0.1	4.0	65.7	**6.3**	8.3	25.4
▲ CITIZENS FIRST BANK	Wartburg	TN	**C+**	C	D	146.2	-1.90	6.1	5.9	32.2	12.5	**7.3**	9.2	14.3
CITIZENS FIRST BANK	Viroqua	WI	**C+**	B-	B-	169.8	2.86	6.6	3.9	10.6	19.8	**9.4**	10.6	14.5
CITIZENS FIRST BANK INC	Bowling Green	KY	**B-**	C	C-	410.9	0.07	7.4	1.2	13.6	15.2	**8.1**	10.0	13.4
CITIZENS FIRST NATIONAL BK	Storm Lake	IA	**A-**	A	A	202.9	-3.82	8.2	5.4	3.9	47.5	**8.2**	9.8	17.7
CITIZENS FIRST ST BK OF WALNUT	Walnut	IL	**E-**	E-	E-	54.5	-1.12	6.1	9.1	22.9	36.7	**3.9**	5.9	10.9
CITIZENS FS&LA	Covington	KY	**B-**	B-	B	35.5	-0.60	0.0	0.0	49.1	35.0	**10.0**	26.9	64.8
CITIZENS FS&LA	Bellefontaine	OH	**C**	C	C	149.6	-1.51	0.0	0.1	57.5	15.9	**8.4**	9.9	20.9
CITIZENS GUARANTY BANK	Irvine	KY	**C+**	C+	C+	135.7	2.29	4.8	8.7	38.9	10.7	**6.5**	8.6	12.6
CITIZENS INDEPENDENT BANK	Saint Louis Park	MN	**D**	D	D+	289.2	-3.48	10.3	9.4	14.3	23.8	**8.3**	9.9	15.8
CITIZENS NATIONAL BK	Greenleaf	KS	**B-**	B-	B	163.4	-5.00	3.2	3.0	12.9	56.4	**7.4**	9.3	21.3
CITIZENS NATIONAL BK	Windsor	VA	**C**	D+	C	55.6	-1.90	12.5	1.7	17.4	9.8	**10.0**	11.8	16.6
CITIZENS NATIONAL BK	Putnam	CT	**B-**	C+	B-	332.7	-17.27	4.1	3.3	14.8	52.3	**10.0**	11.9	22.4
▲ CITIZENS NATIONAL BK	Athens	TN	**C-**	C-	D-	519.0	0.73	5.0	1.7	16.0	25.2	**10.0**	11.3	17.9
▼ CITIZENS NATIONAL BK	Sevierville	TN	**C**	C	C	842.9	2.57	5.6	0.5	14.8	17.0	**9.4**	10.6	15.3
CITIZENS NATIONAL BK	Henderson	TX	**B**	B	B-	1307.9	7.81	8.4	4.1	20.3	30.9	**6.7**	8.7	16.1
CITIZENS NATIONAL BK	Crockett	TX	**C-**	C	D+	91.1	3.99	7.2	7.6	5.9	33.0	**7.6**	9.4	21.0
CITIZENS NATIONAL BK	Cameron	TX	**B-**	B-	B	382.0	2.42	2.9	0.9	4.2	54.7	**8.8**	10.2	22.1
CITIZENS NATIONAL BK LEBANON	Lebanon	KY	**B-**	C+	B-	117.2	4.29	1.6	3.3	11.6	56.3	**9.6**	10.7	21.0
CITIZENS NATIONAL BK NA	Bossier City	LA	**A-**	B+	B+	786.0	8.40	10.6	1.8	15.9	20.8	**9.2**	10.5	15.1
CITIZENS NATIONAL BK OF CROSBY	Crosbyton	TX	**B-**	B	B-	43.8	-0.52	2.9	5.0	5.8	5.6	**10.0**	16.0	31.8
CITIZENS NATIONAL BK OF HILLSB	Hillsboro	TX	**B**	B-	B-	207.1	5.32	1.7	2.1	3.5	81.4	**8.8**	10.2	29.6
CITIZENS NB AT BROWNWOOD	Brownwood	TX	**B+**	A-	A-	198.2	3.95	12.3	5.6	14.3	27.4	**10.0**	11.9	19.4

Asset Quality Index	Adjusted Non-Performing Loans as a % of Total Loans	Adjusted Non-Performing Loans as a % of Capital	Net Charge-Offs Avg Loans	Profitability Index	Net Income ($Mil)	Return on Assets (R.O.A.)	Return on Equity (R.O.E.)	Net Interest Spread	Overhead Efficiency Ratio	Liquidity Index	Liquidity Ratio	Hot Money Ratio	Stability Index
4.1	8.52	14.7	0.17	**4.1**	1.2	0.85	4.82	2.66	55.6	**3.3**	54.2	26.5	**5.9**
3.7	1.41	8.8	-0.08	**2.4**	0.7	0.43	5.05	3.62	86.5	**1.6**	26.3	27.0	**2.9**
6.9	0.80	3.5	-0.01	**3.6**	1.0	0.59	4.92	3.72	85.2	**4.9**	40.8	10.9	**5.8**
4.2	3.07	14.3	0.19	**5.4**	5.4	1.10	10.85	3.74	59.6	**2.3**	39.8	29.7	**5.8**
8.0	0.30	1.5	0.07	**8.3**	6.2	1.87	19.84	4.15	58.6	**4.9**	36.6	8.9	**7.4**
1.2	6.25	48.7	0.29	**4.0**	1.6	1.02	15.72	3.62	80.2	**1.6**	10.1	21.2	**2.4**
3.7	2.91	15.7	0.38	**3.5**	0.8	0.64	6.52	3.77	72.0	**1.9**	14.7	19.5	**5.5**
4.3	2.70	15.3	0.67	**1.4**	-0.2	-0.08	-0.78	3.76	88.1	**4.7**	20.6	4.9	**5.5**
5.3	0.52	3.2	0.06	**7.9**	2.6	1.88	16.99	4.61	53.3	**0.9**	23.8	38.3	**6.5**
5.1	1.07	4.0	0.17	**4.8**	0.6	1.15	11.14	3.70	77.7	**6.0**	45.8	5.0	**4.8**
5.2	0.87	5.2	0.21	**2.7**	133.4	0.57	4.43	2.61	68.7	**5.5**	30.9	6.9	**6.3**
3.6	3.82	16.2	0.73	**4.4**	5.9	0.90	10.88	3.70	70.6	**2.4**	21.4	17.6	**5.5**
3.7	1.66	10.7	0.00	**4.4**	0.7	1.16	12.09	3.88	68.7	**4.4**	24.1	6.9	**4.3**
2.9	3.25	18.2	0.42	**5.9**	1.1	1.01	10.19	4.53	62.7	**1.9**	13.0	19.4	**5.7**
2.1	2.81	16.8	0.21	**2.8**	0.1	0.50	4.71	5.21	90.4	**4.1**	22.3	9.3	**4.2**
4.4	1.65	9.8	0.32	**5.9**	1.9	1.16	11.58	4.05	68.3	**2.7**	18.4	16.1	**5.0**
5.1	1.38	7.6	0.02	**5.4**	1.3	0.94	8.69	3.36	57.8	**4.7**	30.6	7.8	**7.4**
9.2	1.01	0.9	0.56	**8.4**	2.6	1.72	8.11	4.59	40.7	**3.5**	63.3	29.1	**8.3**
8.7	0.29	1.1	0.00	**4.9**	1.7	0.93	7.31	3.10	59.4	**2.2**	37.3	29.1	**7.5**
3.4	2.05	15.8	0.40	**4.7**	8.8	0.94	10.18	3.82	69.0	**3.7**	7.6	10.0	**7.7**
4.8	1.38	7.7	0.56	**7.5**	0.9	1.74	14.91	4.79	59.7	**2.9**	19.8	14.9	**6.9**
3.6	2.53	15.3	0.20	**5.4**	1.5	0.90	9.60	3.83	62.9	**2.2**	30.6	22.7	**4.4**
9.5	0.27	0.9	-0.05	**4.1**	0.2	0.78	4.48	5.06	79.7	**3.2**	29.4	15.3	**7.0**
4.6	1.61	9.3	0.38	**3.7**	0.9	0.56	5.60	4.13	71.6	**1.5**	15.7	24.6	**3.8**
6.1	2.59	8.0	0.18	**4.4**	0.7	0.82	4.01	3.48	61.8	**0.8**	23.2	52.1	**7.0**
5.7	1.74	7.8	-0.02	**9.0**	81.2	1.54	12.93	3.71	44.9	**3.3**	4.5	11.6	**9.6**
0.3	6.80	59.6	0.22	**1.4**	0.2	0.10	2.95	3.18	98.7	**1.5**	20.1	25.7	**0.5**
6.0	0.72	4.2	-0.03	**2.6**	0.6	0.51	3.99	3.79	81.8	**1.4**	12.2	25.4	**5.3**
4.3	2.32	11.8	0.13	**9.8**	2.5	1.75	15.56	5.59	47.6	**1.7**	20.8	22.6	**7.1**
6.2	0.53	3.2	0.20	**5.8**	1.4	1.43	14.89	4.59	70.5	**2.0**	27.8	23.2	**5.5**
4.6	2.01	11.3	0.04	**6.8**	2.7	1.17	11.77	3.50	46.5	**1.3**	11.1	26.0	**5.4**
5.5	0.90	5.7	0.03	**3.7**	0.5	0.64	6.53	3.29	71.3	**3.1**	21.3	14.1	**4.2**
3.3	0.89	6.5	0.32	**3.2**	1.5	0.37	3.69	3.67	77.6	**1.0**	14.3	32.2	**4.9**
5.5	0.65	4.1	0.12	**7.8**	3.4	1.21	11.18	3.78	59.4	**2.2**	10.0	17.3	**5.0**
8.4	0.44	1.7	0.22	**8.0**	2.3	1.78	12.71	3.88	54.6	**1.8**	39.2	51.7	**9.4**
5.0	4.32	15.7	0.00	**2.6**	0.2	0.36	3.24	2.55	82.3	**5.5**	59.4	10.8	**5.6**
4.8	0.86	6.6	0.24	**3.8**	0.7	0.55	5.70	3.62	74.6	**1.6**	17.1	23.5	**6.1**
5.6	9.10	17.1	0.73	**5.6**	10.3	0.84	10.01	2.55	47.4	**7.9**	76.7	2.0	**6.4**
4.0	1.87	13.4	0.53	**3.7**	0.6	0.57	6.49	4.87	79.6	**2.9**	17.5	14.7	**4.0**
3.1	2.50	15.0	-0.01	**4.9**	1.4	1.12	9.66	4.17	74.6	**3.3**	24.7	13.4	**7.8**
4.6	1.12	7.7	0.01	**4.7**	2.6	0.83	7.79	3.91	70.1	**2.0**	7.2	18.4	**5.4**
8.4	0.18	0.9	-0.02	**6.0**	2.1	1.31	12.88	3.08	58.4	**5.8**	52.6	8.9	**8.2**
1.7	3.94	29.4	0.92	**0.7**	0.0	-0.04	-0.76	2.90	95.8	**5.0**	42.2	10.2	**0.3**
10.0	0.08	0.2	0.09	**3.7**	0.2	0.63	2.41	3.12	68.5	**4.0**	58.5	18.1	**7.6**
5.9	1.31	9.5	0.13	**2.4**	0.3	0.29	3.23	2.57	86.1	**1.2**	27.9	37.1	**4.7**
2.8	2.09	18.1	0.04	**3.4**	0.5	0.51	5.91	4.37	88.8	**1.2**	4.3	25.3	**5.1**
1.1	5.54	32.6	0.11	**2.7**	3.8	0.34	3.45	3.34	87.8	**5.8**	29.2	0.1	**4.1**
9.1	0.00	0.0	0.13	**3.9**	1.0	0.79	9.02	3.18	75.0	**5.5**	41.6	7.5	**5.5**
4.7	0.50	3.2	0.56	**2.2**	0.2	0.47	4.03	4.75	89.2	**0.7**	12.0	41.8	**4.5**
7.0	1.93	5.6	0.21	**3.8**	1.9	0.68	6.44	3.52	72.3	**1.0**	19.7	33.1	**5.3**
1.6	6.26	31.7	-0.12	**4.0**	3.7	0.95	8.75	3.31	78.4	**1.8**	22.1	21.6	**6.0**
2.6	2.90	17.6	-0.01	**4.9**	7.4	1.15	11.03	4.11	61.2	**1.4**	15.6	26.4	**6.9**
7.9	0.48	2.9	-0.01	**4.7**	8.4	0.87	8.37	3.70	73.5	**4.2**	24.9	11.6	**8.9**
8.1	0.38	1.3	0.00	**2.5**	0.3	0.45	4.84	3.44	88.9	**5.1**	54.4	11.7	**4.0**
9.4	0.10	0.3	0.00	**3.6**	2.4	0.82	8.59	2.74	73.7	**4.0**	44.8	16.1	**6.3**
9.2	0.11	0.3	0.02	**4.3**	0.9	1.08	10.89	3.06	69.9	**4.9**	43.8	11.3	**5.4**
6.4	0.39	2.5	0.18	**6.4**	6.5	1.15	10.52	4.51	63.6	**3.2**	12.6	12.6	**6.9**
8.8	0.00	0.0	-0.03	**3.8**	0.3	0.84	5.53	2.07	63.2	**3.5**	60.5	22.7	**7.3**
10.0	0.60	0.8	0.00	**5.1**	2.4	1.57	15.30	2.81	56.0	**5.6**	59.3	11.7	**7.0**
4.3	3.01	13.7	0.40	**7.3**	2.4	1.61	13.21	3.72	55.5	**4.1**	33.6	12.6	**8.7**

Name	City	State	Rating	2013 Rating	2012 Rating	Total Assets ($Mil)	One Year Asset Growth	Asset Mix (As a % of Total Assets) Comm-ercial Loans	Cons-umer Loans	Mort-gage Loans	Secur-ities	Capital-ization Index	Lever-age Ratio	Risk-Based Capital Ratio
CITIZENS NB OF ALBION	Albion	IL	A-	A-	A	287.4	4.63	12.8	3.4	13.9	32.4	10.0	15.9	23.6
CITIZENS NB OF BLUFFTON	Bluffton	OH	B+	B+	B-	675.2	2.45	8.5	0.5	7.1	17.8	6.9	9.0	14.7
CITIZENS NB OF CHEBOYGAN	Cheboygan	MI	C+	C	D	263.8	5.64	1.8	2.6	19.0	38.8	6.6	8.7	18.3
▼ CITIZENS NB OF GR ST LOUIS	Maplewood	MO	C-	B-	B-	419.3	-4.15	15.7	2.6	9.9	23.8	10.0	12.4	16.6
CITIZENS NB OF HAMMOND	Hammond	NY	D+	D+	C-	21.2	4.94	5.4	4.9	41.1	26.4	7.4	9.2	24.5
▲ CITIZENS NB OF MCCONNELSVILLE	McConnelsville	OH	B-	C+	C+	85.3	-1.50	1.7	3.8	35.9	26.1	10.0	11.8	26.5
CITIZENS NB OF MERIDIAN	Meridian	MS	B	B	B-	1084.8	0.59	9.0	2.5	16.5	26.0	8.5	12.4	13.7
CITIZENS NB OF MEYERSDALE	Meyersdale	PA	D-	D-	D	76.4	-6.38	0.6	1.3	46.3	26.6	7.7	9.4	21.1
CITIZENS NB OF PAINTSVILLE	Paintsville	KY	C+	C+	C+	513.3	-5.22	3.1	6.2	20.0	31.9	9.4	10.6	18.6
CITIZENS NB OF PARK RAPIDS	Park Rapids	MN	A-	B+	B	222.5	6.05	6.9	14.5	26.5	17.3	8.8	10.2	15.1
▲ CITIZENS NB OF QUITMAN	Quitman	GA	C	C-	D+	91.9	-4.46	2.5	10.4	20.1	16.4	10.0	12.2	19.0
CITIZENS NB OF SOMERSET	Somerset	KY	A-	A-	A-	341.9	4.38	4.2	5.0	20.0	37.7	10.0	11.9	21.5
CITIZENS NB OF SOUTHWESTERN OH	Dayton	OH	B	B	B-	106.8	4.57	15.0	4.5	12.7	7.4	9.8	10.9	15.7
CITIZENS NB OF TEXAS	Waxahachie	TX	C+	C	B-	644.6	2.52	6.4	1.0	8.7	4.0	10.0	11.5	15.6
CITIZENS NB OF WILLS POINT	Wills Point	TX	A	A	A	112.8	11.38	1.0	7.3	29.6	25.7	10.0	11.2	18.8
CITIZENS NB OF WOODSFIELD	Woodsfield	OH	C-	C-	C-	103.1	8.32	1.2	2.6	23.4	47.5	4.9	7.0	21.4
CITIZENS PROGRESSIVE BANK	Winnsboro	LA	C-	C-	C-	99.7	10.80	14.3	8.1	17.2	6.6	7.0	9.7	12.5
CITIZENS S&LA FSB	Leavenworth	KS	C-	C-	B-	200.0	0.17	0.0	0.8	38.8	46.4	10.0	18.5	51.9
CITIZENS SAVINGS BANK	Clarks Summit	PA	B-	B-	B-	324.6	-0.05	0.0	0.1	76.2	12.3	10.0	12.9	25.9
▲ CITIZENS SB	Martins Ferry	OH	B	B-	B-	401.1	0.59	13.3	5.6	21.8	6.5	8.2	9.8	13.8
CITIZENS SB	Bogalusa	LA	C	C+	C	207.3	-3.07	1.1	6.2	39.9	8.3	10.0	12.9	20.9
CITIZENS SB	Anamosa	IA	B	B+	B	130.8	4.68	4.8	0.8	9.2	53.3	5.9	7.9	13.1
CITIZENS SB	Spillville	IA	A-	A-	A-	97.1	10.53	2.2	0.4	3.1	53.2	10.0	11.9	18.0
CITIZENS SB	Marshalltown	IA	C+	C+	C+	57.9	5.80	5.7	1.8	25.0	0.8	5.9	7.9	12.1
CITIZENS SB	Hawkeye	IA	B+	B+	A-	27.9	2.71	0.8	1.8	5.9	49.8	10.0	12.5	24.9
CITIZENS SB & TRUST CO	Nashville	TN	D-	D-	D	99.1	1.90	2.7	1.8	5.6	13.9	5.7	8.3	11.5
CITIZENS SECURITY BANK & TRUST	Bixby	OK	B-	B-	C+	719.1	2.76	21.6	2.7	17.1	18.1	6.2	8.2	12.2
CITIZENS ST BK OF NEW CASTLE	New Castle	IN	B-	B-	C+	443.2	6.37	5.7	12.6	20.0	29.5	7.1	9.0	15.8
CITIZENS ST BK OF TAYLOR CTY	Reynolds	GA	B-	B-	C+	45.6	8.98	6.1	5.1	15.7	28.7	10.0	11.5	22.3
CITIZENS STATE BK	Jasper	TN	C+	C	C-	134.6	1.47	17.4	5.0	22.7	19.1	5.5	7.5	11.7
CITIZENS STATE BK	Vernon	AL	D+	C-	C	82.0	-5.02	6.7	9.8	12.2	33.6	10.0	12.3	24.4
▲ CITIZENS STATE BK	Perry	FL	D	D+	D	240.1	27.65	5.1	48.5	4.2	9.3	7.3	9.9	12.7
▲ CITIZENS STATE BK	Kingsland	GA	D	E	E-	61.5	-5.82	5.0	2.2	14.1	3.2	0.9	5.1	7.8
▲ CITIZENS STATE BK	Lena	IL	B-	B-	C+	230.1	5.01	9.2	4.4	11.8	23.4	9.4	10.6	15.3
CITIZENS STATE BK	Monticello	IA	B+	B+	B-	367.6	6.12	6.7	0.7	3.5	37.1	7.9	9.6	14.1
CITIZENS STATE BK	Hudson	WI	E+	E-	E-	144.1	3.73	8.1	0.5	19.8	19.7	5.8	7.8	12.6
CITIZENS STATE BK	Cadott	WI	B	B	B-	104.8	-0.45	9.2	2.4	18.6	26.2	8.9	10.3	16.3
▲ CITIZENS STATE BK	Carleton	NE	D+	D+	C-	16.7	3.88	7.9	5.8	7.9	0.2	6.6	8.6	14.6
CITIZENS STATE BK	Paola	KS	B-	B-	C	82.8	-6.88	2.6	0.6	9.8	59.3	10.0	13.6	28.3
CITIZENS STATE BK	Hugoton	KS	B	B+	A-	115.7	-3.36	2.2	1.5	5.7	33.3	10.0	12.5	20.2
CITIZENS STATE BK	Moundridge	KS	B-	B	B-	414.9	-1.98	5.3	1.7	7.8	38.6	8.6	10.1	15.0
CITIZENS STATE BK	Marysville	KS	A-	A-	B-	301.6	4.45	17.1	1.4	8.5	16.5	7.8	9.9	13.2
CITIZENS STATE BK	Morland	KS	C-	C-	C-	38.1	9.23	10.7	5.5	9.1	12.9	6.4	8.4	13.3
CITIZENS STATE BK	Okemah	OK	B+	B+	B	296.2	13.02	2.0	0.7	55.1	3.0	4.5	9.4	10.7
▲ CITIZENS STATE BK	Wisner	NE	B-	B	B-	325.4	-1.25	7.6	1.7	4.4	11.7	5.7	9.1	11.5
CITIZENS STATE BK	Buffalo	TX	A-	A-	A-	712.0	10.84	4.6	1.9	3.2	77.9	7.4	9.3	25.2
CITIZENS STATE BK	Tyler	TX	A-	A-	A-	314.4	7.31	8.1	2.9	13.5	2.8	9.1	10.8	14.3
▲ CITIZENS STATE BK	Anton	TX	D+	D	D	31.3	-2.22	10.4	3.0	0.0	24.2	6.4	8.4	14.2
CITIZENS STATE BK	Woodville	TX	B-	B-	C	133.2	12.60	3.4	3.7	31.1	34.9	6.5	8.5	14.8
CITIZENS STATE BK	Ganado	TX	D+	D+	C-	61.4	1.36	2.0	1.0	5.0	75.1	4.6	6.6	26.3
CITIZENS STATE BK	Corrigan	TX	A-	B	C+	119.0	8.66	9.6	11.5	11.6	39.6	9.0	10.3	20.0
CITIZENS STATE BK	Miles	TX	A-	A-	B+	96.3	6.55	10.4	4.1	31.5	2.7	7.6	9.7	13.0
CITIZENS STATE BK	Roma	TX	B	B	B	82.3	1.37	3.1	13.9	15.8	47.4	8.4	9.9	22.2
CITIZENS STATE BK	Sealy	TX	A-	A-	A-	220.4	10.23	4.0	2.6	13.3	58.0	9.5	10.7	25.1
CITIZENS STATE BK	Somerville	TX	B	B	B-	415.7	7.69	8.2	5.6	18.3	29.5	9.0	10.3	18.9
CITIZENS STATE BK	Princeton	TX	C	C-	C	41.4	-4.09	6.3	0.8	2.9	65.7	10.0	14.6	42.8
CITIZENS STATE BK	Wyoming	IA	A	A	A	93.4	-0.62	8.2	3.2	4.0	42.7	10.0	21.2	34.9
CITIZENS STATE BK	Sheldon	IA	A-	A-	A-	113.9	1.01	7.3	5.8	15.9	21.7	10.0	11.1	17.2
▲ CITIZENS STATE BK	Fort Dodge	IA	A-	B+	B+	145.3	1.22	9.1	1.8	10.7	32.4	10.0	11.4	16.2
CITIZENS STATE BK	Gridley	KS	B-	B-	C+	176.6	6.22	12.2	4.4	17.1	21.4	5.6	7.6	12.5

Asset Quality Index	Adjusted Non-Performing Loans as a % of Total Loans	Adjusted Non-Performing Loans as a % of Capital	Net Charge-Offs Avg Loans	Profitability Index	Net Income ($Mil)	Return on Assets (R.O.A.)	Return on Equity (R.O.E.)	Net Interest Spread	Overhead Efficiency Ratio	Liquidity Index	Liquidity Ratio	Hot Money Ratio	Stability Index
7.2	0.91	3.7	0.34	**5.3**	2.2	1.05	6.61	3.41	51.7	**2.8**	30.7	17.7	**8.4**
4.9	1.23	9.3	0.00	**7.5**	8.9	1.78	19.28	3.99	58.5	**1.6**	7.4	20.3	**8.1**
4.3	2.96	14.2	0.52	**3.4**	1.3	0.68	7.98	3.40	88.0	**5.7**	48.4	8.3	**3.9**
1.6	5.52	27.0	0.95	**3.9**	1.5	0.47	3.71	3.53	67.6	**2.5**	20.4	16.9	**7.0**
5.3	1.84	10.9	0.02	**2.9**	0.1	0.40	4.36	3.91	87.2	**5.3**	32.3	2.1	**3.4**
5.3	2.81	12.9	0.11	**3.3**	0.3	0.52	4.46	3.21	74.4	**3.8**	18.5	10.2	**6.1**
5.0	1.98	9.9	0.01	**5.2**	10.7	1.31	11.17	3.74	73.2	**1.9**	17.8	20.7	**8.7**
5.2	1.58	8.8	-0.15	**0.0**	-0.1	-0.19	-2.14	2.35	119.5	**2.2**	36.0	28.0	**2.2**
3.4	2.37	11.3	0.10	**3.9**	3.1	0.77	5.85	3.69	78.8	**3.3**	27.8	14.6	**6.7**
5.8	0.51	3.5	0.09	**7.4**	2.9	1.81	17.46	4.08	58.5	**2.3**	7.2	16.7	**6.8**
2.5	3.76	19.7	0.90	**4.6**	0.7	0.91	8.17	3.76	66.2	**1.1**	11.5	29.3	**5.2**
5.5	2.70	11.9	0.12	**6.1**	3.9	1.54	14.59	3.78	65.2	**3.0**	23.6	14.9	**8.1**
4.7	1.45	8.9	0.06	**5.1**	0.7	0.94	8.63	4.46	71.1	**2.9**	24.0	15.4	**5.8**
3.1	2.30	14.2	-0.05	**8.5**	9.0	1.94	16.52	4.69	63.9	**4.7**	23.1	5.3	**8.9**
8.6	0.00	0.0	0.01	**8.3**	1.5	1.79	15.40	4.05	57.2	**1.9**	28.0	24.8	**8.9**
7.1	1.22	5.4	0.07	**2.2**	0.2	0.26	3.95	2.36	85.0	**7.4**	63.2	1.5	**4.5**
1.4	2.64	20.9	0.29	**7.7**	1.2	1.68	12.19	5.58	67.4	**0.6**	6.7	36.2	**6.8**
7.6	1.83	4.0	0.27	**1.0**	0.0	0.02	0.11	2.24	108.4	**3.5**	54.4	22.5	**6.9**
7.8	0.97	5.9	0.05	**3.5**	1.4	0.56	4.33	3.33	74.3	**2.8**	4.1	13.8	**6.8**
5.0	0.50	3.8	0.22	**5.0**	2.9	0.96	9.91	3.91	65.6	**4.4**	10.8	5.4	**5.1**
1.7	5.63	30.9	0.21	**4.8**	1.2	0.74	5.88	5.02	78.3	**2.0**	16.5	19.1	**6.5**
7.0	0.80	4.0	0.01	**7.1**	1.6	1.70	19.84	3.94	53.6	**5.8**	38.9	4.5	**6.5**
6.7	2.09	7.3	0.06	**7.7**	1.1	1.54	13.26	3.87	44.2	**3.4**	63.0	25.0	**8.0**
8.0	0.28	2.4	0.00	**4.8**	0.5	1.16	14.82	3.39	67.0	**5.0**	26.6	4.1	**4.5**
7.7	3.13	7.5	0.02	**3.1**	0.1	0.58	4.82	2.64	75.9	**6.6**	76.3	6.8	**6.0**
0.3	4.76	39.5	0.11	**2.9**	0.3	0.42	5.64	5.24	85.2	**0.6**	15.3	61.7	**3.0**
5.0	0.64	5.0	-0.30	**5.0**	7.0	1.27	16.25	4.06	71.2	**1.3**	8.3	25.0	**5.8**
6.0	0.67	3.9	0.26	**4.0**	2.0	0.61	6.77	3.68	75.9	**5.3**	41.2	8.1	**3.9**
4.9	4.30	15.0	0.07	**2.2**	0.1	0.15	1.32	3.69	102.0	**3.0**	34.1	17.9	**5.2**
5.4	0.53	4.3	0.07	**3.8**	0.8	0.78	9.77	5.07	84.1	**3.2**	11.6	12.6	**3.8**
0.9	8.61	32.3	0.15	**4.3**	0.6	0.98	8.57	3.03	57.4	**1.7**	37.5	50.6	**5.2**
1.0	2.02	15.2	0.77	**4.9**	1.9	1.16	14.20	6.74	64.1	**0.7**	14.2	40.9	**4.2**
0.3	11.45	117.6	1.37	**0.0**	-0.6	-1.30	-19.88	4.10	150.3	**0.7**	12.5	46.5	**1.7**
4.1	1.61	9.9	0.21	**6.6**	2.8	1.62	14.22	3.88	59.0	**2.5**	11.2	15.9	**7.2**
5.8	0.64	3.6	0.05	**7.6**	4.8	1.79	15.27	3.37	53.1	**3.8**	35.0	14.4	**8.8**
5.9	0.18	1.3	-0.10	**3.0**	0.7	0.60	9.08	3.58	85.9	**3.6**	20.8	11.7	**1.5**
4.1	2.29	13.1	-0.01	**4.8**	0.7	0.86	8.59	4.27	71.1	**4.8**	28.7	6.2	**5.2**
6.4	0.17	1.6	0.00	**4.4**	0.1	0.78	9.41	4.34	76.4	**1.5**	8.0	22.4	**3.0**
5.7	1.35	3.0	0.42	**4.0**	0.5	0.81	4.27	3.37	69.0	**2.8**	41.8	23.5	**7.5**
8.8	0.00	0.0	-0.05	**4.9**	0.8	0.83	7.22	3.63	69.7	**1.2**	11.7	27.9	**7.4**
5.0	1.92	8.6	0.00	**3.7**	2.2	0.68	6.39	3.28	71.3	**4.4**	35.0	11.3	**6.0**
7.5	0.19	1.3	0.01	**8.9**	4.7	2.08	19.91	3.55	37.8	**2.6**	12.1	16.0	**6.6**
6.0	0.33	2.7	0.00	**3.0**	0.2	0.57	6.88	3.42	83.9	**3.1**	14.8	13.7	**4.5**
5.9	0.67	6.0	0.00	**8.0**	3.5	1.81	17.23	3.30	46.6	**0.5**	12.3	67.0	**6.7**
4.0	0.50	4.1	0.34	**6.2**	3.5	1.42	15.11	3.96	59.3	**2.3**	10.3	17.1	**6.3**
9.3	0.69	1.2	-0.20	**6.5**	7.3	1.39	16.72	3.79	44.6	**3.0**	60.7	35.4	**7.1**
7.2	0.04	0.3	0.23	**7.4**	3.3	1.42	13.74	4.12	54.2	**2.0**	10.5	18.6	**6.8**
7.5	0.00	0.0	-0.05	**2.2**	0.1	0.37	4.81	2.60	85.9	**2.1**	33.5	26.4	**2.7**
6.3	0.68	4.2	0.66	**3.5**	0.6	0.63	6.94	4.43	85.1	**3.9**	19.5	9.9	**4.4**
10.0	0.29	0.5	0.06	**0.9**	0.0	-0.06	-1.22	2.05	104.7	**4.0**	83.3	25.2	**1.7**
6.8	0.54	2.4	0.25	**8.2**	1.6	1.82	18.52	4.18	56.6	**2.2**	31.6	23.9	**7.2**
8.3	0.04	0.4	-0.03	**10.0**	2.0	2.84	29.16	5.66	45.9	**1.0**	6.7	29.6	**7.4**
5.1	1.17	4.7	0.11	**6.0**	0.8	1.21	12.63	4.63	73.0	**2.4**	54.1	42.7	**6.4**
9.4	0.02	0.1	0.05	**5.6**	2.1	1.29	12.35	3.54	58.9	**5.1**	67.5	15.4	**6.7**
4.5	1.83	9.0	0.41	**5.7**	3.1	1.02	9.81	4.30	67.3	**4.5**	34.2	10.5	**5.3**
6.5	1.95	2.8	-0.13	**2.0**	0.1	0.31	1.47	2.21	87.6	**5.5**	69.7	12.3	**5.4**
8.3	0.10	0.3	0.09	**8.1**	1.3	1.83	8.57	4.07	51.0	**4.2**	51.4	15.8	**9.7**
8.0	0.35	2.0	0.00	**6.1**	1.2	1.34	11.26	3.55	58.7	**5.3**	33.2	4.7	**8.2**
8.5	0.46	2.3	-0.02	**6.6**	1.3	1.21	10.91	3.74	56.2	**4.7**	35.2	10.1	**7.7**
4.8	0.88	7.0	0.04	**4.4**	1.0	0.77	9.78	4.11	71.6	**3.8**	11.1	9.8	**4.5**

Name	City	State	Rating	2013 Rating	2012 Rating	Total Assets ($Mil)	One Year Asset Growth	Asset Mix (As a % of Total Assets) Comm-ercial Loans	Cons-umer Loans	Mort-gage Loans	Secur-ities	Capital-ization Index	Lever-age Ratio	Risk-Based Capital Ratio
CITIZENS STATE BK & TRUST CO	Hiawatha	KS	**C+**	C+	B-	86.1	6.37	2.3	3.2	10.1	21.4	**10.0**	13.9	29.3
CITIZENS STATE BK & TRUST CO	Woodbine	KS	**D-**	D	C-	15.6	-4.08	14.8	3.0	6.9	21.4	**3.9**	6.7	10.4
CITIZENS STATE BK & TRUST CO	Ellsworth	KS	**B**	B-	B	110.6	-2.65	3.3	3.5	19.1	43.8	**7.2**	9.1	16.9
CITIZENS STATE BK AT MOHALL	Mohall	ND	**B**	B-	C	65.4	4.40	13.1	4.1	13.5	18.8	**6.5**	8.5	12.2
CITIZENS STATE BK MIDWEST	Cavalier	ND	**D+**	D+	D	124.0	14.18	8.6	2.3	6.9	18.8	**8.5**	10.0	14.2
CITIZENS STATE BK NORWOOD	Norwood Young Ame	MN	**C**	C-	D+	80.2	-6.53	14.0	3.1	6.0	0.0	**8.0**	9.6	13.9
CITIZENS STATE BK OF ARLINGTON	Arlington	SD	**C+**	C	C-	104.2	0.47	3.8	1.8	4.3	22.5	**10.0**	12.0	17.3
CITIZENS STATE BK OF CHENEY KS	Cheney	KS	**A-**	A-	A-	59.1	4.93	8.6	12.3	11.6	27.8	**10.0**	11.5	18.6
CITIZENS STATE BK OF FINLEY	Finley	ND	**C**	C	D+	136.1	4.64	8.4	2.0	0.8	28.3	**6.7**	8.7	13.4
CITIZENS STATE BK OF GLENVILLE	Glenville	MN	**C+**	C+	B-	38.1	-12.98	5.1	5.8	7.1	14.7	**9.2**	10.5	31.3
CITIZENS STATE BK OF HAYFIELD	Hayfield	MN	**C-**	C-	C	83.2	4.22	9.2	3.5	10.6	10.0	**4.8**	6.8	11.5
CITIZENS STATE BK OF LA CROSSE	La Crosse	WI	**B+**	B+	B+	157.2	20.36	12.1	1.0	27.0	0.0	**5.9**	8.9	11.7
CITIZENS STATE BK OF LANKIN	Lankin	ND	**C**	C-	C	44.4	-2.33	6.3	4.1	4.0	19.5	**7.1**	9.1	13.5
CITIZENS STATE BK OF LOYAL	Loyal	WI	**B+**	B+	B	183.4	2.85	3.4	0.5	12.8	32.4	**10.0**	11.4	17.9
CITIZENS STATE BK OF LULING	Luling	TX	**B**	B	B-	66.4	5.55	17.3	1.5	8.8	9.2	**10.0**	11.2	15.7
CITIZENS STATE BK OF MILFORD	Milford	IL	**C-**	D+	D	52.7	2.64	13.4	1.5	1.0	32.9	**5.9**	7.9	14.0
CITIZENS STATE BK OF ONTONAGON	Ontonagon	MI	**D+**	C-	C+	50.0	-3.51	4.1	4.6	13.8	43.5	**10.0**	12.9	39.6
CITIZENS STATE BK OF OURAY	Ouray	CO	**B**	B	B-	89.2	-1.15	2.5	0.9	6.7	50.2	**9.4**	10.6	27.0
CITIZENS STATE BK OF ROSEAU	Roseau	MN	**A**	A	A	205.1	1.18	8.3	5.7	5.5	52.4	**10.0**	12.3	21.4
▲ CITIZENS STATE BK OF TYLER INC	Tyler	MN	**D+**	D	D+	19.0	1.70	7.2	4.5	5.4	32.0	**7.6**	9.4	25.8
CITIZENS STATE BK OF WAVERLY	Waverly	MN	**B**	B	B-	68.7	9.37	4.9	1.4	18.9	13.3	**6.6**	8.6	13.3
▲ CITIZENS TRI-COUNTY BANK	Dunlap	TN	**C**	D+	D+	621.5	4.47	0.4	9.5	19.3	37.8	**7.5**	9.3	18.1
CITIZENS TRUST BANK	Atlanta	GA	**C-**	C-	D	400.8	2.33	4.4	1.7	7.8	32.5	**9.3**	10.6	19.5
▲ CITIZENS UNION BK SHELBYVILLE	Shelbyville	KY	**C**	C-	D	530.7	-1.32	4.5	0.5	16.8	10.0	**9.3**	10.6	14.4
CITIZENS-FARMERS BK COLE CAMP	Cole Camp	MO	**A**	A	A-	113.7	8.54	4.3	5.5	30.2	26.3	**10.0**	16.0	16.8
CITY B&TC OF MOBERLY	Moberly	MO	**B-**	B-	B-	149.0	3.10	4.5	9.9	4.9	33.9	**6.2**	8.2	17.2
CITY BANK	Lubbock	TX	**B-**	C+	C-	2268.7	9.88	10.9	5.2	11.0	16.3	**8.0**	9.7	14.7
CITY BANK & TRUST CO	Natchitoches	LA	**B-**	B-	B-	225.5	-1.45	1.9	3.7	15.3	56.9	**8.7**	10.1	22.3
CITY BANK & TRUST CO	Lincoln	NE	**B-**	C+	C-	166.1	-3.15	8.5	1.0	11.3	12.4	**10.0**	13.8	21.4
CITY BANK OF HARTFORD	Hartford	AL	**B-**	C+	C-	53.3	-0.69	3.2	4.9	13.7	22.6	**10.0**	11.5	21.0
CITY FIRST BANK OF DC NA	Washington	DC	**B-**	C+	C+	224.7	5.43	4.5	0.0	4.8	16.3	**10.0**	14.0	18.7
▲ CITY NATIONAL BK	Corsicana	TX	**C**	C-	C-	43.6	3.14	12.2	4.4	29.9	10.8	**9.0**	10.3	20.2
CITY NATIONAL BK	Los Angeles	CA	**B**	B	B-	31698.2	10.43	21.9	2.2	16.0	28.6	**5.4**	7.4	12.0
CITY NATIONAL BK COLORADO CITY	Colorado City	TX	**B+**	B+	B+	128.9	2.27	4.6	7.7	8.0	53.5	**6.8**	8.8	19.0
CITY NATIONAL BK OF FLORIDA	Miami	FL	**B-**	B	B-	5101.9	6.23	11.7	0.5	14.7	21.0	**10.0**	12.6	18.4
CITY NATIONAL BK OF METROPOLIS	Metropolis	IL	**B+**	A-	B+	395.8	5.34	4.0	3.6	17.9	53.2	**10.0**	11.2	25.5
CITY NATIONAL BK OF NEW JERSEY	Newark	NJ	**E-**	E-	E	287.2	-8.34	7.5	0.2	6.7	25.6	**0.2**	3.4	6.4
CITY NATIONAL BK OF SAN SABA	San Saba	TX	**C+**	C+	B-	56.0	5.76	2.5	3.1	0.3	63.0	**10.0**	14.7	35.0
▲ CITY NATIONAL BK OF TAYLOR	Taylor	TX	**C+**	C-	C	195.7	-2.12	2.9	1.3	24.3	49.4	**9.0**	10.3	26.4
CITY NATIONAL BK OF WV	Charleston	WV	**B**	B	B+	3368.6	-0.17	5.0	1.2	36.6	9.9	**7.7**	9.5	13.4
CITY NB OF SULPHUR SPRINGS	Sulphur Springs	TX	**B**	B	B-	451.3	3.13	5.9	6.9	29.7	16.2	**7.6**	9.4	13.3
CITY NB&TC OF GUYMON	Guymon	OK	**B+**	B+	B+	175.5	1.94	4.4	4.1	16.1	50.1	**7.6**	9.4	20.3
CITY NB&TC OF LAWTON OKLAHOMA	Lawton	OK	**A**	A	A-	323.4	-2.95	5.8	2.1	28.8	12.4	**10.0**	12.8	22.0
CITY SB & TRUST CO	De Ridder	LA	**A**	A	A	290.8	11.12	8.5	7.1	29.2	10.3	**10.0**	11.4	16.3
CITY STATE BK	Norwalk	IA	**B**	B	B-	286.7	9.50	5.4	1.2	15.4	22.2	**7.1**	9.1	13.2
CITY STATE BK	Fort Scott	KS	**C+**	C+	B-	38.0	3.89	1.9	3.5	21.8	25.9	**6.3**	8.3	17.3
▲ CITYWIDE BANKS	Aurora	CO	**B**	B-	C+	1260.4	11.52	11.8	0.2	5.8	20.1	**7.0**	9.0	13.5
CIVIC BANK & TRUST	Nashville	TN	**B**	B	C+	137.4	-2.63	5.8	0.5	11.5	44.5	**10.0**	13.7	25.2
CIVIS BANK	Rogersville	TN	**E-**	E-	E-	114.1	-3.96	2.8	1.6	27.2	8.3	**1.8**	4.7	8.8
▲ CLACKAMAS COUNTY BANK	Sandy	OR	**B+**	B-	C+	178.9	4.31	0.7	0.8	9.0	29.3	**10.0**	12.9	22.9
CLARE BANK NA	Platteville	WI	**A-**	A-	A-	281.3	2.28	5.6	2.3	28.3	28.1	**8.5**	10.0	26.5
CLAREMONT SB	Claremont	NH	**C+**	C+	C+	338.6	2.56	4.1	2.6	52.6	17.4	**10.0**	14.5	21.8
CLARENCE STATE BK	Clarence	MO	**B-**	B-	B	18.6	1.42	5.1	2.5	6.7	35.7	**10.0**	21.8	39.1
CLARION COUNTY COMMUNITY BANK	Clarion	PA	**B**	B	B-	125.3	1.71	9.0	2.2	42.1	15.6	**10.0**	11.4	16.8
▲ CLARKE COUNTY STATE BK	Osceola	IA	**B-**	C+	C-	112.2	0.33	4.8	1.3	14.4	24.1	**10.0**	11.2	17.0
CLARKSON BANK	Clarkson	NE	**A-**	A-	A-	59.2	-3.30	4.2	1.0	0.3	56.3	**10.0**	11.3	20.8
CLARKSTON STATE BK	Clarkston	MI	**C**	D+	D-	140.7	11.64	7.0	0.2	4.6	4.1	**4.5**	8.8	10.8
CLASSIC BANK NA	Cameron	TX	**C**	B-	B	278.1	4.35	6.6	3.3	16.9	25.1	**6.8**	8.8	14.5
▲ CLATSOP COMMUNITY BANK	Seaside	OR	**C**	C-	C-	74.0	6.30	7.5	1.2	7.9	22.5	**9.1**	10.4	15.5
CLAXTON BANK	Claxton	GA	**C-**	C	C-	105.9	-1.21	2.2	2.1	13.4	24.5	**8.6**	10.1	15.4

Asset Quality Index	Adjusted Non-Performing Loans as a % of Total Loans	Adjusted Non-Performing Loans as a % of Capital	Net Charge-Offs Avg Loans	Profitability Index	Net Income ($Mil)	Return on Assets (R.O.A.)	Return on Equity (R.O.E.)	Net Interest Spread	Overhead Efficiency Ratio	Liquidity Index	Liquidity Ratio	Hot Money Ratio	Stability Index
9.0	0.06	0.2	0.07	**2.6**	0.3	0.38	2.84	2.26	86.4	**6.3**	47.6	3.2	**7.5**
5.2	0.00	0.0	0.00	**0.6**	0.0	-0.05	-0.52	4.25	100.0	**4.0**	18.4	9.0	**3.5**
5.4	1.39	7.2	0.11	**5.4**	1.2	1.40	16.65	3.39	67.2	**2.4**	32.5	21.3	**6.6**
8.0	0.14	1.2	-0.01	**7.1**	0.8	1.72	20.47	3.71	51.7	**2.8**	8.8	14.5	**5.3**
1.9	3.29	21.4	0.42	**3.7**	0.6	0.67	5.98	3.88	74.7	**3.1**	4.7	12.3	**4.2**
2.9	2.07	13.9	0.24	**4.1**	0.4	0.68	5.41	4.30	71.8	**3.8**	24.7	11.0	**5.0**
3.1	2.39	12.9	0.61	**3.8**	0.5	0.63	5.03	3.37	65.4	**2.8**	21.0	15.5	**6.8**
7.8	0.44	2.2	0.58	**7.0**	0.7	1.57	12.97	4.25	58.8	**2.6**	25.3	17.2	**8.8**
2.7	1.88	12.4	-0.03	**4.8**	1.1	1.10	13.38	3.76	73.5	**2.0**	16.9	19.2	**4.7**
8.2	0.72	2.2	0.01	**3.3**	0.2	0.65	6.65	2.62	76.1	**6.8**	68.6	4.2	**4.9**
2.8	1.90	16.9	0.01	**4.6**	0.7	1.03	15.42	3.66	70.7	**4.2**	16.9	7.3	**4.0**
5.3	0.32	3.2	0.05	**9.8**	3.1	2.78	31.84	4.40	48.2	**0.6**	4.6	39.1	**6.6**
6.1	0.44	3.1	-0.01	**4.3**	0.3	0.89	11.08	4.27	77.2	**4.4**	14.2	5.7	**3.9**
5.7	1.93	9.2	0.00	**5.1**	1.4	1.00	8.85	3.82	68.3	**4.4**	26.3	8.2	**6.6**
6.2	0.65	3.9	0.01	**4.8**	0.4	0.87	7.78	4.56	75.2	**4.3**	29.6	9.8	**6.2**
4.6	2.33	13.7	0.00	**2.5**	0.3	0.62	8.15	3.41	84.5	**5.1**	37.3	8.0	**3.3**
5.5	6.15	12.3	1.57	**1.1**	0.1	0.20	1.60	3.52	92.0	**7.1**	77.2	4.0	**4.5**
7.1	1.59	4.7	-0.95	**4.5**	0.4	0.66	5.96	3.59	83.9	**6.1**	64.0	8.2	**6.1**
6.5	1.37	4.6	0.17	**6.2**	2.3	1.46	12.11	3.18	56.8	**1.6**	22.5	25.5	**8.8**
5.2	3.13	7.7	1.04	**2.7**	0.1	0.55	6.11	2.58	81.7	**6.8**	73.0	3.4	**3.3**
5.0	0.35	2.7	0.07	**6.1**	0.8	1.57	12.06	4.29	60.7	**4.8**	20.8	4.3	**5.6**
2.7	3.12	14.8	0.85	**6.7**	7.3	1.56	15.84	4.61	62.9	**2.5**	35.1	23.0	**6.6**
2.7	4.73	19.6	0.44	**2.9**	1.4	0.46	3.92	3.59	86.7	**1.5**	28.5	31.6	**5.4**
2.2	3.15	19.6	0.04	**3.3**	2.9	0.73	6.32	4.15	75.2	**1.8**	18.0	21.0	**4.7**
6.8	1.27	4.9	0.09	**8.0**	1.2	1.42	8.89	3.81	48.3	**2.4**	24.7	17.9	**8.1**
7.8	0.39	1.8	0.08	**3.9**	0.8	0.72	8.69	2.53	69.0	**5.6**	33.2	2.9	**6.2**
5.1	1.30	8.1	0.14	**4.4**	16.1	0.98	10.19	3.84	79.2	**2.6**	18.0	17.0	**7.4**
8.1	0.59	2.0	0.07	**3.7**	1.5	0.84	8.92	2.70	76.7	**6.0**	63.5	10.6	**5.6**
4.1	4.28	18.9	0.38	**3.3**	0.7	0.52	3.72	3.09	75.5	**4.0**	25.3	9.9	**6.5**
4.1	3.73	17.5	0.09	**5.2**	0.5	1.26	11.17	4.08	67.8	**3.4**	42.3	18.6	**5.0**
3.5	2.23	10.5	-0.05	**5.3**	0.7	0.52	3.60	4.37	79.3	**0.7**	13.5	38.3	**7.8**
8.7	0.00	0.0	0.05	**3.2**	0.2	0.63	6.21	4.00	85.2	**2.0**	22.8	19.7	**4.9**
7.3	0.33	2.6	-0.08	**4.4**	188.1	0.84	9.46	3.02	68.5	**6.3**	30.7	1.5	**7.7**
8.7	0.15	0.6	0.03	**6.0**	1.5	1.52	22.42	3.20	56.1	**3.1**	46.1	23.5	**6.0**
6.6	0.57	2.8	-0.07	**3.8**	32.9	0.87	4.62	3.30	63.8	**4.9**	27.4	8.8	**6.8**
7.0	1.82	6.2	0.65	**4.7**	3.4	1.15	11.08	3.08	52.0	**2.8**	48.4	29.3	**5.6**
0.0	16.15	138.2	0.20	**0.0**	-5.1	-2.40	-90.98	2.68	176.6	**1.1**	18.9	31.1	**1.4**
9.6	0.00	0.0	-0.03	**2.7**	0.2	0.51	3.52	3.19	81.1	**6.5**	73.2	7.0	**6.7**
8.4	0.68	2.8	0.20	**3.4**	1.4	0.94	9.93	3.45	75.7	**4.0**	49.4	17.5	**5.2**
4.8	1.14	9.1	0.19	**8.9**	38.4	1.49	14.78	3.91	54.7	**2.9**	5.0	13.6	**9.3**
4.5	0.99	6.9	0.07	**6.7**	5.4	1.63	16.63	4.47	68.1	**1.9**	23.2	21.0	**6.7**
8.5	0.53	2.3	-0.03	**5.6**	1.9	1.44	16.44	3.40	62.5	**3.5**	37.2	16.6	**6.3**
7.3	0.94	4.2	1.15	**6.2**	3.3	1.39	11.69	4.30	82.3	**4.9**	29.6	6.4	**8.6**
8.3	0.21	1.4	0.13	**9.6**	4.6	2.20	19.76	5.23	56.8	**1.6**	10.6	21.8	**8.4**
6.0	0.69	5.1	0.13	**5.0**	2.5	1.20	12.80	3.47	66.8	**3.6**	24.5	12.2	**5.8**
8.2	0.00	0.0	0.03	**4.3**	0.3	0.88	10.63	3.62	75.1	**3.3**	44.3	19.2	**4.8**
5.7	1.09	6.9	0.04	**4.9**	16.0	1.76	18.74	3.86	77.9	**5.0**	30.9	10.4	**7.5**
9.3	0.00	0.0	1.27	**3.5**	0.9	0.85	6.48	3.32	89.9	**2.4**	49.7	48.6	**6.5**
0.3	7.04	80.2	0.01	**0.3**	-0.8	-0.90	-17.88	4.27	119.0	**1.4**	18.3	27.3	**0.6**
6.7	0.33	1.4	0.08	**5.1**	1.6	1.24	9.72	3.91	72.6	**4.3**	36.8	12.5	**6.5**
7.7	0.53	2.9	0.04	**6.2**	3.1	1.49	14.14	2.87	44.8	**4.8**	32.7	8.4	**7.8**
6.5	1.22	6.1	0.19	**2.4**	1.3	0.54	3.61	3.65	92.2	**2.5**	17.1	16.8	**7.2**
8.9	0.93	1.9	0.05	**3.9**	0.1	0.67	3.21	3.03	71.0	**5.4**	57.1	9.2	**7.0**
5.4	1.93	12.0	0.02	**3.7**	0.6	0.60	5.47	3.70	79.5	**1.8**	19.1	21.1	**6.1**
5.2	2.19	11.4	0.11	**3.5**	0.5	0.62	5.36	3.21	74.5	**4.2**	25.1	8.7	**5.5**
8.7	0.49	1.6	-0.01	**6.2**	0.7	1.62	19.93	3.17	51.1	**3.2**	51.1	23.2	**7.8**
3.1	0.92	7.7	-0.04	**5.0**	1.2	1.21	9.88	4.88	75.4	**4.0**	9.6	8.0	**3.1**
2.8	3.09	20.0	0.01	**4.0**	1.6	0.79	8.73	4.12	80.5	**2.4**	17.6	17.4	**5.7**
5.8	0.62	3.6	0.02	**3.1**	0.2	0.44	4.18	4.16	80.8	**3.4**	24.3	12.8	**5.3**
2.3	3.76	22.1	0.27	**3.2**	0.5	0.54	5.92	4.44	85.4	**2.1**	16.4	18.7	**4.2**

Name	City	State	Rating	2013 Rating	2012 Rating	Total Assets ($Mil)	One Year Asset Growth	Asset Mix (As a % of Total Assets) Commercial Loans	Consumer Loans	Mortgage Loans	Securities	Capitalization Index	Leverage Ratio	Risk-Based Capital Ratio
CLAY CITY BANKING CO	Clay City	IL	**C+**	C+	C	123.9	9.36	11.1	3.1	16.6	14.0	**6.9**	8.9	12.8
CLAY COUNTY BANK INC	Clay	WV	**A-**	A-	A-	81.8	1.59	2.9	13.0	45.2	21.7	**10.0**	13.2	30.0
CLAY COUNTY SAVINGS BANK	Liberty	MO	**C-**	D+	D-	86.8	-6.00	5.2	0.6	39.5	8.3	**10.0**	11.0	18.5
CLAY COUNTY STATE BK	Louisville	IL	**B**	B	B	82.4	3.05	6.6	5.4	11.4	44.1	**10.0**	13.4	27.0
CLAYTON BANK & TRUST	Knoxville	TN	**C+**	C+	C+	672.0	-2.96	21.0	13.1	11.1	10.4	**10.0**	18.6	21.3
CLEAR LAKE BANK & TRUST CO	Clear Lake	IA	**B+**	B+	B+	337.8	24.82	14.7	5.3	17.7	14.7	**5.9**	7.9	11.9
CLEAR MOUNTAIN BANK	Bruceton Mills	WV	**B**	B	B	490.5	3.72	5.7	7.6	37.3	13.0	**9.3**	10.6	17.0
CLEARFIELD BANK & TRUST CO	Clearfield	PA	**B-**	B-	B-	436.1	2.66	10.8	2.9	16.5	22.9	**8.8**	10.2	16.8
CLEARPOINT FEDERAL BANK & TR	Batesville	IN	**U**	U	A-	107.4	3.03	0.0	0.0	0.0	95.1	**10.0**	12.9	33.9
▲ CLEO STATE BK	Cleo Springs	OK	**A**	A-	A	101.7	10.14	11.4	4.8	0.4	60.3	**10.0**	15.4	26.7
CLEVELAND STATE BK	Cleveland	WI	**B-**	B-	B-	106.8	6.47	7.0	2.9	22.9	34.3	**8.1**	9.7	18.7
CLEVELAND STATE BK	Cleveland	MS	**B-**	B-	B	215.4	2.07	8.2	4.9	12.9	35.6	**9.2**	10.5	18.7
CLIFTON SAVINGS BANK	Clifton	NJ	**B**	B	B-	1160.5	7.26	0.0	0.1	47.4	36.7	**10.0**	20.6	48.5
CLINTON BANK	Clinton	KY	**B+**	B+	B+	60.8	4.68	3.3	2.3	6.1	40.9	**10.0**	17.3	26.9
CLINTON NATIONAL BK	Clinton	IA	**B-**	B-	B-	375.0	-0.72	7.7	2.6	9.2	41.7	**10.0**	12.2	21.4
CLINTON SB	Clinton	MA	**C-**	C-	D+	479.8	1.26	4.4	2.5	36.6	18.5	**7.5**	9.4	15.2
CLOVER COMMUNITY BANK	Clover	SC	**B**	C+	C	118.3	0.50	5.0	2.8	7.4	25.4	**8.0**	9.7	16.0
▲ CMMNTY BK OAK PARK RIVER FORE	Oak Park	IL	**D+**	D-	D-	286.1	7.43	8.8	0.2	12.3	2.9	**5.5**	7.5	12.5
▲ CMMNTY BK-WHEATON/GLEN ELLYN	Glen Ellyn	IL	**D+**	D-	D-	335.3	-4.60	6.0	0.4	8.2	30.6	**5.7**	7.7	12.9
CMS BANK	White Plains	NY	**C-**	C-	D	273.3	5.68	14.8	0.0	33.3	14.4	**6.4**	8.4	12.4
▲ CNB	Centreville	MD	**C**	D+	D+	483.2	5.68	2.2	0.7	20.0	22.1	**7.2**	9.2	14.8
CNB BANK	Clearfield	PA	**B-**	B-	B-	2153.2	18.10	10.3	2.1	19.6	32.3	**5.6**	7.6	13.1
CNB BANK & TRUST NA	Carlinville	IL	**B-**	B-	C	779.5	9.29	10.8	1.6	9.1	20.9	**6.1**	8.1	12.2
CNB BANK INC	Berkeley Springs	WV	**C+**	C	C-	294.7	4.45	2.1	3.3	39.1	31.1	**8.8**	10.2	19.1
▲ CNLBANK	Orlando	FL	**D**	D-	E+	1302.6	5.39	8.3	0.8	8.0	29.2	**2.9**	6.2	9.9
COAST NATIONAL BK	San Luis Obispo	CA	**D+**	D+	D-	129.2	4.35	13.6	0.2	3.5	12.0	**7.5**	9.3	15.9
COASTAL BANK & TRUST	Jacksonville	NC	**D**	D	C	63.9	-1.27	11.1	0.5	9.5	7.9	**9.7**	12.0	14.8
COASTAL CAROLINA NATIONAL BK	Myrtle Beach	SC	**D+**	D+	D+	134.0	10.85	6.8	3.6	30.7	15.3	**8.6**	10.0	15.8
COASTAL COMMERCE BANK	Houma	LA	**B+**	B+	B	413.6	5.34	30.6	2.7	13.5	13.9	**7.5**	9.5	12.9
COASTAL COMMUNITY BANK	Everett	WA	**C+**	C+	D+	519.8	23.01	8.2	0.3	8.5	3.0	**8.3**	10.3	13.6
▼ COASTALSTATES BANK	Hilton Head Island	SC	**D-**	D+	D-	376.3	-0.56	18.8	0.6	27.9	12.3	**4.7**	7.0	10.9
COASTWAY COMMUNITY BANK	Warwick	RI	**D**	E+	D-	440.8	15.20	4.5	0.3	35.5	0.0	**10.0**	11.9	15.6
COATESVILLE SB	Coatesville	PA	**D+**	D	D	199.8	-0.91	3.6	0.1	46.6	13.1	**5.6**	7.6	11.9
COBIZ BANK	Denver	CO	**A-**	B+	B	2993.3	7.98	23.1	0.3	7.4	16.3	**8.3**	10.5	13.6
COCONUT GROVE BANK	Miami	FL	**B-**	C+	C	609.9	0.67	1.6	0.3	5.9	37.1	**10.0**	16.0	40.5
COFFEE COUNTY BANK	Manchester	TN	**C+**	C	C-	130.4	8.24	4.4	10.2	39.7	9.5	**10.0**	12.6	19.0
COLCHESTER STATE BK	Colchester	IL	**B+**	B+	B+	60.2	4.82	5.7	5.5	10.8	45.0	**10.0**	12.5	26.8
COLEMAN COUNTY STATE BK	Coleman	TX	**A-**	A-	A-	103.9	11.10	9.9	3.2	15.5	11.1	**8.0**	9.7	14.4
COLFAX BANKING CO	Colfax	LA	**B**	B	B	91.8	6.96	1.7	3.9	26.3	39.7	**8.5**	10.0	20.7
COLLEGE SB	Princeton	NJ	**D+**	C-	D+	476.8	4.14	0.0	48.0	0.0	49.0	**6.4**	8.4	25.4
COLLEGIATE PEAKS BANK	Buena Vista	CO	**B**	B	B	391.3	17.98	9.7	0.6	10.5	8.0	**5.9**	7.9	13.2
▼ COLLINS STATE BK	Collins	WI	**C+**	B-	C+	57.6	5.11	7.1	2.5	24.5	29.5	**8.1**	9.7	17.2
COLLINSVILLE BUILDING & LOAN	Collinsville	IL	**B-**	B-	B	121.4	-3.41	0.0	0.0	71.7	20.4	**10.0**	26.2	70.4
COLLINSVILLE SAVINGS SOCIETY	Collinsville	CT	**D+**	D+	D-	134.7	2.17	7.3	1.4	36.8	13.4	**7.3**	9.2	13.7
COLOMBO BANK	Rockville	MD	**E-**	E-	E-	199.6	211.42	1.6	0.3	39.6	14.0	**8.2**	9.8	17.9
▼ COLONIAL AMERICAN BANK	Middletown	NJ	**E**	D-	D-	153.1	2.82	7.5	0.0	27.7	8.5	**2.5**	6.2	9.6
COLONIAL BANK FSB	Vineland	NJ	**D**	D+	C	552.3	-7.62	3.7	0.4	31.3	42.6	**9.5**	10.6	23.6
COLONIAL CO-OP BANK	Gardner	MA	**E-**	E-	E-	67.5	-0.14	0.1	1.2	73.5	0.0	**4.0**	6.0	11.7
COLONIAL FSB	Quincy	MA	**B-**	B-	B-	285.7	-1.30	0.0	0.9	41.2	42.8	**10.0**	12.5	32.0
COLONIAL SAVINGS FA	Fort Worth	TX	**B+**	B+	B	1065.9	-0.84	0.5	0.3	46.6	4.8	**10.0**	21.3	46.3
▲ COLONY BANK	Fitzgerald	GA	**B-**	C	D+	1110.9	0.08	4.2	2.1	18.1	24.6	**10.0**	11.4	18.3
COLORADO B&TC OF LA JUNTA	La Junta	CO	**C+**	C	C-	106.1	6.31	8.3	3.8	11.8	33.7	**6.2**	8.2	17.5
▲ COLORADO EAST BANK & TRUST	Lamar	CO	**D+**	D	D-	741.0	-3.51	6.6	1.0	4.4	28.6	**8.2**	9.8	16.0
COLORADO FSB	Greenwood Village	CO	**B-**	B-	C+	1798.2	-7.31	0.0	0.0	31.1	30.9	**8.3**	9.9	32.3
COLORADO NATIONAL BK	Palisade	CO	**D-**	D+	C	72.7	9.78	3.1	0.2	4.6	14.2	**8.6**	10.1	32.8
COLUMBIA BANK	Lake City	FL	**D-**	D-	D-	188.8	-0.77	4.8	0.8	15.4	29.9	**8.3**	9.9	19.0
COLUMBIA BANK	Columbia	MD	**B-**	B-	C+	2042.0	1.71	6.3	1.1	11.7	21.8	**7.8**	9.5	13.8
▲ COLUMBIA BANK	Fair Lawn	NJ	**C**	C	C	4639.7	3.42	2.5	0.1	42.2	16.7	**8.7**	10.2	16.2
COLUMBIA NATIONAL BK	Columbia	IL	**C**	C	C+	47.0	0.42	19.5	2.4	25.6	17.5	**10.0**	11.3	19.7
COLUMBIA S&LA	Milwaukee	WI	**D-**	D-	D-	24.4	0.87	1.6	0.9	54.2	0.1	**7.5**	9.3	14.8

Asset Quality Index	Adjusted Non-Performing Loans as a % of Total Loans	Adjusted Non-Performing Loans as a % of Capital	Net Charge-Offs / Avg Loans	Profitability Index	Net Income ($Mil)	Return on Assets (R.O.A.)	Return on Equity (R.O.E.)	Net Interest Spread	Overhead Efficiency Ratio	Liquidity Index	Liquidity Ratio	Hot Money Ratio	Stability Index
3.7	2.03	15.8	0.00	**4.4**	0.7	0.81	8.99	3.78	70.5	**2.3**	12.9	17.4	**4.6**
7.5	0.54	2.3	-0.05	**6.2**	0.7	1.12	8.42	4.20	65.6	**2.9**	29.9	17.1	**8.3**
3.7	2.64	15.1	0.10	**2.1**	0.2	0.26	2.32	3.77	93.5	**3.6**	20.1	11.3	**5.6**
5.1	2.83	9.5	-0.05	**5.0**	0.8	1.29	9.98	2.96	63.0	**4.3**	31.2	10.7	**7.2**
3.2	4.11	16.1	0.16	**10.0**	16.5	3.36	19.12	5.66	41.0	**0.8**	6.5	32.4	**8.5**
7.7	0.13	1.2	0.01	**7.7**	4.3	1.67	19.92	4.02	58.3	**3.4**	16.5	12.0	**6.9**
4.7	1.34	9.1	0.41	**6.3**	3.8	1.05	10.36	4.12	61.2	**1.6**	15.1	22.4	**6.2**
6.0	0.45	2.8	0.08	**3.9**	2.4	0.73	6.11	3.51	77.2	**3.8**	22.4	10.5	**6.6**
10.0	na	0.0	na	**4.2**	0.5	0.63	4.49	2.28	78.3	**8.6**	112.8	0.8	**6.2**
6.3	3.42	5.9	2.45	**8.2**	1.3	1.73	11.43	3.87	41.1	**5.7**	75.5	13.2	**9.3**
4.4	2.51	12.8	1.21	**5.3**	0.8	0.99	10.49	4.26	64.4	**4.5**	45.0	13.8	**5.8**
6.6	0.72	3.4	0.09	**4.0**	1.1	0.68	7.42	3.96	75.9	**4.1**	38.5	14.2	**5.9**
9.7	0.77	2.0	0.08	**3.6**	4.7	0.53	3.04	2.38	61.9	**3.0**	39.1	27.4	**9.3**
8.5	0.95	2.9	0.01	**4.7**	0.5	0.97	5.72	3.71	63.8	**1.7**	20.5	23.7	**7.5**
8.5	0.11	0.5	0.02	**3.2**	1.6	0.56	4.61	3.36	82.6	**5.0**	37.9	9.1	**6.8**
2.6	2.87	21.2	0.07	**3.5**	2.4	0.66	6.56	3.60	77.3	**2.0**	19.7	19.4	**5.3**
6.8	0.54	2.7	0.41	**5.7**	0.9	1.05	10.66	4.18	69.8	**4.8**	36.6	10.0	**4.9**
1.5	7.01	44.2	1.12	**2.7**	1.3	0.62	8.20	3.31	82.6	**4.3**	35.9	12.2	**3.0**
4.4	2.27	15.7	-0.05	**3.3**	5.5	2.17	30.72	3.38	82.9	**4.5**	34.4	10.4	**1.6**
3.5	1.33	12.6	0.06	**2.7**	0.6	0.31	4.00	3.50	82.6	**1.4**	16.9	26.5	**3.4**
4.9	0.84	5.7	0.11	**3.6**	1.8	0.52	5.36	3.59	77.5	**1.9**	21.6	20.0	**5.2**
5.3	0.99	7.4	0.10	**5.4**	16.2	1.02	12.63	3.66	59.8	**4.8**	16.2	3.9	**6.3**
3.9	1.60	12.5	0.27	**4.5**	4.0	0.71	7.99	4.09	67.8	**3.3**	19.7	13.2	**4.7**
3.5	3.31	18.1	0.37	**3.4**	1.3	0.59	6.00	3.82	75.7	**2.0**	27.7	22.2	**5.1**
2.6	3.12	26.2	-0.52	**2.2**	3.6	0.38	4.25	3.22	83.7	**5.4**	31.1	7.5	**5.2**
6.0	0.68	3.6	-1.00	**1.9**	0.1	0.06	0.79	3.66	98.4	**3.7**	30.5	13.4	**3.2**
3.0	0.81	4.8	-1.96	**5.3**	0.8	1.79	19.07	3.94	108.6	**2.3**	16.2	17.4	**3.8**
6.1	0.64	4.3	0.00	**1.5**	0.1	0.10	1.01	3.73	95.1	**1.0**	15.0	31.9	**2.5**
6.3	0.32	2.3	0.08	**8.9**	6.2	2.09	23.80	4.67	56.0	**1.9**	20.0	19.9	**6.6**
3.6	1.16	8.5	0.15	**3.8**	1.7	0.49	5.23	4.57	76.5	**2.6**	14.9	15.9	**3.2**
1.8	3.14	29.9	0.50	**0.2**	-1.7	-0.59	-6.52	3.31	116.4	**3.4**	13.9	11.8	**3.2**
4.0	2.11	15.2	0.04	**0.5**	-1.2	-0.38	-3.28	3.46	109.9	**2.8**	1.7	13.5	**2.2**
2.5	2.80	27.2	-0.02	**2.7**	0.7	0.49	6.38	2.56	80.6	**1.2**	9.2	26.8	**3.7**
5.9	0.81	5.6	0.04	**6.8**	23.7	1.11	10.32	4.09	64.2	**4.0**	10.9	8.4	**8.0**
8.2	2.05	4.2	-0.07	**3.5**	0.5	0.10	0.64	2.29	95.9	**5.0**	64.6	15.3	**7.1**
2.7	3.33	18.6	0.16	**9.7**	2.4	2.51	19.92	5.05	49.1	**1.3**	15.1	27.9	**6.8**
5.4	4.31	13.7	0.92	**4.3**	0.3	0.72	5.41	3.73	42.9	**3.0**	47.4	24.3	**7.0**
7.8	0.22	1.6	0.05	**9.6**	1.7	2.26	24.12	4.81	56.5	**3.5**	17.8	11.8	**7.4**
7.6	0.32	1.6	0.03	**4.7**	0.8	1.16	11.80	4.43	76.4	**1.3**	21.1	29.8	**6.6**
5.6	0.25	1.5	0.02	**1.3**	0.0	0.00	-0.02	1.22	99.1	**1.6**	35.1	48.7	**4.5**
8.2	0.09	0.7	0.00	**5.1**	2.5	0.86	9.03	3.77	61.9	**3.9**	29.1	12.0	**5.9**
8.9	0.12	0.7	0.00	**3.3**	0.2	0.57	5.46	4.02	82.6	**3.4**	39.4	18.1	**5.0**
9.8	0.93	2.5	0.00	**3.8**	0.5	0.59	2.29	2.51	59.2	**3.5**	35.2	16.0	**7.8**
1.6	4.35	34.3	0.05	**1.4**	0.2	0.17	1.64	3.28	99.2	**2.0**	12.5	19.0	**4.6**
2.5	3.74	22.7	0.26	**0.0**	-1.1	-0.72	-6.90	3.14	121.0	**0.8**	17.2	46.0	**1.1**
2.0	1.34	15.6	1.03	**0.0**	-0.7	-0.65	-10.52	2.75	94.0	**0.6**	5.1	40.5	**3.4**
2.9	5.02	22.0	0.82	**1.2**	1.1	0.26	2.50	2.48	85.9	**4.0**	22.2	9.4	**4.2**
0.3	4.51	55.6	0.15	**1.4**	0.1	0.11	1.40	3.74	94.9	**1.4**	11.1	24.8	**2.1**
10.0	0.27	1.0	0.00	**3.4**	1.3	0.62	5.01	2.63	70.8	**4.5**	51.4	15.1	**7.0**
4.4	2.70	5.9	0.18	**10.0**	18.1	2.39	10.52	5.63	79.1	**6.0**	34.3	4.5	**10.0**
4.0	2.56	13.8	0.60	**4.0**	6.1	0.72	6.86	3.66	70.0	**1.8**	19.7	22.9	**6.6**
4.2	3.04	14.0	0.14	**3.2**	0.4	0.54	6.73	3.73	79.5	**4.4**	31.8	10.2	**4.1**
1.6	4.40	22.4	1.46	**1.5**	0.8	0.14	1.19	3.65	88.9	**2.2**	22.3	18.9	**5.8**
5.7	1.65	5.2	0.12	**4.3**	9.8	0.73	7.98	1.65	35.8	**6.2**	49.3	8.2	**7.0**
8.0	0.00	0.0	0.00	**0.0**	-1.5	-2.94	-27.15	2.15	162.3	**2.3**	36.1	26.9	**4.9**
1.7	9.89	45.6	0.93	**0.0**	-0.3	-0.23	-2.34	3.24	100.4	**2.4**	32.0	20.6	**3.7**
3.9	1.35	9.2	0.38	**4.5**	13.0	0.86	5.85	3.51	69.5	**3.2**	18.7	13.9	**7.4**
4.7	2.03	13.7	0.45	**2.9**	19.1	0.56	5.74	2.68	63.1	**3.4**	14.6	12.3	**7.2**
5.2	2.05	10.1	0.16	**2.9**	0.2	0.54	4.79	3.36	80.9	**5.7**	40.5	5.6	**5.3**
0.3	13.39	101.0	0.00	**1.4**	0.0	-0.10	-1.01	5.04	102.4	**0.6**	11.2	41.2	**3.4**

Name	City	State	Rating	2013 Rating	2012 Rating	Total Assets ($Mil)	One Year Asset Growth	Asset Mix (As a % of Total Assets) Commercial Loans	Consumer Loans	Mortgage Loans	Securities	Capitalization Index	Leverage Ratio	Risk-Based Capital Ratio
COLUMBIA STATE BK	Tacoma	WA	**B**	B	B	7462.0	4.40	14.7	0.7	3.1	21.5	**8.6**	10.1	13.9
COLUMBUS BANK & TRUST CO	Columbus	NE	**C+**	C+	C+	110.6	1.76	18.7	2.5	8.1	21.5	**4.8**	9.1	10.9
COLUMBUS COMMUNITY BANK	Columbus	GA	**B**	B-	C-	123.9	5.43	2.9	0.5	16.5	10.4	**10.0**	11.9	16.3
COLUMBUS FIRST BANK	Worthington	OH	**B-**	B-	C+	274.7	8.65	10.1	0.0	26.0	0.0	**7.4**	9.3	13.1
▼ COLUMBUS JUNCTION STATE BK	Columbus Junction	IA	**D-**	D+	C-	51.1	-9.81	7.4	2.8	17.2	41.8	**5.8**	7.8	15.6
COLUMBUS STATE BK	Columbus	TX	**B**	B	B+	92.2	6.28	0.7	0.5	1.0	74.9	**10.0**	13.6	29.0
COMANCHE NATIONAL BK	Comanche	TX	**B+**	B+	A-	317.0	9.29	2.2	3.3	9.7	58.5	**10.0**	11.0	27.4
COMENITY BANK	Wilmington	DE	**C-**	C-	C	7935.9	21.38	0.0	91.5	0.0	2.0	**10.0**	15.4	17.0
COMENITY CAPITAL BANK	Salt Lake City	UT	**C**	C	C+	2246.0	54.93	1.4	89.7	0.0	1.0	**10.0**	14.6	15.4
COMERICA BANK	Dallas	TX	**B**	B	B-	68803.2	6.52	40.6	0.9	2.9	13.7	**6.8**	10.6	12.4
COMERICA BANK & TRUST NA	Ann Arbor	MI	**U**	U	A-	47.7	43.68	0.0	0.0	0.0	0.0	**10.0**	98.7	295.8
COMMENCEMENT BANK	Tacoma	WA	**B**	B-	C	166.5	14.38	26.1	1.1	4.8	1.9	**10.0**	12.8	17.5
COMMERCE BANK	Corinth	MS	**A**	A	A	90.2	1.57	12.8	9.2	24.8	25.8	**10.0**	12.7	23.2
COMMERCE BANK	Kansas City	MO	**A-**	A-	B+	22578.6	1.20	11.8	9.5	9.5	39.1	**6.3**	8.4	13.4
▲ COMMERCE BANK	Edina	MN	**C**	C-	D	174.8	12.44	16.0	0.1	11.2	10.9	**10.0**	15.2	20.0
COMMERCE BANK	Laredo	TX	**A-**	A-	A-	556.1	3.00	4.5	0.8	4.8	72.0	**10.0**	12.0	37.6
COMMERCE BANK & TRUST CO	Worcester	MA	**B-**	B	C+	1807.4	7.51	23.1	4.7	2.9	4.0	**6.2**	8.2	12.3
COMMERCE BANK OF ARIZONA	Tucson	AZ	**E+**	D-	D-	183.2	-15.81	12.8	0.3	7.0	6.0	**1.0**	4.6	7.9
COMMERCE BANK OF OREGON	Portland	OR	**B**	B	B-	87.2	19.74	34.3	0.0	0.6	13.5	**10.0**	15.5	18.3
COMMERCE BANK OF WASHINGTON N	Seattle	WA	**B**	B	B-	906.9	1.63	33.1	2.4	0.8	7.9	**8.7**	11.2	13.9
COMMERCE BANK TEXAS	Stockdale	TX	**B-**	C+	C	47.1	5.26	10.6	1.4	18.4	20.5	**10.0**	12.0	18.7
▲ COMMERCE BK OF TEMECULA VALLEY	Murrieta	CA	**C**	D	D	61.2	16.82	19.5	0.2	1.4	0.0	**10.0**	14.1	18.9
▲ COMMERCE COMMUNITY BANK	Oak Grove	LA	**B-**	C+	B-	54.0	171.10	12.6	4.6	6.0	35.9	**8.6**	10.1	16.2
▲ COMMERCE NATIONAL BK & TRUST	Winter Park	FL	**D+**	D-	D-	80.3	2.69	4.2	0.5	16.7	13.0	**9.4**	10.6	16.0
COMMERCE STATE BK	West Bend	WI	**C**	C-	D+	343.6	9.60	11.6	0.1	20.6	7.3	**6.3**	9.7	12.0
▲ COMMERCE UNION BANK	Springfield	TN	**B+**	B	B	278.5	16.25	11.6	0.6	23.9	9.8	**10.0**	12.6	16.0
COMMERCEWEST BANK	Irvine	CA	**A-**	A-	B	386.2	9.05	22.1	0.0	2.1	11.8	**10.0**	13.1	18.3
COMMERCIAL & SB OF MILLERSBURG	Millersburg	OH	**B-**	B-	C+	610.8	2.88	14.7	1.3	15.4	22.4	**6.4**	8.4	13.3
▲ COMMERCIAL BANK	West Liberty	KY	**A-**	B	B-	140.3	-0.83	13.3	5.3	17.7	42.5	**10.0**	12.0	24.0
COMMERCIAL BANK	Honea Path	SC	**A-**	A-	A-	160.6	-0.62	1.9	2.7	14.8	48.9	**10.0**	14.0	33.6
COMMERCIAL BANK	Harrogate	TN	**C-**	D+	D	802.7	7.36	7.2	1.8	24.8	14.0	**8.9**	10.3	15.7
▲ COMMERCIAL BANK	De Kalb	MS	**C**	C-	D	126.2	-5.25	6.1	11.5	16.0	25.2	**8.4**	10.0	15.4
▲ COMMERCIAL BANK	Crawford	GA	**B-**	C+	C-	111.4	14.25	1.9	2.8	28.5	26.9	**10.0**	12.2	18.0
COMMERCIAL BANK	Whitewater	WI	**D+**	D+	C	97.1	-2.66	0.4	0.4	16.7	41.9	**8.8**	10.2	24.9
COMMERCIAL BANK	Alma	MI	**C+**	C+	D+	374.5	0.27	4.7	1.2	40.5	12.8	**6.4**	8.4	15.3
COMMERCIAL BANK	Saint Louis	MO	**C-**	C-	D+	179.9	7.18	16.3	2.6	13.1	36.3	**5.9**	7.9	12.9
▼ COMMERCIAL BANK	Parsons	KS	**B**	A-	A	319.5	35.09	8.2	4.8	10.2	58.5	**6.9**	8.9	22.5
COMMERCIAL BANK	Mason	TX	**B-**	B-	C+	37.6	12.00	6.6	2.3	23.2	32.1	**7.7**	9.5	16.5
COMMERCIAL BANK & TRUST CO	Paris	TN	**B**	B	B	646.2	-1.30	11.4	3.6	18.4	22.5	**9.8**	10.9	16.3
COMMERCIAL BANK & TRUST CO	Monticello	AR	**B**	B	B-	185.1	1.54	11.4	8.2	14.2	33.4	**8.1**	9.7	15.8
COMMERCIAL BANK & TRUST OF PA	Latrobe	PA	**A**	A	A+	396.0	6.13	3.7	0.3	15.0	47.2	**10.0**	13.2	23.4
COMMERCIAL BANK OF CALIFORNIA	Irvine	CA	**C-**	C-	C	267.6	44.68	20.7	1.3	0.0	13.6	**10.0**	13.2	18.6
COMMERCIAL BANK OF GRAYSON	Grayson	KY	**B-**	B-	B+	163.9	-0.48	3.0	8.8	17.3	51.0	**10.0**	15.9	30.5
COMMERCIAL BANK OF MOTT	Mott	ND	**A-**	B+	B-	99.0	8.41	5.4	1.9	3.4	16.4	**9.4**	11.1	14.5
COMMERCIAL BANK OF NELSON	Nelson	NE	**B**	B	B+	39.0	3.72	15.2	1.6	0.3	46.6	**10.0**	13.9	18.5
COMMERCIAL BANK OF OAK GROVE	Oak Grove	MO	**B**	B-	C+	73.5	-4.42	0.8	0.9	24.9	27.7	**10.0**	14.4	32.5
COMMERCIAL BANK OF OZARK	Ozark	AL	**C-**	C	C-	81.2	2.94	3.1	7.2	18.5	38.4	**6.4**	8.4	18.0
▲ COMMERCIAL BANK OF TEXAS NA	Nacogdoches	TX	**B+**	B	B	538.4	6.45	5.5	6.5	14.4	35.9	**7.1**	9.0	16.7
▲ COMMERCIAL BANKING CO	Valdosta	GA	**B**	B	B-	217.8	-1.44	5.2	2.1	29.8	15.8	**10.0**	12.9	19.9
COMMERCIAL CAPITAL BANK	Delhi	LA	**A-**	A-	A-	80.6	20.51	8.3	2.3	8.3	8.5	**10.0**	12.6	19.2
COMMERCIAL NATIONAL BK BRADY	Brady	TX	**A+**	A+	A+	144.5	8.59	4.0	3.3	16.9	43.4	**10.0**	12.2	23.6
COMMERCIAL NB OF TEXARKANA	Texarkana	TX	**C+**	C+	C+	184.3	-2.90	11.4	3.7	15.9	38.3	**7.2**	9.1	16.9
COMMERCIAL SB	Carroll	IA	**B**	B	B	147.3	6.34	10.8	2.0	20.0	21.1	**4.6**	7.7	10.8
▲ COMMERCIAL SB	Upper Sandusky	OH	**C+**	C-	C-	324.9	5.46	8.2	4.3	17.5	3.8	**7.5**	10.1	12.9
COMMERCIAL STATE BANK	Humble	TX	**B**	C+	B-	289.4	0.24	15.4	1.4	10.2	13.9	**9.8**	10.8	16.3
COMMERCIAL STATE BK	Palmer	TX	**C+**	C+	C+	71.2	7.76	12.4	3.8	8.5	28.2	**6.6**	8.6	16.6
COMMERCIAL STATE BK	Andrews	TX	**C+**	B-	B-	541.4	12.09	28.3	1.3	3.0	7.4	**6.9**	8.9	13.9
COMMERCIAL STATE BK	Wausa	NE	**B**	B	B	83.7	7.48	18.8	5.3	4.1	8.5	**8.0**	10.9	13.3
COMMERCIAL STATE BK	Republican City	NE	**A**	A	A	63.6	5.33	1.3	0.4	0.0	69.7	**10.0**	24.0	38.9
COMMERCIAL STATE BK	Donalsonville	GA	**B-**	B-	B-	100.1	-4.11	13.4	4.9	6.2	28.3	**10.0**	13.3	22.2

Asset Quality Index	Adjusted Non-Performing Loans as a % of Total Loans	Adjusted Non-Performing Loans as a % of Capital	Net Charge-Offs Avg Loans	Profitability Index	Net Income ($Mil)	Return on Assets (R.O.A.)	Return on Equity (R.O.E.)	Net Interest Spread	Overhead Efficiency Ratio	Liquidity Index	Liquidity Ratio	Hot Money Ratio	Stability Index
4.8	0.88	5.5	0.28	**6.4**	63.3	1.17	8.17	4.92	66.8	**5.4**	23.4	3.1	**8.4**
4.1	1.13	7.8	0.12	**4.6**	0.9	1.02	9.14	3.56	64.8	**4.1**	13.5	7.7	**6.0**
4.5	1.53	8.7	0.03	**5.1**	0.9	0.94	8.23	4.16	64.1	**1.2**	13.6	29.2	**5.3**
5.8	0.43	3.4	0.12	**4.6**	1.7	0.84	9.21	3.43	65.4	**1.2**	18.5	29.8	**5.6**
1.7	7.65	40.8	0.27	**1.2**	0.0	0.08	1.19	3.79	99.8	**4.2**	36.2	12.7	**1.8**
9.8	0.85	0.7	0.00	**3.3**	0.4	0.62	4.56	2.58	73.5	**5.1**	101.2	18.6	**6.7**
8.5	0.37	1.0	-0.01	**4.9**	2.4	1.03	8.47	3.70	68.3	**2.0**	38.1	33.5	**8.0**
1.5	3.34	15.3	4.39	**10.0**	301.4	5.46	36.13	24.95	49.1	**0.3**	6.6	78.5	**9.3**
2.0	2.41	12.2	4.48	**10.0**	76.9	5.47	40.74	18.68	31.3	**0.3**	9.1	91.8	**9.3**
6.0	0.76	4.8	0.07	**5.0**	471.2	0.96	8.66	2.75	62.8	**5.1**	23.4	5.3	**9.0**
10.0	na	0.0	na	**9.5**	11.0	33.90	36.09	0.30	55.3	**10.0**	2792.3	0.0	**6.3**
7.2	0.11	0.7	-0.23	**3.6**	0.7	0.56	4.26	3.89	79.1	**1.1**	17.7	30.9	**5.9**
7.4	0.58	2.6	0.49	**7.8**	1.2	1.76	13.77	4.22	59.1	**3.9**	39.8	15.4	**8.7**
6.6	0.70	4.0	0.30	**6.7**	188.4	1.12	12.49	3.07	61.1	**5.2**	27.1	6.7	**8.4**
3.4	3.55	16.8	0.31	**5.9**	1.9	1.53	9.97	4.08	70.5	**0.8**	17.7	46.9	**5.8**
6.7	3.95	7.0	0.20	**7.6**	5.5	1.32	9.80	2.75	38.9	**2.8**	51.4	31.8	**8.4**
5.6	0.93	7.0	0.03	**4.4**	10.4	0.74	8.93	2.74	59.1	**5.2**	32.8	9.5	**6.7**
0.0	11.32	126.7	2.42	**0.0**	-3.0	-2.14	-41.01	3.91	128.1	**2.9**	19.6	15.2	**1.4**
6.1	0.95	3.8	0.36	**0.7**	-0.1	-0.22	-1.25	3.75	112.1	**5.5**	42.7	7.2	**7.0**
5.5	0.86	5.1	-0.11	**5.8**	5.9	0.89	8.31	3.47	56.8	**5.2**	24.1	1.8	**7.1**
7.0	0.01	0.1	0.00	**4.7**	0.3	0.79	5.33	4.75	71.1	**3.6**	19.1	11.2	**6.5**
5.1	1.13	5.3	-0.02	**2.2**	0.2	0.42	2.86	4.44	87.5	**3.3**	26.0	14.1	**4.3**
7.5	0.27	1.3	0.07	**4.1**	0.3	0.67	7.06	3.88	75.3	**2.1**	34.3	28.2	**4.5**
1.5	3.01	16.9	-0.10	**3.3**	0.5	0.81	7.92	3.69	92.0	**1.6**	21.7	25.3	**4.7**
3.2	1.52	11.8	0.17	**3.4**	1.3	0.53	5.38	3.80	71.6	**0.6**	10.9	51.1	**4.4**
7.1	0.74	4.6	0.00	**5.5**	2.0	0.99	7.63	4.24	61.1	**1.3**	7.0	24.9	**7.6**
7.2	0.00	0.0	0.02	**5.5**	3.9	1.39	9.62	4.36	66.9	**2.7**	17.3	15.9	**6.9**
4.0	1.86	13.7	0.12	**5.4**	4.6	1.02	11.37	3.63	61.4	**4.0**	15.4	8.8	**6.3**
6.8	1.15	3.8	0.04	**8.6**	2.9	2.74	21.67	3.59	51.3	**3.2**	41.5	19.3	**8.0**
9.3	0.52	1.4	0.36	**5.5**	1.5	1.30	9.39	3.54	62.8	**4.9**	65.5	16.1	**8.4**
2.4	2.67	17.6	0.13	**4.4**	5.0	0.86	8.29	3.82	68.1	**0.8**	10.7	34.4	**5.6**
6.0	0.40	2.1	0.54	**3.3**	0.6	0.60	6.02	4.15	79.4	**3.5**	26.8	13.4	**3.9**
4.7	2.41	13.3	0.06	**7.4**	1.7	2.13	20.47	4.69	54.5	**3.0**	3.8	13.0	**4.8**
7.7	0.92	2.9	0.00	**1.4**	0.0	0.05	0.55	2.44	97.3	**4.7**	66.5	16.2	**5.5**
4.5	1.81	14.5	0.40	**3.8**	2.0	0.71	8.53	3.26	67.7	**1.2**	21.0	30.8	**4.1**
5.0	0.91	6.0	0.67	**2.4**	0.4	0.28	3.42	3.64	89.9	**3.6**	33.9	14.8	**3.0**
8.4	0.58	1.9	0.06	**4.0**	1.9	0.93	8.86	2.97	75.9	**4.5**	52.1	15.4	**6.5**
9.2	0.00	0.0	0.02	**4.9**	0.3	1.05	10.62	4.16	67.4	**3.8**	38.6	15.6	**4.9**
4.8	1.06	6.2	0.14	**6.5**	7.7	1.55	14.12	3.96	63.7	**3.9**	22.1	10.3	**7.7**
4.4	1.61	9.2	0.32	**6.3**	2.1	1.47	17.99	4.15	62.9	**1.5**	18.3	26.2	**6.7**
9.5	0.14	0.5	0.00	**6.6**	4.8	1.63	12.34	5.14	68.0	**5.6**	52.7	10.0	**9.2**
4.8	3.20	12.0	0.42	**1.5**	0.3	0.14	0.97	3.41	92.9	**4.0**	49.0	17.5	**5.3**
8.7	0.72	1.8	0.01	**3.2**	0.6	0.46	2.91	3.88	86.9	**6.6**	55.7	4.7	**7.5**
7.0	0.18	1.2	0.01	**8.9**	1.5	2.13	19.28	4.13	46.6	**2.2**	12.1	17.6	**7.0**
8.7	0.00	0.0	0.00	**4.2**	0.3	0.85	6.33	3.89	75.4	**3.9**	13.0	8.8	**7.0**
3.7	7.53	21.4	0.03	**1.5**	0.1	0.18	1.23	2.55	91.2	**5.7**	52.0	7.9	**5.6**
4.8	2.55	12.3	0.12	**2.4**	0.1	0.24	2.86	3.84	93.6	**4.7**	39.3	11.1	**3.4**
8.3	0.10	0.6	0.04	**5.4**	4.3	1.08	11.40	3.33	65.9	**3.7**	24.0	11.3	**6.9**
5.0	2.25	11.2	0.03	**4.1**	1.1	0.66	5.10	3.60	74.4	**1.0**	23.9	34.5	**6.9**
7.9	0.37	1.9	0.09	**9.7**	1.3	2.41	19.54	4.82	55.9	**1.5**	24.6	28.0	**7.9**
9.0	0.20	0.8	-0.01	**6.4**	1.5	1.42	11.55	4.19	66.9	**4.6**	33.4	9.5	**9.5**
6.8	0.47	2.7	0.03	**6.3**	2.2	1.56	18.51	3.89	67.4	**3.4**	28.1	13.9	**3.7**
6.6	0.33	2.5	-0.03	**4.4**	1.2	1.08	14.19	3.00	61.2	**5.4**	35.9	5.8	**5.0**
3.3	1.88	14.2	0.13	**6.1**	2.6	1.06	10.67	4.60	66.2	**2.2**	6.4	17.2	**5.7**
8.4	0.00	0.0	0.06	**4.7**	1.8	0.83	7.53	4.63	69.5	**3.9**	22.8	10.5	**4.8**
6.2	0.84	4.7	0.04	**6.5**	0.5	0.99	12.17	4.50	64.4	**1.7**	22.3	23.6	**5.3**
3.1	2.44	16.0	0.21	**8.1**	6.8	1.72	19.17	4.85	56.1	**1.7**	28.6	28.2	**6.5**
6.9	0.06	0.4	0.02	**5.2**	0.7	1.10	10.06	4.58	73.1	**2.2**	9.9	17.7	**6.9**
9.5	0.00	0.0	-0.04	**9.5**	0.9	1.89	8.11	4.28	32.1	**4.0**	85.4	26.0	**9.0**
4.7	3.12	10.4	0.22	**3.6**	0.5	0.63	4.60	3.76	79.9	**2.3**	28.0	19.4	**6.4**

Name	City	State	Rating	2013 Rating	2012 Rating	Total Assets ($Mil)	One Year Asset Growth	Asset Mix (As a % of Total Assets) Comm-ercial Loans	Cons-umer Loans	Mort-gage Loans	Secur-ities	Capital-ization Index	Lever-age Ratio	Risk-Based Capital Ratio
COMMERCIAL STATE BK	Cedar Bluffs	NE	**E-**	E-	E-	24.2	3.74	3.5	1.9	1.3	35.6	**4.9**	6.9	11.7
▼ COMMERCIAL STATE BK OF WAGNER	Wagner	SD	**A-**	A	A-	142.2	6.45	5.9	4.0	5.6	32.5	**9.6**	10.7	17.1
COMMERCIAL TRUST CO OF FAYETTE	Fayette	MO	**C+**	C+	C+	131.4	-0.87	1.4	3.5	34.2	11.9	**7.1**	9.1	22.4
COMMODORE BANK	Somerset	OH	**C-**	C-	C-	83.4	-4.11	7.9	4.4	29.8	36.2	**6.3**	8.3	16.6
▲ COMMONWEALTH BANK & TRUST CO	Louisville	KY	**C**	D	C-	801.7	8.33	7.5	1.8	14.1	26.5	**7.7**	9.4	14.3
COMMONWEALTH BANK FSB	Mount Sterling	KY	**D-**	D+	C-	19.3	0.10	0.0	5.1	74.7	0.0	**6.9**	8.9	14.4
▼ COMMONWEALTH BUSINESS BANK	Los Angeles	CA	**C+**	C	C	628.4	22.68	15.3	0.4	0.5	1.2	**9.8**	11.8	14.8
COMMONWEALTH CO-OPERATIVE BAN	Hyde Park	MA	**B**	B+	B	173.3	-1.17	1.6	0.8	57.0	18.1	**10.0**	13.0	26.3
COMMONWEALTH COMMUNITY BANK	Hartford	KY	**A-**	A-	A-	150.8	-1.02	0.4	2.6	21.8	60.7	**10.0**	13.5	30.9
▼ COMMONWEALTH NATIONAL BK	Mobile	AL	**E**	D-	D-	58.7	-1.22	9.2	2.3	8.0	36.6	**5.8**	7.8	16.2
COMMUNITY & SOUTHERN BANK	Atlanta	GA	**C**	B-	B-	3355.7	25.66	10.7	14.4	5.6	15.7	**9.6**	10.7	15.1
COMMUNITY 1ST BANK	Post Falls	ID	**C+**	C	C-	94.0	13.86	16.7	1.4	4.5	10.9	**10.0**	11.5	15.3
COMMUNITY 1ST BANK	Auburn	CA	**D+**	D+	D	223.2	-7.79	5.7	0.5	6.7	29.3	**8.5**	10.0	15.0
COMMUNITY 1ST BANK LAS VEGAS	Las Vegas	NM	**D-**	D-	D+	134.3	-14.22	8.2	2.1	19.0	21.7	**6.5**	8.5	13.8
COMMUNITY BANK	Alva	OK	**B**	B	B	98.9	12.10	11.3	3.2	5.3	57.9	**6.6**	8.6	12.9
COMMUNITY BANK	Bristow	OK	**B+**	B+	B	83.6	4.40	2.8	4.3	21.4	23.5	**6.0**	8.0	15.5
▼ COMMUNITY BANK	Santa Fe	NM	**C-**	D+	C-	177.6	-0.37	4.0	0.5	18.3	16.0	**9.8**	10.9	18.3
COMMUNITY BANK	Longview	TX	**A-**	A-	B+	221.3	1.13	15.5	3.5	31.7	5.9	**5.9**	8.7	11.7
▼ COMMUNITY BANK	Fort Worth	TX	**B**	B+	B+	639.8	13.81	7.2	1.6	9.8	30.4	**7.3**	9.2	21.4
COMMUNITY BANK	Bridgeport	TX	**C**	C	C-	67.1	8.05	14.9	2.0	9.9	18.3	**6.5**	8.5	16.0
COMMUNITY BANK	Ellisville	MS	**B**	B-	C+	676.4	3.44	4.9	4.9	22.7	13.2	**7.3**	9.2	15.8
▲ COMMUNITY BANK	Raceland	LA	**B**	B-	B-	389.0	-6.74	29.8	1.4	11.4	15.1	**10.0**	12.7	17.8
COMMUNITY BANK	Nevada	IA	**B+**	B+	B	171.9	-0.98	5.8	0.6	4.5	1.9	**7.9**	10.8	13.3
▲ COMMUNITY BANK	Noblesville	IN	**C+**	C-	C-	260.1	0.17	3.2	0.6	12.0	29.8	**10.0**	14.8	23.2
COMMUNITY BANK	Alton	IA	**C**	C+	C	41.2	-2.65	17.3	4.7	7.7	24.4	**7.6**	9.4	14.4
COMMUNITY BANK	Winslow	IL	**A-**	A-	B+	176.8	8.72	5.2	1.6	20.6	40.0	**10.0**	13.2	23.7
COMMUNITY BANK	Hoopeston	IL	**C**	C+	B-	81.1	-7.38	15.6	2.5	11.5	34.1	**6.5**	8.5	20.6
COMMUNITY BANK	Carmichaels	PA	**B-**	B-	C+	555.7	1.19	7.8	12.7	27.5	18.8	**5.6**	7.6	12.3
COMMUNITY BANK	Zanesville	OH	**C+**	C+	C+	373.6	8.63	6.2	3.5	30.7	23.8	**6.2**	8.2	15.1
COMMUNITY BANK	Lexington	TN	**B-**	B-	B-	118.8	11.71	5.2	4.8	30.4	18.1	**7.2**	9.1	14.4
COMMUNITY BANK	Dunlap	IA	**C**	B-	B-	99.7	3.51	2.7	2.6	11.5	37.9	**8.1**	9.8	16.2
COMMUNITY BANK	Indianola	IA	**C+**	C+	C+	156.4	3.26	7.7	1.0	10.3	31.9	**7.5**	9.4	20.5
COMMUNITY BANK	Topeka	KS	**B-**	B	C+	85.1	4.60	14.7	1.3	21.3	8.6	**5.3**	8.9	11.2
▲ COMMUNITY BANK	Alma	NE	**C+**	B-	B-	49.1	-4.50	8.6	3.5	4.9	29.5	**10.0**	11.2	15.9
COMMUNITY BANK	Liberal	KS	**B-**	B	C	97.4	1.12	13.0	9.7	1.5	32.0	**9.8**	10.8	16.0
COMMUNITY BANK	Avon	SD	**B**	B	B	51.6	0.39	5.0	4.3	4.7	58.2	**10.0**	15.3	33.5
COMMUNITY BANK	Joseph	OR	**C+**	C	C-	348.8	-1.22	6.1	0.6	4.1	27.1	**8.0**	9.7	15.5
COMMUNITY BANK	Pasadena	CA	**B-**	B-	C	3502.0	8.22	14.5	0.3	0.7	33.0	**6.1**	8.1	11.9
COMMUNITY BANK & TRUST	Neosho	MO	**B-**	B	B+	297.0	2.72	2.3	2.2	25.3	23.8	**5.9**	7.9	14.4
▲ COMMUNITY BANK & TRUST	Muscatine	IA	**C+**	C	C-	253.6	1.55	12.2	5.4	15.1	25.1	**6.9**	9.0	14.8
COMMUNITY BANK & TRUST	Sheboygan	WI	**B-**	C+	C-	525.5	-0.80	17.1	1.2	10.0	11.1	**6.7**	9.5	12.2
▲ COMMUNITY BANK & TRUST	Ashland City	TN	**D+**	D+	D	197.3	0.66	3.5	1.5	13.1	48.8	**8.8**	10.2	22.2
COMMUNITY BANK & TRUST	Waco	TX	**B+**	A-	B+	387.9	-2.25	28.8	3.4	23.7	26.1	**10.0**	13.0	20.7
COMMUNITY BANK & TRUST - WEST	LaGrange	GA	**E-**	E-	E-	88.7	-1.23	5.4	2.1	22.9	12.6	**0.8**	4.6	7.6
COMMUNITY BANK & TRUST OF FL	Ocala	FL	**B**	B-	B-	598.5	-1.36	4.7	1.5	6.9	47.8	**7.6**	9.4	19.5
▲ COMMUNITY BANK CBD	Delavan	WI	**B**	C+	C	208.0	-1.49	7.3	0.3	21.7	14.9	**10.0**	12.8	19.2
COMMUNITY BANK CHESAPEAKE	Waldorf	MD	**B-**	C	C-	1040.9	4.99	8.6	0.1	15.2	11.6	**10.0**	12.2	15.4
COMMUNITY BANK COAST	Biloxi	MS	**C+**	C+	C	678.0	12.33	3.9	3.4	22.1	9.3	**7.2**	9.1	13.4
COMMUNITY BANK CORP	Chaska	MN	**A-**	B+	B-	182.7	22.78	12.5	0.5	4.7	21.9	**10.0**	12.2	17.4
COMMUNITY BANK DELAWARE	Lewes	DE	**B**	B	B	154.9	8.49	3.6	0.5	25.0	9.0	**10.0**	14.2	18.6
COMMUNITY BANK INC	Ronan	MT	**B-**	B-	C	179.7	-1.71	8.4	1.9	7.4	33.1	**10.0**	11.2	19.8
▼ COMMUNITY BANK MANKATO	Vernon Center	MN	**C-**	C+	C+	212.7	2.25	8.7	2.0	18.9	3.7	**4.1**	8.0	10.5
COMMUNITY BANK NA	Summersville	MO	**B**	B	B-	50.6	-0.46	3.6	4.6	8.8	1.4	**6.8**	8.8	15.1
COMMUNITY BANK NA	De Witt	NY	**B+**	B-	B	7474.1	2.74	5.2	13.8	23.2	33.0	**6.1**	8.1	15.3
COMMUNITY BANK OF BROWARD	Dania Beach	FL	**D-**	D-	D-	499.7	3.38	3.4	0.3	6.0	5.1	**7.2**	9.2	12.7
COMMUNITY BANK OF CAMERON	Cameron	WI	**B**	B	C+	100.6	-1.54	4.5	2.4	42.9	6.2	**7.2**	9.1	15.4
COMMUNITY BANK OF EASTON	Easton	IL	**A-**	A-	A-	31.2	7.08	9.7	7.2	6.2	1.6	**10.0**	15.1	29.2
COMMUNITY BANK OF ELMHURST	Elmhurst	IL	**D**	D	D+	158.2	0.38	6.2	0.2	8.4	47.1	**5.3**	7.3	13.7
COMMUNITY BANK OF FLORIDA INC	Homestead	FL	**D+**	D	E-	474.7	-4.14	3.9	1.5	10.1	14.4	**5.9**	7.9	11.9
COMMUNITY BANK OF GEORGIA	Baxley	GA	**C-**	C-	C-	71.5	1.78	8.2	3.0	9.6	24.0	**10.0**	11.9	19.8

Asset Quality Index	Adjusted Non-Performing Loans as a % of Total Loans	Adjusted Non-Performing Loans as a % of Capital	Net Charge-Offs Avg Loans	Profitability Index	Net Income ($Mil)	Return on Assets (R.O.A.)	Return on Equity (R.O.E.)	Net Interest Spread	Overhead Efficiency Ratio	Liquidity Index	Liquidity Ratio	Hot Money Ratio	Stability Index
5.8	1.82	12.2	0.17	1.8	0.0	0.18	2.79	2.16	90.9	1.9	37.5	26.8	0.3
5.8	0.72	3.8	0.09	10.0	2.8	2.70	23.55	5.12	41.4	1.6	8.3	20.5	7.9
9.1	0.22	1.2	-0.01	3.8	0.9	0.91	10.50	2.47	66.5	5.0	44.5	11.3	5.3
3.2	3.33	19.5	0.23	2.2	0.2	0.33	4.13	3.93	94.7	4.6	37.8	11.3	4.2
4.0	1.52	9.4	0.16	3.0	4.4	0.76	8.73	3.49	85.4	2.3	12.1	17.0	4.0
4.5	1.82	15.5	0.02	0.0	-0.2	-1.05	-11.27	4.40	126.4	1.4	9.0	23.4	3.1
3.1	0.93	6.1	-0.30	10.0	8.8	1.97	17.12	3.83	45.6	0.7	13.7	39.1	7.0
6.5	2.16	11.4	0.00	3.6	0.9	0.67	5.15	3.45	73.8	1.3	24.7	30.4	7.3
9.8	0.65	1.4	0.09	5.8	1.6	1.39	10.50	3.98	62.7	4.0	68.7	24.0	8.1
1.9	6.61	30.4	0.13	0.3	-0.3	-0.70	-9.18	4.59	105.3	1.7	15.9	21.9	2.4
5.9	0.87	5.4	0.29	2.6	5.1	0.22	1.85	5.19	89.6	1.3	14.3	27.9	4.8
8.7	0.00	0.0	0.03	3.2	0.5	0.74	6.49	3.59	84.8	2.5	43.3	29.5	6.5
2.6	3.09	16.8	0.52	1.9	0.4	0.26	2.65	3.14	88.7	2.6	17.0	16.4	3.9
0.3	17.04	93.9	0.68	0.4	-0.9	-0.79	-9.17	4.29	106.6	3.8	29.1	12.4	3.0
8.9	0.00	0.0	-0.31	5.8	1.1	1.50	16.80	3.22	55.8	2.8	61.3	33.0	6.1
8.9	0.08	0.5	-0.01	8.0	0.8	1.32	17.33	4.12	61.5	4.7	48.7	12.9	5.7
1.3	5.22	26.0	-0.02	2.9	0.6	0.44	3.35	3.80	83.9	3.9	26.7	11.0	6.2
8.6	0.00	0.0	0.00	9.4	3.6	2.13	25.17	3.62	47.1	2.9	25.6	15.7	6.3
4.9	0.95	4.9	0.02	3.3	0.7	0.63	6.48	3.25	77.6	6.4	49.5	4.1	6.0
8.8	0.00	0.0	0.01	2.3	0.1	0.30	3.32	3.07	90.2	3.7	50.5	18.3	4.2
4.9	0.86	6.4	0.20	7.3	5.9	1.21	13.08	4.07	56.0	1.8	15.7	20.2	6.5
5.5	1.83	9.4	-0.06	4.3	2.2	0.73	6.29	3.83	69.2	4.2	24.7	8.6	5.8
5.9	0.03	0.3	0.02	8.9	1.8	1.38	13.56	3.62	40.0	0.5	4.1	40.1	7.5
2.2	7.06	25.3	-0.36	5.2	2.6	1.28	9.45	3.77	68.0	4.4	7.1	5.0	6.7
7.4	0.39	2.3	-0.02	3.3	0.2	0.61	6.14	3.74	86.4	5.6	41.3	6.4	4.8
6.2	2.17	8.8	0.00	6.1	2.0	1.56	11.60	3.38	53.3	3.4	35.6	16.7	7.3
6.0	3.34	13.4	0.01	3.0	0.3	0.54	6.39	2.14	77.3	5.5	39.4	6.3	4.3
4.6	0.62	5.3	0.02	4.1	3.3	0.81	10.09	3.36	71.2	4.1	11.0	7.5	5.4
5.1	0.79	5.8	0.55	3.8	1.8	0.64	8.34	4.06	71.9	2.4	5.2	15.9	4.0
4.2	1.57	11.7	0.52	6.3	1.0	1.22	12.66	4.72	63.3	1.3	22.9	30.3	5.0
4.2	1.49	7.7	0.89	3.0	0.3	0.40	4.18	3.53	75.1	2.9	13.3	14.1	6.7
9.0	0.09	0.4	0.28	3.3	0.7	0.58	6.41	3.01	79.0	2.4	35.9	25.0	5.4
8.1	0.08	0.6	0.00	4.6	0.5	0.82	8.26	3.96	72.6	3.5	21.8	11.9	4.9
7.8	0.31	1.4	-0.02	5.5	0.5	1.38	12.81	3.60	65.0	4.0	33.5	12.9	5.0
4.7	1.34	6.9	0.00	3.6	0.5	0.68	6.27	3.58	84.1	1.8	26.0	23.4	6.8
8.9	0.02	0.1	0.37	4.1	0.3	0.88	5.54	3.67	72.8	4.1	65.9	19.0	7.2
3.4	2.64	15.7	0.01	3.7	1.9	0.74	7.54	4.39	83.8	5.3	34.1	5.4	5.7
4.5	1.15	8.0	-0.03	4.6	18.8	0.73	9.19	3.19	64.7	1.8	23.2	28.2	6.8
8.6	0.26	1.6	0.20	4.5	2.3	1.02	11.61	3.30	77.6	5.4	35.8	5.5	6.1
3.6	1.54	9.7	0.26	3.6	1.4	0.75	7.08	3.41	72.6	3.2	30.8	16.1	5.9
3.9	1.97	13.6	0.78	6.2	5.1	1.29	12.36	3.93	56.2	3.4	12.0	11.5	5.8
5.2	2.86	9.9	-0.70	1.4	-0.1	-0.05	-0.50	3.37	94.9	3.2	41.6	19.4	4.3
6.8	1.14	5.6	0.24	4.8	2.6	0.86	6.92	3.90	66.0	2.1	31.8	25.0	6.5
2.5	2.03	23.0	0.02	0.0	-1.1	-1.66	-39.16	3.71	152.2	2.5	17.6	16.8	0.2
5.9	1.38	5.5	-0.03	5.0	4.7	1.02	9.98	3.32	70.4	4.8	54.6	14.8	5.6
5.9	1.76	8.7	0.06	4.3	1.2	0.77	5.95	4.35	69.3	3.6	18.5	11.2	5.7
3.9	1.48	9.2	0.16	4.6	5.7	0.75	6.18	3.70	64.0	0.9	13.1	33.2	7.9
3.7	1.50	11.6	0.22	4.4	3.6	0.73	6.45	4.14	72.0	1.1	15.2	30.1	6.3
5.9	1.07	5.3	0.03	4.3	1.1	0.91	7.14	3.94	77.1	2.4	13.5	17.0	6.6
5.2	1.01	5.7	0.05	4.7	0.8	0.75	5.29	3.87	67.4	1.1	12.0	29.3	6.8
4.3	4.09	17.3	0.13	3.1	0.7	0.51	4.58	3.93	88.4	4.2	27.5	9.7	4.8
1.7	2.11	21.7	0.66	5.1	2.0	1.27	16.03	4.42	58.3	2.6	5.7	15.2	4.1
7.0	0.53	3.2	-0.05	5.7	0.5	1.33	13.43	4.90	83.3	3.2	40.1	18.8	5.8
5.5	0.59	4.1	0.16	5.7	64.8	1.18	9.47	3.90	59.7	5.4	23.2	2.9	9.5
0.5	3.94	32.8	0.02	4.6	2.7	0.74	8.26	4.03	71.8	2.6	12.1	15.9	4.4
5.2	1.14	8.8	0.05	6.2	1.1	1.50	16.71	3.97	60.9	1.8	16.4	20.8	6.4
8.1	0.00	0.0	0.00	8.7	0.4	1.49	10.06	3.08	25.8	4.7	49.8	13.4	8.0
8.0	0.96	5.3	0.03	1.1	0.1	0.07	0.87	2.89	93.9	5.6	53.0	10.2	2.2
1.7	4.68	36.0	0.12	2.6	1.7	0.48	5.28	3.98	85.6	1.5	19.4	25.6	3.6
1.3	9.59	40.9	0.02	5.0	0.5	0.88	8.29	3.95	63.8	1.8	34.2	32.7	5.7

Name	City	State	Rating	2013 Rating	2012 Rating	Total Assets ($Mil)	One Year Asset Growth	Asset Mix (As a % of Total Assets) Comm-ercial Loans	Cons-umer Loans	Mort-gage Loans	Secur-ities	Capital-ization Index	Lever-age Ratio	Risk-Based Capital Ratio
COMMUNITY BANK OF LOUISIANA	Mansfield	LA	B+	B+	B+	357.4	11.96	5.5	2.9	9.7	52.9	6.6	8.6	19.2
COMMUNITY BANK OF MARSHALL	Marshall	MO	B-	B-	B	136.3	4.43	4.6	3.1	13.9	41.8	9.2	10.5	18.4
COMMUNITY BANK OF MEMPHIS	Memphis	MO	C+	C+	B-	41.9	3.52	1.9	3.5	20.8	28.8	7.7	9.5	18.4
COMMUNITY BANK OF MISSISSIPPI	Forest	MS	B	B	B-	688.7	1.56	7.3	3.1	15.3	14.9	6.8	8.8	14.5
COMMUNITY BANK OF MISSOURI	Richmond	MO	B-	B-	C+	50.2	3.56	8.5	0.9	23.5	9.2	10.0	12.1	17.0
COMMUNITY BANK OF NORTHERN WI	Rice Lake	WI	B-	B-	C+	151.0	-3.05	4.4	1.1	17.1	22.7	8.7	10.1	15.8
▲ COMMUNITY BANK OF OELWEIN	Oelwein	IA	B	B-	C+	100.6	3.88	3.3	3.1	7.2	61.1	7.3	9.2	22.8
COMMUNITY BANK OF OKLAHOMA	Verden	OK	B-	B-	B	37.1	9.87	11.5	9.6	8.9	26.7	10.0	12.1	16.7
COMMUNITY BANK OF PARKERSBURG	Parkersburg	WV	B+	B+	B+	239.9	-2.83	3.4	6.7	48.8	22.2	9.8	10.9	19.3
COMMUNITY BANK OF RAYMORE	Raymore	MO	D	D+	C-	177.7	1.75	12.7	1.5	3.0	23.4	6.9	8.9	12.6
COMMUNITY BANK OF SANTA MARIA	Santa Maria	CA	C+	C+	C+	199.6	6.37	14.6	0.8	1.7	31.9	8.9	10.3	14.8
COMMUNITY BANK OF SNYDER	Snyder	TX	C+	C-	D+	132.2	1.36	9.5	2.0	6.5	43.5	6.6	8.6	17.7
COMMUNITY BANK OF THE BAY	Oakland	CA	B-	B-	C	192.0	10.78	30.7	1.1	5.7	4.6	8.5	10.9	13.7
COMMUNITY BANK OF THE MIDWEST	Great Bend	KS	B-	B-	C+	165.0	12.04	14.2	3.1	8.4	11.1	5.5	7.5	12.3
COMMUNITY BANK OF THE SOUTH	Merritt Island	FL	C+	C+	B-	149.3	9.50	3.2	0.1	1.5	24.8	7.8	9.6	24.8
COMMUNITY BANK OF THE SOUTH	Smyrna	GA	E	E	E-	345.8	-1.50	7.7	0.7	10.2	7.2	6.2	8.3	11.9
▼ COMMUNITY BANK OF TRENTON	Trenton	IL	C+	B-	B	74.9	0.15	8.4	3.0	29.5	22.9	10.0	11.9	20.0
COMMUNITY BANK OF WICHITA INC	Wichita	KS	C+	C+	B-	75.3	11.42	25.3	6.2	15.2	15.4	6.9	8.9	12.4
COMMUNITY BANK OWATONNA	Owatonna	MN	C+	C+	C	53.4	0.08	11.6	1.1	11.0	32.2	8.7	10.1	15.7
COMMUNITY BANKERS BANK	Midlothian	VA	C	C	D	147.7	0.66	9.0	1.1	2.1	25.1	9.7	10.8	17.6
COMMUNITY BK & TRUST- ALABAMA	Union Springs	AL	E-	E	E+	63.7	-6.78	7.5	4.8	11.2	29.2	4.3	6.3	12.9
COMMUNITY BK EL DORADO SPRINGS	El Dorado Springs	MO	A	A	A-	103.3	4.02	2.2	2.8	8.2	47.1	10.0	14.3	26.6
COMMUNITY BK NORTH MISSISSIPPI	Amory	MS	B-	B-	C	471.4	-0.72	3.2	2.8	21.5	16.5	8.8	10.2	16.8
▲ COMMUNITY BK OF BERGEN COUNTY	Maywood	NJ	D+	D	D+	296.8	0.32	0.5	1.0	40.7	17.3	6.0	8.0	13.0
COMMUNITY BK OF PICKENS COUNTY	Jasper	GA	E	E-	E-	336.4	1.11	4.0	3.3	17.3	11.1	5.9	8.2	11.7
COMMUNITY BK OF PLEASANT HILL	Pleasant Hill	MO	D	D+	C-	52.7	0.14	6.9	0.8	1.5	38.3	6.2	8.2	14.2
COMMUNITY BK OF SHELBY COUNTY	Cowden	IL	C-	C	C+	49.6	5.84	9.4	4.4	11.0	20.5	9.2	10.5	21.3
▲ COMMUNITY BKG CO OF FITZGERALD	Fitzgerald	GA	B+	B	B-	123.1	0.81	9.8	6.2	22.9	14.0	10.0	11.1	17.7
COMMUNITY BUSINESS BANK	Cumming	GA	B	B	C+	146.1	10.83	6.5	0.3	15.6	10.6	10.0	13.1	20.0
▲ COMMUNITY BUSINESS BANK	West Sacramento	CA	A-	B	C+	191.1	18.42	12.1	0.1	6.4	20.6	10.0	12.8	17.3
COMMUNITY CAPITAL BANK OF VA	Christiansburg	VA	B-	B-	B-	88.3	36.84	12.6	0.0	2.8	1.7	10.0	13.9	24.3
COMMUNITY COMMERCE BANK	Claremont	CA	C	D+	C-	204.5	-12.70	0.0	0.0	4.9	0.4	10.0	22.5	29.2
COMMUNITY DEVELOPMENT BANK FS	Ogema	MN	C+	C	C-	70.9	-1.96	19.3	2.7	10.9	12.8	9.3	10.5	17.3
▼ COMMUNITY FINANCIAL BANK	Prentice	WI	D+	C-	C	27.6	2.71	3.4	2.2	20.4	2.0	10.0	15.4	25.2
COMMUNITY FINANCIAL SVCS BK	Benton	KY	B-	B-	B-	707.9	15.54	12.9	12.0	21.3	8.4	5.9	9.2	11.7
COMMUNITY FIRST BANK	Fairview Heights	IL	A-	A-	B	208.9	0.94	20.4	0.6	16.1	10.0	10.0	14.0	18.9
▲ COMMUNITY FIRST BANK	Harrison	AR	B-	C+	C	463.3	0.74	7.1	4.2	24.9	17.9	10.0	14.4	20.2
▼ COMMUNITY FIRST BANK	Rosholt	WI	B-	B	C+	68.9	2.23	3.8	2.3	14.3	26.9	9.2	10.5	15.6
COMMUNITY FIRST BANK	Boscobel	WI	B-	B-	C	233.3	5.17	5.5	1.7	22.9	28.7	8.5	10.0	18.6
COMMUNITY FIRST BANK	Keosauqua	IA	A-	A-	A	137.1	1.85	15.6	2.6	11.6	32.2	10.0	11.2	17.6
COMMUNITY FIRST BANK	Butler	MO	B-	B-	C+	157.2	4.38	10.5	2.9	22.3	11.2	6.2	8.2	13.0
COMMUNITY FIRST BANK	Kansas City	KS	C	C	D+	120.1	12.74	21.3	1.2	10.4	4.9	5.0	8.9	11.0
COMMUNITY FIRST BANK	Walhalla	SC	D-	D-	D-	341.8	-9.56	3.2	2.3	10.2	42.6	5.5	7.5	14.5
COMMUNITY FIRST BANK	Reynoldsville	PA	C	C+	C	108.7	8.88	9.3	3.6	38.4	5.3	6.9	8.9	12.8
COMMUNITY FIRST BANK	Somerset	NJ	C-	C-	D+	92.4	7.45	7.6	0.8	22.4	10.5	6.1	9.7	11.8
COMMUNITY FIRST BANK	New Iberia	LA	B+	B+	B+	313.6	10.23	12.6	5.7	22.7	16.6	7.2	9.1	13.9
COMMUNITY FIRST BANK	Kennewick	WA	B+	B+	A-	247.2	3.31	8.4	1.0	5.9	27.4	6.8	8.8	15.8
COMMUNITY FIRST BANK & TRUST	Columbia	TN	D+	D-	E	435.5	-2.96	3.5	1.3	19.6	20.1	7.1	9.1	15.8
▼ COMMUNITY FIRST BANK NA	Forest	OH	C-	C	C	52.2	-6.58	4.2	1.8	34.6	17.9	7.8	9.5	18.5
COMMUNITY FIRST BANKING CO	West Plains	MO	A-	A-	B-	148.9	4.84	8.9	3.4	26.0	15.2	10.0	13.1	18.8
COMMUNITY FIRST BK HEARTLAND	Mount Vernon	IL	B+	B+	A-	170.5	4.33	15.4	1.1	17.6	10.1	6.1	8.1	12.2
COMMUNITY FIRST BK OF INDIANA	Kokomo	IN	B-	C+	C-	188.9	2.37	20.1	0.7	8.6	6.6	8.2	10.6	13.5
COMMUNITY FIRST NATIONAL BK	Manhattan	KS	B	B	B-	178.1	5.94	15.0	2.3	23.4	0.1	8.2	10.0	13.5
COMMUNITY FSB	New York	NY	D	D+	C	123.1	29.76	0.6	0.0	7.4	6.5	10.0	13.7	26.5
COMMUNITY GUARANTY SB	Plymouth	NH	C-	C-	C	109.3	0.02	3.0	1.5	36.5	29.4	6.3	8.4	12.0
COMMUNITY NATIONAL BK	Newport	VT	B-	B-	C+	571.7	1.44	10.9	1.4	30.8	13.5	6.5	8.5	13.3
COMMUNITY NATIONAL BK	Melville	NY	C+	C+	C+	945.0	18.52	17.8	0.1	22.9	10.8	6.4	8.4	12.4
COMMUNITY NATIONAL BK	Dayton	TN	C+	C+	D	208.4	3.52	6.9	2.0	13.1	26.2	10.0	11.4	20.4
COMMUNITY NATIONAL BK	Seneca	KS	A-	B+	B	343.4	14.33	4.0	0.6	6.5	51.0	7.3	9.2	19.5
COMMUNITY NATIONAL BK	Monett	MO	B+	B+	B	91.6	7.21	5.7	2.9	18.2	5.8	9.2	10.5	17.2

Asset Quality Index	Adjusted Non-Performing Loans as a % of Total Loans	Adjusted Non-Performing Loans as a % of Capital	Net Charge-Offs Avg Loans	Profitability Index	Net Income ($Mil)	Return on Assets (R.O.A.)	Return on Equity (R.O.E.)	Net Interest Spread	Overhead Efficiency Ratio	Liquidity Index	Liquidity Ratio	Hot Money Ratio	Stability Index
6.1	1.59	7.5	0.13	**6.1**	3.8	1.43	16.24	3.49	63.0	**2.0**	24.0	19.8	**6.2**
7.0	0.83	3.5	0.04	**3.8**	0.8	0.75	7.29	2.70	67.8	**5.3**	42.5	8.8	**6.4**
8.2	0.08	0.4	0.01	**3.6**	0.2	0.56	4.98	2.83	65.9	**3.8**	38.6	15.3	**6.0**
5.0	1.31	9.5	0.05	**6.3**	5.3	1.02	11.74	4.53	65.6	**2.4**	19.3	17.3	**6.3**
7.1	0.48	2.7	0.44	**4.4**	0.3	0.85	7.08	4.96	81.1	**2.9**	13.2	14.2	**5.7**
3.5	2.63	15.9	0.06	**4.2**	1.0	0.83	8.35	3.51	73.0	**2.7**	15.4	15.7	**5.8**
8.4	0.45	1.3	-0.04	**5.8**	1.1	1.40	16.12	2.76	41.7	**3.3**	76.3	46.4	**5.2**
4.3	2.25	10.1	0.51	**4.5**	0.2	0.84	6.47	5.10	80.7	**3.5**	41.3	17.9	**7.0**
5.5	0.86	5.5	0.24	**7.1**	3.1	1.71	16.22	3.96	62.9	**3.2**	15.3	13.3	**7.5**
1.2	2.69	18.4	0.49	**7.9**	3.2	2.33	29.79	3.23	63.8	**4.7**	7.5	3.2	**5.0**
7.1	0.22	1.2	0.11	**3.5**	0.7	0.47	4.63	4.05	82.1	**4.9**	40.1	10.7	**4.7**
5.8	0.00	0.0	0.04	**3.5**	0.5	0.56	6.26	3.09	77.5	**4.6**	60.7	17.2	**3.8**
4.1	1.25	8.3	0.04	**4.5**	1.3	0.91	8.57	4.18	74.6	**1.3**	19.6	29.1	**4.3**
8.4	0.05	0.4	-0.02	**5.0**	1.4	1.20	15.98	3.49	63.5	**4.2**	31.4	11.3	**4.1**
5.7	2.57	6.6	1.40	**2.7**	0.4	0.38	3.75	2.51	83.6	**4.7**	55.8	15.5	**5.3**
0.6	4.38	32.8	0.81	**5.0**	3.7	1.40	18.01	4.14	62.8	**1.6**	17.9	24.0	**3.3**
2.7	5.91	29.7	0.66	**3.7**	0.5	0.82	7.06	3.43	66.3	**3.9**	24.0	10.6	**6.1**
7.3	0.26	2.1	0.13	**4.1**	0.3	0.61	6.70	4.89	77.5	**1.9**	16.6	19.9	**3.9**
5.6	1.00	5.3	-0.13	**4.3**	0.3	0.70	8.00	4.01	71.9	**2.7**	39.0	24.0	**4.1**
4.5	1.80	8.3	0.68	**2.5**	0.4	0.36	3.47	2.74	89.3	**1.0**	26.7	50.4	**5.0**
1.7	8.33	41.6	-1.66	**0.1**	-0.3	-0.49	-10.03	3.85	112.0	**2.2**	34.7	27.0	**0.1**
6.4	2.94	7.8	0.02	**8.0**	1.5	1.96	13.64	3.29	36.6	**5.2**	56.4	13.0	**9.6**
5.0	1.48	8.7	0.15	**3.9**	2.5	0.70	6.64	3.62	71.3	**1.6**	20.1	24.3	**5.9**
2.6	2.74	22.2	0.39	**1.6**	0.7	0.32	3.70	3.91	85.4	**2.7**	21.1	15.9	**2.5**
0.7	4.70	38.9	0.87	**5.8**	2.9	1.12	15.09	4.05	56.7	**0.7**	14.4	45.8	**2.1**
8.3	0.00	0.0	0.02	**1.6**	0.1	0.17	2.05	2.93	96.6	**6.4**	50.0	2.9	**3.5**
7.2	0.67	2.8	-0.01	**2.1**	0.1	0.24	2.35	2.56	91.2	**5.1**	52.4	11.4	**5.0**
7.8	0.37	2.1	0.02	**5.2**	0.9	0.97	8.14	3.84	62.8	**2.1**	16.7	18.6	**7.1**
8.8	0.26	1.3	-0.07	**3.9**	0.7	0.67	5.12	3.21	65.9	**1.1**	23.1	32.7	**7.2**
6.5	0.90	4.8	-0.10	**6.1**	1.6	1.20	9.09	4.44	61.8	**1.2**	28.0	36.2	**6.2**
5.1	3.95	18.3	0.00	**3.3**	0.3	0.45	3.06	3.11	75.6	**1.9**	38.3	35.0	**7.0**
2.5	5.95	15.9	0.24	**8.9**	2.3	1.44	6.35	5.30	71.2	**1.1**	28.8	53.1	**6.9**
4.6	1.59	9.2	0.16	**5.0**	0.4	0.82	7.55	4.31	63.8	**1.6**	21.8	25.3	**4.5**
7.0	1.11	4.4	0.63	**0.7**	-0.1	-0.24	-1.43	4.03	111.2	**5.0**	36.1	8.4	**5.2**
3.6	1.23	10.3	0.65	**5.4**	5.0	1.00	10.90	4.24	64.9	**1.3**	5.8	24.4	**6.3**
6.9	0.85	4.5	0.00	**6.0**	2.3	1.45	10.31	3.65	58.7	**1.4**	17.9	26.1	**8.0**
3.3	3.81	18.4	0.29	**7.1**	4.7	1.35	9.78	4.77	59.5	**2.8**	6.8	14.0	**6.8**
6.7	0.57	3.1	0.04	**3.8**	0.4	0.70	6.58	4.77	88.5	**5.1**	35.8	7.6	**5.2**
6.1	0.99	5.4	-0.03	**4.3**	1.7	1.00	10.21	3.51	76.3	**2.1**	28.1	22.2	**4.2**
6.8	0.93	4.7	0.03	**6.4**	1.4	1.38	11.14	5.32	72.1	**5.0**	34.2	7.7	**7.5**
4.6	0.86	7.7	0.05	**6.4**	1.8	1.50	17.33	3.64	55.3	**1.9**	5.0	18.5	**6.2**
4.3	0.95	8.5	0.03	**4.3**	0.6	0.71	8.21	5.09	73.2	**0.5**	3.7	41.5	**4.4**
1.7	9.66	47.7	2.15	**0.0**	-0.7	-0.27	-4.50	3.12	96.1	**3.3**	35.6	16.9	**1.1**
5.0	0.96	8.3	0.12	**3.2**	0.3	0.38	4.10	3.74	82.7	**1.1**	9.8	29.0	**5.2**
2.6	3.34	27.7	0.01	**2.1**	0.1	0.20	2.02	3.77	92.9	**0.9**	12.0	33.3	**5.0**
6.0	0.44	3.2	-0.02	**8.4**	4.5	1.93	22.97	4.58	57.9	**1.6**	17.9	23.9	**7.3**
7.9	0.22	1.3	0.02	**5.3**	2.0	1.27	14.18	3.40	65.6	**5.9**	42.3	4.8	**6.6**
1.7	6.67	38.1	0.57	**3.5**	2.1	0.64	7.53	3.51	86.4	**1.9**	24.4	21.2	**3.1**
9.3	0.02	0.1	0.00	**2.1**	0.1	0.19	2.03	2.74	91.2	**5.7**	40.6	5.5	**4.4**
6.8	0.78	4.1	0.46	**6.9**	1.8	1.60	12.41	4.26	61.8	**2.7**	8.2	15.0	**8.3**
6.6	0.51	4.6	-0.05	**9.1**	2.7	2.11	22.90	4.98	57.7	**2.8**	9.3	14.5	**7.5**
4.2	1.30	8.4	0.88	**7.4**	1.7	1.20	11.47	4.61	58.1	**3.8**	12.6	9.8	**6.0**
5.1	0.64	5.3	0.09	**4.9**	0.9	0.73	7.25	4.22	80.3	**1.4**	7.9	24.1	**5.9**
7.5	0.72	2.6	0.00	**0.0**	-1.9	-2.45	-15.50	2.87	171.3	**3.4**	57.3	26.3	**6.0**
3.8	2.74	18.9	0.18	**2.4**	0.3	0.39	4.51	3.55	88.6	**4.1**	29.8	11.0	**4.4**
4.0	1.22	10.3	0.11	**4.7**	4.1	0.95	9.19	3.95	70.4	**3.8**	12.0	9.9	**6.9**
5.5	0.67	5.7	0.16	**3.8**	3.4	0.53	6.16	3.68	69.9	**1.6**	7.3	20.1	**5.4**
4.8	2.55	12.0	0.14	**3.3**	1.2	0.78	6.80	4.01	83.1	**3.6**	20.7	11.6	**5.3**
6.7	0.71	2.6	0.16	**9.4**	4.8	1.97	21.66	3.12	52.9	**6.7**	55.7	4.1	**6.0**
7.9	0.24	1.4	0.09	**5.8**	0.9	1.37	13.14	3.66	68.8	**4.0**	29.1	11.2	**6.7**

Name	City	State	Rating	2013 Rating	2012 Rating	Total Assets ($Mil)	One Year Asset Growth	Asset Mix (As a % of Total Assets) Comm-ercial Loans	Cons-umer Loans	Mort-gage Loans	Secur-ities	Capital-ization Index	Lever-age Ratio	Risk-Based Capital Ratio
COMMUNITY NATIONAL BK	Midland	TX	**B**	B	B	1167.9	10.93	29.3	1.0	4.0	25.9	**5.5**	7.5	11.5
COMMUNITY NATIONAL BK	Hondo	TX	**C+**	C+	B-	188.6	5.46	10.2	3.9	11.2	34.0	**7.0**	9.0	16.8
COMMUNITY NATIONAL BK & TRUST	Corsicana	TX	**A-**	A-	A	497.4	0.39	8.2	1.8	12.3	21.6	**9.1**	10.4	15.6
COMMUNITY NATIONAL BK & TRUST	Chanute	KS	**B-**	B-	C+	844.3	3.88	10.1	2.3	18.0	20.8	**6.4**	8.4	12.1
COMMUNITY NATIONAL BK MONMOUT	Monmouth	IL	**C+**	C+	C+	49.0	-4.04	6.7	8.8	13.2	33.0	**10.0**	13.0	24.5
COMMUNITY NATIONAL BK OF NW PA	Albion	PA	**B+**	B+	A-	76.3	-0.05	0.7	1.3	38.2	25.9	**10.0**	20.0	53.9
COMMUNITY NATIONAL BK OKARCHE	Okarche	OK	**A**	A-	A-	82.5	11.09	5.6	4.0	7.5	46.9	**10.0**	13.6	24.5
COMMUNITY NEIGHBOR BANK	Camden	AL	**B+**	A-	B+	105.8	-2.28	10.8	6.6	19.6	13.2	**10.0**	14.3	26.0
▲ COMMUNITY POINT BANK	Russellville	MO	**B-**	C	B-	94.6	2.29	3.1	4.5	26.0	28.8	**10.0**	11.2	19.8
COMMUNITY PRIDE BANK	Isanti	MN	**B-**	C+	C	96.1	-1.86	10.2	0.9	7.6	15.9	**8.7**	10.1	16.5
▲ COMMUNITY RESOURCE BANK	Northfield	MN	**B-**	C	D	241.2	1.81	8.8	1.9	9.8	20.7	**8.1**	9.8	14.0
COMMUNITY SAVINGS	Caldwell	OH	**D**	D+	D	66.4	-5.38	0.0	3.6	33.0	35.9	**6.9**	8.9	22.1
▼ COMMUNITY SAVINGS BANK	Bethel	OH	**C+**	B-	C+	76.2	74.65	1.6	0.1	40.5	15.6	**10.0**	14.2	30.3
COMMUNITY SB	Edgewood	IA	**B-**	B-	B-	318.8	2.21	14.6	1.5	6.8	23.3	**9.6**	11.1	14.7
COMMUNITY SB	Chicago	IL	**D+**	D+	C-	411.8	-1.07	0.0	0.0	30.0	35.2	**10.0**	14.7	37.9
COMMUNITY SHORES BANK	Muskegon	MI	**E-**	E-	E-	189.5	3.59	21.3	1.2	10.7	17.4	**1.9**	5.2	8.9
COMMUNITY SOUTHERN BANK	Lakeland	FL	**C+**	B-	C+	245.5	11.37	13.5	1.3	10.7	24.6	**10.0**	11.2	16.5
▼ COMMUNITY SPIRIT BANK	Red Bay	AL	**C-**	C+	C+	140.6	0.95	12.9	5.2	20.2	19.2	**7.9**	9.6	15.5
COMMUNITY STATE BANK	Ankeny	IA	**B**	B-	C	580.4	3.55	10.6	0.3	11.4	23.8	**8.5**	10.0	15.2
COMMUNITY STATE BK	Tipton	IA	**B**	B	B-	113.3	6.60	7.0	1.8	8.8	43.4	**7.0**	9.0	16.3
COMMUNITY STATE BK	Paton	IA	**B+**	B+	B+	42.9	-1.40	0.4	3.1	3.1	61.7	**10.0**	15.5	33.1
COMMUNITY STATE BK	Union Grove	WI	**D+**	C-	C+	307.6	2.16	14.7	0.8	9.6	32.5	**6.8**	8.8	15.7
COMMUNITY STATE BK	Saint Charles	MI	**D+**	D+	D+	189.6	0.25	4.3	2.6	16.0	48.1	**6.7**	8.7	17.9
COMMUNITY STATE BK	Shelbina	MO	**B-**	B-	B-	52.0	-1.70	4.5	7.9	23.7	37.5	**7.9**	9.6	20.0
▲ COMMUNITY STATE BK	Bradley	AR	**B-**	C+	C+	19.7	-22.15	10.2	4.9	15.3	40.3	**10.0**	11.5	25.2
COMMUNITY STATE BK	Coffeyville	KS	**B**	B	B	163.6	139.83	6.5	1.7	5.9	56.0	**7.6**	9.4	20.9
▲ COMMUNITY STATE BK	Starke	FL	**C-**	D+	C	62.4	3.00	5.8	3.3	18.5	28.1	**10.0**	12.9	25.1
COMMUNITY STATE BK	Avilla	IN	**B+**	B	B-	203.7	-3.40	7.4	2.3	36.2	12.0	**8.7**	10.2	15.6
COMMUNITY STATE BK	Spencer	IA	**B**	B+	B	139.5	3.61	14.3	2.2	4.9	41.9	**7.1**	9.1	16.6
COMMUNITY STATE BK	Royal Center	IN	**B**	B	B-	111.6	4.43	7.3	3.7	16.6	23.6	**7.1**	9.1	14.0
COMMUNITY STATE BK	Brook	IN	**B**	B	B	60.7	1.80	9.1	3.5	19.3	22.1	**10.0**	13.6	21.7
▲ COMMUNITY STATE BK	Galva	IL	**B+**	B+	B	154.4	8.52	9.9	2.1	10.0	28.2	**8.6**	10.0	14.2
COMMUNITY STATE BK	Hennessey	OK	**D**	D+	C	53.7	24.42	10.4	7.6	4.5	6.6	**5.3**	7.3	15.0
COMMUNITY STATE BK	Poteau	OK	**B**	B	B	220.7	10.92	9.7	3.4	21.3	17.4	**7.1**	9.0	13.5
COMMUNITY STATE BK	Lamar	CO	**A-**	B+	B	82.2	-15.92	15.1	4.7	10.3	17.3	**10.0**	13.6	21.2
COMMUNITY STATE BK OF CANTON	Canton	OK	**C**	C+	C+	44.1	15.19	7.8	10.2	6.4	26.4	**7.5**	9.4	13.9
▲ COMMUNITY STATE BK OF MISSOURI	Bowling Green	MO	**A-**	A-	A-	213.9	4.04	8.7	1.1	14.5	35.1	**10.0**	12.8	15.2
COMMUNITY STATE BK ORBISONIA	Orbisonia	PA	**B**	B	B-	320.9	1.24	1.4	7.4	65.1	4.3	**7.9**	9.6	16.2
COMMUNITY STATE BK ROCK FALLS	Rock Falls	IL	**D+**	C-	C+	248.9	-1.80	12.1	2.5	25.7	17.2	**7.0**	9.0	15.8
COMMUNITY STATE BK SW INDIANA	Poseyville	IN	**C+**	C+	B-	71.8	8.08	8.4	1.4	23.2	8.0	**7.1**	9.1	15.2
COMMUNITY TRUST & BANKING CO	Ooltewah	TN	**C**	C-	D	127.8	-2.02	10.8	0.5	15.5	11.1	**10.0**	11.1	19.5
COMMUNITY TRUST BANK	Irvington	IL	**B+**	B+	B	95.1	5.50	5.6	0.9	12.7	31.2	**10.0**	12.3	19.2
COMMUNITY TRUST BANK	Ruston	LA	**B**	B	B-	3581.7	13.19	35.7	0.6	9.4	10.7	**4.8**	9.7	10.9
COMMUNITY TRUST BANK INC	Pikeville	KY	**B-**	B-	C+	3646.3	0.68	7.1	12.6	23.0	17.1	**10.0**	11.4	17.1
▼ COMMUNITY VALLEY BANK	El Centro	CA	**C+**	B-	C	114.0	1.49	11.1	0.2	7.4	1.2	**9.9**	11.3	14.9
COMMUNITY WEST BANK NA	Goleta	CA	**C-**	D+	D+	571.9	7.45	8.6	29.8	4.0	5.5	**10.0**	11.3	15.5
COMMUNITYBANK OF TEXAS NA	Beaumont	TX	**B**	B	C+	2553.9	3.93	19.5	1.9	7.2	3.6	**8.9**	10.5	14.0
COMMUNITYONE BANK NA	Charlotte	NC	**D+**	D	E+	2013.5	-1.05	4.7	3.2	25.7	25.0	**6.0**	8.0	13.0
COMPASS BANK	Birmingham	AL	**C+**	C	C-	78121.4	11.94	21.0	5.0	19.0	13.0	**7.4**	9.3	12.8
▲ COMPASS SB	Wilmerding	PA	**C+**	C	C-	42.7	1.93	0.0	0.9	62.6	29.4	**8.9**	10.2	24.2
COMPUTERSHARE TRUST CO NA	Canton	MA	**U**	U	U	20.5	-15.04	0.0	0.0	0.0	0.0	**10.0**	83.4	144.3
▼ CONCORD BANK	Saint Louis	MO	**D**	D-	E-	123.4	-12.73	17.5	0.4	12.3	4.1	**5.6**	8.2	11.4
CONCORDE BANK	Blomkest	MN	**C-**	C-	C-	52.2	-3.53	9.5	2.8	10.6	13.9	**6.5**	8.5	12.7
▲ CONCORDIA BANK	Concordia	MO	**B+**	B	B	58.8	0.96	14.6	1.7	23.3	11.8	**10.0**	11.3	15.0
▲ CONCORDIA BANK & TRUST CO	Vidalia	LA	**B**	B	B	527.0	-0.01	3.2	2.8	14.3	46.4	**10.0**	11.1	22.7
CONESTOGA BANK	Chester Springs	PA	**C**	C-	D+	689.1	6.96	9.6	1.8	13.8	21.8	**6.3**	8.3	13.0
CONGAREE STATE BK	Cayce	SC	**C**	C	C-	113.1	0.26	8.5	1.2	9.8	22.9	**9.2**	10.5	15.7
CONGRESSIONAL BANK	Bethesda	MD	**C+**	B-	C	422.8	-2.25	30.5	3.2	14.3	9.1	**7.2**	9.1	13.3
▲ CONNEAUT SB	Conneaut	OH	**C-**	C-	D+	80.4	-3.00	0.2	1.0	57.9	18.0	**8.7**	10.1	21.3
CONNECTICUT COMMUNITY BANK NA	Westport	CT	**D-**	D-	D-	508.6	-1.55	13.1	0.1	6.9	9.0	**7.1**	9.0	18.3

Asset Quality Index	Adjusted Non-Performing Loans as a % of Total Loans	Adjusted Non-Performing Loans as a % of Capital	Net Charge-Offs Avg Loans	Profitability Index	Net Income ($Mil)	Return on Assets (R.O.A.)	Return on Equity (R.O.E.)	Net Interest Spread	Overhead Efficiency Ratio	Liquidity Index	Liquidity Ratio	Hot Money Ratio	Stability Index
6.8	0.87	6.1	0.06	**6.2**	9.0	1.07	12.74	3.63	52.4	**4.6**	29.5	11.9	**7.3**
4.9	0.71	3.7	-0.33	**3.9**	1.0	0.72	7.14	4.02	78.3	**4.2**	47.0	15.5	**4.8**
5.8	0.56	3.2	-0.03	**8.3**	5.4	1.44	12.52	4.64	59.5	**3.4**	20.4	12.6	**9.1**
5.3	0.77	5.7	0.04	**4.5**	5.4	0.86	9.70	3.83	70.7	**3.2**	6.1	12.0	**5.9**
8.3	0.16	0.6	-0.24	**2.9**	0.2	0.44	3.48	3.35	79.9	**3.2**	45.5	20.3	**5.6**
9.7	0.66	1.4	0.00	**4.8**	0.5	0.83	4.15	2.99	62.9	**2.7**	32.7	19.3	**8.1**
8.8	0.00	0.0	-0.01	**7.3**	1.0	1.71	12.02	3.52	54.2	**1.9**	28.9	25.0	**9.2**
5.8	1.52	5.6	-0.41	**4.6**	0.6	0.70	5.00	4.22	76.1	**3.1**	36.0	18.0	**7.4**
8.7	0.34	1.8	0.06	**3.5**	0.5	0.77	7.31	3.08	74.9	**2.0**	32.0	26.7	**5.9**
7.5	0.26	1.4	0.02	**6.4**	1.1	1.56	15.77	3.79	63.2	**4.3**	28.2	9.3	**4.5**
4.5	0.86	5.5	0.14	**4.3**	1.3	0.71	6.50	3.97	82.2	**2.8**	23.3	15.7	**5.0**
5.5	2.33	11.3	0.00	**0.7**	-0.1	-0.26	-3.10	3.30	104.1	**5.5**	45.5	7.7	**3.2**
6.3	2.16	9.0	0.05	**2.3**	1.1	0.09	0.57	3.83	98.1	**5.3**	43.6	8.9	**6.6**
5.1	0.85	5.0	0.07	**4.5**	2.4	0.99	9.21	3.75	70.3	**2.0**	25.1	20.0	**5.8**
6.0	3.55	12.0	0.11	**0.7**	-0.1	-0.02	-0.15	2.48	97.5	**3.6**	52.5	20.6	**6.1**
1.7	4.24	44.9	0.84	**2.6**	0.5	0.34	6.77	3.51	91.7	**4.4**	12.8	5.4	**0.3**
6.8	0.83	4.4	0.00	**3.0**	0.9	0.49	4.48	3.33	78.3	**1.0**	25.3	35.4	**5.7**
2.0	4.31	24.3	0.11	**2.0**	-0.1	-0.10	-1.02	4.48	73.9	**1.8**	21.9	21.6	**5.6**
4.4	1.63	9.5	-0.03	**4.4**	3.8	0.87	8.25	3.40	69.1	**5.2**	33.3	6.0	**6.0**
8.8	0.29	1.4	0.08	**4.5**	0.6	0.76	8.77	2.84	66.3	**5.8**	42.4	5.5	**5.7**
9.0	0.23	0.4	0.00	**5.0**	0.4	1.07	7.04	3.24	53.7	**5.2**	64.0	13.0	**7.6**
1.3	8.43	38.8	2.18	**1.1**	-2.9	-1.23	-12.67	3.77	76.6	**5.2**	48.4	11.3	**5.8**
1.7	7.70	30.2	1.72	**2.1**	0.2	0.16	1.58	3.53	89.5	**7.0**	61.3	3.5	**5.3**
8.0	0.29	1.4	0.02	**4.6**	0.3	0.81	8.82	2.67	60.1	**4.8**	27.2	5.6	**4.9**
7.9	0.00	0.0	-0.03	**7.3**	0.3	1.87	13.77	3.92	80.2	**2.5**	52.7	29.4	**5.1**
7.5	0.51	1.7	-0.01	**4.3**	1.0	0.82	8.24	3.38	67.4	**5.4**	38.1	6.6	**6.2**
5.2	3.67	13.3	-0.12	**1.5**	0.1	0.21	1.63	4.20	96.4	**5.6**	42.2	6.4	**4.9**
5.7	1.22	9.0	-0.09	**6.4**	1.6	1.02	10.75	3.92	60.4	**3.2**	15.0	13.0	**5.6**
5.2	1.29	7.0	-0.01	**5.5**	1.3	1.21	12.55	3.34	63.8	**3.4**	33.3	16.0	**6.9**
6.9	0.27	1.9	0.00	**5.0**	0.8	0.98	10.76	4.23	67.1	**4.5**	28.1	7.9	**5.5**
6.1	1.49	6.9	-0.06	**5.8**	0.5	1.01	8.13	3.84	52.2	**1.8**	36.5	35.7	**5.9**
5.7	0.68	4.4	0.13	**6.6**	1.7	1.56	14.94	5.04	61.0	**1.1**	16.2	31.3	**6.3**
2.0	4.20	23.4	0.21	**4.1**	0.3	0.92	12.74	4.09	79.2	**6.6**	58.5	3.7	**2.4**
4.5	1.45	10.9	0.19	**5.3**	1.9	1.16	12.78	5.00	74.6	**1.6**	21.4	24.4	**5.1**
8.3	0.00	0.0	-0.02	**5.9**	0.9	1.46	11.65	3.79	55.2	**1.1**	27.1	45.3	**6.5**
4.4	1.26	5.4	1.20	**3.5**	0.1	0.45	4.96	4.00	71.7	**3.2**	24.9	14.0	**5.2**
8.9	0.09	0.4	0.01	**5.4**	2.1	1.31	10.96	3.44	63.0	**2.1**	16.5	18.9	**7.5**
4.6	1.37	11.2	0.23	**5.0**	2.1	0.86	9.16	3.92	65.0	**1.0**	5.1	28.7	**5.7**
1.7	3.93	24.8	0.09	**3.7**	1.0	0.53	5.77	3.50	65.2	**3.3**	27.4	14.4	**5.3**
8.7	0.10	0.7	-0.04	**3.6**	0.5	0.84	9.37	3.37	76.7	**3.0**	23.9	15.0	**5.5**
4.6	2.52	12.4	-0.25	**3.9**	0.8	0.84	7.85	4.12	78.9	**2.6**	37.7	23.8	**4.6**
4.4	3.82	17.8	0.00	**5.1**	0.8	1.12	9.08	4.27	69.4	**4.6**	26.9	7.0	**6.9**
5.6	0.74	5.7	0.18	**4.5**	19.6	0.79	7.59	3.58	68.6	**1.8**	8.2	19.7	**7.4**
3.3	2.51	15.2	0.27	**6.8**	32.2	1.18	9.31	3.98	57.9	**1.6**	7.8	21.9	**9.4**
1.5	3.73	22.3	0.13	**4.5**	1.0	1.23	10.94	4.79	77.9	**2.2**	22.9	18.8	**4.6**
1.9	2.69	18.2	-0.16	**7.2**	5.2	1.24	10.63	4.55	74.1	**1.4**	5.8	23.7	**6.1**
5.4	0.76	4.9	0.08	**5.2**	17.6	0.93	7.35	3.99	63.7	**4.1**	21.3	9.9	**8.5**
1.9	4.16	30.5	0.13	**2.3**	7.6	0.51	6.70	3.45	95.4	**2.6**	13.9	16.3	**4.3**
4.4	0.79	5.9	0.23	**3.6**	334.0	0.60	3.89	3.07	75.0	**2.3**	19.4	18.5	**7.4**
8.1	0.40	2.5	0.00	**3.3**	0.2	0.65	6.63	2.78	68.7	**2.1**	34.1	27.6	**4.3**
6.5	na	0.0	na	**9.5**	1.8	10.83	11.43	0.76	77.2	**4.0**	806.7	101.0	**5.5**
0.0	4.77	37.7	2.64	**0.6**	-0.6	-0.60	-6.25	3.48	78.2	**1.6**	15.3	23.7	**4.0**
3.4	2.68	16.1	0.00	**2.3**	0.1	0.24	3.01	3.54	91.8	**4.6**	40.2	11.8	**3.8**
7.5	0.00	0.0	0.16	**8.8**	1.0	2.21	21.77	4.57	57.7	**4.4**	15.1	5.8	**6.7**
7.3	0.96	3.6	0.04	**4.1**	3.6	0.90	7.93	2.98	72.4	**2.3**	35.9	26.5	**7.7**
4.4	1.15	8.9	0.35	**3.4**	2.8	0.54	6.40	3.95	74.1	**1.4**	10.7	24.8	**3.7**
3.3	3.04	18.8	0.73	**2.6**	0.4	0.43	3.89	3.99	82.4	**2.9**	17.7	14.6	**5.3**
4.6	1.34	9.9	0.82	**3.3**	1.3	0.41	4.72	4.24	65.0	**1.4**	18.0	26.8	**5.0**
6.2	1.29	8.0	0.32	**2.1**	0.2	0.30	3.50	3.01	84.4	**4.0**	33.2	12.5	**4.1**
2.1	4.33	23.0	2.61	**0.0**	-6.1	-1.56	-17.29	2.77	120.3	**4.3**	46.3	15.3	**3.9**

Name	City	State	Rating	2013 Rating	2012 Rating	Total Assets ($Mil)	One Year Asset Growth	Asset Mix (As a % of Total Assets) Commercial Loans	Consumer Loans	Mortgage Loans	Securities	Capitalization Index	Leverage Ratio	Risk-Based Capital Ratio
CONNECTONE BANK	Englewood Cliffs	NJ	**B**	B-	C	3356.3	197.03	11.3	0.1	7.6	15.8	**5.1**	9.2	11.0
CONSUMERS NATIONAL BK	Minerva	OH	**B-**	B-	C+	388.0	7.85	6.6	2.2	9.4	34.6	**8.1**	9.8	15.5
CONTINENTAL BANK	Salt Lake City	UT	**A**	A-	B+	166.9	18.74	47.8	0.0	0.0	0.5	**10.0**	17.3	19.3
CONTINENTAL BANK	East Norriton	PA	**C**	C	C-	697.5	6.69	12.1	0.6	14.4	30.0	**7.2**	9.1	15.2
CONTINENTAL NATIONAL BANK	Miami	FL	**C+**	C+	C	361.5	8.74	2.7	6.1	10.7	22.1	**7.0**	9.0	18.4
CONVERSE COUNTY BANK	Douglas	WY	**B+**	B+	B+	459.7	8.96	8.1	5.6	4.6	58.4	**6.5**	8.6	19.4
CONWAY BANK NA	Conway Springs	KS	**D-**	D-	D+	60.3	-8.02	10.3	0.9	14.5	14.4	**9.2**	10.5	18.4
CONWAY NATIONAL BK	Conway	SC	**C**	C	C-	1009.1	5.22	4.2	4.5	14.1	46.4	**8.0**	9.7	19.7
COOPER STATE BK	Dublin	OH	**D+**	D+	D	136.2	17.09	0.1	0.1	50.7	0.5	**5.5**	7.6	11.4
COOPERATIVE BANK	Roslindale	MA	**C**	C	C+	291.6	1.48	1.3	0.1	46.7	13.3	**9.4**	10.6	18.3
COOPERATIVE BANK OF CAPE COD	Hyannis	MA	**C+**	C+	C+	757.5	7.54	3.9	0.2	55.7	7.1	**7.9**	9.6	15.4
COPIAH BANK NA	Hazlehurst	MS	**C**	C-	B-	167.7	0.77	5.6	4.4	16.8	17.0	**9.2**	10.5	16.8
CORDER BANK	Corder	MO	**D+**	C-	B-	18.5	11.13	10.0	4.4	15.1	16.2	**8.3**	9.9	17.9
▼ CORE BANK	Omaha	NE	**D+**	C	B-	350.5	0.29	23.0	0.7	12.9	1.4	**6.4**	9.0	12.1
▲ COREFIRST BANK & TRUST	Topeka	KS	**D**	D-	D-	926.4	-0.48	10.6	6.1	6.6	28.5	**6.7**	8.7	13.5
CORN CITY STATE BK	Deshler	OH	**A-**	A-	A	59.5	-0.56	0.1	3.5	30.6	47.7	**10.0**	16.9	39.3
CORN GROWERS STATE BK	Murdock	NE	**D-**	D-	D	27.7	1.89	1.6	4.9	12.5	32.7	**4.7**	6.7	14.9
CORNER STONE BANK	South West City	MO	**C**	C	C-	130.3	4.75	10.8	10.0	26.5	19.8	**10.0**	11.9	19.0
CORNERBANK	Winfield	KS	**C**	C	C	280.6	3.92	8.0	3.0	10.7	45.4	**6.5**	8.5	15.2
CORNERSTONE BANK	Fargo	ND	**D**	D	D-	237.9	1.93	16.0	2.7	17.8	4.5	**9.7**	12.6	14.8
CORNERSTONE BANK	Eureka Springs	AR	**B-**	B-	B	165.6	3.24	3.0	3.3	19.6	23.0	**9.9**	10.9	16.2
CORNERSTONE BANK	Wilson	NC	**E**	E-	E-	115.5	-4.56	11.5	1.8	16.4	24.1	**4.0**	6.0	10.9
▼ CORNERSTONE BANK	Mount Laurel	NJ	**E-**	E-	E-	236.8	-1.63	11.7	0.1	8.1	28.2	**3.2**	5.3	10.1
CORNERSTONE BANK	York	NE	**B+**	B+	B	1326.7	5.55	12.6	2.1	3.5	26.3	**6.0**	8.0	12.1
CORNERSTONE BANK	Overland Park	KS	**D+**	D	D	163.0	-5.84	18.6	0.3	15.2	18.0	**5.7**	9.0	11.5
CORNERSTONE BANK	Watonga	OK	**C+**	C+	C+	153.9	9.33	6.4	5.4	5.9	49.2	**6.2**	8.2	15.3
▼ CORNERSTONE BANK	Clarinda	IA	**C-**	C	C-	39.3	0.04	1.5	4.4	36.9	20.6	**10.0**	13.2	27.2
CORNERSTONE BANK INC	West Union	WV	**B**	B	B	142.0	24.75	4.6	1.2	7.3	51.0	**10.0**	11.9	30.3
▲ CORNERSTONE BANK NA	Lexington	VA	**B+**	B-	C+	113.3	12.07	8.9	3.2	20.4	3.7	**10.0**	11.7	15.5
CORNERSTONE COMMUNITY BANK	Chattanooga	TN	**C**	C	D+	412.3	-3.25	10.1	0.7	11.5	19.0	**7.3**	9.2	13.2
▲ CORNERSTONE COMMUNITY BANK	Saint Petersburg	FL	**D+**	C-	D+	221.2	-3.03	1.7	0.3	15.0	15.4	**9.3**	10.5	14.7
CORNERSTONE COMMUNITY BANK	Grafton	WI	**C**	C-	D+	135.4	2.02	7.1	0.0	12.8	0.6	**6.4**	9.3	12.1
CORNERSTONE COMMUNITY BANK	Red Bluff	CA	**B-**	B-	B-	144.9	18.06	11.3	1.4	5.4	7.9	**6.1**	8.8	11.8
▲ CORNERSTONE NATIONAL BK	Easley	SC	**C+**	D+	D	143.2	-2.72	2.8	0.6	5.3	28.4	**10.0**	12.1	19.2
▲ CORNERSTONE NATIONAL BK & TR	Palatine	IL	**B-**	C-	C-	457.0	1.91	14.2	0.8	8.2	24.3	**10.0**	11.4	15.3
CORNERSTONE STATE BK	Montgomery	MN	**C+**	C+	C-	130.3	3.77	12.4	3.1	20.7	25.5	**8.0**	10.1	13.4
CORNERSTONEBANK	Atlanta	GA	**E-**	E-	E-	256.6	-18.82	10.4	1.2	10.1	12.1	**0.0**	3.0	5.8
CORNHUSKER BANK	Lincoln	NE	**B**	B	B	437.2	6.41	9.0	1.2	15.9	20.6	**6.5**	8.8	12.2
CORTLAND SAVINGS & BANKING CO	Cortland	OH	**B-**	C+	B-	545.7	2.36	8.3	0.7	7.1	29.7	**7.5**	9.3	15.2
CORTRUST BANK NA	Mitchell	SD	**B**	B	B	709.3	-1.84	12.0	4.5	5.1	23.6	**10.0**	11.1	15.8
CORYDON STATE BK	Corydon	IA	**A**	A	A-	94.3	2.79	10.4	5.4	15.4	18.5	**10.0**	17.0	23.2
▲ COTTONPORT BANK	Marksville	LA	**B**	B-	B-	324.7	-1.73	7.7	4.6	18.0	24.4	**10.0**	11.1	18.6
COTTONWOOD VALLEY BANK	Cedar Point	KS	**B-**	C+	C+	34.5	4.45	7.6	3.4	1.7	15.2	**10.0**	13.8	26.8
COULEE BANK	La Crosse	WI	**B**	B	B	291.8	5.61	13.4	0.9	12.4	27.7	**7.8**	9.5	15.4
COUNTRY BANK	New York	NY	**D**	D	D	507.9	0.33	2.8	0.0	8.0	33.8	**6.3**	8.3	13.6
COUNTRY BANK	Prescott	AZ	**B-**	C+	C	183.3	5.03	3.2	0.2	7.0	8.2	**9.6**	10.7	18.3
COUNTRY BANK FOR SAVINGS	Ware	MA	**C+**	C+	B-	1394.9	1.80	1.5	0.4	31.1	31.2	**10.0**	13.9	20.6
COUNTRY CLUB BANK	Kansas City	MO	**B-**	B-	B	1256.2	4.00	14.4	1.2	9.3	38.8	**5.8**	7.8	14.4
COUNTRY CLUB TRUST CO NA	Kansas City	MO	**U**	U	U	15.0	17.42	0.0	0.0	0.0	86.4	**10.0**	102.	381.9
COUNTRY TRUST BANK	Bloomington	IL	**U**	U	A+	29.9	4.99	0.0	0.0	0.0	83.0	**10.0**	91.0	191.5
COUNTRYSIDE BANK	Unadilla	NE	**B**	B+	B+	76.0	0.66	5.3	4.8	16.4	31.9	**10.0**	14.1	25.6
COUNTY BANK	Brunswick	MO	**B-**	B-	C+	76.5	-5.51	6.5	3.7	25.1	12.5	**6.1**	8.1	11.8
COUNTY BANK	Sigourney	IA	**B-**	B-	C+	112.1	1.49	10.9	2.9	9.2	3.8	**9.3**	11.5	14.5
COUNTY BANK	Rehoboth Beach	DE	**D**	D	D-	341.0	1.70	8.2	2.5	13.2	11.5	**6.5**	8.8	12.2
COUNTY COMMERCE BANK	Oxnard	CA	**B+**	B+	B+	252.7	16.39	7.0	0.1	2.4	0.0	**7.0**	9.0	16.6
▼ COUNTY FIRST BANK	La Plata	MD	**C-**	C+	C-	214.0	2.17	7.4	0.2	9.0	22.3	**9.7**	10.8	15.4
COUNTY SAVINGS BANK	Essington	PA	**C-**	C-	D+	62.6	-1.50	0.0	0.3	48.0	11.6	**5.5**	7.5	20.8
COUNTYBANK	Greenwood	SC	**C+**	C+	C-	333.4	2.07	5.2	1.7	32.5	19.8	**6.0**	8.0	13.5
▼ COVENANT BANK	Leeds	AL	**D-**	D-	D-	84.0	0.82	7.5	2.7	22.0	27.3	**6.2**	8.3	14.5
COVENANT BANK	Clarksdale	MS	**C**	C	C-	226.4	0.10	16.0	3.0	14.3	11.5	**8.3**	10.2	13.6

Asset Quality Index	Adjusted Non-Performing Loans as a % of Total Loans	Adjusted Non-Performing Loans as a % of Capital	Net Charge-Offs / Avg Loans	Profitability Index	Net Income ($Mil)	Return on Assets (R.O.A.)	Return on Equity (R.O.E.)	Net Interest Spread	Overhead Efficiency Ratio	Liquidity Index	Liquidity Ratio	Hot Money Ratio	Stability Index
5.3	0.29	2.3	0.04	**4.6**	11.2	0.74	8.05	3.68	72.0	**1.8**	14.8	21.0	**8.0**
5.6	0.82	4.6	0.13	**4.2**	2.3	0.82	8.23	3.88	74.9	**4.4**	28.8	8.8	**5.2**
5.9	1.64	8.3	0.34	**10.0**	7.6	6.60	36.12	11.13	32.3	**0.1**	5.4	96.5	**8.5**
5.1	1.42	8.5	0.13	**3.1**	2.0	0.39	4.32	3.26	73.7	**2.9**	23.8	15.4	**4.9**
5.0	1.13	6.7	0.02	**3.2**	1.0	0.38	4.25	3.52	84.4	**4.8**	41.2	11.2	**4.5**
9.0	0.08	0.3	0.09	**5.6**	4.6	1.38	15.11	2.55	56.8	**2.7**	40.9	25.6	**6.9**
4.6	1.47	8.4	-0.16	**0.2**	-0.1	-0.25	-1.90	3.27	111.4	**3.4**	21.1	12.5	**4.3**
5.0	2.29	9.4	0.64	**3.4**	4.2	0.58	5.97	3.07	69.8	**3.3**	38.6	22.3	**5.6**
6.1	0.54	5.6	0.16	**1.9**	0.2	0.24	2.99	4.15	94.2	**2.8**	7.2	14.3	**2.6**
4.8	1.68	11.3	0.00	**2.9**	0.8	0.36	3.51	3.45	84.3	**3.8**	19.9	10.4	**5.8**
4.1	1.81	14.9	0.08	**3.2**	1.9	0.35	3.52	3.22	81.0	**4.2**	8.9	6.8	**6.1**
3.2	1.95	11.6	0.09	**5.2**	1.1	0.88	8.56	4.87	72.9	**2.9**	18.3	15.0	**6.0**
1.9	3.91	22.6	0.16	**4.6**	0.1	0.94	9.44	3.63	61.1	**4.2**	39.9	11.4	**4.4**
1.3	4.01	29.3	-0.63	**2.9**	1.0	0.37	4.09	3.73	90.0	**4.7**	13.8	3.9	**3.9**
1.0	8.27	47.4	1.33	**1.4**	1.1	0.15	2.04	2.97	93.8	**4.7**	9.9	3.5	**3.8**
9.5	0.19	0.5	0.00	**5.1**	0.5	1.22	7.40	2.87	56.3	**4.3**	46.2	14.8	**8.6**
4.0	2.99	19.6	-0.05	**2.0**	0.1	0.29	4.50	2.85	91.6	**6.0**	50.3	5.4	**1.4**
2.4	3.76	20.6	0.47	**7.1**	1.7	1.75	15.32	5.44	63.9	**1.1**	19.0	31.9	**6.0**
7.5	0.39	2.2	0.13	**2.7**	1.1	0.51	5.93	3.41	81.3	**1.4**	14.2	26.3	**4.2**
1.2	5.00	32.3	-0.20	**6.8**	3.5	1.98	16.77	3.89	91.4	**1.5**	3.3	21.0	**5.2**
4.6	1.92	10.7	0.05	**8.4**	2.7	2.22	21.07	5.00	58.1	**1.4**	9.1	24.5	**6.9**
1.7	5.01	37.6	-0.15	**3.1**	0.9	0.97	18.16	3.34	90.2	**1.2**	14.8	28.4	**0.6**
1.7	4.46	44.2	1.23	**0.3**	-1.0	-0.54	-13.62	4.14	98.3	**2.7**	31.1	18.7	**0.6**
6.8	0.43	3.2	0.05	**7.2**	15.9	1.64	20.72	4.02	62.0	**2.3**	7.4	17.1	**8.1**
3.4	2.04	11.0	-0.86	**1.5**	0.2	0.14	1.52	2.73	95.9	**5.1**	13.7	1.0	**4.0**
6.3	0.91	4.0	0.05	**3.4**	0.7	0.59	7.61	3.74	82.6	**4.5**	47.2	14.4	**3.6**
7.4	1.62	6.1	0.00	**1.3**	0.0	-0.06	-0.46	3.19	98.6	**3.0**	49.8	24.3	**5.4**
9.8	0.10	0.2	0.05	**3.6**	0.7	0.73	6.77	2.97	69.3	**3.7**	77.7	31.8	**5.9**
5.9	0.57	3.8	0.15	**7.8**	2.6	3.31	29.93	4.29	44.6	**1.0**	14.3	32.1	**6.1**
4.2	1.80	12.9	0.11	**3.3**	1.6	0.50	5.39	3.93	78.7	**1.0**	6.4	29.5	**3.2**
2.8	3.28	20.1	0.33	**3.5**	1.1	0.64	5.64	3.86	77.3	**4.6**	25.7	6.1	**4.6**
3.0	1.31	10.9	1.13	**4.4**	0.6	0.56	6.12	4.52	63.2	**1.6**	10.0	21.4	**4.7**
7.3	0.10	0.8	0.02	**3.8**	0.5	0.51	5.41	4.37	78.6	**1.0**	10.5	31.2	**5.1**
6.4	1.62	6.5	0.04	**3.1**	0.7	0.65	5.70	3.69	84.2	**4.1**	36.6	13.6	**5.1**
4.6	2.15	11.5	0.20	**6.1**	3.7	1.09	9.94	3.51	59.8	**4.6**	30.3	8.6	**5.8**
3.4	3.14	17.8	0.13	**5.4**	0.9	0.97	9.72	4.23	65.9	**3.8**	20.7	10.3	**5.7**
0.0	8.55	139.0	0.72	**0.0**	-1.0	-0.47	-16.55	2.97	107.4	**1.0**	20.2	32.8	**0.0**
5.7	0.48	3.7	-0.05	**6.1**	4.4	1.42	16.18	3.89	65.9	**2.7**	19.7	16.1	**5.9**
4.9	1.65	10.1	0.07	**4.2**	3.4	0.85	9.25	3.67	70.5	**2.6**	15.2	16.2	**4.6**
6.9	0.32	1.9	0.39	**4.9**	4.6	0.84	7.52	4.45	70.5	**2.9**	16.8	14.8	**6.5**
5.1	2.25	9.7	0.32	**10.0**	2.1	2.92	16.93	4.92	23.1	**1.3**	25.2	31.0	**8.8**
6.2	0.90	4.9	0.11	**4.2**	1.9	0.80	7.06	4.11	77.1	**3.0**	24.2	14.9	**6.2**
4.9	6.53	15.5	-0.50	**4.5**	0.3	1.16	8.60	3.17	68.2	**5.5**	61.8	11.1	**6.1**
4.6	1.54	10.6	0.21	**5.9**	2.6	1.21	12.09	3.68	65.3	**4.2**	24.5	8.8	**7.0**
1.2	3.22	21.4	0.23	**3.9**	2.8	0.72	8.93	3.80	64.6	**1.7**	31.5	31.0	**4.6**
4.7	2.34	10.9	-0.17	**4.4**	1.4	1.06	10.00	3.55	69.4	**5.9**	45.0	5.5	**5.3**
5.2	3.26	15.0	0.10	**2.9**	4.8	0.47	3.26	3.09	76.8	**2.1**	24.4	24.5	**8.7**
6.6	1.00	6.1	0.10	**3.7**	6.8	0.73	8.92	3.26	86.5	**5.6**	34.3	7.3	**6.9**
10.0	na	0.0	na	**10.0**	1.9	18.29	18.18	0.36	73.5	**4.0**	5373.5	101.0	**5.7**
10.0	na	0.0	na	**10.0**	5.5	25.88	27.43	2.30	71.4	**10.0**	922.8	0.0	**7.0**
8.6	0.08	0.3	-0.03	**4.5**	0.6	0.94	6.90	3.14	67.8	**5.6**	49.2	7.9	**7.6**
8.4	0.00	0.0	0.01	**4.0**	0.5	0.82	10.61	3.76	78.8	**2.6**	8.8	15.3	**4.9**
4.5	1.21	7.8	0.03	**7.2**	0.9	1.08	9.54	4.94	63.4	**3.7**	13.9	10.1	**6.7**
0.6	5.18	37.8	0.70	**3.1**	1.0	0.40	4.08	3.84	80.2	**3.5**	19.3	12.1	**4.3**
8.9	0.00	0.0	0.00	**5.2**	1.4	0.79	8.82	3.01	59.8	**4.9**	49.6	13.0	**5.2**
1.8	6.34	33.8	0.35	**3.0**	0.6	0.37	3.39	3.44	81.0	**4.3**	34.4	11.5	**6.4**
6.9	0.93	6.9	0.18	**2.4**	0.1	0.28	3.87	3.30	86.7	**5.1**	41.2	9.7	**3.4**
4.6	1.36	10.9	0.15	**5.0**	2.9	1.20	15.35	3.90	81.2	**4.4**	8.9	5.2	**3.9**
1.4	6.88	45.1	3.42	**0.1**	-0.6	-0.91	-11.00	3.65	94.0	**3.9**	13.8	9.4	**1.9**
3.1	2.08	13.3	0.60	**3.5**	0.9	0.53	5.01	4.19	77.9	**2.8**	17.2	15.1	**5.0**

Name	City	State	Rating	2013 Rating	2012 Rating	Total Assets ($Mil)	One Year Asset Growth	Asset Mix (As a % of Total Assets) Comm-ercial Loans	Cons-umer Loans	Mort-gage Loans	Secur-ities	Capital-ization Index	Lever-age Ratio	Risk-Based Capital Ratio
COVINGTON COUNTY BANK	Collins	MS	**B-**	B-	B-	67.4	6.87	5.4	4.2	7.8	37.5	**9.8**	10.8	15.2
COVINGTON S&LA	Covington	OH	**C**	C	C+	62.9	-0.22	0.1	0.1	35.2	30.4	**10.0**	15.5	42.0
▲ COWBOY BANK OF TEXAS	Maypearl	TX	**B+**	B	B-	58.7	3.16	1.3	6.8	36.6	19.1	**9.0**	10.3	19.3
COWBOY STATE BK	Ranchester	WY	**D**	C-	D	41.9	-0.22	8.8	3.8	22.6	19.5	**7.2**	9.1	15.9
CRAWFORD COUNTY TRUST & SB	Denison	IA	**B-**	B	B	137.2	4.66	4.6	4.3	11.2	4.4	**5.1**	8.0	11.1
CREDIT FIRST NA	Brook Park	OH	**U**	U	B+	43.9	14.46	0.0	0.0	0.0	0.0	**10.0**	98.2	469.4
CREDIT ONE BANK NA	Las Vegas	NV	**U**	U	A	115.2	8.28	0.0	0.0	0.0	2.7	**10.0**	56.2	135.5
▼ CRESCENT BANK & TRUST	New Orleans	LA	**D**	D+	C+	941.1	9.01	3.0	82.6	1.3	3.5	**8.0**	11.2	13.4
▲ CRESCOM BANK	Charleston	SC	**B+**	B-	C-	1038.0	16.01	6.5	0.3	25.2	24.1	**9.0**	10.4	15.6
CRESSON COMMUNITY BANK	Cresson	PA	**C+**	C+	C+	61.1	-1.14	0.8	3.9	22.7	40.8	**10.0**	11.8	31.2
CREST SAVINGS BANK	Wildwood	NJ	**C+**	C+	C+	432.1	2.06	0.9	0.9	52.6	6.0	**5.6**	7.6	14.5
▼ CRESTMARK BANK	Troy	MI	**C+**	C+	C+	625.5	32.29	63.3	4.7	0.2	3.1	**8.3**	12.9	13.6
CROCKETT NATIONAL BK	San Angelo	TX	**A-**	A-	A	475.1	12.39	2.3	0.2	38.5	2.6	**9.5**	10.7	16.6
CROGHAN COLONIAL BANK	Fremont	OH	**C+**	B-	C+	768.6	24.76	5.3	4.3	17.1	28.5	**6.5**	8.6	13.7
CROOKSTON NATIONAL BK	Crookston	MN	**C+**	C+	C+	59.6	-1.25	6.2	3.0	13.6	28.3	**6.5**	8.5	16.0
CROSS COUNTY BANK	Wynne	AR	**A-**	B+	B-	224.6	5.44	6.5	1.3	11.2	10.7	**10.0**	12.0	16.5
CROSS COUNTY SAVINGS BANK	Middle Village	NY	**B-**	B-	C+	391.7	-3.08	0.0	0.0	46.6	16.4	**9.2**	10.5	20.5
CROSS KEYS BANK	Saint Joseph	LA	**A-**	B+	B-	321.7	2.62	10.5	1.2	11.7	41.3	**10.0**	11.6	18.7
CROSS RIVER BANK	Teaneck	NJ	**A-**	B+	B+	295.2	32.56	3.8	24.1	10.6	10.5	**8.1**	10.9	13.4
CROSSFIRST BANK	Leawood	KS	**C+**	C+	C	1105.5	36.90	22.1	0.5	6.8	31.2	**6.9**	9.5	12.4
CROSSROADS BANK	Effingham	IL	**A-**	A-	A	142.8	1.02	12.1	1.6	11.3	21.5	**10.0**	13.3	18.4
CROSSROADS BANK	Wabash	IN	**C-**	C-	D	340.7	0.05	7.4	3.7	29.4	23.9	**7.6**	9.4	15.4
CROWELL STATE BK	Crowell	TX	**B-**	C+	C+	33.8	2.48	9.1	6.4	7.7	17.7	**8.5**	10.0	17.6
▲ CROWN BANK	Edina	MN	**D+**	D-	E-	195.2	0.99	43.5	1.8	6.7	0.6	**6.2**	8.9	11.9
CROWN BANK	Elizabeth	NJ	**D**	D	C	517.6	-0.78	3.4	0.0	4.1	8.3	**10.0**	13.4	18.3
CRYSTAL LAKE BK & TRUST CO NA	Crystal Lake	IL	**C+**	C+	C-	806.4	1.97	28.8	13.3	3.4	12.7	**7.8**	10.4	13.2
CSB BANK	Capac	MI	**C**	C	C-	238.5	5.19	2.8	1.2	24.6	43.2	**6.5**	8.6	18.6
CTBC BANK CORP (USA)	Los Angeles	CA	**B-**	C+	C+	2280.7	39.16	8.9	0.0	16.8	11.2	**10.0**	13.7	20.7
CULBERTSON BANK	Culbertson	NE	**C-**	C-	C	15.3	-5.22	4.4	0.9	0.4	52.0	**10.0**	14.6	32.3
CULLMAN SAVINGS BANK	Cullman	AL	**A-**	A-	B+	226.6	0.94	4.5	1.3	42.3	10.4	**10.0**	16.4	23.0
CUMBERLAND BANK & TRUST	Clarksville	TN	**C+**	C	C	170.3	6.03	7.9	1.7	15.0	9.8	**8.8**	10.2	14.2
CUMBERLAND COUNTY BANK	Crossville	TN	**B-**	B-	B-	282.7	1.03	1.2	2.2	20.5	34.3	**5.8**	7.8	24.6
CUMBERLAND FEDERAL BANK FSB	Cumberland	WI	**B**	B-	B	101.4	10.39	2.3	2.4	28.6	46.7	**10.0**	11.4	22.9
CUMBERLAND SECURITY BANK	Somerset	KY	**A**	A-	B+	160.1	-0.49	8.2	2.9	27.9	14.6	**10.0**	13.7	19.1
CUMBERLAND VALLEY NB&TC	London	KY	**C**	C	C	422.7	4.49	6.9	2.4	14.4	20.8	**9.0**	10.3	17.8
CURRIE STATE BK	Currie	MN	**C-**	D	D	62.3	17.44	8.5	1.1	9.9	3.4	**4.2**	8.6	10.6
CUSTER FEDERAL STATE BK	Broken Bow	NE	**C+**	C+	C	103.2	15.14	6.0	5.0	16.8	12.4	**6.0**	8.7	11.8
CUSTOMERS BANK	Phoenixville	PA	**C+**	C	D+	6503.0	66.85	5.9	1.4	6.4	6.0	**5.6**	7.6	11.8
CYPRESS BANK SSB	Pittsburg	TX	**C+**	C+	C+	174.8	-0.89	5.6	8.9	37.4	23.3	**7.1**	9.1	16.9
D L EVANS BANK	Burley	ID	**B**	B	B-	1129.7	15.69	10.2	2.0	4.3	23.4	**7.4**	9.2	13.8
DA DAVIDSON TRUST COMPANY	Great Falls	MT	**U**	U	B+	6.1	6.93	0.0	0.0	0.0	89.1	**10.0**	75.0	195.1
DACOTAH BANK	Aberdeen	SD	**B**	B-	C+	2095.1	1.63	12.5	2.7	5.4	13.9	**7.8**	10.2	13.2
DAIRY STATE BK	Rice Lake	WI	**C+**	C+	C	520.7	20.90	8.8	1.3	9.6	59.4	**8.1**	9.7	23.7
DAIRYLAND STATE BK	Bruce	WI	**B-**	B-	C+	83.4	4.00	6.9	2.3	22.5	11.1	**7.4**	9.3	14.4
DAKOTA COMMUNITY BANK & TRUST	Hebron	ND	**B+**	B+	B+	749.8	8.45	10.2	2.2	6.3	21.0	**5.7**	7.7	12.2
DAKOTA HERITAGE BANK OF ND	Hunter	ND	**B+**	B+	B	148.8	6.16	7.0	4.1	1.7	16.8	**5.9**	8.7	11.7
DAKOTA PRAIRIE BANK	Fort Pierre	SD	**B**	B	B	73.0	14.86	14.3	3.6	2.2	10.6	**7.8**	9.7	13.2
▲ DAKOTA STATE BK	Blunt	SD	**B-**	C+	C+	39.0	9.17	5.9	0.3	0.2	25.9	**6.5**	8.5	13.5
DAKOTA WESTERN BANK	Bowman	ND	**A**	A-	B+	251.2	11.38	9.2	3.2	2.4	30.3	**9.2**	10.5	15.3
DALHART FS&LA SSB	Dalhart	TX	**C+**	C+	C+	109.3	5.10	0.4	2.2	51.0	27.7	**8.4**	9.9	22.5
DAMARISCOTTA BANK & TRUST CO	Damariscotta	ME	**C-**	C	C	171.4	1.17	4.3	1.6	29.9	24.7	**8.0**	9.7	16.9
DAMASCUS COMMUNITY BANK	Damascus	MD	**D+**	D+	D	291.5	8.28	11.3	26.9	9.5	15.7	**5.3**	8.5	11.2
DANVILLE STATE SB	Danville	IA	**B+**	A-	A-	142.6	6.74	3.0	3.2	14.0	67.0	**9.6**	10.7	23.3
▲ DARIEN ROWAYTON BANK	Darien	CT	**D+**	D+	D	439.6	50.67	2.1	44.4	25.8	5.5	**3.5**	8.0	10.3
DART BANK	Mason	MI	**C-**	C-	C	280.1	2.31	5.1	0.9	20.7	27.2	**9.1**	10.4	17.1
DAVIS TRUST CO	Elkins	WV	**B-**	C	C-	145.4	-0.63	3.9	3.6	16.5	8.5	**10.0**	13.6	20.5
▼ DE WITT BANK & TRUST CO	De Witt	IA	**B+**	B+	B-	148.0	5.31	9.4	1.9	7.2	30.1	**4.7**	9.7	10.9
DE WITT BANK & TRUST CO	De Witt	AR	**A-**	A-	A-	138.4	-22.50	7.5	0.6	2.5	55.4	**10.0**	15.5	30.4
DEAN CO-OP BANK	Franklin	MA	**C**	C	C-	248.6	1.37	1.7	0.7	49.5	15.7	**6.9**	8.9	15.2
▲ DEARBORN FSB	Dearborn	MI	**B-**	C+	C	256.9	0.39	0.0	0.1	60.6	7.0	**10.0**	26.0	52.0

Asset Quality Index	Adjusted Non-Performing Loans as a % of Total Loans	Adjusted Non-Performing Loans as a % of Capital	Net Charge-Offs / Avg Loans	Profitability Index	Net Income ($Mil)	Return on Assets (R.O.A.)	Return on Equity (R.O.E.)	Net Interest Spread	Overhead Efficiency Ratio	Liquidity Index	Liquidity Ratio	Hot Money Ratio	Stability Index
8.0	0.45	2.0	0.07	3.9	0.3	0.66	6.54	3.78	75.0	2.1	37.7	30.7	4.2
9.8	0.77	2.1	0.00	2.0	0.1	0.11	0.75	2.45	93.8	6.1	55.7	6.5	7.2
6.2	0.56	3.3	0.06	10.0	1.1	2.57	26.02	4.85	55.3	1.3	21.2	29.5	7.3
7.3	0.00	0.0	0.19	1.1	0.0	-0.09	-1.01	4.38	99.5	3.3	33.9	16.5	3.7
7.0	0.02	0.2	0.02	5.9	1.3	1.36	17.18	3.46	61.7	2.9	16.9	14.7	5.4
10.0	na	0.0	na	9.5	10.2	33.62	34.74	0.02	51.8	5.0	1794.1	100.0	6.5
6.9	na	0.0	na	10.0	44.0	56.72	90.30	0.28	78.9	4.3	151.3	100.0	7.0
0.7	2.60	16.4	2.58	8.8	12.0	1.78	15.83	12.20	54.3	0.5	12.2	62.8	8.7
5.6	1.11	6.8	-0.17	6.8	7.1	0.99	9.39	3.62	74.5	2.0	21.6	22.9	5.7
5.8	4.05	11.9	0.33	2.7	0.2	0.34	2.93	2.34	80.8	3.9	69.1	20.7	6.0
6.2	0.52	4.9	0.03	3.3	1.5	0.47	5.62	2.93	76.8	3.2	16.9	13.3	4.6
3.3	1.43	8.5	-0.03	10.0	9.2	3.59	27.82	14.33	60.6	0.3	12.8	95.4	8.9
6.3	0.42	3.1	0.07	9.8	7.1	2.45	25.89	3.87	77.7	0.6	8.2	38.3	8.4
3.0	2.16	14.9	0.08	5.6	6.8	1.13	9.80	4.19	62.9	4.1	16.5	8.2	6.6
8.7	0.00	0.0	0.01	3.8	0.4	0.93	11.54	2.85	67.9	4.8	31.7	7.4	4.4
8.2	0.09	0.5	0.04	8.3	2.3	1.51	12.50	4.81	52.1	1.6	12.2	22.7	6.2
6.3	1.08	6.7	0.01	4.1	1.8	0.59	5.86	3.85	73.0	4.6	26.9	7.2	5.1
8.2	0.65	2.9	0.05	5.5	3.1	1.34	11.51	4.10	71.4	2.5	38.7	26.1	6.8
7.3	0.01	0.1	0.00	8.8	3.9	1.99	18.97	4.64	53.6	2.0	20.2	19.7	6.0
7.6	0.58	3.6	-0.01	3.6	4.8	0.68	6.61	3.54	68.7	3.5	36.2	19.2	6.3
8.3	0.06	0.3	0.00	5.6	1.1	0.97	7.46	3.01	54.9	4.0	30.2	11.7	8.0
2.5	2.87	18.4	-0.66	6.2	3.6	1.42	15.13	3.72	64.9	2.8	22.8	15.9	5.0
8.3	0.17	0.8	0.33	6.2	0.4	1.60	16.50	4.04	63.4	2.1	30.0	22.8	5.1
1.7	2.73	21.3	0.31	2.8	0.9	0.61	6.98	4.46	86.5	2.4	19.9	17.2	3.3
0.0	16.22	75.2	0.54	5.0	5.1	1.38	10.51	5.46	66.2	1.0	24.6	35.2	8.7
3.0	1.74	11.8	0.75	4.1	4.2	0.69	7.23	3.14	54.8	1.6	13.0	23.1	5.4
5.9	1.84	9.3	0.09	3.1	0.9	0.50	5.81	3.15	83.9	6.0	45.4	5.4	3.8
8.7	0.38	1.9	0.51	3.5	10.0	0.63	3.46	3.15	71.1	2.4	20.0	18.2	6.8
8.2	0.20	0.4	-0.06	1.8	0.0	0.23	1.59	3.46	92.6	5.4	66.9	10.6	5.0
6.8	1.12	5.3	-0.06	5.6	1.6	0.96	6.03	4.16	63.8	1.1	9.3	29.5	8.0
3.9	1.28	8.9	0.01	7.2	1.4	1.15	11.36	4.70	60.1	0.8	15.6	34.6	6.3
9.6	0.18	0.9	-0.02	3.6	1.6	0.76	10.01	2.32	72.3	5.4	52.0	10.8	4.7
5.4	2.39	9.9	0.00	4.1	0.5	0.67	5.61	3.01	69.5	2.6	46.2	30.2	6.4
6.9	1.11	5.3	0.05	9.1	2.7	2.19	16.11	4.54	58.3	3.1	20.4	13.9	8.8
5.0	1.65	8.6	0.20	2.6	1.0	0.34	3.15	3.40	89.6	3.1	33.3	17.3	5.9
2.3	0.76	7.4	-0.27	9.9	0.7	1.59	18.92	5.15	49.7	0.5	6.9	49.7	4.3
6.4	0.08	0.7	0.15	4.7	0.6	0.83	9.40	3.60	57.2	0.6	5.9	36.3	5.0
4.8	0.44	5.1	0.06	4.7	34.0	0.88	10.51	3.02	54.3	1.0	5.6	29.2	4.1
4.5	1.18	8.1	0.11	4.0	0.8	0.61	6.79	4.09	77.6	1.3	29.2	35.1	5.1
4.8	2.00	13.0	0.02	5.1	6.6	0.87	8.82	4.01	71.3	3.6	20.5	12.0	7.1
10.0	na	0.0	na	9.5	0.1	2.00	2.56	1.76	96.4	10.0	359.6	0.0	6.4
4.7	1.39	9.7	0.08	5.4	13.8	0.89	8.70	3.98	64.2	3.6	9.1	10.6	8.1
5.2	3.23	10.5	0.21	3.9	2.6	0.69	7.01	3.01	63.3	4.7	51.3	14.3	5.5
4.4	1.51	10.9	0.10	3.8	0.5	0.78	7.82	3.99	78.8	4.3	25.7	8.7	5.4
7.9	0.11	0.9	-0.05	8.2	9.8	1.86	24.36	3.90	57.2	3.4	29.4	14.6	6.9
6.7	0.01	0.1	0.03	6.7	1.7	1.62	17.44	4.27	56.3	3.9	10.0	9.0	7.0
6.6	0.20	1.4	0.01	7.2	0.9	1.68	17.57	4.39	58.9	1.4	11.7	25.5	5.9
8.6	0.00	0.0	0.00	6.4	0.4	1.46	18.04	4.64	64.7	3.3	22.4	13.5	5.7
7.6	0.31	1.8	0.00	8.9	3.8	2.07	20.64	4.11	48.1	3.7	7.4	10.0	7.0
6.7	0.65	4.0	0.10	3.4	0.4	0.49	4.84	4.00	81.4	1.6	35.2	48.2	4.7
4.4	2.25	14.3	0.08	2.6	0.5	0.35	3.63	3.29	85.6	3.3	27.8	14.7	5.2
1.7	2.02	16.7	0.63	2.9	0.8	0.38	4.63	4.16	64.9	1.4	18.8	26.8	4.0
5.5	4.64	12.8	0.04	5.4	1.3	1.26	12.99	2.85	57.9	5.1	74.6	16.1	6.8
5.7	0.22	2.2	0.00	3.9	4.0	1.39	18.35	3.26	71.0	0.8	15.2	34.5	2.1
2.6	4.36	23.0	0.78	4.0	1.5	0.71	7.05	4.16	79.2	4.2	26.5	9.1	5.6
3.6	4.71	18.6	0.67	3.3	0.5	0.45	3.60	4.01	80.8	4.5	30.5	9.3	6.3
5.1	2.12	13.2	0.05	6.1	1.7	1.49	15.54	3.47	65.6	3.8	30.9	13.0	6.9
8.7	1.10	2.2	-0.75	5.5	1.2	1.07	7.26	3.38	53.7	3.0	60.5	35.9	7.7
3.0	2.57	19.9	0.07	3.3	0.7	0.39	4.47	3.69	86.4	3.0	13.9	13.8	4.7
6.0	4.30	10.7	0.43	3.5	1.1	0.57	2.20	3.40	66.6	4.3	34.9	11.7	6.3

Name	City	State	Rating	2013 Rating	2012 Rating	Total Assets ($Mil)	One Year Asset Growth	Asset Mix (As a % of Total Assets) Commercial Loans	Consumer Loans	Mortgage Loans	Securities	Capitalization Index	Leverage Ratio	Risk-Based Capital Ratio
DEARBORN SAVINGS BANK	Lawrenceburg	IN	**B**	B	B	116.0	-1.56	1.6	0.2	49.0	13.4	**10.0**	14.9	23.8
DECATUR COUNTY BANK	Decaturville	TN	**C**	C-	D+	86.1	-4.66	5.1	14.3	15.7	28.5	**8.7**	10.1	16.1
▲ DECATUR STATE BK	Decatur	AR	**C-**	D	E-	128.8	4.32	8.9	1.8	17.9	5.0	**10.0**	11.4	16.8
DECORAH BANK & TRUST CO	Decorah	IA	**A**	A	A-	375.6	4.75	13.3	2.7	11.9	22.1	**9.5**	10.7	14.6
DEDHAM INSTITUTION FOR SAVINGS	Dedham	MA	**C+**	C+	C+	1254.7	3.72	1.1	0.1	46.0	21.9	**9.6**	10.8	16.6
DEDICATED COMMUNITY BANK	Darlington	SC	**C+**	C+	C+	44.4	1.60	12.0	5.1	20.3	20.7	**10.0**	12.5	19.5
DEERWOOD BANK	Deerwood	MN	**C-**	D+	C	264.2	1.84	17.6	2.3	11.6	7.3	**10.0**	11.4	16.3
DEFIANCE STATE BK	Defiance	IA	**C-**	C-	C-	30.0	7.04	8.1	5.0	9.6	1.2	**6.5**	8.6	15.7
DEL NORTE BANK	Del Norte	CO	**C+**	C	C-	53.5	2.34	4.1	1.5	35.1	10.0	**7.4**	9.2	15.7
DELANCO FSB	Delanco	NJ	**D-**	D	D-	126.8	-4.95	1.7	0.6	51.7	21.3	**7.1**	9.0	17.2
DELAWARE COUNTY BK & TRUST CO	Lewis Center	OH	**D+**	D	D	501.4	-1.39	6.1	1.8	28.3	14.9	**7.0**	9.0	13.6
DELAWARE NATIONAL BK OF DELHI	Delhi	NY	**C+**	C+	C+	285.7	2.04	1.0	1.2	14.7	47.7	**6.7**	8.7	25.4
DELAWARE PLACE BANK	Chicago	IL	**D+**	C-	C	239.9	-4.25	30.3	1.3	4.9	11.9	**5.9**	7.9	12.0
DELTA BANK	Vidalia	LA	**B**	B	B	246.4	3.31	7.2	2.7	14.4	20.3	**6.0**	8.0	12.3
▼ DELTA BANK NA	Manteca	CA	**D**	D-	D-	101.6	3.78	4.4	0.1	0.1	33.7	**5.9**	7.9	18.4
DELTA NATIONAL BK & TRUST CO	New York	NY	**C**	C+	B-	454.3	-7.32	14.8	2.3	0.0	29.6	**10.0**	12.0	25.4
DEMOTTE STATE BK	Demotte	IN	**B-**	B-	B-	366.1	-0.60	11.0	1.0	16.0	39.1	**10.0**	12.3	21.3
DENALI STATE BK	Fairbanks	AK	**B-**	B-	B-	274.9	2.40	8.4	1.4	8.1	43.7	**7.9**	9.6	18.1
DENISON STATE BK	Holton	KS	**B**	B	A-	292.0	2.14	7.6	2.7	17.3	33.3	**10.0**	12.0	18.8
DENMARK STATE BK	Denmark	WI	**B**	B	C	410.0	2.09	8.2	2.2	14.6	21.1	**10.0**	11.2	16.8
DENVER SB	Denver	IA	**B-**	B-	B-	137.0	-1.29	4.1	1.8	18.0	42.2	**7.3**	9.2	15.0
▲ DEPARTMENT STORES NATIONAL BK	Sioux Falls	SD	**B**	B	B-	399.6	7.95	0.0	18.1	0.0	0.0	**10.0**	16.4	49.7
DEPOSITORY TRUST CO	New York	NY	**U**	U	U	2864.7	-20.81	0.0	0.0	0.0	0.0	**10.0**	15.7	64.7
DESJARDINS BANK NA	Hallandale	FL	**C+**	C	C	219.2	-0.07	1.1	0.2	54.2	17.5	**10.0**	12.5	28.5
DESOTO COUNTY BANK	Horn Lake	MS	**B**	B-	B-	81.8	4.01	10.4	1.3	23.6	11.6	**10.0**	11.6	15.6
DEUTSCHE BANK TRUST CO NA	New York	NY	**U**	U	U	128.4	-1.06	0.0	0.0	0.0	78.4	**10.0**	88.9	672.8
DEUTSCHE BK NATIONAL TRUST CO	Los Angeles	CA	**U**	U	U	173.2	-8.39	0.0	0.0	0.0	56.2	**10.0**	86.1	461.9
DEUTSCHE BK TRUST CO AMERICAS	New York	NY	**B+**	B+	A-	55325.0	3.94	5.9	0.3	6.6	0.0	**10.0**	15.8	49.2
DEUTSCHE BK TRUST CO DELAWARE	Wilmington	DE	**A-**	A-	A-	435.2	-5.17	5.8	0.1	0.0	7.0	**10.0**	71.1	79.6
DEVON BANK	Chicago	IL	**D**	D	E+	238.8	1.36	8.7	2.2	12.4	18.4	**5.3**	7.5	11.2
DEWEY BANK	Dewey	IL	**C-**	D+	D+	27.5	0.19	1.4	0.8	8.3	41.7	**6.0**	8.0	16.3
DEWITT SB	Clinton	IL	**C+**	C+	B	103.4	-0.09	0.0	9.8	32.9	42.6	**10.0**	11.6	27.7
DIAMOND BANK	Murfreesboro	AR	**B+**	B+	B-	446.2	2.57	3.2	3.3	21.0	31.2	**8.6**	10.1	17.4
DICKINSON COUNTY BANK	Enterprise	KS	**D**	D+	C-	11.1	21.64	2.5	5.7	29.3	7.0	**8.3**	9.8	23.1
DILLEY STATE BK	Dilley	TX	**A-**	B+	A-	137.2	12.56	2.0	1.3	0.4	78.3	**10.0**	13.9	53.7
DIME BANK	Honesdale	PA	**D**	D	D	620.2	2.46	9.1	1.1	13.9	16.2	**8.3**	10.2	13.6
DIME BANK	Norwich	CT	**C**	C	C	763.3	2.57	6.1	0.2	26.3	22.0	**10.0**	11.2	16.1
DIME SB OF WILLIAMSBURGH	Brooklyn	NY	**B**	B-	C+	4369.8	9.17	0.0	0.0	1.6	0.8	**7.4**	9.3	12.8
DISCOVER BANK	Greenwood	DE	**C**	C	C+	79118.0	6.87	0.3	84.5	0.1	5.2	**10.0**	12.0	15.9
DIXON BANK	Dixon	KY	**B**	B	A-	89.5	2.14	2.6	3.7	6.8	70.1	**10.0**	19.2	48.3
DMB COMMUNITY BANK	De Forest	WI	**C+**	C	C-	333.6	9.09	1.7	1.0	16.6	8.1	**10.0**	11.8	15.9
DNB FIRST NA	Downingtown	PA	**C+**	C+	B-	695.5	6.91	7.8	1.0	10.8	28.6	**9.6**	10.8	15.9
DNB NATIONAL BK	Clear Lake	SD	**C+**	C	C+	62.7	1.44	1.8	1.3	8.6	37.9	**9.3**	10.5	18.8
DOLLAR BANK FSB	Pittsburgh	PA	**B**	B	B-	6772.1	1.91	6.7	1.6	58.6	14.3	**10.0**	11.5	18.5
DOLORES STATE BK	Dolores	CO	**A-**	A-	A	152.1	7.56	4.2	5.1	26.2	36.5	**10.0**	12.5	25.7
DONLEY COUNTY STATE BK	Clarendon	TX	**C+**	C	C+	37.6	-9.77	6.6	3.9	0.2	29.7	**10.0**	19.4	37.0
▼ DOOLIN SECURITY SAVINGS BK FSB	New Martinsville	WV	**D**	C	C+	46.5	4.07	0.8	2.3	16.1	43.7	**9.9**	10.9	40.6
DORAL BANK	San Juan	PR	**E+**	D-	D-	6404.2	-19.54	16.6	0.2	32.6	3.2	**0.0**	2.2	4.4
DOUGLAS COUNTY BANK	Lawrence	KS	**B-**	B-	B-	296.4	4.50	4.8	0.7	7.6	41.2	**10.0**	11.8	20.9
DOUGLAS NATIONAL BK	Douglas	GA	**A-**	A-	A-	168.8	17.55	10.8	2.5	17.1	5.9	**10.0**	12.8	17.1
DRAKE BANK	Saint Paul	MN	**B**	B-	D+	86.9	8.79	25.8	2.3	18.6	5.1	**9.9**	10.9	16.7
DRUMMOND COMMUNITY BANK	Chiefland	FL	**A-**	A-	A-	368.9	1.62	3.1	3.1	20.3	37.5	**10.0**	13.0	24.8
DSRM NATIONAL BK	Albuquerque	NM	**U**	U	B	3.6	-1.79	0.0	0.0	0.0	69.0	**10.0**	84.8	403.3
DU QUOIN STATE BK	Du Quoin	IL	**B+**	B	B-	110.3	6.99	4.6	1.4	16.1	56.2	**5.9**	7.9	19.9
▼ DUBLIN NATIONAL BK	Dublin	TX	**D**	D+	B-	27.8	3.26	2.8	4.1	4.4	59.8	**10.0**	12.6	36.4
DUBUQUE BANK & TRUST CO	Dubuque	IA	**B**	B	B	1389.2	-3.39	16.5	0.9	12.5	15.8	**7.0**	9.8	12.5
DURAND STATE BK	Durand	IL	**C+**	C+	C-	89.5	-0.67	8.9	6.2	19.2	34.5	**9.9**	10.9	16.6
DURDEN BANKING CO INC	Twin City	GA	**B+**	B+	B+	152.6	-4.41	10.3	5.8	29.1	25.7	**10.0**	13.5	24.1
DUTTON STATE BK	Dutton	MT	**B-**	B-	C	32.6	9.82	17.9	5.0	11.9	1.8	**9.7**	11.2	14.7
DYSART STATE BK	Dysart	IA	**E+**	E+	C-	15.9	3.26	1.4	1.6	12.3	5.3	**4.9**	6.9	12.0

Arrows denote recent upgrades ▲ or downgrades ▼

Asset Quality Index	Adjusted Non-Performing Loans as a % of Total Loans	Adjusted Non-Performing Loans as a % of Capital	Net Charge-Offs Avg Loans	Profitability Index	Net Income ($Mil)	Return on Assets (R.O.A.)	Return on Equity (R.O.E.)	Net Interest Spread	Overhead Efficiency Ratio	Liquidity Index	Liquidity Ratio	Hot Money Ratio	Stability Index
9.3	0.33	1.6	0.01	**4.9**	0.7	0.82	5.74	3.50	66.6	**1.9**	20.6	20.4	**7.8**
6.2	0.77	4.2	0.12	**4.5**	0.7	1.10	12.12	5.01	80.4	**2.5**	27.0	18.1	**2.8**
1.8	4.42	25.1	0.87	**2.7**	0.2	0.18	1.66	5.57	78.5	**0.7**	14.4	43.2	**4.0**
7.9	0.14	0.9	-0.01	**8.2**	5.1	1.82	14.60	4.05	54.8	**3.7**	23.3	11.4	**8.3**
6.9	0.84	5.6	0.10	**3.8**	6.7	0.72	6.71	3.23	70.8	**3.4**	26.0	16.1	**7.9**
5.1	2.04	10.6	0.00	**3.2**	0.2	0.55	4.65	4.42	84.3	**3.9**	23.1	10.5	**5.6**
3.9	1.21	7.4	0.21	**5.8**	2.7	1.43	11.68	4.28	69.7	**4.7**	21.0	5.1	**6.2**
6.1	1.15	6.5	0.02	**2.6**	0.1	0.47	5.54	3.04	85.1	**4.1**	51.6	16.3	**4.0**
5.4	0.77	6.1	0.00	**4.8**	0.3	0.68	7.63	4.81	73.6	**1.4**	13.4	25.6	**4.6**
2.4	3.52	23.0	1.15	**0.0**	-0.7	-0.71	-6.99	3.36	114.7	**3.1**	12.3	13.1	**3.8**
3.1	2.14	16.1	0.94	**1.5**	0.2	0.05	0.56	3.50	99.4	**3.4**	7.1	11.0	**3.2**
6.8	1.46	5.6	0.05	**3.3**	1.3	0.63	7.55	2.93	73.7	**4.4**	49.1	15.0	**4.9**
1.3	5.17	30.9	-0.01	**1.2**	0.2	0.13	1.27	3.15	93.1	**2.6**	30.5	18.7	**4.0**
5.4	0.81	6.2	0.01	**6.5**	2.9	1.59	20.12	4.44	67.4	**1.7**	21.2	23.1	**6.6**
8.1	0.19	0.8	0.02	**0.6**	0.0	0.01	0.18	3.12	104.8	**5.5**	54.0	10.8	**2.8**
9.7	0.00	0.0	0.00	**2.3**	0.8	0.22	1.92	1.02	90.8	**4.2**	69.1	20.8	**6.5**
3.5	5.21	20.4	0.04	**4.8**	2.5	0.90	7.80	3.60	67.4	**4.4**	35.6	11.6	**6.7**
5.7	1.10	5.2	-0.03	**3.9**	1.5	0.75	7.48	4.30	83.0	**4.6**	48.0	14.3	**5.1**
4.0	3.92	17.9	0.62	**6.5**	3.4	1.54	12.69	3.77	55.5	**3.5**	20.4	11.8	**7.5**
4.7	2.09	12.1	0.19	**4.3**	2.3	0.73	6.70	3.34	66.8	**3.8**	25.9	11.4	**5.9**
8.5	0.00	0.0	0.01	**4.1**	0.9	0.83	8.52	3.16	61.3	**2.2**	45.8	42.1	**5.0**
7.5	1.64	1.7	2.89	**7.8**	3.9	1.37	7.99	3.78	30.0	**3.3**	90.8	99.8	**7.0**
10.0	na	0.0	na	**8.3**	28.8	1.44	8.94	-1.28	83.3	**4.0**	109.3	101.0	**7.0**
8.0	1.21	6.4	0.03	**2.6**	0.7	0.41	3.32	3.30	88.6	**5.2**	33.8	6.0	**4.9**
4.1	2.51	15.4	0.03	**5.2**	0.5	0.78	6.91	4.82	66.2	**0.9**	10.5	32.7	**6.1**
10.0	na	0.0	na	**10.0**	5.4	5.51	6.59	0.42	79.9	**4.0**	622.5	101.0	**7.0**
10.0	na	0.0	na	**8.8**	8.7	6.68	8.22	0.38	83.5	**4.0**	531.1	101.0	**7.0**
9.4	0.51	0.9	0.03	**4.5**	226.0	0.53	3.33	0.87	61.3	**8.2**	83.1	0.8	**10.0**
7.7	0.00	0.0	0.00	**9.5**	7.8	2.34	3.34	1.20	46.5	**1.5**	15.4	25.0	**7.0**
0.3	9.07	65.0	0.29	**2.1**	0.6	0.36	4.58	3.84	94.2	**4.2**	29.8	10.8	**3.0**
4.4	2.77	11.3	-0.24	**2.4**	0.0	0.18	1.95	3.86	99.6	**6.1**	58.1	6.8	**4.3**
6.4	1.59	6.4	0.18	**2.8**	0.3	0.32	2.89	3.29	82.6	**3.8**	43.1	17.0	**6.1**
5.3	1.10	5.9	0.30	**6.2**	5.2	1.53	14.62	4.11	64.4	**1.5**	24.4	27.0	**7.1**
3.7	3.18	16.8	0.89	**1.8**	0.0	0.00	0.00	4.22	95.2	**3.3**	39.1	15.6	**3.4**
10.0	0.44	0.3	0.04	**5.5**	1.0	1.01	7.39	2.62	45.4	**7.2**	89.3	7.0	**7.6**
0.7	4.26	28.0	0.20	**4.9**	4.2	0.92	9.08	4.06	63.1	**1.3**	3.1	24.5	**6.7**
3.2	3.69	21.2	0.26	**2.2**	2.7	0.47	4.31	3.06	86.4	**3.0**	20.8	14.7	**6.4**
4.7	0.51	5.0	-0.01	**7.1**	34.4	1.10	10.44	3.20	44.1	**2.8**	2.3	14.0	**8.9**
2.2	1.70	10.3	2.03	**10.0**	1849.2	3.15	26.62	8.82	34.3	**0.8**	16.0	53.1	**10.0**
8.7	2.70	3.1	0.01	**4.1**	0.5	0.80	4.86	2.80	62.2	**3.4**	81.3	33.6	**7.0**
5.4	0.09	0.6	0.22	**6.9**	2.9	1.20	10.30	3.80	52.6	**1.8**	14.3	20.3	**5.9**
4.8	1.61	9.3	0.21	**3.7**	3.6	0.71	6.83	3.46	72.8	**3.8**	12.5	9.7	**5.8**
7.9	0.00	0.0	0.02	**3.9**	0.4	0.79	7.79	3.70	84.0	**4.1**	41.4	14.8	**4.0**
7.5	0.64	4.2	0.16	**3.6**	28.4	0.56	5.05	2.86	72.4	**4.4**	13.0	6.1	**8.1**
7.1	1.16	4.4	0.11	**5.5**	1.1	1.00	8.07	4.20	66.0	**3.7**	42.1	17.0	**7.9**
9.2	0.00	0.0	0.00	**3.1**	0.2	0.64	3.48	2.62	81.1	**3.7**	65.9	22.0	**6.4**
7.3	0.77	1.3	-0.45	**0.4**	-0.1	-0.15	-1.17	2.40	113.7	**7.3**	84.9	4.2	**6.0**
0.0	11.55	205.6	4.32	**0.0**	-276.2	-4.73	-62.77	3.27	146.0	**0.7**	14.9	55.1	**3.7**
9.1	0.05	0.2	0.13	**3.0**	1.2	0.56	4.71	3.36	83.8	**5.6**	47.3	8.6	**6.7**
5.2	1.63	9.6	-0.09	**9.7**	2.9	2.50	19.28	4.76	53.5	**0.8**	17.0	37.5	**7.8**
4.4	1.33	8.7	0.18	**6.1**	0.9	1.45	12.92	5.41	66.7	**1.8**	14.9	20.1	**5.1**
6.0	1.55	5.8	0.58	**6.7**	4.1	1.51	11.82	5.16	68.5	**3.8**	29.3	12.5	**7.6**
9.5	na	0.0	na	**7.0**	0.0	1.14	1.36	1.37	90.8	**5.0**	632.3	100.0	**5.1**
8.5	0.46	1.8	-0.04	**6.5**	1.1	1.43	15.04	4.57	63.9	**3.7**	52.6	19.6	**7.9**
9.3	0.00	0.0	-1.17	**0.2**	-0.1	-0.65	-5.23	2.86	137.1	**6.4**	76.3	8.1	**4.8**
5.6	0.62	4.1	0.90	**5.8**	11.0	1.05	10.89	3.50	68.0	**3.6**	19.0	11.8	**7.4**
6.5	0.67	3.4	0.20	**3.7**	0.5	0.75	7.38	4.03	74.2	**1.6**	23.4	26.1	**4.6**
4.9	2.97	12.4	0.25	**7.9**	2.2	1.86	14.14	4.58	59.8	**1.5**	23.4	27.2	**8.0**
5.7	0.54	3.5	0.25	**6.4**	0.3	1.00	9.97	4.58	66.1	**4.6**	14.8	4.4	**5.4**
7.7	0.00	0.0	0.00	**1.6**	0.0	0.28	4.20	2.40	88.7	**6.6**	52.3	0.0	**1.6**

Name	City	State	Rating	2013 Rating	2012 Rating	Total Assets ($Mil)	One Year Asset Growth	Asset Mix (As a % of Total Assets): Commercial Loans	Consumer Loans	Mortgage Loans	Securities	Capitalization Index	Leverage Ratio	Risk-Based Capital Ratio
E*TRADE BANK	Arlington	VA	**C**	C-	D+	44509.9	0.26	0.0	1.1	8.5	56.0	**9.1**	10.4	25.9
▲ E*TRADE SAVINGS BANK	Arlington	VA	**C+**	C-	C	1133.4	4.26	0.0	0.0	10.7	76.2	**10.0**	17.6	81.0
EAGLE B&TC OF MISSOURI	Hillsboro	MO	**C**	C-	C-	892.5	0.27	5.5	0.7	12.9	18.8	**8.4**	9.9	14.5
EAGLE BANK	Glenwood	MN	**A-**	A-	A	136.5	15.26	5.0	3.9	15.7	13.3	**10.0**	13.3	20.9
EAGLE BANK	Polson	MT	**C-**	C	C-	47.3	25.48	10.8	5.0	6.0	36.0	**8.1**	9.7	25.9
EAGLE BANK	Everett	MA	**D**	D	C+	432.8	0.14	2.2	0.0	20.6	35.9	**9.1**	10.4	16.1
EAGLE BANK & TRUST CO	Little Rock	AR	**B**	B	B+	373.2	1.27	3.0	1.3	8.5	59.6	**10.0**	11.2	24.4
EAGLE COMMUNITY BANK	Maple Grove	MN	**E-**	E-	E-	22.7	7.85	18.7	1.1	10.6	0.4	**2.5**	5.2	9.5
EAGLE NATIONAL BK	Upper Darby	PA	**C+**	C+	C-	192.2	-0.82	7.6	0.2	13.1	17.3	**10.0**	12.6	19.9
▼ EAGLE SAVINGS BANK	Cincinnati	OH	**B**	B	C+	109.1	1.73	1.5	0.1	50.9	0.0	**9.0**	10.4	15.3
EAGLE STATE BK	Eagle	NE	**D-**	D	C-	21.3	20.89	13.2	3.9	10.5	8.5	**4.8**	8.0	10.9
EAGLE VALLEY BANK NA	Saint Croix Falls	WI	**E-**	E-	E-	135.6	4.83	11.0	1.4	15.0	18.5	**4.2**	6.2	11.2
EAGLEBANK	Bethesda	MD	**B**	B	C+	4151.3	18.96	19.2	0.1	6.1	9.2	**6.0**	10.1	11.8
▲ EAGLEMARK SB	Carson City	NV	**A-**	A-	A	46.3	24.50	0.0	38.6	0.0	59.3	**10.0**	23.8	18.4
EARLHAM SB	West Des Moines	IA	**C+**	C+	C+	263.2	-4.50	15.3	2.0	14.0	26.6	**9.0**	10.3	18.7
EAST BOSTON SB	East Boston	MA	**C-**	D	D+	3170.3	19.73	2.8	0.3	14.8	5.3	**10.0**	12.1	15.4
EAST CAMBRIDGE SB	Cambridge	MA	**C**	C	C+	880.9	3.68	2.2	1.1	33.6	22.2	**7.9**	9.6	16.1
EAST DUBUQUE SB	Dubuque	IA	**C+**	C+	D+	160.7	6.17	19.8	3.6	15.4	9.1	**7.4**	10.0	12.8
EAST RIVER BANK	Philadelphia	PA	**B-**	B-	C	262.7	3.68	3.8	0.1	47.1	3.0	**8.4**	9.9	15.4
EAST WEST BANK	Pasadena	CA	**B+**	B+	B	28350.9	15.85	23.7	1.2	13.4	9.0	**5.8**	8.1	11.6
EAST WISCONSIN SAVINGS BANK SA	Kaukauna	WI	**D+**	C-	C-	225.7	-3.66	0.5	1.1	43.5	38.3	**7.0**	9.0	21.7
▼ EASTBANK NA	New York	NY	**B+**	A-	B+	193.1	-0.33	0.7	0.0	6.0	29.1	**10.0**	14.9	21.9
EASTERN BANK	Boston	MA	**B-**	B-	B-	8811.7	1.22	9.5	9.2	14.9	12.1	**9.0**	10.3	14.2
EASTERN COLORADO BANK	Cheyenne Wells	CO	**B**	B	C+	327.1	0.28	6.6	0.5	7.8	29.6	**7.5**	9.4	13.2
EASTERN INTERNATIONAL BK	Los Angeles	CA	**B**	B	B+	117.9	-5.89	0.0	0.0	0.2	0.0	**10.0**	14.6	22.6
EASTERN MICHIGAN BANK	Croswell	MI	**C+**	C+	C	283.0	3.02	7.7	1.3	9.8	39.6	**8.4**	9.9	19.4
EASTERN NATIONAL BK	Miami	FL	**C-**	C-	D	399.2	4.78	9.1	0.8	15.8	3.8	**7.4**	9.2	16.1
EASTERN SAVINGS BANK	Norwich	CT	**D+**	D+	D+	181.6	8.15	2.9	4.8	37.9	0.6	**6.5**	8.5	12.6
EASTERN SAVINGS BANK FSB	Hunt Valley	MD	**E**	E-	E-	421.3	-4.12	0.0	0.0	45.8	0.4	**10.0**	13.5	26.0
EASTHAMPTON SB	Easthampton	MA	**B**	B	B+	1020.7	2.03	2.1	0.2	54.1	15.5	**10.0**	12.8	21.6
EASTMAN NATIONAL BK OF NEWKIRK	Newkirk	OK	**A-**	A-	B+	227.3	4.53	16.6	2.9	16.1	24.3	**8.9**	10.2	16.7
EASTON BANK & TRUST CO	Easton	MD	**D+**	D+	D-	138.4	-0.85	6.4	2.4	31.5	9.8	**8.9**	10.3	16.1
EASTSIDE COMMERCIAL BANK NA	Bellevue	WA	**E-**	E-	E-	36.0	-14.93	9.1	0.1	5.1	0.0	**0.0**	1.4	3.6
EASTWOOD BANK	Rochester	MN	**B-**	B-	C+	669.6	5.52	5.1	2.8	9.0	25.4	**5.7**	7.7	12.6
▲ EATON FSB	Charlotte	MI	**B-**	C+	C+	307.5	-0.97	0.1	0.0	41.3	34.0	**10.0**	15.8	39.2
ECLIPSE BANK INC	Louisville	KY	**C+**	C+	D+	142.3	4.76	6.0	0.2	11.2	15.8	**9.6**	10.7	15.4
EDGAR COUNTY BANK & TRUST CO	Paris	IL	**B-**	C	D+	398.2	9.83	14.9	0.3	6.8	33.8	**6.1**	8.1	13.1
▼ EDGARTOWN NATIONAL BK	Edgartown	MA	**B-**	B	B	169.0	7.69	3.7	0.1	37.7	9.9	**10.0**	11.0	17.7
EDGEBROOK BANK	Chicago	IL	**E-**	E-	E-	94.8	3.61	8.8	0.2	36.2	5.4	**0.4**	4.1	6.7
EDGEWATER BANK	Saint Joseph	MI	**D-**	D-	D	117.0	-2.46	4.1	0.8	39.9	11.1	**9.4**	10.6	17.9
EDISON NATIONAL BK	Fort Myers	FL	**C**	C-	C-	241.8	4.04	1.9	1.9	28.4	7.9	**6.2**	8.2	19.3
EDMONTON STATE BK	Edmonton	KY	**A-**	A-	A	453.3	1.65	6.4	6.0	20.0	20.0	**10.0**	13.5	21.4
EDON STATE BK CO OF EDON OHIO	Edon	OH	**B**	B	B+	60.2	-4.10	2.0	0.4	9.5	60.4	**10.0**	18.7	64.1
EDWARD JONES TRUST CO	Saint Louis	MO	**U**	U		56.8	16.65	0.0	0.0	0.0	0.2	**10.0**	82.5	342.0
EH NATIONAL BK	Beverly Hills	CA	**D**	D-	D	224.8	6.60	5.8	0.0	1.0	9.2	**10.0**	14.6	20.7
EITZEN STATE BK	Caledonia	MN	**B+**	B	B	86.6	-4.19	7.8	1.4	4.8	27.8	**8.1**	9.7	15.6
EL DORADO SAVINGS BANK FSB	Placerville	CA	**C+**	C+	B-	1884.5	1.50	0.0	0.0	20.9	54.0	**8.2**	9.8	36.7
ELBERFELD STATE BK	Elberfeld	IN	**B-**	B	B+	67.1	5.17	3.7	1.9	9.4	24.6	**10.0**	11.0	19.7
ELBERTON FS&LA	Elberton	GA	**D+**	C-	C+	21.1	8.25	0.0	0.6	60.0	15.0	**10.0**	23.1	44.4
ELDERTON STATE BK	Elderton	PA	**B**	B	C+	225.8	11.15	10.3	1.6	12.8	5.3	**9.5**	11.1	14.6
ELGIN STATE BK	Elgin	IA	**D-**	D-	D+	21.7	-2.62	4.1	2.2	6.2	51.1	**5.7**	7.7	19.3
▼ ELIZABETHTON FSB	Elizabethton	TN	**B+**	A-	B+	332.7	-1.50	0.0	0.8	28.9	51.5	**10.0**	31.7	95.2
ELK STATE BK	Clyde	KS	**C-**	D+	C-	51.5	3.40	4.3	1.7	11.4	47.4	**5.4**	7.4	19.0
ELKHART STATE BK	Elkhart	TX	**D**	D+	B-	53.4	-7.14	9.4	9.3	2.5	58.7	**1.2**	4.3	12.1
ELKHORN VALLEY BANK & TRUST	Norfolk	NE	**A-**	A-	B+	664.3	10.65	10.7	2.7	3.8	44.8	**8.5**	10.0	15.6
ELKTON BANK & TRUST CO	Elkton	KY	**B+**	A-	A-	131.0	2.97	5.6	6.3	15.2	42.9	**10.0**	13.8	18.7
ELMIRA SAVINGS BANK	Elmira	NY	**C+**	C+	B-	533.8	2.69	4.6	5.8	50.9	13.1	**6.6**	8.6	14.3
ELSA STATE BK & TRUST CO	Elsa	TX	**B-**	B-	B-	187.4	3.82	6.3	6.7	12.4	36.5	**7.1**	9.1	16.8
▲ ELYSIAN BANK	Elysian	MN	**C**	C-	D+	40.1	-3.37	10.4	5.7	11.8	4.6	**10.0**	11.0	18.7
EMBASSY BK FOR LEHIGH VALLEY	Bethlehem	PA	**B**	B	B-	717.2	8.29	4.1	0.1	46.8	11.3	**6.5**	8.5	13.5

Asset Quality Index	Adjusted Non-Performing Loans as a % of Total Loans	Adjusted Non-Performing Loans as a % of Capital	Net Charge-Offs / Avg Loans	Profitability Index	Net Income ($Mil)	Return on Assets (R.O.A.)	Return on Equity (R.O.E.)	Net Interest Spread	Overhead Efficiency Ratio	Liquidity Index	Liquidity Ratio	Hot Money Ratio	Stability Index
3.1	4.07	12.6	0.68	**4.8**	341.2	1.01	7.71	2.59	59.4	**3.4**	55.2	30.5	**8.4**
5.6	3.65	4.6	3.17	**4.2**	6.1	0.72	4.28	2.01	45.3	**4.3**	91.6	30.8	**7.2**
2.7	2.31	14.5	0.23	**4.6**	5.5	0.82	7.96	3.51	62.6	**3.6**	17.2	11.2	**6.8**
7.1	0.21	1.0	0.04	**5.9**	1.3	1.40	10.05	3.60	65.4	**4.7**	24.0	5.1	**8.8**
5.4	1.10	3.6	0.27	**2.1**	0.1	0.30	2.83	3.20	88.3	**2.9**	28.6	16.8	**3.7**
9.3	0.20	0.9	0.00	**0.9**	0.6	0.19	1.66	2.37	106.5	**3.9**	49.2	17.8	**6.0**
9.4	0.64	1.8	0.10	**4.5**	2.4	0.86	8.00	3.57	68.0	**4.7**	54.4	15.2	**5.9**
8.5	0.00	0.0	-0.27	**0.9**	0.0	0.08	1.51	4.45	103.1	**1.4**	17.6	25.3	**0.0**
3.4	3.24	16.3	0.32	**2.6**	0.3	0.21	1.61	3.69	98.7	**2.8**	19.9	15.3	**6.0**
4.9	1.94	13.0	0.07	**4.6**	0.6	0.74	7.29	3.31	75.1	**2.5**	17.6	16.6	**5.3**
8.0	0.12	1.1	0.00	**2.7**	0.1	0.56	6.27	3.72	84.5	**4.5**	22.4	6.1	**1.4**
4.0	1.12	9.6	0.13	**1.0**	-0.1	-0.08	-1.44	2.82	96.0	**1.2**	15.3	29.7	**0.3**
4.9	0.79	6.0	0.13	**8.9**	40.4	1.39	13.77	4.56	49.4	**3.6**	8.5	10.6	**8.2**
6.9	0.00	0.0	0.00	**10.0**	3.3	12.75	62.53	17.15	68.1	**4.0**	73.0	20.8	**8.8**
6.2	0.61	3.4	0.13	**3.9**	0.8	0.42	4.18	3.54	74.3	**5.1**	38.8	8.6	**5.7**
3.6	1.37	8.5	0.00	**3.6**	16.4	0.76	8.14	3.23	69.9	**3.0**	19.1	15.1	**7.7**
6.7	0.58	3.8	0.05	**2.6**	2.1	0.33	3.33	2.92	85.8	**2.1**	30.4	24.2	**6.3**
4.6	0.86	6.7	0.08	**3.9**	1.1	0.90	9.05	3.94	74.1	**1.0**	8.1	30.2	**4.3**
6.0	0.51	4.1	0.01	**4.4**	1.4	0.75	7.41	3.81	72.1	**1.2**	7.0	26.8	**5.0**
5.4	0.80	6.9	0.17	**6.9**	212.5	1.05	10.96	4.16	51.4	**1.7**	13.7	22.5	**8.1**
6.0	1.95	10.9	0.00	**1.5**	0.2	0.14	1.59	2.92	101.0	**4.2**	46.4	15.6	**4.2**
7.9	0.00	0.0	0.00	**4.9**	0.9	0.64	4.32	3.78	68.0	**3.3**	49.0	22.1	**8.0**
5.6	0.68	4.2	0.04	**4.0**	45.4	0.69	5.31	2.87	76.9	**5.7**	26.8	2.9	**8.8**
5.4	0.92	5.9	0.27	**6.3**	3.7	1.54	15.24	4.16	60.1	**1.8**	20.7	21.8	**6.2**
7.6	0.00	0.0	0.00	**3.8**	0.5	0.49	3.50	2.88	72.5	**2.0**	38.2	32.7	**7.6**
5.2	1.48	6.7	0.15	**3.6**	1.3	0.64	6.64	3.33	75.7	**6.3**	50.8	4.8	**4.9**
5.4	0.37	3.0	-0.04	**2.4**	0.9	0.31	3.02	3.39	86.5	**0.9**	12.7	32.3	**4.0**
2.2	2.71	25.8	0.12	**1.4**	0.1	0.09	1.03	3.19	95.0	**1.2**	5.5	26.0	**4.4**
0.3	45.11	171.4	1.06	**3.3**	1.9	0.61	7.92	5.77	83.7	**2.6**	36.4	22.2	**2.7**
6.5	1.26	7.1	0.11	**4.1**	5.5	0.73	5.80	3.40	68.0	**1.4**	17.3	28.5	**9.2**
6.1	0.57	3.5	0.10	**8.8**	2.5	1.43	15.19	4.14	50.9	**4.3**	7.6	6.0	**5.9**
1.9	4.13	26.5	0.87	**3.0**	0.6	0.54	5.42	4.24	76.9	**3.6**	18.6	11.3	**4.3**
0.3	5.88	81.1	-0.32	**0.0**	-2.0	-6.74	-201.84	3.19	263.8	**1.6**	34.3	37.4	**1.2**
4.7	1.11	8.1	0.07	**4.1**	4.8	0.95	12.38	3.47	79.7	**4.0**	18.8	9.0	**5.4**
6.8	2.73	8.1	0.48	**3.4**	1.4	0.61	4.01	3.03	73.7	**3.8**	52.2	19.2	**6.6**
4.2	0.90	5.8	0.10	**3.5**	0.5	0.49	4.41	3.77	80.9	**1.1**	22.1	32.0	**5.9**
4.3	1.40	9.6	0.17	**6.9**	4.7	1.62	18.23	3.60	59.0	**2.3**	14.0	17.6	**5.3**
6.7	0.61	4.0	0.00	**3.6**	0.6	0.50	4.50	3.50	77.8	**4.5**	10.9	4.6	**6.6**
0.3	9.30	115.7	0.17	**0.0**	-1.1	-1.62	-47.72	4.76	94.5	**0.7**	16.3	52.5	**0.3**
2.3	3.47	23.4	0.01	**0.0**	-0.5	-0.57	-5.82	3.35	114.8	**4.1**	19.0	8.2	**2.9**
6.0	1.14	6.3	0.38	**2.7**	1.0	0.55	6.85	2.68	84.6	**5.5**	41.2	7.2	**3.6**
6.1	1.27	5.9	0.12	**6.5**	5.0	1.48	11.08	3.71	63.3	**3.4**	25.7	13.2	**8.9**
9.1	0.96	1.6	0.00	**3.6**	0.4	0.81	4.91	2.89	71.7	**6.5**	72.7	7.4	**7.6**
10.0	na	0.0	na	**10.0**	4.4	12.16	13.26	0.05	77.4	**10.0**	529.3	0.0	**6.7**
0.1	6.21	27.7	0.30	**1.0**	-0.1	-0.07	-0.47	3.65	101.3	**0.8**	15.1	36.9	**5.0**
7.7	0.43	2.6	-0.02	**6.5**	1.0	1.53	17.38	3.01	52.9	**3.0**	26.4	15.4	**6.1**
7.9	2.43	5.5	0.14	**3.8**	8.6	0.61	6.20	2.29	64.5	**6.1**	81.8	13.4	**7.4**
6.6	1.35	6.4	-0.02	**3.8**	0.3	0.54	4.78	3.72	82.8	**5.3**	41.9	8.5	**6.1**
9.8	0.44	1.3	0.33	**0.7**	0.0	-0.24	-0.96	4.14	101.2	**3.9**	39.1	12.8	**5.2**
4.8	0.98	7.1	0.09	**7.1**	2.1	1.26	11.49	3.98	46.7	**1.7**	9.4	20.4	**6.4**
9.3	0.21	0.8	0.04	**1.5**	0.0	0.07	1.34	3.16	97.1	**6.1**	61.8	5.1	**1.2**
9.5	1.54	2.0	-0.15	**4.8**	1.9	0.75	2.38	2.68	51.8	**4.0**	78.5	26.4	**8.1**
7.0	0.43	2.6	-0.01	**2.8**	0.2	0.48	6.33	3.33	80.5	**2.9**	25.6	15.7	**4.0**
3.0	4.28	13.2	9.52	**0.0**	-2.7	-6.03	-95.79	3.65	118.6	**7.3**	63.2	0.0	**2.9**
8.8	0.17	0.7	0.13	**5.9**	5.6	1.18	11.89	3.03	48.3	**5.8**	52.3	8.9	**6.4**
8.7	0.33	1.0	0.14	**4.9**	1.1	1.16	8.71	4.12	64.0	**3.1**	40.7	19.9	**7.7**
4.2	1.08	9.3	0.06	**4.0**	2.6	0.68	6.41	3.39	75.6	**1.9**	9.9	18.8	**5.5**
5.2	0.82	4.1	0.56	**4.9**	1.5	1.05	11.83	4.98	76.5	**2.3**	29.1	19.9	**5.0**
3.1	4.60	21.1	0.30	**4.7**	0.3	1.09	10.26	4.44	70.1	**6.2**	42.1	2.8	**4.5**
5.5	0.69	6.3	-0.01	**5.0**	5.0	0.96	11.19	3.57	62.1	**4.1**	7.7	6.8	**5.7**

Name	City	State	Rating	2013 Rating	2012 Rating	Total Assets ($Mil)	One Year Asset Growth	Asset Mix (As a % of Total Assets) Comm-ercial Loans	Cons-umer Loans	Mort-gage Loans	Secur-ities	Capital-ization Index	Lever-age Ratio	Risk-Based Capital Ratio
EMBASSY NATIONAL BK	Lawrenceville	GA	**C+**	C	D+	68.8	22.46	1.8	0.1	0.9	0.0	**10.0**	12.4	18.3
EMERALD BANK	Burden	KS	**D+**	D+	D+	18.1	0.11	4.5	7.8	32.6	4.7	**7.1**	9.1	17.6
EMIGRANT BANK	New York	NY	**C-**	C-	C+	6272.5	-5.62	20.7	0.2	24.8	24.6	**10.0**	16.9	24.6
EMIGRANT MERCANTILE BANK	New York	NY	**U**	U	C-	3.6	-3.97	0.0	0.0	0.0	0.0	**10.0**	85.6	422.7
EMPIRE BANK	Springfield	MO	**B-**	B-	B-	1095.6	4.33	8.5	16.2	9.5	12.6	**4.1**	8.3	10.6
EMPIRE NATIONAL BK	Islandia	NY	**C+**	C	C	514.7	9.50	9.1	0.2	4.3	27.5	**6.7**	8.7	12.9
EMPIRE STATE BK	Newburgh	NY	**C-**	D	D+	164.4	1.66	24.8	0.1	11.7	11.0	**6.5**	8.7	12.1
EMPRISE BANK	Wichita	KS	**B+**	B+	B+	1515.2	-1.76	12.7	2.3	15.5	28.8	**5.7**	7.7	12.5
▼ ENCORE BANK NA	Naples	FL	**D-**	D	C-	328.8	-0.04	2.6	2.6	17.6	26.4	**6.3**	8.3	14.0
ENERBANK USA	Salt Lake City	UT	**B**	B	B-	916.4	37.35	0.0	93.1	0.0	1.2	**6.5**	11.6	12.2
ENGLEWOOD BANK & TRUST	Englewood	FL	**D+**	D+	C-	202.3	5.01	1.9	0.6	23.0	30.4	**7.3**	9.2	17.0
ENLOE STATE BK	Cooper	TX	**B**	B	B-	28.4	10.63	13.7	4.1	20.4	0.0	**10.0**	11.2	16.4
▲ ENNIS STATE BK	Ennis	TX	**B-**	C	C-	148.8	4.05	20.8	1.4	11.3	12.5	**8.6**	10.1	15.4
▲ ENTERPRISE BANK	Houston	TX	**B**	B	C	569.1	10.26	12.3	1.0	6.4	2.5	**10.0**	11.3	15.2
ENTERPRISE BANK	Omaha	NE	**C+**	C+	C-	228.7	14.05	17.4	1.4	10.7	1.4	**5.3**	9.0	11.3
ENTERPRISE BANK	Allison Park	PA	**D**	D	D-	268.0	0.49	14.3	0.0	6.0	0.0	**6.0**	8.0	11.8
ENTERPRISE BANK & TRUST	Clayton	MO	**B+**	B	B-	3190.7	3.24	36.7	0.3	5.5	14.3	**7.6**	10.0	13.0
ENTERPRISE BANK & TRUST CO	Lowell	MA	**C+**	C+	C	1961.8	7.10	17.5	0.5	13.2	12.1	**5.5**	8.5	11.4
ENTERPRISE BANK OF S CAROLINA	Ehrhardt	SC	**E+**	E+	D-	320.5	-6.55	7.0	2.1	7.5	15.8	**0.9**	4.1	9.0
▲ ENTERPRISE NATIONAL BK NJ	Kenilworth	NJ	**A-**	B	C+	162.3	16.76	5.7	0.1	8.9	4.5	**10.0**	13.1	16.8
EPHRATA NATIONAL BK	Ephrata	PA	**B-**	B-	B-	850.4	7.06	3.4	0.5	15.7	35.4	**9.3**	10.6	17.6
EQUITABLE BANK	Grand Island	NE	**C**	C-	D+	185.6	13.56	8.7	1.5	22.2	2.4	**5.7**	9.2	11.5
EQUITABLE BANK SSB	Wauwatosa	WI	**E+**	D-	D-	314.7	-4.77	0.3	0.5	44.7	7.4	**2.8**	5.9	9.9
EQUITABLE CO-OP BANK	Lynn	MA	**C**	C	C	106.4	1.79	0.3	1.8	55.9	21.1	**8.8**	10.2	17.1
EQUITABLE S&LA	Sterling	CO	**B**	B	B	171.1	0.43	0.0	0.6	87.9	5.8	**10.0**	14.5	29.1
EQUITABLE SAVINGS & LOAN CO	Cadiz	OH	**C**	C	C+	13.1	-4.15	0.0	0.8	52.4	25.6	**10.0**	21.3	43.7
EQUITY BANK	Wichita	KS	**B-**	B-	B-	1169.0	1.09	13.4	0.6	14.9	28.5	**9.0**	10.3	15.5
EQUITY BANK	Minnetonka	MN	**C**	C	C	48.9	5.78	10.1	0.5	15.4	0.3	**10.0**	12.8	15.5
ERICSON STATE BK	Ericson	NE	**C+**	C+	C+	70.7	14.66	8.2	8.7	1.8	20.0	**6.7**	8.7	12.8
ESB BANK	Ellwood City	PA	**B**	B	B-	1900.1	2.32	0.8	3.1	21.7	55.8	**7.7**	9.5	17.3
ESB FINANCIAL	Emporia	KS	**B-**	B-	B	190.0	4.94	13.6	10.8	13.1	29.2	**7.2**	9.1	13.2
ESCAMBIA COUNTY BANK	Flomaton	AL	**B-**	C+	C+	79.1	-3.50	2.1	4.4	9.7	67.5	**10.0**	14.3	35.3
ESPIRITO SANTO BANK	Miami	FL	**C**	C	C	676.6	-7.57	19.7	0.6	30.3	2.0	**6.9**	8.9	22.8
ESQUIRE BANK	Garden City	NY	**D+**	D+	D+	295.0	21.46	20.1	2.8	6.9	26.8	**7.9**	9.6	18.8
ESSA BANK & TRUST	Stroudsburg	PA	**C+**	B-	C	1572.5	14.94	2.2	6.0	43.8	24.4	**8.6**	10.0	17.0
ESSEX BANK	Richmond	VA	**C+**	C+	C-	1128.6	1.37	7.8	0.5	15.1	27.1	**8.3**	9.9	15.7
▼ ESSEX SB	Essex	CT	**C**	B-	B	324.1	2.11	4.1	0.6	51.7	0.4	**7.3**	9.2	16.4
EUREKA BANK	Pittsburgh	PA	**A-**	A-	A-	154.2	8.58	15.6	0.5	39.7	7.2	**10.0**	14.3	23.7
▼ EUREKA HOMESTEAD	Metairie	LA	**C-**	C	C-	98.9	5.71	0.0	0.2	60.3	25.5	**10.0**	12.0	27.1
▲ EUREKA SB	La Salle	IL	**C**	C-	C	368.5	-3.40	0.0	0.7	39.0	49.8	**10.0**	18.9	58.1
EVABANK	Cullman	AL	**C+**	C-	D+	330.9	3.01	0.3	8.0	47.8	19.2	**10.0**	14.1	19.0
EVANGELINE BANK & TRUST CO	Ville Platte	LA	**B**	B	B	558.7	-3.10	5.9	4.5	24.3	34.9	**10.0**	18.0	35.4
EVANS BANK NA	Hamburg	NY	**C+**	C+	C+	834.2	1.95	12.8	0.2	13.3	12.2	**8.5**	10.0	14.1
EVANSVILLE COMMERCE BANK	Evansville	IN	**C-**	C	D-	90.7	30.24	20.6	0.6	17.1	3.2	**6.7**	8.7	13.0
▲ EVB	Tappahannock	VA	**C**	D	D	1052.7	1.94	5.1	1.4	22.4	24.0	**7.5**	9.3	15.0
EVERBANK	Jacksonville	FL	**B-**	B-	D+	20504.7	16.43	2.6	0.0	50.1	5.4	**6.5**	8.5	14.0
EVERCORE TRUST CO NA	New York	NY	**U**	U	U	25.3	-11.74	0.0	0.0	0.0	19.3	**10.0**	89.9	284.5
EVERENCE TRUST CO	Goshen	IN	**U**	U	C+	5.8	4.43	0.0	0.0	0.0	72.9	**10.0**	88.5	249.7
EVERETT CO-OP BANK	Everett	MA	**A-**	A-	B+	377.4	13.11	0.7	0.4	42.7	5.3	**10.0**	13.1	19.5
EVERGREEN BANK GROUP	Oak Brook	IL	**B-**	B-	C	537.7	6.10	4.4	42.0	6.2	6.6	**7.3**	10.1	12.8
EVERGREEN FS&LA	Grants Pass	OR	**C+**	C	C-	385.1	-0.46	1.8	0.2	20.0	2.1	**9.9**	10.9	17.5
EVERGREEN NATIONAL BK	Evergreen	CO	**D-**	D	D	99.6	-4.75	5.1	2.2	20.3	20.1	**6.7**	8.7	18.5
EVERTRUST BANK	Pasadena	CA	**B+**	B+	C	672.7	14.40	5.4	0.0	0.5	15.9	**10.0**	15.6	20.7
EVOLVE BANK & TRUST	Memphis	TN	**B-**	B-	C	379.1	38.93	8.9	1.4	41.3	5.4	**5.3**	7.3	12.0
EXCHANGE B&TC NATCHITOCHES	Natchitoches	LA	**A-**	A-	A-	118.0	2.04	2.7	2.0	22.4	52.8	**10.0**	11.2	25.5
▲ EXCHANGE BANK	Skiatook	OK	**C+**	D+	D	89.2	2.29	7.3	3.3	18.3	29.9	**7.7**	9.4	16.5
EXCHANGE BANK	Gibbon	NE	**B+**	A-	A-	561.8	14.28	11.0	1.3	10.8	23.3	**8.5**	10.0	14.2
▲ EXCHANGE BANK	Milledgeville	GA	**B-**	C+	C	220.7	-0.76	3.1	0.9	16.4	41.2	**10.0**	11.2	20.4
▲ EXCHANGE BANK	Santa Rosa	CA	**B-**	C+	C	1802.3	2.90	8.8	0.4	13.3	27.2	**6.9**	8.9	14.0
EXCHANGE BANK & TRUST CO	Perry	OK	**B-**	B-	B-	280.4	12.41	6.5	6.0	20.0	33.8	**6.8**	8.8	15.8

Asset Quality Index	Adjusted Non-Performing Loans as a % of Total Loans	Adjusted Non-Performing Loans as a % of Capital	Net Charge-Offs Avg Loans	Profitability Index	Net Income ($Mil)	Return on Assets (R.O.A.)	Return on Equity (R.O.E.)	Net Interest Spread	Overhead Efficiency Ratio	Liquidity Index	Liquidity Ratio	Hot Money Ratio	Stability Index
4.3	0.92	4.9	-0.01	3.9	0.5	0.96	7.34	4.58	84.9	1.3	20.8	29.2	4.6
5.5	1.10	6.3	-0.12	2.6	0.0	0.29	3.28	4.29	90.1	2.3	38.2	22.0	4.1
1.7	8.22	29.5	-0.16	5.6	31.5	0.69	4.32	3.79	73.8	6.3	32.2	2.2	8.4
10.0	na	0.0	na	0.0	0.0	-1.58	-1.84	0.26	1200.0	10.0	704.5	0.0	5.1
5.9	0.40	3.2	-0.04	6.8	10.0	1.24	13.96	3.87	62.3	4.1	10.6	8.1	6.9
4.6	0.55	4.0	0.01	3.5	1.8	0.48	5.72	3.54	76.1	3.3	14.2	12.3	4.4
3.9	1.35	11.4	0.42	2.7	0.5	0.41	4.46	3.97	87.3	1.6	13.8	23.1	3.9
4.9	1.48	11.4	0.03	6.1	17.0	1.48	15.74	3.65	64.5	5.3	26.6	5.9	8.5
5.6	0.70	4.8	0.04	0.0	-2.1	-0.81	-8.29	3.13	121.3	2.6	26.3	17.2	0.8
4.7	0.24	1.9	0.63	10.0	15.7	2.59	22.56	8.70	40.4	0.1	6.4	99.8	7.3
2.1	4.81	25.2	0.29	4.5	1.6	1.06	11.97	3.54	68.2	6.3	40.6	1.8	4.9
8.2	0.00	0.0	-0.04	7.7	0.3	1.53	14.02	4.99	64.9	1.9	21.4	20.2	5.8
4.2	1.37	9.0	0.23	5.8	1.3	1.29	12.71	4.90	72.4	4.5	27.2	7.6	5.7
4.8	1.05	6.6	-0.05	6.0	4.0	1.00	6.88	4.54	64.5	1.7	25.1	25.2	7.4
4.7	0.45	3.8	0.13	4.9	1.4	0.84	9.53	3.60	61.5	0.7	14.9	41.0	4.5
0.8	2.61	24.3	0.09	3.4	0.9	0.47	5.81	3.87	84.4	0.5	10.3	62.8	4.4
5.6	0.83	5.6	0.10	6.1	23.7	1.01	9.48	4.16	60.0	2.4	11.6	17.0	7.5
3.5	1.39	11.9	0.09	4.7	11.4	0.80	9.07	4.09	72.0	3.5	3.9	10.7	8.0
0.3	19.80	114.0	3.97	2.3	1.9	0.77	31.89	2.86	80.5	3.9	36.1	14.2	2.8
7.2	0.09	0.6	0.00	5.6	1.1	0.94	6.90	4.39	60.1	1.0	10.2	29.8	6.3
8.7	0.35	1.6	-0.01	3.7	5.4	0.86	8.21	3.14	80.0	4.1	34.7	12.5	7.3
3.1	1.73	14.6	-0.05	2.9	0.7	0.52	5.05	3.58	85.2	3.3	6.8	11.6	5.6
0.3	6.68	75.3	0.79	0.0	-4.5	-1.88	-30.21	4.30	122.5	1.6	2.6	19.7	0.9
5.3	2.08	12.7	0.00	2.5	0.3	0.31	3.17	3.11	94.1	2.9	31.0	17.3	4.6
9.9	0.00	0.0	0.00	4.3	0.9	0.67	4.68	3.48	73.0	2.2	11.5	17.6	7.6
8.1	0.70	1.9	0.00	2.5	0.1	0.46	2.21	3.82	87.1	5.7	44.1	3.3	5.8
5.0	1.41	8.0	0.14	4.6	7.8	0.91	7.85	4.04	68.9	1.5	10.3	23.8	7.8
4.9	1.35	8.3	0.00	2.3	0.1	0.15	1.04	4.61	96.4	3.4	11.3	11.5	6.3
6.3	0.02	0.2	0.40	8.8	0.8	1.59	18.29	4.65	43.8	1.0	21.4	33.5	3.6
5.9	1.86	7.3	0.04	4.9	14.7	1.04	8.86	3.03	52.2	2.9	32.0	23.0	9.1
4.8	1.09	6.7	0.13	3.9	1.2	0.88	9.86	3.13	76.3	4.0	24.3	9.9	5.3
9.2	0.89	1.6	-0.01	3.7	0.4	0.73	5.69	3.15	80.6	3.4	70.2	28.8	6.5
5.2	1.44	9.1	0.39	2.9	1.8	0.33	4.09	3.28	92.4	1.7	38.0	51.8	4.3
7.5	0.32	1.7	0.00	2.0	0.3	0.16	1.41	3.86	91.6	6.5	49.9	3.3	5.4
4.4	2.39	15.6	0.18	3.3	7.1	0.64	5.73	3.05	70.3	1.0	19.2	36.9	8.4
5.4	1.49	8.7	0.13	3.8	5.7	0.68	6.68	4.34	78.6	1.5	24.3	34.7	6.6
4.7	0.65	5.3	0.00	2.7	0.5	0.22	1.72	3.33	95.7	3.9	17.1	9.3	7.2
7.5	0.66	3.6	0.00	6.1	1.2	1.07	7.27	4.09	59.8	1.1	10.3	29.0	8.1
7.0	2.38	11.8	0.00	1.2	0.1	0.08	0.66	2.25	101.9	0.5	12.1	64.1	5.9
4.7	8.21	17.6	0.96	1.9	0.7	0.26	1.42	2.24	75.4	5.7	67.6	12.7	6.5
2.8	4.36	21.0	0.36	10.0	8.3	3.33	25.52	8.75	37.8	0.7	19.5	59.5	4.4
5.6	2.58	8.0	0.20	3.7	2.3	0.54	3.07	3.49	74.4	2.8	40.3	22.8	7.9
2.9	1.69	12.1	0.04	4.4	4.8	0.77	7.90	3.96	73.0	4.0	5.1	7.5	6.1
8.6	0.00	0.0	0.00	2.4	0.1	0.22	2.03	3.62	91.0	1.0	23.9	35.1	3.7
4.0	2.62	16.9	0.17	3.2	5.9	0.75	6.94	3.84	75.8	3.3	22.9	14.8	6.1
5.1	0.55	5.4	0.19	4.5	114.7	0.82	8.97	3.26	70.7	1.0	6.9	30.4	5.7
6.5	na	0.0	na	10.0	1.9	10.73	11.88	1.99	78.7	4.0	471.0	101.0	5.6
10.0	na	0.0	na	0.0	-0.6	-14.71	-14.73	1.53	109.4	5.0	681.2	100.0	2.0
6.6	0.82	5.1	-0.02	6.0	2.6	0.94	7.18	3.39	53.1	1.3	14.5	27.9	7.5
4.3	0.53	3.9	0.46	8.1	5.2	1.34	13.68	4.80	52.0	0.8	15.8	41.8	6.4
4.7	1.80	10.0	0.13	3.5	1.6	0.54	5.01	3.72	80.5	5.0	28.6	5.1	5.8
3.7	2.06	12.4	0.37	0.6	-0.1	-0.12	-1.36	3.53	100.3	6.5	40.7	0.2	3.4
5.4	0.76	3.3	0.00	5.7	4.4	0.89	4.64	3.68	53.3	0.8	17.6	42.6	7.3
4.3	0.78	7.6	0.05	6.3	1.6	0.68	7.59	4.17	92.7	0.6	12.3	55.0	4.9
9.1	0.56	2.0	0.02	5.8	1.2	1.34	10.79	3.69	67.3	4.6	21.2	5.2	9.7
4.7	0.51	2.7	0.03	4.0	0.6	0.86	9.16	4.57	83.5	2.6	16.1	16.0	3.6
5.0	0.95	6.1	0.13	8.6	8.2	2.06	20.21	3.76	44.5	1.2	19.6	30.5	7.8
5.0	2.70	10.9	-0.07	4.1	1.4	0.82	7.61	3.79	77.4	2.8	35.9	19.4	5.0
4.1	2.58	15.3	-0.07	5.9	13.2	0.99	11.36	4.01	66.6	4.7	25.3	8.7	7.5
4.3	2.00	12.1	0.20	8.8	4.5	2.22	25.25	4.18	52.6	1.2	17.8	29.3	6.7

Name	City	State	Rating	2013 Rating	2012 Rating	Total Assets ($Mil)	One Year Asset Growth	Asset Mix (As a % of Total Assets) Commercial Loans	Consumer Loans	Mortgage Loans	Securities	Capitalization Index	Leverage Ratio	Risk-Based Capital Ratio
▲ EXCHANGE BANK OF ALABAMA	Altoona	AL	A-	B	C	251.0	1.10	3.7	2.9	14.3	25.4	10.0	12.1	19.4
EXCHANGE BANK OF MISSOURI	Fayette	MO	B+	B+	B	142.2	11.62	6.0	2.2	11.4	9.3	7.8	10.1	13.1
▲ EXCHANGE BANK OF NORTHEAST MO	Kahoka	MO	C	D+	C-	144.1	0.32	2.2	1.5	8.4	39.0	8.1	9.8	15.3
EXCHANGE NATIONAL BK & TRUST	Atchison	KS	B	B	B	372.9	0.56	5.7	19.8	18.1	22.6	6.9	8.9	13.3
EXCHANGE STATE BK	Luverne	MN	B	B	B-	149.2	3.26	3.7	1.7	5.0	18.9	7.1	9.2	12.6
▲ EXCHANGE STATE BK	Collins	IA	B-	C+	C+	103.9	-0.40	10.4	0.8	12.5	17.1	7.8	9.6	13.2
EXCHANGE STATE BK	Carsonville	MI	B	B	B	151.0	2.64	5.9	1.8	15.0	28.6	9.3	10.6	16.9
EXCHANGE STATE BK	Springville	IA	B-	B-	B-	45.7	-1.90	4.9	2.3	10.4	42.6	5.8	7.8	11.7
EXCHANGE STATE BK	Adair	IA	C+	C+	C	36.6	-1.97	4.2	2.3	11.5	30.3	10.0	11.4	18.4
EXCHANGE STATE BK	Lanark	IL	B-	B-	B-	90.4	4.94	7.8	0.8	6.4	53.6	7.7	9.4	19.0
▲ EXCHANGE STATE BK ST PAUL KS	Saint Paul	KS	C+	C	C	69.4	3.86	7.4	3.2	14.4	39.1	6.2	8.2	18.5
▲ EXECUTIVE NATIONAL BK	Miami	FL	B-	C	C	321.4	6.25	3.5	0.1	13.9	16.4	7.7	9.5	17.2
EXTRACO BANKS NA	Temple	TX	C+	C+	B+	1280.6	5.62	3.7	3.8	19.1	23.2	8.3	9.9	17.4
F & C BANK	Holden	MO	B	B	B	159.7	20.98	3.8	2.9	25.0	6.4	8.8	10.4	14.0
F & M BANK & TRUST CO	Manchester	GA	E-	E-	E-	79.1	1.07	2.4	2.4	25.4	4.1	1.0	5.3	8.0
F & M BANK MINNESOTA	Olivia	MN	B-	B-	B-	119.1	24.97	3.6	1.1	2.0	27.1	7.2	9.1	12.9
▲ F & M COMMUNITY BANK NA	Preston	MN	A-	B+	B	108.1	11.42	9.9	2.5	11.7	19.0	7.9	12.3	13.3
F&M BANK	Washington	GA	B-	B-	C	257.6	-0.75	4.0	2.7	16.6	40.6	10.0	16.7	30.3
▲ F&M BANK	Clarksville	TN	C	C-	C-	838.7	6.30	6.0	2.2	19.2	8.3	6.9	9.3	12.4
F&M BANK	Falls City	NE	B-	B-	B-	117.5	5.56	0.9	1.7	5.7	64.3	5.9	7.9	17.6
F&M BANK	West Point	NE	B-	C+	C	271.2	9.54	8.2	0.9	4.9	25.5	5.2	8.8	11.1
▲ F&M BANK	Edmond	OK	C+	C-	C	335.0	16.94	6.8	2.7	13.2	32.8	5.8	7.8	12.9
F&M BANK & TRUST CO	Hannibal	MO	D-	D-	D-	120.5	-8.93	3.7	2.2	37.2	18.1	6.7	8.7	15.2
FAHEY BANKING CO	Marion	OH	B-	B-	C	204.0	3.19	3.0	0.5	9.1	29.0	10.0	22.7	30.1
▲ FAIRFAX STATE SB	Fairfax	IA	C	C	C-	146.0	-2.96	4.9	2.5	8.7	52.8	10.0	11.2	20.4
FAIRFIELD COUNTY BANK	Ridgefield	CT	C+	C+	C-	1538.3	1.87	9.8	0.2	23.3	12.0	9.6	11.2	14.6
FAIRFIELD FS&LA OF LANCASTER	Lancaster	OH	C-	C	D+	252.2	-3.80	0.0	0.5	79.9	1.6	8.5	10.0	19.7
FAIRFIELD NATIONAL BK	Fairfield	IL	B+	B	B	441.7	2.87	21.5	3.1	8.9	40.2	8.4	9.9	22.6
FAIRMOUNT BANK	Rosedale	MD	C	C+	B-	77.7	1.08	2.0	2.3	54.9	15.9	10.0	15.5	29.2
FAIRMOUNT STATE BK	Fairmount	IN	C	C	C+	41.6	-2.90	2.1	4.8	12.4	34.7	10.0	14.1	29.6
FAIRPORT SAVINGS BANK	Fairport	NY	D+	D+	D+	239.4	4.37	0.0	0.0	71.2	15.6	5.3	7.3	15.0
FAIRVIEW S&LA	Fairview	OK	B+	B+	B+	41.0	8.96	1.1	2.3	34.4	1.7	10.0	16.3	27.1
FAIRVIEW STATE BANKING CO	Fairview	IL	C	C+	C+	25.5	-5.05	3.7	6.2	16.2	44.8	10.0	12.0	27.9
FALCON INTERNATIONAL BK	Laredo	TX	B	B-	C-	915.4	11.99	7.6	1.4	10.3	9.0	10.0	11.9	19.4
FALCON NATIONAL BK	Foley	MN	B	B-	C+	170.6	9.78	12.0	0.8	14.8	12.6	6.9	8.9	13.9
FALLS CITY NATIONAL BK	Falls City	TX	C+	C+	C	317.7	12.66	2.9	3.4	12.4	35.1	6.0	8.0	20.5
FAMILY BANK	Pelham	GA	C	C-	D+	88.8	2.00	3.9	8.1	44.1	13.3	9.0	10.3	18.0
FAMILY FEDERAL SAVINGS FA	Fitchburg	MA	C	C	C+	94.5	-0.41	0.0	0.3	53.8	34.0	10.0	11.8	28.8
FANNIN BANK	Bonham	TX	B-	B-	C+	79.8	4.38	7.7	4.8	14.8	35.5	6.6	8.6	15.5
FAR EAST NATIONAL BK	Los Angeles	CA	B	B	C+	1397.3	5.63	14.9	0.0	1.5	13.1	10.0	18.2	24.4
FARM BUREAU BANK FSB	San Antonio	TX	C	C	C	684.0	10.17	5.6	77.9	0.3	0.5	6.6	10.9	12.2
FARMERS & DROVERS BANK	Council Grove	KS	A	A-	A	191.8	-2.35	3.0	6.9	12.1	58.6	10.0	23.4	47.7
FARMERS & MECHANICS BANK	Galesburg	IL	B+	B	C+	278.8	-1.21	11.7	3.0	17.2	30.4	9.3	10.5	17.4
FARMERS & MECHANICS FS&LA	Bloomfield	IN	C-	C-	C+	70.1	1.96	0.0	0.3	43.6	37.8	10.0	17.3	44.0
FARMERS & MERCH BANK & TRUST	Burlington	IA	C+	C	D+	191.0	0.88	8.0	1.2	23.8	26.3	7.4	9.3	16.1
FARMERS & MERCH BANK & TRUST	Marinette	WI	D+	D+	D+	146.3	-4.96	6.4	2.4	26.4	29.9	7.6	9.4	15.5
FARMERS & MERCH BANK ASHLAND	Ashland	NE	B	B	B+	67.1	-5.60	4.4	1.6	17.5	16.4	10.0	11.2	16.8
FARMERS & MERCH BANK OF COLBY	Colby	KS	A	A-	A-	158.9	3.61	6.7	0.8	2.8	35.9	10.0	12.2	15.7
FARMERS & MERCH BANK OF SC	Holly Hill	SC	B+	B+	B+	245.2	2.80	5.2	5.9	15.0	25.5	10.0	17.1	33.4
FARMERS & MERCH BK CENTRAL CA	Lodi	CA	A	A	A	2198.3	11.89	7.4	0.2	9.1	18.5	8.1	10.9	13.4
FARMERS & MERCH BK CRAIG CTY	New Castle	VA	B+	B+	A-	54.6	-4.51	2.5	4.8	36.0	27.4	10.0	18.2	40.7
▲ FARMERS & MERCH BK HUTSONVILLE	Hutsonville	IL	B	B-	B-	42.3	-0.11	7.9	7.0	19.1	8.0	10.0	16.0	37.9
FARMERS & MERCH BK LONG BEACH	Long Beach	CA	A	A	A-	5531.7	7.51	1.3	0.4	8.9	43.6	10.0	14.4	23.8
▼ FARMERS & MERCH BK MOUND CITY	Mound City	KS	D+	C-	C-	37.8	9.48	9.9	8.3	26.7	21.6	4.8	6.8	11.2
▲ FARMERS & MERCH BK OF KENDALL	Kendall	WI	B-	C-	C+	72.9	-0.50	2.6	2.5	9.3	0.4	10.0	12.6	15.3
FARMERS & MERCH BK ORFORDVILLE	Orfordville	WI	B	B	B-	45.7	1.55	3.9	5.9	30.4	29.8	10.0	12.1	22.7
FARMERS & MERCH BK ST CLAIR	Saint Clair	MO	B	B-	C+	164.2	2.29	3.8	3.1	28.8	15.5	10.0	11.5	17.7
FARMERS & MERCH NB NASHVILLE	Nashville	IL	B	B	B	174.9	-0.52	2.9	1.5	15.9	37.3	10.0	12.0	21.9
FARMERS & MERCH NB OF FAIRVIEW	Fairview	OK	A	A	A	103.6	4.41	4.5	3.8	8.2	59.4	10.0	11.5	24.8
▲ FARMERS & MERCH NB OF HATTON	Hatton	ND	D+	D	D+	22.8	-6.19	13.5	2.3	7.5	11.1	9.7	10.8	15.4

Asset Quality Index	Adjusted Non-Performing Loans as a % of Total Loans	Adjusted Non-Performing Loans as a % of Capital	Net Charge-Offs Avg Loans	Profitability Index	Net Income ($Mil)	Return on Assets (R.O.A.)	Return on Equity (R.O.E.)	Net Interest Spread	Overhead Efficiency Ratio	Liquidity Index	Liquidity Ratio	Hot Money Ratio	Stability Index
7.6	0.74	3.7	-0.03	5.5	1.9	1.02	8.92	3.96	63.1	2.4	17.5	17.4	5.4
6.0	0.61	4.5	0.01	5.4	1.0	0.91	8.00	4.52	68.3	2.1	6.7	17.7	6.3
2.9	3.44	17.5	0.17	4.8	1.2	1.09	10.67	3.42	67.4	3.9	29.5	11.9	5.8
5.6	0.27	2.0	0.15	5.8	3.1	1.09	12.63	3.42	55.5	3.9	12.4	9.0	5.0
7.4	0.00	0.0	0.02	4.9	1.3	1.13	12.26	3.59	62.9	1.6	15.2	23.4	5.9
7.1	0.24	1.9	0.10	4.0	0.7	0.85	9.16	3.36	69.5	1.6	16.2	24.1	5.3
5.4	1.14	6.5	0.21	4.7	1.0	0.91	8.95	3.80	66.1	5.1	35.3	7.5	6.3
8.0	0.00	0.0	0.18	3.2	0.2	0.68	8.96	3.37	72.6	5.5	55.0	10.1	3.8
6.8	0.71	3.3	-0.28	3.0	0.2	0.53	4.04	3.04	82.5	4.9	41.2	10.5	5.1
8.2	0.38	1.5	-0.53	4.8	0.8	1.25	12.91	3.55	65.5	2.6	42.6	27.9	4.5
6.0	0.62	3.0	-0.30	4.3	0.4	0.80	9.63	3.64	83.1	3.7	42.1	16.9	3.6
4.1	0.69	4.5	-0.36	4.5	1.9	0.76	8.06	3.65	80.9	4.6	26.2	6.4	5.1
8.6	0.37	2.0	0.08	3.5	6.3	0.68	6.70	3.59	85.3	5.3	22.8	3.0	8.3
4.8	1.06	7.4	0.06	5.8	1.4	1.29	11.95	5.24	73.4	3.2	12.1	12.6	7.5
0.3	10.13	95.3	0.75	0.0	-0.6	-1.05	-18.63	3.70	128.5	0.6	11.9	46.6	1.6
6.4	0.37	2.4	0.01	4.1	0.8	0.89	9.04	3.63	71.0	4.3	23.2	8.0	5.9
6.2	0.55	3.0	0.08	7.8	1.3	1.74	13.82	4.58	63.0	1.9	10.6	18.9	8.4
5.5	3.33	8.8	1.01	4.0	1.6	0.82	4.91	3.98	70.3	2.3	37.3	27.9	6.3
2.8	2.17	18.2	0.04	4.2	3.8	0.69	8.29	3.83	79.5	1.0	8.8	29.9	4.2
9.4	0.00	0.0	0.00	3.8	0.8	0.92	10.78	2.99	68.4	6.3	62.7	8.5	4.7
6.0	0.62	4.2	0.03	4.4	1.9	0.93	9.80	3.66	73.8	3.6	20.8	11.6	4.7
3.7	1.13	7.2	0.32	5.3	3.0	1.23	15.16	3.85	69.5	2.6	21.9	16.4	5.0
1.4	4.21	30.0	1.05	0.0	-0.9	-0.93	-9.07	3.05	140.1	4.6	15.5	4.7	3.3
3.4	4.88	13.4	0.44	5.3	1.5	0.98	4.31	4.14	75.4	1.4	19.2	27.0	7.4
7.9	1.01	3.2	0.17	2.3	0.4	0.37	3.33	2.84	90.6	6.6	64.2	6.6	5.2
4.0	2.65	17.7	0.14	3.8	7.3	0.66	5.69	3.89	78.1	3.7	12.2	10.6	7.7
5.3	1.61	14.2	0.16	2.3	0.4	0.19	1.97	3.39	86.3	1.8	7.6	19.1	4.7
8.2	0.21	1.1	0.05	5.4	3.8	1.15	11.20	3.03	49.3	1.8	34.5	33.0	5.8
4.6	2.49	11.3	2.20	1.9	0.0	0.06	0.38	3.86	64.9	1.5	27.9	30.7	6.6
5.4	3.66	10.7	0.74	2.0	0.0	0.12	0.83	3.79	88.0	4.7	32.4	8.9	5.9
10.0	0.08	0.9	0.00	1.8	0.4	0.24	3.37	3.12	89.5	1.7	18.2	22.7	3.4
9.0	0.28	1.2	0.03	7.5	0.4	1.30	8.01	4.09	54.6	2.3	31.5	21.4	8.0
4.5	6.26	17.8	0.63	0.3	0.0	-0.12	-1.09	3.21	102.0	4.0	48.2	16.3	4.4
4.9	2.26	10.5	-0.15	5.2	5.6	0.90	7.37	3.78	70.7	1.6	30.9	31.7	7.0
7.7	0.33	2.5	-0.03	7.4	2.2	1.85	20.37	4.23	59.1	3.0	17.1	14.0	5.4
4.1	3.74	14.7	0.09	7.7	3.1	1.34	17.17	3.65	29.8	5.0	51.3	12.7	3.9
2.6	2.64	18.2	0.17	3.8	0.4	0.55	5.73	4.20	81.7	1.6	8.7	20.4	4.9
6.3	2.20	10.2	0.43	2.0	0.2	0.26	2.33	2.79	92.3	3.3	42.1	19.1	5.9
8.1	0.11	0.6	0.07	5.7	0.8	1.25	16.44	4.90	73.9	3.7	31.2	13.7	5.1
7.8	0.46	1.7	-0.29	3.8	3.6	0.34	1.53	2.57	77.2	0.8	15.3	41.6	7.0
3.1	0.47	3.8	0.84	3.8	2.8	0.58	5.09	4.20	65.6	0.4	3.8	61.0	5.5
8.8	0.68	1.0	0.00	6.9	1.9	1.32	5.78	3.30	40.4	4.4	56.0	17.2	8.9
6.0	0.35	2.0	0.15	6.2	2.5	1.17	9.07	3.69	63.2	4.6	23.2	5.5	7.8
10.0	0.01	0.0	0.00	1.8	0.2	0.35	2.05	2.76	89.5	3.5	60.5	22.0	7.0
2.9	3.36	20.5	0.31	3.5	0.9	0.66	7.09	3.46	81.8	5.0	24.3	3.2	4.5
3.0	2.94	17.6	0.95	1.1	0.0	0.01	0.06	3.32	95.9	3.3	38.7	18.1	4.2
8.7	0.00	0.0	-0.20	4.4	0.4	0.77	6.99	4.12	73.9	4.3	18.0	7.1	5.8
8.6	0.07	0.3	-0.01	9.0	2.1	1.74	13.92	3.97	33.9	1.4	15.0	26.6	7.2
5.0	4.12	11.6	0.40	4.3	1.6	0.79	5.38	3.41	67.8	3.7	28.7	12.7	7.0
8.6	0.29	1.8	0.00	7.8	19.4	1.22	11.29	3.94	54.2	2.3	4.4	16.6	9.0
8.9	0.33	1.1	0.06	5.4	0.4	0.91	5.03	4.01	63.4	3.4	31.9	15.5	7.4
8.8	0.00	0.0	0.05	4.1	0.3	1.01	6.49	1.95	49.4	2.6	49.9	30.3	7.0
8.7	0.51	1.7	-0.02	6.5	46.6	1.15	7.98	3.46	55.6	3.6	26.9	15.7	9.6
3.3	3.43	34.5	0.00	4.9	0.3	1.14	16.94	3.79	70.3	2.5	6.4	15.8	3.0
4.2	0.90	5.9	0.08	10.0	1.5	2.83	21.84	5.02	48.2	1.7	10.8	20.8	7.6
6.6	0.86	4.1	-0.03	6.0	0.4	1.07	9.18	3.72	59.1	3.7	33.8	14.3	6.3
5.9	1.20	7.2	0.31	3.7	0.7	0.60	5.30	4.45	78.3	2.8	10.5	14.8	5.6
9.1	0.39	1.7	0.00	4.2	1.5	1.10	9.31	3.25	70.7	4.4	20.5	6.5	7.5
9.1	0.00	0.0	0.00	8.4	1.5	1.96	17.31	4.11	50.9	4.3	66.1	19.1	9.0
7.7	0.00	0.0	-0.06	1.3	0.0	0.11	0.84	3.59	99.3	1.5	9.8	21.8	3.8

Name	City	State	Rating	2013 Rating	2012 Rating	Total Assets ($Mil)	One Year Asset Growth	Asset Mix (As a % of Total Assets) Commercial Loans	Consumer Loans	Mortgage Loans	Securities	Capitalization Index	Leverage Ratio	Risk-Based Capital Ratio
FARMERS & MERCH SB	Lone Tree	IA	**C+**	B-	B-	103.6	-3.27	5.1	1.5	16.0	25.9	**10.0**	13.2	23.5
FARMERS & MERCH STATE BK	Neola	IA	**C**	C	C+	63.2	4.61	4.0	3.2	12.9	30.0	**6.8**	8.9	21.1
FARMERS & MERCH STATE BK	Sacred Heart	MN	**D**	D+	C	23.9	-5.04	5.6	2.1	3.2	41.4	**10.0**	12.6	21.8
FARMERS & MERCH STATE BK	Springfield	MN	**C**	C	C-	126.5	2.10	4.0	1.7	3.3	19.4	**5.5**	7.5	11.7
▼ FARMERS & MERCH STATE BK	Pierz	MN	**B-**	A-	B-	179.5	3.48	10.6	2.3	12.2	21.1	**9.6**	10.7	14.9
FARMERS & MERCH STATE BK	Blooming Prairie	MN	**D+**	C-	C	74.5	-0.31	9.7	3.0	13.3	0.0	**6.8**	8.8	13.5
FARMERS & MERCH STATE BK	Appleton	MN	**B**	B	B+	49.8	1.70	4.0	1.8	3.1	22.3	**10.0**	12.3	20.1
FARMERS & MERCH STATE BK	Bloomfield	NE	**B-**	C+	B-	120.0	-4.54	3.3	4.6	0.3	15.4	**5.8**	9.3	11.6
FARMERS & MERCH STATE BK	Argonia	KS	**C-**	C	D+	36.4	7.73	11.2	3.7	13.4	11.2	**5.2**	7.2	11.9
▲ FARMERS & MERCH STATE BK	Bushnell	IL	**C+**	C	C	58.6	0.86	4.5	8.0	14.2	25.9	**7.3**	9.2	15.3
FARMERS & MERCH STATE BK ALPHA	Alpha	MN	**D+**	C	C-	36.8	12.86	6.6	3.8	7.5	7.9	**9.0**	10.3	18.2
FARMERS & MERCH TRUST CO	Chambersburg	PA	**C-**	D+	D	1020.7	2.04	9.1	0.7	17.5	17.3	**7.4**	9.2	14.8
FARMERS & MERCHANTS BANK	Salisbury	NC	**C-**	C-	C-	504.8	1.62	4.4	0.9	23.0	0.5	**10.0**	11.6	16.8
FARMERS & MERCHANTS BANK	Upperco	MD	**B+**	B	C+	317.5	8.94	6.8	0.3	8.4	9.1	**8.1**	10.2	13.4
▲ FARMERS & MERCHANTS BANK	Timberville	VA	**B-**	C-	D+	593.7	6.82	3.1	8.4	28.4	1.9	**10.0**	11.3	16.8
▲ FARMERS & MERCHANTS BANK	Miamisburg	OH	**B**	B-	C+	114.0	0.88	11.1	2.4	25.7	26.0	**7.4**	9.3	17.4
FARMERS & MERCHANTS BANK	Caldwell	OH	**B**	B-	C+	105.4	4.08	10.2	11.0	32.0	25.8	**10.0**	11.7	19.4
FARMERS & MERCHANTS BANK	Boswell	IN	**C**	C	B-	117.1	-1.06	5.7	0.9	12.5	28.5	**9.4**	10.6	19.2
FARMERS & MERCHANTS BANK	Laotto	IN	**B**	B	B+	121.9	3.38	8.2	2.5	27.9	34.5	**7.9**	9.6	16.3
FARMERS & MERCHANTS BANK	Sylvania	GA	**C**	C	C-	112.2	0.67	2.5	4.7	9.7	42.9	**10.0**	13.5	24.0
FARMERS & MERCHANTS BANK	LaFayette	AL	**B+**	B+	A-	134.4	8.10	7.0	4.3	4.9	52.2	**10.0**	13.7	24.7
FARMERS & MERCHANTS BANK	Piedmont	AL	**B**	B	B	191.1	0.32	8.5	2.4	18.2	29.0	**10.0**	13.2	22.0
FARMERS & MERCHANTS BANK	Waterloo	AL	**A-**	A-	A-	72.9	6.28	3.9	2.7	0.8	79.6	**10.0**	21.4	45.0
▲ FARMERS & MERCHANTS BANK	Monticello	FL	**C**	D+	D	423.7	1.19	9.1	0.9	14.3	23.5	**7.4**	9.3	15.2
FARMERS & MERCHANTS BANK	Statesboro	GA	**E-**	E-	E-	156.9	-3.13	8.9	2.0	17.0	17.3	**3.3**	5.6	10.2
FARMERS & MERCHANTS BANK	Lakeland	GA	**E-**	E-	E-	549.9	-3.66	5.7	4.9	22.2	9.8	**0.0**	3.3	5.9
▼ FARMERS & MERCHANTS BANK	Eatonton	GA	**D**	D+	D	187.6	-5.66	3.0	2.6	12.7	31.9	**9.9**	10.9	18.6
FARMERS & MERCHANTS BANK	Axtell	NE	**D-**	D	D+	9.6	-4.94	3.3	4.3	0.8	66.0	**4.7**	6.7	31.7
FARMERS & MERCHANTS BANK	Tomah	WI	**D+**	C	D	192.6	-0.75	12.0	0.9	11.4	31.6	**8.9**	10.3	17.5
FARMERS & MERCHANTS BANK	Rudolph	WI	**B-**	B-	C+	28.7	5.17	7.5	3.3	33.5	13.2	**10.0**	11.6	20.3
▲ FARMERS & MERCHANTS BANK	Berlin	WI	**B**	C+	B-	218.0	5.79	10.2	7.8	24.7	16.9	**10.0**	11.1	16.8
FARMERS & MERCHANTS BANK	Stuttgart	AR	**A**	A	B+	671.9	-1.80	7.9	3.1	10.3	20.2	**10.0**	12.6	16.8
FARMERS & MERCHANTS BANK	Dyer	TN	**C**	C	C+	93.2	-5.97	4.5	2.8	11.9	48.6	**9.8**	10.9	16.1
▲ FARMERS & MERCHANTS BANK	Adamsville	TN	**B-**	C	C+	34.5	-0.04	3.4	8.0	20.3	20.1	**10.0**	11.2	22.4
FARMERS & MERCHANTS BANK	Trezevant	TN	**B-**	B-	C+	307.8	6.10	12.9	5.5	23.6	3.8	**5.4**	8.5	11.3
FARMERS & MERCHANTS BANK	Baldwyn	MS	**A-**	A-	A-	257.6	11.70	2.3	7.5	14.5	33.8	**10.0**	14.5	22.1
FARMERS & MERCHANTS BANK	Maysville	OK	**B-**	B-	B-	21.4	-0.14	24.6	18.3	1.9	20.6	**5.3**	7.3	12.5
FARMERS & MERCHANTS BANK	Duke	OK	**C+**	C-	C-	16.6	-2.74	4.3	3.6	0.8	32.9	**10.0**	11.7	24.9
FARMERS & MERCHANTS BANK	Arnett	OK	**B-**	B-	B	61.1	8.67	5.8	6.6	2.5	31.1	**8.1**	9.7	26.9
FARMERS & MERCHANTS BANK	Milford	NE	**B**	B	B	569.5	5.31	4.6	9.4	6.4	48.8	**6.5**	8.5	13.9
FARMERS & MERCHANTS BANK	Milligan	NE	**B-**	B-	B-	63.4	7.21	4.5	1.6	5.1	0.0	**5.4**	10.1	11.3
FARMERS & MERCHANTS BANK	De Leon	TX	**C-**	C	B-	70.9	14.81	3.3	4.8	24.9	19.7	**10.0**	11.2	19.4
FARMERS & MERCHANTS BANK OF ND	Tolna	ND	**B-**	B-	B-	100.8	61.59	13.1	2.9	1.7	15.9	**7.4**	9.9	12.8
FARMERS & MERCHANTS SB	Manchester	IA	**B**	B	B	389.7	10.03	39.1	0.8	7.0	5.6	**3.9**	9.3	10.4
FARMERS & MERCHANTS SB	Waukon	IA	**A-**	A-	B+	150.2	2.87	4.9	3.9	10.3	34.1	**9.5**	10.6	15.4
FARMERS & MERCHANTS STATE BK	Winterset	IA	**A-**	A-	A-	180.2	1.76	3.8	2.0	8.8	35.8	**10.0**	11.3	17.2
FARMERS & MERCHANTS STATE BK	Waterloo	WI	**C+**	C+	C+	163.1	2.73	2.6	0.8	14.3	11.9	**9.8**	10.9	14.8
FARMERS & MERCHANTS STATE BK	Langdon	ND	**A-**	A-	A-	89.7	12.91	5.8	3.3	1.8	24.8	**10.0**	11.7	15.0
FARMERS & MERCHANTS STATE BK	Scotland	SD	**C+**	C	C-	26.6	1.71	5.4	10.6	2.1	34.2	**8.7**	10.1	19.3
FARMERS & MERCHANTS STATE BK	Plankinton	SD	**B**	B-	B-	96.9	5.79	9.3	6.0	6.8	4.7	**5.8**	9.8	11.6
FARMERS & MERCHANTS STATE BK	Paynesville	MN	**B-**	B-	B	27.4	1.60	7.4	4.0	9.4	42.5	**7.5**	9.3	25.4
FARMERS & MERCHANTS STATE BK	New York Mills	MN	**B-**	B-	B-	60.3	3.96	9.7	2.3	7.5	39.8	**10.0**	13.9	25.9
FARMERS & MERCHANTS STATE BK	Cawker City	KS	**C-**	C-	C-	16.7	8.19	11.0	5.5	5.2	0.0	**5.2**	9.0	11.1
FARMERS & MERCHANTS STATE BK	Archbold	OH	**B**	B	B-	910.1	-1.97	10.2	2.6	7.8	26.2	**8.5**	10.0	14.5
FARMERS & MERCHANTS UNION BANK	Columbus	WI	**B**	B-	C	289.6	14.29	8.6	0.9	10.3	5.3	**8.6**	11.1	13.8
FARMERS & MINERS BANK	Pennington Gap	VA	**B+**	B	B	134.2	1.18	2.2	8.1	21.6	26.1	**10.0**	13.2	29.2
FARMERS & STOCKMENS BANK	Clayton	NM	**B**	B+	B-	169.0	25.69	9.2	0.9	8.5	9.9	**3.9**	8.6	10.5
FARMERS & TRADERS BK CAMPTON	Campton	KY	**B-**	B-	C+	46.8	-0.82	12.2	5.9	22.5	41.0	**7.6**	9.4	19.3
FARMERS & TRADERS SB	Douds	IA	**C-**	D+	D	19.9	-1.41	2.8	12.2	38.8	0.0	**8.6**	10.1	18.3
FARMERS & TRADERS SB	Bancroft	IA	**B-**	B-	B-	54.2	-10.27	5.3	1.9	4.3	34.6	**8.6**	10.1	16.1

Asset Quality Index	Adjusted Non-Performing Loans as a % of Total Loans	Adjusted Non-Performing Loans as a % of Capital	Net Charge-Offs Avg Loans	Profitability Index	Net Income ($Mil)	Return on Assets (R.O.A.)	Return on Equity (R.O.E.)	Net Interest Spread	Overhead Efficiency Ratio	Liquidity Index	Liquidity Ratio	Hot Money Ratio	Stability Index
5.5	2.51	9.3	-0.06	**2.1**	0.5	0.63	4.91	2.86	106.6	**2.6**	38.2	24.7	**6.7**
9.2	0.02	0.1	0.00	**2.6**	0.2	0.41	4.85	2.44	82.5	**5.8**	69.1	10.8	**4.7**
6.3	1.72	5.4	0.07	**0.3**	0.0	-0.20	-1.69	2.62	108.4	**4.2**	57.3	15.1	**3.4**
7.0	0.08	0.6	0.00	**2.6**	0.3	0.29	3.81	3.13	85.2	**4.8**	22.9	4.7	**3.6**
3.9	2.03	13.0	0.00	**8.9**	2.6	2.06	19.98	4.39	53.0	**3.4**	17.8	12.3	**7.4**
1.1	3.11	25.6	0.01	**7.2**	1.0	1.77	20.52	4.24	59.2	**4.2**	17.5	7.4	**5.1**
5.8	0.74	3.4	0.03	**5.3**	0.5	1.38	11.03	3.49	57.2	**5.0**	44.2	10.7	**7.6**
6.3	0.26	1.9	0.00	**5.7**	0.9	0.96	10.64	3.63	59.4	**3.3**	13.6	12.5	**5.2**
5.6	0.35	3.1	0.01	**5.1**	0.1	0.47	6.37	5.02	87.9	**0.9**	18.2	34.0	**3.7**
7.1	0.33	1.9	0.38	**3.7**	0.3	0.68	8.01	3.27	78.4	**4.8**	28.2	6.0	**3.4**
1.3	7.15	39.0	-0.15	**4.1**	0.2	0.69	6.64	3.32	68.8	**3.0**	42.8	21.4	**4.9**
2.4	3.06	21.9	0.23	**4.4**	6.9	0.90	9.61	3.72	71.9	**4.9**	16.0	3.5	**6.8**
1.6	5.53	32.2	0.34	**3.0**	1.2	0.33	2.79	4.03	79.3	**3.5**	19.3	12.1	**6.4**
6.3	0.00	0.0	-0.02	**7.2**	2.6	1.14	11.47	4.57	60.2	**1.6**	9.1	21.0	**6.1**
3.7	1.37	9.7	0.49	**5.4**	4.1	0.97	8.67	4.29	58.1	**2.3**	4.5	16.3	**5.8**
5.2	1.00	6.6	0.45	**4.7**	0.8	0.96	10.39	4.23	64.8	**5.0**	20.8	3.0	**4.9**
3.9	2.95	16.3	0.28	**9.5**	1.2	1.60	13.94	5.10	54.6	**4.3**	25.1	8.2	**6.9**
5.2	1.57	7.0	0.04	**3.1**	0.4	0.44	4.23	3.20	81.4	**2.8**	27.8	17.2	**6.0**
9.3	0.12	0.6	-0.03	**4.9**	1.0	1.11	12.69	3.71	70.4	**6.3**	45.5	3.1	**6.1**
4.6	3.79	12.5	0.60	**2.3**	0.2	0.27	2.20	4.10	84.2	**2.4**	38.4	27.0	**5.3**
6.6	2.39	5.4	0.03	**4.6**	1.0	1.00	7.39	4.30	72.5	**2.9**	40.8	22.4	**7.6**
8.1	0.77	2.8	0.18	**4.1**	1.2	0.84	6.44	4.23	77.7	**4.0**	42.0	15.5	**6.9**
9.7	0.65	0.4	0.44	**8.4**	1.2	2.23	11.14	3.74	32.2	**4.0**	84.0	25.4	**7.2**
3.7	3.01	17.8	0.35	**3.6**	3.0	0.96	11.55	3.80	72.4	**3.4**	30.4	14.7	**2.9**
1.7	4.24	37.0	0.90	**2.0**	0.5	0.43	8.14	3.83	90.8	**3.8**	26.5	11.6	**0.3**
0.3	8.44	121.7	0.38	**2.7**	2.8	0.68	24.83	3.89	72.8	**0.7**	11.7	45.8	**0.8**
0.3	12.30	52.1	0.64	**0.4**	-0.9	-0.58	-5.01	3.50	123.1	**1.3**	19.7	29.0	**3.8**
8.9	0.00	0.0	0.00	**2.0**	0.0	0.13	2.61	2.75	93.6	**4.7**	73.5	15.4	**1.7**
1.6	9.03	42.8	0.03	**2.1**	0.6	0.36	3.51	3.01	82.1	**3.2**	26.3	14.7	**6.0**
5.9	1.68	8.9	-0.03	**4.3**	0.2	0.82	7.54	4.05	73.0	**3.0**	34.9	18.5	**5.1**
4.1	2.09	13.0	0.51	**5.9**	1.6	1.01	9.34	5.34	65.9	**1.2**	13.3	28.0	**6.3**
7.5	0.36	1.9	0.14	**6.5**	5.8	1.18	8.47	4.18	58.5	**1.4**	4.7	22.6	**8.8**
5.1	2.73	8.4	0.20	**2.5**	0.3	0.45	4.73	3.48	90.1	**4.8**	39.1	10.5	**4.9**
3.2	4.17	17.3	0.41	**3.4**	0.2	0.74	6.78	4.56	71.4	**2.7**	32.1	18.9	**4.5**
4.2	0.93	8.4	0.56	**7.4**	2.5	1.10	12.75	5.64	58.8	**1.0**	8.0	29.3	**4.6**
5.9	1.59	5.9	0.10	**7.3**	2.4	1.31	9.05	5.34	64.0	**2.0**	34.3	28.8	**7.3**
7.5	0.01	0.1	0.43	**7.8**	0.3	1.77	25.33	3.87	58.3	**4.3**	41.2	11.3	**5.2**
8.6	1.19	2.9	-0.02	**3.6**	0.1	0.84	7.40	2.60	70.1	**3.6**	70.0	21.2	**5.2**
8.8	0.09	0.2	-0.38	**3.8**	0.4	0.87	8.86	2.06	62.5	**6.3**	62.9	6.5	**5.1**
6.4	0.73	3.6	-0.03	**6.0**	7.1	1.69	18.66	3.14	55.3	**1.9**	38.8	38.1	**7.2**
7.1	0.00	0.0	0.00	**7.7**	0.8	1.83	18.15	4.19	54.0	**1.8**	4.7	19.1	**6.8**
8.9	0.06	0.3	0.04	**1.1**	-0.1	-0.13	-1.12	4.10	98.8	**4.7**	31.0	8.3	**5.3**
3.7	1.12	8.1	0.11	**3.7**	0.5	0.69	6.73	3.77	76.5	**2.7**	21.7	16.1	**6.2**
5.9	0.51	4.2	0.00	**6.6**	4.4	1.55	16.29	4.07	56.1	**1.3**	7.0	24.6	**6.5**
6.6	0.51	2.7	0.16	**8.0**	2.1	1.83	18.04	3.63	49.4	**4.9**	36.0	9.0	**7.8**
8.7	0.03	0.2	0.00	**6.2**	1.6	1.17	10.55	3.50	56.0	**3.7**	35.0	14.7	**7.2**
3.4	1.95	12.6	0.00	**3.9**	0.8	0.67	6.16	3.43	68.7	**3.0**	10.4	13.7	**5.9**
7.2	0.02	0.1	-0.08	**7.2**	1.1	1.70	14.51	3.90	51.2	**3.4**	19.9	12.3	**8.2**
7.4	0.44	2.1	0.00	**3.7**	0.2	0.77	7.77	3.85	78.3	**3.1**	27.6	15.6	**5.2**
5.2	0.27	2.3	0.00	**9.5**	1.4	2.07	21.03	4.49	44.2	**1.4**	6.2	23.1	**7.2**
6.5	2.40	7.6	-0.23	**4.6**	0.2	1.12	11.14	3.63	70.3	**6.9**	68.1	3.5	**5.8**
8.3	0.86	2.8	-0.05	**3.6**	0.4	0.85	6.18	3.24	75.0	**3.3**	37.6	17.8	**6.5**
6.2	0.24	2.3	0.01	**8.8**	0.3	2.15	24.23	4.03	46.4	**1.0**	3.1	29.0	**3.7**
6.6	0.31	1.9	0.10	**4.9**	7.1	1.01	9.95	3.49	63.1	**3.4**	9.6	11.6	**6.3**
4.7	1.29	8.6	0.01	**7.6**	2.4	1.17	10.09	4.55	46.6	**2.0**	11.2	18.7	**5.7**
5.3	2.96	9.1	-0.08	**5.3**	0.9	0.94	7.28	4.57	75.0	**3.4**	54.3	24.3	**6.7**
7.7	0.20	1.6	0.09	**6.3**	1.7	1.40	13.25	4.04	78.9	**1.4**	17.6	27.0	**5.5**
3.9	2.89	13.3	0.86	**3.2**	0.2	0.60	5.81	4.19	83.4	**2.5**	32.7	20.5	**4.9**
6.3	0.72	4.8	0.00	**2.8**	0.1	0.40	4.12	3.52	85.3	**2.0**	31.9	20.9	**4.4**
7.7	0.34	1.9	-0.01	**3.8**	0.4	0.88	8.61	3.18	69.0	**4.1**	39.6	14.3	**5.7**

Name	City	State	Rating	2013 Rating	2012 Rating	Total Assets ($Mil)	One Year Asset Growth	Asset Mix (As a % of Total Assets) Commercial Loans	Consumer Loans	Mortgage Loans	Securities	Capitalization Index	Leverage Ratio	Risk-Based Capital Ratio
FARMERS BANK	Hardinsburg	KY	**A+**	A+	A	103.4	3.95	10.5	3.5	9.8	23.5	**10.0**	19.8	28.7
FARMERS BANK	Parsons	TN	**C+**	C+	C+	36.4	4.94	4.6	5.6	20.9	7.8	**10.0**	12.4	30.1
FARMERS BANK	Greenwood	AR	**B-**	B-	B	184.9	-0.28	4.1	5.2	23.8	38.6	**10.0**	20.1	38.1
FARMERS BANK	Hamburg	AR	**D+**	D+	C+	41.5	5.03	3.7	2.5	10.2	46.8	**10.0**	11.4	21.6
FARMERS BANK	Nicholasville	KY	**B-**	B-	C+	106.0	2.98	2.8	1.1	30.3	21.5	**10.0**	11.6	18.7
FARMERS BANK	Windsor	VA	**C+**	C	C-	409.3	2.69	6.6	0.5	10.6	34.1	**9.5**	10.7	18.1
▼ FARMERS BANK	Forsyth	GA	**E+**	D-	D-	63.6	1.14	6.5	1.4	15.8	17.6	**5.7**	7.7	12.9
▼ FARMERS BANK	Greensboro	GA	**D+**	C-	C-	86.2	-14.09	0.8	0.6	4.3	53.6	**10.0**	12.2	27.4
FARMERS BANK	Portland	TN	**C**	D+	D+	525.4	1.04	3.9	1.6	15.8	30.6	**9.1**	10.4	16.6
▼ FARMERS BANK	Carnegie	OK	**C-**	D+	C	39.8	-5.14	10.9	8.4	1.9	18.5	**9.6**	10.7	15.6
FARMERS BANK	Ault	CO	**B**	C+	C-	216.5	-4.56	8.7	0.8	8.3	0.8	**10.0**	12.3	15.5
FARMERS BANK & CAPITAL TC	Frankfort	KY	**B-**	C+	C-	692.4	-0.59	3.5	1.0	18.6	43.6	**8.5**	10.0	19.9
FARMERS BANK & SAVINGS CO	Pomeroy	OH	**B-**	C+	C+	255.3	1.53	2.2	3.9	45.0	14.7	**9.3**	10.6	17.7
FARMERS BANK & TRUST	Atwood	KS	**C+**	C+	B-	94.3	0.68	3.7	1.0	2.6	58.3	**7.8**	9.5	22.5
FARMERS BANK & TRUST	Great Bend	KS	**A-**	A-	B+	718.7	8.59	2.6	0.3	8.1	58.4	**10.0**	13.5	21.8
FARMERS BANK & TRUST CO	Magnolia	AR	**B-**	B-	C	883.9	8.76	8.0	3.3	26.0	19.0	**8.8**	10.2	14.9
FARMERS BANK & TRUST CO	Blytheville	AR	**B-**	C+	C-	408.0	1.11	19.0	2.4	14.3	4.9	**6.6**	9.5	12.2
FARMERS BANK & TRUST CO	Marion	KY	**A**	A	B	137.7	0.04	6.1	5.3	29.6	17.3	**10.0**	14.1	21.0
FARMERS BANK & TRUST CO	Princeton	KY	**A**	A	A	114.1	-1.25	3.9	3.0	16.9	28.5	**10.0**	17.5	26.8
FARMERS BANK & TRUST CO	Nebraska City	NE	**C**	C	C	51.1	7.30	3.1	1.1	8.8	54.2	**5.6**	7.6	23.2
▲ FARMERS BANK FRANKFORT INDIANA	Frankfort	IN	**B-**	C+	C+	450.5	0.95	8.8	2.4	8.0	27.1	**8.2**	9.8	14.2
FARMERS BANK OF APPOMATTOX	Appomattox	VA	**B+**	B+	B+	211.1	2.75	3.4	9.5	23.1	34.9	**10.0**	12.3	20.4
FARMERS BANK OF COOK	Cook	NE	**B**	B-	B-	89.5	6.27	5.2	2.2	11.1	40.7	**9.0**	10.3	17.1
FARMERS BANK OF GREEN CITY	Green City	MO	**C**	C	C	37.6	-1.48	9.2	3.3	8.2	38.4	**7.8**	9.6	15.0
▼ FARMERS BANK OF LIBERTY	Liberty	IL	**C-**	C+	B-	88.9	0.30	4.8	4.9	15.3	28.1	**7.4**	9.3	14.7
FARMERS BANK OF LINCOLN	Lincoln	MO	**B+**	B+	B+	100.6	3.24	3.1	2.9	39.4	11.0	**8.0**	9.7	16.3
FARMERS BANK OF LOHMAN MO	Lohman	MO	**B-**	B-	B+	65.1	11.95	4.1	3.2	8.0	65.4	**10.0**	13.6	31.9
FARMERS BANK OF MILTON	Milton	KY	**B**	B	B+	220.0	1.12	1.6	4.0	31.2	37.0	**10.0**	13.5	23.6
▲ FARMERS BANK OF MT PULASKI	Mount Pulaski	IL	**B-**	C	C+	43.3	4.60	4.4	7.0	30.5	30.7	**10.0**	14.6	30.9
FARMERS BANK OF NORTHERN MO	Unionville	MO	**B+**	B+	B	318.9	-0.43	3.0	1.9	9.9	35.7	**9.2**	10.4	17.8
FARMERS BANK OF OSBORNE KANSAS	Osborne	KS	**B+**	B+	B	57.5	4.48	6.4	2.1	2.4	27.2	**10.0**	11.7	16.5
FARMERS BANK OF WILLARDS	Willards	MD	**D+**	D	D-	304.8	-0.29	7.0	2.6	36.6	3.2	**9.5**	10.7	15.0
FARMERS BANK WOODLAND MILLS TN	Woodland Mills	TN	**D+**	D+	C+	11.5	3.82	2.4	6.7	2.9	33.6	**10.0**	16.8	39.9
FARMERS BUILDING & SB	Rochester	PA	**B**	B	B+	95.6	-0.78	0.1	0.0	39.5	24.0	**10.0**	16.7	45.3
FARMERS DEPOSIT BANK	Cynthiana	KY	**C**	C-	C-	134.5	0.46	3.7	1.7	13.1	52.9	**10.0**	15.9	35.1
FARMERS DEPOSIT BANK	Middleburg	KY	**C**	C	C	47.0	0.22	7.8	8.1	20.4	2.7	**8.2**	9.8	16.2
FARMERS EXCHANGE BANK	Neshkoro	WI	**B**	B	B-	56.4	-0.08	9.0	1.9	25.7	25.1	**8.0**	9.7	19.0
▲ FARMERS EXCHANGE BANK	Louisville	AL	**C-**	D-	E+	129.9	-3.60	8.9	5.8	20.7	20.2	**7.6**	9.4	14.8
▼ FARMERS EXCHANGE BANK	Cherokee	OK	**B**	B+	B	242.7	15.71	37.2	6.4	7.1	23.6	**3.1**	8.5	10.0
FARMERS NATIONAL BK	Prophetstown	IL	**A-**	A-	B+	524.0	1.07	2.6	0.7	4.7	44.3	**10.0**	13.1	20.7
FARMERS NATIONAL BK	Phillipsburg	KS	**A**	A	A-	121.9	3.68	14.5	4.3	7.4	34.7	**10.0**	14.5	22.3
FARMERS NATIONAL BK CANFIELD	Canfield	OH	**B-**	B-	B-	1122.8	-0.72	7.3	12.3	13.4	35.7	**7.5**	9.3	15.6
FARMERS NATIONAL BK DANVILLE	Danville	KY	**B**	B-	C-	435.5	-1.47	4.7	1.3	27.3	30.0	**10.0**	11.7	19.8
FARMERS NATIONAL BK EMLENTON	Emlenton	PA	**C+**	B-	C+	592.2	12.81	7.2	1.3	30.1	25.0	**5.8**	7.8	14.8
FARMERS NATIONAL BK OF BUHL	Buhl	ID	**B-**	B-	C	414.7	6.14	8.8	1.8	2.3	51.4	**10.0**	12.9	25.4
▲ FARMERS NATIONAL BK OF LEBANON	Lebanon	KY	**B-**	C+	C	102.1	4.05	4.8	3.6	8.1	37.3	**10.0**	11.1	19.0
▼ FARMERS NB OF GRIGGSVILLE	Griggsville	IL	**B-**	B	B-	73.0	3.85	3.3	5.1	12.0	16.0	**7.3**	9.2	13.0
FARMERS NB OF NEW CASTLE	Newcastle	TX	**C**	C	C+	43.4	11.05	5.8	3.7	6.5	43.3	**5.8**	7.8	19.2
FARMERS NB OF SCOTTSVILLE	Scottsville	KY	**B+**	B+	B+	243.2	1.59	3.0	2.6	21.2	33.8	**10.0**	15.4	24.4
FARMERS SB	Mineral Point	WI	**B**	B	C+	251.3	4.26	7.3	13.8	12.7	31.6	**6.4**	8.4	15.6
▲ FARMERS SB	Marshalltown	IA	**B-**	C	C	99.1	-6.75	7.3	1.2	12.7	33.6	**10.0**	13.0	21.6
FARMERS SB	Colesburg	IA	**A-**	A-	B	165.3	6.53	7.2	3.4	6.9	26.2	**10.0**	12.4	18.0
FARMERS SB	Frederika	IA	**B**	B	B	46.5	-4.12	4.7	3.3	13.5	25.9	**10.0**	15.4	24.9
FARMERS SB	Fostoria	IA	**A-**	A-	B	96.8	4.97	6.9	3.1	15.3	26.9	**10.0**	14.5	20.0
FARMERS SB	Wever	IA	**B**	B+	B-	120.4	12.27	9.0	5.0	35.6	9.8	**9.0**	10.3	15.1
FARMERS SB	Victor	IA	**B+**	B+	B+	38.6	-1.44	10.4	5.6	16.9	11.1	**10.0**	16.1	20.9
FARMERS SB	Spencer	OH	**A-**	A-	B+	277.6	1.16	1.1	0.7	15.3	62.0	**10.0**	22.4	62.0
FARMERS SB & TRUST	Traer	IA	**B-**	C+	B-	178.0	0.11	3.5	1.6	13.8	40.5	**5.2**	7.2	12.6
FARMERS SECURITY BANK	Washburn	ND	**B**	B	B	51.0	2.67	6.7	4.3	2.9	22.2	**7.3**	9.2	13.5
▲ FARMERS STATE BANK SPENCER	Spencer	NE	**D+**	D+	C	26.3	57.24	5.3	4.6	0.9	20.2	**10.0**	15.4	17.4

Asset Quality Index	Adjusted Non-Performing Loans as a % of Total Loans	Adjusted Non-Performing Loans as a % of Capital	Net Charge-Offs Avg Loans	Profitability Index	Net Income ($Mil)	Return on Assets (R.O.A.)	Return on Equity (R.O.E.)	Net Interest Spread	Overhead Efficiency Ratio	Liquidity Index	Liquidity Ratio	Hot Money Ratio	Stability Index
8.5	0.33	1.0	0.03	**9.3**	1.5	1.86	9.76	4.34	47.5	**5.1**	37.7	8.1	**8.3**
4.6	3.94	14.4	0.31	**3.3**	0.1	0.47	3.80	4.04	83.1	**3.5**	47.8	19.0	**5.3**
7.9	1.41	2.9	0.52	**3.6**	1.0	0.67	3.30	4.35	82.5	**3.6**	34.0	15.0	**7.1**
9.4	0.83	1.7	0.05	**0.9**	0.0	0.13	1.16	2.52	100.9	**3.6**	58.5	20.6	**4.1**
6.2	1.18	6.6	0.36	**3.8**	0.5	0.60	5.43	4.24	78.1	**2.5**	14.3	16.2	**5.9**
3.6	3.08	14.3	-0.14	**4.4**	2.8	0.88	8.10	3.54	70.4	**2.8**	32.8	18.7	**5.7**
1.6	5.06	34.6	0.45	**0.9**	-0.2	-0.41	-5.38	3.91	110.7	**2.5**	26.0	17.8	**1.3**
5.0	5.49	14.3	0.00	**1.3**	-0.1	-0.09	-0.79	3.11	125.1	**2.6**	27.1	17.5	**4.2**
3.0	2.76	15.4	1.17	**4.1**	3.1	0.77	7.40	4.25	63.0	**1.5**	16.2	24.4	**6.0**
1.4	4.41	21.9	2.52	**1.4**	-0.3	-0.82	-7.70	4.47	84.8	**3.5**	34.6	15.9	**5.3**
4.3	1.93	12.5	0.16	**7.9**	2.5	1.50	11.04	4.36	49.9	**0.8**	8.7	33.6	**6.1**
5.2	2.49	10.8	0.20	**5.0**	5.6	1.07	10.71	3.27	73.5	**4.7**	33.6	9.1	**5.9**
4.3	1.84	11.9	0.34	**4.7**	1.7	0.86	8.21	4.25	73.0	**1.8**	10.2	19.3	**6.5**
6.0	2.29	6.2	0.00	**3.4**	0.5	0.75	7.86	3.03	67.0	**6.3**	52.2	4.3	**4.5**
7.2	1.56	3.8	-0.52	**7.5**	9.3	1.77	12.97	3.45	71.0	**2.5**	44.6	31.2	**7.7**
4.1	1.40	9.1	0.28	**8.5**	12.4	1.92	17.17	4.40	49.1	**0.5**	3.7	38.4	**7.6**
4.5	0.79	6.3	-0.02	**9.0**	6.8	2.19	23.77	4.58	54.5	**1.0**	4.3	29.1	**5.0**
7.8	0.69	3.3	0.23	**8.0**	2.5	2.40	18.06	5.27	64.8	**3.1**	17.2	13.8	**7.9**
8.1	1.13	3.9	0.32	**6.5**	1.3	1.55	9.19	4.01	63.6	**4.4**	26.8	8.0	**9.2**
9.9	0.00	0.0	0.05	**2.7**	0.2	0.49	6.63	2.44	83.1	**7.5**	77.1	1.5	**3.5**
4.1	1.65	10.0	0.36	**5.7**	3.9	1.13	12.00	3.88	64.2	**4.2**	28.0	10.3	**6.0**
8.2	0.43	1.9	0.12	**4.8**	1.5	0.93	7.59	3.92	69.4	**2.9**	38.4	20.3	**6.9**
7.5	0.03	0.2	0.01	**5.5**	0.7	1.11	10.67	4.92	69.4	**3.4**	30.6	15.1	**5.1**
5.3	1.45	7.2	-0.05	**3.7**	0.2	0.63	6.98	3.35	72.7	**2.8**	15.5	15.1	**3.9**
2.2	3.25	20.9	0.16	**5.4**	0.6	0.94	10.47	3.86	63.2	**2.8**	28.6	17.4	**4.6**
5.8	1.03	7.1	0.01	**5.3**	0.9	1.20	12.50	3.79	64.4	**1.9**	18.9	20.0	**7.3**
9.1	0.17	0.2	0.27	**3.3**	0.3	0.61	4.29	2.73	69.7	**6.1**	87.3	11.7	**6.9**
4.2	4.37	17.4	0.43	**3.8**	1.2	0.71	5.39	3.44	61.6	**1.5**	29.2	32.0	**7.3**
5.4	1.93	6.8	0.67	**3.6**	0.2	0.55	3.99	3.82	70.3	**3.5**	34.1	15.6	**6.3**
7.7	0.43	2.2	0.04	**6.1**	2.8	1.16	10.05	3.63	59.3	**4.8**	31.6	7.9	**6.9**
6.3	0.43	2.2	-0.04	**6.3**	0.7	1.53	13.03	4.40	62.7	**3.1**	25.8	14.6	**6.8**
1.5	5.66	38.4	1.43	**3.5**	1.2	0.54	4.94	4.46	60.7	**1.7**	8.8	19.7	**5.1**
5.3	3.49	6.0	1.89	**0.3**	0.0	-0.29	-1.77	2.75	110.6	**7.4**	83.4	1.0	**5.6**
6.4	5.04	12.3	0.25	**4.8**	0.8	1.16	7.15	2.98	50.6	**7.3**	65.3	0.0	**7.7**
3.6	6.17	13.1	-2.19	**2.0**	0.2	0.23	1.52	3.30	93.8	**4.9**	51.0	13.1	**6.3**
2.6	1.81	11.9	0.06	**3.3**	0.2	0.56	4.61	4.28	86.4	**2.5**	23.2	17.4	**4.6**
5.2	1.47	7.5	0.13	**6.7**	0.5	1.16	9.91	4.26	65.7	**5.7**	42.9	6.2	**6.4**
2.3	3.46	21.4	0.73	**2.8**	0.8	0.82	9.49	4.30	76.9	**0.8**	19.2	43.3	**2.3**
5.4	0.54	4.2	-0.06	**9.9**	4.6	2.62	29.21	4.84	41.5	**3.3**	6.9	11.6	**7.1**
6.7	1.76	5.8	-0.07	**6.2**	5.3	1.37	10.28	3.68	42.9	**2.1**	37.7	30.6	**9.1**
8.0	0.05	0.2	0.01	**6.5**	1.0	1.09	7.80	3.34	50.8	**3.9**	39.5	15.4	**8.5**
4.9	1.45	8.3	0.27	**4.2**	6.7	0.80	8.88	3.55	69.9	**4.8**	26.5	8.8	**6.6**
4.9	2.35	11.5	0.02	**4.6**	3.0	0.91	7.65	3.54	77.0	**3.5**	14.8	11.7	**6.2**
4.0	2.18	16.0	0.09	**3.3**	3.0	0.71	8.42	3.33	76.5	**3.6**	15.9	11.1	**5.0**
5.2	3.85	10.5	-1.98	**3.8**	2.1	0.69	5.26	3.04	72.4	**5.7**	65.1	12.0	**6.4**
7.6	0.64	2.6	0.03	**3.4**	0.4	0.58	5.40	3.63	82.2	**3.7**	42.4	17.0	**5.9**
3.7	2.16	15.7	0.13	**7.3**	0.9	1.61	17.55	4.54	61.5	**2.0**	15.2	18.9	**6.6**
7.6	0.97	3.8	0.03	**5.4**	0.4	1.13	14.87	3.50	57.4	**7.5**	68.9	0.0	**3.1**
7.4	0.62	2.3	-0.02	**4.5**	1.6	0.86	5.70	3.84	73.6	**2.7**	25.4	16.6	**7.8**
4.6	0.89	5.6	0.09	**5.1**	2.1	1.14	13.27	3.13	66.3	**5.4**	38.5	6.6	**6.2**
5.0	2.81	11.1	0.31	**3.6**	0.5	0.66	5.22	3.58	76.7	**5.3**	44.2	9.1	**5.5**
6.9	0.84	3.9	0.06	**6.6**	1.8	1.48	11.75	4.47	53.9	**0.8**	16.0	38.1	**8.3**
8.1	1.24	3.9	0.02	**3.8**	0.2	0.64	4.29	2.24	58.9	**5.6**	54.3	9.1	**7.0**
6.8	1.05	4.5	-0.13	**6.0**	0.9	1.25	8.73	3.88	57.0	**4.7**	34.4	9.4	**7.5**
4.6	1.14	8.8	0.04	**9.3**	1.9	2.25	22.05	4.43	45.3	**2.7**	14.5	15.7	**6.5**
8.2	0.00	0.0	0.00	**6.4**	0.4	1.52	9.63	3.66	55.7	**4.3**	29.5	10.1	**8.2**
5.2	11.48	14.3	0.05	**8.7**	4.5	2.14	10.81	3.90	40.5	**4.0**	76.2	26.3	**8.9**
8.9	0.21	1.4	0.02	**4.5**	1.4	1.08	15.68	2.95	66.8	**5.1**	40.0	9.6	**3.8**
8.1	0.00	0.0	0.00	**6.2**	0.5	1.18	13.23	3.93	55.7	**4.2**	11.4	6.7	**5.3**
6.8	0.03	0.2	0.01	**1.2**	0.0	-0.01	-0.06	2.95	100.4	**1.7**	24.4	24.6	**5.5**

Name	City	State	Rating	2013 Rating	2012 Rating	Total Assets ($Mil)	One Year Asset Growth	Asset Mix (As a % of Total Assets) Commercial Loans	Consumer Loans	Mortgage Loans	Securities	Capitalization Index	Leverage Ratio	Risk-Based Capital Ratio
FARMERS STATE BK	Wallace	NE	**D+**	C-	C	47.0	-6.38	8.3	3.1	7.5	34.7	**7.3**	9.2	15.5
FARMERS STATE BK	Maywood	NE	**C**	C	C-	99.9	-2.23	6.2	1.9	3.1	24.7	**7.4**	9.6	12.8
FARMERS STATE BK	Humphrey	NE	**C+**	B-	B-	29.3	5.14	3.0	1.7	0.1	28.2	**9.8**	10.9	20.6
FARMERS STATE BK	Ewing	NE	**B**	B	B	21.9	6.95	15.1	2.8	0.6	0.0	**10.0**	20.3	28.2
▼ FARMERS STATE BK	Pine Bluffs	WY	**D-**	D-	D+	21.5	-13.04	11.0	4.5	0.0	23.8	**6.5**	8.5	18.0
FARMERS STATE BK	Quinton	OK	**B-**	B-	B-	89.2	4.10	4.2	5.1	16.8	35.8	**6.5**	8.5	17.2
FARMERS STATE BK	Center	TX	**A-**	A-	A-	383.7	-3.89	12.5	3.2	6.7	31.9	**10.0**	11.1	18.0
FARMERS STATE BK	Groesbeck	TX	**B+**	B+	B+	126.5	2.19	2.0	5.3	15.4	30.8	**6.8**	8.8	17.9
FARMERS STATE BK	Parkston	SD	**B+**	A-	A-	135.5	-4.89	5.4	2.4	0.0	41.8	**10.0**	12.7	21.8
FARMERS STATE BK	Marion	SD	**C**	B-	B-	79.0	1.64	5.7	2.6	9.5	1.1	**5.1**	9.0	11.1
FARMERS STATE BK	Stickney	SD	**B-**	C+	C+	111.2	6.79	4.8	2.0	0.7	8.1	**6.1**	10.0	11.8
FARMERS STATE BK	Hosmer	SD	**B**	B	B	21.2	8.80	22.5	5.5	0.0	2.2	**10.0**	13.8	16.1
FARMERS STATE BK	Victor	MT	**C+**	C+	D+	329.8	0.14	4.9	2.9	11.2	41.7	**8.9**	10.3	19.3
FARMERS STATE BK	Holton	KS	**C**	D+	C-	53.4	-1.53	3.1	1.7	25.1	30.0	**7.2**	9.1	17.5
FARMERS STATE BK	Dwight	KS	**C**	C	C+	16.4	4.56	2.2	1.6	2.5	24.4	**10.0**	11.9	26.3
FARMERS STATE BK	Fairview	KS	**D**	D-	D+	24.0	-5.89	0.7	3.5	9.4	26.9	**5.6**	7.6	14.6
FARMERS STATE BK	McPherson	KS	**B+**	B+	B	101.2	8.42	7.7	4.7	19.3	40.3	**6.6**	8.6	14.8
FARMERS STATE BK	Atwood	KS	**C+**	C+	C+	23.9	-6.62	6.0	3.1	9.6	30.4	**9.4**	10.6	20.4
FARMERS STATE BK	Wathena	KS	**B**	B	B	60.3	-2.70	12.6	4.6	15.7	44.9	**10.0**	16.0	31.8
FARMERS STATE BK	Phillipsburg	KS	**C-**	C-	C-	35.1	3.64	8.9	7.3	9.3	31.4	**7.4**	9.3	15.8
FARMERS STATE BK	Cameron	MO	**B-**	B-	B-	219.4	14.12	1.4	2.3	48.6	8.4	**7.3**	9.3	12.8
FARMERS STATE BK	Westmoreland	KS	**B+**	B	B	137.9	10.99	4.8	2.5	16.4	30.4	**10.0**	16.1	16.0
FARMERS STATE BK	Dodge	NE	**C**	C-	D-	103.3	20.37	5.9	0.8	5.4	1.8	**4.2**	9.0	10.6
FARMERS STATE BK	Carroll	NE	**C**	C	C-	27.9	-0.31	1.4	1.6	0.7	46.2	**6.1**	8.2	16.3
FARMERS STATE BK	Yale	IA	**C+**	C+	C	46.4	0.89	3.5	2.6	12.8	36.4	**7.0**	9.0	15.7
FARMERS STATE BK	Marcus	IA	**A-**	A-	A-	65.4	-5.17	3.4	3.7	6.6	37.1	**10.0**	13.1	22.7
FARMERS STATE BK	Marion	IA	**A-**	A-	A-	647.8	3.61	9.4	1.6	10.2	20.2	**10.0**	13.1	17.8
FARMERS STATE BK	Mason City	IA	**B**	B	B-	172.6	1.89	2.6	2.8	13.7	43.5	**8.7**	10.1	18.9
FARMERS STATE BK	Lake View	IA	**C+**	C+	C+	32.4	-2.58	9.9	4.9	16.2	35.3	**10.0**	11.0	29.8
FARMERS STATE BK	Waterloo	IA	**B-**	B-	C+	591.4	13.11	13.6	3.0	19.8	7.7	**4.4**	8.1	10.7
FARMERS STATE BK	Markesan	WI	**B**	B-	C+	76.7	1.56	8.3	3.1	11.9	38.4	**10.0**	12.5	21.2
▲ FARMERS STATE BK	Pittsfield	IL	**C+**	C	C+	231.1	-1.25	2.1	1.3	8.0	19.7	**10.0**	11.2	15.3
FARMERS STATE BK	New Madison	OH	**B**	B	B	138.2	6.04	5.5	3.7	25.1	18.7	**10.0**	12.1	18.5
FARMERS STATE BK	West Salem	OH	**C+**	C+	C+	95.6	1.97	2.6	1.8	37.5	19.9	**8.6**	10.0	17.6
FARMERS STATE BK	Booneville	KY	**C+**	C+	C	51.8	-3.29	5.7	6.6	25.9	39.1	**8.3**	9.9	20.4
FARMERS STATE BK	Elmwood	IL	**C-**	C+	C	55.6	-0.87	3.8	1.9	19.3	32.9	**5.8**	7.8	15.1
FARMERS STATE BK	Lagrange	IN	**B**	B	C+	530.7	5.51	5.1	1.6	31.7	14.5	**7.4**	9.3	14.7
FARMERS STATE BK	Mentone	IN	**B**	B	B-	136.0	-2.26	3.9	1.2	23.6	19.6	**8.8**	10.2	16.0
FARMERS STATE BK	Brookston	IN	**D+**	D+	D	69.1	2.84	5.1	3.0	39.0	22.5	**6.4**	8.4	15.1
FARMERS STATE BK	Algona	IA	**B-**	C+	C	100.4	-5.36	9.7	1.6	13.5	16.9	**6.9**	8.9	13.6
FARMERS STATE BK	Dublin	GA	**B+**	B+	B	115.8	0.40	5.1	6.1	14.8	23.5	**10.0**	13.6	20.2
FARMERS STATE BK	Mountain City	TN	**C**	C-	D	133.1	-4.61	3.8	6.9	26.9	28.0	**10.0**	14.7	25.6
FARMERS STATE BK	Lumpkin	GA	**E-**	E-	E-	43.4	2.51	5.2	6.1	9.5	46.3	**0.6**	3.8	9.2
▲ FARMERS STATE BK	Lincolnton	GA	**A-**	B	B-	123.7	1.40	1.8	5.0	22.1	39.7	**10.0**	13.6	29.2
FARMERS STATE BK	Winthrop	WA	**C**	C	B-	29.2	2.66	6.2	2.2	1.8	36.4	**10.0**	12.3	51.2
FARMERS STATE BK & TRUST CO	Church Point	LA	**B**	B-	B-	99.1	6.99	7.8	4.1	14.2	21.3	**7.2**	9.2	14.6
FARMERS STATE BK & TRUST CO	Mount Sterling	IL	**C+**	C+	C	83.1	2.16	18.2	3.0	12.9	17.2	**5.7**	8.5	11.5
FARMERS STATE BK & TRUST CO	Jacksonville	IL	**C+**	C	C	193.4	5.62	9.0	5.2	12.6	41.5	**10.0**	11.6	19.0
▲ FARMERS STATE BK ALLEN OK	Allen	OK	**B**	B-	C+	41.7	1.16	17.6	15.4	16.5	11.0	**10.0**	12.0	15.6
FARMERS STATE BK HILLSBORO	Hillsboro	WI	**A-**	A-	A	142.6	34.91	4.8	2.1	10.7	51.2	**10.0**	13.7	26.9
FARMERS STATE BK OF ALICEVILLE	Westphalia	KS	**A-**	A-	B-	129.9	4.72	2.3	9.6	15.9	9.9	**10.0**	11.1	16.1
FARMERS STATE BK OF ALTO PASS	Harrisburg	IL	**C-**	D+	C-	190.7	1.29	14.1	3.2	18.7	16.5	**7.1**	9.2	12.6
FARMERS STATE BK OF BLUE MOUND	Blue Mound	KS	**D+**	C-	C-	42.6	0.07	4.0	3.7	4.3	14.8	**10.0**	15.3	23.3
FARMERS STATE BK OF BRUSH	Brush	CO	**B+**	B+	A-	106.9	-1.20	2.6	2.4	3.3	31.7	**10.0**	15.7	26.3
▲ FARMERS STATE BK OF BUCKLIN KS	Bucklin	KS	**C**	C-	C	45.1	1.19	6.4	1.7	3.7	40.6	**5.1**	7.1	16.4
FARMERS STATE BK OF CALHAN	Calhan	CO	**B+**	B+	B+	218.0	5.46	3.6	3.0	18.0	44.9	**9.3**	10.6	20.1
▼ FARMERS STATE BK OF CAMP POINT	Camp Point	IL	**C**	C	B-	48.6	-1.78	6.9	2.2	5.8	54.8	**10.0**	11.2	21.8
FARMERS STATE BK OF CANTON	Canton	SD	**C**	C	C	46.5	-5.78	5.5	4.5	22.9	22.5	**9.6**	10.7	17.1
FARMERS STATE BK OF CROSBY ND	Crosby	ND	**C**	C	C+	65.2	-16.87	1.7	0.1	0.8	24.3	**6.5**	8.5	48.3
▲ FARMERS STATE BK OF DANFORTH	Danforth	IL	**B-**	C+	C+	67.0	-1.46	3.7	0.8	6.7	56.1	**7.7**	9.5	19.0

Asset Quality Index	Adjusted Non-Performing Loans as a % of Total Loans	Adjusted Non-Performing Loans as a % of Capital	Net Charge-Offs Avg Loans	Profitability Index	Net Income ($Mil)	Return on Assets (R.O.A.)	Return on Equity (R.O.E.)	Net Interest Spread	Overhead Efficiency Ratio	Liquidity Index	Liquidity Ratio	Hot Money Ratio	Stability Index
6.6	1.28	6.5	0.06	1.4	0.0	-0.04	-0.43	2.91	98.2	4.7	43.9	12.3	2.5
3.1	1.58	10.1	-0.01	5.4	1.0	1.30	13.46	4.33	68.5	2.3	12.0	17.2	5.2
8.9	0.00	0.0	0.00	3.4	0.2	0.73	7.12	2.44	69.9	5.9	50.4	6.2	5.5
6.9	0.63	2.0	0.00	4.6	0.1	0.88	4.26	2.98	59.1	3.1	40.3	17.3	6.8
6.3	1.20	4.3	0.24	1.8	0.0	0.19	2.30	3.66	94.7	5.9	65.5	7.8	1.6
8.3	0.36	1.8	0.11	5.0	0.8	1.20	16.35	4.30	76.4	5.3	44.4	9.1	4.3
6.8	0.89	3.6	0.15	6.2	4.4	1.50	13.09	3.83	57.9	2.7	37.7	22.2	7.7
8.8	0.19	0.9	-0.02	5.3	1.1	1.16	12.26	4.74	74.6	5.0	38.7	9.4	6.6
8.2	0.72	2.8	-0.01	4.8	0.9	0.88	7.54	3.32	61.1	5.4	40.1	7.6	7.5
4.5	0.64	5.9	0.00	6.0	0.8	1.29	12.12	4.65	60.9	4.0	3.0	6.9	4.0
7.0	0.00	0.0	-0.03	8.0	1.1	1.33	13.42	3.95	44.2	3.6	6.8	10.4	6.1
7.0	0.52	2.9	-0.01	8.6	0.3	1.85	13.87	5.21	61.3	0.6	17.6	53.8	6.3
4.8	1.91	8.1	0.56	3.8	1.6	0.63	6.10	3.74	83.0	4.7	46.8	13.2	5.2
5.1	0.60	3.3	0.09	4.1	0.3	0.64	7.47	3.87	74.4	2.1	30.0	23.6	4.5
8.8	0.01	0.1	0.00	2.7	0.1	0.49	4.15	3.07	83.7	5.6	56.7	7.7	5.2
2.2	3.41	20.1	-0.02	2.9	0.1	0.59	8.25	2.93	79.8	5.4	49.1	6.9	1.7
8.8	0.00	0.0	0.00	6.6	1.2	1.59	17.99	4.20	61.7	5.4	45.4	9.2	6.1
6.5	0.75	3.1	0.00	4.4	0.2	0.89	8.86	3.05	58.4	5.0	41.4	7.1	4.3
7.1	0.99	2.7	0.91	4.7	0.6	1.18	7.84	4.06	75.9	5.3	47.4	9.7	6.7
3.0	2.35	13.0	-0.01	4.9	0.3	1.15	12.60	4.09	72.1	2.5	39.4	26.3	4.1
5.7	0.53	4.4	0.09	4.4	1.2	0.70	7.06	4.07	73.2	3.3	11.9	12.3	5.7
4.9	3.46	12.3	0.13	5.5	1.1	1.07	6.83	3.57	59.2	1.9	27.0	23.5	6.2
6.5	0.00	0.0	0.01	3.8	0.7	0.98	9.28	4.16	67.8	1.4	9.6	24.8	5.4
8.1	0.00	0.0	0.00	4.1	0.2	0.73	9.19	2.73	65.7	3.3	54.3	22.3	4.3
6.3	0.57	3.5	0.08	5.1	0.4	1.21	13.76	3.87	64.3	3.5	41.5	17.6	5.0
8.5	0.19	0.7	0.04	5.6	0.7	1.38	11.19	3.12	52.1	5.6	53.8	9.4	6.8
5.4	1.83	9.3	-0.01	6.3	7.2	1.45	11.13	3.64	62.4	3.7	20.6	11.1	8.1
6.0	1.17	5.6	0.03	4.9	1.2	0.96	9.53	3.86	64.0	2.8	41.3	24.7	5.6
8.7	0.00	0.0	0.11	3.2	0.2	0.58	5.55	2.71	74.5	6.6	65.5	4.8	4.6
7.9	0.08	0.8	0.03	7.7	7.2	1.71	21.17	4.09	54.4	2.3	11.1	17.2	6.4
4.6	4.17	16.1	0.22	4.1	0.5	0.79	5.90	4.37	77.3	4.8	45.5	11.9	6.8
3.6	2.15	12.9	-0.01	4.4	1.7	0.99	8.74	3.48	78.8	4.0	17.2	9.0	7.0
5.9	1.26	6.8	0.16	4.6	0.9	0.86	7.27	4.05	69.0	1.4	9.6	23.9	6.6
4.4	1.89	11.7	0.29	3.4	0.4	0.50	5.03	4.07	85.1	4.8	23.8	4.6	5.5
2.9	4.50	20.3	0.35	3.8	0.3	0.70	7.21	4.31	79.8	1.8	26.8	25.2	5.0
3.3	3.37	21.1	2.31	0.8	-0.4	-0.96	-10.74	3.71	90.5	2.0	28.3	23.3	4.0
4.8	1.32	9.4	0.01	5.4	3.9	0.98	10.10	4.04	71.0	4.1	23.0	9.0	6.8
8.1	0.04	0.2	-0.37	4.8	1.0	0.91	9.06	4.02	72.1	4.2	27.2	9.8	6.2
3.3	2.85	20.6	0.21	1.3	0.0	0.01	0.07	3.54	97.8	3.1	30.0	16.1	3.1
4.4	1.38	9.5	0.22	4.3	0.7	0.90	10.52	3.10	70.9	4.7	30.4	8.0	5.4
5.6	1.57	7.1	0.00	4.7	1.0	1.11	8.34	4.13	70.0	2.2	26.3	19.3	7.3
2.6	5.29	20.5	0.65	4.1	0.8	0.79	5.39	4.54	75.1	2.0	22.9	19.7	6.3
2.7	2.07	16.9	0.94	0.2	-0.3	-0.74	-20.08	3.58	111.7	2.0	26.9	22.1	0.0
5.6	2.60	7.9	-0.02	5.3	1.2	1.33	10.48	3.84	69.6	2.1	38.2	32.4	7.1
9.8	0.98	1.6	0.35	2.4	0.1	0.35	2.80	2.86	81.4	7.9	85.8	0.0	5.9
4.8	1.13	6.9	0.04	6.8	1.2	1.61	16.94	4.92	69.0	2.3	23.5	18.3	6.4
6.9	0.37	3.1	-0.01	5.2	0.6	0.91	10.87	4.09	67.0	1.6	14.5	22.7	4.6
5.0	3.45	13.4	0.04	3.2	0.9	0.61	5.45	3.15	80.1	5.8	44.4	6.5	5.8
3.9	1.50	9.2	0.06	9.0	0.6	2.04	17.18	5.48	61.8	1.7	13.1	20.9	7.6
7.0	2.25	7.3	0.05	7.5	1.3	1.46	10.25	3.85	39.3	4.7	59.5	16.6	7.9
7.8	0.22	1.4	-0.04	8.8	1.5	1.54	13.90	3.64	31.1	2.3	14.1	17.5	6.6
1.9	2.89	22.3	0.00	6.1	2.0	1.41	15.64	4.41	71.3	3.2	18.8	13.3	5.5
0.8	6.76	24.9	0.28	3.4	0.2	0.55	3.64	4.49	87.5	3.7	34.1	14.6	6.7
7.0	1.03	3.8	0.02	6.1	0.9	1.14	7.56	4.01	62.7	2.7	14.7	15.3	7.6
7.6	0.00	0.0	0.02	3.7	0.3	0.79	8.65	3.80	75.1	5.1	54.3	11.7	4.7
5.8	1.73	7.7	0.44	5.7	2.2	1.35	13.36	4.12	67.8	3.1	36.9	18.7	5.7
8.0	0.32	1.0	-0.18	4.4	0.3	0.82	5.82	3.23	64.7	5.9	45.2	4.9	3.7
5.3	0.92	4.8	0.24	2.6	0.1	0.38	3.67	3.25	88.1	3.4	15.1	12.1	4.9
10.0	0.00	0.0	0.00	2.3	0.2	0.28	3.30	1.35	80.6	7.5	85.4	2.5	4.6
6.5	0.74	2.9	0.58	4.5	0.5	0.92	10.49	3.47	64.8	5.9	59.4	8.2	4.4

	Name	City	State	Rating	2013 Rating	2012 Rating	Total Assets ($Mil)	One Year Asset Growth	Asset Mix (As a % of Total Assets) Comm-ercial Loans	Cons-umer Loans	Mort-gage Loans	Secur-ities	Capital-ization Index	Lever-age Ratio	Risk-Based Capital Ratio
▲	FARMERS STATE BK OF DARWIN	Darwin	MN	**B-**	C+	B-	38.4	2.76	7.5	4.4	7.4	39.6	**6.7**	8.7	18.5
	FARMERS STATE BK OF DENTON MT	Denton	MT	**C**	C	C-	21.8	6.38	10.8	4.1	1.2	13.2	**10.0**	11.6	15.7
	FARMERS STATE BK OF EMDEN	Emden	IL	**B-**	B-	B-	41.7	2.67	1.6	1.3	4.0	76.1	**10.0**	21.1	47.7
	FARMERS STATE BK OF HAMEL	Hamel	MN	**C+**	C+	B-	114.4	10.26	3.6	0.5	8.9	48.1	**8.9**	10.3	24.0
	FARMERS STATE BK OF HARTLAND	Hartland	MN	**B-**	B	C+	103.2	2.75	10.6	1.1	4.3	11.7	**6.6**	9.6	12.2
	FARMERS STATE BK OF HOFFMAN	Hoffman	MN	**B+**	B+	A-	28.8	-0.30	6.9	4.0	6.8	39.6	**10.0**	12.5	24.1
	FARMERS STATE BK OF HOFFMAN	Hoffman	IL	**B**	B	B+	138.1	-3.21	4.0	1.8	13.1	49.8	**10.0**	13.7	28.1
	FARMERS STATE BK OF MEDORA	Medora	IL	**B-**	B-	B-	20.8	-2.08	2.0	5.9	6.4	58.2	**10.0**	15.3	32.8
▲	FARMERS STATE BK OF MUNITH	Munith	MI	**C**	D+	D-	60.8	-9.02	1.2	3.3	41.4	21.8	**7.4**	9.3	18.6
	FARMERS STATE BK OF OAKLEY KS	Oakley	KS	**A-**	B+	A-	123.2	8.79	10.1	1.4	3.5	37.3	**10.0**	13.0	20.2
▲	FARMERS STATE BK OF SUBLETTE	Sublette	IL	**C-**	D-	D-	41.7	-2.74	10.5	0.7	5.8	54.0	**7.4**	9.2	21.3
	FARMERS STATE BK OF TRIMONT	Trimont	MN	**B+**	B+	A-	62.0	3.47	8.4	1.4	3.6	40.6	**10.0**	13.0	23.6
	FARMERS STATE BK OF TURTON	Turton	SD	**B**	B	B-	29.0	9.58	2.3	4.1	0.2	15.8	**9.7**	10.8	17.5
	FARMERS STATE BK OF UNDERWOOD	Underwood	MN	**B**	B	B-	58.0	10.45	7.1	5.1	17.9	11.1	**6.8**	8.8	12.4
	FARMERS STATE BK OF W CONCORD	West Concord	MN	**C**	C	C-	46.6	-1.98	7.5	5.8	24.9	31.2	**8.6**	10.0	19.0
	FARMERS STATE BK OF WATKINS	Watkins	MN	**B+**	B+	A-	41.3	2.92	6.2	4.6	14.2	34.9	**10.0**	12.6	21.0
	FARMERS STATE BK OF WAUPACA	Waupaca	WI	**A-**	A-	A-	172.4	0.00	9.6	3.6	25.2	33.5	**10.0**	15.1	21.7
	FARMERS STATE BK OF WESTERN IL	Alpha	IL	**B**	B+	A-	128.8	-0.76	4.2	3.0	8.7	33.0	**10.0**	11.8	18.6
▼	FARMERS STATE BK S/B	Bolivar	MO	**C-**	C	C-	65.2	7.65	1.2	2.8	28.3	15.7	**10.0**	15.0	28.4
	FARMERS STATE BK STANBERRY	Stanberry	MO	**A-**	A-	A-	57.9	1.48	1.1	2.2	9.2	37.0	**10.0**	13.3	23.4
	FARMERS TRUST & SB	Earling	IA	**B-**	B-	B-	92.0	2.01	12.5	1.4	8.2	4.6	**6.6**	9.2	12.2
	FARMERS TRUST & SB	Buffalo Center	IA	**B+**	B+	B+	242.6	5.32	10.6	1.5	6.5	2.8	**6.6**	9.7	12.2
	FARMERS TRUST & SB	Williamsburg	IA	**A+**	A+	A+	140.1	5.32	7.8	4.1	15.7	40.7	**10.0**	20.2	32.8
▼	FARMERS TRUST & SB	Spencer	IA	**C+**	B-	C	325.9	-0.74	8.0	1.2	7.2	31.5	**7.3**	9.2	15.0
	FARMERS-MERCHANTS BANK & TRUST	Breaux Bridge	LA	**B-**	C+	B-	292.0	6.04	8.4	3.7	14.5	13.3	**10.0**	11.7	16.6
	FARMERS-MERCHANTS NATIONAL BK	Paxton	IL	**B**	B-	B	114.4	0.52	3.9	1.3	11.9	59.1	**10.0**	11.3	29.0
	FARMINGTON BANK	Farmington	CT	**C**	C-	C-	2393.8	20.31	12.1	0.1	33.5	8.7	**6.3**	8.6	12.0
	FARMINGTON STATE BK	Farmington	WA	**C+**	B-	B-	10.8	-5.67	3.6	0.8	0.8	1.5	**10.0**	15.1	27.8
	FAUQUIER BANK	Warrenton	VA	**B-**	C+	C+	586.0	-1.22	4.2	4.4	24.3	9.4	**7.8**	9.5	14.9
	FAYETTE COUNTY BANK	Saint Elmo	IL	**D**	D+	C	44.8	31.11	17.4	9.3	40.6	13.6	**0.0**	-2.9	-4.8
	FAYETTE COUNTY NB FAYETTEVILLE	Fayetteville	WV	**B**	B	B+	93.7	0.00	0.8	3.6	45.9	30.7	**9.5**	10.6	24.0
	FAYETTE SB SSB	La Grange	TX	**B-**	B-	B-	95.2	5.78	1.5	2.0	43.2	21.6	**6.0**	8.0	15.2
	FAYETTEVILLE BANK	Fayetteville	TX	**A-**	A-	A-	369.1	8.09	2.4	1.7	5.7	77.8	**8.1**	9.7	27.2
	FBT BANK & MORTGAGE	Fordyce	AR	**B+**	B+	B	132.8	1.79	10.3	10.5	24.7	27.9	**10.0**	11.6	20.2
	FCN BANK NA	Brookville	IN	**C+**	C	C	410.9	1.62	5.3	1.3	17.9	40.8	**7.1**	9.0	17.6
	FDS BANK	Mason	OH	**A+**	A+	A+	165.0	23.84	1.3	0.2	0.0	54.6	**10.0**	39.4	152.8
	FEDERAL SAVINGS BANK	Dover	NH	**C+**	C+	C+	296.7	3.95	4.7	0.3	48.8	12.3	**8.1**	9.7	16.7
	FEDERAL SAVINGS BANK	Chicago	IL	**B+**	B+	B+	209.3	32.52	1.6	0.0	82.3	1.4	**10.0**	11.9	22.4
▲	FEDERATED BANK	Onarga	IL	**C-**	D+	D+	83.4	-7.91	4.9	2.8	11.8	31.8	**6.3**	8.3	19.2
	FEDERATION BANK	Washington	IA	**B-**	B-	C+	115.0	8.46	10.0	4.0	14.2	29.3	**6.3**	8.3	12.0
▲	FELICIANA BANK & TRUST CO	Clinton	LA	**C+**	C	D	109.8	5.04	5.3	3.2	31.5	30.7	**9.6**	10.7	20.5
	FIDELITY BANK	Norcross	GA	**C**	C-	C-	2859.6	11.52	3.8	43.0	10.7	5.7	**7.1**	9.9	12.6
	FIDELITY BANK	Fuquay-Varina	NC	**C**	C	C+	1653.0	3.28	2.7	0.9	4.0	15.9	**8.0**	9.6	17.4
	FIDELITY BANK	West Des Moines	IA	**B-**	C+	B-	71.3	23.85	4.9	1.5	27.9	6.5	**6.8**	9.7	12.4
	FIDELITY BANK	Edina	MN	**A**	A	A-	431.9	1.23	20.0	0.8	18.0	16.6	**10.0**	12.9	19.6
	FIDELITY BANK	Wichita Falls	TX	**B**	B-	B	371.4	44.64	16.1	3.9	12.4	5.3	**7.9**	9.6	15.0
	FIDELITY BANK	Wichita	KS	**B**	B	C	1601.2	5.15	5.8	11.8	14.4	7.4	**10.0**	12.2	15.2
	FIDELITY BANK & TRUST	Dubuque	IA	**B-**	B-	C+	594.4	-0.06	10.9	0.7	5.5	16.4	**8.6**	10.5	13.9
	FIDELITY BANK OF FLORIDA NA	Merritt Island	FL	**D+**	D-	E-	254.6	-10.01	1.2	0.0	7.9	28.5	**5.7**	7.7	13.2
	FIDELITY BANK OF TEXAS	Waco	TX	**B**	B-	C+	92.1	2.32	10.5	3.7	39.4	7.1	**10.0**	12.4	22.2
▼	FIDELITY CO-OP BANK	Leominster	MA	**C+**	B-	C+	594.3	5.78	15.7	0.2	27.9	12.0	**6.2**	8.3	13.3
	FIDELITY DEPOSIT & DISCOUNT BK	Dunmore	PA	**B**	C+	C-	673.4	5.24	8.9	4.8	26.2	16.9	**9.0**	10.3	15.2
	FIDELITY FS&LA OF DELAWARE	Delaware	OH	**B-**	B-	B	102.1	-4.76	0.1	1.0	35.3	40.5	**10.0**	20.9	48.8
	FIDELITY HOMESTEAD SB	New Orleans	LA	**C**	C-	C	830.9	-0.16	0.4	0.3	37.1	24.2	**10.0**	14.1	24.2
	FIDELITY NATIONAL BK	West Memphis	AR	**B**	B	C	368.5	4.69	3.6	1.4	6.8	58.3	**9.3**	10.6	22.8
▼	FIDELITY NATIONAL BK	Medford	WI	**D**	D+	D	80.7	-4.29	9.2	2.5	28.8	15.1	**10.0**	11.2	17.5
	FIDELITY PERSONAL TRUST CO FSB	Boston	MA	**U**	U	A+	77.1	21.94	0.0	0.0	0.0	68.3	**10.0**	85.5	85.9
	FIDELITY S&LA OF BUCKS COUNTY	Bristol	PA	**C+**	C+	C+	105.0	-2.49	0.4	0.2	53.3	14.9	**10.0**	12.4	27.0
	FIDELITY STATE BK & TRUST CO	Dodge City	KS	**B+**	B+	A-	163.1	1.64	4.3	0.7	3.0	37.7	**10.0**	16.2	48.6
▲	FIDELITY STATE BK & TRUST CO	Topeka	KS	**B-**	B-	B+	105.2	7.05	13.5	14.1	8.2	25.6	**10.0**	11.2	17.0

Asset Quality Index	Adjusted Non-Performing Loans as a % of Total Loans	Adjusted Non-Performing Loans as a % of Capital	Net Charge-Offs Avg Loans	Profitability Index	Net Income ($Mil)	Return on Assets (R.O.A.)	Return on Equity (R.O.E.)	Net Interest Spread	Overhead Efficiency Ratio	Liquidity Index	Liquidity Ratio	Hot Money Ratio	Stability Index
6.7	1.25	4.7	0.12	**5.2**	0.4	1.29	18.85	3.58	65.6	**6.3**	57.9	5.0	**4.2**
2.8	2.44	14.7	0.19	**6.0**	0.2	1.42	11.86	5.75	62.6	**2.5**	13.7	16.0	**6.1**
9.7	1.05	1.1	0.00	**3.6**	0.2	0.60	2.87	2.24	62.6	**3.8**	78.2	26.3	**7.0**
9.6	0.00	0.0	-0.01	**3.8**	0.8	0.99	9.39	3.13	68.2	**5.6**	59.6	11.8	**4.8**
4.0	1.97	15.9	0.00	**5.4**	0.7	1.57	14.78	5.14	57.0	**2.2**	14.4	18.2	**6.5**
8.7	0.64	2.3	-0.01	**7.2**	0.4	1.74	14.01	3.72	53.2	**4.1**	53.8	16.8	**7.6**
9.3	0.33	0.9	0.07	**4.1**	1.0	0.92	6.73	3.39	67.0	**5.8**	48.5	7.7	**8.1**
9.0	0.07	0.1	0.00	**3.5**	0.1	0.53	3.27	3.14	71.8	**5.3**	85.2	13.9	**6.5**
3.0	2.88	17.7	0.19	**3.4**	0.3	0.69	7.65	4.24	86.5	**4.9**	31.7	6.7	**3.2**
5.6	4.74	19.3	0.07	**6.5**	1.0	1.11	8.21	3.50	49.1	**1.7**	24.2	24.0	**7.5**
5.2	2.60	8.5	0.64	**2.3**	0.2	0.56	6.55	3.17	91.8	**4.2**	46.6	15.2	**2.8**
6.2	2.86	9.3	-0.03	**4.8**	0.4	0.81	6.42	3.34	65.7	**4.0**	35.2	13.3	**7.6**
7.1	0.00	0.0	0.01	**5.2**	0.2	1.07	10.08	4.34	65.1	**2.1**	22.7	19.3	**6.7**
7.4	0.32	2.6	0.04	**8.1**	0.8	1.88	21.35	4.65	60.3	**1.6**	15.3	23.0	**5.8**
5.3	1.23	6.9	0.75	**3.5**	0.3	0.81	8.24	4.07	83.6	**5.7**	37.5	4.4	**4.0**
7.8	0.90	3.8	0.21	**6.6**	0.5	1.61	12.42	4.31	61.1	**4.2**	34.2	12.3	**7.9**
7.1	1.39	4.8	0.15	**6.9**	1.9	1.43	9.91	4.89	58.3	**3.7**	35.6	14.9	**7.3**
6.9	1.23	5.3	0.18	**4.1**	0.7	0.74	6.62	3.60	74.2	**3.9**	27.8	11.5	**6.9**
9.0	0.33	1.3	-0.01	**0.8**	-0.1	-0.21	-1.45	3.62	108.8	**2.3**	26.1	19.1	**6.0**
9.0	0.44	1.4	-0.05	**5.8**	0.6	1.43	10.53	3.25	55.0	**5.2**	51.8	10.8	**8.7**
5.7	0.15	1.2	0.15	**6.2**	1.0	1.45	16.21	3.86	61.3	**3.5**	13.6	11.2	**6.4**
5.6	0.36	3.1	0.02	**7.7**	3.1	1.74	17.07	3.74	51.3	**3.6**	8.1	10.2	**7.6**
7.9	1.15	3.1	-0.05	**8.6**	2.2	2.11	10.59	3.85	45.7	**5.7**	45.4	7.4	**9.5**
2.5	3.27	20.2	0.81	**5.2**	3.0	1.22	13.23	3.16	55.5	**3.8**	16.8	10.2	**5.9**
3.7	2.84	16.1	-0.03	**7.9**	4.2	1.89	16.81	4.88	64.7	**2.9**	23.6	15.2	**7.2**
7.2	1.39	3.8	0.81	**4.3**	0.8	0.93	8.08	3.29	64.9	**4.1**	44.4	15.4	**6.7**
5.3	1.11	10.5	0.12	**2.9**	7.1	0.43	4.95	2.96	77.9	**3.7**	2.4	8.9	**5.4**
8.7	0.00	0.0	0.00	**3.1**	0.1	0.53	3.77	3.45	78.1	**5.5**	62.2	9.7	**6.3**
5.9	0.52	3.6	0.02	**4.3**	3.9	0.88	9.55	3.62	74.7	**3.9**	12.0	8.8	**5.4**
0.3	27.97	294.9	3.17	**0.7**	-5.5	-14.78	-300.05	2.79	62.7	**0.4**	9.2	69.1	**2.9**
4.9	2.07	11.1	0.04	**4.6**	0.6	0.83	7.40	4.24	71.2	**4.4**	13.3	5.8	**6.6**
6.0	0.95	7.4	0.00	**4.0**	0.5	0.70	8.93	3.58	73.7	**3.6**	34.1	15.0	**4.7**
9.6	1.11	1.7	0.05	**6.4**	3.7	1.34	16.79	3.64	46.5	**3.1**	65.7	42.1	**7.6**
5.9	1.37	6.4	0.07	**5.1**	1.2	1.24	12.78	4.47	75.6	**2.3**	33.1	23.1	**6.3**
3.8	2.92	14.8	-0.02	**4.1**	2.4	0.78	8.02	3.08	62.1	**4.7**	46.9	13.2	**5.9**
10.0	0.04	0.0	-0.48	**9.5**	317.1	283.53	632.00	0.15	26.6	**9.3**	152.7	0.0	**8.3**
6.9	0.28	2.1	0.08	**3.3**	0.8	0.36	3.68	3.64	86.3	**2.9**	11.3	14.1	**5.6**
9.8	0.21	1.6	-0.01	**6.5**	1.0	0.89	5.78	3.76	96.6	**0.3**	5.7	77.8	**6.5**
4.4	1.19	5.2	-0.58	**2.1**	0.3	0.46	3.87	2.56	93.1	**6.1**	53.1	5.4	**4.0**
5.0	0.67	4.6	0.13	**4.4**	0.8	0.91	9.81	3.81	75.1	**3.8**	25.2	10.8	**5.1**
5.6	0.78	3.9	0.02	**3.4**	0.8	0.93	9.02	4.16	79.2	**1.2**	28.3	41.9	**6.0**
2.8	1.61	12.7	0.24	**6.9**	22.6	1.14	11.13	3.74	74.6	**2.3**	5.8	16.8	**7.6**
6.3	0.95	4.7	0.04	**2.9**	4.9	0.40	3.75	2.95	80.8	**6.0**	43.9	7.9	**7.9**
7.9	0.00	0.0	0.00	**5.9**	0.7	1.36	11.58	4.95	83.0	**0.9**	9.3	31.9	**5.7**
6.8	0.00	0.0	-0.27	**8.0**	5.6	1.83	9.86	3.38	57.8	**5.1**	9.1	0.4	**9.6**
5.2	0.69	4.6	0.26	**7.4**	3.0	1.23	13.26	4.75	60.1	**4.0**	29.1	11.4	**5.8**
4.4	1.34	7.9	0.19	**4.8**	9.4	0.77	6.56	3.99	70.2	**2.6**	9.2	15.8	**7.0**
4.4	1.07	6.7	-0.03	**5.5**	4.3	0.96	8.00	3.61	57.6	**2.4**	19.4	17.2	**6.5**
2.2	2.22	13.5	1.12	**2.8**	0.8	0.39	3.51	3.56	82.8	**1.5**	29.1	31.2	**3.7**
4.0	2.27	12.5	0.38	**5.6**	0.7	0.96	7.97	4.06	66.0	**4.5**	29.3	8.5	**6.4**
4.8	1.21	10.3	0.24	**3.3**	0.4	0.60	6.88	3.74	81.4	**1.9**	8.5	19.1	**4.7**
4.9	0.95	6.2	0.13	**5.0**	5.0	1.03	9.79	3.87	65.4	**3.9**	9.5	8.4	**6.3**
8.0	1.83	4.1	0.13	**2.9**	0.3	0.42	2.25	3.29	87.0	**6.4**	61.7	7.5	**7.7**
6.1	1.86	8.5	0.13	**2.4**	2.0	0.31	2.12	3.69	93.1	**3.0**	29.3	16.3	**7.5**
7.2	0.54	1.8	0.01	**5.1**	3.4	1.25	13.34	2.94	61.1	**1.6**	24.1	25.3	**6.7**
1.7	4.90	26.8	0.53	**0.1**	-0.7	-1.21	-10.54	4.18	139.6	**1.6**	15.6	23.0	**4.8**
10.0	na	0.0	na	**9.8**	30.8	54.34	70.83	2.21	49.6	**5.0**	470.2	100.0	**6.5**
6.1	2.44	11.8	0.03	**2.7**	0.2	0.27	2.26	2.81	87.3	**2.9**	41.5	22.4	**4.7**
9.4	1.53	2.4	-0.05	**4.6**	1.3	1.05	6.14	3.34	63.9	**7.0**	72.1	5.2	**8.1**
7.8	0.14	0.8	0.06	**3.3**	0.5	0.62	5.57	3.39	82.9	**5.5**	35.7	4.9	**6.2**

Name	City	State	Rating	2013 Rating	2012 Rating	Total Assets ($Mil)	One Year Asset Growth	Asset Mix (As a % of Total Assets) Commercial Loans	Consumer Loans	Mortgage Loans	Securities	Capitalization Index	Leverage Ratio	Risk-Based Capital Ratio
FIELDPOINT PRIVATE BK & TRUST	Greenwich	CT	**D+**	D+	C	699.0	6.16	6.6	2.7	43.0	24.4	**9.8**	10.9	18.6
FIFE COMMERCIAL BANK	Fife	WA	**A**	A	A-	80.2	-1.92	11.2	1.0	12.0	1.5	**10.0**	12.8	20.2
FIFTH DISTRICT SAVINGS BANK	New Orleans	LA	**B**	B	B	389.1	7.40	0.0	0.4	63.2	16.6	**10.0**	16.7	35.5
FIFTH THIRD BANK	Cincinnati	OH	**C+**	C+	B-	131826.2	7.52	26.5	11.5	10.5	17.0	**7.7**	10.8	13.1
FINANCE & THRIFT CO	Porterville	CA	**B+**	B+	B+	121.2	-5.79	0.0	75.1	0.5	3.6	**10.0**	25.5	32.5
FINANCE FACTORS LTD	Honolulu	HI	**B-**	C+	D+	486.6	1.02	0.0	1.2	27.6	22.2	**10.0**	11.4	18.2
FINANCIAL FEDERAL BANK	Memphis	TN	**A**	A	A-	363.1	8.29	7.4	2.8	31.6	0.0	**10.0**	16.2	19.1
FINANCIAL SECURITY BANK	Kerkhoven	MN	**C+**	B-	B	76.2	15.68	14.9	1.1	10.7	5.3	**6.3**	9.1	11.9
FINEMARK NATIONAL BK & TRUST	Fort Myers	FL	**C**	C-	D+	836.2	23.92	5.0	4.8	39.0	22.9	**6.1**	8.1	13.8
FIRST & CITIZENS BANK	Monterey	VA	**B**	B	C+	123.4	2.32	3.7	5.4	35.1	5.7	**10.0**	11.2	27.9
FIRST & FARMERS BANK	Portland	ND	**D**	D	D+	57.4	3.93	10.4	4.3	5.1	24.2	**3.5**	6.7	10.2
FIRST & FARMERS NATIONAL BK	Somerset	KY	**C+**	C+	C+	489.5	1.13	4.7	4.3	22.4	38.7	**8.1**	9.7	17.1
FIRST & PEOPLES BANK & TR CO	Russell	KY	**C**	C	C+	197.2	-0.19	2.7	7.6	15.5	56.0	**10.0**	18.6	43.4
FIRST A NATIONAL BANKING ASSN	Hattiesburg	MS	**B-**	B-	C+	1071.3	12.66	9.4	1.5	17.1	25.5	**6.3**	8.3	12.5
▲ FIRST ADVANTAGE BANK	Coon Rapids	MN	**C-**	D+	D+	70.2	4.52	11.2	0.3	9.1	45.3	**6.6**	8.6	18.9
FIRST ADVANTAGE BANK	Clarksville	TN	**B-**	B	B-	425.1	6.71	8.7	1.0	14.0	9.7	**10.0**	14.3	18.1
▲ FIRST ALLIANCE BANK	Cordova	TN	**D+**	D	D-	120.4	1.22	21.0	1.6	16.1	5.5	**7.3**	9.5	12.7
▲ FIRST AMERICA BANK	Bradenton	FL	**C-**	D	D	261.2	4.39	4.8	2.3	24.8	4.2	**7.4**	10.3	12.8
FIRST AMERICAN BANK	Elk Grove Village	IL	**B-**	B-	C+	3362.8	16.49	9.3	0.5	4.2	59.3	**6.1**	8.1	17.0
▲ FIRST AMERICAN BANK	Fort Dodge	IA	**C-**	C-	D-	1032.4	-9.11	6.6	0.2	11.6	36.0	**6.9**	9.0	18.1
FIRST AMERICAN BANK	Artesia	NM	**B**	B	B-	880.2	7.13	10.3	0.5	7.1	39.2	**6.7**	8.7	16.5
FIRST AMERICAN BANK	Norman	OK	**B**	C+	C+	303.4	-10.54	9.3	2.2	16.4	13.6	**8.6**	10.0	16.2
FIRST AMERICAN BANK	Stonewall	OK	**B-**	B-	B-	29.5	13.85	11.2	13.7	23.3	9.1	**9.3**	10.5	16.2
FIRST AMERICAN BANK	Erick	OK	**C+**	C+	C+	48.6	10.15	3.1	3.6	3.8	47.3	**6.4**	8.4	19.5
FIRST AMERICAN BANK & TRUST	Vacherie	LA	**A-**	A-	B+	772.6	7.56	1.8	1.6	19.3	30.5	**10.0**	12.6	21.5
FIRST AMERICAN BANK & TRUST CO	Athens	GA	**C+**	C+	C	460.9	-11.43	2.3	0.9	13.7	36.0	**8.2**	9.8	19.2
FIRST AMERICAN BANK NA	Hudson	WI	**B-**	C+	D+	175.0	84.50	8.8	1.2	19.6	7.2	**7.0**	9.0	13.5
▲ FIRST AMERICAN INTL BANK	Brooklyn	NY	**B-**	C	C-	571.5	5.69	0.4	0.1	42.1	18.0	**10.0**	13.0	22.5
FIRST AMERICAN NATIONAL BK	Iuka	MS	**C+**	B-	B-	258.3	3.34	2.7	5.3	18.8	41.4	**9.1**	10.4	15.8
▲ FIRST AMERICAN STATE BK	Greenwood Village	CO	**C-**	D+	D	270.9	9.23	3.6	0.5	17.7	21.9	**5.0**	7.0	12.4
FIRST AMERICAN TRUST FSB	Santa Ana	CA	**U**	U	B-	2493.8	35.79	0.0	0.0	0.0	72.0	**5.8**	7.8	34.5
FIRST ARKANSAS BANK & TRUST	Jacksonville	AR	**C+**	B-	B-	652.5	1.32	8.2	18.4	6.7	29.3	**10.0**	15.8	22.8
FIRST AVENUE NATIONAL BK	Ocala	FL	**C**	C+	D+	97.8	-1.12	6.8	5.2	17.8	8.1	**10.0**	12.6	15.2
▼ FIRST B&TC OF ILLINOIS	Palatine	IL	**D-**	D-	D-	249.5	-13.27	13.2	0.0	2.3	0.8	**5.9**	7.9	12.7
▼ FIRST B&TC OF MURPHYSBORO	Murphysboro	IL	**C-**	C+	C+	71.4	5.05	4.6	3.3	19.0	41.9	**7.2**	9.1	12.7
FIRST BANK	Camden	AR	**C+**	B-	C+	317.4	23.79	10.6	4.1	25.8	12.5	**8.4**	9.9	13.9
FIRST BANK	Creve Coeur	MO	**C+**	C	C-	5800.0	-6.71	10.5	0.3	11.2	36.6	**10.0**	11.4	18.6
FIRST BANK	Tomah	WI	**C+**	C+	C-	162.3	29.18	9.0	1.9	20.1	21.3	**7.4**	9.3	13.2
▼ FIRST BANK	Sterling	KS	**B+**	A-	A-	144.2	10.83	6.2	0.8	6.4	39.5	**9.3**	10.5	19.8
▲ FIRST BANK	Clewiston	FL	**C+**	C	D+	266.7	9.77	2.6	2.4	18.8	9.2	**6.7**	8.7	12.8
FIRST BANK	Wadley	AL	**B-**	B-	B-	67.9	4.14	4.7	1.8	5.9	51.4	**9.3**	10.6	24.9
FIRST BANK	McComb	MS	**B-**	B-	B-	386.2	7.41	10.0	1.6	10.8	30.6	**8.5**	10.0	18.3
FIRST BANK	Hamilton	NJ	**C+**	C	D+	643.5	51.16	15.4	0.5	5.8	11.4	**6.8**	10.1	12.4
▲ FIRST BANK	Strasburg	VA	**B-**	C	D+	518.8	-3.21	3.9	1.0	23.9	20.2	**10.0**	11.9	17.7
FIRST BANK	Southern Pines	NC	**B-**	C+	D+	3195.0	0.73	3.9	1.6	26.0	6.6	**10.0**	11.3	17.1
FIRST BANK	Burkburnett	TX	**A-**	B+	B+	332.9	15.16	23.3	2.1	27.8	0.7	**6.8**	8.8	13.3
FIRST BANK	Whitney	TX	**C-**	C-	C	50.3	-3.89	1.3	1.7	2.3	73.0	**10.0**	11.7	35.9
FIRST BANK	Ketchikan	AK	**C+**	C+	B-	504.0	-1.80	4.4	1.0	6.5	40.9	**7.1**	9.1	17.1
FIRST BANK & TRUST	Seymour	TX	**C**	C	C	49.1	-1.27	2.8	1.6	0.0	67.4	**8.0**	9.7	28.8
▲ FIRST BANK & TRUST	New Orleans	LA	**C**	D+	E+	739.9	5.89	11.9	1.7	16.9	2.5	**6.4**	8.9	12.1
FIRST BANK & TRUST	Evanston	IL	**C+**	C+	C	918.1	9.71	25.3	3.3	4.9	18.9	**4.8**	8.1	10.9
▲ FIRST BANK & TRUST	Brookings	SD	**B+**	B	B-	932.7	5.40	9.1	2.0	8.5	18.3	**10.0**	11.6	15.0
▲ FIRST BANK & TRUST	Sioux Falls	SD	**B+**	B	B-	623.8	11.25	20.7	1.4	7.9	7.4	**5.8**	9.7	11.6
▲ FIRST BANK & TRUST CHILDRESS	Childress	TX	**C**	D+	D	80.8	2.07	18.8	4.4	13.0	30.6	**6.1**	8.1	17.4
FIRST BANK & TRUST CO	Perry	OK	**B+**	B+	A-	150.2	9.46	5.8	7.7	12.0	45.0	**9.6**	10.7	21.6
FIRST BANK & TRUST CO	Wagoner	OK	**B-**	B-	C	255.9	-0.06	19.7	6.4	28.9	0.6	**9.4**	10.6	15.1
FIRST BANK & TRUST CO	Clinton	OK	**B-**	B	B-	66.4	2.80	1.1	10.7	22.9	38.5	**7.6**	9.4	27.4
FIRST BANK & TRUST CO	Duncan	OK	**A-**	B	C+	606.0	7.75	4.9	5.1	26.2	10.7	**10.0**	12.2	20.9
FIRST BANK & TRUST CO	Minden	NE	**C+**	C+	C	72.0	-8.11	2.0	1.8	9.3	57.1	**7.7**	9.4	17.6
FIRST BANK & TRUST CO	Dawson	TX	**E+**	E+	E+	40.1	6.29	4.0	4.1	6.1	36.8	**4.5**	6.5	15.7

Asset Quality Index	Adjusted Non-Performing Loans as a % of Total Loans	Adjusted Non-Performing Loans as a % of Capital	Net Charge-Offs Avg Loans	Profitability Index	Net Income ($Mil)	Return on Assets (R.O.A.)	Return on Equity (R.O.E.)	Net Interest Spread	Overhead Efficiency Ratio	Liquidity Index	Liquidity Ratio	Hot Money Ratio	Stability Index
5.2	1.15	6.7	0.00	**1.3**	0.9	0.18	1.53	2.45	91.7	**0.7**	10.0	40.2	**6.4**
7.5	0.19	1.0	0.11	**9.1**	1.3	2.13	16.59	4.62	58.1	**1.5**	25.4	27.2	**8.6**
9.3	0.84	3.5	0.04	**3.7**	1.9	0.67	4.01	3.15	72.1	**2.8**	31.8	18.2	**8.0**
3.3	2.02	12.2	0.56	**7.8**	1111.7	1.16	9.19	3.42	58.5	**4.8**	15.3	3.7	**9.6**
4.6	1.10	2.9	5.63	**5.7**	0.8	0.83	3.32	12.70	63.3	**1.3**	25.5	31.3	**6.7**
6.1	1.31	6.4	0.51	**3.6**	2.5	0.68	5.33	4.23	79.0	**3.3**	25.7	13.7	**5.4**
7.4	0.64	3.3	0.13	**8.8**	5.6	2.09	12.91	3.76	51.4	**0.4**	6.3	65.1	**8.6**
5.7	0.78	6.4	0.03	**5.3**	0.6	1.16	12.48	4.26	71.4	**1.8**	12.4	19.9	**5.0**
7.0	0.35	2.9	0.00	**3.0**	2.8	0.48	6.03	2.86	76.2	**1.6**	10.9	21.2	**4.5**
5.0	2.62	11.7	0.55	**3.5**	0.5	0.58	5.13	3.48	73.9	**4.7**	42.6	12.2	**6.1**
7.5	0.01	0.1	-0.06	**3.2**	0.2	0.46	6.95	3.42	81.2	**3.2**	10.7	12.7	**1.9**
3.4	1.71	8.5	0.28	**4.1**	2.6	0.71	5.42	3.88	70.8	**2.7**	34.7	19.7	**6.6**
6.6	3.00	5.7	-0.11	**2.0**	0.3	0.20	1.17	3.45	93.0	**5.5**	54.2	11.1	**6.3**
6.0	1.11	8.0	0.20	**4.0**	5.2	0.68	7.04	3.74	71.6	**3.0**	14.0	14.1	**6.9**
8.5	0.13	0.6	0.09	**2.2**	0.2	0.32	3.62	2.93	82.6	**1.9**	26.8	23.4	**4.3**
3.5	1.85	10.3	-0.01	**4.5**	2.1	0.68	4.70	4.40	73.3	**1.1**	4.0	26.9	**7.7**
1.4	5.78	42.6	0.22	**2.7**	0.3	0.39	3.75	4.30	88.3	**1.3**	11.4	26.2	**4.7**
2.4	3.09	19.9	0.43	**2.2**	0.6	0.28	2.42	3.42	87.0	**1.8**	22.7	22.0	**4.3**
5.8	2.64	9.9	0.28	**4.0**	22.6	0.90	10.42	2.69	73.0	**3.2**	31.3	19.6	**6.6**
5.2	2.54	11.4	0.05	**2.2**	3.1	0.38	4.45	2.40	93.9	**4.8**	23.0	6.8	**5.0**
6.3	0.61	3.3	-0.02	**5.8**	8.4	1.29	14.54	4.05	70.9	**5.0**	29.2	5.2	**7.9**
6.0	0.56	3.3	0.01	**6.4**	3.8	1.71	17.40	3.86	72.3	**4.9**	31.1	6.7	**4.6**
3.6	1.57	10.3	0.35	**9.5**	0.5	2.03	19.71	4.96	59.1	**1.3**	20.4	29.7	**7.4**
8.7	0.00	0.0	0.01	**3.9**	0.3	0.86	9.98	2.54	69.6	**5.7**	56.4	8.9	**3.8**
7.4	1.04	4.5	0.05	**7.0**	7.5	1.33	10.91	4.21	60.5	**3.9**	29.7	12.0	**7.3**
3.8	3.71	18.0	0.15	**3.7**	2.3	0.65	6.84	3.08	77.3	**4.5**	40.9	12.8	**5.1**
5.6	0.58	4.4	-0.01	**3.6**	0.9	0.82	8.22	4.11	81.1	**2.1**	20.5	19.1	**4.1**
5.1	2.05	9.7	-0.18	**4.2**	1.8	0.42	3.25	4.27	87.2	**2.3**	30.2	21.2	**6.7**
4.8	2.52	10.4	0.14	**3.5**	1.2	0.64	6.00	3.52	84.2	**4.8**	40.3	10.9	**6.0**
6.7	0.00	0.0	0.15	**3.2**	1.1	0.60	8.80	3.29	69.0	**4.1**	27.5	10.4	**2.2**
10.0	na	0.0	na	**5.0**	13.9	0.81	11.77	1.27	43.3	**8.7**	106.7	0.1	**7.0**
2.2	6.06	20.4	0.20	**8.3**	9.7	1.94	10.20	5.00	70.6	**4.5**	25.0	6.5	**9.2**
4.3	2.10	12.2	0.07	**2.0**	0.1	0.13	0.94	4.40	94.5	**3.9**	9.7	8.4	**5.5**
4.1	1.94	12.3	-2.29	**0.0**	-4.1	-2.02	-21.17	3.65	214.3	**1.3**	26.9	32.4	**2.7**
3.1	3.94	19.8	0.92	**1.8**	0.2	0.38	4.05	4.12	92.3	**2.6**	25.2	17.1	**4.7**
3.8	2.03	14.5	0.65	**5.9**	2.4	1.00	10.09	5.00	67.5	**1.1**	8.0	27.9	**5.6**
5.1	3.31	13.8	0.06	**2.9**	24.8	0.57	4.17	3.05	82.1	**6.0**	42.3	7.4	**7.1**
4.4	1.74	11.9	0.02	**4.5**	0.8	0.62	6.59	3.42	74.3	**3.8**	24.1	11.0	**4.8**
8.8	0.25	1.0	-0.06	**5.3**	1.0	0.93	8.30	3.55	63.4	**4.0**	36.9	14.1	**7.9**
3.7	2.03	15.0	0.00	**3.6**	1.1	0.54	6.10	4.25	82.9	**2.3**	16.4	17.7	**3.8**
6.1	4.04	10.5	-0.06	**4.8**	0.5	1.00	8.66	3.78	71.6	**5.6**	58.7	10.1	**5.1**
6.4	0.45	2.2	0.00	**4.6**	3.5	1.19	12.10	2.74	64.0	**4.5**	16.5	5.8	**6.0**
3.9	0.98	7.3	0.20	**5.4**	5.3	1.22	11.51	3.76	59.6	**1.5**	15.3	24.6	**4.7**
4.3	2.99	15.7	0.08	**5.5**	4.2	1.07	9.43	3.87	72.1	**3.6**	24.3	11.8	**6.2**
3.5	3.04	18.4	0.71	**4.1**	19.6	0.81	6.20	4.71	65.6	**2.2**	16.9	18.8	**7.7**
6.7	0.33	2.6	0.02	**8.7**	4.4	1.87	20.69	4.77	70.4	**2.9**	18.9	14.8	**7.0**
9.7	0.09	0.1	0.18	**2.1**	0.1	0.27	2.66	1.92	86.6	**6.9**	86.3	6.5	**4.5**
6.8	1.22	5.6	0.00	**3.5**	2.6	0.72	7.40	3.49	82.5	**4.3**	37.4	12.4	**6.0**
9.6	0.18	0.3	0.00	**2.8**	0.2	0.45	5.58	2.17	78.3	**6.0**	78.1	11.2	**3.8**
2.9	0.99	8.9	0.28	**3.8**	4.3	0.76	8.75	4.54	86.2	**1.1**	7.5	28.8	**3.6**
4.2	1.04	8.4	0.00	**3.6**	3.9	0.58	7.23	3.16	69.9	**2.4**	14.2	17.0	**4.9**
4.8	1.75	10.1	0.04	**8.4**	9.5	1.38	11.81	3.97	60.6	**3.8**	10.7	9.3	**7.8**
7.2	0.05	0.4	-0.03	**8.6**	6.2	1.39	11.84	5.11	62.9	**3.8**	7.4	9.1	**7.9**
3.8	1.98	13.9	0.72	**3.1**	0.5	0.74	11.65	3.45	72.0	**1.3**	31.4	52.3	**3.7**
7.9	0.26	1.0	0.06	**5.8**	1.6	1.40	13.11	3.74	65.8	**5.6**	47.0	8.7	**7.8**
4.3	1.16	8.2	0.07	**9.8**	5.9	2.95	27.64	4.74	46.9	**0.6**	7.6	37.3	**8.7**
6.4	1.02	4.8	0.89	**4.8**	0.6	1.12	11.66	3.35	69.6	**3.0**	18.9	14.6	**6.0**
5.6	1.46	7.0	0.12	**8.3**	9.0	2.07	16.98	3.88	56.9	**3.8**	36.2	14.8	**8.6**
8.1	0.00	0.0	-0.05	**3.3**	0.4	0.68	7.54	3.20	79.7	**6.3**	58.9	5.8	**4.4**
6.6	0.38	1.9	0.14	**1.4**	0.0	0.13	2.41	3.30	93.0	**2.7**	60.1	35.7	**1.0**

Name	City	State	Rating	2013 Rating	2012 Rating	Total Assets ($Mil)	One Year Asset Growth	Asset Mix (As a % of Total Assets) Comm-ercial Loans	Cons-umer Loans	Mort-gage Loans	Secur-ities	Capital-ization Index	Lever-age Ratio	Risk-Based Capital Ratio
FIRST BANK & TRUST CO	Lubbock	TX	**B-**	B-	C-	668.4	9.86	16.5	2.3	19.4	10.4	**7.6**	9.4	13.3
FIRST BANK & TRUST CO	Cozad	NE	**B-**	B-	B-	258.7	-1.63	12.3	2.1	2.5	23.8	**8.6**	10.7	13.9
FIRST BANK & TRUST CO	Lebanon	VA	**A-**	A-	B-	1332.5	3.60	8.1	2.4	16.6	5.8	**10.0**	11.8	17.8
FIRST BANK & TRUST EAST TEXAS	Diboll	TX	**B+**	B+	B	927.4	6.71	9.5	7.1	17.6	25.1	**6.6**	8.6	14.2
FIRST BANK & TRUST FULLERTON	Fullerton	NE	**B**	B	B	72.4	1.28	3.4	2.1	1.1	16.6	**10.0**	16.6	21.3
FIRST BANK & TRUST NA	Pipestone	MN	**B**	B	C+	188.7	-1.52	11.6	2.5	4.5	26.1	**6.4**	9.1	12.1
FIRST BANK & TRUST OF MEMPHIS	Memphis	TX	**B-**	B-	C+	61.0	1.99	18.2	1.0	5.5	4.7	**9.8**	11.0	14.9
▲ FIRST BANK & TRUST OF MILBANK	Milbank	SD	**B+**	B	B	161.0	3.85	6.8	3.2	8.1	22.8	**10.0**	11.0	15.1
FIRST BANK & TRUST SB	Paris	IL	**B**	B-	C	428.7	8.29	9.5	8.1	17.8	13.5	**8.6**	10.1	14.3
▲ FIRST BANK BLUE EARTH	Blue Earth	MN	**A-**	B	B-	187.8	8.44	8.6	2.0	4.2	23.9	**9.2**	10.5	15.9
FIRST BANK FINANCIAL CENTRE	Oconomowoc	WI	**C+**	C+	C	836.9	8.17	9.5	0.6	11.7	20.1	**6.9**	8.9	12.7
FIRST BANK HAMPTON	Hampton	IA	**A**	A-	A	137.9	-0.68	10.8	3.2	8.7	34.3	**10.0**	11.8	16.8
▼ FIRST BANK KANSAS	Salina	KS	**C+**	B-	B-	394.2	55.81	2.9	3.0	11.0	46.0	**5.9**	7.9	19.2
FIRST BANK NA	Conroe	TX	**B**	B	B	367.9	8.09	8.4	2.6	18.2	11.8	**5.6**	7.6	12.0
▲ FIRST BANK OF BALDWIN	Baldwin	WI	**C-**	D+	D-	157.8	-3.36	9.6	1.6	10.0	28.5	**5.6**	7.6	12.9
FIRST BANK OF BERNE	Berne	IN	**A-**	B+	B	540.8	4.51	4.6	1.0	24.1	14.5	**8.0**	9.7	13.9
FIRST BANK OF BOAZ	Boaz	AL	**A+**	A+	A+	190.3	3.51	4.0	2.6	6.7	60.9	**10.0**	16.2	31.9
FIRST BANK OF CELESTE	Celeste	TX	**C+**	C+	C+	41.4	-1.22	5.1	7.9	6.6	16.4	**7.0**	9.0	18.8
FIRST BANK OF CHANDLER	Chandler	OK	**B+**	B+	B+	87.0	3.13	14.6	6.5	13.5	0.3	**6.8**	10.3	12.3
▼ FIRST BANK OF CHARLESTON INC	Charleston	WV	**C**	B	B	210.9	4.78	12.8	1.4	19.4	24.1	**10.0**	11.6	16.4
FIRST BANK OF COASTAL GEORGIA	Pembroke	GA	**C-**	D+	D	119.8	7.30	0.9	1.0	7.7	63.4	**9.7**	10.8	23.2
FIRST BANK OF DALTON	Dalton	GA	**C**	D+	E+	194.8	6.63	12.6	1.7	16.1	17.7	**6.4**	8.4	12.8
FIRST BANK OF FAIRLAND	Fairland	OK	**C-**	C-	C+	11.3	-0.71	5.1	7.1	28.8	4.9	**7.3**	9.2	14.6
FIRST BANK OF GEORGIA	Augusta	GA	**A-**	A-	B-	525.4	5.12	5.1	0.8	11.9	25.5	**10.0**	12.0	16.4
▲ FIRST BANK OF GREENWICH	Cos Cob	CT	**C**	D+	D-	162.1	36.81	10.6	1.6	37.6	8.5	**10.0**	11.9	18.4
FIRST BANK OF HIGHLAND PARK	Highland Park	IL	**B-**	B-	C+	1218.5	17.84	37.3	0.0	4.8	9.3	**5.9**	10.4	11.7
FIRST BANK OF LINCOLN	Lincoln	MT	**C+**	C	C	16.8	3.40	31.9	8.1	24.4	0.0	**10.0**	11.7	17.3
FIRST BANK OF LINDEN	Linden	AL	**B+**	B+	B+	81.2	2.92	6.9	5.2	7.4	46.1	**10.0**	12.6	23.4
FIRST BANK OF MANHATTAN	Manhattan	IL	**C-**	C-	C-	149.2	-0.05	1.9	1.1	15.8	30.3	**8.2**	9.8	23.0
FIRST BANK OF MISSOURI	Gladstone	MO	**B-**	B-	C+	477.8	-2.67	8.7	0.6	4.4	26.0	**10.0**	15.0	23.2
FIRST BANK OF MULESHOE	Muleshoe	TX	**B-**	B-	A-	102.9	3.34	4.8	1.6	0.9	74.0	**10.0**	13.5	56.8
FIRST BANK OF NEWTON	Newton	KS	**B-**	B-	B-	164.6	4.30	9.9	7.9	33.1	19.1	**6.4**	8.4	12.8
FIRST BANK OF OHIO	Tiffin	OH	**A**	A	A	166.5	1.75	0.0	43.5	0.1	44.3	**10.0**	36.3	58.9
FIRST BANK OF OKARCHE	Okarche	OK	**A**	A-	A-	83.8	21.10	8.7	2.4	1.1	24.5	**10.0**	11.4	22.0
▲ FIRST BANK OF OWASSO	Owasso	OK	**B**	C	C+	244.9	6.76	7.5	0.8	8.1	15.3	**10.0**	12.2	16.2
FIRST BANK OF PIKE	Molena	GA	**C+**	C+	C+	41.7	4.39	3.4	10.3	28.4	18.4	**10.0**	11.3	20.1
FIRST BANK OF TENNESSEE	Spring City	TN	**D+**	D+	C-	254.9	8.13	9.5	4.5	24.0	8.1	**9.5**	10.6	15.7
FIRST BANK OF THE LAKE	Osage Beach	MO	**C-**	C	D	47.2	34.28	35.2	1.2	6.5	4.7	**9.2**	10.5	22.3
FIRST BANK OF THE PALM BEACHES	West Palm Beach	FL	**C-**	D+	D-	106.8	27.05	5.5	0.5	21.6	2.6	**10.0**	12.3	18.3
FIRST BANK OF THE SOUTH	Rainsville	AL	**C**	C	C-	85.0	2.12	4.7	8.2	21.0	29.6	**7.1**	9.1	16.7
FIRST BANK OF UTICA	Utica	NE	**D+**	D+	D+	67.2	12.11	7.9	3.2	11.5	10.3	**4.9**	8.1	11.0
FIRST BANK RICHMOND NA	Richmond	IN	**C-**	C-	D+	495.3	-0.21	7.9	0.5	19.3	30.5	**9.1**	10.4	17.9
FIRST BANK TEXAS SSB	Baird	TX	**B-**	B-	B-	390.7	3.71	22.8	3.7	13.2	4.4	**8.0**	10.4	13.3
FIRST BANK UPPER MICHIGAN	Gladstone	MI	**B-**	B-	B-	164.9	-0.52	7.2	10.1	31.2	20.6	**10.0**	19.3	29.8
FIRST BANKERS TRUST CO NA	Quincy	IL	**B-**	B-	C+	837.5	7.63	5.8	4.7	6.6	35.9	**6.0**	8.0	13.1
FIRST BETHANY BANK & TRUST	Bethany	OK	**B-**	B-	C+	187.2	-4.55	4.6	0.5	8.2	54.9	**7.0**	9.0	17.3
FIRST BUSINESS BANK	Madison	WI	**B-**	C+	C	1190.0	13.23	26.5	0.0	1.6	12.5	**6.7**	10.4	12.3
FIRST BUSINESS BANK-MILWAUKEE	Brookfield	WI	**C+**	C+	D+	238.6	7.74	8.9	0.0	3.3	19.1	**5.6**	7.6	14.6
FIRST CAHAWBA BANK	Selma	AL	**B-**	B-	C-	92.7	0.84	14.8	5.8	19.4	18.8	**10.0**	12.7	19.7
FIRST CAPITAL BANK	Glen Allen	VA	**C+**	C	D-	599.5	11.78	10.2	0.3	15.0	13.1	**7.6**	9.6	13.0
FIRST CAPITAL BANK	Germantown	TN	**C+**	C	C-	227.7	6.52	14.8	1.0	12.3	9.1	**6.9**	9.8	12.4
FIRST CAPITAL BANK	Quanah	TX	**C**	C	C-	46.9	-1.82	12.6	6.8	14.4	1.1	**9.5**	10.8	14.6
▼ FIRST CAPITAL BANK	Bennettsville	SC	**C-**	D+	C-	54.1	-7.42	2.9	7.7	31.6	0.0	**10.0**	13.6	20.0
FIRST CAPITAL BANK OF KENTUCKY	Louisville	KY	**C+**	C+	C-	508.5	9.05	2.5	0.4	12.5	12.6	**5.1**	8.8	11.1
FIRST CAROLINA BANK	Rocky Mount	NC	**D-**	D-	D-	103.5	34.97	6.8	0.9	28.2	8.5	**7.4**	9.3	13.8
▲ FIRST CENTRAL BANK	Cambridge	NE	**B**	B-	C-	87.5	4.24	12.8	3.7	4.5	14.1	**8.3**	10.3	13.6
FIRST CENTRAL BANK	Warrensburg	MO	**B**	B	C+	203.7	-1.64	2.9	1.5	13.0	33.1	**10.0**	11.6	17.6
FIRST CENTRAL BANK MCCOOK	McCook	NE	**B-**	B-	C-	92.4	2.63	11.8	2.8	3.0	10.6	**7.7**	10.5	13.1
FIRST CENTRAL NB OF ST PARIS	Saint Paris	OH	**B**	B	B	83.3	-1.00	2.1	2.6	14.3	27.8	**10.0**	17.3	26.8
▲ FIRST CENTRAL SB	Glen Cove	NY	**D+**	E+	E-	510.0	-4.40	10.6	0.0	10.3	27.2	**7.5**	9.3	16.0

Asset Quality Index	Adjusted Non-Performing Loans as a % of Total Loans	Adjusted Non-Performing Loans as a % of Capital	Net Charge-Offs / Avg Loans	Profitability Index	Net Income ($Mil)	Return on Assets (R.O.A.)	Return on Equity (R.O.E.)	Net Interest Spread	Overhead Efficiency Ratio	Liquidity Index	Liquidity Ratio	Hot Money Ratio	Stability Index
4.6	1.22	9.0	0.07	6.4	7.8	1.64	17.68	4.09	73.6	0.7	13.7	39.7	6.2
4.1	1.69	9.1	-0.07	8.1	3.6	1.85	16.13	4.06	51.5	4.3	25.0	8.2	6.5
5.8	0.86	5.3	0.36	8.2	14.1	1.40	12.18	3.94	51.2	2.2	12.7	17.8	9.2
6.1	0.70	4.9	0.11	6.3	7.9	1.17	12.39	4.02	61.9	4.1	23.9	9.3	6.6
6.9	0.01	0.1	0.01	4.3	0.4	0.82	5.00	3.37	66.8	3.1	25.1	14.3	7.8
4.4	1.12	7.3	-0.03	5.4	1.3	0.89	8.63	3.78	66.7	2.9	17.1	14.7	7.6
8.4	0.01	0.1	0.01	4.1	0.4	0.88	8.29	2.56	63.2	1.3	29.4	38.6	6.1
8.0	0.35	2.1	0.00	5.4	1.2	0.99	8.38	3.94	63.7	3.2	17.3	13.1	7.3
5.1	0.55	3.9	0.13	5.0	2.6	0.83	8.17	3.80	64.2	1.6	14.0	23.1	5.3
6.1	0.57	3.4	0.03	8.9	2.7	1.98	18.71	3.63	48.4	2.0	16.7	19.2	7.6
4.0	1.10	8.3	0.19	3.6	3.9	0.63	7.23	3.68	80.5	3.0	15.8	14.2	4.9
8.2	0.34	1.5	0.16	6.7	1.6	1.53	13.25	3.67	51.0	4.6	39.7	11.7	8.1
8.8	0.22	0.9	0.16	3.2	1.5	0.64	7.72	2.99	82.8	4.8	49.5	13.2	4.9
5.7	0.58	4.9	0.05	6.7	3.1	1.18	15.01	4.86	67.3	3.2	20.1	13.6	6.1
4.5	1.03	6.9	0.44	2.0	0.4	0.32	3.81	3.43	91.2	3.8	20.3	10.5	4.0
5.7	0.78	5.8	0.14	9.7	9.2	2.27	23.49	4.18	48.2	4.2	10.6	6.6	8.7
9.5	0.25	0.4	0.00	7.3	2.1	1.46	8.78	3.24	47.6	5.4	69.3	14.3	9.0
8.3	0.00	0.0	-0.01	4.0	0.3	0.85	9.50	3.71	80.3	4.4	50.7	15.0	5.0
5.7	0.45	3.6	0.10	10.0	1.9	3.07	29.85	5.23	37.7	1.5	5.8	21.1	8.0
1.8	6.02	33.0	0.05	6.8	1.5	0.95	8.18	3.61	48.1	1.4	28.5	32.1	6.9
2.4	9.49	24.9	2.76	3.4	0.7	0.75	7.56	3.63	70.2	2.9	25.1	15.8	3.7
4.2	1.91	13.7	-0.72	4.8	1.5	1.05	13.75	4.18	65.1	1.7	22.2	23.4	3.0
6.1	0.06	0.5	0.00	4.8	0.1	0.92	8.45	4.77	80.7	1.9	21.4	19.8	4.3
6.3	1.29	6.3	-0.29	6.3	4.0	1.04	9.08	3.69	76.8	1.7	17.5	21.6	7.4
4.7	1.50	9.7	0.00	2.3	0.4	0.37	2.94	3.34	82.6	0.7	11.0	39.5	3.9
4.4	1.77	13.6	-0.01	4.3	9.7	1.11	10.46	2.71	55.6	0.7	8.6	37.4	8.0
2.8	3.12	19.3	0.00	6.6	0.2	1.85	13.42	4.89	60.0	1.7	16.2	20.9	6.0
8.7	0.00	0.0	0.04	5.0	0.7	1.08	7.91	4.20	68.5	2.6	57.3	36.3	7.3
5.0	2.20	8.5	0.01	2.6	0.5	0.46	4.64	3.27	84.1	3.7	40.8	16.5	4.4
4.9	3.01	10.7	0.72	4.8	2.9	0.79	5.38	3.59	52.4	4.2	31.5	10.9	7.4
9.1	1.29	1.8	0.22	3.0	0.4	0.50	3.67	3.03	83.4	6.1	79.6	12.2	6.9
5.0	0.76	5.7	0.36	4.4	1.1	0.83	10.09	3.72	73.1	3.9	12.4	8.9	5.3
6.8	0.53	0.6	1.00	8.6	2.0	1.62	4.53	4.80	44.3	3.2	74.0	54.9	8.1
8.8	0.00	0.0	0.02	8.2	1.2	2.03	17.99	3.40	40.9	3.7	62.1	20.1	8.5
5.4	0.00	0.0	-0.01	8.3	3.5	1.89	15.71	4.10	56.0	4.8	8.8	2.3	9.0
5.8	1.18	5.8	0.17	3.0	0.1	0.36	3.18	5.65	86.7	3.4	35.5	16.3	4.8
1.3	4.70	32.2	0.05	8.6	3.8	2.04	18.92	5.00	59.8	2.8	6.9	14.2	7.3
1.7	7.27	44.3	2.06	0.2	-0.1	-1.11	-7.82	3.31	78.8	1.3	29.8	42.5	0.2
3.9	2.00	10.0	0.42	2.0	0.1	0.13	1.29	4.04	93.2	4.5	36.4	11.5	3.5
3.5	2.19	12.2	0.24	2.6	0.2	0.35	4.07	4.13	90.2	4.8	38.1	10.3	3.7
2.5	1.48	14.2	0.03	4.3	0.4	0.75	9.43	4.05	68.2	3.1	8.7	12.8	3.6
1.8	5.83	30.4	0.81	3.1	1.6	0.41	3.93	3.70	77.2	2.2	17.5	18.3	4.8
4.8	1.00	7.8	0.12	6.2	2.8	1.00	10.09	5.07	69.2	2.5	5.9	15.8	6.2
3.5	4.53	16.1	0.73	9.6	2.6	2.11	10.71	4.84	58.0	2.1	28.4	21.8	9.0
4.6	0.97	6.0	0.04	4.6	5.3	0.87	9.82	3.13	61.2	2.9	11.2	13.9	6.1
8.6	0.47	1.8	0.00	4.3	1.7	1.17	13.59	3.21	66.7	4.8	36.3	9.8	5.6
4.4	1.65	11.9	0.00	8.4	11.3	1.39	13.28	3.94	53.0	0.9	19.6	40.3	7.3
6.6	0.73	4.5	-0.02	3.0	0.8	0.48	6.32	2.73	75.3	4.6	52.9	15.1	4.4
7.1	0.33	1.7	0.11	4.0	0.5	0.68	5.70	4.00	73.4	4.1	17.1	8.2	5.5
3.8	1.28	9.3	-0.03	3.9	3.6	0.84	8.69	3.68	71.5	1.1	17.5	31.0	4.5
3.4	1.02	8.0	0.36	4.9	1.4	0.85	9.07	3.67	59.6	0.6	11.6	53.7	4.7
4.5	0.66	4.2	0.58	3.0	0.1	0.26	2.45	5.24	91.8	2.8	21.2	15.5	4.1
1.3	5.21	29.2	0.09	4.7	0.3	0.78	6.19	5.40	75.7	0.7	15.0	43.8	5.5
3.5	1.12	9.8	0.36	3.2	1.7	0.46	5.28	3.29	77.5	1.5	15.7	24.7	4.7
4.7	0.66	5.3	0.21	0.0	-0.4	-0.55	-4.83	3.42	111.3	0.9	23.2	38.9	2.7
5.5	0.49	3.2	0.31	5.6	0.7	1.03	10.15	4.21	60.2	1.4	10.6	24.7	5.6
5.8	0.81	3.1	0.10	6.1	1.7	1.06	6.21	3.61	65.0	3.7	29.7	12.9	7.8
4.5	0.69	4.8	0.35	8.5	1.0	1.53	14.95	4.59	49.8	0.8	15.4	39.5	5.9
8.7	0.61	2.1	0.00	3.9	0.5	0.74	4.53	3.41	72.7	4.1	35.5	12.8	7.7
2.1	3.66	19.9	1.45	1.5	-0.6	-0.16	-1.35	2.71	103.7	2.0	39.6	35.1	3.9

Name	City	State	Rating	2013 Rating	2012 Rating	Total Assets ($Mil)	One Year Asset Growth	Asset Mix (As a % of Total Assets) Commercial Loans	Consumer Loans	Mortgage Loans	Securities	Capitalization Index	Leverage Ratio	Risk-Based Capital Ratio
▼ FIRST CENTRAL STATE BK	De Witt	IA	B	B+	B	318.2	13.57	11.9	3.0	12.9	16.9	7.2	10.0	12.7
▲ FIRST CENTURY BANK	Tazewell	TN	C	C-	D+	245.8	0.21	2.4	3.0	19.7	13.8	10.0	11.0	18.3
FIRST CENTURY BANK INC	Bluefield	WV	C+	C-	C-	408.7	-1.96	3.9	3.9	23.8	26.9	9.5	10.7	19.1
FIRST CENTURY BANK NA	Gainesville	GA	D-	D-	D+	97.1	18.11	0.9	0.0	27.5	33.2	5.2	7.2	14.4
FIRST CHATHAM BANK	Savannah	GA	E-	E-	E-	377.5	-2.80	9.3	0.5	9.7	11.8	1.6	5.5	8.6
FIRST CHOICE BANK	Mercerville	NJ	B-	B	B-	1159.4	29.67	4.4	0.4	16.7	44.3	7.9	9.6	19.3
FIRST CHOICE BANK	Cerritos	CA	B-	C+	B-	617.3	61.40	10.2	0.0	13.7	7.0	5.2	8.5	11.2
FIRST CITIZENS BANK	Luverne	AL	B-	B-	C	224.9	-0.75	3.1	5.3	11.2	43.0	10.0	11.4	21.6
FIRST CITIZENS BANK	Elizabethtown	KY	B-	C+	C	316.4	-0.58	2.8	0.6	18.2	25.7	8.2	9.8	14.9
▼ FIRST CITIZENS BANK & TRUST CO	Columbia	SC	C+	B-	C	8213.8	0.75	3.9	8.7	18.9	23.8	7.2	9.1	18.6
FIRST CITIZENS BANK OF BUTTE	Butte	MT	C+	C+	C	62.7	-9.35	15.4	4.1	14.3	16.1	9.8	10.9	21.3
FIRST CITIZENS BANK OF POLSON	Polson	MT	E-	E	E	20.7	4.63	26.9	5.2	21.8	6.1	5.9	7.9	12.6
FIRST CITIZENS COMMUNITY BANK	Mansfield	PA	B	B	B-	911.4	1.58	4.6	1.0	24.6	33.7	9.4	10.6	18.0
FIRST CITIZENS NATIONAL BK	Dyersburg	TN	A-	A-	B+	1210.2	3.97	4.5	2.0	11.3	36.2	7.7	9.5	17.3
FIRST CITIZENS NATIONAL BK	Mason City	IA	A-	A-	A	1178.6	16.25	11.8	1.1	7.8	40.5	10.0	11.0	18.2
FIRST CITIZENS NB UPPER SAND	Upper Sandusky	OH	B-	B-	B-	214.8	-4.26	6.1	1.4	22.8	30.3	10.0	17.9	32.0
FIRST CITIZENS STATE BK	Whitewater	WI	A-	A-	A-	246.5	1.11	5.3	1.4	20.2	30.0	10.0	17.1	29.2
FIRST CITRUS BANK	Tampa	FL	D+	D	D	248.2	14.74	3.9	0.4	7.5	0.7	6.5	9.9	12.2
FIRST CITY BANK	Columbus	OH	B	B	C	53.3	-7.09	4.6	2.1	17.7	11.5	10.0	12.6	19.1
FIRST CITY BANK OF FLORIDA	Fort Walton Beach	FL	E-	E-	E-	227.6	-5.61	6.2	0.6	15.5	11.9	0.0	2.6	4.7
FIRST CLOVER LEAF BANK NA	Edwardsville	IL	C+	C+	B-	631.2	-2.34	9.5	0.2	20.1	17.3	9.7	10.8	17.0
FIRST CMNWLTH BK PRESTONSBURG	Prestonsburg	KY	A-	A-	A-	305.9	0.61	3.5	2.0	29.9	44.1	8.9	10.3	20.7
FIRST COLEBROOK BANK	Colebrook	NH	C+	C+	C	263.6	0.76	14.5	0.5	15.5	16.9	7.3	9.2	13.1
FIRST COLLINSVILLE BANK	Collinsville	IL	B-	B-	B-	680.3	3.38	1.9	3.4	43.4	20.4	7.6	9.4	17.1
FIRST COLONY BANK OF FLORIDA	Maitland	FL	B+	B+	B	169.5	14.95	8.4	0.1	1.8	14.5	10.0	11.0	16.4
▲ FIRST COLORADO NATIONAL BK	Paonia	CO	C	C-	C-	48.9	10.02	11.1	1.2	5.8	0.3	10.0	16.8	19.9
FIRST COLUMBIA BANK & TRUST CO	Bloomsburg	PA	B+	B+	B	628.7	-0.22	5.7	1.0	29.9	26.7	9.7	10.8	20.0
FIRST COMMAND BANK	Fort Worth	TX	B+	B+	B	710.6	7.91	8.9	26.6	0.0	50.0	6.2	8.2	14.7
FIRST COMMERCE BANK	Lakewood	NJ	B	B	C	449.5	45.51	11.8	0.0	23.0	4.8	7.2	10.3	12.7
FIRST COMMERCE BANK	Lewisburg	TN	B+	B+	B	276.1	3.21	11.6	3.1	14.5	18.5	8.4	9.9	14.8
FIRST COMMERCE BANK	Marysville	KS	B	A-	A-	58.1	14.07	8.4	4.0	32.3	2.2	8.2	9.8	14.2
FIRST COMMERCIAL BANK	Jackson	MS	B+	B	B	318.0	17.98	22.6	1.8	8.8	5.8	8.9	12.4	14.1
▲ FIRST COMMERCIAL BANK	Edmond	OK	C+	C-	C-	301.9	-4.22	17.7	1.4	16.2	13.0	10.0	11.0	15.2
▲ FIRST COMMERCIAL BANK	Dexter	MO	C	C	C-	210.7	5.61	10.5	0.8	4.6	32.4	8.4	10.0	15.7
FIRST COMMERCIAL BANK (USA)	Alhambra	CA	C+	C	C+	484.5	-2.07	8.7	0.0	1.0	1.8	10.0	20.9	28.8
FIRST COMMERCIAL BANK NA	Seguin	TX	B-	B-	B-	152.4	10.14	7.2	1.6	14.6	14.4	5.7	7.7	13.4
▲ FIRST COMMONS BANK NA	Newton Centre	MA	C+	C	C-	244.1	-0.89	5.6	0.0	50.9	0.0	7.9	9.6	15.4
FIRST COMMONWEALTH BANK	Indiana	PA	B-	C+	C	6330.0	3.53	15.4	10.2	12.3	20.7	6.9	9.6	12.4
FIRST COMMUNITY BANK	Columbus	OH	C	C-	D-	98.6	-3.59	0.0	0.2	24.9	23.0	10.0	11.8	21.2
FIRST COMMUNITY BANK	Lexington	SC	B-	B-	B-	828.8	30.49	4.0	0.9	11.6	31.5	8.3	9.9	15.9
▲ FIRST COMMUNITY BANK	Chatom	AL	C+	C-	D+	325.7	4.32	10.6	3.4	15.3	21.2	9.0	10.3	15.8
FIRST COMMUNITY BANK	Elgin	IL	B-	C+	C-	173.3	1.91	4.7	0.1	4.4	18.3	10.0	14.6	24.7
FIRST COMMUNITY BANK	Batesville	AR	B-	B-	C	897.8	10.46	9.5	4.3	24.1	16.6	7.1	9.0	13.0
FIRST COMMUNITY BANK	Harbor Springs	MI	B+	B+	B	246.3	3.50	8.1	0.6	17.1	6.9	10.0	12.0	15.8
FIRST COMMUNITY BANK	Milton	WI	B	B+	B-	84.7	7.47	5.0	1.2	18.6	25.2	6.2	10.1	11.9
FIRST COMMUNITY BANK	Newell	IA	B+	B+	B	95.1	0.90	1.8	2.3	5.9	21.0	7.2	9.1	13.4
FIRST COMMUNITY BANK	Bluefield	VA	B-	B-	C-	2526.8	-3.76	3.5	2.8	26.2	14.8	7.4	9.3	14.8
FIRST COMMUNITY BANK	Beemer	NE	C+	B-	B-	134.7	5.21	8.4	2.0	0.9	10.7	5.5	8.5	11.4
FIRST COMMUNITY BANK	Glasgow	MT	C-	C-	D+	263.5	10.77	3.8	1.7	8.1	34.0	8.0	9.7	17.3
FIRST COMMUNITY BANK	Lester Prairie	MN	C+	C	C	52.5	-2.29	7.2	2.3	8.7	38.2	7.3	9.2	17.5
FIRST COMMUNITY BANK	Corpus Christi	TX	B+	B	B-	367.9	0.86	12.6	7.5	16.6	14.7	7.5	9.3	13.9
FIRST COMMUNITY BANK	Santa Rosa	CA	C-	C-	D+	881.5	29.70	5.3	0.1	10.8	2.8	9.4	10.6	16.4
FIRST COMMUNITY BANK & TRUST	Beecher	IL	D+	D+	D+	146.3	0.13	6.1	0.6	16.8	27.9	8.3	9.9	19.9
FIRST COMMUNITY BANK HEARTLAND	Clinton	KY	B+	B+	B	167.9	39.48	3.9	3.9	10.2	31.3	7.3	9.2	16.2
FIRST COMMUNITY BANK MISSOURI	Poplar Bluff	MO	B-	B-	C+	264.1	-2.78	13.3	2.6	9.6	19.5	6.3	8.3	12.4
FIRST COMMUNITY BANK NA	San Benito	TX	B-	B-	C+	322.0	29.65	7.6	1.8	10.9	24.5	6.0	8.0	13.6
▲ FIRST COMMUNITY BANK NA	Sugar Land	TX	C-	D-	D	628.6	-0.32	7.8	3.4	41.1	11.5	8.3	9.9	13.6
FIRST COMMUNITY BANK OF E AR	Marion	AR	A-	A-	B	148.6	11.06	7.3	2.5	18.7	11.8	10.0	11.6	16.1
FIRST COMMUNITY BK CENTRAL AL	Wetumpka	AL	B+	B+	B	315.0	4.91	10.7	4.1	15.2	28.3	6.6	8.6	14.3
FIRST COMMUNITY BK HILLSBORO	Hillsboro	IL	C+	C+	C+	80.5	7.73	11.6	4.5	18.8	19.0	7.1	9.1	18.4

Asset Quality Index	Adjusted Non-Performing Loans as a % of Total Loans	Adjusted Non-Performing Loans as a % of Capital	Net Charge-Offs Avg Loans	Profitability Index	Net Income ($Mil)	Return on Assets (R.O.A.)	Return on Equity (R.O.E.)	Net Interest Spread	Overhead Efficiency Ratio	Liquidity Index	Liquidity Ratio	Hot Money Ratio	Stability Index
4.1	1.68	11.6	-0.01	**7.3**	2.8	1.23	11.72	3.61	54.2	**3.2**	18.7	13.3	**6.7**
2.3	4.99	25.0	0.22	**3.4**	0.8	0.43	3.64	3.96	84.4	**3.8**	29.6	12.4	**5.3**
3.5	1.80	9.1	0.60	**4.2**	2.4	0.77	7.38	3.49	75.2	**3.5**	30.1	14.2	**5.6**
6.7	0.66	4.6	0.24	**0.3**	-0.2	-0.27	-3.99	3.19	102.6	**5.7**	28.8	0.5	**1.0**
0.3	6.51	66.2	0.53	**2.9**	1.4	0.48	9.89	3.14	85.9	**2.5**	16.9	16.8	**0.5**
4.2	3.52	18.0	0.21	**5.8**	7.4	0.96	10.93	2.80	81.5	**2.8**	35.9	27.9	**6.6**
7.5	0.00	0.0	0.00	**5.1**	3.1	0.80	9.49	3.58	57.1	**2.5**	25.6	17.6	**5.3**
5.4	2.54	9.2	0.36	**6.8**	2.4	1.42	12.38	4.01	61.1	**2.6**	37.0	22.4	**5.9**
5.0	1.56	9.6	0.08	**9.8**	5.1	2.13	22.66	3.66	53.6	**3.7**	18.7	10.7	**7.0**
4.0	2.62	14.9	0.12	**0.9**	-121.1	-1.92	-18.41	2.81	141.5	**5.2**	22.2	3.3	**5.5**
4.0	3.30	15.7	0.02	**3.5**	0.4	0.81	8.08	3.39	78.3	**5.0**	30.5	5.5	**4.8**
0.0	12.97	91.9	0.80	**0.3**	-0.1	-0.50	-5.29	4.51	111.1	**2.9**	18.0	14.5	**2.4**
4.8	1.59	8.5	0.19	**8.1**	10.3	1.52	13.53	3.89	52.7	**2.9**	16.7	14.9	**8.6**
6.1	1.28	6.6	0.20	**6.1**	10.9	1.24	11.69	3.86	65.0	**2.6**	27.2	21.0	**8.2**
8.3	0.71	3.3	0.08	**5.9**	11.7	1.46	13.46	3.24	60.8	**3.5**	21.0	12.8	**10.0**
9.0	0.17	0.5	-0.10	**3.1**	1.0	0.57	3.24	3.44	80.5	**4.9**	27.0	4.7	**7.3**
9.1	0.00	0.0	0.11	**6.2**	2.0	1.05	6.37	3.53	60.7	**2.9**	38.7	20.3	**8.0**
1.7	1.90	14.9	0.49	**2.5**	0.4	0.24	2.40	4.37	81.7	**2.2**	14.1	18.1	**4.0**
6.3	0.35	2.0	-0.04	**4.2**	0.4	0.88	6.91	4.23	77.5	**3.3**	19.3	12.9	**5.7**
0.3	12.91	193.3	0.09	**1.0**	0.1	0.08	3.24	3.23	98.4	**1.4**	17.4	26.5	**0.0**
4.5	1.50	8.2	-0.16	**3.8**	3.1	0.65	5.29	2.84	71.8	**3.5**	20.9	12.0	**7.1**
7.1	0.77	3.4	0.25	**5.9**	3.0	1.37	12.31	3.63	65.2	**3.7**	42.8	17.0	**8.1**
5.0	0.85	6.5	0.08	**3.3**	1.2	0.60	6.48	3.42	78.4	**2.0**	16.9	19.0	**4.6**
5.6	1.14	8.2	0.09	**5.2**	4.8	0.96	10.18	3.19	59.8	**3.7**	14.1	10.4	**6.2**
4.3	1.02	5.8	0.00	**5.6**	1.7	1.37	12.63	3.51	60.6	**5.6**	37.1	4.4	**7.2**
2.0	3.13	13.1	0.69	**7.3**	0.7	2.01	10.82	4.74	81.2	**3.7**	13.8	10.2	**5.7**
5.4	0.89	4.9	0.12	**5.3**	4.8	1.02	8.65	3.38	64.8	**2.9**	8.8	13.9	**8.1**
5.3	0.73	3.2	0.39	**6.0**	7.2	1.42	17.43	2.75	66.5	**6.9**	57.0	3.3	**6.3**
5.4	0.61	4.8	-0.01	**5.2**	2.8	0.94	8.52	4.27	52.0	**0.7**	11.1	34.9	**6.0**
6.8	0.46	3.0	0.29	**6.5**	2.5	1.23	12.44	4.28	59.9	**1.0**	11.7	30.9	**6.2**
5.4	0.54	4.5	0.05	**7.4**	0.7	1.63	16.83	3.84	53.6	**3.7**	9.3	9.8	**7.3**
7.5	0.32	2.0	0.02	**4.7**	1.9	0.91	7.39	3.36	64.0	**0.9**	19.0	37.6	**6.7**
4.0	3.05	17.4	0.03	**3.6**	1.5	0.63	5.68	4.18	76.9	**1.6**	21.7	25.7	**4.8**
3.3	2.17	11.7	0.02	**5.5**	1.6	1.04	10.26	3.57	56.9	**2.6**	25.0	16.8	**5.7**
2.7	2.52	10.8	-0.20	**5.0**	2.9	0.83	3.86	3.28	54.9	**0.5**	4.7	44.7	**7.3**
5.9	0.72	5.0	-0.02	**4.4**	1.1	1.02	13.06	4.27	77.1	**5.4**	37.4	6.2	**4.4**
8.1	0.00	0.0	-0.05	**3.6**	1.0	0.52	5.63	3.55	74.9	**0.6**	9.2	42.1	**4.9**
4.6	0.92	6.4	0.37	**4.4**	39.9	0.86	7.88	3.31	64.7	**4.0**	15.2	8.9	**7.7**
4.8	2.97	13.8	0.10	**2.0**	1.0	0.28	2.47	4.08	103.5	**2.9**	38.6	20.4	**5.4**
5.1	1.53	8.6	0.23	**4.0**	4.2	0.73	7.13	3.49	72.8	**3.8**	31.0	12.8	**4.8**
3.5	2.62	16.6	0.03	**4.3**	2.4	0.98	10.17	4.30	77.0	**2.8**	21.6	15.5	**4.6**
3.7	6.32	19.6	-1.07	**3.7**	0.8	0.62	4.24	3.57	77.7	**3.6**	33.5	14.8	**6.4**
4.3	1.56	11.8	0.27	**4.9**	6.1	0.93	10.51	4.15	67.3	**0.9**	9.5	31.8	**5.5**
5.3	1.15	7.4	0.17	**5.7**	2.5	1.38	11.29	5.12	72.9	**3.0**	13.6	13.7	**6.6**
3.0	3.11	19.1	0.24	**6.8**	1.0	1.60	15.28	4.00	63.5	**4.2**	27.1	9.6	**6.4**
6.8	0.42	2.6	0.18	**5.3**	1.0	1.34	11.61	3.46	58.3	**5.6**	35.8	4.4	**7.5**
4.6	1.09	7.8	0.24	**6.0**	19.9	1.04	8.54	4.12	64.0	**2.4**	9.0	16.7	**8.6**
6.4	0.18	1.4	-0.03	**4.0**	0.7	0.75	8.84	4.17	72.9	**1.1**	20.6	32.7	**5.9**
2.3	4.62	22.7	-0.02	**4.9**	1.6	0.85	8.74	3.78	71.3	**5.4**	37.8	6.0	**4.7**
5.0	2.31	10.5	0.56	**3.6**	0.3	0.73	7.72	3.67	75.4	**4.5**	37.2	11.4	**4.2**
5.8	0.36	2.5	0.13	**8.8**	5.7	2.14	24.22	5.67	67.1	**2.5**	25.3	17.9	**6.6**
2.1	2.72	16.0	-0.17	**8.3**	13.2	2.17	20.27	3.68	49.0	**2.2**	31.1	22.5	**5.2**
1.7	10.13	41.7	4.24	**3.1**	0.4	0.40	3.64	4.45	72.6	**4.8**	31.7	7.5	**4.8**
6.4	0.37	2.3	0.07	**5.4**	1.4	1.22	10.13	4.24	68.1	**2.3**	30.2	21.0	**7.5**
7.3	0.19	1.4	0.07	**3.6**	0.8	0.39	4.78	3.51	76.9	**2.2**	12.4	17.6	**4.5**
7.0	0.30	2.0	0.01	**4.5**	1.7	0.75	9.03	4.54	75.3	**2.8**	24.0	15.9	**4.1**
5.3	1.11	7.6	0.05	**2.7**	3.6	0.77	7.91	4.05	82.2	**1.3**	19.3	28.5	**4.1**
8.0	0.14	0.9	0.03	**5.5**	1.0	0.92	8.30	3.83	62.5	**1.5**	11.9	24.1	**6.6**
6.0	1.10	7.0	0.09	**8.2**	4.5	1.90	23.93	4.05	52.4	**1.8**	24.9	22.8	**6.1**
5.0	1.49	8.7	0.05	**3.4**	0.4	0.71	7.99	2.84	75.3	**4.1**	30.8	11.6	**5.1**

Name	City	State	Rating	2013 Rating	2012 Rating	Total Assets ($Mil)	One Year Asset Growth	Asset Mix (As a % of Total Assets) Comm-ercial Loans	Cons-umer Loans	Mort-gage Loans	Secur-ities	Capital-ization Index	Lever-age Ratio	Risk-Based Capital Ratio
FIRST COMMUNITY BK OF BEDFORD	Shelbyville	TN	**A**	A	A	339.5	8.09	8.7	1.4	26.5	20.5	**10.0**	13.0	16.4
FIRST COMMUNITY BK OF CULLMAN	Cullman	AL	**B-**	B	C+	74.4	13.80	4.2	1.8	40.8	9.7	**10.0**	11.1	21.4
FIRST COMMUNITY BK OF EAST TN	Rogersville	TN	**D**	D-	D	187.4	0.97	6.6	0.7	12.6	17.3	**8.7**	10.2	17.4
FIRST COMMUNITY BK THE OZARKS	Branson	MO	**C-**	D+	D-	100.1	2.50	4.8	2.2	13.8	34.4	**6.7**	8.7	15.5
FIRST COMMUNITY BK XENIA-FLORA	Xenia	IL	**B-**	B-	B	41.0	5.45	4.5	7.1	21.7	30.3	**6.8**	11.6	12.3
▲ FIRST COMMUNITY FINANCIAL BANK	Plainfield	IL	**C**	D+	C+	916.2	7.97	19.3	0.6	7.4	17.0	**9.2**	10.8	14.3
FIRST COMMUNITY NATIONAL BK	Cuba	MO	**B-**	C+	C+	223.5	5.12	2.1	2.2	30.0	20.4	**6.7**	8.7	15.3
FIRST COMMUNITY TRUST NA	Dubuque	IA	**U**	U	U	6.3	5.84	0.0	0.0	0.0	74.2	**10.0**	96.8	139.5
▲ FIRST CORNERSTONE BANK	King of Prussia	PA	**D-**	E-	E-	118.0	-14.84	2.3	1.0	14.9	27.5	**5.6**	7.6	13.4
FIRST COUNTY BANK	Stamford	CT	**C**	D+	C-	1411.6	4.19	3.4	0.1	41.7	23.9	**7.4**	9.3	14.7
FIRST COUNTY BANK	New Baden	IL	**C+**	B-	B-	414.9	6.39	1.4	5.4	47.9	10.7	**7.5**	9.4	15.9
FIRST COVENANT BANK	Commerce	GA	**D+**	D-	E-	160.2	-0.51	1.3	0.6	5.4	25.4	**5.7**	7.7	11.9
FIRST CREDIT BANK	Los Angeles	CA	**A-**	B	C+	400.0	7.27	0.7	0.0	12.1	8.9	**10.0**	40.7	47.4
FIRST DAKOTA NATIONAL BK	Yankton	SD	**B+**	B	C+	1057.6	5.44	8.0	1.5	6.1	9.9	**6.2**	9.0	11.9
FIRST DELTA BANK	Marked Tree	AR	**C+**	C+	B-	69.0	-3.81	3.5	1.2	4.2	56.0	**6.8**	8.8	19.4
FIRST EAGLE BANK	Chicago	IL	**A**	A	A	436.4	5.33	0.6	0.1	10.4	30.5	**10.0**	14.3	20.2
▼ FIRST ELECTRONIC BANK	Sandy	UT	**C**	B	B+	9.3	-4.45	0.0	11.4	0.0	1.9	**10.0**	84.6	226.0
FIRST ENTERPRISE BANK	Oklahoma City	OK	**D+**	C-	C	149.5	11.99	11.6	1.6	16.9	0.0	**9.7**	11.8	14.8
FIRST EXCHANGE BANK	Mannington	WV	**D+**	D+	D+	201.0	-0.94	2.7	5.9	42.1	15.8	**7.5**	9.3	15.4
FIRST FARMBANK	Greeley	CO	**B**	B	B+	131.8	25.12	9.8	0.5	5.7	16.3	**6.5**	8.9	12.1
FIRST FARMERS & COMMERCIAL BK	Pikeville	TN	**B-**	B-	C+	108.0	-0.74	4.3	4.6	15.0	28.3	**9.8**	10.9	17.5
FIRST FARMERS & MERCH STATE BK	Grand Meadow	MN	**A-**	A-	B	52.7	18.31	9.5	0.7	6.6	11.8	**8.1**	10.6	13.4
FIRST FARMERS & MERCH STATE BK	Brownsdale	MN	**A-**	A-	B	86.8	-3.92	9.9	2.4	5.0	29.6	**10.0**	12.6	18.1
FIRST FARMERS & MERCHANTS BANK	Cannon Falls	MN	**A-**	B+	B+	270.7	-0.34	9.1	2.7	8.1	15.9	**10.0**	11.8	15.4
FIRST FARMERS & MERCHANTS BANK	Columbia	TN	**B-**	B	C+	1126.3	4.92	8.3	1.4	15.9	35.8	**7.4**	9.3	15.4
FIRST FARMERS & MERCHANTS NB	Fairmont	MN	**A-**	B+	B	100.1	7.94	19.1	4.9	15.2	8.9	**9.9**	11.9	14.9
FIRST FARMERS & MERCHANTS NB	Luverne	MN	**A-**	A-	B+	165.1	4.40	15.2	3.6	3.0	13.3	**10.0**	13.3	16.5
▼ FIRST FARMERS BANK & TRUST	Converse	IN	**B**	B+	B	1253.2	8.22	14.0	0.5	4.7	17.8	**8.2**	10.1	13.5
FIRST FARMERS BANK & TRUST CO	Owenton	KY	**C**	C-	C+	108.1	-3.30	3.8	1.9	27.8	10.3	**10.0**	12.8	18.8
FIRST FARMERS NB OF WAURIKA	Waurika	OK	**B+**	B+	A-	46.0	2.74	2.3	3.4	3.4	59.4	**10.0**	19.1	55.5
FIRST FARMERS STATE BK	Minier	IL	**B-**	B	B-	162.3	2.56	6.4	0.6	8.4	42.3	**9.4**	10.6	21.1
▲ FIRST FEDERAL BANK	Dickson	TN	**B+**	B+	B	456.3	0.41	2.4	3.3	18.9	45.4	**9.5**	10.6	25.1
▲ FIRST FEDERAL BANK	Harrison	AR	**C**	C-	D+	601.4	13.48	8.6	0.7	20.5	11.5	**6.8**	8.9	12.4
FIRST FEDERAL BANK	Dunn	NC	**C**	C	C-	163.6	-3.63	1.2	1.7	45.8	6.9	**10.0**	12.0	24.3
▲ FIRST FEDERAL BANK A FSB	Tuscaloosa	AL	**B-**	C-	D+	128.3	-5.84	0.0	0.9	63.6	1.2	**10.0**	12.6	20.5
FIRST FEDERAL BANK FSB	Kansas City	MO	**C**	C+	C+	417.1	18.24	0.0	0.1	63.2	16.7	**10.0**	14.6	28.1
FIRST FEDERAL BANK LITTLEFIELD	Littlefield	TX	**C+**	C+	C+	50.4	6.06	5.3	5.6	19.9	11.1	**10.0**	16.2	24.0
FIRST FEDERAL BANK OF FLORIDA	Lake City	FL	**B**	B	B-	1021.6	7.51	10.2	4.6	19.6	22.3	**10.0**	12.3	19.0
FIRST FEDERAL BANK OF OHIO	Galion	OH	**D**	D+	C-	238.1	-2.91	0.1	0.7	26.1	28.4	**10.0**	14.7	33.9
FIRST FEDERAL BK OF LOUISIANA	Lake Charles	LA	**C-**	C-	C+	827.2	12.85	1.5	1.2	22.8	41.1	**10.0**	11.6	24.6
FIRST FEDERAL BK OF MIDWEST	Defiance	OH	**C+**	C+	C	2136.2	4.52	16.3	0.7	10.8	11.2	**9.9**	11.8	14.9
▲ FIRST FEDERAL BK OF WISCONSIN	Waukesha	WI	**C+**	C-	C+	248.0	114.19	2.6	0.1	37.2	21.0	**10.0**	13.3	24.3
FIRST FEDERAL CMNTY BK BUCYRUS	Bucyrus	OH	**C-**	C-	D+	131.6	6.73	3.9	5.3	51.5	10.9	**6.3**	8.3	13.8
FIRST FEDERAL COMMUNITY BANK	Paris	TX	**B-**	B	C+	339.7	2.23	4.3	2.8	46.0	13.7	**10.0**	11.3	19.2
FIRST FEDERAL COMMUNITY BANK N	Dover	OH	**B-**	B-	C+	261.5	5.08	11.8	2.8	23.2	4.4	**6.6**	9.0	12.2
▲ FIRST FEDERAL OF NORTHERN MI	Alpena	MI	**C**	C-	C-	311.6	45.76	5.2	0.4	23.8	36.7	**6.8**	8.8	16.7
FIRST FEDERAL SOUTH CAROLINA	Walterboro	SC	**E-**	E-	E-	72.8	-27.90	0.4	1.3	33.6	20.8	**5.4**	7.4	14.6
FIRST FEDERAL SVGS & LOAN BK	Olathe	KS	**B-**	B-	C	67.4	0.87	0.0	0.1	76.2	0.0	**10.0**	12.4	23.2
FIRST FEDERAL SVGS MIDDLETOWN	Middletown	NY	**C-**	C-	B-	154.7	-0.74	0.1	0.0	1.8	33.4	**10.0**	35.8	120.2
▲ FIRST FIDELITY BANK	Burke	SD	**B+**	B+	A-	340.2	6.27	3.6	2.5	1.2	49.8	**7.5**	9.3	15.7
FIRST FIDELITY BANK	Fort Payne	AL	**C**	C	C-	89.1	-3.06	6.7	2.4	26.3	32.0	**6.7**	8.7	23.2
FIRST FIDELITY BANK NA	Oklahoma City	OK	**C-**	C-	C	1378.0	-1.38	5.9	15.3	7.7	32.4	**6.7**	8.7	14.4
FIRST FINANCIAL BANK	Aneta	ND	**B**	B	B-	43.6	0.79	7.8	2.4	2.0	32.8	**6.7**	8.7	14.9
FIRST FINANCIAL BANK	El Dorado	AR	**C+**	C+	C+	902.5	6.09	4.6	2.2	4.4	3.1	**9.1**	10.4	21.8
FIRST FINANCIAL BANK	Bessemer	AL	**D+**	D+	D-	180.3	-6.12	2.5	2.2	15.1	29.0	**7.1**	9.1	16.6
FIRST FINANCIAL BANK IN WINNEB	Winnebago	MN	**B+**	B+	B+	43.1	7.61	8.4	3.8	5.3	27.0	**10.0**	15.2	21.8
FIRST FINANCIAL BANK NA	Terre Haute	IN	**B**	B	B-	2963.5	1.23	16.1	7.2	11.8	30.2	**10.0**	11.6	16.6
FIRST FINANCIAL BANK NA	Cincinnati	OH	**B**	B	B-	7346.7	17.70	16.2	0.8	10.2	24.9	**6.7**	8.7	12.6
FIRST FINANCIAL BANK NA	Abilene	TX	**A-**	A-	B+	5542.8	9.79	8.4	6.4	14.7	40.4	**6.2**	8.2	14.2
FIRST FINANCIAL TRUST & ASSET	Abilene	TX	**U**	U	U	10.5	26.74	0.0	0.0	0.0	21.6	**10.0**	102.	332.1

Asset Quality Index	Adjusted Non-Performing Loans as a % of Total Loans	Adjusted Non-Performing Loans as a % of Capital	Net Charge-Offs Avg Loans	Profitability Index	Net Income ($Mil)	Return on Assets (R.O.A.)	Return on Equity (R.O.E.)	Net Interest Spread	Overhead Efficiency Ratio	Liquidity Index	Liquidity Ratio	Hot Money Ratio	Stability Index
7.6	0.39	1.8	0.39	**6.3**	2.4	1.00	6.91	4.05	83.4	**1.0**	20.1	33.4	**8.3**
9.4	0.00	0.0	0.06	**3.0**	0.2	0.46	4.02	3.43	82.9	**1.4**	22.8	28.3	**4.1**
3.7	4.51	21.1	0.53	**1.3**	0.5	0.36	3.60	3.37	89.9	**2.5**	21.1	16.9	**4.2**
3.7	1.96	10.9	-0.02	**2.4**	0.2	0.31	3.81	3.58	83.0	**1.8**	28.8	26.1	**3.6**
7.2	0.35	1.8	-0.01	**6.3**	0.5	1.52	13.34	3.78	59.2	**3.6**	29.0	13.2	**5.7**
3.2	1.43	8.9	0.92	**4.7**	4.8	0.72	5.82	3.63	60.8	**1.4**	18.0	27.6	**6.0**
3.6	2.67	18.5	1.24	**5.3**	2.2	1.36	16.58	4.14	71.3	**1.3**	15.3	28.1	**4.8**
10.0	na	0.0	na	**10.0**	0.8	18.02	18.25	3.80	68.4	**4.0**	2671.4	101.0	**5.8**
0.3	20.30	124.3	0.55	**0.0**	-2.5	-2.65	-35.85	2.75	205.3	**3.4**	33.1	15.6	**0.0**
4.4	2.90	20.0	0.13	**2.9**	4.5	0.43	5.21	3.04	80.1	**2.3**	22.9	19.9	**5.4**
3.1	2.49	20.1	0.16	**5.6**	2.7	0.90	9.55	3.39	64.2	**3.4**	10.5	11.3	**6.5**
6.3	0.65	3.7	-0.76	**2.9**	0.5	0.41	5.21	4.33	96.6	**5.5**	27.2	0.8	**2.0**
5.8	2.35	4.3	0.00	**10.0**	17.7	6.11	14.97	7.75	13.2	**1.2**	31.3	61.9	**10.0**
6.2	0.54	4.4	0.02	**7.6**	9.9	1.28	13.87	4.51	60.4	**3.5**	8.5	11.0	**8.7**
7.1	0.70	2.8	-0.01	**5.0**	0.5	1.02	13.11	3.38	62.8	**4.4**	49.2	14.5	**4.0**
6.8	1.18	5.1	0.06	**8.7**	6.2	1.95	13.12	4.14	47.7	**1.2**	24.7	31.8	**8.8**
9.0	0.00	0.0	0.00	**1.8**	-0.1	-1.69	-1.95	4.36	102.4	**5.2**	395.3	68.5	**8.1**
1.4	2.70	19.1	0.00	**8.1**	2.3	2.09	17.93	5.56	64.6	**1.2**	7.0	26.7	**7.2**
1.7	3.79	27.3	0.64	**3.9**	1.4	0.94	10.19	3.49	71.3	**3.3**	22.2	13.1	**4.6**
7.2	0.00	0.0	0.01	**4.0**	0.5	0.53	5.95	4.08	73.4	**0.7**	10.0	40.9	**5.1**
6.7	0.19	0.8	0.25	**4.1**	0.6	0.67	6.39	4.02	73.2	**1.6**	31.8	32.5	**5.6**
5.2	1.20	8.6	0.19	**5.1**	0.5	1.28	11.62	4.24	68.8	**2.1**	6.7	17.8	**6.9**
7.0	0.74	3.6	0.04	**5.3**	0.9	1.29	9.65	3.81	63.8	**2.5**	23.2	17.5	**7.8**
5.8	1.06	6.2	0.02	**7.5**	3.4	1.73	13.79	4.22	63.9	**4.0**	15.9	8.6	**7.8**
6.7	0.93	5.2	0.07	**4.5**	7.7	0.92	9.85	3.52	70.9	**3.5**	18.3	12.4	**7.9**
2.4	3.68	23.9	0.10	**5.8**	0.8	1.01	8.27	4.32	59.6	**1.2**	4.2	25.6	**8.8**
6.9	0.33	1.8	0.01	**8.4**	2.4	1.97	15.03	4.35	65.7	**4.2**	11.1	7.0	**8.9**
4.3	1.69	11.8	0.02	**7.4**	12.1	1.31	12.63	4.06	55.9	**2.2**	13.3	18.0	**8.7**
4.8	2.47	14.0	0.09	**6.9**	1.1	1.26	8.66	4.43	59.5	**2.0**	13.1	18.6	**4.3**
8.7	0.83	1.3	-0.24	**5.6**	0.4	1.14	6.49	3.61	64.4	**2.9**	50.6	27.4	**8.0**
7.0	0.53	2.4	0.01	**4.1**	1.1	0.94	8.64	3.35	69.4	**5.0**	38.4	9.6	**5.8**
6.0	1.26	4.2	0.30	**7.0**	5.7	1.67	14.72	3.77	57.4	**3.1**	37.8	18.7	**6.8**
3.9	2.18	14.8	0.18	**3.2**	21.5	5.02	45.73	3.19	98.1	**0.8**	14.5	34.2	**5.7**
8.7	0.52	2.8	0.15	**2.1**	0.3	0.21	1.74	3.49	90.7	**1.6**	25.6	25.9	**5.8**
4.8	1.83	10.8	0.31	**3.8**	1.1	1.13	9.04	3.33	87.8	**0.6**	11.3	46.6	**3.7**
9.0	0.52	2.6	0.03	**2.4**	0.6	0.23	1.45	2.95	92.1	**1.7**	22.2	23.8	**7.1**
8.4	0.12	0.5	0.00	**3.0**	0.1	0.33	1.96	3.67	83.9	**0.8**	13.9	34.0	**7.1**
4.0	2.64	11.6	0.10	**4.4**	6.7	0.89	7.13	4.00	83.9	**4.3**	24.6	10.8	**9.1**
5.5	4.90	13.1	0.11	**0.2**	-0.9	-0.47	-3.37	2.53	115.8	**5.7**	60.3	11.6	**5.7**
7.9	1.22	5.1	0.00	**1.6**	0.9	0.15	1.31	2.48	92.3	**1.9**	21.8	21.0	**6.8**
3.6	2.12	12.9	0.11	**5.6**	17.3	1.08	7.96	3.65	64.5	**3.8**	10.6	9.9	**9.2**
4.9	1.81	9.1	0.21	**3.3**	0.6	0.46	3.60	3.53	75.2	**3.4**	31.0	14.8	**5.0**
2.2	2.93	24.7	0.71	**3.4**	0.5	0.49	5.96	4.11	80.5	**3.9**	12.3	8.7	**3.5**
6.8	0.89	5.3	0.16	**3.6**	1.1	0.45	4.01	4.02	83.6	**1.4**	23.5	27.9	**5.8**
4.7	1.04	8.8	-0.01	**6.1**	2.1	1.09	12.11	3.82	58.8	**3.0**	12.6	13.7	**5.6**
5.0	1.57	9.1	0.25	**3.9**	2.1	1.16	11.71	3.42	71.9	**4.3**	31.2	10.7	**2.9**
1.7	7.41	47.7	0.57	**1.2**	0.2	0.28	4.69	3.45	100.3	**4.6**	41.7	12.5	**0.6**
3.6	3.89	22.9	0.15	**9.5**	1.2	2.25	17.85	4.26	43.4	**0.7**	18.9	59.1	**5.6**
10.0	0.00	0.0	0.00	**1.3**	0.1	0.06	0.16	1.58	97.8	**6.6**	134.4	14.6	**7.0**
8.2	0.40	1.7	0.02	**5.2**	3.1	1.23	14.59	3.12	62.7	**5.8**	51.3	8.5	**5.4**
4.5	3.40	15.7	0.02	**2.6**	0.2	0.32	3.78	2.96	83.7	**3.4**	54.2	20.4	**3.8**
2.1	3.30	20.4	0.00	**7.4**	19.7	1.87	19.19	4.13	61.9	**4.9**	23.5	6.1	**7.6**
7.1	0.27	1.5	-0.06	**4.4**	0.2	0.75	8.62	3.72	68.6	**4.0**	27.9	10.7	**5.3**
3.7	1.12	7.6	0.17	**9.8**	16.5	2.50	23.62	4.17	56.8	**0.9**	19.9	35.7	**8.6**
2.0	7.72	34.9	0.41	**1.8**	0.3	0.25	3.11	2.74	91.5	**5.0**	33.4	7.4	**2.2**
7.2	0.78	3.1	-0.01	**6.2**	0.4	1.36	8.86	4.08	66.1	**4.8**	30.6	6.9	**9.3**
4.8	1.69	8.4	0.30	**5.6**	21.9	0.99	7.94	3.87	66.2	**4.6**	20.0	6.3	**9.3**
5.1	1.14	8.5	0.27	**5.9**	50.5	1.03	11.46	3.79	64.7	**3.7**	10.8	10.5	**7.6**
5.9	0.79	4.8	0.06	**8.9**	63.3	1.61	15.81	4.29	51.5	**4.3**	21.3	8.7	**9.1**
10.0	na	0.0	na	**9.5**	5.3	78.74	82.99	0.91	42.4	**4.0**	1083.0	101.0	**7.0**

I. Index of Banks

Name	City	State	Rating	2013 Rating	2012 Rating	Total Assets ($Mil)	One Year Asset Growth	Asset Mix (As a % of Total Assets) Comm-ercial Loans	Cons-umer Loans	Mort-gage Loans	Secur-ities	Capital-ization Index	Lever-age Ratio	Risk-Based Capital Ratio
FIRST FINANCIAL TRUST NA	Wellesley	MA	**U**	U	U	7.8	6.69	0.0	0.0	0.0	41.2	**10.0**	98.1	198.8
FIRST FLORIDA BANK	Destin	FL	**B**	B	B	268.6	13.20	4.8	1.0	13.2	34.7	**10.0**	11.4	22.3
▲ FIRST FLORIDA INTEGRITY BANK	Naples	FL	**C-**	C-	D-	865.9	29.72	3.0	1.2	24.8	20.5	**7.0**	9.0	13.6
FIRST FOUNDATION BANK	Irvine	CA	**B**	B-	C+	1281.5	33.82	6.5	1.5	25.2	10.5	**6.4**	8.4	13.6
▲ FIRST FREEDOM BANK	Lebanon	TN	**B**	C+	C-	285.0	8.08	12.6	2.1	16.1	3.6	**8.6**	11.0	13.8
FIRST FS&LA	Hazard	KY	**B-**	B-	B	79.0	-7.61	0.0	2.3	62.2	2.5	**10.0**	20.1	43.2
FIRST FS&LA	Morehead	KY	**C**	C	C-	34.3	-2.87	0.6	1.8	57.7	0.1	**10.0**	27.1	51.3
FIRST FS&LA	Aberdeen	MS	**B**	B	B	30.3	-2.64	0.0	1.9	54.1	16.4	**10.0**	21.7	60.6
FIRST FS&LA	Delta	OH	**C-**	C-	C+	161.2	0.30	0.4	0.8	48.9	0.0	**10.0**	11.8	28.8
FIRST FS&LA	Newark	OH	**C**	C	C-	178.5	9.07	0.0	0.2	54.9	5.0	**10.0**	18.3	30.4
FIRST FS&LA CENTRAL ILLINOIS	Shelbyville	IL	**B-**	B-	C+	100.9	1.46	5.6	6.1	31.9	23.2	**9.3**	10.5	17.9
FIRST FS&LA OF BATH	Bath	ME	**C+**	C+	C+	121.0	1.68	1.2	1.1	71.8	0.0	**10.0**	15.1	27.8
FIRST FS&LA OF BUCKS COUNTY	Bristol	PA	**B-**	B-	B-	739.4	5.38	3.9	0.7	43.5	23.5	**10.0**	11.1	18.5
FIRST FS&LA OF CENTERBURG	Centerburg	OH	**C+**	C+	C+	25.9	-2.77	0.0	0.5	43.7	30.6	**10.0**	16.3	36.9
FIRST FS&LA OF GREENE COUNTY	Waynesburg	PA	**C+**	C+	C+	893.3	2.29	0.0	1.2	63.1	25.7	**10.0**	12.9	29.3
FIRST FS&LA OF GREENSBURG	Greensburg	IN	**C-**	C	C+	157.9	4.05	1.0	2.1	32.8	9.7	**6.8**	8.8	22.6
FIRST FS&LA OF INDEPENDENCE	Independence	KS	**D+**	D-	D	136.9	-2.43	0.3	4.1	49.3	18.8	**8.3**	9.8	20.9
FIRST FS&LA OF KEWANEE	Kewanee	IL	**D-**	D	D+	63.7	-7.61	0.6	0.1	37.7	50.5	**9.8**	10.8	28.5
FIRST FS&LA OF LAKEWOOD	Lakewood	OH	**C**	C	C	1565.8	7.02	0.2	1.9	61.0	5.0	**8.5**	10.0	18.0
FIRST FS&LA OF LORAIN	Lorain	OH	**C-**	C+	C-	423.1	-9.01	0.0	0.3	54.8	6.1	**10.0**	14.0	31.5
FIRST FS&LA OF MATTOON	Mattoon	IL	**B-**	B-	B-	87.8	1.08	4.3	0.8	24.6	34.7	**10.0**	28.6	66.4
FIRST FS&LA OF MCMINNVILLE	McMinnville	OR	**C**	C-	C	362.1	1.59	0.0	0.1	38.5	27.1	**10.0**	14.9	28.7
FIRST FS&LA OF PASCAGOULA-MOSS	Pascagoula	MS	**C**	C	C-	276.8	0.68	0.0	0.5	78.3	9.4	**6.5**	8.5	17.4
▲ FIRST FS&LA OF PORT ANGELES	Port Angeles	WA	**C-**	C-	D	788.2	-0.86	1.8	1.3	33.2	28.5	**8.9**	10.2	20.3
FIRST FS&LA OF RAVENSWOOD	Ravenswood	WV	**C-**	D+	C	16.0	2.25	0.0	0.1	67.0	0.3	**6.6**	8.6	17.2
FIRST FS&LA OF SAN RAFAEL	San Rafael	CA	**B-**	B	B-	173.0	-0.28	0.0	0.0	3.8	0.0	**10.0**	21.6	28.9
FIRST FS&LA OF VALDOSTA	Valdosta	GA	**C-**	C-	C	164.2	-2.03	0.0	1.6	67.2	3.2	**10.0**	16.9	30.1
FIRST FS&LA OF VAN WERT	Van Wert	OH	**B-**	B-	B-	113.5	-2.96	0.0	0.2	35.7	47.5	**10.0**	15.2	42.7
FIRST FS&LA OF WAKEENEY	WaKeeney	KS	**D+**	C-	C+	30.6	-0.65	0.3	1.3	20.5	46.4	**10.0**	11.6	36.1
▲ FIRST FSB	Sheridan	WY	**C+**	C	C+	219.4	-0.56	8.2	1.3	18.4	36.1	**10.0**	18.3	30.4
FIRST FSB	Ottawa	IL	**C-**	C	D-	374.1	0.33	0.0	0.1	61.9	7.1	**7.7**	9.5	18.5
FIRST FSB	Huntington	IN	**C**	C-	C-	271.2	1.41	10.6	3.4	17.2	26.8	**9.0**	10.3	17.1
FIRST FSB	Rochester	IN	**C**	C-	C	354.3	-3.14	0.2	0.2	64.8	0.0	**10.0**	12.3	18.8
FIRST FSB	Evansville	IN	**C**	C	C	372.5	1.33	15.0	4.6	16.1	25.1	**7.0**	9.0	13.5
FIRST FSB OF ANGOLA	Angola	IN	**B**	B	B-	132.0	-0.38	0.6	2.9	64.3	0.1	**10.0**	17.1	37.3
FIRST FSB OF BOSTON	Andover	MA	**C+**	C+	C	58.6	-6.48	0.0	0.0	52.2	0.0	**10.0**	21.1	37.5
FIRST FSB OF CHAMPAIGN-URBANA	Champaign	IL	**B-**	C+	B-	173.0	2.04	3.7	1.9	30.2	0.2	**7.2**	9.1	20.5
FIRST FSB OF ELIZABETHTOWN	Elizabethtown	KY	**D**	D	D-	753.7	-11.33	3.2	2.4	16.5	27.6	**7.1**	9.0	15.8
FIRST FSB OF FRANKFORT	Frankfort	KY	**B-**	B-	B	225.7	-6.02	0.8	0.5	64.3	3.1	**10.0**	15.2	27.1
▼ FIRST FSB OF LINCOLNTON	Lincolnton	NC	**B-**	B	C+	340.4	3.47	1.3	0.5	59.3	10.7	**10.0**	14.0	25.1
FIRST FSB OF MASCOUTAH	Mascoutah	IL	**C**	C	C+	97.7	-12.89	0.0	0.5	31.9	54.1	**10.0**	13.2	37.1
FIRST FSB OF TWIN FALLS	Twin Falls	ID	**C+**	B-	C+	535.9	4.52	5.3	3.8	38.0	3.3	**9.6**	10.8	18.2
▼ FIRST FSB OF WASHINGTON	Washington	IN	**C+**	B-	B-	74.8	-5.70	0.7	3.2	47.0	17.3	**10.0**	12.4	28.8
▲ FIRST GENERAL BANK	Rowland Heights	CA	**C**	C+	C-	573.0	9.71	11.4	0.0	14.6	1.0	**10.0**	11.5	15.2
FIRST GREEN BANK	Mount Dora	FL	**B-**	C+	C	304.2	20.02	6.8	1.0	8.7	8.6	**8.8**	11.5	14.0
FIRST GUARANTY BANK	Hammond	LA	**B-**	C+	C	1473.7	3.57	11.6	1.0	7.0	44.7	**7.2**	9.1	14.3
FIRST GUARANTY BANK	Martin	KY	**B**	B	B	56.2	-3.79	5.5	6.6	16.1	14.7	**10.0**	18.0	46.4
FIRST HARRISON BANK	Corydon	IN	**B-**	C+	C	458.7	2.46	6.0	6.9	21.1	21.9	**9.6**	10.8	15.8
FIRST HAWAIIAN BANK	Honolulu	HI	**A-**	A-	B+	18056.7	8.18	14.0	6.1	13.1	23.3	**9.0**	10.3	17.7
FIRST HERITAGE BANK	Centralia	KS	**B+**	B+	A-	114.5	-0.97	6.6	1.6	5.9	57.0	**10.0**	11.4	21.7
FIRST HERITAGE BANK	Shenandoah	IA	**C+**	C+	C	41.4	1.42	9.3	3.7	17.4	37.3	**7.9**	9.6	16.5
FIRST HOME BANK	Seminole	FL	**E+**	E-	E-	76.4	9.45	4.0	1.1	19.4	3.2	**6.7**	8.7	13.0
FIRST HOME BANK	Mountain Grove	MO	**D+**	D+	D+	189.9	1.32	3.0	1.3	28.4	32.2	**6.4**	8.4	16.6
FIRST HOPE BANK A NATL BKG ASN	Hope	NJ	**C**	C	C+	472.5	5.57	3.7	0.3	13.3	24.7	**6.3**	8.4	13.6
FIRST ILLINOIS BANK	East Saint Louis	IL	**A**	A-	B+	45.1	-8.95	5.5	2.2	3.3	82.8	**10.0**	11.6	88.4
FIRST INDEPENDENCE BANK	Detroit	MI	**C+**	C+	C	247.1	6.72	20.0	0.2	13.9	3.6	**8.3**	9.9	15.0
▼ FIRST INDEPENDENT BANK	Aurora	MO	**C+**	C+	C-	92.5	3.08	6.6	6.8	25.1	20.7	**8.6**	10.1	17.9
FIRST INDEPENDENT BANK	Russell	MN	**B-**	B-	C+	276.8	-2.01	6.8	4.1	8.5	22.1	**6.3**	9.0	12.0
▲ FIRST INTERCONTINENTAL BANK	Doraville	GA	**C**	D+	D+	294.0	3.26	24.0	0.2	0.0	10.1	**10.0**	14.5	20.6
FIRST INTERNATIONAL BK & TRUST	Watford City	ND	**B+**	B+	B-	1821.3	21.91	14.7	5.7	11.3	18.3	**5.7**	8.1	11.5

Asset Quality Index	Adjusted Non-Performing Loans as a % of Total Loans	Adjusted Non-Performing Loans as a % of Capital	Net Charge-Offs Avg Loans	Profitability Index	Net Income ($Mil)	Return on Assets (R.O.A.)	Return on Equity (R.O.E.)	Net Interest Spread	Overhead Efficiency Ratio	Liquidity Index	Liquidity Ratio	Hot Money Ratio	Stability Index
6.5	na	0.0	na	8.0	0.2	4.10	4.11	2.01	85.9	4.0	1304.4	101.0	4.3
6.3	2.49	10.2	0.03	5.0	2.1	1.08	9.74	3.76	66.9	4.7	49.8	14.2	4.5
3.5	1.26	9.2	0.19	2.1	1.4	0.22	2.15	3.45	84.7	1.8	8.8	19.2	6.4
4.8	0.77	7.6	0.00	5.6	7.4	0.87	9.94	3.87	63.4	1.4	13.9	26.7	7.0
4.7	0.86	5.7	-0.11	6.5	2.2	1.06	9.71	4.63	57.6	0.7	12.3	37.8	5.7
4.1	4.21	15.8	0.23	3.1	0.2	0.29	1.51	3.56	79.6	1.7	22.9	24.5	6.3
4.9	4.67	12.9	0.09	2.4	0.1	0.21	0.77	3.63	87.9	2.9	22.3	15.2	6.2
9.7	0.00	0.0	0.00	3.9	0.1	0.60	2.86	3.04	67.0	2.4	53.7	36.2	7.4
10.0	0.03	0.1	0.03	1.4	0.1	0.05	0.47	2.61	99.5	6.2	48.3	5.0	7.0
5.8	2.33	10.3	0.18	2.3	0.4	0.27	1.40	3.39	88.1	1.0	12.1	31.8	6.8
6.3	1.17	6.9	0.17	4.0	0.6	0.76	7.42	3.70	73.5	2.7	29.0	18.0	5.4
3.5	4.31	24.0	0.20	2.6	0.1	0.15	0.91	4.28	87.4	3.8	11.6	9.3	7.5
8.9	0.46	2.7	-0.01	3.8	3.7	0.69	6.44	3.35	72.0	3.0	19.4	14.3	7.2
10.0	0.00	0.0	0.00	2.5	0.1	0.29	1.81	2.66	86.5	3.7	49.4	18.0	6.7
9.8	0.42	2.1	0.02	2.7	2.7	0.39	3.11	2.42	79.8	2.2	32.3	23.9	7.7
0.3	10.01	58.9	0.17	2.9	0.4	0.31	3.66	2.67	80.1	6.1	44.7	3.9	5.0
4.8	1.60	8.8	0.26	1.7	0.4	0.39	4.05	3.34	89.1	4.8	34.4	8.6	3.9
3.4	3.60	12.3	1.02	0.0	-0.2	-0.44	-4.03	3.39	101.8	6.4	63.6	6.1	4.6
6.0	1.07	8.0	0.19	2.9	4.7	0.42	4.06	2.79	80.7	2.3	12.9	17.9	7.6
3.7	4.76	21.3	0.90	1.3	0.2	0.05	0.33	3.24	92.0	2.4	29.8	19.5	6.9
9.7	0.25	0.4	0.01	3.9	0.5	0.79	2.82	3.41	68.6	5.4	70.3	12.8	7.6
6.5	2.13	7.8	0.12	2.7	1.2	0.45	3.07	3.46	80.9	5.1	45.3	10.6	6.2
6.4	1.03	9.5	0.26	2.8	0.9	0.44	5.18	3.42	77.1	0.7	12.8	46.8	3.9
4.9	1.96	11.0	0.19	2.3	2.0	0.33	3.28	3.10	84.3	4.2	28.2	10.2	4.3
9.8	0.00	0.0	0.00	3.7	0.1	0.63	6.53	3.64	75.4	1.8	17.7	19.8	5.1
7.3	0.00	0.0	0.00	3.0	0.4	0.27	1.27	3.68	87.5	0.8	18.2	40.8	7.9
5.7	2.60	12.3	0.30	1.7	0.1	0.12	0.67	4.00	94.2	1.6	13.0	21.7	7.0
10.0	0.00	0.0	0.03	2.9	0.5	0.54	3.76	2.60	78.9	4.8	53.8	14.4	7.8
10.0	0.15	0.4	0.00	0.5	-0.1	-0.28	-2.42	2.17	114.5	6.1	65.6	8.4	4.9
5.4	3.50	10.1	-0.23	2.9	0.7	0.44	2.52	3.19	84.4	3.6	26.5	12.3	6.7
4.2	2.31	16.2	0.02	2.5	1.2	0.41	4.41	2.80	88.8	2.3	21.7	18.3	4.3
2.4	3.59	19.2	0.13	6.1	2.3	1.14	10.95	3.92	59.8	3.8	31.7	13.2	5.5
1.9	4.91	29.7	0.24	3.9	1.1	0.39	3.34	3.73	88.6	1.7	7.4	19.7	5.2
3.6	1.45	9.7	0.16	2.7	1.2	0.42	4.00	3.14	84.9	3.1	20.0	14.0	4.0
9.6	0.00	0.0	0.11	3.9	0.6	0.61	3.64	2.79	67.2	3.4	31.8	15.1	7.7
2.9	3.03	11.4	0.15	3.2	0.1	0.12	0.52	5.65	99.4	2.0	3.4	18.0	8.1
5.2	1.26	7.9	-0.01	3.9	0.7	0.54	6.06	3.00	80.8	5.4	37.5	6.5	5.4
2.1	4.99	27.7	-0.06	1.0	1.1	0.18	2.36	2.96	110.5	2.3	17.9	17.7	3.0
3.1	3.22	17.9	0.01	4.7	1.3	0.75	3.77	4.23	70.1	1.4	6.8	24.1	6.8
6.2	1.70	9.4	0.02	2.7	0.8	0.33	2.40	3.46	84.3	1.0	17.3	33.4	7.4
7.5	2.55	6.9	-0.01	1.7	0.1	0.13	1.01	2.10	86.3	5.3	64.6	12.6	4.5
6.1	0.49	3.1	-0.11	3.5	2.0	0.51	4.58	3.39	83.9	4.0	22.3	9.8	6.9
8.0	0.64	2.8	0.00	2.7	0.2	0.28	2.46	3.06	84.2	2.3	46.6	34.1	5.7
2.9	1.99	14.7	-0.04	10.0	8.0	1.91	16.93	4.34	31.6	0.5	6.2	46.4	7.7
6.4	0.38	2.5	0.02	4.3	1.4	0.69	5.99	4.56	69.8	1.0	15.3	32.1	6.4
5.2	1.88	9.8	0.51	4.4	8.7	0.80	8.84	3.08	61.9	0.8	12.8	35.2	6.4
6.7	2.00	4.9	0.17	3.6	0.3	0.75	4.28	3.04	73.8	4.3	46.4	14.5	8.0
4.1	1.36	7.8	0.03	6.7	4.4	1.30	10.99	4.18	60.9	5.1	31.2	5.4	6.9
6.5	0.49	2.6	0.10	7.3	165.0	1.27	8.28	2.90	45.9	2.1	21.5	20.3	8.3
9.0	0.10	0.3	-0.06	4.6	1.0	1.11	9.09	3.19	66.2	1.7	23.9	23.4	7.8
6.2	1.00	5.5	0.01	5.5	0.4	1.39	14.24	4.18	67.0	4.2	29.7	10.7	5.1
3.6	1.36	9.2	0.27	3.2	0.4	0.80	10.02	4.20	82.7	4.3	28.4	9.4	1.8
6.8	0.77	4.9	-0.01	1.9	0.4	0.30	4.20	2.83	90.7	3.9	36.8	14.6	3.2
3.9	2.17	14.9	0.14	2.6	1.0	0.29	3.46	3.39	91.5	4.0	15.7	8.8	4.6
8.8	5.39	5.9	1.66	3.9	0.4	1.05	9.15	3.39	63.5	3.7	38.8	16.0	6.5
4.9	1.79	10.8	1.38	2.8	-0.1	0.26	3.18	4.04	93.6	2.7	35.2	20.3	2.9
4.7	1.30	7.2	0.12	3.4	0.3	0.41	4.15	3.72	80.9	3.3	36.5	17.1	5.3
5.3	0.49	3.6	0.16	6.1	2.3	1.12	12.38	4.02	55.2	3.4	23.1	12.9	5.8
5.3	0.52	2.3	0.52	8.2	3.7	1.83	12.99	3.88	53.2	3.3	33.3	16.2	6.2
5.8	0.83	6.9	0.16	9.4	30.1	2.35	30.36	4.76	54.1	4.2	8.0	7.0	7.3

Name	City	State	Rating	2013 Rating	2012 Rating	Total Assets ($Mil)	One Year Asset Growth	Asset Mix (As a % of Total Assets) Comm-ercial Loans	Cons-umer Loans	Mort-gage Loans	Secur-ities	Capital-ization Index	Lever-age Ratio	Risk-Based Capital Ratio
FIRST INTERNET BANK OF INDIANA	Indianapolis	IN	**C+**	C+	C-	924.9	25.45	7.4	11.1	27.0	13.9	**6.3**	8.9	11.9
FIRST INTERSTATE BK	Billings	MT	**C+**	C+	C-	7844.0	5.00	8.1	9.4	12.1	27.3	**7.0**	9.0	14.8
FIRST IOWA STATE BK	Albia	IA	**A-**	A-	A-	141.1	2.94	8.1	1.5	11.4	31.2	**10.0**	13.7	21.2
FIRST IPSWICH BANK	Ipswich	MA	**B-**	B-	C+	329.8	4.86	11.4	0.1	15.9	20.5	**8.7**	10.1	14.7
FIRST JACKSON BANK	Stevenson	AL	**C+**	C+	C-	221.8	0.15	4.1	6.1	14.2	33.1	**8.9**	10.2	16.9
FIRST KANSAS BANK	Hoisington	KS	**C+**	C+	B-	170.2	52.72	1.5	0.8	2.5	70.1	**6.3**	8.4	31.1
FIRST KENTUCKY BANK INC	Mayfield	KY	**B**	B	B	371.1	-2.30	3.0	5.8	29.3	25.7	**8.3**	9.8	16.2
FIRST KEYSTONE COMMUNITY BANK	Berwick	PA	**B+**	B+	B+	903.9	7.74	4.9	0.6	20.4	37.6	**6.7**	8.7	14.5
FIRST LANDMARK BANK	Marietta	GA	**B**	B-	B-	205.5	-1.45	17.7	0.4	3.4	22.8	**10.0**	11.5	15.9
FIRST LIBERTY BANK	Oklahoma City	OK	**B+**	B	B-	247.2	11.11	19.7	0.7	5.0	14.5	**8.4**	11.2	13.7
FIRST LIBERTY NATIONAL BK	Liberty	TX	**B**	B	A-	307.8	-4.42	9.7	15.9	7.6	43.3	**10.0**	11.0	26.7
FIRST MADISON BANK & TRUST	Athens	GA	**B**	B-	B-	166.7	5.37	9.1	2.3	20.9	1.3	**9.0**	10.3	14.3
FIRST MADISON VALLEY BANK	Ennis	MT	**B-**	C+	D+	142.9	4.95	5.8	4.7	14.0	30.8	**6.9**	8.9	15.5
FIRST MARINER BANK	Baltimore	MD	**E**	E-	E-	875.7	-19.15	2.7	2.3	25.4	10.7	**7.4**	9.3	14.6
FIRST MERCHANTS BANK NA	Muncie	IN	**B**	B	B-	5569.1	29.14	16.2	1.2	11.9	21.6	**9.2**	10.4	14.3
FIRST METRO BANK	Muscle Shoals	AL	**A**	A	A-	529.7	5.42	6.9	3.2	21.6	29.8	**10.0**	11.2	19.6
FIRST MID-ILLINOIS BK & TR NA	Mattoon	IL	**B+**	B+	B+	1584.1	3.12	13.3	1.0	10.0	27.1	**8.5**	10.0	15.1
FIRST MIDWEST BANK	Itasca	IL	**B-**	B-	C	8975.6	7.12	20.3	0.8	5.5	11.2	**5.9**	9.4	11.7
FIRST MIDWEST BANK OF DEXTER	Dexter	MO	**B-**	B-	B-	277.1	6.95	14.6	2.2	10.7	15.4	**6.5**	9.7	12.1
FIRST MIDWEST BK OF THE OZARKS	Piedmont	MO	**B**	B	B-	112.9	-0.81	11.7	4.6	13.8	17.6	**7.5**	9.8	12.9
FIRST MIDWEST BK POPLAR BLUFF	Poplar Bluff	MO	**B-**	B-	C	319.6	8.90	19.4	4.2	16.7	8.5	**5.9**	8.6	11.7
▲ FIRST MINNESOTA BANK	Minnetonka	MN	**B**	C	C-	415.2	-0.20	3.8	0.8	9.3	53.3	**10.0**	11.8	22.1
FIRST MINNETONKA CITY BANK	Minnetonka	MN	**B**	B	B	195.5	-3.33	9.6	1.9	12.4	41.0	**8.8**	10.2	18.1
▲ FIRST MISSOURI BANK	Brookfield	MO	**B+**	B	B-	155.0	1.96	8.2	4.5	20.9	10.5	**10.0**	11.3	15.9
FIRST MISSOURI STATE BK	Poplar Bluff	MO	**C+**	C-	C	154.8	-0.84	8.3	5.0	32.0	6.4	**10.0**	11.3	15.4
▲ FIRST MO STATE BK OF CAPE CTY	Cape Girardeau	MO	**C+**	C-	C-	125.7	3.27	10.4	2.5	23.5	8.3	**6.9**	8.9	12.8
FIRST MONTANA BANK INC	Missoula	MT	**B-**	B-	C+	287.0	-0.88	10.4	6.5	9.3	27.4	**8.8**	10.2	15.6
FIRST MOUNTAIN BANK	Big Bear Lake	CA	**D-**	D-	D-	136.2	2.63	7.6	1.1	3.7	8.5	**7.5**	9.3	13.8
FIRST NATIONAL B&T ELK CITY	Elk City	OK	**A-**	A	A	323.3	3.25	11.4	1.6	16.7	28.9	**8.6**	10.0	17.9
FIRST NATIONAL BANK	Alamogordo	NM	**A**	A	A-	308.8	-1.99	3.2	1.8	5.6	47.4	**10.0**	11.8	22.4
FIRST NATIONAL BANK OF SONORA	Sonora	TX	**B-**	B-	C+	349.3	3.68	5.9	4.4	17.7	22.0	**8.6**	10.1	17.5
FIRST NATIONAL BANKERS BANK	Baton Rouge	LA	**B-**	B-	B	818.5	-6.82	7.8	0.0	0.5	13.0	**10.0**	17.0	28.4
FIRST NATIONAL BK	Lenoir City	TN	**B-**	B-	C	419.8	6.44	3.9	0.7	16.5	32.7	**9.1**	10.4	17.0
FIRST NATIONAL BK	Hamilton	AL	**A**	A	A	284.1	2.83	2.6	8.5	12.8	49.5	**10.0**	14.7	29.5
FIRST NATIONAL BK	Davenport	IA	**C+**	C	C	64.1	0.70	10.3	13.9	10.0	20.3	**10.0**	13.5	17.6
FIRST NATIONAL BK	Cloverdale	IN	**C+**	C+	C+	254.8	2.12	2.8	1.3	23.8	18.5	**7.8**	9.5	19.5
FIRST NATIONAL BK	Orrville	OH	**B**	B	C+	525.8	13.47	7.1	5.3	20.0	15.8	**6.4**	8.4	12.6
FIRST NATIONAL BK	Ronceverte	WV	**D+**	D+	D+	254.0	0.39	3.7	1.2	18.8	34.6	**9.2**	10.5	18.5
FIRST NATIONAL BK	Altavista	VA	**C+**	C+	C	361.1	2.26	7.0	14.8	16.6	8.3	**7.2**	9.6	12.7
FIRST NATIONAL BK	Milnor	ND	**B+**	B+	A-	72.3	-3.62	9.6	3.7	3.2	36.7	**10.0**	14.1	22.0
FIRST NATIONAL BK	Fort Pierre	SD	**A**	A	A-	758.0	5.38	6.8	16.5	6.5	17.0	**10.0**	23.3	31.7
FIRST NATIONAL BK	Slayton	MN	**C+**	C+	C+	198.2	0.11	5.7	6.0	3.6	21.9	**8.6**	10.1	14.4
FIRST NATIONAL BK	Goodland	KS	**C+**	C	C-	187.3	0.37	1.9	1.1	1.8	46.8	**10.0**	12.6	23.7
FIRST NATIONAL BK	Camdenton	MO	**D**	D	C	225.1	-11.08	0.3	0.7	12.7	59.2	**10.0**	15.0	42.1
▲ FIRST NATIONAL BK	Malden	MO	**B**	B-	C+	173.8	4.86	10.8	2.0	26.2	4.7	**7.4**	9.4	12.8
FIRST NATIONAL BK	Mattoon	IL	**C**	C+	C+	71.7	0.26	15.5	3.5	12.3	29.4	**9.6**	10.8	16.5
FIRST NATIONAL BK	Vandalia	IL	**B-**	B-	B	308.6	4.24	7.0	1.4	16.9	37.5	**8.5**	10.0	17.7
FIRST NATIONAL BK	Paragould	AR	**A**	A	A	848.6	14.30	5.6	3.4	25.2	12.9	**10.0**	11.9	16.2
FIRST NATIONAL BK	Hot Springs	AR	**B**	A-	B+	619.2	-10.36	6.4	3.4	15.9	15.9	**6.8**	9.2	12.3
▼ FIRST NATIONAL BK	Waupaca	WI	**D-**	D+	C	777.9	-2.20	7.2	2.1	17.1	8.6	**8.7**	10.6	13.9
FIRST NATIONAL BK	Fontanelle	IA	**B+**	B+	C+	210.9	0.43	7.0	1.0	6.9	19.6	**8.9**	10.4	14.1
FIRST NATIONAL BK	Waverly	IA	**C+**	C+	C+	324.7	2.01	17.8	1.3	11.5	12.4	**10.0**	11.4	15.0
FIRST NATIONAL BK	Spearman	TX	**B+**	B	B	196.5	1.72	10.1	2.3	6.0	30.0	**8.5**	10.0	15.5
FIRST NATIONAL BK	Fabens	TX	**A**	A	A-	322.7	0.15	15.0	0.7	8.0	25.4	**9.8**	10.9	17.4
FIRST NATIONAL BK	Groesbeck	TX	**C+**	C+	C	55.3	5.46	2.3	4.4	30.3	30.7	**9.0**	10.3	24.2
FIRST NATIONAL BK	Wichita Falls	TX	**B+**	B	B-	358.0	13.17	7.6	2.4	21.8	9.5	**7.0**	9.4	12.5
FIRST NATIONAL BK	Arcadia	LA	**B+**	B	B-	211.2	6.46	6.6	2.1	21.9	4.9	**6.0**	8.5	11.8
FIRST NATIONAL BK	Rotan	TX	**B**	B-	B-	75.3	-3.55	9.0	4.5	1.0	48.9	**9.4**	10.6	19.7
FIRST NATIONAL BK	Heavener	OK	**B+**	B+	B+	75.8	0.45	3.4	4.3	15.2	11.4	**8.4**	9.9	18.4
FIRST NATIONAL BK & TRUST	Phillipsburg	KS	**B+**	B+	A-	198.2	3.12	6.9	4.9	11.7	38.6	**10.0**	13.7	19.6

Asset Quality Index	Adjusted Non-Performing Loans as a % of Total Loans	Adjusted Non-Performing Loans as a % of Capital	Net Charge-Offs Avg Loans	Profitability Index	Net Income ($Mil)	Return on Assets (R.O.A.)	Return on Equity (R.O.E.)	Net Interest Spread	Overhead Efficiency Ratio	Liquidity Index	Liquidity Ratio	Hot Money Ratio	Stability Index
6.8	0.13	1.2	-0.02	3.8	3.8	0.59	6.44	2.67	76.2	0.8	17.6	37.6	4.5
3.7	1.86	11.1	0.13	7.2	68.2	1.20	11.18	3.57	62.4	4.5	22.2	8.2	8.5
6.0	1.37	5.9	0.03	8.7	2.1	1.94	14.31	4.63	46.3	3.3	37.8	17.7	8.1
3.3	2.20	14.8	0.01	3.1	1.1	0.46	4.07	3.45	78.1	4.6	6.8	3.3	6.6
4.4	1.88	9.1	0.21	4.3	1.4	0.87	9.57	3.83	61.6	1.6	30.9	32.5	4.2
9.9	0.00	0.0	0.00	3.9	0.9	0.89	11.61	2.38	68.7	6.1	56.3	8.0	4.7
5.1	1.19	7.3	0.07	5.1	3.6	1.29	13.22	3.94	71.7	2.1	27.3	20.1	6.6
5.0	1.15	6.7	0.13	4.7	7.5	1.12	10.30	3.49	67.1	3.9	16.1	9.3	7.6
6.0	1.51	7.6	0.00	4.3	1.1	0.72	6.31	3.94	70.5	3.0	17.5	14.4	6.3
8.4	0.00	0.0	-0.70	6.2	1.9	1.14	10.54	4.17	57.4	2.5	31.1	19.3	5.3
8.0	0.04	0.2	0.17	4.6	2.6	1.10	10.37	2.98	66.7	3.8	30.7	13.2	7.2
4.7	0.54	3.1	0.13	7.8	1.7	1.37	13.70	4.63	44.2	2.2	18.5	18.3	6.2
5.0	1.32	7.5	0.07	4.4	1.1	1.08	12.41	4.18	75.0	5.0	44.8	11.3	4.4
1.7	3.72	25.0	-0.20	0.6	-2.4	-0.87	-11.44	2.84	112.6	0.9	19.6	38.5	0.5
4.6	1.31	7.9	0.14	6.2	49.1	1.20	8.75	4.12	63.2	3.3	17.1	13.3	8.2
8.8	0.08	0.4	0.19	9.1	5.8	1.49	14.86	3.95	45.0	1.8	14.1	19.9	8.0
7.6	0.37	2.2	0.01	6.0	12.4	1.04	9.80	3.57	61.1	3.9	13.3	9.2	8.6
4.1	1.44	11.0	0.67	5.2	64.3	1.03	7.86	3.84	62.4	4.4	11.0	5.6	8.3
4.2	1.48	10.4	0.13	5.3	1.8	0.88	9.31	3.67	66.5	1.3	12.4	27.5	5.6
5.2	0.88	6.2	0.03	5.6	0.8	1.00	10.22	4.19	67.3	1.5	12.0	23.9	5.6
4.6	0.77	6.9	0.10	6.7	3.7	1.58	18.39	4.22	59.6	1.0	2.7	28.9	6.4
6.9	3.08	8.0	0.01	4.3	2.5	0.82	7.40	3.38	63.6	2.5	34.3	21.5	5.7
7.5	0.58	2.6	0.18	5.3	1.9	1.28	12.64	3.52	65.9	5.4	50.5	10.6	6.2
6.1	0.84	5.7	0.14	5.3	1.4	1.22	11.47	4.52	68.8	1.1	14.4	30.4	6.3
4.1	1.75	12.5	0.18	9.0	2.6	2.28	21.12	4.24	46.0	1.1	4.8	26.9	6.5
3.3	1.64	13.6	0.25	5.1	1.1	1.17	13.31	3.92	69.1	1.3	5.2	24.3	5.8
4.5	1.34	7.5	0.00	4.3	1.4	0.67	6.31	3.99	73.3	4.3	25.6	8.5	5.2
0.0	10.69	63.5	-0.14	2.5	0.4	0.43	4.67	4.02	90.8	2.9	26.6	16.1	4.6
6.2	0.70	3.9	0.10	8.8	5.3	2.15	20.46	3.83	44.8	2.2	22.1	18.6	8.4
8.9	0.70	2.5	0.01	6.4	3.6	1.54	13.90	4.31	66.5	4.9	32.1	7.5	8.3
3.9	2.51	13.9	0.07	4.5	2.8	1.06	10.16	3.92	76.9	2.2	28.8	21.4	5.6
6.6	1.61	4.6	0.13	3.2	2.9	0.49	2.83	2.63	83.9	6.8	46.6	0.0	7.1
8.3	0.39	2.1	0.21	3.7	2.0	0.65	6.15	3.37	74.5	2.9	27.2	16.1	5.2
8.6	0.56	1.5	0.21	6.8	3.2	1.53	10.45	4.17	60.9	3.8	48.7	18.4	8.8
6.9	0.69	3.0	2.44	3.1	0.2	0.39	2.94	7.20	62.9	4.4	14.2	6.2	5.9
5.2	1.61	8.3	0.25	3.2	0.9	0.47	4.96	3.12	80.1	5.4	42.3	8.2	5.6
6.4	0.44	3.7	0.04	5.5	4.3	1.14	12.02	3.72	59.8	4.1	11.6	7.7	6.0
1.7	7.78	35.4	0.01	3.4	1.2	0.65	5.87	3.21	80.6	4.6	42.6	12.8	5.0
3.9	1.08	8.0	0.17	4.2	1.8	0.69	7.22	3.62	76.1	3.6	19.4	11.5	4.9
8.3	0.64	2.5	0.00	4.7	0.6	1.07	7.48	4.04	72.5	3.6	20.5	11.7	8.3
7.0	0.60	1.6	3.25	10.0	15.4	2.73	11.67	9.01	40.3	3.6	15.5	11.0	9.2
5.2	0.95	5.0	0.70	3.9	0.7	0.49	4.75	4.64	69.6	4.8	24.0	4.5	5.5
2.7	6.49	22.8	0.56	4.1	0.9	0.60	4.71	3.12	84.2	4.9	35.8	9.1	4.3
5.4	7.44	12.4	0.31	0.0	-3.2	-1.79	-12.58	2.66	179.7	4.3	48.3	15.7	4.7
6.1	0.30	2.6	0.04	5.6	1.3	0.96	11.10	3.92	61.9	2.2	6.4	17.4	5.1
6.4	0.57	2.9	0.19	2.6	0.3	0.53	4.82	3.44	91.3	2.5	28.0	18.4	5.9
6.1	0.92	4.7	-0.01	4.5	2.0	0.88	7.93	3.51	69.3	4.0	33.5	12.7	6.8
8.1	0.42	2.7	0.15	8.0	7.9	1.36	11.07	4.05	50.1	1.3	3.0	24.0	8.0
5.8	0.52	3.8	0.01	5.4	2.6	1.41	8.78	4.76	49.0	3.8	11.2	9.5	7.6
0.0	7.43	50.6	0.65	4.5	5.4	0.93	8.27	4.48	59.3	0.7	12.8	35.4	7.3
6.7	0.04	0.2	-0.01	5.7	2.1	1.33	11.07	3.79	60.9	1.7	13.0	20.3	7.4
3.6	2.16	13.9	0.00	5.3	2.3	0.95	8.22	3.61	62.6	3.8	19.9	10.4	6.8
5.4	1.29	7.4	-0.02	6.7	2.4	1.66	16.86	4.22	59.0	1.2	24.3	32.4	6.3
8.5	0.11	0.6	0.03	9.8	6.7	2.77	26.40	4.24	50.2	1.1	13.8	29.8	7.7
4.8	2.18	9.5	-0.13	2.8	0.1	0.30	2.89	3.60	89.9	2.7	39.3	24.4	5.1
5.7	0.40	3.3	-0.03	5.9	3.2	1.30	12.88	4.93	75.7	2.6	8.1	15.5	6.4
4.9	0.89	7.8	0.05	9.0	3.3	2.13	24.97	5.45	61.7	2.7	11.4	15.2	6.9
6.8	0.22	0.9	-0.01	5.3	0.7	1.24	12.76	3.90	65.2	3.5	31.7	14.9	6.1
8.0	0.28	1.7	0.08	7.8	0.7	1.13	11.89	5.04	70.5	3.2	27.1	14.7	6.2
8.1	0.39	1.5	0.11	4.4	1.5	1.01	7.28	3.70	71.7	3.3	30.5	15.1	7.9

Name	City	State	Rating	2013 Rating	2012 Rating	Total Assets ($Mil)	One Year Asset Growth	Asset Mix (As a % of Total Assets) Comm-ercial Loans	Cons-umer Loans	Mort-gage Loans	Secur-ities	Capital-ization Index	Lever-age Ratio	Risk-Based Capital Ratio
FIRST NATIONAL BK & TRUST	London	KY	**C**	C	D+	205.7	6.73	5.2	3.8	16.2	39.1	**9.3**	10.5	18.5
FIRST NATIONAL BK & TRUST	Atmore	AL	**C-**	C+	D+	126.2	-5.01	3.3	4.3	14.2	38.7	**10.0**	12.1	21.4
FIRST NATIONAL BK & TRUST CO	Rochelle	IL	**C+**	C+	C	260.3	5.39	1.2	1.5	9.4	64.2	**6.0**	8.0	19.6
FIRST NATIONAL BK & TRUST CO	Clinton	IL	**C+**	C+	B-	115.2	-4.52	4.8	1.1	11.7	35.6	**10.0**	11.2	25.0
▼ FIRST NATIONAL BK & TRUST CO	Newtown	PA	**C+**	C+	C	815.6	0.98	0.8	1.7	11.9	49.3	**8.2**	9.8	22.9
FIRST NATIONAL BK & TRUST CO	Iron Mountain	MI	**C+**	C+	C+	321.8	4.48	7.3	2.6	14.1	36.4	**6.3**	8.3	14.6
FIRST NATIONAL BK & TRUST CO	Williston	ND	**A-**	B	B-	465.5	10.98	7.0	1.4	5.4	46.7	**6.1**	8.1	16.1
FIRST NATIONAL BK & TRUST CO	Bottineau	ND	**C-**	C	B-	146.6	0.89	4.0	3.5	6.9	35.5	**8.4**	9.9	17.5
FIRST NATIONAL BK & TRUST CO	Beloit	WI	**B-**	B-	B-	805.1	-1.57	11.3	1.5	16.9	21.2	**9.6**	10.7	15.0
FIRST NATIONAL BK & TRUST CO	McAlester	OK	**C+**	C+	B-	449.2	0.64	4.2	1.8	8.2	47.3	**10.0**	11.6	23.0
FIRST NATIONAL BK & TRUST CO	Miami	OK	**C**	C+	C+	131.2	3.03	5.8	6.1	14.7	22.2	**8.3**	9.9	17.5
▲ FIRST NATIONAL BK & TRUST CO	Okmulgee	OK	**B**	C	C-	267.2	13.97	10.8	3.8	16.4	38.0	**10.0**	11.5	17.8
FIRST NATIONAL BK & TRUST CO	Chickasha	OK	**C+**	C+	B-	471.8	6.80	19.5	3.4	8.6	24.6	**9.6**	10.7	17.3
FIRST NATIONAL BK & TRUST CO	Ardmore	OK	**B**	B	B-	502.5	5.37	8.2	4.0	8.3	52.2	**6.1**	8.2	16.9
FIRST NATIONAL BK & TRUST CO	Broken Arrow	OK	**D+**	D	D+	187.8	3.40	11.2	1.0	20.2	25.4	**6.6**	8.6	15.6
FIRST NATIONAL BK & TRUST CO	Weatherford	OK	**B**	B	A-	221.7	7.23	14.4	3.6	8.1	11.0	**6.3**	9.5	12.0
FIRST NATIONAL BK & TRUST CO	Vinita	OK	**B-**	B-	C	353.1	2.35	11.5	4.9	9.3	45.3	**6.6**	8.6	13.5
▲ FIRST NATIONAL BK & TRUST CO	Shawnee	OK	**C+**	C	C	240.1	2.73	11.3	1.1	7.7	46.7	**10.0**	11.3	20.5
FIRST NATIONAL BK - FOX VALLEY	Neenah	WI	**B**	B-	B-	369.3	3.50	19.1	2.6	20.6	7.9	**9.3**	10.7	14.4
FIRST NATIONAL BK ALASKA	Anchorage	AK	**A**	A	A-	3244.3	3.39	7.0	0.5	3.1	52.6	**10.0**	14.5	22.6
FIRST NATIONAL BK AMES IOWA	Ames	IA	**A-**	A-	A-	680.9	12.09	3.4	0.2	9.0	47.2	**8.6**	10.1	15.2
FIRST NATIONAL BK ARENZVILLE	Arenzville	IL	**C+**	C+	C	81.1	18.79	9.3	5.4	14.0	17.5	**6.6**	8.6	16.2
▲ FIRST NATIONAL BK ASSUMPTION	Assumption	IL	**C**	C-	C	22.2	3.13	1.6	5.1	13.9	42.3	**8.0**	9.7	22.0
FIRST NATIONAL BK AT PARIS	Paris	AR	**A-**	A-	B+	124.4	1.74	3.0	6.0	25.6	9.2	**10.0**	12.0	18.7
FIRST NATIONAL BK BATTLE LAKE	Battle Lake	MN	**A**	A	A-	74.8	6.87	2.2	4.1	13.3	50.6	**10.0**	11.0	20.6
FIRST NATIONAL BK BEARDSTOWN	Beardstown	IL	**B**	B	B	109.0	4.11	5.9	10.0	17.4	7.0	**10.0**	11.6	16.3
FIRST NATIONAL BK BLANCHESTER	Blanchester	OH	**B+**	B+	B+	56.1	-1.93	0.8	7.8	51.1	22.3	**10.0**	12.1	20.6
FIRST NATIONAL BK BOSQUE CTY	Valley Mills	TX	**B-**	B-	C+	109.2	1.73	10.8	7.6	19.2	6.0	**7.9**	9.6	19.8
FIRST NATIONAL BK BROOKFIELD	Brookfield	IL	**E-**	E-	E-	146.9	-2.63	1.4	0.3	32.2	14.0	**2.0**	4.8	9.0
FIRST NATIONAL BK BROOKSVILLE	Brooksville	KY	**C**	C	C+	62.5	-1.19	1.1	3.8	41.7	27.4	**9.7**	10.8	21.8
FIRST NATIONAL BK BROWNSTOWN	Brownstown	IL	**C**	C	C	36.1	0.47	3.0	6.8	13.3	37.0	**8.5**	10.0	21.2
FIRST NATIONAL BK CARROLLTON	Carrollton	KY	**B**	B-	B	103.6	3.29	2.1	1.5	34.3	26.5	**10.0**	11.2	20.6
FIRST NATIONAL BK CENTRAL TX	Waco	TX	**B**	B	B	742.8	2.28	12.6	1.8	12.7	13.2	**6.0**	8.1	12.2
FIRST NATIONAL BK CHILLICOTHE	Chillicothe	TX	**B**	B	B+	47.8	2.65	3.3	4.5	7.6	52.5	**10.0**	12.2	26.1
▼ FIRST NATIONAL BK CLARKSDALE	Clarksdale	MS	**B+**	A-	A-	365.7	2.18	8.0	3.3	8.9	31.9	**9.7**	10.8	16.5
FIRST NATIONAL BK COFFEE CTY	Douglas	GA	**B+**	B	B	130.0	0.05	5.4	1.3	12.6	17.3	**10.0**	12.9	21.3
FIRST NATIONAL BK CORTEZ	Cortez	CO	**C**	C	C	94.6	-2.38	3.5	2.8	12.7	49.1	**7.3**	9.2	18.9
FIRST NATIONAL BK CUNNINGHAM	Cunningham	KS	**B-**	B-	B	33.2	0.89	3.5	3.0	8.1	55.4	**8.1**	9.8	19.9
FIRST NATIONAL BK DARLINGTON	Darlington	WI	**A-**	A-	A-	99.2	2.80	4.3	5.3	7.9	23.9	**10.0**	14.0	19.7
▲ FIRST NATIONAL BK DECATUR CTY	Bainbridge	GA	**B-**	B-	C	102.3	-6.95	7.9	4.9	15.2	29.6	**10.0**	11.7	21.2
▲ FIRST NATIONAL BK EAGLE LAKE	Eagle Lake	TX	**B-**	C	C	109.8	1.34	12.8	1.3	4.8	16.2	**7.8**	9.6	13.3
▲ FIRST NATIONAL BK EAGLE RIVER	Eagle River	WI	**D+**	D	D	140.5	-3.00	2.3	0.7	42.0	27.3	**7.0**	9.0	16.9
FIRST NATIONAL BK EASTERN AR	Forrest City	AR	**C+**	C+	B-	374.2	5.05	4.3	2.4	5.2	38.7	**8.4**	9.9	21.5
FIRST NATIONAL BK FALFURRIAS	Falfurrias	TX	**C**	C	C+	71.0	6.31	9.2	9.3	0.5	60.5	**10.0**	11.2	42.5
FIRST NATIONAL BK FORT SMITH	Fort Smith	AR	**B+**	B+	B	1180.3	10.48	16.4	1.5	7.8	22.2	**10.0**	12.0	17.9
FIRST NATIONAL BK GEORGETOWN	Georgetown	IL	**C+**	C	C	51.2	7.72	8.4	0.6	4.1	11.9	**4.2**	8.9	10.6
▲ FIRST NATIONAL BK GERMANTOWN	Germantown	OH	**C**	D+	D-	53.4	6.13	8.4	2.6	26.9	16.3	**7.2**	9.1	14.8
FIRST NATIONAL BK HARTFORD	Hartford	WI	**C+**	C	B-	180.7	3.81	9.4	0.7	11.7	23.6	**10.0**	11.9	18.3
▼ FIRST NATIONAL BK HARVEYVILLE	Harveyville	KS	**C-**	C+	C-	14.0	18.04	5.4	4.2	26.4	6.5	**8.0**	9.6	22.9
FIRST NATIONAL BK HEBBRONVILLE	Hebbronville	TX	**A-**	A-	A-	142.8	5.97	3.6	8.9	6.8	62.8	**10.0**	11.4	30.5
FIRST NATIONAL BK HUNTSVILLE	Huntsville	TX	**B-**	B-	B	432.0	5.07	7.5	5.8	18.0	48.6	**8.2**	9.8	22.8
FIRST NATIONAL BK HUTCHINSON	Hutchinson	KS	**B-**	B-	B-	615.2	6.06	7.9	1.5	6.5	39.5	**10.0**	11.1	17.8
▲ FIRST NATIONAL BK IN ALTUS	Altus	OK	**B+**	B	B-	283.5	-2.91	16.4	0.8	2.4	46.7	**8.1**	9.8	17.6
FIRST NATIONAL BK IN AMBOY	Amboy	IL	**C+**	B-	C+	181.8	4.48	6.0	1.6	8.1	48.4	**8.8**	10.2	20.5
FIRST NATIONAL BK IN CARLYLE	Carlyle	IL	**B+**	B+	B+	147.4	-0.38	2.4	1.9	10.1	41.2	**10.0**	13.5	25.1
FIRST NATIONAL BK IN CIMARRON	Cimarron	KS	**B-**	B-	B-	84.7	-3.34	4.2	3.5	8.7	47.0	**6.2**	8.2	15.7
FIRST NATIONAL BK IN COOPER	Cooper	TX	**B-**	B-	C+	47.7	-0.64	5.3	6.6	19.6	22.2	**8.1**	12.4	13.4
FIRST NATIONAL BK IN CRESTON	Creston	IA	**B**	B	B-	234.5	6.68	12.0	5.5	15.8	12.6	**5.6**	8.4	11.5
FIRST NATIONAL BK IN DALHART	Dalhart	TX	**B**	B	B	73.9	8.32	7.6	0.8	0.8	19.9	**8.9**	10.3	15.7
FIRST NATIONAL BK IN DE RIDDER	DeRidder	LA	**A-**	A-	A-	200.6	8.52	2.5	3.3	28.9	35.5	**10.0**	12.9	20.9

Asset Quality Index	Adjusted Non-Performing Loans as a % of Total Loans	Adjusted Non-Performing Loans as a % of Capital	Net Charge-Offs Avg Loans	Profitability Index	Net Income ($Mil)	Return on Assets (R.O.A.)	Return on Equity (R.O.E.)	Net Interest Spread	Overhead Efficiency Ratio	Liquidity Index	Liquidity Ratio	Hot Money Ratio	Stability Index
4.4	2.61	11.5	0.11	2.9	1.0	0.60	5.54	3.82	82.2	1.8	18.7	21.4	5.5
5.9	2.04	7.2	-0.16	1.5	0.2	0.15	1.47	3.81	97.5	4.0	37.8	14.2	5.4
6.2	1.22	4.0	0.07	3.4	1.7	0.87	9.85	3.12	77.4	4.6	38.7	11.4	4.6
9.5	0.65	1.9	0.00	3.1	0.5	0.54	5.10	2.49	77.9	5.8	41.1	5.3	6.7
2.7	6.72	25.5	0.00	4.0	4.8	0.78	8.26	2.96	72.9	6.2	47.1	4.5	6.4
4.1	2.02	12.5	0.32	3.5	1.4	0.59	6.66	3.52	77.7	3.3	38.8	18.3	4.5
8.9	0.00	0.0	-0.29	8.1	6.7	2.03	23.83	2.99	43.8	6.5	52.2	4.1	6.0
2.7	3.30	16.2	0.10	3.5	0.6	0.55	5.78	2.77	71.7	4.5	30.3	8.9	7.2
5.9	0.66	4.1	0.15	4.4	5.6	0.91	7.79	3.90	74.6	3.3	17.7	12.6	6.8
2.8	6.25	22.6	0.01	7.6	6.2	1.84	15.75	3.52	48.5	3.8	41.5	16.5	9.1
6.4	0.38	2.1	0.35	3.3	0.5	0.45	4.94	3.50	80.1	4.4	17.2	6.1	4.4
5.0	2.44	11.0	-0.50	6.1	2.3	1.25	11.45	4.53	74.5	2.4	28.4	19.4	7.6
3.5	1.85	10.3	0.92	8.1	4.7	1.35	11.13	4.89	53.9	3.8	26.0	11.1	8.2
8.2	0.23	1.1	-0.03	4.4	4.0	1.08	12.19	3.31	70.8	4.0	43.6	15.7	6.0
3.5	2.14	13.1	0.11	1.7	0.3	0.24	2.83	3.39	92.5	5.6	34.5	3.5	3.8
5.0	1.33	9.9	0.17	6.5	2.4	1.49	14.73	4.53	66.1	2.4	17.7	17.2	6.8
5.4	0.88	4.5	0.17	5.4	3.2	1.24	15.33	3.59	63.7	1.3	15.3	26.9	5.7
7.5	0.80	2.8	-0.06	2.7	0.7	0.40	3.24	3.70	88.4	5.4	50.1	10.7	6.1
4.9	0.68	5.0	0.22	4.9	2.3	0.84	7.88	3.99	66.9	1.4	8.6	24.1	4.9
8.6	0.94	2.7	0.00	6.2	25.2	1.06	7.27	3.42	61.5	5.8	30.0	4.5	10.0
7.9	0.61	2.7	0.03	6.3	5.9	1.23	11.69	3.00	48.1	5.3	36.3	6.5	8.1
4.9	0.92	5.8	0.03	3.7	0.6	0.89	10.98	3.06	71.1	4.4	34.7	11.3	4.1
9.4	0.29	0.9	-0.09	3.3	0.1	0.69	8.03	3.04	75.0	5.5	48.5	6.0	3.8
6.5	0.24	1.4	0.04	7.5	1.5	1.59	10.57	5.09	68.6	1.3	15.0	27.4	8.9
8.5	0.00	0.0	0.06	7.3	1.0	1.87	15.24	3.82	56.3	5.0	44.0	10.8	7.7
6.9	0.73	4.5	0.05	4.7	0.8	1.05	9.04	3.98	75.6	1.6	19.5	24.5	6.6
8.8	0.16	0.9	0.02	5.2	0.4	0.94	7.60	3.92	68.6	2.5	15.4	16.5	6.7
5.0	1.10	5.6	0.16	3.6	0.7	0.79	8.15	3.35	75.0	4.8	41.7	11.4	5.9
2.7	2.03	22.8	-0.01	1.8	0.2	0.22	4.56	4.24	92.9	3.8	23.0	10.9	0.3
5.5	1.81	10.0	0.13	3.0	0.3	0.57	5.48	3.44	82.0	4.0	18.3	9.2	5.3
5.3	1.55	6.5	0.33	3.2	0.2	0.54	5.44	3.13	76.3	4.3	39.8	13.5	4.9
4.8	2.42	13.2	0.07	6.1	1.1	1.46	13.29	3.85	65.8	1.5	25.7	28.6	6.1
4.8	0.82	6.5	0.07	7.4	9.6	1.76	22.69	3.89	52.1	3.1	19.6	14.1	7.3
8.2	0.93	2.8	0.07	5.1	0.5	1.21	9.87	4.16	70.6	2.9	51.4	27.5	6.7
5.4	1.04	5.3	0.01	5.4	2.8	1.01	9.94	3.58	64.1	2.8	27.1	16.8	6.7
5.1	2.47	11.8	0.08	7.3	1.6	1.69	13.93	3.93	62.2	2.8	33.0	18.7	6.8
5.8	1.76	7.2	0.02	3.0	0.2	0.33	3.67	3.65	85.0	1.8	17.9	21.4	4.8
8.3	0.54	2.0	0.00	5.0	0.3	1.29	13.95	3.93	69.1	5.2	44.8	9.7	5.8
7.6	0.76	3.5	0.01	6.4	0.8	1.09	7.87	3.94	61.5	4.1	33.3	12.4	7.5
4.6	2.58	11.1	0.31	3.3	0.5	0.64	5.83	3.20	72.6	2.2	32.6	25.2	5.3
6.1	0.18	1.2	0.12	5.1	1.0	1.26	13.55	5.17	73.3	4.5	19.5	6.2	4.6
2.7	4.32	26.8	0.31	1.5	0.3	0.27	3.14	3.08	92.3	4.6	17.3	5.3	3.3
8.9	0.11	0.4	0.02	3.5	1.9	0.69	6.98	2.80	75.0	3.7	47.8	18.7	6.1
5.9	5.17	10.0	0.59	2.6	0.3	0.46	4.34	2.32	82.1	4.8	28.9	6.2	4.6
4.6	1.97	10.0	0.08	8.1	11.2	1.26	9.49	3.96	57.4	4.1	25.0	11.9	9.0
2.8	2.21	18.1	0.00	6.9	0.4	0.96	8.63	3.80	56.7	2.4	9.5	16.5	5.7
3.8	2.43	16.9	0.40	3.1	0.2	0.57	6.04	4.01	86.0	4.5	25.2	6.8	3.4
5.7	0.95	4.6	0.91	3.1	0.7	0.50	4.22	3.40	80.5	5.3	36.3	6.6	6.6
6.4	1.06	5.7	0.02	2.6	0.0	0.28	2.68	3.55	90.1	3.5	39.4	15.1	4.1
7.9	1.42	3.1	0.04	6.2	1.6	1.60	12.97	3.20	52.2	2.9	59.5	48.0	8.4
8.4	0.07	0.3	0.01	4.0	2.3	0.71	6.30	2.82	71.0	4.1	33.9	12.3	7.0
6.6	1.30	5.6	0.16	3.7	3.8	0.79	7.28	3.10	78.7	4.3	26.3	8.8	6.9
9.0	0.18	0.8	0.00	5.4	2.9	1.34	13.09	3.84	57.9	1.0	19.2	32.8	6.4
5.4	1.57	6.0	0.06	3.7	1.1	0.84	8.71	3.45	72.5	5.8	44.8	6.2	5.4
9.0	0.17	0.6	0.00	4.2	0.9	0.75	5.90	2.92	67.7	5.4	35.5	5.2	7.5
8.8	0.09	0.5	0.05	5.0	0.8	1.22	14.89	3.94	68.7	4.1	28.2	10.4	5.2
7.9	0.83	2.6	-0.01	3.8	0.3	0.89	7.24	3.34	64.0	3.3	57.9	23.8	6.8
5.9	0.21	1.9	0.50	6.3	2.3	1.32	15.32	3.80	67.4	2.4	13.2	17.0	6.9
8.6	0.00	0.0	0.04	5.8	0.7	1.41	14.17	4.27	61.6	4.4	29.8	9.7	5.6
7.6	0.60	2.5	-0.21	5.3	1.7	1.08	8.65	4.17	70.3	3.2	21.2	13.7	8.0

Name	City	State	Rating	2013 Rating	2012 Rating	Total Assets ($Mil)	One Year Asset Growth	Asset Mix (As a % of Total Assets) Commercial Loans	Consumer Loans	Mortgage Loans	Securities	Capitalization Index	Leverage Ratio	Risk-Based Capital Ratio
FIRST NATIONAL BK IN FAIRFIELD	Fairfield	IA	B-	C+	C+	134.1	2.10	14.3	1.5	16.4	6.9	4.0	8.4	10.5
FIRST NATIONAL BK IN FRANKFORT	Frankfort	KS	B-	C+	B-	37.7	2.47	5.2	3.3	9.0	50.7	8.8	10.2	19.7
FIRST NATIONAL BK IN FREDONIA	Fredonia	KS	A	A-	A-	98.3	2.34	3.7	6.9	9.8	69.5	10.0	14.6	34.3
FIRST NATIONAL BK IN HOMINY	Hominy	OK	C	C	C+	41.9	6.89	13.8	8.4	8.0	41.3	6.4	8.4	18.8
▲ FIRST NATIONAL BK IN HOWELL	Howell	MI	D	E	E-	321.0	6.38	4.1	2.0	6.7	42.9	7.3	9.2	16.5
FIRST NATIONAL BK IN MAHNOMEN	Mahnomen	MN	B-	C+	C	89.7	1.90	17.0	7.0	9.0	12.8	7.7	9.5	13.2
FIRST NATIONAL BK IN MARLOW	Marlow	OK	B-	B-	B-	66.4	0.97	9.9	8.1	16.8	27.7	6.2	8.2	13.5
FIRST NATIONAL BK IN OKEENE	Okeene	OK	A-	A-	A-	61.5	11.50	5.2	0.6	0.2	30.7	10.0	18.3	31.6
FIRST NATIONAL BK IN OLNEY	Olney	IL	B	B	B-	304.9	-3.23	6.2	3.3	16.8	32.0	7.1	9.1	15.3
FIRST NATIONAL BK IN ORD	Ord	NE	C	C-	C+	124.5	2.20	3.9	2.5	12.0	30.0	5.9	7.9	15.5
FIRST NATIONAL BK IN PAWHUSKA	Pawhuska	OK	C-	C	C	30.8	7.77	1.6	6.4	9.8	46.7	9.8	10.9	31.8
FIRST NATIONAL BK IN PAXTON	Paxton	IL	C+	C	C+	80.2	-1.70	6.7	2.0	10.7	32.8	7.8	9.5	21.1
FIRST NATIONAL BK IN PHILIP	Philip	SD	A	A	A	244.1	14.17	6.0	1.1	0.4	19.0	8.9	10.3	15.9
FIRST NATIONAL BK IN PRATT	Pratt	KS	C	C	C	109.9	4.12	8.6	1.2	4.7	37.2	7.6	9.4	16.0
▲ FIRST NATIONAL BK IN STAUNTON	Staunton	IL	B+	B	B	473.1	-2.63	2.6	3.3	28.5	24.4	10.0	11.4	18.8
FIRST NATIONAL BK IN TIGERTON	Tigerton	WI	B-	B-	B-	20.8	-4.56	0.9	2.4	36.6	20.1	10.0	16.1	42.3
FIRST NATIONAL BK IN TREMONT	Tremont	IL	C+	C+	C	112.1	-2.09	4.8	2.5	18.0	46.1	9.3	10.5	22.8
▲ FIRST NATIONAL BK IN TRINIDAD	Trinidad	CO	C+	C	C+	190.8	-0.08	0.9	1.4	32.9	10.6	10.0	12.3	31.5
▲ FIRST NATIONAL BK IN WADENA	Wadena	MN	C+	C	C	54.8	-3.74	5.2	1.6	20.1	40.8	6.6	8.6	14.9
FIRST NATIONAL BK IZARD COUNTY	Calico Rock	AR	A+	A+	A+	156.9	6.19	2.1	4.9	16.4	34.0	10.0	32.0	60.0
FIRST NATIONAL BK JEANERETTE	Jeanerette	LA	B	B	B-	216.5	6.16	6.1	4.1	29.1	19.2	4.8	9.3	10.9
FIRST NATIONAL BK LAKE JACKSON	Lake Jackson	TX	B	B	A-	233.9	5.86	1.9	1.1	0.8	77.0	8.3	9.9	44.4
FIRST NATIONAL BK LAS ANIMAS	Las Animas	CO	A-	A-	A-	318.0	5.37	3.9	1.5	12.4	21.6	8.3	9.8	14.8
FIRST NATIONAL BK LAWRENCE CTY	Walnut Ridge	AR	A-	A-	A-	191.6	6.79	9.7	3.7	17.2	21.1	9.0	10.4	15.5
FIRST NATIONAL BK LITCHFIELD	Litchfield	IL	B	B	B-	104.3	9.25	5.8	3.1	11.4	23.9	7.4	9.3	13.8
FIRST NATIONAL BK LIVINGSTON	Livingston	TX	A-	A	A+	327.9	3.22	3.9	5.2	13.9	40.1	10.0	13.8	35.2
FIRST NATIONAL BK LONG ISLAND	Glen Head	NY	B	B	B+	2570.7	8.84	2.8	0.2	27.7	31.7	6.6	8.6	16.6
FIRST NATIONAL BK MANCHESTER	Manchester	KY	B-	B-	C+	141.7	-1.21	2.4	2.6	14.1	45.3	10.0	15.8	31.4
FIRST NATIONAL BK MANCHESTER	Manchester	TN	B+	B+	B+	228.6	0.53	11.6	6.4	19.6	25.3	10.0	12.7	23.6
FIRST NATIONAL BK MCMINNVILLE	McMinnville	TN	B	B-	C+	478.2	-1.39	6.3	0.6	22.7	32.7	10.0	12.6	24.6
FIRST NATIONAL BK MENAHGA	Menahga	MN	A-	A-	B+	87.7	-2.65	7.7	4.2	19.3	29.3	10.0	13.1	26.4
FIRST NATIONAL BK MERCERSBURG	Mercersburg	PA	C+	C+	C-	171.1	-1.69	3.1	1.7	34.5	9.1	9.4	10.6	16.5
FIRST NATIONAL BK MIFFLINTOWN	Mifflintown	PA	B	B	B	443.8	2.84	5.5	1.0	29.6	30.2	7.7	9.4	18.2
FIRST NATIONAL BK MINERSVILLE	Minersville	PA	C-	C+	B	80.3	-3.48	2.4	2.2	28.0	33.8	10.0	14.3	30.3
FIRST NATIONAL BK MINNESOTA	Saint Peter	MN	C+	C+	C-	195.6	0.78	11.4	2.4	7.7	18.5	9.2	10.5	17.1
FIRST NATIONAL BK MOOSE LAKE	Moose Lake	MN	B+	B	B	79.7	8.85	8.4	3.0	24.5	11.0	10.0	12.6	17.9
▲ FIRST NATIONAL BK MOUNT DORA	Mount Dora	FL	B	C+	C-	201.7	3.98	1.9	1.3	21.2	37.1	10.0	14.3	23.5
FIRST NATIONAL BK MOUNT VERNON	Mount Vernon	TX	B+	B+	A-	204.2	0.36	1.0	2.3	19.5	68.1	8.0	9.7	31.2
FIRST NATIONAL BK NEVADA MO	Nevada	MO	B	B	B	98.8	5.13	6.5	1.6	17.8	44.2	10.0	13.1	25.7
FIRST NATIONAL BK NEW BREMEN	New Bremen	OH	B	B	B	260.0	3.80	6.2	2.9	14.3	31.0	7.3	9.2	19.6
FIRST NATIONAL BK NEW MEXICO	Clayton	NM	B	B	B-	193.0	6.18	4.4	2.7	7.7	23.7	6.8	8.8	13.2
FIRST NATIONAL BK NORTHEAST	Lyons	NE	B+	B+	B	276.8	5.19	7.2	7.9	1.9	33.3	8.8	10.3	14.0
▲ FIRST NATIONAL BK NORTHERN CA	South San Francisc	CA	B-	C+	C	905.7	-2.23	5.4	0.2	9.6	29.6	8.7	10.2	14.3
FIRST NATIONAL BK NORTHFIELD	Northfield	MN	B	B-	C	152.1	2.73	7.4	1.1	21.5	14.6	7.9	9.6	14.9
FIRST NATIONAL BK NORTHWEST FL	Panama City	FL	C	C-	D	112.7	-0.04	2.2	0.1	13.6	13.2	10.0	13.4	25.5
FIRST NATIONAL BK OF ABSECON	Absecon	NJ	C-	C-	C	149.5	-3.65	0.3	0.2	19.3	58.7	7.7	9.5	31.7
FIRST NATIONAL BK OF ALBANY	Albany	TX	A-	A-	A-	480.6	3.81	14.0	5.5	8.8	49.0	7.7	9.4	17.6
FIRST NATIONAL BK OF ALLENDALE	Allendale	IL	B+	B+	B+	184.8	2.66	9.5	7.5	21.6	28.1	9.7	10.8	17.9
FIRST NATIONAL BK OF ALVIN	Alvin	TX	A-	A-	A+	114.8	1.50	1.7	0.9	2.2	70.4	10.0	14.1	40.1
▼ FIRST NATIONAL BK OF AMERICA	East Lansing	MI	C-	C	C	649.3	9.78	0.6	3.1	61.4	9.4	10.0	11.6	17.4
FIRST NATIONAL BK OF ANDERSON	Anderson	TX	B	B	B	166.8	8.13	7.6	6.6	10.7	24.9	7.9	9.6	18.6
FIRST NATIONAL BK OF ANSON	Anson	TX	C	C	C+	56.0	1.31	8.8	10.1	20.9	37.1	7.5	9.4	18.2
FIRST NATIONAL BK OF ASPERMONT	Aspermont	TX	A-	A-	A-	57.8	-11.32	5.1	2.1	1.7	75.5	10.0	17.8	50.4
FIRST NATIONAL BK OF AVA	Ava	IL	A-	A-	A-	62.2	1.05	6.8	3.5	17.2	44.3	10.0	12.4	20.8
FIRST NATIONAL BK OF BAGLEY	Bagley	MN	C+	C+	C	81.2	3.75	9.5	9.2	15.6	25.3	5.8	7.8	13.1
FIRST NATIONAL BK OF BALLINGER	Ballinger	TX	B-	B	B-	141.1	5.15	6.3	3.1	19.1	19.1	7.4	9.3	16.5
FIRST NATIONAL BK OF BANCROFT	Bancroft	NE	B-	B-	B-	21.8	4.89	3.7	2.7	6.9	31.4	10.0	15.2	32.2
▲ FIRST NATIONAL BK OF BANGOR	Bangor	WI	B+	B	B-	207.0	1.62	2.7	1.6	19.4	36.3	10.0	22.4	37.0
▼ FIRST NATIONAL BK OF BARRY	Barry	IL	C	B	B-	115.7	-5.38	9.8	5.4	13.2	16.8	10.0	14.5	21.3
FIRST NATIONAL BK OF BASTROP	Bastrop	TX	B+	B+	B	451.4	15.22	3.1	2.4	15.5	39.3	9.3	10.5	20.2

Asset Quality Index	Adjusted Non-Performing Loans as a % of Total Loans	Adjusted Non-Performing Loans as a % of Capital	Net Charge-Offs Avg Loans	Profitability Index	Net Income ($Mil)	Return on Assets (R.O.A.)	Return on Equity (R.O.E.)	Net Interest Spread	Overhead Efficiency Ratio	Liquidity Index	Liquidity Ratio	Hot Money Ratio	Stability Index
4.2	1.24	11.5	0.15	5.6	1.0	0.98	11.53	4.01	63.3	2.1	5.1	17.4	5.5
7.0	0.11	0.4	-0.60	5.4	0.4	1.41	14.05	3.50	68.3	5.0	57.5	12.7	6.1
7.7	1.85	3.5	0.40	7.2	1.4	1.76	12.55	3.58	47.6	3.9	57.0	18.5	7.9
6.1	1.14	4.9	0.02	4.1	0.3	0.95	17.29	3.21	75.2	4.9	61.6	14.3	3.4
1.9	6.53	28.3	-0.20	4.5	2.8	1.19	14.02	3.58	96.6	4.8	35.9	9.6	2.8
6.5	0.41	3.1	0.18	3.8	0.5	0.67	7.59	3.95	81.4	2.2	16.8	18.3	4.7
8.4	0.12	0.8	0.10	5.5	0.6	1.24	14.57	4.56	75.5	4.1	34.8	12.7	5.5
8.7	0.00	0.0	0.00	7.0	0.7	1.58	9.70	3.64	59.6	2.6	33.4	20.0	8.7
5.5	0.67	4.4	0.07	5.1	2.3	0.98	9.64	3.39	59.4	3.9	17.6	9.4	6.3
8.8	0.00	0.0	-0.06	3.0	0.5	0.56	7.07	2.73	77.9	3.7	27.6	12.2	4.0
2.3	10.19	21.8	-0.49	3.2	0.1	0.54	4.99	3.01	86.4	3.8	65.8	20.1	5.1
7.3	0.44	1.9	0.07	3.8	0.5	0.83	8.44	2.63	70.1	4.9	40.3	10.7	5.1
7.3	0.00	0.0	0.00	7.4	2.8	1.63	16.07	3.78	55.1	2.4	28.5	19.2	8.7
8.3	0.00	0.0	0.00	2.8	0.4	0.53	5.18	3.01	83.4	5.6	38.3	4.9	6.0
7.6	0.39	2.0	0.09	5.5	4.9	1.36	11.48	3.51	63.6	4.0	18.7	9.4	7.7
9.4	0.00	0.0	0.01	3.6	0.1	0.75	4.88	3.27	79.1	4.6	32.0	6.5	7.0
4.9	2.42	9.3	0.03	3.5	0.6	0.63	5.85	3.47	77.3	5.8	49.4	7.9	5.3
6.8	2.50	9.0	0.05	3.1	0.9	0.64	5.29	3.25	83.4	3.8	40.5	16.1	6.9
7.6	0.23	1.1	-0.38	3.4	0.3	0.74	7.89	3.37	79.8	5.1	40.9	9.3	4.3
8.9	1.15	1.6	0.06	9.8	2.1	1.81	5.80	4.55	44.9	3.8	56.7	21.0	9.1
6.8	0.35	2.4	0.13	7.2	2.8	1.74	19.06	4.93	56.6	1.8	18.1	20.7	6.2
10.0	0.00	0.0	0.20	4.7	2.2	1.14	11.99	2.28	49.7	2.0	28.5	22.9	7.2
7.3	0.33	2.0	-0.11	9.4	5.4	2.29	21.69	4.84	50.3	2.2	15.6	18.0	8.6
6.6	0.58	3.6	0.27	6.2	2.1	1.47	15.10	4.06	63.7	1.1	9.9	28.8	7.5
8.1	0.17	1.2	0.03	5.1	0.9	1.22	12.77	3.66	65.1	2.1	26.0	19.7	6.3
8.8	0.08	0.2	0.10	5.8	3.4	1.38	9.27	3.19	67.4	6.8	69.1	6.1	9.3
9.2	0.15	1.1	0.07	4.8	18.3	0.99	11.08	3.10	52.9	4.0	21.7	10.6	7.9
6.3	2.91	7.1	0.12	2.9	0.6	0.56	3.57	3.37	84.0	2.9	51.1	30.6	7.5
5.8	1.81	7.1	0.22	5.7	1.8	1.01	8.24	3.29	56.7	2.3	33.3	23.6	7.3
5.1	2.50	11.0	0.34	4.5	3.7	1.02	8.47	3.00	63.2	1.3	23.9	29.9	6.5
7.2	1.24	4.5	0.00	6.3	1.0	1.56	11.24	3.95	61.9	3.7	43.6	17.0	8.5
4.6	1.76	11.6	0.10	3.4	0.7	0.57	5.03	3.97	84.4	3.2	15.1	13.1	5.7
5.2	0.92	5.8	-0.01	4.6	3.1	0.96	10.18	3.54	70.1	2.7	23.8	16.2	5.7
8.5	0.61	2.2	0.00	1.2	-0.5	-0.89	-6.28	3.05	100.4	5.1	35.7	7.8	6.8
3.8	2.44	12.6	-0.06	3.5	0.8	0.53	4.81	3.73	80.5	4.1	25.5	9.3	5.8
5.4	1.42	8.2	-0.05	7.9	1.0	1.82	14.23	4.60	62.4	2.4	15.4	16.9	7.8
4.6	5.31	17.5	0.10	3.9	1.0	0.68	4.91	3.84	80.0	5.2	40.8	9.2	6.4
9.8	0.03	0.1	0.00	5.1	2.4	1.57	15.83	3.12	61.1	4.0	57.8	19.2	7.5
8.4	0.80	2.9	0.04	4.2	0.7	0.87	6.92	3.76	71.6	4.9	55.2	13.2	7.0
6.7	0.80	3.6	0.23	4.7	2.3	1.17	12.80	3.20	62.2	5.2	49.1	11.4	6.2
5.2	0.72	4.9	0.15	4.9	1.6	1.09	12.33	4.89	76.4	2.7	15.1	15.7	5.5
6.2	0.60	3.2	0.03	4.7	2.2	1.07	10.15	3.03	59.5	3.9	25.0	10.7	7.1
4.8	1.75	9.9	-0.19	4.8	5.5	0.82	7.73	4.27	72.5	4.3	27.4	8.9	7.2
7.6	0.26	1.7	-0.06	5.3	1.5	1.32	14.64	3.91	69.3	4.4	23.9	7.5	4.8
4.4	2.34	8.8	1.25	2.5	0.4	0.53	3.85	3.23	84.9	4.0	51.8	18.0	6.1
6.1	2.96	8.1	0.12	2.2	0.3	0.26	2.90	3.12	86.7	7.3	77.9	4.0	4.5
7.6	0.53	2.1	0.34	8.3	7.0	1.93	19.01	3.79	39.4	4.3	56.2	17.6	8.6
5.3	0.97	5.2	0.17	5.4	1.3	0.96	8.96	3.52	60.6	2.3	18.1	17.7	6.6
9.9	0.00	0.0	-0.01	4.8	1.0	1.14	7.67	2.91	63.5	5.7	81.8	14.3	8.4
1.7	5.50	35.6	0.42	9.9	9.4	1.97	16.86	6.56	50.4	0.6	13.6	52.6	8.6
5.7	0.95	4.6	0.08	4.8	0.9	0.76	8.66	3.55	67.3	2.1	39.8	33.5	5.4
8.3	0.00	0.0	-0.04	2.9	0.2	0.49	5.68	4.31	89.2	3.9	17.6	9.4	4.7
9.8	0.00	0.0	-0.04	6.3	0.7	1.40	8.95	2.81	45.6	2.7	60.8	34.2	8.5
6.4	1.51	6.0	-0.08	7.0	0.6	1.35	10.75	4.73	58.9	4.1	45.2	15.1	7.5
4.4	1.39	9.8	0.56	3.6	0.4	0.62	7.34	4.13	82.2	4.2	16.5	7.8	4.1
8.6	0.06	0.3	0.00	4.5	1.1	1.00	11.06	3.89	74.7	1.8	23.9	22.6	6.3
8.9	0.19	0.5	0.08	3.5	0.1	0.68	4.54	3.36	75.9	5.7	63.0	8.5	6.5
3.8	7.09	18.6	-0.07	9.8	3.0	1.90	8.87	4.08	27.4	6.0	40.1	3.6	8.7
2.0	5.67	25.5	0.06	4.0	0.8	0.88	5.85	3.74	74.6	2.6	25.9	17.1	6.7
5.5	1.28	5.9	0.08	6.9	5.3	1.66	15.42	3.99	63.1	3.5	34.6	15.5	7.6

Name	City	State	Rating	2013 Rating	2012 Rating	Total Assets ($Mil)	One Year Asset Growth	Asset Mix (As a % of Total Assets) Commercial Loans	Consumer Loans	Mortgage Loans	Securities	Capitalization Index	Leverage Ratio	Risk-Based Capital Ratio
FIRST NATIONAL BK OF BEEVILLE	Beeville	TX	**C+**	C+	C+	305.5	0.89	11.3	0.8	3.9	23.2	**6.2**	8.2	16.7
FIRST NATIONAL BK OF BELLEVUE	Bellevue	OH	**B-**	C	D+	163.3	11.70	10.1	1.4	7.6	21.2	**6.2**	8.4	11.9
FIRST NATIONAL BK OF BELLVILLE	Bellville	TX	**A-**	A-	A-	538.8	11.01	2.5	1.9	10.2	64.7	**8.6**	10.0	24.7
FIRST NATIONAL BK OF BELOIT	Beloit	KS	**C+**	B-	B-	74.1	0.60	10.1	3.0	9.0	25.6	**10.0**	11.5	18.2
FIRST NATIONAL BK OF BEMIDJI	Bemidji	MN	**A**	A	A	612.9	4.12	10.5	7.6	15.2	43.8	**10.0**	13.5	23.1
FIRST NATIONAL BK OF BENTON	Benton	LA	**B**	B	B-	51.4	-10.95	6.3	1.8	26.1	27.1	**10.0**	17.3	40.6
FIRST NATIONAL BK OF BERLIN	Berlin	WI	**B-**	B-	B-	351.7	18.56	8.5	1.9	16.0	15.5	**6.6**	8.6	13.1
FIRST NATIONAL BK OF BRUNDIDGE	Brundidge	AL	**B-**	B-	B-	95.5	-2.33	4.6	3.6	14.3	33.0	**10.0**	12.3	21.5
FIRST NATIONAL BK OF BUHL	Mountain Iron	MN	**E-**	E-	E-	23.5	-1.55	11.1	14.6	28.6	0.0	**5.5**	7.5	12.0
FIRST NATIONAL BK OF BURLESON	Burleson	TX	**A-**	B+	A-	176.6	-4.97	15.6	2.3	0.9	54.2	**7.6**	9.4	25.4
FIRST NATIONAL BK OF CARMI	Carmi	IL	**C+**	C+	C+	393.8	4.23	15.2	1.5	7.1	14.4	**5.9**	8.4	11.6
▲ FIRST NATIONAL BK OF CATLIN	Catlin	IL	**C**	D+	D-	43.7	-0.30	9.8	1.8	25.0	24.3	**7.9**	9.6	16.8
FIRST NATIONAL BK OF CHADRON	Chadron	NE	**B+**	B	A-	122.8	2.88	5.1	2.3	0.7	22.6	**9.3**	10.5	16.4
FIRST NATIONAL BK OF CHISHOLM	Chisholm	MN	**C**	C-	C-	81.5	-1.09	3.3	2.1	7.1	76.1	**6.2**	8.2	20.3
FIRST NATIONAL BK OF CHRISMAN	Chrisman	IL	**C**	C	C+	38.5	-10.86	1.5	5.3	6.0	33.0	**8.3**	9.8	16.4
FIRST NATIONAL BK OF CLINTON	Clinton	MO	**B-**	B-	B+	68.2	1.69	7.8	6.3	10.6	32.8	**10.0**	14.0	28.2
FIRST NATIONAL BK OF COKATO	Cokato	MN	**C**	C	C-	43.9	-5.28	7.0	3.1	10.4	31.6	**6.2**	8.2	16.0
FIRST NATIONAL BK OF COLERAINE	Coleraine	MN	**C**	C	C	82.3	7.62	3.6	3.2	16.0	52.8	**5.2**	7.2	16.4
FIRST NATIONAL BK OF COLORADO	Colorado City	TX	**C-**	D+	C	36.4	4.02	21.4	4.1	1.5	41.4	**9.5**	10.7	23.4
FIRST NATIONAL BK OF COWETA	Coweta	OK	**C-**	C-	C-	68.8	0.95	7.2	4.7	12.8	47.1	**6.5**	8.5	20.0
FIRST NATIONAL BK OF CRESTVIEW	Crestview	FL	**E-**	E-	E-	79.7	-14.39	0.7	0.5	4.8	26.9	**0.0**	1.4	3.6
▲ FIRST NATIONAL BK OF CROSSETT	Crossett	AR	**C-**	D	D-	140.4	6.20	11.4	6.1	8.5	42.6	**10.0**	11.9	21.9
FIRST NATIONAL BK OF DENNISON	Dennison	OH	**C+**	C+	C+	213.6	1.60	5.2	17.7	15.4	33.4	**7.4**	9.2	15.8
FIRST NATIONAL BK OF DIETERICH	Dieterich	IL	**B**	B	B	551.3	4.37	8.0	1.6	9.6	32.0	**8.1**	9.7	14.0
▼ FIRST NATIONAL BK OF DIGHTON	Dighton	KS	**C+**	B-	B-	66.9	9.65	5.7	1.6	1.7	51.3	**10.0**	18.4	43.7
FIRST NATIONAL BK OF DOZIER	Dozier	AL	**B-**	C+	C+	39.5	5.63	3.1	3.0	2.7	71.6	**10.0**	12.1	35.9
FIRST NATIONAL BK OF DRYDEN	Dryden	NY	**A-**	A-	A-	137.4	9.49	4.0	5.6	15.4	45.4	**10.0**	11.5	33.0
FIRST NATIONAL BK OF DUBLIN	Dublin	TX	**B**	B	B	75.7	3.79	15.0	9.3	9.7	3.2	**9.2**	10.4	15.2
FIRST NATIONAL BK OF DURANGO	Durango	CO	**B-**	B	B	465.1	4.15	2.3	0.5	4.4	58.7	**6.9**	8.9	15.7
▲ FIRST NATIONAL BK OF DWIGHT	Dwight	IL	**C+**	B-	C+	123.8	-5.24	1.2	0.6	6.0	47.6	**10.0**	11.4	30.4
FIRST NATIONAL BK OF EDGEWOOD	Edgewood	TX	**C-**	C-	C	20.6	3.97	3.2	5.6	13.5	46.6	**7.8**	9.6	24.8
FIRST NATIONAL BK OF ELDORADO	Eldorado	TX	**B+**	B	B	66.7	3.63	12.5	3.6	9.6	34.1	**10.0**	12.1	24.2
FIRST NATIONAL BK OF ELK RIVER	Elk River	MN	**C-**	D+	D+	301.0	0.86	13.1	0.6	4.0	44.3	**7.5**	9.4	17.5
FIRST NATIONAL BK OF ELKHART	Elkhart	KS	**B**	B	B	74.0	-4.02	3.2	4.3	3.6	29.7	**10.0**	11.4	19.4
FIRST NATIONAL BK OF ELMER	Elmer	NJ	**B-**	B-	C+	219.6	0.44	7.8	2.0	28.7	6.5	**8.6**	10.1	14.1
FIRST NATIONAL BK OF ELY	Ely	NV	**A**	A	A-	88.1	2.87	1.5	0.6	4.0	78.4	**10.0**	12.2	31.7
FIRST NATIONAL BK OF EMORY	Emory	TX	**B**	B	A-	111.1	5.17	3.9	3.2	10.0	48.6	**10.0**	11.6	35.7
FIRST NATIONAL BK OF EVANT	Evant	TX	**C+**	C+	C+	70.6	7.76	5.3	7.7	31.9	13.4	**6.6**	8.6	15.8
FIRST NATIONAL BK OF FAIRBURY	Fairbury	NE	**B+**	B+	A	139.7	-2.29	3.8	2.7	2.4	51.0	**10.0**	17.4	26.1
FIRST NATIONAL BK OF FAIRFAX	Fairfax	MN	**B-**	C	C+	28.6	2.34	11.8	0.9	2.3	1.7	**10.0**	38.2	39.5
FIRST NATIONAL BK OF FLEMING	Fleming	CO	**D+**	D	D-	22.5	-1.93	8.2	4.2	5.7	6.9	**9.6**	10.8	19.6
FIRST NATIONAL BK OF FLETCHER	Fletcher	OK	**B+**	A-	B	18.2	-0.18	7.5	6.5	5.4	46.7	**10.0**	11.4	22.9
FIRST NATIONAL BK OF FLOYDADA	Floydada	TX	**B+**	A-	A-	98.1	2.88	3.4	1.6	2.5	30.9	**10.0**	12.3	15.9
▲ FIRST NATIONAL BK OF FREDERICK	Frederick	SD	**C+**	C	C	20.6	7.16	2.7	0.4	0.0	33.7	**10.0**	12.7	26.0
FIRST NATIONAL BK OF GIDDINGS	Giddings	TX	**B**	B	B-	179.1	12.39	4.6	3.3	12.4	46.0	**8.4**	9.9	22.2
▲ FIRST NATIONAL BK OF GILBERT	Gilbert	MN	**B-**	C+	C+	32.6	0.35	2.2	4.7	25.9	27.5	**10.0**	11.6	27.6
FIRST NATIONAL BK OF GILLETTE	Gillette	WY	**B-**	B	B	547.0	5.69	6.3	2.6	4.6	64.5	**8.4**	9.9	28.3
FIRST NATIONAL BK OF GILMER	Gilmer	TX	**B-**	B-	B	323.0	15.50	10.0	6.7	21.3	20.2	**9.9**	11.0	17.0
FIRST NATIONAL BK OF GIRARD	Girard	KS	**B**	B	B	76.4	4.57	9.1	2.7	22.1	34.0	**9.7**	10.8	19.1
FIRST NATIONAL BK OF GORDON	Gordon	NE	**B+**	B+	A-	175.6	3.96	6.4	3.4	0.2	40.5	**10.0**	12.9	22.5
FIRST NATIONAL BK OF GRANBURY	Granbury	TX	**B-**	B-	B	473.0	0.44	2.8	3.2	18.2	41.0	**9.4**	10.6	22.0
FIRST NATIONAL BK OF GRAYSON	Grayson	KY	**B**	B	B	211.3	0.92	4.5	11.5	27.6	23.2	**9.5**	10.6	19.1
FIRST NATIONAL BK OF GRIFFIN	Griffin	GA	**E-**	E-	E-	236.6	0.88	3.5	2.9	7.2	37.4	**2.5**	4.8	10.4
FIRST NATIONAL BK OF GROTON	Groton	NY	**A**	A	A-	154.0	7.65	6.8	9.1	20.4	43.4	**10.0**	13.6	28.9
▲ FIRST NATIONAL BK OF HARTFORD	Hartford	AL	**C+**	C-	C-	121.0	-0.95	3.8	5.4	15.7	48.6	**10.0**	12.7	25.6
FIRST NATIONAL BK OF HENNING	Ottertail	MN	**A**	A	A-	102.7	-1.00	10.2	5.0	15.7	26.5	**10.0**	12.0	16.6
FIRST NATIONAL BK OF HEREFORD	Hereford	TX	**C**	C+	C	139.9	3.49	18.3	1.3	10.1	13.7	**8.1**	9.8	13.6
FIRST NATIONAL BK OF HOLDREGE	Holdrege	NE	**C**	C	C	112.3	4.89	9.8	1.3	2.8	44.2	**6.4**	8.4	15.3
FIRST NATIONAL BK OF HOOKER	Hooker	OK	**A-**	A-	A-	70.8	3.15	7.2	2.6	7.1	47.8	**10.0**	12.2	21.2
FIRST NATIONAL BK OF HOPE	Hope	KS	**B**	B	B-	73.3	1.16	6.6	1.9	2.9	26.4	**10.0**	13.1	16.1

Asset Quality Index	Adjusted Non-Performing Loans as a % of Total Loans	Adjusted Non-Performing Loans as a % of Capital	Net Charge-Offs Avg Loans	Profitability Index	Net Income ($Mil)	Return on Assets (R.O.A.)	Return on Equity (R.O.E.)	Net Interest Spread	Overhead Efficiency Ratio	Liquidity Index	Liquidity Ratio	Hot Money Ratio	Stability Index
8.8	0.01	0.1	0.00	**5.1**	2.1	0.95	11.72	3.43	57.4	**5.6**	46.2	8.0	**3.8**
4.8	1.15	8.5	-0.02	**4.8**	1.0	0.90	10.31	4.41	73.3	**3.9**	9.2	8.9	**4.9**
8.1	0.03	0.1	0.04	**7.7**	6.1	1.53	12.65	3.93	48.3	**2.4**	49.7	43.4	**9.0**
5.2	1.59	7.4	0.60	**2.9**	0.2	0.28	2.52	3.68	77.0	**3.2**	15.2	13.2	**5.6**
8.0	0.66	2.5	0.00	**7.6**	8.6	1.94	13.69	3.95	50.9	**2.4**	29.8	19.6	**9.7**
7.3	1.24	3.7	-0.27	**4.1**	0.3	0.68	3.95	3.51	72.1	**4.4**	37.5	12.2	**7.1**
4.8	1.19	8.8	0.02	**3.6**	1.4	0.52	6.20	4.01	83.2	**3.2**	23.0	13.8	**3.6**
6.8	1.15	4.7	0.05	**3.6**	0.5	0.69	5.61	3.80	81.2	**2.2**	38.4	29.7	**5.4**
0.4	4.91	45.7	0.72	**0.4**	-0.2	-0.85	-9.13	4.22	112.4	**2.6**	17.0	16.1	**0.3**
6.4	1.80	6.9	-0.02	**7.7**	2.5	1.91	20.69	3.51	49.8	**6.1**	54.0	7.7	**6.4**
7.2	0.30	2.4	0.08	**3.9**	2.0	0.66	7.50	3.39	71.3	**3.6**	18.9	11.4	**5.0**
5.4	1.05	6.1	0.08	**3.6**	0.2	0.66	7.19	4.30	85.4	**3.3**	26.6	14.0	**3.7**
7.8	0.10	0.5	0.03	**5.0**	1.1	1.21	9.68	3.55	66.5	**4.1**	30.9	11.4	**7.9**
9.4	0.40	0.8	-0.63	**2.9**	0.5	0.78	8.77	2.83	81.5	**5.7**	55.9	8.8	**4.3**
5.3	2.60	13.2	-0.02	**2.4**	0.1	0.30	3.22	2.51	88.4	**5.3**	41.0	8.5	**4.8**
8.7	0.00	0.0	0.16	**3.5**	0.3	0.66	4.58	3.78	80.9	**5.2**	56.2	11.6	**6.2**
8.8	0.00	0.0	0.02	**3.8**	0.3	0.92	12.35	3.67	76.5	**5.3**	46.6	9.6	**3.7**
9.4	0.06	0.3	0.07	**2.7**	0.3	0.43	5.94	3.03	83.1	**4.0**	46.2	16.3	**3.3**
8.8	0.00	0.0	0.01	**2.6**	0.1	0.41	4.32	2.66	81.9	**3.0**	42.6	20.7	**3.9**
5.4	1.62	6.9	-0.01	**2.6**	0.3	0.48	6.28	3.36	88.0	**4.8**	51.1	13.1	**3.4**
3.4	2.19	23.3	-1.09	**0.0**	-1.7	-2.57	-107.01	3.00	654.2	**5.2**	40.4	8.9	**0.6**
4.0	3.23	10.7	0.32	**4.1**	0.9	0.88	8.42	3.68	73.0	**2.5**	31.2	19.4	**4.8**
6.9	0.23	1.3	0.07	**3.4**	0.8	0.51	5.65	3.26	78.6	**5.0**	31.7	6.3	**5.5**
5.3	1.00	6.0	0.19	**4.6**	3.5	0.85	8.79	3.16	59.9	**3.7**	29.1	12.8	**6.3**
8.6	2.17	3.4	-0.10	**2.7**	0.2	0.37	2.12	2.24	79.0	**6.5**	58.1	4.1	**7.0**
9.7	0.00	0.0	0.06	**3.9**	0.2	0.77	6.65	3.21	68.4	**3.6**	62.6	21.8	**5.4**
6.8	3.14	8.3	0.15	**5.2**	1.2	1.19	10.23	3.84	61.2	**6.3**	46.7	3.4	**7.6**
4.8	0.67	4.4	-0.02	**5.6**	0.7	1.31	12.64	4.64	73.4	**4.2**	22.0	8.0	**6.5**
8.6	0.46	1.5	-0.11	**4.5**	3.9	1.13	11.62	3.38	73.3	**6.7**	61.8	5.4	**5.8**
6.5	2.70	6.5	-0.28	**3.1**	0.7	0.74	6.67	2.07	76.0	**5.6**	59.9	12.0	**5.8**
8.9	0.00	0.0	0.00	**2.2**	0.1	0.34	3.55	3.28	88.8	**5.7**	53.3	6.5	**3.7**
9.1	0.04	0.1	-0.32	**5.5**	0.7	1.40	11.92	4.35	67.5	**4.8**	39.0	10.5	**6.7**
4.2	2.79	11.9	-0.02	**2.6**	1.2	0.54	6.82	2.97	84.4	**1.4**	21.4	27.7	**2.9**
5.4	1.38	7.1	0.23	**5.2**	0.6	1.00	8.69	4.10	67.4	**1.1**	15.1	30.7	**5.9**
4.2	1.72	13.3	0.03	**4.2**	1.1	0.63	6.40	4.30	73.7	**3.3**	11.7	12.3	**6.0**
10.0	1.40	1.6	0.01	**7.8**	1.2	1.90	16.73	3.53	55.3	**7.5**	69.1	0.0	**6.8**
6.9	1.79	4.5	0.45	**4.1**	0.8	0.92	7.39	3.23	72.6	**3.6**	50.1	19.4	**7.3**
5.3	1.21	8.6	0.04	**6.9**	0.9	1.67	20.41	4.14	62.7	**3.4**	27.7	14.2	**5.5**
8.9	0.01	0.0	0.00	**4.3**	0.8	0.72	4.62	3.19	72.8	**3.9**	42.9	16.3	**7.8**
4.0	3.71	7.0	-0.05	**4.8**	0.3	1.17	3.10	3.53	67.6	**6.1**	39.1	2.3	**6.3**
1.9	1.51	10.0	0.28	**6.8**	0.2	1.30	12.68	4.60	54.6	**0.6**	6.4	38.6	**4.4**
9.0	0.31	0.6	0.24	**3.2**	0.1	0.60	5.44	3.54	84.5	**5.6**	65.5	9.4	**6.5**
4.7	3.12	14.1	0.00	**6.1**	1.2	1.48	13.12	3.07	48.4	**2.8**	28.7	17.1	**8.2**
7.0	1.28	3.5	0.04	**3.0**	0.1	0.53	3.95	3.32	80.0	**5.4**	63.7	10.2	**6.7**
6.5	0.64	2.6	0.16	**4.3**	1.2	0.91	9.47	3.42	66.5	**4.0**	48.3	17.0	**5.7**
9.2	0.52	1.9	0.48	**3.6**	0.2	0.71	6.14	3.51	75.0	**4.9**	40.8	10.8	**6.0**
6.8	1.42	3.3	-0.06	**4.6**	4.5	1.10	10.96	2.47	61.8	**4.0**	68.8	22.9	**6.6**
2.5	3.19	17.9	0.30	**6.6**	3.7	1.53	12.82	4.82	67.2	**1.9**	20.4	20.7	**7.1**
5.9	0.92	4.8	0.03	**5.3**	0.7	1.26	11.42	3.69	65.4	**2.0**	10.0	18.6	**6.4**
4.3	3.50	13.5	0.28	**8.7**	2.7	2.09	16.43	4.56	42.7	**1.3**	12.6	26.5	**8.4**
6.8	0.98	4.2	-0.01	**4.2**	2.9	0.82	7.96	3.41	65.1	**5.6**	46.2	8.3	**5.8**
4.6	1.21	6.8	0.08	**6.7**	1.7	1.10	10.72	3.98	65.4	**2.7**	20.1	16.2	**6.6**
4.8	1.52	11.0	0.44	**2.5**	1.2	0.70	17.02	3.21	96.2	**5.3**	45.2	9.6	**0.2**
5.8	2.28	8.0	0.74	**7.0**	1.4	1.21	9.42	4.52	59.2	**4.6**	32.8	9.2	**7.7**
6.2	1.75	5.4	0.56	**3.0**	0.6	0.65	5.48	4.00	76.7	**2.9**	43.8	24.2	**5.0**
5.2	2.11	10.8	0.05	**7.4**	1.4	1.84	15.08	4.27	60.9	**3.3**	23.0	13.2	**8.0**
3.2	2.29	15.7	0.17	**5.1**	1.3	1.20	12.58	4.13	64.6	**1.6**	24.4	26.1	**6.0**
8.9	0.00	0.0	-0.02	**2.9**	0.5	0.57	7.70	2.56	81.7	**4.7**	20.0	4.9	**3.6**
6.7	2.22	8.4	0.04	**6.9**	0.8	1.40	11.26	4.76	61.3	**4.3**	45.9	14.4	**8.1**
4.3	1.67	7.6	0.11	**5.7**	0.8	1.39	11.12	4.05	64.6	**2.4**	22.5	17.8	**7.9**

Name	City	State	Rating	2013 Rating	2012 Rating	Total Assets ($Mil)	One Year Asset Growth	Asset Mix (As a % of Total Assets) Commercial Loans	Consumer Loans	Mortgage Loans	Securities	Capitalization Index	Leverage Ratio	Risk-Based Capital Ratio
FIRST NATIONAL BK OF HOWARD	Howard	KS	**B-**	B-	B-	8.1	-0.96	0.3	1.6	1.7	4.3	**10.0**	21.8	40.3
FIRST NATIONAL BK OF HUGO	Hugo	CO	**A-**	A-	A-	108.6	0.72	2.6	1.6	5.0	31.3	**10.0**	12.1	25.0
FIRST NATIONAL BK OF JACKSON	Jackson	KY	**C-**	C-	C+	109.1	5.39	5.5	6.0	18.4	47.3	**10.0**	13.9	32.6
FIRST NATIONAL BK OF JASPER	Jasper	TX	**B-**	B	B	257.9	14.50	2.7	3.9	9.3	59.6	**9.4**	10.6	38.2
FIRST NATIONAL BK OF JOHNSON	Johnson	NE	**C**	C	B-	71.4	-4.47	3.3	2.1	4.2	54.9	**10.0**	19.4	46.5
FIRST NATIONAL BK OF KANSAS	Burlington	KS	**D+**	C-	C	69.7	-1.31	4.7	1.5	8.8	66.1	**7.7**	9.5	26.1
FIRST NATIONAL BK OF KEMP	Kemp	TX	**C**	C	B-	53.9	-0.71	1.9	2.9	12.9	30.5	**10.0**	11.6	24.9
FIRST NATIONAL BK OF KINMUNDY	Kinmundy	IL	**B**	B	B	42.6	6.75	5.6	16.5	27.7	20.4	**8.4**	9.9	16.2
FIRST NATIONAL BK OF LA GRANGE	La Grange	IL	**C-**	C-	C-	335.6	3.99	3.3	0.3	21.3	38.4	**7.1**	9.1	18.6
FIRST NATIONAL BK OF LACON	Lacon	IL	**C-**	C-	C	64.1	7.32	9.0	4.1	13.2	9.8	**6.1**	8.5	11.8
▼ FIRST NATIONAL BK OF LAYTON	Layton	UT	**B-**	A-	C+	276.2	1.68	8.9	0.9	6.8	25.6	**10.0**	13.3	22.2
FIRST NATIONAL BK OF LE CENTER	Le Center	MN	**B+**	B+	B	79.8	-2.87	9.0	4.4	19.0	11.4	**10.0**	13.6	19.5
FIRST NATIONAL BK OF LIBERAL	Liberal	KS	**B-**	B-	C+	302.4	10.05	7.6	2.3	2.9	43.9	**6.3**	8.3	14.6
FIRST NATIONAL BK OF LILLY	Lilly	PA	**C**	C	C+	22.1	-2.87	2.3	6.4	13.2	64.5	**10.0**	16.2	38.5
▲ FIRST NATIONAL BK OF LINDSAY	Lindsay	OK	**C+**	C	C-	52.7	18.41	10.4	2.6	5.5	28.5	**6.9**	8.9	18.0
FIRST NATIONAL BK OF LIPAN	Lipan	TX	**D-**	D-	D+	19.6	2.55	5.0	17.5	12.8	25.2	**6.6**	8.6	18.2
FIRST NATIONAL BK OF LOUISBURG	Louisburg	KS	**B-**	B-	B+	92.8	10.30	3.7	1.5	17.4	56.1	**10.0**	17.1	38.5
FIRST NATIONAL BK OF LOUISIANA	Crowley	LA	**A-**	A-	B+	321.8	5.18	17.5	1.4	17.0	15.3	**8.0**	9.7	13.7
FIRST NATIONAL BK OF MANNING	Manning	IA	**B**	B	B+	77.0	-0.96	4.2	1.1	4.8	28.0	**10.0**	13.9	26.7
FIRST NATIONAL BK OF MCGEHEE	McGehee	AR	**C+**	C	D+	50.7	1.19	8.2	4.6	6.1	50.7	**10.0**	11.8	25.8
FIRST NATIONAL BK OF MCGREGOR	McGregor	TX	**B**	B	B-	149.3	12.22	10.2	8.1	43.8	0.0	**6.9**	8.9	12.9
FIRST NATIONAL BK OF MCHENRY	McHenry	IL	**C-**	C-	C-	159.4	3.00	1.2	0.7	14.0	57.3	**7.9**	9.6	23.7
FIRST NATIONAL BK OF MCINTOSH	McIntosh	MN	**C**	C+	B-	27.2	5.19	4.3	3.5	6.0	25.3	**10.0**	23.9	75.0
FIRST NATIONAL BK OF MERTZON	Mertzon	TX	**D+**	C-	C+	339.8	-2.56	4.0	1.4	2.6	48.7	**3.5**	5.5	26.9
FIRST NATIONAL BK OF MICHIGAN	Kalamazoo	MI	**B**	B	B	354.8	18.97	11.7	1.2	5.3	21.2	**7.6**	9.4	14.5
FIRST NATIONAL BK OF MILACA	Milaca	MN	**A-**	B+	B-	184.5	3.66	12.4	5.1	15.8	29.1	**10.0**	11.3	22.1
FIRST NATIONAL BK OF MONTEREY	Monterey	IN	**B-**	B-	B-	314.8	-3.63	3.5	1.3	10.8	39.7	**9.4**	10.6	18.0
FIRST NATIONAL BK OF MOODY	Moody	TX	**B**	B	B+	45.3	-1.63	4.3	4.7	18.8	28.7	**10.0**	19.1	35.8
▲ FIRST NATIONAL BK OF MUSCATINE	Muscatine	IA	**B**	C+	C	294.4	-1.46	16.3	4.6	29.8	5.9	**9.8**	10.8	16.1
FIRST NATIONAL BK OF NASH	Nash	OK	**D-**	D	D+	19.1	7.11	5.7	4.8	0.8	0.0	**4.6**	6.6	17.9
FIRST NATIONAL BK OF NIAGARA	Niagara	WI	**C-**	C-	C	65.3	-7.52	7.1	6.7	23.8	34.3	**9.5**	10.6	22.0
FIRST NATIONAL BK OF NOKOMIS	Nokomis	IL	**A-**	A-	A-	139.8	-7.00	4.6	3.1	17.4	23.9	**10.0**	11.6	19.6
FIRST NATIONAL BK OF NORTH AR	Berryville	AR	**B-**	B	B	182.6	7.53	7.7	7.4	36.4	1.3	**9.2**	10.5	15.0
FIRST NATIONAL BK OF NORWAY	Norway	MI	**B+**	B+	B	93.7	2.36	10.6	3.1	30.6	21.0	**10.0**	11.6	19.3
FIRST NATIONAL BK OF ODON	Odon	IN	**C+**	C+	C	84.5	6.33	5.2	3.3	16.8	43.2	**5.9**	7.9	17.0
FIRST NATIONAL BK OF OKAWVILLE	Okawville	IL	**C+**	B-	B-	61.7	12.04	1.8	2.2	8.3	56.2	**9.3**	10.5	18.7
FIRST NATIONAL BK OF OKLAHOMA	Oklahoma City	OK	**B**	B	B-	323.1	19.13	7.1	1.9	15.0	4.5	**7.0**	9.0	12.5
FIRST NATIONAL BK OF OMAHA	Omaha	NE	**C+**	C+	C+	16998.8	19.24	10.6	30.5	4.0	15.6	**7.9**	9.6	13.2
FIRST NATIONAL BK OF ONEIDA	Oneida	TN	**B**	B-	C	204.7	0.75	2.2	3.2	25.5	23.8	**9.8**	10.8	19.1
FIRST NATIONAL BK OF ORWELL	Orwell	VT	**D+**	D+	C-	48.7	7.80	5.9	2.7	63.1	0.0	**6.5**	8.5	14.0
FIRST NATIONAL BK OF OSAKIS	Osakis	MN	**B+**	B	B-	62.7	-3.29	3.2	3.4	23.0	28.6	**10.0**	12.5	22.1
FIRST NATIONAL BK OF OTTAWA	Ottawa	IL	**C**	C	D+	286.2	-0.96	11.6	1.0	13.9	22.9	**7.4**	9.3	17.5
FIRST NATIONAL BK OF PADUCAH	Paducah	TX	**D**	D	D-	43.0	0.41	3.6	9.3	3.0	40.5	**8.1**	9.8	21.4
FIRST NATIONAL BK OF PANA	Pana	IL	**A-**	A-	A-	144.0	3.97	6.3	2.5	20.4	20.8	**10.0**	12.6	18.7
FIRST NATIONAL BK OF PANDORA	Pandora	OH	**C**	C	C	143.7	2.18	5.3	2.3	15.5	22.6	**6.4**	8.5	12.7
FIRST NATIONAL BK OF PASCO	Dade City	FL	**C**	C	D	139.0	-0.90	0.4	11.5	26.6	38.9	**8.7**	10.1	20.5
FIRST NATIONAL BK OF PAWNEE	Pawnee	OK	**B-**	B-	B-	68.6	2.76	4.3	2.6	5.7	52.3	**10.0**	11.2	24.0
FIRST NATIONAL BK OF PICAYUNE	Picayune	MS	**B**	B	B	199.9	-1.37	2.6	4.9	29.4	16.3	**10.0**	12.7	20.7
FIRST NATIONAL BK OF PONTOTOC	Pontotoc	MS	**B**	B	B	258.7	0.83	2.7	4.9	17.3	44.3	**10.0**	13.5	28.1
FIRST NATIONAL BK OF PRIMGHAR	Primghar	IA	**B-**	B-	B-	32.0	0.50	4.7	3.1	6.5	36.3	**10.0**	16.0	24.2
FIRST NATIONAL BK OF PROCTOR	Proctor	MN	**C-**	C-	C-	22.0	-7.50	2.1	5.4	38.4	12.5	**9.0**	10.3	20.9
FIRST NATIONAL BK OF PULASKI	Pulaski	TN	**B**	B-	C+	705.6	1.98	5.2	3.5	11.1	39.9	**8.1**	9.8	17.0
FIRST NATIONAL BK OF QUITAQUE	Quitaque	TX	**C+**	B-	B-	49.4	8.00	4.7	4.5	0.0	23.1	**10.0**	15.0	27.2
FIRST NATIONAL BK OF RAYMOND	Raymond	IL	**B-**	B	B+	144.6	-1.78	3.5	3.2	10.2	37.7	**8.9**	10.3	14.9
FIRST NATIONAL BK OF REMBRANDT	Rembrandt	IA	**B**	B	B+	55.7	2.62	7.6	4.5	9.8	23.9	**10.0**	16.8	29.4
▲ FIRST NATIONAL BK OF SANDOVAL	Sandoval	IL	**C+**	C	C-	46.2	-0.82	1.5	11.5	26.6	38.6	**8.7**	10.2	21.1
▲ FIRST NATIONAL BK OF SANTA FE	Albuquerque	NM	**D+**	D	B-	1669.6	97.46	5.1	0.2	8.0	25.9	**10.0**	11.2	16.6
FIRST NATIONAL BK OF SCOTIA	Scotia	NY	**C+**	C+	C+	456.8	9.87	10.1	31.6	16.7	10.8	**4.6**	8.0	10.8
▲ FIRST NATIONAL BK OF SEDAN	Sedan	KS	**C+**	C	B-	57.3	4.69	3.6	1.4	5.8	52.0	**9.6**	10.8	24.1
FIRST NATIONAL BK OF SEILING	Seiling	OK	**C+**	C+	B-	89.9	11.90	7.1	3.4	6.7	34.0	**8.3**	9.8	14.3

Asset Quality Index	Adjusted Non-Performing Loans as a % of Total Loans	Adjusted Non-Performing Loans as a % of Capital	Net Charge-Offs Avg Loans	Profitability Index	Net Income ($Mil)	Return on Assets (R.O.A.)	Return on Equity (R.O.E.)	Net Interest Spread	Overhead Efficiency Ratio	Liquidity Index	Liquidity Ratio	Hot Money Ratio	Stability Index
9.0	0.00	0.0	0.00	**3.3**	0.0	0.65	3.05	2.65	78.9	**6.1**	64.3	6.0	**5.9**
6.1	1.66	6.4	0.08	**5.2**	0.9	1.05	8.63	3.87	72.9	**4.4**	31.6	10.2	**7.3**
8.6	0.92	2.6	0.14	**1.7**	0.2	0.25	1.87	2.93	89.4	**3.0**	53.6	30.7	**5.9**
8.0	0.32	0.8	0.65	**3.4**	1.2	0.65	5.52	2.89	71.9	**3.5**	42.6	18.1	**6.2**
9.3	0.02	0.0	-0.09	**1.9**	0.1	0.15	0.79	2.02	92.3	**6.9**	79.1	5.4	**6.6**
9.3	0.36	0.8	-0.06	**1.8**	0.2	0.44	5.38	2.74	98.5	**3.2**	33.3	16.8	**4.7**
7.5	0.77	2.2	0.05	**2.4**	0.2	0.43	3.86	3.15	90.7	**4.9**	42.9	11.2	**5.2**
6.2	0.33	2.3	0.02	**9.3**	0.6	1.90	14.35	5.14	43.7	**3.1**	22.6	14.3	**7.8**
3.9	2.93	14.8	0.19	**5.2**	3.1	1.25	13.60	2.96	69.4	**6.0**	47.1	5.8	**6.0**
4.6	0.64	5.5	0.34	**4.0**	0.4	0.80	9.03	4.03	70.8	**2.8**	12.8	14.9	**2.8**
7.2	0.87	3.3	-0.06	**3.9**	1.7	0.82	6.12	3.90	90.3	**5.1**	43.2	10.2	**6.3**
4.7	2.66	12.9	0.00	**6.2**	0.9	1.52	11.71	4.04	59.3	**4.1**	16.7	8.2	**7.2**
8.7	0.00	0.0	0.01	**4.6**	2.1	0.95	11.61	3.48	66.3	**1.8**	26.9	24.9	**4.2**
8.2	1.95	3.2	0.00	**1.9**	0.0	0.25	1.46	3.33	91.6	**5.7**	84.4	12.3	**6.1**
5.0	2.89	10.9	0.14	**6.6**	0.5	1.31	15.58	3.52	54.1	**5.5**	48.4	8.4	**4.3**
4.3	1.28	6.2	0.11	**2.0**	0.1	0.32	3.81	3.10	89.3	**3.2**	57.2	20.6	**1.7**
9.7	0.00	0.0	0.06	**3.5**	0.5	0.74	4.30	3.00	78.2	**5.6**	54.8	9.0	**7.2**
7.9	0.02	0.2	0.03	**7.4**	4.1	1.74	18.29	4.17	60.2	**4.2**	14.5	7.5	**7.8**
9.0	0.00	0.0	-0.01	**3.9**	0.4	0.73	5.24	2.93	65.9	**5.7**	55.7	9.1	**8.0**
3.6	5.35	16.4	0.96	**3.0**	0.3	0.72	6.52	3.20	79.1	**5.5**	51.9	9.1	**5.0**
8.1	0.02	0.2	0.12	**5.3**	0.9	0.89	10.11	4.96	70.0	**0.6**	6.9	44.4	**5.0**
5.6	4.24	12.8	0.22	**2.1**	0.4	0.32	3.34	3.15	91.1	**5.8**	52.8	8.8	**4.1**
9.2	0.00	0.0	0.00	**2.0**	0.0	0.18	0.75	1.85	90.8	**5.0**	78.9	15.9	**7.0**
8.8	0.62	1.4	0.00	**2.7**	1.0	0.37	6.46	1.38	65.9	**6.5**	71.0	8.4	**1.8**
5.8	0.00	0.0	0.08	**6.6**	3.2	1.24	13.26	3.65	51.6	**1.3**	16.8	27.5	**6.0**
5.8	1.32	6.4	0.23	**6.8**	2.3	1.70	14.80	3.82	59.9	**5.3**	37.5	6.8	**6.7**
6.5	1.02	4.7	0.05	**3.8**	1.8	0.74	7.54	3.01	64.2	**5.3**	44.0	9.6	**6.1**
7.3	1.11	2.7	-0.34	**5.2**	0.4	1.27	6.46	4.10	66.6	**3.1**	42.1	20.0	**6.9**
5.4	0.40	2.6	-0.28	**6.0**	2.4	1.05	10.05	3.20	58.4	**3.8**	15.5	9.8	**6.5**
9.0	0.00	0.0	0.00	**2.6**	0.1	0.33	4.92	2.13	81.1	**7.1**	78.1	2.2	**1.7**
4.3	3.12	13.4	0.13	**2.6**	0.2	0.42	4.01	4.03	92.5	**3.9**	49.3	16.9	**4.9**
6.4	1.48	7.3	0.02	**6.1**	1.6	1.44	12.55	3.52	59.2	**4.4**	32.5	10.5	**7.9**
3.6	1.97	14.8	0.07	**5.0**	1.5	1.09	10.45	5.30	79.3	**1.5**	8.1	22.6	**6.8**
4.8	2.65	14.3	0.10	**4.8**	0.6	0.86	7.34	4.19	73.4	**3.7**	30.6	13.5	**6.8**
7.9	0.00	0.0	0.00	**3.9**	0.5	0.80	10.12	3.41	73.3	**7.0**	60.4	1.2	**3.7**
9.4	0.19	0.6	0.01	**2.9**	0.2	0.54	5.29	3.35	81.7	**6.2**	53.7	5.3	**4.2**
5.2	0.76	5.8	-0.01	**7.2**	3.7	1.65	17.86	4.35	58.7	**1.2**	20.3	29.9	**6.9**
3.8	1.24	7.9	1.55	**6.5**	124.5	1.02	10.11	5.75	62.0	**4.1**	12.8	8.0	**8.0**
5.4	1.15	5.7	0.39	**5.4**	2.0	1.26	11.87	4.03	63.1	**1.7**	26.5	25.6	**6.2**
2.8	1.95	19.3	0.10	**3.9**	0.2	0.55	6.34	4.62	76.3	**2.4**	4.8	15.9	**4.4**
4.6	2.72	12.8	0.16	**7.2**	0.8	1.73	13.49	4.40	59.6	**4.6**	28.1	7.3	**7.4**
4.9	1.65	8.7	-0.11	**3.3**	1.1	0.54	5.16	3.59	79.8	**4.7**	32.1	8.3	**4.4**
3.6	4.02	13.4	-0.07	**1.0**	0.0	-0.05	-0.58	2.37	102.4	**3.4**	55.4	22.0	**1.8**
6.8	0.79	4.1	0.10	**6.2**	1.2	1.09	9.05	3.77	56.5	**4.0**	21.4	9.7	**7.4**
4.0	2.12	14.9	0.10	**2.9**	0.4	0.40	4.75	3.76	87.7	**2.0**	10.1	18.8	**4.8**
3.5	3.57	16.4	2.06	**3.3**	0.5	0.47	4.73	3.52	81.2	**3.7**	37.7	15.6	**4.8**
7.4	1.05	2.8	0.22	**3.3**	0.4	0.68	6.44	3.39	73.9	**5.1**	46.4	10.5	**5.7**
3.7	3.73	19.0	0.19	**9.7**	3.6	2.36	18.28	4.91	55.4	**1.9**	26.3	23.2	**8.7**
7.4	1.37	4.1	0.20	**4.0**	1.4	0.71	5.57	3.73	74.4	**2.4**	36.1	25.4	**7.1**
8.7	0.00	0.0	0.00	**3.1**	0.1	0.48	3.02	3.71	84.4	**3.7**	45.6	17.7	**7.0**
9.0	0.20	1.1	0.00	**1.9**	0.0	0.11	1.02	3.51	96.8	**4.2**	29.5	8.4	**3.6**
4.6	2.30	11.0	0.13	**5.5**	5.3	0.98	10.64	3.56	63.9	**2.2**	30.2	22.3	**5.7**
8.3	0.36	1.3	0.12	**2.7**	0.2	0.45	3.01	3.27	81.2	**3.5**	38.7	17.2	**7.2**
6.9	0.43	2.3	0.32	**3.8**	0.9	0.81	8.77	3.36	73.9	**3.3**	37.8	17.9	**6.3**
6.1	1.79	5.7	-0.03	**4.1**	0.3	0.74	4.52	2.72	53.0	**5.7**	48.1	6.9	**7.5**
4.9	2.43	10.0	-0.07	**4.1**	0.3	0.78	7.84	3.83	75.1	**4.8**	51.0	12.6	**5.2**
1.1	4.34	22.4	0.05	**2.4**	2.7	0.22	1.38	3.95	87.9	**3.5**	30.4	17.8	**6.9**
4.5	0.43	4.1	0.05	**3.8**	1.7	0.53	6.80	3.58	75.0	**4.5**	7.8	4.1	**4.3**
7.8	0.43	1.1	0.09	**3.3**	0.4	0.96	9.47	2.76	80.0	**4.5**	57.9	15.5	**5.2**
7.7	0.56	2.7	0.03	**3.6**	0.5	0.70	6.52	3.55	81.5	**0.9**	21.8	36.3	**6.5**

Name	City	State	Rating	2013 Rating	2012 Rating	Total Assets ($Mil)	One Year Asset Growth	Asset Mix (As a % of Total Assets) Comm-ercial Loans	Cons-umer Loans	Mort-gage Loans	Secur-ities	Capital-ization Index	Lever-age Ratio	Risk-Based Capital Ratio
FIRST NATIONAL BK OF SHINER	Shiner	TX	B+	B+	B+	479.0	39.32	1.3	0.8	2.4	81.9	6.1	8.1	22.7
▲ FIRST NATIONAL BK OF SPARTA	Sparta	IL	B	B-	B-	81.1	-0.30	6.0	7.2	21.9	42.6	10.0	11.1	24.2
FIRST NATIONAL BK OF ST IGNACE	Saint Ignace	MI	C+	C+	C+	253.7	3.09	3.0	1.4	10.7	48.3	8.7	10.1	19.1
FIRST NATIONAL BK OF ST LOUIS	Clayton	MO	B-	B-	C+	1483.6	0.31	13.0	2.8	10.8	15.6	8.2	9.9	13.5
FIRST NATIONAL BK OF STANTON	Stanton	TX	B	B	B-	133.3	14.99	9.8	5.2	1.9	51.1	6.9	8.9	18.5
▼ FIRST NATIONAL BK OF STIGLER	Stigler	OK	B	B+	B+	104.3	5.03	7.3	2.7	5.8	42.5	5.3	7.3	16.8
FIRST NATIONAL BK OF SUFFIELD	Suffield	CT	B	B	B	246.1	4.88	11.5	0.5	40.6	12.9	8.6	10.1	19.5
▲ FIRST NATIONAL BK OF SULLIVAN	Sullivan	IL	D+	D	C-	58.2	-13.30	8.2	6.1	35.7	10.5	8.0	9.6	15.9
FIRST NATIONAL BK OF SYCAMORE	Sycamore	OH	B-	B-	B-	118.5	2.86	3.4	2.1	16.2	49.2	10.0	12.2	24.1
FIRST NATIONAL BK OF SYRACUSE	Syracuse	KS	B+	B+	B	237.2	13.66	8.7	1.4	6.6	25.6	8.7	10.1	14.2
FIRST NATIONAL BK OF TAHOKA	Tahoka	TX	C	C	C+	54.8	-9.65	6.1	3.0	3.5	38.9	9.5	10.7	26.8
▲ FIRST NATIONAL BK OF TALLADEGA	Talladega	AL	B+	C+	C	388.9	1.10	4.5	1.4	10.5	52.9	10.0	13.6	26.5
FIRST NATIONAL BK OF TENNESSEE	Livingston	TN	B-	B-	B-	713.1	3.50	7.3	2.9	15.3	22.4	8.1	9.7	18.4
FIRST NATIONAL BK OF THE LAKES	Navarre	MN	C-	D+	C-	70.4	3.02	8.4	3.7	5.2	6.6	6.5	8.5	20.8
FIRST NATIONAL BK OF THOMAS	Thomas	OK	B+	B+	B+	41.9	4.41	2.3	2.0	8.3	40.2	10.0	14.8	25.8
FIRST NATIONAL BK OF TOM BEAN	Tom Bean	TX	C	C-	C-	64.4	4.62	15.5	11.9	19.1	22.5	6.5	8.5	16.4
▼ FIRST NATIONAL BK OF TRENTON	Trenton	TX	C-	C+	C+	165.9	8.11	1.2	0.9	34.2	41.9	8.7	10.1	22.5
FIRST NATIONAL BK OF TRINITY	Trinity	TX	B-	B-	C+	54.1	-0.63	3.0	11.6	8.1	57.0	7.5	9.3	21.6
FIRST NATIONAL BK OF WAKEFIELD	Wakefield	MI	C	C	C	49.3	-0.94	2.9	8.3	18.7	37.4	8.2	9.8	21.3
FIRST NATIONAL BK OF WALKER	Walker	MN	B	B	B+	367.8	-0.71	5.5	4.0	21.7	29.2	8.4	9.9	17.4
▼ FIRST NATIONAL BK OF WASECA	Waseca	MN	B	B+	C+	125.1	6.66	4.6	2.8	27.1	6.8	4.3	9.2	10.7
FIRST NATIONAL BK OF WATERLOO	Waterloo	IL	C+	C+	C+	384.2	3.86	1.4	0.6	14.0	51.6	7.5	9.3	20.3
FIRST NATIONAL BK OF WAUCHULA	Wauchula	FL	D+	D	D-	77.7	5.18	13.1	2.4	25.8	22.5	8.9	10.2	21.3
FIRST NATIONAL BK OF WAVERLY	Waverly	OH	C+	B-	B	168.4	-3.97	5.2	1.3	16.2	19.5	7.1	9.1	17.3
▲ FIRST NATIONAL BK OF WINNSBORO	Winnsboro	TX	B-	C-	C-	139.8	4.57	2.7	2.7	12.8	16.2	10.0	17.5	27.4
FIRST NATIONAL BK OF WOODSBORO	Woodsboro	TX	C	C-	C-	61.8	10.58	8.3	6.8	13.3	47.6	6.4	8.4	13.8
FIRST NATIONAL BK OF WYNNE	Wynne	AR	C	C	C	277.1	-2.03	7.2	2.2	6.3	26.0	9.0	10.3	15.2
FIRST NATIONAL BK PARK FALLS	Park Falls	WI	B	B	B+	129.8	9.58	10.0	1.4	24.4	36.0	8.5	10.0	18.8
FIRST NATIONAL BK PENNSYLVANIA	Hermitage	PA	C+	C+	C+	15572.3	23.54	14.2	6.1	17.8	18.7	5.9	8.4	11.7
FIRST NATIONAL BK PETERSTOWN	Peterstown	WV	B-	C+	C+	64.3	-1.59	1.3	4.2	32.0	44.7	9.9	10.9	25.9
FIRST NATIONAL BK PORT LAVACA	Port Lavaca	TX	C+	C+	C+	255.3	8.82	3.6	2.9	19.2	51.0	9.0	10.4	26.7
FIRST NATIONAL BK RIVER FALLS	River Falls	WI	C+	C	C+	271.2	0.34	5.9	3.6	13.4	31.6	9.8	10.9	20.3
FIRST NATIONAL BK S CAROLINA	Holly Hill	SC	B-	B-	B-	167.7	1.69	4.0	3.3	11.4	22.1	10.0	14.4	25.8
FIRST NATIONAL BK SAINT JAMES	Saint James	MN	C-	D+	D	30.4	6.17	3.8	4.1	24.7	19.7	6.5	8.5	16.2
▲ FIRST NATIONAL BK SCOTT CITY	Scott City	KS	B	B-	B-	117.3	1.63	12.8	6.5	3.6	27.7	7.2	10.7	12.6
FIRST NATIONAL BK SIOUX FALLS	Sioux Falls	SD	B	B	B	1041.6	3.86	14.4	0.6	19.4	23.0	10.0	13.3	18.7
FIRST NATIONAL BK SOUTH	Alma	GA	B	C+	C-	319.4	2.45	9.1	5.0	15.8	5.7	10.0	14.5	22.8
▲ FIRST NATIONAL BK SOUTH MIAMI	South Miami	FL	C	C-	D+	582.4	16.64	4.7	0.1	3.9	42.7	6.4	8.4	18.2
▼ FIRST NATIONAL BK SOUTHERN CA	Riverside	CA	D	C-	D+	165.1	14.28	1.4	0.2	0.3	20.8	10.0	13.7	24.3
FIRST NATIONAL BK SPEARVILLE	Spearville	KS	B	B	B+	30.4	5.16	5.0	2.3	0.0	14.0	10.0	14.7	23.3
▲ FIRST NATIONAL BK STEELEVILLE	Steeleville	IL	A-	B	B	197.7	-1.19	3.9	4.1	20.3	50.2	10.0	12.6	28.3
FIRST NATIONAL BK TAYLORVILLE	Taylorville	IL	A	A	A-	204.2	3.41	4.5	4.4	10.9	54.3	10.0	13.0	18.6
FIRST NATIONAL BK TEXAS	Killeen	TX	B	B	B	1219.0	7.26	0.3	11.7	11.1	48.8	5.8	7.8	25.1
FIRST NATIONAL BK THROCKMORTON	Throckmorton	TX	C	C	C+	32.3	8.62	5.2	2.7	1.2	4.6	6.8	8.8	15.8
FIRST NATIONAL BK USA	Boutte	LA	C	C-	D	131.1	-4.63	5.5	0.9	26.0	0.8	10.0	12.2	20.3
FIRST NATIONAL BK WASHINGTON	Washington	KS	B+	B+	A-	75.0	5.39	0.9	2.2	12.4	52.7	10.0	21.1	43.9
FIRST NATIONAL BK WAYNESBORO	Waynesboro	GA	A	A	A-	111.1	2.38	5.7	9.1	22.0	15.0	10.0	16.5	31.1
FIRST NATIONAL BK WEATHERFORD	Weatherford	TX	B-	B-	C+	199.0	2.73	13.9	3.9	9.7	7.9	9.3	10.7	14.4
FIRST NATIONAL BK WILLIAMSON	Williamson	WV	A-	A-	A-	92.3	-1.96	4.9	7.1	30.4	36.7	10.0	14.7	33.1
FIRST NATIONAL COMMUNITY BANK	Dunmore	PA	C+	C	D-	981.8	0.37	13.8	9.6	12.7	22.1	8.6	10.1	15.3
▲ FIRST NATIONAL COMMUNITY BANK	Chatsworth	GA	C-	D-	D-	123.8	-0.11	8.0	1.7	15.0	27.8	9.0	10.4	18.2
FIRST NATIONAL COMMUNITY BANK	New Richmond	WI	C-	C	C+	169.4	3.82	5.9	3.6	17.5	23.5	7.3	9.2	14.4
FIRST NATIONAL TRUST CO	Pittsburgh	PA	U	U	U	22.1	10.89	0.0	0.0	0.0	0.0	10.0	78.1	122.8
FIRST NATIONS BANK	Chicago	IL	B	B	B	304.1	0.55	5.4	1.5	7.0	7.5	10.0	12.8	16.4
FIRST NB IN PINCKNEYVILLE	Pinckneyville	IL	A-	A	A	81.6	3.59	0.8	7.1	23.4	46.7	10.0	15.1	35.3
FIRST NB MCCONNELSVILLE	McConnelsville	OH	C	C-	D+	142.1	2.08	1.1	4.3	39.3	23.9	5.2	7.2	16.7
FIRST NB MUHLENBERG COUNTY	Central City	KY	B+	B+	B	144.1	-0.52	3.8	3.4	30.3	31.3	9.5	10.6	21.5
FIRST NB OF CRYSTAL FALLS	Crystal Falls	MI	C-	C-	C	71.1	0.52	5.1	3.1	18.5	5.2	10.0	12.6	23.5
FIRST NB OF FORT STOCKTON	Fort Stockton	TX	B-	B-	B	81.0	27.74	7.0	3.4	11.4	44.8	9.2	10.5	24.5
FIRST NB OF FREDERICKSBURG	Fredericksburg	PA	C-	C-	D+	225.0	4.58	2.9	13.7	15.8	13.6	5.5	7.5	11.6

Asset Quality Index	Adjusted Non-Performing Loans as a % of Total Loans	Adjusted Non-Performing Loans as a % of Capital	Net Charge-Offs Avg Loans	Profitability Index	Net Income ($Mil)	Return on Assets (R.O.A.)	Return on Equity (R.O.E.)	Net Interest Spread	Overhead Efficiency Ratio	Liquidity Index	Liquidity Ratio	Hot Money Ratio	Stability Index
9.8	0.05	0.1	-0.11	**5.4**	4.2	1.27	17.26	3.55	46.4	**3.8**	66.9	26.0	**6.4**
5.7	1.63	6.3	-0.13	**4.6**	0.6	1.02	9.42	3.96	72.3	**4.0**	26.0	10.4	**6.1**
4.5	4.97	16.7	0.00	**3.1**	1.0	0.55	5.39	3.28	80.1	**4.3**	63.1	18.9	**5.5**
4.1	1.42	9.5	0.08	**7.1**	14.9	1.30	11.86	3.71	57.5	**4.1**	9.8	7.5	**8.0**
7.4	0.97	3.8	0.57	**4.5**	0.9	0.88	10.25	3.65	59.0	**4.4**	44.2	14.1	**5.2**
6.4	1.24	6.3	2.68	**4.5**	0.5	0.58	7.66	3.58	56.8	**5.0**	46.2	11.8	**6.7**
5.0	1.75	11.4	0.00	**4.3**	1.2	0.65	6.28	3.01	70.7	**2.9**	25.5	15.9	**6.3**
3.3	2.31	15.2	0.31	**2.6**	0.2	0.45	5.04	3.70	85.6	**4.2**	16.2	7.7	**2.1**
5.5	2.18	8.0	1.14	**3.3**	0.6	0.69	5.39	3.27	77.2	**4.7**	43.6	12.4	**7.6**
5.7	0.74	4.9	0.00	**6.2**	1.9	1.09	10.05	4.27	60.5	**1.5**	27.1	29.3	**5.2**
5.8	1.89	5.4	-0.03	**3.2**	0.3	0.64	6.64	2.51	75.5	**3.6**	69.7	26.1	**4.6**
5.7	3.63	9.6	1.21	**5.0**	3.5	1.19	8.86	3.64	53.7	**2.3**	32.9	24.2	**6.2**
5.0	1.56	8.9	-0.07	**4.3**	5.3	1.01	10.59	3.07	69.9	**3.2**	37.9	18.2	**6.7**
6.0	1.48	6.4	0.17	**2.1**	0.2	0.33	3.82	3.23	90.3	**6.6**	58.1	3.3	**3.1**
8.4	0.82	2.3	-0.03	**5.9**	0.5	1.44	9.62	4.21	65.0	**3.7**	56.2	19.3	**7.3**
7.2	0.20	1.3	0.09	**3.4**	0.3	0.67	8.00	4.11	77.7	**1.9**	32.7	29.7	**4.4**
5.2	1.98	9.6	0.00	**2.2**	0.2	0.15	1.50	2.88	98.0	**5.1**	39.5	9.0	**5.4**
6.0	1.17	4.1	0.22	**4.6**	0.4	1.05	14.84	3.62	75.8	**5.6**	54.5	9.1	**4.0**
6.0	1.04	4.3	0.00	**3.3**	0.2	0.63	7.13	4.31	83.4	**4.2**	55.9	16.6	**4.0**
4.8	1.58	8.7	0.09	**5.8**	3.9	1.43	13.74	3.37	60.4	**2.9**	33.8	18.3	**7.4**
7.2	0.14	1.1	-0.02	**7.4**	1.5	1.62	16.19	4.93	66.2	**4.1**	7.1	6.9	**7.8**
6.6	1.19	4.7	0.08	**3.2**	1.8	0.64	6.53	3.04	77.0	**4.9**	47.3	12.2	**5.3**
1.6	7.97	39.4	0.73	**2.6**	0.3	0.45	4.89	4.24	90.4	**1.3**	29.6	39.5	**4.7**
3.8	3.60	18.1	0.76	**4.7**	1.1	0.83	9.04	3.61	64.2	**4.1**	28.0	10.5	**5.8**
3.6	6.50	20.7	-0.10	**4.2**	1.1	1.04	6.07	4.36	68.8	**1.9**	27.0	23.6	**5.7**
8.9	0.01	0.0	-0.01	**2.5**	0.3	0.59	7.30	3.01	79.3	**5.1**	53.2	11.5	**3.5**
3.2	2.57	13.9	0.01	**4.0**	1.5	0.70	6.17	3.77	75.6	**2.5**	20.5	16.9	**5.8**
5.6	1.76	8.9	0.13	**5.0**	1.3	1.29	12.73	3.91	67.3	**2.7**	40.5	25.0	**7.5**
3.9	0.97	8.1	0.19	**4.9**	98.3	0.94	7.55	3.40	61.8	**4.0**	8.7	8.1	**8.6**
5.5	2.56	10.2	-0.01	**4.5**	0.5	0.94	9.43	3.51	66.0	**3.4**	55.6	22.1	**5.8**
8.8	0.47	1.8	-0.01	**3.9**	1.3	0.73	6.85	2.82	64.9	**2.9**	42.5	23.8	**6.2**
3.8	2.04	10.5	0.55	**5.0**	2.3	1.13	10.24	3.50	70.9	**4.7**	23.4	5.2	**6.5**
5.3	2.94	9.7	0.13	**3.5**	0.6	0.49	3.56	3.61	80.1	**5.0**	43.3	11.0	**7.1**
6.3	0.77	4.9	0.06	**4.3**	0.3	1.11	13.22	4.08	72.4	**2.4**	32.9	21.8	**3.8**
5.4	0.42	2.4	0.68	**5.2**	0.8	0.89	8.79	3.60	58.7	**3.5**	19.9	11.9	**6.0**
7.4	0.78	3.8	-0.09	**4.5**	6.8	0.87	6.43	3.44	73.4	**2.5**	11.6	16.6	**9.6**
4.5	2.08	9.0	1.61	**7.8**	4.4	1.82	12.91	5.33	50.3	**1.8**	18.4	20.4	**6.8**
7.1	0.59	2.7	-0.02	**3.0**	1.5	0.37	4.87	2.64	74.7	**5.1**	42.9	10.2	**2.9**
5.4	1.51	4.9	0.00	**0.0**	-0.8	-0.77	-5.77	2.78	114.1	**6.0**	53.1	7.5	**4.6**
6.1	0.00	0.0	-0.06	**6.2**	0.2	1.01	5.88	3.61	52.3	**2.0**	25.9	20.2	**7.6**
7.9	1.23	3.9	0.17	**5.6**	2.2	1.47	11.74	3.25	58.4	**4.3**	39.6	13.4	**7.2**
8.5	1.04	3.2	0.00	**8.5**	3.2	2.12	16.35	3.63	42.1	**4.7**	57.4	15.7	**8.3**
7.3	1.06	3.8	2.21	**5.3**	13.1	1.36	18.54	3.40	91.4	**7.1**	58.8	3.8	**6.9**
7.1	0.80	4.4	0.00	**2.4**	0.1	0.34	3.92	2.61	88.1	**4.8**	49.2	12.6	**3.9**
1.8	6.37	32.4	0.63	**2.2**	0.4	0.38	3.13	4.14	91.2	**1.9**	21.5	20.0	**4.7**
9.4	0.28	0.5	0.01	**4.2**	0.4	0.77	3.66	2.61	58.3	**3.1**	39.2	19.3	**8.4**
7.4	1.12	3.7	0.22	**6.6**	1.1	1.28	8.03	4.40	62.3	**3.1**	31.6	16.8	**8.0**
3.3	2.10	13.7	0.21	**4.8**	1.4	0.93	9.11	4.69	72.5	**2.4**	18.5	17.5	**6.0**
6.3	1.58	5.4	0.49	**5.5**	0.9	1.30	9.29	4.17	68.0	**2.7**	42.4	25.0	**8.2**
5.4	0.69	4.3	-0.71	**5.2**	15.4	2.11	22.75	3.44	84.5	**2.6**	5.9	15.0	**3.8**
3.1	2.71	13.1	-0.30	**3.0**	0.9	0.95	11.25	4.19	76.2	**3.4**	27.2	13.5	**2.8**
1.9	3.70	24.9	0.15	**4.3**	1.2	0.92	9.83	4.12	81.8	**4.2**	15.5	7.7	**5.6**
6.5	na	0.0	na	**10.0**	2.7	17.42	20.85	na	81.8	**4.0**	127.0	101.0	**5.7**
6.4	0.66	3.4	0.30	**4.8**	1.9	0.83	6.58	3.49	47.1	**0.7**	12.7	36.7	**6.4**
8.2	1.23	3.2	0.09	**5.4**	0.7	1.14	7.05	4.38	68.9	**5.5**	32.0	2.9	**8.5**
2.7	1.75	13.5	0.08	**3.5**	0.6	0.54	4.83	3.68	79.1	**3.8**	17.5	10.1	**6.1**
6.2	1.19	6.0	0.55	**5.1**	1.1	0.97	9.33	3.61	65.7	**1.6**	29.1	30.9	**6.7**
2.4	6.74	24.8	0.39	**1.2**	0.0	-0.02	-0.17	2.95	99.9	**5.5**	52.1	9.1	**5.7**
8.9	0.00	0.0	0.06	**3.4**	0.4	0.73	6.79	3.71	77.3	**4.6**	42.7	12.5	**5.1**
3.3	1.35	10.8	0.13	**2.1**	0.3	0.17	2.68	3.90	91.8	**4.3**	20.4	7.1	**3.0**

	Name	City	State	Rating	2013 Rating	2012 Rating	Total Assets ($Mil)	One Year Asset Growth	Comm-ercial Loans	Cons-umer Loans	Mort-gage Loans	Secur-ities	Capital-ization Index	Lever-age Ratio	Risk-Based Capital Ratio
									Asset Mix (As a % of Total Assets)						
	FIRST NB OF HUGHES SPRINGS	Hughes Springs	TX	**A+**	A+	A	238.9	15.40	12.1	6.6	14.5	27.8	**10.0**	12.7	21.7
	FIRST NB OF PORT ALLEGANY	Port Allegany	PA	**B**	B	B-	94.9	0.08	2.6	4.5	31.6	40.9	**10.0**	11.5	25.8
	FIRST NB OF POWHATAN POINT	Powhatan Point	OH	**C+**	C+	C+	44.8	4.39	5.4	3.1	7.9	56.0	**6.7**	8.7	23.9
▲	FIRST NB OF RUSSELL SPRINGS	Russell Springs	KY	**C+**	B-	A-	202.0	6.89	5.4	2.5	10.2	46.1	**10.0**	12.4	24.5
	FIRST NB OF S PADRE ISLAND	South Padre Island	TX	**C+**	C	C-	59.8	-6.54	2.4	0.5	21.6	30.2	**7.4**	9.3	23.5
	FIRST NB OF STERLING CITY	Sterling City	TX	**B-**	B-	C+	158.1	22.36	5.2	4.0	4.9	65.9	**6.2**	8.2	23.0
	FIRST NBC BANK	New Orleans	LA	**B-**	B-	B-	3628.6	14.97	27.9	0.6	8.0	9.3	**7.4**	10.6	12.8
	FIRST NEBRASKA BANK	Valley	NE	**B-**	B-	C+	265.8	2.48	9.6	2.7	10.4	24.3	**4.9**	8.9	11.0
	FIRST NEBRASKA BANK OF WAYNE	Wayne	NE	**D+**	D+	D+	44.7	11.15	14.8	3.2	4.0	20.7	**7.0**	9.0	16.1
	FIRST NEIGHBOR BANK NA	Toledo	IL	**B**	B	B	296.5	7.49	17.1	6.5	17.4	16.0	**10.0**	12.3	15.8
	FIRST NEIGHBORHOOD BANK	Spencer	WV	**C+**	C+	C	143.8	-1.10	9.4	1.9	32.0	21.4	**8.5**	10.0	17.9
	FIRST NEODESHA BANK	Neodesha	KS	**B**	B	B-	81.7	4.42	8.2	5.3	23.8	14.6	**6.8**	8.8	14.2
	FIRST NEW MEXICO BANK	Deming	NM	**A-**	A-	A-	211.8	2.89	1.5	2.7	11.7	42.6	**10.0**	11.3	22.4
	FIRST NEW MEXICO BK LAS CRUCES	Las Cruces	NM	**A**	A	A-	114.2	4.61	5.0	6.2	11.7	26.8	**10.0**	12.5	22.6
	FIRST NEWTON NATIONAL BK	Newton	IA	**C**	C+	C+	78.0	0.69	11.4	0.8	13.9	27.9	**6.7**	8.7	15.2
	FIRST NIAGARA BANK NA	Buffalo	NY	**C**	C	C-	37905.4	1.58	12.2	7.0	10.2	30.4	**5.4**	7.8	11.3
	FIRST NM BANK OF SILVER CITY	Silver City	NM	**A-**	A-	A-	98.7	3.97	2.0	1.8	12.5	43.7	**10.0**	11.3	22.3
▼	FIRST NORTHERN BANK & TRUST CO	Palmerton	PA	**C**	B-	B-	714.9	7.13	4.0	0.7	26.0	39.8	**10.0**	13.3	23.9
	FIRST NORTHERN BANK OF DIXON	Dixon	CA	**C+**	C+	C+	954.1	8.91	10.8	0.2	5.7	15.1	**7.3**	9.2	16.4
	FIRST NORTHERN BANK OF WYOMING	Buffalo	WY	**B**	B	C+	269.0	13.27	9.8	3.3	10.3	29.4	**6.9**	8.9	13.1
	FIRST OKLAHOMA BANK	Tulsa	OK	**C**	C	D+	317.1	27.05	10.3	1.2	21.0	3.4	**6.9**	9.8	12.5
	FIRST OPTION BANK	Osawatomie	KS	**B**	B	B	269.6	16.29	2.0	1.5	24.2	52.1	**6.1**	8.1	21.1
	FIRST PALMETTO BANK	Camden	SC	**C-**	C-	C-	565.9	0.94	1.4	0.9	16.8	2.7	**10.0**	13.5	21.3
	FIRST PARTNERS BANK	Birmingham	AL	**A-**	A-	B	206.2	21.41	19.8	2.2	6.5	11.0	**10.0**	13.0	17.3
	FIRST PEOPLES BANK	Pine Mountain	GA	**C+**	C	C-	72.0	3.89	4.9	6.7	31.5	9.2	**10.0**	16.2	26.7
	FIRST PEOPLES BANK INC	Mullens	WV	**C+**	C+	B-	123.3	-0.79	0.8	4.5	18.1	49.2	**10.0**	15.4	27.2
	FIRST PEOPLES BANK OF TENNESSE	Jefferson City	TN	**C+**	C	C	143.8	4.27	12.5	2.3	18.1	20.8	**6.3**	8.6	12.0
	FIRST PERSONAL BANK	Orland Park	IL	**C-**	D+	D-	162.8	-2.56	14.0	0.0	29.4	13.0	**5.9**	7.9	15.3
	FIRST PIEDMONT FS&LA GAFFNEY	Gaffney	SC	**A+**	A+	A	330.6	3.28	2.7	1.0	32.6	3.3	**10.0**	23.5	36.7
	FIRST PIONEER NATIONAL BK	Wray	CO	**B+**	B+	B	170.8	2.66	2.2	3.3	3.0	36.8	**10.0**	11.7	20.5
	FIRST PORT CITY BANK	Bainbridge	GA	**A-**	A-	B+	140.6	-2.30	6.9	1.3	16.4	24.6	**10.0**	11.8	16.6
	FIRST PREMIER BANK	Sioux Falls	SD	**A-**	A-	A-	1388.4	13.91	7.3	31.5	3.8	16.7	**10.0**	14.2	19.8
▲	FIRST PRIORITY BANK	Malvern	PA	**C**	D+	D+	470.2	10.04	11.4	2.2	25.5	13.6	**7.1**	9.2	12.6
	FIRST PROGRESSIVE BANK	Brewton	AL	**C**	C	C+	31.5	0.52	8.9	3.3	9.8	58.5	**10.0**	25.3	66.6
	FIRST PRYORITY BANK	Pryor	OK	**C**	C	C-	130.1	11.76	12.5	11.7	2.7	13.2	**10.0**	11.4	18.7
▲	FIRST RELIANCE BANK	Florence	SC	**C-**	D-	D	367.1	1.56	8.5	6.2	12.7	12.7	**9.9**	11.3	15.0
	FIRST REPUBLIC BANK	San Francisco	CA	**B+**	B+	B+	46680.9	13.99	5.8	1.3	43.5	12.7	**7.8**	9.5	14.5
	FIRST RESOURCE BANK	Exton	PA	**C**	C	C-	171.2	6.10	7.4	0.3	24.1	5.7	**8.0**	10.6	13.4
	FIRST RESOURCE BANK	Lino Lakes	MN	**B+**	B	B	82.8	-0.64	7.0	0.6	1.3	12.3	**10.0**	34.1	80.6
	FIRST ROBINSON SB NA	Robinson	IL	**B**	B	B-	279.9	17.94	5.9	4.5	21.0	28.4	**6.2**	8.2	15.4
▲	FIRST S&LA	Mebane	NC	**B**	B-	B-	58.0	-6.48	0.0	0.0	48.4	31.4	**10.0**	19.9	55.1
	FIRST SAFETY BANK	Saint Bernard	OH	**B-**	B-	B-	49.7	-3.91	1.6	1.6	38.8	20.7	**10.0**	19.9	35.0
	FIRST SAVANNA SB	Savanna	IL	**D**	D	D	15.3	8.25	0.0	6.0	48.4	30.0	**8.6**	10.1	22.8
	FIRST SAVINGS BANK	Beresford	SD	**B-**	B-	B-	499.8	8.02	3.3	14.5	7.4	16.9	**10.0**	15.6	21.2
	FIRST SAVINGS BANK FSB	Clarksville	IN	**B-**	B-	B-	707.2	7.86	2.9	1.1	25.8	26.9	**7.2**	9.1	14.9
	FIRST SB	Danville	IL	**C+**	C+	B-	35.5	0.60	0.0	0.8	22.2	68.9	**10.0**	24.7	93.4
	FIRST SB NORTHWEST	Renton	WA	**A-**	B	C-	909.3	2.92	0.2	0.0	30.2	13.7	**10.0**	19.0	29.2
	FIRST SB OF HEGEWISCH	Chicago	IL	**B**	B	B+	559.5	-0.64	0.0	0.1	58.9	20.8	**10.0**	12.8	35.9
	FIRST SB OF PERKASIE	Perkasie	PA	**C+**	C+	C-	1054.3	12.94	2.1	0.2	36.0	24.8	**10.0**	14.1	23.7
	FIRST SCOTTSDALE BANK NA	Scottsdale	AZ	**C-**	C+	D+	94.7	-17.52	11.4	0.9	12.1	9.9	**10.0**	18.2	27.1
	FIRST SECURITY BANK	Mackinaw	IL	**B-**	B-	C	78.0	1.63	8.7	0.7	15.3	11.4	**8.1**	9.7	14.0
	FIRST SECURITY BANK	Searcy	AR	**A+**	A+	A	4593.4	7.24	6.4	1.3	8.0	49.9	**10.0**	13.1	18.2
	FIRST SECURITY BANK	Batesville	MS	**B**	B-	C	491.8	0.63	3.8	3.9	18.8	32.7	**10.0**	11.9	20.8
	FIRST SECURITY BANK	Overbrook	KS	**C+**	C+	C	53.2	1.94	8.7	1.7	11.2	18.3	**6.3**	8.4	12.0
▲	FIRST SECURITY BANK	Union Star	MO	**D**	E+	E+	25.3	5.31	7.6	5.2	25.6	34.5	**5.8**	7.8	16.5
	FIRST SECURITY BANK	Bozeman	MT	**B-**	C+	C-	690.8	7.88	8.2	1.7	15.1	27.4	**7.4**	9.3	14.4
	FIRST SECURITY BANK	Byron	MN	**C**	C	C	55.4	2.55	4.9	2.5	14.2	21.0	**6.4**	8.4	13.4
▼	FIRST SECURITY BANK	Beaver	OK	**C**	B-	B-	112.8	-1.97	16.9	2.8	11.6	23.6	**6.4**	8.4	12.9
▼	FIRST SECURITY BANK & TRUST CO	Oklahoma City	OK	**D**	D+	D-	48.8	-3.19	20.8	1.4	38.6	2.7	**5.4**	8.2	11.3
	FIRST SECURITY BANK & TRUST CO	Charles City	IA	**B-**	B-	C	456.4	1.04	8.4	2.1	10.1	28.6	**6.5**	8.5	12.6

Asset Quality Index	Adjusted Non-Performing Loans as a % of Total Loans	as a % of Capital	Net Charge-Offs Avg Loans	Profitability Index	Net Income ($Mil)	Return on Assets (R.O.A.)	Return on Equity (R.O.E.)	Net Interest Spread	Overhead Efficiency Ratio	Liquidity Index	Liquidity Ratio	Hot Money Ratio	Stability Index
7.9	0.71	3.1	0.38	**9.4**	3.6	2.05	14.58	5.53	58.5	**3.3**	15.3	12.7	**9.5**
5.5	2.46	9.7	0.04	**4.3**	0.6	0.84	7.75	4.01	74.7	**3.5**	32.6	15.0	**5.9**
9.7	0.00	0.0	0.14	**3.2**	0.2	0.66	7.71	2.19	65.6	**7.0**	83.9	5.4	**4.6**
2.3	7.98	24.6	0.36	**3.4**	0.8	0.53	4.19	3.96	82.0	**3.2**	44.3	20.2	**6.8**
5.3	2.58	9.9	-0.36	**3.2**	0.3	0.61	6.54	3.12	78.8	**5.5**	59.9	11.0	**4.5**
8.9	0.23	0.6	0.03	**3.8**	1.0	0.87	12.58	2.94	66.5	**5.9**	55.3	9.4	**4.1**
6.1	0.83	5.9	0.04	**4.5**	40.6	1.55	14.41	3.38	62.2	**1.1**	2.7	27.8	**8.8**
7.4	0.21	1.4	0.04	**4.2**	1.7	0.85	9.67	3.33	73.3	**4.6**	21.8	5.5	**5.2**
6.0	1.47	7.3	-0.15	**2.3**	0.1	0.21	2.61	3.26	87.8	**6.1**	38.1	2.0	**1.4**
4.1	2.05	12.1	0.08	**5.6**	2.1	0.94	7.31	4.06	66.9	**3.4**	4.2	11.0	**7.5**
9.0	0.04	0.2	0.15	**3.5**	0.7	0.62	6.48	3.84	78.0	**4.6**	31.5	9.1	**5.1**
8.2	0.01	0.1	0.00	**7.0**	1.0	1.56	17.58	3.85	60.6	**2.0**	7.6	18.0	**6.3**
9.8	0.66	2.0	0.01	**6.2**	1.9	1.16	10.54	3.87	59.4	**6.2**	52.3	5.8	**7.6**
9.0	0.05	0.2	0.06	**7.1**	1.1	1.25	9.97	4.91	60.9	**4.9**	56.9	14.8	**8.3**
8.3	0.01	0.1	0.03	**3.0**	0.3	0.45	5.20	3.62	86.5	**5.2**	34.2	6.3	**4.8**
3.6	1.45	10.6	0.27	**1.3**	-756.4	-2.65	-19.65	3.42	173.2	**4.2**	16.6	8.3	**4.1**
9.8	0.40	1.2	0.05	**5.7**	0.9	1.20	10.98	4.46	65.5	**6.4**	65.2	6.2	**7.6**
5.6	2.52	10.1	0.72	**1.7**	1.8	0.35	2.48	3.46	92.3	**3.7**	36.8	15.2	**7.6**
4.7	1.78	10.0	0.66	**3.7**	4.3	0.62	6.89	3.36	71.0	**5.6**	41.7	6.8	**5.0**
5.1	1.04	6.4	0.06	**6.2**	2.9	1.50	17.08	4.50	67.9	**2.5**	17.4	16.9	**5.4**
5.9	0.49	3.8	0.04	**2.8**	0.6	0.29	2.91	3.89	86.3	**0.8**	16.6	41.2	**5.1**
6.7	0.79	3.9	0.61	**5.5**	2.7	1.36	16.93	3.37	64.5	**4.2**	27.8	9.9	**5.0**
1.5	5.63	26.7	0.30	**3.7**	2.9	0.68	4.87	3.29	66.5	**1.6**	27.2	28.9	**6.9**
5.0	1.34	7.9	0.25	**6.6**	1.7	1.16	8.85	4.80	64.7	**1.6**	22.0	25.5	**6.1**
2.9	4.53	17.7	0.62	**4.6**	0.4	0.69	4.26	5.32	80.3	**3.6**	20.4	11.3	**6.1**
9.4	0.65	1.3	0.13	**2.9**	0.4	0.45	2.93	2.00	74.2	**4.9**	56.3	14.6	**7.0**
5.0	0.76	5.8	0.57	**3.2**	0.4	0.36	4.53	4.30	86.9	**3.6**	19.0	11.5	**3.5**
2.2	4.60	30.4	-0.15	**3.0**	0.6	0.44	5.45	3.51	80.0	**3.6**	34.4	15.3	**3.2**
9.0	0.45	1.4	0.00	**7.7**	2.8	1.15	4.25	4.40	64.6	**4.0**	30.2	11.5	**9.2**
8.6	0.00	0.0	0.00	**3.8**	1.0	0.76	6.49	3.02	69.7	**3.0**	28.4	15.9	**6.3**
5.6	1.56	8.1	0.20	**6.3**	1.2	1.13	9.80	4.07	61.3	**2.6**	27.5	18.0	**6.7**
5.6	0.85	3.4	0.17	**7.1**	17.1	1.66	11.52	3.95	61.4	**1.8**	13.2	20.3	**9.8**
4.3	1.13	9.7	0.21	**3.1**	1.9	0.59	5.97	3.74	79.8	**0.9**	11.5	32.2	**3.6**
7.1	2.82	3.2	1.35	**2.3**	0.1	0.31	1.25	3.22	85.3	**4.9**	94.5	18.8	**6.7**
4.3	3.35	13.4	0.04	**1.5**	0.3	0.27	2.18	3.08	86.7	**2.6**	32.1	19.3	**4.0**
2.9	2.45	14.5	0.05	**3.8**	4.6	1.75	15.67	4.54	87.4	**3.3**	16.4	12.6	**3.8**
8.9	0.16	1.3	0.00	**5.9**	371.6	1.10	11.00	3.36	56.1	**4.1**	9.3	7.8	**7.0**
2.4	2.28	18.1	0.18	**4.2**	0.9	0.69	6.51	3.88	69.2	**0.5**	2.0	38.1	**5.6**
8.9	1.58	1.6	-0.25	**10.0**	5.8	9.49	32.34	8.25	35.8	**5.9**	76.1	11.5	**5.1**
6.3	0.70	4.8	0.29	**4.9**	1.7	0.82	10.23	3.28	64.5	**4.2**	14.9	7.2	**4.1**
8.1	2.43	6.1	0.00	**4.1**	0.3	0.74	3.88	3.74	71.1	**2.6**	60.1	43.2	**7.1**
7.5	1.73	5.5	-0.02	**3.3**	0.2	0.62	3.09	3.33	83.9	**5.0**	41.8	10.3	**6.7**
3.5	2.39	13.4	0.02	**1.5**	0.0	0.05	0.62	3.50	96.5	**2.2**	31.4	19.6	**3.4**
2.9	2.41	9.2	2.99	**8.8**	6.0	1.64	10.59	8.77	53.9	**2.9**	12.3	14.5	**6.9**
4.2	1.78	11.3	0.21	**5.0**	5.1	0.97	8.73	4.04	64.2	**2.6**	30.5	19.0	**7.0**
7.0	6.26	5.8	1.92	**2.6**	0.1	0.46	1.80	2.26	86.3	**4.2**	99.9	27.7	**7.2**
7.4	0.92	3.5	0.08	**6.6**	8.4	1.24	6.67	3.79	51.5	**0.8**	22.1	48.1	**6.3**
9.7	0.63	2.9	0.13	**4.0**	2.5	0.58	4.66	2.66	63.2	**3.0**	42.3	21.1	**7.6**
4.0	4.15	18.4	0.26	**3.2**	4.0	0.55	3.62	2.72	80.0	**3.9**	24.5	12.6	**7.3**
8.7	0.07	0.3	-0.08	**1.1**	-0.1	-0.12	-0.71	4.42	99.9	**1.8**	33.5	31.7	**5.7**
5.7	0.73	5.1	0.03	**3.7**	0.4	0.76	7.27	3.47	78.1	**2.3**	12.6	17.2	**5.0**
8.5	0.80	2.4	0.21	**10.0**	75.6	2.28	16.76	5.44	40.5	**3.9**	29.4	15.2	**10.0**
7.2	0.71	3.1	-0.31	**4.6**	3.6	0.94	7.68	3.94	73.8	**3.9**	20.1	9.9	**6.2**
7.2	0.00	0.0	0.00	**3.5**	0.3	0.64	7.08	4.03	82.2	**3.3**	23.8	13.6	**4.7**
2.4	3.07	19.7	0.69	**2.6**	0.1	0.44	5.86	3.42	88.8	**4.2**	33.1	11.7	**2.3**
4.7	1.17	7.0	-0.25	**4.8**	5.7	1.14	11.29	3.67	70.6	**4.8**	26.2	5.1	**6.5**
4.4	1.74	11.7	0.00	**3.9**	0.4	0.89	10.70	3.93	77.1	**3.8**	27.9	12.0	**4.0**
3.8	1.47	10.4	1.43	**2.4**	0.2	0.25	3.22	2.65	58.2	**0.8**	18.1	36.3	**5.3**
1.6	3.09	29.8	0.77	**3.2**	0.1	0.15	1.74	5.39	86.7	**1.0**	5.4	28.5	**4.7**
4.1	1.58	10.9	0.03	**6.0**	4.7	1.38	12.89	4.07	61.8	**4.3**	31.7	10.8	**6.3**

Name	City	State	Rating	2013 Rating	2012 Rating	Total Assets ($Mil)	One Year Asset Growth	Asset Mix (As a % of Total Assets) Commercial Loans	Consumer Loans	Mortgage Loans	Securities	Capitalization Index	Leverage Ratio	Risk-Based Capital Ratio
▲ FIRST SECURITY BANK - CANBY	Canby	MN	**A**	B+	A-	64.3	-1.16	10.4	2.2	3.0	20.5	**10.0**	13.2	21.7
FIRST SECURITY BANK - WEST	Beulah	ND	**A**	A	A	68.2	7.97	9.4	1.0	1.2	26.4	**10.0**	12.5	23.9
FIRST SECURITY BANK DEER LODGE	Deer Lodge	MT	**B-**	B-	C+	29.1	-0.02	8.4	5.1	22.7	2.4	**7.6**	9.4	16.1
▲ FIRST SECURITY BANK INC	Owensboro	KY	**C+**	C	C+	528.9	15.78	7.5	2.6	27.3	11.5	**5.6**	7.9	11.5
FIRST SECURITY BANK KENTUCKY	Central City	KY	**C+**	C+	D+	93.2	7.32	13.6	5.3	31.3	10.0	**6.5**	8.5	12.8
FIRST SECURITY BANK OF HELENA	Helena	MT	**D**	D	D	37.9	-0.51	20.0	4.5	43.1	5.2	**9.2**	10.5	16.7
FIRST SECURITY BANK OF MALTA	Malta	MT	**C+**	C	D+	32.5	4.95	8.0	8.9	1.5	23.4	**9.9**	10.9	18.1
FIRST SECURITY BANK OF NEVADA	Las Vegas	NV	**B-**	C	C	169.3	42.48	2.9	0.0	1.3	6.8	**10.0**	13.5	19.8
FIRST SECURITY BANK OF ROUNDUP	Roundup	MT	**B-**	B-	B-	47.9	-2.26	10.3	4.3	4.6	30.8	**9.7**	10.8	17.8
FIRST SECURITY BANK-HENDRICKS	Hendricks	MN	**B**	B	B-	22.9	8.80	8.1	3.0	9.5	20.8	**10.0**	11.7	23.6
▲ FIRST SECURITY BANK-SLEEPY EYE	Sleepy Eye	MN	**A**	B+	A-	201.2	2.39	6.0	2.4	8.9	18.7	**10.0**	12.1	17.0
FIRST SECURITY BUSINESS BANK	Orange	CA	**B**	B	B-	61.7	-34.69	0.6	0.0	0.0	0.0	**10.0**	26.0	35.1
FIRST SECURITY STATE BK	Evansdale	IA	**B**	B	C+	88.2	5.80	23.9	30.5	12.5	10.4	**6.4**	9.9	12.1
FIRST SECURITY STATE BK	Cranfills Gap	TX	**B**	B	B	116.2	6.45	2.1	3.9	12.1	50.8	**5.0**	7.0	16.8
▼ FIRST SECURITY TRUST & SB	Elmwood Park	IL	**D-**	D-	D-	236.1	-5.73	8.7	0.2	9.6	28.4	**7.4**	9.3	17.4
FIRST SENTINEL BANK	Richlands	VA	**C+**	C+	C-	167.6	0.20	4.2	13.5	34.5	1.1	**8.0**	9.7	15.5
FIRST SENTRY BANK INC	Huntington	WV	**C+**	C-	D+	490.7	-0.97	16.4	2.0	17.9	18.5	**7.0**	9.0	14.7
FIRST SERVICE BANK	Greenbrier	AR	**B**	B	B-	234.4	10.56	7.6	3.3	27.2	7.5	**10.0**	11.2	15.8
FIRST SHORE FS&LA	Salisbury	MD	**B**	B-	B-	290.5	-1.42	1.2	4.8	59.4	6.7	**10.0**	13.8	22.9
FIRST SOUND BANK	Seattle	WA	**D+**	D+	E-	96.5	-2.13	53.6	0.4	0.2	0.0	**7.9**	9.9	13.3
FIRST SOUTH BANK	Jackson	TN	**B-**	B-	B	434.9	2.87	5.7	2.0	12.4	33.5	**9.6**	10.8	18.3
FIRST SOUTH BANK	Spartanburg	SC	**E-**	E-	E-	259.7	-11.94	10.2	0.1	1.6	23.0	**0.2**	3.6	6.4
▲ FIRST SOUTH BANK	Washington	NC	**B-**	B-	C-	733.9	7.74	3.3	0.5	17.7	25.6	**10.0**	11.0	16.2
FIRST SOUTHEAST BANK	Harmony	MN	**B-**	B-	B-	92.3	5.05	10.1	3.5	10.1	8.0	**5.9**	8.8	11.7
▼ FIRST SOUTHERN BANK	Marion	IL	**B+**	B+	B+	595.3	70.52	6.2	6.0	15.6	27.1	**8.3**	9.8	13.6
FIRST SOUTHERN BANK	Columbia	MS	**B-**	B-	C+	193.8	-7.20	7.1	5.8	17.3	20.5	**8.0**	9.6	14.6
FIRST SOUTHERN BANK	Florence	AL	**B-**	B-	C+	205.8	4.52	12.7	2.9	28.8	11.5	**7.4**	9.3	14.3
FIRST SOUTHERN BANK	Patterson	GA	**E-**	E-	E-	86.4	-8.57	8.7	1.4	13.5	9.6	**1.6**	5.8	8.6
▲ FIRST SOUTHERN NATIONAL BK	Lancaster	KY	**B-**	C+	B-	663.9	-6.76	4.1	2.5	23.3	24.9	**7.6**	9.4	16.2
FIRST SOUTHERN STATE BK	Stevenson	AL	**B**	B	B-	351.8	1.03	1.7	7.1	17.6	40.6	**8.3**	9.9	17.0
FIRST SOUTHWEST BANK	Alamosa	CO	**D+**	C-	D	242.8	3.45	4.5	1.0	8.4	14.1	**8.0**	9.6	14.8
FIRST STAR BANK SSB	Bremond	TX	**B+**	A-	B+	236.4	5.62	4.9	3.1	13.6	24.4	**10.0**	11.9	16.9
FIRST STATE B&TC OF LARNED	Larned	KS	**A**	A	A-	126.9	2.42	7.1	1.4	3.9	24.2	**10.0**	12.6	20.2
FIRST STATE BK	Ness City	KS	**A-**	A-	A-	66.5	3.55	7.7	2.8	0.5	55.3	**10.0**	14.8	24.7
FIRST STATE BK	Norton	KS	**B+**	B+	B+	310.9	-1.42	10.1	2.4	2.3	44.0	**7.7**	9.4	16.1
FIRST STATE BK	Buxton	ND	**B**	B	C+	167.2	5.41	14.5	1.0	13.5	4.4	**7.8**	10.8	13.2
FIRST STATE BK	Wilmot	SD	**B-**	B-	B-	42.2	11.67	9.8	2.9	0.9	31.4	**9.9**	11.0	17.8
FIRST STATE BK	Armour	SD	**B**	B	B	112.7	11.72	4.6	3.4	1.0	21.2	**5.3**	7.3	12.8
FIRST STATE BK	Lonoke	AR	**D+**	D+	C-	254.1	-1.88	2.4	0.4	8.8	27.1	**9.7**	10.8	19.8
FIRST STATE BK	Crossett	AR	**C+**	C+	C	37.4	-5.09	5.2	11.5	11.9	32.8	**10.0**	12.3	26.6
FIRST STATE BK	Russellville	AR	**A-**	A-	B	208.0	8.60	7.9	1.7	19.4	14.5	**9.8**	10.9	16.8
FIRST STATE BK	Union City	TN	**A-**	B+	B	1929.0	3.03	6.9	7.2	14.9	34.1	**8.7**	10.1	17.3
FIRST STATE BK	Irvington	KY	**B+**	B+	A-	163.0	1.23	0.2	3.9	28.0	40.1	**9.3**	10.5	25.4
FIRST STATE BK	Holly Springs	MS	**C-**	C-	C-	113.9	1.96	6.4	2.5	17.0	35.6	**8.8**	10.2	17.2
FIRST STATE BK	Ida Grove	IA	**B+**	B+	B	134.5	-6.09	6.3	3.7	9.7	26.8	**8.7**	10.4	13.9
FIRST STATE BK	Hawarden	IA	**C**	C+	B-	46.5	-3.77	11.3	1.8	9.4	3.6	**5.9**	8.2	11.7
FIRST STATE BK	Britt	IA	**A**	A	A	103.6	5.97	3.2	1.1	11.4	46.1	**9.9**	11.0	19.8
▲ FIRST STATE BK	Belmond	IA	**B**	B-	B-	96.5	1.14	8.9	2.7	7.8	54.8	**9.8**	10.9	24.0
FIRST STATE BK	Lynnville	IA	**A-**	A-	B-	158.8	49.75	5.7	2.1	11.8	24.5	**9.0**	10.4	14.4
FIRST STATE BK	Webster City	IA	**B+**	B	C+	348.4	11.53	10.6	0.7	8.9	14.7	**7.6**	11.3	13.0
FIRST STATE BK	Sioux Rapids	IA	**B**	B	B+	35.9	-0.40	1.6	1.0	4.8	47.6	**10.0**	14.4	35.4
FIRST STATE BK	Stuart	IA	**C+**	C+	C+	99.1	1.69	9.1	3.1	8.9	30.3	**6.0**	8.0	17.5
FIRST STATE BK	Sumner	IA	**B-**	B-	B-	103.0	-0.92	5.5	2.5	11.4	37.1	**10.0**	11.5	19.9
FIRST STATE BK	New London	WI	**C+**	C+	C	258.9	0.42	3.6	0.5	10.1	42.0	**10.0**	13.7	23.2
FIRST STATE BK	Saint Clair Shores	MI	**B-**	C+	C-	649.1	13.03	8.2	0.5	12.9	24.1	**8.2**	9.8	14.3
FIRST STATE BK	Nashua	IA	**B**	B	B-	46.4	2.30	8.4	2.4	13.5	12.6	**9.9**	10.9	15.0
FIRST STATE BK	Wrens	GA	**E+**	E	E-	90.2	3.58	5.2	5.9	34.1	19.0	**5.6**	7.6	13.2
FIRST STATE BK	Waynesboro	MS	**B+**	B+	B	541.0	6.08	7.7	3.0	26.4	31.3	**9.0**	10.3	16.7
FIRST STATE BK	Monticello	IL	**C+**	C	C-	231.3	-5.30	5.2	2.7	15.3	29.2	**6.5**	8.5	13.7
FIRST STATE BK	Mendota	IL	**C**	C-	C-	863.3	-8.20	7.4	1.2	24.0	19.5	**6.4**	8.5	12.8

Asset Quality Index	Adjusted Non-Performing Loans as a % of Total Loans	Adjusted Non-Performing Loans as a % of Capital	Net Charge-Offs / Avg Loans	Profitability Index	Net Income ($Mil)	Return on Assets (R.O.A.)	Return on Equity (R.O.E.)	Net Interest Spread	Overhead Efficiency Ratio	Liquidity Index	Liquidity Ratio	Hot Money Ratio	Stability Index
7.1	0.31	1.2	0.01	**9.4**	1.1	2.30	14.38	4.45	44.6	**6.2**	36.9	0.5	**7.9**
9.2	0.33	0.9	0.08	**7.2**	0.7	1.48	10.40	3.72	53.5	**6.8**	53.9	1.4	**8.3**
8.6	0.03	0.2	-0.10	**4.8**	0.2	0.76	7.75	4.10	73.1	**4.7**	30.9	8.2	**4.3**
4.5	0.89	8.4	0.08	**4.2**	2.5	0.66	7.56	3.67	69.8	**1.7**	13.4	21.2	**4.6**
6.2	0.41	3.4	0.05	**5.2**	0.7	1.02	12.63	4.90	72.2	**1.3**	8.9	25.6	**4.5**
1.2	6.08	37.8	0.17	**2.3**	0.1	0.25	2.43	4.69	94.4	**1.9**	22.6	20.8	**3.7**
4.2	1.61	8.7	0.04	**6.6**	0.3	1.37	13.04	4.22	63.3	**3.6**	34.2	15.0	**4.7**
3.8	1.95	9.0	-0.06	**6.0**	1.8	1.53	8.70	4.50	67.3	**3.2**	29.7	15.6	**5.1**
4.0	3.12	14.7	0.19	**7.4**	0.6	1.69	16.77	4.31	62.7	**4.3**	26.6	8.7	**7.3**
8.9	0.08	0.3	0.00	**9.1**	0.4	2.37	21.07	3.96	46.5	**5.4**	58.1	9.0	**6.3**
6.7	0.70	3.5	0.45	**8.2**	2.9	1.91	13.72	4.42	55.8	**5.0**	27.8	4.5	**8.4**
0.6	10.30	27.0	-0.01	**9.3**	0.8	1.38	5.97	4.22	43.3	**1.5**	11.8	23.5	**8.5**
5.7	0.26	2.2	0.02	**6.4**	0.9	1.45	14.24	4.13	63.9	**1.3**	12.9	26.3	**5.6**
9.0	0.10	0.4	0.10	**4.6**	1.0	1.18	15.80	3.30	68.7	**6.4**	70.2	8.8	**4.6**
2.3	4.75	22.8	6.43	**0.0**	-3.6	-2.20	-19.04	3.74	115.9	**5.0**	51.9	12.8	**4.7**
3.3	1.72	12.6	0.54	**6.6**	1.3	0.98	10.14	5.16	64.3	**1.8**	13.4	19.8	**5.3**
4.5	0.89	6.4	0.55	**4.8**	3.2	0.87	9.33	3.70	55.6	**0.9**	18.1	35.5	**4.2**
4.6	2.09	13.1	0.09	**4.9**	1.9	1.12	9.24	5.44	80.8	**1.7**	9.1	19.7	**6.1**
4.2	2.57	14.9	0.02	**4.0**	1.6	0.71	5.20	3.46	69.6	**1.5**	10.2	22.8	**6.9**
6.1	0.39	3.0	0.09	**1.8**	0.0	0.02	0.16	3.79	98.4	**0.8**	10.6	33.4	**2.2**
3.8	2.23	11.2	-0.53	**7.1**	5.4	1.64	13.51	3.73	70.7	**2.8**	23.5	15.6	**7.3**
0.3	8.61	83.2	0.03	**1.5**	0.5	0.23	10.83	3.09	95.5	**1.1**	19.9	32.5	**0.0**
5.7	1.20	6.7	0.33	**3.7**	3.9	0.75	6.00	4.22	74.5	**2.5**	30.8	19.6	**6.1**
3.5	0.96	8.3	0.07	**6.2**	1.0	1.44	16.43	4.33	66.5	**2.0**	5.2	18.1	**6.4**
4.0	1.54	9.7	0.04	**5.4**	3.1	0.98	9.84	3.44	57.4	**2.0**	18.6	19.6	**7.9**
3.8	2.44	15.2	-0.25	**4.4**	1.4	0.97	10.20	4.27	79.6	**2.2**	17.1	18.3	**4.8**
5.5	0.64	4.9	0.01	**4.5**	1.1	0.74	8.27	4.14	69.4	**2.9**	16.4	14.6	**5.1**
0.3	15.56	135.1	1.22	**0.8**	0.0	0.00	-0.03	4.24	100.0	**2.6**	7.6	15.4	**0.0**
4.0	1.53	9.6	-0.20	**6.1**	5.2	1.01	8.97	3.96	67.9	**3.3**	24.2	13.3	**7.6**
8.6	0.15	0.7	0.28	**5.8**	2.8	1.04	10.76	3.74	60.7	**2.8**	38.1	20.9	**4.9**
3.9	0.89	6.0	0.11	**1.1**	-0.4	-0.20	-1.73	4.26	104.8	**2.2**	16.8	18.4	**4.9**
6.7	0.76	4.1	0.07	**6.1**	1.5	0.86	7.81	4.08	69.6	**1.5**	5.4	21.5	**7.0**
8.7	0.00	0.0	0.01	**7.2**	1.5	1.63	13.12	3.93	57.6	**4.7**	31.5	8.5	**8.0**
8.9	0.21	0.5	-0.02	**7.1**	0.9	1.80	12.72	3.90	47.7	**4.5**	48.4	14.0	**8.9**
6.8	0.36	1.8	0.20	**6.4**	3.5	1.50	13.80	4.05	57.1	**1.8**	22.9	23.0	**7.1**
5.3	0.52	4.0	0.00	**5.6**	1.7	1.35	12.63	3.57	63.3	**0.9**	2.9	29.6	**7.3**
7.6	0.00	0.0	-0.05	**7.3**	0.6	1.96	18.96	4.25	50.7	**4.2**	32.5	11.2	**4.2**
7.1	0.05	0.5	0.02	**5.3**	1.0	1.24	17.62	3.11	66.1	**4.3**	21.6	7.4	**5.2**
6.2	2.11	9.5	0.49	**1.8**	0.5	0.24	2.29	3.26	95.0	**2.0**	29.2	23.5	**4.1**
3.8	4.58	14.3	0.33	**4.5**	0.2	0.62	5.10	4.81	81.1	**3.4**	55.6	22.4	**4.8**
6.3	0.57	3.1	-0.11	**5.4**	1.3	0.85	7.54	3.67	67.4	**2.3**	22.9	18.2	**6.4**
7.3	0.63	3.4	0.19	**6.6**	17.4	1.20	12.09	3.74	59.0	**1.2**	19.4	32.5	**7.8**
9.3	0.15	0.6	0.06	**5.1**	1.2	0.94	9.78	3.58	69.2	**5.6**	44.0	7.1	**7.2**
5.1	2.06	9.5	-0.06	**2.2**	0.2	0.26	2.66	3.22	91.8	**1.8**	18.2	20.4	**3.8**
5.3	1.42	8.4	0.10	**7.1**	1.8	1.79	17.35	4.25	53.1	**2.4**	32.5	21.1	**6.8**
1.6	2.76	24.3	0.00	**4.0**	0.3	0.81	9.36	3.62	66.5	**2.7**	11.0	15.3	**4.9**
9.1	0.19	0.8	-0.09	**6.8**	1.1	1.37	12.20	3.21	38.8	**4.3**	49.7	15.8	**8.3**
7.4	0.09	0.3	0.39	**4.4**	0.8	1.05	9.64	2.82	61.9	**5.6**	63.9	10.8	**6.2**
5.6	1.19	7.4	-0.02	**7.4**	1.5	1.60	14.69	4.20	53.0	**2.5**	28.9	18.8	**6.5**
8.0	0.11	0.7	0.04	**7.3**	3.1	1.23	10.51	3.57	63.5	**2.5**	15.9	16.8	**7.0**
9.7	0.00	0.0	0.04	**4.0**	0.2	0.81	5.79	3.01	65.0	**6.7**	80.2	6.8	**7.4**
8.6	0.00	0.0	-0.15	**3.5**	0.4	0.47	6.09	3.16	71.7	**5.1**	39.9	9.4	**4.1**
8.4	0.56	2.3	0.00	**4.6**	0.7	0.93	7.16	3.71	63.9	**3.9**	46.3	17.1	**6.1**
6.2	2.54	7.7	0.14	**3.3**	1.2	0.63	4.60	3.29	76.8	**5.0**	52.4	13.1	**5.7**
4.2	2.62	15.1	-0.02	**4.7**	4.1	0.89	8.37	4.13	73.1	**3.7**	30.1	13.4	**5.8**
5.2	0.67	4.1	0.02	**7.6**	0.5	1.28	12.01	3.48	47.7	**0.9**	20.4	35.1	**6.2**
2.3	2.48	20.3	0.32	**4.2**	0.5	0.73	9.75	5.07	78.0	**1.6**	18.7	23.7	**2.2**
8.4	0.29	1.7	-0.01	**5.6**	4.3	1.08	10.57	4.20	61.8	**1.6**	12.4	22.6	**6.8**
3.9	2.25	14.6	0.04	**5.8**	2.5	1.41	15.89	4.24	65.1	**3.2**	19.3	13.6	**4.7**
3.1	1.96	15.4	0.18	**3.0**	0.9	0.14	1.55	3.55	94.7	**2.0**	14.9	19.1	**4.5**

Name	City	State	Rating	2013 Rating	2012 Rating	Total Assets ($Mil)	One Year Asset Growth	Asset Mix (As a % of Total Assets) Commercial Loans	Consumer Loans	Mortgage Loans	Securities	Capitalization Index	Leverage Ratio	Risk-Based Capital Ratio
FIRST STATE BK	Winchester	OH	**B**	B	B+	318.3	20.89	2.0	5.6	23.2	29.4	**6.9**	9.0	15.5
FIRST STATE BK	Danville	VA	**E-**	E-	E-	39.2	1.14	5.8	6.4	17.3	17.9	**0.7**	4.0	7.4
FIRST STATE BK	Barboursville	WV	**D-**	D-	D-	252.9	-8.88	13.9	2.1	33.4	6.0	**5.5**	7.5	11.5
FIRST STATE BK	Chico	TX	**C**	C	C+	205.3	1.10	12.8	4.8	12.6	39.2	**8.4**	9.9	18.6
▲ FIRST STATE BK	Clute	TX	**C+**	C	C	167.2	21.26	10.7	8.6	6.6	21.2	**6.3**	8.3	16.7
FIRST STATE BK	Socorro	NM	**B+**	B+	B+	124.4	6.86	0.2	0.8	5.3	78.7	**9.1**	10.4	48.9
FIRST STATE BK	Abernathy	TX	**B-**	B-	C+	31.2	12.07	5.3	8.9	0.2	16.7	**10.0**	12.2	15.7
FIRST STATE BK	Athens	TX	**A-**	A-	B	376.5	6.61	6.6	4.7	25.6	24.8	**9.6**	10.7	20.1
FIRST STATE BK	Commerce	OK	**C+**	C	C	11.0	-10.62	9.5	15.2	17.7	26.7	**10.0**	12.5	17.4
FIRST STATE BK	Ryan	OK	**C+**	C	D+	28.3	-5.04	4.1	5.9	18.4	0.1	**10.0**	12.5	22.5
FIRST STATE BK	Tahlequah	OK	**B-**	C+	C	64.1	-0.97	6.5	1.0	14.4	15.2	**10.0**	13.5	18.8
▲ FIRST STATE BK	Valliant	OK	**B-**	C+	C-	42.3	-4.77	6.1	7.9	12.8	34.5	**10.0**	12.1	22.4
FIRST STATE BK	Waynoka	OK	**D+**	C-	C+	22.9	-2.97	6.0	2.9	2.9	52.9	**9.8**	10.9	31.1
FIRST STATE BK	Watonga	OK	**B**	B	C	56.2	3.11	16.2	6.4	2.3	33.2	**7.7**	9.5	16.8
FIRST STATE BK	Noble	OK	**C**	C-	D+	55.0	-5.61	2.0	7.8	15.8	23.8	**7.0**	9.0	22.2
▼ FIRST STATE BK	Grandfield	OK	**D-**	D	C-	37.9	-7.86	3.0	4.1	12.2	33.7	**5.6**	7.6	14.7
▲ FIRST STATE BK	Boise City	OK	**B-**	C	C-	62.3	4.15	1.9	11.8	2.6	16.9	**7.1**	10.3	12.6
FIRST STATE BK	Anadarko	OK	**A**	A-	A	93.6	6.46	2.0	4.2	4.2	65.2	**10.0**	15.6	37.6
FIRST STATE BK	Yukon	OK	**C-**	C-	C	21.6	-2.02	19.6	9.4	30.6	0.0	**7.2**	9.1	12.7
FIRST STATE BK	Elmore City	OK	**E+**	D-	D	10.8	8.87	18.6	4.1	22.2	4.4	**4.5**	7.1	10.8
FIRST STATE BK	Oklahoma City	OK	**C+**	C+	B-	181.4	7.22	32.3	0.6	11.5	3.4	**4.7**	9.2	10.8
FIRST STATE BK	Randolph	NE	**A-**	B+	A-	51.6	4.87	1.5	1.6	2.6	13.5	**10.0**	13.8	16.9
FIRST STATE BK	Scottsbluff	NE	**B+**	B+	B	272.2	15.32	7.9	1.5	8.3	14.9	**6.3**	8.7	12.0
FIRST STATE BK	Hordville	NE	**C+**	C+	C+	40.6	11.30	4.3	1.0	7.3	6.6	**7.4**	9.9	12.8
FIRST STATE BK	Loomis	NE	**B**	B	A-	140.8	3.90	5.5	4.7	5.3	13.1	**5.2**	8.2	11.1
▲ FIRST STATE BK	Gothenburg	NE	**C+**	B-	C+	311.6	5.54	9.0	1.3	4.3	20.3	**9.7**	12.8	14.7
FIRST STATE BK	Farnam	NE	**C+**	B-	B-	55.0	3.89	8.2	4.0	7.4	22.3	**10.0**	12.3	20.8
FIRST STATE BK	Columbus	TX	**B**	B	A-	138.1	6.69	1.3	3.0	2.4	46.3	**10.0**	13.3	39.6
FIRST STATE BK	Junction	TX	**B-**	B-	B-	45.3	7.86	6.3	3.3	11.7	47.7	**7.1**	9.1	17.6
FIRST STATE BK	Gainesville	TX	**B-**	B-	B-	762.9	11.84	5.1	1.9	9.3	50.5	**6.5**	8.5	18.5
FIRST STATE BK	Hemphill	TX	**B-**	B-	B-	53.8	1.37	3.0	2.3	3.8	72.5	**10.0**	15.4	41.4
FIRST STATE BK	Spearman	TX	**B-**	B-	C+	123.2	2.61	10.9	1.3	2.1	26.7	**7.2**	9.2	19.2
FIRST STATE BK	Shallowater	TX	**A-**	A-	B+	88.3	44.82	9.8	2.7	3.8	20.1	**10.0**	12.3	20.0
FIRST STATE BK	Rice	TX	**C+**	C-	C	131.2	-1.63	13.1	4.1	12.6	30.1	**9.5**	10.6	18.3
FIRST STATE BK	Mesquite	TX	**D-**	D-	D	173.2	-2.33	2.5	0.6	6.7	19.1	**7.5**	9.3	26.7
FIRST STATE BK	Abilene	TX	**C-**	C-	C-	40.4	-1.11	13.1	2.5	7.8	2.3	**4.7**	6.7	15.4
FIRST STATE BK	Louise	TX	**B+**	B+	B+	347.2	7.04	11.0	1.5	9.8	21.7	**5.2**	7.9	11.1
FIRST STATE BK	Three Rivers	TX	**C+**	C+	C+	176.6	17.45	2.6	2.9	14.6	35.0	**6.5**	8.5	23.8
▲ FIRST STATE BK	Stratford	TX	**B+**	B	B	226.6	4.40	6.0	1.4	6.8	31.5	**7.3**	9.2	16.9
FIRST STATE BK	Graham	TX	**B+**	B+	B	144.7	1.48	13.7	4.2	14.9	2.2	**6.9**	8.9	18.0
FIRST STATE BK	Yoakum	TX	**A-**	A-	A-	178.9	13.49	5.4	8.1	16.6	43.8	**8.3**	9.8	21.6
FIRST STATE BK & TRUST	Bayport	MN	**B-**	B-	C+	203.0	-2.07	8.9	4.1	33.6	23.2	**6.7**	8.7	14.8
FIRST STATE BK & TRUST	Tonganoxie	KS	**C-**	D+	D-	227.4	2.07	4.3	2.5	21.6	13.3	**6.4**	8.4	12.9
FIRST STATE BK & TRUST CO	Fremont	NE	**B-**	B-	C+	210.9	-0.74	16.9	4.0	12.1	14.7	**6.8**	8.8	14.0
FIRST STATE BK & TRUST CO	Carthage	TX	**A**	A	A	483.9	8.05	2.1	6.6	16.2	57.8	**10.0**	14.7	34.0
FIRST STATE BK & TRUST CO INC	Caruthersville	MO	**A-**	A-	B+	359.2	7.25	5.9	4.1	17.7	24.8	**10.0**	11.1	16.2
FIRST STATE BK BOURBON INDIANA	Bourbon	IN	**B**	B	B+	85.8	0.37	4.3	1.3	20.4	33.7	**10.0**	19.6	37.6
FIRST STATE BK CAMPBELL HILL	Campbell Hill	IL	**C+**	C	C	106.6	2.24	5.3	3.5	25.5	28.5	**7.6**	9.4	16.4
FIRST STATE BK CENTRAL TEXAS	Austin	TX	**B+**	B-	C-	1354.8	5.53	6.6	0.8	3.0	50.2	**7.8**	9.5	18.1
FIRST STATE BK FLORIDA KEYS	Key West	FL	**C**	C-	D	780.7	-4.23	1.3	0.5	21.6	38.8	**7.8**	9.5	18.5
FIRST STATE BK IN TEMPLE	Temple	OK	**B-**	B-	B-	22.7	7.28	3.7	5.2	7.8	46.4	**10.0**	20.2	40.5
FIRST STATE BK KIOWA KANSAS	Kiowa	KS	**A-**	A-	B-	80.6	1.25	10.1	2.6	5.2	30.6	**10.0**	12.9	20.1
FIRST STATE BK MINNESOTA	Le Roy	MN	**C+**	B-	C+	63.9	-5.11	11.5	3.5	6.0	24.7	**6.9**	8.9	16.7
▲ FIRST STATE BK NEBRASKA	Lincoln	NE	**C+**	C	C	421.2	5.92	12.3	2.3	15.5	12.4	**7.4**	9.3	13.1
FIRST STATE BK OF ARCADIA	Arcadia	FL	**D+**	C-	C-	134.6	0.19	2.6	2.5	21.4	30.9	**10.0**	11.9	22.2
FIRST STATE BK OF ASHBY	Ashby	MN	**C-**	C-	C-	31.6	0.32	9.6	5.5	20.7	23.3	**5.9**	7.9	14.7
FIRST STATE BK OF BEDIAS	Bedias	TX	**A**	A	A	161.4	10.63	7.6	4.0	7.0	42.2	**10.0**	12.4	24.3
FIRST STATE BK OF BEECHER CITY	Beecher City	IL	**B**	B-	B-	68.6	-1.06	11.6	12.5	20.4	12.8	**10.0**	14.3	20.2
FIRST STATE BK OF BEN WHEELER	Ben Wheeler	TX	**A**	A	A-	130.2	4.41	4.2	4.9	14.6	50.9	**10.0**	12.1	24.9
FIRST STATE BK OF BIGFORK	Bigfork	MN	**D+**	D+	C-	65.8	0.64	6.3	6.6	34.0	10.2	**9.4**	10.6	18.5

Asset Quality Index	Adjusted Non-Performing Loans as a % of Total Loans	Adjusted Non-Performing Loans as a % of Capital	Net Charge-Offs Avg Loans	Profitability Index	Net Income ($Mil)	Return on Assets (R.O.A.)	Return on Equity (R.O.E.)	Net Interest Spread	Overhead Efficiency Ratio	Liquidity Index	Liquidity Ratio	Hot Money Ratio	Stability Index
5.6	0.71	4.4	0.14	5.5	2.7	1.16	11.92	3.89	65.7	2.8	23.5	15.9	6.6
0.3	12.90	182.8	0.20	1.8	0.0	0.07	1.78	4.82	98.0	0.6	12.6	55.9	0.4
0.3	11.46	100.5	2.61	0.6	-2.9	-1.47	-19.45	3.86	107.1	0.6	13.0	54.5	3.5
2.9	3.82	16.8	0.29	4.5	1.5	0.98	10.62	4.52	78.8	1.8	25.6	23.6	4.1
3.9	1.97	9.8	0.57	3.7	1.0	0.88	10.07	3.41	76.6	4.7	50.0	14.2	3.7
10.0	0.25	0.2	0.78	4.9	0.8	0.86	8.15	4.44	68.8	4.9	41.3	10.8	5.6
5.3	0.31	1.9	na	2.8	0.1	0.29	2.57	na	58.8	1.7	3.4	19.6	7.1
8.2	0.28	1.5	0.05	7.4	3.4	1.22	11.56	4.53	60.7	3.9	25.0	10.6	7.4
5.8	1.22	4.8	0.09	5.4	0.1	1.04	8.88	6.52	77.9	4.2	28.1	8.6	3.8
5.7	1.47	6.2	-0.09	3.6	0.1	0.63	5.14	3.70	77.5	3.1	44.4	21.3	3.6
3.4	4.54	19.8	0.06	3.7	0.4	0.91	6.77	3.38	75.9	2.5	35.0	23.1	6.3
6.5	0.51	2.2	-0.80	4.3	0.3	1.01	8.08	4.28	91.6	2.5	33.8	21.7	5.3
4.5	7.44	10.5	11.83	0.0	-0.4	-2.18	-20.32	2.54	107.6	6.4	86.3	8.7	4.7
6.3	0.70	3.2	0.08	6.8	0.6	1.45	14.62	4.68	60.3	4.2	39.9	14.1	7.6
4.4	3.16	11.7	0.56	3.9	0.3	0.58	6.61	4.69	81.7	5.7	48.0	6.9	3.7
1.4	5.47	33.8	na	0.8	-0.2	-0.68	-9.44	na	469.8	2.6	42.1	26.5	3.0
4.6	0.36	2.6	0.03	9.4	0.9	1.94	23.00	5.32	48.6	0.8	9.2	33.4	4.9
8.7	1.10	1.6	-0.06	6.9	1.2	1.71	14.96	3.54	54.6	5.0	50.0	11.8	8.7
2.9	1.78	15.5	0.00	6.7	0.2	1.46	16.91	5.76	74.1	2.3	14.6	17.2	5.0
8.5	0.00	0.0	0.00	1.3	0.0	0.07	0.93	5.29	98.9	5.9	38.3	0.0	1.0
4.2	1.07	9.2	0.00	4.3	0.9	0.68	7.01	4.23	75.2	0.7	8.4	35.8	4.8
7.5	0.00	0.0	-0.02	7.2	0.7	1.76	13.31	3.60	49.0	3.7	34.0	14.4	7.0
5.0	1.28	9.2	-0.46	9.7	4.9	2.64	28.42	4.40	48.4	1.5	29.4	32.5	6.5
7.2	0.03	0.2	0.00	3.8	0.2	0.59	6.13	3.03	68.4	4.3	22.4	7.7	4.7
5.9	0.07	0.6	0.00	6.6	1.1	1.12	10.51	3.88	58.6	3.0	9.7	13.3	7.0
2.5	3.46	18.2	0.29	7.3	3.4	1.48	10.93	3.87	49.3	1.2	11.1	27.1	6.8
7.4	0.43	1.7	-0.01	6.0	0.7	1.60	10.76	3.46	66.2	2.8	19.5	15.6	5.0
9.7	0.17	0.2	0.07	4.2	1.0	0.96	7.19	2.28	59.7	2.7	54.3	36.4	8.4
9.1	0.00	0.0	0.10	4.0	0.3	0.95	10.29	4.06	78.5	4.1	18.6	8.4	5.0
7.4	0.11	0.5	-0.10	4.1	5.4	0.99	12.01	3.47	73.3	5.7	52.1	9.3	5.3
9.9	1.97	1.7	0.00	3.0	0.2	0.53	3.57	2.47	75.2	4.0	77.2	22.7	6.3
7.0	0.00	0.0	-0.21	4.3	1.0	1.06	13.37	3.11	69.0	2.9	47.8	27.1	5.3
7.4	0.00	0.0	0.00	8.3	1.0	1.87	12.04	4.95	59.4	2.1	28.7	22.7	8.6
7.8	0.36	1.7	-0.07	3.9	0.8	0.80	7.07	4.26	75.8	1.8	22.2	21.9	4.8
3.0	11.20	26.4	-0.44	0.0	-1.1	-0.82	-9.60	2.21	132.3	6.9	70.5	6.0	3.4
8.4	0.00	0.0	0.00	2.4	0.1	0.27	3.40	2.88	87.2	5.4	50.0	9.7	3.9
8.2	0.15	1.2	0.03	7.2	4.0	1.58	20.04	4.81	64.2	4.3	21.8	7.6	6.8
7.1	1.22	5.0	0.05	3.8	1.1	0.85	9.98	2.27	63.9	6.1	67.9	10.6	4.3
8.7	0.00	0.0	0.00	5.4	2.3	1.35	14.06	3.27	61.8	4.0	43.5	16.1	6.4
8.3	0.29	1.6	0.04	5.8	1.5	1.39	15.59	3.84	63.5	3.3	49.1	22.4	5.8
7.5	0.89	3.5	0.11	7.3	2.4	1.84	18.12	3.63	51.8	5.8	58.5	10.8	7.1
5.9	0.72	5.4	0.00	4.4	1.5	0.96	10.88	4.06	81.5	3.4	20.6	12.8	4.8
6.1	0.42	3.0	0.05	2.5	0.7	0.42	4.26	4.06	89.6	3.8	9.0	9.4	4.1
4.3	1.87	12.0	0.02	6.7	2.7	1.62	18.92	3.92	61.7	3.4	19.7	12.5	5.3
8.8	0.97	2.3	0.06	7.8	5.4	1.48	10.05	3.60	43.4	2.3	37.8	27.8	8.8
8.5	0.18	1.0	0.14	6.0	3.6	1.42	13.86	4.34	67.7	1.3	14.9	27.5	6.4
6.0	3.33	7.7	0.29	4.4	0.6	0.85	4.58	3.98	66.5	4.9	62.9	14.3	7.3
3.0	3.13	19.1	0.23	4.1	0.6	0.70	7.45	3.65	67.7	3.9	31.6	12.9	4.9
5.6	1.85	7.5	-0.07	6.6	15.1	1.51	14.98	3.64	55.3	3.2	36.2	21.6	9.3
2.9	3.52	18.6	0.24	3.8	5.4	0.88	9.60	3.09	74.3	4.4	24.0	7.4	4.2
8.1	1.32	2.6	-0.02	5.7	0.3	1.45	7.28	4.29	65.1	2.0	42.6	28.9	5.7
8.3	0.00	0.0	0.02	5.5	0.8	1.31	10.72	3.89	54.2	4.5	33.9	10.5	7.0
6.1	0.71	4.4	0.00	3.6	0.4	0.75	8.66	3.10	75.3	6.2	37.3	0.9	4.8
3.5	0.76	6.1	0.24	4.9	3.6	1.16	10.19	3.76	67.3	3.7	6.4	9.3	6.5
1.3	12.45	47.8	2.19	3.3	0.5	0.52	4.55	3.85	72.4	3.2	37.0	18.0	5.8
6.9	0.15	1.1	-0.01	2.6	0.1	0.33	4.08	3.65	89.6	4.9	40.6	10.5	3.6
7.7	1.38	4.6	-0.17	9.1	2.4	2.10	16.93	3.98	46.3	3.1	59.0	32.9	7.5
4.1	2.50	12.5	-0.03	9.6	1.2	2.32	17.09	4.34	49.3	2.1	10.6	18.2	8.6
8.0	0.81	2.8	0.01	9.3	2.4	2.47	21.50	3.83	46.3	2.4	45.0	32.6	8.4
1.2	4.66	28.9	-0.11	3.7	0.3	0.56	5.33	4.18	74.3	4.0	18.4	9.1	5.6

Name	City	State	Rating	2013 Rating	2012 Rating	Total Assets ($Mil)	One Year Asset Growth	Asset Mix (As a % of Total Assets) Commercial Loans	Consumer Loans	Mortgage Loans	Securities	Capitalization Index	Leverage Ratio	Risk-Based Capital Ratio
FIRST STATE BK OF BLAKELY	Blakely	GA	**A-**	A-	A-	404.9	6.77	5.0	2.7	11.9	6.5	**10.0**	12.1	17.6
FIRST STATE BK OF BLOOMINGTON	Bloomington	IL	**C+**	C	C-	112.4	3.37	9.3	2.2	23.3	22.3	**5.8**	7.8	12.0
▲ FIRST STATE BK OF BROWNSBORO	Brownsboro	TX	**B-**	C+	C-	97.5	1.35	4.3	9.4	18.2	37.7	**8.0**	9.6	17.3
FIRST STATE BK OF BURNET	Burnet	TX	**A-**	A	A	234.0	2.53	4.5	2.3	8.6	65.4	**10.0**	11.8	28.4
FIRST STATE BK OF CANDO	Cando	ND	**C**	C	C-	58.5	8.67	5.1	5.3	4.1	35.9	**6.7**	8.7	14.0
FIRST STATE BK OF CLAREMONT	Groton	SD	**B+**	B+	B+	56.6	-1.66	11.4	2.3	0.0	9.5	**9.5**	11.2	14.6
FIRST STATE BK OF CLEARBROOK	Clearbrook	MN	**B-**	B-	B-	42.8	3.01	6.0	6.1	7.3	32.7	**7.0**	9.0	16.9
FIRST STATE BK OF COLFAX	Colfax	IA	**A**	A	A-	70.3	0.34	3.2	0.9	15.1	48.3	**10.0**	15.2	19.5
FIRST STATE BK OF COLORADO	Hotchkiss	CO	**C**	C+	C+	189.2	4.51	4.0	1.0	10.5	18.1	**10.0**	12.1	18.3
FIRST STATE BK OF DE QUEEN	De Queen	AR	**B**	B-	B-	202.0	8.08	7.6	6.1	13.7	21.7	**6.9**	8.9	14.0
FIRST STATE BK OF DECATUR	Decatur	MI	**B**	B	B+	56.0	-0.62	9.0	2.8	39.7	32.6	**10.0**	19.2	42.0
FIRST STATE BK OF DEKALB CNTY	Fort Payne	AL	**B-**	B	B-	88.7	5.62	5.3	5.9	20.1	26.4	**10.0**	16.6	28.4
FIRST STATE BK OF DONGOLA	Dongola	IL	**D+**	D+	D+	23.3	0.91	3.9	17.8	39.8	4.3	**8.2**	9.8	15.7
FIRST STATE BK OF FERTILE	Fertile	MN	**B-**	B-	B-	35.1	-0.90	7.6	6.5	8.2	43.5	**10.0**	14.5	27.9
▼ FIRST STATE BK OF FORREST	Forrest	IL	**B**	B+	B-	150.3	7.39	10.9	4.3	39.9	6.4	**7.5**	9.4	13.7
▲ FIRST STATE BK OF FORSYTH	Forsyth	MT	**A-**	B	B	119.7	0.74	3.2	4.3	8.5	48.0	**10.0**	11.1	21.0
▼ FIRST STATE BK OF FOUNTAIN	Fountain	MN	**C-**	C+	C+	34.5	-0.91	3.1	1.7	12.2	39.3	**7.7**	9.5	17.4
FIRST STATE BK OF GOLVA	Golva	ND	**B+**	B+	B-	79.0	1.63	7.0	1.9	5.4	42.1	**7.1**	9.1	15.4
FIRST STATE BK OF GROVE CITY	Grove City	MN	**B**	B-	C+	24.5	4.28	8.3	4.9	15.3	12.4	**10.0**	19.5	39.0
FIRST STATE BK OF HARVEY	Harvey	ND	**B-**	B-	C+	79.0	4.72	4.2	2.4	5.5	48.1	**7.6**	9.4	18.7
FIRST STATE BK OF HEALY	Healy	KS	**A-**	A	A-	83.3	0.51	16.1	1.5	1.6	43.7	**10.0**	16.8	26.6
FIRST STATE BK OF ILLINOIS	La Harpe	IL	**C+**	C+	C+	300.6	9.13	8.9	1.4	14.6	13.9	**6.1**	8.4	11.8
▲ FIRST STATE BK OF KIESTER	Kiester	MN	**E**	E-	E-	18.7	-0.21	12.0	1.1	5.3	2.7	**5.6**	7.6	13.9
FIRST STATE BK OF LE CENTER	Le Center	MN	**B+**	B+	B+	69.9	1.14	16.0	7.0	18.0	20.5	**9.2**	10.5	16.0
FIRST STATE BK OF LIVINGSTON	Livingston	TX	**B**	B+	A-	317.1	6.77	2.4	4.6	5.0	53.3	**10.0**	14.0	35.6
FIRST STATE BK OF MALTA	Malta	MT	**A-**	A-	A-	127.9	6.28	4.2	2.2	0.4	45.8	**10.0**	14.9	25.5
FIRST STATE BK OF MIDDLEBURY	Middlebury	IN	**B-**	B-	C	422.3	3.40	12.3	2.3	22.9	18.9	**8.5**	10.0	14.6
▲ FIRST STATE BK OF MOBEETIE	Mobeetie	TX	**C**	C-	C-	90.5	6.37	5.3	3.3	1.0	68.2	**7.1**	9.0	30.2
FIRST STATE BK OF NEWCASTLE	Newcastle	WY	**B+**	B+	A	150.4	3.33	3.8	3.9	8.5	56.4	**10.0**	12.4	39.5
FIRST STATE BK OF NORTH DAKOTA	Arthur	ND	**B-**	C+	C-	340.6	10.61	9.2	2.5	4.1	2.0	**3.5**	9.3	10.2
FIRST STATE BK OF ODEM	Odem	TX	**C+**	C-	D	135.2	4.50	12.0	3.1	6.8	35.6	**7.4**	9.2	18.6
FIRST STATE BK OF OLMSTED	Olmsted	IL	**B-**	B-	C+	47.0	8.94	6.1	4.8	26.7	31.1	**8.6**	10.1	19.1
FIRST STATE BK OF PAINT ROCK	Paint Rock	TX	**B+**	B+	B-	87.5	8.57	7.4	4.7	4.3	36.5	**10.0**	11.1	19.5
FIRST STATE BK OF PORTER	Porter	OK	**A-**	A-	A-	34.7	2.68	13.0	10.9	23.6	0.0	**10.0**	14.3	22.3
FIRST STATE BK OF PORTER	Porter	IN	**C+**	C	C	151.5	-7.24	2.3	0.3	22.8	42.9	**10.0**	11.4	21.6
FIRST STATE BK OF PURDY	Monett	MO	**C**	D+	C	172.4	-1.23	8.3	1.0	4.7	23.4	**5.5**	7.5	12.9
▲ FIRST STATE BK OF RANDOLPH CTY	Cuthbert	GA	**C**	C-	C-	70.8	4.82	9.1	4.3	4.1	42.0	**8.0**	9.6	16.3
FIRST STATE BK OF RANSOM	Ransom	KS	**B+**	B+	B+	46.5	0.40	15.8	1.0	0.6	54.4	**10.0**	19.7	39.8
FIRST STATE BK OF RED WING	Red Wing	MN	**C**	C-	C-	71.9	0.48	4.3	4.0	10.6	57.5	**6.8**	8.8	21.7
FIRST STATE BK OF ROSCOE	Roscoe	SD	**B+**	B	B-	96.8	6.64	14.5	0.6	0.2	8.3	**8.7**	11.2	13.9
FIRST STATE BK OF ROSEMOUNT	Rosemount	MN	**D-**	D-	D-	63.6	-0.18	5.3	3.9	9.5	58.2	**4.9**	7.0	16.9
FIRST STATE BK OF SAN DIEGO	San Diego	TX	**B-**	B-	B-	75.3	3.42	14.8	9.4	5.9	32.2	**5.3**	7.3	16.7
▼ FIRST STATE BK OF SAUK CENTRE	Sauk Centre	MN	**B+**	A-	B	96.9	-9.07	7.0	3.5	9.3	37.7	**8.3**	9.9	19.1
FIRST STATE BK OF SHELBY	Shelby	MT	**A**	A-	A	135.9	3.87	5.4	0.9	0.0	75.7	**10.0**	17.3	32.4
▲ FIRST STATE BK OF ST CHARLES	Saint Charles	MO	**B**	B-	B	290.4	10.21	5.9	0.1	40.1	27.1	**10.0**	11.9	17.3
FIRST STATE BK OF ST PETER	Saint Peter	IL	**A-**	A-	A-	30.2	-11.17	4.8	5.7	6.0	60.9	**10.0**	15.1	30.2
FIRST STATE BK OF ST ROBERT	Saint Robert	MO	**B**	B	B	95.1	-1.37	3.3	4.6	25.3	26.5	**10.0**	11.4	21.3
▲ FIRST STATE BK OF SWANVILLE	Swanville	MN	**C**	D	C-	27.1	-5.69	12.7	4.8	9.7	6.8	**10.0**	11.7	17.3
FIRST STATE BK OF THE SOUTH	Sulligent	AL	**B+**	B+	B+	96.3	1.11	5.9	6.5	12.5	49.5	**10.0**	15.2	27.4
FIRST STATE BK OF UVALDE	Uvalde	TX	**B**	B	B-	1297.1	27.46	2.9	0.8	5.3	53.5	**4.7**	6.7	28.6
FIRST STATE BK OF VAN ORIN	Van Orin	IL	**C-**	C-	C-	43.3	-1.41	2.8	1.5	3.7	41.5	**5.7**	7.7	19.4
FIRST STATE BK OF WABASHA	Wabasha	MN	**B-**	B-	C+	123.4	1.04	4.1	1.8	9.7	47.7	**9.0**	10.3	26.0
FIRST STATE BK OF WARNER SOUTH	Warner	SD	**C**	C-	D+	57.7	4.53	10.5	3.0	2.0	9.2	**7.0**	9.5	12.5
FIRST STATE BK OF WARREN	Warren	AR	**B-**	B-	B	101.8	0.60	15.2	3.4	6.4	50.6	**9.3**	10.5	18.6
FIRST STATE BK OF WEST SALEM	West Salem	IL	**C**	C	B-	18.9	0.34	1.8	2.3	10.7	43.5	**10.0**	17.4	46.5
FIRST STATE BK OF WYOMING	Wyoming	MN	**B**	B	B-	158.2	5.03	4.8	1.5	13.8	52.7	**10.0**	15.8	34.7
FIRST STATE BK OKABENA (INC)	Okabena	MN	**C+**	C+	C-	18.2	-2.15	6.6	1.3	6.3	30.6	**10.0**	16.6	38.6
FIRST STATE BK POND CREEK OKLA	Pond Creek	OK	**B-**	B-	C	58.8	6.80	15.4	3.8	5.3	23.2	**6.1**	8.1	17.0
FIRST STATE BK SHANNON-POLO	Shannon	IL	**B-**	B-	C+	160.0	-0.86	5.4	2.4	9.4	30.0	**6.4**	8.4	14.5
FIRST STATE BK SOUTHWEST	Pipestone	MN	**A**	A	A	228.6	4.12	9.7	3.9	3.7	38.1	**8.9**	10.2	17.5

Arrows denote recent upgrades ▲ or downgrades ▼

Asset Quality Index	Adjusted Non-Performing Loans as a % of Total Loans	Adjusted Non-Performing Loans as a % of Capital	Net Charge-Offs Avg Loans	Profitability Index	Net Income ($Mil)	Return on Assets (R.O.A.)	Return on Equity (R.O.E.)	Net Interest Spread	Overhead Efficiency Ratio	Liquidity Index	Liquidity Ratio	Hot Money Ratio	Stability Index
8.3	0.13	0.7	0.03	**7.3**	3.8	1.30	10.51	4.29	52.9	**0.8**	18.2	46.9	**7.1**
4.4	0.82	7.0	0.00	**6.1**	1.1	1.40	16.61	4.56	68.2	**1.6**	10.3	21.9	**4.7**
5.0	1.14	5.9	0.37	**5.3**	1.0	1.34	16.01	4.01	68.3	**2.8**	28.1	17.0	**5.7**
6.1	4.43	11.6	-0.09	**6.0**	2.4	1.40	11.77	3.23	58.6	**4.2**	67.7	20.3	**9.1**
5.5	1.03	6.6	0.00	**4.0**	0.4	0.89	10.21	3.64	71.7	**2.6**	19.1	16.2	**3.7**
5.1	1.00	6.0	-0.02	**5.7**	0.6	1.32	11.79	4.45	64.7	**4.1**	22.3	9.1	**7.9**
8.6	0.00	0.0	0.02	**4.9**	0.4	1.27	15.32	3.60	70.7	**5.9**	46.1	5.7	**5.7**
4.0	6.74	19.8	0.00	**8.3**	1.1	2.07	14.02	4.24	37.6	**4.5**	57.6	15.5	**8.7**
2.0	4.36	23.1	0.78	**3.5**	0.7	0.49	3.69	4.30	77.0	**2.9**	19.4	15.0	**5.9**
4.8	0.95	6.4	0.19	**7.5**	2.7	1.77	23.90	4.50	57.9	**0.7**	13.9	50.4	**6.1**
5.8	3.96	10.9	-0.05	**3.5**	0.3	0.59	3.09	3.54	81.7	**3.9**	53.6	17.9	**7.0**
5.1	2.60	8.3	0.06	**3.4**	0.4	0.53	3.26	3.63	82.0	**1.5**	19.4	25.9	**6.8**
3.6	0.97	6.7	0.17	**1.0**	-0.1	-0.46	-4.84	3.72	96.1	**2.2**	19.4	18.0	**4.5**
7.6	0.45	1.2	0.01	**3.0**	0.1	0.48	3.69	3.63	85.8	**6.0**	57.8	7.6	**6.2**
4.6	1.26	10.6	0.01	**7.9**	1.9	1.70	17.98	3.64	55.1	**1.7**	7.4	19.5	**7.3**
8.3	0.82	2.9	0.07	**6.1**	1.1	1.23	11.11	3.50	51.8	**3.4**	50.6	21.9	**6.8**
9.1	0.00	0.0	0.00	**2.2**	0.1	0.31	3.32	3.45	94.3	**5.8**	50.7	7.3	**4.6**
7.5	0.65	3.6	0.00	**7.0**	1.0	1.73	18.73	4.12	51.4	**3.7**	25.1	11.6	**7.0**
6.7	1.70	4.7	0.00	**7.1**	0.3	1.67	8.72	3.67	57.3	**5.0**	49.2	9.8	**5.7**
8.7	0.09	0.4	-0.47	**4.4**	0.6	1.07	11.40	3.12	67.7	**5.7**	57.7	9.6	**5.4**
8.4	0.80	2.3	-0.02	**9.0**	1.7	2.60	15.41	4.25	32.7	**1.8**	37.0	36.2	**7.7**
3.4	1.12	9.3	0.31	**4.1**	1.4	0.67	5.64	3.50	70.2	**1.3**	15.0	27.1	**6.3**
4.7	0.34	2.8	-0.02	**2.9**	0.1	0.62	8.68	3.69	77.3	**4.3**	28.9	7.6	**0.0**
5.0	1.18	6.4	-0.08	**7.9**	1.0	1.87	17.36	4.58	58.6	**3.8**	21.9	10.7	**7.3**
6.9	1.80	4.6	0.01	**4.8**	2.4	1.04	6.73	3.48	69.6	**4.1**	42.0	14.9	**7.8**
7.5	0.95	2.9	-0.06	**6.1**	1.2	1.24	8.32	3.35	46.9	**3.9**	34.4	13.8	**7.7**
4.5	1.49	10.1	0.20	**4.4**	2.6	0.85	8.45	4.29	78.2	**2.6**	21.1	16.6	**5.8**
6.1	2.83	5.7	0.02	**4.1**	0.6	0.92	10.10	2.83	58.1	**4.4**	88.3	21.4	**2.7**
8.6	1.06	1.9	0.25	**4.3**	1.0	0.92	7.33	2.93	65.4	**3.6**	62.9	27.8	**7.5**
5.5	0.14	1.3	-0.05	**7.3**	3.8	1.64	14.56	4.75	64.0	**3.5**	2.4	10.3	**7.3**
6.8	0.54	2.5	0.25	**4.1**	0.7	0.76	8.15	4.03	72.9	**5.2**	40.7	9.0	**3.3**
4.9	2.37	13.1	0.00	**5.1**	0.3	0.91	9.04	3.97	65.6	**2.9**	11.3	14.0	**5.7**
5.7	2.59	10.5	-0.06	**5.5**	0.9	1.34	12.20	3.78	64.6	**3.1**	40.7	19.4	**6.3**
7.9	0.11	0.5	-0.03	**9.5**	0.6	2.02	13.98	6.68	69.8	**2.9**	24.3	15.2	**8.9**
3.1	5.74	23.3	0.20	**3.9**	1.1	0.95	8.55	3.47	64.8	**2.6**	46.2	31.1	**5.6**
4.1	2.07	13.2	0.24	**3.8**	1.3	0.94	16.95	3.48	72.0	**2.5**	33.6	20.6	**3.3**
5.6	0.66	2.9	0.06	**2.7**	0.3	0.56	7.31	3.31	84.6	**4.7**	38.7	11.1	**3.8**
8.1	0.05	0.1	0.02	**5.9**	0.5	1.25	6.59	3.33	48.8	**6.5**	62.6	5.0	**7.7**
6.0	2.02	6.0	-0.01	**2.6**	0.2	0.29	3.71	2.86	85.2	**4.6**	62.3	15.8	**3.2**
7.0	0.00	0.0	0.12	**7.7**	1.4	1.90	17.76	3.94	44.6	**2.7**	8.7	15.0	**6.7**
3.0	5.75	24.5	-0.05	**0.5**	0.0	-0.07	-0.98	2.78	103.4	**5.5**	52.5	9.4	**1.1**
7.4	0.56	3.0	0.08	**5.4**	0.8	1.31	18.14	3.08	63.7	**3.6**	29.9	13.4	**5.4**
5.4	1.99	9.3	-0.05	**4.8**	0.2	1.73	12.38	3.64	50.9	**4.9**	44.4	11.3	**7.3**
9.9	1.01	1.1	0.06	**7.5**	1.4	1.38	8.05	3.65	42.1	**6.0**	96.6	14.7	**7.8**
6.1	2.26	11.2	0.08	**4.8**	2.0	0.95	7.80	3.98	87.2	**3.1**	27.5	15.5	**6.9**
9.3	0.31	0.7	0.87	**6.3**	0.3	1.21	8.89	4.28	59.3	**6.1**	62.9	7.9	**7.5**
8.3	0.79	3.5	-0.02	**2.9**	0.3	0.35	3.10	3.83	87.1	**3.5**	25.1	12.7	**6.1**
3.9	1.39	7.4	0.61	**3.0**	0.1	0.61	5.28	5.17	84.6	**3.9**	30.7	12.5	**3.8**
8.9	0.81	1.9	0.04	**4.2**	0.6	0.85	5.51	4.10	76.5	**3.4**	56.7	22.8	**7.7**
7.4	2.77	7.1	-0.01	**4.5**	8.4	0.95	13.34	2.26	46.8	**3.5**	63.6	32.5	**5.3**
5.9	1.72	5.4	0.04	**2.5**	0.1	0.43	5.07	2.56	80.6	**6.3**	61.1	6.0	**4.2**
6.2	2.57	7.4	0.85	**4.3**	0.9	1.02	10.01	2.83	57.0	**3.5**	52.3	21.5	**5.2**
5.3	0.32	2.4	-0.74	**7.4**	0.8	1.91	21.52	4.95	60.7	**3.3**	6.2	11.7	**3.1**
6.1	1.59	5.9	0.20	**3.9**	0.6	0.76	7.47	3.81	75.2	**3.4**	45.5	19.3	**6.1**
9.0	1.14	1.8	0.25	**2.0**	0.0	0.26	1.51	2.58	89.4	**6.4**	83.3	7.7	**5.9**
4.8	5.91	13.7	0.84	**6.4**	1.4	1.24	7.78	3.58	53.3	**5.4**	59.4	12.6	**6.9**
9.2	0.13	0.3	-0.08	**2.4**	0.1	0.35	1.90	2.66	87.0	**5.3**	71.3	12.2	**4.6**
8.5	0.23	1.1	0.00	**4.9**	0.5	1.19	14.98	3.41	67.7	**3.9**	51.1	17.1	**5.4**
8.0	0.29	1.6	0.02	**3.8**	1.0	0.84	9.10	2.79	73.1	**4.0**	25.2	10.0	**5.0**
8.4	0.02	0.1	0.00	**7.9**	3.0	1.79	17.38	3.77	58.6	**4.4**	31.6	10.2	**7.8**

Name	City	State	Rating	2013 Rating	2012 Rating	Total Assets ($Mil)	One Year Asset Growth	Asset Mix (As a % of Total Assets) Commercial Loans	Consumer Loans	Mortgage Loans	Securities	Capitalization Index	Leverage Ratio	Risk-Based Capital Ratio
FIRST STATE COMMUNITY BANK	Farmington	MO	**B**	B	B	1695.4	3.51	4.2	2.9	27.5	19.4	**7.0**	9.0	13.8
FIRST STATE FINANCIAL INC	Middlesboro	KY	**D**	D	D-	361.6	-0.36	8.8	3.7	24.3	12.1	**9.0**	10.3	15.1
▲ FIRST TENNESSEE BANK NA	Memphis	TN	**B**	C	C+	23766.7	-0.82	17.4	1.4	14.1	14.2	**10.0**	13.4	18.3
FIRST TEXAS BANK	Lampasas	TX	**B-**	B-	B+	113.8	2.92	2.5	1.7	5.8	63.6	**10.0**	12.8	32.6
FIRST TEXAS BANK	Georgetown	TX	**C+**	B	B+	542.4	5.13	3.6	0.8	4.0	55.3	**7.5**	9.3	20.2
▼ FIRST TEXAS BANK	Killeen	TX	**C+**	B-	A-	283.6	8.20	1.3	0.6	6.9	59.8	**10.0**	11.5	28.0
▲ FIRST TEXOMA NATIONAL BK	Durant	OK	**C**	D+	D+	156.7	2.55	5.3	6.7	21.9	18.2	**9.9**	11.0	18.3
FIRST TRI-COUNTY BANK	Swanton	NE	**C+**	C+	C	58.3	7.28	9.3	4.9	14.6	9.3	**7.2**	9.1	13.5
FIRST TRUST & SB	Marcus	IA	**C-**	C-	C	42.1	-5.07	6.0	9.2	3.8	49.2	**8.6**	10.0	18.8
FIRST TRUST & SB	Wheatland	IA	**B-**	C+	C+	141.1	3.88	15.1	3.8	8.3	5.7	**6.9**	10.3	12.4
FIRST TRUST & SB	Moville	IA	**A-**	A-	B+	120.9	1.09	1.0	0.8	2.6	52.4	**10.0**	19.0	33.3
FIRST TRUST & SB	Coralville	IA	**C-**	C-	D+	51.2	3.32	6.6	1.1	6.7	52.3	**8.9**	10.2	17.7
FIRST TRUST & SB OF ALBANY IL	Albany	IL	**B+**	B	B	208.3	6.65	10.3	4.9	25.6	15.1	**7.1**	9.1	13.6
FIRST TRUST & SB OF WATSEKA IL	Watseka	IL	**A**	A	A	235.9	1.43	6.3	1.3	7.7	36.2	**10.0**	12.8	25.2
▲ FIRST TRUST BANK OF ILLINOIS	Kankakee	IL	**B+**	B	B-	221.9	-3.87	14.8	1.9	6.5	51.0	**8.5**	10.0	19.0
FIRST TUSKEGEE BANK	Tuskegee	AL	**E+**	E+	E+	55.5	-6.27	3.9	1.0	14.2	29.2	**6.0**	8.0	13.9
FIRST UNITED BANK	Park River	ND	**B**	B	B-	192.9	9.24	8.4	3.5	5.2	19.8	**5.7**	8.7	11.5
FIRST UNITED BANK	Dimmitt	TX	**B+**	B+	B+	1177.0	4.24	11.5	0.8	5.9	32.4	**7.5**	9.3	14.6
FIRST UNITED BANK & TRUST	Oakland	MD	**B-**	B-	C-	1326.4	-0.76	6.3	1.8	21.6	24.8	**10.0**	11.4	15.7
FIRST UNITED BANK & TRUST CO	Madisonville	KY	**A**	A	A-	202.7	-1.16	8.2	2.6	29.3	32.2	**10.0**	12.5	22.4
▲ FIRST UNITED BANK & TRUST CO	Durant	OK	**B**	B-	C+	2521.1	9.86	9.7	5.1	16.3	28.7	**6.7**	8.7	14.3
FIRST UNITED NATIONAL BK	Fryburg	PA	**B**	B	B-	263.2	3.47	4.3	8.8	39.7	25.2	**6.1**	8.1	16.2
FIRST UNITED SECURITY BANK	Thomasville	AL	**C**	C	D+	562.7	0.49	2.3	11.6	8.4	38.3	**10.0**	11.6	22.0
▲ FIRST UTAH BANK	Salt Lake City	UT	**D+**	D	E+	325.1	16.13	11.2	0.8	3.4	14.2	**5.1**	7.1	11.6
FIRST VIRGINIA COMMUNITY BANK	Fairfax	VA	**B**	B-	C	571.7	20.49	11.5	0.7	15.2	10.6	**9.0**	11.5	14.1
FIRST VISION BANK OF TENNESSEE	Tullahoma	TN	**A-**	A-	B+	156.6	6.99	6.6	2.6	20.0	9.5	**10.0**	12.5	17.8
FIRST VOLUNTEER BANK	Chattanooga	TN	**C+**	C	C+	872.9	-2.08	7.1	2.1	18.8	11.2	**7.2**	9.2	14.1
FIRST WESTERN BANK	Booneville	AR	**C+**	C+	C+	322.6	12.08	3.4	1.9	38.0	4.8	**6.1**	8.1	12.2
▲ FIRST WESTERN BANK & TRUST	Minot	ND	**B+**	B	B-	893.7	10.08	14.3	2.2	4.2	38.4	**6.9**	8.9	13.6
FIRST WESTERN FSB	Rapid City	SD	**A-**	A-	B+	41.4	15.56	0.0	1.0	73.6	0.1	**10.0**	16.9	30.5
FIRST WESTERN TRUST BANK	Denver	CO	**C-**	C-	D-	687.7	6.86	17.8	6.5	16.5	12.8	**5.9**	8.6	11.7
FIRST WESTROADS BANK INC	Omaha	NE	**B+**	B+	A-	245.4	2.89	12.0	0.4	7.7	16.7	**9.1**	10.4	15.0
FIRST WHITNEY BANK & TRUST	Atlantic	IA	**A+**	A+	A	201.7	7.55	11.9	1.5	5.9	40.4	**8.7**	10.5	13.9
▼ FIRST-CITIZENS BANK & TRUST CO	Raleigh	NC	**C+**	B+	B	21608.3	2.10	5.7	1.8	6.6	25.4	**7.4**	9.3	14.7
FIRST-LOCKHART NATIONAL BK	Lockhart	TX	**B-**	B	B+	203.5	10.27	3.8	1.8	25.5	14.7	**6.8**	8.8	13.4
FIRSTAR BANK NA	Sallisaw	OK	**B-**	B	C+	473.7	5.77	18.2	2.2	19.0	8.0	**6.2**	8.2	12.1
▲ FIRSTATLANTIC BANK	Jacksonville	FL	**C**	C-	C	380.2	-1.89	7.1	0.5	12.1	19.1	**10.0**	12.8	18.3
▼ FIRSTBANK	Antlers	OK	**B**	B+	B	268.4	10.60	7.8	14.2	33.3	0.2	**5.5**	7.9	11.4
FIRSTBANK	Lexington	TN	**C+**	C-	D+	2343.4	7.02	11.5	1.4	16.9	27.5	**6.1**	8.1	12.9
FIRSTBANK	Lakewood	CO	**A-**	A-	B+	14016.1	6.67	0.7	0.7	33.8	37.3	**5.9**	7.9	16.1
FIRSTBANK OF NEBRASKA	Wahoo	NE	**B**	B-	B-	217.0	2.50	4.2	1.4	8.2	45.6	**7.0**	9.4	12.5
FIRSTBANK PUERTO RICO	San Juan	PR	**D**	D	D+	12626.5	-1.13	7.7	13.9	21.6	15.7	**10.0**	12.1	18.2
FIRSTBANK SOUTHWEST	Amarillo	TX	**B-**	B-	B	976.3	8.19	13.2	2.7	6.5	41.7	**5.6**	7.6	13.4
FIRSTCAPITAL BANK OF TEXAS NA	Midland	TX	**B**	B+	B	848.1	5.43	18.4	0.9	15.3	13.2	**7.1**	9.1	13.3
FIRSTCITY BANK OF COMMERCE	Palm Beach Gardens	FL	**C-**	D+	D+	65.3	8.20	19.3	0.0	11.7	13.2	**8.9**	10.3	15.2
▲ FIRSTIER BANK	Kimball	NE	**C**	D+	D	233.0	4.11	4.8	2.8	3.0	21.4	**10.0**	13.2	18.4
FIRSTMERIT BANK NA	Akron	OH	**C+**	C+	C-	24589.3	2.10	19.7	12.5	5.4	26.0	**6.7**	8.7	12.6
▲ FIRSTOAK BANK	Independence	KS	**B+**	B	B-	93.4	3.60	14.8	2.4	18.6	6.7	**8.7**	10.3	13.9
▼ FIRSTRUST SB	Conshohocken	PA	**B+**	B	B	2560.2	7.31	22.8	1.7	14.7	9.7	**10.0**	13.0	16.2
FIRSTSECURE BANK & TRUST CO	Palos Hills	IL	**E-**	E-	E-	55.8	-5.39	1.6	0.2	21.8	1.8	**9.3**	10.6	21.7
FIRSTSTATE BK	Lineville	AL	**B**	B	B-	213.0	4.78	3.8	4.8	11.8	37.1	**9.0**	10.3	16.1
▲ FISHER NATIONAL BK	Fisher	IL	**B+**	B	B	106.6	11.29	4.9	3.8	33.9	22.3	**8.9**	10.2	15.1
FIVE POINTS BANK	Grand Island	NE	**B+**	B+	A-	928.9	8.71	19.4	1.9	6.7	23.8	**6.2**	9.6	11.9
FIVE POINTS BANK OF HASTINGS	Hastings	NE	**B+**	B+	B+	251.3	3.55	8.5	0.8	5.0	40.6	**9.0**	10.3	15.3
▲ FIVE STAR BANK	Rocklin	CA	**B-**	C+	C-	623.7	9.39	6.5	0.7	4.5	7.3	**5.7**	8.2	11.6
FIVE STAR BANK	Warsaw	NY	**B**	B	B	3035.8	6.02	7.1	22.3	12.2	28.9	**5.2**	7.2	11.5
▲ FLAGLER BANK	West Palm Beach	FL	**D**	D	D-	158.7	4.90	8.6	0.1	4.0	31.3	**9.2**	10.5	16.0
FLAGSHIP BANK MINNESOTA	Wayzata	MN	**D**	D-	E-	101.7	5.20	11.8	0.7	11.8	9.2	**6.5**	8.5	12.9
FLAGSHIP COMMUNITY BANK	Clearwater	FL	**D**	D	D-	97.6	3.46	14.0	0.5	5.8	0.0	**10.0**	11.9	15.4
FLAGSTAR BANK FSB	Troy	MI	**D**	D+	C-	9560.7	-18.93	3.5	0.3	48.6	14.4	**10.0**	12.4	24.1

Asset Quality Index	Adjusted Non-Performing Loans as a % of Total Loans	Adjusted Non-Performing Loans as a % of Capital	Net Charge-Offs / Avg Loans	Profitability Index	Net Income ($Mil)	Return on Assets (R.O.A.)	Return on Equity (R.O.E.)	Net Interest Spread	Overhead Efficiency Ratio	Liquidity Index	Liquidity Ratio	Hot Money Ratio	Stability Index
5.0	1.17	8.5	0.22	**6.4**	15.1	1.19	11.22	3.85	60.7	**3.0**	4.9	13.1	**9.0**
1.3	5.18	35.3	0.84	**3.4**	1.8	0.65	6.32	4.24	71.9	**1.4**	8.8	24.3	**4.9**
4.5	2.46	11.5	0.31	**4.4**	198.7	1.12	8.45	3.05	66.9	**4.3**	13.7	6.7	**8.1**
9.9	0.00	0.0	-0.27	**3.0**	0.3	0.37	2.89	2.49	84.5	**7.1**	82.3	6.6	**5.9**
7.7	0.21	0.7	1.99	**3.2**	1.6	0.41	4.41	2.68	67.3	**6.5**	63.4	6.9	**5.2**
10.0	0.10	0.2	-0.01	**2.6**	0.6	0.28	2.44	2.29	87.2	**7.6**	82.8	3.4	**5.4**
5.0	1.00	5.4	-0.16	**3.2**	0.8	0.66	5.91	3.88	87.1	**4.3**	25.7	8.4	**4.9**
6.1	0.33	2.5	0.35	**3.5**	0.2	0.44	4.52	3.33	75.9	**4.2**	24.3	8.8	**4.7**
6.1	1.38	5.1	0.08	**2.1**	0.1	0.32	3.30	3.10	90.8	**6.1**	58.1	6.5	**4.1**
4.2	0.45	3.6	0.11	**6.1**	1.5	1.46	14.33	3.97	57.8	**2.0**	9.4	18.4	**6.8**
9.7	0.22	0.2	-0.03	**5.5**	1.1	1.19	6.23	3.22	46.8	**6.9**	97.7	10.1	**8.5**
4.7	3.58	12.9	0.02	**2.3**	0.2	0.56	5.37	3.80	90.5	**1.4**	31.8	35.4	**4.6**
4.1	1.32	10.4	0.02	**7.0**	2.7	1.75	17.40	3.92	49.1	**1.5**	15.2	25.1	**8.3**
7.3	1.15	3.9	0.02	**7.1**	2.4	1.32	10.89	3.25	43.5	**4.5**	36.8	11.5	**8.1**
5.6	1.72	6.7	0.00	**5.4**	1.8	1.07	10.72	3.62	59.8	**2.8**	35.8	19.5	**6.3**
1.7	6.36	37.4	0.37	**0.2**	-0.4	-0.83	-10.39	4.61	118.3	**0.8**	13.2	34.2	**1.8**
5.6	0.25	2.0	-0.03	**6.8**	2.1	1.56	17.90	4.06	59.3	**3.1**	15.5	13.4	**6.3**
6.8	0.66	3.9	0.00	**6.5**	14.2	1.63	16.85	3.70	57.5	**1.2**	12.6	29.7	**9.2**
4.9	2.25	11.4	0.51	**3.3**	5.3	0.52	4.51	3.18	77.1	**2.8**	15.1	15.5	**7.2**
8.3	0.58	2.6	0.04	**7.6**	2.6	1.70	13.04	4.46	62.0	**3.9**	9.6	8.9	**7.7**
5.1	0.76	5.0	0.12	**6.3**	27.0	1.47	15.44	3.73	74.1	**2.0**	4.8	17.9	**8.6**
6.8	0.63	4.4	0.06	**4.4**	1.6	0.81	10.08	3.15	64.2	**3.9**	31.1	12.7	**5.0**
4.1	2.60	9.9	0.94	**4.4**	3.1	0.73	5.74	5.60	82.3	**3.4**	38.3	17.6	**6.6**
2.9	2.34	17.2	0.25	**3.8**	2.4	1.09	15.05	4.03	83.6	**1.1**	19.3	31.4	**2.2**
4.7	0.51	3.6	0.03	**4.3**	2.9	0.73	6.13	3.64	67.0	**1.1**	15.8	30.1	**6.8**
6.0	0.85	4.8	0.02	**5.5**	1.1	0.89	7.56	4.42	65.9	**0.9**	12.2	32.8	**6.7**
3.7	1.37	9.7	0.40	**5.8**	6.5	0.99	10.05	4.50	65.8	**3.2**	16.0	13.0	**6.3**
6.6	0.36	3.4	0.01	**3.7**	1.2	0.53	6.49	4.36	81.4	**0.9**	7.2	31.2	**3.5**
7.2	0.17	1.0	0.06	**6.6**	8.1	1.26	13.58	3.67	53.9	**3.4**	12.7	11.8	**5.3**
8.1	0.91	4.7	0.00	**10.0**	1.0	3.27	19.19	5.94	47.1	**0.5**	6.9	55.0	**8.0**
3.7	0.86	7.3	0.01	**2.3**	1.4	0.30	2.69	3.63	94.0	**1.6**	24.7	25.7	**5.4**
5.0	0.52	3.3	-0.02	**7.3**	3.1	1.69	15.97	4.13	61.6	**3.4**	25.2	13.2	**8.2**
8.6	0.00	0.0	0.01	**9.1**	2.9	1.99	18.80	3.83	37.4	**4.9**	39.4	10.5	**8.5**
6.2	1.10	6.9	0.24	**3.3**	79.7	0.49	5.21	3.30	84.0	**4.4**	19.3	7.2	**7.0**
6.0	0.52	3.8	0.12	**4.1**	1.2	0.86	9.89	4.06	81.1	**1.7**	12.7	21.5	**5.9**
3.3	1.35	11.5	1.01	**5.0**	2.1	0.58	5.28	4.45	72.8	**1.6**	9.6	21.1	**8.9**
2.9	1.60	8.4	0.84	**4.9**	2.1	0.73	5.66	4.83	65.4	**2.9**	25.0	15.7	**4.4**
4.6	0.80	7.9	0.22	**9.0**	3.9	2.00	24.20	7.00	71.0	**0.6**	9.0	42.1	**6.3**
3.9	1.69	12.1	0.02	**5.9**	25.2	1.47	14.79	3.98	73.7	**3.8**	7.4	8.9	**8.3**
8.5	0.49	3.2	0.04	**7.8**	135.5	1.32	16.31	3.65	53.5	**5.8**	34.5	6.0	**7.5**
6.3	0.59	2.8	0.00	**5.0**	1.6	1.00	9.92	3.10	57.6	**4.8**	22.8	4.7	**6.2**
0.0	9.69	52.5	1.99	**2.9**	67.0	0.70	6.09	4.38	65.1	**0.8**	15.2	46.1	**6.3**
8.7	0.08	0.5	-0.02	**3.9**	6.2	0.85	11.44	2.60	70.3	**4.3**	31.5	10.9	**5.8**
8.6	0.09	0.6	0.02	**4.9**	5.0	0.79	8.79	3.86	69.1	**1.3**	30.1	35.9	**5.1**
2.3	3.60	24.5	0.21	**2.2**	0.1	0.27	2.73	3.85	91.5	**1.4**	29.2	32.8	**3.6**
3.0	5.69	21.0	0.15	**6.8**	3.1	1.74	14.15	3.83	63.2	**3.4**	26.7	13.7	**4.8**
3.7	1.29	9.0	0.40	**5.6**	189.6	1.04	8.98	3.87	61.2	**4.6**	17.0	5.6	**8.1**
7.3	0.10	0.7	0.06	**6.3**	1.0	1.43	13.65	5.62	71.1	**1.6**	13.2	21.9	**6.8**
6.2	0.76	4.3	-0.04	**5.0**	22.7	1.22	9.42	4.45	73.3	**4.2**	9.1	6.8	**9.3**
0.3	11.89	50.2	-0.02	**0.0**	-2.3	-5.72	-128.91	2.44	175.4	**2.8**	49.5	28.2	**0.0**
5.1	1.45	7.2	0.23	**6.2**	2.0	1.29	13.32	4.29	61.8	**1.1**	16.8	31.4	**5.2**
5.6	0.76	5.2	-0.03	**7.8**	1.3	1.75	16.84	4.14	58.5	**2.0**	17.0	19.2	**6.5**
8.4	0.02	0.2	0.00	**6.7**	9.8	1.42	14.86	3.54	52.5	**3.6**	23.7	11.9	**8.7**
6.3	0.62	2.7	-0.01	**4.9**	1.8	0.94	9.44	3.25	57.1	**4.9**	38.6	9.8	**7.3**
4.5	0.52	4.1	0.09	**9.2**	9.4	2.11	24.97	3.80	42.1	**4.3**	28.3	9.5	**6.4**
5.5	0.34	2.7	0.38	**5.2**	22.7	1.02	11.98	3.49	57.3	**3.4**	4.2	11.1	**7.4**
2.1	3.72	18.1	-0.01	**6.6**	2.1	1.73	18.54	4.04	55.6	**1.5**	34.1	43.5	**4.0**
3.0	2.38	17.3	-0.51	**1.4**	0.2	0.23	1.83	4.07	89.7	**1.7**	16.1	22.4	**4.1**
0.2	5.65	35.8	1.74	**1.6**	-0.1	-0.10	-0.74	3.99	84.7	**1.4**	19.1	27.5	**5.9**
2.3	4.40	19.8	0.67	**0.0**	-74.9	-1.03	-6.43	3.24	96.7	**3.7**	18.5	11.2	**6.8**

Name	City	State	Rating	2013 Rating	2012 Rating	Total Assets ($Mil)	One Year Asset Growth	Comm-ercial Loans	Cons-umer Loans	Mort-gage Loans	Secur-ities	Capital-ization Index	Lever-age Ratio	Risk-Based Capital Ratio
								Asset Mix (As a % of Total Assets)						
FLANAGAN STATE BK	Flanagan	IL	**B**	B	B-	165.7	2.44	4.8	2.0	16.4	34.8	**7.1**	9.1	15.1
FLATHEAD BANK OF BIGFORK MT	Bigfork	MT	**C-**	D+	D-	218.8	6.65	4.0	1.1	13.9	49.1	**8.9**	10.3	22.5
FLATIRONS BANK	Boulder	CO	**B**	B-	B-	123.6	9.97	22.3	0.2	22.2	27.8	**8.3**	9.8	13.7
FLEETWOOD BANK	Fleetwood	PA	**C**	C+	C+	228.6	-0.20	1.2	0.2	37.8	29.5	**7.2**	9.1	16.9
FLINT COMMUNITY BANK	Albany	GA	**B-**	C+	C	163.2	4.40	8.3	0.9	34.5	1.8	**6.6**	8.6	12.8
FLINT HILLS BANK	Eskridge	KS	**B**	B+	B+	120.6	-4.12	5.8	3.6	11.2	42.6	**9.0**	10.3	19.9
FLORA BANK & TRUST	Flora	IL	**C**	C	C+	69.5	-1.00	3.8	9.1	15.9	23.0	**8.8**	10.2	19.2
FLORA SB	Flora	IL	**D+**	D+	D+	28.6	-4.52	10.3	7.0	45.2	15.1	**9.4**	10.6	18.9
FLORENCE SB	Florence	MA	**C+**	C+	B-	1074.2	-0.95	3.2	0.0	48.1	16.3	**9.2**	10.4	16.5
▲ FLORIDA BANK	Tampa	FL	**C-**	D-	E+	518.1	-4.81	4.7	0.8	12.7	22.6	**9.8**	10.8	18.7
FLORIDA BANK OF COMMERCE	Orlando	FL	**C+**	C-	D	245.3	2.52	8.6	0.5	9.6	9.6	**9.2**	10.5	14.4
▲ FLORIDA BUSINESS BANK	Melbourne	FL	**B-**	C+	C-	108.1	-2.25	5.4	0.0	1.6	24.4	**10.0**	12.8	20.4
FLORIDA CAPITAL BANK NA	Jacksonville	FL	**E-**	E-	E-	392.8	-22.99	5.4	0.4	24.3	16.1	**3.8**	6.1	10.4
▲ FLORIDA CITIZENS BANK	Gainesville	FL	**C-**	D	E+	238.3	-6.61	22.4	1.9	6.4	16.4	**6.4**	8.4	13.1
FLORIDA COMMUNITY BANK NA	Weston	FL	**C+**	C+	C	5929.3	67.37	13.1	0.1	16.1	28.1	**9.3**	10.6	14.6
FLORIDA PARISHES BANK	Hammond	LA	**B**	B-	C	223.9	11.62	3.5	3.9	17.6	28.7	**8.6**	10.0	17.5
FLORIDIAN BANK	Daytona Beach	FL	**D+**	D	D-	406.2	200.60	10.1	0.7	4.5	14.0	**9.5**	10.7	14.8
FLORIDIAN COMMUNITY BANK INC	Davie	FL	**D**	C-	C-	330.5	18.86	10.0	0.1	19.0	6.9	**6.4**	9.0	12.1
FLOWERS NATIONAL BK	Cainsville	MO	**C-**	D+	C	41.1	11.20	1.3	0.9	6.1	48.2	**8.5**	10.0	19.0
▲ FLUSHING BANK	Flushing	NY	**B-**	C+	B+	4895.5	3.34	6.5	0.0	14.9	19.3	**7.9**	9.6	15.3
▲ FMB BANK	Wright City	MO	**C**	D+	D	37.5	2.22	3.8	3.4	18.5	38.5	**8.0**	9.7	17.1
▲ FMS BANK	Fort Morgan	CO	**D+**	D+	B-	153.7	3.97	10.6	12.1	10.3	23.9	**7.2**	9.1	13.6
FNB BANK	Scottsboro	AL	**B**	B+	B-	359.9	2.59	8.0	3.4	9.8	27.0	**10.0**	12.2	19.4
FNB BANK INC	Romney	WV	**C**	C	C-	166.2	4.44	5.3	1.9	23.5	28.1	**8.1**	9.7	16.5
FNB BANK INC	Mayfield	KY	**B**	B	B	420.3	4.13	8.3	2.2	15.2	25.8	**6.0**	8.0	12.2
FNB BANK NA	Danville	PA	**B**	B	C+	350.7	-2.09	2.7	5.7	27.7	20.9	**9.8**	10.8	17.6
FNB COMMUNITY BANK	Midwest City	OK	**C+**	C+	B	450.8	2.12	3.9	3.4	8.3	52.6	**9.1**	10.4	21.1
▲ FNB OF CENTRAL ALABAMA	Tuscaloosa	AL	**C+**	C	C-	223.1	0.03	6.8	0.8	11.7	29.8	**10.0**	11.7	20.2
FNB OXFORD	Oxford	MS	**B+**	B+	B+	244.0	3.19	4.7	2.1	19.0	32.9	**10.0**	13.3	22.5
FNBC BANK	Ash Flat	AR	**B-**	C+	B-	366.8	-2.23	7.5	3.3	20.5	29.4	**9.8**	10.8	17.5
FNBT.COM BANK	Fort Walton Beach	FL	**B**	B	B-	368.3	-0.65	1.5	1.0	11.1	1.9	**10.0**	11.6	24.2
FOCUS BANK	Charleston	MO	**C+**	C+	C-	689.6	7.27	7.2	2.8	24.2	7.9	**9.1**	10.4	14.3
FOCUS BUSINESS BANK	San Jose	CA	**C**	C	B	407.1	44.90	10.4	0.6	0.7	22.6	**5.2**	7.2	15.2
FOLSOM LAKE BANK	Folsom	CA	**C-**	D+	D	146.8	7.18	6.6	0.1	6.0	28.9	**8.5**	10.0	15.8
FOOTHILLS BANK	Yuma	AZ	**D**	D	C	292.3	5.05	3.4	0.3	3.2	18.1	**8.3**	10.3	13.5
FOOTHILLS BANK & TRUST	Maryville	TN	**C**	C	C-	195.7	7.66	6.5	1.0	15.9	25.2	**8.1**	9.7	15.1
FOOTHILLS COMMUNITY BANK	Dawsonville	GA	**E-**	E-	E-	81.8	-14.92	4.1	3.3	9.4	15.8	**0.0**	2.7	4.7
▲ FORCHT BANK NA	Lexington	KY	**B-**	C	C-	902.3	-4.91	3.2	2.6	26.4	35.0	**10.0**	11.5	22.0
FORD COUNTY STATE BK	Spearville	KS	**B-**	B-	B-	37.6	8.28	15.6	1.7	4.5	30.4	**10.0**	13.0	19.7
FORESIGHT BANK	Plainview	MN	**B-**	B-	C-	170.6	8.29	4.0	2.3	40.0	10.5	**7.3**	9.3	12.8
FOREST PARK NATIONAL BK & TR	Forest Park	IL	**D+**	C-	C-	216.9	2.01	6.0	0.5	23.1	9.4	**5.4**	8.2	11.3
FORREST CITY BANK NA	Forrest City	AR	**D-**	D-	D	50.9	-0.91	2.6	2.0	16.6	35.8	**6.7**	8.7	17.0
▲ FORRESTON STATE BK	Forreston	IL	**B**	B-	B-	100.9	3.01	3.5	0.4	6.2	25.1	**10.0**	13.0	18.1
FORT DAVIS STATE BK	Fort Davis	TX	**D**	D+	D	70.1	1.04	9.2	4.9	7.9	28.7	**9.2**	10.5	20.2
FORT GIBSON STATE BK	Fort Gibson	OK	**C-**	C-	C-	62.1	4.98	4.5	14.9	15.0	25.8	**4.9**	6.9	11.3
FORT HOOD NATIONAL BK	Fort Hood	TX	**B-**	B	B	232.5	0.82	0.0	1.1	10.2	62.2	**5.6**	7.6	37.4
FORT JENNINGS STATE BK	Fort Jennings	OH	**B**	B	B-	166.2	5.02	9.4	4.0	27.6	9.0	**6.7**	8.9	12.3
FORT MADISON BANK & TRUST CO	Fort Madison	IA	**C+**	C+	B-	152.9	1.83	29.2	1.1	23.7	22.2	**6.6**	8.6	13.2
FORT SILL NATIONAL BK	Fort Sill	OK	**A**	A	A	384.9	-2.21	0.0	4.8	9.2	51.5	**10.0**	11.8	26.5
FORTUNEBANK	Arnold	MO	**D**	D	D-	150.0	6.01	20.1	0.9	20.3	10.2	**7.4**	9.3	13.6
FORWARD FINANCIAL BANK	Marshfield	WI	**C+**	C+	C+	322.2	1.49	11.9	2.1	18.3	3.0	**6.1**	8.8	11.8
FOUNDATION BANK	Bellevue	WA	**D**	D	D	394.2	7.98	25.5	0.1	4.0	15.0	**8.4**	9.9	13.9
▲ FOUNDATION BANK	Cincinnati	OH	**B+**	B	B	209.8	6.71	1.2	0.6	31.2	0.0	**10.0**	14.4	19.1
▲ FOUNDATION ONE BANK	Waterloo	NE	**C**	C	C	65.4	10.52	12.1	1.8	24.1	10.5	**5.1**	9.9	11.1
FOUNDATIONS BANK	Pewaukee	WI	**C-**	D+	E+	128.7	2.74	11.6	0.2	13.8	19.3	**10.0**	13.1	21.4
FOUNDERS BANK & TRUST	Grand Rapids	MI	**B**	B+	B	477.4	4.84	11.1	0.6	27.5	16.6	**6.7**	8.8	13.0
FOUNDERS COMMUNITY BANK	San Luis Obispo	CA	**B**	B	B	169.0	7.68	13.8	0.2	2.9	5.7	**7.8**	9.5	15.0
FOUNTAIN TRUST CO	Covington	IN	**B**	B	B	267.0	-1.31	4.4	2.6	22.9	36.8	**10.0**	13.4	25.2
FOUR CORNERS COMMUNITY BANK	Farmington	NM	**B**	B	B	310.5	33.77	10.0	1.0	6.1	27.5	**7.9**	9.6	16.3
FOUR COUNTY BANK	Allentown	GA	**B-**	C+	C-	59.4	-4.14	7.8	8.0	17.4	20.4	**10.0**	11.6	17.7

Asset Quality Index	Adjusted Non-Performing Loans as a % of Total Loans	Adjusted Non-Performing Loans as a % of Capital	Net Charge-Offs Avg Loans	Profitability Index	Net Income ($Mil)	Return on Assets (R.O.A.)	Return on Equity (R.O.E.)	Net Interest Spread	Overhead Efficiency Ratio	Liquidity Index	Liquidity Ratio	Hot Money Ratio	Stability Index
4.8	1.25	7.3	0.00	4.2	1.1	0.84	9.26	3.65	78.6	3.6	34.7	15.5	6.3
3.2	6.58	20.4	0.60	2.3	0.8	0.52	5.20	3.24	82.3	6.0	53.6	7.7	5.1
8.4	0.29	1.8	-0.82	6.3	1.6	1.68	16.72	3.93	71.7	2.5	27.6	18.2	4.9
4.7	1.97	12.3	0.16	2.9	0.7	0.42	4.69	3.40	82.2	3.8	31.1	12.9	4.9
4.9	0.95	8.8	0.13	5.3	1.0	0.89	10.52	4.04	63.6	0.7	9.1	38.8	4.5
7.6	0.14	0.7	0.17	4.9	1.2	1.23	12.78	3.04	58.9	1.7	22.4	23.4	7.6
6.7	0.65	3.3	0.00	3.0	0.2	0.42	4.19	3.03	82.9	4.9	29.9	6.1	4.8
3.3	1.80	11.4	0.13	1.9	0.1	0.27	2.55	3.37	91.0	1.5	27.4	30.4	3.6
6.1	1.19	8.4	0.09	3.6	4.7	0.60	5.80	3.27	73.5	3.4	16.1	12.5	7.0
6.6	0.39	2.0	-0.42	2.8	3.9	0.97	9.49	3.53	93.3	4.3	36.9	12.5	4.1
3.6	1.16	7.7	-0.02	4.5	1.4	0.74	6.71	4.29	70.9	4.5	17.5	5.8	5.1
4.1	1.72	7.9	-0.18	3.4	0.5	0.57	4.31	3.31	75.4	5.3	35.0	5.9	5.4
2.1	2.76	26.5	1.03	0.0	-3.4	-1.16	-21.41	3.38	120.0	0.7	7.3	33.9	0.0
4.6	0.79	5.5	0.01	2.0	0.7	0.38	4.91	3.51	89.2	1.7	22.9	23.4	2.7
5.7	1.73	10.2	0.06	3.1	22.8	0.59	4.93	3.54	71.4	2.0	17.8	19.6	5.3
5.0	1.79	9.5	0.29	6.3	1.7	1.05	10.63	5.19	72.1	3.6	32.7	14.7	6.4
3.8	1.49	8.7	0.70	5.1	11.8	5.07	48.98	4.67	82.2	1.9	26.1	23.2	3.9
0.7	3.93	32.3	0.30	2.6	0.8	0.34	3.99	3.58	72.2	3.8	14.6	9.9	3.2
7.9	0.32	1.2	0.02	2.7	0.2	0.50	3.86	3.79	85.5	2.2	39.7	32.0	4.1
4.3	1.12	8.3	0.02	5.2	33.4	0.93	9.56	3.19	56.8	1.2	12.9	29.3	7.7
4.9	3.14	12.9	0.34	3.7	0.3	0.83	9.41	3.41	74.4	3.4	16.8	12.0	4.0
2.3	1.99	12.1	0.60	4.2	0.9	0.79	8.60	4.39	74.9	1.8	23.2	22.3	5.6
6.5	1.03	4.7	0.36	4.5	2.5	0.93	7.94	4.18	72.5	2.8	27.3	16.7	5.8
3.4	3.14	17.4	0.70	2.8	0.7	0.55	5.39	3.71	74.9	1.7	24.2	23.5	5.4
4.4	0.94	7.1	0.14	5.8	3.2	1.05	9.60	3.92	59.6	2.9	18.3	15.0	6.8
4.8	0.99	6.3	0.10	5.1	2.5	0.97	8.43	3.47	71.2	3.9	11.5	8.9	6.9
8.9	0.16	0.6	0.01	3.7	2.7	0.80	7.34	3.18	72.9	4.8	34.9	9.1	6.1
4.9	2.77	12.0	-0.24	3.3	1.1	0.64	5.76	3.06	89.8	3.7	26.8	12.0	5.4
7.3	1.08	4.3	0.11	4.8	1.7	0.97	7.17	4.08	69.3	3.6	33.9	14.8	7.2
4.1	1.50	7.9	0.24	4.8	3.3	1.20	11.75	4.41	72.0	3.5	25.2	12.4	5.6
6.8	2.43	6.4	0.20	4.3	2.7	0.97	8.01	2.83	80.0	6.7	63.5	5.7	6.7
2.8	2.43	18.0	0.29	3.9	2.6	0.51	5.11	3.49	68.3	0.6	5.9	39.3	6.8
7.7	0.00	0.0	0.15	2.8	0.8	0.32	4.07	2.87	80.8	6.7	60.6	5.6	5.3
2.1	4.86	25.8	-0.01	3.3	0.7	0.67	6.88	3.63	82.6	2.1	27.4	20.7	4.7
1.0	3.17	19.5	0.21	4.1	1.4	0.64	5.58	4.76	76.6	5.0	28.6	4.8	4.7
5.5	0.89	5.6	0.31	3.2	0.8	0.55	5.79	3.35	71.8	2.9	23.5	15.3	5.0
0.3	4.15	61.8	1.07	2.7	0.4	0.61	42.14	4.60	88.9	1.6	14.6	22.2	0.0
4.1	3.64	16.3	0.16	3.6	5.8	0.82	6.66	3.97	79.1	4.1	22.3	9.0	6.9
4.5	4.21	17.5	0.04	3.9	0.2	0.72	5.88	3.42	68.9	3.9	34.9	13.9	6.3
4.6	1.40	12.0	-0.05	6.2	1.9	1.54	16.84	3.75	59.9	1.6	10.8	22.2	6.0
0.2	4.16	37.7	0.10	4.4	1.6	0.97	11.69	4.70	77.2	3.7	7.4	9.6	4.6
5.0	2.94	11.8	0.27	0.1	-0.1	-0.31	-3.42	2.70	113.8	3.8	33.5	13.8	3.0
5.7	1.56	7.9	-0.15	7.9	1.5	2.03	16.56	3.69	51.7	1.5	22.5	26.6	5.9
1.0	8.56	34.2	0.06	0.5	-0.1	-0.14	-1.34	3.84	105.9	5.0	44.5	10.5	4.0
7.5	0.00	0.0	0.18	4.3	0.4	0.79	12.97	4.87	80.5	1.3	19.9	29.1	2.9
10.0	0.01	0.0	0.51	3.9	1.3	0.82	10.89	2.43	90.2	7.3	75.3	3.7	5.5
7.4	0.25	2.2	0.53	6.3	1.5	1.19	13.26	4.47	55.6	1.7	12.3	21.1	5.1
7.8	0.38	2.4	0.04	3.4	0.8	0.71	7.83	3.12	81.7	5.6	38.4	5.6	4.4
9.4	0.80	1.9	6.59	9.4	7.1	2.85	25.23	3.27	75.6	6.5	54.7	5.1	8.4
2.0	2.62	19.2	0.86	1.2	0.1	0.13	1.27	3.35	87.4	1.0	9.6	30.7	4.3
4.3	0.82	6.7	0.00	3.7	1.3	0.53	5.18	3.77	81.6	4.1	14.3	7.8	5.5
1.2	4.81	31.3	0.00	3.4	1.4	0.49	4.43	3.81	81.3	4.9	10.4	2.4	4.7
5.1	0.79	4.5	0.09	5.2	1.7	1.18	6.98	3.85	64.3	1.3	11.7	26.6	9.1
7.7	0.17	1.5	0.05	3.8	0.4	0.77	7.29	3.55	80.9	0.5	2.3	36.0	6.0
5.7	1.54	6.5	0.00	4.5	6.1	6.73	43.03	3.23	74.0	1.8	27.2	25.0	4.4
5.4	0.83	6.6	0.00	6.1	3.9	1.11	12.31	3.65	67.9	2.1	15.0	18.4	5.6
8.6	0.00	0.0	0.13	5.9	1.2	0.98	10.08	4.49	62.3	4.7	37.6	10.9	4.4
6.2	1.77	6.7	0.59	4.7	1.8	0.86	6.48	3.84	66.9	5.9	48.3	6.6	7.0
4.3	2.11	11.7	0.00	6.4	3.5	1.57	17.46	3.90	54.8	1.8	20.7	21.9	6.5
7.3	0.85	4.3	0.07	5.5	0.6	1.34	12.31	4.24	62.7	1.6	27.3	28.2	3.5

	Name	City	State	Rating	2013 Rating	2012 Rating	Total Assets ($Mil)	One Year Asset Growth	Comm-ercial Loans	Cons-umer Loans	Mort-gage Loans	Secur-ities	Capital-ization Index	Lever-age Ratio	Risk-Based Capital Ratio
▲	FOUR OAKS BANK & TRUST CO	Four Oaks	NC	**D-**	E-	E-	837.4	3.47	2.5	1.1	12.6	12.4	**5.1**	7.1	15.0
	FOWLER STATE BK	Fowler	IN	**B+**	B+	B+	138.7	2.45	4.8	4.1	9.7	49.8	**10.0**	13.6	21.1
	FOWLER STATE BK	Fowler	CO	**B**	B	B	69.7	2.03	3.3	2.0	9.0	32.8	**10.0**	14.0	29.5
	FOWLER STATE BK	Fowler	KS	**B-**	B-	C+	65.3	2.29	14.0	6.8	4.1	41.8	**10.0**	11.3	18.9
	FOX CHASE BANK	Hatboro	PA	**B-**	B-	C	1076.5	-3.00	12.5	0.0	15.7	28.1	**10.0**	13.4	20.2
▲	FOX RIVER STATE BK	Burlington	WI	**D**	D-	D-	74.8	-1.88	8.6	1.8	15.3	9.3	**7.6**	9.4	14.6
	FOX VALLEY SAVINGS BANK	Fond Du Lac	WI	**B-**	B-	C+	305.0	1.83	0.8	0.6	28.5	39.5	**10.0**	13.2	25.9
	FOXBORO FEDERAL SAVINGS	Foxboro	MA	**B-**	B-	B-	151.1	1.48	0.0	0.6	51.2	28.7	**10.0**	15.4	35.5
	FRANDSEN BANK & TRUST	Lonsdale	MN	**C+**	C+	C	1547.5	2.73	10.2	1.7	14.7	30.3	**6.6**	8.6	14.0
▲	FRANKLIN BANK	Franklin	IL	**B+**	B	B	40.8	4.94	2.5	5.2	17.6	43.3	**10.0**	12.2	23.3
	FRANKLIN BANK	Pilesgrove	NJ	**C-**	C-	D+	247.1	-2.57	1.0	3.7	48.6	21.5	**6.2**	8.2	16.5
	FRANKLIN BANK & TRUST CO	Franklin	KY	**A-**	B+	A-	369.7	1.83	22.1	1.9	21.4	3.6	**10.0**	11.8	15.5
	FRANKLIN COMMUNITY BANK NA	Rocky Mount	VA	**B-**	C	C	166.7	-4.16	6.2	0.7	24.7	11.4	**10.0**	13.9	20.2
	FRANKLIN COUNTY UNITED BANK	Decherd	TN	**D-**	D-	C-	85.7	-3.07	10.1	2.6	15.6	11.1	**8.6**	10.1	14.0
	FRANKLIN FSB	Glen Allen	VA	**B**	B-	B-	1078.4	6.52	1.6	0.0	6.2	24.2	**10.0**	19.2	33.7
▼	FRANKLIN GROVE BANK	Franklin Grove	IL	**B**	B+	A-	30.7	-1.98	6.3	3.3	5.9	27.0	**10.0**	16.8	31.6
	FRANKLIN SB	Farmington	ME	**A-**	A-	A-	347.8	3.79	6.3	3.5	38.3	4.5	**10.0**	26.7	38.2
	FRANKLIN SB	Franklin	NH	**C+**	C+	C	382.0	4.02	1.9	0.8	32.6	23.9	**10.0**	11.3	19.8
	FRANKLIN STATE BK	Franklin	MN	**B**	B	B	27.0	5.23	3.1	3.2	14.3	15.2	**10.0**	13.8	21.4
	FRANKLIN STATE BK	Franklin	NE	**B+**	B+	B+	49.7	1.53	3.4	3.0	2.0	49.3	**10.0**	17.0	29.6
	FRANKLIN STATE BK & TRUST CO	Winnsboro	LA	**B+**	B+	B-	150.4	6.54	6.5	7.4	17.1	13.8	**7.2**	9.1	13.8
▲	FRANKLIN SYNERGY BANK	Franklin	TN	**B**	B-	C+	1238.3	87.75	5.7	0.3	12.5	32.5	**6.8**	8.8	13.0
	FRATERNITY FS&LA	Baltimore	MD	**D+**	D+	C-	162.8	-1.46	0.0	0.0	57.2	14.7	**10.0**	14.5	27.3
	FREDERICK COUNTY BANK	Frederick	MD	**C+**	C	C	333.7	5.91	12.4	0.6	11.6	7.3	**7.8**	10.2	13.2
	FREDONIA VALLEY BANK	Fredonia	KY	**B+**	B+	B+	75.0	2.97	2.8	3.7	44.9	21.2	**10.0**	13.5	23.2
	FREEDOM BANK	Huntingburg	IN	**A-**	A-	B+	344.5	2.74	6.4	5.2	39.3	0.8	**7.5**	9.7	12.9
	FREEDOM BANK	Columbia Falls	MT	**D+**	D	D-	51.0	14.58	16.2	2.8	15.6	0.0	**9.0**	10.4	15.5
	FREEDOM BANK	Maywood	NJ	**B-**	B-	B-	248.8	22.78	11.0	0.3	7.8	2.0	**6.3**	9.5	12.0
	FREEDOM BANK	Overland Park	KS	**B**	B	B	160.0	7.16	18.7	0.2	7.1	29.7	**9.6**	10.7	16.3
	FREEDOM BANK INC	Belington	WV	**D+**	D+	D	153.4	2.03	8.6	3.8	38.3	10.1	**7.3**	9.2	15.0
▲	FREEDOM BANK OF AMERICA	Saint Petersburg	FL	**C-**	D	D	124.4	27.11	10.4	2.2	4.3	2.3	**5.5**	10.0	11.4
	FREEDOM BANK OF OKLAHOMA	Tulsa	OK	**D-**	D+	C	41.5	-4.09	10.1	4.4	32.6	12.2	**6.8**	8.8	14.5
▲	FREEDOM BANK OF SOUTHERN MO	Cassville	MO	**B-**	B-	C+	206.9	8.21	7.6	3.6	20.0	17.3	**5.9**	7.9	13.4
	FREEDOM BANK OF VIRGINIA	Fairfax	VA	**C+**	C+	B-	305.3	12.99	14.2	2.5	17.6	8.4	**6.6**	9.2	12.2
	FREEDOM FINANCIAL BANK	West Des Moines	IA	**B+**	B+	B-	161.8	0.42	10.8	1.1	7.6	0.0	**8.9**	10.6	14.1
▲	FREEDOM NATIONAL BK	Greenville	RI	**D+**	D+	D+	107.1	4.42	9.2	0.1	9.2	17.8	**8.0**	9.7	13.5
	FREEDOMBANK	Elkader	IA	**B**	B	B	265.8	6.78	8.4	2.0	16.4	25.6	**7.8**	9.6	15.3
	FREEHOLD SAVINGS BANK	Freehold	NJ	**B-**	B-	B-	288.4	7.65	0.0	0.0	17.4	74.5	**10.0**	12.2	41.4
	FREELAND STATE BK	Freeland	MI	**C-**	C-	C	56.8	-1.32	0.2	4.2	15.8	60.8	**10.0**	16.2	52.0
▼	FREEPORT STATE BK	Harper	KS	**D-**	D	E+	26.1	11.69	3.5	1.4	10.3	25.0	**4.7**	6.7	12.0
	FREEPORT STATE BK	Freeport	MN	**B-**	B-	B-	99.5	4.06	12.2	3.6	11.4	11.1	**7.0**	9.1	12.5
	FREMONT BANK	Fremont	CA	**A-**	A-	B-	2740.7	6.57	5.2	0.1	29.5	7.4	**7.1**	9.2	12.6
	FRESNO FIRST BANK	Fresno	CA	**C+**	C+	B-	258.3	16.05	21.3	0.0	5.6	25.0	**7.9**	9.6	18.8
▲	FRIEND BANK	Slocomb	AL	**B**	C+	C	70.0	0.79	4.4	3.4	33.7	16.6	**10.0**	11.2	17.7
▲	FRIENDLY HILLS BANK	Whittier	CA	**C+**	C	C	113.3	7.40	8.3	0.1	10.3	34.2	**10.0**	13.0	19.3
	FRIENDS BANK	New Smyrna Beach	FL	**E-**	E-	E-	98.3	-3.92	0.2	0.6	18.6	3.7	**3.3**	6.2	10.1
	FRIENDSHIP STATE BK	Friendship	IN	**B**	B	B-	326.6	3.79	2.1	3.5	46.1	20.3	**7.3**	9.2	17.0
	FRONT RANGE BANK	Lakewood	CO	**C+**	C+	D+	208.1	9.20	9.9	4.4	13.5	41.9	**6.5**	8.5	14.7
▲	FRONTENAC BANK	Earth City	MO	**D**	D-	D-	267.8	0.28	3.1	0.4	10.4	14.1	**7.8**	9.6	13.9
	FRONTIER BANK	Lamar	CO	**A**	A-	A-	265.0	15.08	2.3	0.8	11.2	39.3	**10.0**	11.7	20.6
	FRONTIER BANK	Madison	NE	**B-**	B-	C	289.4	36.11	12.7	1.6	14.8	10.7	**4.5**	8.6	10.7
	FRONTIER BANK	Rock Rapids	IA	**C+**	C	C-	173.3	9.05	5.3	1.4	10.1	29.0	**6.9**	8.9	13.0
	FRONTIER BANK OF TEXAS	Elgin	TX	**B-**	C+	C+	144.6	7.38	4.3	5.0	22.4	31.1	**10.0**	18.1	33.8
	FRONTIER COMMUNITY BANK	Waynesboro	VA	**C-**	C	C	93.4	3.26	7.4	1.4	23.2	2.1	**9.3**	10.5	15.4
	FRONTIER SB	Council Bluffs	IA	**C-**	C	B-	35.6	6.84	3.6	0.3	6.8	0.0	**10.0**	12.2	24.9
▲	FRONTIER STATE BK	Oklahoma City	OK	**B-**	C	D+	662.9	6.80	21.1	0.9	11.9	13.8	**10.0**	11.7	15.2
	FROST BANK	San Antonio	TX	**B+**	B+	B+	27397.4	16.36	16.9	1.4	2.5	35.9	**5.5**	7.5	13.3
	FROST STATE BK	Frost	MN	**D+**	D+	C	41.6	8.41	11.1	4.6	6.6	3.4	**8.3**	11.3	13.6
▲	FSGBANK NA	Chattanooga	TN	**D+**	D-	E-	1027.7	1.63	6.6	2.6	11.7	22.4	**6.9**	8.9	12.5
	FULLERTON NATIONAL BK	Fullerton	NE	**B**	B	B-	42.6	3.23	9.8	3.7	4.1	9.2	**8.5**	10.6	13.7

Asset Mix columns (Commercial Loans, Consumer Loans, Mortgage Loans, Securities) are As a % of Total Assets.

Asset Quality Index	Adjusted Non-Performing Loans as a % of Total Loans	Adjusted Non-Performing Loans as a % of Capital	Net Charge-Offs Avg Loans	Profitability Index	Net Income ($Mil)	Return on Assets (R.O.A.)	Return on Equity (R.O.E.)	Net Interest Spread	Overhead Efficiency Ratio	Liquidity Index	Liquidity Ratio	Hot Money Ratio	Stability Index
2.0	4.24	28.1	2.84	**0.0**	-4.1	-0.66	-11.00	3.00	84.2	**2.2**	31.0	22.2	**2.4**
7.8	0.81	2.5	0.03	**5.1**	1.1	1.08	7.77	4.54	73.2	**5.9**	51.2	7.5	**7.2**
5.1	3.65	10.9	0.37	**4.6**	0.5	0.89	6.44	2.99	47.9	**2.8**	55.4	30.1	**6.6**
7.2	1.15	5.1	0.07	**3.5**	0.4	0.80	7.82	3.28	73.7	**2.9**	15.5	14.5	**6.0**
6.7	0.85	3.9	0.37	**3.9**	6.2	0.75	5.82	3.27	60.3	**2.7**	11.0	15.6	**8.4**
1.6	4.09	24.4	3.31	**1.0**	0.1	0.12	0.88	3.70	94.1	**2.2**	15.0	17.8	**4.5**
6.4	1.82	6.4	0.42	**3.3**	1.2	0.53	3.95	2.85	73.6	**4.5**	41.1	12.9	**6.2**
10.0	0.08	0.3	0.01	**3.2**	0.6	0.49	3.29	2.62	79.6	**4.6**	48.6	14.1	**8.0**
3.8	1.88	12.1	0.29	**5.5**	14.7	1.25	10.19	3.92	70.3	**4.7**	14.8	4.3	**9.3**
9.0	0.39	1.4	0.00	**7.2**	0.5	1.68	22.65	3.61	52.5	**3.3**	40.2	18.6	**5.4**
5.3	1.37	9.7	0.27	**1.9**	0.5	0.29	3.40	3.05	89.6	**4.0**	35.2	13.3	**4.0**
7.6	0.35	2.3	0.27	**5.3**	2.6	0.98	8.38	4.17	64.8	**3.7**	13.7	10.2	**6.2**
4.7	2.21	11.2	0.26	**3.9**	0.9	0.73	5.13	3.92	73.8	**2.0**	25.3	20.1	**5.7**
0.3	10.11	58.3	-0.06	**2.5**	0.3	0.53	4.63	4.43	75.3	**1.2**	17.5	30.4	**4.5**
4.4	5.37	13.3	0.19	**4.2**	8.8	1.11	5.79	2.80	64.2	**2.8**	27.8	20.2	**8.8**
8.1	0.39	1.0	2.92	**3.0**	0.1	0.28	1.65	3.45	60.1	**3.9**	56.6	18.2	**7.6**
7.1	1.16	3.5	0.07	**6.2**	2.7	1.06	4.12	4.70	67.5	**3.7**	6.7	9.8	**7.7**
5.7	2.01	11.0	-0.06	**3.0**	1.3	0.46	3.98	3.28	84.5	**2.9**	21.6	15.0	**5.7**
8.5	0.16	0.7	0.02	**4.4**	0.2	0.77	5.82	3.42	63.4	**4.4**	29.2	9.5	**6.7**
6.2	2.77	6.5	-0.11	**6.9**	0.5	1.44	9.43	3.73	45.7	**5.2**	48.9	10.3	**7.2**
6.9	0.37	2.7	0.04	**7.7**	2.1	1.87	21.50	4.77	62.4	**1.5**	15.3	24.4	**6.3**
7.7	0.48	3.3	0.12	**5.0**	6.4	0.88	11.09	3.67	63.5	**1.7**	8.2	20.7	**6.1**
6.0	3.28	15.1	-0.11	**0.8**	-0.1	-0.05	-0.39	2.85	101.1	**1.5**	26.7	28.9	**6.4**
3.3	1.60	11.2	0.07	**3.7**	1.5	0.60	5.99	3.71	76.8	**2.0**	16.3	19.2	**5.6**
5.1	2.84	13.0	0.49	**6.7**	0.8	1.38	10.80	4.59	56.9	**4.3**	27.3	9.2	**7.5**
5.8	0.50	3.9	0.00	**9.8**	6.2	2.37	24.52	3.59	40.5	**3.4**	7.3	11.1	**8.4**
1.5	4.48	28.6	0.10	**6.2**	0.6	1.52	15.02	5.38	70.5	**0.8**	16.8	35.3	**3.3**
6.4	0.21	1.8	0.05	**4.3**	1.2	0.73	7.43	4.19	65.6	**0.7**	11.7	37.2	**4.5**
4.9	1.25	6.8	0.00	**5.2**	1.1	0.94	8.96	3.76	67.6	**4.1**	22.2	9.2	**5.8**
1.6	6.45	44.1	0.63	**3.0**	0.5	0.40	4.15	3.64	76.3	**3.1**	16.3	13.6	**4.5**
3.0	1.58	12.3	-0.06	**3.6**	3.0	3.69	30.58	4.24	88.8	**1.6**	10.4	21.1	**3.4**
0.3	9.89	71.9	1.83	**0.0**	-0.8	-2.41	-25.69	3.73	123.1	**0.8**	14.6	36.2	**2.5**
5.5	0.46	4.0	0.58	**5.6**	2.1	1.34	18.92	4.02	63.3	**0.9**	9.0	31.1	**4.7**
3.7	0.84	7.1	0.21	**3.3**	1.3	0.59	6.45	3.90	81.7	**0.6**	10.4	48.6	**4.2**
5.0	0.44	3.3	0.06	**5.4**	1.5	1.28	11.98	3.41	56.7	**0.6**	12.7	53.8	**6.5**
2.7	1.33	9.7	0.62	**0.5**	0.0	-0.01	-0.07	3.25	98.7	**1.7**	15.2	22.3	**3.2**
4.7	0.95	6.2	0.03	**6.3**	2.8	1.45	14.37	3.24	55.9	**1.9**	25.5	21.4	**7.9**
10.0	0.78	1.1	-0.01	**2.8**	0.6	0.29	2.39	1.64	73.3	**2.6**	43.3	28.5	**6.8**
5.9	6.67	9.6	0.05	**1.6**	0.0	0.08	0.51	2.12	96.4	**6.6**	90.0	9.4	**5.5**
3.7	2.75	20.2	0.19	**2.1**	0.1	0.32	4.85	3.73	86.7	**5.4**	35.2	5.4	**1.5**
4.5	1.45	11.6	-0.01	**5.3**	0.6	0.86	9.50	5.14	73.8	**3.1**	15.6	13.3	**5.0**
5.8	1.41	11.1	-0.10	**7.1**	24.8	1.30	13.74	3.92	77.4	**4.6**	12.3	4.8	**9.2**
7.9	0.30	1.7	-0.13	**4.6**	1.6	0.91	9.27	4.29	63.5	**4.2**	41.2	14.3	**3.3**
7.8	0.35	2.2	0.37	**4.2**	0.5	0.92	8.39	4.33	76.3	**3.5**	11.0	11.2	**4.7**
6.4	1.07	3.9	-0.32	**4.1**	1.7	2.10	17.56	3.73	87.3	**6.4**	49.1	3.5	**5.6**
0.0	9.24	80.2	-0.03	**1.4**	0.2	0.26	4.47	3.60	92.9	**2.2**	22.6	18.7	**1.5**
6.6	0.63	4.5	0.18	**6.3**	2.6	1.08	11.52	3.99	63.8	**2.9**	26.7	15.8	**5.5**
3.6	2.89	17.0	-0.04	**3.6**	1.4	0.94	11.19	3.72	79.4	**4.4**	32.3	10.6	**4.6**
0.7	5.37	34.9	0.51	**1.7**	0.3	0.17	1.84	3.17	95.1	**1.6**	18.2	23.3	**4.0**
7.9	1.10	4.6	0.07	**7.5**	3.7	1.82	15.14	3.91	50.0	**3.8**	32.8	13.7	**8.5**
7.6	0.14	1.3	-0.01	**7.7**	3.7	1.80	18.76	3.63	47.9	**1.5**	7.8	23.1	**6.2**
4.0	1.93	12.2	-0.05	**3.3**	0.8	0.65	6.51	3.35	80.1	**1.6**	23.2	24.9	**5.4**
8.8	0.04	0.1	0.17	**3.5**	0.5	0.49	2.70	3.72	78.0	**4.3**	52.7	16.5	**6.9**
5.6	0.55	4.0	0.63	**1.9**	0.1	0.10	0.93	3.02	82.5	**1.2**	18.0	30.0	**5.2**
9.1	0.00	0.0	0.00	**3.0**	0.1	0.31	2.53	3.73	87.4	**6.3**	52.8	4.0	**5.6**
3.7	3.91	20.7	0.02	**4.0**	5.5	1.14	10.40	2.58	56.9	**0.8**	16.4	44.0	**5.7**
7.1	0.71	3.7	0.08	**5.3**	207.1	1.11	10.73	3.32	64.2	**7.1**	50.6	2.8	**8.7**
1.6	1.95	14.6	0.38	**9.3**	0.4	1.46	13.27	4.13	32.3	**0.5**	7.2	56.5	**6.6**
6.0	0.92	6.7	0.14	**1.8**	3.3	0.44	5.46	3.36	94.0	**1.6**	9.4	22.1	**4.0**
7.0	0.00	0.0	0.00	**6.9**	0.5	1.57	14.50	3.86	57.2	**2.7**	22.6	16.3	**6.3**

Name	City	State	Rating	2013 Rating	2012 Rating	Total Assets ($Mil)	One Year Asset Growth	Asset Mix (As a % of Total Assets) Comm-ercial Loans	Cons-umer Loans	Mort-gage Loans	Secur-ities	Capital-ization Index	Lever-age Ratio	Risk-Based Capital Ratio
FULTON BANK NA	Lancaster	PA	**B-**	B-	C+	9624.9	-0.12	14.6	1.6	11.9	10.8	**8.0**	10.5	13.4
▲ FULTON BANK OF NEW JERSEY	Mount Laurel	NJ	**B-**	C	C-	3464.3	2.98	12.6	1.7	8.6	16.4	**7.5**	9.5	12.9
FULTON SB	Fulton	NY	**A-**	A	A	377.3	1.23	0.6	1.0	30.3	34.6	**10.0**	23.9	37.6
FULTON STATE BK	Fulton	SD	**B**	B	B	63.4	12.25	13.4	2.0	0.0	49.0	**9.6**	10.7	18.5
G W JONES EXCHANGE BANK	Marcellus	MI	**C**	C	C-	63.7	-1.20	3.4	1.2	30.6	29.1	**8.4**	9.9	26.5
GALENA STATE BK & TRUST CO	Galena	IL	**B**	B-	C+	293.4	-0.99	12.0	1.0	13.5	32.8	**6.7**	8.8	13.8
GALION BUILDING & LOAN BANK	Galion	OH	**C-**	C-	C	66.1	-0.32	1.2	2.2	60.4	17.0	**9.0**	10.3	23.7
GARDEN PLAIN STATE BK	Wichita	KS	**A-**	A	A-	93.6	5.25	12.2	2.2	14.4	31.2	**10.0**	11.8	17.9
GARDNER BANK	Gardner	KS	**C+**	C+	B-	119.0	14.95	10.4	6.2	11.5	46.3	**5.9**	7.9	14.3
▼ GARFIELD COUNTY BANK	Jordan	MT	**C-**	C+	C+	61.8	3.48	6.4	3.5	3.6	10.1	**9.3**	11.9	14.4
GARNAVILLO SB	Garnavillo	IA	**C**	C+	C	40.0	4.40	12.8	4.6	10.7	7.6	**10.0**	11.6	15.3
GARRETT STATE BK	Garrett	IN	**B**	B	B	199.5	3.77	4.9	3.5	51.7	21.1	**7.3**	9.2	17.9
GARRISON STATE BK & TRUST	Garrison	ND	**B**	B	B-	118.8	8.25	6.3	4.8	2.9	14.9	**7.0**	9.5	12.5
GARY STATE BK	Gary	MN	**B-**	B-	B-	12.7	-7.86	11.3	7.0	2.3	0.0	**10.0**	13.5	17.6
GATE CITY BANK	Fargo	ND	**B**	B	B+	1720.0	6.47	0.7	25.1	52.4	7.3	**10.0**	11.1	18.0
GATES BANKING & TRUST CO	Gates	TN	**B-**	B-	B	43.9	5.37	3.1	1.2	2.5	63.4	**9.2**	10.5	23.3
GATEWAY BANK	Mendota Heights	MN	**A-**	A-	B+	123.1	7.27	30.4	3.0	12.8	1.2	**8.4**	9.9	13.8
GATEWAY BANK FSB	Oakland	CA	**E-**	E	E-	203.5	-2.85	0.1	0.0	49.8	10.1	**1.6**	4.7	8.6
GATEWAY BANK OF CENTRAL FL	Ocala	FL	**C+**	C	D	191.6	4.36	6.7	1.0	15.1	11.8	**8.6**	10.2	13.8
GATEWAY BANK OF FLORIDA	Daytona Beach	FL	**C+**	C+	C	227.2	-13.09	5.4	0.5	4.7	42.1	**8.7**	10.1	22.1
GATEWAY BANK OF SOUTHWEST FL	Sarasota	FL	**C+**	C+	C	218.3	-5.86	5.3	0.2	8.4	32.8	**8.4**	9.9	13.8
GATEWAY COMMERCIAL BANK	Mesa	AZ	**B**	B	B-	96.5	10.23	9.5	0.1	4.5	35.1	**10.0**	14.3	20.2
GATEWAY COMMUNITY BANK	Roscoe	IL	**C-**	C-	D+	91.4	5.90	8.8	1.5	15.4	30.4	**8.5**	10.0	16.3
GATEWAY STATE BK	Clinton	IA	**B**	B	C+	136.1	3.08	10.2	1.7	13.0	21.4	**6.5**	8.5	13.5
GBC INTERNATIONAL BK	Los Angeles	CA	**C+**	C	C-	479.1	2.61	19.2	0.0	0.7	9.9	**9.6**	10.7	16.7
GE CAPITAL BANK	Salt Lake City	UT	**A**	A	A	19886.4	18.54	54.0	0.0	0.0	0.4	**10.0**	14.9	15.9
▲ GEAUGA SB	Newbury	OH	**C-**	D	D+	364.9	-5.74	1.5	0.1	26.2	49.5	**10.0**	12.0	25.0
GEDDES FS&LA	Syracuse	NY	**B+**	B+	B	521.3	1.32	0.0	0.1	90.6	0.6	**10.0**	14.0	27.2
GENERATIONS BANK	Seneca Falls	NY	**B-**	B-	C+	277.7	3.57	7.8	17.5	34.2	11.6	**7.3**	9.7	12.7
GENERATIONS BANK	Exeter	NE	**C**	C	D+	34.8	7.45	9.5	1.4	10.0	24.5	**6.7**	8.7	12.5
GENESEE REGIONAL BANK	Rochester	NY	**B-**	B-	B-	421.2	11.34	21.4	0.5	7.0	25.9	**6.2**	8.2	13.1
GENOA BANKING CO	Genoa	OH	**C+**	C+	C+	278.5	7.80	4.2	5.6	25.0	18.8	**6.9**	8.9	14.2
GENOA COMMUNITY BANK	Genoa	NE	**D**	D+	D-	61.7	6.19	5.3	1.6	4.6	23.1	**8.6**	10.2	13.8
▲ GEO D WARTHEN BANK	Sandersville	GA	**C-**	D-	D-	159.4	1.45	9.2	7.9	21.9	24.5	**7.1**	9.1	13.4
GEORGETOWN BANK	Georgetown	MA	**C+**	C+	C+	269.7	9.05	6.6	0.1	37.4	7.7	**8.4**	9.9	14.5
GEORGIA B&TC OF AUGUSTA	Augusta	GA	**B**	B	C+	1749.9	3.61	4.9	1.0	12.4	37.8	**7.7**	9.5	15.4
GEORGIA BANKING CO	Atlanta	GA	**C+**	B-	D+	245.0	19.01	1.6	2.4	64.9	16.9	**10.0**	11.1	21.4
▲ GEORGIA COMMERCE BANK	Atlanta	GA	**B+**	B-	B-	1004.8	36.76	27.5	0.9	9.8	14.6	**8.8**	10.7	14.0
GEORGIA HERITAGE BANK	Dallas	GA	**E-**	E-	E-	69.0	8.82	7.6	0.9	15.4	13.2	**1.1**	5.3	8.1
GEORGIA PRIMARY BANK	Atlanta	GA	**D-**	D-	E+	157.5	-19.80	6.1	0.1	5.3	14.5	**9.0**	10.3	15.5
GERBER STATE BK	Argenta	IL	**C+**	C+	C+	82.9	-0.15	0.6	1.2	10.3	57.5	**7.7**	9.5	21.5
GERMAN AMERICAN BANCORP	Jasper	IN	**B+**	B+	B+	2200.3	7.22	14.5	1.2	8.4	26.0	**6.6**	8.6	12.7
GERMAN-AMERICAN STATE BK	German Valley	IL	**B-**	B-	C	203.5	5.84	11.6	2.7	11.7	21.8	**8.1**	9.7	14.0
GERMANTOWN TRUST & SB	Breese	IL	**A**	A	A+	343.0	2.46	1.8	0.9	13.3	50.1	**10.0**	12.8	25.4
▼ GIBRALTAR BANK	Whippany	NJ	**C**	C+	C+	103.1	-3.14	0.0	0.0	78.5	8.0	**10.0**	12.3	24.2
▲ GIBRALTAR PRIVATE BANK & TRUST	Coral Gables	FL	**D+**	D-	D-	1567.7	0.10	3.1	1.8	56.3	1.8	**6.6**	8.6	13.9
GIBSLAND BANK & TRUST CO	Gibsland	LA	**B-**	B-	B-	325.0	21.05	13.6	4.7	17.4	9.2	**7.8**	9.6	13.6
GIFFORD STATE BK	Gifford	IL	**B**	B	B-	142.6	7.99	6.8	4.0	17.8	6.2	**6.7**	8.7	12.7
GILMER NATIONAL BK	Gilmer	TX	**B+**	B	B	225.9	7.56	4.5	11.8	17.4	26.0	**10.0**	12.2	21.7
GIRARD NATIONAL BK	Girard	KS	**B-**	B-	C+	565.3	5.11	11.8	2.5	8.0	30.4	**9.6**	10.7	15.1
GLACIER BANK	Kalispell	MT	**B**	B	C+	8090.2	0.76	7.1	1.7	10.6	36.0	**10.0**	12.4	18.4
GLADEWATER NATIONAL BK	Gladewater	TX	**C+**	C	C+	55.8	7.02	13.0	5.1	40.2	24.0	**10.0**	13.0	26.4
GLASFORD STATE BK	Glasford	IL	**C**	C+	B-	36.4	-0.64	1.4	7.6	26.0	40.6	**6.2**	8.2	23.9
GLEN BURNIE MUTUAL SB	Glen Burnie	MD	**D+**	D+	C-	82.6	3.33	0.0	0.0	71.5	3.5	**6.0**	8.0	17.6
GLEN ROCK SB	Glen Rock	NJ	**C**	C	C	134.3	-0.66	0.0	0.1	74.8	17.8	**7.0**	9.0	18.0
GLENMEDE TRUST CO NA	Philadelphia	PA	**U**	U	U	70.4	-5.14	0.0	0.0	0.0	9.9	**10.0**	44.8	65.9
GLENNVILLE BANK	Glennville	GA	**B+**	B-	B-	209.5	2.33	5.8	3.4	17.2	25.4	**9.0**	10.3	17.1
GLENS FALLS NATIONAL BK & TR	Glens Falls	NY	**B+**	B+	B+	1871.2	1.71	2.8	17.1	17.8	32.7	**7.5**	9.3	15.4
GLENVIEW STATE BK	Glenview	IL	**C+**	C+	B-	1192.6	-1.32	5.9	20.2	6.9	52.4	**8.9**	10.2	14.7
GLENWOOD STATE BK	Glenwood	MN	**C**	C+	C+	227.1	3.98	21.7	2.0	14.3	0.7	**5.6**	9.4	11.5

Asset Quality Index	Adjusted Non-Performing Loans as a % of Total Loans	Adjusted Non-Performing Loans as a % of Capital	Net Charge-Offs Avg Loans	Profitability Index	Net Income ($Mil)	Return on Assets (R.O.A.)	Return on Equity (R.O.E.)	Net Interest Spread	Overhead Efficiency Ratio	Liquidity Index	Liquidity Ratio	Hot Money Ratio	Stability Index
4.8	1.11	7.9	0.21	**6.0**	82.7	1.17	9.78	3.43	61.6	**4.0**	6.1	7.9	**7.9**
3.0	2.02	14.1	0.33	**4.1**	18.5	0.73	5.24	3.66	74.8	**4.0**	9.7	8.3	**7.0**
7.3	3.24	5.8	0.15	**6.0**	3.4	1.20	5.16	4.42	68.3	**6.3**	66.7	9.0	**8.6**
8.8	0.05	0.2	-0.01	**4.4**	0.3	0.75	7.15	3.76	68.7	**4.4**	53.8	15.1	**5.8**
9.7	0.32	1.3	0.16	**2.5**	0.2	0.38	3.88	3.43	87.2	**5.9**	57.2	8.1	**4.5**
6.0	0.63	4.2	-0.09	**6.4**	2.6	1.20	13.66	3.61	64.0	**4.0**	15.3	8.5	**6.2**
6.0	1.33	8.4	0.23	**2.3**	0.1	0.22	2.13	3.14	86.6	**3.8**	30.9	12.8	**4.8**
8.7	0.15	0.6	2.31	**5.9**	0.5	0.71	5.85	3.67	52.5	**4.4**	51.9	15.0	**7.2**
4.9	1.84	9.8	0.19	**2.8**	0.3	0.33	4.29	3.12	82.3	**5.8**	38.1	4.0	**3.5**
1.7	2.93	18.0	0.00	**7.8**	0.6	1.31	11.59	4.60	53.2	**0.7**	5.1	33.0	**7.4**
2.3	2.87	19.2	0.03	**5.6**	0.4	1.28	11.06	4.07	59.6	**3.0**	14.9	14.1	**5.6**
4.8	1.74	12.5	0.18	**6.5**	2.3	1.56	17.41	3.64	53.1	**1.0**	25.7	38.4	**6.7**
5.2	0.60	4.5	0.00	**7.8**	1.2	1.36	14.97	4.26	52.9	**3.8**	12.0	9.3	**5.9**
6.7	0.00	0.0	0.11	**6.3**	0.1	1.27	9.66	4.79	74.3	**5.1**	17.1	1.0	**5.7**
7.2	0.05	0.4	0.03	**4.2**	7.7	0.61	5.50	2.85	76.3	**4.0**	15.4	9.2	**8.6**
6.3	2.05	5.8	0.00	**5.0**	0.3	1.09	9.46	3.91	63.6	**2.0**	44.4	48.7	**6.8**
7.3	0.00	0.0	0.15	**6.9**	1.5	1.67	16.55	4.08	57.7	**3.7**	22.3	11.0	**7.4**
0.3	6.41	83.8	0.10	**0.0**	-3.2	-2.00	-35.58	3.55	148.1	**1.6**	10.8	22.3	**0.5**
4.4	1.87	12.1	0.15	**3.7**	1.1	0.81	7.91	4.25	75.2	**3.8**	20.7	10.4	**5.3**
6.9	1.18	4.2	-0.13	**3.3**	1.4	0.74	7.86	3.24	125.2	**2.8**	55.6	37.4	**5.0**
5.4	1.97	10.4	0.00	**3.6**	1.0	0.61	6.80	3.87	81.4	**3.0**	37.4	19.2	**5.3**
6.8	1.25	4.8	0.00	**4.7**	0.6	0.83	5.86	3.70	61.9	**4.7**	42.9	11.9	**7.0**
1.9	5.66	30.7	0.08	**2.2**	0.2	0.30	3.12	3.81	82.5	**2.4**	38.6	26.9	**4.1**
4.9	0.91	6.9	0.26	**3.7**	0.6	0.60	6.29	3.23	73.5	**1.9**	25.3	22.2	**6.1**
3.5	1.19	8.1	-0.01	**6.0**	3.7	1.02	9.63	3.92	62.9	**0.7**	14.1	47.3	**5.9**
7.7	0.35	1.8	0.22	**7.7**	147.9	1.08	6.72	3.08	60.7	**0.6**	16.3	74.8	**10.0**
1.7	13.48	46.9	0.64	**2.1**	0.9	0.32	2.71	2.49	81.1	**1.5**	33.1	39.6	**4.2**
8.3	0.61	4.1	0.04	**4.9**	3.0	0.78	5.64	2.74	51.1	**0.6**	5.2	35.3	**8.2**
4.3	0.83	5.8	0.05	**4.3**	1.6	0.78	8.08	4.23	73.2	**2.6**	15.3	16.0	**5.2**
7.1	0.30	1.9	0.45	**4.1**	0.2	0.68	6.46	3.82	68.1	**4.1**	23.5	9.3	**3.6**
4.7	1.15	8.6	0.08	**5.8**	2.9	0.97	11.84	3.81	62.5	**1.8**	36.6	34.3	**4.2**
5.0	0.82	6.0	0.10	**3.7**	1.2	0.60	6.88	3.80	77.3	**1.7**	15.4	21.0	**4.6**
0.9	4.23	26.9	0.02	**4.0**	0.5	1.12	11.60	3.32	74.1	**3.6**	13.6	11.0	**5.4**
3.9	1.48	9.4	0.18	**2.4**	0.6	0.50	5.79	4.48	88.7	**2.9**	24.3	15.4	**2.5**
5.8	0.58	4.7	0.15	**3.8**	1.1	0.55	5.60	3.81	78.3	**1.3**	3.8	23.6	**5.5**
5.7	1.50	7.6	0.37	**5.3**	12.8	0.98	10.85	3.28	59.7	**3.0**	31.2	20.5	**6.9**
5.3	2.23	15.1	-0.07	**2.2**	0.0	-0.01	-0.07	2.99	104.6	**0.5**	3.8	43.4	**4.3**
8.0	0.27	1.8	0.02	**5.5**	7.0	0.97	8.69	4.77	61.9	**2.8**	18.1	15.6	**6.1**
0.3	4.96	51.9	-0.03	**5.3**	0.9	1.73	38.89	4.50	67.6	**1.4**	14.4	26.6	**0.1**
0.0	15.95	83.9	3.41	**0.3**	-0.8	-0.58	-5.85	3.79	119.6	**2.8**	27.9	16.8	**4.2**
5.6	3.54	11.0	-0.01	**3.4**	0.4	0.67	7.45	2.46	70.0	**5.8**	57.2	8.3	**4.5**
6.8	0.49	3.5	-0.04	**7.2**	20.8	1.29	13.86	3.79	59.0	**5.0**	26.3	7.2	**8.2**
3.9	1.84	12.1	0.20	**6.7**	1.8	1.19	12.04	3.84	53.3	**2.3**	15.8	17.5	**5.9**
9.4	0.10	0.4	0.04	**7.0**	4.4	1.71	13.57	2.71	37.4	**4.8**	45.2	12.3	**9.6**
8.9	0.51	3.3	0.04	**2.0**	0.1	0.08	0.69	2.80	97.4	**1.1**	6.8	27.7	**6.6**
2.3	3.24	28.4	-0.29	**2.6**	7.9	0.66	8.21	3.22	96.3	**1.7**	13.2	21.9	**6.2**
4.8	0.80	6.2	0.15	**8.1**	3.0	1.29	13.70	5.49	57.9	**0.8**	14.9	39.5	**5.2**
5.8	0.43	3.2	0.17	**4.7**	1.1	1.01	12.24	3.58	66.4	**2.2**	19.0	18.2	**5.2**
5.0	2.12	9.3	0.39	**4.7**	1.5	0.93	7.71	3.88	61.4	**2.4**	45.5	33.7	**6.6**
4.2	1.48	7.6	0.05	**4.9**	3.7	0.87	7.47	3.55	64.4	**3.0**	18.2	14.1	**6.9**
4.9	2.34	9.7	0.05	**8.2**	88.8	1.52	11.09	4.51	55.8	**3.9**	23.6	12.5	**8.9**
4.6	2.85	14.1	0.03	**6.7**	0.6	1.37	10.90	4.59	85.5	**3.0**	35.3	18.3	**5.4**
8.4	0.38	2.0	0.01	**2.7**	0.1	0.47	5.75	2.46	82.4	**6.3**	41.3	2.0	**3.7**
6.4	0.76	6.8	0.00	**1.6**	0.1	0.13	1.57	0.86	85.9	**5.5**	25.2	0.0	**4.0**
5.1	1.37	11.1	0.13	**2.6**	0.3	0.25	2.99	3.09	84.2	**2.1**	2.6	17.1	**4.3**
10.0	na	0.0	na	**10.0**	14.4	29.00	60.13	1.45	78.7	**4.0**	77.6	101.0	**6.7**
4.0	2.92	14.7	0.06	**7.0**	2.0	1.25	11.44	4.49	55.0	**1.7**	27.9	27.1	**6.1**
6.6	0.55	3.5	0.06	**5.7**	14.9	1.08	11.17	3.14	62.2	**4.8**	8.7	3.1	**8.2**
7.7	0.40	1.5	0.01	**3.3**	6.0	0.67	6.70	1.89	75.9	**6.6**	49.4	5.5	**8.5**
2.4	2.07	18.4	-0.13	**7.2**	3.0	1.80	18.86	4.22	59.1	**3.1**	2.4	12.5	**6.4**

Name	City	State	Rating	2013 Rating	2012 Rating	Total Assets ($Mil)	One Year Asset Growth	Asset Mix (As a % of Total Assets) Commercial Loans	Consumer Loans	Mortgage Loans	Securities	Capitalization Index	Leverage Ratio	Risk-Based Capital Ratio
GLENWOOD STATE BK	Glenwood	IA	**C-**	C-	C	173.3	3.65	1.5	2.1	7.3	57.7	**7.1**	9.1	23.1
GLOBAL BANK	New York	NY	**B-**	B-	C	125.4	11.31	0.5	0.1	15.8	8.9	**10.0**	13.8	18.8
▲ GNB BANK	Grundy Center	IA	**B**	B-	B-	344.3	0.35	10.6	1.3	4.6	27.2	**7.5**	10.4	12.9
GOGEBIC RANGE BANK	Ironwood	MI	**B**	B-	B-	68.7	4.53	21.7	6.7	9.9	16.5	**10.0**	12.8	17.3
GOLD COAST BANK	Chicago	IL	**A-**	A-	B-	334.5	16.43	7.4	0.1	25.9	0.0	**7.9**	9.7	13.2
GOLD COAST BANK	Islandia	NY	**C-**	C	C	276.2	18.71	7.2	0.6	0.0	17.7	**8.6**	10.1	14.4
GOLDEN BANK NA	Houston	TX	**B**	B	C	570.4	-2.53	3.5	0.1	5.2	16.8	**10.0**	14.2	20.0
GOLDEN BELT BANK FSA	Ellis	KS	**C+**	C+	B-	147.4	4.32	10.9	5.2	30.9	10.5	**7.7**	12.1	13.1
GOLDEN EAGLE COMMUNITY BANK	Woodstock	IL	**D**	D	E+	135.5	0.06	7.7	0.6	14.7	12.3	**8.5**	10.1	13.7
▼ GOLDEN PACIFIC BANK NA	Sacramento	CA	**D-**	D	D-	120.6	-9.86	12.8	0.4	23.1	5.5	**7.8**	9.5	14.7
GOLDEN STATE BK	Upland	CA	**E-**	E-	E-	100.0	21.05	8.8	0.0	0.7	0.0	**10.0**	13.6	20.6
GOLDEN VALLEY BANK	Chico	CA	**A-**	A-	B	164.9	17.53	8.6	0.1	7.7	20.0	**10.0**	11.4	18.5
▲ GOLDMAN SACHS BANK USA	New York	NY	**A**	A-	A-	111758.0	0.58	8.2	1.1	3.7	0.0	**10.0**	17.9	16.6
GOLDMAN SACHS TRUST CO NA	New York	NY	**U**	U	U	62.0	14.46	0.0	0.0	0.0	56.9	**10.0**	74.1	386.5
GOLDWATER BANK NA	Scottsdale	AZ	**E**	E-	E-	76.4	-32.10	3.2	9.1	23.0	19.1	**5.7**	7.7	15.3
▼ GOODFIELD STATE BK	Goodfield	IL	**A-**	A	A-	97.9	19.09	13.0	2.7	23.7	14.2	**8.4**	11.5	13.7
GOOSE RIVER BANK	Mayville	ND	**C+**	C+	C	118.7	2.94	15.6	5.5	2.2	28.3	**6.1**	8.1	12.7
GOPPERT FINANCIAL BANK	Lathrop	MO	**C**	C	C+	81.7	3.21	9.7	1.2	8.7	12.3	**8.2**	9.8	14.0
GOPPERT STATE SERVICE BANK	Garnett	KS	**C**	C	C	154.7	1.80	13.1	3.8	15.3	28.6	**9.2**	10.4	18.6
GORHAM SB	Gorham	ME	**C-**	C-	C-	973.8	3.99	8.1	0.5	24.2	18.7	**7.2**	9.2	13.9
GORHAM STATE BK	Gorham	KS	**C**	C	C	31.4	7.89	8.6	3.8	6.7	1.5	**5.8**	7.8	16.6
GOTHENBURG STATE BK	Gothenburg	NE	**A-**	A-	A-	147.3	17.71	16.2	3.0	3.2	16.2	**8.8**	11.5	14.0
GOUVERNEUR S&LA	Gouverneur	NY	**A**	A	A-	144.9	0.63	1.4	2.8	59.1	13.2	**10.0**	18.5	32.5
GRAHAM SAVINGS & LOAN SSB	Graham	TX	**B+**	B+	B+	125.8	0.44	0.8	1.1	49.1	10.0	**10.0**	11.2	23.9
GRAND BANK	Tulsa	OK	**A-**	A-	B+	228.4	6.73	20.7	0.8	10.9	14.0	**10.0**	11.6	15.6
GRAND BANK	Dallas	TX	**C**	C	C	538.9	0.06	9.1	0.6	8.8	16.8	**5.7**	7.7	16.5
GRAND BANK & TRUST OF FLORIDA	West Palm Beach	FL	**C-**	D	E-	207.6	-4.87	5.2	1.0	5.7	22.7	**8.7**	10.1	15.3
▲ GRAND BANK FOR SAVINGS FSB	Hattiesburg	MS	**C**	C-	D+	92.7	-16.28	0.0	0.7	66.6	0.0	**10.0**	13.4	26.7
GRAND BANK NA	Hamilton	NJ	**D-**	D-	D-	201.0	-6.33	7.7	0.5	15.9	5.0	**7.5**	9.4	14.4
▲ GRAND BANK OF TEXAS	Grand Prairie	TX	**C+**	C	D+	210.5	21.68	18.6	1.3	26.7	2.2	**6.1**	8.3	11.8
GRAND MARAIS STATE BK	Grand Marais	MN	**B**	B	B	86.0	6.14	8.8	1.3	25.6	42.1	**5.5**	7.5	14.7
GRAND MARSH STATE BK	Grand Marsh	WI	**A-**	A-	A-	132.4	-0.17	1.6	2.0	19.8	55.5	**10.0**	13.0	32.8
GRAND MOUNTAIN BANK FSB	Granby	CO	**E+**	E-	E-	93.7	-3.72	2.8	0.4	41.0	7.4	**3.9**	5.9	11.5
▼ GRAND RAPIDS STATE BK	Grand Rapids	MN	**B-**	B	B	229.3	-0.71	10.1	4.3	12.4	33.1	**7.8**	9.5	16.0
GRAND RIDGE NATIONAL BK	Wheaton	IL	**A-**	A-	B-	93.4	16.03	10.2	0.1	11.6	6.3	**10.0**	12.5	17.3
▲ GRAND RIVER BANK	Grandville	MI	**D**	D-	D-	124.8	8.56	12.2	0.1	9.6	4.3	**6.6**	9.9	12.2
▲ GRAND RIVERS COMMUNITY BANK	Grand Chain	IL	**D**	D-	E+	30.6	16.58	20.7	5.6	20.6	2.8	**5.6**	8.1	11.4
▲ GRAND SB	Grove	OK	**B**	B-	D+	236.0	9.44	6.2	10.3	23.5	4.1	**8.7**	10.1	15.0
GRAND TIMBER BANK	McGregor	MN	**C**	C-	C-	41.6	-1.39	5.0	4.7	23.8	18.5	**10.0**	13.7	22.7
▲ GRAND VALLEY BANK	Heber City	UT	**B-**	C+	C+	321.2	4.36	2.5	0.4	11.8	51.4	**7.1**	9.1	19.9
GRANDPOINT BANK	Los Angeles	CA	**C+**	C	C-	2485.9	23.70	10.2	0.5	10.2	9.5	**8.4**	10.4	13.7
GRANDSOUTH BANK	Greenville	SC	**B**	B	B-	388.1	0.14	17.0	12.2	11.9	9.2	**10.0**	11.6	16.9
GRANDVIEW BANK	Grandview	TX	**A-**	B+	B	144.0	6.25	12.3	8.1	18.6	15.7	**8.2**	9.8	15.5
GRANGER NATIONAL BK	Granger	TX	**B-**	B-	B	32.7	5.60	1.2	2.8	4.7	49.4	**10.0**	14.6	39.1
GRANITE COMMUNITY BANK	Cold Spring	MN	**C+**	C+	C+	97.1	12.07	14.0	1.6	9.5	5.1	**5.0**	8.7	11.0
▼ GRANITE FALLS BANK	Granite Falls	MN	**B-**	B	B	251.6	30.01	2.9	0.4	1.2	47.9	**5.0**	7.0	19.3
GRANITE MOUNTAIN BANK INC	Philipsburg	MT	**C**	D+	C-	64.1	-1.68	12.2	2.9	13.1	14.1	**7.5**	9.3	17.3
GRANITE SB	Rockport	MA	**D**	D+	D+	67.2	-2.80	0.1	0.5	30.5	18.4	**10.0**	13.5	24.2
GRANT COUNTY BANK	Petersburg	WV	**C+**	C	C-	234.3	-0.23	4.6	3.7	31.9	10.2	**10.0**	12.8	18.5
▲ GRANT COUNTY BANK	Ulysses	KS	**B**	B	C+	230.2	3.41	5.3	2.7	19.4	38.2	**10.0**	11.3	17.1
GRANT COUNTY BANK	Medford	OK	**B**	B-	B	79.2	-0.91	5.1	5.6	2.8	51.2	**10.0**	11.9	25.4
GRANT COUNTY STATE BK	Carson	ND	**B+**	B+	B-	36.4	8.98	3.6	0.8	0.0	0.0	**8.7**	10.7	13.9
▲ GRANT COUNTY STATE BK	Swayzee	IN	**B+**	B	B	120.0	7.91	4.1	5.5	37.1	8.8	**7.5**	9.4	14.9
GRANVILLE NATIONAL BK	Granville	IL	**C**	C	C+	52.5	-1.39	3.0	3.7	19.7	40.9	**6.9**	8.9	21.5
GRAPELAND STATE BK	Grapeland	TX	**C**	C	C	31.4	0.51	14.3	17.9	12.5	29.6	**10.0**	11.9	18.4
▼ GRATIOT STATE BK	Gratiot	WI	**D+**	C+	B-	43.8	-6.38	2.0	0.8	7.3	65.1	**5.2**	7.2	15.0
GRATZ BANK	Gratz	PA	**A+**	A+	A	213.1	13.40	7.0	0.6	37.0	11.3	**10.0**	11.1	20.3
▲ GRAYSON NATIONAL BK	Independence	VA	**C-**	D	D-	333.0	1.65	2.8	1.2	29.8	19.5	**7.0**	9.0	14.1
GREAT AMERICAN BANK	Lawrence	KS	**C**	C-	D+	149.2	107.13	8.0	0.8	20.4	2.6	**7.4**	10.2	12.8
GREAT LAKES BANK NA	Blue Island	IL	**C**	C	C-	558.8	-4.23	6.1	0.1	10.1	39.8	**9.8**	10.8	20.3

Asset Quality Index	Adjusted Non-Performing Loans as a % of Total Loans	Adjusted Non-Performing Loans as a % of Capital	Net Charge-Offs Avg Loans	Profitability Index	Net Income ($Mil)	Return on Assets (R.O.A.)	Return on Equity (R.O.E.)	Net Interest Spread	Overhead Efficiency Ratio	Liquidity Index	Liquidity Ratio	Hot Money Ratio	Stability Index
9.5	0.30	0.9	-0.17	**2.0**	0.3	0.24	2.67	2.04	88.2	**6.7**	63.7	6.0	**4.9**
6.0	0.44	2.4	0.00	**3.6**	0.4	0.49	3.44	4.21	78.7	**0.7**	12.2	41.1	**6.8**
6.5	0.58	3.4	0.00	**5.5**	3.6	1.40	11.76	3.48	64.9	**2.0**	26.1	21.3	**6.6**
3.7	3.33	17.1	1.08	**6.5**	0.6	1.10	9.39	5.03	57.5	**2.6**	23.8	17.1	**6.3**
7.2	0.37	2.7	0.00	**9.8**	4.2	1.75	18.73	4.72	38.3	**0.5**	12.0	67.8	**6.8**
7.4	0.00	0.0	0.00	**2.3**	0.4	0.21	1.97	3.20	84.5	**4.3**	16.3	6.9	**6.2**
4.3	1.83	7.8	-0.61	**7.0**	6.0	1.40	10.24	3.80	56.7	**3.1**	38.4	19.1	**8.1**
3.5	2.25	13.3	0.24	**8.0**	2.0	1.77	13.43	3.41	56.1	**4.4**	16.3	6.3	**8.8**
2.7	2.46	15.8	0.88	**2.8**	0.6	0.59	6.32	3.73	84.6	**0.9**	22.2	37.4	**4.1**
4.6	0.70	5.1	-0.08	**0.0**	-0.8	-0.86	-9.96	4.63	112.2	**4.0**	18.5	9.3	**3.0**
0.6	10.83	44.8	0.53	**0.0**	-0.9	-1.34	-10.27	3.99	133.0	**2.4**	41.5	30.5	**1.9**
8.8	0.14	0.7	-0.15	**5.6**	1.1	0.93	8.02	4.06	64.6	**5.2**	41.3	9.2	**7.1**
9.5	0.17	0.3	0.00	**7.5**	960.0	1.13	6.25	0.90	29.9	**3.6**	77.4	47.1	**10.0**
10.0	na	0.0	na	**10.0**	8.7	21.39	28.39	0.19	63.5	**4.0**	289.8	101.0	**7.0**
0.3	10.04	69.1	2.67	**0.0**	-1.5	-2.32	-33.98	3.19	120.3	**1.2**	30.3	52.7	**0.0**
6.7	0.91	5.7	0.59	**9.7**	1.6	2.27	18.94	4.42	54.7	**2.9**	17.5	14.9	**8.0**
4.9	0.80	5.5	0.03	**3.8**	0.8	0.90	11.13	3.25	71.6	**3.4**	19.0	12.2	**4.4**
8.5	0.01	0.1	0.00	**3.6**	0.3	0.53	5.50	3.70	77.5	**3.6**	22.3	11.5	**5.0**
5.7	0.80	4.2	0.04	**2.9**	0.5	0.44	4.24	3.00	81.1	**3.4**	25.3	13.0	**5.3**
4.4	1.71	12.7	0.04	**2.6**	3.1	0.42	4.80	2.93	81.6	**2.0**	2.6	17.9	**5.4**
8.7	0.17	1.1	0.00	**4.0**	0.2	0.80	10.59	3.10	64.9	**6.0**	51.6	6.1	**3.7**
7.5	0.16	1.0	-0.03	**7.7**	2.0	1.86	15.73	4.36	59.4	**1.1**	7.3	28.2	**8.5**
5.6	2.66	10.8	0.10	**7.1**	1.3	1.22	6.65	4.89	65.1	**3.9**	14.1	9.4	**8.5**
9.4	0.12	0.7	0.01	**6.2**	1.4	1.48	13.58	3.71	60.2	**1.3**	29.8	35.7	**7.0**
7.9	0.31	1.8	-0.05	**6.5**	2.1	1.25	10.04	5.04	68.3	**0.9**	3.8	29.5	**7.4**
9.3	0.00	0.0	0.00	**2.9**	1.9	0.50	6.74	1.97	76.6	**6.8**	54.8	3.0	**4.8**
2.1	6.70	34.6	-0.27	**3.1**	1.0	0.62	6.47	3.88	99.1	**4.2**	29.6	10.5	**3.1**
3.1	4.21	22.2	0.41	**4.3**	0.5	0.73	5.67	5.68	87.9	**0.9**	17.9	34.3	**5.9**
0.0	4.34	30.6	-0.07	**0.0**	-2.9	-1.96	-19.92	3.80	163.1	**1.5**	15.8	24.6	**3.0**
6.6	0.34	2.9	0.02	**3.8**	1.3	0.85	10.30	4.93	80.2	**3.9**	15.9	9.4	**3.4**
6.6	1.23	8.2	-0.16	**5.6**	0.7	1.23	17.69	3.46	66.7	**4.2**	17.2	7.4	**5.9**
5.7	4.60	12.2	0.83	**4.2**	0.7	0.69	5.33	2.38	54.1	**5.2**	71.5	15.3	**7.4**
1.7	6.59	46.1	-0.06	**1.5**	0.1	0.07	1.19	3.83	98.2	**4.6**	27.1	7.2	**2.8**
5.2	1.09	6.0	0.03	**4.4**	1.6	0.96	8.43	4.32	77.1	**4.6**	33.3	9.5	**5.5**
7.2	0.00	0.0	0.00	**8.2**	0.9	1.38	10.24	5.61	55.1	**1.7**	23.6	23.6	**6.8**
7.3	0.00	0.0	0.07	**0.7**	-0.1	-0.14	-1.52	3.34	97.5	**3.1**	9.5	13.2	**2.0**
4.1	0.82	7.2	-0.01	**4.2**	0.1	0.66	7.82	4.37	72.7	**0.7**	16.0	50.7	**2.6**
5.4	0.29	2.1	0.02	**4.9**	1.5	0.87	8.58	4.68	69.4	**2.0**	25.8	20.2	**6.1**
2.3	6.91	27.5	0.25	**4.4**	0.3	0.90	6.20	4.54	80.6	**4.7**	17.3	4.1	**6.1**
6.4	1.02	4.5	-0.03	**4.2**	1.7	0.73	7.91	3.93	72.6	**5.7**	48.5	8.2	**4.8**
3.6	1.00	7.1	0.10	**4.5**	13.3	0.74	5.77	4.40	66.5	**2.7**	20.3	16.5	**7.1**
4.8	1.46	9.0	0.42	**6.3**	3.3	1.10	9.36	6.22	59.8	**2.1**	13.5	18.5	**5.8**
7.9	0.18	1.2	0.01	**7.9**	1.4	1.37	13.63	4.77	59.8	**2.2**	26.9	19.5	**6.8**
9.6	0.00	0.0	0.00	**3.6**	0.2	0.76	5.18	3.17	75.4	**5.1**	85.3	16.4	**7.4**
8.3	0.04	0.4	0.00	**4.1**	0.6	0.85	9.80	4.12	79.3	**1.3**	13.9	27.2	**4.4**
7.9	0.71	2.4	0.00	**6.0**	2.4	1.43	17.18	3.05	44.0	**6.4**	59.6	7.5	**6.3**
3.9	0.84	5.3	0.12	**3.9**	0.3	0.57	6.31	4.42	78.7	**5.0**	28.7	5.0	**4.6**
9.7	0.09	0.3	0.00	**0.0**	-0.4	-0.81	-5.78	2.32	136.1	**3.2**	46.0	20.0	**6.5**
3.5	3.39	19.0	-0.02	**5.7**	1.7	0.95	7.62	4.55	67.8	**2.3**	13.7	17.3	**5.9**
6.2	1.66	7.5	0.66	**5.7**	2.6	1.46	12.93	3.52	62.1	**1.7**	12.7	21.5	**7.3**
5.8	3.10	6.9	0.72	**4.2**	0.7	1.17	10.46	2.92	62.0	**2.7**	45.1	27.7	**6.0**
6.8	0.00	0.0	0.00	**9.8**	0.6	2.46	23.16	4.76	47.3	**2.6**	2.3	14.6	**7.2**
5.3	0.60	4.7	0.43	**8.0**	1.7	1.84	19.61	3.87	44.6	**1.6**	17.9	23.9	**6.8**
6.1	1.02	4.2	0.17	**2.6**	0.2	0.44	5.11	2.56	78.7	**5.9**	55.9	7.6	**4.3**
4.9	1.41	6.6	0.24	**2.0**	0.1	0.19	1.70	4.41	91.1	**2.2**	36.4	28.4	**4.5**
9.7	0.00	0.0	-0.01	**1.4**	-0.5	-1.41	-16.12	2.35	99.3	**5.8**	61.7	9.7	**2.0**
8.0	1.06	5.9	-0.04	**5.2**	1.0	0.67	5.39	3.79	71.9	**4.4**	31.4	10.2	**7.8**
2.1	5.19	33.8	0.32	**2.4**	1.2	0.48	5.35	3.46	83.0	**2.4**	20.9	17.4	**3.6**
5.5	0.08	0.6	0.03	**7.5**	1.5	2.04	15.76	7.62	69.5	**1.2**	6.5	25.9	**6.2**
4.2	4.40	15.2	0.38	**2.9**	3.0	0.70	6.84	3.20	85.1	**6.6**	54.0	4.0	**5.8**

	Name	City	State	Rating	2013 Rating	2012 Rating	Total Assets ($Mil)	One Year Asset Growth	Asset Mix (As a % of Total Assets): Commercial Loans	Consumer Loans	Mortgage Loans	Securities	Capitalization Index	Leverage Ratio	Risk-Based Capital Ratio
	GREAT LAKES BANKERS BANK	Worthington	OH	**C**	C	C-	101.1	-0.54	7.8	0.4	0.5	30.3	**8.1**	9.8	18.9
	GREAT MIDWEST BANK SSB	Brookfield	WI	**B-**	B-	B	531.5	3.35	0.1	0.2	65.9	12.6	**10.0**	19.7	32.3
▼	GREAT NATIONS BANK	Norman	OK	**D**	D	D	53.5	15.36	21.5	0.4	9.5	4.7	**10.0**	12.9	16.9
▲	GREAT PLAINS BANK	Eureka	SD	**B**	B	C+	99.8	-3.54	9.5	1.4	2.3	5.6	**6.8**	10.5	12.4
	GREAT PLAINS NATIONAL BK	Elk City	OK	**B**	B-	B	605.9	30.71	13.7	6.0	29.6	4.4	**5.4**	7.9	11.3
	GREAT SOUTHERN BANK	Springfield	MO	**B**	B	B-	3907.8	8.52	7.4	9.3	12.8	10.8	**7.6**	9.4	13.3
	GREAT SOUTHERN NATIONAL BK	Meridian	MS	**B+**	B+	A-	272.6	1.93	5.9	10.8	13.4	49.1	**7.7**	9.5	22.2
	GREAT STATE BK	Wilkesboro	NC	**B**	B-	C+	92.9	10.16	9.6	0.3	11.5	15.1	**10.0**	11.2	17.4
	GREAT WESTERN BANK	Sioux Falls	SD	**C+**	C+	C-	9367.1	2.59	13.5	1.0	5.3	14.3	**7.6**	9.5	13.0
▲	GREATER COMMUNITY BANK	Rome	GA	**C-**	D	D-	123.8	2.03	13.8	2.7	19.7	10.5	**8.1**	9.7	14.1
	GREATER HUDSON BANK NA	Middletown	NY	**B**	B	B	389.9	22.29	20.0	0.0	0.2	30.9	**9.9**	10.9	15.2
	GREATER STATE BANK	Falfurrias	TX	**D+**	C-	D+	63.8	4.00	12.6	3.3	15.6	12.5	**7.5**	9.3	13.8
▲	GREEN BANK NA	Houston	TX	**B+**	B-	C+	1870.1	10.47	34.8	0.4	5.3	13.1	**10.0**	14.3	16.3
	GREEN BELT BANK & TRUST	Iowa Falls	IA	**B-**	B	B-	370.3	8.47	9.5	3.0	8.3	10.4	**4.6**	9.0	10.8
	GREEN DOT BANK DBA BONNEVILLE	Provo	UT	**B+**	B+	A-	702.2	86.51	0.4	0.1	0.2	7.1	**10.0**	17.6	150.1
	GREENE COUNTY COMMERCIAL BANK	Catskill	NY	**U**	U	B+	206.1	5.95	0.0	0.0	0.0	100.0	**6.2**	8.2	43.4
	GREENEVILLE FEDERAL BANK FSB	Greeneville	TN	**C-**	D+	D-	161.8	-1.76	8.2	1.3	27.1	2.2	**8.1**	9.7	16.3
	GREENFIELD BANKING CO	Greenfield	IN	**B-**	B-	B-	437.3	1.39	3.4	2.5	6.1	33.5	**8.7**	10.2	22.7
▼	GREENFIELD BANKING CO	Greenfield	TN	**C+**	B-	C+	50.3	-1.29	11.3	14.4	23.8	9.0	**9.0**	12.7	14.2
	GREENFIELD CO-OP BANK	Greenfield	MA	**C+**	C+	B-	345.1	3.62	4.4	0.9	36.7	26.0	**10.0**	11.1	19.8
▲	GREENFIELD SB	Greenfield	MA	**C+**	C	C	685.9	3.67	3.6	0.1	49.0	15.8	**10.0**	11.0	19.2
	GREENLEAF WAYSIDE BANK	Greenleaf	WI	**C+**	C	B-	77.3	2.75	5.1	0.8	18.8	26.7	**7.0**	9.0	17.5
	GREENSBURG STATE BK	Greensburg	KS	**B+**	A-	A	56.0	0.30	1.7	4.0	1.5	80.0	**10.0**	18.7	57.3
	GREENVILLE BANKING CO	Greenville	GA	**C+**	B-	B	25.8	-6.27	6.0	1.8	10.8	33.5	**10.0**	15.9	22.4
	GREENVILLE FEDERAL	Greenville	OH	**B**	B-	C+	148.0	-3.01	3.9	1.1	72.2	5.2	**10.0**	11.5	19.6
	GREENVILLE NATIONAL BK	Greenville	OH	**B**	B	B	383.6	-0.46	3.1	7.5	24.7	25.4	**9.4**	10.6	17.8
	GREENVILLE SB	Greenville	PA	**B**	B-	B-	234.8	-1.20	3.2	0.9	50.0	21.2	**10.0**	11.3	18.7
▲	GREENWOODS STATE BK	Lake Mills	WI	**C+**	C-	C-	152.5	13.81	14.0	2.3	23.7	10.7	**5.8**	8.6	11.6
	GREER STATE BK	Greer	SC	**B-**	C+	C-	359.0	-1.39	4.7	0.8	12.1	39.2	**8.0**	9.7	16.5
	GRINNELL STATE BK	Grinnell	IA	**B+**	B+	C+	274.0	5.61	5.8	0.5	6.4	26.5	**10.0**	11.4	16.9
	GRUNDY BANK	Morris	IL	**B-**	C	D+	269.8	-3.05	5.4	0.5	13.5	23.5	**6.8**	8.8	19.8
▼	GRUNDY NATIONAL BK	Grundy	VA	**B+**	A-	A	325.4	0.74	7.7	5.7	6.0	45.2	**10.0**	20.8	42.9
	GRUVER STATE BK	Gruver	TX	**B+**	B+	B+	67.5	3.31	11.1	2.2	5.2	30.4	**10.0**	11.0	17.6
	GSL SB	Guttenberg	NJ	**C-**	C-	B-	98.0	-2.25	0.0	0.0	30.1	57.9	**10.0**	14.8	44.9
	GUADALUPE NATIONAL BK	Kerrville	TX	**B-**	B-	C	117.5	3.75	11.3	2.3	19.3	3.1	**7.4**	9.2	13.8
	GUARANTY B&TC OF DELHI LA	Delhi	LA	**A-**	A-	A-	185.5	7.04	10.0	4.0	21.1	11.0	**6.8**	8.8	12.6
	GUARANTY BANK	Milwaukee	WI	**E-**	E-	E-	1060.2	-5.39	0.0	1.8	30.9	1.1	**0.0**	2.8	6.8
	GUARANTY BANK	Springfield	MO	**C**	C-	D+	616.0	-3.72	13.7	0.5	15.9	15.7	**10.0**	11.4	15.2
	GUARANTY BANK & TRUST CO	Denver	CO	**B**	B	B-	2076.0	9.85	10.8	0.2	9.6	21.3	**8.6**	10.9	13.9
	GUARANTY BANK & TRUST CO	Cedar Rapids	IA	**B**	C+	C	248.7	5.65	11.0	0.6	16.4	32.7	**10.0**	11.5	18.2
	GUARANTY BANK & TRUST CO	Belzoni	MS	**B**	B	B	599.3	2.93	12.6	2.2	14.1	23.9	**10.0**	11.4	16.3
▼	GUARANTY BANK & TRUST CO	New Roads	LA	**A-**	A	B+	140.1	3.09	3.1	3.8	31.4	13.2	**8.0**	9.6	16.5
	GUARANTY BANK & TRUST NA	Mount Pleasant	TX	**B+**	B+	B+	1288.6	5.60	9.7	3.5	19.2	25.7	**8.2**	9.8	16.0
▲	GUARANTY STATE BK & TRUST CO	Beloit	KS	**A-**	B+	B+	239.4	26.02	4.4	1.1	6.2	23.4	**9.9**	11.1	14.9
	GUARDIAN BANK	Valdosta	GA	**B**	B-	B-	239.1	5.40	7.0	1.2	22.3	14.3	**9.8**	10.8	16.1
	GUARDIAN SAVINGS BANK	Granite City	IL	**C**	C+	B-	37.6	-2.69	0.0	0.4	27.3	51.6	**10.0**	20.7	73.5
	GUARDIAN SAVINGS BANK FSB	West Chester	OH	**C-**	C	C-	800.9	-1.83	0.0	0.0	62.4	1.1	**9.6**	10.8	20.5
	GUIDE ROCK STATE BK	Guide Rock	NE	**B**	B	B-	27.6	-4.78	8.6	5.4	1.1	12.5	**10.0**	13.7	19.3
	GUILFORD SB	Guilford	CT	**B**	B-	B	576.9	3.21	1.3	0.1	43.0	28.3	**10.0**	13.3	24.1
	GULF COAST BANK	Abbeville	LA	**A-**	A-	A-	370.3	0.19	5.5	8.9	16.1	25.9	**10.0**	12.6	22.6
	GULF COAST BANK & TRUST CO	New Orleans	LA	**C**	C-	D+	1197.6	22.01	16.9	2.4	21.3	17.6	**7.2**	9.2	12.6
	GULF COAST COMMUNITY BANK	Pensacola	FL	**E-**	E-	E-	141.9	-11.07	6.0	0.7	11.0	14.4	**0.5**	4.4	7.1
	GULFSHORE BANK	Tampa	FL	**C**	C	D+	298.9	23.65	8.4	0.6	12.0	5.7	**6.8**	8.8	14.5
	GUNNISON BANK & TRUST CO	Gunnison	CO	**B-**	B-	C	77.6	5.16	5.7	0.9	11.3	12.3	**7.7**	9.5	15.6
	GUNNISON S&LA	Gunnison	CO	**D+**	D+	D+	109.2	1.21	0.0	0.7	49.0	2.4	**7.5**	9.3	22.6
	GUNNISON VALLEY BANK	Gunnison	UT	**D-**	D-	D-	78.7	4.30	22.6	28.3	3.0	3.1	**9.9**	12.0	14.9
	GUTHRIE COUNTY STATE BK	Panora	IA	**B**	B	B-	113.1	-1.02	9.1	4.4	19.5	22.7	**8.1**	9.7	15.9
	GWINNETT COMMUNITY BANK	Duluth	GA	**E-**	E-	E-	384.3	-10.54	5.9	0.4	9.4	18.4	**0.4**	3.7	6.8
	H F GEHANT BANKING CO	West Brooklyn	IL	**B**	B	B	59.5	-2.40	4.3	5.0	23.3	14.8	**10.0**	11.8	19.7
	H&R BLOCK BANK	Kansas City	MO	**B-**	C+	C	1090.5	-11.77	0.0	1.2	24.3	34.9	**10.0**	54.3	199.4

Asset Quality Index	Adjusted Non-Performing Loans as a % of Total Loans	Adjusted Non-Performing Loans as a % of Capital	Net Charge-Offs Avg Loans	Profitability Index	Net Income ($Mil)	Return on Assets (R.O.A.)	Return on Equity (R.O.E.)	Net Interest Spread	Overhead Efficiency Ratio	Liquidity Index	Liquidity Ratio	Hot Money Ratio	Stability Index
5.8	1.22	5.2	-0.39	**2.8**	0.4	0.49	5.29	2.91	89.7	**7.4**	58.4	0.0	**4.2**
6.7	1.97	8.1	0.01	**3.2**	1.6	0.41	2.01	2.96	83.8	**2.1**	17.3	18.8	**8.0**
8.3	0.19	1.1	0.49	**0.3**	-0.1	-0.29	-2.07	3.90	107.6	**0.8**	19.9	53.0	**1.9**
6.3	0.13	1.0	0.00	**10.0**	1.7	2.35	22.56	4.57	45.3	**2.0**	3.8	18.0	**8.1**
5.4	0.22	2.3	0.12	**10.0**	12.3	2.88	35.76	6.40	66.4	**1.9**	3.2	18.4	**7.0**
4.4	1.62	11.9	0.30	**6.1**	32.6	1.15	11.55	4.90	65.6	**1.9**	8.7	18.9	**7.3**
6.2	0.82	3.3	0.33	**5.1**	1.7	0.80	8.63	4.92	77.6	**5.2**	57.7	13.3	**5.5**
7.7	0.10	0.5	0.03	**4.1**	0.6	0.83	7.43	3.32	63.0	**2.4**	35.8	25.3	**6.7**
3.8	0.98	7.7	0.20	**6.6**	78.9	1.14	6.94	4.19	53.4	**2.6**	5.9	15.5	**9.0**
2.2	2.95	18.9	0.34	**2.3**	0.5	0.50	5.09	4.80	91.9	**4.4**	23.7	7.4	**3.7**
4.3	1.95	10.6	0.29	**4.5**	2.2	0.82	7.38	3.59	70.7	**1.7**	14.6	21.7	**6.5**
3.5	2.07	14.4	0.10	**1.0**	-0.1	-0.20	-2.35	4.39	104.5	**1.0**	22.9	35.1	**3.8**
6.4	0.43	2.4	0.24	**5.5**	13.5	1.01	8.45	3.98	60.5	**1.4**	14.9	27.8	**8.1**
5.2	0.25	2.1	0.12	**7.8**	4.9	1.80	19.27	3.59	46.7	**1.5**	12.9	24.0	**6.7**
9.5	7.29	0.4	0.94	**7.6**	7.2	1.27	7.36	0.45	21.7	**8.5**	112.1	1.2	**7.0**
10.0	na	0.0	na	**6.0**	1.7	1.09	13.49	2.15	13.6	**5.0**	0.1	0.1	**7.0**
2.1	3.16	20.2	0.19	**2.8**	0.4	0.33	3.22	4.15	80.6	**2.4**	22.9	17.6	**4.5**
5.6	1.90	6.5	0.34	**3.9**	2.6	0.78	7.92	3.33	73.9	**7.2**	62.3	2.5	**5.5**
4.0	1.40	8.4	0.33	**4.2**	0.2	0.51	4.06	4.51	75.6	**1.2**	18.7	29.6	**6.0**
6.1	1.63	9.0	0.04	**2.7**	0.8	0.32	2.92	2.88	84.0	**3.0**	28.3	16.1	**6.5**
7.3	0.80	5.2	0.11	**3.0**	2.8	0.56	5.01	3.30	80.0	**2.5**	20.4	17.0	**7.1**
8.8	0.28	1.5	-0.02	**3.1**	0.3	0.52	5.73	3.10	83.4	**6.1**	50.2	5.1	**5.1**
9.8	2.83	2.2	0.25	**4.5**	0.4	0.84	5.21	2.79	63.8	**6.2**	57.0	5.6	**8.2**
8.7	0.00	0.0	0.00	**2.5**	0.1	0.26	1.79	3.87	93.2	**4.6**	36.2	11.0	**6.4**
7.5	0.70	5.1	0.06	**3.7**	0.7	0.60	5.48	3.48	77.8	**1.4**	8.4	23.8	**6.1**
5.2	1.05	6.2	0.14	**4.6**	2.7	0.92	8.80	3.47	63.9	**3.3**	21.2	13.3	**6.0**
7.8	0.77	4.4	0.10	**4.2**	1.3	0.75	6.78	2.88	59.3	**3.7**	32.1	13.9	**6.4**
4.1	1.03	9.1	0.02	**4.5**	2.1	1.89	19.09	4.08	81.6	**3.6**	9.5	10.3	**4.4**
5.9	1.06	5.4	-0.26	**4.5**	2.8	1.04	10.41	3.21	74.3	**3.0**	28.5	16.2	**4.7**
5.8	1.45	7.7	-0.02	**5.2**	1.9	0.89	7.94	4.12	68.8	**4.7**	30.3	7.7	**7.8**
3.5	3.32	17.0	0.52	**5.1**	2.5	1.23	12.05	2.73	64.1	**2.7**	23.1	16.5	**6.0**
4.3	7.74	13.9	0.05	**5.0**	2.2	0.87	4.60	3.52	66.1	**4.0**	63.0	21.1	**8.0**
8.6	0.00	0.0	0.00	**6.7**	0.8	1.61	14.75	3.64	55.3	**1.0**	23.0	34.3	**7.7**
7.8	1.16	2.6	0.00	**0.9**	-0.1	-0.07	-0.46	2.69	103.9	**3.7**	66.1	22.5	**7.2**
5.4	0.99	6.8	0.01	**4.4**	0.9	1.06	12.08	3.88	82.8	**4.3**	26.0	8.2	**5.1**
8.6	0.06	0.4	0.07	**9.4**	2.9	2.20	26.38	4.67	53.8	**2.1**	23.0	19.5	**7.0**
0.3	15.64	160.3	3.18	**1.9**	4.4	0.53	19.40	2.57	91.1	**6.8**	39.0	0.8	**1.3**
4.5	1.26	7.8	0.65	**4.7**	4.7	0.99	9.37	3.59	62.9	**3.1**	11.6	13.1	**6.1**
4.5	1.46	8.9	-0.13	**4.9**	13.2	0.90	8.24	3.83	68.9	**4.3**	13.3	7.2	**7.5**
8.8	0.18	0.9	0.02	**4.3**	2.0	1.11	9.90	3.83	76.9	**5.0**	29.5	5.1	**4.8**
3.7	3.12	16.6	0.56	**6.6**	6.8	1.46	13.08	4.06	63.8	**1.6**	17.5	24.4	**7.8**
6.1	0.67	4.8	0.07	**7.9**	1.4	1.32	12.08	4.80	58.5	**3.4**	14.9	11.9	**6.5**
7.0	0.52	3.1	0.11	**4.9**	8.2	0.87	8.61	3.54	65.2	**2.5**	16.1	17.0	**9.0**
7.2	0.11	0.7	-0.24	**7.1**	2.2	1.26	11.74	3.70	56.6	**2.8**	13.4	14.8	**6.4**
5.4	0.84	5.3	0.00	**7.3**	3.2	1.80	16.67	3.87	52.6	**1.3**	14.6	26.7	**6.9**
9.9	1.32	1.8	-0.01	**1.7**	0.0	0.14	0.69	2.40	93.0	**5.4**	87.8	15.5	**7.2**
2.6	3.10	19.0	0.03	**7.5**	9.8	1.58	15.47	2.45	56.5	**2.8**	26.3	16.4	**4.6**
6.9	0.48	2.0	-0.09	**5.3**	0.2	1.01	7.74	4.12	67.9	**3.3**	36.2	17.2	**6.2**
7.2	1.11	5.1	0.00	**4.2**	3.4	0.84	6.15	3.56	75.0	**4.7**	32.7	8.8	**8.1**
6.4	1.06	4.8	-0.09	**6.1**	3.0	1.08	8.97	4.23	69.9	**4.9**	35.4	8.7	**7.6**
2.9	2.53	18.8	0.14	**9.3**	13.2	1.60	16.92	6.75	66.3	**1.4**	23.1	34.1	**6.8**
0.3	5.77	54.0	-0.02	**1.5**	0.3	0.27	8.55	4.26	94.3	**1.9**	18.2	20.1	**0.0**
4.8	0.93	6.5	0.14	**2.9**	0.7	0.37	4.15	3.47	78.8	**5.4**	39.6	6.8	**3.3**
7.0	0.16	1.0	-0.03	**5.7**	0.6	0.98	10.23	4.58	67.4	**3.8**	30.4	12.9	**5.0**
7.7	0.39	2.2	0.15	**1.7**	0.1	0.09	0.94	2.19	92.4	**3.1**	46.4	23.9	**5.0**
0.3	7.87	49.3	1.20	**7.5**	1.2	2.11	18.78	6.46	48.2	**1.6**	12.7	22.4	**4.1**
6.4	0.57	3.5	0.00	**4.2**	0.8	0.87	8.84	3.90	76.4	**3.5**	24.2	12.5	**5.2**
0.3	17.95	223.4	0.34	**1.7**	0.8	0.25	8.38	2.30	90.3	**0.9**	24.6	41.6	**0.0**
4.7	2.12	11.2	0.05	**6.3**	0.7	1.51	13.19	3.53	53.2	**2.7**	31.5	18.7	**6.8**
3.4	35.75	16.4	1.53	**10.0**	52.1	4.58	12.36	3.60	42.5	**8.4**	117.5	3.3	**9.5**

Name	City	State	Rating	2013 Rating	2012 Rating	Total Assets ($Mil)	One Year Asset Growth	Asset Mix (As a % of Total Assets) Commercial Loans	Consumer Loans	Mortgage Loans	Securities	Capitalization Index	Leverage Ratio	Risk-Based Capital Ratio
HABIB AMERICAN BANK	New York	NY	**B-**	B-	C	950.4	14.44	6.8	1.3	4.8	3.9	**7.3**	9.2	18.1
HADDON SB	Haddon Heights	NJ	**D+**	D+	C-	308.1	-1.87	0.2	0.1	27.6	63.9	**8.1**	9.7	27.2
HALSTEAD BANK	Halstead	KS	**C+**	C+	C	90.8	6.56	9.9	7.9	16.5	12.7	**5.3**	8.3	11.2
HAMILTON BANK	Hamilton	MO	**C-**	C-	C	67.3	13.86	3.9	3.7	15.1	26.9	**7.1**	9.1	14.7
HAMILTON BANK	Towson	MD	**D**	D	C-	285.3	-6.08	6.5	0.1	25.2	35.2	**10.0**	14.6	26.3
HAMILTON STATE BK	Hoschton	GA	**B+**	A-	B	1612.4	3.78	6.3	0.5	7.2	29.1	**10.0**	14.2	25.1
HAMLER STATE BK	Hamler	OH	**B+**	B+	B+	73.8	0.94	4.2	1.0	14.4	41.9	**10.0**	15.1	27.6
HAMLIN BANK & TRUST CO	Smethport	PA	**A**	A	A	444.8	0.86	1.9	4.6	34.0	46.5	**10.0**	14.9	27.9
HAMLIN NATIONAL BK	Hamlin	TX	**B+**	B+	B	98.1	2.08	12.4	3.1	3.6	53.1	**10.0**	16.2	32.1
HAMPDEN BANK	Springfield	MA	**B-**	B	B	703.5	1.52	6.9	4.8	21.4	20.2	**9.8**	10.8	15.9
▼ HAMPTON STATE BK	Hampton	IA	**B**	A-	A-	69.3	-4.09	3.1	2.6	14.9	30.1	**8.8**	10.2	15.7
HANCOCK BANK & TRUST CO	Hawesville	KY	**D**	D-	D-	283.4	-8.06	9.2	1.9	27.8	11.2	**8.0**	9.6	15.1
HANCOCK COUNTY SAVINGS BK FSB	Chester	WV	**B**	B	B	337.8	1.74	0.2	1.8	71.9	13.5	**10.0**	16.5	37.3
▲ HANMI BANK	Los Angeles	CA	**B+**	B	B-	4231.7	49.03	5.5	0.1	2.6	26.7	**10.0**	12.7	16.2
▲ HANOVER COMMUNITY BANK	Garden City Park	NY	**C-**	D	D	141.8	52.58	5.4	0.3	29.6	0.0	**10.0**	12.7	22.8
HANTZ BANK	Southfield	MI	**B**	B-	C	171.0	32.43	19.0	0.9	18.3	4.2	**9.4**	10.6	14.8
HAPPY STATE BK	Happy	TX	**B-**	B-	C+	2555.3	13.74	15.8	1.9	11.5	12.7	**5.7**	8.7	11.5
▼ HARBOR BANK OF MARYLAND	Baltimore	MD	**D-**	D	D-	233.6	-3.73	12.5	0.9	10.9	13.2	**6.1**	8.1	12.8
HARBOR COMMUNITY BANK	Indiantown	FL	**B-**	B-	B-	926.2	49.18	5.3	4.0	13.3	40.2	**10.0**	14.5	21.6
HARBOR NATIONAL BK	Charleston	SC	**C+**	C	C-	325.4	16.09	3.0	0.2	32.1	4.1	**9.3**	10.5	14.6
HARBORONE BANK	Brockton	MA	**U**	U		1996.4	3.45	1.7	22.9	40.6	10.5	**7.1**	9.0	13.2
HARDIN COUNTY BANK	Savannah	TN	**D**	D+	C+	422.9	2.10	18.9	4.5	25.4	8.6	**7.2**	9.2	12.7
HARDIN COUNTY SB	Eldora	IA	**C+**	C+	C	177.6	-2.55	2.9	1.0	4.5	50.5	**6.9**	8.9	15.6
HARDWARE STATE BK	Lovington	IL	**D+**	D	D	23.8	0.88	3.1	5.1	9.5	19.0	**6.9**	8.9	25.3
HARFORD BANK	Aberdeen	MD	**C**	C	C-	301.9	2.66	3.6	5.3	18.8	13.6	**9.2**	10.5	14.9
HARLEYSVILLE SB	Harleysville	PA	**C+**	C+	C+	798.2	-2.67	1.6	0.1	39.4	29.5	**6.0**	8.0	13.8
HARMONY BANK	Jackson	NJ	**C+**	C+	C+	245.1	23.15	4.6	0.0	9.4	8.0	**9.7**	10.9	14.8
HARRISON BUILDING & LOAN ASSN	Harrison	OH	**C**	C	C-	224.1	-0.41	2.0	0.3	34.3	42.9	**10.0**	13.3	30.6
HARRISON COUNTY BANK	Lost Creek	WV	**B-**	B-	B-	98.5	5.79	1.7	7.4	27.1	38.8	**8.2**	9.8	21.2
HART COUNTY BANK & TRUST CO	Munfordville	KY	**B**	B	B	27.2	-0.33	6.2	1.4	0.2	34.2	**10.0**	19.7	32.6
HARTSBURG STATE BK	Hartsburg	IL	**E+**	E	E+	18.9	13.18	4.7	2.3	7.8	28.1	**7.0**	9.0	15.7
HARTWICK STATE BK	Hartwick	IA	**C**	C-	C	24.3	-8.58	1.1	4.0	14.1	40.6	**6.7**	8.7	19.4
▼ HARVARD SB	Harvard	IL	**D+**	C-	C-	169.4	1.57	3.9	5.6	23.1	5.4	**1.4**	6.0	8.4
HARVARD STATE BK	Harvard	IL	**C-**	C-	D+	221.1	-2.74	5.1	2.2	16.2	34.5	**7.3**	9.2	17.0
HARVEST BANK	Kimball	MN	**B**	B	B	127.0	-0.32	10.2	3.0	17.8	18.0	**7.3**	9.2	15.0
HARVEST COMMUNITY BANK	Pennsville	NJ	**D-**	D-	D-	181.1	-2.78	15.5	0.9	20.2	19.5	**5.3**	7.3	11.3
HARWOOD STATE BK	Harwood	ND	**C-**	C	C	34.6	6.25	14.8	4.4	4.8	4.2	**6.1**	8.2	12.1
▲ HASKELL NATIONAL BK	Haskell	TX	**C+**	C	C+	75.7	5.55	4.4	5.9	10.4	42.1	**9.2**	10.4	21.4
HASTINGS CITY BANK	Hastings	MI	**C**	C	C	294.0	7.70	2.8	3.0	23.4	24.2	**6.5**	8.5	18.2
HATBORO FEDERAL SAVINGS FA	Hatboro	PA	**B**	B-	B	493.7	-4.84	0.0	0.0	59.8	23.8	**10.0**	20.4	42.0
HAVANA NATIONAL BK	Havana	IL	**B-**	B-	C+	223.1	3.32	4.7	3.2	10.4	29.1	**6.7**	8.7	13.2
HAVEN SB	Hoboken	NJ	**C+**	C+	B-	841.1	17.66	0.8	0.0	59.2	11.3	**9.1**	10.4	17.2
HAVERFORD TRUST CO	Radnor	PA	**A**	A	A	109.0	0.57	7.5	38.0	0.2	23.1	**10.0**	14.3	15.8
HAVERHILL BANK	Haverhill	MA	**C**	C+	C+	338.1	6.37	4.4	1.3	49.4	11.7	**9.2**	10.5	18.8
HAVILAND STATE BK	Haviland	KS	**B-**	B-	B-	39.6	5.88	4.3	1.5	2.4	29.6	**10.0**	11.6	18.2
HAWAII NATIONAL BK	Honolulu	HI	**D**	D	C-	627.3	1.02	14.0	2.1	11.6	19.6	**6.6**	8.6	15.5
HAWTHORN BANK	Jefferson City	MO	**B-**	C+	C	1144.6	2.42	10.5	1.6	18.7	18.0	**8.9**	10.2	14.7
HBANK TEXAS	Grapevine	TX	**A-**	A-	B	121.3	1.63	10.6	5.8	12.5	12.6	**10.0**	11.3	24.0
▼ HEADWATERS STATE BK	Land OLakes	WI	**B+**	A-	A-	66.6	0.32	1.6	3.3	32.1	24.3	**10.0**	13.7	24.2
HEARTLAND BANK	Bryant	AR	**B**	B	B	225.1	16.21	45.7	0.7	5.6	4.5	**10.0**	13.3	16.0
HEARTLAND BANK	Somers	IA	**A**	A	A	122.3	4.72	8.7	3.4	8.5	20.3	**10.0**	13.3	16.5
HEARTLAND BANK	Gahanna	OH	**B-**	C+	C-	635.4	8.99	6.5	1.3	17.5	17.5	**7.2**	9.2	14.0
HEARTLAND BANK	Geneva	NE	**B-**	B-	B-	379.0	44.70	5.8	1.2	3.2	19.2	**4.4**	8.3	10.7
HEARTLAND BANK	Saint Louis	MO	**D+**	D+	C-	900.8	3.91	9.9	0.4	8.2	8.3	**6.9**	8.9	13.6
▲ HEARTLAND BANK & TRUST CO	Bloomington	IL	**B+**	B-	B-	2430.8	-12.34	11.0	0.5	12.5	25.7	**8.7**	10.1	15.5
HEARTLAND NATIONAL BK	Sebring	FL	**C**	C	D+	302.1	2.87	3.9	2.7	9.9	21.9	**7.7**	9.4	18.4
▲ HEARTLAND STATE BK	Edgeley	ND	**B-**	C+	C+	63.3	2.74	9.8	2.5	1.3	24.5	**8.4**	9.9	14.4
HEARTLAND STATE BK	Redfield	SD	**B+**	A-	B	71.6	-10.49	9.6	3.5	3.3	6.8	**9.5**	11.9	14.6
HEBRON SB	Hebron	MD	**C**	C	C-	546.8	7.53	7.2	0.7	29.7	6.0	**6.2**	8.2	11.9
▼ HELENA NATIONAL BK	Helena	AR	**B-**	B	B	198.4	0.98	5.5	2.1	3.8	36.2	**10.0**	14.0	25.4

Asset Quality Index	Adjusted Non-Performing Loans as a % of Total Loans	Adjusted Non-Performing Loans as a % of Capital	Net Charge-Offs Avg Loans	Profitability Index	Net Income ($Mil)	Return on Assets (R.O.A.)	Return on Equity (R.O.E.)	Net Interest Spread	Overhead Efficiency Ratio	Liquidity Index	Liquidity Ratio	Hot Money Ratio	Stability Index
4.8	1.21	6.8	-0.01	**5.2**	5.6	0.82	8.80	2.10	62.6	**2.2**	44.3	38.2	**6.0**
9.2	0.63	1.9	0.09	**1.4**	0.2	0.08	0.80	1.47	97.3	**5.1**	58.6	14.3	**4.5**
6.7	0.57	4.5	0.04	**3.9**	0.5	0.68	8.52	3.85	81.5	**2.9**	14.1	14.3	**4.8**
2.5	3.13	18.7	-0.34	**5.8**	0.7	1.46	16.76	3.91	65.1	**2.3**	29.0	20.0	**4.7**
5.2	3.89	13.4	1.20	**0.0**	-0.8	-0.38	-2.40	2.89	114.7	**2.9**	47.2	27.4	**4.7**
5.9	2.08	8.0	0.20	**4.6**	6.8	0.55	3.92	5.91	78.2	**3.7**	28.7	16.0	**7.3**
9.1	0.01	0.0	-0.09	**5.3**	0.8	1.35	9.80	2.97	52.9	**4.2**	45.2	15.0	**7.5**
6.7	2.49	7.2	0.26	**8.5**	5.1	1.59	9.10	3.93	42.9	**5.1**	52.3	12.8	**8.5**
5.3	5.32	11.7	1.68	**4.4**	0.9	1.16	7.27	3.69	70.0	**4.4**	47.2	14.1	**7.2**
4.7	1.64	10.3	0.05	**4.0**	3.6	0.68	6.23	3.13	66.4	**1.7**	8.6	20.1	**7.4**
8.9	0.03	0.2	0.00	**1.7**	-0.3	-0.55	-4.55	3.41	116.1	**3.1**	39.7	19.3	**6.6**
2.1	2.68	18.2	1.90	**0.6**	-0.6	-0.28	-2.90	3.63	87.9	**1.7**	15.0	21.1	**2.9**
7.2	1.52	6.6	0.16	**3.8**	1.5	0.58	3.59	3.34	68.3	**3.6**	19.9	11.5	**7.6**
5.3	0.90	4.9	-0.06	**8.6**	32.3	1.36	10.57	3.91	56.4	**2.8**	33.3	25.4	**7.5**
4.9	1.12	6.5	0.00	**2.0**	0.6	0.55	4.92	3.42	81.0	**0.8**	18.7	46.4	**4.1**
6.4	0.35	2.5	-0.02	**4.8**	0.6	0.54	4.77	4.58	80.2	**2.2**	25.2	18.9	**4.8**
5.8	0.59	4.7	0.11	**4.1**	13.2	0.73	7.35	3.99	70.9	**2.7**	5.5	14.8	**7.0**
1.8	4.28	30.4	1.79	**0.1**	-1.2	-0.64	-6.12	4.11	99.7	**3.7**	20.1	10.9	**4.0**
6.0	1.38	5.9	0.17	**3.2**	2.0	0.39	3.17	4.05	83.1	**3.2**	33.1	16.6	**5.4**
3.7	1.06	7.8	-0.14	**4.9**	2.2	0.96	8.97	3.68	75.1	**2.0**	7.9	18.1	**5.9**
1.1	2.84	24.3	0.21	**1.6**	1.7	0.11	1.24	2.29	91.5	**2.5**	3.8	15.6	**3.8**
0.5	5.83	47.5	0.38	**5.8**	3.4	1.09	12.71	4.31	62.8	**0.6**	5.7	37.0	**5.1**
7.8	0.02	0.1	-1.19	**4.4**	1.7	1.21	18.61	3.26	71.5	**3.8**	41.4	16.2	**3.7**
8.9	0.00	0.0	0.00	**1.8**	0.0	0.14	1.59	2.04	100.0	**4.1**	63.7	17.0	**3.6**
2.4	3.38	22.6	-0.12	**4.9**	1.9	0.84	8.22	4.02	68.4	**2.9**	13.5	14.5	**5.4**
3.6	2.32	17.8	0.23	**3.8**	4.1	0.68	8.61	2.63	61.6	**4.4**	24.9	7.4	**4.2**
6.8	0.14	1.0	0.00	**3.2**	0.7	0.39	4.25	3.56	75.4	**2.6**	22.4	16.5	**6.5**
4.9	5.09	17.9	0.38	**2.0**	0.4	0.21	1.53	2.79	84.4	**4.6**	53.8	15.5	**6.3**
7.6	0.43	2.1	-0.15	**4.4**	0.5	0.66	7.05	3.70	69.0	**4.5**	44.4	13.1	**4.6**
9.8	0.00	0.0	0.00	**4.5**	0.2	0.91	4.66	4.61	73.6	**6.5**	75.1	7.3	**7.4**
3.3	3.76	18.1	-0.25	**2.7**	0.1	0.58	6.86	2.72	78.7	**3.6**	37.5	13.9	**1.4**
9.2	0.00	0.0	0.00	**2.9**	0.1	0.60	7.45	2.80	78.0	**5.6**	66.7	9.6	**3.2**
0.3	14.99	102.2	0.27	**0.7**	-4.7	-3.67	-34.21	3.37	68.1	**1.5**	12.7	24.2	**6.0**
2.2	3.85	21.2	0.90	**2.6**	0.7	0.39	3.84	4.02	82.0	**2.6**	25.5	17.1	**4.1**
4.9	1.23	8.2	0.06	**5.6**	1.3	1.30	14.21	3.72	62.0	**4.5**	22.0	6.3	**6.3**
0.0	15.12	123.3	0.22	**0.7**	-0.9	-0.63	-7.34	3.44	102.6	**2.8**	22.1	15.4	**4.0**
8.0	0.11	0.9	-0.01	**2.9**	0.1	0.37	4.47	3.44	83.8	**4.6**	26.8	6.6	**3.0**
8.0	0.00	0.0	-0.62	**3.7**	0.3	0.59	5.64	3.50	80.6	**5.1**	41.1	9.4	**5.0**
5.3	1.58	9.2	0.03	**3.0**	1.1	0.51	5.53	3.24	84.2	**6.2**	41.9	2.9	**4.7**
6.4	3.60	11.4	0.04	**3.7**	2.3	0.61	3.08	2.56	70.0	**2.2**	32.4	24.6	**8.5**
4.3	1.45	10.1	0.15	**5.3**	1.6	1.00	11.50	3.45	58.4	**2.8**	14.4	15.0	**5.2**
5.8	1.07	8.0	0.03	**3.1**	2.9	0.46	4.21	3.12	73.9	**1.2**	9.3	26.9	**6.5**
6.8	0.00	0.0	0.00	**10.0**	4.4	5.40	30.17	1.90	79.7	**2.4**	55.3	87.6	**10.0**
6.2	0.66	4.5	0.00	**2.9**	0.9	0.35	3.30	3.16	83.1	**1.7**	21.5	23.7	**6.1**
3.7	2.51	11.4	0.00	**7.3**	0.5	1.54	12.71	4.77	56.5	**4.2**	33.3	11.7	**6.9**
6.5	0.72	4.5	0.00	**0.6**	-0.2	-0.04	-0.47	3.27	106.7	**2.0**	26.1	20.5	**5.0**
4.2	2.46	16.2	0.27	**4.8**	7.1	0.83	8.26	3.86	70.3	**2.8**	7.0	14.4	**7.2**
8.6	0.00	0.0	0.00	**6.3**	1.0	1.12	9.96	3.88	55.7	**3.1**	54.0	28.5	**6.8**
4.0	3.77	17.3	0.08	**6.6**	0.7	1.41	10.06	4.89	65.3	**2.7**	37.2	21.2	**8.6**
4.8	1.21	6.3	-0.03	**10.0**	5.3	3.30	22.25	6.96	48.2	**3.7**	14.4	10.7	**9.1**
6.0	0.89	4.8	0.02	**9.0**	1.8	2.04	14.33	4.77	52.4	**1.4**	9.1	24.7	**9.8**
3.8	0.85	6.6	0.10	**5.1**	4.5	0.99	10.83	4.01	63.1	**1.5**	10.3	23.4	**5.8**
5.8	0.23	1.9	0.00	**6.0**	3.1	1.20	12.14	4.17	61.2	**3.3**	9.5	12.1	**5.0**
1.1	2.92	20.0	-0.36	**4.3**	1.3	0.21	2.09	3.45	98.0	**4.3**	18.5	6.9	**4.8**
5.4	1.13	6.8	0.33	**8.5**	37.7	1.98	17.28	4.40	59.0	**4.5**	18.2	6.4	**9.1**
4.5	2.21	10.2	0.09	**3.3**	1.3	0.56	6.09	3.19	74.1	**4.6**	48.5	14.0	**4.4**
5.9	0.22	1.4	0.00	**4.4**	0.5	1.08	10.19	3.44	74.9	**1.8**	14.8	19.9	**5.7**
5.0	0.59	4.0	0.24	**10.0**	1.3	2.30	20.32	5.92	53.1	**2.3**	5.7	16.7	**7.5**
2.6	2.69	25.2	0.77	**4.8**	3.5	0.87	10.86	4.14	49.0	**1.4**	5.8	22.8	**4.4**
8.7	0.34	1.1	1.15	**3.0**	0.5	0.36	2.79	3.63	70.4	**1.4**	23.6	29.0	**7.4**

Name	City	State	Rating	2013 Rating	2012 Rating	Total Assets ($Mil)	One Year Asset Growth	Asset Mix (As a % of Total Assets) Comm-ercial Loans	Cons-umer Loans	Mort-gage Loans	Secur-ities	Capital-ization Index	Lever-age Ratio	Risk-Based Capital Ratio
▼ HELM BANK USA	Miami	FL	**C**	C	C	763.9	-2.57	2.8	2.3	45.9	35.8	**10.0**	11.0	28.0
HENDERSON FSB	Henderson	TX	**A-**	B+	B+	114.7	1.63	2.6	3.0	48.9	23.2	**10.0**	17.0	37.2
HENDERSON STATE BK	Henderson	NE	**B-**	C+	C+	206.6	12.52	13.3	1.2	0.2	11.0	**3.4**	8.3	10.2
HENDRICKS COUNTY BANK & TRUST	Brownsburg	IN	**D+**	D+	C	150.2	1.72	6.0	0.8	16.1	26.0	**10.0**	11.7	21.4
HENRY COUNTY BANK	Napoleon	OH	**C+**	C+	B-	262.3	3.00	4.6	3.5	13.0	46.4	**8.7**	10.2	19.9
HENRY STATE BK	Henry	IL	**B**	B-	C+	103.7	-6.99	5.5	7.0	8.4	41.5	**10.0**	13.1	23.4
HERGET BANK NA	Pekin	IL	**C+**	C+	C-	274.6	0.84	2.9	1.0	15.1	41.9	**8.5**	10.0	23.9
HERITAGE BANK	Hinesville	GA	**E-**	E-	E-	526.7	-11.38	5.5	2.3	11.8	20.7	**2.0**	5.2	9.0
▲ HERITAGE BANK	Jonesboro	GA	**E**	E-	E-	367.9	-2.38	2.5	0.4	11.6	13.7	**5.0**	7.0	11.6
HERITAGE BANK	Norfolk	VA	**B-**	B-	B	337.8	9.33	8.9	0.2	7.1	9.3	**9.2**	10.6	14.4
HERITAGE BANK	Marion	IA	**D+**	D+	C	37.1	2.50	9.4	1.8	13.4	48.6	**8.5**	10.0	20.1
HERITAGE BANK	Spencer	WI	**B**	B	B-	103.1	-0.08	11.5	1.4	29.3	13.7	**10.0**	11.1	17.7
HERITAGE BANK	Wood River	NE	**A**	A	A+	595.1	7.24	5.0	1.3	3.6	46.6	**10.0**	13.8	22.6
HERITAGE BANK	Topeka	KS	**E-**	E-	E+	49.4	0.52	18.4	0.5	23.5	4.3	**4.1**	6.1	10.6
HERITAGE BANK	Olympia	WA	**B**	B-	C+	3450.7	106.14	9.5	3.6	5.7	20.9	**8.7**	10.1	15.7
▼ HERITAGE BANK	Pearland	TX	**B-**	B-	C	181.4	88.92	9.2	4.9	11.9	9.9	**8.4**	9.9	14.8
HERITAGE BANK	Saint George	UT	**C+**	C+	B-	87.2	-4.94	0.0	0.0	1.3	75.9	**10.0**	14.7	61.6
▲ HERITAGE BANK & TRUST	Columbia	TN	**D-**	E+	E	102.5	-1.15	9.9	2.2	19.6	15.0	**5.8**	7.8	12.2
▼ HERITAGE BANK INC	Erlanger	KY	**C+**	C+	C-	510.3	7.77	7.7	1.2	18.9	17.1	**9.8**	10.9	15.0
HERITAGE BANK NA	Jonesboro	AR	**B-**	B+	B	308.2	22.69	8.8	2.7	26.6	7.4	**7.3**	9.7	12.8
HERITAGE BANK NA	Spicer	MN	**B-**	B	B	385.8	-3.90	17.1	2.7	7.8	14.1	**8.8**	11.1	14.0
HERITAGE BANK OF CENTRAL IL	Trivoli	IL	**D+**	D+	C-	271.2	-8.47	22.5	0.8	11.6	20.4	**8.8**	10.2	15.4
▲ HERITAGE BANK OF COMMERCE	San Jose	CA	**B+**	B	B-	1559.7	11.51	24.9	0.9	0.4	18.3	**9.2**	10.9	14.3
▲ HERITAGE BANK OF NEVADA	Reno	NV	**C+**	C-	C-	543.4	2.92	8.1	0.2	3.5	15.9	**10.0**	11.0	15.5
▲ HERITAGE BANK OF SCHAUMBURG	Schaumburg	IL	**C-**	D+	C-	133.9	4.44	1.7	0.1	15.2	4.0	**5.8**	7.8	14.7
HERITAGE BANK OF ST TAMMANY	Covington	LA	**D**	D-	D-	89.6	0.94	0.0	0.3	48.0	14.2	**8.5**	10.0	20.3
HERITAGE BANK OF THE OZARKS	Lebanon	MO	**C**	C	C	88.6	37.08	9.8	3.6	25.6	6.5	**5.9**	8.0	11.6
HERITAGE BANK USA INC	Hopkinsville	KY	**C**	C	C	927.9	-0.04	5.4	1.6	16.2	33.6	**10.0**	11.3	18.9
HERITAGE COMMUNITY BANK	Chamois	MO	**B-**	B-	B-	78.2	6.93	12.3	2.5	17.2	6.6	**10.0**	11.8	15.6
HERITAGE COMMUNITY BANK	Greeneville	TN	**E-**	E-	E-	97.2	-1.54	4.4	4.9	32.9	5.9	**3.5**	6.1	10.3
HERITAGE COMMUNITY BANK	Hartsville	SC	**B-**	B	C	100.1	0.42	6.4	2.2	15.0	3.9	**8.6**	10.1	13.9
HERITAGE FIRST BANK	Rome	GA	**B-**	C+	D	94.7	-3.14	6.4	6.4	23.2	1.5	**10.0**	12.0	18.5
HERITAGE OAKS BANK	Paso Robles	CA	**B-**	B	B-	1714.3	48.83	8.3	0.5	7.4	22.3	**8.2**	9.8	13.8
▼ HERITAGE STATE BK	Lawrenceville	IL	**B+**	A-	B+	76.8	3.31	7.2	0.1	1.5	0.0	**7.3**	10.8	12.7
HERITAGE STATE BK	Nevada	MO	**B**	B	B+	131.0	7.00	6.1	3.9	28.6	16.0	**7.0**	9.0	13.5
HERITAGEBANK OF THE SOUTH	Albany	GA	**B-**	B-	C+	1750.0	32.77	6.8	1.5	23.7	19.4	**6.6**	9.7	12.2
HERRIN SECURITY BANK	Herrin	IL	**B-**	C+	C+	101.9	-1.77	10.5	5.6	17.3	43.7	**9.7**	10.8	22.6
HERRING BANK	Amarillo	TX	**B**	B+	B	458.7	-6.07	10.9	2.4	7.5	23.5	**10.0**	11.7	19.4
HERSHEY STATE BK	Hershey	NE	**B+**	A-	A-	71.2	8.60	15.5	10.2	11.8	4.9	**10.0**	13.8	17.3
HERTFORD SB SSB	Hertford	NC	**C**	C	C	14.4	-2.90	0.0	2.0	44.4	0.1	**10.0**	13.9	30.4
HIAWATHA BANK & TRUST CO	Hiawatha	IA	**B-**	B-	B+	43.4	5.63	13.2	2.2	16.7	4.6	**8.9**	11.7	14.1
HIAWATHA NATIONAL BK	Hager City	WI	**C**	C-	C-	135.6	8.11	7.8	1.3	14.6	28.0	**9.9**	10.9	18.8
HIBERNIA BANK	New Orleans	LA	**C**	C	C	103.2	-5.27	4.0	0.1	51.1	9.4	**10.0**	18.8	28.6
HICKORY POINT BANK & TRUST FSB	Decatur	IL	**C+**	C	C+	638.4	4.57	7.0	7.1	7.4	31.2	**6.4**	8.4	13.8
▲ HICKSVILLE BANK	Hicksville	OH	**C+**	C	C-	111.2	-3.32	4.0	2.5	20.9	32.0	**10.0**	11.1	17.9
HIGH COUNTRY BANK	Salida	CO	**B+**	B+	B+	206.0	3.21	9.2	1.9	25.9	14.6	**9.1**	10.4	17.1
HIGH DESERT BANK	Bend	OR	**E-**	E-	D-	28.1	-3.87	12.1	0.4	29.4	4.8	**5.0**	7.0	12.9
HIGH PLAINS BANK	Flagler	CO	**B**	B	C+	126.3	10.69	7.7	2.0	15.6	10.8	**7.5**	9.3	13.3
HIGH PLAINS BANK	Keyes	OK	**D+**	D+	C	76.0	18.47	8.2	3.9	4.7	3.7	**5.6**	9.7	11.4
▲ HIGH POINT BANK & TRUST CO	High Point	NC	**C+**	D+	D+	799.6	-2.47	10.7	0.3	10.3	20.1	**10.0**	11.0	16.4
HIGHLAND BANK	Saint Michael	MN	**C+**	C	C-	470.4	3.94	12.1	0.6	8.2	44.0	**6.6**	8.6	15.5
▲ HIGHLAND COMMERCIAL BANK	Marietta	GA	**C+**	D+	D-	123.8	-1.66	12.3	1.4	6.0	15.2	**9.9**	10.9	16.3
HIGHLAND COMMUNITY BANK	Chicago	IL	**E-**	E-	E-	58.3	-20.40	4.9	0.4	15.3	33.7	**0.0**	1.9	5.3
HIGHLAND FS&LA	Crossville	TN	**C-**	C	C+	63.8	-1.37	0.0	0.2	44.7	8.1	**10.0**	21.3	45.0
HIGHLAND STATE BK	Highland	WI	**C**	C	C	30.8	2.60	11.7	6.5	28.6	9.2	**7.8**	9.5	17.3
HIGHLANDS BANK	Jackson	LA	**A-**	B+	B+	142.5	5.67	13.5	1.3	12.6	20.9	**10.0**	11.9	19.5
HIGHLANDS COMMUNITY BANK	Covington	VA	**B**	B	B-	130.1	2.88	2.5	8.1	19.7	41.0	**9.5**	10.6	19.2
▲ HIGHLANDS STATE BK	Vernon	NJ	**D+**	D	D	253.2	21.08	11.1	0.2	10.8	4.9	**6.6**	9.7	12.2
▲ HIGHLANDS UNION BANK	Abingdon	VA	**D+**	E+	E-	609.4	2.06	5.2	3.4	31.5	13.7	**5.6**	7.6	13.9
HILL BANK & TRUST CO	Weimar	TX	**B**	B	B	125.3	2.10	1.0	1.0	3.5	83.3	**10.0**	17.1	36.2

Asset Quality Index	Adjusted Non-Performing Loans as a % of Total Loans	Adjusted Non-Performing Loans as a % of Capital	Net Charge-Offs Avg Loans	Profitability Index	Net Income ($Mil)	Return on Assets (R.O.A.)	Return on Equity (R.O.E.)	Net Interest Spread	Overhead Efficiency Ratio	Liquidity Index	Liquidity Ratio	Hot Money Ratio	Stability Index
3.4	4.68	20.4	0.05	2.4	1.9	0.32	3.00	3.75	99.5	6.3	50.8	5.3	4.9
5.3	3.06	11.2	0.03	5.7	0.8	0.92	5.48	3.75	57.9	0.7	12.7	40.9	8.3
6.2	0.20	1.8	0.01	9.3	2.4	1.56	18.46	4.25	42.4	0.8	2.4	32.0	5.7
3.4	5.05	23.3	0.48	1.3	0.1	0.05	0.43	3.29	90.3	5.1	43.4	10.4	5.1
3.4	3.79	15.3	1.21	3.3	1.2	0.60	6.07	3.69	67.9	0.8	20.7	43.8	5.7
5.5	2.45	8.8	-0.27	4.2	0.8	1.03	8.34	3.05	61.6	3.8	42.5	16.8	6.1
3.3	5.57	21.6	0.83	2.7	0.8	0.38	3.64	2.79	79.7	5.2	49.1	11.4	4.9
0.3	16.34	130.2	0.36	2.7	2.9	0.67	17.41	3.25	86.7	1.8	24.0	21.9	1.2
0.0	8.15	71.9	0.52	1.9	0.3	0.12	2.39	3.97	90.9	1.7	12.1	20.1	0.9
8.6	0.04	0.2	-0.01	4.4	2.3	0.94	8.83	3.06	65.2	5.7	28.8	0.1	7.1
8.5	0.36	1.5	0.00	1.5	0.0	0.03	0.32	3.78	98.4	6.3	61.4	6.2	3.5
6.5	0.78	4.5	-0.03	4.6	0.6	0.74	6.92	3.59	68.7	3.3	18.2	13.0	6.3
8.3	0.57	1.9	0.02	7.8	8.4	1.84	12.91	3.02	45.1	4.2	26.1	8.9	10.0
3.4	1.88	18.8	0.61	0.5	-0.1	-0.12	-2.11	3.75	101.6	1.4	14.8	26.6	0.9
4.4	1.35	8.2	0.17	5.1	17.5	0.88	6.89	4.45	71.7	4.5	24.4	9.9	8.2
7.2	0.29	1.9	0.00	3.5	0.4	0.42	2.75	4.77	82.1	3.9	27.1	11.4	6.2
10.0	2.58	0.3	-0.49	2.8	0.5	0.62	5.00	2.08	75.4	1.4	18.6	27.4	6.4
1.5	4.77	35.4	1.74	3.2	0.6	0.83	11.43	3.94	85.7	1.4	14.9	25.3	3.2
2.7	3.28	20.4	0.70	6.1	4.1	1.09	9.95	4.34	60.1	1.8	11.7	19.9	7.0
3.0	1.51	12.4	0.00	5.0	1.2	1.38	11.48	5.65	53.2	2.8	7.9	14.5	6.0
3.8	1.61	10.5	0.26	4.3	2.8	0.94	8.72	3.97	79.7	2.2	14.0	18.2	6.2
0.3	7.81	50.4	0.14	2.7	1.5	0.72	6.88	3.48	77.5	4.1	12.6	7.4	3.5
6.5	0.66	3.7	0.05	5.4	10.7	0.96	8.70	4.07	64.7	2.6	20.9	17.2	7.4
3.9	1.95	11.5	0.15	8.8	6.5	1.64	15.10	4.51	45.0	3.6	22.1	11.9	7.0
1.9	2.10	14.6	0.31	4.1	1.0	0.96	7.02	3.32	70.0	5.2	41.2	8.9	7.8
2.3	4.64	28.1	0.23	1.1	0.2	0.22	2.17	3.11	93.6	1.2	28.9	41.2	4.1
5.4	0.46	4.4	0.00	3.0	0.2	0.32	3.97	4.42	85.1	1.7	8.3	20.1	4.3
6.4	1.16	5.5	-0.05	2.9	3.9	0.54	4.90	3.21	86.1	1.5	14.0	24.2	6.3
6.9	0.86	5.5	0.48	3.4	0.3	0.59	4.74	4.10	81.1	3.1	10.3	13.1	6.8
1.7	3.49	33.3	0.61	0.7	-0.1	-0.07	-1.13	3.83	100.9	2.1	16.1	18.5	0.3
5.7	0.71	4.9	0.02	4.1	0.4	0.56	5.50	4.78	80.8	3.2	13.5	12.8	6.0
5.2	1.29	7.9	0.00	4.0	0.7	0.97	8.33	4.88	81.4	2.9	17.6	14.6	3.8
5.4	1.03	6.7	0.14	3.6	5.3	0.44	3.78	4.11	85.0	3.5	23.9	14.4	7.6
4.8	0.83	6.0	0.26	10.0	1.4	2.47	23.55	5.29	52.9	4.1	11.2	7.3	8.1
8.5	0.01	0.1	0.00	4.8	1.0	1.07	12.13	4.07	76.1	2.9	12.8	14.3	6.3
5.2	1.19	9.5	0.05	3.7	5.5	0.51	6.08	5.29	86.3	1.9	11.0	19.6	6.1
3.7	3.44	14.6	0.22	4.9	0.9	1.15	10.67	3.94	68.7	4.2	34.2	11.9	6.1
6.6	0.98	4.7	0.09	4.3	3.4	0.96	8.08	4.32	82.1	3.2	28.0	14.8	6.5
4.7	0.61	3.6	0.00	9.9	0.9	1.72	13.18	5.14	50.3	0.6	7.7	46.7	8.9
5.5	3.76	15.3	0.00	3.4	0.1	0.71	5.11	3.83	72.8	3.8	45.7	14.8	5.8
8.2	0.00	0.0	0.00	7.9	0.4	1.27	10.91	4.29	54.5	2.5	9.8	16.2	5.7
2.1	4.52	23.2	0.10	2.0	0.3	0.32	2.77	3.74	93.1	2.4	37.5	26.3	5.8
9.3	0.29	1.2	0.00	1.9	0.1	0.09	0.48	3.35	93.1	0.7	13.3	37.7	6.5
6.0	0.78	5.1	0.05	3.0	1.9	0.42	4.64	2.88	81.9	4.5	23.3	6.6	5.3
3.6	4.00	19.6	0.70	4.0	0.6	0.69	5.97	3.99	80.0	2.8	28.0	17.0	5.7
5.4	1.13	6.8	0.09	6.1	1.6	1.03	9.51	4.80	69.4	3.6	23.0	11.8	6.7
0.3	10.10	82.3	0.09	0.0	-0.6	-2.79	-38.31	5.17	153.5	1.6	20.4	24.2	0.0
5.8	0.72	5.2	0.00	7.0	1.5	1.63	17.51	4.94	69.7	2.6	13.6	16.1	5.0
1.9	1.83	15.3	0.01	8.3	1.2	2.21	19.15	4.50	49.5	0.7	12.6	42.4	6.6
4.6	1.96	10.3	0.58	3.2	3.4	0.56	4.75	3.57	80.6	1.9	25.3	22.2	5.9
4.8	1.74	9.7	-0.11	3.7	2.3	0.68	7.18	3.93	84.7	3.7	38.9	16.0	3.2
5.4	0.00	0.0	0.75	4.2	0.6	0.65	6.16	3.82	69.8	1.8	26.4	23.8	5.3
0.3	11.62	120.4	0.08	0.0	-0.4	-0.83	-47.51	2.98	109.0	1.6	25.0	26.1	0.0
9.7	0.89	2.3	0.26	1.7	0.0	0.06	0.27	3.16	96.3	3.6	45.5	18.1	7.5
6.2	0.29	1.8	0.39	3.4	0.2	0.75	8.05	3.46	74.0	5.1	33.8	6.8	4.3
5.9	0.87	4.9	0.13	6.4	1.7	1.60	13.65	4.10	61.9	1.3	18.3	28.0	6.9
4.9	2.29	10.4	0.07	5.8	1.2	1.21	11.28	4.06	59.6	3.0	51.8	28.3	6.5
2.0	1.42	12.0	0.32	3.1	0.7	0.40	3.90	4.01	80.9	0.9	5.0	30.0	5.0
1.9	4.39	34.8	0.84	2.2	2.3	0.52	6.79	3.46	83.8	3.7	19.1	11.0	3.1
9.8	0.08	0.1	-0.04	3.8	0.7	0.70	4.14	2.64	62.4	4.7	94.8	22.6	7.5

Name	City	State	Rating	2013 Rating	2012 Rating	Total Assets ($Mil)	One Year Asset Growth	Comm-ercial Loans	Cons-umer Loans	Mort-gage Loans	Secur-ities	Capital-ization Index	Lever-age Ratio	Risk-Based Capital Ratio
								Asset Mix (As a % of Total Assets)						
HILL-DODGE BANKING CO	Warsaw	IL	**B+**	B	B+	37.3	-5.53	19.7	5.2	8.2	13.1	**10.0**	12.5	19.7
HILLS BANK & TRUST CO	Hills	IA	**A**	A	A-	2307.8	8.13	7.8	0.9	31.1	10.6	**10.0**	12.6	17.4
HILLSBORO BANK	Plant City	FL	**B**	B	B-	111.5	-8.71	6.4	1.0	7.1	50.9	**10.0**	13.0	27.5
HILLSBORO STATE BK	Hillsboro	KS	**D**	D	C-	17.0	-1.98	3.4	3.4	17.2	14.8	**6.9**	8.9	16.1
HILLSDALE COUNTY NATIONAL BK	Hillsdale	MI	**C-**	C	D+	473.8	7.62	13.0	2.9	25.4	5.6	**5.8**	7.8	12.4
HILLTOP NATIONAL BK	Casper	WY	**B+**	A-	A-	690.7	5.20	4.3	4.0	13.6	48.1	**8.4**	9.9	23.0
HINGHAM INSTITUTION FOR SAVING	Hingham	MA	**B+**	B+	B	1506.0	15.49	0.0	0.0	45.8	5.5	**6.0**	8.0	13.9
HINSDALE BANK & TRUST CO	Hinsdale	IL	**B-**	C+	C	1556.8	-1.60	31.0	10.4	3.4	7.2	**6.3**	9.7	11.9
▲ HNB FIRST BANK	Headland	AL	**C+**	C-	C-	101.5	-0.38	10.9	3.6	16.7	15.9	**10.0**	12.2	18.1
HNB NATIONAL BK	Hannibal	MO	**B+**	B	B	390.9	-3.22	9.7	2.7	25.2	2.6	**10.0**	11.9	15.7
HOCKING VALLEY BANK	Athens	OH	**B**	B	B-	238.2	-0.50	20.3	2.1	25.7	20.8	**9.7**	10.8	18.0
HODGE BANK & TRUST CO	Hodge	LA	**A-**	A-	A-	66.4	-0.92	17.4	9.6	25.4	24.8	**10.0**	15.0	27.2
HOLBROOK CO-OP BANK	Holbrook	MA	**C**	C-	D+	95.1	5.79	3.3	7.5	31.6	12.4	**7.1**	9.1	15.0
HOLCOMB STATE BK	Holcomb	IL	**C+**	C+	C+	188.1	3.63	9.8	2.3	10.8	24.5	**6.5**	8.6	12.9
HOLLADAY BANK & TRUST	Salt Lake City	UT	**B-**	C+	C-	51.5	6.75	8.2	3.4	20.5	0.8	**10.0**	12.2	19.9
HOLMES COUNTY BANK & TRUST CO	Lexington	MS	**C-**	C	C	109.8	-1.41	15.4	5.8	9.4	28.3	**10.0**	12.0	22.3
HOME BANK	Lafayette	LA	**B**	B	B	1259.0	30.88	7.5	3.7	19.1	15.3	**10.0**	11.3	17.5
HOME BANK & TRUST CO	Eureka	KS	**C+**	C+	C+	89.2	0.96	11.8	2.6	19.1	10.7	**5.2**	7.5	11.1
HOME BANK OF CALIFORNIA	San Diego	CA	**A**	A	B+	115.5	12.40	0.6	0.0	31.0	0.5	**10.0**	19.5	27.0
HOME BANK SB	Martinsville	IN	**C**	C-	C+	243.3	-0.11	1.7	0.9	40.2	24.4	**10.0**	12.9	22.6
▲ HOME BANKING CO	Selmer	TN	**C+**	C	C	84.7	3.68	4.7	7.6	17.5	36.7	**7.6**	9.4	17.7
HOME CITY FSB OF SPRINGFIELD	Springfield	OH	**B**	B-	C+	147.4	1.51	5.4	0.5	51.6	7.8	**9.0**	10.4	17.5
HOME EXCHANGE BANK	Jamesport	MO	**B+**	B+	B	125.1	14.89	3.1	0.7	2.7	60.1	**9.0**	10.3	21.5
HOME FEDERAL BANK	Sioux Falls	SD	**C+**	C+	C+	1254.3	0.56	5.6	1.6	6.5	27.5	**8.1**	9.7	14.5
HOME FEDERAL BANK	Shreveport	LA	**A**	A-	A-	340.7	16.27	7.9	0.1	31.8	16.3	**10.0**	12.3	20.6
HOME FEDERAL BANK CORP	Middlesboro	KY	**C+**	C+	C+	337.4	1.70	2.3	1.7	39.1	20.2	**9.3**	10.6	18.1
▲ HOME FEDERAL BANK OF HOLLYWOO	Hallandale Beach	FL	**E**	E-	E-	46.1	-14.07	0.4	0.1	45.1	0.0	**4.8**	6.8	12.8
HOME FEDERAL BANK OF TENNESSEE	Knoxville	TN	**B-**	B-	B	2169.1	4.30	1.9	0.4	18.7	49.5	**10.0**	16.4	33.1
HOME FS&LA	Collinsville	IL	**C-**	D	D+	94.2	-3.19	0.1	0.2	63.4	15.5	**10.0**	11.3	25.4
HOME FS&LA	Bamberg	SC	**C+**	C+	C	41.7	1.29	0.2	3.5	72.1	3.8	**9.6**	10.8	20.0
▲ HOME FS&LA OF GRAND ISLAND	Grand Island	NE	**C**	C	B-	235.5	1.97	8.3	2.3	14.5	39.1	**8.5**	10.0	18.9
HOME FS&LA OF NEBRASKA	Lexington	NE	**D+**	C	C	54.4	11.88	7.3	27.5	18.5	1.6	**9.1**	10.8	14.2
HOME FS&LA OF NILES OHIO	Niles	OH	**C-**	D+	C+	97.4	0.45	0.1	0.4	16.3	64.4	**10.0**	13.2	37.4
▲ HOME FSB	Rochester	MN	**B-**	C	D	593.2	5.50	10.2	0.7	14.0	23.7	**10.0**	11.7	18.4
HOME LOAN INVESTMENT BANK FSB	Warwick	RI	**D-**	D-	D-	216.2	5.60	0.3	31.2	27.9	2.0	**8.0**	9.7	14.3
HOME LOAN SB	Coshocton	OH	**A-**	B	B-	177.6	8.33	13.3	4.0	44.8	1.7	**10.0**	11.7	16.7
▲ HOME LOAN STATE BK	Grand Junction	CO	**C**	D	D+	74.0	3.96	11.4	4.8	5.5	47.5	**8.0**	9.6	18.5
HOME NATIONAL BK	Racine	OH	**D+**	C-	C+	58.7	-6.45	8.2	10.3	39.1	16.3	**10.0**	14.3	21.8
HOME NATIONAL BK OF THORNTOWN	Thorntown	IN	**C**	C	C-	102.7	-1.13	11.0	2.8	17.7	36.9	**5.8**	7.8	15.0
HOME S&LA OF NORBORNE FA	Norborne	MO	**C-**	C	C-	83.1	-3.49	1.2	5.2	51.1	10.0	**10.0**	16.3	32.6
▲ HOME SAVINGS & LOAN CO	Youngstown	OH	**C+**	C-	D-	1801.0	2.46	2.2	1.5	43.0	28.2	**10.0**	12.1	21.2
HOME SAVINGS & LOAN KENTON OH	Kenton	OH	**C**	C+	B	118.2	-1.55	2.7	0.8	39.5	28.4	**10.0**	27.0	56.3
HOME SAVINGS BANK	Jefferson City	MO	**E**	E	E-	25.5	-4.84	0.0	2.7	60.6	0.0	**5.6**	7.6	15.4
HOME SAVINGS BANK	Chanute	KS	**C-**	C-	C	68.4	6.46	0.4	1.9	17.3	60.1	**10.0**	17.0	44.4
▲ HOME SAVINGS BANK FSB	Ludlow	KY	**C-**	D	C	27.9	-3.59	0.0	0.1	39.3	17.1	**10.0**	14.9	38.0
HOME SAVINGS BK OF WAPAKONETA	Wapakoneta	OH	**C+**	C	C+	36.6	-1.06	0.0	0.4	57.1	21.5	**10.0**	11.4	24.0
HOME SB	Madison	WI	**D-**	D-	D	119.4	3.67	1.4	1.8	34.1	9.9	**8.1**	9.7	15.8
HOME SB	Salt Lake City	UT	**B-**	B	B-	114.1	-3.49	0.5	0.0	33.5	4.3	**10.0**	11.5	16.9
▲ HOME STATE BK	Loveland	CO	**B**	B-	C+	810.0	11.35	7.1	0.5	5.8	42.3	**6.5**	8.5	14.8
▲ HOME STATE BK	Litchfield	MN	**A-**	B	B	137.5	3.02	12.9	2.7	8.9	32.0	**10.0**	11.7	19.4
HOME STATE BK	Jefferson	IA	**B**	B	B	190.3	3.18	14.7	1.3	6.7	12.2	**4.5**	8.3	10.7
HOME STATE BK	Royal	IA	**A-**	A-	A-	47.6	5.72	2.0	1.0	2.2	43.4	**10.0**	26.2	41.3
HOME STATE BK	Louisville	NE	**A**	A	A-	82.2	6.04	10.3	3.1	18.8	12.5	**10.0**	12.4	16.1
HOME STATE BK NA	Crystal Lake	IL	**C+**	C+	C-	595.6	-4.03	7.2	3.9	18.6	14.3	**10.0**	11.5	16.3
HOME TRUST & SB	Osage	IA	**B+**	B+	B+	217.7	0.77	7.7	1.5	11.4	40.3	**7.4**	9.3	17.0
HOMEBANC NA	Lake Mary	FL	**C+**	C+	C+	890.9	36.36	0.8	33.6	20.2	24.1	**6.0**	8.0	20.6
HOMEBANK	Palmyra	MO	**B+**	B+	B	164.5	4.37	10.1	3.1	12.1	9.0	**7.2**	9.9	12.7
▲ HOMEBANK OF ARKANSAS	Portland	AR	**C+**	C-	D	69.6	3.07	10.4	5.1	25.4	7.5	**10.0**	11.1	16.0
HOMEBANK TEXAS	Seagoville	TX	**C**	D+	D+	122.7	4.42	11.7	1.4	15.5	26.1	**6.7**	8.7	14.6
HOMELAND COMMUNITY BANK	McMinnville	TN	**D-**	D-	D+	140.9	1.37	5.0	2.6	18.9	27.9	**7.4**	9.3	16.4

Asset Quality Index	Adjusted Non-Performing Loans as a % of Total Loans	Adjusted Non-Performing Loans as a % of Capital	Net Charge-Offs Avg Loans	Profitability Index	Net Income ($Mil)	Return on Assets (R.O.A.)	Return on Equity (R.O.E.)	Net Interest Spread	Overhead Efficiency Ratio	Liquidity Index	Liquidity Ratio	Hot Money Ratio	Stability Index
7.8	0.37	1.7	0.15	7.6	0.5	1.83	15.29	4.15	50.1	4.3	28.9	9.6	7.0
6.4	0.95	6.0	-0.01	7.1	21.9	1.33	10.55	3.44	55.3	3.5	12.1	11.4	9.8
9.5	0.36	1.0	0.00	4.9	0.9	1.02	8.32	3.57	60.4	4.4	67.1	19.0	6.2
8.7	0.16	0.8	0.00	2.0	0.0	0.18	2.13	3.23	93.9	4.2	48.4	13.4	2.5
2.2	2.55	22.1	0.12	4.9	3.1	0.89	10.78	4.00	71.4	4.4	19.4	6.5	5.5
7.3	0.76	2.7	0.03	5.9	7.5	1.47	16.56	3.04	63.1	6.1	62.4	9.7	7.9
6.9	0.59	5.6	0.00	8.8	17.7	1.64	20.90	3.28	37.0	1.5	12.4	24.4	7.0
4.3	0.81	6.0	0.20	5.3	10.5	0.88	6.83	3.60	58.8	2.2	16.2	18.7	6.8
5.2	1.71	8.6	-0.09	3.1	0.5	0.63	5.24	3.54	84.0	2.4	27.2	18.6	5.4
5.5	1.17	7.7	0.36	9.7	6.5	2.19	18.65	4.54	51.4	3.8	6.2	9.1	7.0
8.0	0.43	2.4	0.03	4.6	1.5	0.88	8.31	3.71	69.1	3.2	9.8	12.6	6.4
6.0	1.37	5.2	0.05	9.9	1.2	2.31	16.31	4.71	49.4	2.8	31.7	18.0	8.9
4.2	1.45	11.1	-0.27	2.9	0.3	0.38	4.06	3.99	95.6	3.3	21.0	13.0	4.0
4.0	1.57	11.8	1.16	3.7	1.1	0.75	9.04	3.92	69.8	1.2	22.5	31.4	3.9
4.2	3.62	16.5	0.42	4.1	0.3	0.66	5.42	4.90	78.8	2.5	34.3	21.1	4.6
2.2	8.78	28.9	0.72	1.8	0.2	0.25	2.25	2.94	92.4	2.6	36.4	22.9	5.5
4.8	1.41	8.6	0.22	5.1	7.1	0.83	6.63	4.92	71.3	3.7	5.6	9.9	8.7
8.6	0.04	0.3	0.08	4.0	0.5	0.79	10.65	3.91	79.9	3.2	22.0	13.8	3.7
7.5	0.12	0.5	0.02	10.0	2.1	2.60	13.02	5.06	48.9	0.6	12.7	51.9	9.0
4.5	3.16	14.1	-0.42	1.8	0.4	0.20	1.61	3.18	99.5	3.1	32.9	17.2	3.8
6.3	1.50	6.7	0.17	3.7	0.4	0.59	6.47	4.08	79.9	2.8	40.8	22.8	4.8
7.1	0.37	2.5	0.00	4.5	1.0	0.88	8.65	3.69	63.0	1.0	12.9	31.5	5.6
6.0	1.51	4.8	0.00	7.2	1.6	1.81	16.33	3.19	40.4	1.4	30.9	35.2	6.6
4.2	1.88	11.8	0.13	3.8	6.5	0.69	7.16	2.95	73.0	2.6	1.9	14.5	7.5
8.9	0.04	0.2	0.09	6.1	2.3	1.02	7.45	3.99	65.1	1.2	17.1	29.5	8.0
4.6	1.72	10.5	0.20	3.8	1.6	0.64	6.30	4.03	77.9	2.6	20.2	16.6	5.5
6.0	0.00	0.0	0.23	0.8	0.0	-0.08	-1.21	4.60	131.6	0.7	18.4	54.0	2.1
8.7	1.20	3.1	0.04	3.7	9.3	0.58	3.56	2.68	68.5	4.3	52.4	18.6	8.8
5.7	2.59	14.5	0.57	1.7	0.3	0.35	3.40	2.62	91.2	1.9	29.6	25.9	4.7
5.2	1.12	9.0	0.04	4.1	0.2	0.61	5.87	4.05	74.7	0.6	10.6	49.6	5.1
6.0	0.89	4.0	0.03	2.9	0.7	0.40	4.13	2.66	97.7	5.0	36.5	8.5	6.2
3.7	1.10	8.0	0.28	1.7	0.0	0.06	0.50	4.80	98.9	1.4	11.1	24.8	4.6
6.8	6.03	10.5	0.86	1.5	0.3	0.37	3.16	2.08	81.6	2.5	52.3	33.5	4.7
4.2	2.85	14.1	-0.45	7.7	5.9	1.28	9.45	3.31	74.8	5.3	33.6	4.9	6.2
0.3	6.65	50.7	0.61	2.7	0.6	0.37	3.91	5.15	90.9	1.0	9.7	30.1	4.3
5.5	1.06	7.4	0.23	10.0	2.2	1.76	14.79	4.99	50.6	2.9	9.1	13.7	7.7
6.5	1.46	5.9	-0.48	3.5	0.5	0.92	9.98	3.51	68.0	1.8	25.4	23.7	2.9
1.1	5.51	25.6	0.40	6.0	0.6	1.43	10.21	5.27	68.5	1.4	15.7	26.2	7.0
2.8	3.58	21.5	0.11	3.8	0.5	0.65	9.07	3.67	72.9	3.5	36.8	16.7	4.1
5.6	2.17	8.6	0.26	1.4	0.0	0.02	0.15	2.15	86.0	2.5	34.2	22.0	6.5
5.0	2.88	14.2	0.18	3.7	45.9	3.42	33.72	3.03	85.0	4.7	25.2	8.8	6.3
8.1	1.45	3.0	0.13	2.1	0.1	0.09	0.34	2.84	76.5	4.6	53.4	15.4	7.0
2.4	3.16	27.2	0.02	0.0	-0.3	-1.61	-18.13	3.24	173.4	1.6	18.7	24.2	2.5
9.9	0.51	0.8	0.00	1.3	-0.7	-1.40	-6.88	2.87	88.3	4.2	48.5	15.3	5.9
8.2	0.28	1.0	0.00	1.6	0.1	0.38	2.57	3.45	89.3	2.7	48.0	27.8	5.5
10.0	0.00	0.0	0.00	2.3	0.1	0.24	2.10	3.40	90.5	2.8	30.8	17.7	6.4
5.3	0.94	6.2	0.15	0.0	-1.0	-1.11	-14.13	3.27	124.5	4.0	21.8	9.3	2.4
3.6	2.01	12.9	0.34	4.6	0.6	0.73	6.57	4.47	62.9	0.6	12.8	50.8	5.6
6.5	0.45	2.6	0.18	4.9	7.0	1.20	13.94	3.55	67.4	4.7	33.6	8.9	5.1
8.2	0.37	1.5	0.00	6.6	1.9	1.82	16.27	3.89	72.9	3.7	30.5	13.3	7.2
6.9	0.27	2.3	0.00	6.8	2.2	1.54	18.78	3.64	54.9	2.6	11.7	15.6	6.4
7.5	0.07	0.1	0.02	8.1	0.7	1.92	7.53	3.67	41.9	5.9	52.5	6.6	9.1
8.4	0.38	2.2	-0.01	7.4	1.1	1.79	14.44	3.35	62.4	2.9	17.0	14.6	9.0
3.9	3.16	17.7	0.57	2.9	2.2	0.48	4.26	3.81	85.1	3.2	12.0	12.5	5.8
5.1	1.63	9.0	0.09	6.0	2.2	1.39	14.69	2.73	40.2	4.0	44.2	15.9	7.0
5.2	0.57	4.8	0.01	3.8	3.2	0.54	6.26	2.52	75.7	1.5	8.1	22.1	3.7
5.1	0.78	5.8	-0.01	5.8	1.7	1.38	14.28	4.07	65.6	3.4	11.8	11.7	7.1
5.6	0.95	5.9	0.07	2.9	0.2	0.33	3.04	5.10	87.5	0.8	18.8	41.8	4.7
4.8	1.55	10.1	-0.01	3.5	0.8	0.89	10.10	4.08	75.3	4.8	37.3	10.1	4.5
0.3	10.36	54.1	0.17	2.5	0.2	0.24	2.65	3.11	81.4	2.3	36.0	26.3	5.3

Name	City	State	Rating	2013 Rating	2012 Rating	Total Assets ($Mil)	One Year Asset Growth	Asset Mix (As a % of Total Assets): Comm-ercial Loans	Cons-umer Loans	Mort-gage Loans	Secur-ities	Capital-ization Index	Lever-age Ratio	Risk-Based Capital Ratio
HOMELAND FSB	Columbia	LA	**B**	B	C	161.7	3.10	10.1	14.3	29.2	6.1	**10.0**	11.2	16.9
▼ HOMEPRIDE BANK	Mansfield	MO	**B-**	B	B	94.7	5.43	7.4	4.4	41.0	11.4	**6.7**	8.7	13.5
HOMESTAR BANK & FINANCIAL SVCS	Manteno	IL	**E-**	E-	E-	333.4	-1.95	2.7	3.6	19.7	31.7	**2.3**	4.7	9.7
▲ HOMESTEAD BANK	Cozad	NE	**A-**	B+	A-	247.9	-10.41	7.8	1.7	2.7	24.1	**10.0**	11.6	17.1
▼ HOMESTEAD SAVINGS BANK	Albion	MI	**E+**	D-	D-	71.0	-3.52	0.9	1.7	64.9	4.7	**4.9**	6.9	12.6
▲ HOMESTREET BANK	Seattle	WA	**C-**	C-	C-	3454.6	22.05	4.3	0.1	41.7	12.8	**8.0**	9.6	14.0
HOMETOWN BANK	Kent	OH	**D+**	D+	C	164.1	-0.47	11.4	2.3	32.1	3.2	**6.1**	8.2	12.3
HOMETOWN BANK	Roanoke	VA	**B-**	B-	C	417.9	8.54	8.4	2.0	17.7	13.6	**7.9**	9.8	13.3
HOMETOWN BANK	Fond Du Lac	WI	**B-**	B-	B	244.3	15.95	23.2	0.9	4.3	2.8	**10.0**	14.3	21.0
HOMETOWN BANK	Redwood Falls	MN	**A-**	A-	B+	226.9	3.94	11.9	3.3	15.5	18.1	**9.6**	10.7	16.1
▼ HOMETOWN BANK A COOPERATIVE BK	Oxford	MA	**C-**	C+	B-	392.8	8.92	3.6	0.3	45.5	6.3	**9.3**	10.5	15.8
HOMETOWN BANK NA	Carthage	MO	**D**	D+	C-	158.5	-4.09	9.9	2.3	16.2	10.8	**10.0**	11.8	18.5
▲ HOMETOWN BANK NA	Galveston	TX	**B+**	B	B	513.4	9.79	3.6	2.7	17.9	36.2	**7.9**	9.6	16.9
HOMETOWN BANK OF ALABAMA	Oneonta	AL	**A-**	B	B-	301.5	-0.03	5.5	9.1	26.3	29.9	**10.0**	11.9	21.0
HOMETOWN BANK OF CORBIN INC	Corbin	KY	**C-**	C-	C	138.4	3.55	4.1	4.0	23.9	23.0	**7.4**	9.3	15.0
HOMETOWN BANK OF PENNSYLVANIA	Bedford	PA	**B**	B	B	129.0	4.41	8.3	1.5	37.7	5.0	**9.3**	10.5	15.4
▼ HOMETOWN BK HUDSON VALLEY	Walden	NY	**E-**	D-	D	130.8	-11.71	5.6	0.3	50.7	3.4	**2.0**	5.6	9.0
HOMETOWN COMMUNITY BANK	Cyrus	MN	**D**	D	D-	25.4	-0.75	5.9	4.0	23.0	18.5	**6.2**	8.2	13.6
HOMETOWN NATIONAL BK	LaSalle	IL	**B**	B	B-	214.2	8.52	13.2	0.6	8.9	22.3	**8.1**	9.7	16.2
HOMETOWN NATIONAL BK	Longview	WA	**E+**	D-	C-	14.3	-32.40	14.7	1.8	15.3	0.0	**4.6**	6.6	14.5
HOMETRUST BANK NA	Asheville	NC	**B-**	B-	C-	2188.2	33.70	4.2	1.0	30.2	8.1	**10.0**	11.5	16.4
▲ HOMEWOOD FSB	Baltimore	MD	**B**	B-	C+	66.3	-4.52	0.0	7.2	65.4	8.8	**10.0**	21.5	42.4
HONDO NATIONAL BK	Hondo	TX	**B+**	B+	B-	221.5	10.68	6.7	3.5	10.9	42.1	**7.3**	9.2	18.2
HONESDALE NATIONAL BK	Honesdale	PA	**A**	A	A	591.3	1.25	9.9	4.6	26.8	20.0	**10.0**	13.9	19.4
HONOR BANK	Honor	MI	**C**	C-	D+	192.3	0.29	8.2	4.5	15.2	10.7	**8.5**	10.0	15.4
HOOSIER HEARTLAND STATE BK	Crawfordsville	IN	**C+**	C+	C	147.9	0.43	4.6	4.0	12.5	33.2	**7.6**	9.4	15.4
HOPETON STATE BK	Hopeton	OK	**C+**	C+	C+	29.2	16.47	3.7	4.8	0.0	64.4	**10.0**	17.2	39.1
HOPEWELL VALLEY COMMUNITY BANK	Pennington	NJ	**C**	D+	C+	484.4	7.87	4.4	0.2	12.0	20.2	**7.2**	9.2	13.7
HOPKINS FSB	Baltimore	MD	**B**	B	C+	266.6	-11.58	0.5	0.4	14.9	39.5	**10.0**	12.5	31.8
HORATIO STATE BK	Horatio	AR	**A-**	A-	B	146.3	5.42	3.3	19.2	35.0	13.9	**10.0**	11.2	19.2
HORICON BANK	Horicon	WI	**B-**	B-	C+	585.5	8.28	12.8	1.2	18.6	3.3	**8.4**	11.3	13.7
HORIZON BANK	Fyffe	AL	**B-**	B	C	90.3	-2.30	2.5	4.8	21.4	18.5	**10.0**	17.2	27.9
HORIZON BANK	Waverly	NE	**A**	A	A-	230.7	-0.97	24.5	4.4	7.9	19.7	**10.0**	11.7	15.9
HORIZON BANK NA	Michigan City	IN	**B**	B-	B-	2039.9	14.53	5.8	7.9	14.3	24.5	**6.6**	8.6	13.3
HORIZON BANK SSB	Austin	TX	**B+**	A-	B+	511.5	26.50	19.6	0.6	12.4	4.2	**5.4**	8.5	11.3
▲ HORIZON COMMUNITY BANK	Lake Havasu City	AZ	**C**	C-	D	172.0	1.45	10.6	0.6	12.3	9.8	**6.4**	8.4	12.8
HORIZON FINANCIAL BANK	Munich	ND	**A-**	A-	B-	137.2	9.87	5.2	2.0	4.3	12.3	**8.0**	11.0	13.3
▼ HORIZON STATE BK	Cameron	MO	**E+**	D	C-	21.0	10.49	7.7	2.0	14.9	2.9	**4.5**	6.6	12.7
HORRY COUNTY STATE BK	Loris	SC	**E-**	E-	E-	434.8	-4.38	5.8	1.5	15.6	27.8	**0.0**	2.5	4.8
HOUGHTON STATE BK	Red Oak	IA	**B+**	B-	C+	170.5	5.18	22.0	0.9	5.1	14.0	**6.3**	8.3	12.8
HOWARD BANK	Ellicott City	MD	**C+**	C+	C+	575.0	23.24	19.3	0.3	17.7	4.7	**4.2**	9.1	10.6
HOWARD STATE BANK	Howard	KS	**C+**	B-	B	51.5	10.29	9.4	4.3	6.9	24.7	**7.4**	9.3	21.7
HOYNE SB	Chicago	IL	**D**	D+	C-	279.5	-3.18	0.0	0.0	47.0	27.2	**10.0**	18.7	58.4
HSBC BANK USA NA	McLean	VA	**D+**	D+	C	168428.1	-6.36	17.8	0.7	9.9	24.7	**8.6**	10.1	18.0
HSBC TRUST CO (DELAWARE) NA	Wilmington	DE	**U**	U	C+	55.4	-97.09	0.0	0.0	0.0	0.0	**10.0**	96.7	1453
HUDSON CITY SAVINGS BANK	Paramus	NJ	**C+**	C	C	37157.5	-5.18	0.0	0.1	59.8	22.8	**10.0**	11.5	27.9
HUDSON VALLEY BANK NA	Yonkers	NY	**C**	C	C+	3113.8	3.24	7.3	0.2	9.3	27.0	**6.8**	8.9	15.3
HUNTINGDON SB	Huntingdon	PA	**C+**	C+	B-	16.0	3.14	0.0	0.0	70.4	0.0	**10.0**	18.6	23.8
▲ HUNTINGDON VALLEY BANK	Huntingdon Valley	PA	**D**	D	D+	169.9	6.71	0.4	0.0	43.8	22.9	**4.7**	6.7	12.6
HUNTINGTON FSB	Huntington	WV	**B**	B	B-	548.0	-0.59	0.0	0.2	32.2	53.6	**10.0**	14.1	41.9
HUNTINGTON NATIONAL BK	Columbus	OH	**B-**	B-	C	64107.3	13.60	20.0	13.9	13.5	18.5	**7.3**	9.5	12.8
▲ HUNTINGTON STATE BK	Huntington	TX	**C+**	C-	C-	223.1	-0.47	11.2	7.1	15.2	17.1	**9.0**	10.4	16.8
HURON COMMUNITY BANK	East Tawas	MI	**B-**	B-	B	205.9	2.19	13.1	1.5	16.0	11.2	**10.0**	11.4	15.2
HURON NATIONAL BK	Rogers City	MI	**B**	B	B+	62.2	5.37	5.5	6.7	36.7	7.1	**10.0**	14.2	22.5
HURON VALLEY STATE BK	Milford	MI	**B-**	B-	B-	97.9	12.82	10.7	0.8	3.2	3.6	**8.1**	11.3	13.4
HUSTISFORD STATE BK	Hustisford	WI	**B+**	B+	B+	55.6	-2.42	3.1	2.6	56.6	9.2	**10.0**	15.4	24.8
HYDEN CITIZENS BANK	Hyden	KY	**B-**	B-	C+	127.2	-0.97	23.4	4.4	21.8	37.6	**6.6**	8.6	15.1
▲ HYPERION BANK	Philadelphia	PA	**E+**	E-	E+	79.5	-11.15	5.3	0.0	32.3	6.3	**4.9**	7.1	11.0
IAB FINANCIAL BANK	Fort Wayne	IN	**B-**	C+	C+	945.5	0.31	10.5	0.6	10.7	20.0	**9.7**	10.8	15.6
▲ IBERIABANK	Lafayette	LA	**B-**	C+	C+	15442.6	18.07	18.4	5.5	13.9	14.4	**5.3**	8.3	11.2

Asset Quality Index	Adjusted Non-Performing Loans as a % of Total Loans	Adjusted Non-Performing Loans as a % of Capital	Net Charge-Offs Avg Loans	Profitability Index	Net Income ($Mil)	Return on Assets (R.O.A.)	Return on Equity (R.O.E.)	Net Interest Spread	Overhead Efficiency Ratio	Liquidity Index	Liquidity Ratio	Hot Money Ratio	Stability Index
4.4	1.41	8.5	0.24	**9.5**	2.7	2.25	20.40	5.34	58.6	**0.7**	13.5	38.6	**7.8**
3.1	2.39	18.6	1.86	**2.8**	-0.3	-0.46	-4.71	4.69	63.5	**1.4**	10.7	24.7	**6.2**
1.7	3.83	35.4	0.36	**2.4**	1.4	0.54	13.57	3.13	89.9	**4.5**	24.5	6.4	**0.0**
8.3	0.08	0.4	-0.25	**5.8**	2.7	1.44	12.38	3.61	62.5	**4.4**	18.9	6.4	**7.6**
0.3	5.62	59.4	0.21	**0.9**	-0.1	-0.19	-2.80	3.90	97.0	**4.4**	12.0	5.8	**1.4**
2.7	2.35	18.9	0.03	**5.0**	18.9	0.81	7.88	3.44	88.1	**3.8**	12.4	10.0	**5.7**
0.3	7.03	50.3	0.88	**0.6**	-1.1	-0.88	-10.54	4.07	85.7	**1.6**	12.4	22.0	**3.6**
5.1	0.98	7.0	0.17	**4.3**	2.5	0.81	8.29	3.91	69.3	**1.6**	16.4	23.2	**4.4**
5.1	1.72	8.4	0.00	**8.0**	2.0	1.25	8.52	3.92	51.0	**4.5**	30.2	8.8	**6.5**
7.2	0.37	2.2	-0.04	**7.4**	1.9	1.12	8.97	4.93	64.5	**4.7**	16.0	4.4	**7.3**
2.1	3.23	23.5	0.06	**5.1**	2.3	0.79	7.40	3.71	63.6	**1.4**	13.3	25.0	**6.5**
6.8	0.57	2.7	0.12	**0.0**	-0.8	-0.70	-6.01	3.33	117.7	**3.6**	20.6	11.5	**5.1**
7.0	0.53	3.0	0.01	**6.4**	4.6	1.25	12.87	4.23	60.3	**2.5**	36.1	23.2	**7.0**
5.9	1.49	7.0	0.05	**8.9**	3.8	1.68	15.28	4.55	57.6	**1.7**	18.4	22.0	**6.1**
3.4	2.00	12.7	0.58	**2.5**	0.3	0.31	3.33	4.22	85.4	**3.5**	27.9	13.2	**3.9**
4.5	1.67	12.4	0.00	**5.0**	0.8	0.84	8.04	3.81	61.3	**1.5**	13.2	23.9	**6.0**
0.3	6.55	73.4	1.86	**0.0**	-2.6	-2.56	-38.81	3.95	123.3	**2.0**	11.2	18.4	**2.2**
5.0	0.97	7.3	0.02	**3.0**	0.1	0.48	6.42	3.82	82.1	**3.3**	15.5	12.4	**2.8**
4.7	1.93	10.6	0.17	**4.8**	1.3	0.86	8.69	3.55	68.4	**5.6**	40.5	6.1	**5.4**
0.3	8.80	52.4	1.55	**0.0**	-0.6	-4.26	-50.07	4.62	227.2	**2.6**	36.2	18.4	**3.3**
4.0	2.90	17.8	0.04	**3.0**	5.9	0.43	2.57	3.83	91.5	**2.2**	17.7	18.6	**7.6**
6.4	1.12	4.1	0.14	**4.2**	0.3	0.65	3.19	3.58	54.4	**1.4**	21.8	28.2	**6.8**
8.2	0.37	1.8	0.02	**5.1**	1.9	1.20	12.52	3.79	68.4	**3.5**	50.2	20.7	**5.5**
7.9	0.62	2.9	0.05	**6.6**	5.4	1.23	8.95	3.89	60.3	**2.7**	22.0	16.2	**9.2**
2.9	2.27	14.4	0.40	**3.5**	0.7	0.49	4.81	4.19	81.0	**4.4**	25.8	7.6	**4.6**
4.4	1.22	7.0	0.05	**4.0**	0.9	0.77	8.22	4.26	77.6	**4.5**	32.1	9.7	**4.5**
9.0	0.00	0.0	-0.61	**2.7**	0.1	0.60	3.14	3.38	87.5	**3.9**	88.2	28.7	**6.2**
4.1	1.09	7.5	0.03	**3.2**	1.9	0.55	5.88	3.65	75.4	**2.6**	21.2	16.4	**4.3**
5.4	7.28	15.1	-1.47	**3.5**	1.7	0.81	6.74	2.48	65.6	**4.6**	83.0	20.2	**5.6**
6.0	0.63	3.7	0.28	**7.7**	1.3	1.21	11.05	4.19	47.5	**0.8**	19.1	44.6	**6.8**
4.0	1.78	12.5	0.27	**6.0**	5.8	1.37	11.77	4.30	65.9	**3.1**	6.4	12.8	**8.1**
6.4	2.19	6.5	0.00	**3.6**	0.5	0.77	4.70	4.22	80.7	**3.7**	38.3	15.8	**6.7**
8.2	0.33	1.7	0.00	**9.0**	3.2	1.79	15.59	4.05	44.1	**2.5**	34.9	21.9	**8.4**
4.7	1.24	8.9	0.22	**5.6**	13.9	0.97	9.53	3.99	69.5	**3.7**	14.2	10.9	**7.8**
7.2	0.02	0.1	0.04	**8.7**	5.8	1.58	18.07	4.78	57.7	**3.8**	10.7	9.7	**6.9**
2.8	2.48	17.5	-0.06	**3.6**	1.0	0.76	9.28	3.98	83.6	**2.4**	20.8	17.5	**3.2**
6.3	0.12	0.8	0.02	**7.4**	1.2	1.24	10.95	4.14	50.3	**1.3**	6.3	25.4	**7.5**
9.0	0.00	0.0	0.03	**0.4**	-0.1	-0.50	-8.11	3.75	110.3	**5.8**	49.8	4.3	**0.7**
0.3	7.70	117.1	2.27	**2.0**	1.2	0.36	21.99	3.14	89.5	**0.9**	22.3	41.6	**0.4**
7.5	0.06	0.4	0.00	**6.0**	1.2	0.97	8.98	3.45	56.8	**5.3**	34.8	5.6	**7.5**
4.9	0.42	4.0	0.62	**3.4**	1.4	0.37	3.91	3.99	75.3	**1.0**	4.8	28.6	**4.3**
8.3	0.47	1.9	0.05	**3.7**	0.3	0.68	7.29	3.41	77.7	**5.9**	43.1	4.8	**5.3**
6.3	3.72	9.6	0.65	**0.4**	-0.9	-0.41	-2.20	3.08	102.9	**4.2**	56.1	17.9	**6.0**
5.8	2.12	8.2	0.21	**2.0**	510.5	0.39	3.66	1.39	79.2	**4.8**	51.0	16.3	**6.8**
10.0	na	0.0	na	**2.3**	0.1	0.27	0.28	0.43	85.2	**10.0**	2810.7	0.0	**5.0**
4.7	4.00	20.0	0.17	**3.0**	114.0	0.40	3.43	1.25	63.2	**1.8**	20.6	24.6	**7.7**
5.3	2.04	12.0	-0.04	**3.1**	7.0	0.31	3.32	3.10	85.6	**6.1**	30.9	3.0	**5.8**
7.2	1.69	6.3	0.00	**3.3**	0.1	0.46	2.45	2.74	76.5	**1.2**	32.0	33.5	**7.9**
4.5	2.06	16.2	0.49	**1.2**	0.2	0.14	2.13	2.82	92.0	**3.0**	24.7	14.7	**2.1**
8.9	0.83	2.3	0.15	**4.3**	3.0	0.72	5.31	2.92	55.5	**4.1**	68.8	21.7	**7.5**
3.9	1.63	11.6	0.30	**5.7**	492.4	1.07	11.34	3.32	61.2	**5.0**	16.1	2.7	**6.0**
5.7	0.74	4.2	-0.35	**4.9**	2.2	1.29	12.91	4.38	77.6	**3.1**	21.4	14.0	**4.5**
3.8	2.83	16.2	0.60	**4.7**	1.3	0.88	7.63	3.73	67.1	**4.6**	25.7	6.6	**5.9**
4.6	2.84	13.8	0.32	**6.6**	0.5	1.23	8.70	4.75	49.7	**3.6**	31.5	14.4	**7.1**
5.7	0.65	4.7	-0.01	**4.2**	0.5	0.70	6.25	4.34	70.9	**2.8**	9.6	14.5	**5.6**
5.9	1.21	6.1	0.99	**6.5**	0.5	1.08	7.20	4.69	56.4	**2.9**	10.9	14.0	**7.5**
5.3	1.24	7.5	0.29	**4.3**	0.9	0.93	10.61	4.42	77.4	**2.1**	16.5	18.8	**5.2**
3.0	2.49	23.3	0.06	**2.6**	0.3	0.54	8.33	4.92	88.9	**0.8**	19.1	49.8	**1.3**
4.5	1.13	6.6	0.19	**4.8**	6.1	0.85	7.04	3.61	68.6	**3.1**	21.9	14.1	**7.4**
4.6	0.82	6.8	0.05	**4.2**	73.1	0.69	6.06	3.59	75.2	**3.3**	10.5	12.2	**8.2**

Name	City	State	Rating	2013 Rating	2012 Rating	Total Assets ($Mil)	One Year Asset Growth	Asset Mix (As a % of Total Assets) Commercial Loans	Consumer Loans	Mortgage Loans	Securities	Capitalization Index	Leverage Ratio	Risk-Based Capital Ratio
IBERVILLE BANK	Plaquemine	LA	**C-**	C-	D+	240.0	2.51	0.8	1.5	12.9	37.3	**8.5**	10.0	17.1
ICON BANK OF TEXAS NA	Houston	TX	**B**	B	B-	625.2	18.93	16.6	2.3	12.1	0.0	**6.7**	9.1	12.3
IDABEL NATIONAL BK	Idabel	OK	**B+**	B+	B+	123.0	2.14	6.1	4.6	18.2	44.9	**6.7**	8.7	17.2
IDAHO FIRST BANK	McCall	ID	**D-**	E+	E-	103.0	12.92	18.0	4.3	19.1	5.0	**7.8**	10.1	13.2
▼ IDAHO INDEPENDENT BANK	Coeur DAlene	ID	**C-**	C	C-	500.8	-1.03	6.8	1.8	4.3	12.0	**9.9**	10.9	16.1
IDAHO TRUST BANK	Boise	ID	**B+**	B+	B-	76.8	1.65	26.7	0.4	3.6	1.5	**10.0**	20.8	32.2
▼ ILLINI BANK	Springfield	IL	**C**	C	B-	287.1	7.51	12.4	0.5	7.3	26.7	**7.3**	9.2	13.5
ILLINI STATE BK	Oglesby	IL	**B-**	B-	B+	108.6	0.82	3.5	1.0	10.9	50.3	**10.0**	12.7	25.4
ILLINOIS BANK & TRUST	Rockford	IL	**C+**	C+	C+	505.5	9.81	14.7	1.2	6.1	44.8	**5.3**	7.3	14.2
▲ ILLINOIS NATIONAL BK	Springfield	IL	**C+**	C	C-	664.8	3.89	13.1	0.6	8.5	11.4	**7.3**	9.2	13.3
ILLINOIS-SERVICE FS&LA	Chicago	IL	**E-**	E	D-	113.5	-3.73	0.6	0.4	27.5	32.5	**3.0**	5.0	12.0
IMPACT BANK	Wellington	KS	**B-**	B-	C+	131.4	2.96	12.1	3.6	7.3	27.2	**9.2**	10.5	17.2
INCOMMONS BANK NA	Mexia	TX	**B+**	B+	B-	104.1	1.71	7.4	7.4	32.6	20.9	**8.6**	10.1	17.4
INDEPENDENCE BANK	Havre	MT	**A**	A-	A-	539.6	9.58	6.5	2.6	6.4	11.5	**9.9**	12.4	14.9
INDEPENDENCE BANK	East Greenwich	RI	**B**	B	B-	41.3	-27.81	30.7	0.6	11.0	2.6	**10.0**	14.4	28.8
INDEPENDENCE BANK	Independence	OH	**B**	B	C+	175.0	-0.60	22.1	1.2	6.0	25.5	**10.0**	11.6	19.8
INDEPENDENCE BANK	Newport Beach	CA	**B-**	B-	C+	426.2	36.71	13.3	0.3	1.8	13.3	**7.9**	11.0	13.2
INDEPENDENCE BANK OF GEORGIA	Braselton	GA	**B**	B	B-	163.7	3.73	5.0	1.4	10.0	21.6	**10.0**	12.8	19.0
INDEPENDENCE BANK OF KENTUCKY	Owensboro	KY	**A-**	A-	B+	1485.5	10.72	6.2	0.8	16.6	35.9	**6.0**	8.0	12.9
▲ INDEPENDENCE NATIONAL BK	Greenville	SC	**D+**	D-	D-	99.9	-2.79	15.6	1.4	12.9	19.8	**9.6**	10.7	15.4
INDEPENDENCE STATE BK	Independence	WI	**D+**	D+	D+	64.4	-4.72	14.3	1.3	9.5	16.6	**6.3**	8.4	12.4
INDEPENDENCE TRUST CO	Franklin	TN	**U**	U	B+	4.0	1.26	0.0	0.0	0.0	56.0	**10.0**	83.1	206.4
▲ INDEPENDENT BANK	Memphis	TN	**C**	C-	C	881.1	14.07	7.9	57.6	1.6	1.4	**7.2**	11.4	12.7
INDEPENDENT BANK	Ionia	MI	**C-**	D+	D+	2214.7	1.94	8.0	9.0	21.4	24.1	**8.8**	10.2	16.6
INDEPENDENT BANK	McKinney	TX	**B+**	B+	B	3742.2	92.60	14.9	1.0	12.7	6.3	**7.1**	10.0	12.6
▲ INDEPENDENT BANK OF TEXAS	Irving	TX	**C+**	C	D	128.1	10.99	16.2	2.0	6.0	7.3	**7.0**	9.0	15.1
INDEPENDENT BANKERS BANK OF FL	Lake Mary	FL	**E-**	E-	E	165.1	-20.19	0.0	0.0	13.6	28.9	**1.7**	4.5	9.1
INDEPENDENT FARMERS BANK	Maysville	MO	**B**	B	B-	103.7	2.64	4.3	2.9	8.0	51.4	**7.0**	9.0	18.9
▲ INDIANA BUSINESS BANK	Indianapolis	IN	**D+**	D	C-	65.9	4.84	15.4	0.8	7.4	11.9	**10.0**	15.4	20.5
INDIANA FIRST SB	Indiana	PA	**B-**	B-	B-	313.5	4.90	4.6	0.7	63.7	6.5	**8.3**	9.9	16.3
INDUS AMERICAN BANK	Iselin	NJ	**D+**	D	D-	234.8	11.40	9.1	0.2	8.6	21.2	**6.5**	8.5	13.7
▲ INDUSTRIAL & COMMERCIAL BANK	New York	NY	**D+**	D+	C-	1097.2	22.33	17.8	0.0	3.3	0.4	**6.6**	8.9	12.2
INDUSTRIAL BANK	Washington	DC	**D+**	D+	D-	365.2	3.21	6.0	0.4	26.3	23.6	**8.2**	9.8	16.8
INDUSTRIAL STATE BK	Kansas City	KS	**B-**	B-	B-	141.5	-1.61	5.7	2.3	2.4	33.9	**10.0**	24.9	35.6
INDUSTRY STATE BK	Industry	TX	**A-**	A-	A-	607.9	11.13	5.3	1.5	4.4	73.0	**8.1**	9.7	25.2
INEZ DEPOSIT BANK	Inez	KY	**C**	C	C-	154.7	-6.72	1.0	4.5	24.5	46.4	**10.0**	11.8	30.9
▲ INLAND BANK & TRUST	Oak Brook	IL	**C-**	D+	E	1098.6	5.72	23.8	0.1	7.3	20.8	**9.0**	10.3	14.2
▲ INLAND NORTHWEST BANK	Spokane	WA	**C+**	C-	D+	420.3	7.08	16.6	1.3	9.0	10.1	**8.1**	11.2	13.4
INSBANK	Nashville	TN	**B**	B-	C	254.5	22.78	14.3	1.7	7.0	6.3	**6.1**	10.4	11.8
▼ INSIGNIA BANK	Sarasota	FL	**B-**	B	C	179.2	16.15	0.7	0.8	26.7	10.7	**9.6**	11.1	14.7
INSOUTH BANK	Brownsville	TN	**C-**	C-	D-	286.0	-0.54	5.1	2.0	19.1	19.6	**7.1**	9.1	14.3
INST FOR SVGS IN NEWBURYPORT	Newburyport	MA	**B**	B	B	1991.9	25.11	0.8	0.2	52.6	19.5	**10.0**	11.4	18.6
INTEGRITY BANK	Camp Hill	PA	**C+**	C+	C	860.4	18.10	17.8	4.2	13.0	1.4	**6.2**	9.2	11.9
▲ INTEGRITY BANK & TRUST	Monument	CO	**B-**	C	D+	138.1	13.49	8.1	0.7	15.3	10.9	**7.2**	9.2	14.5
▼ INTEGRITY BANK PLUS	Wabasso	MN	**C+**	B-	C-	62.3	3.56	3.3	1.3	6.5	9.2	**7.0**	9.4	12.5
INTEGRITY BANK SSB	Houston	TX	**B+**	B	B-	606.8	24.12	19.2	1.0	10.8	7.2	**8.5**	10.0	14.0
▲ INTEGRITY FIRST BANK	Wausau	WI	**C**	C-	D	73.8	-7.44	14.3	0.3	25.3	6.7	**10.0**	11.0	16.0
INTEGRITY FIRST BANK NA	Mountain Home	AR	**B+**	A-	A	407.1	0.87	3.3	2.0	26.7	22.0	**10.0**	11.1	16.1
INTER NATIONAL BK	McAllen	TX	**B-**	C+	C-	1843.0	-1.02	5.2	0.5	7.8	27.6	**10.0**	13.4	23.1
INTER-STATE FS&LA KANSAS CITY	Kansas City	KS	**C-**	C-	B-	230.3	-4.77	0.0	0.1	18.9	75.9	**10.0**	23.0	98.1
INTERAMERICAN BANK A FSB	Miami	FL	**D-**	D-	D-	216.3	-4.07	0.9	0.5	28.1	0.0	**8.5**	10.0	15.7
INTERAUDI BANK	New York	NY	**C+**	C+	C	1627.4	14.35	6.6	0.6	13.7	21.3	**4.8**	6.8	15.9
INTERBANK	Oklahoma City	OK	**C+**	B	B	2540.7	19.81	11.0	1.9	7.1	2.5	**6.8**	10.5	12.3
INTERCITY STATE BK	Schofield	WI	**A-**	B+	B-	157.9	-0.73	5.1	1.0	19.3	27.1	**10.0**	18.3	28.3
INTERCONTINENTAL BANK	West Miami	FL	**C+**	B-	B-	163.6	0.33	4.1	0.8	4.7	64.5	**10.0**	11.7	25.8
INTERCREDIT BANK NA	Miami	FL	**D-**	D-	D-	316.0	-2.21	17.9	1.3	12.3	26.2	**7.7**	9.4	15.9
INTERNATIONAL BK	Raton	NM	**C+**	C	C	292.3	0.31	8.6	0.8	12.6	25.1	**10.0**	12.9	21.3
INTERNATIONAL BK OF AMHERST	Amherst	WI	**A-**	A-	B+	52.3	0.28	7.9	2.0	21.5	31.5	**10.0**	14.6	26.3
▲ INTERNATIONAL BK OF CHICAGO	Chicago	IL	**C**	C	B-	526.5	10.23	3.1	1.1	10.2	38.2	**9.1**	10.4	18.7
INTERNATIONAL BK OF COMMERCE	Brownsville	TX	**A-**	A-	A-	1048.2	0.46	6.9	0.6	4.4	51.6	**10.0**	13.7	28.6

Asset Quality Index	Adjusted Non-Performing Loans as a % of Total Loans	Adjusted Non-Performing Loans as a % of Capital	Net Charge-Offs Avg Loans	Profitability Index	Net Income ($Mil)	Return on Assets (R.O.A.)	Return on Equity (R.O.E.)	Net Interest Spread	Overhead Efficiency Ratio	Liquidity Index	Liquidity Ratio	Hot Money Ratio	Stability Index
5.0	2.09	10.2	0.00	**2.3**	0.5	0.28	2.95	3.70	92.5	**5.5**	39.4	6.3	**4.5**
5.3	0.47	3.6	0.03	**5.3**	3.7	0.84	9.04	5.35	72.7	**1.4**	17.9	27.0	**5.6**
7.8	0.20	1.1	-0.10	**7.6**	1.7	1.85	19.67	3.83	56.6	**2.1**	35.5	29.0	**7.6**
4.2	0.89	6.4	0.26	**4.0**	1.1	1.55	14.79	4.31	88.3	**0.6**	10.6	54.9	**2.3**
5.1	1.25	5.3	-0.31	**2.1**	1.2	0.33	2.83	3.43	92.3	**6.1**	42.2	3.5	**5.1**
8.0	1.18	3.4	0.24	**6.5**	1.4	2.60	10.39	3.18	78.3	**3.5**	35.2	15.9	**5.6**
1.6	4.49	27.8	0.66	**4.7**	1.6	0.75	8.08	3.70	73.4	**4.8**	25.4	5.0	**5.5**
5.5	1.91	5.6	-0.02	**3.7**	0.7	0.85	5.47	3.11	66.3	**5.1**	45.2	10.9	**7.7**
3.8	2.86	16.0	0.55	**2.5**	1.7	0.46	6.19	3.45	76.6	**4.8**	18.7	3.8	**4.8**
4.2	1.44	10.9	-0.01	**3.3**	3.4	0.67	7.48	3.26	83.5	**3.7**	14.3	10.5	**5.3**
0.3	21.09	133.9	2.79	**0.0**	-1.5	-1.72	-26.67	3.65	121.1	**3.8**	44.2	16.9	**2.2**
6.5	0.20	1.0	0.01	**4.0**	0.8	0.80	7.81	3.56	75.8	**2.0**	26.9	22.1	**5.3**
7.0	0.77	4.8	0.00	**5.1**	0.7	0.92	9.02	5.01	77.4	**4.3**	23.5	8.0	**6.3**
6.5	0.24	1.5	0.05	**10.0**	7.2	1.86	14.33	4.81	36.9	**0.7**	4.7	32.8	**9.9**
3.9	5.65	17.4	-0.21	**4.3**	0.2	0.61	4.54	4.60	80.5	**3.0**	37.8	19.5	**5.1**
5.0	2.70	11.6	0.56	**3.8**	0.9	0.71	6.23	3.52	63.9	**1.3**	28.9	33.7	**6.3**
4.8	0.85	5.8	0.13	**4.4**	2.6	0.83	7.48	4.69	80.1	**3.5**	17.6	11.9	**5.7**
7.6	0.33	1.7	0.00	**4.9**	1.1	0.85	6.86	3.99	63.5	**2.1**	30.3	23.1	**6.7**
8.8	0.22	1.6	0.03	**8.3**	16.3	1.54	19.88	4.43	54.1	**2.7**	3.2	14.5	**7.7**
5.7	1.13	6.5	0.01	**1.5**	0.2	0.27	2.74	4.08	94.5	**1.9**	29.9	26.2	**3.4**
4.3	1.51	11.8	0.30	**2.5**	0.5	0.95	11.61	4.18	92.6	**3.3**	19.7	13.1	**2.7**
10.0	na	0.0	na	**9.5**	0.2	6.21	7.29	2.58	83.7	**5.0**	394.6	100.0	**5.8**
2.6	0.64	4.6	0.48	**6.1**	6.2	0.97	7.56	4.83	63.0	**1.3**	4.2	24.4	**6.9**
1.9	4.84	27.5	0.27	**4.9**	15.0	0.90	7.92	3.87	78.0	**5.0**	30.6	10.0	**7.0**
6.3	0.10	0.8	0.04	**6.1**	24.1	1.05	8.23	4.23	59.1	**1.7**	9.7	20.8	**9.5**
4.2	0.84	6.5	-0.01	**3.6**	0.9	0.92	10.55	3.75	80.2	**4.3**	24.9	7.8	**3.9**
0.3	20.14	144.0	-0.16	**0.0**	-0.9	-0.64	-17.31	1.94	114.3	**0.6**	19.9	78.3	**1.1**
5.3	2.13	9.1	0.04	**4.5**	0.7	0.92	9.91	3.80	68.2	**4.0**	38.5	14.6	**5.6**
1.5	3.77	18.8	0.72	**3.9**	0.5	0.96	6.08	4.20	81.3	**2.5**	5.3	15.4	**6.1**
5.6	1.21	9.7	0.09	**4.1**	1.4	0.58	5.84	3.53	72.1	**2.2**	4.7	17.2	**6.0**
2.3	2.96	20.2	0.46	**2.4**	0.7	0.42	5.20	3.73	90.8	**1.5**	19.6	25.7	**2.8**
1.9	0.57	5.1	0.10	**1.7**	1.2	0.15	0.96	3.32	91.3	**0.9**	15.9	34.7	**8.1**
2.0	4.76	30.2	0.04	**3.1**	1.1	0.39	3.81	4.55	89.9	**1.0**	19.3	34.0	**4.6**
6.4	2.21	4.8	-0.01	**7.0**	1.3	1.24	5.06	4.46	59.8	**5.8**	54.6	9.6	**5.7**
8.7	1.00	2.0	0.02	**7.9**	7.2	1.62	18.85	3.78	46.7	**3.2**	71.0	38.4	**7.4**
6.4	3.27	9.4	0.09	**2.3**	0.4	0.33	3.09	3.13	88.1	**3.5**	51.3	21.3	**5.5**
2.6	3.26	19.7	0.24	**3.5**	5.0	0.64	5.77	3.58	71.7	**1.7**	10.6	21.5	**6.5**
3.6	0.87	5.5	0.16	**5.0**	2.7	0.90	7.99	4.60	71.4	**2.7**	19.1	15.8	**5.5**
5.9	0.29	2.2	0.04	**5.1**	1.5	0.85	8.32	3.69	61.9	**0.6**	5.0	39.8	**6.2**
7.5	0.08	0.5	-0.06	**3.5**	0.5	0.40	3.18	3.74	84.5	**1.8**	14.7	19.9	**5.8**
2.4	3.29	22.0	0.53	**3.9**	1.4	0.63	6.19	4.25	82.2	**1.9**	13.1	19.4	**3.5**
8.8	0.37	2.3	0.01	**4.1**	22.8	1.74	13.41	2.25	80.4	**1.5**	24.9	36.3	**10.0**
3.5	0.93	8.3	0.08	**7.7**	8.2	1.38	15.91	3.71	45.0	**2.2**	6.2	16.9	**4.2**
4.4	1.98	12.7	0.25	**4.8**	1.3	1.31	14.17	4.19	75.3	**2.6**	25.5	17.3	**4.0**
0.7	4.94	39.7	-0.53	**7.2**	0.8	1.67	17.34	4.75	64.3	**3.1**	4.7	12.6	**6.7**
7.6	0.24	1.8	0.06	**6.4**	4.7	1.17	11.85	4.25	56.5	**2.9**	20.0	14.8	**5.7**
4.5	1.62	9.4	-0.04	**2.8**	0.2	0.43	3.97	4.01	88.2	**1.8**	19.6	20.6	**3.6**
7.9	0.36	2.1	0.04	**5.2**	2.8	0.91	6.91	3.85	72.1	**3.7**	5.4	9.3	**8.1**
5.0	1.08	3.9	0.10	**3.9**	11.0	0.78	3.50	3.32	67.4	**1.4**	24.7	37.4	**8.0**
10.0	1.24	1.0	0.03	**1.8**	0.9	0.49	2.29	1.82	85.9	**6.9**	94.9	9.6	**7.3**
0.3	13.76	84.5	0.01	**2.7**	0.6	0.36	3.27	3.58	90.0	**3.9**	20.1	10.2	**5.1**
7.1	1.79	10.1	0.00	**3.2**	5.3	0.45	6.46	1.63	63.4	**3.3**	60.6	35.9	**4.8**
2.9	2.81	21.3	0.04	**9.6**	41.7	2.19	17.26	4.08	48.0	**3.0**	10.7	14.1	**10.0**
6.9	2.23	7.2	0.01	**6.5**	1.3	1.09	6.17	3.14	49.8	**4.4**	41.0	13.3	**7.6**
8.0	2.30	4.4	3.38	**1.2**	-0.3	-0.20	-1.83	1.95	75.8	**3.5**	84.5	48.9	**5.4**
3.2	2.07	13.4	0.37	**0.4**	0.0	-0.02	-0.20	3.33	104.3	**0.9**	20.1	37.2	**3.2**
3.2	4.73	18.5	0.84	**3.5**	0.9	0.40	3.21	4.51	74.2	**2.4**	19.5	17.5	**6.5**
6.5	1.50	6.3	0.00	**5.3**	0.5	1.27	8.94	4.18	68.5	**5.0**	36.4	8.1	**8.2**
3.1	2.90	13.7	0.24	**6.0**	4.7	1.21	11.76	3.84	49.9	**2.3**	44.7	34.7	**7.0**
7.0	1.91	5.2	0.18	**9.1**	11.7	1.51	10.75	3.48	45.0	**3.2**	47.8	30.2	**8.9**

Name	City	State	Rating	2013 Rating	2012 Rating	Total Assets ($Mil)	One Year Asset Growth	Asset Mix (As a % of Total Assets) Comm-ercial Loans	Cons-umer Loans	Mort-gage Loans	Secur-ities	Capital-ization Index	Lever-age Ratio	Risk-Based Capital Ratio
INTERNATIONAL BK OF COMMERCE	Laredo	TX	**B+**	B+	C+	9845.3	0.07	12.0	0.7	7.8	35.1	**9.9**	11.0	17.1
INTERNATIONAL BK OF COMMERCE	Zapata	TX	**A-**	A-	A-	560.9	3.46	4.2	1.5	6.9	70.8	**9.5**	10.7	32.7
INTERNATIONAL CITY BANK NA	Long Beach	CA	**B+**	B+	C+	143.4	7.48	9.2	0.0	5.6	22.4	**10.0**	13.1	21.2
INTERNATIONAL FINANCE BANK	Miami	FL	**D-**	D-	D-	344.8	-0.06	5.3	2.4	34.0	16.9	**8.3**	9.8	17.4
▲ INTERSTATE BK SSB	Perryton	TX	**B-**	C+	C-	198.2	0.14	11.7	5.1	9.4	39.8	**6.0**	8.1	15.3
INTERSTATE FS&LA OF MCGREGOR	McGregor	IA	**D+**	C-	C	8.6	-1.90	0.0	0.8	74.8	0.1	**10.0**	19.2	46.3
INTERVEST NATIONAL BK	New York	NY	**C+**	C	C-	1505.0	-4.25	0.1	0.0	4.0	20.3	**10.0**	16.4	21.5
INTRACOASTAL BANK	Palm Coast	FL	**B+**	B+	B	221.4	11.33	4.7	0.2	1.9	34.2	**6.9**	8.9	13.8
INTRUST BANK NA	Wichita	KS	**B-**	B-	C	4380.8	7.33	22.5	5.1	4.0	39.0	**6.7**	8.7	13.2
INVESCO NATIONAL TRUST COMPANY	Atlanta	GA	**U**			39.2	-9999	0.0	0.0	0.0	0.0	**10.0**	67.9	183.1
INVESTAR BANK	Baton Rouge	LA	**B-**	B-	B-	783.6	39.18	5.7	21.0	16.2	11.8	**5.3**	9.0	11.2
INVESTMENT SB	Altoona	PA	**B-**	B-	B-	115.7	4.22	0.8	0.8	45.1	40.9	**10.0**	16.9	35.9
INVESTORS BANK	Short Hills	NJ	**B**	B-	C	17760.7	29.22	2.3	0.1	34.3	14.6	**10.0**	13.1	19.0
INVESTORS COMMUNITY BANK	Manitowoc	WI	**B**	B	C-	742.3	-0.48	6.8	0.0	3.2	10.5	**10.0**	13.7	17.8
INVESTORS COMMUNITY BANK	Chillicothe	MO	**A-**	A-	B+	67.0	2.82	0.6	2.5	20.5	59.3	**10.0**	12.5	29.9
INVESTRUST NA	Oklahoma City	OK	**U**	U	U	3.6	-0.27	0.0	0.0	0.0	83.4	**10.0**	87.0	120.5
INWOOD NATIONAL BK	Dallas	TX	**A+**	A+	A	1786.4	15.37	6.7	0.6	17.0	20.1	**9.0**	10.3	14.1
ION BANK	Naugatuck	CT	**C**	C-	C-	1047.0	7.32	5.0	6.9	35.3	10.1	**8.0**	9.6	14.0
IOWA FALLS STATE BK	Iowa Falls	IA	**B**	B	B	126.6	1.77	16.1	2.7	5.0	41.3	**6.8**	10.6	12.4
IOWA PRAIRIE BANK	Brunsville	IA	**D**	D+	C	68.5	5.16	8.7	2.5	3.4	43.8	**6.1**	8.1	14.4
IOWA SB	Carroll	IA	**B-**	B-	B-	172.5	0.73	18.8	1.2	5.3	27.9	**6.6**	8.6	13.5
IOWA STATE BK	Clarksville	IA	**C+**	C+	C+	300.8	16.25	11.5	1.0	2.7	23.1	**4.8**	8.2	10.9
IOWA STATE BK	Des Moines	IA	**A**	A	A-	342.5	4.88	2.5	0.4	10.3	52.5	**10.0**	15.0	25.9
IOWA STATE BK	Hull	IA	**A-**	B+	B	509.1	33.52	10.6	1.6	5.6	17.7	**10.0**	12.4	15.6
IOWA STATE BK	Sac City	IA	**B-**	C	C-	113.4	3.35	8.7	4.2	19.5	18.8	**8.0**	9.6	14.2
IOWA STATE BK	Wapello	IA	**B**	B-	B-	80.8	1.57	3.0	5.6	22.0	0.9	**10.0**	12.9	16.6
IOWA STATE BK	Algona	IA	**B+**	B	B-	288.2	1.53	6.8	1.8	9.2	34.9	**8.5**	10.0	15.3
IOWA STATE BK & TRUST CO	Fairfield	IA	**C+**	C+	C+	115.7	34.21	13.1	2.3	16.9	7.4	**7.6**	9.4	15.4
IOWA STATE SB	Knoxville	IA	**B-**	B-	B-	121.9	4.58	11.8	6.0	6.3	26.2	**6.5**	8.5	13.4
IOWA STATE SB	Creston	IA	**C+**	B-	B-	218.4	0.64	5.8	3.0	12.9	18.5	**5.3**	7.3	11.3
IOWA TRUST & SB	Centerville	IA	**A-**	A-	A-	174.1	-1.73	4.3	2.3	8.3	51.0	**8.8**	10.2	15.0
IOWA TRUST & SB	Emmetsburg	IA	**B+**	B+	B	188.7	7.99	5.5	1.2	6.7	28.9	**7.2**	9.3	12.7
IOWA-NEBRASKA STATE BK	South Sioux City	NE	**C**	C	D+	203.0	4.16	5.7	3.1	12.9	34.9	**6.7**	8.7	14.9
IPAVA STATE BK	Lewistown	IL	**B+**	B+	B	102.5	0.89	11.5	3.5	11.9	17.7	**7.4**	9.6	12.9
▲ IPSWICH STATE BK	Ipswich	SD	**B**	B-	A-	55.7	5.91	6.1	1.9	0.0	27.0	**10.0**	12.5	17.7
▲ IRELAND BANK	Malad City	ID	**C**	C-	D+	215.9	-1.90	15.4	1.4	3.9	30.4	**7.7**	9.5	15.5
IRON WORKERS SB	Aston	PA	**C**	C	C	179.9	6.33	0.5	0.0	51.2	7.3	**6.6**	8.6	13.3
IROQUOIS FARMERS STATE BK	Iroquois	IL	**C+**	C+	B-	87.6	-2.15	6.1	3.7	11.4	31.3	**7.7**	9.5	15.7
IROQUOIS FS&LA	Watseka	IL	**B**	B	B-	539.5	0.06	5.7	1.6	27.5	31.8	**10.0**	12.5	22.2
ISABELLA BANK	Mount Pleasant	MI	**B-**	B-	B-	1496.2	6.68	6.3	2.2	17.3	38.2	**5.9**	7.9	14.2
ISLANDERS BANK	Friday Harbor	WA	**A-**	B+	B-	250.9	5.07	4.2	1.8	17.9	8.1	**10.0**	13.5	19.4
ISRAEL DISCOUNT BK OF NEW YORK	New York	NY	**C**	C	C-	9774.3	0.57	26.2	0.7	0.0	38.3	**6.2**	8.2	13.0
ITASCA BANK & TRUST CO	Itasca	IL	**C**	C-	D-	441.6	3.24	19.6	0.2	10.4	24.0	**7.1**	9.1	13.2
ITS BANK	Johnston	IA	**U**	U	B+	6.2	4.82	0.0	0.0	0.0	26.0	**10.0**	91.9	444.1
▼ IUKA STATE BK	Iuka	IL	**C**	C+	C+	62.7	23.75	13.6	5.1	12.6	2.2	**5.3**	8.4	11.3
▲ IXONIA BANK	Ixonia	WI	**D+**	D	D-	269.3	-4.48	6.0	0.3	6.5	34.4	**9.9**	10.9	18.0
JACKSBORO NATIONAL BK	Jacksboro	TX	**B**	B	A-	241.2	10.67	10.5	2.5	9.1	49.8	**6.8**	8.8	17.7
JACKSON COUNTY BANK	Black River Falls	WI	**A-**	B	B	201.3	-4.27	1.8	3.7	19.1	17.1	**10.0**	11.8	16.8
▲ JACKSON COUNTY BANK	Seymour	IN	**B-**	C+	C-	440.4	2.69	4.3	0.8	21.2	17.8	**9.2**	10.4	17.2
JACKSON COUNTY BANK	McKee	KY	**A**	A	A	130.0	-0.27	1.9	10.3	20.5	40.2	**10.0**	24.7	47.9
JACKSON FS&LA	Jackson	MN	**B**	B	B	37.6	2.90	3.9	3.3	29.7	44.3	**10.0**	20.5	33.8
JACKSON PARISH BANK	Jonesboro	LA	**B-**	C+	C	63.2	4.18	5.1	6.1	11.9	63.2	**10.0**	12.4	32.5
JACKSON SB SSB	Sylva	NC	**C+**	C+	B-	34.3	-2.99	0.0	0.7	63.2	0.0	**10.0**	18.6	34.4
JACKSONVILLE BANK	Jacksonville	FL	**D**	D	D-	509.8	-0.59	9.4	0.4	9.3	16.2	**8.7**	10.1	15.1
JACKSONVILLE SB	Jacksonville	IL	**A-**	A-	B-	314.2	-2.00	7.9	4.1	16.6	33.7	**10.0**	12.7	19.5
JAMES POLK STONE COMMUNITY BK	Portales	NM	**B-**	B	B-	200.8	10.78	6.0	5.6	22.0	29.8	**8.4**	9.9	18.1
▲ JAMESTOWN STATE BK	Jamestown	KS	**C**	C-	B-	19.2	0.75	1.8	2.3	1.9	62.2	**10.0**	14.8	36.4
JANESVILLE STATE BK	Janesville	MN	**A-**	A-	A-	63.6	6.22	1.9	2.0	17.5	22.1	**10.0**	12.4	17.0
JARRETTSVILLE FS&LA	Jarrettsville	MD	**B-**	B+	A-	115.9	5.04	0.0	0.2	70.5	12.4	**10.0**	13.4	26.3
JD BANK	Jennings	LA	**B**	B	B-	750.8	3.82	9.0	6.3	18.6	25.7	**6.7**	8.7	14.3

Asset Quality Index	Adjusted Non-Performing Loans as a % of Total Loans	Adjusted Non-Performing Loans as a % of Capital	Net Charge-Offs Avg Loans	Profitability Index	Net Income ($Mil)	Return on Assets (R.O.A.)	Return on Equity (R.O.E.)	Net Interest Spread	Overhead Efficiency Ratio	Liquidity Index	Liquidity Ratio	Hot Money Ratio	Stability Index
5.7	1.42	6.5	0.17	**6.2**	88.9	1.20	9.36	3.42	58.0	**2.9**	25.0	18.1	**9.1**
9.1	0.79	1.5	0.41	**7.0**	5.1	1.24	10.48	2.85	52.1	**1.8**	31.7	30.1	**8.0**
5.7	2.11	8.8	-0.43	**5.7**	0.8	0.76	5.45	5.14	88.1	**1.2**	19.2	30.4	**5.8**
0.3	9.33	53.3	0.58	**2.2**	0.7	0.28	2.28	3.85	92.1	**1.9**	28.6	24.7	**5.1**
4.4	2.45	11.9	0.21	**4.4**	1.6	1.11	13.19	3.26	68.7	**5.7**	57.5	11.0	**4.5**
9.9	0.00	0.0	0.00	**0.8**	0.0	-0.24	-1.21	3.14	104.6	**2.9**	25.2	15.3	**6.1**
3.1	3.31	13.9	-0.03	**7.8**	15.2	1.29	8.16	3.22	34.2	**1.2**	22.2	37.3	**8.1**
8.9	0.06	0.3	0.00	**5.6**	2.3	1.40	17.07	3.42	56.3	**3.2**	37.3	18.2	**6.1**
4.4	2.29	13.3	0.45	**4.0**	34.6	1.08	12.59	2.69	67.7	**5.3**	24.8	4.8	**6.6**
10.0	na	0.0	na	**9.5**	1.9	2.49	4.06	0.00	94.6	**4.0**	236.7	101.0	**7.0**
5.4	0.24	2.1	0.06	**4.0**	3.6	0.68	7.56	3.93	73.1	**4.2**	12.9	7.2	**4.9**
10.0	0.05	0.1	0.02	**2.9**	0.4	0.41	2.44	2.83	82.8	**4.1**	47.3	16.5	**7.6**
6.1	0.95	5.5	0.09	**4.6**	95.1	0.75	7.00	3.37	58.9	**3.6**	16.5	11.8	**7.0**
4.4	1.45	7.7	0.03	**6.6**	6.2	1.11	8.32	3.32	53.7	**0.6**	12.1	50.1	**7.3**
8.5	1.65	4.5	-0.01	**5.0**	0.6	1.13	8.79	3.84	68.0	**4.3**	69.4	18.3	**6.7**
10.0	na	0.0	na	**0.7**	0.0	-1.28	-1.42	2.35	101.5	**4.0**	588.2	101.0	**2.7**
7.1	0.22	1.5	-0.01	**8.4**	25.0	2.02	16.38	3.89	49.1	**3.4**	20.2	13.0	**10.0**
3.8	2.40	18.5	0.06	**2.7**	3.3	0.43	4.40	3.32	83.2	**3.9**	10.4	9.3	**7.1**
4.7	2.32	10.7	0.08	**6.2**	1.3	1.37	12.03	4.01	60.8	**4.6**	49.9	14.4	**8.1**
1.5	4.93	29.3	0.02	**3.7**	0.4	0.78	11.05	3.26	74.0	**3.8**	10.6	9.3	**2.6**
4.7	1.19	7.7	0.25	**4.2**	1.2	0.91	10.53	3.14	69.9	**5.1**	33.9	6.9	**6.0**
4.1	0.77	6.2	0.16	**6.5**	3.2	1.48	18.67	3.30	41.4	**3.6**	27.5	12.6	**5.0**
6.8	2.60	6.5	-0.02	**9.1**	5.2	2.04	14.10	3.80	52.7	**6.5**	63.9	7.5	**9.4**
6.8	0.58	3.1	0.02	**7.6**	4.9	1.34	11.09	3.84	50.9	**4.3**	28.6	9.8	**7.2**
4.4	0.82	5.4	0.14	**6.0**	1.2	1.44	13.85	3.25	55.7	**4.3**	27.7	9.4	**7.0**
4.6	2.11	12.4	0.00	**5.5**	0.8	1.27	9.93	3.69	70.3	**3.9**	8.8	8.7	**6.1**
5.2	1.16	6.4	0.00	**6.5**	2.9	1.30	12.45	3.89	57.7	**3.6**	27.9	13.1	**6.4**
7.3	0.67	4.4	0.02	**4.4**	0.6	0.79	8.59	3.64	74.9	**5.4**	35.8	5.6	**4.0**
4.6	1.68	10.0	0.96	**5.1**	1.0	1.07	12.84	4.02	71.1	**5.4**	32.4	4.3	**4.8**
6.6	0.03	0.3	0.00	**3.2**	0.3	0.20	2.51	3.86	77.3	**4.1**	14.5	8.0	**5.1**
8.9	0.04	0.2	0.01	**5.6**	1.7	1.29	12.41	2.96	57.9	**4.0**	39.1	14.9	**7.4**
8.3	0.04	0.2	-0.01	**6.6**	1.7	1.25	12.84	3.89	52.3	**4.0**	10.4	8.3	**5.7**
3.0	3.52	18.6	0.21	**2.7**	0.6	0.41	4.85	2.92	89.5	**4.5**	20.9	5.9	**4.2**
8.2	0.02	0.1	0.05	**5.9**	1.1	1.37	14.36	4.28	70.0	**1.7**	12.3	20.9	**6.8**
7.2	0.00	0.0	-0.03	**4.6**	0.5	1.21	10.13	3.38	62.1	**1.8**	24.2	22.3	**7.4**
4.2	1.51	9.2	0.22	**2.9**	0.8	0.49	5.52	4.36	86.1	**4.3**	23.0	7.7	**4.5**
5.6	1.01	9.0	0.19	**2.8**	0.4	0.34	3.93	3.31	84.7	**2.7**	15.1	15.4	**4.5**
5.9	0.88	4.9	0.13	**3.3**	0.4	0.65	7.19	2.83	75.8	**4.6**	37.6	11.4	**4.6**
6.6	1.31	6.1	0.10	**3.9**	2.6	0.62	5.26	2.94	67.9	**1.2**	28.6	37.1	**7.5**
5.3	1.80	11.7	0.08	**4.8**	11.7	1.07	13.46	3.42	66.6	**2.5**	26.8	22.6	**7.0**
4.3	3.39	17.3	0.26	**7.3**	2.2	1.21	8.71	4.19	59.3	**4.0**	25.3	10.2	**8.7**
7.1	0.62	3.6	0.25	**3.1**	28.2	0.35	4.54	1.99	63.7	**2.2**	35.4	38.3	**4.8**
2.7	2.95	19.5	0.27	**3.6**	2.1	0.63	7.08	3.66	76.3	**1.8**	20.7	22.4	**4.2**
10.0	na	0.0	na	**9.5**	0.2	4.83	5.30	2.46	18.4	**5.0**	1142.8	100.0	**5.8**
4.0	1.81	16.2	0.04	**6.7**	0.6	1.22	14.94	3.58	51.6	**0.7**	14.0	45.0	**4.3**
3.4	3.80	15.2	1.62	**1.4**	0.3	0.14	1.31	3.08	96.9	**4.6**	42.7	12.4	**3.9**
7.9	0.35	1.6	-0.19	**4.5**	1.7	0.98	10.60	3.85	77.3	**5.1**	42.6	10.1	**6.0**
6.4	0.79	4.4	0.09	**8.3**	3.1	2.05	17.61	4.01	50.5	**1.6**	12.1	22.3	**8.5**
4.1	2.22	13.1	0.06	**4.7**	3.2	0.96	9.73	3.18	70.8	**3.7**	26.4	12.2	**5.3**
7.9	1.60	3.1	0.49	**5.9**	1.1	1.06	4.44	3.85	60.0	**3.0**	46.4	24.5	**7.8**
9.4	0.47	1.0	0.00	**4.3**	0.2	0.86	4.17	4.40	66.5	**4.4**	38.9	12.8	**7.4**
5.4	5.65	13.0	0.11	**3.8**	0.5	0.97	7.80	3.40	74.0	**5.1**	38.7	8.7	**4.8**
9.4	0.00	0.0	0.09	**2.4**	0.0	0.17	0.90	3.04	89.2	**1.3**	20.8	29.4	**6.7**
0.6	5.16	28.3	0.32	**3.2**	2.6	0.70	7.10	4.00	81.4	**2.1**	28.1	21.2	**4.3**
6.1	1.08	4.8	0.37	**5.5**	2.7	1.15	8.95	3.88	67.1	**2.9**	28.8	16.8	**6.9**
3.9	3.02	14.4	-0.08	**6.0**	2.1	1.45	14.96	4.99	72.6	**5.7**	37.2	4.1	**5.6**
7.0	3.52	7.3	-0.02	**2.1**	0.1	0.43	2.70	3.03	83.4	**6.9**	74.3	3.0	**5.5**
8.9	0.11	0.5	-0.01	**5.5**	0.7	1.41	11.78	3.33	58.6	**3.9**	15.5	9.1	**7.9**
5.7	2.03	11.3	0.14	**1.5**	-0.5	-0.59	-4.51	3.14	127.2	**3.1**	20.5	14.2	**7.4**
5.3	0.85	5.7	0.06	**4.6**	4.8	0.87	9.12	4.45	77.4	**2.8**	18.5	15.3	**6.8**

Name	City	State	Rating	2013 Rating	2012 Rating	Total Assets ($Mil)	One Year Asset Growth	Asset Mix (As a % of Total Assets) Commercial Loans	Consumer Loans	Mortgage Loans	Securities	Capitalization Index	Leverage Ratio	Risk-Based Capital Ratio
JEFF BANK	Jeffersonville	NY	**B-**	C+	C+	447.7	3.40	6.9	1.0	23.6	24.6	**10.0**	11.3	18.9
JEFFERSON BANK	Fayette	MS	**A**	A	A-	113.1	5.54	13.4	0.8	0.7	36.2	**10.0**	14.8	23.7
JEFFERSON BANK	San Antonio	TX	**B+**	B+	B	1325.5	14.87	7.4	1.7	16.3	40.5	**5.7**	7.7	13.2
JEFFERSON BANK & TRUST CO	Eureka	MO	**C+**	C-	D-	478.5	-0.34	13.9	0.4	4.2	15.9	**10.0**	12.0	15.4
▲ JEFFERSON BANK OF FLORIDA	Oldsmar	FL	**C+**	C+	C	216.8	17.29	10.1	1.2	6.7	26.3	**10.0**	11.5	18.4
JEFFERSON BANK OF MISSOURI	Jefferson City	MO	**B-**	B-	B-	499.4	1.25	8.5	27.4	13.6	14.0	**5.1**	8.0	11.1
JEFFERSON COUNTY BANK	Daykin	NE	**B+**	B+	B+	46.5	2.73	1.6	2.2	1.7	21.7	**10.0**	12.1	23.6
JEFFERSON SECURITY BANK	Shepherdstown	WV	**C-**	C-	D+	284.7	-0.44	0.8	0.9	20.3	44.2	**6.0**	8.0	15.8
JERSEY SHORE STATE BK	Williamsport	PA	**B-**	C+	C	888.2	1.54	3.7	1.8	29.3	21.3	**6.4**	8.5	12.1
JERSEY STATE BK	Jerseyville	IL	**A-**	A-	B+	150.8	2.33	6.9	1.0	10.3	46.6	**10.0**	11.4	23.7
▼ JEWETT CITY SB	Jewett City	CT	**C+**	B-	C+	246.9	-1.25	3.1	0.9	38.2	22.0	**10.0**	16.1	30.6
JIM THORPE NATIONAL BK	Jim Thorpe	PA	**C+**	C+	C+	174.0	0.80	0.8	0.5	32.7	43.6	**6.7**	8.7	20.3
JOHN DEERE FINANCIAL FSB	Madison	WI	**A-**	A-	A-	2540.0	0.33	6.5	14.5	0.0	0.0	**10.0**	22.2	23.2
▲ JOHN MARSHALL BANK	Reston	VA	**A-**	B-	C+	758.3	20.85	10.2	0.2	2.1	7.7	**9.3**	13.2	14.4
JOHNSON BANK	Racine	WI	**B-**	B	C-	3762.9	2.50	15.3	1.4	21.0	11.2	**9.2**	10.5	15.3
JOHNSON CITY BANK	Johnson City	TX	**A-**	A-	B+	103.0	1.84	9.2	10.5	26.9	3.2	**10.0**	12.9	20.0
▼ JOHNSON COUNTY BANK	Mountain City	TN	**C**	C	C-	121.6	1.82	0.6	3.8	34.0	25.9	**10.0**	13.4	28.1
JOHNSON STATE BK	Johnson	KS	**C+**	C+	B-	74.8	1.53	6.5	1.5	3.6	43.3	**10.0**	14.3	22.2
JONAH BANK OF WYOMING	Casper	WY	**B+**	B+	B	267.9	11.58	16.2	0.3	8.6	25.3	**7.1**	9.0	15.8
JONES NATIONAL BK & TRUST CO	Seward	NE	**B-**	B-	B	233.8	2.56	20.7	1.8	6.6	31.0	**6.8**	8.8	13.2
JONESBORO STATE BK	Jonesboro	LA	**A-**	A-	A-	172.5	9.26	3.2	2.8	6.9	74.3	**10.0**	12.6	36.7
▼ JONESBURG STATE BK	Jonesburg	MO	**B-**	B	B-	69.1	1.65	5.5	2.1	29.5	4.1	**6.5**	8.5	14.0
JONESTOWN BANK & TRUST CO	Jonestown	PA	**C-**	D+	C-	451.0	7.65	3.5	17.8	26.0	6.7	**7.4**	9.8	12.9
JOURDANTON STATE BK	Jourdanton	TX	**B-**	B-	B+	168.4	15.72	3.4	2.3	2.0	63.9	**8.9**	10.3	26.7
JOY STATE BK	Joy	IL	**D**	C-	D	42.1	-7.63	5.2	6.1	22.5	14.9	**6.9**	8.9	15.2
▲ JPMORGAN BANK & TRUST CO NA	San Francisco	CA	**C-**	D+	D+	6608.8	-33.37	0.0	0.9	65.3	0.0	**5.8**	21.9	11.6
▲ JPMORGAN CHASE BANK DEARBORN	Dearborn	MI	**C**	C-	C+	60.3	-4.19	0.0	0.0	0.0	0.0	**10.0**	88.7	454.9
▲ JPMORGAN CHASE BANK NA	Columbus	OH	**C-**	C-	C-	2008808.0	0.95	6.2	4.5	7.0	17.4	**6.0**	8.0	12.1
JUNCTION NATIONAL BK	Junction	TX	**B+**	B+	A-	54.6	-0.44	6.7	4.1	6.2	54.3	**10.0**	11.5	25.5
JUNIATA VALLEY BANK	Mifflintown	PA	**B-**	B-	C+	477.5	5.69	4.6	0.9	27.1	31.2	**7.7**	9.5	15.8
JUSTIN STATE BK	Justin	TX	**A-**	B	C+	73.2	5.85	6.0	1.0	30.0	1.4	**10.0**	13.7	26.8
▲ KAHOKA STATE BK	Kahoka	MO	**C**	C-	C-	47.0	2.39	6.2	4.2	22.8	34.1	**8.2**	9.8	19.2
KALAMAZOO COUNTY STATE BK	Schoolcraft	MI	**C**	C	C+	94.1	4.42	2.2	7.5	14.2	39.0	**10.0**	12.1	25.4
KANSAS STATE BK	Ottawa	KS	**C+**	C+	C+	113.8	10.98	2.9	1.4	8.7	68.8	**6.9**	8.9	22.7
KANSAS STATE BK OF MANHATTAN	Manhattan	KS	**A-**	A-	A-	1192.3	17.24	14.7	0.7	15.7	19.5	**7.1**	9.1	14.2
KANSAS STATE BK OVERBROOK KS	Overbrook	KS	**B**	B-	B-	54.8	1.18	7.0	4.0	5.6	44.0	**10.0**	11.7	21.4
▲ KANSASLAND BANK	Quinter	KS	**C**	C-	D+	52.8	4.18	6.7	2.0	14.5	32.1	**6.6**	8.6	15.8
KANZA BANK	Kingman	KS	**B-**	B-	B	208.6	-1.89	9.4	0.8	17.9	18.7	**8.3**	9.9	14.3
KAPLAN STATE BK	Kaplan	LA	**A**	A	A	96.0	-0.36	1.5	3.7	12.1	55.7	**10.0**	12.2	31.6
KARNES COUNTY NATIONAL BK	Karnes City	TX	**B-**	C+	C+	325.4	14.24	4.1	2.0	5.7	61.6	**5.2**	7.2	17.9
▼ KASSON STATE BK	Kasson	MN	**D**	D+	C	58.6	-6.28	12.7	7.4	12.4	26.6	**6.3**	8.3	13.1
KATAHDIN TRUST CO	Patten	ME	**C+**	C+	C+	643.4	4.49	19.7	2.4	20.3	8.7	**8.1**	9.7	13.8
▲ KAW VALLEY BANK	Topeka	KS	**D**	D-	D-	355.7	-3.02	19.8	2.2	13.8	25.3	**7.5**	9.3	14.6
KAW VALLEY STATE BK	Eudora	KS	**C-**	C-	C	42.9	7.55	9.6	6.3	18.3	32.4	**6.1**	8.1	12.1
KAW VALLEY STATE BK & TRUST CO	Wamego	KS	**A-**	A-	A	151.8	1.81	9.7	2.6	15.9	35.8	**10.0**	11.3	20.6
▲ KCB BANK	Kearney	MO	**A-**	A-	B+	209.3	5.66	8.4	0.8	9.4	33.2	**10.0**	12.3	19.2
KEARNEY TRUST CO	Kearney	MO	**A-**	A-	A-	151.8	2.07	6.1	4.5	18.6	18.0	**9.7**	10.8	18.6
KEARNY COUNTY BANK	Lakin	KS	**A**	A	A	187.1	1.21	13.6	3.1	12.4	24.5	**10.0**	14.8	21.0
KEARNY FSB	Fairfield	NJ	**C-**	C-	C+	3513.5	9.10	2.1	0.1	18.5	38.3	**9.3**	10.5	19.9
KENDALL STATE BK	Valley Falls	KS	**E**	E-	E-	37.9	3.72	7.9	1.6	8.8	1.1	**4.8**	6.8	12.0
KENNEBEC FS&LA OF WATERVILLE	Waterville	ME	**C-**	C	C	83.8	3.39	0.4	0.3	71.6	3.2	**6.7**	8.7	13.7
KENNEBEC SB	Augusta	ME	**B-**	B-	B-	789.8	-1.15	3.7	0.4	56.4	13.0	**10.0**	12.9	20.1
KENNEBUNK SB	Kennebunk	ME	**B+**	B	B-	949.0	5.92	3.0	0.2	28.4	8.2	**10.0**	11.7	15.1
KENNETT NATIONAL BK	Kennett	MO	**B-**	B	B	104.5	12.83	22.6	4.1	18.5	26.5	**10.0**	11.7	16.5
KENNEY BANK & TRUST	Kenney	IL	**C-**	C	C+	25.4	-56.87	11.2	0.0	20.3	1.1	**10.0**	24.7	75.4
▲ KENSINGTON BANK	Kensington	MN	**B-**	C-	D-	142.0	32.21	13.1	1.9	13.2	14.5	**7.5**	9.3	13.8
▲ KENTLAND BANK	Kentland	IN	**A-**	B	B-	299.3	2.90	5.9	2.0	10.2	37.1	**10.0**	12.1	20.4
KENTLAND FS&LA	Kentland	IN	**D**	D	D	4.8	0.60	0.7	0.3	83.6	3.9	**10.0**	13.3	28.4
KENTUCKY BANK	Paris	KY	**B-**	C+	C+	792.7	6.96	3.8	2.1	19.1	27.0	**6.7**	8.7	13.5
▼ KENTUCKY FARMERS BANK CORP	Ashland	KY	**A-**	A	A+	168.3	1.44	7.8	5.8	16.5	47.4	**10.0**	21.7	36.1

Arrows denote recent upgrades ▲ or downgrades ▼

Asset Quality Index	Adjusted Non-Performing Loans as a % of Total Loans	Adjusted Non-Performing Loans as a % of Capital	Net Charge-Offs / Avg Loans	Profitability Index	Net Income ($Mil)	Return on Assets (R.O.A.)	Return on Equity (R.O.E.)	Net Interest Spread	Overhead Efficiency Ratio	Liquidity Index	Liquidity Ratio	Hot Money Ratio	Stability Index
3.7	4.17	20.9	0.07	**5.4**	3.8	1.13	10.06	4.44	66.5	**3.7**	17.1	10.8	**6.4**
8.5	0.04	0.1	0.04	**9.4**	1.1	1.42	9.38	4.53	51.4	**0.6**	9.9	43.3	**8.0**
6.7	0.69	4.6	0.06	**5.4**	13.1	1.40	18.51	3.48	67.5	**6.3**	44.6	6.3	**7.2**
4.7	1.23	6.7	0.30	**3.3**	2.3	0.66	5.01	3.06	68.8	**2.9**	14.0	14.2	**5.2**
8.0	0.66	3.6	0.09	**2.8**	0.5	0.33	3.13	3.23	85.3	**1.5**	20.6	25.6	**5.7**
3.4	1.04	8.4	0.19	**9.5**	5.9	1.59	19.22	4.15	49.2	**3.8**	12.6	9.9	**6.9**
8.8	0.00	0.0	0.01	**6.3**	0.5	1.46	12.41	3.68	53.5	**5.0**	54.4	12.3	**7.3**
3.4	5.77	31.0	0.01	**2.0**	0.4	0.20	2.86	2.90	89.1	**2.9**	17.2	14.8	**2.6**
4.9	1.10	8.4	0.48	**6.9**	9.8	1.48	16.45	3.81	62.8	**3.7**	10.7	10.2	**7.4**
6.9	1.50	5.1	0.28	**7.3**	1.4	1.33	11.29	3.49	52.8	**5.3**	42.9	8.7	**6.5**
6.5	1.93	7.0	0.26	**2.6**	0.9	0.46	2.71	3.46	88.2	**5.1**	37.7	8.4	**7.4**
7.5	0.52	2.6	0.05	**2.9**	0.7	0.54	6.94	3.30	80.0	**4.6**	23.2	6.0	**4.3**
5.8	0.11	0.5	0.57	**10.0**	69.5	4.27	16.84	7.98	37.0	**0.0**	0.0	99.3	**10.0**
7.0	0.22	1.4	0.06	**6.7**	5.8	1.10	8.26	4.22	56.3	**0.6**	6.6	45.0	**7.5**
5.6	1.33	8.4	0.24	**3.8**	19.8	0.68	5.39	3.46	79.0	**4.4**	10.4	5.5	**7.5**
5.8	1.47	8.3	0.09	**7.0**	1.3	1.65	12.98	4.54	60.7	**1.2**	24.7	32.3	**7.6**
1.7	10.61	39.0	0.71	**3.9**	0.6	0.69	5.18	3.45	70.2	**2.1**	39.6	32.9	**6.8**
8.9	0.61	1.7	0.02	**3.3**	0.4	0.64	4.73	3.49	81.0	**5.4**	47.0	8.8	**7.3**
7.2	0.03	0.2	0.00	**5.7**	2.5	1.26	14.15	4.04	69.0	**4.2**	35.7	12.8	**6.7**
6.1	0.35	2.3	0.51	**3.9**	1.5	0.88	10.30	3.30	69.9	**3.5**	10.2	11.1	**5.1**
6.7	4.14	6.1	0.10	**7.3**	2.1	1.65	12.60	3.65	41.9	**2.6**	52.4	38.3	**8.8**
5.6	1.26	10.4	0.00	**7.5**	0.9	1.79	21.27	4.47	63.1	**2.5**	19.9	16.8	**6.1**
2.2	2.04	16.5	0.27	**5.1**	2.9	0.87	8.94	3.69	63.5	**2.3**	5.6	16.5	**5.9**
8.3	0.04	0.1	0.06	**3.7**	0.9	0.74	7.36	2.90	73.9	**7.6**	79.6	2.4	**5.7**
2.3	3.34	19.1	0.20	**1.8**	0.0	0.01	0.07	3.56	76.7	**4.4**	31.1	10.2	**4.3**
1.7	12.06	44.3	0.01	**9.3**	106.5	1.87	9.66	3.44	8.2	**0.2**	6.5	100.0	**7.7**
10.0	0.00	0.0	0.00	**1.9**	0.1	0.12	0.13	0.19	3.6	**5.0**	828.1	95.2	**7.7**
5.0	2.63	10.2	0.33	**4.2**	11453.0	0.80	8.67	1.98	69.5	**7.3**	62.9	3.6	**6.5**
9.1	0.21	0.5	0.31	**4.7**	0.5	1.18	10.30	3.42	70.5	**5.7**	71.4	11.5	**7.1**
4.4	1.99	12.2	0.09	**4.0**	3.1	0.88	9.05	3.49	73.1	**4.7**	29.5	7.3	**6.2**
6.4	1.62	6.9	-0.04	**9.2**	1.2	2.33	17.65	4.95	63.2	**5.7**	40.1	5.2	**8.1**
4.6	1.29	6.1	0.87	**3.1**	0.2	0.54	5.56	3.10	76.2	**3.0**	42.5	22.0	**4.1**
8.8	0.44	1.5	0.24	**2.1**	0.2	0.24	1.98	3.53	96.2	**5.6**	61.1	10.7	**5.9**
9.8	0.00	0.0	0.26	**3.2**	0.6	0.69	8.21	2.49	75.4	**4.3**	21.7	7.4	**4.6**
7.8	0.47	3.5	0.01	**9.2**	16.4	1.93	21.59	3.94	50.0	**0.8**	14.5	43.5	**9.5**
8.0	0.45	1.6	-0.01	**4.5**	0.4	0.94	8.04	3.98	66.5	**4.4**	44.7	14.0	**5.7**
5.8	0.37	2.3	0.08	**3.0**	0.2	0.60	6.71	3.32	80.7	**1.0**	25.8	36.2	**4.7**
6.6	0.07	0.5	-0.15	**4.1**	1.4	0.90	8.62	4.07	79.1	**2.1**	10.4	17.9	**5.6**
9.4	0.13	0.3	0.00	**6.9**	1.1	1.56	11.51	3.75	60.7	**4.1**	55.5	17.0	**8.9**
9.0	0.23	0.8	0.06	**5.5**	2.8	1.19	18.67	3.15	47.2	**6.5**	67.2	7.7	**3.7**
1.6	5.90	36.9	0.83	**1.3**	-0.1	-0.11	-1.35	3.18	88.5	**5.6**	41.7	6.5	**2.7**
3.9	1.16	9.2	0.08	**4.2**	3.3	0.68	6.89	3.93	73.4	**1.3**	8.7	25.0	**7.2**
1.1	8.62	49.7	0.04	**2.2**	1.8	0.67	6.23	3.26	78.4	**0.9**	21.5	36.2	**4.1**
5.3	0.59	3.6	0.00	**5.0**	0.4	1.20	14.58	4.25	75.5	**4.1**	23.0	9.1	**3.7**
6.6	1.10	5.2	0.09	**7.1**	1.8	1.55	14.13	3.31	60.1	**4.1**	30.5	11.5	**8.1**
5.7	2.50	11.3	0.01	**5.3**	1.8	1.16	9.58	4.11	72.5	**3.3**	21.8	13.1	**7.6**
7.2	0.41	2.1	0.09	**6.6**	1.8	1.59	14.81	3.72	59.2	**4.1**	32.5	11.9	**6.9**
6.2	1.08	4.8	-0.04	**9.1**	2.9	2.07	13.14	4.74	50.6	**3.5**	15.1	11.4	**9.2**
5.5	1.42	6.8	0.13	**2.1**	7.7	0.30	2.22	2.51	81.4	**3.3**	37.7	21.0	**8.8**
3.0	1.98	16.0	0.66	**2.8**	0.1	0.43	5.99	3.73	88.7	**5.4**	36.0	5.4	**1.0**
4.7	0.96	9.6	0.22	**1.7**	0.1	0.12	1.38	3.41	94.9	**1.6**	4.2	20.5	**4.5**
5.9	1.62	10.0	0.05	**3.5**	4.5	0.76	5.86	3.06	74.6	**2.3**	12.9	17.5	**7.5**
5.9	1.40	9.4	0.11	**5.1**	6.0	0.88	7.72	4.13	73.2	**4.7**	7.9	3.3	**7.0**
5.6	2.11	11.0	0.32	**3.7**	0.5	0.61	5.07	4.19	83.8	**1.8**	28.3	26.2	**5.3**
7.3	2.25	3.0	9.64	**0.0**	-1.5	-5.98	-24.06	1.93	187.2	**3.2**	81.2	43.4	**5.4**
4.0	1.36	9.8	0.44	**4.2**	1.0	1.13	10.07	4.03	75.5	**4.2**	21.3	8.3	**4.2**
5.7	1.88	7.5	0.08	**5.5**	2.5	1.12	9.52	3.85	60.7	**3.1**	42.5	20.9	**6.5**
3.7	5.06	30.9	0.00	**1.3**	0.0	-0.03	-0.21	4.21	100.7	**0.8**	14.5	34.8	**1.9**
4.3	1.48	10.3	0.06	**4.3**	5.6	0.94	9.47	3.79	76.1	**2.6**	7.4	15.1	**6.1**
5.2	5.89	10.7	0.35	**9.9**	3.7	2.91	12.26	5.79	56.1	**5.8**	67.1	11.8	**9.6**

Name	City	State	Rating	2013 Rating	2012 Rating	Total Assets ($Mil)	One Year Asset Growth	Asset Mix (As a % of Total Assets) Commercial Loans	Consumer Loans	Mortgage Loans	Securities	Capitalization Index	Leverage Ratio	Risk-Based Capital Ratio
KENTUCKY FS&LA	Covington	KY	D	D	D	36.8	-3.74	0.0	1.0	55.2	10.1	6.4	8.4	19.9
KENTUCKY HOME BANK INC	Bardstown	KY	B	B-	B	108.5	-1.53	4.1	3.2	27.3	15.7	10.0	14.7	22.9
KENTUCKY NEIGHBORHOOD BANK	Elizabethtown	KY	C	C	C	130.9	1.91	4.5	1.2	29.7	11.7	9.0	11.3	14.2
▲ KERNDT BROTHERS SB	Lansing	IA	B+	B	B+	242.3	-3.97	4.2	0.8	9.0	20.7	10.0	11.4	15.8
▲ KEY COMMUNITY BANK	Inver Grove Height	MN	D	E-	E	42.9	0.45	19.2	1.9	8.8	0.0	7.9	9.6	16.3
KEY NATIONAL TRUST CO DELAWARE	Wilmington	DE	U	U	B-	3.6	-3.47	0.0	0.0	0.0	0.0	10.0	99.0	468.6
KEYBANK NA	Cleveland	OH	B	B	B-	87398.3	-0.79	23.8	6.3	7.2	19.6	8.7	10.5	13.9
KEYSAVINGS BANK	Wisconsin Rapids	WI	D+	D+	B-	80.0	1.53	0.0	0.5	38.0	42.7	10.0	13.7	36.0
KEYSTONE BANK	Auburn	AL	B+	B+	B+	239.1	1.74	5.8	3.7	21.3	16.5	9.8	10.9	15.2
KEYSTONE SB	Keystone	IA	B	B	B-	92.1	2.93	5.5	4.5	24.9	27.4	9.2	10.7	14.3
KEYWORTH BANK	Johns Creek	GA	B-	B-	C	390.8	16.70	10.0	0.3	2.0	27.1	9.9	10.9	15.8
KILGORE NATIONAL BK	Kilgore	TX	B-	B-	C+	92.4	2.78	8.4	3.9	24.1	3.3	8.8	10.2	18.5
KILLBUCK SB CO	Killbuck	OH	B-	B-	C+	480.0	4.40	7.8	1.2	21.2	35.1	8.3	9.9	16.5
▲ KINDRED STATE BK	Kindred	ND	D	D-	D+	28.0	0.27	4.1	5.2	2.3	16.5	5.2	7.2	15.6
KING SOUTHERN BANK	Chaplin	KY	B	B-	B-	183.8	4.68	5.9	1.1	27.0	12.8	9.0	10.3	14.4
KINGSLEY STATE BK	Kingsley	IA	A-	B+	A	174.3	14.03	6.3	2.3	10.8	32.9	10.0	12.5	19.0
KINGSTON NATIONAL BK	Kingston	OH	B	B	B	244.1	7.51	10.2	2.3	22.1	26.4	8.2	9.8	16.4
KINGSTREE S&LA	Kingstree	SC	C+	C+	C	34.2	2.61	0.5	0.6	39.5	20.7	10.0	14.4	34.1
KIRKPATRICK BANK	Edmond	OK	B-	C+	C-	627.3	1.03	8.3	0.5	4.6	25.0	7.6	9.4	13.7
KIRKWOOD BANK & TRUST CO	Bismarck	ND	C+	C	C-	214.1	-0.77	10.4	3.2	10.5	16.0	5.6	7.6	12.1
KIRKWOOD BANK OF NEVADA	Las Vegas	NV	C+	C	C-	72.4	34.11	17.2	0.0	3.1	0.0	10.0	12.6	18.3
KISH BANK	Belleville	PA	C+	C+	C+	655.6	3.77	8.5	1.1	20.6	28.8	6.9	8.9	13.3
KITSAP BANK	Port Orchard	WA	C+	C+	C+	954.6	1.97	4.4	0.7	6.2	41.0	7.3	9.2	16.2
KLEBERG BANK NA	Kingsville	TX	B-	B-	C+	499.6	6.21	6.5	12.8	10.5	37.1	6.0	8.0	15.0
KLEINBANK	Big Lake	MN	C+	C+	C	1601.4	1.25	4.4	1.4	5.3	48.8	6.9	9.0	16.3
KODABANK	Drayton	ND	B+	B+	B	141.5	0.99	11.8	9.5	7.8	19.9	8.2	9.8	14.6
KOPERNIK FEDERAL BANK	Baltimore	MD	C+	C	C	68.5	-2.24	0.0	0.1	55.9	10.8	10.0	11.8	29.3
KOSCIUSZKO FSB	Baltimore	MD	C+	C+	C	12.2	0.52	0.0	0.1	66.3	3.1	10.0	21.0	44.6
KRESS NATIONAL BK	Kress	TX	B-	B-	B-	43.1	-1.65	6.8	4.6	0.7	32.6	8.6	10.0	17.3
▼ KS BANK INC	Smithfield	NC	D+	C-	D+	312.1	2.78	3.3	0.8	24.8	23.1	7.8	9.6	15.1
KSB BANK	Keokuk	IA	B-	C+	C-	114.7	5.09	6.3	1.6	16.9	27.9	5.7	7.7	13.3
LA MONTE COMMUNITY BANK	La Monte	MO	B	B-	B-	27.7	-2.09	3.7	2.3	18.7	20.8	9.6	10.8	18.5
LA PORTE SAVINGS BANK	La Porte	IN	B	B	B-	503.5	2.61	3.4	1.0	10.0	30.5	10.0	12.4	19.2
LA SALLE STATE BK	La Salle	IL	C	C	C-	117.1	2.56	9.1	2.1	12.9	37.9	6.7	8.7	17.8
LABETTE BANK	Altamont	KS	B	B	B-	354.5	3.12	3.5	3.3	22.4	30.0	8.3	9.9	17.6
LADYSMITH FS&LA	Ladysmith	WI	D+	D+	D+	47.1	1.81	7.1	3.5	37.6	29.4	9.4	10.6	22.2
LAFAYETTE AMBASSADOR BANK	Bethlehem	PA	B-	B-	B-	1449.3	2.75	7.8	1.5	10.9	16.7	9.8	10.9	15.4
LAFAYETTE COMMUNITY BANK	Lafayette	IN	C+	C+	C	157.6	3.63	4.9	0.1	17.2	27.3	9.9	11.0	15.3
▼ LAFAYETTE STATE BK	Mayo	FL	D-	D	C-	93.3	-2.79	5.1	3.5	14.4	6.0	2.0	5.5	9.0
LAGRANGE BANKING CO	LaGrange	GA	B-	B	B-	140.1	12.54	6.9	0.9	16.6	13.9	10.0	11.2	16.2
LAKE AREA BANK	Lindstrom	MN	D-	D-	D-	270.4	-0.67	8.6	0.6	14.8	26.7	6.8	8.8	13.4
▲ LAKE BANK	Two Harbors	MN	D-	E+	E+	109.9	8.33	7.6	1.4	28.0	21.5	6.5	8.5	15.3
LAKE CITY BANK	Warsaw	IN	B+	B	B-	3345.5	10.25	30.8	1.4	4.7	14.2	8.7	10.8	14.0
LAKE CITY FEDERAL BANK	Lake City	MN	D+	D+	D-	67.7	-5.69	1.4	2.4	41.5	12.8	9.7	10.8	17.2
LAKE COMMUNITY BANK	Long Lake	MN	C+	C-	D+	110.4	1.14	6.4	0.8	7.8	24.4	10.0	12.7	18.5
LAKE COUNTRY COMMUNITY BANK	Morristown	MN	D-	D-	E	29.7	-1.10	12.1	2.0	30.3	1.0	4.0	6.0	11.8
▼ LAKE COUNTY BANK	Saint Ignatius	MT	D+	D+	C-	30.7	1.39	7.2	8.9	3.2	2.0	10.0	11.5	20.4
LAKE ELMO BANK	Lake Elmo	MN	C+	C+	C-	309.5	2.37	4.0	2.0	22.1	32.5	6.9	8.9	15.4
LAKE FEDERAL BANK FSB	Hammond	IN	C+	C+	C+	66.6	-4.07	0.4	0.7	59.2	3.7	10.0	21.5	44.8
LAKE FOREST BANK & TRUST CO	Lake Forest	IL	B+	B-	B-	2506.6	7.25	47.7	3.5	3.8	9.1	6.0	8.9	11.7
LAKE NATIONAL BK	Mentor	OH	C	C+	C	140.8	1.78	12.1	0.8	26.2	1.1	7.4	9.2	13.2
LAKE REGION BANK	New London	MN	C	C	C-	108.0	5.08	13.7	4.2	5.3	34.4	6.1	8.1	15.2
LAKE SHORE SAVINGS BANK	Dunkirk	NY	B	B	B	486.1	0.31	2.0	0.3	37.0	29.0	10.0	13.3	26.5
LAKE SUNAPEE BANK FSB	Newport	NH	B-	B-	C+	1482.3	19.60	4.6	0.6	45.6	7.2	6.3	8.3	12.9
LAKE-OSCEOLA STATE BK	Baldwin	MI	C	C-	C-	192.0	0.74	2.8	6.0	35.5	10.4	8.1	9.8	15.3
LAKELAND BANK	Oak Ridge	NJ	B	B	C+	3493.5	6.08	6.5	0.8	17.4	15.6	6.4	8.4	12.2
LAKES STATE BK	Pequot Lakes	MN	B+	B+	B+	119.7	1.83	5.8	7.4	26.6	15.5	9.6	10.8	16.8
▲ LAKESIDE BANK	Chicago	IL	C	D+	D+	1184.0	5.95	4.5	0.1	8.7	4.6	10.0	13.4	16.1
LAKESIDE BANK	Lake Charles	LA	C	C-	D+	126.9	5.76	9.7	3.7	13.0	19.1	10.0	16.2	24.0
LAKESIDE BANK OF SALINA	Salina	OK	C	C	C+	33.1	3.25	12.1	20.2	39.5	3.2	9.5	10.7	15.8

Asset Quality Index	Adjusted Non-Performing Loans as a % of Total Loans	Adjusted Non-Performing Loans as a % of Capital	Net Charge-Offs Avg Loans	Profitability Index	Net Income ($Mil)	Return on Assets (R.O.A.)	Return on Equity (R.O.E.)	Net Interest Spread	Overhead Efficiency Ratio	Liquidity Index	Liquidity Ratio	Hot Money Ratio	Stability Index
8.6	0.37	2.5	0.06	**0.7**	0.0	-0.02	-0.26	3.23	104.4	**2.0**	34.1	28.6	**2.1**
4.6	2.40	10.6	1.15	**4.8**	0.7	0.80	5.62	3.90	67.2	**3.2**	28.3	14.9	**7.2**
2.6	2.96	20.2	0.09	**4.8**	0.8	0.85	7.57	4.41	75.4	**1.3**	13.3	27.2	**6.8**
8.4	0.15	0.8	-0.05	**5.1**	2.3	1.24	10.39	3.38	62.6	**3.9**	34.6	13.6	**6.8**
3.0	2.77	14.9	-0.05	**2.3**	0.2	0.48	5.08	3.54	108.3	**6.0**	41.4	3.8	**2.6**
10.0	na	0.0	na	**0.0**	-0.1	-3.08	-3.09	na	136.6	**4.0**	19994.1	101.0	**7.0**
5.5	0.84	5.0	0.23	**5.3**	650.2	1.04	9.49	2.93	64.9	**4.8**	14.1	3.9	**8.9**
8.9	0.75	2.3	0.06	**0.8**	0.0	-0.05	-0.35	2.49	100.3	**5.1**	60.3	12.8	**6.2**
5.5	0.86	4.9	0.15	**6.1**	2.0	1.13	10.77	3.88	60.9	**2.7**	29.7	18.0	**5.9**
6.7	0.52	3.0	0.09	**4.8**	0.7	1.05	10.21	4.09	74.6	**4.3**	28.9	9.9	**5.7**
7.3	0.23	1.2	0.04	**4.1**	2.0	0.70	6.54	3.41	67.2	**1.7**	30.0	29.4	**5.4**
7.9	0.56	2.8	0.02	**3.6**	0.3	0.49	4.77	4.05	83.0	**3.9**	40.8	15.8	**6.0**
6.5	0.65	3.5	0.19	**4.2**	3.0	0.87	8.71	3.05	62.1	**2.9**	31.6	17.8	**6.0**
6.7	0.50	2.8	-0.15	**3.1**	0.2	0.66	10.58	2.82	80.7	**6.0**	45.0	4.2	**2.6**
5.4	0.56	3.8	0.23	**6.2**	2.0	1.47	14.45	4.75	60.1	**0.8**	16.2	38.4	**6.1**
8.8	0.06	0.3	-0.04	**6.6**	2.0	1.55	12.37	3.53	49.3	**3.3**	45.3	20.1	**7.9**
6.2	0.57	3.5	0.03	**4.7**	1.6	0.89	9.21	3.67	66.0	**1.8**	21.2	22.4	**6.4**
6.6	1.99	7.5	0.18	**2.7**	0.1	0.38	2.58	2.91	83.6	**2.4**	44.6	31.1	**6.6**
5.1	0.35	2.2	0.11	**4.2**	5.2	1.06	11.66	3.28	59.9	**2.3**	10.7	16.9	**6.4**
4.6	1.73	12.0	-0.01	**4.0**	1.2	0.74	9.86	3.28	71.3	**5.0**	31.3	6.3	**4.6**
4.2	2.13	11.3	0.34	**3.0**	0.3	0.61	4.20	4.05	79.0	**1.5**	33.7	46.1	**4.9**
4.9	1.15	7.4	0.07	**3.7**	3.6	0.74	8.51	3.40	77.7	**2.8**	21.6	15.5	**6.5**
8.2	0.25	1.3	0.07	**3.3**	5.3	0.75	7.02	3.19	80.8	**5.4**	42.1	8.4	**6.1**
4.4	0.52	3.1	0.27	**4.3**	3.7	0.97	8.64	3.80	76.8	**4.2**	32.8	11.5	**7.0**
6.4	1.34	5.6	-0.05	**3.5**	9.2	0.77	7.56	3.34	81.3	**5.9**	35.8	5.9	**7.2**
4.9	1.18	7.9	0.20	**7.8**	1.9	1.82	17.78	3.97	46.5	**2.1**	13.6	18.2	**7.4**
2.8	6.01	30.8	0.28	**4.4**	0.4	0.74	6.54	3.44	54.7	**2.6**	41.3	26.3	**5.8**
5.5	4.48	15.4	0.00	**3.6**	0.1	0.55	2.65	3.83	78.8	**2.7**	30.9	16.6	**7.7**
8.5	0.02	0.1	0.00	**4.6**	0.3	1.07	10.56	3.66	71.2	**1.8**	27.0	25.3	**5.2**
1.6	4.76	31.8	0.00	**2.8**	0.9	0.39	3.70	3.66	86.5	**1.6**	15.2	22.9	**5.0**
7.2	0.43	2.9	-0.03	**4.0**	0.9	1.01	10.96	3.25	79.6	**5.1**	34.9	7.0	**4.9**
8.4	0.30	1.8	0.00	**3.5**	0.1	0.52	4.95	3.46	76.3	**4.0**	13.6	8.3	**6.1**
4.7	2.48	11.3	0.07	**4.0**	2.8	0.73	5.05	3.41	74.5	**3.5**	27.3	13.4	**7.9**
3.9	1.60	8.3	-0.03	**2.9**	0.5	0.58	6.34	3.34	86.0	**3.8**	23.9	10.7	**5.1**
7.0	0.43	2.4	0.05	**5.2**	2.9	1.06	10.61	3.69	68.6	**2.1**	21.5	18.9	**6.1**
1.3	7.36	36.8	0.32	**2.3**	0.1	0.29	2.76	2.97	81.3	**2.1**	36.4	29.8	**4.4**
4.8	1.34	8.7	0.16	**6.2**	10.5	1.01	8.82	3.55	63.5	**3.9**	10.0	8.9	**7.9**
2.7	3.94	20.9	0.03	**3.1**	0.5	0.39	3.54	3.24	80.8	**4.8**	34.4	8.7	**5.6**
0.0	16.98	120.3	2.96	**1.0**	-4.1	-5.46	-94.95	5.10	54.0	**0.8**	17.7	35.2	**3.9**
6.0	0.70	4.1	0.23	**3.2**	0.4	0.42	3.80	3.91	80.2	**1.7**	14.3	21.1	**5.7**
0.3	8.81	51.8	0.58	**3.0**	1.3	0.64	6.76	4.21	84.7	**3.3**	29.8	15.2	**4.0**
2.7	2.76	20.4	0.00	**3.8**	0.4	0.55	6.16	3.55	75.7	**1.5**	17.1	25.2	**3.6**
5.5	0.87	5.8	0.12	**8.0**	34.0	1.38	12.70	3.39	47.6	**1.5**	11.5	24.3	**9.1**
1.9	4.67	28.1	0.18	**2.2**	0.1	0.26	2.43	3.39	88.0	**3.3**	19.6	13.1	**4.7**
3.1	2.77	13.3	0.03	**4.7**	0.9	1.08	9.07	3.93	58.1	**4.5**	32.2	9.6	**4.7**
3.7	1.63	12.6	1.13	**1.1**	-0.1	-0.24	-3.06	3.23	118.4	**5.8**	37.9	4.0	**1.0**
2.0	6.89	21.8	1.21	**0.6**	-0.1	-0.40	-3.30	4.05	109.2	**6.0**	61.4	8.0	**4.9**
5.9	0.87	5.1	-0.03	**3.8**	1.4	0.63	7.01	3.16	74.0	**4.9**	31.5	7.0	**4.6**
9.9	0.18	0.6	0.05	**2.7**	0.1	0.28	1.31	3.37	85.4	**3.1**	31.1	16.4	**7.1**
5.4	0.69	5.6	0.16	**9.0**	27.9	1.52	14.78	3.29	50.2	**3.0**	9.8	13.9	**7.4**
3.6	2.33	17.1	1.23	**3.2**	0.4	0.32	3.59	3.83	66.7	**2.3**	17.3	17.5	**5.5**
3.0	3.01	17.4	-0.06	**3.5**	0.5	0.64	7.45	3.76	88.8	**6.3**	47.8	3.9	**3.4**
6.8	2.00	8.5	0.04	**3.6**	2.5	0.69	5.10	3.47	76.1	**3.5**	40.4	17.6	**7.4**
4.5	0.96	9.2	0.10	**4.0**	7.9	0.72	6.20	3.21	75.5	**2.1**	3.2	17.3	**8.4**
2.7	2.39	17.5	0.34	**4.7**	1.3	0.89	8.96	4.47	68.8	**3.3**	16.0	12.4	**5.4**
5.0	0.88	7.4	0.21	**5.6**	25.1	0.99	8.72	3.71	57.7	**4.6**	9.9	4.1	**8.1**
6.3	0.39	2.4	0.12	**6.1**	1.3	1.47	12.16	4.45	70.0	**2.2**	18.1	18.4	**6.9**
2.1	2.78	15.7	1.12	**8.4**	15.6	1.84	13.66	4.19	39.3	**0.8**	14.0	37.0	**9.4**
8.5	0.15	0.6	0.02	**2.7**	0.4	0.38	2.29	3.49	75.7	**1.9**	26.9	23.4	**4.7**
3.1	2.18	12.7	-0.01	**9.7**	0.4	1.51	14.44	5.87	58.8	**2.2**	17.1	18.2	**5.8**

Name	City	State	Rating	2013 Rating	2012 Rating	Total Assets ($Mil)	One Year Asset Growth	Asset Mix (As a % of Total Assets): Commercial Loans	Consumer Loans	Mortgage Loans	Securities	Capitalization Index	Leverage Ratio	Risk-Based Capital Ratio
LAKESIDE NATIONAL BK	Rockwall	TX	**B**	B-	B-	60.4	8.20	5.9	5.1	10.8	28.1	**7.0**	9.0	20.5
LAKESIDE STATE BK	Oologah	OK	**B-**	B-	B-	61.6	3.53	4.1	11.8	17.1	45.2	**7.8**	9.5	21.6
LAKESIDE STATE BK	New Town	ND	**B-**	B-	B-	414.5	26.50	7.4	3.1	2.4	31.8	**3.9**	5.9	13.0
LAKEVIEW BANK	Lakeville	MN	**C-**	D+	D-	61.3	8.65	17.4	1.2	26.5	9.5	**7.4**	9.3	13.5
LAMAR BANK & TRUST CO	Lamar	MO	**A-**	A-	A-	133.6	4.11	7.7	2.4	24.6	25.4	**7.9**	9.6	15.9
LAMAR NATIONAL BK	Paris	TX	**A-**	A-	A-	127.0	3.17	13.3	7.1	28.7	21.3	**10.0**	12.1	23.1
▲ LAMESA NATIONAL BK	Lamesa	TX	**B-**	C+	B-	308.6	7.02	7.1	0.2	0.0	51.6	**9.1**	10.4	19.5
▲ LAMONT BANK OF ST JOHN	Saint John	WA	**C**	D+	D+	45.9	-11.07	3.4	4.0	0.6	65.6	**9.2**	10.5	28.5
LANDMANDS BANK	Audubon	IA	**B-**	B-	B	61.2	-5.07	7.2	2.7	5.7	5.3	**4.6**	8.8	10.8
▼ LANDMARK BANK	Clinton	LA	**C+**	C+	B-	107.3	3.80	7.0	2.9	23.3	25.7	**9.2**	10.5	18.9
LANDMARK BANK NA	Fort Lauderdale	FL	**D**	D	D+	348.2	36.67	11.7	0.7	6.9	0.8	**10.0**	12.8	17.2
LANDMARK BANK NA	Columbia	MO	**B+**	B+	B+	2088.7	13.15	7.1	3.2	17.8	30.3	**6.5**	8.5	13.7
LANDMARK COMMUNITY BANK	Collierville	TN	**B-**	C+	C	659.1	14.27	5.7	1.7	61.2	12.3	**6.9**	8.9	16.2
▼ LANDMARK COMMUNITY BANK	Pittston	PA	**C-**	C	C-	276.4	5.68	10.8	2.3	8.6	19.1	**7.3**	9.2	13.6
LANDMARK COMMUNITY BANK NA	Isanti	MN	**E-**	E-	D-	81.2	-16.97	8.4	1.2	20.7	6.9	**2.9**	6.0	9.9
LANDMARK NATIONAL BK	Manhattan	KS	**C+**	C+	B-	849.9	35.26	7.7	0.7	16.2	38.2	**6.3**	8.4	14.7
LAONA STATE BK	Laona	WI	**C-**	C-	D+	165.3	3.59	5.4	4.0	30.3	29.7	**9.5**	10.7	18.2
LAPEER COUNTY BANK & TRUST CO	Lapeer	MI	**B**	C+	C-	317.1	2.84	4.7	0.7	12.4	42.8	**9.6**	10.7	21.4
LATIMER STATE BK	Wilburton	OK	**B**	B	B+	81.0	4.52	8.7	2.9	7.1	20.3	**10.0**	16.7	29.4
LAUDERDALE COUNTY BANK	Halls	TN	**C**	C-	C-	49.6	2.49	16.5	6.3	14.2	36.2	**7.3**	9.2	18.5
LAURA STATE BK	Williamsfield	IL	**D+**	C-	C+	16.1	-8.19	3.0	7.9	7.6	7.0	**10.0**	11.1	27.8
LAURENS STATE BK	Laurens	IA	**B**	B	A-	67.6	5.06	3.9	2.6	8.0	47.4	**9.5**	10.7	21.5
LAWRENCEBURG FEDERAL BANK	Lawrenceburg	TN	**B+**	B+	B	55.4	2.92	0.0	3.1	80.3	0.0	**10.0**	23.1	45.1
LAWSON BANK	Lawson	MO	**C+**	C+	B-	120.0	-1.84	2.8	0.7	11.1	35.6	**8.4**	9.9	20.1
LAYTON STATE BK	West Allis	WI	**D-**	D-	D	136.3	-10.60	10.1	0.1	8.8	12.1	**7.0**	9.0	13.5
LCA BANK CORP	Park City	UT	**A**	A	A-	101.4	27.54	2.4	0.0	0.0	0.7	**10.0**	15.9	16.7
LCNB NATIONAL BK	Lebanon	OH	**B-**	B-	B-	1121.4	19.36	3.1	1.7	19.1	27.7	**6.0**	8.0	14.0
LEA COUNTY STATE BK	Hobbs	NM	**C+**	C	C+	296.5	10.53	9.7	0.8	0.9	74.9	**6.5**	8.5	23.4
LEAD BANK	Garden City	MO	**D**	D-	D-	133.4	37.35	13.0	0.6	19.0	5.5	**6.8**	8.8	12.7
LEADER BANK NA	Arlington	MA	**A**	A	A	813.0	28.75	3.1	0.1	37.3	5.7	**10.0**	11.3	16.3
LEADERS BANK	Oak Brook	IL	**E+**	E	E-	355.0	-1.08	16.7	0.2	4.2	8.5	**3.5**	7.6	10.3
LEDYARD NATIONAL BK	Norwich	VT	**B-**	B-	C+	426.0	6.78	5.5	3.0	25.1	27.7	**6.8**	8.8	14.5
LEE BANK	Lee	MA	**D+**	D+	C	295.5	7.34	4.9	0.3	31.4	9.2	**8.0**	9.7	13.4
LEE BANK & TRUST CO	Pennington Gap	VA	**C-**	C-	C-	153.8	-4.19	11.9	8.7	26.3	12.9	**10.0**	14.5	21.7
LEE COUNTY BANK & TRUST NA	Fort Madison	IA	**B**	C+	C-	138.4	-1.58	8.1	1.7	33.2	0.4	**10.0**	11.9	21.6
LEGACY BANK	Altoona	IA	**D-**	D-	D-	89.2	0.17	14.4	2.4	26.2	10.8	**5.4**	7.4	12.3
LEGACY BANK	Wiley	CO	**B-**	C	C-	253.9	0.11	10.9	0.9	11.8	15.5	**10.0**	12.6	17.5
LEGACY BANK	Wichita	KS	**C-**	C-	C	293.8	7.90	8.0	0.9	20.8	10.3	**8.3**	10.4	13.6
LEGACY BANK	Hinton	OK	**C-**	C	C	466.6	-7.42	19.3	0.9	8.3	10.0	**5.6**	8.4	11.4
▼ LEGACY BANK & TRUST CO	Rogersville	MO	**C**	C+	C-	123.3	6.27	7.8	1.9	32.1	3.4	**7.1**	9.0	12.7
▲ LEGACY BANK OF FLORIDA	Boca Raton	FL	**D-**	E-	E-	274.9	7.44	8.9	0.2	4.8	24.7	**6.4**	8.7	12.1
▲ LEGACY NATIONAL BK	Springdale	AR	**B**	C	D+	318.8	19.57	8.3	1.4	14.5	3.1	**10.0**	12.2	15.6
LEGACY STATE BK	Loganville	GA	**E-**	E-	E-	70.4	0.83	4.0	0.3	6.9	15.2	**2.1**	6.1	9.1
LEGACY TRUST CO NA	Houston	TX	**U**	U	U	20.1	2.59	0.0	0.0	0.0	81.0	**10.0**	91.2	123.6
LEGACYTEXAS BANK	Plano	TX	**A-**	B+	B-	1833.0	7.15	15.5	0.9	16.0	11.7	**8.6**	10.1	13.8
LEGENCE BANK	Eldorado	IL	**C+**	B-	B	292.4	3.95	8.0	4.5	6.6	34.5	**6.8**	8.8	17.7
▲ LEGEND BANK NA	Bowie	TX	**A-**	B-	C+	606.5	6.23	11.3	1.5	10.2	29.6	**8.9**	10.3	15.2
LEGENDS BANK	Linn	MO	**B+**	B+	A-	295.1	9.00	4.7	7.5	21.4	17.7	**10.0**	15.7	22.3
LEGENDS BANK	Clarksville	TN	**B-**	B-	C	385.0	0.98	8.2	0.4	7.5	24.5	**8.0**	9.6	14.0
LEIGHTON STATE BK	Pella	IA	**A-**	A-	A-	150.7	27.71	9.0	2.5	16.0	18.6	**8.8**	10.2	14.4
LEITCHFIELD DEPOSIT BANK & TR	Leitchfield	KY	**A**	A	A	117.2	3.61	8.2	1.8	10.3	18.2	**10.0**	14.9	21.6
▲ LEMONT NATIONAL BK	Lemont	IL	**C-**	D-	D	58.1	-1.64	0.0	0.1	10.2	38.9	**3.5**	5.5	23.6
LENA STATE BK	Lena	IL	**C+**	C+	C+	84.3	5.88	14.9	0.5	3.7	37.5	**9.0**	10.4	17.4
LENOX NATIONAL BK	Lenox	MA	**B**	B	B-	70.2	5.98	2.3	1.0	20.7	48.7	**10.0**	12.3	30.2
LEONARDVILLE STATE BK	Leonardville	KS	**C-**	C+	D+	38.6	26.50	8.4	2.9	17.2	11.0	**10.0**	12.7	19.1
▼ LEVEL ONE BANK	Farmington Hills	MI	**B-**	A-	B+	680.7	14.22	25.7	0.2	9.6	14.6	**8.2**	10.4	13.5
LEWIS & CLARK BANK	Oregon City	OR	**B-**	B-	C+	129.6	8.24	5.8	0.1	12.1	0.0	**10.0**	12.4	16.0
LEWISBURG BANKING CO	Lewisburg	KY	**A-**	A-	B+	111.0	8.02	12.6	3.9	23.0	30.0	**8.0**	9.6	16.7
LEWISTON STATE BK	Lewiston	UT	**B**	B-	C	284.3	9.18	9.9	2.4	7.7	21.6	**9.3**	10.6	14.7
LIBERTY BANK	Springfield	MO	**A**	A-	A-	1065.9	0.10	11.8	1.7	19.3	9.1	**10.0**	11.7	18.8

Asset Quality Index	Adjusted Non-Performing Loans as a % of Total Loans	Adjusted Non-Performing Loans as a % of Capital	Net Charge-Offs / Avg Loans	Profitability Index	Net Income ($Mil)	Return on Assets (R.O.A.)	Return on Equity (R.O.E.)	Net Interest Spread	Overhead Efficiency Ratio	Liquidity Index	Liquidity Ratio	Hot Money Ratio	Stability Index
6.3	1.15	4.5	0.02	**3.4**	0.3	0.74	8.01	3.32	75.3	**6.2**	65.4	7.8	**5.9**
5.6	0.89	3.6	0.17	**4.6**	0.4	0.84	9.05	3.99	81.1	**2.7**	28.8	17.6	**5.9**
8.6	0.12	0.7	0.04	**5.9**	4.4	1.52	25.55	2.85	39.5	**5.8**	47.1	7.4	**4.8**
2.4	3.41	25.4	-0.09	**4.5**	0.3	0.69	6.64	4.89	71.8	**4.5**	20.1	6.1	**4.1**
6.9	0.73	4.6	0.01	**9.2**	2.3	2.22	24.22	3.89	49.1	**2.4**	20.3	17.4	**7.9**
8.6	0.17	0.8	0.02	**5.6**	1.3	1.41	11.72	4.39	68.5	**4.7**	42.9	12.1	**8.5**
6.6	0.99	3.3	-0.23	**4.6**	2.7	1.17	11.73	2.30	40.1	**3.0**	47.1	25.5	**5.9**
6.8	2.30	3.5	0.22	**3.1**	0.2	0.45	5.13	2.50	58.0	**7.9**	86.2	0.0	**2.6**
2.6	1.52	13.7	0.15	**6.5**	0.7	1.41	15.41	3.98	67.7	**2.7**	10.5	15.0	**5.9**
3.0	2.98	16.2	0.13	**4.1**	0.8	0.96	9.13	4.09	75.8	**4.0**	30.4	12.0	**6.7**
0.0	11.86	68.9	0.02	**8.7**	3.7	1.59	11.65	4.13	49.4	**0.8**	15.0	35.5	**5.5**
6.6	0.82	5.5	0.03	**6.5**	18.2	1.21	13.92	4.34	68.3	**1.8**	15.3	20.5	**7.2**
6.2	0.62	5.3	0.21	**5.8**	4.7	1.00	10.90	3.72	50.6	**0.5**	6.2	47.7	**4.2**
1.7	3.54	26.0	0.28	**3.6**	1.5	0.72	7.84	4.02	75.7	**3.5**	7.0	10.7	**4.8**
1.5	3.35	33.9	0.07	**0.0**	-1.2	-1.72	-28.19	4.07	144.7	**1.6**	9.5	21.6	**1.1**
3.6	1.90	11.1	0.29	**5.6**	6.4	1.03	10.01	3.59	68.2	**4.1**	20.6	8.9	**6.5**
2.3	3.99	21.4	-0.05	**4.3**	1.0	0.84	7.44	3.70	67.6	**2.8**	35.4	19.3	**6.0**
4.9	1.72	7.1	0.51	**5.3**	2.4	0.98	10.34	3.69	69.7	**5.5**	44.7	8.4	**5.3**
6.7	5.74	7.2	0.27	**3.8**	0.5	0.89	5.33	1.98	60.0	**3.5**	79.0	31.0	**7.1**
4.2	2.30	11.1	0.15	**3.5**	0.3	0.67	7.47	3.77	81.0	**2.5**	45.2	30.9	**3.7**
7.0	1.60	4.2	0.00	**0.6**	0.0	-0.23	-2.03	1.99	110.3	**6.8**	72.5	2.8	**4.8**
8.3	0.14	0.5	0.14	**4.7**	0.6	1.15	13.39	3.00	63.7	**5.5**	57.7	10.7	**6.2**
7.4	1.91	6.9	0.09	**5.4**	0.4	1.04	4.62	3.37	65.5	**1.7**	12.3	20.1	**7.9**
8.1	0.06	0.2	-0.03	**3.1**	0.5	0.58	7.05	3.47	82.8	**5.1**	43.1	10.4	**4.6**
0.9	3.93	27.1	1.00	**0.1**	-0.7	-0.71	-7.30	3.77	126.1	**3.5**	25.9	12.6	**3.1**
9.0	0.23	1.3	0.71	**10.0**	1.5	2.31	14.00	9.28	49.0	**0.2**	9.5	99.2	**8.1**
4.3	1.98	14.8	0.20	**4.5**	6.7	0.80	7.78	3.62	71.1	**4.2**	15.5	8.2	**7.8**
9.8	0.32	0.7	-0.04	**3.8**	2.2	1.04	10.84	3.12	71.6	**6.0**	62.8	10.3	**5.7**
2.7	2.70	19.9	0.03	**1.4**	0.1	0.08	0.87	4.54	89.4	**1.8**	19.5	21.6	**2.7**
8.2	0.21	1.5	0.01	**7.6**	6.6	1.19	10.15	3.18	56.9	**0.9**	9.9	31.6	**8.1**
0.0	12.42	93.9	0.98	**1.0**	-0.1	-0.03	-0.34	3.34	89.5	**0.7**	15.8	46.7	**3.3**
5.1	1.33	8.6	0.04	**4.4**	3.1	0.98	10.79	3.39	77.7	**4.5**	24.1	6.9	**5.5**
2.1	3.41	26.8	0.10	**2.4**	0.5	0.24	2.38	3.49	92.3	**3.1**	11.5	13.3	**5.0**
1.5	6.05	27.2	1.03	**3.9**	0.7	0.59	4.25	4.32	72.0	**1.2**	19.0	30.1	**6.4**
6.0	1.09	5.2	0.13	**4.8**	1.3	1.22	10.39	3.49	70.2	**6.1**	40.0	2.5	**5.2**
0.3	7.42	59.1	0.10	**0.5**	-0.2	-0.26	-3.48	3.65	101.4	**4.4**	23.1	6.9	**2.3**
3.4	3.83	19.1	0.31	**4.5**	1.9	1.03	7.10	4.38	68.4	**1.7**	21.3	24.0	**6.2**
2.0	3.82	27.0	0.92	**4.3**	1.4	0.66	6.36	4.08	69.5	**1.2**	8.3	27.5	**5.9**
0.9	4.82	39.7	1.04	**1.6**	-1.2	-0.33	-3.90	4.66	95.2	**4.2**	5.8	6.2	**3.6**
2.3	2.08	17.7	0.12	**4.7**	0.7	0.79	6.97	4.68	71.8	**2.7**	4.2	14.4	**5.8**
2.4	1.81	13.0	0.41	**3.3**	10.2	5.35	65.66	3.39	87.7	**3.9**	26.4	10.9	**2.4**
4.7	2.34	13.5	0.29	**4.5**	1.5	0.73	5.37	4.08	68.4	**2.0**	21.9	19.8	**5.6**
2.0	2.65	20.1	-0.28	**4.1**	0.9	1.68	30.31	3.19	131.0	**2.4**	22.7	17.9	**0.3**
10.0	na	0.0	na	**9.5**	1.4	9.22	10.13	1.93	76.9	**4.0**	917.1	101.0	**6.7**
7.2	0.13	0.9	0.00	**8.1**	26.9	2.01	19.59	4.31	59.5	**2.6**	11.6	16.0	**8.1**
3.7	2.60	14.7	0.44	**8.2**	4.2	1.91	18.39	5.45	64.0	**3.6**	28.4	13.1	**6.5**
6.4	0.25	1.4	0.12	**6.8**	7.3	1.65	13.55	4.62	64.4	**3.5**	21.4	12.1	**7.5**
4.6	2.49	11.2	0.33	**6.3**	2.3	1.09	6.93	3.77	57.5	**3.0**	9.4	13.5	**8.2**
5.2	0.86	5.2	0.31	**4.4**	2.5	0.86	9.25	4.23	73.2	**2.0**	22.0	19.5	**4.9**
6.3	0.58	3.8	0.11	**7.7**	1.7	1.66	13.38	3.98	63.1	**3.3**	25.9	13.6	**7.9**
6.3	1.11	4.7	0.05	**7.5**	1.2	1.38	9.49	4.30	54.6	**2.1**	17.7	18.6	**8.4**
10.0	0.00	0.0	0.00	**2.6**	0.3	0.74	10.55	1.77	72.3	**7.0**	82.2	5.5	**3.1**
5.1	0.55	2.5	1.10	**5.3**	0.7	1.10	10.62	3.63	54.3	**2.1**	28.6	21.6	**6.1**
6.4	2.54	7.2	0.18	**3.4**	0.2	0.40	3.23	2.86	74.4	**3.4**	69.9	28.7	**6.8**
8.5	0.01	0.0	0.00	**1.1**	0.0	0.07	0.63	4.86	90.6	**0.7**	13.8	41.4	**4.1**
6.1	0.54	3.8	0.31	**3.2**	1.7	0.34	3.28	3.84	84.4	**1.2**	6.1	26.8	**6.0**
3.8	2.05	12.2	0.00	**5.2**	0.8	0.87	7.19	4.71	70.1	**1.1**	15.2	30.8	**6.9**
5.5	0.97	5.7	0.02	**6.5**	1.2	1.47	15.12	3.82	63.2	**3.4**	21.9	12.8	**7.8**
2.5	3.11	19.0	-0.06	**4.5**	1.5	0.71	6.50	4.73	75.6	**3.6**	30.0	13.7	**6.5**
6.3	0.82	4.9	0.27	**9.9**	13.6	1.71	14.79	4.57	52.7	**4.3**	14.5	7.2	**9.3**

Name	City	State	Rating	2013 Rating	2012 Rating	Total Assets ($Mil)	One Year Asset Growth	Asset Mix (As a % of Total Assets) Commercial Loans	Consumer Loans	Mortgage Loans	Securities	Capitalization Index	Leverage Ratio	Risk-Based Capital Ratio
▲ LIBERTY BANK	Alton	IL	B-	C+	C-	287.3	-1.34	16.4	1.3	10.5	36.5	10.0	11.0	18.3
LIBERTY BANK	Middletown	CT	B	B	B	3700.5	4.95	10.8	0.6	15.7	19.2	10.0	15.6	19.8
LIBERTY BANK	Geraldine	AL	B+	B+	B+	107.2	1.77	2.1	11.6	14.0	40.2	10.0	13.7	21.7
▲ LIBERTY BANK	Hurst	TX	B-	C+	C	372.7	11.80	16.3	1.2	14.9	11.3	7.0	9.0	13.3
LIBERTY BANK	Salt Lake City	UT	E+	E+	D	10.1	2.91	5.9	2.0	26.3	2.5	10.0	12.7	25.2
▲ LIBERTY BANK	South San Francisc	CA	C	C-	C-	237.8	6.62	9.2	0.5	0.5	31.1	10.0	12.9	15.7
LIBERTY BANK	Ironton	OH	C+	C+	C+	60.0	9.84	5.2	2.7	39.3	22.2	10.0	11.5	26.4
LIBERTY BANK & TRUST CO	New Orleans	LA	C+	C+	C-	552.1	-1.77	4.0	4.5	22.9	42.5	6.3	8.3	16.9
LIBERTY BANK FOR SAVINGS	Chicago	IL	C+	C+	B-	824.1	-1.15	0.0	0.0	35.2	56.0	10.0	21.7	59.8
LIBERTY BANK NA	Beachwood	OH	B-	C	D	200.5	-1.42	16.9	11.3	6.9	1.0	10.0	13.8	17.6
LIBERTY BANK OF MARYLAND	Baltimore	MD	C-	C-	C-	38.7	-5.37	0.0	0.0	57.8	12.1	10.0	15.6	37.5
LIBERTY BAY BANK	Poulsbo	WA	D+	D	C-	74.9	20.66	10.3	0.6	6.5	19.0	10.0	11.0	15.7
LIBERTY BELL BANK	Marlton	NJ	E-	E-	E-	148.7	-12.71	9.5	0.1	11.5	16.1	5.0	7.0	11.5
LIBERTY CAPITAL BANK	Addison	TX	B	B	B-	136.5	22.58	24.7	0.3	16.2	0.0	8.7	10.2	14.8
LIBERTY FIRST BANK	Monroe	GA	C-	D+	D+	114.0	0.47	2.6	0.8	21.1	33.0	9.7	10.8	18.5
LIBERTY FSB	Enid	OK	E-	E-	E-	96.5	-6.50	1.2	0.4	31.5	17.4	2.2	4.7	11.6
▲ LIBERTY NATIONAL BK	Ada	OH	C+	C+	C	234.3	5.91	7.8	0.6	17.0	13.6	7.2	9.1	14.0
LIBERTY NATIONAL BK	Sioux City	IA	B-	B-	C+	290.4	3.20	15.3	1.1	9.4	21.2	6.6	8.7	12.3
LIBERTY NATIONAL BK	Lawton	OK	B-	B-	B-	449.0	76.58	8.0	2.3	11.7	22.9	8.5	10.0	16.0
LIBERTY NATIONAL BK IN PARIS	Paris	TX	B+	A-	A	251.6	-1.39	2.6	3.9	21.5	48.2	10.0	17.8	38.5
LIBERTY SAVINGS ASSN FSA	Fort Scott	KS	C-	C-	C+	36.5	-2.42	0.6	2.4	19.4	66.4	10.0	17.5	75.6
▲ LIBERTY SAVINGS BANK FSB	Saint Cloud	MN	A+	A	A-	184.9	-2.13	0.0	2.8	38.9	26.6	9.9	11.0	19.3
LIBERTY SAVINGS BANK FSB	Whiting	IN	E+	E+	E+	56.6	-3.28	0.0	0.0	50.8	15.4	4.5	6.5	16.8
LIBERTY SAVINGS BANK FSB	Wilmington	OH	C	C-	D+	578.8	4.20	0.6	0.0	59.2	16.2	10.0	12.6	25.3
LIBERTY STATE BK	Powers Lake	ND	A-	B+	B+	82.7	13.01	4.3	3.7	6.8	44.3	7.9	9.6	16.4
LIBERTY TRUST & SB	Durant	IA	A	A	A	142.2	2.17	4.2	2.4	8.7	47.5	10.0	17.0	32.0
LIBERTYVILLE BANK & TRUST CO	Libertyville	IL	B-	C+	C	1163.6	2.42	26.6	11.0	3.0	12.3	5.7	9.3	11.5
▲ LIBERTYVILLE SB	Fairfield	IA	A-	B+	B-	315.9	54.71	6.2	1.4	8.5	33.0	10.0	11.6	16.2
LIFESTORE BANK	West Jefferson	NC	C-	C-	D+	253.1	-3.86	5.1	1.0	36.8	10.5	8.4	10.0	15.0
LIGHTHOUSE BANK	Santa Cruz	CA	A	A	B+	163.5	1.74	3.0	0.0	12.1	8.3	10.0	15.2	18.5
▲ LINCOLN COMMUNITY BANK	Merrill	WI	B-	C+	C	56.5	-0.49	3.2	6.5	22.8	12.4	10.0	12.5	19.9
▲ LINCOLN FSB OF NEBRASKA	Lincoln	NE	C+	C-	D+	286.6	-1.17	0.0	0.0	41.9	21.1	10.0	12.3	24.1
LINCOLN NB OF HODGENVILLE	Hodgenville	KY	A-	A-	A-	179.4	3.03	2.3	5.1	38.2	12.2	10.0	16.0	24.6
▲ LINCOLN PARK SB	Lincoln Park	NJ	C	C-	C	224.9	7.49	2.8	0.1	26.7	60.1	5.4	7.4	19.9
LINCOLN SB	Reinbeck	IA	C+	C	C-	760.2	14.21	7.3	1.0	12.8	17.8	3.7	7.5	10.3
LINCOLN STATE BK	Hankinson	ND	C	C	C	63.2	-1.61	8.1	6.8	1.7	41.0	5.8	7.8	13.2
LINCOLNWAY COMMUNITY BANK	New Lenox	IL	D+	D+	D-	162.9	26.49	10.5	0.0	16.5	4.0	8.0	9.6	13.8
LINDELL BANK & TRUST CO	Saint Louis	MO	A	A-	B	471.3	-4.09	8.6	0.3	13.2	45.5	10.0	12.8	28.6
LINN COUNTY STATE BK	Coggon	IA	C+	C+	C+	35.3	15.19	5.5	5.4	32.2	5.9	8.8	10.2	14.4
LISLE SB	Lisle	IL	B-	C+	C	528.8	1.45	0.9	0.0	34.6	44.8	10.0	18.8	43.5
LITCHFIELD BANCORP	Litchfield	CT	C-	C-	C-	219.6	1.73	3.6	1.5	35.2	29.5	6.1	8.2	15.1
LITCHFIELD NATIONAL BK	Litchfield	IL	C+	C	C-	76.1	-9.25	3.3	5.3	19.2	18.1	7.8	9.6	14.6
LITTLE BANK INC	Kinston	NC	B	B	B	338.5	9.44	6.0	0.6	16.3	18.4	7.7	9.5	13.8
LITTLE HORN STATE BK	Hardin	MT	C	D+	C	71.5	14.10	5.0	2.4	7.2	17.5	8.7	10.2	15.3
▲ LITTLE RIVER BANK	Lepanto	AR	D+	D	D+	35.9	-12.97	3.4	3.5	15.4	49.1	10.0	12.2	28.7
▲ LIVE OAK BANKING CO	Wilmington	NC	C	C-	C	565.0	32.35	22.9	0.0	0.0	8.7	10.0	11.0	15.6
LIVERPOOL COMMUNITY BANK	Liverpool	PA	B-	B-	B-	43.4	0.13	1.9	2.7	58.7	14.3	10.0	19.2	35.6
▲ LIVINGSTON STATE BK	Livingston	WI	A-	B+	B-	159.0	-0.85	4.4	1.8	20.0	13.0	10.0	11.4	17.0
LLANO NATIONAL BK	Llano	TX	B-	B-	C	145.9	4.62	2.9	6.9	17.9	30.5	9.8	10.9	19.1
LLEWELLYN-EDISON SVGS BANK FSB	West Orange	NJ	D+	C-	C+	124.5	-2.57	1.0	0.0	10.4	55.7	10.0	17.7	52.3
LOGAN BANK & TRUST CO	Logan	WV	C+	C+	B-	259.7	-1.69	7.8	3.7	20.5	48.2	6.9	8.9	23.7
LOGAN COUNTY BANK	Scranton	AR	A-	A-	A-	78.1	4.81	2.6	5.3	16.9	62.8	10.0	18.8	51.6
LOGAN STATE BANK	Logan	IA	B+	B+	B	30.5	6.10	3.8	1.7	5.5	8.4	10.0	13.0	18.9
LOGANSPORT SAVINGS BANK FSB	Logansport	IN	A-	A-	B	161.7	-2.29	9.6	0.6	21.8	23.1	10.0	12.3	19.0
LONE STAR BANK	Houston	TX	D-	D-	D-	98.3	-6.96	8.9	0.3	25.6	0.7	9.3	10.5	16.8
LONE STAR BANK SSB	Moulton	TX	B+	A-	B+	311.0	13.50	6.1	0.8	19.8	11.1	5.5	8.3	11.4
LONE STAR CAPITAL BANK NA	San Antonio	TX	C	C-	C-	239.6	-1.03	12.8	1.5	13.0	15.3	7.1	9.1	14.5
LONE STAR NATIONAL BK	McAllen	TX	B	B	B-	2125.5	-0.47	7.8	1.4	12.0	30.0	9.3	10.5	19.1
LONE STAR STATE BK OF WEST TX	Lubbock	TX	B+	B+	B-	704.7	28.97	24.3	1.5	4.5	3.4	7.6	11.9	13.0
LONGVIEW BANK	Ogden	IL	C+	C	C-	170.7	175.28	7.4	1.4	14.1	16.9	7.2	9.1	13.9

Asset Quality Index	Adjusted Non-Performing Loans as a % of Total Loans	Adjusted Non-Performing Loans as a % of Capital	Net Charge-Offs Avg Loans	Profitability Index	Net Income ($Mil)	Return on Assets (R.O.A.)	Return on Equity (R.O.E.)	Net Interest Spread	Overhead Efficiency Ratio	Liquidity Index	Liquidity Ratio	Hot Money Ratio	Stability Index
3.8	3.65	17.5	0.51	4.5	1.7	0.80	6.42	3.90	70.2	3.5	21.9	12.3	6.3
6.3	1.03	4.8	0.06	4.3	23.4	0.87	5.31	3.56	75.0	4.5	24.3	9.4	9.5
5.2	2.28	7.6	0.18	5.2	0.8	0.97	7.15	5.11	70.0	4.1	50.9	17.3	7.4
5.5	0.34	2.6	0.06	4.0	1.9	0.70	5.63	4.33	72.3	1.1	20.4	32.3	6.9
1.7	17.67	48.6	-1.91	0.0	-0.3	-3.68	-32.89	3.26	182.8	2.0	53.6	55.3	3.4
4.5	1.85	8.0	-0.09	3.3	1.1	0.67	5.20	3.38	97.8	5.4	41.8	7.7	5.5
6.0	2.34	11.5	0.00	3.0	0.1	0.32	2.73	4.52	88.5	4.2	32.7	11.8	6.5
4.2	2.39	11.8	0.77	4.4	4.2	1.00	12.45	4.41	78.4	2.6	11.5	15.7	4.6
7.6	3.32	6.0	0.04	2.9	2.7	0.44	2.00	2.61	75.4	5.3	73.6	15.0	7.5
3.0	1.40	7.6	-0.05	7.4	2.6	1.63	12.91	3.93	63.6	2.8	17.7	15.2	5.2
3.7	5.04	20.8	0.69	1.8	0.1	0.35	2.20	3.54	99.9	3.6	37.3	15.9	5.1
7.5	0.00	0.0	0.00	1.1	0.0	0.07	0.65	4.22	100.0	2.5	22.5	17.3	1.4
1.7	4.19	35.3	1.43	0.0	-2.4	-2.06	-35.02	3.40	137.5	2.2	19.6	18.3	1.0
8.5	0.00	0.0	0.00	5.3	1.4	1.35	13.87	3.80	61.5	5.2	28.1	3.6	6.5
2.0	6.55	32.3	1.00	4.3	0.9	1.03	10.36	3.56	65.8	2.7	41.7	26.4	6.4
0.3	8.79	69.7	-0.65	0.9	0.0	0.00	-0.10	2.49	115.2	2.9	48.3	25.3	0.8
4.0	2.00	14.6	0.03	4.4	1.4	0.78	8.08	3.94	69.8	2.1	7.4	17.6	6.1
7.5	0.02	0.1	0.00	4.5	1.7	0.80	6.55	3.86	64.9	3.1	14.0	13.4	7.0
4.3	2.15	12.8	0.07	6.2	3.3	1.40	15.14	7.02	72.8	3.0	24.0	15.0	5.9
9.5	0.61	1.2	0.16	5.0	2.0	1.03	5.86	3.14	59.5	5.7	55.1	10.1	8.0
10.0	0.00	0.0	0.00	1.6	0.0	0.10	0.61	2.16	95.3	3.9	69.8	20.8	6.3
8.2	0.13	0.6	0.05	9.0	3.2	2.28	21.53	3.05	59.3	6.0	40.9	4.0	8.4
4.0	2.69	19.3	0.06	0.0	-0.3	-0.77	-11.84	2.91	129.2	3.0	40.5	20.0	1.8
2.5	4.35	23.4	0.16	2.8	2.0	0.47	3.65	3.10	92.0	1.2	19.9	30.7	5.9
8.6	0.01	0.1	-0.03	9.6	1.4	2.29	25.57	4.09	39.3	4.1	24.6	9.1	6.9
8.9	0.03	0.1	-0.06	6.4	1.3	1.26	7.51	3.80	53.5	6.2	61.1	8.7	8.5
4.6	0.81	6.4	0.22	5.0	8.2	0.94	10.17	3.14	55.8	1.8	8.3	19.4	5.6
6.9	0.82	4.0	0.09	5.3	2.3	1.33	12.17	4.11	66.5	5.2	47.7	10.9	5.9
2.2	3.46	22.9	0.47	2.1	0.4	0.23	2.25	3.82	88.6	2.5	15.9	16.6	4.0
7.7	0.00	0.0	0.00	9.2	1.8	1.43	9.87	5.28	50.1	3.0	18.8	14.6	7.9
4.2	2.77	13.5	1.39	3.9	0.3	0.67	5.51	3.90	68.8	4.3	27.5	9.4	5.6
3.5	3.71	17.7	-0.16	4.4	1.8	0.81	6.37	2.96	94.7	2.4	34.2	23.9	6.8
8.7	0.13	0.6	0.04	5.5	1.3	1.00	6.30	4.12	66.4	1.6	19.9	23.7	8.4
3.7	3.52	15.8	0.64	3.3	0.8	0.50	6.89	2.77	62.2	2.5	33.9	21.9	3.2
4.9	0.49	4.5	0.06	4.4	4.6	0.85	8.54	4.15	76.9	2.4	3.3	16.0	5.7
5.8	0.87	5.4	-0.17	4.0	0.5	0.94	13.52	3.03	63.9	3.5	27.3	13.1	4.4
1.6	5.02	35.6	-0.18	5.9	1.1	0.94	9.42	4.63	65.6	0.8	18.2	37.0	3.9
7.8	1.04	3.1	-0.18	6.9	6.3	1.76	11.50	4.15	52.2	5.3	34.5	5.9	8.0
0.5	4.30	31.8	0.26	6.1	0.3	1.10	7.26	5.77	65.8	4.3	13.0	6.2	5.7
3.7	9.77	21.3	0.30	4.0	2.6	0.66	3.64	2.92	60.0	3.9	60.2	20.8	7.2
3.7	2.66	20.1	0.03	1.7	0.2	0.13	1.54	3.23	96.2	4.2	32.9	11.6	4.4
4.3	1.44	10.3	-0.04	4.6	0.5	0.72	8.39	3.77	72.7	4.3	23.2	7.5	3.8
8.4	0.06	0.4	0.01	5.1	2.2	0.88	9.38	3.65	63.3	1.6	19.8	24.5	5.5
7.7	0.09	0.5	-0.10	3.2	0.2	0.46	4.27	4.11	86.5	5.2	35.2	6.5	4.4
4.8	5.01	15.7	0.35	0.8	0.0	-0.07	-0.77	3.43	101.6	3.5	52.5	19.5	3.3
3.6	0.85	5.5	0.20	10.0	22.9	5.94	55.64	3.86	56.1	0.8	17.9	42.4	8.1
8.2	0.61	2.3	0.05	7.5	0.4	1.17	6.13	4.45	59.9	3.4	22.5	12.8	5.7
6.4	1.00	6.1	0.02	5.4	1.1	0.87	7.34	3.82	64.5	2.8	17.5	15.0	6.3
3.6	3.25	15.7	0.54	5.6	1.1	0.99	8.90	4.59	61.5	3.3	42.8	19.0	6.9
6.9	4.07	7.4	0.47	0.5	-0.3	-0.34	-1.92	2.40	116.3	5.9	73.3	12.0	6.6
6.4	1.03	3.9	-0.14	3.2	0.9	0.46	5.39	2.51	78.3	4.1	48.0	16.7	5.0
8.0	2.66	4.3	0.11	5.0	0.6	0.98	5.52	3.30	54.1	4.5	65.3	16.5	8.3
7.1	0.00	0.0	0.04	5.7	0.3	1.19	9.01	4.64	69.0	5.1	2.7	0.0	7.5
6.5	1.17	6.0	0.13	6.1	1.4	1.11	9.48	3.81	57.5	3.5	20.1	12.2	6.9
8.5	0.00	0.0	-0.17	0.5	0.0	0.03	0.28	3.40	99.1	1.3	18.4	28.2	3.5
7.4	0.06	0.5	0.08	6.5	2.2	0.98	12.03	4.74	67.9	1.8	10.7	19.7	6.3
7.7	0.02	0.1	0.00	3.0	0.7	0.37	3.24	3.68	81.0	2.0	26.0	20.7	5.9
5.1	2.48	11.8	0.15	4.1	10.1	0.61	5.43	3.57	78.8	1.0	10.6	31.4	7.6
6.2	0.49	3.6	0.05	7.5	8.6	1.87	16.16	4.24	53.6	0.9	5.8	30.3	8.3
4.3	1.28	9.8	0.02	5.6	1.1	1.06	13.85	4.41	63.8	2.9	9.6	13.8	4.7

Name	City	State	Rating	2013 Rating	2012 Rating	Total Assets ($Mil)	One Year Asset Growth	Asset Mix (As a % of Total Assets) Commercial Loans	Consumer Loans	Mortgage Loans	Securities	Capitalization Index	Leverage Ratio	Risk-Based Capital Ratio
LOOMIS FS&LA	Chicago	IL	**B**	B-	B-	85.0	-6.04	2.6	0.0	39.4	22.9	**10.0**	20.7	65.3
LORAIN NATIONAL BK	Lorain	OH	**C-**	D+	D	1240.4	2.51	6.1	18.3	6.8	17.6	**6.6**	8.9	12.2
▲ LORRAINE STATE BK	Lorraine	KS	**B**	B-	C	25.0	6.13	2.7	8.3	8.1	25.9	**10.0**	11.4	17.5
LOS ALAMOS NATIONAL BK	Los Alamos	NM	**D-**	D-	D+	1463.7	-2.66	8.1	2.0	19.6	14.0	**6.8**	8.8	15.4
LOTUS BANK	Novi	MI	**B**	B	B	101.8	20.29	16.1	0.3	7.2	13.8	**10.0**	11.3	15.6
LOUISA COMMUNITY BANK	Louisa	KY	**C+**	C+	C	31.2	8.27	16.1	3.6	17.5	2.7	**10.0**	15.4	19.6
LOVELADY STATE BK	Lovelady	TX	**C**	C	C	45.9	10.86	7.9	11.3	13.3	8.9	**7.1**	9.1	18.7
▲ LOWELL FIVE CENT SB	Lowell	MA	**C+**	C	C+	949.1	2.88	6.7	0.3	28.9	17.5	**10.0**	12.0	17.3
▲ LOWRY STATE BK	Lowry	MN	**D+**	D	C-	42.7	0.91	17.7	6.7	18.1	1.2	**7.3**	10.3	12.8
LUANA SB	Luana	IA	**B+**	B+	B	674.6	17.40	1.3	2.5	21.3	16.6	**5.3**	8.8	11.2
▲ LUBBOCK NATIONAL BK	Lubbock	TX	**B**	B-	C	917.1	13.85	18.0	0.7	4.1	38.3	**7.9**	9.6	16.0
LUMBEE GUARANTY BANK	Pembroke	NC	**C**	C	C	314.4	0.07	3.6	2.8	16.5	27.1	**9.0**	10.3	17.8
LUSITANIA SAVINGS BANK	Newark	NJ	**B+**	B+	B	275.8	0.30	0.2	1.4	37.9	20.3	**10.0**	14.1	34.9
LUSK STATE BK	Lusk	WY	**B+**	B+	A-	59.5	9.17	2.3	3.8	1.8	5.6	**8.6**	10.1	18.4
▲ LUTHER BURBANK SAVINGS	Santa Rosa	CA	**A-**	B-	C	3957.0	9.11	0.0	0.0	30.1	6.1	**10.0**	12.3	23.9
LUZERNE BANK	Luzerne	PA	**B-**	C+	B-	337.2	0.60	17.9	1.4	15.5	9.7	**4.2**	9.1	10.6
LYNDON STATE BK	Lyndon	KS	**C+**	C+	C	79.5	2.04	5.3	2.4	29.4	31.5	**8.2**	9.8	14.7
LYNNVILLE NATIONAL BK	Lynnville	IN	**C+**	C+	B-	98.3	-1.60	1.2	4.6	52.0	10.4	**9.4**	10.6	18.9
▼ LYON COUNTY STATE BK	Emporia	KS	**C**	C+	B-	151.0	27.94	3.2	1.7	8.5	56.3	**5.9**	7.9	22.3
LYONS FEDERAL BANK	Lyons	KS	**C**	C	C+	88.4	5.87	4.2	4.1	19.7	1.1	**8.6**	10.1	15.4
LYONS NATIONAL BK	Lyons	NY	**B**	B	B-	803.0	11.46	9.1	3.2	21.4	25.1	**6.2**	8.2	12.4
LYONS STATE BK	Lyons	KS	**B-**	B	B-	99.4	4.95	10.7	4.8	7.6	34.0	**8.1**	9.8	15.4
LYTLE STATE BK OF LYTLE TEXAS	Lytle	TX	**B+**	B+	B+	83.1	1.29	4.4	16.6	7.0	57.1	**10.0**	16.2	36.8
M C BANK & TRUST CO	Morgan City	LA	**A-**	A-	A-	343.1	1.77	7.3	3.0	8.0	54.4	**10.0**	16.6	36.0
M Y SAFRA BANK FSB	New York	NY	**U**	U	C+	174.3	10.83	0.0	0.0	3.5	84.9	**10.0**	22.0	57.2
▲ MACATAWA BANK	Holland	MI	**B-**	C	C	1488.6	-4.45	18.5	0.8	16.1	13.0	**10.0**	11.4	16.0
MACHIAS SB	Machias	ME	**B-**	B-	C+	1099.4	12.04	14.2	1.0	19.8	2.9	**10.0**	11.9	15.0
▼ MACKINAC SAVINGS BANK FSB	Boynton Beach	FL	**D**	D+	D+	110.9	-1.95	0.0	0.0	38.3	0.0	**5.7**	7.7	35.0
MACON BANK & TRUST CO	Lafayette	TN	**B-**	B-	B	344.7	2.31	2.8	4.7	12.7	48.9	**10.0**	12.7	27.1
MACON BANK INC	Franklin	NC	**D+**	D+	D-	883.9	13.74	1.3	0.3	26.0	24.3	**10.0**	12.0	21.2
MACON-ATLANTA STATE BK	Macon	MO	**B**	B	B	269.7	16.15	3.2	2.1	8.0	39.6	**6.8**	8.9	15.6
MADISON BANK	Richmond	KY	**C-**	C-	D-	120.6	-2.36	3.4	0.7	18.1	20.7	**7.8**	9.5	15.9
▼ MADISON BANK OF MARYLAND	Forest Hill	MD	**D**	D	D	136.1	-8.73	0.0	0.0	62.7	11.0	**10.0**	12.7	23.1
MADISON COUNTY BANK	Madison	NE	**A**	A	A	301.9	8.99	2.2	1.2	12.4	15.1	**10.0**	17.2	17.9
MADISON COUNTY COMMUNITY BANK	Madison	FL	**C-**	C-	D	111.2	9.24	6.2	2.5	9.9	34.9	**6.5**	8.5	18.1
MADISON SQUARE FSB	Baltimore	MD	**D+**	D+	D+	137.2	-6.67	3.7	0.2	37.7	31.7	**7.4**	9.2	20.7
MAGNA BANK	Memphis	TN	**B+**	B	B-	563.3	11.68	13.1	1.5	22.0	9.8	**10.0**	12.1	16.0
MAGNOLIA BANK	Hodgenville	KY	**B**	A-	B+	154.9	7.42	6.6	1.2	20.8	13.3	**6.2**	10.1	11.9
MAGNOLIA STATE BK	Bay Springs	MS	**B+**	B+	B+	315.7	6.84	7.6	6.0	24.6	17.9	**7.9**	9.6	13.9
MAGYAR BANK	New Brunswick	NJ	**D+**	D+	D-	530.4	-1.36	6.6	2.0	29.9	11.5	**6.4**	8.4	12.7
MAHOPAC BANK	Brewster	NY	**B-**	C+	C+	1020.2	4.15	7.5	1.0	16.6	29.7	**7.9**	9.6	15.3
MAIN BANK	Albuquerque	NM	**A-**	B+	A-	103.0	-10.76	7.9	0.2	13.7	18.6	**10.0**	11.3	17.6
MAIN STREET BANK	Bingham Farms	MI	**B-**	B-	C	176.1	13.13	17.8	0.5	29.3	4.3	**5.2**	8.9	11.2
▲ MAIN STREET BANK CORP	Wheeling	WV	**C+**	C-	D+	314.6	8.63	13.0	3.7	41.7	9.2	**6.7**	8.7	13.5
MAINLAND BANK	Texas City	TX	**B+**	B	B-	120.0	2.56	33.9	1.4	11.4	19.9	**8.7**	10.1	14.7
MAINSOURCE BANK	Greensburg	IN	**B**	B	B-	2884.2	2.64	5.7	1.4	18.6	29.1	**8.4**	9.9	15.8
MAINSTREET BANK	Fairfax	VA	**C-**	C	D	322.4	18.73	4.4	6.1	14.6	14.0	**4.3**	8.5	10.7
▼ MAINSTREET BANK	Ashland	MO	**D+**	C	C-	49.7	-12.47	9.3	2.0	20.1	41.1	**9.6**	10.7	19.4
MAINSTREET COMMUNITY BK OF FL	Deland	FL	**B-**	C+	C	247.7	7.66	10.8	1.6	11.0	16.4	**6.4**	9.5	12.0
MALAGA BANK FSB	Palos Verdes Estat	CA	**A**	A	A	935.8	7.46	0.3	0.0	16.2	0.0	**10.0**	13.2	23.3
MALVERN FSB	Paoli	PA	**D+**	D	C-	533.3	-9.85	1.0	0.5	52.6	17.4	**10.0**	12.1	20.8
MALVERN NATIONAL BK	Malvern	AR	**C+**	C+	C+	462.5	1.09	5.8	1.3	8.7	35.3	**9.5**	10.6	17.9
MALVERN TRUST & SB	Malvern	IA	**C-**	C-	C-	82.2	11.52	10.6	11.4	23.5	2.6	**4.1**	7.6	10.6
MANASQUAN SB	Manasquan	NJ	**B-**	B-	C+	887.5	3.10	6.8	0.1	39.7	11.2	**9.3**	10.5	15.5
MANCOS VALLEY BANK	Mancos	CO	**C**	C	C	73.2	-3.30	1.8	1.1	10.2	41.5	**9.1**	10.4	20.0
MANHATTAN BANK	Manhattan	MT	**C+**	B-	C	143.5	9.08	4.4	2.4	9.2	39.0	**7.1**	9.1	15.7
MANOR BANK	Manor	PA	**D**	D	C	29.0	13.04	1.0	0.3	40.4	27.3	**9.2**	10.5	24.9
MANSFIELD CO-OP BANK	Mansfield	MA	**C**	C+	C	440.9	8.45	1.5	0.1	28.1	12.9	**8.0**	9.7	14.7
MANSON STATE BK	Manson	IA	**C+**	C+	C+	38.5	-1.82	4.4	1.3	8.2	55.0	**8.3**	9.8	19.7
MANUFACTURERS & TRADERS TRUST	Buffalo	NY	**C**	C	B-	96469.5	15.37	16.3	5.0	9.1	13.4	**6.9**	8.9	13.2

Arrows denote recent upgrades ▲ or downgrades ▼

Asset Quality Index	Adjusted Non-Performing Loans as a % of Total Loans	Adjusted Non-Performing Loans as a % of Capital	Net Charge-Offs Avg Loans	Profitability Index	Net Income ($Mil)	Return on Assets (R.O.A.)	Return on Equity (R.O.E.)	Net Interest Spread	Overhead Efficiency Ratio	Liquidity Index	Liquidity Ratio	Hot Money Ratio	Stability Index
6.4	5.29	11.4	0.43	**3.8**	0.4	0.60	3.01	3.47	65.0	**5.9**	66.7	10.1	**7.3**
2.6	2.17	16.1	0.38	**3.7**	6.4	0.69	6.87	3.30	69.7	**1.3**	5.6	24.5	**7.3**
7.9	0.04	0.2	-0.01	**6.0**	0.2	1.13	10.03	3.59	51.3	**4.2**	39.8	13.8	**6.4**
0.3	8.71	51.4	0.82	**1.6**	0.5	0.04	0.47	3.40	98.3	**4.0**	31.2	15.5	**5.9**
5.1	1.45	8.4	0.15	**3.8**	0.4	0.47	4.10	3.72	79.3	**1.2**	29.0	40.7	**6.9**
4.6	2.35	11.9	0.28	**5.2**	0.3	1.24	7.94	4.58	69.4	**0.8**	15.1	40.9	**5.7**
3.6	2.50	12.0	0.62	**3.9**	0.3	0.80	8.59	3.70	80.2	**3.2**	51.2	22.9	**4.7**
5.8	1.34	7.4	0.14	**2.7**	3.1	0.44	3.66	3.04	80.4	**4.2**	28.2	10.2	**7.8**
1.9	2.03	16.2	-0.08	**9.8**	0.8	2.32	23.88	4.91	52.1	**4.0**	6.3	7.8	**6.6**
7.5	0.25	2.0	0.01	**9.0**	9.8	2.03	22.65	3.64	36.3	**0.7**	18.8	61.7	**7.8**
7.3	0.10	0.5	-0.12	**4.6**	5.7	0.89	9.05	3.81	68.3	**2.9**	43.8	25.0	**5.3**
2.4	4.42	22.7	0.60	**4.0**	1.7	0.72	7.22	4.24	74.9	**2.5**	17.0	16.8	**6.0**
5.3	3.41	12.9	0.39	**5.6**	1.9	0.89	6.48	3.02	46.9	**4.2**	44.2	15.0	**7.3**
6.8	0.30	1.5	0.03	**7.1**	0.7	1.58	15.20	3.50	61.4	**6.0**	47.2	5.0	**7.6**
5.8	0.56	3.6	0.11	**5.6**	34.9	1.25	10.10	2.88	55.5	**0.6**	13.2	65.3	**10.0**
3.1	1.27	11.1	0.01	**4.4**	1.8	0.70	5.33	3.76	68.2	**4.1**	12.1	7.9	**6.7**
5.7	0.72	4.1	0.03	**3.4**	0.4	0.58	5.51	4.83	85.9	**3.2**	21.7	13.8	**5.2**
5.1	1.71	10.7	0.10	**3.7**	0.6	0.71	6.86	4.08	84.4	**4.1**	14.6	7.7	**6.5**
9.6	0.23	0.7	0.24	**2.1**	0.4	0.37	4.76	3.00	91.2	**6.5**	58.4	6.2	**4.2**
7.4	0.21	1.4	0.01	**3.3**	0.3	0.50	4.92	3.30	77.0	**2.4**	24.6	18.1	**6.0**
5.5	0.65	4.9	0.03	**5.4**	5.7	0.99	12.65	3.51	64.5	**2.6**	14.6	16.1	**5.5**
5.9	0.85	4.6	-0.05	**4.4**	0.4	0.56	6.03	3.71	70.0	**2.1**	26.1	20.2	**6.3**
7.6	1.41	2.8	0.20	**5.1**	0.6	0.99	6.35	3.99	70.4	**3.6**	49.3	18.5	**7.0**
6.3	4.43	9.2	1.10	**5.9**	3.0	1.17	7.20	3.75	56.3	**4.2**	66.2	19.9	**7.5**
10.0	0.00	0.0	0.00	**0.0**	-0.7	-0.56	-2.56	1.05	252.5	**4.2**	117.8	44.5	**1.7**
3.9	3.08	17.2	-0.20	**4.4**	9.1	0.82	7.06	3.22	75.9	**5.2**	23.8	4.3	**7.1**
3.7	2.67	17.1	0.32	**4.5**	6.2	0.78	6.35	4.25	71.6	**1.3**	8.9	25.9	**8.7**
5.3	1.08	5.6	-0.04	**0.6**	-0.3	-0.33	-4.21	2.23	110.5	**6.7**	61.6	6.0	**2.3**
7.6	0.81	2.5	0.11	**4.0**	2.0	0.80	6.41	3.56	73.3	**2.7**	53.1	34.3	**6.9**
3.6	3.99	18.6	0.62	**3.4**	4.9	0.79	10.79	3.55	71.7	**2.8**	36.7	19.7	**3.1**
4.4	2.18	11.8	0.40	**4.2**	1.7	0.86	9.63	2.97	67.2	**3.1**	27.6	15.4	**5.3**
2.8	3.35	20.4	0.18	**1.9**	0.1	0.15	1.53	3.86	94.6	**1.7**	15.9	21.9	**4.6**
2.2	6.15	34.6	0.98	**0.0**	-1.2	-1.09	-8.43	2.90	99.6	**1.5**	18.2	24.9	**4.9**
7.3	0.18	0.7	0.00	**6.4**	2.3	1.06	5.90	3.85	56.7	**5.0**	16.8	2.5	**9.0**
2.8	3.60	19.6	0.27	**2.9**	0.4	0.49	6.10	3.03	68.6	**2.9**	45.8	26.6	**3.2**
4.7	2.41	14.3	0.09	**1.3**	0.1	0.06	0.72	2.60	97.2	**2.4**	42.3	30.9	**3.5**
4.9	1.68	10.5	0.04	**5.8**	4.3	1.05	8.49	3.60	71.4	**1.5**	6.7	21.4	**7.8**
5.3	0.79	5.7	0.32	**4.8**	1.1	1.00	9.67	3.82	88.6	**1.5**	9.9	23.2	**6.8**
7.7	0.27	2.1	0.02	**5.3**	2.9	1.24	13.50	4.44	71.7	**2.4**	9.3	16.4	**6.3**
1.8	3.28	28.4	0.45	**1.6**	0.5	0.14	1.58	3.34	86.9	**1.5**	5.4	22.1	**4.0**
4.0	1.89	11.7	0.07	**5.1**	6.9	0.93	8.12	3.71	65.2	**3.6**	13.0	11.0	**7.4**
6.2	0.43	2.7	-0.04	**6.2**	1.2	1.48	12.82	4.03	71.5	**3.0**	23.9	15.1	**6.3**
4.9	0.70	6.9	0.09	**8.3**	1.5	1.22	13.40	4.32	80.8	**0.6**	10.5	42.9	**4.6**
3.5	1.50	13.0	-0.01	**6.6**	2.7	1.17	13.88	4.24	53.9	**1.5**	8.6	22.7	**5.2**
7.1	0.12	0.8	0.27	**6.3**	1.4	1.51	15.65	4.84	62.9	**3.4**	22.5	12.6	**6.0**
5.2	1.38	8.2	0.36	**6.3**	26.3	1.24	10.20	3.90	63.9	**5.0**	22.3	4.8	**8.4**
3.4	0.74	6.4	0.14	**3.0**	1.2	0.51	5.99	4.12	78.6	**0.7**	17.3	47.6	**3.7**
1.7	11.06	43.8	0.49	**1.5**	0.0	0.10	0.92	4.08	95.9	**2.1**	43.7	43.3	**4.6**
4.7	1.45	9.7	0.18	**5.9**	2.7	1.47	15.75	4.10	66.3	**3.3**	22.8	13.4	**4.8**
7.4	0.00	0.0	0.00	**9.1**	9.0	1.32	9.90	3.50	34.2	**0.8**	7.3	32.1	**9.1**
7.8	0.74	4.2	0.15	**0.9**	0.4	0.09	0.83	2.78	95.9	**1.6**	23.8	25.0	**3.3**
3.5	4.58	17.5	0.15	**3.3**	1.8	0.53	4.84	3.69	79.0	**2.7**	30.5	18.3	**5.5**
6.0	0.24	2.5	0.31	**3.6**	0.4	0.66	8.92	3.61	70.5	**1.4**	10.6	23.9	**4.1**
6.4	0.48	3.3	0.07	**4.2**	5.0	0.74	7.21	3.19	60.6	**2.0**	15.2	19.2	**6.7**
2.9	5.72	19.9	-0.14	**4.1**	0.5	1.00	9.46	3.21	77.3	**5.3**	55.0	10.9	**5.1**
3.9	2.75	14.5	-0.06	**4.5**	1.1	1.08	12.31	3.89	73.8	**5.5**	44.8	8.4	**4.9**
7.0	1.54	7.1	0.16	**0.8**	0.0	-0.16	-1.46	3.57	102.7	**5.5**	34.9	4.3	**4.8**
5.3	0.55	4.3	0.00	**3.0**	1.4	0.44	4.43	3.44	82.7	**1.6**	17.5	24.2	**5.6**
8.8	0.08	0.3	0.00	**3.4**	0.2	0.74	7.08	2.75	73.3	**6.5**	69.5	6.6	**4.7**
3.1	1.76	13.1	0.18	**7.5**	814.1	1.22	9.67	3.44	58.6	**5.3**	21.6	2.5	**10.0**

Name	City	State	Rating	2013 Rating	2012 Rating	Total Assets ($Mil)	One Year Asset Growth	Asset Mix (As a % of Total Assets) Comm-ercial Loans	Cons-umer Loans	Mort-gage Loans	Secur-ities	Capital-ization Index	Lever-age Ratio	Risk-Based Capital Ratio
MANUFACTURERS BANK	Los Angeles	CA	**B-**	C+	C	2442.0	6.51	41.3	0.0	0.2	25.4	**10.0**	12.4	15.5
MANUFACTURERS BANK & TRUST CO	Forest City	IA	**A-**	B+	B	297.5	8.10	9.7	2.7	11.0	29.3	**10.0**	11.1	15.6
MAPLE BANK	Champlin	MN	**D**	D+	D	47.7	-12.81	13.4	2.2	10.8	0.0	**8.8**	10.2	16.0
MAPLE CITY SAVINGS BANK FSB	Hornell	NY	**C**	C+	C+	63.0	12.34	4.6	1.0	65.8	0.1	**9.0**	10.3	15.6
MAQUOKETA STATE BK	Maquoketa	IA	**A-**	A-	B+	312.9	-0.48	8.0	2.6	6.1	35.9	**10.0**	14.6	22.6
MARATHON SB	Wausau	WI	**D-**	D-	C-	150.6	-13.55	1.6	0.8	32.0	43.6	**8.8**	10.2	22.8
MARBLEHEAD BANK	Marblehead	MA	**C-**	D+	C-	182.4	3.01	0.6	0.5	56.8	2.2	**8.3**	9.9	16.5
MARBLEHEAD BANK	Marblehead	OH	**C**	C-	C	45.6	12.97	3.1	5.4	18.9	66.6	**7.8**	9.5	22.6
MARIES COUNTY BANK	Vienna	MO	**B**	B	B+	353.6	3.57	2.4	4.9	15.4	39.0	**10.0**	13.0	20.5
▲ MARINE BANK	Springfield	IL	**C-**	D+	C-	621.6	6.77	7.1	0.9	7.7	14.0	**7.5**	10.3	12.9
MARINE BANK & TRUST	Carthage	IL	**B+**	B+	A-	247.1	3.10	8.0	7.0	11.6	27.5	**7.2**	9.1	14.6
MARINE BANK & TRUST CO	Vero Beach	FL	**D-**	E	E-	149.2	7.75	11.8	0.6	26.3	11.1	**6.6**	8.6	13.7
MARINERS BANK	Edgewater	NJ	**D+**	D	D	263.3	2.53	8.9	1.0	20.4	8.1	**7.7**	10.0	13.1
MARION BANK & TRUST CO	Marion	AL	**B**	B+	B	252.9	-3.05	2.0	4.7	11.1	26.1	**9.7**	10.8	16.0
▼ MARION CENTER BANK	Indiana	PA	**D**	D	D	294.0	1.18	8.8	1.3	21.2	41.0	**4.8**	6.8	12.9
MARION COUNTY SB	Salem	IL	**C+**	C+	C+	158.0	0.71	2.3	14.7	28.1	33.9	**8.3**	9.9	18.7
MARION COUNTY STATE BK	Pella	IA	**A**	A	A	274.3	6.32	10.2	0.9	12.4	32.6	**8.9**	10.3	15.9
▲ MARION NATIONAL BK	Marion	KS	**C**	C-	C-	22.7	-2.96	3.9	1.6	8.9	46.6	**8.9**	10.2	21.4
▲ MARION STATE BK	Marion	TX	**A-**	B+	A-	86.5	12.47	6.5	7.8	1.2	58.4	**10.0**	13.1	26.0
MARION STATE BK	Marion	LA	**B**	B	C+	148.1	9.07	8.5	6.9	24.6	18.8	**8.9**	10.2	15.8
▲ MARKESAN STATE BK	Markesan	WI	**C+**	C-	C-	159.8	0.37	8.1	3.1	9.2	9.4	**10.0**	11.2	15.0
▲ MARLBOROUGH SB	Marlborough	MA	**B-**	C+	C+	486.0	3.11	3.9	0.6	30.7	16.1	**10.0**	11.0	17.5
MARLIN BUSINESS BANK	Salt Lake City	UT	**A**	A	B+	677.8	14.58	8.5	0.0	0.0	2.9	**10.0**	16.7	19.2
MARQUETTE BANK	Orland Park	IL	**C**	C-	D+	1511.4	0.26	1.1	0.1	16.0	24.1	**7.7**	9.5	15.4
MARQUETTE FARMERS STATE BK	Marquette	KS	**C+**	C+	C	34.2	1.99	4.5	5.8	14.0	33.4	**10.0**	12.5	23.5
MARQUETTE SB	Erie	PA	**B+**	B+	A-	810.0	0.59	2.6	0.6	43.2	37.8	**10.0**	15.5	29.0
MARQUIS BANK	Coral Gables	FL	**B-**	B-	B-	256.9	28.96	7.4	0.3	2.7	6.1	**10.0**	11.5	15.5
MARS NATIONAL BK	Mars	PA	**C-**	C-	C	352.8	-1.14	5.1	1.1	22.1	39.3	**8.3**	9.8	16.9
MARSEILLES BANK	Marseilles	IL	**B-**	B-	C+	52.4	8.20	0.6	5.7	30.0	49.9	**7.2**	9.2	22.5
MARSHALL COUNTY STATE BK	Newfolden	MN	**B**	B	B	33.3	8.19	3.3	5.0	15.8	19.9	**10.0**	16.5	51.6
MARTHAS VINEYARD SAVINGS BANK	Edgartown	MA	**B+**	B+	A-	582.6	5.90	1.0	0.3	53.0	11.7	**10.0**	12.9	22.2
MARTINSBURG BANK & TRUST	Mexico	MO	**B+**	B+	A-	189.9	-0.40	6.7	0.8	13.9	19.2	**10.0**	12.3	18.1
MARTINSVILLE FIRST SAVINGS BK	Martinsville	VA	**C**	C-	C-	44.2	-4.31	0.0	0.4	50.3	29.5	**10.0**	13.2	31.3
MARYLAND FINANCIAL BANK	Towson	MD	**D**	D-	D-	60.3	0.72	6.0	5.0	8.0	15.9	**8.9**	10.3	16.5
MASCOMA SAVINGS BANK	Lebanon	NH	**C**	C-	C+	1425.6	28.15	7.7	0.6	36.0	12.7	**5.3**	7.3	11.3
MASON BANK	Mason	TX	**A**	A-	A	100.4	12.07	4.6	4.4	10.5	59.8	**10.0**	16.5	38.7
MASON CITY NATIONAL BK	Mason City	IL	**B**	B	B	76.0	4.90	0.8	1.6	10.3	51.1	**10.0**	14.5	36.6
MASON STATE BK	Mason	MI	**C+**	C+	C	128.0	-0.11	4.7	0.4	37.6	18.6	**9.1**	10.4	21.2
MASPETH FS&LA	Maspeth	NY	**B**	B	B-	1732.9	-0.31	0.0	0.0	54.5	5.9	**10.0**	30.4	39.2
MASSENA SAVINGS & LOAN	Massena	NY	**B**	B	B-	136.4	-0.78	0.7	7.1	73.2	0.0	**10.0**	12.6	20.7
MASSMUTUAL TRUST CO FSB	Enfield	CT	**U**	U	B-	69.8	2.64	0.0	0.0	0.0	81.6	**10.0**	20.7	101.8
MAUCH CHUNK TRUST CO	Jim Thorpe	PA	**B**	B	B-	347.1	6.49	2.0	0.8	16.0	55.8	**8.8**	10.2	20.2
MAXWELL STATE BK	Maxwell	IA	**A**	A	A+	28.4	1.83	3.5	0.7	4.6	64.0	**10.0**	13.8	27.8
MAYNARD SB	Maynard	IA	**B+**	B+	A-	59.0	7.96	5.4	9.3	22.8	22.1	**10.0**	13.0	18.3
▲ MAYVILLE SB	Mayville	WI	**C+**	C	C-	56.1	-3.23	7.8	2.3	55.0	12.0	**8.4**	10.0	17.3
MAYVILLE STATE BK	Mayville	MI	**C+**	C+	C+	89.9	-0.13	0.6	2.1	35.4	36.8	**8.1**	9.8	23.4
MAZON STATE BK	Mazon	IL	**C-**	C-	C	87.1	2.01	1.4	1.3	24.4	50.1	**6.6**	8.6	13.0
MB FINANCIAL BANK NA	Chicago	IL	**C+**	C+	C	14476.5	56.65	27.7	2.3	8.8	19.4	**7.8**	11.8	13.1
MBANK	Manistique	MI	**C+**	C+	C-	604.4	7.09	15.0	2.6	15.7	8.1	**7.6**	10.4	13.0
▲ MBANK	Gresham	OR	**D-**	E-	E-	164.5	-3.49	5.4	1.1	16.9	8.9	**7.3**	9.2	13.1
MBL BANK	Minden	LA	**A**	A	A-	285.2	4.13	6.7	4.9	20.7	34.0	**10.0**	15.1	28.1
▲ MCCLAIN BANK	Purcell	OK	**B**	B-	B-	198.0	6.66	4.2	2.5	19.4	19.0	**8.6**	10.0	18.3
▲ MCCLAVE STATE BK	McClave	CO	**B-**	C	C-	25.4	1.85	8.1	1.8	3.8	18.3	**10.0**	12.5	18.5
MCCOOK NATIONAL BK	McCook	NE	**A-**	A-	B+	325.6	5.90	8.3	1.1	5.9	18.5	**10.0**	14.0	17.9
MCCURTAIN COUNTY NATIONAL BK	Broken Bow	OK	**B+**	B+	B	197.7	-1.44	3.1	10.1	18.4	14.6	**9.1**	10.4	19.8
MCFARLAND STATE BK	McFarland	WI	**C**	D+	D+	426.4	4.40	8.4	0.1	8.3	4.6	**10.0**	12.9	17.5
MCGEHEE BANK	McGehee	AR	**B**	B+	A-	127.2	8.26	12.9	1.0	2.5	17.9	**10.0**	14.5	17.0
MCHENRY SB	McHenry	IL	**E-**	E-	E-	257.1	2.27	2.0	6.9	38.9	21.5	**0.5**	3.7	7.7
MCINTOSH COUNTY BANK	Ashley	ND	**C-**	C-	C	87.2	3.23	3.8	2.9	0.7	24.7	**9.6**	10.8	15.2
MCKENZIE BANKING CO	McKenzie	TN	**A-**	B	B-	119.6	-0.33	7.2	5.0	18.4	17.4	**10.0**	13.9	28.0

Asset Quality Index	Adjusted Non-Performing Loans as a % of Total Loans	Adjusted Non-Performing Loans as a % of Capital	Net Charge-Offs Avg Loans	Profitability Index	Net Income ($Mil)	Return on Assets (R.O.A.)	Return on Equity (R.O.E.)	Net Interest Spread	Overhead Efficiency Ratio	Liquidity Index	Liquidity Ratio	Hot Money Ratio	Stability Index
8.3	0.13	0.7	-0.15	3.4	8.5	0.48	3.91	2.38	65.6	1.2	19.4	31.3	8.2
8.2	0.25	1.3	-0.04	6.6	3.2	1.45	12.70	3.97	63.8	3.6	31.2	14.0	7.2
0.9	6.07	37.9	0.07	0.6	-0.2	-0.53	-4.31	3.91	109.2	0.9	24.8	47.5	4.1
3.4	2.58	20.6	0.06	1.5	0.0	0.00	-0.02	4.09	96.9	4.8	10.7	2.8	5.5
5.6	2.24	7.9	-0.80	6.1	3.1	1.31	9.15	3.48	56.6	4.6	39.2	11.9	8.0
3.0	6.26	24.1	1.36	0.1	-2.4	-2.04	-21.59	3.48	83.2	4.3	51.6	16.4	3.8
5.6	1.09	8.9	0.05	2.0	0.3	0.20	1.94	3.59	94.0	4.4	13.0	5.6	5.2
9.3	0.00	0.0	0.00	2.7	0.2	0.53	5.70	2.91	82.3	5.5	62.6	11.2	4.3
8.2	0.89	3.5	0.24	4.8	2.6	0.99	7.81	4.13	67.2	2.9	28.8	16.9	7.1
2.0	2.33	16.0	0.30	4.1	4.0	0.83	8.27	3.27	78.3	3.7	14.5	10.4	6.0
5.9	0.68	4.3	0.15	6.1	2.6	1.42	13.71	3.42	56.9	2.8	15.9	14.9	7.9
3.8	1.13	8.6	0.03	3.4	0.7	0.62	6.63	3.67	76.3	4.1	21.0	8.6	3.8
1.9	2.02	16.3	0.64	3.0	1.7	0.90	9.29	3.78	80.1	1.2	15.3	29.7	3.3
4.5	1.26	7.3	0.02	5.3	2.4	1.28	11.93	3.59	58.4	1.2	19.9	31.2	6.3
2.1	3.66	26.6	0.09	2.8	1.0	0.47	8.25	3.11	84.9	3.7	42.0	17.0	2.8
4.3	1.48	8.3	0.06	2.9	0.5	0.40	4.06	3.19	84.1	3.6	22.9	12.0	5.2
8.6	0.04	0.3	0.00	9.3	4.3	2.11	20.17	3.86	43.0	4.2	27.6	9.8	8.3
6.9	0.82	2.8	-0.05	2.8	0.1	0.46	3.35	3.45	84.7	4.1	39.8	12.2	6.2
8.1	0.07	0.2	0.15	6.0	1.0	1.67	12.86	3.70	56.1	2.7	51.0	29.2	6.9
5.5	0.68	4.4	0.23	5.4	1.1	1.00	9.98	4.94	69.1	1.4	8.7	24.5	5.6
2.8	2.75	18.6	1.36	4.6	1.1	0.89	7.92	4.47	54.4	2.1	17.6	18.8	6.8
7.2	0.81	4.5	-0.03	3.4	2.4	0.67	5.99	3.30	76.6	3.5	31.4	14.7	6.3
9.0	0.26	1.3	1.50	10.0	15.7	3.19	20.27	10.68	44.2	0.3	12.6	90.0	8.8
3.3	3.19	19.6	0.23	3.5	6.4	0.56	4.78	3.74	83.7	4.9	22.2	5.7	7.5
4.0	3.65	13.1	-0.05	3.7	0.2	0.81	6.66	3.79	73.5	2.9	54.2	28.0	5.7
7.4	1.36	4.8	0.13	4.7	5.7	0.94	6.15	3.32	60.5	4.5	43.4	13.5	8.8
5.0	1.02	6.6	-0.01	3.6	1.0	0.57	4.82	3.26	69.9	1.4	23.1	28.1	5.7
6.9	0.54	2.8	-0.04	2.0	0.8	0.32	3.29	3.06	93.1	5.8	37.2	3.6	5.6
7.6	0.38	1.7	0.29	6.5	0.6	1.50	16.54	3.92	60.4	3.1	54.9	26.6	5.7
9.2	0.14	0.3	0.01	4.2	0.2	0.98	5.71	2.46	62.4	6.6	61.7	4.3	7.9
5.9	1.68	10.0	-0.01	4.6	3.0	0.71	5.22	3.55	71.4	4.4	19.7	6.9	8.3
7.6	0.69	3.6	-0.01	4.8	1.7	1.16	9.71	3.48	69.2	3.8	8.9	9.4	7.9
2.5	8.53	33.6	0.24	3.5	0.1	0.34	2.67	2.96	65.1	2.4	49.0	33.0	5.9
1.8	2.16	13.4	0.49	0.5	-0.1	-0.11	-1.09	3.48	94.6	1.2	33.9	91.6	3.0
5.5	1.11	10.5	0.05	2.6	3.6	0.38	4.15	3.24	84.0	3.0	7.1	13.6	6.1
9.0	0.28	0.6	0.00	7.1	1.2	1.72	10.04	3.89	58.0	5.6	68.6	13.0	9.2
9.4	0.91	2.1	0.00	4.2	0.7	1.13	8.12	2.74	62.1	5.0	71.1	15.2	7.9
6.7	0.71	4.2	-0.01	3.4	0.7	0.74	7.16	2.72	76.2	1.6	27.2	27.7	5.6
4.1	6.31	17.5	0.03	9.1	15.9	1.22	4.09	4.03	40.7	3.6	15.2	11.5	10.0
4.0	2.54	17.9	0.24	4.2	0.7	0.70	5.79	3.64	67.4	0.7	2.8	33.6	6.3
10.0	na	0.0	na	5.1	0.6	1.16	5.48	1.01	91.3	3.7	123.5	100.0	6.5
5.5	2.54	8.9	0.34	4.1	2.5	1.02	9.92	3.56	75.6	4.9	32.4	7.0	5.7
9.2	0.00	0.0	0.00	8.0	0.4	1.68	12.03	3.92	42.2	5.1	72.9	14.8	8.7
5.1	0.93	5.0	0.21	9.4	0.9	2.06	15.33	4.52	46.9	4.7	29.7	7.4	8.1
5.9	0.74	5.7	0.15	3.4	0.2	0.51	5.21	3.62	76.5	1.7	19.5	22.6	4.4
6.1	1.71	7.2	0.39	3.1	0.3	0.42	4.38	3.26	77.3	5.8	56.7	8.3	5.1
5.8	2.02	8.8	0.38	1.7	0.2	0.30	3.61	3.09	98.8	5.6	40.7	6.4	3.5
3.2	1.96	12.9	0.20	4.5	55.7	0.72	5.07	3.64	79.2	3.0	13.1	14.2	8.1
3.7	0.83	6.4	-0.02	5.1	3.7	0.83	7.47	4.16	67.9	2.0	12.3	18.8	6.8
4.4	0.15	1.0	-0.06	6.1	4.8	3.83	46.86	4.27	66.9	1.3	13.8	27.1	1.2
8.7	0.26	1.0	0.00	7.6	3.0	1.39	9.68	3.46	42.5	1.7	21.9	23.8	8.0
4.6	1.25	6.7	2.06	4.8	1.2	0.83	8.50	3.95	73.2	4.1	25.6	9.6	5.0
6.1	0.22	1.2	0.36	6.9	0.2	1.20	10.05	4.94	62.3	0.8	14.2	36.1	5.5
6.2	0.58	2.8	0.00	7.4	3.2	1.35	9.58	4.01	49.9	2.2	13.7	18.1	7.9
5.9	0.79	3.8	0.16	5.5	1.5	0.96	9.59	3.28	55.5	2.8	38.6	21.9	6.5
2.6	2.53	13.8	0.37	6.3	5.2	1.67	12.63	4.03	61.0	1.6	10.9	21.8	7.5
8.4	0.03	0.2	-0.03	4.5	1.0	1.06	7.39	3.44	68.4	3.0	19.6	14.6	8.7
0.3	5.72	73.1	0.21	1.9	0.6	0.30	11.41	3.43	91.3	0.8	19.1	42.6	0.4
2.6	2.83	15.5	-0.11	7.6	1.2	1.79	18.23	4.02	51.3	3.7	12.8	10.1	5.7
5.0	4.85	13.9	0.18	8.9	1.4	1.58	11.84	4.74	64.1	5.2	61.2	14.2	8.0

Name	City	State	Rating	2013 Rating	2012 Rating	Total Assets ($Mil)	One Year Asset Growth	Asset Mix (As a % of Total Assets) Comm-ercial Loans	Cons-umer Loans	Mort-gage Loans	Secur-ities	Capital-ization Index	Lever-age Ratio	Risk-Based Capital Ratio
MCKENZIE COUNTY BANK	Watford City	ND	**B**	B	B	158.3	32.42	5.1	5.6	17.8	18.9	**4.4**	6.4	12.8
MCNB BANK & TRUST CO	Welch	WV	**C-**	C	C+	300.0	-3.32	5.9	1.1	11.5	22.2	**9.1**	10.4	15.8
MEADE COUNTY BANK	Brandenburg	KY	**A-**	A-	A-	179.5	7.25	0.6	2.9	33.4	36.2	**7.0**	9.0	19.8
▲ MEADOWS BANK	Las Vegas	NV	**A**	B+	B	484.8	49.98	27.5	0.1	2.2	6.5	**10.0**	12.7	17.5
MECHANICS & FARMERS BANK	Durham	NC	**D**	D	C-	289.2	-0.89	2.8	0.4	8.2	24.5	**10.0**	11.6	17.8
MECHANICS BANK	Mansfield	OH	**C+**	C+	B-	414.2	2.15	1.2	1.1	62.0	8.5	**8.1**	9.7	18.2
▼ MECHANICS BANK	Water Valley	MS	**C**	B	B-	214.0	0.90	11.1	3.9	25.7	22.3	**8.7**	10.1	17.4
▲ MECHANICS BANK	Richmond	CA	**B-**	C+	C-	3345.3	1.37	5.5	5.8	3.5	37.0	**8.9**	10.3	17.3
MECHANICS COOPERATIVE BANK	Taunton	MA	**C+**	C+	C	443.0	5.46	5.0	1.8	34.7	14.7	**6.3**	8.3	12.6
▲ MECHANICS SB	Auburn	ME	**C+**	C-	D+	370.1	2.45	7.8	1.5	51.4	12.6	**10.0**	11.6	17.5
MEDALLION BANK	Salt Lake City	UT	**B+**	A-	A-	957.5	18.99	44.6	49.3	0.0	2.9	**10.0**	15.7	17.0
MEDIAPOLIS SB	Mediapolis	IA	**B**	B	B-	125.6	-1.74	6.1	2.1	15.7	27.2	**10.0**	11.7	16.5
MEDINA BANKING CO	Medina	TN	**B-**	B	B	42.8	2.32	14.9	7.1	4.7	58.7	**10.0**	15.6	29.9
MEDINA S&LA	Medina	NY	**D**	D	C-	46.7	4.48	1.0	2.6	42.4	11.9	**7.1**	9.1	20.5
MEETINGHOUSE BANK	Dorchester	MA	**D+**	D+	C+	107.8	40.80	2.7	1.2	50.8	15.4	**6.1**	8.1	13.3
MEGA BANK	San Gabriel	CA	**C+**	B-	C	269.7	7.45	3.0	0.0	16.1	13.3	**10.0**	13.1	19.9
MELROSE CO-OP BANK	Melrose	MA	**C**	C	C+	212.7	7.53	0.0	0.1	55.2	19.0	**9.6**	10.7	18.2
MELVIN SB	Melvin	IA	**B**	B	B+	64.9	6.09	6.8	2.4	5.3	45.6	**10.0**	16.4	21.8
MEMBERS TRUST CO	Tampa	FL	**U**	U	B+	29.5	4.54	0.0	0.0	0.0	76.1	**10.0**	93.1	458.0
MEMORIAL CITY BANK	Houston	TX	**B-**	C+	C+	279.1	-5.28	26.0	0.5	8.2	0.0	**6.6**	8.7	12.3
MEMPHIS STATE BK	Memphis	TX	**C**	C-	C-	31.9	-5.07	7.7	3.4	0.4	72.7	**9.2**	10.5	28.5
MENARD BANK	Menard	TX	**B-**	B-	B-	33.9	4.78	4.3	0.5	9.1	43.2	**10.0**	13.2	22.7
MENNO STATE BK	Menno	SD	**C+**	C+	B-	35.6	1.72	5.2	1.4	2.1	35.3	**8.6**	10.1	18.0
MER ROUGE STATE BK	Mer Rouge	LA	**C+**	B-	B-	45.3	-1.07	11.8	1.0	5.0	22.2	**10.0**	11.9	20.3
▲ MERAMEC VALLEY BANK	Ellisville	MO	**C-**	D	D	93.9	-1.79	7.6	0.8	19.1	18.2	**6.9**	8.9	15.6
MERCANTIL COMMERCEBANK NA	Coral Gables	FL	**C**	C	C	7784.6	13.34	29.9	1.5	2.4	30.0	**8.0**	9.6	13.9
MERCANTIL COMMERCEBANK TR CO	Coral Gables	FL	**U**	U	U	8.9	0.65	0.0	0.0	0.0	69.6	**10.0**	95.2	187.0
MERCANTILE BANK	Quincy	IL	**D+**	D	E+	334.1	-7.08	8.7	16.2	26.1	14.6	**6.5**	8.5	12.4
MERCANTILE BANK OF MICHIGAN	Grand Rapids	MI	**B**	B-	C-	2842.9	100.79	16.5	2.2	9.2	16.0	**8.8**	10.9	14.0
MERCANTILE BK OF LOUISIANA MO	Louisiana	MO	**B**	B	B+	101.9	-0.25	2.2	1.2	20.7	27.8	**10.0**	21.8	38.2
▲ MERCER COUNTY STATE BK	Sandy Lake	PA	**B**	B-	B-	352.3	1.58	4.9	2.3	19.5	37.5	**8.4**	9.9	15.9
MERCER SAVINGS BANK	Celina	OH	**D+**	D+	D+	108.1	-0.97	1.2	1.9	50.2	22.4	**8.4**	9.9	18.4
MERCHANTS & CITIZENS BANK	McRae	GA	**B**	B-	C+	101.9	5.58	3.3	5.0	12.8	50.3	**10.0**	14.2	31.4
▼ MERCHANTS & FARMERS BANK	Eutaw	AL	**C+**	B-	C+	57.4	-3.48	6.3	6.9	8.9	43.0	**9.7**	10.8	22.7
▲ MERCHANTS & FARMERS BANK	Holly Springs	MS	**C+**	C-	C	91.8	1.39	5.7	5.0	14.1	36.5	**9.8**	10.9	21.5
▲ MERCHANTS & FARMERS BANK	Dumas	AR	**B-**	C+	C+	108.1	6.82	11.8	3.0	9.2	21.6	**10.0**	11.0	15.8
MERCHANTS & FARMERS BANK	Salisbury	MO	**C+**	C+	C	96.2	0.25	4.7	2.2	19.1	28.6	**6.5**	8.5	13.7
MERCHANTS & FARMERS BANK & TR	Leesville	LA	**B-**	B	B	319.3	7.56	3.0	1.2	16.1	43.5	**10.0**	13.0	22.8
MERCHANTS & MANUFACTURERS BAN	Joliet	IL	**C+**	C+	C	207.3	12.31	29.1	25.2	3.4	3.1	**5.5**	8.8	11.4
MERCHANTS & MARINE BANK	Pascagoula	MS	**B**	B-	B-	566.4	-2.68	4.8	4.2	10.6	47.3	**10.0**	11.2	23.2
MERCHANTS & PLANTERS BANK	Raymond	MS	**C-**	D+	D	86.7	3.16	3.6	1.6	8.5	45.7	**6.9**	8.9	20.5
MERCHANTS & PLANTERS BANK	Clarendon	AR	**C+**	C+	C+	44.7	-5.37	6.0	2.8	4.7	64.2	**9.3**	10.6	26.4
MERCHANTS & PLANTERS BANK	Newport	AR	**C+**	C+	C+	245.0	2.48	7.6	5.7	10.5	32.7	**6.6**	8.6	13.6
▲ MERCHANTS & PLANTERS BANK	Bolivar	TN	**B**	B	D+	84.1	-6.24	3.8	3.6	15.5	27.5	**10.0**	12.0	20.0
▲ MERCHANTS & SOUTHERN BANK	Gainesville	FL	**C+**	C-	D+	397.9	-1.55	3.4	0.7	5.9	36.4	**9.4**	10.6	17.8
MERCHANTS BANK	Jackson	AL	**C**	C	C-	201.9	-2.41	4.8	3.5	16.4	33.9	**9.4**	10.6	18.3
MERCHANTS BANK	South Burlington	VT	**B**	B	B	1651.8	-1.59	9.8	0.3	28.4	19.8	**6.8**	8.8	16.9
MERCHANTS BANK	Rugby	ND	**B**	B	B-	105.5	8.38	10.1	2.9	2.9	29.4	**6.2**	8.2	13.1
MERCHANTS BANK NA	Winona	MN	**B+**	B+	B	1471.6	9.46	17.0	3.0	9.3	17.7	**7.6**	10.4	13.0
▲ MERCHANTS BANK OF ALABAMA	Cullman	AL	**C**	D+	D+	249.7	1.69	6.0	4.2	19.6	23.1	**7.8**	9.5	16.5
MERCHANTS BANK OF BANGOR	Bangor	PA	**C+**	C+	C+	356.4	8.22	2.8	0.9	22.6	36.1	**6.4**	8.4	15.9
▲ MERCHANTS BANK OF INDIANA	Lynn	IN	**B+**	A-	A-	1716.4	25.90	2.4	0.2	2.8	14.2	**6.2**	8.2	12.3
▲ MERCHANTS BK OF CALIFORNIA NA	Carson	CA	**B+**	B	B+	80.9	-7.66	7.9	0.0	0.4	19.7	**10.0**	23.8	59.8
▼ MERCHANTS COMMERCIAL BANK	Saint Thomas	VI	**D-**	D+	C-	116.7	0.76	7.0	0.4	27.7	5.6	**8.7**	10.1	19.1
MERCHANTS NATIONAL BK	Hillsboro	OH	**C+**	C+	C	624.5	6.30	4.1	3.1	27.3	6.3	**7.5**	9.3	13.1
MERCHANTS NB OF SACRAMENTO	Sacramento	CA	**B-**	B-	B	222.3	14.37	0.9	0.2	12.4	55.9	**6.8**	8.8	30.6
MERCHANTS STATE BK	Freeman	SD	**B**	B-	B-	146.4	2.81	7.2	1.8	1.8	31.8	**7.2**	9.2	13.6
MEREDITH VILLAGE SB	Meredith	NH	**B-**	B-	C+	748.8	6.85	4.1	2.7	41.4	8.3	**9.6**	10.8	16.5
▲ MERIDIAN BANK	Malvern	PA	**C**	D+	D+	584.5	25.11	18.7	0.2	21.3	5.2	**6.0**	8.1	11.8
MERIDIAN BANK NA	Scottsdale	AZ	**B+**	B	B	720.3	-1.12	34.8	0.1	9.6	19.4	**10.0**	13.2	15.6

Asset Quality Index	Adjusted Non-Performing Loans as a % of Total Loans	Adjusted Non-Performing Loans as a % of Capital	Net Charge-Offs Avg Loans	Profitability Index	Net Income ($Mil)	Return on Assets (R.O.A.)	Return on Equity (R.O.E.)	Net Interest Spread	Overhead Efficiency Ratio	Liquidity Index	Liquidity Ratio	Hot Money Ratio	Stability Index
5.0	1.16	8.7	0.00	8.0	1.9	1.80	25.98	3.93	50.5	4.0	39.5	15.0	5.4
3.6	3.19	16.7	0.12	2.3	0.6	0.27	2.70	3.45	89.2	3.1	24.9	14.4	5.4
8.5	0.28	1.6	0.02	5.7	1.4	1.08	12.72	3.38	57.9	5.8	49.4	7.7	5.4
8.2	0.20	1.1	-0.01	7.1	4.4	1.25	10.20	4.29	62.9	4.7	27.6	6.9	6.5
0.0	12.02	58.2	0.06	3.5	1.2	0.53	4.53	3.76	80.3	1.0	25.4	43.8	6.2
5.7	1.20	9.2	0.13	3.4	1.9	0.61	6.39	3.42	77.3	3.8	11.3	9.4	5.6
2.5	5.33	29.7	1.09	3.6	0.7	0.46	4.60	4.18	62.1	1.3	24.1	29.6	6.1
4.7	2.07	9.3	0.02	4.1	16.9	0.68	7.24	3.78	71.8	5.5	39.4	9.6	6.9
5.6	0.84	7.5	0.14	4.3	2.5	0.75	9.64	3.56	66.8	1.1	17.6	30.5	4.4
2.6	3.57	23.9	0.26	4.0	1.8	0.66	5.93	4.00	67.9	0.7	12.7	36.1	6.4
4.9	0.50	2.7	0.75	10.0	18.9	2.89	18.37	7.92	28.0	0.1	6.0	100.0	8.9
5.3	1.82	9.3	-0.08	5.0	1.1	1.15	10.22	3.48	60.6	3.0	29.3	16.3	6.8
5.5	6.28	11.4	0.06	3.1	0.1	0.35	2.27	4.15	88.1	6.1	72.4	10.0	6.8
5.5	1.44	7.5	0.20	1.0	0.1	0.13	1.58	3.00	97.6	5.0	50.6	12.0	2.6
8.5	0.26	2.6	0.00	1.2	0.0	0.01	0.07	3.34	96.8	0.9	23.1	43.4	2.6
4.9	1.17	6.0	0.88	2.8	0.7	0.36	2.82	3.38	68.1	0.7	18.2	50.3	6.3
8.4	0.63	4.0	0.00	3.0	0.5	0.36	3.27	2.31	76.1	3.1	37.3	18.7	5.6
8.9	0.11	0.3	-0.02	3.9	0.4	0.89	5.44	3.07	65.5	6.5	70.5	7.1	7.4
9.1	na	0.0	na	9.3	1.5	7.25	8.10	2.78	85.2	10.0	970.8	0.0	7.0
8.4	0.00	0.0	-0.01	4.6	1.1	0.53	6.16	3.99	67.7	2.0	25.8	21.1	4.6
8.5	0.05	0.1	0.03	1.6	0.0	0.02	0.19	2.12	100.0	4.2	35.1	12.4	4.5
9.6	0.00	0.0	0.00	3.4	0.1	0.58	4.37	3.64	82.1	3.1	54.3	25.1	6.5
6.0	1.02	4.6	0.00	4.0	0.2	0.68	7.05	2.81	63.6	6.6	49.4	1.7	5.0
7.2	1.05	4.2	0.01	2.7	0.1	0.43	3.65	3.28	84.5	2.9	44.9	23.7	5.9
7.6	0.43	2.5	-0.49	2.7	0.5	0.64	7.05	3.25	91.8	4.0	26.7	10.5	3.2
6.1	0.97	6.3	0.13	3.0	19.7	0.37	3.58	2.22	77.2	4.8	27.3	9.3	5.9
10.0	na	0.0	na	10.0	0.4	5.29	5.58	2.13	74.5	4.0	2680.5	101.0	5.0
4.3	0.56	4.4	0.31	3.1	2.2	0.85	10.37	4.29	73.9	2.6	11.2	15.5	7.0
4.7	1.59	10.1	-0.05	6.1	14.3	1.01	7.17	4.15	70.6	1.6	16.2	25.0	8.1
5.5	5.06	11.8	-0.45	4.7	0.9	1.10	4.73	3.09	63.8	3.5	45.4	19.0	7.7
5.5	1.50	8.0	0.03	4.7	2.4	0.95	9.43	3.94	72.2	4.2	35.5	12.3	5.7
5.5	2.01	11.9	0.04	1.6	0.0	0.05	0.49	2.97	97.8	5.0	34.3	7.5	4.1
4.8	3.37	8.4	-0.30	5.3	0.9	1.12	8.19	3.56	61.2	2.2	34.6	27.3	7.5
5.1	2.25	8.5	0.04	3.1	0.3	0.55	5.06	3.92	88.0	4.8	23.9	4.7	5.3
3.5	3.09	12.1	0.25	3.6	0.5	0.70	7.01	3.81	80.0	2.4	35.9	24.5	5.0
8.2	0.19	1.1	0.07	3.5	0.5	0.66	6.37	3.86	82.0	1.9	14.6	19.3	6.1
7.1	0.00	0.0	-0.32	3.8	0.7	0.92	10.52	3.35	73.2	2.2	19.0	18.6	4.3
9.3	0.40	1.5	0.18	3.3	1.4	0.58	4.74	3.38	81.4	4.2	38.7	13.7	7.3
6.3	0.00	0.0	-0.18	4.1	1.0	0.64	7.36	4.14	74.5	1.2	8.9	26.7	4.1
6.3	1.79	5.9	0.31	4.8	4.2	0.92	9.87	3.23	65.6	2.6	20.6	16.3	6.2
5.5	1.95	6.2	-0.70	2.0	0.2	0.31	3.61	2.68	102.3	5.5	43.3	7.4	3.0
7.4	0.63	1.2	1.37	3.3	0.2	0.58	6.01	3.12	78.1	3.4	59.9	23.9	5.0
5.0	0.94	5.8	0.17	4.1	1.5	0.77	9.89	3.58	77.2	1.7	13.9	20.8	4.2
8.6	0.54	2.4	-0.02	3.9	0.4	0.69	5.50	4.55	78.5	3.2	37.4	18.3	5.2
3.4	2.94	13.9	0.35	4.5	3.7	1.19	12.12	3.37	67.0	4.3	15.1	6.5	5.1
2.7	4.10	19.2	0.04	3.3	1.2	0.76	7.74	3.98	77.9	2.4	32.5	22.0	4.6
8.9	0.05	0.4	0.01	4.4	10.3	0.82	9.70	3.12	71.0	4.4	12.7	6.4	7.6
8.2	0.15	1.1	-0.01	6.1	0.9	1.14	13.52	3.90	51.6	4.2	16.7	7.5	5.3
5.4	0.98	6.5	0.03	6.3	10.7	1.01	8.89	3.99	66.3	4.1	3.4	6.4	9.0
3.1	2.56	14.8	0.33	3.9	1.2	0.64	6.86	3.80	78.1	3.2	30.3	15.7	4.0
4.3	2.68	15.6	0.14	3.1	1.4	0.52	6.60	3.21	80.4	4.3	17.8	7.2	4.1
7.4	0.03	0.2	0.01	7.8	-1.6	-0.14	-1.79	2.14	27.9	4.8	27.0	9.5	8.7
5.0	8.65	9.5	-1.47	10.0	1.7	2.46	11.64	4.21	71.0	5.6	61.4	10.6	7.1
0.3	10.55	57.8	0.06	3.0	0.6	0.65	6.97	3.34	76.1	5.4	33.1	4.0	5.4
3.7	1.74	14.3	0.17	6.3	5.0	1.06	11.66	3.96	57.8	2.6	7.5	15.3	6.3
9.6	0.48	1.3	0.00	4.0	1.2	0.77	8.36	2.65	64.0	4.1	71.5	22.4	5.3
4.8	1.37	8.8	-0.01	5.8	1.4	1.31	14.40	4.18	61.8	4.4	20.8	6.8	4.8
4.1	1.47	10.6	0.75	3.6	3.1	0.56	5.14	3.60	76.8	1.9	5.6	18.6	6.7
3.7	0.89	9.3	0.40	4.8	2.9	0.74	9.40	4.17	80.5	0.6	7.7	42.8	4.4
8.4	0.06	0.3	-0.29	6.6	8.2	1.50	11.12	5.71	80.8	0.9	23.2	36.5	7.0

Name	City	State	Rating	2013 Rating	2012 Rating	Total Assets ($Mil)	One Year Asset Growth	Asset Mix (As a % of Total Assets) Commercial Loans	Consumer Loans	Mortgage Loans	Securities	Capitalization Index	Leverage Ratio	Risk-Based Capital Ratio
MERIDIAN BANK TEXAS	Fort Worth	TX	**B**	B	B	433.1	63.95	18.5	1.0	10.1	18.5	**9.3**	10.5	14.6
▼ MERIT BANK	Overland Park	KS	**C**	C+	C+	81.6	16.43	25.1	2.3	19.7	6.4	**3.4**	8.0	10.2
MERRICK BANK	South Jordan	UT	**C**	C	C+	2083.4	12.12	0.0	94.0	0.0	2.1	**10.0**	23.7	26.9
MERRILL FS&LA	Merrill	WI	**B**	B	B-	47.0	2.61	7.9	5.3	38.1	0.0	**10.0**	12.1	17.4
MERRIMAC SB	Merrimac	MA	**E+**	E+	D-	74.9	7.78	2.5	2.9	42.2	35.8	**4.3**	6.3	14.5
MERRIMACK COUNTY SB	Concord	NH	**B-**	B-	C+	709.9	7.25	7.1	2.5	31.3	13.2	**7.0**	9.0	12.8
METABANK	Sioux Falls	SD	**B-**	B-	B-	2050.6	21.39	1.3	0.7	4.9	69.2	**6.6**	8.6	21.6
METAIRIE BANK & TRUST CO	Metairie	LA	**B-**	B-	B	348.9	-0.49	2.0	1.9	30.7	24.1	**9.4**	10.6	20.1
▲ METAMORA STATE BK	Metamora	OH	**C**	D+	C-	62.0	1.10	20.4	1.0	29.0	12.7	**7.3**	9.2	14.9
METCALF BANK	Lees Summit	MO	**C+**	C+	C+	1322.2	11.28	11.9	5.8	5.9	8.2	**6.1**	9.1	11.8
METHUEN CO-OP BANK	Methuen	MA	**C-**	C-	C-	89.0	0.07	0.5	1.7	49.2	17.6	**8.9**	10.3	20.9
METRO BANK	Lemoyne	PA	**B-**	C+	C	2960.2	7.44	13.3	0.4	10.3	29.6	**6.9**	8.9	13.5
METRO BANK	Pell City	AL	**A-**	B+	A-	652.6	0.23	5.0	3.6	16.1	21.6	**10.0**	12.7	20.0
METRO BANK	Douglasville	GA	**B**	B	C+	223.5	22.43	3.9	0.2	7.2	19.2	**10.0**	11.5	15.6
METRO BANK	Louisville	KY	**C-**	C-	C	32.1	-5.90	10.6	0.1	4.9	13.2	**10.0**	16.8	33.1
METRO CITY BANK	Doraville	GA	**B-**	B-	C+	569.3	13.46	5.0	2.5	14.0	6.8	**10.0**	12.1	17.0
▼ METRO PHOENIX BANK	Phoenix	AZ	**C**	C	D+	96.5	13.45	23.4	0.3	5.8	4.4	**9.7**	11.3	14.7
METROPOLITAN BANK	Ridgeland	MS	**C+**	C+	C	892.3	15.27	21.0	2.1	12.9	18.4	**5.9**	7.9	11.7
▲ METROPOLITAN BANK	Oakland	CA	**C-**	C-	D	144.9	11.24	3.7	0.1	21.4	8.3	**8.8**	10.2	17.1
METROPOLITAN CAPITAL BANK & TR	Chicago	IL	**C+**	C	C	188.6	8.11	50.4	0.3	9.4	9.2	**4.8**	8.2	10.9
▲ METROPOLITAN COMMERCIAL BANK	New York	NY	**C-**	C-	C-	757.4	21.26	21.0	0.0	9.6	7.9	**8.4**	9.9	13.8
▲ METROPOLITAN NATIONAL BK	Springfield	MO	**C+**	C-	C-	449.4	1.54	6.5	1.1	20.2	15.8	**10.0**	11.7	17.6
METUCHEN SB	Metuchen	NJ	**C-**	C-	C	259.2	-0.68	3.2	0.0	38.1	28.2	**10.0**	11.0	24.8
▲ METZ BANKING CO	Nevada	MO	**B**	B	B	71.9	5.65	9.2	1.5	9.8	19.0	**9.0**	10.4	15.2
▲ MIAMI SAVINGS BANK	Miamitown	OH	**B**	B-	C+	113.2	-0.66	4.8	0.4	45.9	2.3	**10.0**	13.5	21.8
MID AMERICA BANK	Linn	MO	**B-**	B-	B-	356.3	8.10	8.8	2.0	25.6	15.2	**5.5**	7.5	11.6
MID AMERICA BANK	Janesville	WI	**D**	D	D	93.6	-6.70	31.6	0.1	13.3	16.7	**8.3**	9.9	16.8
MID AMERICA BANK & TRUST CO	Dixon	MO	**A**	A-	B	146.2	2.39	5.6	4.0	18.7	23.1	**10.0**	13.5	20.0
▲ MID PENN BANK	Millersburg	PA	**C+**	C-	C-	764.4	9.52	10.5	0.3	14.5	19.4	**5.6**	7.6	11.5
MID-AMERICA BANK	Baldwin City	KS	**B+**	B	B-	97.2	26.84	4.8	2.0	50.3	0.0	**5.7**	10.7	11.5
MID-CENTRAL FSB	Wadena	MN	**C+**	C+	C	94.1	-2.33	3.1	13.9	53.6	1.1	**7.3**	9.2	15.1
MID-MISSOURI BANK	Springfield	MO	**B-**	B-	C+	556.7	8.37	5.7	1.2	19.6	1.8	**7.2**	9.1	13.3
▼ MID-SOUTHERN SAVINGS BANK FSB	Salem	IN	**D+**	C	C+	193.0	-6.85	2.1	1.7	43.1	10.2	**9.5**	10.6	17.6
MIDAMERICA NATIONAL BK	Canton	IL	**B**	B	B+	336.8	2.30	4.2	3.3	13.1	43.5	**10.0**	12.0	23.4
▼ MIDCOAST COMMUNITY BANK	Wilmington	DE	**D-**	D	D+	231.2	-12.18	10.4	0.0	19.0	0.0	**6.0**	8.4	11.7
MIDCOUNTRY BANK	Bloomington	MN	**C+**	C	C-	693.6	2.57	7.4	4.5	18.1	12.3	**10.0**	13.4	18.0
MIDDLEBURG BANK	Middleburg	VA	**C+**	C+	C	1201.6	-0.64	11.3	1.4	17.8	27.8	**7.5**	9.4	16.7
MIDDLEFIELD BANKING CO	Middlefield	OH	**C+**	C+	C-	678.4	17.68	8.2	0.6	22.8	22.9	**7.3**	9.2	13.5
▲ MIDDLESEX FEDERAL SAVINGS FA	Somerville	MA	**C**	D+	D	340.3	1.11	1.5	0.0	41.1	22.1	**9.8**	10.9	18.5
MIDDLESEX SB	Natick	MA	**B**	B	B-	4213.7	4.65	6.9	0.3	28.4	30.4	**10.0**	12.1	18.6
MIDDLETON COMMUNITY BANK	Middleton	WI	**A-**	A-	B+	263.5	3.80	11.9	1.0	7.2	30.5	**10.0**	12.6	19.0
MIDDLETOWN STATE BK	Middletown	IL	**B+**	B	B	30.1	12.28	4.7	2.9	26.0	9.4	**10.0**	11.6	16.1
MIDDLETOWN VALLEY BANK	Middletown	MD	**C+**	C+	B	168.0	7.53	8.5	0.3	34.0	24.4	**10.0**	11.0	19.7
MIDFIRST BANK	Oklahoma City	OK	**B**	B-	B-	9797.1	1.85	7.3	0.4	45.5	3.9	**10.0**	12.1	17.3
MIDLAND COMMUNITY BANK	Kincaid	IL	**C+**	C	C	51.9	4.28	8.5	2.5	38.1	31.9	**6.9**	8.9	16.4
MIDLAND FS&LA	Bridgeview	IL	**D+**	D+	D+	119.3	-3.83	0.0	0.2	47.4	25.6	**7.1**	9.1	25.4
MIDLAND NATIONAL BK	Newton	KS	**C-**	C-	C-	137.8	3.97	4.4	2.5	9.8	48.9	**8.3**	9.9	15.7
MIDLAND STATES BANK	Effingham	IL	**B**	B	B-	1817.1	6.24	12.7	6.3	5.7	16.7	**5.9**	9.0	11.7
MIDSOUTH BANK	Dothan	AL	**C-**	C-	C-	368.0	-1.22	12.3	1.0	12.2	8.6	**9.7**	10.8	16.8
MIDSOUTH BANK NA	Lafayette	LA	**B+**	B	B	1888.3	1.50	23.1	6.2	7.3	22.9	**7.1**	9.1	13.0
MIDSTATE COMMUNITY BANK	Baltimore	MD	**B-**	C	C-	179.4	-1.20	0.0	0.2	51.3	23.5	**10.0**	12.9	29.6
MIDSTATES BANK NA	Council Bluffs	IA	**A-**	A-	B+	365.0	6.59	2.0	0.7	9.8	29.5	**9.1**	10.4	15.1
MIDWEST BANK	Detroit Lakes	MN	**A-**	A-	B+	345.9	2.71	18.1	2.9	17.6	5.4	**6.4**	9.8	12.1
▲ MIDWEST BANK NA	Pierce	NE	**A-**	B+	B+	635.2	7.80	6.9	2.7	2.7	20.0	**8.1**	9.7	13.9
MIDWEST BANK OF WESTERN IL	Monmouth	IL	**B**	B	B-	413.2	0.42	6.2	2.0	7.2	32.3	**7.9**	9.6	16.2
MIDWEST BANKCENTRE	Saint Louis	MO	**B-**	B-	C+	1124.9	-2.43	7.9	1.6	16.0	21.3	**10.0**	11.1	15.2
MIDWEST COMMUNITY BANK	Plainville	KS	**C-**	C	C-	67.9	-6.75	13.7	0.6	8.6	53.3	**9.6**	10.7	25.7
MIDWEST COMMUNITY BANK	Freeport	IL	**D**	D	D-	202.0	0.51	6.8	0.1	19.3	0.9	**8.6**	10.1	15.1
MIDWEST HERITAGE BANK FSB	West Des Moines	IA	**A-**	A-	B+	187.5	10.30	3.6	18.9	24.0	26.5	**9.9**	10.9	17.2
▲ MIDWEST INDEPENDENT BANK	Jefferson City	MO	**C**	C-	C-	281.4	0.20	1.0	0.0	0.6	18.5	**10.0**	12.6	25.8

Asset Quality Index	Adjusted Non-Performing Loans as a % of Total Loans	Adjusted Non-Performing Loans as a % of Capital	Net Charge-Offs / Avg Loans	Profitability Index	Net Income ($Mil)	Return on Assets (R.O.A.)	Return on Equity (R.O.E.)	Net Interest Spread	Overhead Efficiency Ratio	Liquidity Index	Liquidity Ratio	Hot Money Ratio	Stability Index
3.6	1.41	9.2	0.05	**4.1**	2.3	0.89	6.16	4.02	78.9	**1.7**	25.1	24.3	**7.8**
7.9	0.00	0.0	0.03	**4.0**	0.3	0.48	5.22	4.70	80.7	**0.6**	8.9	44.3	**4.9**
2.1	3.77	10.6	7.73	**10.0**	111.5	7.23	31.52	21.40	28.4	**0.4**	7.3	75.4	**9.5**
6.0	0.90	6.0	0.22	**5.3**	0.3	0.74	6.07	3.77	67.0	**1.2**	12.5	27.5	**6.4**
3.9	2.07	16.7	-0.04	**1.7**	0.2	0.35	5.82	3.64	97.1	**3.5**	45.3	18.3	**1.5**
4.2	0.95	8.2	0.00	**4.3**	2.5	0.48	4.60	3.52	77.5	**3.5**	9.0	11.0	**6.5**
9.4	0.65	1.8	0.00	**4.0**	12.0	0.81	9.91	2.88	79.5	**6.2**	43.9	6.3	**5.1**
8.5	0.33	1.8	0.05	**3.4**	1.3	0.49	4.77	3.21	81.4	**5.5**	35.2	4.7	**6.6**
4.0	1.82	13.4	0.51	**3.8**	0.3	0.57	6.38	4.17	79.6	**2.2**	17.2	18.3	**3.2**
2.5	2.25	16.6	0.11	**6.5**	9.1	0.97	6.20	4.52	68.0	**4.6**	13.1	4.6	**7.8**
4.4	2.93	16.2	0.05	**2.1**	0.1	0.17	1.66	2.80	90.8	**3.7**	41.6	16.8	**5.3**
4.5	1.92	12.8	0.19	**4.2**	16.6	0.77	8.89	3.70	70.9	**4.4**	9.9	5.9	**6.1**
6.2	0.81	3.8	0.31	**7.4**	6.7	1.36	11.09	5.09	54.4	**2.0**	28.7	23.8	**6.9**
5.5	0.98	5.1	-0.06	**4.1**	1.0	0.67	5.64	4.23	74.7	**2.1**	30.3	23.7	**6.7**
8.2	0.61	1.5	-2.03	**1.9**	0.0	0.17	1.07	2.53	102.2	**2.2**	56.4	79.8	**5.7**
3.4	1.53	9.3	0.45	**10.0**	9.3	2.24	18.91	4.63	41.8	**0.8**	16.8	37.1	**8.8**
2.2	1.76	12.0	2.47	**3.5**	0.4	0.51	3.43	5.08	67.3	**2.3**	13.8	17.4	**4.9**
7.3	0.25	2.0	-0.01	**3.5**	3.8	0.55	6.86	3.02	72.1	**1.7**	15.1	20.8	**4.9**
2.4	3.39	20.0	0.00	**5.6**	1.4	1.39	13.20	4.12	66.3	**2.9**	21.5	15.0	**5.7**
5.9	0.00	0.0	0.19	**3.9**	0.7	0.48	5.74	6.04	79.0	**0.7**	14.5	50.0	**4.8**
2.8	1.13	8.6	0.00	**2.6**	1.2	0.24	2.05	3.46	88.5	**2.9**	18.3	14.6	**6.5**
5.3	1.44	8.3	0.09	**2.8**	1.9	0.56	4.36	3.44	95.3	**4.1**	13.1	8.0	**5.4**
9.1	0.72	3.3	0.00	**1.6**	0.4	0.18	1.77	2.54	99.6	**5.3**	49.1	10.6	**4.7**
4.8	1.12	6.9	-0.04	**7.4**	1.0	1.82	17.95	4.06	53.9	**2.7**	26.6	17.2	**6.5**
6.5	1.22	6.9	0.04	**4.0**	0.6	0.69	5.10	3.22	68.3	**0.8**	16.2	40.6	**6.9**
6.5	0.38	3.3	0.00	**6.7**	4.3	1.63	21.77	3.82	52.3	**2.2**	18.3	18.4	**4.5**
4.3	2.09	11.5	-0.17	**0.7**	0.0	0.06	0.54	3.88	106.9	**1.7**	18.5	22.3	**3.9**
6.9	1.19	5.6	0.11	**10.0**	3.2	2.97	22.08	4.29	40.6	**4.7**	31.4	8.3	**7.5**
3.3	1.62	14.7	0.27	**4.5**	4.9	0.90	11.64	4.02	66.8	**4.0**	4.0	7.5	**4.4**
7.4	0.38	2.8	0.07	**8.6**	1.2	1.86	16.73	4.75	64.6	**0.7**	10.5	39.3	**6.4**
3.7	1.19	10.6	0.43	**3.8**	0.5	0.74	8.08	4.38	80.5	**3.4**	7.7	11.3	**4.5**
4.9	0.92	7.3	0.21	**4.3**	3.8	0.93	9.98	3.85	73.9	**1.5**	13.0	23.6	**5.7**
1.7	6.44	36.4	0.23	**1.5**	0.2	0.13	1.28	3.26	78.8	**2.4**	25.6	18.0	**4.5**
5.4	1.67	6.3	0.02	**4.1**	1.9	0.75	5.38	3.51	70.8	**5.1**	34.0	6.5	**6.8**
0.4	5.71	45.9	1.25	**0.2**	-0.6	-0.33	-3.79	3.09	74.5	**1.0**	15.3	32.3	**3.8**
3.1	3.52	17.9	0.27	**2.6**	0.7	0.13	0.82	4.13	97.8	**3.6**	21.1	11.7	**6.6**
5.3	1.32	7.7	0.59	**3.9**	6.2	0.68	7.19	3.47	74.1	**2.5**	23.1	18.9	**6.8**
3.8	2.37	16.3	0.04	**6.0**	5.9	1.18	12.54	3.91	62.0	**2.8**	20.0	15.3	**5.7**
6.0	1.24	7.3	-0.71	**2.8**	1.1	0.42	3.68	2.73	93.9	**1.0**	25.8	36.1	**4.8**
6.3	1.28	6.3	0.00	**4.4**	24.7	0.82	6.55	2.84	64.7	**4.3**	39.0	15.7	**8.4**
5.1	2.63	11.1	0.21	**5.8**	1.9	1.01	8.30	3.63	62.4	**2.9**	40.8	22.6	**7.0**
8.6	0.03	0.2	0.00	**7.8**	0.4	1.85	16.39	3.40	43.6	**4.0**	15.4	9.0	**6.8**
5.0	2.07	11.1	0.00	**2.9**	0.5	0.39	3.67	3.56	89.7	**4.8**	13.7	3.3	**6.0**
4.2	0.91	5.8	0.01	**9.4**	170.4	2.26	20.12	3.80	61.3	**1.6**	5.8	20.1	**10.0**
4.9	1.72	11.6	-0.05	**4.0**	0.2	0.52	6.12	3.27	76.5	**2.7**	31.5	18.7	**4.2**
3.5	4.02	23.3	0.21	**0.9**	-0.1	-0.12	-1.34	2.86	102.0	**5.1**	44.2	10.6	**4.5**
4.2	3.68	12.8	0.25	**2.3**	0.4	0.42	4.53	3.19	89.9	**6.5**	60.5	6.8	**4.2**
4.4	1.33	9.9	1.21	**5.1**	11.9	0.91	8.94	4.48	72.3	**1.9**	10.9	19.6	**7.8**
8.5	0.10	0.5	0.06	**1.8**	0.5	0.16	1.46	2.62	93.8	**2.0**	26.2	22.0	**5.4**
6.5	0.53	3.7	0.25	**6.4**	16.6	1.18	10.28	4.84	66.6	**4.2**	12.5	7.6	**8.0**
3.8	4.32	19.9	0.01	**3.7**	0.8	0.61	4.91	2.95	61.9	**1.9**	40.1	43.1	**6.2**
6.6	0.31	1.7	-0.15	**6.9**	4.3	1.59	14.13	3.86	53.7	**3.9**	34.8	14.0	**8.2**
7.6	0.12	1.0	0.01	**9.5**	5.5	2.16	22.28	3.99	50.2	**3.7**	9.2	9.7	**7.6**
7.3	0.36	2.4	0.09	**7.0**	6.2	1.31	13.44	3.72	53.3	**1.5**	11.1	23.7	**7.2**
6.3	0.29	1.6	0.06	**4.8**	2.9	0.92	7.50	3.45	61.0	**2.6**	19.0	16.4	**6.3**
6.3	0.92	5.2	-0.01	**3.9**	6.1	0.71	6.56	3.01	71.0	**3.3**	6.2	11.6	**8.3**
5.5	1.31	4.8	2.21	**2.2**	0.2	0.34	3.07	3.20	69.7	**1.8**	29.5	27.4	**3.3**
0.8	3.15	22.7	0.69	**3.9**	1.1	0.80	7.81	3.64	80.8	**1.7**	4.4	19.3	**5.0**
6.6	0.33	1.9	0.07	**6.6**	1.6	1.08	9.47	3.25	75.7	**5.9**	34.4	1.5	**7.1**
7.0	1.48	3.9	-3.59	**2.7**	0.8	0.33	2.83	1.87	86.1	**4.2**	64.3	19.7	**5.9**

Name	City	State	Rating	2013 Rating	2012 Rating	Total Assets ($Mil)	One Year Asset Growth	Asset Mix (As a % of Total Assets) Commercial Loans	Consumer Loans	Mortgage Loans	Securities	Capitalization Index	Leverage Ratio	Risk-Based Capital Ratio
MIDWEST REGIONAL BANK	Festus	MO	**C**	C	C	319.5	24.92	20.6	0.7	7.9	2.2	**3.4**	8.7	10.2
▲ MIDWESTONE BANK	Iowa City	IA	**A-**	B+	B	1802.8	4.40	12.0	1.2	13.5	29.5	**8.6**	10.1	13.8
MIFFLIN COUNTY SB	Lewistown	PA	**B-**	B	B	130.8	6.94	4.6	8.1	40.3	15.7	**10.0**	13.0	16.5
MIFFLINBURG BANK & TRUST CO	Mifflinburg	PA	**B+**	B+	A-	372.6	10.61	9.8	3.0	22.4	19.6	**8.6**	10.1	16.0
MILESTONE BANK	Doylestown	PA	**B-**	B-	B	235.3	19.06	29.3	0.1	8.5	14.2	**10.0**	13.5	18.4
MILFORD BANK	Milford	CT	**C+**	C	C+	404.1	2.66	7.7	3.1	44.7	3.0	**10.0**	11.0	17.0
MILFORD BUILDING & LOAN ASN SB	Milford	IL	**D+**	C-	C-	25.0	-1.44	0.0	0.0	70.2	0.1	**6.3**	8.3	16.2
▼ MILFORD FS&LA	Milford	MA	**C**	B-	B-	351.9	1.73	0.0	0.4	77.8	7.7	**10.0**	12.1	20.6
MILFORD NATIONAL BK & TRUST CO	Milford	MA	**C-**	C-	C-	290.0	4.39	6.1	3.6	26.5	8.8	**6.6**	8.6	12.9
MILLBURY NATIONAL BK	Millbury	MA	**B-**	C+	C	80.8	8.31	12.6	1.6	18.6	19.4	**9.3**	10.5	16.1
MILLBURY SB	Millbury	MA	**C+**	C+	C	203.0	0.86	3.1	0.8	26.3	24.6	**10.0**	11.7	18.9
MILLEDGEVILLE STATE BK	Milledgeville	IL	**A**	A-	B+	106.4	9.64	13.6	1.2	6.7	29.7	**9.3**	10.5	14.6
MILLENNIUM BANK	Des Plaines	IL	**C-**	C-	D+	58.5	11.14	6.8	1.0	24.7	0.0	**7.2**	9.7	12.7
MILLENNIUM BANK	Junction City	KS	**C+**	B-	B	35.8	3.21	9.6	2.5	23.0	0.5	**10.0**	13.5	19.1
▲ MILLINGTON SB	Millington	NJ	**C-**	D+	D	345.5	-0.42	2.8	0.3	46.0	21.7	**9.2**	10.5	18.7
MILLS COUNTY STATE BK	Goldthwaite	TX	**B**	B	B	279.1	-1.23	5.6	5.6	14.3	45.9	**7.5**	9.3	19.4
▲ MILLVILLE S&LA	Millville	NJ	**C**	C-	C+	146.4	-3.01	0.0	0.0	14.5	51.7	**10.0**	11.0	30.1
MILTON BANKING CO	Wellston	OH	**B-**	C+	C+	134.7	0.54	8.9	16.6	37.2	4.5	**8.4**	9.9	14.0
MILTON SAVINGS BANK	Milton	PA	**B+**	B+	A-	66.1	-4.13	0.0	0.6	57.3	16.8	**10.0**	19.9	49.4
MINDEN EXCHANGE BANK & TRUST	Minden	NE	**B+**	B+	A-	148.8	4.02	6.3	3.3	2.0	45.7	**10.0**	14.4	25.0
MINEOLA COMMUNITY BANK SSB	Mineola	TX	**B**	B	B+	178.9	16.76	1.9	2.5	45.9	24.4	**10.0**	15.5	26.8
MINER COUNTY BANK	Howard	SD	**C+**	C+	C+	43.5	8.92	5.1	1.9	0.5	43.4	**9.8**	10.9	21.5
MINERS & MERCHANTS BANK	Thomas	WV	**B**	B	B+	50.8	1.47	0.2	2.5	28.6	48.8	**10.0**	16.1	47.8
MINERS BANK	Minersville	PA	**C**	C	C	140.0	2.80	16.7	1.2	28.2	8.2	**9.0**	10.3	14.4
MINERS EXCHANGE BANK	Coeburn	VA	**C+**	C	D+	103.5	-26.05	0.8	8.2	30.7	25.2	**8.3**	9.9	18.9
MINERS NATIONAL BK OF EVELETH	Eveleth	MN	**D+**	C-	C-	60.5	7.59	1.8	3.2	17.1	27.9	**6.6**	8.7	21.4
MINERS STATE BK	Iron River	MI	**D+**	C	C	122.5	-1.31	11.9	0.4	7.8	22.2	**8.0**	9.7	13.6
MINNESOTA BANK & TRUST	Edina	MN	**C+**	C+	C+	165.6	-0.45	30.3	1.3	6.1	25.7	**6.6**	8.7	13.8
MINNESOTA FIRST CREDIT & SVG	Rochester	MN	**B-**	B-	C+	28.5	-1.68	1.8	31.9	56.4	0.0	**10.0**	12.8	19.5
MINNESOTA LAKES BANK	Delano	MN	**C+**	C+	B-	85.4	2.86	6.5	1.8	9.6	42.5	**7.2**	9.1	18.4
MINNESOTA NATIONAL BK	Sauk Centre	MN	**B**	B	B-	211.8	3.54	14.8	3.1	15.0	25.5	**6.9**	8.9	13.2
MINNSTAR BANK NA	Lake Crystal	MN	**C+**	C	C-	117.4	4.08	7.4	1.2	19.5	14.4	**7.1**	9.1	13.0
MINNWEST BANK	Redwood Falls	MN	**B-**	C+	C-	1483.4	200.54	6.6	1.1	4.9	5.8	**7.8**	10.4	13.2
MINSTER BANK	Minster	OH	**B+**	B+	B	393.4	5.55	7.2	0.8	11.2	21.6	**6.5**	8.5	16.0
MINT NATIONAL BK	Kingwood	TX	**B-**	B-	C+	63.0	-1.61	8.2	0.4	26.5	0.0	**10.0**	14.5	21.0
MISSION BANK	Bakersfield	CA	**B**	B	A-	421.4	7.96	6.9	0.1	9.3	15.3	**6.7**	8.7	13.3
MISSION BANK	Mission	KS	**B-**	B-	C+	545.9	-1.70	7.1	0.3	0.5	41.2	**10.0**	15.0	25.5
MISSION BANK	Kingman	AZ	**C-**	C	C-	95.4	9.54	4.6	0.6	7.0	9.4	**7.3**	9.2	13.2
MISSION NATIONAL BK	San Francisco	CA	**B-**	B-	D+	186.5	2.30	2.0	0.1	1.8	0.3	**10.0**	12.3	17.4
MISSION VALLEY BANK	Sun Valley	CA	**B-**	B-	C+	259.8	-3.49	20.3	0.3	1.3	8.1	**10.0**	14.7	19.5
MISSISSIPPI COUNTY S&LA	Charleston	MO	**D+**	C	B-	9.7	-4.34	0.0	0.3	29.1	17.1	**10.0**	25.4	58.0
MISSISSIPPI RIVER BANK	Belle Chasse	LA	**A-**	B+	B+	133.4	-5.96	15.2	1.6	10.7	32.2	**10.0**	12.1	22.5
MISSOURI B&TC OF KANSAS CITY	Kansas City	MO	**C+**	C+	C+	540.1	-8.31	26.9	0.9	9.3	14.8	**5.2**	7.2	11.3
▲ MISSOURI BANK	Warrenton	MO	**B+**	B	B	188.1	-3.39	6.3	1.5	19.7	27.2	**10.0**	11.3	16.9
▲ MISSOURI BANK II	Sedalia	MO	**B+**	B	C+	82.3	-0.47	3.1	1.4	31.5	24.0	**10.0**	11.3	19.2
MITCHELL BANK	Milwaukee	WI	**C+**	C-	C	55.7	-0.04	11.2	0.3	17.7	0.1	**10.0**	13.9	26.8
MITSUBISHI UFJ TRUST & BANKING	New York	NY	**U**	U	B+	752.8	139.56	0.0	0.0	0.0	0.0	**10.0**	80.5	136.1
MIZUHO BANK (USA)	New York	NY	**B-**	B-	B-	5115.4	6.52	43.6	0.0	0.1	2.3	**10.0**	20.9	16.6
MIZUHO TRUST & BANKING CO USA	New York	NY	**U**	U	B-	880.1	35.16	0.0	0.0	0.0	0.0	**4.8**	6.8	39.6
▲ MODERN BANK NA	New York	NY	**C**	C	D	692.0	-1.59	30.9	0.0	4.2	37.5	**7.4**	9.3	15.8
MOHAVE STATE BK	Lake Havasu City	AZ	**D**	D	D-	317.7	10.82	5.9	0.2	6.2	11.5	**9.0**	10.3	14.8
MONARCH BANK	Chesapeake	VA	**A**	A-	B+	1018.9	0.77	11.4	0.5	23.6	2.5	**9.0**	11.5	14.2
MONARCH COMMUNITY BANK	Coldwater	MI	**E+**	E-	E	175.4	4.43	1.1	0.6	35.6	6.3	**8.8**	10.2	15.8
MONITOR BANK	Big Prairie	OH	**C+**	C+	C+	44.5	1.26	13.8	3.7	9.9	6.9	**10.0**	11.9	22.3
MONONA STATE BK	Monona	WI	**C**	C-	D-	410.3	12.78	10.4	0.6	15.8	7.7	**9.5**	11.8	14.6
▲ MONROE BANK & TRUST	Monroe	MI	**C**	C-	D-	1251.1	4.52	5.0	0.9	12.5	40.0	**7.6**	9.4	16.7
MONROE FS&LA	Tipp City	OH	**B-**	C	C	91.8	-3.51	4.8	0.3	35.3	17.4	**10.0**	11.7	20.3
MONROE SAVINGS BANK	Williamstown	NJ	**C+**	C+	C	94.9	3.78	0.2	5.7	48.0	25.5	**10.0**	11.3	23.6
MONSON SB	Monson	MA	**C+**	B-	B-	278.1	2.48	9.7	0.6	27.6	16.6	**8.3**	9.9	16.6
MONTANA STATE BK	Plentywood	MT	**B-**	B-	B-	79.7	7.25	5.8	2.3	0.4	2.9	**6.3**	8.3	16.6

Asset Quality Index	Adjusted Non-Performing Loans as a % of Total Loans	Adjusted Non-Performing Loans as a % of Capital	Net Charge-Offs Avg Loans	Profitability Index	Net Income ($Mil)	Return on Assets (R.O.A.)	Return on Equity (R.O.E.)	Net Interest Spread	Overhead Efficiency Ratio	Liquidity Index	Liquidity Ratio	Hot Money Ratio	Stability Index
7.0	0.04	0.4	0.04	**4.9**	1.7	0.79	8.58	3.61	67.4	**2.0**	15.7	19.0	**3.2**
6.0	1.03	6.0	0.08	**6.2**	15.5	1.19	11.35	3.62	58.9	**2.8**	25.3	18.9	**8.4**
4.8	2.47	13.2	0.36	**3.6**	0.6	0.57	4.42	3.41	73.2	**2.3**	24.8	18.5	**7.2**
6.6	0.51	3.1	0.01	**5.4**	2.9	1.10	10.86	3.37	59.9	**2.8**	15.3	14.9	**6.7**
3.5	3.25	18.1	0.10	**5.0**	1.3	0.79	5.80	4.31	71.9	**2.9**	23.5	15.3	**6.2**
4.8	1.77	12.4	0.04	**2.7**	0.8	0.27	2.55	3.60	89.3	**4.0**	13.4	8.6	**5.8**
3.3	3.07	27.6	0.30	**2.8**	0.1	0.27	3.29	3.18	76.3	**2.7**	17.8	15.3	**4.1**
5.7	1.51	10.4	0.15	**2.0**	0.2	0.06	0.51	2.82	96.2	**3.3**	11.0	12.2	**6.7**
2.7	2.10	17.2	0.14	**2.6**	0.7	0.31	3.67	3.35	85.2	**3.9**	9.9	8.9	**4.8**
6.0	1.63	10.1	0.00	**4.2**	0.4	0.65	6.44	4.28	74.5	**0.7**	14.7	42.9	**5.1**
7.7	0.78	4.0	0.05	**2.8**	0.6	0.40	3.42	3.26	83.6	**2.9**	33.1	18.0	**6.2**
7.5	0.55	3.2	0.03	**8.6**	1.5	1.88	16.47	3.91	46.0	**1.3**	26.0	31.6	**7.7**
3.9	1.88	16.5	1.17	**5.5**	0.7	1.67	17.32	3.83	60.6	**0.6**	8.1	44.9	**2.1**
2.6	4.12	22.8	0.47	**3.1**	0.1	0.30	2.16	4.38	80.0	**1.5**	19.4	25.4	**7.3**
2.3	4.99	29.7	0.25	**2.2**	0.8	0.31	2.94	2.95	78.7	**3.1**	28.9	15.6	**4.5**
6.3	0.68	3.2	-0.01	**4.8**	2.4	1.13	11.02	3.79	69.8	**3.5**	41.7	17.7	**6.7**
8.6	1.85	3.7	-0.57	**2.0**	0.3	0.29	2.73	2.07	85.1	**6.0**	73.3	11.9	**5.5**
3.7	1.50	11.6	0.05	**6.1**	1.0	1.02	10.31	5.39	70.1	**1.7**	10.2	20.1	**5.4**
9.9	0.61	1.9	0.03	**4.7**	0.4	0.80	4.17	3.46	60.6	**5.1**	43.6	9.9	**7.7**
8.6	0.04	0.1	0.00	**4.9**	1.2	1.06	7.89	3.09	59.3	**5.0**	28.3	4.7	**8.2**
9.2	0.33	1.4	0.00	**3.5**	0.8	0.61	3.79	4.11	81.2	**2.0**	34.7	29.0	**7.1**
6.4	2.15	7.3	0.00	**3.5**	0.2	0.70	6.96	3.51	77.3	**4.2**	44.4	14.8	**5.7**
6.2	5.06	10.5	-0.01	**3.4**	0.2	0.61	3.88	2.99	73.5	**5.1**	76.2	15.3	**7.4**
5.8	0.36	2.7	0.05	**2.8**	0.4	0.41	3.74	4.28	86.1	**3.0**	4.1	12.8	**5.9**
2.7	3.97	20.9	0.29	**3.7**	0.5	0.56	6.37	4.97	86.1	**1.7**	18.9	22.2	**4.0**
8.0	0.30	1.1	0.00	**1.8**	0.1	0.14	1.57	3.09	93.3	**4.7**	52.0	13.6	**4.0**
1.4	3.58	23.6	0.21	**3.9**	0.6	0.68	7.20	3.96	77.2	**3.8**	30.5	12.7	**5.0**
8.6	0.00	0.0	0.00	**2.0**	0.3	0.24	2.72	3.81	99.9	**4.9**	34.2	8.3	**6.1**
4.2	1.42	8.8	0.64	**4.4**	0.2	0.69	5.54	6.74	75.5	**4.2**	6.7	6.4	**5.8**
5.1	1.52	6.1	na	**1.6**	0.0	-0.01	-0.12	na	104.1	**6.1**	41.1	3.1	**5.3**
4.5	0.92	6.6	0.01	**4.6**	1.8	1.18	10.62	3.36	66.7	**3.3**	15.4	12.5	**6.3**
4.2	2.09	14.9	-0.01	**4.0**	0.8	0.87	10.37	4.02	75.5	**3.7**	16.6	10.6	**4.1**
4.5	1.57	11.4	0.10	**7.2**	9.1	1.06	11.62	5.06	65.8	**3.2**	9.3	12.8	**8.3**
6.6	0.64	3.6	0.03	**5.5**	3.0	1.04	12.33	3.39	63.3	**5.1**	30.3	5.0	**6.0**
4.5	1.42	7.7	0.00	**3.8**	0.4	0.80	5.68	4.00	79.8	**0.7**	14.6	45.2	**6.4**
8.7	0.20	1.2	0.14	**4.7**	2.2	0.72	8.14	3.89	68.6	**5.7**	40.7	5.4	**4.3**
5.4	3.06	8.8	-0.08	**4.8**	4.0	0.97	6.10	3.62	57.2	**5.7**	50.2	8.9	**6.9**
6.9	0.26	1.6	0.50	**2.1**	0.1	0.14	1.45	3.82	95.5	**4.5**	37.4	11.7	**4.2**
2.9	2.75	14.7	-0.04	**6.2**	1.4	1.04	8.52	4.75	67.9	**1.4**	25.1	29.4	**7.0**
4.0	1.67	7.3	-0.39	**3.9**	1.1	0.57	4.05	4.35	82.3	**2.4**	28.5	19.3	**6.6**
9.4	3.21	3.8	0.00	**0.2**	0.0	-0.53	-2.14	2.67	121.3	**6.0**	91.7	11.3	**6.9**
6.2	1.21	5.4	0.18	**8.4**	2.1	2.04	17.51	4.46	55.5	**4.9**	32.2	7.5	**8.6**
7.6	0.03	0.3	0.42	**4.6**	4.8	1.17	16.80	3.48	69.4	**4.5**	24.1	6.3	**3.8**
5.6	2.35	12.4	0.28	**6.3**	2.2	1.48	13.23	4.39	58.9	**4.0**	15.3	8.6	**7.3**
4.9	2.25	11.9	0.33	**8.2**	1.6	2.60	24.10	4.33	49.1	**3.5**	22.2	12.4	**6.3**
2.4	7.71	26.5	1.09	**2.2**	0.1	0.25	1.73	3.98	92.1	**5.8**	44.2	5.8	**5.4**
9.6	na	0.0	0.00	**10.0**	17.5	8.69	10.66	0.33	44.0	**9.1**	137.1	0.0	**6.3**
8.0	0.00	0.0	-0.01	**3.8**	22.6	0.55	2.68	1.35	47.5	**0.6**	12.5	58.5	**8.6**
10.0	na	0.0	0.00	**4.1**	3.6	0.54	8.48	0.28	79.8	**8.5**	100.5	0.2	**5.5**
4.5	1.39	6.9	-0.12	**3.2**	4.2	0.79	8.99	2.97	72.7	**0.4**	8.0	70.4	**6.3**
0.7	7.26	42.8	0.69	**5.0**	4.9	2.22	20.31	4.28	72.3	**3.3**	23.4	13.1	**4.2**
8.5	0.34	2.3	0.01	**7.6**	8.9	1.23	10.87	4.23	82.3	**3.0**	11.4	14.1	**8.0**
1.7	7.48	48.6	0.20	**1.5**	0.2	0.18	1.75	4.53	97.8	**3.2**	16.0	13.0	**2.7**
7.1	1.59	6.5	0.57	**3.2**	0.2	0.50	4.23	2.76	70.3	**4.4**	48.3	14.3	**5.8**
3.4	0.53	3.4	0.19	**5.0**	2.5	0.84	7.05	4.02	69.3	**1.5**	11.6	23.3	**6.6**
3.5	4.01	18.3	0.58	**3.4**	5.2	0.56	5.75	3.17	79.4	**5.7**	37.8	7.9	**5.3**
5.0	2.20	13.1	-0.10	**3.8**	0.5	0.65	5.88	3.35	75.2	**4.1**	24.3	9.3	**5.7**
5.9	0.76	4.4	0.18	**3.1**	0.3	0.39	3.40	3.32	77.6	**1.6**	31.0	32.7	**6.1**
5.3	0.83	5.6	0.13	**3.4**	1.2	0.58	5.96	3.45	80.0	**1.9**	23.3	20.8	**5.7**
8.6	0.15	0.9	0.00	**4.5**	0.7	1.17	14.62	2.89	60.0	**5.8**	48.5	6.3	**5.4**

Name	City	State	Rating	2013 Rating	2012 Rating	Total Assets ($Mil)	One Year Asset Growth	Asset Mix (As a % of Total Assets) Commercial Loans	Consumer Loans	Mortgage Loans	Securities	Capitalization Index	Leverage Ratio	Risk-Based Capital Ratio
MONTECITO BANK & TRUST	Santa Barbara	CA	**B**	B	C	1161.0	7.06	9.5	2.8	0.7	41.2	**7.9**	9.6	14.1
▲ MONTEREY COUNTY BANK	Monterey	CA	**E**	E-	E-	196.7	-6.26	17.7	0.1	10.1	2.6	**3.9**	6.7	10.5
MONTEZUMA STATE BK	Montezuma	IA	**D+**	C-	C	37.5	-8.74	10.5	4.2	8.2	17.9	**7.4**	9.3	18.7
MONTGOMERY BANK NA	Sikeston	MO	**C+**	C+	C	874.0	-2.14	18.1	0.8	21.6	8.4	**6.7**	8.7	12.4
MONTICELLO BANKING CO	Monticello	KY	**B-**	C+	C-	540.4	-2.04	7.3	7.8	18.9	21.9	**8.4**	9.9	15.6
MONTROSE SB	Montrose	MO	**B**	B	B+	44.1	3.77	4.6	3.5	14.7	39.7	**10.0**	12.9	21.0
▲ MONTROSEBANK	Montrose	CO	**B**	C+	C-	235.3	4.63	1.5	1.4	9.2	54.1	**7.9**	9.6	23.8
▲ MONUMENT BANK	Doylestown	PA	**C**	C-	C-	258.5	6.50	0.7	0.0	18.1	37.7	**5.5**	7.5	14.7
MONUMENT BANK	Bethesda	MD	**C**	C+	C	457.5	11.08	7.4	0.4	11.1	16.5	**7.5**	9.7	12.9
MOODY NATIONAL BK	Galveston	TX	**B**	B	B	995.6	6.03	7.6	0.9	4.8	42.3	**9.2**	10.5	19.1
MORGAN FEDERAL BANK	Fort Morgan	CO	**B-**	C+	B-	106.0	0.14	0.8	0.7	29.1	43.3	**9.9**	10.9	19.6
▲ MORGAN STANLEY BANK NA	Salt Lake City	UT	**B+**	B+	A-	116771.0	16.58	9.6	7.9	0.0	42.4	**9.0**	10.5	14.2
▲ MORGAN STANLEY PRIVATE BANK NA	New York	NY	**B-**	B-	B	25182.0	16.00	1.7	0.2	56.2	12.2	**8.7**	10.1	21.8
MORGANTON SAVINGS BANK SSB	Morganton	NC	**C+**	C+	C	79.5	-2.88	0.0	0.5	21.0	6.0	**10.0**	30.6	47.0
MORGANTOWN BANK & TRUST CO INC	Morgantown	KY	**B-**	B-	C	157.3	3.47	2.5	4.2	40.2	20.7	**7.1**	9.1	14.8
MORRILL & JANES BANK & TRUST	Merriam	KS	**B-**	B-	B	867.4	10.16	16.4	0.6	3.6	44.4	**5.7**	7.7	12.9
MORRIS BANK	Dublin	GA	**C**	C+	C+	479.0	10.08	10.1	3.8	15.0	11.1	**9.4**	10.8	14.5
MORRIS COUNTY NATIONAL BK	Naples	TX	**B-**	B-	C	88.3	0.52	8.8	7.7	16.6	36.3	**7.6**	9.4	18.8
MORRIS PLAN CO OF TERRE HAUTE	Terre Haute	IN	**B**	B	B-	74.2	2.00	0.7	76.4	8.4	6.6	**10.0**	25.6	30.5
MORRIS STATE BK	Morris	OK	**B-**	B-	C+	69.4	1.52	4.4	12.9	37.5	13.3	**6.4**	8.4	14.3
▲ MORTON COMMUNITY BANK	Morton	IL	**B+**	B	C+	2862.9	1.47	13.8	0.8	11.9	24.6	**10.0**	12.0	18.5
MOTHER LODE BANK	Sonora	CA	**D-**	D	D-	64.1	-2.80	10.5	0.5	15.6	12.7	**6.1**	8.1	13.2
MOUND CITY BANK	Platteville	WI	**B**	B	C+	280.5	3.75	3.4	0.8	21.7	12.5	**8.2**	9.8	13.5
MOUNT VERNON BANK	Vidalia	GA	**B-**	B-	C+	128.4	-2.62	3.3	2.9	14.9	30.5	**9.6**	10.7	20.0
MOUNT VERNON BANK & TRUST CO	Mount Vernon	IA	**A**	A	A	103.6	6.47	6.2	3.5	32.3	27.7	**10.0**	13.7	20.2
▲ MOUNTAIN COMMERCE BANK	Erwin	TN	**C**	D+	D-	402.1	18.50	9.9	1.5	19.7	8.8	**7.2**	9.2	12.9
▲ MOUNTAIN PACIFIC BANK	Everett	WA	**C-**	D+	D+	150.0	8.14	12.2	1.2	6.3	5.6	**9.7**	12.3	14.7
MOUNTAIN VALLEY BANK	Dunlap	TN	**D+**	D+	D	89.8	-3.94	0.3	6.4	38.4	21.1	**7.8**	9.5	17.1
MOUNTAIN VALLEY BANK	Walden	CO	**B-**	C+	D+	156.4	3.59	10.8	1.0	10.3	15.9	**7.3**	9.2	13.1
MOUNTAIN VALLEY BANK NA	Elkins	WV	**B**	B	B	132.2	1.79	9.6	2.4	29.3	27.9	**10.0**	13.2	24.2
MOUNTAIN VALLEY COMMUNITY BANK	Cleveland	GA	**C+**	C	C-	162.7	9.50	3.8	1.3	8.5	20.6	**9.1**	10.4	15.8
MOUNTAIN VIEW BANK OF COMMERCE	Westminster	CO	**C+**	C+	C	66.1	6.45	9.6	0.0	4.1	0.0	**10.0**	11.7	16.5
▲ MOUNTAINONE BANK	North Adams	MA	**C**	C-	D+	800.2	4.95	8.3	0.2	32.8	11.9	**7.8**	9.6	13.2
MRV BANKS	Sainte Genevieve	MO	**B**	B	C	120.6	22.44	25.5	0.8	13.3	6.6	**8.0**	10.8	13.4
MT MCKINLEY BANK	Fairbanks	AK	**A-**	A-	A	345.2	1.44	6.6	0.2	4.9	52.3	**10.0**	20.8	40.4
MT VICTORY STATE BK	Mount Victory	OH	**C**	C	C	16.6	0.65	3.2	12.4	8.6	53.8	**10.0**	11.6	24.6
MT WASHINGTON SAVINGS BANK	Cincinnati	OH	**D-**	D-	D	90.3	8.62	0.3	0.1	64.2	7.3	**8.3**	9.9	18.7
MUENSTER STATE BK	Muenster	TX	**A+**	A+	A+	170.6	7.79	2.8	2.0	7.9	71.4	**10.0**	13.5	37.7
MUFG UNION BANK NA	San Francisco	CA	**C+**	C+	B-	110319.8	5.11	17.3	0.3	26.0	20.4	**9.8**	11.3	14.8
▲ MULESHOE STATE BK	Muleshoe	TX	**C**	C	C	108.4	3.48	9.8	4.7	6.0	40.0	**5.0**	7.0	13.7
MUNCY BANK & TRUST CO	Muncy	PA	**B+**	B+	B+	362.3	2.55	3.8	3.4	46.7	13.5	**8.6**	10.1	15.9
▼ MUNICIPAL TRUST & SB	Bourbonnais	IL	**B+**	A-	A-	275.4	2.95	0.3	0.4	24.2	4.8	**10.0**	21.6	47.2
MURPHY BANK	Fresno	CA	**B**	B	B-	179.4	29.64	25.0	27.7	21.1	0.0	**10.0**	12.6	16.6
MURPHY-WALL STATE BK & TRUST	Pinckneyville	IL	**B**	B	B	114.2	-3.69	4.5	1.5	16.2	42.9	**10.0**	12.2	25.1
MURRAY BANK	Murray	KY	**B-**	B-	B-	257.0	3.16	7.0	3.1	24.1	27.9	**6.9**	8.9	16.2
MURRAY STATE BK	Murray	NE	**C**	C+	B-	53.1	4.88	8.6	2.6	16.2	20.9	**7.9**	9.6	15.3
MUTUAL BANK	Whitman	MA	**C-**	C-	C-	436.5	1.19	2.0	4.5	47.5	22.8	**6.7**	8.7	16.9
MUTUAL FEDERAL BANK	Chicago	IL	**D**	D+	D	81.5	8.36	2.1	0.1	29.4	5.2	**10.0**	15.8	22.3
MUTUAL FEDERAL SAVINGS BANK	Sidney	OH	**C-**	C-	D+	114.4	-0.21	6.0	7.4	27.8	27.1	**9.0**	10.3	18.1
MUTUAL OF OMAHA BANK	Omaha	NE	**C+**	C+	C	6894.7	6.20	12.1	0.8	26.1	16.5	**5.9**	8.5	11.7
MUTUAL S&LA	Metairie	LA	**B**	B	B	38.5	11.95	0.0	0.3	82.8	0.1	**10.0**	31.4	55.2
MUTUAL SAVINGS ASSN FSA	Leavenworth	KS	**B**	B-	C	195.2	-6.68	5.6	1.3	31.8	23.9	**10.0**	28.5	42.6
MUTUAL SAVINGS BANK	Hartsville	SC	**D+**	D+	C+	38.1	-5.85	1.5	2.7	25.1	11.9	**10.0**	36.8	67.0
MUTUAL SB	Franklin	IN	**C+**	C+	C	123.8	-2.45	2.7	2.2	36.2	7.1	**10.0**	12.5	19.6
MUTUALBANK	Muncie	IN	**C+**	C+	C	1415.1	0.77	6.2	8.8	38.2	18.7	**6.6**	8.6	13.5
MUTUALONE BANK	Framingham	MA	**A-**	A-	A-	582.7	4.50	18.2	0.9	20.2	7.9	**10.0**	20.1	26.2
▲ MVB BANK INC	Fairmont	WV	**B-**	C+	C+	1084.4	29.51	8.7	1.6	14.3	11.8	**10.0**	11.1	16.1
MWABANK	Rock Island	IL	**C-**	C	C	271.2	10.49	0.8	2.7	62.5	20.6	**8.6**	10.0	20.7
MY BANK	Belen	NM	**C+**	C-	C-	159.7	1.89	1.7	1.3	10.1	40.4	**8.8**	10.2	20.5
NANTAHALA BANK & TRUST CO	Franklin	NC	**E-**	E-	E-	151.6	-1.51	4.6	0.6	19.4	14.2	**1.4**	4.8	8.4

Asset Quality Index	Adjusted Non-Performing Loans as a % of Total Loans	Adjusted Non-Performing Loans as a % of Capital	Net Charge-Offs Avg Loans	Profitability Index	Net Income ($Mil)	Return on Assets (R.O.A.)	Return on Equity (R.O.E.)	Net Interest Spread	Overhead Efficiency Ratio	Liquidity Index	Liquidity Ratio	Hot Money Ratio	Stability Index
6.3	0.83	4.0	0.10	**4.6**	9.8	1.16	11.52	3.63	79.7	**6.2**	40.4	5.5	**8.7**
2.0	4.48	32.4	0.59	**3.3**	1.4	0.96	15.42	4.06	75.5	**1.9**	23.5	21.4	**1.6**
1.3	8.53	40.2	0.06	**2.3**	0.1	0.37	3.63	3.33	81.4	**6.0**	50.9	5.5	**4.8**
4.2	1.63	13.5	0.27	**3.8**	6.0	0.91	10.44	3.60	71.9	**4.3**	6.3	5.6	**4.9**
4.1	1.76	10.8	0.45	**4.6**	4.2	1.01	10.20	4.13	67.0	**1.5**	20.1	25.4	**5.4**
7.7	0.60	2.4	0.01	**5.8**	0.5	1.37	10.97	3.77	58.0	**3.7**	44.7	17.5	**7.8**
4.8	3.60	12.4	0.41	**5.9**	2.4	1.38	13.25	3.82	65.7	**6.8**	65.3	5.8	**7.6**
4.3	1.99	13.6	0.07	**2.8**	1.2	0.59	7.70	3.06	75.9	**1.2**	29.3	44.5	**4.7**
2.9	1.87	13.6	0.16	**3.9**	1.5	0.44	4.56	3.98	74.7	**3.4**	16.0	12.3	**5.1**
6.0	1.24	5.4	0.51	**4.4**	4.9	0.68	6.49	3.73	70.4	**4.0**	35.7	13.5	**6.7**
9.8	0.27	1.0	0.04	**3.6**	0.5	0.62	5.75	3.14	79.8	**4.7**	45.1	12.8	**5.8**
8.6	0.01	0.0	0.00	**6.5**	795.0	0.95	9.34	0.93	17.0	**3.6**	62.8	31.0	**8.3**
9.9	0.24	1.7	0.00	**3.4**	86.0	0.51	5.13	1.59	45.7	**2.3**	36.4	35.8	**7.0**
5.6	5.79	10.3	0.07	**2.8**	0.2	0.38	1.26	3.56	85.0	**2.6**	39.1	24.5	**6.7**
5.3	0.95	7.1	0.03	**3.8**	0.8	0.64	7.33	3.94	80.3	**3.4**	14.2	12.0	**4.7**
8.4	0.15	1.0	-0.04	**4.1**	4.6	0.73	8.22	3.39	64.7	**4.4**	23.6	7.2	**6.0**
2.9	2.29	15.3	0.40	**9.7**	7.9	2.33	21.96	4.90	48.5	**0.7**	13.1	36.6	**6.9**
6.5	0.56	2.9	0.24	**6.1**	1.1	1.58	16.50	4.38	67.1	**2.0**	23.9	20.1	**5.8**
4.1	1.38	4.0	2.31	**10.0**	2.3	4.15	15.43	13.19	30.1	**1.1**	6.8	28.8	**8.1**
5.3	0.41	3.4	0.00	**10.0**	1.3	2.55	31.20	4.81	54.0	**1.1**	11.5	30.2	**6.4**
5.2	1.52	8.1	0.14	**6.3**	34.4	1.61	13.99	3.34	50.3	**1.7**	11.0	20.8	**9.9**
4.1	2.02	14.3	-0.03	**0.5**	-0.2	-0.48	-6.21	3.57	109.7	**5.2**	28.7	3.7	**2.8**
5.1	0.96	7.1	0.10	**5.6**	2.0	0.98	10.17	3.75	60.7	**2.7**	5.2	14.6	**5.2**
4.9	1.95	8.3	-0.01	**4.4**	1.2	1.20	12.67	3.48	69.1	**3.1**	44.5	21.8	**5.4**
8.9	0.00	0.0	-0.06	**6.5**	0.9	1.22	8.73	3.54	57.7	**5.3**	36.7	6.4	**8.5**
3.4	1.35	10.6	0.79	**3.8**	1.5	0.56	5.74	3.90	66.5	**1.0**	11.7	31.3	**4.4**
6.6	0.90	5.4	-0.01	**2.7**	0.6	0.49	4.15	4.22	86.9	**1.6**	15.7	23.3	**5.4**
1.4	7.74	48.0	0.52	**2.0**	0.1	0.21	2.24	4.19	90.2	**2.1**	14.2	18.3	**3.7**
5.1	1.05	7.8	0.05	**2.7**	0.2	0.61	6.01	4.47	70.1	**1.3**	22.2	30.4	**6.0**
8.5	0.59	2.8	-0.03	**4.2**	0.7	0.71	5.75	3.76	74.2	**3.4**	22.7	12.8	**7.0**
4.9	1.34	6.8	0.08	**3.2**	0.6	0.52	5.28	3.77	76.1	**1.9**	21.7	21.1	**4.5**
5.0	1.25	7.9	0.04	**3.2**	0.2	0.39	3.12	4.24	80.6	**3.6**	17.3	11.1	**6.0**
3.3	2.14	16.2	0.11	**2.7**	1.8	0.30	2.95	2.86	83.4	**0.9**	6.1	30.8	**5.9**
6.7	0.10	0.8	0.02	**4.9**	0.7	0.84	7.84	3.84	57.9	**0.9**	2.8	29.5	**5.9**
8.3	2.90	5.2	0.00	**5.0**	2.7	1.07	5.18	4.24	73.0	**6.4**	59.6	7.3	**8.8**
8.3	0.68	2.0	0.14	**2.9**	0.1	0.47	5.44	3.12	81.2	**4.8**	45.3	9.6	**3.7**
3.9	2.28	16.3	0.20	**0.6**	0.2	0.36	3.38	2.59	99.2	**1.2**	14.1	29.2	**5.1**
8.5	2.37	3.6	0.03	**7.9**	2.9	2.31	17.48	3.37	38.1	**5.6**	76.7	14.2	**9.3**
6.0	0.76	4.5	0.02	**3.9**	624.6	0.76	5.63	2.95	73.6	**4.0**	22.4	11.0	**9.2**
4.5	1.58	9.4	0.14	**3.1**	0.4	0.46	6.42	3.59	83.5	**4.0**	38.1	14.3	**3.8**
5.6	1.00	6.8	-0.02	**7.4**	3.6	1.32	13.46	3.94	54.6	**1.4**	7.3	23.6	**7.0**
4.8	5.31	13.7	0.06	**7.4**	3.8	1.84	8.65	2.94	41.7	**4.4**	48.7	15.2	**8.4**
4.6	0.74	5.0	0.21	**10.0**	2.9	2.38	18.14	5.65	47.6	**0.5**	13.1	68.6	**8.4**
7.0	1.33	4.6	-0.09	**3.8**	0.7	0.75	5.96	4.01	78.5	**4.9**	31.1	6.6	**6.7**
5.4	0.96	5.9	0.04	**4.4**	1.6	0.82	9.44	3.18	63.4	**2.6**	25.7	17.3	**5.6**
8.6	0.00	0.0	0.00	**2.8**	0.1	0.39	4.03	3.16	77.5	**4.3**	36.3	12.4	**5.1**
6.0	0.78	5.7	0.06	**2.2**	1.3	0.41	4.87	2.76	90.8	**3.0**	16.3	14.0	**4.8**
0.4	8.38	39.5	0.06	**2.0**	0.2	0.28	1.72	3.78	90.9	**1.3**	21.2	29.6	**5.5**
4.1	2.19	12.5	0.03	**3.4**	0.4	0.51	4.72	3.91	86.0	**3.4**	37.0	17.0	**5.2**
4.7	1.07	8.9	0.07	**3.3**	24.8	0.49	4.59	3.45	78.0	**3.8**	17.8	10.7	**5.6**
9.6	0.44	1.3	0.00	**4.6**	0.2	0.76	2.36	4.17	71.9	**0.5**	3.0	38.9	**7.9**
4.9	7.17	14.1	1.38	**3.7**	0.7	0.49	1.69	3.69	68.3	**3.3**	28.2	14.8	**6.8**
6.7	6.66	8.8	-0.02	**0.7**	-0.1	-0.21	-0.58	2.82	106.4	**3.6**	70.3	26.7	**4.5**
5.9	1.46	8.1	0.16	**2.6**	0.3	0.29	2.32	3.48	87.6	**3.9**	17.5	9.9	**5.7**
5.3	1.04	7.9	0.13	**3.8**	7.7	0.73	8.12	3.37	72.8	**3.3**	22.1	14.5	**7.0**
4.6	3.08	12.1	0.00	**5.9**	5.2	1.24	6.01	3.89	61.5	**1.1**	18.9	31.4	**8.4**
6.0	0.97	6.2	0.03	**3.4**	4.4	0.56	5.13	3.20	79.9	**1.7**	8.1	20.1	**6.9**
4.6	1.79	12.4	0.40	**2.0**	0.2	0.12	1.09	3.07	96.6	**4.8**	26.3	5.0	**5.3**
4.2	3.32	14.2	0.05	**3.8**	0.8	0.69	6.84	4.04	77.7	**4.7**	44.8	12.5	**5.0**
0.3	5.67	58.1	0.38	**0.4**	-0.1	-0.05	-1.07	3.35	101.5	**1.7**	20.5	23.3	**0.4**

Name	City	State	Rating	2013 Rating	2012 Rating	Total Assets ($Mil)	One Year Asset Growth	Asset Mix (As a % of Total Assets) Comm-ercial Loans	Cons-umer Loans	Mort-gage Loans	Secur-ities	Capital-ization Index	Lever-age Ratio	Risk-Based Capital Ratio
NAPOLEON STATE BK	Napoleon	IN	**B**	B	B-	195.0	0.85	7.7	8.0	24.3	13.1	**8.4**	9.9	14.1
NASHVILLE SB	Nashville	IL	**B-**	B-	B-	53.5	4.84	5.0	2.8	24.4	17.6	**9.5**	10.7	18.0
NATBANK NA	Hollywood	FL	**C**	C-	D	166.0	10.53	0.7	0.9	62.4	3.9	**8.3**	9.9	21.4
NATIONAL ADVISORS TRUST CO FSB	Overland Park	KS	**U**	U	B+	6.9	2.91	0.0	0.0	0.0	49.7	**10.0**	82.6	261.4
NATIONAL B&TC OF SYCAMORE	Sycamore	IL	**C-**	C-	C	661.1	-0.39	6.5	8.4	8.4	20.3	**6.6**	8.6	13.4
NATIONAL BK	Hillsboro	IL	**B-**	C+	B-	343.1	0.63	6.5	0.7	14.0	25.4	**6.7**	8.7	13.4
NATIONAL BK	Gatesville	TX	**B+**	B+	B+	558.5	3.11	7.0	8.0	13.9	29.0	**9.0**	10.4	17.6
NATIONAL BK & TRUST	La Grange	TX	**B**	B	B+	221.1	4.94	1.0	4.2	11.3	70.4	**7.4**	9.3	28.0
NATIONAL BK & TRUST CO	Wilmington	OH	**B-**	C+	B-	649.7	0.71	5.7	0.6	19.1	24.3	**10.0**	11.1	18.0
▼ NATIONAL BK OF ADAMS COUNTY	West Union	OH	**C+**	B-	B-	84.8	2.76	1.4	2.6	27.0	13.0	**9.6**	10.8	25.5
NATIONAL BK OF ANDREWS	Andrews	TX	**A-**	A-	B+	197.6	28.81	20.7	3.1	8.6	19.5	**8.0**	9.7	15.3
NATIONAL BK OF ARIZONA	Phoenix	AZ	**B**	B	B-	4716.3	1.75	14.8	0.7	11.3	8.3	**10.0**	11.8	15.2
NATIONAL BK OF BLACKSBURG	Blacksburg	VA	**A**	A-	A	1114.0	3.66	2.7	2.5	11.5	33.4	**10.0**	14.4	24.8
NATIONAL BK OF CALIFORNIA	Los Angeles	CA	**D-**	E+	D-	339.9	-3.54	8.1	0.4	3.3	2.6	**3.7**	5.7	10.3
NATIONAL BK OF COMMERCE	Birmingham	AL	**B-**	B-	C+	897.5	33.26	17.8	0.9	14.0	3.8	**6.0**	9.3	11.8
NATIONAL BK OF COMMERCE	Superior	WI	**B+**	B	B	520.6	0.46	12.1	0.6	15.7	20.8	**10.0**	11.8	17.3
NATIONAL BK OF COXSACKIE	Coxsackie	NY	**C+**	C+	B-	286.2	13.67	3.1	3.6	22.8	39.9	**6.9**	8.9	17.5
NATIONAL BK OF DELAWARE COUNTY	Walton	NY	**C-**	C	C+	369.4	39.09	2.2	1.7	14.5	55.2	**10.0**	11.3	19.9
NATIONAL BK OF GEORGIA	Athens	GA	**B**	B	C	352.7	9.61	6.1	0.9	24.2	3.6	**7.4**	9.8	12.9
▲ NATIONAL BK OF HARVEY	Harvey	ND	**C+**	C-	C-	50.1	7.69	5.6	1.1	4.7	48.7	**10.0**	11.7	22.6
NATIONAL BK OF INDIANAPOLIS	Indianapolis	IN	**C+**	C+	C	1649.0	2.73	14.6	2.3	12.3	18.5	**5.0**	7.0	11.7
NATIONAL BK OF KANSAS CITY	Overland Park	KS	**B**	A-	B-	598.2	6.05	2.9	4.1	25.5	37.1	**10.0**	12.1	20.1
NATIONAL BK OF MALVERN	Malvern	PA	**A-**	A-	B+	145.7	3.00	0.6	0.1	33.2	25.0	**10.0**	15.8	27.3
NATIONAL BK OF MIDDLEBURY	Middlebury	VT	**C+**	C+	B-	307.9	2.81	4.6	0.4	31.5	28.5	**6.8**	8.8	14.9
NATIONAL BK OF NEW YORK CITY	Flushing	NY	**C+**	C	C-	180.5	-4.24	2.2	0.0	0.0	4.7	**10.0**	21.5	27.5
NATIONAL BK OF PETERSBURG	Petersburg	IL	**B-**	B-	B	149.7	2.37	2.2	5.0	16.8	42.0	**9.7**	10.8	21.1
NATIONAL BK OF ST ANNE	Saint Anne	IL	**C+**	C	C-	48.6	0.71	3.5	9.0	16.8	6.5	**7.3**	9.2	15.3
NATIONAL BK OF TENNESSEE	Newport	TN	**E+**	E+	D-	147.7	-5.52	1.4	1.7	15.9	39.6	**3.8**	5.8	12.4
NATIONAL BK OF TEXAS FT WORTH	Fort Worth	TX	**C**	C	C	206.0	17.73	12.3	6.3	1.8	41.8	**6.0**	8.0	17.8
▲ NATIONAL BK OF WAUPUN	Waupun	WI	**B-**	C	D+	135.6	0.63	14.3	3.6	13.1	23.3	**9.5**	10.6	16.8
NATIONAL CAPITAL BANK OF WA	Washington	DC	**B-**	B	A-	428.2	5.17	9.4	1.1	33.7	35.7	**7.4**	9.3	18.0
NATIONAL EXCHANGE BANK & TRUST	Fond Du Lac	WI	**A**	A-	A-	1341.8	8.05	9.0	1.8	8.3	31.5	**10.0**	18.0	26.8
NATIONAL GRAND BK MARBLEHEAD	Marblehead	MA	**A-**	A-	B+	290.2	2.02	2.1	1.6	50.3	22.9	**10.0**	11.1	20.7
NATIONAL IRON BANK	Salisbury	CT	**C-**	C	C	111.3	0.37	1.2	1.0	45.0	36.8	**6.3**	8.3	19.7
NATIONAL PENN BANK	Allentown	PA	**B+**	B-	B+	8607.4	2.49	9.3	2.6	12.4	27.2	**6.9**	8.9	13.0
NATIONAL PENN WEALTH MGMT NA	Wyomissing	PA	**U**	U	U	17.0	19.32	0.0	0.0	0.0	5.9	**10.0**	82.3	254.4
NATIONAL UNION BANK KINDERHOOK	Kinderhook	NY	**B**	B	B-	372.2	11.08	8.4	1.0	17.3	20.0	**8.5**	10.0	16.1
NATIONWIDE BANK	Columbus	OH	**B**	B	B+	6023.5	11.71	1.2	21.4	21.5	37.0	**6.3**	8.3	12.6
NATIVE AMERICAN BANK NA	Denver	CO	**D-**	D-	D-	62.8	0.55	55.0	2.5	3.0	7.7	**6.9**	8.9	20.1
NATURE COAST BANK	Hernando	FL	**C-**	D+	D-	54.8	-4.17	5.0	1.4	5.8	10.2	**9.3**	10.8	14.4
▲ NAUGATUCK VALLEY SVGS & LOAN	Naugatuck	CT	**D**	D	D	490.9	0.34	5.3	1.8	41.0	19.0	**10.0**	11.1	18.6
NBC OKLAHOMA	Oklahoma City	OK	**C+**	C-	C-	584.0	8.21	21.8	1.4	11.6	12.8	**5.8**	7.8	11.8
▼ NBH BANK NA	Kansas City	MO	**C+**	B	B+	4793.3	-6.33	13.1	0.7	11.1	44.0	**10.0**	11.9	23.8
NBT BANK NA	Norwich	NY	**B-**	B-	C+	7791.4	2.43	11.0	18.5	17.3	19.1	**6.6**	8.6	12.6
NCB FSB	Hillsboro	OH	**B**	B-	C+	1748.4	14.19	18.9	1.3	21.1	5.1	**10.0**	12.8	15.7
NEBRASKA BANK OF COMMERCE	Lincoln	NE	**C+**	C+	C-	101.8	18.74	12.6	1.2	15.0	0.2	**6.3**	8.6	12.0
NEBRASKA STATE BK	Bristow	NE	**C+**	C+	C+	15.3	-2.92	11.5	3.3	2.5	0.0	**10.0**	16.0	25.8
NEBRASKA STATE BK	Lynch	NE	**C+**	C+	C+	13.5	-2.09	3.9	2.0	4.6	0.0	**10.0**	15.8	30.4
NEBRASKA STATE BK	Oshkosh	NE	**B+**	B	B+	48.1	-1.09	0.2	0.1	0.1	2.2	**9.7**	11.5	14.8
NEBRASKA STATE BK & TRUST CO	Broken Bow	NE	**B+**	B+	B+	191.8	-0.35	8.6	2.9	10.4	11.4	**7.4**	10.7	12.8
NEBRASKALAND NATIONAL BK	North Platte	NE	**A-**	A-	B+	588.6	15.86	26.8	1.1	4.1	18.9	**7.5**	10.2	13.0
NECEDAH BANK	Necedah	WI	**C**	C	C-	33.6	-1.61	6.2	1.2	17.1	22.0	**10.0**	12.3	17.5
NEEDHAM BANK	Needham	MA	**A-**	A-	B+	1584.8	29.00	1.5	0.2	47.5	11.2	**10.0**	14.8	22.4
NEFFS NATIONAL BK	Neffs	PA	**A**	A	A	309.6	3.38	1.2	1.7	23.3	47.0	**10.0**	17.4	33.0
NEHAWKA BANK	Nehawka	NE	**C-**	C	C	16.1	-6.81	0.8	7.5	40.9	0.1	**10.0**	15.0	23.1
NEIGHBORHOOD NATIONAL BANK	Mora	MN	**B-**	B-	B-	168.7	6.58	5.0	2.4	16.0	44.3	**10.0**	11.2	20.5
▲ NEIGHBORHOOD NATIONAL BK	Alexandria	MN	**B-**	C	D+	51.2	6.33	10.3	2.5	13.1	24.3	**8.7**	10.3	13.9
NEIGHBORHOOD NATIONAL BK	San Diego	CA	**E-**	E-	E	76.4	-14.29	6.3	0.1	9.3	3.9	**3.0**	5.0	12.1
NEKOMA STATE BK	La Crosse	KS	**C-**	C-	C	44.2	12.19	4.3	1.8	2.5	58.9	**6.4**	8.4	20.5
NEKOOSA PORT EDWARDS STATE BK	Nekoosa	WI	**B+**	B+	B+	203.9	1.06	2.9	1.5	32.6	27.8	**10.0**	12.7	26.4

Asset Quality Index	Adjusted Non-Performing Loans as a % of Total Loans	Adjusted Non-Performing Loans as a % of Capital	Net Charge-Offs / Avg Loans	Profitability Index	Net Income ($Mil)	Return on Assets (R.O.A.)	Return on Equity (R.O.E.)	Net Interest Spread	Overhead Efficiency Ratio	Liquidity Index	Liquidity Ratio	Hot Money Ratio	Stability Index
4.7	0.94	6.9	0.20	**5.6**	1.3	0.88	9.41	3.84	60.3	**2.4**	20.7	17.4	**5.6**
7.0	0.07	0.4	0.20	**4.6**	0.3	0.79	7.57	2.91	58.4	**1.7**	19.6	23.5	**5.7**
5.7	1.87	12.5	-0.06	**3.1**	0.8	0.68	7.13	3.75	86.7	**2.4**	35.2	24.4	**4.1**
9.3	na	0.0	na	**5.1**	0.0	0.30	0.35	1.22	99.7	**5.0**	461.4	100.0	**4.6**
2.4	2.58	17.9	0.18	**2.5**	1.7	0.35	3.88	3.26	86.9	**3.6**	14.6	11.1	**4.6**
5.0	1.60	10.8	0.11	**4.2**	1.8	0.69	8.11	3.19	65.0	**4.3**	12.5	6.4	**4.6**
5.5	0.94	5.0	0.19	**5.4**	3.9	0.95	9.03	4.00	67.5	**4.2**	30.9	10.8	**7.0**
9.0	0.29	0.7	0.00	**4.2**	1.6	0.99	11.88	2.45	60.2	**3.8**	59.6	22.7	**5.9**
6.5	0.98	5.2	0.22	**4.2**	3.9	0.79	7.11	3.79	74.8	**5.0**	21.7	2.9	**6.5**
2.9	5.28	21.7	0.07	**1.8**	0.1	0.10	0.87	2.55	78.4	**4.2**	42.7	14.7	**6.8**
8.2	0.16	0.8	-0.03	**9.3**	3.5	2.76	29.46	4.02	53.8	**5.8**	49.5	7.7	**7.0**
5.9	0.91	5.6	0.04	**5.6**	33.5	0.96	8.09	3.74	74.1	**4.9**	17.1	3.7	**7.6**
6.2	1.87	6.6	0.30	**8.7**	13.1	1.55	11.45	4.01	48.6	**5.2**	32.7	9.3	**10.0**
3.7	0.76	6.4	-0.23	**0.0**	-1.9	-0.75	-12.68	3.48	118.4	**5.8**	34.7	2.2	**2.2**
6.8	0.18	1.5	0.06	**3.8**	3.9	0.70	6.04	3.46	71.6	**2.1**	11.4	17.9	**6.0**
5.2	1.41	8.1	0.02	**7.4**	7.0	1.80	14.33	4.46	62.4	**1.8**	18.3	21.6	**7.6**
4.3	2.62	13.2	0.21	**2.9**	0.7	0.36	4.12	3.22	84.8	**2.9**	22.9	15.1	**4.7**
7.0	1.25	3.6	0.16	**1.2**	0.7	0.32	3.11	3.14	104.9	**5.1**	44.9	10.6	**5.1**
5.0	0.88	7.0	-0.02	**6.5**	3.0	1.14	12.17	3.96	56.1	**3.0**	10.7	13.6	**5.3**
6.5	0.51	1.5	-0.74	**3.3**	0.3	0.88	7.77	3.24	76.4	**4.9**	48.6	12.2	**4.0**
4.9	1.43	11.9	0.03	**4.0**	9.5	0.77	10.91	3.07	71.1	**4.5**	12.9	5.5	**5.1**
6.0	2.47	9.4	0.24	**4.4**	1.8	0.40	3.08	1.67	97.0	**2.2**	14.6	18.1	**7.2**
6.1	2.80	10.9	0.01	**5.4**	1.0	0.97	6.20	3.91	64.4	**3.3**	31.6	15.5	**7.9**
4.8	1.43	9.5	0.29	**3.3**	1.1	0.49	5.33	3.37	85.1	**4.8**	27.9	5.9	**5.3**
3.2	2.52	9.0	-0.10	**6.3**	2.2	1.53	7.26	3.54	63.5	**0.6**	18.0	65.0	**7.7**
7.9	0.54	2.3	0.17	**3.5**	0.8	0.70	7.37	2.46	71.8	**5.3**	47.8	10.3	**5.8**
7.0	0.00	0.0	0.28	**3.9**	0.2	0.60	4.76	3.79	72.8	**2.1**	34.9	28.2	**5.1**
1.7	5.45	38.2	-0.31	**0.0**	-0.6	-0.54	-11.15	3.10	117.9	**4.2**	31.5	11.2	**0.8**
8.5	0.27	1.2	-0.17	**2.8**	0.8	0.56	7.47	3.06	84.4	**4.4**	61.5	18.1	**4.1**
4.3	1.79	9.6	0.10	**5.5**	1.1	1.06	10.11	4.29	59.2	**2.9**	30.3	17.4	**4.9**
6.3	0.54	3.1	2.01	**2.1**	-0.2	-0.05	-0.51	2.86	67.4	**4.4**	33.2	10.7	**5.0**
6.6	1.69	4.6	-1.61	**8.4**	15.7	1.55	8.85	3.84	43.6	**5.8**	34.2	6.2	**9.3**
7.6	0.81	4.9	0.03	**5.3**	2.0	0.93	8.33	3.41	61.9	**5.1**	30.6	5.5	**7.0**
6.1	1.32	8.6	0.01	**2.6**	0.3	0.36	4.20	2.99	88.6	**3.1**	44.1	20.9	**4.9**
5.7	0.76	5.1	0.24	**5.8**	76.0	1.19	9.45	3.47	59.8	**4.5**	7.2	4.8	**7.9**
10.0	na	0.0	na	**10.0**	3.1	29.91	36.99	0.56	66.3	**4.0**	350.3	101.0	**7.0**
5.2	0.79	5.5	0.32	**4.4**	1.8	0.67	6.92	3.61	69.9	**3.8**	8.3	8.8	**5.7**
7.9	0.16	1.2	0.50	**4.8**	36.6	0.87	9.54	2.26	79.2	**1.8**	27.9	35.2	**5.9**
2.6	1.67	13.3	0.20	**0.8**	0.0	-0.08	-0.94	4.57	101.4	**0.6**	11.8	55.4	**2.6**
2.5	2.41	13.9	0.30	**2.8**	0.2	0.41	3.15	4.03	82.4	**2.2**	19.9	18.4	**5.6**
4.7	1.76	10.5	0.77	**0.5**	0.4	0.11	1.02	3.61	110.9	**2.7**	19.0	15.9	**4.5**
4.3	0.58	4.7	0.08	**5.3**	5.0	1.20	15.63	4.61	70.8	**3.6**	29.6	13.7	**5.5**
6.0	2.25	8.4	0.06	**2.6**	8.0	0.22	1.65	3.86	87.5	**5.2**	45.7	13.0	**5.6**
4.1	1.03	8.0	0.31	**5.3**	54.4	0.95	8.28	3.65	64.5	**3.7**	3.3	8.9	**8.2**
4.5	1.32	7.8	-0.01	**4.5**	13.0	0.96	8.07	3.61	82.9	**2.0**	18.4	19.6	**8.3**
5.7	0.26	2.4	0.01	**3.9**	0.8	1.09	12.84	3.44	73.9	**2.7**	14.5	15.4	**3.7**
8.3	0.00	0.0	0.00	**4.1**	0.1	0.84	5.34	4.06	78.6	**2.5**	53.0	29.0	**6.5**
8.7	0.23	0.6	0.75	**2.7**	0.1	0.44	2.95	3.24	83.5	**3.3**	64.9	23.1	**6.2**
6.9	0.00	0.0	0.00	**10.0**	1.1	3.11	29.12	4.15	43.1	**1.7**	16.4	22.2	**7.7**
6.9	0.06	0.5	0.01	**5.5**	1.9	1.29	11.94	3.73	63.0	**1.0**	5.9	28.8	**7.7**
6.8	0.61	3.9	0.00	**5.9**	4.3	1.02	9.80	3.85	60.9	**0.8**	8.8	33.4	**7.4**
7.3	0.61	3.2	0.16	**1.5**	0.1	0.35	2.83	3.40	91.0	**4.3**	29.4	10.0	**4.1**
8.5	0.37	2.1	0.02	**5.3**	8.3	0.77	4.96	3.73	64.8	**0.9**	15.0	35.2	**8.5**
7.1	2.45	6.9	0.45	**6.7**	2.9	1.26	7.32	3.71	42.9	**3.8**	52.3	19.3	**9.1**
3.1	4.29	22.1	0.00	**1.7**	0.0	0.08	0.52	4.01	96.9	**3.0**	13.4	13.4	**6.0**
5.3	1.98	7.9	-0.10	**3.9**	0.8	0.62	5.31	4.03	78.5	**4.4**	30.4	9.7	**5.6**
7.6	0.13	0.8	0.00	**5.7**	0.5	4.18	41.20	3.87	45.3	**3.1**	28.5	15.7	**4.7**
2.4	3.53	20.4	0.51	**0.0**	-1.4	-2.25	-39.56	3.56	151.1	**2.3**	43.2	32.4	**1.9**
6.8	0.63	2.1	-0.03	**2.7**	0.2	0.54	6.57	3.10	86.2	**6.8**	60.4	2.6	**3.8**
7.5	0.80	3.3	0.16	**5.1**	2.0	1.27	10.08	2.85	50.6	**2.3**	45.8	38.3	**8.0**

Name	City	State	Rating	2013 Rating	2012 Rating	Total Assets ($Mil)	One Year Asset Growth	Asset Mix (As a % of Total Assets)				Capital-ization Index	Lever-age Ratio	Risk-Based Capital Ratio
								Comm-ercial Loans	Cons-umer Loans	Mort-gage Loans	Secur-ities			
NELSONVILLE HOME & SAVINGS	Nelsonville	OH	C+	C+	C	27.4	6.39	0.0	2.8	60.3	7.3	8.4	9.9	20.7
NEUBERGER BERMAN TRUST CO DE	Wilmington	DE	U	U	U	8.1	11.21	0.0	0.0	0.0	0.0	10.0	120.	168.8
NEUBERGER BERMAN TRUST CO NA	New York	NY	U	U	U	29.5	4.25	0.0	0.0	0.0	0.0	10.0	86.3	226.5
NEVADA BANK & TRUST CO	Caliente	NV	C+	C+	B-	106.1	8.33	4.8	3.9	10.5	45.9	9.7	10.8	24.1
NEVADA STATE BK	Las Vegas	NV	B-	B	B-	4050.2	1.69	12.3	1.9	16.7	20.3	6.9	8.9	16.6
NEW ALBIN SB	New Albin	IA	A+	A+	A+	207.9	3.98	2.7	1.2	9.7	68.8	10.0	16.0	49.5
NEW BUFFALO SAVINGS BANK A FSB	New Buffalo	MI	D	D	D+	86.9	-13.22	0.9	1.5	36.4	0.8	10.0	13.5	20.8
NEW CARLISLE FSB	New Carlisle	OH	C	C	D+	85.0	-0.65	9.2	1.6	33.9	3.2	10.0	11.5	15.7
▲ NEW CENTURY BANK	Belleville	KS	B	B-	B-	26.4	10.50	8.0	5.8	31.3	3.3	9.2	11.2	14.3
NEW COVENANT TRUST CO NA	Jeffersonville	IN	U	U	U	5.7	5.01	0.0	0.0	0.0	49.3	10.0	96.2	360.8
NEW ERA BANK	Fredericktown	MO	A+	A+	A	324.4	22.67	3.9	1.2	31.3	26.3	7.5	9.3	17.0
▲ NEW FOUNDATION SAVINGS BANK	Cincinnati	OH	C	C-	C	20.0	-9.74	0.0	0.1	65.2	1.8	10.0	13.0	23.9
▲ NEW FRONTIER BANK	Saint Charles	MO	C-	D-	E-	95.6	-8.86	7.9	0.4	10.4	21.5	6.3	8.3	13.9
NEW HORIZON BANK NA	Powhatan	VA	C	C	C-	55.0	6.93	17.5	2.1	12.1	17.8	10.0	12.3	18.7
▼ NEW JERSEY COMMUNITY BANK	Freehold	NJ	D+	C+	C+	128.2	-5.27	1.0	0.2	5.2	13.5	8.7	10.2	14.4
NEW MARKET BANK	Elko New Market	MN	D+	C-	D+	93.4	8.04	7.7	1.4	6.6	22.2	6.5	8.5	16.6
NEW MEXICO BANK & TRUST	Albuquerque	NM	B	B-	C+	1069.7	7.02	13.8	0.4	5.6	35.3	6.7	8.7	13.9
NEW MILLENNIUM BANK	New Brunswick	NJ	E-	E-	E-	184.5	2.04	5.3	0.0	10.5	9.3	8.6	10.1	14.9
NEW OMNI BANK NA	Alhambra	CA	B-	C+	C	276.4	18.78	4.1	0.3	42.3	0.0	10.0	12.6	21.8
NEW PEOPLES BANK INC	Honaker	VA	D+	D	E+	668.9	-3.18	3.1	3.9	35.5	14.5	5.8	7.8	15.1
NEW REPUBLIC SAVINGS BANK	Roanoke Rapids	NC	B-	B-	C	65.4	12.25	0.6	0.2	57.5	0.0	8.3	9.9	17.1
NEW RESOURCE BANK	San Francisco	CA	B-	C+	C-	230.7	5.22	25.5	0.1	3.0	12.5	10.0	13.0	17.5
▲ NEW TRADITIONS BANK	Orlando	FL	B-	C+	B-	522.7	1.20	10.0	0.7	4.2	0.6	8.6	10.1	13.9
NEW TRIPOLI BANK	New Tripoli	PA	A-	A-	A-	378.1	6.18	3.9	0.6	45.9	24.5	10.0	12.0	21.1
▼ NEW WASHINGTON STATE BK	New Washington	IN	B	B+	B	246.9	2.37	8.7	14.5	22.1	9.8	9.8	11.1	14.8
NEW WINDSOR STATE BK	Taneytown	MD	C+	C-	D+	281.3	2.38	3.5	1.2	20.6	12.7	6.7	8.7	12.3
NEW YORK COMMERCIAL BANK	Westbury	NY	B	C+	B-	4079.4	22.23	12.4	0.1	0.3	21.7	8.4	10.1	13.7
NEW YORK COMMUNITY BANK	Westbury	NY	B	C+	C	44619.4	4.66	1.1	0.0	7.2	15.0	5.7	7.7	12.3
NEWBANK	Flushing	NY	A-	B+	B	195.8	16.20	33.9	0.0	1.0	1.2	10.0	13.8	19.0
NEWBRIDGE BANK	Greensboro	NC	C	C+	D+	2441.2	35.56	4.8	1.1	17.0	19.6	6.7	9.0	12.3
NEWBURYPORT FIVE CENTS SB	Newburyport	MA	B+	B+	B+	704.7	6.87	2.4	0.2	40.3	15.7	10.0	15.5	21.2
NEWDOMINION BANK	Charlotte	NC	E-	E-	E-	287.0	4.34	8.4	0.2	13.3	8.3	1.2	5.9	8.2
NEWFIELD NATIONAL BK	Newfield	NJ	C+	C+	C+	566.3	7.19	6.7	0.8	15.3	41.2	7.0	9.0	17.0
NEWFIRST NATIONAL BK	El Campo	TX	B	B+	B	572.3	10.83	12.9	1.4	11.3	8.3	8.3	9.9	14.8
NEWPORT FEDERAL BANK	Newport	TN	B	B	B-	190.1	3.20	0.6	1.4	39.8	41.0	8.4	9.9	24.9
NEWTON COUNTY BANK	Newton	MS	A-	A-	B+	158.0	1.70	2.1	7.0	18.3	29.3	10.0	13.6	19.8
NEWTON FEDERAL BANK	Covington	GA	C	C-	D+	222.8	0.00	5.2	0.7	62.1	3.1	10.0	16.2	32.2
▲ NEWTOWN SB	Newtown	CT	C-	C-	D+	1000.7	2.90	7.1	2.1	48.7	7.9	6.0	8.0	12.6
NEXBANK SSB	Dallas	TX	B+	B	C+	1621.6	49.63	23.6	0.6	38.1	11.0	7.6	9.4	13.6
NEXTIER BANK NA	Butler	PA	B-	B-	C	436.1	4.83	12.0	1.1	32.0	13.8	9.4	10.6	16.8
▲ NICOLET NATIONAL BK	Green Bay	WI	B	B-	C	1155.7	3.09	22.1	0.5	15.3	12.9	7.6	9.4	13.5
▲ NICOLLET COUNTY BK OF ST PETER	Saint Peter	MN	C+	C	C+	160.8	2.15	9.6	2.8	7.5	31.3	5.5	7.5	15.8
▼ NJM BANK FSB	Ewing	NJ	C-	C	C	459.8	-26.68	0.0	0.3	56.8	0.0	10.0	15.0	35.7
NOA BANK	Duluth	GA	A	A	B+	183.8	25.58	4.3	0.0	1.0	16.8	10.0	12.5	16.1
NOAH BANK	Elkins Park	PA	D	D+	C-	317.3	25.81	20.4	0.1	0.0	0.6	5.9	9.9	11.7
NOBLEBANK & TRUST	Anniston	AL	C+	C+	C	176.1	5.14	8.8	1.8	14.3	30.4	8.9	10.3	16.9
NODAWAY VALLEY BANK	Maryville	MO	B-	B-	B-	807.1	2.12	9.1	1.3	8.5	19.5	9.4	10.6	14.9
NOKOMIS SB	Nokomis	IL	B-	B-	B-	28.2	-2.77	20.6	0.9	2.3	40.2	10.0	15.2	128.3
NORDSTROM FSB	Scottsdale	AZ	A-	A-	A-	233.3	3.09	0.0	55.2	0.0	0.1	10.0	51.7	71.1
▼ NORMANGEE STATE BK	Normangee	TX	B+	A	A	110.7	10.59	0.6	20.0	24.8	31.3	10.0	13.7	27.0
NORSTATES BANK	Waukegan	IL	D-	E+	D-	422.9	4.25	2.2	0.3	7.2	31.3	8.9	10.3	19.1
NORTH ADAMS STATE BK	Ursa	IL	B-	B-	C+	33.5	-6.92	15.9	5.1	11.7	14.2	10.0	12.3	19.6
NORTH ALABAMA BANK	Hazel Green	AL	C-	D+	D-	97.4	-2.64	3.6	1.8	11.8	10.0	6.7	8.7	13.1
NORTH AMERICAN BANKING CO	Roseville	MN	C+	C+	C+	360.7	9.23	11.8	0.6	7.6	15.0	6.1	8.9	11.8
NORTH AMERICAN SAVINGS BK FSB	Grandview	MO	B	C+	C-	1148.0	2.08	0.8	0.1	45.5	17.5	10.0	17.4	22.9
NORTH AMERICAN STATE BK	Belgrade	MN	D+	D+	D	105.5	1.06	4.1	1.4	12.8	24.0	8.1	9.7	14.7
NORTH ARUNDEL SAVINGS BK FSB	Pasadena	MD	B-	B-	C+	43.3	5.42	0.0	0.7	60.5	18.3	10.0	11.3	23.3
NORTH BANK	Chicago	IL	C	C	C-	112.9	-0.40	7.1	0.7	12.4	46.0	7.6	9.4	18.6
NORTH BROOKFIELD SB	North Brookfield	MA	B-	B-	B	258.6	20.26	0.8	1.0	42.2	30.5	10.0	11.4	24.0
NORTH CAMBRIDGE CO-OP BANK	Cambridge	MA	B-	B-	B-	89.8	4.09	0.0	0.1	47.9	17.6	10.0	20.8	57.5

Asset Quality Index	Adjusted Non-Performing Loans as a % of Total Loans	Adjusted Non-Performing Loans as a % of Capital	Net Charge-Offs / Avg Loans	Profitability Index	Net Income ($Mil)	Return on Assets (R.O.A.)	Return on Equity (R.O.E.)	Net Interest Spread	Overhead Efficiency Ratio	Liquidity Index	Liquidity Ratio	Hot Money Ratio	Stability Index
9.5	0.00	0.0	0.00	4.0	0.1	0.67	6.93	3.32	61.9	1.6	26.9	27.9	4.6
10.0	na	0.0	na	9.5	0.4	8.21	6.74	2.39	88.5	4.0	402.7	101.0	5.4
10.0	na	0.0	na	8.8	1.5	7.56	8.67	2.69	91.0	4.0	314.6	101.0	7.0
8.0	0.53	1.8	-0.07	3.7	0.5	0.57	5.41	3.51	81.2	6.9	55.0	2.5	5.6
5.0	2.18	12.5	-0.03	3.5	15.6	0.52	5.55	2.97	87.5	6.2	32.8	2.8	6.9
9.6	0.74	1.4	-0.14	7.7	2.5	1.63	9.45	3.19	25.9	4.2	73.6	22.1	9.8
3.7	4.18	21.1	0.28	0.0	-0.7	-1.07	-8.01	2.92	144.7	1.8	19.4	20.7	4.4
5.2	1.52	10.0	0.36	2.4	0.1	0.18	1.53	3.80	92.5	2.9	12.5	14.1	4.9
8.2	0.09	0.6	-0.01	8.2	0.4	1.81	16.94	6.08	74.6	1.6	12.9	22.9	7.0
10.0	na	0.0	na	10.0	0.1	1.86	1.94	0.38	92.4	4.0	2244.0	101.0	5.8
5.3	1.24	7.7	0.03	8.3	3.7	1.75	14.96	3.18	53.3	5.0	32.8	6.6	7.4
8.3	0.23	1.4	0.37	3.0	0.1	0.45	5.35	2.78	89.0	1.4	17.9	26.1	4.1
5.9	0.86	4.8	-0.22	3.7	0.9	1.23	15.72	4.00	91.7	2.1	25.9	20.1	2.9
5.3	2.69	15.2	0.08	2.7	0.1	0.32	2.46	4.30	87.8	1.4	23.8	28.8	6.4
2.5	1.14	6.7	1.39	1.1	0.1	0.05	0.50	3.47	86.8	1.0	25.1	35.9	4.4
3.3	3.21	16.5	0.61	1.8	0.2	0.23	2.76	2.96	92.9	6.2	50.0	4.1	3.4
5.7	0.96	6.0	0.14	5.3	8.3	1.06	11.20	3.86	65.9	3.5	17.8	12.2	6.7
1.7	2.29	14.3	0.48	0.0	-1.7	-1.24	-19.31	2.75	147.1	1.2	20.4	30.8	0.9
8.9	0.00	0.0	0.00	3.9	1.1	0.58	4.39	3.91	66.6	0.8	19.0	51.5	7.1
1.6	5.66	41.7	0.73	1.9	0.7	0.14	1.81	3.79	96.6	2.0	21.3	19.6	4.0
4.4	1.12	8.6	0.57	4.9	0.2	0.46	4.44	4.82	72.9	0.6	15.3	62.0	5.9
7.4	0.90	4.6	0.00	3.8	1.3	0.78	6.00	4.40	82.6	3.5	27.1	13.4	5.6
8.4	0.00	0.0	0.09	4.3	3.3	0.86	8.34	3.43	48.5	5.5	34.7	4.4	5.7
5.4	2.95	15.4	0.29	6.4	3.7	1.35	11.26	4.04	50.4	1.6	13.1	22.4	8.1
4.2	0.98	6.6	0.16	6.8	2.9	1.58	14.24	4.66	68.9	4.3	17.1	7.1	7.7
3.0	1.20	9.9	0.03	3.7	1.1	0.53	6.18	3.57	77.6	3.4	9.1	11.5	4.3
4.7	0.47	3.4	0.00	5.5	27.7	0.99	6.25	3.14	48.4	4.1	13.2	8.1	8.2
4.9	0.32	3.1	0.01	6.4	343.7	1.04	8.49	2.71	41.8	2.1	7.5	17.9	9.3
5.4	1.21	5.8	-0.19	10.0	4.5	3.25	24.93	4.38	39.3	1.9	33.8	30.7	7.4
6.8	0.52	3.8	0.24	3.5	11.0	0.65	6.51	3.80	75.8	1.9	16.8	20.3	6.5
7.7	0.98	4.8	0.08	4.2	3.8	0.74	4.55	3.53	69.3	1.5	20.4	26.7	8.7
1.8	3.32	34.2	0.06	0.5	-0.3	-0.12	-2.07	3.51	103.4	1.1	9.0	28.9	0.3
4.2	2.19	11.6	0.19	3.3	2.2	0.53	6.06	3.64	81.3	4.9	41.3	10.8	5.6
4.5	1.78	11.8	0.05	9.1	8.6	2.05	20.55	4.84	60.3	4.8	28.3	5.9	8.2
7.3	1.11	4.9	0.49	4.7	1.1	0.74	7.72	3.54	57.0	1.6	33.6	33.9	5.0
6.3	1.05	4.1	0.00	5.6	1.7	1.40	10.47	4.15	70.1	2.9	25.4	15.6	7.8
5.0	2.72	11.7	0.02	4.4	1.4	0.83	5.23	4.28	68.6	1.6	20.6	24.7	5.4
4.6	1.36	13.1	0.32	2.2	2.1	0.29	3.68	3.42	84.2	4.1	8.8	7.5	4.1
8.6	0.05	0.4	-0.01	6.2	17.7	1.63	17.82	3.06	48.2	2.5	16.5	17.2	6.2
4.2	1.52	9.6	0.06	3.7	2.1	0.65	6.12	3.49	84.9	4.4	14.2	6.2	6.6
5.3	0.99	7.4	0.19	4.6	7.6	0.87	9.12	4.08	68.1	3.7	16.8	10.9	6.4
5.1	1.72	9.9	0.00	3.5	0.9	0.72	10.28	2.55	72.0	4.4	27.9	8.8	4.0
7.0	2.11	8.7	0.11	0.1	-6.2	-1.39	-11.59	1.89	154.4	3.1	42.4	20.5	6.0
6.6	0.71	3.9	0.03	9.8	4.3	3.31	26.26	4.27	48.4	0.7	21.6	60.7	8.5
1.0	1.71	12.7	0.64	9.7	5.5	2.48	24.00	4.88	58.3	0.6	13.7	52.3	1.9
5.4	1.15	6.0	0.07	3.7	1.0	0.72	7.20	3.75	77.1	5.3	33.4	4.8	4.6
4.0	1.40	8.6	0.03	9.2	13.8	2.26	19.87	3.93	49.5	3.7	16.1	10.6	9.5
8.5	0.02	0.1	0.00	4.1	0.2	0.90	5.93	3.35	64.9	4.3	44.9	14.3	7.1
5.7	1.48	1.6	1.98	10.0	88.4	44.47	102.84	7.55	38.6	3.3	58.7	28.9	8.5
5.0	2.10	8.6	0.34	10.0	1.5	1.88	13.77	4.86	40.8	2.6	35.6	22.0	8.5
0.3	12.42	52.2	0.44	0.9	0.6	0.20	2.42	3.02	95.4	4.1	29.3	10.8	3.6
6.2	0.73	4.1	0.04	4.2	0.2	0.68	5.46	4.08	74.2	4.4	23.0	7.0	6.2
2.3	4.33	27.8	1.22	3.6	0.3	0.43	4.14	4.67	81.8	1.1	19.0	31.7	3.6
8.2	0.16	1.2	0.06	5.0	2.3	0.91	10.62	3.74	63.9	0.9	24.0	38.4	3.7
4.6	3.15	13.2	0.13	9.7	15.1	1.74	9.82	4.02	74.1	2.2	21.5	19.8	9.2
5.0	1.09	5.9	-0.42	3.5	0.7	0.90	10.57	3.67	77.1	2.7	26.9	17.0	4.8
5.2	2.70	16.1	0.00	4.0	0.2	0.62	5.69	3.85	70.4	1.5	32.5	36.1	5.6
3.9	3.94	18.2	0.37	3.2	0.4	0.48	5.37	3.84	80.4	3.0	44.1	22.8	4.5
6.9	1.58	7.9	0.02	3.6	1.1	0.64	4.94	3.39	78.8	4.2	37.7	13.3	6.6
10.0	0.57	1.4	0.00	2.9	0.3	0.43	1.95	3.03	77.9	3.1	59.7	27.8	7.6

Name	City	State	Rating	2013 Rating	2012 Rating	Total Assets ($Mil)	One Year Asset Growth	Asset Mix (As a % of Total Assets) Commercial Loans	Consumer Loans	Mortgage Loans	Securities	Capitalization Index	Leverage Ratio	Risk-Based Capital Ratio
NORTH CENTRAL BANK	Hennepin	IL	**B**	B	B	133.4	2.85	8.0	4.2	13.8	33.5	**8.3**	9.9	16.1
NORTH COMMUNITY BANK	Chicago	IL	**E**	E	E-	2453.6	-0.43	2.2	0.1	9.8	26.6	**5.6**	7.6	13.8
NORTH COUNTRY BANK	McClusky	ND	**B+**	B+	B	64.0	3.58	5.3	4.2	0.9	33.6	**6.8**	8.8	13.4
▲ NORTH COUNTRY SB	Canton	NY	**B-**	C	C+	241.6	3.96	0.2	1.8	71.5	2.1	**10.0**	14.5	24.4
NORTH COUNTY SB	Red Bud	IL	**C**	C	C	45.8	2.44	0.2	3.7	51.2	18.8	**6.2**	8.2	18.5
NORTH DALLAS BANK & TRUST CO	Dallas	TX	**C+**	C+	C+	1246.5	3.69	5.5	0.7	15.7	37.4	**9.4**	10.6	30.5
NORTH EASTON SB	South Easton	MA	**C-**	C-	C-	489.4	1.50	0.6	0.7	49.3	24.7	**6.9**	8.9	17.1
▲ NORTH GEORGIA NATIONAL BK	Calhoun	GA	**C-**	D	D	114.3	-4.41	4.8	1.2	14.9	16.9	**9.6**	10.7	19.7
NORTH LOUP VALLEY BANK	North Loup	NE	**D**	D	D	19.7	-6.21	5.3	4.1	2.8	16.8	**8.5**	10.0	17.2
NORTH MIDDLESEX SB	Ayer	MA	**C-**	C-	D+	372.3	6.92	5.7	3.0	30.7	15.9	**6.7**	8.7	13.6
NORTH MILWAUKEE STATE BK	Milwaukee	WI	**E-**	E+	E+	77.1	-11.16	3.5	1.4	12.7	15.5	**4.7**	7.2	10.8
NORTH SALEM STATE BK	North Salem	IN	**C+**	C	C	209.5	9.83	8.2	5.2	16.9	15.3	**6.4**	8.5	12.7
NORTH SHORE BANK A CO-OP BANK	Peabody	MA	**C+**	B-	B-	690.5	45.55	10.8	0.1	19.9	13.6	**9.1**	10.4	15.0
NORTH SHORE BANK FSB	Brookfield	WI	**C**	C	C-	1770.6	-0.22	1.2	13.4	26.2	7.2	**10.0**	11.3	18.4
NORTH SHORE BANK OF COMMERCE	Duluth	MN	**C+**	C+	C	243.4	2.60	4.3	0.8	38.0	11.3	**4.4**	6.4	11.2
NORTH SHORE TRUST & SAVINGS	Waukegan	IL	**C-**	C-	C	247.9	-2.01	0.1	0.0	36.2	37.3	**10.0**	17.3	55.9
NORTH SIDE BANK & TRUST CO	Cincinnati	OH	**B+**	B+	B	493.5	-2.32	23.8	1.5	10.6	20.5	**10.0**	14.0	21.5
NORTH SIDE FS&LA OF CHICAGO	Chicago	IL	**D+**	C-	C-	44.8	3.81	0.2	0.1	44.2	9.6	**9.8**	10.9	24.9
NORTH STAR BANK	Roseville	MN	**C**	C	D-	242.7	1.68	10.8	0.9	4.7	35.4	**7.2**	9.1	16.7
▲ NORTH STATE BK	Raleigh	NC	**B-**	C	D+	678.6	0.50	6.5	0.4	30.9	5.3	**6.9**	8.9	13.1
NORTH TEXAS BANK NA	Decatur	TX	**A-**	A-	B+	157.9	9.11	14.6	2.1	19.1	5.4	**8.8**	10.2	16.2
NORTH VALLEY BANK	Zanesville	OH	**C+**	C	C-	172.8	2.48	6.4	4.7	20.4	22.4	**7.6**	9.4	14.9
▲ NORTH VALLEY BANK	Thornton	CO	**B+**	B-	C	141.9	3.12	3.2	0.3	28.8	8.6	**9.6**	10.8	16.9
NORTHAMPTON CO-OP BANK	Northampton	MA	**C+**	C+	B-	171.8	4.80	0.8	0.1	40.8	30.8	**10.0**	14.1	27.5
NORTHBROOK BANK & TRUST CO	Northbrook	IL	**B-**	B-	C	1317.7	-19.30	29.7	3.8	5.3	12.9	**5.4**	8.7	11.3
▲ NORTHEAST BANK	Minneapolis	MN	**B**	C+	C-	369.0	7.28	19.2	0.3	4.5	10.8	**10.0**	13.0	15.9
▲ NORTHEAST BANK	Lewiston	ME	**B**	B-	C	779.9	8.26	2.7	1.2	17.3	14.2	**10.0**	13.3	19.6
NORTHEAST COMMUNITY BANK	White Plains	NY	**C**	C	C-	490.6	16.98	6.6	0.0	2.6	1.5	**10.0**	17.1	21.8
▲ NORTHEAST GEORGIA BANK	Lavonia	GA	**C+**	C	D+	401.6	1.43	4.6	4.1	9.0	24.8	**9.3**	10.5	17.4
NORTHEAST MISSOURI STATE BK	Kirksville	MO	**A-**	A	A-	96.9	4.72	0.6	4.3	9.8	50.9	**9.8**	10.8	21.1
▲ NORTHEAST SECURITY BANK	Sumner	IA	**A-**	B+	B	123.5	0.48	8.9	1.0	9.1	27.3	**10.0**	11.1	16.7
▲ NORTHERN BANK & TRUST CO	Woburn	MA	**B+**	B-	D+	1240.6	20.32	27.2	0.1	10.0	3.3	**5.7**	9.2	11.5
NORTHERN CALIFORNIA NATL BK	Chico	CA	**B-**	B-	B-	162.9	18.46	11.6	1.3	8.7	17.4	**8.3**	9.9	23.7
NORTHERN HANCOCK BANK & TRUST	Newell	WV	**C-**	D+	C	27.3	-6.89	4.8	12.0	40.2	3.9	**10.0**	11.7	18.7
NORTHERN MICHIGAN BANK & TRUST	Escanaba	MI	**D-**	D-	D-	244.8	7.87	14.9	2.2	8.6	23.5	**6.0**	8.0	11.7
NORTHERN ST BK THIEF RVR FALLS	Thief River Falls	MN	**C+**	B-	B-	295.7	5.69	6.7	4.8	10.6	14.3	**8.5**	10.0	27.9
NORTHERN STAR BANK	Mankato	MN	**E-**	E-	E-	18.8	-19.25	8.7	2.9	26.3	5.6	**0.0**	2.4	4.6
NORTHERN STATE BK	Ashland	WI	**B-**	B	B-	246.5	2.97	5.3	1.6	25.5	41.6	**5.9**	7.9	16.4
NORTHERN STATE BK OF GONVICK	Gonvick	MN	**C-**	C-	C+	35.2	-0.01	2.8	4.8	3.9	25.9	**10.0**	16.7	90.8
NORTHERN STATE BK OF VIRGINIA	Virginia	MN	**D+**	D+	D	57.6	-3.32	8.2	4.7	36.8	8.6	**6.1**	8.1	13.1
▲ NORTHERN TRUST CO	Chicago	IL	**B-**	B-	B-	110796.2	15.86	5.3	0.2	7.3	27.8	**4.8**	6.8	13.6
NORTHERN TRUST CO OF NEW YORK	New York	NY	**U**	U	U	7.1	-1.29	0.0	0.0	0.0	79.5	**10.0**	105.	115.1
NORTHFIELD BANK	Staten Island	NY	**B**	B	B-	2919.9	6.95	1.3	0.1	11.9	27.7	**10.0**	17.4	24.7
NORTHFIELD SB	Northfield	VT	**B**	B	B-	773.0	3.28	4.2	0.2	37.6	22.9	**10.0**	12.8	21.4
NORTHLAND FINANCIAL	Steele	ND	**B-**	B-	C+	196.6	4.67	8.7	2.6	4.8	13.4	**5.8**	8.7	11.6
NORTHMARK BANK	North Andover	MA	**B+**	B+	B	331.3	5.06	7.8	0.3	39.1	7.8	**10.0**	11.7	18.6
NORTHPOINTE BANK	Grand Rapids	MI	**D+**	D-	D-	360.6	18.99	0.3	0.0	41.9	2.5	**6.0**	8.9	11.7
NORTHRIM BANK	Anchorage	AK	**A**	A-	A-	1413.4	20.55	15.7	0.9	4.1	16.8	**9.6**	11.6	14.6
NORTHSIDE BANK	Adairsville	GA	**E-**	E-	E-	137.5	1.46	5.9	1.0	12.3	12.8	**1.0**	5.3	8.0
NORTHSIDE COMMUNITY BANK	Gurnee	IL	**C**	D+	D	256.6	-13.16	8.4	0.1	9.7	2.7	**10.0**	16.9	23.6
NORTHSTAR BANK	Tampa	FL	**D+**	C-	C	204.1	3.32	13.0	1.0	4.3	54.1	**7.3**	9.2	17.3
▲ NORTHSTAR BANK	Estherville	IA	**B**	B-	B	181.6	0.43	3.8	1.7	15.6	8.0	**7.5**	9.3	13.1
NORTHSTAR BANK	Bad Axe	MI	**C-**	C-	C-	487.5	78.92	12.1	1.9	18.3	7.6	**6.8**	9.6	12.3
NORTHSTAR BANK OF COLORADO	Denver	CO	**C+**	C	C-	619.2	-7.32	7.7	0.4	5.6	11.7	**9.4**	10.6	14.9
NORTHSTAR BANK OF TEXAS	Denton	TX	**B**	C+	C+	1104.9	0.83	10.0	1.8	9.1	14.9	**8.6**	10.2	13.9
NORTHUMBERLAND NATIONAL BK	Northumberland	PA	**B-**	B	B-	479.0	-1.94	9.2	0.9	36.1	36.8	**7.9**	9.6	21.1
NORTHVIEW BANK	Sandstone	MN	**B-**	B-	C+	248.3	5.34	6.3	3.6	21.6	20.3	**7.5**	9.3	13.1
▲ NORTHWAY BANK	Berlin	NH	**C+**	C	C-	936.2	4.23	8.1	0.9	17.6	24.8	**7.7**	9.5	16.0
NORTHWEST BANK	Spencer	IA	**B-**	B-	B-	1348.6	26.97	17.9	3.0	18.6	8.3	**5.4**	8.4	11.3
NORTHWEST BANK	Boise	ID	**B+**	B+	B+	335.6	35.21	19.4	0.5	1.8	4.4	**10.0**	14.5	16.2

Asset Quality Index	Adjusted Non-Performing Loans as a % of Total Loans	Adjusted Non-Performing Loans as a % of Capital	Net Charge-Offs Avg Loans	Profitability Index	Net Income ($Mil)	Return on Assets (R.O.A.)	Return on Equity (R.O.E.)	Net Interest Spread	Overhead Efficiency Ratio	Liquidity Index	Liquidity Ratio	Hot Money Ratio	Stability Index
4.2	1.50	8.3	0.24	**4.4**	1.1	1.10	9.54	3.31	68.0	**2.7**	25.9	17.0	**7.2**
0.3	14.95	94.3	0.15	**1.1**	-1.0	-0.05	-0.56	4.00	97.2	**5.3**	35.5	9.7	**4.5**
6.8	0.22	1.4	0.04	**3.7**	0.3	0.50	4.59	3.74	74.1	**4.4**	25.3	7.6	**7.2**
8.6	0.44	2.4	0.17	**3.5**	1.0	0.57	4.14	3.90	77.5	**4.6**	10.1	3.9	**6.7**
9.2	0.06	0.4	0.11	**2.9**	0.1	0.39	4.94	2.66	79.0	**2.7**	40.8	25.3	**3.7**
8.9	0.71	2.6	0.00	**3.2**	4.3	0.47	4.37	2.16	68.7	**5.3**	58.9	14.5	**7.9**
6.1	1.49	10.1	0.02	**2.2**	1.0	0.28	3.32	2.60	89.5	**4.1**	32.4	11.8	**4.4**
2.0	6.29	27.6	-0.46	**3.7**	1.0	1.13	11.04	3.23	95.1	**2.3**	31.1	21.2	**4.7**
5.5	1.23	4.8	-1.03	**1.1**	0.0	0.02	0.20	2.36	99.8	**3.1**	59.5	23.5	**2.0**
2.5	2.49	19.3	0.35	**3.2**	1.2	0.45	4.72	3.58	80.1	**1.7**	15.9	21.4	**4.4**
0.0	13.55	93.7	2.11	**0.0**	-0.2	-0.38	-4.91	4.10	79.6	**0.7**	15.1	48.2	**2.8**
3.6	0.95	7.7	0.44	**5.1**	1.5	1.01	11.90	4.29	60.9	**1.6**	19.8	24.1	**4.9**
6.8	0.50	3.3	0.04	**3.0**	1.4	0.35	3.45	3.18	83.8	**3.4**	22.0	12.7	**5.8**
3.2	2.19	14.0	0.17	**2.4**	2.9	0.22	1.77	3.22	88.9	**4.3**	17.1	7.5	**7.3**
4.4	1.41	14.5	0.07	**4.0**	1.5	0.82	13.09	3.59	84.8	**5.0**	24.0	3.3	**3.9**
6.7	4.05	9.4	0.48	**1.4**	0.2	0.10	0.61	2.51	89.9	**4.1**	60.8	19.5	**6.5**
6.8	0.77	3.5	0.47	**4.5**	3.1	0.83	5.91	3.31	60.1	**3.1**	21.0	14.0	**6.9**
1.7	6.76	35.1	-0.01	**1.4**	0.0	-0.06	-0.56	3.38	102.6	**4.2**	38.7	13.8	**6.1**
4.7	2.58	11.9	-0.02	**3.2**	1.4	0.77	9.26	3.19	86.1	**5.6**	47.2	8.4	**3.4**
5.5	0.61	5.0	0.14	**4.4**	3.9	0.73	8.61	3.53	75.3	**3.9**	12.5	8.8	**4.6**
8.6	0.00	0.0	0.00	**7.0**	1.9	1.64	16.03	5.26	63.4	**2.6**	28.6	18.3	**6.5**
4.7	1.29	8.2	0.06	**3.8**	0.9	0.69	7.42	4.07	75.9	**3.5**	18.9	12.1	**4.5**
7.2	0.04	0.3	0.20	**7.7**	2.1	2.04	19.53	4.96	63.3	**4.3**	13.7	6.6	**6.0**
9.3	0.66	2.6	0.00	**2.7**	0.4	0.29	2.06	2.60	85.5	**4.6**	38.8	11.5	**7.5**
4.8	1.03	8.3	-0.25	**6.4**	11.2	1.00	11.00	3.67	58.2	**1.2**	7.9	27.4	**6.0**
4.4	1.42	7.7	0.13	**5.3**	2.6	0.97	7.31	4.63	70.0	**5.0**	16.3	2.1	**6.5**
5.4	1.80	9.4	0.13	**4.2**	3.6	0.63	4.89	4.67	80.4	**0.9**	23.6	41.3	**7.0**
2.9	3.56	17.2	-0.02	**2.3**	1.1	0.31	1.62	3.77	90.1	**0.8**	7.5	33.2	**6.2**
3.4	3.48	15.5	0.08	**3.6**	2.7	0.88	9.80	3.38	75.6	**3.8**	31.0	13.1	**4.0**
8.1	0.06	0.2	0.00	**5.6**	1.0	1.38	11.30	3.40	58.7	**3.6**	46.3	18.0	**9.6**
6.8	0.62	3.3	0.00	**6.8**	1.2	1.22	10.51	3.88	52.2	**3.7**	23.3	11.6	**6.8**
6.9	0.34	2.8	0.35	**8.2**	10.7	1.24	14.15	4.22	47.1	**1.1**	10.0	29.4	**7.9**
7.5	0.47	1.7	0.88	**3.5**	0.6	0.47	5.07	2.28	62.3	**4.4**	50.1	15.3	**5.8**
1.3	5.46	29.4	1.14	**3.6**	0.1	0.56	4.65	7.26	80.2	**1.2**	24.2	31.6	**5.5**
0.3	9.66	68.4	0.08	**3.4**	1.1	0.60	7.40	3.87	84.4	**2.4**	31.9	20.5	**4.7**
5.8	1.80	6.4	-0.06	**3.4**	1.5	0.69	6.92	1.89	67.3	**6.8**	60.6	5.0	**5.9**
1.7	2.81	46.6	0.22	**0.0**	-0.1	-0.73	-33.18	4.29	113.8	**1.5**	21.7	24.9	**0.0**
5.2	1.58	10.3	0.13	**3.7**	1.5	0.86	10.68	2.69	71.4	**4.8**	35.5	9.2	**5.7**
9.4	0.67	0.6	-0.13	**1.1**	0.0	-0.04	-0.26	1.30	103.1	**7.3**	93.4	5.6	**6.4**
2.7	2.80	22.9	0.31	**2.4**	0.2	0.36	4.57	4.18	88.5	**3.6**	13.7	10.7	**3.3**
8.0	0.95	4.0	0.06	**4.3**	577.5	0.75	10.63	1.07	72.6	**6.8**	49.5	4.2	**5.2**
10.0	na	0.0	na	**1.0**	0.0	-0.12	-0.11	0.07	433.3	**4.0**	na	101.0	**7.0**
5.1	2.04	7.0	0.03	**4.2**	15.4	0.76	3.97	2.99	60.3	**4.0**	15.8	9.4	**8.7**
8.2	0.75	3.9	0.04	**3.6**	3.7	0.66	5.25	3.29	76.8	**1.8**	16.4	20.2	**8.0**
5.3	0.48	4.0	0.00	**6.5**	2.4	1.61	19.57	4.49	64.1	**1.7**	14.1	20.9	**5.3**
9.0	0.10	0.6	0.00	**5.1**	1.9	0.77	6.59	3.55	64.0	**1.2**	13.4	29.2	**7.1**
1.6	4.40	39.4	0.30	**8.6**	5.4	2.29	27.20	4.73	64.8	**0.4**	4.7	56.5	**3.1**
7.3	0.63	3.5	-0.13	**7.5**	12.4	1.31	10.94	4.56	65.2	**5.3**	25.0	5.0	**9.4**
0.3	8.01	86.2	1.05	**0.6**	-0.5	-0.45	-8.51	3.93	96.8	**1.3**	10.0	26.7	**0.8**
3.2	5.82	20.7	-0.02	**2.8**	0.6	0.30	1.42	3.91	83.8	**3.9**	26.6	11.1	**5.3**
6.1	1.63	6.7	0.21	**1.4**	0.1	0.05	0.53	3.39	92.4	**2.0**	38.9	33.8	**3.8**
7.7	0.14	1.1	-0.01	**5.0**	1.7	1.25	11.31	3.28	60.3	**3.5**	20.3	11.8	**6.6**
2.3	2.39	18.6	0.04	**6.7**	4.4	1.25	12.29	4.20	72.7	**1.7**	8.5	20.0	**7.4**
0.9	3.92	21.8	0.31	**3.3**	1.8	0.38	2.30	4.60	80.8	**2.6**	22.1	16.8	**5.8**
5.3	0.71	4.7	0.03	**6.3**	9.3	1.19	8.37	4.28	66.1	**2.8**	19.4	15.9	**6.6**
6.9	0.64	3.5	0.04	**4.1**	2.8	0.77	8.20	2.87	69.7	**3.5**	24.9	12.5	**5.4**
3.6	2.04	14.5	0.06	**7.6**	2.4	1.33	13.75	4.72	62.4	**2.4**	18.7	17.5	**6.3**
3.5	2.15	13.8	0.51	**3.6**	5.2	0.76	7.44	3.50	76.6	**3.1**	16.7	13.4	**6.2**
5.1	0.72	6.4	0.81	**3.5**	3.3	0.32	3.48	3.52	73.9	**3.5**	12.5	11.3	**5.8**
8.3	0.18	0.9	-0.09	**4.8**	1.3	0.65	3.92	4.65	72.0	**2.4**	34.9	23.6	**6.1**

Name	City	State	Rating	2013 Rating	2012 Rating	Total Assets ($Mil)	One Year Asset Growth	Asset Mix (As a % of Total Assets) Comm-ercial Loans	Cons-umer Loans	Mort-gage Loans	Secur-ities	Capital-ization Index	Lever-age Ratio	Risk-Based Capital Ratio
NORTHWEST BANK & TRUST CO	Davenport	IA	**C-**	C-	C-	191.4	-2.84	12.8	1.9	13.7	8.3	**7.2**	9.2	14.6
NORTHWEST BANK OF ROCKFORD	Rockford	IL	**C+**	C+	C-	241.7	2.37	17.2	0.6	15.4	19.4	**7.9**	9.6	14.2
▲ NORTHWEST COMMUNITY BANK	Winsted	CT	**C**	C-	C	325.9	0.62	3.4	2.9	38.5	24.3	**10.0**	11.3	21.1
NORTHWEST GEORGIA BANK	Ringgold	GA	**E-**	E-	E-	294.7	-20.28	2.5	0.5	6.8	49.4	**0.2**	3.2	8.0
NORTHWEST SB	Warren	PA	**B**	B	B	7850.2	-0.87	4.3	3.2	43.5	13.3	**10.0**	11.2	17.8
NORTHWESTERN BANK	Orange City	IA	**A-**	A-	B+	213.0	6.94	7.4	0.9	7.3	5.6	**8.6**	10.5	13.9
NORTHWESTERN BANK	Chippewa Falls	WI	**A-**	B+	B-	385.8	1.99	12.1	0.9	8.4	34.0	**10.0**	11.9	18.0
NORTHWESTERN BANK NA	Dilworth	MN	**C+**	C+	C	129.2	-0.48	13.1	3.6	11.6	17.8	**8.7**	10.1	14.7
NORTHWESTERN MUTUAL WEALTH M	Milwaukee	WI	**U**	U	A+	192.1	3.51	0.0	0.0	0.0	95.9	**10.0**	65.1	265.1
NORTHWOODS BANK OF MINNESOTA	Park Rapids	MN	**C+**	C	C	103.8	-5.12	3.6	1.6	23.3	38.0	**10.0**	12.1	19.2
NORWAY SB	Norway	ME	**B**	B	B-	996.2	-0.18	4.3	3.8	28.0	9.0	**10.0**	12.6	16.0
NORWOOD CO-OP BANK	Norwood	MA	**C+**	C	C	394.4	8.61	1.0	0.1	30.5	21.1	**10.0**	15.4	23.2
NSB BANK	Mason City	IA	**B+**	B+	B	182.2	6.32	18.7	1.0	5.3	23.3	**6.6**	8.6	12.2
NUVO BANK & TRUST CO	Springfield	MA	**C**	C	D+	154.7	16.15	19.9	7.4	17.1	3.6	**5.0**	8.8	11.0
▲ NVE BANK	Englewood	NJ	**B-**	C+	C	679.6	-1.71	0.1	0.1	36.4	18.3	**10.0**	12.8	22.2
NXT BANK	Central City	IA	**C**	C+	C+	251.5	41.25	8.1	0.7	13.3	18.2	**8.1**	9.8	13.4
OAK BANK	Fitchburg	WI	**A-**	B+	C	232.5	1.25	14.8	0.5	17.3	12.5	**9.8**	11.0	14.8
OAK BANK	Chicago	IL	**B-**	B-	B	191.7	-3.42	6.8	0.4	10.8	1.6	**10.0**	15.9	21.4
OAK CREEK VALLEY BANK	Valparaiso	NE	**A**	A	A+	75.4	3.07	7.6	0.9	9.5	33.0	**10.0**	12.7	18.7
OAK VALLEY COMMUNITY BANK	Oakdale	CA	**B**	B	B-	706.8	7.23	6.8	0.1	2.5	17.6	**8.9**	10.2	14.7
OAK VIEW NATIONAL BK	Warrenton	VA	**C**	C	C-	168.4	15.07	8.0	1.7	37.7	0.6	**7.1**	9.1	14.3
OAKDALE STATE BK	Oakdale	IL	**C**	C	C-	19.4	1.20	5.0	3.5	27.1	11.1	**7.6**	9.4	16.4
OAKSTAR BANK	Springfield	MO	**B**	B+	B+	307.1	23.20	16.6	0.6	25.1	0.0	**6.6**	9.5	12.2
OAKWOOD STATE BK	Oakwood	TX	**B**	B	B	5.7	13.12	4.8	12.2	0.0	31.8	**10.0**	22.7	75.4
▲ OAKWORTH CAPITAL BANK	Birmingham	AL	**A**	A-	B	310.6	21.63	24.9	2.7	2.2	12.1	**10.0**	15.6	17.7
OBANNON BANKING CO	Buffalo	MO	**B-**	B-	C+	165.9	3.57	6.6	3.4	23.4	17.2	**6.8**	8.9	14.4
OCEAN BANK	Miami	FL	**D**	D-	E+	3256.6	-1.38	7.1	0.7	7.4	19.9	**7.4**	9.3	14.2
OCEAN CITY HOME BANK	Ocean City	NJ	**C+**	C+	C+	1035.0	-0.15	0.8	0.1	59.6	10.9	**7.8**	9.5	19.1
▲ OCEANFIRST BANK	Toms River	NJ	**B-**	C+	C+	2315.9	1.21	3.2	0.0	38.1	22.2	**7.9**	9.6	15.3
OCONEE FS&LA	Seneca	SC	**A**	A-	A-	357.2	-2.30	0.0	0.2	60.7	26.2	**10.0**	20.1	42.8
OCONEE STATE BK	Watkinsville	GA	**C**	D+	D-	270.4	1.87	3.2	1.6	8.3	41.7	**7.5**	9.4	17.7
▲ OCULINA BANK	Fort Pierce	FL	**C**	D	D+	175.4	15.25	5.3	0.6	51.7	1.9	**8.1**	9.8	16.3
ODIN STATE BK	Odin	MN	**B**	B	B-	40.2	2.58	10.7	4.9	6.3	22.4	**10.0**	11.9	19.7
OGLESBY STATE BK	Oglesby	TX	**C-**	C	C-	13.6	-7.54	5.1	19.4	32.1	0.0	**9.9**	10.9	17.4
OHANA PACIFIC BANK	Honolulu	HI	**B-**	B-	C+	116.6	9.90	7.0	1.0	5.3	0.0	**10.0**	12.4	19.9
OHIO STATE BK	Marion	OH	**E-**	E-	E-	84.7	-18.09	5.4	1.7	29.5	8.3	**0.8**	4.7	7.6
OHIO VALLEY BANK CO	Gallipolis	OH	**C+**	C+	C+	763.5	3.86	8.6	10.5	26.9	13.7	**9.8**	10.9	15.5
OHIO VALLEY FINANCIAL GROUP	Henderson	KY	**A-**	A-	B+	259.8	4.89	12.2	3.8	25.0	4.8	**7.1**	9.7	12.6
OHNWARD BANK & TRUST	Cascade	IA	**B+**	B+	B	218.7	11.26	9.4	3.1	8.5	16.5	**9.0**	11.0	14.2
OJAI COMMUNITY BANK	Ojai	CA	**C+**	C	C	154.1	4.12	11.9	0.4	11.2	3.9	**8.5**	10.3	13.8
OKEY-VERNON FIRST NATIONAL BK	Corning	IA	**B**	B	B+	73.2	12.21	3.2	1.5	5.8	44.8	**10.0**	13.8	21.4
OKLAHOMA BANK & TRUST CO	Clinton	OK	**B**	B	A-	168.6	5.23	1.7	1.5	9.4	58.8	**10.0**	12.2	28.9
OKLAHOMA HERITAGE BANK	Stratford	OK	**C**	C	C-	92.6	9.16	7.1	14.8	27.5	24.4	**5.4**	7.4	13.4
OKLAHOMA STATE BK	Vinita	OK	**B**	B-	C+	127.8	5.94	26.2	3.3	9.4	13.6	**8.7**	10.2	14.6
OKLAHOMA STATE BK	Buffalo	OK	**B-**	B-	B-	56.1	0.81	4.1	10.8	3.8	46.0	**5.4**	7.4	14.1
OKLAHOMA STATE BK	Guthrie	OK	**D+**	C-	C	95.4	38.01	19.7	2.2	20.4	2.4	**4.8**	8.3	10.9
OLD DOMINION NATIONAL BK	North Garden	VA	**E**	E	E-	50.5	18.99	8.4	3.2	17.4	17.3	**10.0**	14.3	31.9
OLD EXCHANGE NB OF OKAWVILLE	Okawville	IL	**C+**	C+	C+	61.6	0.58	1.6	0.9	7.8	42.7	**7.7**	9.5	18.0
OLD FLORIDA BANK	Orlando	FL	**C+**	C+	B-	886.0	10.76	23.4	0.4	7.1	7.7	**5.5**	9.6	11.4
OLD FORT BANKING CO	Old Fort	OH	**B**	B	B-	438.9	3.16	9.9	1.6	10.3	30.3	**6.8**	8.8	14.4
OLD LINE BANK	Bowie	MD	**B-**	C+	C	1200.9	2.39	8.4	0.8	13.6	13.6	**6.5**	9.1	12.1
OLD MISSION BANK	Sault Sainte Marie	MI	**C+**	C+	B-	108.3	-0.57	10.1	3.9	13.7	34.9	**8.8**	10.2	17.1
OLD MISSOURI BANK	Springfield	MO	**B-**	B	B-	177.6	11.68	14.1	2.9	16.1	6.9	**6.2**	8.7	11.9
OLD NATIONAL BK	Evansville	IN	**C+**	C+	C-	11035.8	16.15	9.9	7.7	16.1	30.7	**6.2**	8.2	12.7
OLD PLANK TRAIL COMMUNITY BANK	Mokena	IL	**B-**	B-	C	1175.0	7.73	32.5	5.8	3.4	17.4	**5.9**	8.1	11.7
OLD POINT NATIONAL BK PHOEBUS	Hampton	VA	**C**	C	C-	860.6	-1.30	4.1	2.2	11.9	27.1	**8.6**	10.1	14.5
OLD POINT TRUST & FINANCIAL	Newport News	VA	**U**	U	U	5.7	1.66	0.0	0.0	0.0	66.7	**10.0**	98.8	168.8
OLD SECOND NATIONAL BK	Aurora	IL	**B-**	C	D+	2012.0	-0.12	5.4	0.2	8.9	31.1	**10.0**	11.7	18.5
▲ OLDTOWN BANK	Waynesville	NC	**C+**	C-	D	111.0	15.73	0.9	0.4	23.5	33.1	**6.9**	8.9	15.4
▲ OLMSTED NATIONAL BK	Rochester	MN	**D+**	D	D-	54.3	4.84	14.8	1.1	20.6	5.4	**8.4**	9.9	14.6

Asset Quality Index	Adjusted Non-Performing Loans as a % of Total Loans	Adjusted Non-Performing Loans as a % of Capital	Net Charge-Offs Avg Loans	Profitability Index	Net Income ($Mil)	Return on Assets (R.O.A.)	Return on Equity (R.O.E.)	Net Interest Spread	Overhead Efficiency Ratio	Liquidity Index	Liquidity Ratio	Hot Money Ratio	Stability Index
2.4	4.26	23.9	0.07	**6.6**	2.3	1.60	17.42	3.55	69.1	**4.4**	31.2	10.0	**5.0**
1.9	3.20	20.9	0.90	**3.1**	1.1	0.60	6.16	4.07	74.6	**1.6**	15.9	23.6	**5.1**
6.1	1.70	9.4	0.03	**2.2**	0.9	0.37	3.15	3.02	89.8	**3.1**	25.2	14.5	**5.7**
0.3	10.47	76.6	1.50	**0.0**	-2.6	-0.99	-57.87	2.85	126.2	**5.1**	31.7	5.4	**0.0**
4.4	1.83	11.7	0.43	**4.4**	44.9	0.76	5.68	3.67	67.9	**4.3**	9.5	6.3	**9.0**
5.7	0.37	2.6	-0.02	**10.0**	2.6	1.73	14.16	3.88	39.4	**3.2**	18.7	13.3	**8.6**
5.9	1.66	8.0	0.11	**8.1**	3.8	1.30	11.01	3.92	46.7	**5.0**	28.4	5.0	**6.4**
4.6	0.86	5.8	0.02	**3.6**	0.7	0.73	6.59	4.12	83.5	**3.9**	11.4	8.7	**5.9**
10.0	na	0.0	na	**9.5**	18.8	12.73	20.99	1.73	88.2	**5.0**	279.2	100.0	**6.5**
3.2	5.31	21.9	0.15	**3.6**	0.5	0.66	5.36	4.23	87.7	**4.5**	31.8	9.8	**5.8**
6.1	1.18	7.0	0.18	**4.1**	6.5	0.87	6.63	4.11	75.5	**3.9**	11.9	9.2	**8.5**
6.8	1.15	5.0	0.00	**2.9**	1.3	0.46	2.87	3.01	78.0	**1.8**	15.7	19.9	**6.4**
5.6	0.55	4.1	0.17	**7.3**	2.4	1.72	19.78	3.49	50.9	**4.3**	16.8	6.9	**6.4**
7.5	0.15	1.3	0.48	**2.7**	0.2	0.21	2.12	3.63	74.6	**0.6**	8.5	38.1	**4.1**
8.0	0.95	4.8	-0.12	**3.4**	3.1	0.59	4.70	3.25	74.0	**4.6**	24.3	5.8	**7.2**
6.9	0.64	4.6	-0.02	**2.8**	0.7	0.34	3.51	3.23	85.3	**1.2**	17.8	30.1	**5.3**
7.2	0.32	2.1	-0.02	**7.0**	2.1	1.24	11.36	4.06	53.1	**3.9**	18.1	9.5	**6.2**
3.2	4.15	18.3	0.19	**3.9**	0.9	0.58	3.68	3.43	68.4	**1.6**	21.4	25.3	**7.6**
7.7	0.81	4.0	0.00	**10.0**	1.4	2.70	22.53	4.68	38.8	**3.4**	29.2	14.2	**8.8**
5.1	0.86	4.8	-0.55	**6.3**	5.7	1.11	11.08	4.11	68.2	**4.9**	27.9	5.3	**7.0**
8.6	0.18	1.5	0.00	**2.6**	0.3	0.23	2.33	3.56	87.3	**1.5**	16.6	25.3	**3.6**
7.5	0.62	3.8	0.00	**4.8**	0.1	0.82	8.94	3.97	68.0	**3.0**	26.1	14.6	**4.3**
5.5	0.48	4.0	0.00	**5.5**	1.8	0.85	8.69	3.68	69.2	**0.5**	5.2	42.2	**5.2**
8.4	0.32	0.3	0.11	**10.0**	0.1	2.90	13.23	3.53	49.6	**7.5**	79.3	0.0	**6.3**
8.3	0.00	0.0	0.00	**6.3**	2.5	1.19	7.33	3.83	59.9	**4.4**	28.2	8.6	**7.8**
5.5	0.87	5.9	0.31	**4.4**	0.9	0.75	8.49	4.16	67.8	**3.6**	13.0	10.6	**4.9**
0.7	4.86	32.9	-0.08	**4.7**	19.7	0.81	6.84	3.77	70.4	**2.5**	27.6	23.6	**6.3**
6.9	1.09	8.4	0.13	**3.8**	5.0	0.66	6.43	2.95	66.7	**4.2**	13.2	7.7	**7.6**
4.6	1.76	12.2	0.53	**4.8**	15.0	0.87	9.31	3.41	63.1	**4.6**	4.6	3.6	**7.4**
9.5	0.67	2.2	0.00	**6.4**	3.0	1.11	5.57	3.40	48.3	**2.7**	38.1	22.7	**8.2**
2.9	3.69	17.8	0.03	**3.7**	1.3	0.62	6.89	3.32	76.7	**3.7**	37.4	15.5	**3.7**
7.6	0.25	2.0	-0.32	**3.4**	1.3	0.98	10.26	3.48	83.0	**2.3**	10.4	17.0	**3.1**
6.9	0.75	3.6	0.20	**6.4**	0.5	1.58	13.70	3.79	57.0	**2.5**	36.6	23.6	**6.3**
5.1	0.45	2.9	0.40	**4.7**	0.1	0.85	8.29	5.14	82.7	**0.9**	23.4	36.3	**4.3**
8.4	0.32	1.7	0.00	**3.4**	0.8	0.95	7.22	3.22	82.9	**2.4**	35.6	25.2	**5.9**
0.3	4.50	55.6	0.35	**0.7**	0.0	-0.04	-0.80	3.50	113.0	**1.5**	6.7	22.7	**0.0**
3.6	2.31	15.0	0.06	**5.4**	6.3	1.06	10.25	4.20	66.9	**3.2**	11.0	12.8	**6.5**
7.3	0.18	1.4	0.15	**6.1**	2.6	1.36	14.07	4.31	74.6	**3.2**	7.5	12.1	**7.4**
6.8	0.26	1.7	0.01	**5.4**	1.6	0.99	8.44	3.83	62.5	**1.8**	17.5	21.4	**6.8**
3.3	1.59	10.4	0.00	**3.3**	0.5	0.43	4.08	3.85	80.2	**3.9**	23.1	10.2	**5.2**
6.6	2.99	9.2	0.00	**4.5**	0.6	1.06	7.63	3.15	63.2	**6.1**	61.4	7.7	**7.7**
9.4	0.28	0.8	0.05	**4.8**	1.5	1.19	9.76	2.66	57.3	**3.2**	47.8	23.2	**7.7**
4.8	0.94	7.3	0.19	**4.6**	0.5	0.81	10.86	3.85	69.1	**0.9**	20.6	41.1	**3.7**
4.9	1.18	7.9	0.29	**6.6**	1.5	1.64	16.23	4.71	62.7	**1.3**	21.8	28.9	**6.2**
7.8	0.03	0.2	0.11	**7.1**	0.7	1.73	23.52	3.87	60.6	**4.4**	37.8	12.2	**5.8**
3.9	0.79	8.1	0.00	**2.7**	0.2	0.37	3.33	4.37	83.8	**0.7**	10.7	37.9	**5.3**
4.9	5.37	16.2	1.22	**0.0**	-2.3	-5.93	-35.78	2.59	291.8	**5.5**	57.1	10.3	**3.9**
7.0	0.81	4.2	0.00	**3.9**	0.5	1.00	10.61	3.01	64.6	**3.1**	44.9	21.3	**5.6**
3.3	1.18	9.3	0.16	**5.4**	5.6	0.88	9.44	4.28	65.7	**4.4**	13.8	5.9	**5.1**
6.1	0.71	4.4	0.12	**5.0**	3.2	0.98	10.13	3.69	68.4	**3.5**	25.9	13.0	**4.8**
4.5	0.67	5.4	0.52	**4.0**	5.7	0.64	6.07	4.02	72.3	**1.8**	14.4	20.6	**7.5**
4.3	2.30	11.9	0.04	**3.4**	0.4	0.50	4.86	4.14	87.9	**3.5**	39.8	17.5	**6.6**
6.2	0.70	6.3	0.35	**5.6**	1.2	0.89	10.25	4.40	59.6	**0.5**	6.5	46.2	**5.0**
3.5	2.01	14.2	0.03	**5.5**	72.0	0.96	8.83	4.42	72.7	**5.2**	22.5	3.8	**8.2**
4.5	1.32	9.6	0.03	**7.1**	9.1	1.10	11.54	4.79	57.5	**4.2**	21.0	9.6	**6.1**
4.4	1.99	11.2	0.16	**2.7**	2.5	0.39	4.31	3.53	87.0	**2.8**	17.1	15.2	**4.8**
10.0	na	0.0	na	**9.5**	0.4	9.76	9.86	1.02	81.6	**4.0**	3799.3	101.0	**4.3**
4.7	2.76	12.5	0.23	**3.6**	10.1	0.67	5.15	3.46	79.9	**4.0**	20.3	10.3	**7.5**
3.9	2.40	13.7	0.50	**3.4**	0.6	0.74	8.23	3.58	75.4	**1.3**	30.7	47.6	**3.4**
7.7	0.17	1.3	0.01	**1.8**	0.1	0.22	2.27	4.67	95.4	**1.2**	20.8	30.5	**4.1**

	Name	City	State	Rating	2013 Rating	2012 Rating	Total Assets ($Mil)	One Year Asset Growth	Comm-ercial Loans	Cons-umer Loans	Mort-gage Loans	Secur-ities	Capital-ization Index	Lever-age Ratio	Risk-Based Capital Ratio
									Asset Mix (As a % of Total Assets)						
	OLPE STATE BK	Olpe	KS	**B**	B	B	36.5	-3.50	5.6	3.3	18.1	26.5	**10.0**	15.3	26.8
	OLYMPIA FS&LA	Olympia	WA	**B-**	B-	B-	542.4	-1.26	0.0	0.1	56.3	21.2	**10.0**	15.8	29.2
	OMNIAMERICAN BANK	Fort Worth	TX	**B-**	B-	C+	1338.3	-7.60	5.1	16.8	21.6	32.9	**10.0**	14.8	23.8
▲	OMNIBANK	Bay Springs	MS	**D**	D+	D-	47.8	-0.36	13.7	10.0	15.2	17.1	**10.0**	11.0	19.0
	ONB BANK & TRUST CO	Tulsa	OK	**C+**	C+	C+	636.7	5.40	14.9	0.5	9.5	2.9	**9.8**	12.3	14.8
	ONE AMERICAN BANK	Sioux Falls	SD	**C+**	B	C	77.3	-4.59	10.6	3.0	5.1	9.0	**10.0**	16.6	20.3
	ONE BANK & TRUST NA	Little Rock	AR	**E-**	E-	E-	358.0	-8.90	9.8	2.6	24.0	21.0	**1.7**	4.5	8.7
▲	ONE SOUTH BANK	Chipley	FL	**B-**	C+	C-	37.5	5.57	8.0	1.7	19.8	1.8	**10.0**	15.1	23.5
▲	ONE WORLD BANK	Dallas	TX	**D+**	D+	D-	83.9	0.32	5.2	0.1	0.3	20.0	**10.0**	12.1	20.9
	ONEIDA SB	Oneida	NY	**B**	B	B	786.7	10.28	6.8	5.1	18.4	37.8	**7.9**	9.6	16.9
	ONEUNITED BANK	Boston	MA	**D**	D-	E+	619.9	1.23	0.1	0.1	5.8	32.8	**4.1**	6.1	12.4
	ONEWEST BANK NA	Pasadena	CA	**A-**	B+	B-	21955.6	-9.36	13.0	0.0	31.0	5.4	**10.0**	11.8	24.9
	OOSTBURG STATE BK	Oostburg	WI	**C**	B-	B+	180.9	0.51	14.2	2.8	18.3	22.5	**10.0**	14.2	17.6
▲	OPEN BANK	Los Angeles	CA	**B+**	C+	C+	447.4	51.04	12.4	1.4	11.4	5.2	**10.0**	14.9	18.8
	OPPORTUNITY BANK OF MONTANA	Helena	MT	**C-**	C	C+	548.7	8.07	6.3	2.6	23.5	31.8	**6.4**	8.4	13.8
	OPTIMA BANK & TRUST CO	Portsmouth	NH	**C**	C	C	308.0	15.27	5.7	0.0	44.9	12.6	**5.7**	7.7	13.5
	OPTIMUMBANK	Plantation	FL	**E**	E-	D-	122.6	-3.90	12.3	0.0	17.6	23.3	**3.9**	6.7	10.5
	OPTUM BANK INC	Salt Lake City	UT	**A+**	A+	A+	3297.6	19.26	8.0	0.0	0.0	78.0	**7.9**	9.8	13.2
▲	OPUS BANK	Irvine	CA	**B+**	C+	C-	4722.8	35.89	10.4	0.0	5.8	4.0	**9.5**	11.7	14.6
▲	ORANGE COUNTY BUSINESS BANK	Irvine	CA	**C**	C	D+	201.6	-5.41	9.9	0.2	0.8	25.8	**10.0**	20.8	34.0
	ORANGE COUNTY TRUST CO	Middletown	NY	**B**	B	B+	702.7	3.67	12.6	0.1	8.1	43.6	**10.0**	13.0	23.3
▲	OREGON COAST BANK	Newport	OR	**A**	A-	B+	184.3	-0.51	3.4	1.5	14.2	41.6	**10.0**	11.5	19.4
	OREGON COMMUNITY BANK & TRUST	Oregon	WI	**B-**	B-	C-	193.3	11.17	4.1	0.5	15.8	7.8	**10.0**	13.3	17.4
	OREGON PACIFIC BANKING CO	Florence	OR	**D**	D+	D+	179.6	1.01	8.2	0.7	10.5	10.3	**8.2**	9.8	16.7
	OREGON TRAIL BANK	Guernsey	WY	**D+**	D+	D+	35.2	11.42	4.5	3.4	6.0	23.9	**5.7**	7.7	14.8
▼	ORIENTAL BANK	San Juan	PR	**D-**	D	D-	7619.7	-8.49	5.0	16.8	21.2	18.5	**8.5**	10.0	16.7
	ORITANI BANK	Township of Washin	NJ	**A-**	B+	A-	3183.0	14.13	0.3	0.2	5.7	13.1	**10.0**	14.4	17.9
	ORMSBY STATE BK	Ormsby	MN	**B+**	B+	B+	27.1	-4.38	2.6	2.4	3.4	40.8	**10.0**	13.6	24.0
▲	ORRSTOWN BANK	Shippensburg	PA	**C+**	C-	D-	1183.0	-2.39	2.9	0.5	16.9	34.0	**6.9**	8.9	16.2
	OSB COMMUNITY BANK	Brooklyn	MI	**D-**	D-	D+	78.8	3.42	18.1	0.4	13.3	2.3	**3.7**	6.5	10.3
	OSGOOD STATE BK	Osgood	OH	**B-**	B-	B-	156.5	6.57	11.5	3.9	13.2	36.9	**8.0**	9.7	16.7
	OSSIAN STATE BK	Ossian	IN	**C+**	C+	C+	96.2	-2.13	7.4	1.0	9.3	24.8	**8.7**	10.1	17.0
	OTTAWA SAVINGS BANK	Ottawa	IL	**C**	C-	D	160.5	-6.48	5.8	6.4	43.5	18.8	**10.0**	12.7	20.9
	OTTOVILLE BANK CO	Ottoville	OH	**A-**	A-	A	82.8	1.25	6.0	0.8	12.2	43.0	**10.0**	18.2	32.3
	OUACHITA INDEPENDENT BANK	Monroe	LA	**A-**	A-	A-	640.2	-3.60	8.9	1.1	10.8	16.6	**10.0**	11.4	15.3
	OUR COMMUNITY BANK	Spencer	IN	**B-**	B-	C	67.0	-6.78	0.0	1.8	62.6	9.9	**10.0**	12.3	24.6
	OWEN COUNTY STATE BK	Spencer	IN	**C+**	B-	C+	170.7	2.59	4.5	4.4	30.2	18.5	**9.1**	10.4	18.3
▲	OWINGSVILLE BANKING CO	Owingsville	KY	**C**	D+	D	59.6	-4.74	2.5	6.5	42.4	24.5	**10.0**	11.3	16.7
	OXFORD BANK	Oxford	MI	**D-**	E+	E-	263.4	1.52	4.5	0.7	17.0	2.5	**3.6**	6.2	10.3
	OXFORD BANK & TRUST	Oak Brook	IL	**D**	D	D-	433.4	-2.27	2.1	9.6	4.3	24.0	**6.9**	8.9	13.5
▲	OXFORD UNIVERSITY BANK	Oxford	MS	**C+**	B-	C+	113.7	3.39	8.2	2.7	28.1	17.7	**7.7**	9.5	14.5
	OZARK BANK	Ozark	MO	**B-**	B-	C+	191.1	8.52	8.9	0.5	18.4	23.0	**10.0**	12.7	18.9
▲	OZARK HERITAGE BANK NA	Mountain View	AR	**B-**	C	D+	83.6	26.92	16.3	2.1	28.2	9.7	**10.0**	11.3	17.9
	OZARK MOUNTAIN BANK	Branson	MO	**B-**	B-	B-	294.3	-8.80	6.9	4.4	16.4	25.0	**6.3**	9.1	12.0
	OZARKS FS&LA	Farmington	MO	**C+**	C+	C+	208.9	-2.02	0.0	0.6	56.1	14.7	**10.0**	14.9	25.6
	OZONA NATIONAL BK	Ozona	TX	**B**	C+	C+	229.6	9.56	6.3	1.8	12.4	26.1	**9.1**	10.4	17.9
▲	PACIFIC ALLIANCE BANK	Rosemead	CA	**C**	D	D+	212.1	63.31	11.4	0.0	3.1	5.4	**10.0**	12.1	15.0
	PACIFIC CITY BANK	Los Angeles	CA	**C**	C+	C	854.8	16.97	11.4	3.6	13.6	7.9	**8.0**	9.8	13.4
	PACIFIC COAST BANKERS BANK	Walnut Creek	CA	**B**	B-	C+	627.8	10.65	5.3	0.0	1.5	13.7	**10.0**	11.6	25.8
	PACIFIC COMMERCE BANK	Los Angeles	CA	**B**	B-	C-	209.2	26.40	21.3	0.1	7.0	0.3	**9.6**	12.4	14.7
▲	PACIFIC CONTINENTAL BANK	Eugene	OR	**A**	A-	B	1491.4	2.58	26.4	0.2	2.6	23.3	**10.0**	11.1	15.6
	PACIFIC CREST SB	Lynnwood	WA	**C**	C	C-	179.6	10.08	0.0	0.2	21.2	8.3	**9.1**	10.4	15.6
	PACIFIC ENTERPRISE BANK	Irvine	CA	**A-**	A-	B-	348.7	3.94	40.8	0.0	7.9	2.1	**10.0**	12.4	19.5
▲	PACIFIC GLOBAL BANK	Chicago	IL	**B-**	C-	D-	156.7	0.33	0.4	0.0	54.5	12.8	**9.5**	10.7	22.5
	PACIFIC MERCANTILE BANK	Costa Mesa	CA	**D+**	C	C+	1063.3	15.94	24.4	0.5	9.2	5.7	**9.9**	11.0	14.9
	PACIFIC NATIONAL BK	Miami	FL	**C-**	D+	D+	352.7	-0.57	3.4	0.1	4.0	30.2	**10.0**	11.6	20.7
▲	PACIFIC PREMIER BANK	Irvine	CA	**A-**	A-	B+	2029.6	29.68	15.4	0.1	6.0	13.9	**8.1**	11.5	13.4
	PACIFIC RIM BANK	Honolulu	HI	**D**	D	C-	121.1	-10.44	24.0	2.0	6.6	6.4	**6.0**	8.0	13.6
	PACIFIC VALLEY BANK	Salinas	CA	**C**	B-	C	230.6	13.05	17.9	1.7	5.8	0.8	**8.4**	9.9	13.7
	PACIFIC WEST BANK	West Linn	OR	**E-**	E-	E-	49.8	-0.18	13.7	0.8	13.5	0.0	**3.9**	6.8	10.5

Asset Quality Index	Adjusted Non-Performing Loans as a % of Total Loans	Adjusted Non-Performing Loans as a % of Capital	Net Charge-Offs Avg Loans	Profitability Index	Net Income ($Mil)	Return on Assets (R.O.A.)	Return on Equity (R.O.E.)	Net Interest Spread	Overhead Efficiency Ratio	Liquidity Index	Liquidity Ratio	Hot Money Ratio	Stability Index
7.4	0.41	1.5	0.00	**4.8**	0.3	1.16	7.72	3.40	64.7	**4.3**	36.4	12.3	**7.1**
9.1	0.70	3.0	0.04	**3.3**	2.1	0.52	3.40	3.26	77.8	**2.1**	27.8	21.2	**8.5**
6.6	0.73	2.8	0.36	**3.4**	5.9	0.57	3.99	3.20	75.4	**3.8**	31.7	16.4	**8.2**
4.1	1.30	5.9	-0.09	**0.2**	-0.3	-0.87	-7.69	4.26	122.3	**3.5**	35.9	16.3	**3.7**
1.7	1.40	8.6	0.20	**6.0**	4.8	1.04	5.04	4.22	54.8	**1.1**	10.1	29.7	**7.1**
5.7	0.91	3.9	0.03	**1.0**	-0.2	-0.31	-1.87	3.78	94.6	**1.9**	12.5	19.3	**5.0**
0.3	6.08	59.7	0.99	**1.2**	1.3	0.46	11.30	2.57	92.3	**1.2**	27.9	40.0	**1.0**
8.6	0.00	0.0	0.00	**2.9**	0.2	0.54	3.51	4.34	85.2	**0.8**	20.0	49.3	**5.0**
1.9	6.37	24.6	0.17	**1.6**	0.1	0.22	1.77	3.46	90.8	**1.9**	40.4	45.0	**5.1**
7.5	0.28	1.3	0.03	**3.9**	5.1	0.88	7.54	3.11	86.3	**4.2**	21.0	8.5	**6.6**
1.0	3.32	29.3	-0.09	**1.2**	0.7	0.16	2.04	2.58	109.0	**2.8**	26.1	16.3	**4.2**
8.8	0.22	1.2	0.13	**5.7**	101.9	0.85	6.22	3.81	52.9	**2.1**	28.0	31.2	**10.0**
1.9	6.31	26.8	0.02	**4.0**	0.9	0.67	4.68	3.97	73.0	**3.7**	25.1	11.4	**7.6**
6.9	0.27	1.4	0.00	**7.1**	3.5	1.19	9.80	4.30	66.8	**1.7**	13.0	21.4	**5.7**
7.9	0.16	1.1	0.15	**2.5**	1.7	0.43	4.61	3.48	89.5	**3.7**	34.0	14.4	**5.6**
5.4	0.76	7.6	0.00	**3.1**	0.9	0.39	5.50	3.25	76.9	**0.5**	7.9	54.6	**3.6**
0.3	10.03	72.9	-0.05	**5.6**	2.1	2.19	40.77	4.25	59.1	**2.7**	23.1	16.4	**1.8**
10.0	0.08	0.1	0.09	**9.5**	48.4	2.05	20.47	2.51	36.5	**8.6**	98.5	0.0	**9.2**
5.6	0.24	1.7	0.01	**5.6**	31.3	0.99	5.72	4.26	57.5	**3.4**	12.9	12.0	**8.0**
4.0	3.36	9.3	-2.58	**5.3**	2.4	1.60	8.16	3.19	94.5	**6.0**	34.6	1.2	**5.3**
4.2	5.43	19.1	-0.04	**4.3**	4.3	0.81	6.47	3.52	70.2	**3.1**	13.4	13.3	**8.4**
9.1	0.00	0.0	-0.08	**6.9**	2.6	1.91	16.68	4.12	61.4	**4.6**	39.3	11.8	**7.0**
3.9	1.14	6.6	0.32	**9.5**	2.3	1.60	12.19	4.21	42.4	**1.0**	14.1	32.4	**5.6**
1.2	5.63	34.2	1.31	**0.7**	-0.1	-0.05	-0.48	3.33	91.7	**4.3**	26.3	8.8	**4.7**
5.6	1.27	7.2	-0.01	**2.1**	0.0	0.17	2.21	3.79	94.5	**4.5**	43.4	13.1	**2.4**
0.0	6.75	38.9	0.76	**5.4**	64.6	1.11	9.58	6.31	59.2	**1.5**	12.9	25.0	**7.1**
5.3	1.11	5.9	-0.03	**8.0**	29.8	1.31	9.01	3.30	39.6	**1.6**	4.6	20.1	**9.6**
5.9	4.95	13.0	0.11	**5.8**	0.3	1.43	10.43	3.04	53.4	**3.7**	66.7	23.4	**8.1**
4.9	1.93	10.9	0.40	**3.7**	10.7	1.22	14.60	3.21	82.9	**2.5**	17.2	17.1	**6.0**
1.6	4.52	38.9	0.49	**0.5**	-0.7	-1.23	-16.38	4.52	114.0	**2.8**	30.9	18.2	**0.3**
5.5	1.09	5.4	0.08	**4.2**	0.8	0.74	6.95	3.82	79.2	**5.5**	38.7	6.0	**5.9**
8.8	0.00	0.0	0.00	**3.3**	0.4	0.48	4.89	2.86	80.2	**4.8**	37.4	10.0	**6.0**
2.1	5.19	25.9	0.69	**3.6**	0.7	0.54	4.21	3.67	63.7	**1.7**	24.0	24.7	**5.6**
9.3	0.10	0.2	-0.03	**6.0**	0.9	1.39	7.67	4.25	55.1	**2.4**	33.1	22.5	**8.5**
5.8	1.28	7.8	0.08	**8.0**	9.8	2.00	17.82	4.22	58.9	**3.1**	8.2	12.7	**8.9**
5.0	3.13	17.3	0.96	**3.6**	0.3	0.57	4.81	4.69	84.1	**1.6**	25.1	26.7	**4.5**
5.4	1.02	5.9	0.09	**3.8**	0.7	0.55	5.22	3.92	81.2	**2.6**	29.5	18.4	**5.6**
2.3	4.45	24.1	1.08	**2.4**	0.1	0.16	1.68	4.90	85.0	**1.7**	21.4	22.8	**3.8**
0.0	5.53	50.5	0.07	**4.1**	1.8	0.90	14.80	3.91	76.7	**4.5**	25.4	6.8	**1.7**
1.2	4.57	30.1	0.17	**1.7**	0.7	0.21	2.42	3.93	94.3	**5.3**	28.3	3.0	**2.8**
4.3	1.82	13.0	0.48	**4.1**	0.5	0.64	6.84	3.74	76.3	**0.9**	20.8	43.1	**5.2**
8.9	0.00	0.0	0.00	**3.5**	1.1	0.77	6.19	3.70	76.1	**1.7**	10.9	20.1	**5.9**
3.7	2.18	13.5	0.74	**8.1**	1.1	1.89	15.14	5.38	56.5	**0.4**	6.4	65.9	**4.4**
4.6	1.83	11.1	0.02	**5.0**	2.2	0.94	10.39	3.81	67.4	**3.8**	12.3	9.8	**6.2**
5.3	3.66	15.9	0.18	**2.6**	0.5	0.29	2.09	2.97	85.7	**3.0**	26.3	15.2	**7.0**
6.9	0.14	0.8	0.02	**5.2**	2.2	1.32	13.30	4.27	73.0	**4.7**	40.3	11.5	**5.6**
2.7	1.43	8.5	0.00	**2.6**	0.7	0.51	4.63	3.14	73.4	**0.9**	25.7	56.4	**5.4**
2.9	0.95	7.5	0.19	**9.4**	9.6	1.62	16.12	4.12	55.1	**0.6**	6.7	39.9	**4.6**
5.8	2.54	8.0	0.22	**4.5**	3.4	0.77	6.34	2.37	65.6	**5.7**	46.3	7.6	**5.6**
5.6	0.28	1.8	-0.10	**4.8**	1.6	1.09	7.84	4.22	89.4	**1.0**	7.2	30.4	**5.6**
7.0	0.53	3.1	0.03	**6.6**	12.8	1.16	9.12	4.31	58.8	**4.1**	26.5	12.6	**8.7**
3.0	1.19	8.5	0.20	**5.2**	1.7	1.32	12.73	3.67	61.0	**1.6**	20.0	24.6	**4.7**
6.7	0.82	4.8	0.11	**9.9**	4.4	1.72	14.84	5.52	55.7	**1.0**	23.4	35.7	**7.2**
4.2	2.35	12.5	0.37	**5.6**	1.9	1.57	15.15	3.82	63.1	**2.6**	26.1	17.4	**5.0**
2.9	3.37	22.1	-0.05	**1.2**	2.1	0.03	0.24	3.26	93.7	**1.2**	22.8	43.9	**4.8**
5.3	3.08	12.0	0.06	**1.9**	0.8	0.30	2.72	3.56	94.0	**1.5**	19.8	25.9	**4.0**
7.0	0.12	0.8	0.07	**6.6**	13.7	1.03	9.13	4.43	60.0	**2.2**	17.3	18.8	**7.7**
4.5	1.51	9.9	-0.03	**0.7**	-0.4	-0.37	-4.49	3.34	110.5	**2.3**	28.0	19.6	**3.1**
1.1	5.27	34.3	0.19	**3.1**	0.4	0.25	2.06	3.89	88.7	**2.1**	26.3	20.2	**5.2**
3.3	1.43	12.9	-0.46	**2.7**	0.2	0.43	6.69	4.30	106.5	**1.0**	20.8	34.0	**0.3**

Name	City	State	Rating	2013 Rating	2012 Rating	Total Assets ($Mil)	One Year Asset Growth	Asset Mix (As a % of Total Assets) Comm-ercial Loans	Cons-umer Loans	Mort-gage Loans	Secur-ities	Capital-ization Index	Lever-age Ratio	Risk-Based Capital Ratio
PACIFIC WESTERN BANK	Los Angeles	CA	**B-**	B-	C+	15676.2	137.19	25.7	0.7	2.2	9.8	**8.1**	11.7	13.4
PADUCAH BANK & TRUST CO	Paducah	KY	**A**	A	B+	533.0	0.51	8.9	2.5	24.1	23.5	**10.0**	12.0	18.9
PALM BEACH COMMUNITY BANK	West Palm Beach	FL	**A-**	B+	B+	263.7	9.70	8.5	0.3	20.9	14.7	**10.0**	12.3	17.8
▲ PALMETTO BANK	Greenville	SC	**B-**	C	D-	1097.7	-0.22	6.7	4.8	10.7	19.6	**10.0**	12.0	16.6
PALMETTO HERITAGE BANK & TRUST	Pawleys Island	SC	**C**	C-	D	143.6	-0.98	3.7	2.9	31.1	2.3	**7.1**	9.0	13.8
▲ PALMETTO STATE BK	Hampton	SC	**A-**	B	B	485.2	12.59	4.0	2.6	8.4	48.5	**10.0**	13.5	30.1
PALMYRA STATE BK	Palmyra	WI	**A-**	A-	A-	38.8	1.45	7.5	1.4	8.8	57.5	**10.0**	18.4	40.1
PALO SB	Palo	IA	**A-**	A-	A-	32.8	2.14	1.9	2.7	29.3	39.6	**10.0**	12.5	25.6
▼ PAN AMERICAN BANK	Melrose Park	IL	**C-**	C	C-	288.7	26.98	6.7	0.5	18.6	17.5	**5.2**	7.2	11.7
▲ PAN AMERICAN BANK	Los Angeles	CA	**E**	E-	E-	40.2	6.47	24.9	2.5	40.4	0.0	**10.0**	14.8	29.6
▲ PAN PACIFIC BANK	Fremont	CA	**B-**	C	C	119.1	11.12	14.2	0.1	4.4	9.3	**10.0**	13.1	16.5
PANOLA NATIONAL BK	Carthage	TX	**B-**	B-	B-	128.7	1.18	4.6	7.6	21.3	39.5	**6.7**	8.7	17.3
PANORA STATE BK	Panora	IA	**A**	A	A-	71.9	0.89	2.8	1.3	18.3	58.6	**10.0**	12.9	27.9
PAPER CITY SAVINGS ASSN	Wisconsin Rapids	WI	**B-**	B-	B-	166.1	1.16	0.0	2.0	54.5	3.4	**9.4**	10.6	21.2
▲ PARADISE BANK	Boca Raton	FL	**B**	C+	C	322.6	8.51	9.8	0.6	10.1	8.9	**10.0**	11.8	17.2
PARAGON BANK	Memphis	TN	**C-**	C-	D	281.3	3.09	14.5	4.5	16.5	15.8	**9.7**	10.8	15.6
PARAGON BANK	Wells	MN	**C-**	C-	D+	31.7	0.22	9.6	3.9	13.1	7.4	**6.9**	8.9	13.8
PARAGON COMMERCIAL BANK	Raleigh	NC	**B-**	C+	D	1140.6	14.32	9.2	0.5	12.4	16.3	**8.3**	9.8	13.6
PARIS NATIONAL BK	Paris	MO	**B**	B	B-	79.9	5.50	2.6	1.3	6.7	45.4	**10.0**	12.5	24.9
▼ PARK BANK	Holmen	WI	**C+**	B	B	49.0	3.60	13.8	2.8	23.4	26.3	**10.0**	15.6	27.3
PARK BANK	Milwaukee	WI	**C+**	C-	C	860.8	5.98	26.9	1.1	2.6	18.9	**8.6**	10.0	15.1
PARK BANK	Fitchburg	WI	**D**	D+	C-	720.8	1.24	10.1	1.2	16.4	8.9	**9.8**	11.7	14.8
PARK FSB	Chicago	IL	**E-**	E-	E-	163.7	-8.55	0.4	0.2	41.3	15.3	**0.6**	3.8	8.7
PARK NATIONAL BK	Newark	OH	**C**	C-	C-	6917.4	4.96	8.2	12.3	21.2	20.5	**5.1**	7.1	11.7
PARK RIDGE COMMUNITY BANK	Park Ridge	IL	**A-**	A-	B+	283.9	1.60	2.1	0.0	14.4	39.3	**10.0**	12.3	21.2
PARK STATE BK	Duluth	MN	**E-**	E-	E	33.5	1.17	8.2	8.5	40.4	8.6	**2.9**	6.4	9.9
▲ PARK STATE BK & TRUST	Woodland Park	CO	**D**	D-	D-	90.1	4.36	1.7	0.7	26.0	25.1	**6.2**	8.2	14.5
PARK STERLING BANK	Charlotte	NC	**B-**	B-	D+	2317.8	20.17	6.4	0.8	11.4	20.4	**7.6**	9.5	13.0
PARKE BANK	Sewell	NJ	**D**	D	C-	813.5	8.94	3.8	2.1	19.2	3.9	**10.0**	14.0	17.5
PARKSIDE FINANCIAL BANK & TR	Clayton	MO	**B**	B-	B-	357.3	26.22	34.9	0.6	3.0	6.5	**5.9**	9.0	11.7
PARKWAY BANK	Rogers	AR	**C+**	C+	C	123.0	-0.59	6.2	1.8	11.7	18.3	**8.5**	10.3	13.7
PARKWAY BANK & TRUST CO	Harwood Heights	IL	**D**	D	D-	2105.6	10.54	2.0	0.1	2.4	7.0	**9.1**	10.5	14.2
▲ PARTNERS BANK OF CALIFORNIA	Mission Viejo	CA	**C**	D+	D+	130.1	2.37	27.0	0.8	2.8	17.1	**10.0**	11.8	15.6
PASCACK COMMUNITY BANK	Waldwick	NJ	**C+**	C+	C-	354.5	-11.16	8.7	0.3	6.2	1.4	**7.7**	9.7	13.1
▼ PASSUMPSIC SB	Saint Johnsbury	VT	**C-**	C-	C-	590.6	2.12	4.5	9.0	29.4	14.7	**7.0**	9.0	15.0
PATAPSCO BANK	Dundalk	MD	**C**	D+	D	231.2	2.56	3.0	0.7	40.1	19.0	**7.2**	9.1	16.6
PATASKALA BANKING CO	Pataskala	OH	**D**	D+	C-	30.0	-2.18	3.3	1.1	35.8	21.0	**7.1**	9.1	17.7
PATHFINDER BANK	Oswego	NY	**C+**	C+	C+	569.0	15.85	7.6	0.7	31.3	24.2	**6.4**	8.4	13.3
PATHFINDER COMMERCIAL BANK	Oswego	NY	**U**	U	B-	86.2	38.95	0.0	0.0	0.0	83.7	**6.8**	8.8	38.8
PATHWAY BANK	Cairo	NE	**B-**	C+	C	137.1	-7.13	7.5	3.0	2.3	17.9	**10.0**	11.6	15.4
PATRIOT BANK	Millington	TN	**B-**	B-	B-	281.2	4.93	6.7	2.1	13.3	43.8	**6.7**	8.7	16.0
▲ PATRIOT BANK	Trinity	FL	**C-**	D	D-	130.7	4.85	8.3	2.9	6.2	3.0	**6.5**	8.8	12.2
PATRIOT BANK	Tulsa	OK	**B**	B	C+	137.6	19.60	23.6	0.1	23.4	0.0	**8.7**	11.0	13.9
PATRIOT BANK	Houston	TX	**C+**	C+	C-	1368.5	10.29	24.1	0.2	6.3	23.8	**8.6**	10.3	13.9
PATRIOT COMMUNITY BANK	Woburn	MA	**A-**	A	A-	149.6	4.55	11.6	0.1	15.6	0.0	**10.0**	12.0	18.3
PATRIOT FEDERAL BANK	Canajoharie	NY	**D+**	D+	D	122.4	15.80	6.5	4.6	40.8	23.8	**7.3**	9.2	16.8
▲ PATRIOT NATIONAL BK	Stamford	CT	**C-**	D-	D-	623.9	16.53	7.4	0.7	19.5	6.3	**8.6**	10.6	13.8
PATRIOTS BANK	Garnett	KS	**C**	C+	C	89.1	3.26	4.2	2.7	21.3	27.9	**8.6**	10.0	16.9
PATTERSON STATE BK	Patterson	LA	**B**	B	B-	226.7	3.34	7.3	2.6	46.7	27.9	**8.5**	10.0	20.8
PAULS VALLEY NATIONAL BK	Pauls Valley	OK	**B**	B	C+	233.0	3.54	15.6	10.2	7.2	38.4	**6.9**	8.9	14.9
PAVILLION BANK	Richardson	TX	**B-**	C+	C	81.9	0.62	8.1	1.1	20.5	8.4	**10.0**	12.3	21.2
PAYNE COUNTY BANK	Perkins	OK	**A+**	A+	A+	151.1	13.39	13.0	9.3	15.8	36.6	**10.0**	16.7	23.7
PBI BANK INC	Louisville	KY	**D-**	D-	E+	1029.4	-0.70	5.6	1.2	17.9	22.9	**4.1**	6.1	11.0
PBK BANK INC	Stanford	KY	**C**	C	C-	104.8	-1.62	3.0	2.3	20.7	14.3	**9.7**	10.8	19.3
PCSB BANK	Clarinda	IA	**B+**	A-	B+	195.9	4.30	11.1	4.6	10.1	33.9	**10.0**	11.4	16.0
PCSB COMMERCIAL BANK	Brewster	NY	**U**	U	C+	36.0	-8.09	0.0	0.0	0.0	85.9	**10.0**	20.8	174.0
▲ PEABODY STATE BK	Peabody	KS	**C+**	C	D+	40.3	4.50	5.7	2.7	10.9	32.4	**8.5**	10.0	18.6
PEACH STATE BANK & TRUST	Gainesville	GA	**D+**	D+	D	142.1	3.05	9.2	1.1	13.3	20.1	**7.1**	9.0	13.8
PEAPACK-GLADSTONE BANK	Bedminster	NJ	**C+**	C+	C+	2513.7	39.88	3.3	0.5	19.5	10.7	**5.2**	7.2	12.8
PEARLAND STATE BK	Pearland	TX	**A-**	A	A	174.5	5.77	2.4	1.1	3.5	71.5	**10.0**	11.7	32.4

Asset Quality Index	Adjusted Non-Performing Loans as a % of Total Loans	Adjusted Non-Performing Loans as a % of Capital	Net Charge-Offs Avg Loans	Profitability Index	Net Income ($Mil)	Return on Assets (R.O.A.)	Return on Equity (R.O.E.)	Net Interest Spread	Overhead Efficiency Ratio	Liquidity Index	Liquidity Ratio	Hot Money Ratio	Stability Index
4.2	1.10	7.6	0.17	7.4	105.8	1.16	6.67	6.20	61.5	1.2	12.2	29.6	7.6
6.0	1.51	8.0	0.12	8.1	7.8	1.93	14.92	4.47	61.6	4.1	16.5	8.4	9.7
6.0	0.70	4.1	0.05	5.9	2.7	1.47	11.64	4.44	66.7	1.6	22.3	24.6	7.9
3.7	2.94	15.8	0.11	3.9	6.5	0.79	6.73	3.88	76.4	4.2	14.4	7.4	6.1
5.5	0.67	5.1	0.43	3.4	0.5	0.48	5.34	3.82	73.0	0.8	15.2	41.3	4.0
5.6	3.44	8.4	-0.39	5.3	3.6	1.06	7.46	3.76	59.2	3.8	43.1	17.0	6.2
9.3	0.62	1.0	0.00	2.3	0.1	0.28	1.62	2.14	86.2	5.0	75.8	15.8	7.3
7.5	1.23	5.1	0.00	8.1	0.5	1.92	14.97	3.90	49.0	3.9	46.4	16.7	8.6
3.4	2.16	17.5	0.07	3.6	1.3	0.69	9.28	3.90	77.1	1.2	29.1	39.3	2.5
1.1	9.40	43.2	-0.19	0.0	-1.0	-3.16	-72.12	4.59	151.0	0.9	23.5	46.2	1.8
7.0	0.44	2.4	-0.01	4.0	3.0	3.54	24.66	4.03	92.9	2.3	24.1	18.2	5.2
8.6	0.28	1.3	0.00	4.0	0.9	0.92	10.08	3.58	80.0	4.4	52.6	16.1	6.0
8.3	0.00	0.0	0.02	9.4	1.2	2.16	13.52	4.42	31.5	3.6	57.5	20.0	9.0
4.9	1.61	10.9	0.11	4.0	0.7	0.58	5.52	2.76	69.7	2.6	26.5	17.4	5.3
5.2	1.56	8.6	0.63	7.7	4.1	1.79	18.61	3.84	68.3	4.7	29.5	7.1	4.9
4.6	0.95	6.2	-0.19	2.6	0.6	0.30	2.68	3.73	87.7	2.8	12.5	14.6	5.6
3.6	1.65	12.7	0.40	4.6	0.2	0.67	7.85	4.74	77.4	3.8	18.1	10.2	3.6
7.6	0.18	1.3	0.08	4.4	5.8	0.73	7.23	3.57	63.0	0.8	16.6	42.8	6.1
5.5	3.87	12.5	-0.09	4.3	0.5	0.80	6.34	3.55	68.0	4.5	45.4	13.6	5.7
3.4	6.32	22.9	1.39	2.3	0.2	0.43	2.82	4.79	89.8	4.4	9.7	5.3	5.6
3.9	1.86	10.7	0.12	3.7	5.3	0.84	8.42	3.31	67.4	4.5	28.0	8.2	5.7
0.9	3.57	23.1	0.46	4.8	4.1	0.75	6.64	4.16	68.6	3.7	11.2	9.9	6.7
0.3	6.75	64.4	0.42	0.0	-1.3	-1.00	-24.88	2.77	142.5	2.3	29.1	20.1	0.7
2.9	2.10	18.6	0.28	6.6	61.0	1.21	15.57	3.55	57.8	2.6	6.0	15.4	6.7
6.6	1.60	6.6	0.19	7.3	3.8	1.81	14.80	3.73	46.7	3.6	24.5	12.0	8.6
5.5	0.52	6.3	0.00	2.1	0.1	0.35	5.99	5.48	94.3	2.3	17.3	17.8	0.0
2.3	4.11	25.6	0.43	1.1	0.1	0.12	1.48	3.96	97.5	4.2	23.3	8.8	2.3
6.3	0.66	4.7	-0.17	3.8	10.4	0.64	5.15	4.04	79.1	2.9	18.7	15.4	7.3
0.2	7.13	37.5	0.60	9.0	8.5	1.71	12.43	4.29	45.7	1.8	11.4	19.7	8.1
8.1	0.00	0.0	0.06	5.5	2.1	0.88	9.51	3.55	63.9	2.1	28.7	22.9	5.0
3.8	2.07	12.7	0.11	3.7	0.6	0.62	5.08	3.98	78.5	1.4	22.8	28.9	5.3
0.7	4.74	30.0	0.57	3.4	7.2	0.48	4.11	3.10	60.1	1.1	14.0	30.9	6.6
3.5	3.24	17.8	-0.20	2.6	0.6	0.66	5.67	3.63	82.4	1.5	10.3	23.6	4.2
3.9	0.94	6.5	0.04	4.6	2.2	0.80	8.23	4.44	68.1	3.3	16.7	12.8	4.1
1.5	2.55	18.7	0.29	3.0	2.6	0.60	5.27	3.60	89.9	2.8	16.4	15.3	6.2
4.1	2.10	14.8	-0.32	3.4	2.1	1.19	13.17	3.35	81.6	4.1	24.7	9.2	3.3
5.0	2.54	14.8	0.02	0.6	-0.1	-0.58	-6.69	3.82	108.9	6.2	40.1	1.8	2.5
4.2	2.09	15.4	0.30	3.5	2.1	0.54	5.99	3.54	74.5	1.6	15.3	22.4	5.3
10.0	na	0.0	na	3.9	0.4	0.72	8.13	1.32	23.0	2.3	29.3	19.9	5.1
6.0	0.43	2.4	0.15	3.7	0.6	0.56	4.62	3.59	79.8	1.9	23.6	20.4	5.0
5.4	1.68	8.4	0.36	5.1	2.1	1.02	11.78	3.54	68.7	1.0	19.9	33.0	5.7
3.4	0.35	2.8	0.01	2.4	0.3	0.28	2.23	4.33	86.1	2.3	16.4	17.5	4.9
5.7	0.27	2.1	0.00	6.0	1.4	1.51	11.48	4.47	56.5	0.4	1.0	46.4	5.5
5.1	1.03	6.5	0.25	3.6	6.5	0.67	6.23	3.07	78.3	1.9	29.4	37.6	7.2
8.8	0.00	0.0	0.00	5.7	0.9	0.81	6.77	3.12	61.3	1.1	26.9	42.3	7.0
5.0	1.38	9.7	0.54	1.2	-0.1	-0.06	-0.61	3.60	91.4	1.6	14.1	23.3	2.2
3.0	2.13	15.8	0.25	3.3	18.5	4.56	46.03	3.39	88.4	1.4	16.0	25.7	3.7
2.8	3.46	20.1	-0.02	4.0	0.6	0.98	9.80	4.25	76.4	2.9	25.8	15.7	5.1
8.6	0.40	2.5	0.15	5.9	1.9	1.12	11.39	4.26	66.7	3.7	12.9	10.4	5.2
5.1	1.12	5.7	0.26	4.4	1.5	0.85	8.61	4.41	72.6	3.5	46.1	19.1	5.6
5.2	0.90	4.4	0.55	4.6	0.6	0.97	7.86	3.85	67.3	3.8	35.3	14.6	5.4
8.0	0.51	1.5	0.07	9.8	2.7	2.45	14.16	4.56	50.3	3.9	51.6	18.6	9.1
0.3	8.92	65.6	2.03	0.0	-5.5	-0.70	-11.74	3.15	102.6	2.0	26.4	28.8	4.3
3.4	2.76	15.0	-0.08	3.1	0.3	0.38	3.58	3.82	86.7	4.0	30.3	11.9	5.3
6.5	1.49	7.3	0.22	4.4	1.0	0.68	6.12	3.85	72.7	6.2	42.9	3.0	7.1
10.0	na	0.0	na	1.8	0.0	0.09	0.42	0.38	61.0	5.4	17.6	0.0	3.1
5.9	1.15	5.8	0.10	4.8	0.3	1.02	9.57	3.98	68.5	4.8	36.7	10.0	4.1
1.6	5.28	33.9	0.57	3.5	0.8	0.72	7.70	3.80	73.4	2.6	25.0	17.0	3.4
5.1	0.75	7.8	0.05	4.0	11.0	0.65	8.47	3.06	67.1	3.9	14.4	9.6	4.7
9.8	0.01	0.0	0.00	6.2	2.0	1.50	12.17	2.80	48.2	3.9	78.4	28.7	8.9

Name	City	State	Rating	2013 Rating	2012 Rating	Total Assets ($Mil)	One Year Asset Growth	Asset Mix (As a % of Total Assets) Commercial Loans	Consumer Loans	Mortgage Loans	Securities	Capitalization Index	Leverage Ratio	Risk-Based Capital Ratio
PECOS COUNTY STATE BK	Fort Stockton	TX	**B**	B	B-	200.7	5.21	6.3	5.4	10.2	50.3	**6.0**	8.0	17.8
PEE DEE FSB	Marion	SC	**D**	D+	C	38.0	0.21	12.0	6.8	16.2	2.6	**10.0**	19.2	36.0
PEGASUS BANK	Dallas	TX	**B-**	B-	B-	339.2	21.78	12.4	9.1	15.7	21.9	**4.2**	8.2	10.6
PEKIN NATIONAL BK	Pekin	IL	**D**	D+	C	23.3	4.21	3.3	0.3	27.2	54.7	**10.0**	13.2	30.9
PELHAM BANKING CO	Pelham	GA	**B+**	B+	A-	68.5	4.44	3.9	4.3	7.9	47.1	**10.0**	15.3	29.5
PENDER STATE BK	Pender	NE	**B**	B	B-	160.4	6.25	4.5	1.2	1.4	9.5	**7.1**	9.6	12.6
PENDLETON COMMUNITY BANK INC	Franklin	WV	**C+**	C	C-	269.0	0.93	3.7	4.1	25.1	15.9	**10.0**	12.0	18.4
▼ PENINSULA BANK OF ISHPEMING	Ishpeming	MI	**C-**	C	C	126.4	-5.24	2.0	2.7	23.5	18.1	**10.0**	13.4	23.7
PENN LIBERTY BANK	Wayne	PA	**C+**	C+	C	597.9	6.69	14.8	0.0	15.1	2.6	**8.7**	10.8	13.9
PENNSVILLE NATIONAL BK	Pennsville	NJ	**C+**	C+	B-	181.6	-2.08	0.7	1.2	20.5	57.7	**7.2**	9.1	13.9
PENTUCKET BANK	Haverhill	MA	**C+**	C+	C	651.8	1.61	8.7	0.2	36.8	20.2	**10.0**	11.5	18.2
PEOPLEFIRST BANK	Joliet	IL	**D+**	D+	C-	100.2	-5.67	3.4	0.1	11.5	21.2	**10.0**	13.2	20.0
PEOPLES B&TC OF CLINTON CNTY	Albany	KY	**D**	D	E+	32.7	3.97	4.0	19.6	26.6	7.1	**6.4**	8.4	13.2
PEOPLES B&TC OF HAZARD	Hazard	KY	**C-**	C-	D+	282.4	2.29	23.2	5.4	22.6	9.3	**6.9**	8.9	13.0
PEOPLES B&TC OF MADISON COUNTY	Berea	KY	**D**	D+	C	380.8	-1.41	2.3	1.8	21.0	32.0	**8.4**	9.9	18.4
PEOPLES B&TC OF PICKETT COUNTY	Byrdstown	TN	**D**	D	D-	112.0	-3.01	14.3	12.2	20.6	13.9	**8.1**	9.7	15.7
PEOPLES B&TC OF POINTE COUPEE	New Roads	LA	**C+**	C+	C-	223.8	9.26	7.0	2.0	25.9	3.8	**9.3**	10.5	16.0
PEOPLES BANK	Mendenhall	MS	**C+**	C+	C+	245.8	8.13	11.4	7.0	16.5	11.5	**7.8**	9.6	14.5
PEOPLES BANK	Covington	GA	**E+**	E+	E-	96.2	-7.61	0.8	0.9	18.1	11.7	**0.1**	3.8	6.3
PEOPLES BANK	Lyons	GA	**C-**	C-	D-	57.2	14.58	6.3	2.8	11.5	4.3	**6.2**	8.9	11.9
PEOPLES BANK	Willacoochee	GA	**B**	B	B	69.5	5.04	1.6	5.2	15.1	31.1	**10.0**	11.8	22.8
PEOPLES BANK	Clifton	TN	**D+**	D	D	139.8	3.73	17.1	12.5	16.3	13.1	**6.9**	8.9	12.7
PEOPLES BANK	Eatonton	GA	**D-**	D-	D-	133.0	2.23	1.9	3.2	22.6	10.4	**5.9**	7.9	14.3
PEOPLES BANK	Gambier	OH	**C**	C+	C	53.6	0.57	2.7	7.2	38.9	28.4	**7.7**	9.4	19.6
PEOPLES BANK	Chestertown	MD	**D+**	D	D-	233.6	-3.33	4.3	0.6	24.2	5.1	**6.8**	8.8	16.0
PEOPLES BANK	Newton	NC	**B**	C+	C	1052.3	1.16	7.2	1.0	15.6	26.5	**8.9**	10.2	15.8
PEOPLES BANK	Iva	SC	**C-**	C-	D-	268.4	3.93	2.0	2.5	17.2	30.9	**8.5**	10.0	17.6
▲ PEOPLES BANK	Rose Hill	VA	**C+**	C-	D	97.2	6.08	16.4	1.8	29.9	12.3	**8.3**	9.8	15.3
▲ PEOPLES BANK	Pratt	KS	**B**	C+	C-	348.1	0.57	15.8	1.7	9.9	39.4	**10.0**	12.3	21.0
PEOPLES BANK	Lawrence	KS	**B**	B	C+	425.3	3.31	9.5	0.6	32.1	8.3	**8.0**	9.7	15.2
▲ PEOPLES BANK	Coldwater	KS	**B+**	B	B-	47.1	3.45	4.0	2.2	7.7	50.6	**10.0**	11.2	20.6
PEOPLES BANK	Elkhorn	WI	**C-**	C-	C-	206.2	5.17	3.7	0.3	21.2	4.4	**8.4**	10.5	13.6
PEOPLES BANK	Rock Valley	IA	**B+**	B+	B	420.2	4.81	11.5	1.4	3.5	6.8	**7.3**	10.2	12.8
▲ PEOPLES BANK	Marion	KY	**C-**	D	D	35.5	-0.39	28.7	5.9	22.1	8.6	**8.7**	10.1	14.1
PEOPLES BANK	Taylorsville	KY	**C**	C-	C+	104.7	-2.94	3.3	2.7	21.8	31.8	**10.0**	11.9	23.8
PEOPLES BANK	Ripley	MS	**B**	B-	B	360.4	2.87	11.7	8.2	14.3	52.7	**8.9**	10.2	22.5
▼ PEOPLES BANK	Cuba	MO	**B**	A-	A-	192.8	4.05	3.5	3.0	38.3	20.4	**8.3**	9.9	16.2
PEOPLES BANK	Sheridan	AR	**A**	A	A	118.3	7.47	15.9	4.6	8.6	35.5	**10.0**	15.0	25.3
PEOPLES BANK	Sardis	TN	**C+**	C+	C	71.2	0.78	6.1	5.6	22.0	29.6	**7.2**	9.1	15.3
PEOPLES BANK	Magnolia	AR	**B**	B	B+	136.3	10.06	1.1	6.7	32.7	23.9	**7.7**	9.4	22.3
▲ PEOPLES BANK	Lebanon	KY	**C+**	C	C-	52.8	2.07	7.1	4.0	12.6	26.1	**8.6**	10.1	14.3
PEOPLES BANK	Brownstown	IN	**B-**	B-	B-	188.8	7.90	2.7	6.6	16.8	52.9	**8.0**	9.7	21.0
PEOPLES BANK	Tulsa	OK	**C**	C+	D+	100.6	-3.20	29.2	5.9	14.0	2.1	**6.4**	8.4	12.8
PEOPLES BANK	Westville	OK	**B+**	B	B	49.0	-4.88	9.1	3.6	10.7	31.6	**10.0**	11.6	19.3
PEOPLES BANK	Paris	TX	**B+**	B+	B+	121.9	5.30	6.9	1.7	31.4	35.5	**6.5**	8.5	17.1
PEOPLES BANK	Chatham	LA	**B-**	C+	C+	40.8	49.01	1.0	14.0	24.5	0.3	**9.1**	11.6	14.3
PEOPLES BANK	Lubbock	TX	**B**	B+	B+	377.9	8.24	8.9	3.2	5.4	13.7	**6.6**	9.3	12.2
PEOPLES BANK	Bellingham	WA	**B+**	B+	B	1360.7	4.12	6.1	8.1	10.6	0.3	**7.9**	10.3	13.3
PEOPLES BANK & TRUST	Buford	GA	**E**	E-	E-	275.1	-2.75	2.7	1.5	18.2	17.7	**3.8**	6.4	10.4
PEOPLES BANK & TRUST	Pana	IL	**B**	B	B-	384.2	0.10	19.1	0.7	6.5	21.9	**6.8**	8.8	12.6
PEOPLES BANK & TRUST CO	Manchester	TN	**C-**	D+	C-	85.5	-0.42	7.0	5.7	15.8	27.0	**9.9**	10.9	18.5
PEOPLES BANK & TRUST CO	Troy	MO	**C-**	D+	D-	418.9	5.27	6.8	0.6	8.5	36.5	**5.7**	7.7	13.1
PEOPLES BANK & TRUST CO	North Carrollton	MS	**B+**	B+	A-	64.1	0.85	0.4	5.3	15.3	60.9	**10.0**	14.0	39.6
PEOPLES BANK & TRUST CO	Owenton	KY	**B**	B	B+	55.0	-8.61	3.0	3.5	29.3	17.4	**10.0**	20.0	31.6
PEOPLES BANK & TRUST CO	McPherson	KS	**A-**	A-	B+	445.3	5.96	15.9	2.2	3.8	41.1	**10.0**	11.3	17.3
PEOPLES BANK & TRUST CO	Ryan	OK	**B**	B-	B-	31.5	5.12	6.0	1.7	22.4	0.2	**10.0**	13.1	18.4
PEOPLES BANK CO	Coldwater	OH	**A-**	A-	A-	430.9	3.39	4.0	1.9	16.3	44.4	**7.7**	9.4	19.1
PEOPLES BANK KANKAKEE COUNTY	Bourbonnais	IL	**C+**	C-	C-	191.3	2.79	4.8	1.7	16.7	35.4	**6.1**	8.1	15.9
▲ PEOPLES BANK MIDWEST	Hayward	WI	**A-**	B+	C+	312.2	31.63	8.1	0.6	8.5	18.0	**10.0**	17.5	23.4
PEOPLES BANK MONITEAU COUNTY	Jamestown	MO	**D+**	D+	C-	56.9	5.34	4.9	4.6	20.7	32.5	**6.3**	8.3	14.6

Asset Quality Index	Adjusted Non-Performing Loans as a % of Total Loans	Adjusted Non-Performing Loans as a % of Capital	Net Charge-Offs Avg Loans	Profitability Index	Net Income ($Mil)	Return on Assets (R.O.A.)	Return on Equity (R.O.E.)	Net Interest Spread	Overhead Efficiency Ratio	Liquidity Index	Liquidity Ratio	Hot Money Ratio	Stability Index
8.1	0.24	1.2	0.21	**5.7**	2.1	1.41	18.48	3.97	65.0	**2.9**	12.1	14.4	**5.6**
5.4	3.53	8.2	0.39	**0.3**	-0.1	-0.29	-1.51	3.56	112.6	**4.6**	57.4	14.7	**4.9**
8.3	0.00	0.0	0.00	**3.9**	1.5	0.64	7.48	2.86	62.5	**6.4**	43.5	1.7	**4.2**
8.6	1.15	3.3	2.20	**0.0**	-0.1	-0.60	-4.65	3.58	107.2	**2.1**	43.9	29.6	**5.4**
5.5	3.31	8.1	0.32	**4.6**	0.6	1.18	8.04	3.49	67.0	**3.7**	52.8	18.5	**8.0**
5.1	0.38	2.9	0.00	**8.1**	2.1	1.73	13.28	3.44	46.8	**0.9**	22.3	35.7	**8.2**
2.8	4.19	23.7	0.11	**6.1**	2.3	1.18	9.79	4.42	60.0	**2.1**	17.0	18.6	**6.3**
2.2	6.66	26.5	-0.02	**1.1**	-0.2	-0.24	-1.77	3.91	95.2	**5.2**	38.4	8.1	**5.5**
4.8	0.94	6.8	0.17	**3.4**	2.0	0.47	4.35	3.71	77.0	**4.1**	14.2	8.0	**5.9**
7.8	0.50	1.8	0.26	**2.9**	0.5	0.36	3.83	2.68	83.1	**7.2**	61.7	2.5	**4.7**
5.8	1.67	10.0	0.00	**2.6**	2.9	0.61	5.13	2.97	87.7	**1.6**	22.5	24.7	**6.9**
0.4	7.40	33.6	0.30	**0.7**	-0.1	-0.16	-1.25	3.37	100.0	**1.6**	31.1	31.8	**5.7**
2.5	0.94	7.3	0.29	**2.9**	0.2	0.65	8.03	5.11	82.1	**0.8**	20.4	52.7	**1.8**
1.6	3.34	26.6	0.43	**4.1**	1.7	0.82	8.77	4.13	70.6	**1.5**	20.0	26.3	**5.0**
0.4	8.93	48.1	0.90	**2.3**	0.5	0.17	1.38	3.94	79.5	**2.7**	24.4	16.5	**5.5**
0.5	6.63	38.5	0.93	**4.4**	0.9	1.05	11.49	4.70	64.3	**0.9**	22.6	36.4	**3.9**
5.9	0.75	5.3	-0.01	**9.0**	2.4	1.59	15.45	4.27	47.6	**2.0**	25.9	21.6	**5.8**
3.6	1.70	12.9	0.66	**9.8**	4.0	2.21	22.92	5.84	57.5	**1.5**	5.1	21.3	**7.3**
0.3	15.60	211.2	0.13	**0.1**	-0.4	-0.56	-17.83	3.70	112.5	**3.2**	17.8	13.3	**0.3**
4.8	0.89	7.2	-0.01	**3.0**	0.2	0.38	3.88	4.33	85.2	**2.9**	12.9	14.5	**2.9**
8.9	0.23	0.9	0.02	**4.3**	0.5	1.03	9.09	3.59	73.0	**2.0**	33.7	28.5	**6.3**
1.1	3.95	28.1	0.27	**2.9**	0.4	0.41	4.76	4.55	77.2	**1.0**	15.0	31.5	**3.6**
0.3	11.93	73.2	1.05	**0.0**	-0.6	-0.63	-7.94	3.10	111.5	**4.3**	31.9	10.6	**2.3**
8.9	0.06	0.4	0.11	**2.5**	0.1	0.32	3.34	3.88	91.4	**2.8**	31.6	18.4	**4.8**
1.9	5.76	32.8	0.43	**1.7**	0.4	0.22	2.30	3.07	94.4	**4.5**	34.0	10.7	**4.7**
5.4	1.78	9.7	0.24	**5.0**	7.9	1.03	9.95	3.91	70.3	**4.4**	27.8	12.0	**7.2**
2.0	6.06	30.7	0.13	**4.3**	2.0	0.98	10.31	3.72	72.4	**2.7**	36.0	20.8	**4.7**
4.9	0.90	6.6	-1.38	**6.3**	1.2	1.69	17.99	4.46	82.1	**2.5**	19.4	17.0	**3.4**
4.0	2.95	12.7	0.78	**6.2**	3.5	1.31	9.35	4.27	57.0	**1.4**	23.5	28.7	**7.7**
4.7	1.00	7.2	0.22	**6.1**	3.2	1.03	10.76	4.74	91.1	**4.8**	10.5	2.9	**5.1**
6.2	2.72	9.1	-0.06	**4.2**	0.3	0.91	7.39	4.23	75.1	**3.7**	44.9	17.2	**6.5**
1.9	3.60	25.7	0.06	**4.1**	0.9	0.58	5.48	3.78	73.8	**3.0**	10.3	13.7	**5.9**
4.6	0.48	3.7	-0.03	**8.9**	6.5	2.08	18.76	4.27	50.3	**2.6**	7.8	15.1	**8.8**
2.6	2.32	16.5	0.00	**2.8**	0.1	0.35	3.81	4.73	91.0	**2.4**	12.1	16.8	**3.5**
2.5	6.12	25.1	-0.19	**5.7**	1.2	1.52	12.73	3.77	68.6	**4.3**	36.9	12.3	**6.6**
7.2	1.25	4.6	-0.20	**5.2**	3.0	1.12	10.94	3.13	60.0	**3.3**	50.5	23.7	**5.6**
4.1	2.10	14.6	0.16	**7.4**	2.3	1.60	15.45	4.52	61.3	**2.2**	6.8	17.3	**8.3**
8.5	0.22	0.8	0.00	**8.6**	1.2	1.35	9.25	3.86	49.1	**3.4**	32.2	15.5	**8.9**
5.0	1.09	6.6	0.61	**3.9**	0.4	0.77	9.42	4.68	79.9	**1.9**	28.5	25.4	**4.2**
5.5	1.32	6.7	0.09	**5.8**	1.4	1.42	14.47	3.68	62.0	**1.6**	34.4	44.3	**5.8**
6.6	0.25	1.5	0.02	**3.6**	0.3	0.66	7.06	3.72	78.7	**2.3**	26.0	18.7	**3.8**
4.8	2.15	8.8	0.53	**4.1**	1.2	0.88	9.35	3.35	62.8	**6.5**	62.9	7.4	**5.7**
4.3	1.09	9.0	0.23	**2.9**	0.4	0.49	5.91	4.35	88.2	**2.0**	18.0	19.3	**4.1**
6.1	1.75	8.9	0.00	**8.5**	0.8	2.15	18.69	4.69	64.6	**2.4**	40.3	28.4	**7.2**
6.8	1.02	6.3	-0.02	**5.7**	1.2	1.33	16.34	3.76	74.7	**5.2**	39.8	8.4	**6.6**
4.3	0.55	4.0	0.00	**5.8**	0.3	0.99	8.17	5.70	73.5	**0.7**	14.9	53.4	**6.7**
8.1	0.01	0.0	0.02	**5.1**	2.3	0.90	9.25	4.29	70.9	**1.8**	19.2	20.6	**5.7**
6.2	0.51	3.8	0.02	**5.3**	8.4	0.85	8.24	3.99	72.2	**1.8**	14.9	21.5	**8.3**
0.3	6.58	55.7	-0.02	**4.2**	2.4	1.14	20.13	3.40	70.1	**0.8**	14.4	34.6	**0.6**
4.8	0.94	7.0	0.06	**6.7**	4.5	1.58	16.71	4.03	63.9	**2.8**	7.4	14.3	**5.9**
2.1	4.64	21.3	0.01	**3.7**	0.4	0.63	6.04	4.16	77.9	**3.6**	31.5	14.3	**5.9**
1.7	7.39	44.5	0.37	**3.4**	3.1	0.98	15.40	3.28	74.0	**3.6**	16.2	11.2	**3.1**
8.6	0.19	0.4	0.00	**5.1**	0.5	1.02	7.56	2.58	45.5	**2.8**	59.0	32.4	**7.7**
5.0	2.45	7.6	0.02	**6.1**	0.6	1.30	6.66	4.82	68.3	**3.3**	7.8	11.9	**6.3**
8.3	0.69	2.8	0.00	**5.1**	2.9	0.87	7.54	3.68	66.5	**5.1**	36.9	7.7	**7.1**
3.8	4.04	19.4	0.79	**8.7**	1.2	5.16	41.95	5.05	82.8	**0.9**	24.2	49.2	**6.9**
9.0	0.03	0.2	0.00	**6.5**	3.9	1.22	13.35	3.01	46.4	**5.3**	38.2	7.5	**6.9**
3.0	3.34	20.1	0.67	**3.1**	0.8	0.57	6.84	3.09	84.8	**4.8**	30.1	7.2	**4.5**
5.6	1.70	6.2	0.29	**6.9**	3.5	1.57	8.61	4.55	58.3	**3.9**	22.5	10.3	**7.9**
5.4	0.23	1.5	0.35	**2.0**	0.2	0.49	5.92	3.48	86.3	**2.9**	33.8	18.6	**3.8**

Name	City	State	Rating	2013 Rating	2012 Rating	Total Assets ($Mil)	One Year Asset Growth	Asset Mix (As a % of Total Assets) Comm-ercial Loans	Cons-umer Loans	Mort-gage Loans	Secur-ities	Capital-ization Index	Lever-age Ratio	Risk-Based Capital Ratio
▼ PEOPLES BANK MT WASHINGTON	Mount Washington	KY	**D+**	D+	D-	77.9	-0.10	2.0	0.6	12.1	13.9	**10.0**	11.3	16.0
PEOPLES BANK NA	Marietta	OH	**B**	B	B-	2426.9	27.03	10.3	7.4	17.1	27.7	**7.1**	9.1	13.5
PEOPLES BANK OF ALABAMA	Cullman	AL	**C**	C-	D+	600.4	13.24	15.2	2.5	13.5	16.3	**7.7**	9.5	13.1
PEOPLES BANK OF ALTENBURG	Altenburg	MO	**C-**	D+	C-	57.2	5.28	3.8	3.4	26.0	22.3	**8.0**	9.7	15.1
PEOPLES BANK OF BEDFORD COUNTY	Shelbyville	TN	**B**	B	B	101.1	1.22	5.6	6.3	20.3	24.4	**10.0**	12.4	19.9
PEOPLES BANK OF BULLITT COUNTY	Shepherdsville	KY	**C+**	C	C-	228.7	1.90	0.0	1.9	17.1	60.1	**10.0**	13.0	32.5
PEOPLES BANK OF COMMERCE	Cambridge	MN	**C+**	C	C-	286.9	2.78	13.2	0.4	9.6	37.3	**10.0**	11.6	18.9
▼ PEOPLES BANK OF COMMERCE	Medford	OR	**B-**	B-	C+	209.6	22.82	13.2	2.1	8.7	11.7	**9.0**	10.4	15.3
PEOPLES BANK OF DEER LODGE	Deer Lodge	MT	**C+**	C+	C	29.9	14.56	5.2	3.8	19.6	31.7	**9.1**	10.4	22.4
▼ PEOPLES BANK OF EAST TENNESSEE	Madisonville	TN	**D+**	C-	D	216.7	-0.38	3.6	4.7	30.2	19.1	**7.8**	9.5	16.1
PEOPLES BANK OF GRACEVILLE	Graceville	FL	**A-**	A-	A-	90.1	9.72	1.7	2.1	15.8	52.5	**10.0**	13.7	41.1
PEOPLES BANK OF GREENSBORO	Greensboro	AL	**B-**	B-	B-	92.9	-1.15	5.7	7.6	12.9	43.5	**6.8**	8.9	17.0
PEOPLES BANK OF KENTUCKY INC	Flemingsburg	KY	**C+**	C+	B	256.6	1.08	6.8	7.3	21.1	9.1	**10.0**	11.0	15.5
PEOPLES BANK OF MACON	Macon	IL	**C+**	C+	B-	19.1	1.41	7.5	5.2	13.0	44.9	**10.0**	13.9	33.7
PEOPLES BANK OF RED LEVEL	Red Level	AL	**B-**	B-	C+	15.9	6.88	3.4	17.4	12.5	34.0	**10.0**	12.5	26.9
PEOPLES BANK OF SENECA	Seneca	MO	**B**	B	B-	125.5	24.19	10.0	4.2	28.2	18.4	**6.9**	8.9	12.6
PEOPLES BANK OF TALBOTTON	Talbotton	GA	**C-**	C-	C+	47.6	17.55	5.7	8.9	25.2	25.6	**7.9**	9.6	15.7
▲ PEOPLES BANK OF THE OZARKS	Nixa	MO	**B**	C+	C-	264.4	-3.85	5.2	2.1	24.0	11.5	**8.6**	10.1	15.3
PEOPLES BANK OF THE SOUTH	LaFollette	TN	**C-**	C-	C-	140.2	-5.62	2.6	2.6	33.6	2.4	**10.0**	13.9	19.1
PEOPLES BANK OF WYACONDA	Kahoka	MO	**B**	B	B	84.9	10.93	3.2	3.7	14.4	30.2	**6.9**	8.9	14.9
▲ PEOPLES BANK SB	Munster	IN	**B-**	C	C-	781.7	12.73	8.1	0.1	21.3	27.7	**7.1**	9.1	14.6
PEOPLES BK BILOXI MISSISSIPPI	Biloxi	MS	**D+**	D+	D	749.6	-5.42	4.1	0.9	9.2	37.1	**10.0**	13.6	22.4
PEOPLES BK OF ARLINGTON HGHTS	Arlington Heights	IL	**B-**	C+	C-	103.4	-3.63	8.4	0.1	11.0	33.9	**10.0**	12.0	20.3
PEOPLES COMMUNITY BANK	Montross	VA	**C**	C	C	158.4	3.44	1.6	0.9	36.8	16.4	**6.5**	8.5	14.5
PEOPLES COMMUNITY BANK	Greenville	MO	**A+**	A+	A	314.4	93.30	2.4	6.0	36.5	23.8	**10.0**	15.8	22.4
▲ PEOPLES COMMUNITY BANK	Mazomanie	WI	**A-**	B	C+	251.0	0.63	5.9	2.2	10.7	16.3	**10.0**	12.2	16.2
PEOPLES COMMUNITY NATIONAL BK	Bremen	GA	**B-**	C	D	91.7	19.09	3.0	0.3	7.8	5.5	**10.0**	24.2	30.1
PEOPLES EXCH BK OF MONROE CNTY	Monroeville	AL	**B-**	C+	B-	61.8	-4.50	14.7	3.2	17.6	21.8	**10.0**	14.2	20.5
PEOPLES EXCHANGE BANK	Stanton	KY	**B-**	C+	C+	325.1	0.07	5.0	2.1	30.0	2.7	**7.8**	9.5	13.6
▲ PEOPLES EXCHANGE BANK	Belleville	KS	**B-**	C+	C+	65.5	3.25	11.0	1.8	7.2	18.8	**9.4**	11.6	14.5
PEOPLES FIRST SAVINGS BANK	Mason	OH	**C**	C+	C+	59.9	2.42	0.0	0.1	66.5	3.0	**9.8**	10.9	18.3
PEOPLES FS&LA	Sidney	OH	**C-**	C-	C-	110.8	-7.42	3.0	1.9	51.0	7.2	**10.0**	13.5	25.5
PEOPLES FSB	Brighton	MA	**B**	B	B-	600.7	2.79	1.6	0.7	53.5	7.6	**10.0**	15.4	25.3
▲ PEOPLES FSB OF DEKALB COUNTY	Auburn	IN	**B-**	C+	C+	470.2	3.98	3.1	0.8	30.1	38.4	**10.0**	11.0	22.1
PEOPLES INDEPENDENT BANK	Boaz	AL	**B-**	B-	C+	185.9	1.38	4.6	1.7	7.5	39.0	**8.1**	9.8	16.7
PEOPLES NATIONAL BK	Niceville	FL	**C-**	D+	D	112.9	-0.44	3.1	1.5	17.6	33.6	**8.1**	9.7	22.3
PEOPLES NATIONAL BK	Colorado Springs	CO	**B**	B+	B-	316.3	19.20	1.1	0.1	39.5	22.0	**7.8**	9.5	17.8
PEOPLES NATIONAL BK NA	Mount Vernon	IL	**B-**	C+	C	957.8	9.85	19.1	0.5	6.0	7.7	**5.5**	9.5	11.4
PEOPLES NATIONAL BK CHECOTAH	Checotah	OK	**B+**	A	A	130.0	4.39	0.9	13.1	11.3	42.6	**10.0**	15.4	32.4
▲ PEOPLES NATIONAL BK OF KEWANEE	Kewanee	IL	**A-**	B+	B+	255.1	0.75	4.5	2.7	8.9	44.8	**10.0**	15.1	25.4
PEOPLES NB OF MOUNT PLEASANT	Mount Pleasant	OH	**C+**	B-	C	61.5	10.00	1.0	31.3	18.6	3.1	**10.0**	11.3	24.7
PEOPLES NB OF NEW LEXINGTON	New Lexington	OH	**C+**	C+	C+	113.2	1.38	4.6	10.5	39.7	15.5	**6.7**	8.7	14.8
PEOPLES S&LA OF MONTICELLO IN	Monticello	IN	**C-**	C-	C+	35.2	-3.84	0.0	0.3	58.9	13.9	**10.0**	36.1	87.8
PEOPLES SAVINGS & LOAN CO	West Liberty	OH	**C+**	C+	B	49.7	-2.79	1.0	2.2	52.9	10.0	**10.0**	12.9	26.5
PEOPLES SAVINGS & LOAN CO	Bucyrus	OH	**B-**	B-	B-	142.5	-0.69	0.0	0.7	38.9	33.1	**10.0**	18.0	48.5
PEOPLES SB	New Matamoras	OH	**B**	B+	B	63.1	16.74	5.7	3.1	27.3	44.5	**9.3**	10.5	23.7
PEOPLES SB	Urbana	OH	**D**	D+	D+	105.4	4.45	1.5	3.1	56.0	3.1	**9.0**	10.4	16.2
PEOPLES SB	Indianola	IA	**C+**	C+	C+	178.0	8.23	6.4	1.0	10.0	45.8	**8.0**	9.7	18.6
PEOPLES SB	Montezuma	IA	**C-**	C	C	34.5	-0.61	6.4	3.9	5.6	57.6	**8.5**	10.0	22.3
PEOPLES SB	Wellsburg	IA	**C+**	C+	C+	101.6	0.53	12.9	2.3	5.8	33.0	**6.4**	8.4	12.1
PEOPLES SB	Crawfordsville	IA	**B-**	B-	B+	36.1	-1.44	9.6	1.9	11.7	43.7	**6.9**	8.9	14.6
▼ PEOPLES SB	Elma	IA	**C+**	B-	C+	59.2	0.66	9.8	1.5	9.8	0.3	**7.8**	10.3	13.1
PEOPLES SB OF RHINELAND	Rhineland	MO	**B-**	B	B-	194.4	4.42	7.8	1.7	33.5	11.1	**7.9**	9.6	14.3
PEOPLES SECURITY BANK	Louisa	KY	**C**	C+	B-	47.3	-0.25	1.1	3.5	22.7	39.4	**10.0**	14.4	31.1
PEOPLES SECURITY BANK & TRUST	Scranton	PA	**B-**	B-	C+	1719.7	140.23	15.7	4.1	20.1	21.3	**8.9**	10.2	15.0
PEOPLES SOUTHERN BANK	Clanton	AL	**B+**	B+	B+	160.6	6.19	1.6	3.8	9.8	55.5	**10.0**	14.1	32.6
PEOPLES STATE BK	Lake City	FL	**D-**	D-	D-	69.2	2.11	5.3	1.8	15.1	7.1	**6.8**	8.8	13.0
PEOPLES STATE BK	Albia	IA	**B+**	B+	B+	89.9	1.75	15.7	2.0	11.1	40.5	**10.0**	13.7	25.9
PEOPLES STATE BK	Ellettsville	IN	**B+**	B-	C+	208.5	5.82	5.8	1.3	4.8	43.1	**10.0**	11.6	19.5
PEOPLES STATE BK	Winfield	IA	**C-**	D+	C-	27.8	-1.52	2.6	6.3	16.6	52.9	**7.4**	9.3	20.2

Asset Quality Index	Adjusted Non-Performing Loans as a % of Total Loans	Adjusted Non-Performing Loans as a % of Capital	Net Charge-Offs / Avg Loans	Profitability Index	Net Income ($Mil)	Return on Assets (R.O.A.)	Return on Equity (R.O.E.)	Net Interest Spread	Overhead Efficiency Ratio	Liquidity Index	Liquidity Ratio	Hot Money Ratio	Stability Index
0.6	7.34	40.9	-0.11	**3.2**	0.5	0.78	7.07	4.26	85.6	**4.2**	23.4	8.6	**5.1**
5.4	0.67	4.7	-0.03	**5.4**	14.7	0.92	8.76	3.40	72.8	**3.5**	15.3	11.7	**7.8**
2.9	1.73	11.7	0.08	**4.5**	4.0	0.94	10.47	4.70	82.7	**3.7**	11.5	10.4	**4.9**
4.1	1.75	11.6	0.00	**4.9**	0.5	1.13	11.65	3.99	70.5	**4.6**	27.4	7.1	**3.7**
4.6	2.71	13.1	0.50	**4.9**	0.6	0.83	6.80	4.05	64.8	**1.7**	31.4	30.6	**6.4**
4.5	4.57	9.2	0.08	**3.4**	2.1	1.23	10.86	3.36	79.6	**6.3**	59.8	8.1	**5.9**
3.6	3.10	13.1	0.20	**5.0**	2.5	1.20	9.92	3.89	74.2	**5.2**	34.9	6.3	**6.5**
4.7	1.62	9.8	0.16	**3.9**	0.9	0.59	5.42	4.19	82.9	**4.6**	28.4	7.7	**5.8**
3.3	3.80	18.7	-0.14	**3.3**	0.1	0.46	4.40	4.30	84.0	**5.5**	31.1	2.5	**4.1**
1.0	5.85	36.6	1.01	**2.6**	0.4	0.27	2.88	4.93	88.2	**2.2**	25.1	19.1	**3.9**
6.6	4.12	9.4	0.01	**6.6**	1.0	1.68	12.26	3.18	52.2	**5.0**	78.4	16.1	**8.3**
5.9	0.70	3.6	0.02	**6.4**	1.1	1.59	18.46	3.76	58.4	**2.8**	42.1	24.3	**5.8**
3.6	2.09	13.7	0.13	**5.1**	1.8	0.90	7.97	4.08	66.1	**1.5**	6.8	22.4	**7.5**
9.0	0.00	0.0	0.00	**2.5**	0.1	0.33	2.47	2.63	84.2	**4.3**	40.7	11.3	**6.2**
7.6	0.79	2.3	0.05	**6.1**	0.1	1.18	9.70	5.31	69.7	**6.8**	68.6	2.2	**4.3**
4.5	1.53	10.8	0.45	**6.6**	1.0	1.09	12.43	3.86	62.4	**4.1**	20.2	8.4	**5.0**
4.1	1.68	10.2	-0.11	**3.2**	0.2	0.48	4.96	4.89	88.0	**1.0**	15.4	32.1	**2.8**
4.1	2.12	14.2	-0.11	**3.2**	0.3	0.69	6.44	4.54	60.7	**3.1**	21.0	14.1	**6.5**
0.0	6.90	38.7	0.15	**6.1**	1.5	1.39	10.22	4.98	65.3	**1.2**	6.8	26.4	**7.1**
8.5	0.03	0.2	0.01	**4.7**	0.5	0.76	9.10	3.03	60.7	**2.7**	16.5	15.4	**5.3**
5.9	0.50	3.2	0.43	**5.0**	5.7	1.02	10.86	3.87	67.2	**3.5**	29.7	14.2	**5.6**
1.9	10.07	32.5	0.93	**0.6**	-0.8	-0.15	-1.13	3.34	89.7	**3.6**	18.8	11.5	**5.6**
7.2	0.59	2.4	0.25	**3.5**	0.4	0.54	4.77	3.58	82.2	**4.6**	42.3	12.8	**5.0**
5.0	1.68	12.0	0.04	**3.1**	0.6	0.55	6.55	3.87	83.8	**2.6**	18.2	16.4	**4.6**
7.9	0.83	3.4	-0.12	**10.0**	7.1	3.05	20.15	5.39	44.4	**2.2**	18.3	18.5	**9.0**
5.4	1.36	7.5	0.12	**7.0**	2.0	1.07	8.32	4.00	61.0	**2.6**	8.6	15.1	**6.9**
5.1	1.61	5.4	0.18	**4.2**	0.8	1.17	4.80	4.29	75.2	**0.6**	10.4	52.4	**4.9**
7.3	0.73	3.0	-0.04	**3.7**	0.4	0.78	5.96	4.69	87.2	**4.1**	34.1	12.7	**5.9**
4.9	1.11	8.9	0.06	**4.9**	2.1	0.87	9.14	4.17	74.2	**2.6**	10.1	15.5	**4.7**
2.6	1.40	8.3	0.00	**7.6**	0.7	1.37	9.86	4.65	65.7	**3.1**	9.5	12.7	**7.4**
5.5	1.06	7.8	0.05	**2.9**	0.2	0.32	3.02	3.55	82.6	**2.1**	7.9	18.0	**6.3**
2.1	5.33	27.6	0.97	**1.2**	-0.2	-0.24	-1.85	3.77	83.7	**4.2**	25.8	9.0	**6.2**
8.9	0.40	2.0	0.00	**4.2**	3.1	0.69	4.59	3.12	64.7	**2.9**	13.6	14.5	**8.4**
9.4	0.20	0.9	0.34	**3.4**	2.6	0.75	6.29	3.11	76.5	**4.8**	48.2	13.1	**6.5**
4.4	2.65	12.5	0.42	**6.0**	1.7	1.20	11.41	4.33	65.1	**4.6**	45.6	13.3	**5.2**
3.6	3.11	13.0	0.10	**3.1**	0.7	0.84	11.16	3.78	82.8	**3.7**	47.2	18.5	**2.6**
4.5	2.08	14.6	-0.02	**8.8**	2.8	1.33	12.89	3.60	84.7	**4.3**	10.2	5.8	**5.5**
4.2	1.08	9.0	0.14	**5.7**	9.9	1.44	15.20	4.46	67.3	**1.5**	2.0	20.4	**6.0**
7.8	1.41	3.1	0.25	**4.7**	1.0	1.05	6.90	3.24	71.9	**4.8**	60.6	16.2	**9.1**
7.2	1.81	4.6	0.15	**5.2**	1.8	0.93	5.61	4.67	64.5	**5.9**	53.9	8.4	**6.8**
5.5	0.66	3.1	0.16	**3.1**	0.2	0.46	3.96	3.77	79.9	**4.8**	49.9	12.5	**5.5**
4.0	1.54	12.3	0.05	**3.1**	0.4	0.41	4.45	4.00	84.7	**2.9**	4.7	13.6	**5.6**
6.5	4.99	8.1	0.09	**1.7**	0.0	0.11	0.33	2.72	89.2	**5.8**	57.3	8.4	**6.9**
9.1	0.15	0.7	0.06	**3.0**	0.2	0.42	3.48	3.41	81.2	**3.4**	30.2	14.8	**6.3**
9.7	1.18	2.8	0.21	**3.4**	0.8	0.73	4.17	3.23	73.7	**4.7**	62.9	16.7	**7.7**
7.8	0.51	1.9	0.26	**4.4**	0.4	0.86	8.06	4.32	72.9	**6.4**	57.9	4.5	**6.0**
1.7	4.28	35.2	1.60	**0.5**	-0.3	-0.40	-4.03	4.41	84.1	**1.5**	8.3	22.9	**4.0**
6.5	1.01	4.0	0.01	**3.7**	1.0	0.83	8.96	3.29	70.5	**6.1**	54.2	7.6	**3.9**
6.8	1.67	4.5	-0.08	**1.9**	0.0	0.16	1.61	3.49	93.1	**6.2**	77.9	9.9	**3.5**
2.8	2.89	18.2	0.16	**3.8**	0.6	0.80	11.58	3.25	71.9	**1.4**	23.0	28.5	**3.6**
5.5	1.40	5.7	0.65	**4.3**	0.3	0.92	11.37	3.22	61.5	**5.9**	54.1	7.5	**3.9**
3.3	1.00	7.9	0.00	**8.0**	0.8	1.84	18.71	4.26	52.6	**2.1**	5.8	17.5	**7.0**
4.5	1.68	12.5	-0.05	**3.9**	1.0	0.66	7.45	4.17	79.5	**3.9**	9.4	8.5	**5.1**
8.3	0.91	2.4	0.02	**2.3**	0.1	0.22	1.56	4.26	94.8	**5.1**	49.5	10.9	**6.1**
4.1	1.05	6.9	0.13	**5.5**	13.1	1.01	7.36	3.94	64.1	**4.0**	12.3	8.7	**7.5**
8.5	1.71	3.6	0.07	**4.5**	1.3	1.10	7.81	3.12	69.4	**5.1**	61.0	14.5	**8.2**
0.3	8.21	56.9	0.01	**2.3**	0.2	0.30	3.07	4.23	89.6	**4.1**	21.4	8.9	**4.1**
8.5	0.74	2.6	-0.01	**4.5**	0.8	1.12	8.21	3.87	71.5	**2.5**	47.6	30.8	**7.3**
4.7	2.86	10.8	0.61	**5.7**	2.0	1.30	12.43	3.78	73.4	**4.0**	36.0	13.7	**5.6**
2.6	6.98	29.2	0.21	**2.5**	0.1	0.58	6.23	3.42	87.5	**5.0**	53.1	12.4	**3.7**

Name	City	State	Rating	2013 Rating	2012 Rating	Total Assets ($Mil)	One Year Asset Growth	Asset Mix (As a % of Total Assets) Commercial Loans	Consumer Loans	Mortgage Loans	Securities	Capitalization Index	Leverage Ratio	Risk-Based Capital Ratio
PEOPLES STATE BK	Prairie Du Chien	WI	B	B	B-	632.5	15.73	10.3	1.2	11.9	29.3	7.0	9.0	14.2
PEOPLES STATE BK	Wausau	WI	B	B	C+	729.5	3.48	11.6	0.5	22.7	19.9	7.9	9.6	14.3
PEOPLES STATE BK	Cherryvale	KS	B-	B-	B-	16.3	4.30	14.9	11.7	27.1	2.8	10.0	28.8	36.2
PEOPLES STATE BK	McDonald	KS	C-	C+	B-	133.3	7.65	14.5	1.9	8.5	4.0	5.9	9.0	11.7
PEOPLES STATE BK	Summit	SD	B	B	B-	60.0	6.19	13.8	4.2	4.2	18.7	8.7	11.1	13.9
PEOPLES STATE BK	Westhope	ND	B	B	B	73.2	6.47	4.8	2.8	1.7	41.0	9.0	10.3	20.5
PEOPLES STATE BK	Blair	OK	B-	B-	B-	17.0	3.27	24.7	14.7	4.4	14.6	7.0	9.0	13.2
PEOPLES STATE BK	Rocksprings	TX	A	A	A	72.1	8.59	1.5	1.9	9.4	49.7	10.0	11.8	26.8
▲ PEOPLES STATE BK	Shepherd	TX	B-	C+	C	108.7	4.04	2.6	3.9	14.1	45.6	6.3	8.3	18.3
PEOPLES STATE BK & TRUST	Baxley	GA	D+	D+	C-	79.1	1.22	3.2	1.8	4.5	7.2	10.0	12.4	16.8
PEOPLES STATE BK FAIRMOUNT ND	Fairmount	ND	D+	D	C-	23.7	-5.20	11.1	5.3	4.4	28.2	5.2	7.2	11.6
PEOPLES STATE BK HALLETTSVILLE	Hallettsville	TX	C+	C+	B-	278.6	20.96	2.0	2.0	6.1	49.3	8.7	10.1	38.9
PEOPLES STATE BK MADISON LAKE	Madison Lake	MN	E	E	E+	24.1	5.29	14.2	5.8	6.6	11.7	6.2	8.2	13.9
PEOPLES STATE BK OF COLFAX	Colfax	IL	B	B	B	36.6	-0.11	4.7	7.0	18.4	26.6	9.5	10.7	22.1
PEOPLES STATE BK OF COMMERCE	Nolensville	TN	E-	E-	E-	148.5	2.49	12.5	8.9	12.5	18.2	2.1	5.5	9.1
▼ PEOPLES STATE BK OF MUNISING	Munising	MI	B-	B	B-	120.6	1.75	8.6	6.3	22.2	24.5	8.0	9.7	14.6
PEOPLES STATE BK OF NEWTON IL	Newton	IL	B	B	B-	347.5	2.47	12.3	2.5	9.8	30.6	7.8	9.5	14.1
PEOPLES STATE BK OF PLAINVIEW	Plainview	MN	B-	C+	C+	190.6	0.78	7.9	2.8	15.8	30.9	6.8	8.9	15.1
PEOPLES STATE BK OF VELVA	Velva	ND	C	C	C-	111.2	27.72	8.7	2.9	8.7	8.0	3.7	8.1	10.4
PEOPLES STATE BK OF WELLS	Wells	MN	B+	B+	B	28.7	0.91	3.4	2.2	11.7	9.6	10.0	12.4	16.8
PEOPLES TRUST & SAVINGS BANK	Boonville	IN	B-	B-	B	160.2	12.47	3.7	1.1	32.1	30.7	10.0	16.4	26.2
PEOPLES TRUST & SB	Riverside	IA	B-	B-	B	29.2	11.82	10.6	3.3	19.0	38.2	5.8	7.8	15.2
PEOPLES TRUST & SB	Clive	IA	C+	C+	C-	284.1	12.95	6.8	2.5	14.5	18.1	6.3	8.4	11.9
▲ PEOPLES TRUST CO OF ST ALBANS	Saint Albans	VT	C+	C-	C-	258.6	4.40	1.8	0.9	25.7	25.7	10.0	11.9	21.9
PEOPLES UNITED BANK	Bridgeport	CT	C+	C+	C	34531.1	10.43	16.3	0.2	15.3	13.2	6.8	8.8	13.3
PEOPLESBANK	Holyoke	MA	C+	C+	C+	1840.2	-0.35	3.0	0.1	22.9	26.5	8.3	9.9	14.9
PEOPLESBANK A CODORUS VLY CO	York	PA	B	B	B	1200.4	7.79	8.8	0.7	9.6	19.1	8.4	9.9	14.0
▲ PEOPLESSOUTH BANK	Colquitt	GA	B+	B-	C+	481.0	2.19	3.1	5.1	12.8	21.9	10.0	11.4	16.8
PEOPLESTRUST BANK	Hamilton	AL	C+	C-	C	83.3	-5.23	17.2	5.5	11.6	30.9	8.5	10.0	15.2
PERPETUAL FSB	Urbana	OH	B	B	C+	346.0	-1.60	0.6	1.7	37.7	0.0	10.0	17.7	27.7
PERRYTON NATIONAL BK	Perryton	TX	B	B	B	185.4	15.38	6.8	5.1	3.0	55.2	8.6	10.0	26.1
PERU FSB	Peru	IL	B-	C+	C+	138.4	-0.21	2.4	2.7	33.3	39.9	10.0	12.1	26.0
PESHTIGO NATIONAL BK	Peshtigo	WI	A-	A-	B+	184.6	6.87	5.1	2.5	20.8	16.2	10.0	11.7	20.7
PETEFISH SKILES & CO	Virginia	IL	A-	B+	B-	172.0	-4.88	4.1	8.3	13.7	29.5	10.0	11.3	17.2
PETERSBURG STATE BK	Petersburg	NE	D+	D+	C-	37.4	11.18	11.6	5.8	0.1	7.5	4.9	8.5	11.0
PETIT JEAN STATE BK	Morrilton	AR	A-	A-	B	172.1	7.23	8.9	3.6	17.4	36.6	10.0	11.7	23.7
PHELPS COUNTY BANK	Rolla	MO	B	B	B	337.1	7.64	2.6	2.2	31.2	42.9	5.5	7.5	15.9
PHENIX-GIRARD BANK	Phenix City	AL	B+	B+	A-	170.8	4.95	1.8	0.6	10.0	43.9	10.0	14.9	27.8
PHILADELPHIA TRUST CO	Philadelphia	PA	A-	A-	A-	16.6	14.10	0.6	5.4	7.4	3.9	10.0	81.0	142.3
PHILO EXCHANGE BANK	Philo	IL	C+	C+	B-	87.3	-0.21	2.7	1.3	7.3	36.6	7.9	9.6	17.5
PHOENIXVILLE FEDERAL BANK & TR	Phoenixville	PA	C+	C	C	386.8	0.65	3.2	0.1	37.5	23.3	10.0	12.1	21.8
PICKENS S&LA FA	Pickens	SC	C-	D+	D	91.8	-2.22	2.3	1.1	36.6	25.9	7.9	9.6	17.4
PIEDMONT BANK	Norcross	GA	D-	E-	E-	396.1	15.49	12.2	1.0	2.2	6.2	6.9	9.4	12.4
PIEDMONT FSB	Winston-Salem	NC	C+	C+	B-	927.0	-0.75	0.0	0.0	55.2	27.9	10.0	23.7	61.6
PIGEON FALLS STATE BK	Pigeon Falls	WI	B	B	B-	75.5	3.88	3.3	1.1	10.3	9.0	9.3	10.6	16.4
PIGGOTT STATE BK	Piggott	AR	B+	A-	A-	76.9	-0.85	5.0	4.0	14.7	51.9	9.2	10.4	24.8
PIKE NATIONAL BK	McComb	MS	B	B-	C+	203.5	0.13	7.4	6.8	18.0	22.8	10.0	13.8	21.7
PIKES PEAK NATIONAL BK	Colorado Springs	CO	C-	C-	C-	86.6	9.09	5.8	2.3	5.4	0.0	8.9	10.3	26.1
▼ PILGRIM BANK	Cohasset	MA	D+	D+	D-	194.5	13.19	0.7	1.4	46.5	6.6	5.4	7.4	14.3
PILGRIM BANK	Pittsburg	TX	B-	B-	B-	387.4	0.14	4.2	1.2	9.9	32.7	8.2	9.8	17.5
PILOT BANK	Tampa	FL	E-	E+	E	220.7	12.47	16.8	14.7	7.5	14.7	2.3	6.4	9.3
PILOT GROVE SB	Pilot Grove	IA	B+	A-	B+	559.8	22.17	6.4	3.5	22.7	21.4	6.9	8.9	12.8
PINE COUNTRY BANK	Little Falls	MN	C+	C	C-	160.8	-0.96	8.0	1.5	6.1	28.3	6.4	8.4	12.8
PINE ISLAND BANK	Pine Island	MN	B-	B-	B-	77.8	4.70	4.6	1.3	21.6	22.5	7.9	9.6	13.5
PINE RIVER STATE BK	Pine River	MN	C	C	C+	107.4	3.73	4.3	2.0	12.7	23.1	5.9	7.9	16.1
PINE RIVER VALLEY BANK	Bayfield	CO	D-	D-	D-	142.1	-4.58	3.4	1.0	15.0	30.2	7.2	9.1	16.9
PINELAND STATE BK	Metter	GA	D+	D+	D	54.5	-1.74	6.9	4.2	15.2	11.3	7.1	9.1	15.9
PINERIES BANK	Stevens Point	WI	B	B	B-	72.7	3.48	3.2	2.3	35.2	6.5	8.4	9.9	17.7
PINNACLE BANK	Marshalltown	IA	B	B	B	184.6	11.27	9.2	3.1	5.9	53.4	5.6	7.6	16.6
▲ PINNACLE BANK	Rogers	AR	C	D+	D+	90.8	0.68	0.8	0.2	12.4	23.7	9.4	10.6	20.2

Asset Quality Index	Adjusted Non-Performing Loans as a % of Total Loans	Adjusted Non-Performing Loans as a % of Capital	Net Charge-Offs Avg Loans	Profitability Index	Net Income ($Mil)	Return on Assets (R.O.A.)	Return on Equity (R.O.E.)	Net Interest Spread	Overhead Efficiency Ratio	Liquidity Index	Liquidity Ratio	Hot Money Ratio	Stability Index
4.8	1.01	6.6	0.05	**6.9**	6.8	1.54	15.09	3.59	55.9	**2.0**	25.6	20.9	**7.9**
4.5	1.68	12.0	0.20	**5.3**	4.9	0.92	9.60	3.54	64.4	**2.4**	16.7	17.4	**6.2**
4.5	3.19	9.3	0.38	**10.0**	0.5	4.20	14.79	6.66	43.5	**3.3**	11.8	11.8	**7.1**
2.4	1.74	14.5	-0.27	**9.6**	2.0	2.06	22.80	5.45	51.9	**1.0**	5.4	29.2	**6.3**
5.4	0.71	4.2	0.03	**10.0**	1.2	2.74	24.91	4.88	39.1	**1.0**	10.4	30.4	**7.2**
8.8	0.00	0.0	-0.03	**4.4**	0.6	1.08	10.44	3.28	63.1	**3.1**	46.7	21.3	**7.4**
7.3	0.18	1.2	0.96	**6.1**	0.1	1.07	12.31	4.72	71.7	**4.2**	34.2	10.3	**5.7**
9.5	0.04	0.1	-0.01	**7.1**	0.9	1.73	14.69	3.21	44.3	**3.9**	58.6	18.6	**8.7**
8.7	0.14	0.7	0.02	**4.0**	0.6	0.75	10.03	3.53	74.0	**1.8**	26.6	25.0	**4.6**
3.6	2.21	11.8	-0.01	**9.2**	1.0	1.63	13.62	5.00	59.5	**3.1**	21.2	14.3	**3.0**
8.4	0.00	0.0	-0.04	**3.7**	0.1	0.69	9.77	3.83	77.3	**4.7**	15.4	3.9	**2.1**
9.7	0.12	0.3	0.01	**3.3**	1.3	0.69	6.55	2.23	61.8	**3.8**	67.7	25.9	**5.3**
3.7	2.34	15.1	0.67	**1.1**	0.0	-0.16	-1.97	3.69	99.7	**4.4**	36.6	9.6	**1.0**
8.7	0.00	0.0	0.00	**4.7**	0.2	0.90	8.57	3.34	62.2	**5.6**	43.1	6.9	**5.9**
1.1	4.63	43.6	1.26	**1.3**	0.3	0.30	5.78	4.04	79.5	**1.0**	16.6	32.3	**0.3**
2.7	2.74	15.3	0.13	**5.1**	0.9	0.99	7.39	4.55	72.3	**2.1**	26.2	20.1	**7.2**
5.3	0.81	5.2	0.00	**5.7**	2.7	1.06	10.61	3.20	53.9	**3.0**	13.4	14.0	**5.8**
4.0	1.72	11.0	0.02	**4.5**	1.5	1.07	12.01	3.45	71.5	**3.3**	23.2	13.4	**6.1**
5.3	0.32	3.0	0.00	**6.4**	1.2	1.54	18.47	4.66	59.7	**1.2**	7.3	26.1	**4.9**
7.4	0.14	0.8	0.00	**5.6**	0.3	1.35	11.10	3.67	62.5	**4.2**	23.6	8.5	**7.2**
8.1	1.24	4.5	0.07	**4.0**	1.2	0.97	5.97	3.79	78.5	**4.1**	42.3	15.2	**7.5**
9.1	0.00	0.0	0.00	**6.1**	0.2	1.14	14.25	3.59	54.5	**5.2**	51.2	10.9	**4.0**
5.4	0.49	4.0	0.16	**4.2**	1.5	0.74	8.16	3.83	72.0	**2.6**	16.1	16.1	**3.9**
3.0	5.06	23.4	0.10	**2.8**	0.9	0.47	3.86	4.10	83.5	**4.8**	35.1	9.0	**5.0**
3.3	1.32	11.2	0.12	**4.5**	197.0	0.79	5.67	3.26	67.1	**3.3**	13.2	12.8	**9.7**
8.7	0.23	1.5	0.22	**3.3**	8.3	0.60	6.49	2.91	74.9	**4.2**	19.2	8.4	**7.3**
5.3	1.07	7.3	0.05	**5.5**	9.4	1.06	10.56	3.87	62.5	**2.1**	8.0	18.2	**8.0**
5.1	1.45	8.1	0.29	**5.7**	4.2	1.18	11.50	4.15	58.8	**1.8**	13.8	19.8	**5.5**
4.0	2.45	13.4	0.04	**3.9**	0.4	0.62	5.98	3.61	72.9	**3.1**	39.0	19.0	**4.4**
4.2	3.72	16.4	1.46	**4.5**	1.6	0.61	3.48	3.27	30.4	**0.9**	18.8	36.0	**7.6**
9.0	0.00	0.0	0.05	**4.7**	1.6	1.22	12.24	2.71	53.8	**4.1**	66.2	20.2	**6.4**
7.1	1.58	6.2	0.19	**3.6**	0.7	0.65	5.67	2.90	69.3	**4.3**	44.4	14.7	**6.1**
8.3	0.33	1.8	0.04	**6.6**	2.0	1.51	12.98	4.09	61.2	**3.0**	28.4	16.2	**7.4**
7.1	0.71	3.7	0.03	**5.5**	1.6	1.23	9.28	3.93	67.6	**4.0**	21.3	9.6	**7.5**
1.8	1.43	13.7	0.17	**7.2**	0.5	1.82	21.16	4.04	48.9	**1.8**	4.0	19.0	**4.8**
6.9	1.19	4.1	0.20	**7.2**	1.6	1.26	11.03	3.70	50.7	**2.7**	38.7	23.0	**6.1**
8.1	0.30	2.0	0.06	**4.9**	3.1	1.23	18.07	3.26	69.6	**4.8**	23.5	4.8	**4.9**
6.4	3.13	8.3	0.14	**4.5**	1.7	1.28	10.12	3.10	70.8	**3.7**	19.1	10.9	**7.6**
9.2	0.00	0.0	0.00	**10.0**	1.9	16.66	21.89	2.06	62.2	**5.4**	223.8	46.6	**8.0**
5.0	1.09	5.5	-0.10	**3.5**	0.5	0.72	6.92	2.42	72.0	**5.4**	36.6	5.8	**7.0**
4.3	2.44	11.5	0.15	**3.3**	1.6	0.56	4.92	3.25	85.9	**4.1**	36.1	13.3	**5.4**
2.6	3.51	21.0	0.15	**3.0**	0.3	0.49	5.10	3.73	83.6	**2.4**	34.5	23.0	**4.2**
2.4	1.10	8.2	0.15	**4.3**	2.3	0.79	6.22	4.15	61.1	**0.9**	19.0	38.3	**4.6**
10.0	0.25	0.6	0.03	**2.9**	2.3	0.34	1.41	2.61	77.1	**2.7**	53.3	36.0	**8.2**
6.1	0.41	2.8	-0.01	**5.3**	0.5	0.92	8.51	4.14	65.7	**1.0**	14.0	31.9	**6.0**
9.2	0.00	0.0	0.00	**5.1**	0.6	0.99	9.22	3.75	68.0	**3.8**	56.6	18.6	**7.4**
4.0	3.67	15.6	0.08	**5.1**	1.3	0.84	6.23	4.69	71.8	**2.8**	21.0	15.5	**6.8**
2.6	5.65	20.4	-0.07	**2.9**	0.4	0.58	5.55	3.27	92.9	**5.6**	63.9	11.2	**5.1**
2.7	3.10	29.8	0.00	**2.7**	0.4	0.34	4.52	3.14	84.3	**2.1**	27.7	21.8	**2.7**
4.3	1.52	8.5	0.00	**4.3**	3.0	1.02	8.96	3.27	68.4	**1.2**	22.6	31.6	**6.8**
1.8	2.21	21.3	0.72	**0.2**	-0.6	-0.39	-4.08	3.53	115.2	**1.5**	15.7	25.3	**2.7**
6.5	0.44	3.2	0.12	**6.2**	5.3	1.30	12.26	3.54	56.7	**4.2**	22.9	8.3	**7.7**
3.5	2.59	18.0	0.27	**4.2**	0.7	0.60	7.29	4.15	72.9	**3.6**	22.4	11.7	**4.1**
3.9	1.82	12.0	-0.01	**4.5**	0.6	0.98	8.64	3.81	70.2	**2.9**	15.7	14.5	**5.7**
3.9	2.88	16.7	0.21	**2.8**	0.4	0.48	5.90	3.38	83.4	**5.2**	38.1	7.6	**4.0**
5.7	1.04	5.1	0.02	**0.0**	-0.7	-0.62	-6.25	3.89	116.8	**3.3**	30.9	15.6	**3.5**
1.4	5.89	34.8	0.51	**1.6**	0.1	0.16	1.67	3.81	86.4	**2.3**	30.7	21.1	**3.0**
5.8	1.02	6.2	0.00	**6.1**	0.7	1.42	13.71	3.56	61.3	**2.7**	36.1	21.3	**6.6**
5.6	1.28	4.6	-0.04	**4.3**	1.0	0.74	8.54	2.86	62.9	**7.3**	64.3	2.2	**6.4**
5.6	1.91	7.9	-0.38	**2.8**	0.4	0.58	5.85	3.00	80.3	**0.4**	11.2	71.9	**4.5**

Name	City	State	Rating	2013 Rating	2012 Rating	Total Assets ($Mil)	One Year Asset Growth	Asset Mix (As a % of Total Assets) Comm-ercial Loans	Cons-umer Loans	Mort-gage Loans	Secur-ities	Capital-ization Index	Lever-age Ratio	Risk-Based Capital Ratio
PINNACLE BANK	Nashville	TN	B+	B	C+	5846.6	8.82	29.2	3.0	7.4	12.8	7.3	10.6	12.8
▲ PINNACLE BANK	Elberton	GA	C+	C-	C	595.7	7.30	4.9	1.7	9.2	26.3	9.3	10.5	15.1
PINNACLE BANK	Jasper	AL	B	B	B	218.2	-2.57	5.9	1.9	7.6	51.8	9.9	10.9	19.7
PINNACLE BANK	Orange City	FL	E-	E-	E-	163.7	-3.25	3.3	2.6	2.7	36.3	0.0	2.1	4.8
PINNACLE BANK	Keene	TX	B	B	B-	606.8	3.97	7.1	2.6	10.6	32.2	6.8	8.8	15.2
PINNACLE BANK	Lincoln	NE	B+	B+	B	3899.7	3.09	6.8	1.6	9.7	24.3	7.6	9.4	13.5
PINNACLE BANK	Scottsdale	AZ	B+	B-	B-	121.1	6.86	6.2	0.1	28.0	0.0	10.0	16.2	19.9
▲ PINNACLE BANK	Gilroy	CA	C+	C-	D+	222.1	17.97	15.5	0.4	6.2	2.8	5.2	8.8	11.2
PINNACLE BANK - WYOMING	Torrington	WY	B	B	B-	683.8	2.38	5.3	2.6	14.7	24.2	7.4	9.2	13.5
PINNACLE BANK INC	Vanceburg	KY	B-	C+	C+	45.6	14.27	7.4	10.2	38.7	8.7	10.0	12.2	17.8
PINNACLE BANK SIOUX CITY	Sioux City	IA	B	B	B+	79.9	6.38	5.8	2.2	25.0	24.0	10.0	12.5	20.9
PINNACLE BK OF SOUTH CAROLINA	Greenville	SC	B	B	B-	151.4	1.46	6.1	2.2	13.1	10.1	10.0	12.6	17.4
▼ PIONEER BANK	Stanley	VA	D	C-	C	171.9	1.41	4.6	11.6	34.5	5.6	9.9	10.9	15.6
PIONEER BANK	Sioux City	IA	B-	B-	B	146.9	2.82	9.9	1.2	19.8	19.6	5.9	8.8	11.7
PIONEER BANK	Auburndale	WI	C	C+	B-	124.0	4.36	5.6	1.0	13.0	12.2	9.6	11.2	14.6
▲ PIONEER BANK	Saint James	MN	B	C+	C-	358.3	20.98	12.5	1.6	14.0	5.6	7.5	9.3	13.0
PIONEER BANK	Roswell	NM	C+	C+	B	662.0	1.56	3.3	0.6	29.2	45.3	9.0	10.3	24.2
PIONEER BANK & TRUST	Belle Fourche	SD	A-	A-	A-	604.5	6.84	8.8	1.8	5.0	44.0	7.6	9.4	17.5
PIONEER BANK OF WISCONSIN	Ladysmith	WI	B	B	B-	64.2	-2.88	6.0	1.2	3.1	54.4	9.8	10.9	20.6
PIONEER BANK SSB	Dripping Springs	TX	B	B	B+	364.3	44.92	9.7	1.3	15.4	7.6	9.9	11.0	15.8
PIONEER COMMERCIAL BANK	Troy	NY	U	U	C-	95.1	-15.17	0.0	0.0	0.0	29.6	4.3	6.3	33.3
PIONEER COMMUNITY BANK INC	Iaeger	WV	B	B	C	118.0	-4.82	2.0	5.8	61.9	6.2	10.0	12.7	22.7
PIONEER FS&LA	Dillon	MT	B	B	B	94.9	-0.10	1.5	1.8	54.9	26.0	10.0	15.4	36.0
PIONEER NATIONAL BK OF DULUTH	Duluth	MN	B-	B	B-	80.7	2.25	17.9	3.1	21.8	3.3	9.6	10.7	14.8
PIONEER SB	Cleveland	OH	B-	C+	C+	31.3	-1.12	0.0	0.3	40.3	40.3	10.0	19.7	49.8
PIONEER SB	Troy	NY	B-	B-	B-	791.9	4.52	11.0	2.5	24.9	9.0	10.0	12.7	16.2
PIONEER STATE BANK	Earlville	IL	D	D	C-	71.5	204.06	3.3	1.4	17.4	24.8	10.0	16.4	27.9
PIONEER TRUST BANK NA	Salem	OR	A	A-	B+	377.8	10.91	12.6	0.6	8.2	25.4	10.0	11.9	18.9
▼ PIQUA STATE BK	Piqua	KS	D	D+	C-	26.5	0.16	6.5	4.3	8.0	35.4	7.3	9.2	20.9
PISCATAQUA SB	Portsmouth	NH	B-	B-	B-	235.4	4.31	0.0	0.3	56.9	24.0	10.0	17.4	27.5
PITNEY BOWES BANK INC	Salt Lake City	UT	B-	C+	B-	748.6	-4.33	45.7	0.0	0.0	47.9	9.6	10.7	19.1
PITTSFIELD CO-OP BANK	Pittsfield	MA	C+	C+	C+	254.4	1.97	5.2	0.6	44.5	15.4	10.0	15.5	26.0
▼ PLAINS COMMERCE BANK	Hoven	SD	B+	B+	B-	553.9	12.37	8.3	1.0	8.7	9.0	7.7	12.2	13.1
PLAINS STATE BK	Plains	KS	C+	C+	B-	137.4	-1.63	7.4	1.6	2.9	64.4	7.8	9.5	22.7
PLAINS STATE BK	Humble	TX	B+	B+	B	311.6	15.67	11.7	0.3	7.9	12.6	8.6	10.0	14.8
PLAINSCAPITAL BANK	Dallas	TX	A-	A-	B-	8604.7	0.35	12.3	0.5	22.0	12.1	8.4	10.0	14.2
PLANTERS & CITIZENS BANK	Camilla	GA	C-	C-	C	97.7	0.82	4.4	2.2	2.9	25.1	8.4	9.9	23.8
PLANTERS BANK & TRUST CO	Indianola	MS	B	B	B	791.8	6.17	9.7	3.6	16.6	41.2	6.6	8.6	16.0
PLANTERS BANK INC	Hopkinsville	KY	B+	B+	B+	835.6	7.71	7.4	1.2	15.9	22.4	7.3	9.2	13.5
PLANTERSFIRST	Cordele	GA	E	E	E-	266.8	0.14	3.5	2.8	17.2	10.0	6.1	8.1	12.4
PLAQUEMINE BANK & TRUST CO	Plaquemine	LA	B-	B-	B-	129.2	7.43	10.8	4.5	14.8	33.7	10.0	12.1	21.4
PLATINUM BANK	Brandon	FL	B-	B-	C-	464.0	3.09	19.6	0.7	6.6	8.6	10.0	11.3	15.4
PLATINUM BANK	Oakdale	MN	A-	B+	B-	144.0	5.80	20.3	5.0	10.7	17.1	10.0	11.6	17.4
PLATINUM BANK	Lubbock	TX	B-	C	D	221.2	28.31	20.3	0.7	10.7	10.5	7.3	9.3	12.7
PLATTE VALLEY BANK	North Bend	NE	B	B	B+	70.8	7.73	13.5	3.7	3.7	24.1	10.0	13.3	19.3
PLATTE VALLEY BANK	Torrington	WY	B+	B+	B	318.8	36.32	26.2	3.2	17.9	6.6	7.9	10.6	13.2
PLATTE VALLEY BANK	Scottsbluff	NE	B	B+	B	448.3	4.26	12.6	2.6	22.7	10.5	7.3	9.2	13.7
PLATTE VALLEY BANK OF MISSOURI	Platte City	MO	B+	B	B-	427.7	7.28	5.8	1.2	19.3	26.6	6.9	8.9	13.9
▲ PLATTSMOUTH STATE BK	Plattsmouth	NE	C	D	D-	92.7	1.71	11.8	7.5	5.6	42.1	7.8	9.5	14.4
▲ PLAZA BANK	Seattle	WA	D	E+	E+	80.2	-2.20	8.3	0.1	3.0	21.5	10.0	11.1	17.9
PLAZA BANK	Irvine	CA	C-	C	C	524.5	10.75	18.0	5.1	3.3	3.2	7.5	10.1	12.9
PLAZA PARK STATE BK	Waite Park	MN	C-	C-	C-	173.8	-1.32	7.6	2.5	21.7	12.6	8.6	10.1	14.5
PLEASANT HILL BANK	Pleasant Hill	MO	C	C	C	70.9	-3.86	2.0	2.7	24.1	27.0	10.0	11.6	22.8
PLEASANTS COUNTY BANK	Saint Marys	WV	B	B	B	66.1	5.95	15.6	7.6	19.5	19.4	9.4	10.6	19.1
PLUMAS BANK	Quincy	CA	C+	C	C-	542.0	3.49	6.2	8.4	5.1	15.6	8.2	9.8	14.2
▲ PLUS INTERNATIONAL BK	Miami	FL	B	B-	C+	101.8	12.23	13.3	0.0	8.3	43.4	10.0	14.5	28.7
PNA BANK	Chicago	IL	E-	E-	E-	99.0	-8.32	0.0	0.0	36.0	10.1	1.6	5.3	8.6
PNC BANK NA	Wilmington	DE	C	C	C	324117.0	8.59	19.4	8.2	9.2	17.0	7.8	9.5	14.1
POCA VALLEY BANK INC	Walton	WV	B-	B-	C+	318.7	0.94	13.6	8.9	28.4	15.6	8.5	10.0	16.0
POCAHONTAS STATE BK	Pocahontas	IA	A	A	A+	100.3	2.79	5.3	0.4	3.4	57.0	10.0	17.2	30.6

Asset Quality Index	Adjusted Non-Performing Loans as a % of Total Loans	Adjusted Non-Performing Loans as a % of Capital	Net Charge-Offs Avg Loans	Profitability Index	Net Income ($Mil)	Return on Assets (R.O.A.)	Return on Equity (R.O.E.)	Net Interest Spread	Overhead Efficiency Ratio	Liquidity Index	Liquidity Ratio	Hot Money Ratio	Stability Index
5.3	0.58	4.0	0.11	**7.1**	54.2	1.28	8.97	3.83	53.5	**3.9**	7.3	8.7	**8.6**
3.7	1.70	9.4	0.70	**5.3**	5.8	1.30	11.48	4.47	67.4	**4.0**	19.8	9.4	**5.9**
7.8	0.72	2.4	-0.25	**4.7**	1.6	0.93	8.13	3.67	70.5	**3.7**	47.3	18.3	**5.8**
0.3	11.68	154.9	1.53	**0.0**	-0.8	-0.62	-44.60	2.76	124.9	**1.2**	30.2	52.7	**0.5**
3.8	1.07	6.6	0.21	**6.8**	6.6	1.48	10.68	4.14	66.4	**3.5**	31.7	15.0	**8.7**
6.1	0.71	4.8	0.05	**7.4**	47.6	1.65	16.71	3.52	54.8	**3.7**	13.7	10.8	**8.6**
3.9	1.87	9.6	-0.03	**7.5**	1.0	1.19	7.35	4.24	66.6	**2.5**	10.9	16.2	**5.8**
4.6	1.25	8.9	-0.04	**3.4**	0.7	0.48	4.24	4.29	81.9	**2.7**	24.2	16.5	**4.9**
4.4	1.16	7.9	0.06	**5.7**	6.6	1.30	14.11	3.91	68.4	**2.7**	13.9	15.5	**8.2**
5.0	1.18	7.4	0.13	**4.0**	0.2	0.68	4.36	5.16	79.4	**1.0**	5.3	29.8	**5.9**
8.6	0.34	1.7	0.00	**4.8**	0.7	1.17	9.91	3.46	67.2	**2.5**	34.0	21.7	**7.3**
4.6	1.18	6.7	0.24	**4.2**	1.0	0.89	6.90	4.07	76.5	**1.3**	16.2	27.3	**6.9**
0.9	4.80	32.6	0.19	**6.7**	1.3	1.03	9.24	5.41	70.7	**2.0**	13.6	18.6	**6.6**
7.6	0.40	3.0	-0.02	**5.9**	1.5	1.42	15.64	3.89	63.2	**1.9**	17.5	19.8	**5.0**
3.8	2.22	14.0	-0.04	**3.1**	0.3	0.35	3.11	4.11	86.0	**4.6**	24.9	5.8	**6.2**
5.1	0.52	4.2	0.07	**5.8**	3.9	1.43	14.08	4.16	61.9	**1.5**	7.4	21.6	**5.3**
9.1	0.04	0.2	0.09	**3.7**	3.7	0.75	8.23	2.91	81.4	**4.3**	36.3	12.2	**5.7**
9.0	0.12	0.6	0.06	**7.5**	8.3	1.88	20.78	3.11	45.8	**4.4**	37.7	12.3	**8.1**
7.1	0.95	3.2	-0.03	**4.9**	0.5	0.93	8.81	3.64	65.7	**6.1**	58.2	6.4	**5.2**
8.6	0.15	1.0	0.10	**5.0**	1.9	0.84	7.86	4.16	64.3	**1.5**	24.8	26.9	**6.8**
10.0	na	0.0	na	**2.0**	0.2	0.28	4.57	0.78	45.1	**7.6**	74.1	0.0	**3.0**
4.1	3.43	19.9	0.18	**6.3**	0.9	0.94	7.43	5.28	72.8	**4.4**	12.9	5.9	**7.5**
9.5	0.03	0.1	0.01	**4.1**	0.4	0.61	3.99	3.62	73.7	**2.8**	41.6	23.4	**6.9**
5.3	0.98	7.0	0.04	**4.1**	0.6	0.93	8.63	4.42	78.6	**4.5**	16.3	5.3	**6.4**
6.2	5.43	12.5	0.65	**3.9**	0.3	1.20	6.16	3.74	71.8	**3.1**	21.2	13.9	**6.5**
6.3	0.92	5.5	0.06	**3.6**	3.2	0.54	4.57	3.73	79.3	**4.5**	6.9	4.3	**7.1**
6.0	4.89	15.3	-0.05	**0.3**	-0.3	-0.49	-3.48	3.91	116.8	**4.5**	31.4	9.8	**4.2**
6.6	1.27	6.1	0.24	**9.7**	4.9	1.78	14.39	3.63	40.9	**5.8**	41.2	5.4	**8.7**
4.6	3.78	14.8	0.06	**0.8**	-0.1	-0.30	-3.13	3.61	108.0	**6.4**	61.9	5.6	**3.7**
10.0	0.31	1.2	0.00	**3.1**	0.8	0.45	2.65	2.51	79.8	**3.1**	38.5	19.1	**7.8**
4.3	2.02	8.0	1.87	**10.0**	50.4	8.90	96.55	12.41	2.9	**7.4**	57.9	0.0	**7.0**
6.4	1.93	8.6	0.13	**3.0**	0.9	0.46	2.95	3.34	80.2	**1.7**	20.7	23.0	**7.1**
4.9	1.44	9.4	-0.04	**10.0**	9.4	2.43	17.82	5.11	57.5	**0.9**	5.5	31.2	**9.4**
9.3	0.05	0.2	0.06	**3.2**	0.7	0.63	6.56	2.83	76.4	**3.1**	48.2	24.6	**5.1**
4.8	1.03	7.2	-0.12	**6.2**	2.5	1.09	10.51	4.52	63.0	**1.1**	24.2	33.9	**6.2**
5.7	0.76	5.1	0.11	**8.0**	84.4	1.34	10.94	4.97	79.5	**1.6**	9.4	21.7	**9.5**
6.8	2.63	7.0	0.33	**2.1**	0.2	0.23	2.42	2.83	89.2	**6.3**	61.7	6.4	**4.5**
5.2	1.57	8.5	0.19	**6.1**	6.9	1.18	14.03	3.44	54.7	**1.9**	26.1	23.0	**6.6**
7.8	0.21	1.5	0.00	**6.6**	9.1	1.52	15.74	3.85	57.4	**0.8**	4.7	31.8	**7.8**
0.3	7.12	53.3	-0.19	**6.2**	3.4	1.64	23.05	4.19	74.7	**2.9**	14.2	14.3	**1.9**
4.6	3.00	12.6	0.35	**3.2**	0.5	0.49	4.23	3.25	76.2	**2.3**	32.7	23.5	**5.8**
3.8	1.67	10.9	0.15	**4.0**	3.0	0.89	7.89	4.00	74.1	**1.3**	18.2	28.1	**5.6**
7.1	0.60	3.5	0.00	**6.2**	1.7	1.56	14.79	3.76	57.0	**2.0**	18.2	19.1	**6.2**
3.9	1.39	10.4	0.08	**4.5**	1.2	0.77	6.36	4.92	68.6	**0.7**	16.9	47.8	**6.9**
8.2	0.27	1.1	0.00	**4.0**	0.4	0.75	5.67	3.38	71.2	**5.5**	35.2	4.4	**7.2**
5.5	0.65	4.7	0.18	**9.8**	3.7	1.65	15.18	5.81	54.4	**0.8**	11.3	34.6	**6.6**
5.0	0.93	7.0	0.12	**6.1**	3.5	1.03	11.04	3.79	63.9	**1.8**	13.8	19.9	**6.2**
7.4	0.36	2.4	0.16	**6.4**	4.9	1.56	18.28	4.19	67.9	**3.5**	10.0	11.0	**6.0**
6.3	0.11	0.6	-0.10	**2.9**	0.4	0.56	6.04	3.85	82.0	**2.5**	34.1	20.9	**4.1**
2.9	2.84	12.6	0.71	**0.0**	-0.7	-1.16	-12.60	3.56	131.8	**1.6**	36.6	60.0	**4.1**
2.9	1.10	8.4	-0.01	**6.4**	3.6	0.94	8.47	4.76	66.6	**0.9**	13.4	32.8	**6.6**
2.3	2.92	20.0	0.00	**6.1**	1.9	1.44	14.79	4.48	68.0	**3.7**	18.0	10.9	**6.8**
6.6	1.51	6.5	0.33	**1.9**	0.1	0.16	1.47	2.71	90.6	**5.1**	32.8	6.1	**4.8**
5.7	1.11	5.3	0.02	**4.2**	0.3	0.68	6.38	3.69	74.4	**4.8**	43.7	11.7	**5.4**
3.8	1.91	12.1	0.39	**5.8**	4.1	1.03	10.49	4.29	64.2	**4.7**	18.2	4.7	**5.0**
9.2	0.00	0.0	0.26	**4.1**	0.8	1.08	7.71	4.45	77.5	**2.8**	67.1	80.3	**6.2**
0.0	10.90	110.9	0.19	**3.4**	0.8	1.05	22.11	3.74	100.1	**2.6**	17.1	16.3	**1.1**
3.2	1.91	11.8	0.27	**5.7**	2555.0	1.10	9.29	3.14	64.2	**5.7**	26.2	2.8	**9.2**
4.4	1.41	9.4	0.30	**4.9**	2.2	0.92	9.10	4.21	70.8	**3.3**	24.8	13.4	**5.0**
8.2	0.00	0.0	0.00	**10.0**	1.9	2.52	12.88	4.69	23.0	**4.3**	73.6	20.1	**9.3**

Name	City	State	Rating	2013 Rating	2012 Rating	Total Assets ($Mil)	One Year Asset Growth	Asset Mix (As a % of Total Assets) Comm-ercial Loans	Cons-umer Loans	Mort-gage Loans	Secur-ities	Capital-ization Index	Lever-age Ratio	Risk-Based Capital Ratio
POINTBANK	Pilot Point	TX	**B-**	B-	B-	436.6	18.44	4.7	1.3	5.2	33.8	**7.2**	9.1	18.6
POINTS WEST COMMUNITY BANK	Sidney	NE	**B+**	B+	B	370.5	11.07	3.6	2.5	7.2	42.6	**7.3**	9.2	19.7
POINTS WEST COMMUNITY BANK	Julesburg	CO	**B+**	B+	B	218.3	6.70	5.9	0.9	10.4	34.4	**7.1**	9.1	15.9
POINTWEST BANK	West	TX	**C**	C+	B-	98.7	-5.99	0.8	8.2	12.7	44.4	**5.7**	7.7	20.9
POLONIA BANK	Huntingdon Valley	PA	**C-**	C-	C-	298.4	4.66	0.1	0.9	65.6	20.0	**10.0**	11.5	22.5
PONCE DE LEON FEDERAL BANK	Bronx	NY	**C-**	D	C	707.9	-4.03	2.3	0.1	40.5	14.4	**10.0**	13.4	20.1
PONY EXPRESS BANK	Liberty	MO	**B**	B	B	142.5	7.08	18.0	1.9	19.9	8.2	**10.0**	11.6	16.2
PONY EXPRESS COMMUNITY BANK	Saint Joseph	MO	**C+**	C+	C	91.1	-2.66	4.4	3.9	13.6	40.6	**7.7**	9.4	15.7
▲ POPLAR GROVE STATE BK	Poplar Grove	IL	**A**	A-	A-	92.8	20.42	6.0	1.0	9.0	50.9	**10.0**	22.7	44.8
PORT AUSTIN STATE BK	Port Austin	MI	**B+**	B+	B+	50.0	9.24	3.5	5.1	38.9	13.0	**10.0**	17.0	30.1
PORT BYRON STATE BK	Port Byron	IL	**D-**	D-	D-	75.4	-8.31	4.7	2.2	7.8	34.0	**6.9**	8.9	16.6
PORT RICHMOND SAVINGS	Philadelphia	PA	**B**	B	B	68.3	0.80	0.0	0.0	73.7	0.0	**10.0**	17.2	29.6
PORT WASHINGTON STATE BK	Port Washington	WI	**C-**	C-	D+	465.1	2.72	10.3	2.3	16.8	28.7	**6.3**	8.3	13.4
PORTAGE COMMUNITY BANK	Ravenna	OH	**B-**	C+	C	278.5	1.45	6.6	1.0	26.4	18.0	**8.7**	10.1	15.2
PORTAGE COUNTY BANK	Almond	WI	**B-**	C+	B-	95.0	0.34	8.8	0.9	18.1	14.7	**10.0**	12.3	18.0
POST OAK BANK NA	Houston	TX	**B+**	B+	B	849.4	16.12	16.1	1.0	15.5	1.7	**7.3**	9.7	12.7
POTTER STATE BK OF POTTER	Potter	NE	**B-**	B-	B	36.3	-1.55	10.8	3.7	0.8	28.4	**10.0**	12.1	19.3
▲ POWELL STATE BK	Powell	TX	**C-**	D+	C-	29.0	-0.24	10.4	17.4	7.2	34.6	**10.0**	11.2	19.1
▲ POWELL VALLEY NATIONAL BK	Jonesville	VA	**A-**	B+	B+	256.3	5.56	3.0	4.8	25.4	26.1	**10.0**	16.0	26.2
PRAIRIE BANK OF KANSAS	Stafford	KS	**C-**	C	C-	107.8	-2.02	10.2	2.0	6.4	37.3	**6.4**	8.4	14.4
PRAIRIE COMMUNITY BANK	Marengo	IL	**D-**	E+	E	105.4	-6.22	9.3	1.5	27.4	7.4	**5.4**	7.4	12.5
PRAIRIE MOUNTAIN BANK	Great Falls	MT	**B-**	C+	C-	75.6	2.49	13.8	3.9	6.6	4.0	**9.4**	10.6	15.2
PRAIRIE NATIONAL BK	Stewardson	IL	**C+**	C+	C+	52.9	-3.50	10.7	2.9	15.4	30.3	**8.4**	9.9	16.6
PRAIRIE STATE BK & TRUST	Springfield	IL	**A-**	A-	A-	717.0	4.05	8.3	1.0	18.3	19.6	**8.7**	10.2	14.6
PRAIRIE SUN BANK	Milan	MN	**D**	D-	D+	36.3	6.55	5.1	4.3	3.6	33.5	**5.3**	7.4	11.2
PREFERRED BANK	Rothville	MO	**B+**	A-	B	107.8	1.38	3.2	2.6	10.0	50.6	**6.0**	8.0	19.7
PREFERRED BANK	Casey	IL	**C-**	C-	D+	50.3	7.32	23.1	4.9	19.2	22.7	**8.4**	9.9	15.8
PREFERRED BANK	Houston	TX	**B**	B	B-	215.1	13.34	7.5	0.4	15.4	20.6	**10.0**	15.5	27.1
PREFERRED BANK	Los Angeles	CA	**B**	B-	C-	1996.3	17.34	22.8	0.0	5.6	8.6	**8.8**	11.6	14.0
▲ PREFERRED COMMUNITY BANK	Fort Myers	FL	**C**	C-	E+	89.4	11.79	2.4	0.1	40.6	12.3	**8.6**	10.1	16.5
PREMIER BANK	Dubuque	IA	**C+**	C-	C	260.9	8.98	16.2	1.2	11.5	21.8	**7.7**	9.4	13.4
PREMIER BANK	Rock Valley	IA	**B**	B-	B-	297.8	4.73	11.3	2.1	5.4	3.6	**8.4**	11.5	13.6
PREMIER BANK	Denver	CO	**E-**	E-	E-	44.8	1.75	1.6	0.2	0.5	23.6	**0.0**	2.5	6.7
PREMIER BANK	Maplewood	MN	**D**	D	D-	593.4	5.54	9.8	0.3	6.5	6.9	**8.7**	10.9	13.9
▼ PREMIER BANK	Omaha	NE	**B-**	B+	A	141.4	4.71	16.2	2.3	6.1	10.4	**7.8**	13.3	13.2
▲ PREMIER BANK & TRUST	North Canton	OH	**C+**	C	D+	268.0	19.46	16.7	2.1	21.4	4.3	**7.1**	9.8	12.6
PREMIER BANK INC	Huntington	WV	**C+**	C	C-	881.0	19.30	10.2	2.8	19.5	17.6	**8.3**	9.9	15.8
PREMIER BANK MINNESOTA	Hastings	MN	**C+**	C	D	174.8	0.79	9.7	0.1	4.9	13.8	**7.5**	9.4	13.0
PREMIER BANK OF JACKSONVILLE	Jacksonville	IL	**C-**	D+	C-	191.7	-8.32	5.9	6.8	10.9	45.9	**9.4**	10.6	21.4
PREMIER BANK OF THE SOUTH	Cullman	AL	**B**	B	B-	151.0	8.73	9.9	5.5	19.0	20.9	**8.0**	9.6	14.7
▲ PREMIER BANK ROCHESTER	Rochester	MN	**B-**	C+	D+	149.8	4.90	7.4	0.1	4.8	4.3	**7.0**	9.9	12.5
▼ PREMIER BUSINESS BANK	Los Angeles	CA	**C**	B-	C+	209.3	31.59	10.5	0.0	15.7	0.0	**9.9**	11.5	14.9
PREMIER COMMERCIAL BANK	Greensboro	NC	**C-**	C-	D	171.6	8.32	7.5	0.8	9.8	28.4	**7.6**	9.4	15.8
PREMIER COMMUNITY BANK	Marion	WI	**C+**	C+	B-	261.3	0.01	4.0	1.2	15.8	23.3	**8.6**	10.0	15.6
PREMIER COMMUNITY BANK	Hillsboro	OR	**C-**	C-	D+	343.0	1.21	21.9	0.3	4.4	11.6	**9.5**	11.1	14.6
PREMIER VALLEY BANK	Fresno	CA	**C**	C-	C	618.6	8.92	8.7	0.4	6.9	34.6	**7.2**	9.1	14.4
PREMIERBANK	Fort Atkinson	WI	**B**	B	B	291.5	0.71	9.8	1.4	12.6	26.6	**10.0**	12.5	19.4
▲ PRESCOTT STATE BK	Prescott	KS	**C+**	C	C	15.0	-4.27	9.0	3.0	13.0	28.7	**10.0**	11.6	22.9
PRESIDENTIAL BANK FSB	Bethesda	MD	**D+**	D+	C-	522.6	-9.23	2.4	0.4	36.3	10.1	**8.0**	9.7	19.8
PRESIDIO BANK	San Francisco	CA	**B-**	B-	C+	510.3	20.50	19.7	3.0	1.4	2.2	**8.1**	9.7	13.5
PRESTON NATIONAL BK	Dallas	TX	**A-**	A-	A-	61.9	14.17	14.9	2.8	29.4	0.0	**10.0**	14.1	18.3
▲ PRESTON STATE BANK	Dallas	TX	**A-**	B-	C	121.6	0.50	21.3	1.4	15.1	2.8	**10.0**	19.4	24.1
PRIME ALLIANCE BANK	Woods Cross	UT	**B**	B-	C+	163.3	19.39	23.3	0.2	1.5	10.7	**10.0**	13.9	16.0
PRIME BANK	Edmond	OK	**A-**	B+	B+	214.4	10.79	16.0	0.7	22.7	0.0	**6.1**	9.5	11.9
PRIME BANK	Orange	CT	**C**	C	C+	78.7	12.68	20.6	7.0	1.6	47.9	**10.0**	11.1	21.4
PRIME MERIDIAN BANK	Tallahassee	FL	**C**	B-	C	204.4	7.39	13.6	1.2	14.1	21.2	**7.1**	9.1	13.8
▲ PRIME PACIFIC BANK NA	Lynnwood	WA	**D+**	D-	E-	128.3	2.10	5.7	0.6	11.3	4.0	**7.2**	9.1	13.9
PRIME SECURITY BANK	Karlstad	MN	**D-**	E+	E-	62.0	5.33	3.2	1.0	13.0	1.7	**6.2**	8.2	12.1
PRIMEBANK	Le Mars	IA	**B**	C+	C	331.0	4.03	10.1	1.3	14.1	22.7	**10.0**	11.5	17.7
PRIMESOUTH BANK	Tallassee	AL	**B-**	C+	C+	188.2	4.73	6.9	2.8	20.5	13.8	**8.7**	10.1	14.9

Asset Quality Index	Adjusted Non-Performing Loans as a % of Total Loans	Adjusted Non-Performing Loans as a % of Capital	Net Charge-Offs / Avg Loans	Profitability Index	Net Income ($Mil)	Return on Assets (R.O.A.)	Return on Equity (R.O.E.)	Net Interest Spread	Overhead Efficiency Ratio	Liquidity Index	Liquidity Ratio	Hot Money Ratio	Stability Index
6.8	0.42	1.9	0.01	**4.6**	3.4	1.12	11.92	4.09	74.6	**4.4**	29.1	8.9	**5.5**
7.6	0.50	2.3	0.03	**5.2**	3.5	1.28	13.32	3.32	61.2	**3.0**	26.5	15.4	**7.0**
4.8	1.89	11.1	0.06	**10.0**	4.0	2.52	25.64	4.53	45.3	**2.3**	30.2	20.5	**7.3**
7.4	0.61	2.0	0.16	**2.9**	0.4	0.47	7.11	2.78	85.8	**5.6**	49.9	8.4	**3.3**
6.9	1.32	7.9	0.03	**1.3**	0.2	0.09	0.80	2.88	95.4	**1.5**	25.1	27.6	**5.4**
1.6	6.89	36.8	0.41	**3.3**	2.0	0.37	3.01	4.41	79.1	**0.9**	18.8	35.6	**7.0**
4.7	1.16	7.6	0.11	**9.3**	2.3	2.19	15.65	4.79	56.1	**3.6**	13.9	11.0	**8.5**
5.1	0.91	4.3	1.33	**3.5**	0.3	0.48	4.99	3.73	72.8	**5.3**	43.3	9.1	**5.0**
8.0	2.32	3.1	0.01	**8.3**	1.3	2.14	9.46	4.28	44.8	**6.4**	73.6	8.2	**7.6**
7.8	0.66	2.6	0.06	**5.5**	0.5	1.23	7.20	3.35	62.6	**3.4**	32.7	15.4	**8.6**
0.3	10.97	57.0	-1.06	**0.3**	-0.1	-0.13	-1.41	3.02	118.5	**4.7**	31.2	8.2	**3.2**
4.5	2.72	14.1	0.63	**8.4**	0.9	1.82	10.97	4.97	53.1	**1.5**	1.4	21.0	**7.9**
2.9	2.66	17.0	0.31	**3.0**	1.5	0.42	5.27	3.05	74.8	**3.7**	13.7	10.3	**3.9**
4.0	2.03	13.4	0.16	**4.5**	1.8	0.87	8.74	3.58	65.8	**3.6**	19.1	11.6	**5.2**
5.4	1.68	8.9	0.00	**3.7**	0.5	0.74	6.20	4.21	78.0	**1.8**	28.4	25.8	**5.2**
6.2	0.24	1.9	0.13	**5.5**	5.7	0.95	9.54	4.22	59.4	**1.0**	15.7	32.0	**6.3**
6.4	2.04	7.7	0.00	**4.0**	0.2	0.79	6.78	4.29	74.9	**3.0**	42.2	20.7	**6.5**
2.7	4.02	17.8	1.00	**3.4**	0.1	0.60	5.71	4.43	77.9	**2.7**	36.9	21.6	**4.7**
6.5	1.21	4.2	0.10	**6.2**	2.3	1.25	7.47	4.36	60.8	**2.2**	33.3	25.8	**7.3**
3.5	2.51	14.5	1.62	**2.1**	0.2	0.25	2.93	3.62	83.0	**3.9**	37.4	14.8	**4.1**
0.3	12.02	79.8	1.21	**1.5**	0.3	0.33	4.47	3.53	80.8	**2.1**	22.1	19.1	**3.2**
4.8	0.80	4.6	-0.01	**6.2**	0.6	1.01	9.81	4.71	69.7	**3.4**	27.6	13.7	**6.3**
6.2	0.75	4.1	0.02	**3.9**	0.4	0.91	9.76	3.28	72.6	**4.3**	34.3	11.5	**4.9**
6.7	0.50	3.6	0.00	**8.1**	9.1	1.72	16.84	3.63	57.6	**3.4**	6.2	11.0	**8.0**
3.7	1.12	8.1	0.44	**3.8**	0.2	0.85	14.49	3.94	76.2	**3.6**	13.1	11.0	**2.8**
7.9	0.66	3.0	0.07	**5.3**	1.1	1.25	15.55	3.37	63.7	**6.0**	46.4	5.8	**6.4**
2.5	3.10	18.0	0.82	**3.2**	0.2	0.61	6.12	3.80	77.3	**4.3**	33.7	11.2	**3.9**
6.9	1.18	4.4	-0.04	**4.8**	1.2	0.86	4.90	4.43	71.9	**3.9**	43.7	16.3	**6.3**
5.3	0.72	4.4	-0.03	**7.4**	17.7	1.28	10.82	3.90	42.3	**0.8**	14.8	38.6	**6.9**
7.5	0.00	0.0	-0.02	**2.8**	0.3	0.45	3.71	3.96	84.8	**0.7**	13.6	38.8	**5.0**
8.2	0.20	1.4	0.00	**4.0**	1.7	0.90	9.48	3.26	70.0	**2.8**	9.3	14.7	**4.0**
4.4	0.64	4.4	-0.01	**9.8**	5.9	2.70	23.38	4.34	34.4	**0.8**	9.8	33.2	**8.9**
0.3	9.75	97.4	0.59	**0.0**	-0.7	-2.17	-80.50	3.13	155.0	**4.8**	48.6	12.3	**0.1**
1.1	3.11	20.4	0.14	**8.1**	9.2	2.18	21.12	4.01	40.0	**4.1**	14.6	8.0	**5.3**
6.7	0.08	0.4	0.41	**4.0**	0.6	0.56	4.11	4.02	76.8	**4.3**	22.9	7.4	**8.6**
5.5	0.56	4.5	-0.06	**4.1**	4.2	2.27	21.13	3.30	83.8	**1.5**	10.6	23.6	**4.0**
2.0	2.49	16.3	0.18	**7.6**	7.7	1.21	9.46	4.62	57.8	**2.5**	17.6	16.7	**7.6**
4.8	0.65	4.7	0.00	**5.5**	1.8	1.39	15.17	3.96	69.2	**4.3**	13.1	6.2	**3.6**
2.2	4.75	18.0	0.75	**4.3**	1.2	0.80	8.24	3.50	58.3	**2.0**	37.7	32.1	**4.0**
5.1	0.83	5.4	0.22	**4.8**	1.1	1.01	10.79	4.67	73.4	**1.8**	10.7	19.8	**4.9**
4.0	0.92	6.8	0.07	**6.5**	1.9	1.71	17.80	3.92	62.2	**4.4**	18.2	6.6	**4.1**
6.8	0.00	0.0	0.00	**2.6**	0.4	0.27	2.33	3.32	86.0	**0.9**	23.9	43.7	**6.6**
6.5	0.48	2.8	0.13	**2.0**	0.2	0.12	1.15	2.79	94.9	**1.4**	28.3	32.6	**5.4**
5.3	1.25	7.0	-0.01	**3.5**	1.2	0.58	5.76	3.70	81.9	**4.3**	32.3	10.8	**5.8**
2.1	2.19	12.9	-0.02	**3.5**	1.2	0.46	3.93	3.67	80.5	**3.3**	19.4	13.0	**5.4**
2.6	2.89	17.4	-0.05	**6.7**	5.5	1.24	10.81	3.75	58.1	**5.8**	40.9	5.0	**7.8**
3.3	3.98	17.0	0.10	**4.9**	1.7	0.75	5.15	3.56	70.9	**4.3**	22.1	7.4	**7.2**
8.9	0.30	1.2	-0.26	**2.8**	0.1	0.51	4.53	3.00	91.9	**1.8**	35.8	28.1	**4.5**
1.7	5.98	38.7	0.01	**2.0**	0.7	0.17	1.90	3.04	96.1	**4.4**	23.4	7.4	**4.2**
4.1	0.86	6.7	0.00	**4.2**	2.4	0.68	7.08	3.98	70.7	**3.6**	22.2	11.5	**5.7**
7.1	0.24	1.5	0.12	**8.2**	0.9	1.94	13.45	5.90	69.1	**1.6**	4.2	20.1	**8.9**
7.2	0.00	0.0	-0.73	**5.4**	1.1	1.29	6.42	4.50	81.9	**3.8**	18.1	10.3	**6.1**
4.0	2.55	14.7	0.36	**9.9**	3.1	2.78	20.10	5.36	47.3	**0.6**	16.8	59.2	**5.2**
7.3	0.00	0.0	0.00	**9.8**	4.0	2.55	26.82	4.45	42.6	**1.5**	7.6	22.6	**7.6**
2.6	6.92	25.5	0.05	**2.5**	0.3	0.48	4.58	3.01	83.0	**2.0**	32.5	26.8	**6.2**
8.7	0.06	0.4	0.51	**2.8**	0.5	0.33	3.75	3.59	73.8	**4.7**	24.7	5.4	**5.0**
1.5	1.99	14.5	0.51	**7.1**	1.7	1.78	18.24	4.45	66.8	**0.8**	19.7	48.1	**4.0**
4.4	1.89	13.3	-0.03	**0.7**	-0.1	-0.22	-3.09	4.04	113.4	**4.5**	21.6	6.4	**2.1**
4.4	2.02	11.5	0.44	**5.3**	3.4	1.37	11.71	3.46	58.8	**3.6**	25.9	12.2	**5.9**
5.0	1.13	7.0	0.63	**4.4**	1.1	0.78	7.71	4.19	57.3	**1.4**	7.9	24.0	**5.0**

Name	City	State	Rating	2013 Rating	2012 Rating	Total Assets ($Mil)	One Year Asset Growth	Asset Mix (As a % of Total Assets) Commercial Loans	Consumer Loans	Mortgage Loans	Securities	Capitalization Index	Leverage Ratio	Risk-Based Capital Ratio
▲ PRIMESOUTH BANK	Blackshear	GA	**D**	E	E-	331.4	1.81	5.3	2.9	18.9	15.6	**5.8**	7.8	13.8
PRINCEVILLE STATE BK	Princeville	IL	**C+**	C	C	76.9	10.51	15.5	6.7	3.6	50.6	**6.8**	8.8	16.7
PRINCIPAL BANK	Des Moines	IA	**B**	B-	C-	2152.5	0.84	0.0	1.3	16.7	69.1	**7.1**	9.0	20.0
▼ PRINSBANK	Prinsburg	MN	**C**	C-	C	122.3	0.47	4.2	0.5	3.9	1.7	**8.7**	10.7	13.9
PRIORITY BANK	Ozark	AR	**B**	B	B-	82.4	-7.93	0.0	0.3	83.5	0.0	**8.7**	10.1	21.0
PRIORITYONE BANK	Magee	MS	**B-**	C	C	554.4	4.22	6.0	5.2	17.6	20.0	**10.0**	11.1	15.6
PRIVATE BANK OF BUCKHEAD	Atlanta	GA	**D+**	D	D-	231.3	12.41	8.0	0.6	13.9	12.4	**9.2**	10.7	14.4
PRIVATE TRUST CO NA	Cleveland	OH	**U**	U	U	18.6	8.89	0.0	0.0	0.0	80.5	**10.0**	91.3	237.4
PRIVATEBANK & TRUST CO	Chicago	IL	**B+**	B	C	15159.7	9.56	38.3	1.0	3.1	17.2	**6.9**	10.8	12.4
PROAMÉRICA BANK	Los Angeles	CA	**B-**	B-	C-	161.4	9.35	9.7	0.0	1.9	0.0	**10.0**	16.5	20.1
PROBANK	Tallahassee	FL	**E-**	E-	E	48.9	-22.16	2.7	1.4	5.2	25.7	**4.0**	6.0	10.8
PRODUCE STATE BK	Hollandale	MN	**B-**	B	B-	60.1	44.31	12.6	4.0	8.0	9.0	**6.4**	8.4	17.2
PROFESSIONAL BANK	Coral Gables	FL	**C**	C	C-	251.3	23.28	9.7	0.1	29.1	20.8	**6.4**	8.4	13.1
▼ PROFICIO BANK	Cottonwood Heights	UT	**C+**	B	D+	179.5	-4.11	25.8	0.0	23.9	11.2	**9.5**	10.7	15.2
PROFILE BANK	Rochester	NH	**C+**	C+	C+	183.7	0.93	1.5	0.4	40.8	13.4	**10.0**	12.7	19.1
PROFINIUM INC	Truman	MN	**C-**	C-	C-	313.9	-2.05	8.2	1.8	6.9	23.0	**7.1**	9.1	13.5
PROGRESS BANK & TRUST	Huntsville	AL	**C+**	C+	C+	570.4	8.94	13.1	1.6	8.4	18.1	**5.9**	10.0	11.7
PROGRESSIVE BANK	Monroe	LA	**B**	B	B	467.5	-1.84	13.2	0.7	16.3	7.9	**10.0**	12.3	15.7
PROGRESSIVE BANK NA	Wheeling	WV	**C+**	C+	B-	332.9	-5.46	1.7	0.9	7.4	59.1	**8.1**	9.7	21.9
PROGRESSIVE NB DESOTO PARISH	Mansfield	LA	**C**	C	C	38.4	7.37	2.6	3.9	15.7	23.2	**6.9**	8.9	17.2
PROGRESSIVE OZARK BANK	Salem	MO	**A-**	B+	B-	113.2	-3.17	1.2	7.3	51.2	9.3	**8.9**	10.3	18.1
▲ PROGRESSIVE SB	Jamestown	TN	**C**	C-	D+	251.4	-3.69	1.4	3.6	30.6	13.4	**7.0**	9.0	12.8
PROGRESSIVE-HOME FS&LA	Pittsburgh	PA	**C**	C	C	52.8	1.54	0.0	0.3	48.6	35.9	**10.0**	11.6	26.1
▼ PROGROWTH BANK	Nicollet	MN	**C-**	C-	C-	139.6	12.50	4.6	1.4	10.9	27.6	**6.2**	8.2	14.6
PROSPECT FSB	Worth	IL	**D**	D	C-	248.5	-5.56	0.0	0.0	12.2	52.9	**10.0**	13.3	42.4
PROSPER BANK	Prosper	TX	**C+**	C+	C	78.4	9.17	12.1	0.4	8.3	39.8	**7.5**	9.4	16.1
PROSPERITY BANK	El Campo	TX	**B+**	B+	B+	21112.2	31.55	8.2	0.8	11.5	41.8	**5.3**	7.3	13.7
PROVIDENCE BANK	Columbia	MO	**C-**	D+	C	679.9	1.68	13.8	0.2	9.7	22.8	**10.0**	11.5	18.9
PROVIDENCE BANK	Rocky Mount	NC	**B-**	C	C-	242.6	13.68	6.1	0.3	11.3	0.8	**8.4**	9.9	15.1
PROVIDENCE BANK	Alpharetta	GA	**E-**	E-	E-	117.2	2.14	1.0	0.8	5.6	3.5	**1.5**	6.4	8.5
PROVIDENCE BANK & TRUST	South Holland	IL	**B-**	B-	B-	495.4	12.17	12.3	0.1	9.3	22.0	**6.8**	8.9	12.3
▼ PROVIDENCE BANK OF TEXAS	Southlake	TX	**C-**	C	C+	106.2	-5.32	3.4	0.3	17.8	0.0	**10.0**	14.0	20.6
PROVIDENT BANK	Amesbury	MA	**B-**	C+	B-	646.4	4.86	13.6	0.5	16.3	19.6	**10.0**	11.3	15.7
PROVIDENT BANK	Iselin	NJ	**C**	C	C-	8418.8	14.67	6.4	0.7	18.7	18.8	**6.2**	8.2	12.0
PROVIDENT SAVINGS BANK FSB	Riverside	CA	**C**	C	C+	1106.8	-4.00	0.1	0.0	50.4	1.4	**9.3**	10.5	16.5
PROVIDENT STATE BK INC	Preston	MD	**C+**	C+	C	298.2	3.84	5.2	1.2	21.0	19.3	**6.5**	8.5	12.5
PROVINCIAL BANK	Lakeville	MN	**B-**	B-	B-	78.2	9.66	16.6	4.2	23.1	0.3	**8.2**	10.4	13.5
PRUDENTIAL BANK & TRUST FSB	Hartford	CT	**U**	U	B+	25.9	-51.56	0.0	0.0	0.0	86.3	**10.0**	50.2	144.4
PRUDENTIAL SAVINGS BANK	Philadelphia	PA	**C+**	C+	C	524.9	-13.60	0.4	0.1	52.4	26.1	**10.0**	18.0	41.6
PS BANK	Wyalusing	PA	**B-**	B-	C	300.1	11.55	7.7	1.1	25.8	26.3	**6.1**	8.1	13.5
PUEBLO BANK & TRUST CO	Pueblo	CO	**C**	C	C-	329.7	3.90	3.2	0.5	4.1	33.6	**10.0**	11.0	18.7
PUGET SOUND BANK	Bellevue	WA	**B**	B	B	382.1	17.62	31.5	1.0	2.4	10.3	**9.8**	12.3	14.8
PULASKI BANK	Creve Coeur	MO	**C**	C-	D	1379.3	8.19	15.5	0.3	27.0	4.4	**8.1**	9.7	13.5
PULASKI SB	Chicago	IL	**D**	C-	D+	44.4	-3.63	0.0	0.9	47.5	40.4	**10.0**	12.1	33.4
PUTNAM 1ST MERCANTILE BANK	Cookeville	TN	**B**	B	C+	101.3	4.44	20.6	2.6	18.2	17.0	**10.0**	12.5	17.0
PUTNAM BANK	Putnam	CT	**C**	C	D+	470.8	4.46	0.4	0.1	37.0	41.8	**6.7**	8.7	18.5
▲ PUTNAM COUNTY BANK	Hurricane	WV	**B+**	B	B-	627.2	-0.10	6.4	1.0	32.9	24.9	**10.0**	13.2	24.9
PUTNAM COUNTY NB OF CARMEL	Carmel	NY	**D**	D+	C	159.4	-1.81	3.2	0.3	18.4	10.8	**10.0**	20.8	44.5
PUTNAM COUNTY SB	Brewster	NY	**C**	C	C	988.2	2.92	3.6	0.1	16.6	39.8	**10.0**	11.8	23.0
PUTNAM COUNTY STATE BK	Unionville	MO	**B+**	B	B-	160.9	3.43	11.8	3.6	8.6	2.4	**10.0**	11.9	15.0
PYRAMAX BANK FSB	Greenfield	WI	**D+**	D+	D	420.8	-2.58	3.5	0.4	29.7	15.8	**6.3**	8.3	12.2
QNB BANK	Quakertown	PA	**C+**	C	C-	987.9	5.78	12.3	0.4	11.0	36.0	**6.1**	8.1	13.2
QUAD CITY BANK & TRUST CO	Bettendorf	IA	**B-**	B-	B-	1293.9	2.51	10.8	0.5	7.3	31.1	**5.2**	7.2	11.4
▼ QUAIL CREEK BANK NA	Oklahoma City	OK	**C**	C+	C+	560.9	5.52	4.7	1.4	11.9	14.8	**7.4**	9.3	13.7
QUAINT OAK BANK	Southampton	PA	**B**	B	B	147.2	22.79	0.3	0.0	43.7	1.2	**10.0**	11.1	17.2
▼ QUALITY BANK	Page	ND	**D+**	D+	C	26.6	6.70	7.0	4.5	1.7	8.5	**6.1**	9.8	11.8
▲ QUANTUM NATIONAL BK	Suwanee	GA	**D+**	D+	D	331.2	-1.29	16.3	0.1	11.4	1.8	**9.6**	11.2	14.7
QUARRY CITY S&LA	Warrensburg	MO	**B-**	B-	C+	46.8	6.88	1.3	1.7	42.7	0.0	**10.0**	16.9	25.9
QUEENSBOROUGH NATIONAL BK & TR	Louisville	GA	**D+**	D	D+	807.9	-2.97	5.1	1.5	12.3	23.9	**9.0**	10.3	16.3
QUEENSTOWN BANK OF MARYLAND	Queenstown	MD	**D+**	D+	D+	443.7	-1.58	3.2	2.0	35.7	2.3	**9.4**	10.6	15.2

Asset Quality Index	Adjusted Non-Performing Loans as a % of Total Loans	Adjusted Non-Performing Loans as a % of Capital	Net Charge-Offs / Avg Loans	Profitability Index	Net Income ($Mil)	Return on Assets (R.O.A.)	Return on Equity (R.O.E.)	Net Interest Spread	Overhead Efficiency Ratio	Liquidity Index	Liquidity Ratio	Hot Money Ratio	Stability Index
2.0	4.45	28.1	0.79	**6.3**	4.4	1.74	24.70	4.88	63.0	**1.7**	21.8	23.5	**3.0**
6.0	0.86	3.7	-0.01	**3.9**	0.4	0.82	8.62	3.73	75.6	**3.6**	36.0	15.8	**3.8**
6.0	4.86	12.8	1.02	**5.3**	15.4	0.95	10.80	2.53	34.0	**6.0**	80.0	13.5	**6.5**
2.6	2.36	14.0	0.16	**10.0**	4.0	4.39	39.66	4.58	46.6	**2.9**	24.3	15.3	**7.4**
4.6	2.35	17.1	0.15	**6.5**	1.0	1.52	15.36	4.42	77.0	**1.5**	11.5	24.0	**7.3**
3.5	3.46	19.9	0.29	**7.2**	6.9	1.67	14.79	4.18	64.0	**2.7**	16.8	15.9	**7.8**
1.7	2.44	16.8	0.01	**4.4**	1.5	0.93	9.44	4.74	85.2	**3.7**	15.6	10.5	**5.2**
6.8	na	0.0	na	**10.0**	1.3	9.62	10.50	0.37	65.3	**4.0**	1093.9	101.0	**6.0**
5.6	0.75	5.0	0.03	**7.1**	132.8	1.24	10.90	3.43	49.1	**2.3**	21.3	19.1	**7.9**
7.0	0.29	1.3	0.52	**3.4**	0.4	0.39	2.14	4.24	86.6	**1.0**	27.2	48.0	**5.9**
0.0	12.63	105.6	0.51	**0.0**	-0.3	-0.65	-13.30	3.62	116.6	**1.2**	24.2	31.6	**0.0**
4.6	1.82	8.9	0.51	**4.4**	0.5	1.01	11.57	2.71	66.1	**6.1**	52.6	5.3	**5.3**
7.7	0.15	1.2	0.00	**2.3**	0.8	0.47	5.79	3.31	89.5	**1.9**	29.1	24.9	**4.0**
4.7	1.74	10.3	0.46	**1.6**	-5.6	-4.29	-32.35	3.45	115.0	**0.2**	11.0	98.2	**4.5**
8.2	0.75	3.7	0.03	**2.2**	0.3	0.23	1.82	3.40	92.0	**3.9**	30.7	12.2	**7.1**
2.3	2.59	17.6	0.14	**4.1**	1.5	0.63	6.34	3.54	71.3	**3.7**	7.7	9.9	**4.9**
7.5	0.21	1.4	0.18	**2.8**	2.0	0.49	4.98	3.13	81.7	**1.0**	8.5	29.6	**5.5**
8.6	0.06	0.4	0.02	**4.1**	2.3	0.66	5.45	4.08	79.7	**3.8**	12.3	9.9	**6.6**
7.2	1.33	3.8	0.08	**3.0**	1.8	0.71	7.22	3.01	85.9	**5.9**	52.2	7.9	**6.0**
8.6	0.20	1.0	0.04	**3.9**	0.2	0.60	6.78	4.00	82.4	**2.2**	31.7	23.5	**4.1**
6.3	0.54	3.8	0.04	**9.6**	2.0	2.22	21.99	4.38	62.8	**4.5**	13.6	5.4	**8.0**
2.7	2.71	18.8	0.24	**3.1**	0.9	0.45	5.03	4.04	90.7	**1.6**	17.1	23.4	**4.0**
7.5	1.52	7.2	0.03	**2.1**	0.1	0.26	1.98	2.96	87.5	**3.7**	46.6	17.6	**6.6**
5.0	1.76	10.1	0.17	**2.2**	0.1	0.06	0.74	3.60	94.2	**5.6**	41.2	6.3	**2.4**
6.4	7.99	11.4	0.36	**0.2**	-0.6	-0.30	-2.40	1.59	115.2	**4.6**	88.4	21.2	**4.6**
8.7	0.00	0.0	-0.06	**2.8**	0.2	0.36	3.83	4.35	89.3	**2.4**	41.6	29.2	**3.7**
6.4	0.48	3.0	0.02	**8.7**	225.2	1.47	9.69	3.80	40.4	**3.9**	22.8	11.8	**10.0**
5.9	1.35	6.8	0.69	**1.1**	-0.1	-0.03	-0.24	4.82	93.0	**1.7**	12.0	21.2	**4.8**
4.4	0.73	5.1	-0.01	**5.4**	1.6	0.92	8.97	3.46	56.5	**0.9**	20.3	41.4	**6.7**
1.7	5.31	40.5	-0.01	**1.5**	0.2	0.17	1.88	3.21	91.4	**1.1**	11.8	29.2	**0.7**
2.6	2.95	20.2	0.24	**6.7**	4.3	1.25	13.95	3.94	59.6	**3.4**	28.6	14.3	**5.0**
1.2	5.77	25.7	0.00	**3.8**	0.5	0.62	4.49	3.52	73.2	**1.3**	29.5	35.4	**6.3**
6.0	1.43	8.8	0.08	**3.9**	3.6	0.74	6.57	3.59	72.1	**1.9**	6.2	18.5	**7.3**
3.3	1.58	13.1	0.11	**4.8**	51.6	0.87	6.85	3.35	62.5	**4.4**	11.1	5.8	**8.4**
1.7	4.48	35.0	-0.03	**5.8**	6.2	0.74	6.02	2.90	82.4	**1.8**	8.8	19.9	**8.6**
4.5	1.21	9.1	0.67	**3.6**	1.4	0.62	7.96	3.80	72.7	**3.5**	24.3	12.3	**4.1**
4.9	0.57	4.1	0.02	**5.3**	0.6	1.09	10.14	4.28	82.0	**2.8**	10.7	14.4	**5.8**
8.6	na	0.0	na	**9.2**	2.5	8.75	22.02	3.10	28.0	**4.7**	183.0	100.0	**6.7**
6.7	2.07	7.1	0.07	**2.8**	1.7	0.44	2.49	2.65	82.1	**3.0**	42.4	21.5	**6.7**
5.1	1.11	7.5	-0.03	**5.5**	2.2	1.02	12.60	3.93	71.5	**3.9**	28.3	11.6	**3.5**
5.2	2.68	10.2	-0.02	**2.4**	0.9	0.39	3.69	3.51	90.5	**5.6**	36.3	4.4	**5.0**
7.3	0.24	1.5	0.07	**4.8**	2.3	0.87	6.62	4.16	63.8	**3.7**	13.0	10.0	**6.5**
2.5	3.03	23.7	0.33	**5.2**	9.1	0.94	9.02	3.57	64.6	**1.6**	8.2	21.1	**7.0**
6.7	2.45	9.8	0.00	**0.0**	-0.2	-0.60	-6.06	3.05	123.9	**4.0**	53.5	17.3	**3.8**
5.8	1.17	6.7	0.37	**4.4**	0.8	1.00	8.73	3.67	66.9	**0.7**	12.8	37.0	**5.6**
4.1	2.97	16.3	0.16	**2.4**	0.9	0.25	2.50	2.36	87.1	**2.4**	21.7	17.4	**4.8**
7.6	1.31	6.0	0.00	**5.1**	4.7	0.99	7.82	2.69	44.8	**1.2**	29.6	48.0	**7.5**
1.8	12.61	28.7	0.48	**0.0**	-3.0	-2.44	-10.69	2.70	166.8	**5.5**	46.0	8.5	**5.3**
4.3	4.26	18.1	0.23	**2.0**	1.4	0.18	1.62	2.49	87.0	**5.5**	46.8	9.1	**6.1**
5.4	0.38	2.6	0.03	**9.4**	1.8	1.51	13.36	3.97	34.2	**0.7**	10.4	40.9	**7.8**
2.9	2.19	17.1	-0.02	**0.0**	-3.3	-1.02	-11.65	2.85	127.6	**1.8**	23.7	22.5	**3.5**
4.0	2.14	13.5	0.14	**4.3**	5.9	0.85	10.70	3.10	68.0	**3.7**	20.1	10.9	**5.1**
4.7	2.09	15.4	0.14	**4.5**	8.5	0.87	12.68	3.19	61.2	**3.7**	15.4	11.0	**5.7**
2.1	2.44	17.2	0.01	**9.5**	9.1	2.18	23.10	4.30	50.1	**3.3**	29.2	14.8	**8.3**
5.0	1.95	14.2	0.15	**5.3**	0.9	0.89	7.69	4.38	68.1	**0.8**	12.6	34.6	**6.9**
5.7	0.13	0.9	-0.31	**6.2**	0.3	1.51	15.22	3.33	90.7	**1.4**	15.1	25.9	**3.0**
2.9	1.07	7.3	0.74	**6.6**	2.9	1.15	10.98	4.92	55.7	**0.8**	10.6	33.2	**4.9**
6.5	0.82	3.8	-0.24	**3.9**	0.2	0.53	3.04	4.07	80.5	**3.0**	16.2	14.0	**6.0**
1.6	5.33	29.9	0.41	**3.9**	4.0	0.64	6.38	3.92	74.7	**1.9**	19.7	20.2	**5.5**
1.9	3.54	25.2	0.59	**4.5**	2.8	0.83	7.96	3.93	55.4	**1.0**	10.7	31.1	**5.0**

Name	City	State	Rating	2013 Rating	2012 Rating	Total Assets ($Mil)	One Year Asset Growth	Asset Mix (As a % of Total Assets): Comm-ercial Loans	Cons-umer Loans	Mort-gage Loans	Secur-ities	Capital-ization Index	Lever-age Ratio	Risk-Based Capital Ratio
QUOIN FINANCIAL BANK	Miller	SD	B-	B-	C	147.5	4.14	10.6	3.0	2.4	19.9	10.0	11.4	15.0
QUONTIC BANK	Astoria	NY	B	B-	B-	135.1	1.61	0.7	0.2	57.0	0.1	10.0	11.2	21.2
▲ R BANK	Round Rock	TX	C+	D+	C	304.6	20.81	11.9	0.6	9.4	18.9	7.9	9.6	14.4
RABOBANK NA	Roseville	CA	C-	C-	C-	14662.0	6.20	4.4	0.1	9.2	20.0	8.7	10.2	14.6
RABUN COUNTY BANK	Clayton	GA	D+	D+	E	154.1	-9.75	0.9	2.5	34.4	3.1	8.2	9.8	18.0
RACCOON VALLEY BANK	Perry	IA	B-	B-	B-	225.2	2.35	10.3	1.6	2.8	29.5	4.5	7.6	10.7
RADIUS BANK	Boston	MA	C	C	D+	699.6	5.44	9.8	8.5	37.7	10.8	6.3	8.4	13.9
RAMSEY NATIONAL BK	Devils Lake	ND	A-	B+	B-	261.6	0.70	11.4	1.0	6.5	26.3	9.7	10.8	16.9
RANCHO SANTA FE THRIFT & LOAN	San Marcos	CA	A-	A-	A+	27.8	2.55	0.0	26.8	18.2	44.7	10.0	97.1	176.9
RANDALL STATE BK	Randall	MN	B	B	B-	35.0	0.89	4.3	2.2	19.9	14.9	10.0	13.7	22.4
▲ RANDOLPH SB	Stoughton	MA	D+	D-	C-	350.6	-8.23	0.6	0.3	43.0	23.9	8.0	9.7	17.7
RANGE BANK NA	Marquette	MI	B-	B-	B-	326.3	9.71	7.3	1.0	11.0	22.8	7.8	9.5	14.0
RARITAN STATE BK	Raritan	IL	B-	C+	C-	164.4	-1.85	5.2	5.1	22.6	32.3	8.1	9.7	16.7
RAWLINS NATIONAL BK	Rawlins	WY	D	D	D	158.1	1.96	8.1	1.5	4.0	24.4	7.4	9.3	19.7
▼ RAYMOND FEDERAL BANK	Raymond	WA	C-	C	C	52.9	1.37	0.0	1.1	72.7	10.2	9.9	11.0	24.1
RAYMOND JAMES BANK NA	Saint Petersburg	FL	B	B	B-	12547.9	19.35	51.9	6.7	13.9	2.9	7.0	10.7	12.5
RAYMOND JAMES TRUST NA	Saint Petersburg	FL	U	U	U	24.8	35.55	0.0	0.0	0.0	4.2	10.0	73.5	150.4
RAYNE BUILDING & LOAN ASSN	Rayne	LA	A-	A-	B+	66.4	2.57	1.0	0.9	25.1	55.0	10.0	19.4	63.2
RAYNE STATE BK & TRUST CO	Rayne	LA	A-	A-	B+	359.4	10.46	10.7	0.8	17.6	18.8	7.7	9.5	14.9
RBC BANK (GEORGIA) NA	Raleigh	NC	C-	D+	C-	3015.5	3.66	0.0	2.1	15.5	70.4	5.8	7.8	41.6
RCB BANK	Claremore	OK	B+	B+	B+	2360.8	15.21	5.6	5.6	9.2	36.2	5.4	7.4	13.0
▲ RCSBANK	New London	MO	C-	C-	C-	55.2	0.96	15.0	2.0	8.6	19.2	5.8	9.2	11.6
READING CO-OP BANK	Reading	MA	C+	B-	B-	448.4	16.94	3.0	1.4	53.7	16.1	6.4	8.4	13.8
READLYN SB	Readlyn	IA	A	A	A	71.3	6.39	8.3	1.3	15.9	36.9	10.0	11.7	17.9
RECONTRUST CO NA	Simi Valley	CA	U	U	U	358.8	-10.38	0.0	0.0	0.0	0.0	10.0	99.2	445.2
RED RIVER BANK	Alexandria	LA	B+	B+	B	1380.1	6.18	13.8	1.8	17.9	25.3	7.2	9.1	14.3
RED RIVER STATE BK	Halstad	MN	B	B-	B-	41.4	-7.45	40.8	27.2	3.2	0.0	10.0	13.4	15.5
▲ RED ROCK BANK	Sanborn	MN	C	C-	D-	19.9	-4.91	12.9	4.0	16.7	0.0	10.0	11.3	18.6
REDDING BANK OF COMMERCE	Redding	CA	C	C	C-	977.2	5.28	15.8	3.0	7.9	23.2	10.0	11.8	15.9
REDSTONE BANK	Centennial	CO	B+	B	C	80.5	11.55	17.5	0.3	13.8	0.9	10.0	12.3	17.1
REDWOOD CAPITAL BANK	Eureka	CA	B	B	B-	273.7	9.05	4.3	0.6	9.6	9.6	8.1	9.7	14.3
▲ REELFOOT BANK	Union City	TN	C+	C	C+	145.2	-1.66	10.9	5.8	17.1	34.0	9.2	10.4	18.0
REGAL BANK	Livingston	NJ	C+	C+	C+	344.9	10.25	1.0	0.1	1.6	6.7	5.5	9.1	11.3
REGAL BANK & TRUST	Owings Mills	MD	C-	D+	D	139.6	-6.40	1.5	0.3	19.1	18.5	8.3	9.9	15.4
REGAL FINANCIAL BANK	Seattle	WA	D	D	D	95.3	-6.94	31.4	3.5	0.8	6.7	10.0	11.5	15.8
REGENT BANK	Davie	FL	D-	D-	E+	352.0	-7.98	6.8	0.1	15.1	6.8	5.7	7.7	12.0
▲ REGENT BANK	Nowata	OK	C	D+	D	209.4	11.46	19.1	1.5	13.1	6.8	6.7	9.6	12.2
REGIONAL MISSOURI BANK	Marceline	MO	C+	C-	C-	191.7	16.66	6.8	2.1	19.2	18.6	4.9	8.2	11.0
REGIONS BANK	Birmingham	AL	C	C-	C	118289.8	1.91	18.7	4.8	12.6	20.3	9.5	10.7	14.6
RELIABANK DAKOTA	Estelline	SD	B+	B+	B	265.5	6.29	12.9	2.6	4.1	22.4	6.6	9.3	12.2
▲ RELIANCE BANK	Faribault	MN	B-	C+	B-	84.3	11.33	18.1	1.3	11.6	13.5	7.4	11.6	12.8
▲ RELIANCE BANK	Saint Louis	MO	C+	C-	E+	1110.5	10.02	5.4	0.1	5.8	26.0	9.4	10.6	14.6
RELIANCE BANK	Athens	AL	B-	C+	C	153.0	8.53	8.7	0.3	10.0	23.4	10.0	12.2	17.7
RELIANCE SB	Altoona	PA	C+	B-	B-	398.9	1.50	4.0	2.2	33.5	12.8	10.0	11.2	15.0
RELIANCE STATE BK	Story City	IA	A-	A-	A-	214.6	0.87	4.9	1.3	8.7	38.3	7.6	9.4	13.6
RELIANT BANK	Brentwood	TN	C+	C	D+	451.5	16.26	16.1	2.3	18.2	17.0	8.0	9.6	13.8
▲ RELIANZBANK	Wichita	KS	B-	C+	C+	51.6	0.30	20.4	1.1	12.5	1.9	9.2	10.4	15.9
RELYANCE BANK NA	Pine Bluff	AR	B+	B+	B	535.4	28.47	5.1	2.1	9.9	14.6	10.0	13.5	17.5
RENASANT BANK	Tupelo	MS	B-	B-	C+	5736.4	0.27	7.6	1.6	16.1	17.1	7.0	9.0	13.0
REPUBLIC BANK	Philadelphia	PA	C-	D+	D+	1126.3	19.95	9.4	0.1	5.2	20.2	8.0	10.0	13.4
▼ REPUBLIC BANK	Bountiful	UT	B+	B+	B	304.9	-39.60	15.5	1.9	0.0	1.2	8.9	11.0	14.0
REPUBLIC BANK & TRUST	Norman	OK	B+	B+	B+	450.8	6.23	14.2	1.6	16.2	18.8	7.5	9.6	13.0
REPUBLIC BANK & TRUST CO	Louisville	KY	A-	A-	A-	3620.7	12.78	3.5	0.8	37.9	13.8	10.0	12.7	18.6
REPUBLIC BANK INC	Duluth	MN	C	C-	D	328.8	6.33	21.1	1.5	12.0	2.8	7.5	10.1	12.9
REPUBLIC BANK OF CHICAGO	Oak Brook	IL	C-	C-	C-	1548.0	18.28	16.3	0.1	7.6	15.1	8.5	11.0	13.7
▼ REPUBLIC BANKING CO	Republic	OH	C+	B-	C+	42.8	4.25	4.7	5.9	40.8	8.2	10.0	14.1	21.2
▲ REPUBLICBANKAZ NA	Phoenix	AZ	C-	C-	B-	90.2	0.21	10.2	0.5	16.4	5.2	10.0	11.8	15.0
RESOURCE BANK	Covington	LA	B	B	B-	541.0	6.91	5.8	2.1	18.1	9.5	7.6	10.3	13.0
RESOURCE BANK NA	DeKalb	IL	C-	C-	C-	379.3	3.09	6.7	0.6	11.9	32.9	7.8	9.5	15.0
▲ RESURGENS BANK	Atlanta	GA	B+	B	B-	122.2	35.97	10.4	1.2	8.5	5.0	10.0	12.7	16.6

Asset Quality Index	Adjusted Non-Performing Loans as a % of Total Loans	Adjusted Non-Performing Loans as a % of Capital	Net Charge-Offs Avg Loans	Profitability Index	Net Income ($Mil)	Return on Assets (R.O.A.)	Return on Equity (R.O.E.)	Net Interest Spread	Overhead Efficiency Ratio	Liquidity Index	Liquidity Ratio	Hot Money Ratio	Stability Index
4.6	1.15	6.6	-0.04	**6.7**	1.4	1.29	11.76	4.33	57.6	**1.8**	21.2	21.9	**5.5**
6.6	0.33	2.4	-0.16	**4.9**	0.8	0.79	6.21	5.28	89.3	**0.6**	11.9	51.5	**5.2**
8.4	0.00	0.0	0.01	**3.5**	1.3	0.61	5.82	3.68	70.9	**2.1**	27.4	21.1	**4.3**
2.5	2.67	16.8	0.00	**3.1**	37.0	0.35	2.16	2.78	76.3	**3.8**	9.2	9.7	**7.8**
1.8	5.59	31.9	0.60	**2.8**	0.6	0.47	4.95	3.67	87.4	**3.9**	28.0	11.5	**3.2**
6.3	0.32	2.5	0.04	**4.6**	1.9	1.10	15.05	3.18	65.5	**3.3**	20.0	12.8	**4.4**
4.9	0.62	5.5	0.06	**2.9**	2.3	0.44	5.23	3.14	79.5	**1.5**	3.1	21.7	**4.2**
6.8	0.36	2.2	-0.09	**6.9**	3.3	1.66	15.71	3.48	56.7	**3.9**	15.3	9.4	**7.5**
7.5	0.54	0.3	-3.70	**6.2**	0.3	1.30	1.34	4.96	89.1	**5.0**	1331.5	100.0	**8.6**
4.2	3.88	18.0	-0.01	**8.3**	0.5	1.93	13.93	4.58	58.0	**3.4**	32.2	15.4	**8.3**
2.8	3.35	21.8	0.26	**1.4**	1.0	0.36	3.48	3.23	95.0	**4.2**	27.1	9.9	**3.4**
5.3	1.01	6.0	0.25	**4.0**	1.5	0.67	6.41	3.79	77.7	**4.8**	41.1	11.4	**5.6**
3.7	2.74	16.9	0.07	**5.7**	1.2	0.98	10.52	3.47	53.6	**3.4**	36.3	16.6	**4.4**
6.0	0.98	4.3	-0.04	**0.9**	0.0	0.00	-0.03	3.11	100.1	**4.1**	40.8	14.7	**3.3**
6.7	0.84	5.8	0.43	**2.3**	0.1	0.16	1.43	3.55	89.2	**1.6**	19.5	24.9	**4.5**
5.1	0.83	6.3	0.03	**8.5**	120.9	1.34	13.14	2.99	26.7	**4.8**	11.0	3.2	**9.0**
10.0	na	0.0	na	**9.5**	2.8	17.40	24.78	0.29	79.7	**4.0**	187.5	101.0	**7.0**
8.9	1.15	1.9	0.00	**5.2**	0.5	0.98	4.95	3.33	60.7	**3.0**	78.7	59.0	**8.0**
8.4	0.22	1.5	0.04	**7.0**	4.4	1.71	18.53	4.41	60.2	**4.2**	26.8	9.4	**7.5**
8.7	1.36	3.4	0.41	**2.2**	7.5	0.34	4.18	1.60	77.1	**7.5**	61.8	2.2	**6.4**
7.6	0.42	2.9	0.03	**5.3**	22.0	1.30	13.74	3.49	66.3	**3.2**	18.7	14.0	**8.7**
7.8	0.34	2.4	0.02	**2.3**	0.1	0.18	1.93	3.55	93.5	**4.7**	6.2	2.8	**3.0**
7.5	0.14	1.2	0.50	**3.1**	1.3	0.40	4.83	3.73	74.1	**2.5**	19.0	16.9	**4.1**
8.4	0.64	3.1	0.00	**6.8**	0.8	1.55	13.42	3.32	46.0	**3.3**	45.7	19.4	**8.5**
10.0	na	0.0	na	**0.7**	-4.8	-1.77	-1.80	0.10	117.3	**4.0**	8266.2	101.0	**5.2**
7.1	0.75	5.0	0.00	**4.7**	9.5	0.93	10.36	3.39	67.4	**2.9**	23.3	17.4	**7.9**
6.8	0.17	1.0	-0.69	**9.1**	0.7	2.19	16.80	4.52	52.4	**0.6**	8.3	37.2	**7.1**
2.7	4.27	24.0	0.37	**2.7**	0.1	0.30	2.47	3.70	75.5	**3.0**	30.0	15.1	**5.5**
2.5	4.47	22.7	1.35	**4.2**	6.1	0.83	7.06	3.77	64.6	**1.5**	25.4	28.2	**6.9**
8.7	0.00	0.0	0.02	**5.5**	0.9	1.60	12.90	5.35	74.4	**1.7**	22.9	24.1	**6.4**
4.8	0.67	4.6	0.12	**5.3**	1.9	0.96	9.80	4.10	63.3	**3.0**	20.1	14.6	**5.5**
4.4	2.71	13.1	-0.73	**3.9**	0.9	0.78	8.36	3.91	71.3	**3.5**	38.4	16.8	**3.6**
6.0	0.00	0.0	0.02	**3.7**	1.2	0.48	5.35	3.67	73.3	**0.9**	17.1	34.3	**5.3**
3.8	1.22	8.0	-0.11	**2.3**	0.3	0.28	3.10	3.79	92.7	**1.1**	15.6	30.7	**3.3**
0.3	10.75	64.6	-0.09	**1.8**	0.3	0.34	3.05	3.55	93.1	**0.6**	10.2	44.8	**3.0**
0.0	9.34	69.9	1.00	**2.1**	1.2	0.44	6.00	3.80	89.8	**1.6**	17.9	23.2	**2.4**
2.6	1.43	12.1	0.48	**3.7**	0.9	0.56	5.23	4.45	74.3	**0.6**	6.7	41.4	**5.3**
3.6	0.91	7.6	0.00	**6.6**	1.9	1.38	15.87	4.04	60.3	**1.8**	9.3	19.2	**7.0**
3.2	2.21	12.8	0.39	**6.0**	1015.8	1.16	8.40	3.30	61.5	**4.5**	16.4	6.2	**8.9**
7.1	0.48	3.3	0.11	**6.4**	2.9	1.47	15.78	4.09	62.6	**3.6**	19.3	11.4	**5.9**
5.3	1.45	8.4	0.06	**5.2**	0.9	1.46	13.15	4.08	61.8	**2.8**	27.8	16.9	**4.8**
6.3	0.01	0.0	0.01	**4.2**	41.3	5.22	46.01	2.78	74.6	**2.4**	24.3	20.2	**5.4**
7.2	0.79	4.0	-0.27	**3.3**	0.6	0.54	4.26	3.40	85.9	**2.4**	27.9	19.2	**5.2**
5.5	0.65	4.3	0.06	**3.5**	1.6	0.53	4.58	3.45	79.7	**2.7**	8.9	14.8	**6.5**
7.9	0.07	0.4	0.00	**5.8**	1.9	1.14	9.72	3.49	50.5	**5.2**	39.0	8.5	**8.0**
4.1	1.65	11.3	-0.12	**3.8**	2.9	0.52	5.14	4.05	87.4	**1.0**	14.8	31.8	**5.1**
4.8	1.27	8.3	0.54	**3.9**	0.3	0.81	7.97	3.82	75.7	**1.0**	25.9	46.2	**6.4**
5.3	1.48	7.9	0.14	**6.0**	3.5	0.97	6.99	4.38	70.8	**1.7**	9.2	19.8	**7.8**
3.9	1.29	9.6	0.28	**5.6**	46.0	1.05	8.11	4.17	66.7	**2.8**	9.4	14.7	**8.5**
2.2	3.35	20.7	0.12	**2.0**	2.3	0.30	3.22	3.76	91.4	**4.8**	17.7	4.1	**5.0**
5.1	1.44	9.2	0.24	**9.8**	9.7	3.39	25.39	4.02	20.3	**0.2**	7.8	90.2	**8.3**
5.1	0.99	6.7	-0.03	**7.6**	6.0	1.83	18.33	4.67	67.1	**3.3**	29.7	15.2	**7.6**
5.4	1.65	10.3	0.05	**5.8**	24.9	0.95	7.47	3.47	67.1	**4.2**	7.7	6.5	**9.5**
2.9	1.66	12.7	0.20	**5.9**	3.4	1.44	13.79	4.19	64.4	**1.4**	14.8	26.4	**6.4**
2.2	4.41	26.1	-0.69	**7.1**	20.9	1.94	17.79	3.77	64.3	**1.8**	21.9	26.5	**8.2**
2.2	5.61	31.6	0.21	**5.1**	0.3	0.99	7.12	4.04	55.7	**1.7**	8.7	19.8	**6.3**
3.9	1.05	6.0	2.25	**4.9**	0.5	0.80	6.74	5.13	39.1	**0.7**	13.1	39.8	**5.0**
4.6	0.54	3.9	0.02	**6.2**	4.2	1.05	10.16	4.87	65.4	**3.7**	12.1	10.2	**7.1**
2.5	3.74	21.8	-0.16	**3.3**	1.8	0.65	6.70	3.77	86.0	**3.9**	25.3	10.4	**5.4**
6.8	0.61	3.4	0.00	**5.0**	1.0	1.18	9.00	4.25	72.6	**1.8**	22.0	21.4	**7.1**

Name	City	State	Rating	2013 Rating	2012 Rating	Total Assets ($Mil)	One Year Asset Growth	Asset Mix (As a % of Total Assets) Commercial Loans	Consumer Loans	Mortgage Loans	Securities	Capitalization Index	Leverage Ratio	Risk-Based Capital Ratio
REUNION BANK OF FLORIDA	Tavares	FL	**C+**	C+	C	267.0	20.34	11.7	1.2	2.0	15.0	**6.3**	9.7	12.0
REVERE BANK	Laurel	MD	**B-**	C+	C-	597.0	26.87	8.0	0.1	21.4	6.3	**4.4**	8.6	10.7
REYNOLDS STATE BK	Reynolds	IL	**A+**	A+	A+	93.7	3.94	0.3	0.2	0.3	82.3	**10.0**	24.2	69.9
RHINEBECK BANK	Poughkeepsie	NY	**D**	D	D-	657.0	8.74	6.4	32.3	8.2	12.4	**4.5**	8.0	10.8
RICHARDSON COUNTY BANK & TRUST	Falls City	NE	**B-**	B-	B-	133.3	9.44	8.7	5.9	15.6	26.2	**5.5**	7.5	12.0
RICHLAND COUNTY BANK	Richland Center	WI	**B**	B	B+	101.3	-1.05	3.3	4.4	12.2	47.0	**10.0**	20.6	42.7
RICHLAND STATE BK	Bruce	SD	**A-**	A-	A-	42.8	5.64	2.2	4.8	3.3	48.1	**10.0**	23.7	56.8
RICHLAND STATE BK	Rayville	LA	**A-**	A-	A	289.0	8.36	13.1	2.3	11.2	36.1	**7.9**	9.6	17.0
RICHTON BANK & TRUST CO	Richton	MS	**B-**	B-	B-	63.6	0.47	5.9	4.1	17.0	30.0	**10.0**	14.9	23.8
RICHWOOD BANKING CO	Richwood	OH	**B-**	B-	B-	441.3	8.16	4.8	0.8	11.9	43.8	**6.4**	8.4	14.4
RIDDELL NATIONAL BK	Brazil	IN	**D+**	D+	D+	190.9	4.34	8.6	6.0	35.6	14.6	**6.8**	8.8	12.9
RIDGESTONE BANK	Brookfield	WI	**C-**	C-	D+	386.9	-1.68	25.6	0.0	1.1	7.7	**10.0**	13.1	17.0
RIDGEWOOD SB	Ridgewood	NY	**C**	C	C+	5072.5	0.92	0.1	0.1	34.8	42.4	**10.0**	12.5	25.9
RILEY STATE BK OF RILEY KANSAS	Riley	KS	**B**	B	B-	79.8	3.36	11.2	4.9	7.0	27.1	**7.8**	9.5	14.9
RIO BANK	McAllen	TX	**B-**	B-	C+	261.3	15.79	19.8	1.6	4.8	23.6	**6.7**	8.8	14.0
RIO GRANDE S&LA	Monte Vista	CO	**C+**	C+	C-	92.8	-1.72	1.0	2.3	60.9	11.4	**10.0**	11.4	22.6
RIPLEY FSB	Ripley	OH	**D+**	D+	D+	66.7	-3.46	0.4	0.8	42.6	1.1	**10.0**	11.0	17.9
RIVER BANK	Stoddard	WI	**B**	B-	C	434.5	0.13	7.0	0.8	12.6	12.1	**9.8**	11.1	14.9
RIVER BANK & TRUST	Prattville	AL	**B-**	B-	B-	431.2	3.43	10.5	3.0	11.7	32.2	**7.8**	9.6	15.8
▲ RIVER CITIES BANK	Wisconsin Rapids	WI	**A-**	B	B-	199.0	-1.48	12.1	0.3	11.6	16.3	**10.0**	13.2	19.9
RIVER CITY BANK	Rome	GA	**C-**	C-	D+	157.3	-2.77	6.7	1.3	13.9	24.9	**10.0**	11.3	18.3
RIVER CITY BANK	Sacramento	CA	**B+**	A-	B+	1245.3	4.35	6.1	0.1	11.7	33.9	**10.0**	11.5	18.0
RIVER CITY BANK INC	Louisville	KY	**A-**	A-	A-	273.4	-4.80	0.4	0.5	39.0	38.5	**10.0**	18.4	40.9
RIVER COMMUNITY BANK NA	Martinsville	VA	**C+**	C	D+	108.5	10.34	21.9	1.3	28.6	5.3	**6.9**	8.9	12.5
RIVER FALLS STATE BK	River Falls	WI	**B-**	B-	B-	80.5	-0.72	2.0	2.3	27.2	31.6	**10.0**	15.9	32.6
RIVER TOWN BANK	Dardanelle	AR	**D+**	D	D+	150.0	-7.35	3.5	2.4	25.2	28.1	**8.9**	10.3	19.0
RIVER VALLEY BANK	Wausau	WI	**C+**	C	C-	1006.5	-0.45	14.0	0.8	15.3	12.3	**7.4**	9.3	13.1
▼ RIVER VALLEY COMMUNITY BANK	Yuba City	CA	**B-**	B+	B+	197.5	33.39	5.7	0.4	3.5	31.6	**9.8**	10.9	17.5
RIVER VALLEY FINANCIAL BANK	Madison	IN	**C-**	C-	D+	504.3	3.72	2.4	0.8	23.4	27.3	**6.9**	8.9	14.4
RIVERBANK	Spokane	WA	**D**	D	E+	118.4	13.19	9.2	1.6	9.5	0.0	**10.0**	11.0	15.4
▼ RIVERBANK S&LA	Corning	AR	**C**	C	C+	45.6	-0.39	5.1	2.6	20.4	5.6	**10.0**	12.9	17.7
RIVERBEND BANK	Fort Worth	TX	**B+**	B+	B+	45.2	2.39	11.9	2.0	5.3	8.7	**10.0**	12.1	18.5
RIVERHILLS BANK	Milford	OH	**D**	D	D	129.6	1.99	5.0	14.2	10.4	19.5	**8.0**	10.3	13.3
RIVERHILLS BANK	Port Gibson	MS	**B-**	B-	B-	283.2	1.85	7.5	1.9	14.4	31.4	**8.0**	9.7	16.1
▲ RIVERLAND BANK	Jordan	MN	**D**	E	E-	44.3	11.23	17.7	2.2	11.8	7.7	**10.0**	11.1	15.2
RIVERSIDE BANK	Sparkman	AR	**B**	B	B	59.9	6.92	21.5	9.4	47.2	1.2	**6.9**	8.9	13.1
RIVERSIDE BANK	Poughkeepsie	NY	**B-**	B-	C	231.6	5.99	31.8	0.1	3.9	6.3	**9.0**	11.7	14.2
RIVERVIEW BANK	Marysville	PA	**C+**	C+	C	434.7	37.28	7.0	0.5	23.0	13.5	**5.8**	7.8	11.8
RIVERVIEW COMMUNITY BANK	Vancouver	WA	**D+**	D	D-	838.1	6.51	5.7	3.5	12.7	16.8	**10.0**	11.0	16.8
RIVERWOOD BANK	Bemidji	MN	**C**	C-	D	317.3	5.68	6.9	5.1	18.6	3.4	**7.4**	9.3	12.9
ROANOKE RAPIDS SB SSB	Roanoke Rapids	NC	**C**	C	C+	58.1	-1.92	1.2	3.4	32.8	17.2	**10.0**	14.7	30.5
ROANOKE VALLEY SB SSB	Roanoke Rapids	NC	**C-**	C-	C-	39.1	-2.70	0.0	1.0	35.9	5.6	**10.0**	24.7	52.8
ROBERT LEE STATE BK	Robert Lee	TX	**C+**	C+	C+	42.6	-0.40	5.3	8.4	15.5	48.3	**10.0**	12.7	26.7
ROBERTS COUNTY NB OF SISSETON	Sisseton	SD	**A-**	A-	A	57.4	0.01	5.2	0.7	2.0	64.5	**10.0**	14.7	34.8
ROBERTSON BANKING CO	Demopolis	AL	**A-**	A-	B+	262.7	2.97	9.0	2.2	23.2	15.2	**10.0**	11.0	15.8
ROCHELLE STATE BK	Rochelle	GA	**C+**	C+	B-	27.4	2.98	6.6	5.2	2.5	56.9	**10.0**	15.4	32.4
ROCHESTER STATE BK	Rochester	IL	**C**	C+	B	88.5	9.61	2.2	3.8	8.0	66.8	**10.0**	11.2	28.8
ROCK BRANCH COMMUNITY BANK INC	Nitro	WV	**C+**	C-	D+	70.4	-1.80	9.1	5.1	43.1	15.6	**9.5**	10.7	19.1
ROCK CANYON BANK	Provo	UT	**B**	B	C	200.3	13.28	9.3	0.8	11.4	0.0	**9.3**	11.0	14.4
ROCKEFELLER TRUST CO NA	New York	NY	**U**	U	U	10.4	7.71	0.0	0.0	0.0	83.2	**10.0**	89.1	540.3
ROCKFORD BANK & TRUST CO	Rockford	IL	**C+**	C+	C+	346.5	3.80	17.3	0.7	14.3	14.4	**7.1**	9.1	12.8
▲ ROCKHOLD BROWN & CO BANK	Bainbridge	OH	**D**	E+	E+	32.9	0.16	4.0	2.3	44.9	1.7	**7.2**	9.2	14.6
ROCKLAND SAVINGS BANK FSB	Rockland	ME	**C-**	D+	C+	83.4	0.75	4.3	3.4	46.9	0.4	**10.0**	13.3	19.9
ROCKLAND TRUST CO	Rockland	MA	**B**	B	B-	6384.7	8.27	13.3	0.2	17.2	11.5	**6.5**	8.5	12.1
ROCKWOOD BANK	Eureka	MO	**B-**	C+	C-	246.2	-3.60	4.0	1.1	15.8	2.0	**10.0**	11.6	15.2
ROCKY MOUNTAIN BANK	Jackson	WY	**D**	D-	E+	218.4	-1.14	3.5	1.0	29.2	5.2	**9.4**	10.6	17.2
ROCKY MOUNTAIN BANK	Billings	MT	**B-**	B-	B-	480.3	3.46	13.4	2.0	13.3	16.3	**7.5**	9.7	12.9
ROCKY MOUNTAIN BANK & TRUST FL	Florence	CO	**D-**	E+	D-	70.4	-18.59	10.7	0.1	14.4	35.7	**6.5**	8.5	13.6
ROLETTE STATE BK	Rolette	ND	**D**	C-	C-	39.6	6.65	22.3	4.8	5.1	9.8	**6.4**	8.4	12.6
ROLFE STATE BK	Rolfe	IA	**A-**	A-	A-	48.8	1.30	7.6	2.4	5.4	36.1	**8.8**	10.2	17.4

Asset Quality Index	Adjusted Non-Performing Loans as a % of Total Loans	Adjusted Non-Performing Loans as a % of Capital	Net Charge-Offs Avg Loans	Profitability Index	Net Income ($Mil)	Return on Assets (R.O.A.)	Return on Equity (R.O.E.)	Net Interest Spread	Overhead Efficiency Ratio	Liquidity Index	Liquidity Ratio	Hot Money Ratio	Stability Index
4.4	0.97	7.2	0.12	**3.8**	1.1	0.58	6.25	3.82	72.2	**1.3**	23.0	29.8	**4.5**
7.2	0.18	1.7	0.01	**4.6**	3.2	0.79	8.84	3.98	61.4	**0.6**	8.3	42.5	**4.7**
10.0	0.43	0.1	0.02	**9.3**	1.5	2.21	8.99	3.86	21.8	**5.9**	109.3	15.4	**9.3**
0.8	2.50	21.6	0.54	**2.7**	1.7	0.35	4.02	3.97	84.5	**2.5**	14.4	16.6	**4.4**
2.1	2.07	17.3	0.16	**7.5**	1.6	1.66	14.31	4.10	42.3	**2.1**	24.9	19.3	**7.9**
8.7	1.32	2.6	0.00	**3.5**	0.4	0.55	2.75	3.03	76.3	**5.9**	62.0	10.5	**7.8**
8.9	0.00	0.0	-0.01	**7.1**	0.5	1.70	7.09	2.74	61.2	**3.9**	85.2	27.4	**8.8**
7.0	0.66	3.4	-0.08	**5.9**	3.0	1.43	14.95	4.37	69.5	**3.5**	35.9	16.0	**6.9**
9.0	0.00	0.0	0.10	**3.8**	0.4	0.85	5.95	3.59	80.1	**4.7**	45.6	12.5	**6.7**
9.1	0.13	0.7	-0.01	**4.2**	3.2	0.95	11.71	3.49	66.5	**2.0**	18.1	19.5	**4.2**
1.8	3.08	24.9	0.50	**3.9**	1.0	0.69	8.57	3.67	74.6	**1.6**	11.3	21.6	**4.5**
1.6	2.67	13.9	1.38	**9.6**	9.6	3.31	25.16	5.30	48.4	**0.7**	10.5	38.1	**6.1**
6.8	1.17	4.7	-0.02	**2.1**	13.8	0.36	2.83	2.16	88.1	**5.0**	49.4	14.7	**8.3**
8.0	0.17	1.0	0.03	**4.4**	0.6	0.97	10.22	3.58	70.3	**2.3**	15.5	17.8	**6.1**
4.8	1.15	7.4	0.26	**4.7**	1.6	0.86	9.88	5.22	75.6	**4.0**	32.6	12.7	**4.4**
6.8	1.13	6.8	0.45	**2.2**	0.1	0.07	0.58	4.32	84.5	**1.7**	23.5	23.5	**5.7**
1.7	7.50	44.0	0.23	**1.3**	0.0	0.00	0.02	3.16	99.9	**1.7**	18.7	22.6	**4.2**
4.4	0.75	5.1	0.03	**6.2**	4.9	1.49	12.79	3.41	49.7	**1.2**	15.6	28.7	**8.3**
6.0	0.59	3.4	0.46	**4.5**	2.7	0.82	8.94	3.64	62.8	**3.0**	29.4	16.3	**4.2**
5.6	1.48	6.6	0.01	**6.4**	1.6	1.05	7.83	3.83	56.4	**4.2**	25.1	9.0	**7.8**
1.6	6.55	32.7	0.29	**2.8**	0.5	0.40	2.76	3.25	82.2	**2.2**	27.2	19.8	**5.6**
4.9	2.35	10.4	0.69	**5.6**	8.2	0.89	7.74	3.07	56.7	**3.1**	13.2	13.5	**8.5**
8.3	1.33	3.5	0.01	**8.8**	3.7	1.66	10.24	3.71	64.4	**6.4**	54.6	5.3	**8.0**
4.2	0.99	8.6	0.56	**7.2**	1.1	1.43	16.17	5.53	79.1	**0.7**	8.9	34.8	**3.4**
9.4	0.00	0.0	0.09	**2.7**	0.3	0.41	2.58	2.94	87.4	**5.8**	52.3	7.7	**7.1**
2.5	4.02	20.1	0.20	**1.5**	0.2	0.18	1.69	3.53	90.9	**3.0**	34.6	18.3	**3.9**
3.3	2.12	16.1	0.70	**5.2**	9.7	1.28	12.03	4.35	64.1	**4.0**	11.0	8.4	**8.0**
9.3	0.00	0.0	-0.01	**3.6**	0.8	0.58	5.19	2.84	73.9	**6.1**	48.8	5.6	**6.9**
2.0	4.01	26.8	0.38	**4.9**	3.6	0.98	11.18	3.85	67.1	**3.4**	26.3	13.2	**5.1**
3.3	2.18	13.3	0.40	**0.0**	-0.8	-1.01	-9.17	3.50	111.9	**1.0**	25.4	43.8	**3.9**
2.0	1.63	10.5	0.50	**6.8**	0.4	1.09	7.78	4.75	57.5	**1.2**	6.8	26.4	**7.1**
7.4	0.07	0.3	0.00	**6.6**	0.5	1.57	12.50	4.24	74.4	**5.3**	39.1	7.3	**6.2**
1.1	4.44	25.4	-0.08	**3.0**	0.6	0.67	6.58	3.21	83.2	**2.8**	19.2	15.7	**5.2**
4.7	2.24	12.1	0.02	**5.3**	3.1	1.43	15.72	3.08	54.4	**1.6**	22.6	25.6	**6.6**
7.5	0.54	3.0	-0.31	**2.4**	0.2	0.52	5.02	4.47	93.1	**1.0**	23.1	35.2	**1.4**
6.7	0.24	2.2	0.05	**10.0**	1.3	2.94	31.97	5.35	48.4	**0.7**	3.6	33.3	**6.3**
4.1	1.15	7.8	0.44	**5.4**	1.6	0.91	8.15	3.95	57.0	**1.8**	9.1	19.3	**6.1**
3.6	1.75	15.5	0.12	**3.9**	2.3	0.71	7.75	4.18	78.2	**3.7**	4.3	9.5	**4.7**
2.0	3.15	17.4	0.05	**4.2**	17.4	2.87	19.54	3.64	88.4	**3.8**	28.1	11.9	**6.5**
3.3	1.74	13.1	0.12	**3.0**	0.7	0.29	2.72	3.70	88.0	**2.4**	12.7	16.8	**4.9**
7.9	0.81	3.5	0.05	**2.0**	0.1	0.14	0.94	3.44	89.2	**3.0**	31.6	17.4	**6.4**
7.2	4.02	7.3	0.76	**1.0**	0.0	-0.02	-0.10	2.04	103.2	**2.5**	56.8	42.1	**6.6**
7.9	1.42	4.1	-0.04	**3.2**	0.2	0.61	5.41	3.69	85.7	**1.8**	25.1	22.8	**6.1**
9.5	0.00	0.0	-0.01	**5.9**	0.7	1.47	9.92	3.28	50.8	**6.5**	70.2	7.1	**8.4**
8.5	0.13	0.8	0.07	**6.3**	2.9	1.48	13.97	3.88	62.4	**1.7**	19.7	22.5	**7.0**
8.9	0.00	0.0	1.72	**2.8**	0.1	0.56	4.07	3.31	84.9	**2.5**	56.0	35.8	**7.1**
9.3	1.19	2.1	1.31	**2.6**	0.3	0.43	3.74	2.31	75.6	**6.6**	79.5	7.8	**6.8**
3.6	2.35	15.0	0.22	**3.4**	0.2	0.42	3.93	4.71	80.2	**0.9**	24.0	47.7	**5.2**
4.5	1.01	6.7	0.00	**7.7**	1.5	1.05	9.63	5.32	71.9	**1.2**	15.5	28.4	**4.6**
10.0	na	0.0	na	**10.0**	0.5	6.54	7.35	0.08	86.4	**4.0**	696.7	101.0	**6.8**
4.1	1.46	10.6	0.21	**3.2**	1.6	0.60	6.65	3.33	73.9	**1.1**	13.5	30.2	**5.4**
2.3	2.88	22.9	0.68	**3.2**	0.2	0.64	7.81	5.30	87.7	**2.8**	13.7	14.8	**2.4**
4.6	3.55	19.0	0.85	**1.2**	0.0	0.02	0.18	2.93	91.0	**1.2**	21.6	31.0	**5.2**
4.9	0.87	7.5	0.19	**5.1**	45.9	0.98	9.10	3.55	63.9	**4.5**	11.0	5.3	**8.2**
5.1	0.85	4.7	0.99	**3.7**	1.0	0.54	4.13	3.81	78.5	**4.1**	16.8	8.3	**5.3**
3.0	2.04	12.8	0.04	**3.9**	2.1	1.30	10.97	3.91	66.3	**2.4**	18.7	17.1	**3.4**
4.6	1.00	7.3	-0.01	**4.9**	2.9	0.83	7.85	4.30	81.9	**3.3**	13.4	12.2	**6.5**
3.5	3.00	13.5	1.85	**3.4**	-0.5	-0.83	-12.48	3.76	85.3	**1.1**	23.7	33.8	**0.0**
1.5	2.79	23.8	0.05	**3.6**	0.2	0.70	8.98	4.10	84.5	**1.6**	9.2	21.1	**4.0**
4.3	2.79	13.8	-0.02	**5.3**	0.5	1.24	12.57	4.00	67.2	**5.9**	48.5	5.7	**6.7**

Name	City	State	Rating	2013 Rating	2012 Rating	Total Assets ($Mil)	One Year Asset Growth	Asset Mix (As a % of Total Assets) Comm-ercial Loans	Cons-umer Loans	Mort-gage Loans	Secur-ities	Capital-ization Index	Lever-age Ratio	Risk-Based Capital Ratio
ROLLING HILLS BANK & TRUST	Atlantic	IA	C	C+	C+	231.5	2.46	6.4	0.8	2.6	2.3	5.5	10.1	11.4
ROLLSTONE BANK & TRUST	Fitchburg	MA	C	C	C	601.0	1.99	4.8	0.3	31.7	25.2	7.6	9.4	16.0
RONDOUT SB	Kingston	NY	B-	B-	B	305.6	11.93	7.7	0.4	41.6	13.7	10.0	11.1	17.4
ROOT RIVER STATE BK	Chatfield	MN	C+	C+	B-	67.2	-3.34	6.1	1.2	9.9	38.5	9.7	10.8	18.0
ROSCOE STATE BK	Roscoe	TX	B	B-	B	147.6	-1.64	6.1	3.0	9.8	55.2	7.4	9.3	19.5
▲ ROSE HILL BANK	Rose Hill	KS	B-	C+	C+	250.1	0.26	10.6	5.3	16.1	26.6	9.4	10.6	15.2
ROSEDALE FS&LA	Baltimore	MD	A	A	A-	799.3	2.29	0.0	0.1	36.6	28.3	10.0	23.6	44.1
ROSELLE SB	Roselle	NJ	C+	C+	B-	405.4	-2.38	0.0	0.0	18.4	70.5	10.0	16.2	60.2
ROUND TOP STATE BK	Round Top	TX	B+	B+	A-	432.3	5.89	3.5	2.4	17.6	40.9	8.4	9.9	19.2
ROUNDBANK	Waseca	MN	C	C-	C	283.3	-2.30	12.7	1.6	18.7	26.2	10.0	11.4	16.4
ROWLEY SB	Rowley	IA	D	D	C-	16.6	2.57	7.0	5.2	14.8	0.0	5.0	7.0	19.2
ROXBORO SB SSB	Roxboro	NC	B+	B+	B+	214.9	2.06	1.0	0.6	29.6	44.4	10.0	17.3	37.2
ROXBURY BANK	Roxbury	KS	C-	D+	C-	15.0	8.98	5.2	1.4	14.7	4.5	8.4	9.9	21.3
ROYAL BANK	Elroy	WI	B-	B-	C+	324.5	1.82	8.5	4.0	18.0	23.1	9.2	10.5	15.6
▲ ROYAL BANK AMERICA	Narberth	PA	C	D	D-	716.9	-1.79	5.3	0.3	7.8	36.9	9.1	10.4	16.5
ROYAL BANKS OF MISSOURI	Saint Louis	MO	D	D	C-	414.4	-1.30	6.0	2.3	7.3	13.8	10.0	13.0	17.0
ROYAL BUSINESS BANK	Los Angeles	CA	A-	A-	B-	849.6	16.47	16.8	0.0	24.5	3.9	10.0	15.5	19.3
ROYAL SB	Chicago	IL	C+	C+	C-	136.3	21.91	3.4	0.3	16.6	28.1	10.0	15.1	26.4
RSI BANK	Rahway	NJ	C+	C+	B-	494.2	-3.48	1.1	0.1	46.1	34.0	10.0	15.7	34.9
RSNB BANK	Rock Springs	WY	B+	A-	B+	365.8	4.20	3.6	1.5	3.9	70.5	9.3	10.5	28.3
▲ RUBY VALLEY NATIONAL BK	Twin Bridges	MT	D+	C-	B-	84.6	4.97	12.5	2.2	6.4	24.0	10.0	14.1	19.5
RUSHFORD STATE BK (INC)	Rushford	MN	D+	D+	D+	56.6	5.85	6.8	5.6	15.8	9.3	2.3	6.8	9.3
RUSHVILLE STATE BK	Rushville	IL	B+	B+	B+	95.8	-1.15	6.2	2.0	4.2	52.3	10.0	14.3	28.9
RUTH STATE BK	Ruth	MI	D+	D+	D+	34.7	5.39	5.2	2.4	7.5	43.5	6.9	9.0	24.6
▼ S BANK	Glennville	GA	D	C-	D	94.5	-2.04	7.3	3.7	13.0	15.2	8.1	9.7	16.4
S&T BANK	Indiana	PA	B-	C+	C	4887.3	7.02	15.1	1.4	13.6	12.4	7.1	9.1	13.3
S-BANK	Weymouth	MA	C-	C+	C-	190.1	0.17	11.1	0.2	35.3	20.9	7.9	9.6	14.2
SABADELL UNITED BANK NA	Miami	FL	B	B	C+	4587.4	21.67	20.2	0.3	23.7	12.5	7.6	9.4	15.0
▲ SABAL PALM BANK	Sarasota	FL	C-	D-	D-	107.2	19.65	6.2	0.2	18.9	13.5	8.8	10.2	15.8
SABINE STATE BK & TRUST CO	Many	LA	A-	A-	A-	768.9	5.32	15.7	2.5	8.5	17.7	7.7	9.4	13.5
SACO & BIDDEFORD SAVINGS INST	Saco	ME	C+	C+	C	821.0	3.47	2.0	0.9	51.0	12.8	8.8	10.2	15.7
SACRAMENTO DEPOSIT BANK	Sacramento	KY	A-	A-	A-	69.4	-2.54	4.7	6.0	15.6	41.7	10.0	12.7	21.4
SAFRA NATIONAL BK OF NEW YORK	New York	NY	B-	B-	B	6093.2	-7.50	13.8	0.0	0.6	25.8	8.3	9.9	18.2
SAGE BANK	Lowell	MA	D+	D+	C-	207.8	2.76	2.5	0.1	52.2	0.6	3.2	6.3	10.1
SAGE CAPITAL BANK NA	Gonzales	TX	B-	B	B-	344.4	9.64	6.7	1.1	7.8	23.3	6.8	8.8	16.4
SAIGON NATIONAL BK	Westminster	CA	D	D+	D+	47.5	-1.82	7.6	0.0	1.5	4.9	10.0	24.6	37.5
SAINT CASIMIRS SB	Baltimore	MD	C-	C-	B-	95.2	-4.38	0.0	0.1	18.3	61.2	10.0	21.6	78.1
SAINTE MARIE STATE BK	Sainte Marie	IL	D+	D+	C+	18.9	-3.46	4.8	1.6	1.6	23.9	10.0	22.5	34.3
SALEM CO-OP BANK	Salem	NH	C+	B	B	398.2	0.06	2.0	0.0	55.6	25.2	10.0	15.3	31.0
SALEM FIVE CENTS SB	Salem	MA	B	B	B-	3577.2	17.17	9.3	1.6	27.0	27.7	8.8	10.2	16.0
▲ SALIN BANK & TRUST CO	Indianapolis	IN	A-	B	C	776.6	-0.48	11.1	1.7	11.2	23.4	10.0	11.8	17.5
SALISBURY BANK & TRUST CO	Lakeville	CT	C-	C-	C-	638.1	9.03	6.9	0.6	38.0	13.4	6.3	8.3	13.8
SALLIE MAE BANK	Salt Lake City	UT	A-	A-	A-	11477.8	18.07	0.0	79.8	0.0	1.3	10.0	12.3	16.5
SALYERSVILLE NATIONAL BK	Salyersville	KY	B+	B+	B+	145.5	29.64	3.0	2.2	14.6	39.6	10.0	12.1	28.1
SAMSON BANKING CO INC	Samson	AL	B	B	B-	57.7	2.00	3.6	5.9	16.7	45.5	10.0	16.4	34.5
SAN DIEGO PRIVATE BANK	Coronado	CA	B+	A-	B	343.4	5.56	12.2	0.2	12.0	5.4	10.0	13.9	17.3
SAN LUIS VALLEY FEDERAL BANK	Alamosa	CO	B	B	B	253.5	1.15	0.6	1.1	39.9	26.4	10.0	14.9	24.7
SANBORN SB	Sanborn	IA	B	B	B-	59.4	5.20	5.9	3.3	12.9	21.2	9.6	10.8	15.2
SANDHILLS BANK	North Myrtle Beach	SC	C+	C	C-	99.8	25.05	1.7	4.6	27.6	22.6	6.1	8.1	15.0
SANDHILLS STATE BK	Bassett	NE	C	C-	D+	141.8	7.91	8.9	1.5	0.1	13.0	6.9	10.0	12.4
SANDY SPRING BANK	Olney	MD	B	B	C+	4245.8	4.82	7.5	0.5	17.4	21.5	8.8	10.2	15.3
▲ SANFORD INSTITUTION FOR SVGS	Sanford	ME	B-	C+	B-	454.6	1.44	4.3	1.2	39.1	8.2	9.0	11.7	14.2
SANGER BANK	Sanger	TX	A	A	A	119.5	7.15	9.0	3.0	19.7	29.9	10.0	12.7	23.7
SANIBEL CAPTIVA COMMUNITY BANK	Sanibel	FL	D+	D+	D+	260.9	14.21	2.4	0.9	43.8	2.1	9.0	10.3	15.7
SANTA ANNA NATIONAL BK	Santa Anna	TX	A-	A-	A-	44.7	-5.48	10.8	8.9	4.0	46.4	10.0	12.1	23.5
SANTA CLARA VALLEY BANK NA	Santa Paula	CA	D+	D+	C-	129.4	-5.00	4.3	0.1	3.0	34.8	10.0	11.1	21.1
SANTA CRUZ COUNTY BANK	Santa Cruz	CA	B	B-	B-	457.2	13.41	11.5	0.4	4.4	13.2	6.3	8.3	13.3
SANTANDER BANK NA	Boston	MA	C+	C+	C-	77335.4	4.20	19.9	2.2	10.9	19.5	9.9	12.1	14.9
SARATOGA NATIONAL BK & TRUST	Saratoga Springs	NY	B	B	B+	337.3	7.05	4.0	31.7	16.3	18.6	7.9	9.6	13.3
SARGENT COUNTY BANK	Forman	ND	A+	A+	A+	115.2	4.71	3.0	2.2	0.1	50.4	10.0	14.1	20.6

Asset Quality Index	Adjusted Non-Performing Loans as a % of Total Loans	Adjusted Non-Performing Loans as a % of Capital	Net Charge-Offs Avg Loans	Profitability Index	Net Income ($Mil)	Return on Assets (R.O.A.)	Return on Equity (R.O.E.)	Net Interest Spread	Overhead Efficiency Ratio	Liquidity Index	Liquidity Ratio	Hot Money Ratio	Stability Index
2.7	0.92	7.1	0.17	**5.2**	1.6	0.93	7.26	3.75	61.3	**4.6**	11.2	3.9	**6.5**
5.5	1.14	7.6	0.01	**2.8**	2.2	0.50	5.17	2.63	81.0	**0.7**	11.7	36.4	**6.5**
5.6	1.72	11.1	0.08	**3.5**	1.1	0.50	4.56	3.81	79.8	**1.7**	17.5	21.5	**6.3**
6.4	1.06	4.7	0.10	**2.8**	0.2	0.47	4.50	3.20	82.4	**5.3**	43.7	8.6	**5.7**
9.1	0.01	0.0	0.02	**4.8**	1.3	1.18	12.24	4.12	67.8	**3.5**	43.2	18.3	**6.3**
4.3	1.00	6.2	0.49	**4.1**	1.3	0.69	5.82	4.06	69.1	**2.5**	7.5	15.6	**7.0**
5.9	3.82	10.0	-0.04	**8.6**	7.9	1.32	5.70	3.82	40.8	**4.3**	45.9	14.9	**9.5**
9.5	1.44	1.7	0.43	**2.5**	0.9	0.29	1.73	2.01	77.1	**4.2**	82.2	24.7	**6.9**
9.0	0.00	0.0	0.01	**5.1**	3.3	1.02	10.64	3.08	55.6	**2.7**	45.2	29.0	**6.3**
2.3	5.05	25.8	0.08	**7.8**	3.9	1.84	16.71	4.83	63.0	**2.7**	22.1	16.4	**6.9**
8.6	0.47	1.9	0.00	**2.4**	0.0	0.30	4.41	2.33	86.4	**6.8**	71.7	2.7	**2.3**
6.9	3.01	7.5	0.00	**4.7**	1.5	0.95	5.67	3.25	61.4	**3.8**	60.0	23.6	**8.0**
4.5	1.85	8.5	1.53	**4.3**	0.1	1.10	11.08	4.03	79.8	**5.8**	44.7	2.7	**2.8**
4.1	2.08	12.2	0.02	**6.3**	2.6	1.08	9.59	4.28	64.9	**3.7**	23.9	11.1	**7.1**
3.6	3.65	16.9	0.51	**3.1**	4.2	0.82	12.60	3.27	80.6	**2.8**	25.6	16.4	**3.1**
0.2	7.26	39.8	0.45	**5.7**	3.3	1.04	8.36	3.68	61.0	**1.5**	10.7	23.4	**6.9**
8.2	0.17	0.9	0.01	**7.1**	7.1	1.22	7.73	4.27	51.4	**0.5**	5.9	49.8	**6.8**
7.0	1.08	4.3	0.17	**3.2**	0.6	0.61	3.24	4.29	77.3	**1.2**	21.4	31.3	**5.0**
7.2	1.89	6.4	0.00	**3.0**	1.6	0.43	2.78	2.86	70.8	**4.4**	45.0	14.1	**6.6**
8.4	0.77	1.5	0.15	**5.1**	3.5	1.25	11.99	3.29	63.3	**5.3**	50.5	11.1	**6.9**
0.9	10.83	49.1	1.62	**8.6**	1.1	1.74	12.40	4.96	56.3	**2.9**	28.5	16.7	**9.3**
4.1	1.17	11.8	-0.01	**4.0**	0.4	0.81	12.21	4.22	73.5	**3.3**	16.8	12.6	**3.3**
6.9	2.05	5.3	-0.01	**5.1**	1.0	1.33	9.55	3.29	58.4	**4.0**	49.9	16.8	**7.7**
7.0	1.58	4.3	0.00	**1.9**	0.1	0.23	2.85	2.30	89.2	**4.8**	74.2	16.6	**3.9**
4.6	2.33	12.4	0.06	**0.5**	-0.5	-0.74	-6.71	3.96	120.2	**2.1**	19.9	19.0	**4.1**
4.5	0.84	6.9	-0.02	**6.2**	45.5	1.30	10.63	3.54	59.2	**2.7**	10.1	15.3	**8.9**
5.5	0.81	5.6	0.00	**1.7**	0.1	0.07	0.79	3.26	98.5	**3.3**	18.1	12.8	**5.0**
4.1	1.79	12.6	0.01	**4.2**	20.0	0.63	5.05	3.52	73.1	**3.3**	17.4	13.2	**6.8**
5.9	0.00	0.0	0.36	**2.3**	0.3	0.40	2.90	3.65	78.6	**1.2**	20.2	31.2	**4.2**
5.9	0.48	3.5	0.19	**7.5**	9.6	1.64	17.72	4.34	69.1	**3.5**	9.6	10.8	**7.6**
4.8	1.22	9.2	0.01	**3.8**	4.5	0.74	7.17	3.15	74.5	**0.9**	7.2	31.9	**6.2**
8.8	0.31	1.2	0.14	**8.7**	1.1	2.09	17.66	4.93	52.9	**2.5**	49.6	32.0	**7.8**
9.0	0.21	0.9	-0.01	**3.5**	22.1	0.47	4.95	1.54	69.4	**1.9**	31.9	64.3	**7.5**
5.8	0.58	7.4	0.03	**1.7**	-0.4	-0.24	-3.10	3.62	105.3	**0.5**	4.8	45.9	**1.7**
7.9	0.12	0.7	-0.01	**4.4**	1.9	0.76	7.96	3.56	68.7	**3.6**	39.8	16.9	**5.6**
4.2	3.78	7.8	-1.66	**0.0**	-0.9	-2.44	-10.32	3.30	170.3	**2.1**	43.1	34.7	**4.8**
10.0	0.50	0.5	0.00	**0.2**	-0.3	-0.42	-1.97	2.17	120.4	**7.0**	98.1	8.2	**6.5**
6.2	2.46	5.9	0.00	**0.6**	0.0	-0.12	-0.56	2.32	105.8	**3.0**	48.3	19.4	**5.7**
9.3	0.85	3.6	0.00	**2.4**	0.5	0.16	1.07	3.01	93.1	**2.6**	31.2	18.8	**7.9**
5.9	0.97	6.1	0.12	**4.6**	19.3	0.74	7.06	2.79	67.6	**2.4**	24.5	20.4	**7.9**
6.1	0.97	5.0	0.26	**6.0**	8.5	1.44	12.24	3.92	70.9	**4.9**	23.7	4.1	**6.7**
2.4	2.77	22.6	0.08	**3.8**	2.9	0.63	5.95	3.56	76.4	**4.2**	12.3	6.8	**6.2**
5.6	0.21	1.3	0.87	**10.0**	187.7	2.26	19.37	5.35	33.9	**0.8**	15.5	46.9	**9.7**
9.5	0.20	0.5	0.22	**4.2**	0.9	0.93	8.30	3.45	68.4	**2.9**	52.8	30.5	**5.9**
8.1	1.13	3.0	0.02	**4.5**	0.4	1.05	6.32	3.70	71.6	**5.0**	54.5	12.2	**7.1**
7.3	0.35	2.0	0.02	**4.8**	1.8	0.71	4.82	4.21	67.5	**2.9**	17.4	14.6	**7.5**
5.2	3.91	15.3	0.01	**4.4**	1.3	0.70	4.66	3.56	74.4	**4.1**	39.9	14.7	**7.6**
7.3	0.38	2.3	-0.01	**4.7**	0.4	1.05	9.31	3.54	68.0	**3.9**	31.1	12.7	**5.5**
5.0	1.62	10.7	-0.03	**4.2**	3.3	4.66	46.86	3.95	83.6	**1.0**	20.2	33.3	**5.0**
6.7	0.09	0.7	-0.01	**3.1**	0.5	0.52	4.90	3.50	81.1	**1.1**	8.4	29.0	**5.0**
5.2	1.39	9.0	0.01	**5.3**	29.6	0.95	7.92	3.44	67.9	**4.4**	15.9	6.8	**8.6**
7.0	0.30	2.0	0.09	**3.9**	2.3	0.68	5.86	3.86	79.6	**2.2**	8.1	17.2	**6.1**
8.0	0.73	3.1	0.02	**7.1**	1.1	1.29	10.13	4.30	60.1	**2.4**	31.3	20.3	**7.9**
1.9	3.49	27.7	0.61	**5.4**	1.8	0.97	9.74	4.18	63.0	**1.2**	15.2	29.1	**4.4**
7.9	0.85	3.0	0.04	**9.1**	0.6	1.75	14.26	4.73	51.0	**3.2**	47.4	20.3	**7.8**
7.5	0.51	2.1	0.02	**0.4**	-0.4	-0.38	-3.56	3.48	109.9	**5.6**	46.4	8.4	**4.2**
8.7	0.01	0.1	0.03	**5.8**	3.1	0.96	11.71	4.24	63.7	**4.0**	23.9	9.8	**4.8**
3.6	1.65	8.9	0.71	**3.1**	273.9	0.49	2.82	2.56	80.1	**4.5**	20.1	7.0	**7.8**
4.0	0.62	4.5	0.05	**5.5**	2.3	0.91	9.42	3.03	56.4	**4.2**	6.0	6.5	**7.5**
8.8	0.00	0.0	0.02	**9.9**	2.2	2.52	18.35	4.38	30.0	**4.5**	44.7	13.5	**9.8**

Name	City	State	Rating	2013 Rating	2012 Rating	Total Assets ($Mil)	One Year Asset Growth	Asset Mix (As a % of Total Assets) Comm-ercial Loans	Cons-umer Loans	Mort-gage Loans	Secur-ities	Capital-ization Index	Lever-age Ratio	Risk-Based Capital Ratio
SAUK VALLEY BANK & TRUST CO	Sterling	IL	**B-**	B-	C+	310.6	9.87	11.2	0.9	10.0	25.7	**6.2**	8.3	12.4
▲ SAVANNA-THOMSON STATE BK	Savanna	IL	**B**	C+	C-	95.8	-3.95	24.2	1.0	12.8	23.2	**8.5**	10.0	15.3
SAVANNAH BANK NA	Savannah	NY	**C+**	C+	B-	137.5	5.64	8.5	1.2	16.3	47.7	**5.5**	7.5	15.6
SAVERS CO-OP BANK	Southbridge	MA	**C+**	C+	C	462.4	7.90	1.9	6.1	46.5	13.5	**9.6**	10.7	17.7
SAVINGS BANK	Wakefield	MA	**C+**	C+	C+	485.3	5.53	2.7	0.1	45.2	16.4	**10.0**	11.7	20.7
SAVINGS BANK	Circleville	OH	**B**	B	B+	313.3	0.50	2.2	5.0	34.1	35.0	**10.0**	11.1	22.6
SAVINGS BANK	Primghar	IA	**B+**	A-	B+	168.3	10.22	12.7	2.9	10.3	23.4	**6.8**	9.2	12.4
▲ SAVINGS BANK OF DANBURY	Danbury	CT	**C+**	C	C-	864.1	7.72	3.8	0.1	45.9	8.7	**8.6**	10.1	15.6
SAVINGS BANK OF MENDOCINO CNTY	Ukiah	CA	**B+**	B	B-	974.8	3.59	3.4	0.8	7.4	53.5	**10.0**	16.0	26.5
SAVINGS BANK OF WALPOLE	Walpole	NH	**C-**	C-	C-	343.9	2.01	3.3	0.3	36.2	27.8	**5.9**	7.9	17.4
SAVINGS INSTITUTE BANK & TRUST	Willimantic	CT	**C-**	C-	C+	1332.4	-1.56	11.8	0.5	34.2	12.6	**7.5**	9.3	15.9
SAVOY BANK	New York	NY	**D**	D	D	120.0	20.51	14.6	0.0	9.8	5.7	**9.4**	10.7	14.5
SAWYER SB	Saugerties	NY	**C+**	C+	C	197.1	3.18	2.8	0.2	35.3	37.4	**10.0**	11.4	24.5
SCHAUMBURG BANK & TRUST CO NA	Schaumburg	IL	**C+**	C+	C-	781.2	7.25	27.4	7.3	3.1	7.0	**5.7**	8.8	11.5
▲ SCHERTZ BANK & TRUST	Schertz	TX	**B**	B-	C+	229.2	15.33	4.2	0.4	3.9	17.7	**9.0**	10.9	14.1
SCHUYLER SAVINGS BANK	Kearny	NJ	**C**	C	C+	110.2	-2.41	0.0	0.1	49.0	26.2	**10.0**	15.8	40.0
SCHWERTNER STATE BK	Schwertner	TX	**C+**	C+	C	41.3	-0.60	6.5	1.7	3.9	60.3	**10.0**	12.2	30.0
SCITUATE FSB	Scituate	MA	**C-**	C-	C	282.4	1.15	0.4	0.9	53.7	21.3	**6.3**	8.3	16.6
SCOTIABANK DE PUERTO RICO	San Juan	PR	**D+**	D+	C	4944.4	-12.06	6.5	11.2	42.3	1.9	**10.0**	14.0	27.5
SCOTT COUNTY STATE BK	Scottsburg	IN	**B**	B	B-	134.0	1.54	7.8	2.4	24.8	27.6	**8.0**	9.7	16.9
SCOTT STATE BK	Bethany	IL	**B-**	B-	B+	107.5	3.17	7.5	3.8	15.8	39.4	**10.0**	13.4	21.4
SCOTT VALLEY BANK	Yreka	CA	**B-**	B-	B-	572.1	0.77	11.7	0.5	1.4	32.6	**8.8**	10.7	14.0
SCOTTDALE BANK & TRUST CO	Scottdale	PA	**B**	B	B+	260.3	0.17	0.7	0.6	10.3	67.4	**10.0**	17.1	37.2
SCOTTRADE BANK	Saint Louis	MO	**B-**	B-	B-	19258.1	-0.24	1.1	0.4	8.8	84.8	**5.2**	7.2	23.0
SCOTTSBURG BUILDING & LOAN ASN	Scottsburg	IN	**C**	C	C	91.6	1.29	2.3	0.2	42.9	38.9	**10.0**	12.2	27.4
SCRIBNER BANK	Scribner	NE	**B+**	B+	B	69.9	5.62	8.9	1.7	5.1	20.5	**9.2**	10.5	17.0
SEACOAST COMMERCE BANK	San Diego	CA	**C+**	C+	C	367.0	33.52	0.4	0.0	0.0	1.5	**6.1**	8.1	16.5
SEACOAST NATIONAL BK	Stuart	FL	**C**	C+	C-	2359.2	9.93	3.1	2.0	24.6	32.9	**8.8**	10.2	17.1
▼ SEAMENS BANK	Provincetown	MA	**D+**	C	C-	348.6	2.24	2.0	0.2	33.7	23.5	**9.8**	10.9	16.4
SEASIDE NATIONAL BK & TRUST	Orlando	FL	**C-**	C-	D	1039.7	15.03	34.0	0.7	8.6	21.3	**6.7**	8.9	12.2
SEATTLE BANK	Seattle	WA	**D+**	C	D	195.5	-20.73	14.5	0.1	4.0	0.9	**10.0**	23.6	36.3
SEAWAY BANK & TRUST CO	Chicago	IL	**D-**	D	D-	522.4	-5.30	4.8	0.7	19.2	19.7	**4.6**	6.6	15.1
SEBREE DEPOSIT BANK	Sebree	KY	**D**	D+	C	23.3	3.46	6.9	5.4	31.6	22.0	**10.0**	11.1	23.2
SECOND FS&LA OF PHILADELPHIA	Philadelphia	PA	**B**	B	B	14.4	-3.03	0.0	0.0	34.7	59.5	**10.0**	45.3	58.9
SECURANT BANK & TRUST	Milwaukee	WI	**E-**	E-	E-	192.0	0.56	17.0	0.5	24.4	12.9	**1.4**	5.2	8.4
SECURIAN TRUST CO NA	Saint Paul	MN	**U**	U	U	13.4	-0.10	0.0	0.0	0.0	86.8	**10.0**	90.0	100.1
SECURITY BANK	Dyersburg	TN	**B**	B-	B	170.8	-0.66	2.1	2.1	5.7	54.4	**10.0**	11.4	23.1
▲ SECURITY BANK	Stephens	AR	**B**	B-	C	55.3	1.84	9.2	8.0	37.2	21.1	**6.4**	8.4	15.4
SECURITY BANK	Rich Hill	MO	**C**	C	C-	46.3	2.15	9.4	3.9	23.8	10.7	**6.8**	8.8	12.8
SECURITY BANK	New Auburn	WI	**C+**	C	C-	81.8	9.33	8.2	2.1	20.3	13.4	**10.0**	12.1	15.3
SECURITY BANK	Midland	TX	**B+**	B+	B+	942.3	21.17	29.2	0.7	5.6	10.7	**6.2**	8.2	13.3
▲ SECURITY BANK	Laurel	NE	**B**	B	A-	184.4	5.16	8.6	3.0	3.1	22.8	**10.0**	11.0	15.3
SECURITY BANK	Tulsa	OK	**B**	C+	B-	495.5	11.97	22.0	1.2	7.0	7.4	**9.6**	10.7	14.7
SECURITY BANK & TRUST CO	Miami	OK	**B**	B-	B-	79.0	6.63	11.7	3.0	9.4	48.1	**9.9**	11.0	20.7
SECURITY BANK & TRUST CO	Glencoe	MN	**B**	B	B-	448.6	71.00	7.5	0.6	6.6	33.1	**8.1**	9.7	15.5
SECURITY BANK & TRUST CO	Paris	TN	**A-**	A-	A-	173.1	-0.79	9.4	2.2	22.1	20.7	**8.1**	10.0	13.4
SECURITY BANK & TRUST CO	Maysville	KY	**B+**	A-	A-	50.8	-2.59	4.4	3.2	25.5	29.7	**10.0**	20.7	21.4
SECURITY BANK MINNESOTA	Albert Lea	MN	**A-**	A-	B	101.5	1.39	34.1	7.0	6.0	19.8	**10.0**	11.3	15.3
SECURITY BANK OF CALIFORNIA	Riverside	CA	**B**	B	C	599.1	11.65	19.5	0.4	2.9	23.1	**8.5**	10.0	13.8
SECURITY BANK OF CRAWFORD	Crawford	TX	**D**	D	D-	23.8	-57.13	1.1	5.8	41.6	8.6	**10.0**	19.1	35.0
SECURITY BANK OF KANSAS CITY	Kansas City	KS	**C+**	C+	C-	829.4	3.34	13.4	0.4	1.6	22.7	**10.0**	11.0	16.8
SECURITY BANK OF PULASKI COUNT	Waynesville	MO	**C-**	C-	D-	95.6	-1.13	9.2	4.4	21.1	15.3	**7.0**	9.0	13.2
SECURITY BANK OF SOUTHWEST MO	Cassville	MO	**C+**	B-	C+	79.5	5.53	6.6	4.0	25.2	25.4	**8.9**	10.3	15.9
SECURITY BANK OF THE OZARKS	Eminence	MO	**C-**	D+	D	44.6	-0.21	2.8	13.2	13.5	13.8	**4.6**	7.9	10.8
SECURITY BANK SB	Springfield	IL	**D**	D-	C-	141.7	-3.92	3.0	9.0	49.1	14.7	**7.6**	9.4	16.2
SECURITY BANK USA	Bemidji	MN	**B**	B	C	126.3	13.63	16.0	5.0	19.1	9.1	**6.5**	9.2	12.1
SECURITY FEDERAL BANK	Aiken	SC	**C+**	C	C-	828.6	-2.77	1.1	1.5	12.9	51.7	**8.9**	10.3	23.6
SECURITY FEDERAL BANK	Elizabethton	TN	**B+**	B+	B+	57.3	2.94	2.8	2.6	39.8	21.1	**10.0**	22.8	41.8
SECURITY FINANCIAL BANK	Durand	WI	**B**	B	C	416.3	42.73	8.0	0.5	10.2	36.9	**8.1**	9.7	18.3
SECURITY FIRST BANK	Cheyenne	WY	**B+**	B+	B	68.1	4.80	5.6	1.9	8.3	15.1	**8.1**	9.7	13.4

Asset Quality Index	Adjusted Non-Performing Loans as a % of Total Loans	Adjusted Non-Performing Loans as a % of Capital	Net Charge-Offs Avg Loans	Profitability Index	Net Income ($Mil)	Return on Assets (R.O.A.)	Return on Equity (R.O.E.)	Net Interest Spread	Overhead Efficiency Ratio	Liquidity Index	Liquidity Ratio	Hot Money Ratio	Stability Index
4.5	1.27	9.5	0.00	4.5	1.5	0.69	8.54	3.72	69.4	1.8	8.7	19.5	4.8
6.7	0.34	2.2	0.00	5.1	1.0	1.36	11.36	3.60	57.6	5.0	22.6	3.3	5.0
9.1	0.04	0.2	0.03	3.6	0.7	0.70	9.40	3.61	77.3	1.7	15.4	22.1	4.5
4.2	1.82	12.6	0.08	3.0	1.4	0.41	3.78	3.34	79.5	2.4	17.6	17.4	6.2
8.8	0.26	1.6	0.06	2.2	1.4	0.39	2.88	3.23	91.3	3.5	22.9	12.1	6.9
5.2	2.49	12.0	0.35	4.3	1.8	0.73	6.61	3.54	65.8	3.4	23.4	12.7	6.2
8.1	0.16	1.2	0.23	7.9	2.1	1.74	20.37	3.65	41.7	2.4	17.1	17.4	6.1
3.8	1.73	13.9	0.28	3.5	3.8	0.61	5.89	3.40	71.8	1.4	2.4	22.2	5.7
6.5	3.10	6.8	0.06	5.0	6.2	0.86	5.33	3.11	62.3	6.0	59.5	9.8	8.1
6.0	1.03	7.2	0.07	1.9	0.6	0.22	2.74	2.48	92.6	5.1	37.6	8.0	4.3
6.1	0.61	5.0	0.06	2.5	3.2	0.32	3.05	3.15	84.0	2.7	15.8	16.2	7.3
1.2	2.69	17.0	0.00	3.8	0.8	1.01	9.32	5.08	79.5	1.0	26.4	40.6	5.0
6.3	1.93	9.1	0.43	3.3	0.9	0.66	5.76	3.88	85.4	2.1	40.7	34.5	5.9
3.1	1.56	13.2	0.17	4.1	3.3	0.58	5.42	3.54	72.7	1.4	10.6	24.3	6.0
5.6	0.31	1.9	-0.11	5.1	1.6	0.98	9.13	4.03	65.2	1.4	14.0	26.0	6.1
6.0	3.07	10.3	0.07	2.2	0.2	0.29	1.79	3.17	85.2	3.1	47.4	24.2	7.0
8.4	2.13	4.0	0.01	2.6	0.1	0.46	4.04	2.57	83.9	6.6	83.2	8.4	5.2
6.3	0.65	5.2	0.04	2.1	0.4	0.19	2.19	3.05	92.4	2.5	26.4	18.2	3.9
0.4	7.52	36.0	0.37	4.8	25.1	0.63	3.67	5.88	65.9	1.0	7.2	29.5	7.1
4.4	2.24	13.1	0.37	4.7	0.9	0.84	7.23	4.41	72.5	5.0	36.1	8.6	5.2
6.7	1.62	5.1	0.25	3.3	0.5	0.66	4.88	3.32	82.6	5.9	50.2	7.3	7.8
4.5	2.25	11.8	0.00	3.9	2.6	0.63	5.83	3.63	72.8	4.0	33.4	12.7	6.7
10.0	0.67	0.9	0.02	3.5	1.6	0.81	4.62	3.06	75.4	8.0	88.0	1.5	8.0
10.0	0.12	0.2	0.01	3.8	132.0	0.90	12.65	1.24	25.1	2.4	38.9	37.4	7.2
9.5	0.87	3.5	0.16	1.8	0.2	0.26	2.13	2.55	84.1	1.4	32.0	46.9	6.0
7.7	0.39	1.9	-0.02	6.4	0.7	1.21	11.61	3.43	63.5	6.0	40.0	3.6	6.5
4.6	0.51	4.8	0.01	6.8	3.5	1.34	16.33	4.63	66.9	3.9	7.8	8.6	3.4
4.9	2.37	13.5	-0.11	3.0	8.2	0.48	4.27	3.16	85.4	5.2	26.1	6.0	6.6
1.7	6.54	36.0	0.01	2.9	1.0	0.41	3.60	3.17	80.0	5.2	39.0	8.4	6.4
5.4	1.18	9.0	-0.04	2.2	2.0	0.27	2.80	3.11	84.8	1.7	22.3	27.2	5.7
4.0	6.33	16.5	0.11	0.6	-0.9	-0.53	-2.59	2.91	165.9	2.2	34.1	26.0	5.1
0.3	29.86	149.9	2.11	0.7	-5.4	-1.35	-18.59	4.99	101.9	0.9	20.2	40.3	4.8
8.8	0.62	2.5	-0.21	0.0	-0.1	-0.38	-3.47	3.09	113.0	2.6	44.5	21.9	4.5
10.0	0.00	0.0	-0.08	3.8	0.0	0.40	0.91	6.49	80.8	4.7	116.9	23.3	8.0
0.3	8.64	83.6	1.57	2.5	0.6	0.45	9.38	3.53	87.3	1.9	11.6	19.2	1.6
10.0	na	0.0	na	8.9	0.3	2.69	2.89	4.24	88.0	4.0	737.5	101.0	6.5
5.8	4.04	11.2	0.09	4.8	1.4	1.05	9.15	3.68	72.4	4.1	43.7	15.6	6.9
5.3	0.35	2.5	0.64	3.8	0.3	0.81	10.27	4.48	71.5	0.9	24.6	52.2	4.8
6.7	0.22	1.8	0.20	3.8	0.1	0.27	2.92	5.11	77.6	3.6	20.9	11.4	4.0
3.8	1.89	11.8	0.00	7.2	0.7	1.19	8.89	4.34	57.6	1.8	18.2	21.2	5.5
5.8	0.51	3.5	-0.02	9.8	14.1	2.38	21.57	5.48	58.2	5.2	36.2	6.7	8.1
5.5	1.19	6.5	0.17	7.7	2.7	1.98	18.04	4.46	58.7	3.2	24.1	14.1	6.6
4.3	0.65	4.1	-0.08	9.7	9.0	2.55	23.66	4.25	32.4	0.9	23.0	44.3	7.4
7.1	0.00	0.0	-0.01	4.7	0.7	1.13	11.75	3.67	69.0	3.8	44.1	16.5	5.6
5.8	1.01	5.4	0.12	7.8	5.3	2.04	21.06	4.45	58.5	4.8	32.4	8.1	5.1
8.8	0.01	0.1	0.02	9.6	2.9	2.23	23.03	4.24	43.7	1.6	16.0	23.3	7.7
7.0	1.51	4.4	-0.05	4.8	0.4	1.11	5.42	3.46	68.4	4.2	31.7	11.4	8.5
7.8	0.07	0.4	0.31	7.5	1.4	1.80	15.81	4.67	55.8	1.5	14.2	24.5	6.9
6.0	0.59	3.7	0.07	4.2	2.9	0.68	7.22	3.73	67.0	3.3	31.1	15.5	5.2
7.0	1.19	4.0	0.38	0.0	-0.1	-0.66	-3.44	3.02	121.7	0.8	24.0	43.5	4.4
1.6	4.54	19.3	0.78	3.9	4.6	0.73	4.86	3.69	65.4	4.6	30.5	8.4	6.9
3.8	2.22	15.8	0.33	2.3	0.2	0.31	3.40	4.39	89.1	1.2	11.0	27.4	3.6
2.2	4.00	23.4	0.13	8.4	1.2	1.92	21.22	4.17	57.0	2.1	27.6	20.7	7.3
6.9	0.22	1.9	-0.04	5.8	0.5	1.52	16.21	4.97	74.8	1.4	4.7	23.3	3.7
4.7	0.81	6.3	-0.01	0.7	-0.1	-0.10	-1.16	3.91	102.5	4.3	17.8	6.9	3.0
7.2	0.33	2.5	-0.02	6.6	1.5	1.62	18.18	3.94	64.4	4.2	11.4	7.2	5.6
3.6	4.94	18.7	0.67	3.9	4.8	0.76	7.13	3.10	69.5	3.1	42.1	19.8	5.6
4.6	5.06	14.7	0.00	6.5	0.5	1.06	4.72	4.59	68.9	1.1	26.4	37.8	7.7
6.6	0.66	3.4	0.07	6.1	3.9	1.56	15.62	3.42	67.1	4.5	27.7	8.3	4.9
6.3	0.45	2.5	0.09	4.1	0.4	0.84	8.43	3.75	78.1	1.8	36.3	34.9	5.7

Name	City	State	Rating	2013 Rating	2012 Rating	Total Assets ($Mil)	One Year Asset Growth	Comm-ercial Loans	Cons-umer Loans	Mort-gage Loans	Secur-ities	Capital-ization Index	Lever-age Ratio	Risk-Based Capital Ratio
								Asset Mix (As a % of Total Assets)						
▲ SECURITY FIRST BANK	Lincoln	NE	**C+**	C+	C+	857.8	-3.79	7.1	2.1	9.5	26.6	**6.6**	8.6	12.9
▲ SECURITY FIRST BANK	Fresno	CA	**C+**	C	C-	104.1	5.80	16.1	0.1	2.6	24.1	**10.0**	12.9	18.5
▼ SECURITY FIRST BANK OF ND	Center	ND	**A-**	A-	A-	173.7	4.27	16.6	3.5	11.0	5.4	**7.7**	10.8	13.1
SECURITY FIRST NB OF HUGO	Hugo	OK	**B+**	B	B	105.3	0.93	3.0	5.1	22.0	9.6	**7.0**	9.0	13.9
SECURITY FSB	Jasper	AL	**C+**	C+	C	37.8	0.88	2.7	10.4	22.4	31.7	**10.0**	11.4	21.6
SECURITY FSB	Logansport	IN	**B-**	C+	B-	207.7	2.27	5.3	1.0	45.6	13.2	**10.0**	12.5	20.8
SECURITY FSB OF MCMINNVILLE	McMinnville	TN	**B-**	B-	B-	174.5	7.57	10.9	5.8	28.1	12.9	**8.5**	10.0	14.7
SECURITY HOME BANK	Malmo	NE	**B-**	B-	C+	39.5	10.50	4.2	2.7	20.8	6.8	**8.0**	9.6	13.6
SECURITY NATIONAL BK	Witt	IL	**B-**	B-	C+	74.7	4.25	4.8	7.0	25.3	34.3	**9.8**	10.9	18.1
SECURITY NATIONAL BK OF ENID	Enid	OK	**A-**	A-	B+	318.2	0.46	6.7	1.5	17.1	36.2	**6.8**	8.8	15.7
SECURITY NATIONAL BK OF OMAHA	Omaha	NE	**A-**	A-	A-	799.7	-1.07	15.4	2.8	5.9	27.9	**8.8**	10.2	15.3
SECURITY NATIONAL BK OF SD	Dakota Dunes	SD	**B+**	B+	B+	183.1	14.93	7.4	2.1	6.1	40.4	**6.0**	8.0	16.9
SECURITY NATIONAL TRUST CO	Wheeling	WV	**U**	U	U	4.8	2.19	0.0	0.0	0.0	78.7	**10.0**	113.	126.9
SECURITY NB OF SIOUX CITY IA	Sioux City	IA	**A-**	A-	B+	828.9	3.66	7.0	1.2	14.1	27.8	**8.8**	10.2	19.1
▲ SECURITY SB	Canton	SD	**B**	B-	B-	180.5	5.23	5.9	2.1	8.4	3.4	**6.2**	9.6	11.9
SECURITY SB	Gowrie	IA	**B**	B	B-	125.1	8.15	3.8	2.0	10.7	39.3	**6.9**	8.9	14.9
SECURITY SB	Eagle Grove	IA	**B**	B	B	113.1	-7.50	33.2	0.5	3.4	20.9	**8.8**	10.2	14.1
SECURITY SB	Monmouth	IL	**C+**	C+	C+	177.6	0.74	2.7	4.8	12.5	14.6	**8.1**	9.8	15.4
▲ SECURITY STATE BK	Independence	IA	**A-**	B+	B	101.7	3.36	5.3	1.2	8.2	51.8	**10.0**	11.6	21.9
SECURITY STATE BK	Algona	IA	**A-**	A-	B+	102.9	8.27	9.8	2.9	3.5	19.5	**9.9**	11.9	14.9
SECURITY STATE BK	Sutherland	IA	**B-**	B-	C+	101.3	3.58	9.5	3.8	5.9	0.6	**4.0**	8.7	10.5
▼ SECURITY STATE BK	Radcliffe	IA	**C**	C+	C+	103.2	0.52	7.4	2.2	13.8	32.0	**2.9**	9.4	10.0
SECURITY STATE BK	Waverly	IA	**B+**	B+	B+	79.9	1.48	0.9	3.4	14.2	45.6	**8.0**	9.7	16.3
SECURITY STATE BK	Tyndall	SD	**C+**	C	C+	131.0	40.39	11.4	2.4	3.1	4.8	**3.3**	8.5	10.2
SECURITY STATE BK	Alexandria	SD	**B-**	B-	B	72.2	-6.87	6.1	3.7	4.1	32.8	**9.7**	10.8	16.8
SECURITY STATE BK	Emery	SD	**B-**	C+	B-	39.9	-1.26	12.3	4.6	0.7	34.1	**10.0**	13.7	22.2
SECURITY STATE BK	Iron River	WI	**C**	C-	C-	82.8	3.93	11.2	1.9	12.8	20.5	**10.0**	17.5	25.2
SECURITY STATE BK	Scott City	KS	**A-**	A-	B	177.3	23.12	22.4	1.4	1.9	12.4	**10.0**	15.3	16.6
▼ SECURITY STATE BK	Wellington	KS	**C+**	C+	B	65.7	6.72	5.7	3.8	15.6	41.5	**9.9**	10.9	21.8
SECURITY STATE BK	Ansley	NE	**C+**	C+	C+	144.1	9.67	15.6	1.4	17.1	4.7	**6.7**	8.9	12.2
SECURITY STATE BK	McRae	GA	**B+**	B+	B	41.1	4.72	12.5	3.8	7.7	32.5	**10.0**	14.5	24.9
▲ SECURITY STATE BK	Cheyenne	OK	**A**	A-	B+	190.4	7.40	4.5	4.2	12.6	49.4	**9.3**	10.5	21.2
SECURITY STATE BK	Anahuac	TX	**C+**	B-	C-	162.3	13.15	11.3	2.3	8.7	32.7	**6.5**	8.5	13.6
SECURITY STATE BK	Basin	WY	**A-**	B+	B	326.8	6.42	9.8	4.5	11.5	24.9	**10.0**	11.3	17.3
SECURITY STATE BK	Winters	TX	**C+**	C+	C+	51.2	18.04	7.0	8.0	8.5	37.5	**6.0**	8.0	17.2
▼ SECURITY STATE BK	Littlefield	TX	**B**	B	C+	118.0	-6.47	11.1	3.6	12.8	16.5	**9.1**	10.5	14.3
SECURITY STATE BK	Pearsall	TX	**A-**	A-	B+	480.1	8.99	9.2	2.7	1.6	29.7	**8.0**	9.6	17.1
SECURITY STATE BK	Farwell	TX	**A**	A	A	111.3	1.93	7.7	1.1	12.4	12.9	**10.0**	14.6	20.0
SECURITY STATE BK	Centralia	WA	**B**	B-	C+	379.5	3.18	10.8	2.0	7.1	3.1	**10.0**	11.5	21.5
SECURITY STATE BK & TRUST	Fredericksburg	TX	**B**	B	B	766.5	6.71	6.9	3.2	11.1	35.2	**10.0**	14.7	25.3
SECURITY STATE BK FERGUS FALLS	Fergus Falls	MN	**C+**	C+	C	131.3	-3.23	10.4	0.7	8.5	19.8	**9.4**	10.6	14.6
SECURITY STATE BK OF AITKIN	Aitkin	MN	**B-**	C+	C+	92.3	-0.09	11.1	1.8	10.8	25.3	**9.0**	10.4	17.2
▲ SECURITY STATE BK OF HIBBING	Hibbing	MN	**C+**	C	C-	127.2	5.42	17.5	1.3	9.3	26.7	**7.8**	9.5	19.4
▼ SECURITY STATE BK OF KENYON	Kenyon	MN	**D**	D+	D	52.4	-0.85	9.6	1.9	13.5	3.1	**7.8**	10.1	13.2
▲ SECURITY STATE BK OF LEWISTON	Lewiston	MN	**D+**	D-	D-	63.8	-1.55	6.1	2.1	7.1	31.2	**5.8**	7.8	12.9
▲ SECURITY STATE BK OF MARINE	Marine On Saint Cr	MN	**B**	B-	B	115.1	2.37	4.3	2.0	35.6	8.9	**8.2**	9.8	17.8
SECURITY STATE BK OF OKLEE	Oklee	MN	**C+**	B-	B-	29.6	-7.19	1.8	6.5	8.4	32.6	**10.0**	16.0	51.3
SECURITY STATE BK OF WANAMINGO	Wanamingo	MN	**B**	B	B	67.3	-5.85	4.8	1.5	6.8	22.5	**9.4**	10.6	17.1
▼ SECURITY STATE BK OF WARROAD	Warroad	MN	**B-**	B	C	91.0	0.76	14.3	13.0	5.4	40.8	**10.0**	18.3	29.1
SECURITY STATE BK OF WEWOKA OK	Wewoka	OK	**B-**	B-	B-	160.1	5.11	9.7	12.2	16.0	23.1	**7.2**	9.2	14.2
SECURITY STATE BK WISHEK ND	Wishek	ND	**B-**	B-	B-	68.0	-0.65	4.2	5.2	2.5	34.0	**9.4**	10.6	15.7
SECURITY TRUST & SB	Storm Lake	IA	**B-**	B-	B+	194.4	11.22	3.3	1.3	8.2	62.0	**8.6**	10.1	25.4
SEI PRIVATE TRUST CO	Oaks	PA	**U**	U	A+	126.8	7.91	0.0	0.0	0.0	76.1	**10.0**	82.7	305.0
SELECT BANK	Forest	VA	**C+**	C	D+	130.7	12.93	14.5	2.0	29.9	0.1	**7.1**	9.0	12.8
SELECT BANK & TRUST CO	Dunn	NC	**B-**	B-	D+	782.5	43.72	6.4	0.5	11.7	13.2	**10.0**	13.3	16.3
SENATH STATE BK	Senath	MO	**A**	A	A	66.6	2.07	6.5	9.4	35.3	0.6	**10.0**	14.6	30.1
SENECA FS&LA	Baldwinsville	NY	**D+**	D	D+	126.1	-7.47	4.7	0.7	55.0	29.3	**8.5**	10.0	20.1
▲ SENTRY BANK	Saint Joseph	MN	**B+**	B	B-	184.7	8.78	10.4	1.7	11.0	27.8	**6.5**	8.5	15.8
SERVISFIRST BANK	Birmingham	AL	**B+**	B+	B	3952.7	16.39	33.7	1.0	4.9	8.4	**6.5**	9.3	12.1
SETTLERS BANK	Marietta	OH	**B**	B	B	120.9	9.56	6.2	4.9	38.9	3.6	**9.1**	10.4	15.8

Asset Quality Index	Adjusted Non-Performing Loans as a % of Total Loans	Adjusted Non-Performing Loans as a % of Capital	Net Charge-Offs / Avg Loans	Profitability Index	Net Income ($Mil)	Return on Assets (R.O.A.)	Return on Equity (R.O.E.)	Net Interest Spread	Overhead Efficiency Ratio	Liquidity Index	Liquidity Ratio	Hot Money Ratio	Stability Index
5.9	0.40	2.6	0.05	**3.7**	4.5	0.70	7.05	3.42	76.4	**3.1**	21.4	14.2	**6.5**
6.9	0.00	0.0	-1.35	**4.2**	0.8	1.02	8.86	4.30	91.8	**2.1**	27.9	20.7	**5.3**
6.3	0.72	5.3	0.02	**9.5**	2.8	2.22	20.45	4.90	56.3	**2.9**	5.4	13.7	**8.5**
5.0	0.43	3.4	0.05	**10.0**	1.5	1.95	23.46	5.60	51.7	**1.5**	12.5	23.2	**6.6**
8.7	0.14	0.5	0.09	**2.9**	0.2	0.61	5.22	3.70	87.5	**2.9**	56.7	30.5	**3.9**
5.0	2.42	13.0	0.16	**3.9**	1.1	0.72	5.72	4.56	79.6	**3.9**	19.1	9.9	**6.5**
6.2	0.44	3.2	0.28	**4.5**	1.1	0.85	8.57	3.45	65.7	**1.3**	10.1	25.3	**5.6**
7.2	0.04	0.3	0.00	**5.6**	0.3	1.02	10.39	4.01	58.0	**2.0**	16.2	19.4	**4.8**
5.9	0.91	4.8	0.28	**5.1**	0.5	0.90	8.10	3.90	64.9	**3.8**	35.1	14.5	**6.2**
7.0	0.53	2.8	-0.01	**8.4**	4.7	1.91	20.22	3.54	47.6	**4.4**	31.5	10.1	**7.1**
7.4	0.25	1.3	-0.05	**5.7**	8.2	1.42	13.55	3.34	66.3	**5.2**	33.5	5.5	**8.5**
9.1	0.02	0.1	0.00	**6.7**	1.7	1.25	16.22	2.26	48.6	**5.5**	51.8	10.2	**6.3**
10.0	na	0.0	na	**9.8**	0.4	13.82	12.92	1.43	85.3	**4.0**	1320.1	101.0	**5.7**
6.8	0.62	2.9	0.01	**6.6**	7.6	1.18	12.01	2.82	59.3	**4.6**	24.9	6.3	**8.3**
5.0	0.27	2.2	0.00	**4.8**	1.2	0.91	8.04	3.95	58.1	**1.5**	8.4	22.7	**7.2**
8.6	0.22	1.2	0.00	**5.5**	1.2	1.27	15.40	3.52	58.0	**3.3**	36.9	17.5	**4.9**
8.0	0.15	1.0	0.00	**5.9**	1.2	1.33	12.53	3.88	59.9	**2.6**	23.3	16.8	**6.4**
5.4	0.69	4.6	0.05	**3.0**	0.5	0.39	4.12	2.73	77.7	**1.6**	21.5	24.9	**4.9**
7.8	0.98	3.3	-0.02	**5.6**	0.8	1.06	9.87	3.63	65.3	**5.6**	53.1	10.4	**7.1**
6.7	0.47	2.5	0.49	**6.1**	0.8	1.15	9.74	3.59	53.5	**2.6**	36.1	22.5	**7.3**
6.7	0.01	0.1	0.03	**9.8**	2.0	2.58	29.31	4.40	36.3	**1.7**	2.2	19.4	**7.6**
2.0	4.41	23.1	0.03	**4.1**	0.7	0.95	10.52	2.99	61.1	**6.0**	49.9	6.5	**4.0**
9.0	0.04	0.2	0.05	**5.0**	0.7	1.20	12.13	3.20	60.3	**5.4**	45.2	8.5	**6.5**
4.9	0.35	3.4	-0.01	**4.2**	0.8	0.84	8.61	3.93	71.7	**3.6**	3.6	9.7	**5.4**
5.8	0.41	2.2	0.01	**4.7**	0.6	1.11	10.73	3.69	64.8	**2.3**	31.9	22.7	**6.0**
8.5	0.00	0.0	0.00	**3.8**	0.2	0.69	5.22	3.07	68.4	**6.1**	50.7	5.0	**6.4**
1.3	9.44	32.3	0.56	**8.8**	1.0	1.66	9.63	4.08	56.6	**1.9**	29.5	26.1	**5.4**
6.0	0.48	2.5	-0.01	**7.3**	1.6	1.30	8.34	4.14	55.6	**0.9**	8.6	31.7	**7.1**
3.0	5.18	19.5	0.68	**1.5**	-0.1	-0.17	-1.40	4.31	76.9	**4.0**	35.2	13.1	**5.7**
3.6	1.35	11.8	0.22	**5.7**	1.2	1.14	13.22	4.70	72.3	**0.5**	5.6	51.0	**5.4**
8.7	0.01	0.0	0.12	**5.6**	0.4	1.34	9.59	4.50	69.9	**3.9**	45.3	16.2	**7.1**
8.3	0.13	0.5	0.17	**8.8**	3.3	2.33	21.46	3.50	42.8	**1.6**	25.5	26.3	**8.2**
8.3	0.00	0.0	0.02	**3.1**	0.7	0.58	6.30	4.10	82.4	**2.7**	35.0	19.8	**3.9**
7.9	0.33	1.7	-0.04	**5.8**	2.4	1.02	9.22	3.96	63.9	**1.7**	15.8	21.2	**6.5**
8.3	0.32	1.4	0.22	**4.0**	0.3	0.91	10.64	3.40	76.3	**4.4**	42.9	13.7	**4.1**
8.2	0.01	0.0	0.05	**4.2**	1.4	0.84	8.10	5.04	81.4	**1.6**	13.5	22.8	**5.8**
5.5	1.00	5.1	0.03	**7.9**	5.3	1.47	15.14	3.59	51.6	**2.2**	29.2	20.8	**6.0**
6.1	2.12	10.1	-0.02	**7.8**	1.6	1.90	13.93	4.14	39.3	**0.9**	20.8	35.3	**8.6**
5.3	2.33	9.1	0.21	**4.6**	3.3	1.17	10.10	3.15	65.8	**5.7**	47.9	7.8	**5.6**
4.8	3.51	12.4	0.06	**5.6**	6.1	1.07	7.47	4.01	69.0	**4.3**	30.1	10.2	**8.0**
1.8	2.87	19.1	0.00	**4.1**	1.0	1.03	9.03	3.42	69.2	**3.0**	11.7	13.8	**5.7**
7.3	0.86	4.3	0.00	**4.4**	0.7	1.05	10.49	3.95	66.3	**5.2**	27.9	3.6	**4.9**
4.4	2.76	12.1	0.09	**4.5**	0.7	0.78	9.25	3.68	67.2	**4.2**	41.2	14.1	**3.6**
0.9	4.69	32.9	-0.06	**4.1**	0.4	1.03	10.45	5.17	76.1	**2.4**	10.7	16.5	**3.3**
5.8	0.91	5.8	0.15	**2.1**	0.2	0.44	5.81	3.28	87.8	**5.4**	31.1	3.7	**1.3**
6.9	0.48	3.0	-0.07	**5.0**	1.0	1.23	12.47	3.96	66.6	**2.7**	26.1	16.7	**5.3**
8.7	1.59	2.9	0.00	**3.1**	0.1	0.55	3.57	1.79	75.0	**6.3**	65.0	7.1	**7.0**
6.6	0.87	4.3	0.02	**4.7**	0.6	1.11	10.82	3.25	66.9	**4.5**	42.5	12.9	**6.4**
3.3	7.88	19.8	0.44	**3.5**	0.3	0.49	2.80	3.68	77.3	**5.4**	45.1	8.6	**6.1**
4.1	1.67	11.0	0.69	**6.6**	1.5	1.30	15.02	4.65	57.4	**1.2**	22.5	31.0	**4.5**
5.8	0.85	3.2	0.02	**3.9**	0.4	0.86	8.17	2.77	69.2	**5.6**	47.6	8.0	**6.2**
7.9	0.91	2.8	0.24	**4.3**	1.4	0.96	9.50	3.04	59.5	**5.5**	59.6	12.3	**5.3**
10.0	na	0.0	na	**10.0**	26.2	28.38	32.03	2.71	75.0	**5.0**	443.2	100.0	**7.0**
4.7	0.75	7.0	0.53	**3.8**	0.6	0.61	6.16	3.96	68.8	**0.5**	4.3	52.5	**3.9**
4.6	1.80	9.9	0.05	**3.1**	0.9	0.21	1.68	3.74	89.7	**1.4**	19.6	27.5	**5.6**
7.3	0.56	2.1	0.17	**7.6**	0.9	1.65	11.77	3.70	59.5	**5.9**	46.6	5.4	**9.2**
4.4	1.92	11.5	0.04	**1.7**	0.3	0.34	3.91	3.24	89.0	**2.2**	20.8	18.4	**3.7**
6.1	0.06	0.4	0.03	**7.6**	2.3	1.75	14.22	3.75	51.1	**3.0**	38.5	19.3	**8.6**
6.5	0.58	4.7	0.17	**8.1**	38.2	1.40	15.09	3.76	41.5	**3.9**	12.8	9.5	**7.4**
4.7	1.31	9.0	0.06	**5.5**	0.9	0.99	9.34	3.46	58.0	**1.6**	15.2	22.8	**6.8**

Name	City	State	Rating	2013 Rating	2012 Rating	Total Assets ($Mil)	One Year Asset Growth	Asset Mix (As a % of Total Assets) Comm-ercial Loans	Cons-umer Loans	Mort-gage Loans	Secur-ities	Capital-ization Index	Lever-age Ratio	Risk-Based Capital Ratio
SETTLERS BANK	Windsor	WI	**B-**	B-	C+	141.1	14.62	21.8	0.4	10.6	1.9	**7.2**	10.0	12.7
SEVERN SAVINGS BANK FSB	Annapolis	MD	**C-**	D+	C	765.4	-5.58	2.3	0.1	39.9	8.2	**10.0**	13.7	20.3
SEVIER COUNTY BANK	Sevierville	TN	**E-**	E-	E-	299.9	-4.26	1.3	0.7	8.2	10.5	**0.2**	3.8	6.4
SEWICKLEY SB	Sewickley	PA	**B-**	B-	B	315.6	-2.80	0.4	0.1	4.1	69.9	**10.0**	24.6	65.9
▼ SEYMOUR BANK	Seymour	MO	**B**	B+	A-	135.8	-1.73	1.3	5.3	18.2	33.6	**10.0**	13.0	21.1
SHAMROCK BANK NA	Coalgate	OK	**B**	A-	A-	271.4	5.52	6.1	6.6	13.3	41.6	**10.0**	11.3	18.2
SHARON SB	Darby	PA	**D**	D+	C	191.3	-16.06	0.2	0.1	24.2	52.4	**8.6**	10.1	18.8
SHELBY COUNTY STATE BK	Shelbyville	IL	**B-**	B-	B-	215.0	-2.30	5.1	3.0	15.1	31.2	**8.2**	9.8	16.9
SHELBY COUNTY STATE BK	Harlan	IA	**B**	B-	C+	256.3	3.94	3.9	1.9	5.9	21.1	**6.5**	8.5	13.1
SHELBY SB SSB	Center	TX	**A-**	A	A-	261.0	-1.03	13.5	6.0	18.7	15.6	**10.0**	11.5	18.4
SHELBY STATE BK	Shelby	MI	**C**	C+	C	209.8	-3.66	5.1	1.7	13.6	28.7	**7.4**	9.3	15.0
SHELL LAKE STATE BK	Shell Lake	WI	**A**	A	A	170.0	9.00	4.9	2.1	19.1	53.6	**10.0**	17.0	37.1
▲ SHERBURNE STATE BK	Becker	MN	**B+**	B	C+	85.9	6.12	7.5	1.3	12.9	21.6	**8.1**	9.7	16.3
SHERIDAN STATE BK	Sheridan	IL	**C+**	C+	C+	30.6	0.23	3.4	6.0	29.5	15.8	**8.4**	9.9	18.8
SHERWOOD COMMUNITY BANK	Creighton	MO	**C-**	C-	C-	43.8	15.65	2.3	1.7	27.9	22.5	**6.7**	8.7	15.4
▼ SHERWOOD STATE BK	Sherwood	OH	**C+**	B-	C	56.1	8.94	9.8	10.3	25.2	23.0	**9.3**	10.5	15.9
SHINHAN BANK AMERICA	New York	NY	**B+**	B+	C+	991.4	0.63	21.5	0.4	10.8	8.5	**10.0**	12.8	19.4
SHORE BANK	Onley	VA	**C**	C-	D+	336.4	-0.97	5.9	4.5	24.8	12.7	**9.5**	10.7	15.0
SHORE COMMUNITY BANK	Toms River	NJ	**C-**	C	C-	226.0	-0.11	3.3	0.1	15.1	23.4	**8.5**	10.0	16.6
SIBLEY STATE BK	Sibley	IA	**B-**	B-	B-	91.9	7.45	1.0	1.8	4.0	17.6	**5.8**	8.1	11.6
SICILY ISLAND STATE BK	Sicily Island	LA	**B+**	B+	B	46.8	19.35	14.5	12.1	28.0	7.4	**10.0**	13.6	19.6
SIDELL STATE BK	Sidell	IL	**D+**	D+	C	22.1	-5.95	4.9	4.3	1.8	27.1	**8.6**	10.0	22.1
▼ SIDNEY FS&LA	Sidney	NE	**D-**	D+	C	23.1	-10.95	0.0	1.6	26.4	62.5	**8.4**	9.9	39.4
SIDNEY STATE BK	Sidney	MI	**C+**	C+	C	50.3	2.80	2.7	4.7	59.3	9.3	**10.0**	12.4	22.7
SIERRA VISTA BANK	Folsom	CA	**C+**	C	D	121.4	31.66	6.6	0.2	12.9	13.3	**10.0**	11.2	16.2
SIGNATURE BANK	Bad Axe	MI	**D+**	D+	D+	233.5	2.86	5.7	1.4	25.7	14.7	**7.8**	9.6	14.3
▼ SIGNATURE BANK	Chicago	IL	**C-**	C+	B-	515.1	23.08	38.3	0.2	4.2	6.2	**8.5**	10.0	13.8
SIGNATURE BANK	Minnetonka	MN	**C+**	C	D+	303.3	27.10	26.5	2.4	12.2	6.9	**5.8**	8.4	11.6
SIGNATURE BANK	New York	NY	**A-**	A-	A-	25950.5	23.54	12.5	0.6	1.6	31.7	**7.7**	9.5	16.5
SIGNATURE BANK NA	Toledo	OH	**B**	B	B-	662.2	9.00	20.6	1.8	11.7	4.6	**7.5**	9.7	12.9
▲ SIGNATURE BANK OF ARKANSAS	Fayetteville	AR	**D**	D-	D-	491.9	0.67	15.1	1.7	24.2	9.8	**8.9**	10.3	14.2
SIGNATURE BANK OF GEORGIA	Sandy Springs	GA	**D-**	E+	E-	98.7	-23.28	10.4	0.3	2.9	23.1	**5.5**	7.5	11.6
SILEX BANKING CO	Silex	MO	**B+**	B+	B+	72.4	4.63	1.4	0.4	10.7	47.2	**10.0**	14.4	29.1
SILICON VALLEY BANK	Santa Clara	CA	**B+**	B+	B	34371.9	53.81	22.8	0.1	2.8	58.0	**5.1**	7.1	13.1
▲ SILVER LAKE BANK	Topeka	KS	**C**	D+	C-	237.7	-0.24	13.2	0.9	16.5	32.1	**10.0**	11.3	20.0
SILVERGATE BANK	La Jolla	CA	**B+**	B+	B-	761.8	23.57	0.7	0.0	26.3	5.6	**8.6**	10.1	15.4
SIMMESPORT STATE BK	Simmesport	LA	**B+**	B+	B	66.5	4.16	7.1	17.7	37.3	5.7	**10.0**	14.8	23.0
SIMMONS FIRST NATIONAL BK	Pine Bluff	AR	**C+**	C+	B-	4248.1	113.52	6.7	7.0	13.0	25.3	**7.0**	9.0	14.9
SIMMONS FIRST TRUST CO NA	Pine Bluff	AR	**U**	U	A-	2.5	38.91	0.0	0.0	0.0	0.0	**10.0**	80.5	243.0
SIMPLICITY BANK	Covina	CA	**B**	B	C+	863.3	3.44	0.0	6.8	33.2	6.3	**10.0**	14.6	23.2
SIMSBURY BANK & TRUST CO	Simsbury	CT	**C-**	C-	C	410.2	0.79	5.4	3.9	36.9	20.9	**4.8**	6.8	12.8
SIOUXLAND NATIONAL BK	South Sioux City	NE	**C**	C	C-	50.5	1.39	11.7	2.2	22.9	0.3	**7.3**	9.2	17.5
SIUSLAW BANK	Florence	OR	**C**	C-	C+	399.3	12.03	6.5	1.7	6.0	3.2	**10.0**	12.6	18.8
SJN BANK OF KANSAS	Saint John	KS	**A-**	A-	A-	89.4	7.25	17.1	3.2	5.6	17.4	**10.0**	11.7	17.1
SKAGIT BANK	Burlington	WA	**B-**	B-	C	784.9	0.42	7.1	2.8	6.9	32.0	**7.4**	9.3	16.3
SKOWHEGAN SB	Skowhegan	ME	**B-**	B-	B-	534.5	11.58	5.7	7.1	36.6	16.3	**10.0**	12.2	18.8
SLOAN STATE BK	Sloan	IA	**B+**	A-	B+	51.4	2.39	3.8	2.1	14.4	50.5	**9.4**	10.6	23.0
▲ SLOVAK SB	Pittsburgh	PA	**D+**	D	D+	120.1	13.26	2.2	0.7	71.0	2.0	**6.5**	8.5	14.4
SLOVENIAN S&LA FRANKLIN-CONEMA	Conemaugh	PA	**C**	C+	C	130.7	-3.31	0.0	1.1	52.7	27.1	**9.7**	10.8	24.0
SLOVENIAN S&LA OF CANONSBURG	Strabane	PA	**A-**	A-	B+	329.5	6.44	0.0	0.3	40.2	47.2	**10.0**	13.0	28.0
SMACKOVER STATE BK	Smackover	AR	**B**	B	B+	193.0	2.66	1.3	5.3	16.7	53.9	**10.0**	11.3	24.5
▲ SMALL TOWN BANK	Wedowee	AL	**A**	A-	B+	213.7	-4.52	4.3	2.5	8.6	47.0	**10.0**	15.0	26.5
SMARTBANK	Pigeon Forge	TN	**B**	B	B-	535.4	9.69	7.0	0.4	13.7	19.5	**9.3**	10.5	15.1
SNB BANK NA	Shattuck	OK	**C**	C	C	88.2	23.76	25.0	3.9	2.2	27.9	**6.1**	8.1	17.8
SOLERA NATIONAL BK	Lakewood	CO	**D**	D+	C-	148.0	-14.12	7.4	0.0	14.5	39.5	**9.0**	10.3	16.9
SOLOMON STATE BK	Solomon	KS	**A**	A	A	202.6	3.11	4.5	2.3	53.4	4.3	**10.0**	13.4	22.9
SOLON STATE BK	Solon	IA	**B**	B	B	88.4	1.54	18.8	1.9	10.4	30.8	**10.0**	22.0	33.8
SOLVAY BANK	Solvay	NY	**B**	B	B	762.6	14.15	8.7	6.6	29.6	36.2	**7.8**	9.5	19.1
▲ SOMERSET SAVINGS BANK SLA	Bound Brook	NJ	**B-**	C+	B-	569.6	-2.12	0.0	0.0	42.2	42.2	**10.0**	19.1	51.0
SOMERSET TRUST CO	Somerset	PA	**B**	B	B-	900.3	8.26	18.6	3.6	9.6	30.3	**7.1**	9.1	13.5

Asset Quality Index	Adjusted Non-Performing Loans as a % of Total Loans	Adjusted Non-Performing Loans as a % of Capital	Net Charge-Offs Avg Loans	Profitability Index	Net Income ($Mil)	Return on Assets (R.O.A.)	Return on Equity (R.O.E.)	Net Interest Spread	Overhead Efficiency Ratio	Liquidity Index	Liquidity Ratio	Hot Money Ratio	Stability Index
7.1	0.15	1.2	0.01	**3.7**	0.4	0.43	4.32	4.04	79.5	**0.7**	13.1	39.2	**5.8**
3.4	3.91	21.8	0.61	**1.7**	2.2	0.37	2.83	3.31	87.4	**1.6**	13.4	23.2	**5.3**
1.0	2.09	23.5	-0.40	**0.0**	-12.2	-5.25	-75.63	3.28	115.2	**0.7**	12.8	37.4	**2.3**
10.0	0.19	0.1	0.00	**3.7**	1.8	0.73	3.12	1.92	46.7	**4.6**	108.8	28.5	**7.5**
8.7	0.11	0.5	0.56	**4.1**	0.8	0.77	6.27	3.71	75.6	**4.3**	40.2	13.5	**7.1**
7.5	0.88	3.8	1.90	**3.4**	0.9	0.42	3.65	4.08	72.5	**4.2**	48.5	16.3	**7.7**
7.0	1.67	4.7	0.74	**0.8**	-0.2	-0.15	-1.44	2.49	103.1	**4.9**	64.9	16.0	**4.4**
8.7	0.05	0.3	-0.01	**4.6**	1.9	1.15	11.78	3.37	66.4	**4.3**	23.8	7.7	**6.3**
5.3	0.64	4.3	0.00	**4.8**	1.6	0.83	8.61	3.41	63.2	**5.3**	33.6	5.0	**6.4**
7.6	0.31	1.7	0.04	**5.2**	2.1	1.08	9.47	3.63	67.6	**2.0**	14.7	19.0	**8.3**
3.2	2.57	15.5	0.18	**4.1**	1.1	0.71	7.38	4.05	81.4	**4.4**	25.2	7.3	**5.7**
6.3	3.62	8.0	0.07	**6.2**	1.8	1.45	8.01	3.95	57.8	**5.2**	52.0	12.1	**9.5**
4.7	1.75	9.9	0.21	**6.4**	1.0	1.53	16.26	5.14	67.6	**3.8**	25.7	11.2	**5.5**
5.9	0.41	2.3	-0.01	**3.8**	0.1	0.63	5.12	3.22	66.6	**5.3**	39.2	7.6	**5.8**
5.3	1.55	10.4	0.05	**2.6**	0.2	0.44	5.13	4.37	88.5	**3.4**	19.9	12.5	**3.8**
3.1	2.54	16.1	0.13	**5.6**	0.4	1.07	10.21	4.85	72.5	**3.4**	20.7	12.6	**4.9**
6.0	0.69	4.1	0.07	**4.2**	4.9	0.63	4.58	3.16	80.0	**1.6**	17.5	24.2	**6.8**
4.1	1.49	10.3	0.22	**3.6**	1.7	0.70	6.52	3.83	82.2	**3.3**	12.4	12.1	**5.2**
4.9	1.70	9.2	0.08	**2.5**	0.7	0.38	3.84	3.28	80.7	**3.1**	26.9	15.0	**4.9**
7.2	0.13	1.1	0.01	**5.8**	0.6	0.96	11.52	3.43	56.5	**1.5**	11.8	23.4	**4.7**
6.4	0.67	3.9	0.08	**9.3**	0.7	2.37	16.91	6.84	66.1	**0.7**	15.2	48.4	**7.6**
8.7	0.00	0.0	-0.03	**1.4**	0.0	0.05	0.57	2.49	97.8	**6.8**	61.7	0.5	**4.2**
6.7	2.63	7.5	0.34	**0.0**	-0.2	-0.95	-9.43	2.34	152.3	**5.0**	72.6	14.0	**3.7**
3.4	4.12	25.4	0.52	**4.0**	0.3	0.67	5.67	4.49	77.4	**4.2**	19.2	7.6	**5.3**
4.1	1.74	10.2	-0.07	**3.1**	0.4	0.46	3.25	4.50	82.2	**0.8**	19.2	43.3	**5.0**
1.7	5.29	36.1	0.49	**2.6**	0.6	0.32	3.48	4.12	92.4	**3.9**	14.8	9.0	**4.3**
1.9	2.87	18.6	1.58	**3.6**	0.5	0.13	1.17	3.70	44.8	**3.3**	28.4	14.7	**6.1**
3.4	1.97	16.1	0.16	**6.0**	3.0	1.52	17.65	4.12	60.3	**4.5**	28.0	8.0	**4.5**
7.4	0.22	1.5	0.02	**7.6**	215.3	1.20	13.66	3.36	36.2	**4.7**	14.3	4.6	**7.7**
6.8	0.24	1.9	-0.01	**5.4**	4.5	0.92	9.64	3.40	58.1	**2.7**	20.1	16.1	**6.4**
1.4	6.70	44.6	0.57	**3.4**	1.9	0.53	4.69	4.03	71.4	**0.7**	13.3	45.0	**4.8**
3.8	2.16	12.8	0.73	**0.0**	-0.6	-0.80	-11.11	3.80	117.7	**4.4**	28.1	9.0	**1.1**
9.2	0.00	0.0	-0.32	**4.7**	0.6	1.03	7.21	3.10	56.5	**5.8**	61.3	9.6	**8.1**
8.8	0.10	0.5	0.40	**5.2**	194.3	0.87	12.95	2.95	57.9	**7.8**	62.8	0.4	**5.0**
3.7	4.51	21.2	-0.01	**2.9**	1.1	0.58	5.27	2.94	71.6	**2.6**	11.1	15.7	**5.2**
5.8	0.65	5.6	0.01	**4.7**	3.4	0.67	6.35	3.22	73.5	**0.7**	11.1	38.4	**5.9**
4.6	1.53	8.0	0.19	**8.8**	0.9	1.71	12.14	5.15	54.4	**0.8**	17.7	40.2	**7.1**
3.4	2.45	15.0	0.26	**6.0**	28.8	1.02	10.69	5.15	72.9	**3.8**	22.3	12.1	**6.5**
8.1	na	0.0	na	**10.0**	0.6	42.20	54.66	na	79.3	**9.5**	174.5	0.0	**5.0**
4.7	1.61	8.7	-0.01	**4.2**	4.4	0.68	4.69	3.21	73.0	**1.8**	18.2	20.2	**8.4**
5.2	0.80	7.3	0.04	**2.2**	0.6	0.19	2.77	3.03	94.7	**4.3**	24.2	7.6	**3.2**
7.0	0.37	2.2	-0.08	**2.8**	0.2	0.47	5.23	3.04	80.9	**3.0**	35.6	18.6	**4.5**
1.8	4.52	22.1	0.03	**5.6**	3.3	1.22	9.61	3.86	72.7	**5.6**	33.4	2.8	**7.4**
8.2	0.24	1.3	0.00	**8.9**	1.2	1.71	14.77	4.58	46.7	**1.8**	18.8	21.4	**7.1**
5.7	0.87	4.4	-0.06	**4.2**	4.6	0.78	8.69	2.99	70.3	**4.5**	42.0	12.9	**5.9**
4.8	1.64	9.7	0.06	**3.7**	2.3	0.58	4.28	3.68	75.3	**4.2**	16.9	7.4	**7.7**
5.5	4.30	14.8	-0.06	**6.8**	0.6	1.59	15.15	3.56	47.4	**6.3**	64.4	6.6	**7.7**
1.7	4.10	40.7	0.10	**3.4**	0.5	0.59	6.87	2.93	64.9	**0.6**	9.8	48.9	**4.5**
6.2	1.25	6.3	0.00	**3.0**	0.4	0.40	3.92	2.89	79.3	**3.8**	45.5	17.6	**5.3**
6.2	3.32	11.9	0.00	**6.0**	2.4	0.98	7.64	2.70	36.6	**2.8**	58.6	45.1	**7.4**
6.5	2.37	7.2	0.03	**4.9**	1.5	1.02	9.18	3.35	56.8	**2.9**	46.4	26.2	**6.7**
7.1	1.74	4.7	0.21	**7.7**	2.5	1.55	10.05	4.62	51.9	**3.5**	49.7	20.3	**7.4**
5.7	1.38	8.3	0.21	**4.0**	1.6	0.41	3.90	4.13	81.0	**1.2**	13.6	29.1	**6.0**
6.0	1.05	7.1	-0.15	**2.6**	0.2	0.39	4.82	3.13	89.3	**1.1**	16.2	31.5	**4.4**
9.1	0.20	0.9	-0.08	**0.6**	-0.3	-0.28	-2.82	3.52	101.6	**1.1**	27.5	45.6	**4.4**
9.0	0.27	1.5	0.37	**8.3**	2.1	1.34	10.94	3.90	35.2	**1.7**	12.5	20.7	**8.0**
4.3	4.05	11.0	1.66	**10.0**	2.2	3.25	14.67	5.67	40.3	**5.4**	44.4	8.3	**8.6**
5.4	1.14	6.6	0.07	**4.8**	4.9	0.91	9.73	3.11	64.3	**2.6**	21.9	16.5	**5.8**
10.0	0.02	0.1	0.03	**3.4**	2.1	0.49	2.66	2.45	68.3	**6.2**	64.5	9.7	**8.3**
5.3	0.92	5.7	0.14	**5.0**	7.5	1.18	13.49	4.33	75.8	**2.6**	29.0	18.2	**5.7**

Name	City	State	Rating	2013 Rating	2012 Rating	Total Assets ($Mil)	One Year Asset Growth	Asset Mix (As a % of Total Assets) Commercial Loans	Consumer Loans	Mortgage Loans	Securities	Capitalization Index	Leverage Ratio	Risk-Based Capital Ratio
SOMERVILLE NATIONAL BK	Somerville	OH	**B-**	B-	B	168.3	-2.96	2.6	1.7	23.1	32.2	**10.0**	11.0	22.1
▲ SONABANK	McLean	VA	**A-**	B+	A-	882.7	24.74	13.0	0.2	15.2	10.3	**10.0**	12.7	17.2
SOONER STATE BK	Tuttle	OK	**A**	A	A-	178.3	6.86	11.6	3.5	12.2	24.1	**10.0**	11.2	16.8
SOUND BANKING CO	Morehead City	NC	**C+**	C+	C+	151.0	18.12	5.0	1.9	26.2	11.7	**6.3**	8.3	12.8
SOUND BANKING CO	Tacoma	WA	**C+**	C+	C	53.7	20.79	15.5	0.5	23.5	0.0	**7.9**	9.6	15.1
SOUND COMMUNITY BANK	Seattle	WA	**B-**	C+	C	479.2	10.83	5.0	5.8	29.2	2.7	**8.8**	10.3	14.0
SOUTH ATLANTIC BANK	Myrtle Beach	SC	**C+**	C+	C	338.0	8.39	5.2	1.0	17.1	21.0	**6.1**	8.2	11.9
SOUTH CAROLINA COMMUNITY BANK	Columbia	SC	**E-**	E-	E-	61.8	-11.25	2.9	1.1	14.7	19.2	**0.8**	4.5	7.7
SOUTH CENTRAL BANK INC	Glasgow	KY	**B-**	B-	C+	274.6	2.61	4.7	2.6	15.8	24.7	**10.0**	12.2	18.8
SOUTH CENTRAL BANK NA	Chicago	IL	**C-**	C-	D+	256.0	4.90	16.5	2.1	15.3	39.4	**6.3**	8.3	15.9
SOUTH CENTRAL BK BOWLING GREEN	Bowling Green	KY	**B-**	B-	C+	216.7	-0.81	1.7	2.4	21.2	31.3	**10.0**	13.6	22.5
SOUTH CENTRAL BK HARDIN CNTY	Elizabethtown	KY	**B-**	B-	C+	84.7	6.37	2.7	2.0	28.6	19.3	**10.0**	11.0	16.5
SOUTH CENTRAL BK MONROE CNTY	Tompkinsville	KY	**B-**	B-	C+	119.3	1.34	4.9	5.4	17.2	31.8	**10.0**	11.9	18.5
SOUTH CENTRAL BK OF DAVIESS	Owensboro	KY	**C+**	C+	C	174.4	-1.51	6.5	3.2	15.3	32.3	**7.4**	9.2	18.6
SOUTH CENTRAL STATE BK	Campbell	NE	**B**	B	C+	111.6	2.57	4.1	9.1	1.9	23.5	**7.3**	9.9	12.8
▲ SOUTH COAST BANK & TRUST	Brunswick	GA	**D-**	E	D-	26.6	-3.45	3.6	8.8	13.7	26.8	**5.8**	7.8	21.2
SOUTH COUNTY BANK NA	Irvine	CA	**E**	E-	E-	141.4	-3.75	8.7	0.4	1.6	31.0	**3.7**	5.7	12.9
SOUTH END SAVINGS SB	Homewood	IL	**D+**	D+	C+	34.7	-5.70	0.0	0.0	36.2	49.9	**10.0**	15.1	46.6
SOUTH GEORGIA BANK	Glennville	GA	**C+**	C	D-	123.1	-2.21	3.2	6.1	21.2	17.3	**9.5**	10.6	16.8
SOUTH GEORGIA BANKING CO	Tifton	GA	**B-**	B-	C+	430.6	25.84	4.8	3.3	11.6	23.2	**9.3**	10.5	18.8
SOUTH LAFOURCHE BANK & TRUST	Larose	LA	**C+**	C	C-	168.6	-2.78	17.0	5.4	41.2	4.6	**8.5**	10.0	16.7
SOUTH LOUISIANA BANK	Houma	LA	**A**	A	A-	457.7	6.70	16.2	2.8	9.8	8.7	**10.0**	12.3	19.4
SOUTH OTTUMWA SB	Ottumwa	IA	**C+**	C+	C+	297.6	0.59	3.7	0.5	13.5	51.0	**8.9**	10.3	20.2
▼ SOUTH PORTE BANK	Marion	IL	**D**	D+	C	40.2	53.12	6.0	2.2	32.7	1.3	**9.1**	10.4	17.2
SOUTH SHORE BANK	South Weymouth	MA	**C-**	C	C	996.8	-1.39	2.6	0.2	32.7	21.2	**9.2**	10.5	15.3
SOUTH SIDE TRUST & SB PEORIA	Peoria	IL	**B+**	B+	A-	659.6	-1.08	4.3	2.1	26.5	35.5	**10.0**	11.7	22.4
SOUTH SOUND BANK	Olympia	WA	**C**	C	C	166.6	-0.64	15.1	0.9	4.5	19.4	**10.0**	13.5	20.5
SOUTH STATE BANK	Columbia	SC	**C+**	C+	C	7893.1	-1.61	4.5	6.3	25.0	10.3	**7.1**	9.0	13.9
SOUTH STORY BANK & TRUST	Slater	IA	**B**	B	B	126.1	28.56	16.7	1.9	18.0	9.4	**4.3**	7.7	10.7
SOUTHBANK A FSB	Palm Beach Gardens	FL	**D-**	D-	D-	22.5	0.27	0.0	0.0	1.4	35.0	**7.4**	9.2	30.5
SOUTHBANK A FSB	Huntsville	AL	**D-**	D-	D-	162.6	-4.64	0.8	0.8	11.6	18.5	**5.1**	9.0	11.1
SOUTHBRIDGE SB	Southbridge	MA	**C**	C+	C+	441.8	1.16	6.5	3.3	48.6	5.2	**6.7**	8.7	13.3
SOUTHCOAST COMMUNITY BANK	Mount Pleasant	SC	**C+**	C	D+	459.5	5.04	4.4	0.5	43.5	7.7	**9.7**	10.8	15.9
SOUTHCREST BANK NA	Tyrone	GA	**D**	D	D+	551.7	265.74	3.1	2.8	18.7	29.5	**6.2**	8.2	14.0
▼ SOUTHEAST BANK	Athens	TN	**C-**	C+	C	623.3	24.57	3.7	46.1	13.1	2.3	**7.9**	9.6	16.8
SOUTHEAST FIRST NATIONAL BK	Summerville	GA	**C**	C	C-	60.9	-7.77	0.5	2.5	7.7	67.5	**9.5**	10.7	37.0
SOUTHEAST NATIONAL BK	Moline	IL	**C**	C	C+	182.6	19.44	9.1	1.3	16.6	36.0	**9.0**	10.3	17.5
▲ SOUTHEASTERN BANK	Darien	GA	**C-**	D+	D-	382.6	8.72	3.8	1.8	8.7	24.6	**8.0**	9.6	19.1
SOUTHERN BANCORP BANK	Arkadelphia	AR	**B-**	B-	B-	1155.8	-3.52	8.9	3.5	18.5	17.3	**6.4**	8.4	12.9
SOUTHERN BANK	Poplar Bluff	MO	**A-**	A-	A-	1046.2	27.01	7.8	1.5	22.1	12.1	**7.8**	9.6	13.6
SOUTHERN BANK	Sardis	GA	**C**	C	D+	80.1	-1.44	0.7	9.1	29.4	20.2	**9.0**	10.3	17.0
SOUTHERN BANK & TRUST	Clarkesville	GA	**B**	B	C+	101.9	3.60	2.7	3.5	20.6	23.6	**10.0**	12.1	18.5
SOUTHERN BANK & TRUST CO	Mount Olive	NC	**C+**	B-	C	2156.5	-4.86	5.2	1.2	10.8	21.9	**7.2**	9.2	18.0
SOUTHERN BANK CO	Gadsden	AL	**D**	D	D+	95.7	-0.07	5.9	1.0	9.1	53.7	**10.0**	14.5	31.1
▼ SOUTHERN BANK OF TENNESSEE	Mount Juliet	TN	**D-**	D	C	191.6	28.48	7.6	1.4	18.1	18.6	**9.7**	10.8	16.1
▲ SOUTHERN COMMERCE BANK NA	Tampa	FL	**B**	C+	D+	77.2	9.34	14.5	0.6	2.6	16.5	**10.0**	19.2	37.8
SOUTHERN COMMERCIAL BANK	Saint Louis	MO	**B-**	C+	C-	510.3	0.44	8.0	0.3	10.7	34.4	**10.0**	11.1	19.6
SOUTHERN COMMUNITY BANK	Tullahoma	TN	**C**	C	B-	154.9	7.31	7.3	1.9	19.8	12.6	**8.6**	10.0	14.1
SOUTHERN FIRST BANK	Greenville	SC	**C+**	C+	C+	1005.2	18.53	10.7	1.2	21.0	5.7	**6.4**	9.1	12.0
SOUTHERN HERITAGE BANK	Cleveland	TN	**A-**	A-	A-	240.5	1.90	8.9	0.7	8.8	33.7	**10.0**	11.5	18.3
SOUTHERN HERITAGE BANK	Jonesville	LA	**A-**	A-	A-	275.3	6.27	7.6	6.3	26.0	28.7	**10.0**	11.8	21.8
▼ SOUTHERN HILLS COMMUNITY BANK	Leesburg	OH	**C+**	B-	B-	82.4	-4.11	2.1	5.6	47.5	0.0	**10.0**	15.6	30.1
SOUTHERN ILLINOIS BANK	Johnston City	IL	**B**	B	B-	104.0	7.12	6.4	3.0	17.4	36.1	**7.2**	9.1	15.0
SOUTHERN INDEPENDENT BANK	Opp	AL	**B-**	B-	B-	195.2	2.25	14.5	2.5	15.4	35.1	**8.5**	10.0	17.5
▲ SOUTHERN MICHIGAN BANK & TRUST	Coldwater	MI	**B-**	C+	C	542.6	1.34	8.6	1.4	13.5	15.7	**8.0**	9.7	13.3
SOUTHERN MO BK OF MARSHFIELD	Marshfield	MO	**B-**	B	B-	93.6	-2.03	3.0	2.6	29.0	10.1	**9.0**	10.4	15.0
SOUTHERN STATES BANK	Anniston	AL	**B-**	C+	C+	289.8	11.06	12.1	2.0	9.6	6.1	**10.0**	15.7	17.9
▼ SOUTHERNTRUST BANK	Goreville	IL	**D**	D+	D	50.1	3.59	4.5	2.5	25.3	22.5	**7.0**	9.0	17.4
SOUTHFIRST BANK	Sylacauga	AL	**C-**	C	D	93.0	-7.84	1.3	1.0	38.0	5.9	**9.1**	10.4	17.2
▲ SOUTHPOINT BANK	Birmingham	AL	**C**	D	E+	206.9	2.06	15.1	1.7	15.4	14.1	**6.6**	8.9	12.2

Asset Quality Index	Adjusted Non-Performing Loans as a % of Total Loans	Adjusted Non-Performing Loans as a % of Capital	Net Charge-Offs Avg Loans	Profitability Index	Net Income ($Mil)	Return on Assets (R.O.A.)	Return on Equity (R.O.E.)	Net Interest Spread	Overhead Efficiency Ratio	Liquidity Index	Liquidity Ratio	Hot Money Ratio	Stability Index
5.3	2.47	11.9	0.08	**3.7**	1.0	0.76	7.35	2.96	73.5	**4.3**	47.9	15.3	**6.0**
6.6	0.21	1.3	0.52	**5.8**	5.6	0.98	6.93	4.72	59.2	**0.6**	8.7	49.1	**6.8**
8.5	0.30	1.6	0.04	**6.7**	2.1	1.60	13.84	4.25	64.1	**2.5**	31.0	19.4	**8.6**
4.0	2.02	16.6	0.07	**4.3**	0.8	0.73	9.11	4.28	72.3	**1.5**	22.2	26.3	**3.3**
4.3	1.56	11.2	0.09	**8.2**	0.7	2.02	20.03	4.87	59.4	**3.2**	28.3	15.2	**4.6**
4.4	1.01	8.3	0.18	**6.2**	3.5	1.05	10.14	4.69	64.6	**1.1**	8.2	28.3	**4.6**
7.9	0.11	0.8	0.08	**3.5**	1.5	0.58	7.67	4.00	78.0	**3.2**	22.3	13.6	**3.8**
0.0	28.66	256.1	0.29	**0.0**	-0.5	-0.93	-20.70	3.50	120.2	**1.2**	20.5	30.8	**0.1**
4.4	2.74	12.9	0.31	**4.1**	1.4	0.66	5.73	3.77	77.8	**2.8**	26.6	16.8	**6.1**
2.4	4.37	19.7	0.16	**2.7**	0.9	0.48	5.97	3.71	90.5	**4.0**	48.9	17.3	**4.2**
5.2	2.32	9.4	0.10	**4.0**	1.2	0.71	5.49	3.30	78.3	**4.0**	32.3	12.6	**6.7**
4.9	1.44	8.8	0.10	**2.3**	0.2	0.30	2.92	3.43	87.3	**1.3**	28.9	34.2	**5.6**
7.8	0.56	2.8	0.26	**4.2**	0.7	0.77	6.84	3.64	75.6	**1.8**	21.0	21.9	**6.7**
6.3	0.73	3.6	0.09	**2.9**	0.7	0.48	5.46	3.29	83.0	**4.5**	40.6	12.7	**5.2**
4.3	1.51	9.2	0.01	**5.3**	0.9	1.11	10.66	3.44	61.6	**4.4**	34.0	10.9	**6.8**
1.9	7.05	27.0	0.03	**0.6**	0.0	0.04	0.60	2.78	98.4	**4.5**	40.4	12.6	**3.2**
4.9	0.93	5.3	-0.15	**1.6**	0.4	0.41	7.90	3.10	99.1	**2.5**	35.9	24.0	**1.7**
8.8	0.69	1.7	0.00	**0.5**	-0.1	-0.31	-2.03	2.66	106.8	**3.6**	70.8	25.9	**5.8**
5.5	0.85	4.8	0.43	**6.4**	1.5	1.58	16.26	5.50	66.2	**1.1**	19.4	32.4	**3.8**
4.0	2.69	12.1	0.03	**6.9**	4.6	1.38	11.58	3.98	57.6	**3.4**	43.3	18.7	**6.9**
3.2	2.37	16.8	0.24	**5.0**	1.5	1.15	11.98	4.03	73.9	**1.4**	17.5	26.2	**7.3**
6.3	1.47	6.4	0.12	**7.2**	4.1	1.21	10.06	4.09	60.4	**2.6**	33.1	19.7	**7.8**
6.3	0.92	3.5	0.07	**4.0**	2.2	0.95	8.75	3.29	70.9	**3.3**	48.8	22.3	**5.2**
6.3	0.86	6.3	0.05	**0.7**	0.0	0.13	1.05	2.98	88.5	**0.9**	23.3	39.8	**4.0**
4.2	2.05	13.3	0.04	**2.4**	2.1	0.28	2.60	2.90	89.1	**3.2**	18.1	13.5	**7.0**
6.1	1.75	7.5	0.13	**4.9**	4.6	0.92	7.98	3.17	61.9	**3.6**	31.5	14.4	**7.6**
6.9	0.95	3.7	0.33	**2.4**	0.4	0.34	2.48	3.68	88.5	**4.8**	31.6	7.8	**6.1**
3.5	1.33	10.5	0.10	**5.8**	59.8	1.00	7.66	4.87	70.3	**4.2**	12.8	7.3	**8.4**
7.5	0.02	0.2	0.00	**5.2**	1.0	1.15	11.01	4.26	67.5	**1.4**	8.2	24.0	**7.1**
7.0	0.00	0.0	0.00	**0.0**	-0.3	-1.57	-21.66	1.12	219.9	**4.8**	90.8	17.6	**2.3**
1.7	10.33	43.2	-0.03	**0.0**	-2.1	-1.67	-21.39	2.60	154.3	**2.9**	44.1	24.1	**2.3**
4.0	1.80	16.4	0.37	**2.6**	0.8	0.25	2.82	3.66	86.6	**2.3**	8.3	16.9	**4.4**
3.5	2.28	15.0	0.04	**4.3**	2.5	0.76	6.99	3.70	71.3	**1.8**	9.6	19.5	**4.4**
3.5	3.44	20.0	0.40	**0.8**	-1.3	-0.31	-3.97	4.96	106.7	**4.0**	26.6	10.8	**3.2**
1.7	1.10	9.8	0.21	**6.7**	5.2	1.17	11.44	4.73	64.7	**1.2**	6.1	26.2	**3.2**
4.2	6.16	9.4	-0.01	**2.9**	0.2	0.39	3.79	2.83	79.2	**6.3**	67.5	7.7	**3.9**
5.8	1.10	6.0	0.06	**2.6**	0.5	0.46	4.17	3.45	87.0	**5.4**	40.0	7.1	**5.1**
2.2	6.02	24.3	0.42	**2.5**	1.7	0.58	6.25	3.40	84.2	**4.6**	38.1	11.6	**4.1**
4.4	1.13	8.6	0.27	**5.1**	8.6	1.00	9.16	4.43	66.6	**2.4**	5.8	16.3	**8.0**
7.4	0.43	3.4	0.12	**6.7**	8.7	1.15	11.07	3.92	58.2	**1.4**	6.9	23.8	**8.5**
5.2	0.73	4.2	0.07	**2.9**	0.2	0.33	3.24	5.21	89.0	**1.4**	16.9	26.6	**4.3**
4.6	2.68	13.8	0.00	**4.5**	0.6	0.83	7.12	4.13	72.1	**2.7**	28.6	17.8	**6.6**
5.7	2.06	11.3	0.32	**3.1**	5.2	0.32	3.32	4.44	82.8	**4.6**	26.2	10.3	**6.3**
8.0	1.45	3.9	0.02	**0.1**	-0.2	-0.31	-2.07	2.83	125.3	**1.7**	27.3	26.7	**6.4**
5.8	0.68	4.1	-0.13	**0.1**	-0.1	-0.09	-0.70	3.18	104.6	**1.2**	26.5	32.9	**4.3**
7.8	2.65	6.0	0.85	**2.5**	0.4	0.68	2.17	2.46	82.2	**3.5**	57.5	21.4	**7.5**
5.5	2.37	10.0	1.19	**3.9**	3.0	0.77	6.92	3.39	71.6	**5.3**	44.8	9.4	**6.6**
8.3	0.02	0.2	0.00	**3.1**	0.4	0.31	2.74	4.04	86.4	**1.1**	15.0	30.2	**6.4**
4.8	1.37	11.6	0.37	**4.2**	5.3	0.75	8.32	3.73	62.3	**1.2**	9.7	27.8	**5.6**
5.9	2.14	9.7	0.03	**5.7**	2.2	1.21	9.51	3.67	67.5	**3.7**	45.2	17.8	**7.0**
7.2	0.73	3.6	0.01	**6.4**	3.0	1.48	12.47	4.27	68.5	**3.2**	24.2	13.8	**7.3**
7.3	0.80	3.4	0.55	**2.8**	0.2	0.29	1.88	4.47	81.9	**4.3**	30.7	10.4	**6.4**
6.6	0.96	5.4	0.06	**5.2**	0.7	0.92	10.26	3.69	60.7	**5.1**	19.9	2.1	**4.8**
5.6	1.17	5.5	-0.08	**4.5**	1.4	0.90	9.82	3.26	56.5	**2.2**	37.4	29.4	**5.1**
4.0	0.94	6.6	0.11	**4.8**	3.8	0.91	7.86	3.88	71.0	**4.2**	16.0	7.8	**6.6**
8.2	0.29	1.9	0.01	**3.9**	0.5	0.76	7.10	4.30	83.8	**0.9**	13.0	32.6	**6.1**
3.5	2.09	10.5	-0.03	**6.7**	2.1	1.05	6.61	5.03	69.1	**1.6**	7.2	21.4	**6.5**
2.5	3.62	21.0	-0.08	**1.7**	0.0	0.07	0.74	3.88	95.6	**2.4**	33.0	22.4	**3.8**
3.5	3.12	18.9	0.05	**2.3**	0.2	0.23	2.33	3.76	94.5	**1.9**	20.9	20.6	**3.3**
4.9	0.94	7.3	0.02	**4.7**	2.2	1.40	16.70	3.59	76.2	**1.8**	2.9	18.9	**2.7**

	Name	City	State	Rating	2013 Rating	2012 Rating	Total Assets ($Mil)	One Year Asset Growth	Asset Mix (As a % of Total Assets) Comm-ercial Loans	Cons-umer Loans	Mort-gage Loans	Secur-ities	Capital-ization Index	Lever-age Ratio	Risk-Based Capital Ratio
	SOUTHPORT BANK	Kenosha	WI	**D**	D	E+	269.3	4.95	7.5	0.2	10.6	5.5	**5.6**	8.6	11.5
	SOUTHSIDE BANK	Tyler	TX	**B**	B	B	3362.3	-2.96	3.6	4.4	11.8	49.2	**8.6**	10.0	21.5
	SOUTHTRUST BANK NA	George West	TX	**B+**	B+	B+	334.0	14.87	7.2	3.1	10.1	28.2	**7.7**	9.5	14.0
▲	SOUTHWEST BANK	Fort Worth	TX	**B**	B-	C	1492.8	25.00	17.6	0.9	12.6	5.0	**7.0**	11.2	12.5
	SOUTHWEST BANK	Odessa	TX	**B-**	B-	C+	314.4	11.86	32.4	2.0	8.6	18.2	**5.6**	8.2	11.5
	SOUTHWEST CAPITAL BANK	Las Vegas	NM	**A-**	A-	A-	276.0	24.90	7.1	0.8	13.0	17.2	**7.7**	9.4	13.4
	SOUTHWEST GEORGIA BANK	Moultrie	GA	**C+**	C+	C+	379.9	2.29	3.7	0.8	17.5	29.0	**6.8**	8.8	15.0
	SOUTHWEST MISSOURI BANK	Carthage	MO	**B**	B	B	620.4	3.10	6.3	7.4	25.1	25.2	**8.0**	9.6	16.0
	SOUTHWEST NATIONAL BK	Wichita	KS	**B+**	B+	B	442.4	2.38	4.9	41.1	4.8	15.0	**6.5**	9.0	12.1
	SOUTHWEST NATIONAL BK	Weatherford	OK	**B+**	A-	B+	70.6	9.23	3.4	5.2	12.4	31.5	**10.0**	11.0	18.2
	SOUTHWEST SECURITIES FSB	Dallas	TX	**C+**	C+	C	1228.6	-2.96	4.1	0.4	5.4	37.4	**10.0**	14.6	25.6
	SOUTHWEST STATE BK	Sentinel	OK	**A-**	A-	B-	95.9	-9.19	4.9	2.4	2.3	41.4	**7.8**	9.5	13.3
	SOUTHWESTERN NATIONAL BK	Houston	TX	**B**	C+	C	348.1	-1.01	1.4	0.1	0.5	43.0	**10.0**	11.6	25.5
	SOUTHWIND BANK	Natoma	KS	**C+**	C+	C+	122.7	9.67	4.6	2.7	7.8	54.3	**5.9**	7.9	16.7
▲	SOVEREIGN BANK	Dallas	TX	**B-**	C	C+	1045.9	-3.46	29.1	0.2	1.7	31.2	**10.0**	11.1	15.1
▲	SOY CAPITAL BANK & TRUST CO	Decatur	IL	**A**	A-	A	389.5	1.84	9.7	4.0	2.4	23.5	**10.0**	13.8	22.3
	SPENCER COUNTY BANK	Santa Claus	IN	**C+**	C+	C+	106.9	-5.58	3.3	3.4	24.6	43.6	**8.1**	9.8	22.0
	SPENCER SAVINGS BANK SLA	Elmwood Park	NJ	**B**	B	B	2075.5	6.54	0.7	0.0	27.2	23.6	**10.0**	13.8	17.7
	SPENCER SB	Spencer	MA	**B-**	B-	B-	458.3	15.76	2.7	0.5	41.6	8.2	**10.0**	12.3	18.9
	SPIRIT OF TEXAS BANK SSB	College Station	TX	**B**	B	B-	661.8	22.07	12.2	1.0	25.9	3.6	**8.3**	10.8	13.5
	SPIRITBANK	Tulsa	OK	**D+**	D	D-	626.8	-22.11	16.3	0.6	39.6	5.2	**10.0**	12.4	18.0
	SPIRO STATE BK	Spiro	OK	**C-**	C	B-	49.7	-2.93	2.9	4.6	13.7	54.2	**10.0**	12.5	29.8
	SPIVEY STATE BK	Swainsboro	GA	**D-**	D-	D+	90.9	2.64	6.9	10.6	16.7	16.5	**9.9**	11.0	16.2
	SPRATT S&LA	Chester	SC	**C+**	C+	B-	112.9	5.69	1.7	0.3	8.4	49.8	**10.0**	24.2	67.8
▲	SPRING BANK	Bronx	NY	**B-**	B-	B	105.2	11.23	22.9	0.0	11.2	10.6	**10.0**	13.4	20.6
	SPRING BANK	Brookfield	WI	**C-**	C+	B-	197.6	9.84	15.0	0.1	13.9	10.5	**9.6**	11.0	14.7
	SPRING HILL STATE BK	Longview	TX	**B-**	B-	C+	186.1	5.45	7.5	5.6	49.1	2.2	**6.9**	9.0	16.0
	SPRING VALLEY BANK	Wyoming	OH	**B-**	B-	B-	67.2	-9.87	3.3	0.1	16.8	2.3	**10.0**	41.8	54.8
	SPRING VALLEY CITY BANK	Spring Valley	IL	**B+**	B+	B+	206.8	1.39	4.3	3.2	17.3	48.0	**10.0**	12.4	30.8
▲	SPRINGFIELD FIRST COMMUNITY BK	Springfield	MO	**B**	C+	C+	330.9	1.79	14.9	1.0	16.6	0.3	**6.8**	8.8	13.0
	SPRINGFIELD STATE BK	Springfield	KY	**A-**	A-	A-	283.8	4.46	1.9	2.0	23.3	44.4	**10.0**	13.5	24.0
▲	SPRINGFIELD STATE BK	Springfield	NE	**B**	B-	C+	42.2	-1.44	4.0	3.7	11.7	30.5	**10.0**	11.2	21.4
▼	SPRINGS VALLEY BANK & TRUST CO	French Lick	IN	**B-**	B	C+	276.5	12.98	5.6	2.3	28.2	17.1	**9.0**	10.4	15.7
	SPUR SECURITY BANK	Spur	TX	**C**	C	C	42.5	-4.10	1.8	6.0	3.9	68.8	**9.3**	10.5	26.9
	SQUARE 1 BANK	Durham	NC	**B+**	B	B-	2984.3	37.91	36.4	0.0	0.0	49.3	**8.3**	9.8	14.5
	SSB COMMUNITY BANK	Strasburg	OH	**B-**	B-	B-	57.2	23.07	7.3	1.0	51.7	0.0	**8.3**	9.8	16.4
▲	SSBBANK	Stockbridge	MI	**D**	D-	E+	60.1	1.10	6.4	5.4	31.1	27.8	**6.5**	8.5	15.9
	ST ANSGAR STATE BK	Saint Ansgar	IA	**A-**	A-	A-	99.2	-4.03	10.5	2.0	9.9	19.5	**10.0**	13.3	19.3
	ST CHARLES BANK & TRUST CO	Saint Charles	IL	**C+**	C+	C	705.9	1.94	21.5	12.2	4.2	5.0	**5.7**	9.7	11.5
	ST CLAIR COUNTY STATE BK	Osceola	MO	**A-**	A-	A-	127.6	4.58	6.6	4.8	23.3	14.1	**10.0**	11.9	19.1
	ST CLAIR STATE BK (INC)	Saint Clair	MN	**A-**	A-	A-	80.6	0.23	7.4	6.3	14.3	3.3	**10.0**	12.9	19.0
	ST HENRY BANK	Saint Henry	OH	**A+**	A+	A+	265.5	4.58	4.0	1.0	15.1	41.1	**10.0**	14.9	27.9
▼	ST JAMES FS&LA	Saint James	MN	**C**	C+	C	26.6	-1.53	5.0	5.3	24.7	4.6	**8.8**	10.2	16.8
▲	ST JOHNS BANK & TRUST CO	Saint Louis	MO	**D**	D	D-	303.2	-1.38	5.6	0.5	7.3	22.2	**6.9**	8.9	13.2
	ST LANDRY BANK & TRUST CO	Opelousas	LA	**C+**	C+	B-	281.4	5.83	3.4	1.0	2.9	59.3	**10.0**	11.3	29.7
	ST LANDRY HOMESTEAD FSB	Opelousas	LA	**C**	C	C	232.6	1.66	1.3	2.1	54.9	11.5	**10.0**	18.4	33.3
	ST LOUIS BANK	Town And Country	MO	**D+**	D	D-	373.6	-1.87	9.5	0.1	12.2	15.7	**5.7**	7.7	12.7
	ST MARTIN BANK & TRUST CO	Saint Martinville	LA	**B-**	B-	B-	466.6	10.97	6.5	5.1	23.3	10.4	**8.4**	9.9	14.3
	ST MARTIN NATIONAL BK	Saint Martin	MN	**B**	B	B+	21.0	5.21	4.5	3.7	16.0	18.7	**10.0**	13.4	28.9
	ST MARYS STATE BK	Saint Marys	KS	**B-**	B-	B-	91.2	5.22	10.1	3.0	14.6	33.8	**9.2**	10.4	14.7
	STAFFORD SB	Stafford Springs	CT	**B**	B	B	253.1	6.71	0.0	0.3	27.7	49.5	**10.0**	28.1	53.2
	STANDARD BANK & TRUST CO	Hickory Hills	IL	**C-**	D+	D	2280.1	5.85	15.9	0.2	6.4	6.5	**8.9**	10.4	14.0
	STANDARD BANK PASB	Monroeville	PA	**B**	B	B-	443.8	1.84	3.0	0.3	49.2	20.1	**10.0**	14.2	22.7
	STANDING STONE NATIONAL BK	Lancaster	OH	**C**	C	C	95.5	12.26	5.0	5.9	19.0	25.6	**6.0**	8.0	14.2
	STANLEY BANK	Overland Park	KS	**C**	C	C	94.0	3.00	34.3	2.8	4.7	0.0	**10.0**	18.0	29.0
	STANTON STATE BK	Stanton	NE	**C-**	C-	C-	45.5	7.88	6.9	3.0	16.2	26.2	**6.4**	8.4	16.0
▼	STAR BANK	Maple Lake	MN	**B-**	B	B	217.2	1.23	9.6	3.2	14.2	3.2	**4.1**	8.5	10.6
	STAR BANK OF TEXAS	Fort Worth	TX	**B**	B	A-	143.7	2.98	2.7	1.7	21.6	28.1	**8.6**	10.1	21.0
	STAR FINANCIAL BANK	Fort Wayne	IN	**B**	B	B-	1708.2	2.64	19.6	6.7	13.0	16.5	**8.4**	10.3	13.7
	STARION FINANCIAL	Bismarck	ND	**B+**	B	B	1060.9	3.89	9.4	2.3	13.5	30.6	**8.1**	9.7	14.4

Asset Quality Index	Adjusted Non-Performing Loans as a % of Total Loans	Adjusted Non-Performing Loans as a % of Capital	Net Charge-Offs Avg Loans	Profitability Index	Net Income ($Mil)	Return on Assets (R.O.A.)	Return on Equity (R.O.E.)	Net Interest Spread	Overhead Efficiency Ratio	Liquidity Index	Liquidity Ratio	Hot Money Ratio	Stability Index
0.7	3.80	28.9	0.37	3.1	1.4	0.70	7.90	3.67	83.2	2.9	11.6	14.0	3.9
8.4	0.49	2.1	1.65	4.8	27.5	1.08	11.12	3.97	58.5	2.8	26.3	19.2	8.0
4.9	1.20	7.4	0.11	6.9	3.4	1.40	14.46	4.57	65.4	2.6	22.9	17.0	7.4
6.4	0.07	0.5	0.01	4.8	8.7	0.83	6.27	4.16	68.7	3.3	2.8	11.2	8.9
5.8	0.35	2.7	0.76	5.8	3.1	1.37	16.74	4.33	70.0	4.9	29.3	5.9	6.0
6.6	0.22	1.6	0.00	9.2	4.0	2.07	21.40	4.82	53.4	1.2	8.4	27.2	7.2
7.0	0.49	3.1	0.08	3.9	2.3	0.80	9.92	3.95	78.4	4.2	21.5	8.3	4.8
7.1	0.41	2.5	0.18	4.5	3.9	0.83	8.96	4.10	77.8	3.8	18.0	10.4	5.6
6.3	0.18	1.5	0.36	8.2	6.1	1.87	21.73	4.45	54.7	1.1	19.4	31.7	6.8
6.7	0.87	3.7	0.10	7.0	0.6	1.19	10.31	4.47	60.0	2.9	45.2	24.1	7.6
5.7	2.31	8.2	-0.10	2.3	3.0	0.32	2.36	2.87	94.6	7.4	50.4	1.1	7.3
8.0	0.55	3.0	0.01	7.6	1.2	1.66	17.47	3.65	55.1	2.1	27.6	20.3	7.0
8.2	0.00	0.0	-0.07	4.5	2.8	1.06	9.27	2.93	80.0	4.2	70.2	21.4	6.0
6.6	0.95	3.8	-0.01	3.4	0.7	0.73	9.04	2.97	70.5	5.2	54.6	12.9	5.0
4.9	1.54	8.2	0.50	3.7	4.9	0.64	5.86	3.59	76.3	2.4	37.9	37.2	8.4
6.3	1.12	3.9	-0.02	7.6	3.8	1.22	8.30	2.83	74.0	4.7	25.3	5.5	8.3
6.0	1.02	4.5	0.08	3.4	0.4	0.51	5.11	3.26	75.8	2.4	37.5	26.5	4.5
6.6	1.28	6.2	0.03	4.1	8.3	0.54	4.03	2.92	64.7	3.4	23.9	14.8	9.1
6.9	1.06	6.6	0.09	3.1	1.6	0.50	4.01	3.44	79.6	1.7	18.1	22.3	5.7
6.7	0.35	2.8	0.03	4.8	3.8	0.82	6.88	5.19	80.4	1.1	13.7	30.1	6.7
2.7	4.36	22.8	0.00	6.5	9.0	1.61	13.54	4.86	80.8	0.6	11.0	52.3	4.7
9.4	0.78	1.7	0.07	1.6	0.1	0.16	1.28	3.42	95.6	6.3	59.3	5.7	5.7
0.7	5.50	35.6	0.32	4.8	0.8	1.10	10.56	4.10	73.7	2.0	12.5	19.0	3.0
9.8	0.16	0.2	0.00	2.6	0.3	0.33	1.29	2.29	82.1	5.2	91.3	17.9	7.8
4.6	0.60	3.5	0.56	9.6	1.8	2.35	18.89	5.53	61.7	0.6	14.2	54.9	6.3
1.7	2.94	19.2	0.00	6.5	1.6	1.11	10.22	3.81	45.0	0.9	19.9	37.7	6.1
4.6	1.48	11.5	0.05	4.9	1.1	0.80	9.17	3.99	67.1	2.5	16.4	16.6	5.1
2.8	8.12	12.8	0.37	9.5	1.1	1.95	4.92	4.76	51.7	5.8	50.8	7.1	8.2
5.4	3.54	10.7	0.21	4.8	1.5	0.96	8.02	2.91	55.5	4.4	53.9	16.7	6.7
7.0	0.20	1.7	0.00	4.6	2.8	1.16	13.70	3.41	60.7	2.3	12.1	17.0	5.1
9.4	0.56	1.9	-0.02	5.1	2.2	1.07	8.53	3.55	61.0	2.6	40.0	25.4	7.2
6.5	1.32	5.8	0.04	4.8	0.4	1.21	10.94	3.53	67.8	5.1	25.4	3.0	6.3
3.0	2.79	17.4	0.08	6.0	2.1	1.09	9.87	3.84	68.0	2.0	27.3	22.4	5.8
9.0	0.50	1.1	0.01	3.2	0.3	0.88	8.57	3.11	77.1	2.6	60.5	41.7	4.9
6.8	0.93	3.9	0.49	6.7	24.5	1.25	12.73	4.14	52.1	7.4	50.1	0.6	5.6
4.7	1.66	13.6	-0.01	4.2	0.3	0.88	8.60	3.84	78.3	1.8	18.2	20.4	5.8
1.9	5.02	32.4	0.28	2.1	0.1	0.26	3.16	3.77	96.7	4.5	29.1	8.2	2.7
8.4	0.26	1.3	0.23	6.3	1.1	1.46	11.35	3.56	57.2	4.7	31.3	8.1	7.2
3.3	0.72	5.7	0.21	6.1	5.1	0.97	8.79	3.93	56.8	1.5	10.7	22.9	5.7
7.9	0.43	2.5	0.04	5.8	1.0	1.04	8.85	3.36	56.2	2.5	12.1	16.3	7.5
8.2	0.12	0.6	0.05	8.2	1.3	2.13	17.18	3.28	35.7	3.7	33.1	14.2	7.9
9.2	0.31	1.0	0.01	9.5	4.3	2.23	14.90	3.58	35.1	5.4	49.4	10.2	10.0
6.0	0.66	4.0	0.00	2.7	0.1	0.27	2.72	3.79	87.6	3.8	33.5	14.0	4.8
1.3	3.29	22.4	0.51	1.9	0.3	0.13	1.35	3.49	90.3	4.6	20.4	5.3	3.9
9.5	0.42	1.0	0.01	3.1	1.4	0.64	5.88	1.76	73.2	6.4	57.9	6.7	6.1
1.9	7.59	30.8	0.13	4.3	1.1	0.66	3.62	3.61	69.3	0.6	10.4	42.8	3.9
2.2	2.85	20.8	1.04	1.1	2.3	0.80	8.72	2.95	103.5	0.8	22.3	48.7	3.5
4.1	1.16	8.6	0.02	10.0	9.2	2.73	25.65	5.64	47.0	3.9	13.3	9.0	8.4
9.0	0.00	0.0	0.00	6.5	0.2	1.61	12.26	3.15	63.3	5.8	54.7	5.5	6.3
8.3	0.19	1.0	1.11	4.6	0.8	1.08	10.83	3.59	68.9	4.2	29.8	10.8	5.4
9.9	1.55	2.0	-0.01	4.0	1.8	1.08	2.93	2.97	70.7	6.7	97.6	11.3	8.2
2.3	3.12	19.8	0.16	4.1	12.7	0.75	6.65	3.65	68.1	2.5	13.5	16.5	6.6
8.6	0.20	1.0	0.13	4.2	2.7	0.82	5.01	3.07	66.2	3.4	20.7	12.5	7.4
8.7	0.06	0.4	-0.23	3.1	0.4	0.56	7.17	3.60	86.2	3.7	31.2	13.3	3.4
2.1	6.07	21.0	0.38	4.3	0.7	1.01	5.56	3.15	52.9	5.6	37.4	5.1	5.4
8.8	0.00	0.0	0.00	2.5	0.1	0.40	4.74	2.84	85.4	4.6	28.6	7.6	4.3
6.0	0.32	3.1	0.18	6.7	2.6	1.57	17.72	4.96	64.7	4.1	3.1	6.2	4.7
9.2	0.05	0.2	0.01	4.6	0.9	0.80	8.40	4.37	72.8	3.0	49.6	27.2	5.6
5.7	0.93	5.7	0.07	4.5	9.0	0.71	7.09	3.50	74.2	4.7	22.8	7.0	7.3
5.8	1.31	8.2	-0.01	8.0	14.3	1.84	19.19	3.93	58.9	2.7	13.4	15.6	9.1

Name	City	State	Rating	2013 Rating	2012 Rating	Total Assets ($Mil)	One Year Asset Growth	Asset Mix (As a % of Total Assets) Comm-ercial Loans	Cons-umer Loans	Mort-gage Loans	Secur-ities	Capital-ization Index	Lever-age Ratio	Risk-Based Capital Ratio
START COMMUNITY BANK	New Haven	CT	**D**	D	C-	70.9	29.92	10.8	2.5	42.0	7.6	**10.0**	12.2	17.5
STATE BANK	New Hampton	IA	**B+**	B+	B	363.5	-0.01	2.8	1.9	9.9	45.0	**6.6**	8.6	13.1
STATE BK	Spirit Lake	IA	**C+**	C	C	69.0	-3.63	6.6	1.2	11.8	39.8	**9.8**	10.8	19.1
STATE BK	Spencer	IA	**C**	C	C-	69.6	-1.78	8.2	4.2	17.0	13.8	**4.5**	7.3	10.8
STATE BK	Fenton	MI	**C+**	C+	D+	370.8	17.17	11.9	0.9	22.7	8.8	**7.1**	9.4	12.6
STATE BK	Gresham	WI	**B**	B	B+	22.6	-0.23	5.9	5.0	12.1	0.0	**10.0**	22.5	41.5
STATE BK	Freeport	IL	**B-**	B-	C+	220.1	2.77	23.8	0.2	7.3	22.8	**8.8**	10.2	14.3
STATE BK	Hoxie	KS	**C+**	C+	C+	147.6	-1.24	9.6	1.7	0.2	5.2	**9.8**	11.2	14.8
STATE BK	Richmond	MO	**B**	B	C+	33.5	3.87	3.5	5.1	25.2	39.9	**6.9**	8.9	21.1
STATE BK	La Junta	CO	**C+**	B-	C	99.6	3.47	3.0	2.2	6.2	11.1	**10.0**	11.9	22.1
STATE BK	Wonder Lake	IL	**B**	B-	D	165.7	-0.66	5.4	0.7	33.8	25.4	**10.0**	12.1	23.5
STATE BK	Green River	WY	**C**	C	C-	39.2	-2.44	5.7	3.0	9.3	14.9	**10.0**	11.8	19.9
STATE BK & TRUST	Winfield	AL	**B+**	A-	A-	219.6	8.74	1.5	6.2	11.9	53.0	**10.0**	11.9	25.0
STATE BK & TRUST CO	Golden Meadow	LA	**B**	B	B-	127.3	6.52	25.1	4.3	16.0	19.0	**6.8**	8.9	13.3
▲ STATE BK & TRUST CO	Macon	GA	**A-**	B	A	2647.5	4.58	2.3	0.4	4.5	20.1	**10.0**	14.1	21.9
STATE BK & TRUST CO	Defiance	OH	**C+**	C+	C	666.7	5.50	13.2	1.2	18.2	12.2	**6.5**	8.7	12.1
STATE BK & TRUST CO	Ridgeland	MS	**C+**	C+	C-	973.1	-0.60	5.4	1.7	16.9	12.4	**5.6**	8.9	11.5
STATE BK & TRUST CO	Nevada	IA	**A-**	A-	B+	157.4	0.34	11.4	0.7	14.4	35.1	**9.7**	10.8	16.0
STATE BK & TRUST OF KENMARE	Kenmare	ND	**B**	B-	C+	121.4	9.54	16.2	3.4	11.1	26.6	**6.9**	8.9	12.9
STATE BK FINANCIAL	La Crosse	WI	**B-**	C+	B-	331.7	3.60	8.1	0.1	6.7	28.7	**8.7**	10.1	17.9
STATE BK IN EDEN VALLEY	Eden Valley	MN	**B-**	B-	C	31.0	5.56	6.5	2.1	9.6	33.9	**8.1**	9.7	17.0
STATE BK NORTHWEST	Spokane Valley	WA	**B-**	B-	C+	111.0	8.75	24.9	0.4	13.1	7.6	**9.4**	11.1	14.5
STATE BK OF ALCESTER	Alcester	SD	**B-**	B-	B-	119.6	5.17	4.0	5.4	12.7	19.1	**6.5**	8.6	12.1
STATE BK OF ARCADIA	Arcadia	WI	**B-**	B-	B-	167.8	31.97	3.1	2.1	18.7	25.8	**8.1**	9.7	20.5
STATE BK OF ARTHUR	Arthur	IL	**A-**	A-	A-	121.6	8.32	17.1	8.6	12.2	31.7	**10.0**	13.8	23.9
STATE BK OF BARTLEY	Colorado Springs	CO	**B-**	C+	C-	88.1	3.83	20.2	0.6	11.2	0.4	**7.1**	9.1	18.6
STATE BK OF BELLE PLAINE	Belle Plaine	MN	**B**	B	B	100.4	-3.07	2.2	1.1	7.7	56.9	**10.0**	11.3	26.2
STATE BK OF BELLINGHAM	Bellingham	MN	**C+**	C+	C+	43.1	12.49	2.0	1.2	0.4	3.2	**5.8**	8.5	11.6
STATE BK OF BEMENT	Bement	IL	**B-**	B-	C+	82.2	3.62	13.8	3.9	8.7	34.2	**10.0**	13.9	21.0
STATE BK OF BERN	Bern	KS	**A-**	A-	A-	89.1	8.45	3.6	2.2	4.5	54.5	**10.0**	13.0	21.7
STATE BK OF BLUE MOUND	Blue Mound	IL	**E-**	E-	D-	34.4	10.14	14.3	2.4	10.9	10.3	**1.7**	4.5	12.6
▲ STATE BK OF BLUE RAPIDS	Blue Rapids	KS	**C**	C-	C	46.2	-0.37	9.1	9.6	18.7	41.7	**8.8**	10.2	18.5
STATE BK OF BOTTINEAU	Bottineau	ND	**C-**	C	D+	68.3	16.25	6.3	4.2	23.7	6.6	**4.3**	8.1	10.7
STATE BK OF BROOKS	Corning	IA	**C+**	C+	C	17.6	10.10	2.7	4.7	9.4	41.3	**10.0**	11.2	22.6
▼ STATE BK OF BURNETTSVILLE	Burnettsville	IN	**C-**	C+	C+	48.6	11.47	7.2	10.6	22.5	22.1	**7.5**	9.4	15.3
STATE BK OF BURRTON	Burrton	KS	**D+**	D+	C	10.5	-6.89	2.6	2.0	19.8	8.9	**9.1**	10.4	23.5
▲ STATE BK OF BUSSEY	Bussey	IA	**D+**	D	D-	44.9	-3.87	8.8	3.8	21.0	7.1	**6.8**	8.8	12.9
STATE BK OF CANTON	Canton	KS	**B-**	B-	B-	33.3	-2.76	7.8	2.2	4.8	46.1	**10.0**	16.6	44.6
STATE BK OF CAZENOVIA	Cazenovia	WI	**C+**	C+	B-	35.3	4.05	3.2	3.2	15.0	23.7	**10.0**	17.5	33.7
STATE BK OF CERRO GORDO	Cerro Gordo	IL	**B-**	B-	C+	27.7	-1.30	10.4	3.8	14.0	33.2	**10.0**	13.2	29.4
STATE BK OF CEYLON	Ceylon	MN	**D**	C-	C-	12.2	-5.54	7.9	4.5	1.8	11.7	**8.0**	9.7	23.8
STATE BK OF CHANDLER	Chandler	MN	**B-**	B-	B	44.4	11.33	6.1	3.0	2.1	21.4	**10.0**	11.0	16.7
STATE BK OF CHERRY	Cherry	IL	**B-**	B-	B-	90.6	1.31	1.7	2.7	11.4	51.9	**9.9**	10.9	30.1
STATE BK OF CHILTON	Chilton	WI	**B-**	B-	C+	171.6	13.82	11.9	1.3	10.7	6.0	**10.0**	15.7	20.8
STATE BK OF CHITTENANGO	Chittenango	NY	**U**	U	A-	203.8	35.47	0.0	0.0	0.0	99.6	**7.8**	9.5	50.7
▼ STATE BK OF CHRISMAN	Chrisman	IL	**C+**	C	C-	82.4	1.46	9.0	2.9	10.3	14.2	**5.9**	8.4	11.6
STATE BK OF COCHRAN	Cochran	GA	**B**	B	B	202.9	-2.66	5.3	7.4	21.7	6.3	**10.0**	13.9	27.0
STATE BK OF COLD SPRING	Cold Spring	MN	**C-**	C	C	52.7	1.65	4.0	5.3	20.4	12.7	**7.3**	9.2	18.9
STATE BK OF COLON	Colon	NE	**E+**	D-	C	18.3	0.79	4.9	0.7	1.9	8.7	**6.5**	8.5	13.4
STATE BK OF COUNTRYSIDE	Countryside	IL	**C-**	D	E-	591.3	1.82	9.5	0.1	7.7	22.2	**8.1**	9.8	13.5
STATE BK OF CROSS PLAINS	Cross Plains	WI	**D+**	D+	C-	742.4	-4.56	7.9	1.8	16.3	19.5	**9.8**	10.9	15.6
STATE BK OF DANVERS	Benson	MN	**B**	B	B+	45.9	-1.03	7.2	1.8	1.2	45.5	**10.0**	11.6	21.3
STATE BK OF DAVIS	Davis	IL	**C+**	C+	C+	144.5	3.57	18.1	0.7	11.1	28.2	**8.4**	9.9	15.3
STATE BK OF DE KALB	De Kalb	TX	**A**	A	A-	160.6	16.36	16.2	3.2	14.4	1.3	**10.0**	12.3	17.2
STATE BK OF DELANO	Delano	MN	**E**	E-	E-	76.7	3.23	10.5	1.2	9.8	17.7	**4.3**	6.3	11.1
STATE BK OF DELPHOS	Delphos	KS	**B-**	B-	C+	43.5	-3.47	7.3	2.3	12.2	18.7	**8.5**	10.0	14.7
▲ STATE BK OF DOWNS	Downs	KS	**B**	B-	B-	86.0	15.34	18.9	1.4	21.2	2.5	**9.2**	10.8	14.4
STATE BK OF DRUMMOND	Drummond	WI	**C+**	C+	B-	42.7	-7.20	3.5	1.2	25.6	26.0	**10.0**	13.9	28.6
STATE BK OF EAGLE BUTTE	Eagle Butte	SD	**B-**	B-	B-	53.0	9.72	8.2	29.5	2.4	25.7	**9.6**	10.7	15.3
STATE BK OF EASTON	Easton	MN	**C-**	C-	C-	20.9	5.95	11.9	4.1	7.5	12.4	**10.0**	13.1	18.9

Asset Quality Index	Adjusted Non-Performing Loans as a % of Total Loans	Adjusted Non-Performing Loans as a % of Capital	Net Charge-Offs Avg Loans	Profitability Index	Net Income ($Mil)	Return on Assets (R.O.A.)	Return on Equity (R.O.E.)	Net Interest Spread	Overhead Efficiency Ratio	Liquidity Index	Liquidity Ratio	Hot Money Ratio	Stability Index
6.9	0.77	5.2	0.01	**0.0**	-1.8	-3.66	-29.94	2.85	259.6	**0.6**	10.7	53.4	**1.0**
8.0	0.03	0.2	0.02	**5.0**	3.4	1.25	11.38	3.33	61.6	**6.0**	52.9	7.6	**5.9**
5.4	1.79	7.8	0.19	**3.9**	0.5	0.91	9.82	3.19	67.6	**2.7**	39.6	23.6	**4.9**
6.5	0.37	3.4	0.03	**5.2**	0.6	1.15	15.70	3.76	71.8	**1.6**	11.7	22.5	**4.3**
5.3	0.60	4.7	0.05	**5.0**	2.4	0.93	9.47	4.02	73.7	**2.8**	7.6	14.3	**3.6**
8.5	0.00	0.0	0.00	**5.5**	0.2	1.32	6.01	3.13	55.8	**2.7**	50.0	24.2	**7.9**
4.7	1.44	8.7	0.01	**6.8**	2.1	1.26	12.34	3.70	44.2	**2.3**	12.2	17.1	**6.3**
3.5	1.00	6.4	0.00	**8.0**	2.2	1.94	18.45	3.49	44.8	**2.5**	20.2	17.1	**8.5**
3.5	4.14	21.0	0.02	**4.1**	0.2	0.86	10.35	3.03	72.9	**3.4**	34.8	16.1	**5.5**
5.0	2.59	9.2	0.20	**2.5**	0.3	0.43	3.33	3.43	94.1	**4.1**	40.4	14.6	**6.3**
4.7	3.82	17.1	-0.03	**4.5**	1.3	0.96	8.54	3.90	73.3	**4.8**	27.3	5.9	**5.1**
5.6	1.84	7.8	0.04	**2.6**	0.1	0.33	2.78	3.68	90.4	**5.3**	44.0	8.8	**4.9**
6.0	3.03	8.6	0.22	**4.7**	1.7	1.07	9.00	3.57	63.2	**3.1**	65.5	46.3	**7.8**
4.9	0.83	6.1	0.14	**5.4**	1.2	1.30	15.54	4.35	67.9	**1.5**	13.9	23.8	**5.6**
6.9	1.16	4.5	0.53	**6.8**	24.3	1.26	8.41	6.38	64.7	**5.6**	37.3	8.8	**8.0**
4.0	0.78	6.4	0.15	**6.0**	5.2	1.06	9.50	3.75	69.4	**2.8**	5.2	14.1	**6.8**
4.2	0.86	6.9	0.35	**4.0**	4.7	0.65	5.80	4.18	70.5	**2.3**	5.1	16.5	**6.5**
7.7	0.24	1.2	0.01	**8.0**	1.7	1.46	13.18	3.63	44.4	**4.2**	30.7	10.9	**8.6**
8.3	0.00	0.0	-0.12	**7.3**	1.7	1.87	21.71	3.30	52.1	**3.7**	23.3	11.1	**5.5**
4.5	2.29	11.0	-0.21	**4.1**	2.2	0.90	8.00	3.53	76.4	**4.3**	28.7	10.0	**5.9**
5.9	0.68	3.5	0.06	**5.5**	0.3	1.15	13.20	3.77	73.4	**5.1**	38.8	8.7	**4.3**
4.1	1.38	9.7	0.02	**4.8**	0.9	1.10	10.20	4.92	75.1	**2.0**	5.8	18.3	**5.4**
7.1	0.06	0.5	0.02	**4.1**	0.9	0.99	11.48	3.28	73.6	**1.8**	17.1	21.0	**5.6**
7.6	0.62	3.2	-0.02	**3.5**	0.9	0.69	6.75	2.72	73.3	**5.1**	42.0	10.0	**5.1**
5.1	5.13	18.5	0.23	**6.0**	1.0	1.11	7.95	4.14	58.5	**5.6**	47.0	8.2	**7.5**
6.3	0.40	3.0	-0.09	**6.2**	1.0	1.51	16.52	4.32	61.1	**1.8**	24.6	22.6	**5.1**
8.3	1.43	4.2	-0.03	**4.4**	0.8	1.02	8.64	3.88	71.7	**5.8**	51.6	8.4	**6.6**
7.0	0.00	0.0	0.00	**6.3**	0.3	0.80	9.49	4.26	61.6	**1.1**	2.5	27.2	**4.3**
6.6	0.93	3.6	0.10	**3.5**	0.4	0.55	4.00	3.80	81.3	**3.8**	34.1	14.0	**6.6**
8.0	1.11	3.3	0.00	**6.9**	0.8	1.21	9.10	3.68	44.4	**3.6**	54.0	19.3	**8.1**
1.3	5.48	37.8	1.82	**0.0**	-0.3	-1.03	-21.75	2.44	140.6	**5.7**	51.1	7.5	**0.0**
4.6	1.82	9.0	-0.09	**2.8**	0.2	0.45	4.59	2.66	83.8	**5.0**	46.6	11.1	**3.6**
6.9	0.00	0.0	-0.08	**4.9**	0.6	1.29	15.10	4.35	70.6	**2.4**	4.1	16.0	**3.0**
5.4	5.97	12.3	-0.06	**2.9**	0.1	0.51	4.67	2.39	75.1	**6.3**	84.9	8.8	**4.7**
3.2	2.90	18.6	0.13	**1.7**	0.0	-0.11	-1.10	3.46	91.5	**2.1**	35.1	27.9	**4.6**
6.7	0.00	0.0	0.00	**1.2**	0.0	-0.08	-0.72	2.74	102.6	**4.4**	53.5	13.4	**4.1**
5.6	0.55	4.4	0.04	**2.9**	0.2	0.44	5.13	3.97	88.6	**3.5**	21.8	12.0	**2.5**
8.4	1.46	2.1	0.25	**2.7**	0.1	0.34	2.07	2.47	82.1	**7.4**	85.9	3.5	**6.9**
8.8	0.02	0.1	0.01	**3.1**	0.1	0.54	3.11	3.70	83.9	**5.5**	53.8	9.5	**6.9**
6.5	2.54	7.2	-0.03	**2.0**	0.0	0.17	1.13	3.39	94.7	**4.3**	47.1	14.6	**6.1**
2.5	9.70	34.7	0.05	**0.5**	-0.1	-0.56	-5.72	3.00	83.6	**2.4**	54.3	31.6	**4.2**
4.1	1.08	5.7	-0.01	**5.5**	0.3	1.04	9.12	3.88	58.0	**3.6**	30.9	13.7	**5.8**
9.3	0.06	0.2	0.16	**3.9**	0.6	0.85	7.45	2.64	61.0	**5.6**	74.6	12.7	**6.9**
3.2	2.77	14.0	0.21	**6.6**	2.0	1.65	10.61	4.20	52.7	**3.7**	18.3	10.9	**6.2**
10.0	na	0.0	na	**8.1**	2.2	1.43	17.69	2.43	4.1	**4.7**	8.9	3.4	**6.0**
2.0	2.06	17.2	0.00	**5.8**	0.6	1.02	12.60	4.01	59.2	**3.9**	18.8	10.1	**4.8**
4.1	3.95	14.6	0.65	**6.6**	2.4	1.51	10.83	4.51	55.1	**2.7**	36.7	21.8	**7.1**
7.9	0.04	0.2	0.69	**2.2**	0.1	0.27	2.83	3.23	92.3	**5.9**	44.3	5.1	**4.0**
1.6	2.60	16.6	-0.08	**0.1**	0.0	-0.26	-2.98	2.15	107.4	**4.4**	36.5	9.6	**2.8**
1.8	2.88	17.6	0.81	**6.5**	7.6	1.74	18.12	5.02	52.9	**2.9**	18.6	15.1	**4.4**
1.3	5.71	32.5	0.33	**4.3**	3.7	0.66	5.65	3.55	70.1	**4.0**	20.2	9.1	**5.9**
8.7	0.24	0.9	0.35	**4.5**	0.4	1.00	9.09	3.53	67.1	**3.9**	26.3	11.0	**6.9**
3.6	1.80	10.7	0.60	**6.6**	1.3	1.23	12.41	3.82	41.1	**1.7**	23.6	24.7	**5.7**
7.9	0.31	1.9	0.03	**8.6**	2.4	2.09	16.84	4.60	56.1	**2.1**	15.6	18.8	**9.0**
3.0	2.56	17.7	0.08	**3.3**	0.5	0.79	15.02	4.37	81.0	**5.8**	34.3	1.8	**1.2**
6.4	0.43	2.8	0.11	**4.6**	0.3	0.99	9.98	4.21	73.0	**3.5**	8.3	10.9	**6.4**
6.1	0.04	0.3	-0.06	**5.0**	0.8	1.28	12.29	4.19	66.5	**3.4**	22.0	12.7	**5.9**
3.7	5.30	16.4	0.29	**2.8**	0.1	0.33	2.30	4.06	92.2	**4.1**	54.4	16.7	**5.5**
6.8	0.13	0.7	1.56	**4.7**	0.3	0.79	7.27	6.87	73.3	**3.0**	10.1	13.4	**5.7**
4.0	3.95	18.2	0.00	**3.8**	0.1	0.91	6.89	3.88	75.4	**2.0**	31.5	21.7	**5.0**

Name	City	State	Rating	2013 Rating	2012 Rating	Total Assets ($Mil)	One Year Asset Growth	Asset Mix (As a % of Total Assets) Commercial Loans	Consumer Loans	Mortgage Loans	Securities	Capitalization Index	Leverage Ratio	Risk-Based Capital Ratio
STATE BK OF EWEN	Ewen	MI	**B+**	B+	B+	57.9	4.81	4.7	6.1	18.6	46.4	**10.0**	16.1	36.3
▼ STATE BK OF FAIRMONT	Fairmont	MN	**C+**	C+	B-	100.8	-1.58	19.7	7.4	5.1	22.1	**10.0**	11.7	15.4
STATE BK OF FARIBAULT	Faribault	MN	**B-**	B-	C+	183.0	6.10	6.5	2.3	10.7	31.7	**9.4**	11.3	14.5
STATE BK OF FLORENCE	Florence	WI	**D+**	D	D+	83.8	4.05	10.8	6.1	22.5	21.8	**7.4**	9.3	16.7
▼ STATE BK OF GENEVA	Geneva	IL	**D+**	D+	D+	84.8	2.08	4.0	0.7	10.1	31.2	**7.2**	9.1	16.6
STATE BK OF GEORGIA	Fayetteville	GA	**C**	C	D	69.5	-3.08	4.0	0.5	11.2	12.9	**10.0**	13.6	19.0
STATE BK OF GRAYMONT	Graymont	IL	**B**	B	B-	211.8	3.31	7.0	2.1	6.2	34.1	**6.7**	8.7	12.7
STATE BK OF HAMBURG	Hamburg	MN	**D-**	D-	C-	21.8	-2.53	6.1	2.0	10.2	26.0	**6.0**	8.0	16.2
STATE BK OF HAWLEY	Hawley	MN	**B**	B	B	96.4	1.57	12.2	4.5	14.6	34.4	**7.8**	9.5	16.6
STATE BK OF HERSCHER	Herscher	IL	**E-**	E-	E-	138.5	-9.66	14.3	1.3	20.5	26.6	**0.0**	2.6	5.4
STATE BK OF HILDRETH	Hildreth	NE	**C-**	C-	C+	31.1	-1.27	3.9	0.6	0.9	7.6	**8.7**	10.1	13.9
STATE BK OF ILLINOIS	West Chicago	IL	**C-**	D+	D+	186.7	-4.30	1.2	0.2	28.9	21.0	**6.2**	8.2	15.6
STATE BK OF INDIA (CALIFORNIA)	Los Angeles	CA	**C+**	C	D+	684.1	-7.33	23.8	0.1	0.0	19.5	**10.0**	18.7	24.5
STATE BK OF INDUSTRY	Industry	IL	**B**	B	B-	46.5	3.02	7.2	7.2	22.9	28.8	**10.0**	13.6	21.5
STATE BK OF JEFFERS	Jeffers	MN	**C+**	C+	B-	25.1	1.26	8.4	4.1	4.8	26.1	**10.0**	11.8	20.4
STATE BK OF KANSAS	Fredonia	KS	**A-**	A-	A	65.6	2.86	3.2	1.5	9.7	10.4	**10.0**	12.3	20.3
STATE BK OF LAKE PARK	Lake Park	MN	**C-**	C	C+	35.9	-0.19	11.4	8.1	21.1	26.8	**6.4**	8.4	15.7
STATE BK OF LAKOTA	Lakota	ND	**C+**	C	C+	52.7	-1.57	5.8	4.9	8.1	27.0	**8.0**	9.7	14.9
STATE BK OF LIMA	Lima	IL	**B+**	B	B+	32.7	-11.25	11.4	0.7	1.8	43.6	**10.0**	12.0	19.7
STATE BK OF LINCOLN	Lincoln	IL	**B**	B	B	328.3	-6.57	15.0	0.6	5.2	44.4	**6.1**	8.1	18.3
STATE BK OF LISMORE	Lismore	MN	**C**	C+	C+	46.7	8.67	9.2	2.8	0.2	1.1	**5.8**	10.8	11.6
STATE BK OF LIZTON	Lizton	IN	**B**	C+	C	375.7	0.01	5.8	0.8	6.9	23.0	**10.0**	11.3	16.0
STATE BK OF MARIETTA	Marietta	MN	**C-**	C-	C	13.1	2.35	13.7	3.0	2.2	27.2	**5.5**	7.5	13.1
STATE BK OF MEDORA	Medora	IN	**B+**	B+	B+	69.3	5.64	2.4	6.5	24.9	46.2	**10.0**	16.2	33.4
STATE BK OF MISSOURI	Concordia	MO	**B-**	B-	B-	79.9	-1.98	3.9	2.1	26.7	37.4	**6.8**	8.8	19.9
STATE BK OF NAUVOO	Nauvoo	IL	**D-**	E+	E+	32.9	-1.96	5.9	10.5	35.7	5.1	**4.7**	6.7	11.6
▲ STATE BK OF NEW PRAGUE	New Prague	MN	**B**	C	C-	112.0	-0.59	2.6	1.1	17.2	51.1	**10.0**	12.9	23.0
STATE BK OF NEW RICHLAND	New Richland	MN	**C+**	C+	C+	96.5	9.56	6.1	1.9	16.9	16.8	**7.7**	9.4	13.1
STATE BK OF NEWBURG	Newburg	WI	**B**	B	B-	162.1	0.00	0.9	0.7	33.8	16.0	**10.0**	17.2	23.5
STATE BK OF ODELL	Odell	NE	**C**	C	C	25.7	-3.20	1.0	19.4	5.8	15.0	**7.8**	9.5	15.8
STATE BK OF OSKALOOSA	Oskaloosa	KS	**D+**	D+	C-	28.0	5.24	1.6	5.0	16.5	16.1	**6.3**	8.3	43.0
STATE BK OF PARK RAPIDS	Park Rapids	MN	**B-**	C+	C	98.4	-1.31	9.3	1.4	7.8	46.0	**9.3**	10.6	19.4
STATE BK OF PEARL CITY	Pearl City	IL	**C**	C	C	47.6	1.58	3.1	31.4	9.1	32.9	**9.7**	10.8	15.7
▼ STATE BK OF REESEVILLE	Reeseville	WI	**C+**	B-	B-	60.5	7.24	5.1	2.1	13.5	32.8	**10.0**	12.6	20.9
STATE BK OF RICHMOND	Richmond	MN	**B**	B-	B	87.4	1.40	2.3	2.0	16.1	35.0	**10.0**	11.2	18.0
STATE BK OF SAUNEMIN	Saunemin	IL	**C**	C	C+	35.9	2.68	7.3	2.5	8.6	39.7	**6.4**	8.4	17.1
STATE BK OF SCHALLER	Schaller	IA	**B+**	B+	A-	33.0	-0.82	2.6	1.2	1.1	69.3	**9.0**	10.4	27.3
STATE BK OF SCOTIA	Scotia	NE	**D+**	C-	C+	35.6	10.19	7.7	3.4	7.3	24.8	**10.0**	23.8	31.3
STATE BK OF SOUTHERN UTAH	Cedar City	UT	**A-**	A-	B	813.9	8.62	5.6	2.2	2.2	34.5	**10.0**	12.4	18.8
STATE BK OF SOUTHWEST MISSOURI	Springfield	MO	**C**	C+	B-	101.8	6.90	1.4	5.2	46.8	5.6	**4.1**	6.7	10.6
STATE BK OF SPEER	Speer	IL	**C+**	C+	C	180.4	-6.72	7.8	1.1	12.5	48.3	**6.7**	8.7	15.9
STATE BK OF SPRING HILL	Spring Hill	KS	**C-**	D+	C-	35.9	-5.97	5.1	2.2	8.0	61.6	**9.3**	10.5	27.1
STATE BK OF ST JACOB	Saint Jacob	IL	**B+**	B+	A-	56.1	-0.83	6.2	6.4	18.7	34.1	**10.0**	14.8	31.4
STATE BK OF TABLE ROCK	Table Rock	NE	**C**	C	C	58.1	0.88	7.5	5.8	7.2	3.0	**6.3**	8.4	12.1
▲ STATE BK OF TAUNTON	Taunton	MN	**E**	E-	C	56.6	-16.30	10.8	3.0	9.9	22.2	**5.5**	7.5	12.3
STATE BK OF TEXAS	Houston	TX	**C-**	C-	D	158.8	7.77	14.4	15.7	5.6	33.9	**6.7**	8.7	23.2
STATE BK OF TEXAS	Dallas	TX	**B+**	B-	C+	376.3	-12.11	1.7	0.1	0.2	2.0	**10.0**	25.3	31.3
STATE BK OF THE LAKES	Antioch	IL	**C+**	C+	C	883.2	18.11	21.6	21.6	4.1	10.7	**5.6**	8.4	11.5
STATE BK OF TOLEDO	Toledo	IA	**C**	B-	C+	102.8	-1.18	7.7	4.5	30.5	3.9	**5.1**	9.1	11.1
STATE BK OF TOULON	Toulon	IL	**B**	B	C+	199.1	-1.19	6.4	1.9	4.9	32.9	**7.1**	9.1	13.7
STATE BK OF TOWNSEND	Townsend	MT	**B-**	B	C+	53.6	2.31	1.9	1.7	2.4	21.5	**9.2**	10.5	19.7
STATE BK OF WAPELLO	Wapello	IA	**C+**	C+	B-	39.1	5.06	1.3	4.7	10.8	32.9	**10.0**	11.0	22.9
▼ STATE BK OF WATERLOO	Waterloo	IL	**D**	C	C-	143.9	8.74	3.3	1.2	24.9	26.3	**6.9**	8.9	13.7
STATE BK OF WHEATON	Wheaton	MN	**B+**	B	B	73.2	-0.81	7.8	0.9	2.8	12.2	**10.0**	20.2	26.2
STATE BK OF WHITTINGTON	Benton	IL	**B-**	B-	C+	121.5	4.07	3.2	13.7	16.2	32.3	**6.4**	8.4	17.0
STATE BK OF WYNNEWOOD	Wynnewood	OK	**A**	A	A	80.4	-2.38	8.8	2.2	7.8	39.0	**10.0**	14.4	22.6
STATE CENTRAL BANK	Bonaparte	IA	**E-**	E-	E-	59.0	-51.47	20.6	1.2	11.8	2.3	**9.5**	10.6	17.2
STATE EXCHANGE BANK	Mankato	KS	**C+**	C	C	34.4	-0.52	4.8	6.5	4.6	50.7	**9.9**	10.9	22.3
STATE EXCHANGE BANK	Lamont	OK	**B+**	B	B-	50.2	19.13	20.1	1.0	5.1	7.4	**10.0**	12.4	20.0
STATE FARM BANK FSB	Bloomington	IL	**C**	C	C-	17018.7	14.02	0.7	41.2	16.1	34.2	**8.4**	9.9	15.9

Asset Quality Index	Adjusted Non-Performing Loans as a % of Total Loans	Adjusted Non-Performing Loans as a % of Capital	Net Charge-Offs Avg Loans	Profitability Index	Net Income ($Mil)	Return on Assets (R.O.A.)	Return on Equity (R.O.E.)	Net Interest Spread	Overhead Efficiency Ratio	Liquidity Index	Liquidity Ratio	Hot Money Ratio	Stability Index
6.4	3.60	7.1	0.11	**5.2**	0.5	1.21	7.27	4.29	60.7	**4.0**	75.9	22.7	**6.8**
2.4	3.98	22.5	0.04	**7.3**	1.4	1.83	16.25	3.95	50.4	**3.2**	26.5	14.4	**7.4**
5.8	1.12	4.8	0.14	**4.1**	1.2	0.90	7.89	4.08	79.5	**4.8**	28.3	6.4	**6.1**
1.5	4.56	29.5	0.49	**3.7**	0.4	0.68	7.90	4.26	75.6	**0.9**	22.0	38.0	**4.7**
2.4	5.96	26.9	0.51	**1.4**	0.9	-0.32	-4.27	2.57	112.1	**2.6**	37.9	24.2	**3.3**
2.4	4.72	23.1	0.06	**3.1**	0.4	0.71	5.54	4.03	81.9	**0.9**	22.2	36.9	**4.7**
6.4	0.54	3.5	-0.03	**4.5**	1.5	0.93	9.87	3.08	57.9	**4.3**	33.6	11.1	**5.4**
3.5	3.43	18.6	0.87	**1.4**	0.0	-0.01	-0.16	3.05	98.8	**5.0**	49.1	9.8	**1.0**
6.7	0.45	2.6	0.01	**4.7**	0.8	1.06	10.84	3.85	73.1	**5.4**	37.5	6.3	**6.3**
0.3	11.30	130.1	2.81	**0.0**	-1.7	-1.58	-82.33	3.62	129.3	**3.8**	15.7	10.0	**0.2**
4.8	1.29	7.6	-0.45	**2.4**	0.1	0.27	2.82	3.01	89.3	**4.1**	32.3	11.8	**5.6**
1.3	6.82	43.3	-0.14	**0.4**	-0.7	-0.49	-5.43	3.62	112.5	**4.9**	29.6	6.2	**4.0**
4.7	2.57	9.5	0.55	**2.3**	2.5	0.49	2.61	3.17	103.0	**0.8**	20.4	46.3	**6.4**
7.5	0.67	3.2	-0.15	**7.8**	0.7	2.04	15.76	3.97	47.4	**1.2**	25.6	32.9	**6.8**
8.3	0.00	0.0	0.01	**2.8**	0.1	0.55	4.84	3.22	79.2	**5.8**	40.8	5.0	**6.5**
8.3	0.14	0.6	0.00	**6.3**	0.7	1.37	10.17	3.28	57.8	**4.3**	34.8	11.9	**9.3**
2.6	4.00	22.2	0.10	**3.8**	0.2	0.63	7.84	4.10	64.5	**4.5**	37.0	11.3	**5.3**
5.8	1.21	7.2	0.01	**4.5**	0.4	1.04	11.83	3.32	65.5	**4.4**	32.5	10.3	**4.4**
8.9	0.00	0.0	0.00	**6.3**	0.4	1.47	12.99	3.61	55.5	**4.5**	49.6	14.4	**6.3**
4.9	2.51	11.3	-0.28	**7.6**	4.5	1.79	21.71	3.19	64.9	**5.6**	44.7	7.9	**5.0**
5.8	0.27	2.2	0.00	**5.5**	0.5	1.30	12.25	4.54	69.0	**2.3**	4.9	16.3	**4.3**
4.8	2.18	11.4	0.09	**4.4**	2.5	0.89	7.97	3.62	73.4	**3.3**	25.4	13.7	**6.3**
8.1	0.04	0.2	-0.14	**5.4**	0.1	1.32	13.89	3.70	59.7	**6.2**	61.8	4.6	**4.3**
5.5	4.20	11.0	0.10	**4.9**	0.5	0.90	5.49	3.63	61.2	**3.7**	59.5	19.6	**7.1**
7.0	0.68	3.4	-0.20	**4.0**	0.6	0.99	11.56	3.36	72.0	**5.0**	34.7	7.9	**5.4**
5.5	0.39	3.7	0.17	**1.7**	0.1	0.22	3.25	3.85	92.8	**3.5**	20.6	11.9	**1.6**
7.9	0.00	0.0	1.44	**7.8**	1.5	1.81	11.79	4.43	58.8	**2.9**	31.3	17.7	**7.0**
2.8	2.04	16.0	0.02	**9.5**	1.6	2.29	23.04	3.80	39.3	**0.7**	12.1	39.9	**7.5**
4.2	4.67	20.0	0.00	**9.2**	1.8	1.45	8.67	3.95	34.8	**1.8**	21.5	22.5	**8.5**
4.8	0.86	4.6	0.08	**3.7**	0.1	0.72	8.04	3.78	81.1	**5.7**	46.0	7.0	**3.8**
8.2	0.73	2.2	0.13	**1.3**	0.0	0.04	0.51	2.10	98.3	**5.2**	61.3	12.5	**3.5**
4.6	3.01	12.1	0.00	**6.1**	1.2	1.59	16.35	3.80	65.1	**3.0**	27.2	15.9	**4.9**
3.1	1.96	9.6	0.46	**3.8**	0.3	0.72	7.37	4.58	71.5	**3.2**	33.6	17.1	**4.2**
7.6	1.12	4.9	-0.12	**2.7**	0.3	0.63	5.16	3.90	90.6	**2.9**	44.7	23.9	**5.6**
8.3	0.01	0.0	0.00	**4.2**	0.6	0.91	8.39	3.05	65.6	**5.1**	41.3	9.7	**6.6**
7.6	0.21	1.0	-0.02	**4.1**	0.3	1.02	13.19	2.96	65.4	**5.7**	48.8	7.3	**4.2**
9.5	0.10	0.2	-0.02	**6.0**	0.3	1.29	13.70	3.33	60.9	**5.4**	79.4	14.3	**7.1**
0.6	8.23	23.2	-0.04	**7.1**	0.3	1.28	5.36	4.03	46.5	**4.7**	37.9	10.6	**6.2**
6.7	0.97	4.1	0.10	**7.8**	8.0	1.35	11.17	3.69	53.1	**3.5**	35.0	15.7	**7.2**
5.4	0.55	6.4	0.02	**4.8**	0.8	1.04	15.62	3.93	75.3	**3.4**	12.7	11.9	**4.0**
4.5	3.32	16.2	0.20	**3.9**	1.4	1.03	11.58	3.14	63.3	**3.0**	31.1	17.0	**4.5**
8.3	0.29	0.7	-0.29	**1.9**	0.1	0.37	3.52	2.85	87.6	**5.4**	46.5	8.6	**5.1**
7.6	1.62	4.5	0.15	**4.8**	0.5	1.22	8.32	3.09	54.0	**4.9**	53.8	12.8	**7.6**
4.7	0.38	3.2	-0.07	**3.5**	0.3	0.65	7.84	3.56	82.2	**4.0**	19.6	9.2	**3.8**
1.7	3.37	22.4	2.92	**0.1**	-0.2	-0.35	-5.03	3.49	95.2	**1.9**	26.4	22.5	**1.6**
6.6	0.22	1.2	0.01	**2.2**	0.3	0.23	2.68	2.53	86.8	**2.3**	49.2	51.9	**4.0**
5.4	0.91	2.6	-0.06	**10.0**	17.1	5.56	24.52	6.34	21.5	**1.8**	23.6	21.9	**8.3**
3.2	1.03	8.9	0.08	**4.4**	4.4	0.74	4.89	3.31	65.1	**2.3**	13.0	17.3	**7.1**
3.8	1.80	15.3	0.08	**6.3**	1.1	1.46	16.37	4.30	65.8	**3.8**	12.4	9.8	**5.5**
8.1	0.05	0.3	0.02	**5.1**	2.0	1.29	13.19	3.62	63.6	**1.7**	11.5	19.9	**6.0**
5.4	1.54	7.7	0.00	**4.0**	0.4	0.85	8.41	4.23	81.1	**3.2**	39.8	18.9	**6.5**
8.5	0.32	0.9	0.08	**2.3**	0.1	0.29	2.59	2.45	85.6	**7.2**	62.6	0.4	**6.1**
2.0	5.39	32.4	2.79	**0.7**	-0.7	-0.63	-6.71	3.19	82.9	**3.5**	31.0	14.3	**4.1**
7.2	0.27	1.0	-0.05	**6.8**	1.0	1.72	8.55	3.46	51.8	**2.0**	20.2	19.7	**6.6**
4.3	1.87	9.5	0.22	**4.1**	0.8	0.88	10.91	3.85	75.5	**4.9**	40.7	10.4	**4.9**
8.7	0.50	1.8	0.09	**6.9**	1.0	1.61	11.86	4.36	61.9	**3.0**	39.6	20.1	**9.5**
0.0	38.28	153.1	2.38	**0.9**	-0.7	-1.39	-12.22	2.96	143.2	**1.7**	23.2	24.2	**2.5**
8.6	0.36	1.3	0.03	**4.2**	0.3	1.09	10.75	3.41	68.0	**5.2**	32.7	5.5	**3.5**
8.3	0.22	0.9	-0.22	**7.7**	0.6	1.58	12.62	4.57	57.3	**3.6**	32.9	14.6	**6.4**
3.2	2.04	11.7	0.60	**2.8**	46.7	0.37	3.62	2.75	69.8	**0.9**	20.5	51.7	**6.5**

Name	City	State	Rating	2013 Rating	2012 Rating	Total Assets ($Mil)	One Year Asset Growth	Asset Mix (As a % of Total Assets) Comm-ercial Loans	Cons-umer Loans	Mort-gage Loans	Secur-ities	Capital-ization Index	Lever-age Ratio	Risk-Based Capital Ratio
STATE GUARANTY BANK	Okeene	OK	B	B	B+	44.6	10.42	7.3	1.5	1.5	16.0	10.0	12.1	17.5
STATE NATIONAL BK BIG SPRING	Big Spring	TX	C-	C-	C+	316.3	1.56	3.6	1.1	0.3	65.4	6.8	8.8	28.9
STATE NATIONAL BK IN WEST	West	TX	C-	D+	C	75.7	-4.05	5.9	2.8	1.5	64.1	6.0	8.0	24.2
▼ STATE NATIONAL BK OF GROOM	Groom	TX	D-	C-	D+	38.6	-2.37	12.7	2.0	0.4	8.8	5.2	8.6	11.2
STATE NATIONAL BK OF TEXAS	Iowa Park	TX	C+	B-	B	229.1	4.77	3.8	3.3	14.2	48.1	6.8	8.9	19.8
STATE NEBRASKA BANK & TRUST	Wayne	NE	B	B	B	147.5	5.68	6.9	1.3	6.4	43.4	9.8	10.9	18.0
STATE SAVINGS BANK	West Des Moines	IA	A-	B+	B+	104.4	5.15	7.7	0.9	23.9	1.9	8.4	10.1	13.7
STATE SAVINGS BANK	Creston	IA	B+	B+	B+	97.1	4.62	11.4	5.3	19.3	0.8	7.4	9.5	12.8
▲ STATE SAVINGS BANK	Rake	IA	C-	D+	D	62.8	-4.92	8.8	1.1	1.1	9.8	6.6	10.1	12.2
STATE SAVINGS BANK	Frankfort	MI	B-	B-	B	103.3	-2.09	1.6	0.7	12.4	24.4	10.0	14.3	32.4
STATE SB OF MANISTIQUE	Manistique	MI	C+	C	C-	114.8	-4.05	15.7	4.4	16.1	36.3	10.0	11.8	17.8
▼ STATE STREET BANK & TRUST CO	Quincy	IL	C	B-	B	183.3	-1.04	5.1	21.9	19.3	29.3	5.7	7.7	14.3
STATE STREET BANK & TRUST CO	Boston	MA	B-	B	B	270372.3	27.12	0.7	0.1	0.0	42.6	4.1	6.1	16.1
STATE STREET BANK & TRUST CO	Los Angeles	CA	U	U	U	14.8	0.56	0.0	0.0	0.0	0.0	10.0	99.0	394.4
STATE STREET BANK & TRUST CO	New York	NY	U	U	U	29.4	5.49	0.0	0.0	0.0	0.0	10.0	99.6	155.8
STATE-INVESTORS BANK	Metairie	LA	B-	C+	C+	268.8	5.00	0.2	0.4	49.6	14.0	10.0	14.1	24.2
STC CAPITAL BANK	Saint Charles	IL	C+	C+	C-	192.4	22.21	8.9	0.5	15.8	7.8	10.0	12.5	16.5
STEARNS BANK HOLDINGFORD NA	Holdingford	MN	A	A	A-	101.6	-14.27	43.8	0.2	3.3	6.6	10.0	11.7	16.7
STEARNS BANK NA	Saint Cloud	MN	A	A	A-	1601.4	14.15	42.1	0.5	4.8	5.4	10.0	14.7	17.3
STEARNS BANK UPSALA NA	Upsala	MN	A	A	B+	81.5	-9.88	42.6	0.3	3.2	3.5	10.0	11.0	15.8
STEELE STREET BANK & TRUST	Denver	CO	A-	A-	A-	567.2	15.87	9.4	0.5	12.6	13.8	8.6	10.4	13.8
STEPHENS FEDERAL BANK	Toccoa	GA	E-	E-	E-	147.2	-8.31	0.7	1.4	36.4	2.0	0.6	4.3	7.3
▲ STEPHENSON NATIONAL BK & TRUST	Marinette	WI	B	B	B-	322.8	1.45	17.3	1.9	14.6	17.5	7.8	9.5	14.1
STERLING BANK	Barron	WI	B+	B+	A-	213.6	3.55	5.0	0.4	14.1	28.6	6.9	8.9	13.6
STERLING BANK	Poplar Bluff	MO	B+	B+	B+	540.0	5.89	27.9	0.4	9.0	2.8	5.2	9.6	11.1
STERLING BANK & TRUST FSB	Southfield	MI	A-	B	C+	1195.1	25.97	0.7	0.0	71.1	2.7	7.2	9.1	15.8
▲ STERLING FEDERAL BANK FSB	Sterling	IL	C-	D+	C-	437.6	-2.12	0.1	0.7	32.6	45.1	8.8	10.2	17.2
STERLING NATIONAL BANK	Montebello	NY	C+	C	C	7311.4	80.76	25.8	0.3	8.4	23.2	7.3	9.3	12.7
STERLING STATE BK	Austin	MN	C	C-	D+	306.7	4.35	9.6	1.1	8.8	34.4	7.0	9.0	15.6
STEUBEN TRUST CO	Hornell	NY	B+	B+	B+	467.5	8.97	4.2	3.5	15.7	38.1	8.3	9.9	18.1
▲ STIFEL BANK & TRUST	Saint Louis	MO	B+	B	B	4984.7	9.24	21.3	9.7	8.7	55.0	6.0	8.0	13.9
STIFEL TRUST CO NA	Saint Louis	MO	U	U	B	9.0	18.17	0.0	0.0	0.0	95.8	10.0	93.4	245.7
STILLMAN BANCCORP NA	Stillman Valley	IL	C-	C-	C	408.0	-3.39	3.9	1.0	8.1	49.1	7.4	9.3	20.9
STOCK EXCHANGE BANK	Caldwell	KS	D+	D+	D+	49.1	6.38	4.5	4.9	29.9	24.5	5.3	7.3	13.0
STOCK EXCHANGE BANK	Woodward	OK	B+	B	B	268.6	0.10	8.3	3.6	7.1	60.4	9.3	10.6	23.3
STOCK GROWERS BANK	Napoleon	ND	A-	A-	A	60.4	6.63	1.6	2.1	4.5	33.4	10.0	12.2	18.8
STOCK YARDS BANK & TRUST CO	Louisville	KY	B+	B	B	2405.2	5.37	19.8	1.2	8.8	18.7	8.2	10.1	13.5
▲ STOCKGROWERS STATE BK	Ashland	KS	B+	B	B-	122.0	4.51	10.6	0.9	2.0	46.3	10.0	13.6	22.7
STOCKGROWERS STATE BK	Maple Hill	KS	A-	A-	A-	74.4	2.28	6.6	1.0	8.4	50.0	10.0	13.0	24.8
STOCKMAN BANK OF MONTANA	Miles City	MT	A-	A-	A-	2805.4	14.80	6.4	1.1	6.7	23.3	7.3	9.2	13.2
STOCKMANS BANK	Altus	OK	D+	D+	D	161.5	7.98	6.5	1.9	8.7	6.6	5.1	7.7	11.1
STOCKMENS BANK	Cascade	MT	B-	B-	B-	34.4	7.34	2.8	2.8	5.1	21.6	10.0	11.3	19.3
▼ STOCKMENS NATIONAL BK COTULLA	Cotulla	TX	C+	B-	B-	115.7	20.00	6.1	4.9	2.0	50.9	5.4	7.4	24.7
STOCKTON NATIONAL BK	Stockton	KS	B-	B-	B-	165.5	50.84	8.4	2.6	4.0	19.3	3.4	11.2	10.2
STONEBRIDGE BANK	Minneapolis	MN	C+	C+	C	171.2	23.69	11.8	3.5	20.7	6.1	4.4	8.1	10.7
STONEBRIDGE BANK	West Chester	PA	E-	E-	E-	153.6	-15.33	7.0	0.2	27.6	24.9	4.5	6.5	10.9
STONEGATE BANK	Pompano Beach	FL	B-	B+	B-	1676.2	54.19	10.5	0.5	12.5	5.7	9.6	10.8	14.7
STONEHAMBANK	Stoneham	MA	C+	C+	B-	471.1	2.14	8.0	0.3	35.9	13.8	7.7	9.5	16.8
STOUGHTON CO-OP BANK	Stoughton	MA	C-	C-	C	97.6	6.43	0.1	0.5	53.1	30.0	7.2	9.1	17.4
STRASBURG STATE BK	Strasburg	ND	B-	B-	B-	58.8	-1.54	3.7	1.2	0.1	27.5	7.0	9.0	15.2
STRATFORD STATE BK	Stratford	WI	B	B	B-	102.9	0.33	6.9	2.7	7.3	37.5	10.0	12.4	20.9
STREATOR HOME BUILDING & LOAN	Streator	IL	B	B	B+	167.6	2.79	0.0	1.2	28.0	62.4	10.0	22.1	77.9
STROUD NATIONAL BK	Stroud	OK	C+	C+	C+	83.7	4.10	8.8	4.6	20.9	25.2	9.0	10.3	17.4
STURDY SB	Cape May Court Hou	NJ	C	C+	C+	573.4	0.19	1.8	0.0	31.3	22.1	10.0	11.3	18.3
STURGIS BANK & TRUST CO	Sturgis	MI	D+	D+	D	318.2	-0.05	7.4	1.6	30.8	2.8	8.1	9.7	15.8
▲ SUBURBAN BANK & TRUST CO	Elmhurst	IL	D	D-	D-	471.1	-4.85	2.8	0.1	3.3	22.8	6.0	8.0	13.4
▼ SUCCESS BANK	Bloomfield	IA	B	A-	A-	133.6	5.10	6.4	2.4	9.3	6.7	9.6	12.0	14.7
▲ SUFFOLK COUNTY NATIONAL BANK	Riverhead	NY	B-	C+	C	1792.3	3.93	10.0	0.4	10.4	20.8	8.7	10.1	14.0
SUGAR RIVER BANK	Newport	NH	C-	C-	C	255.9	0.98	4.3	0.6	45.6	25.6	10.0	13.8	20.2
SUMITOMO MITSUI TRUST BK (USA)	Hoboken	NJ	U	U	A	2453.4	36.62	0.0	0.0	0.0	0.1	10.0	12.1	17.0

Asset Quality Index	Adjusted Non-Performing Loans as a % of Total Loans	Adjusted Non-Performing Loans as a % of Capital	Net Charge-Offs Avg Loans	Profitability Index	Net Income ($Mil)	Return on Assets (R.O.A.)	Return on Equity (R.O.E.)	Net Interest Spread	Overhead Efficiency Ratio	Liquidity Index	Liquidity Ratio	Hot Money Ratio	Stability Index
7.2	0.83	4.0	-0.03	**5.8**	0.5	1.42	11.20	3.36	61.9	**2.0**	30.9	26.5	**4.8**
9.9	0.00	0.0	-1.11	**2.6**	1.1	0.45	5.18	1.70	77.6	**6.5**	78.9	9.8	**5.2**
8.5	0.44	1.1	0.17	**2.5**	0.2	0.35	4.50	2.26	79.7	**7.1**	80.7	4.7	**3.2**
0.3	4.08	34.8	1.04	**2.9**	0.1	0.43	5.17	4.18	87.3	**2.3**	8.8	16.7	**3.9**
6.4	0.89	3.6	0.06	**3.6**	1.2	0.68	7.37	3.14	80.7	**5.1**	44.0	10.4	**6.0**
4.8	2.24	10.1	0.10	**4.9**	1.0	0.97	8.80	3.24	56.6	**3.1**	20.1	14.2	**7.1**
6.4	0.66	5.0	-0.06	**7.6**	1.3	1.68	17.23	4.18	60.5	**3.5**	10.8	11.3	**7.4**
6.4	0.50	4.1	-0.05	**7.7**	1.2	1.77	19.26	4.09	54.2	**3.2**	14.5	12.9	**6.5**
2.6	1.43	11.1	0.63	**5.4**	0.5	0.95	10.27	3.35	43.0	**0.8**	17.2	42.6	**4.8**
6.0	4.19	10.9	0.16	**2.9**	0.3	0.36	2.46	2.50	87.5	**6.9**	69.5	5.5	**5.9**
2.8	4.62	20.6	0.62	**3.7**	0.7	0.77	6.36	3.88	77.8	**5.0**	39.8	9.7	**6.1**
2.8	2.16	15.8	0.16	**4.2**	1.2	0.88	9.54	3.07	77.7	**5.1**	36.5	7.8	**4.8**
8.8	0.35	0.5	0.00	**4.4**	1409.6	0.83	9.26	1.33	76.1	**6.7**	68.7	8.3	**6.5**
10.0	na	0.0	na	**9.5**	0.2	1.95	1.97	0.06	88.6	**4.0**	6676.8	101.0	**5.7**
10.0	na	0.0	na	**10.0**	3.0	14.03	14.55	0.06	80.8	**4.0**	1434.0	101.0	**5.7**
6.8	1.07	5.9	0.10	**3.9**	1.2	0.62	4.14	3.62	70.5	**1.5**	18.6	26.0	**7.3**
6.4	0.89	5.0	-0.03	**2.9**	0.8	0.62	4.86	4.29	82.1	**1.4**	23.7	28.2	**5.8**
8.5	0.17	1.0	0.33	**6.2**	1.2	1.55	10.80	3.63	61.5	**1.1**	29.4	60.8	**8.4**
6.0	1.15	6.1	0.10	**10.0**	46.4	4.07	26.05	7.53	48.8	**0.5**	3.4	48.7	**9.4**
8.5	0.15	0.9	0.36	**5.5**	0.9	1.46	11.21	3.53	60.7	**1.1**	30.2	61.6	**8.1**
7.7	0.00	0.0	0.08	**8.1**	7.9	1.92	18.87	4.14	52.3	**3.9**	21.8	10.3	**8.0**
1.7	3.83	48.7	0.63	**0.5**	-0.4	-0.31	-7.56	3.53	123.3	**1.2**	16.2	30.1	**0.0**
4.7	1.04	7.2	0.02	**6.9**	3.9	1.63	16.61	3.89	67.0	**3.5**	11.7	11.2	**6.8**
5.6	0.94	6.1	0.00	**7.3**	2.5	1.59	18.05	4.04	59.9	**2.3**	34.7	25.3	**7.4**
7.5	0.00	0.0	0.00	**6.9**	5.0	1.29	13.84	4.21	53.7	**0.6**	6.4	38.8	**6.2**
7.9	0.45	4.1	-0.09	**8.7**	13.5	1.68	16.09	4.43	39.6	**2.6**	4.2	14.8	**7.2**
5.1	2.66	11.0	0.04	**2.3**	-0.4	-0.13	-1.20	3.04	83.5	**3.4**	51.7	22.4	**5.2**
4.0	1.25	8.8	0.19	**4.2**	47.5	0.91	6.34	3.93	62.0	**4.2**	9.1	6.9	**7.5**
3.5	2.49	14.4	0.08	**3.2**	1.7	0.73	9.55	3.43	82.8	**3.9**	22.5	10.4	**4.1**
6.7	0.65	3.4	0.04	**5.9**	3.6	1.05	10.81	3.86	64.9	**1.4**	7.4	24.4	**6.8**
8.4	0.29	1.4	0.03	**7.5**	51.3	1.35	19.06	2.73	22.2	**2.1**	35.6	54.1	**6.2**
10.0	na	0.0	na	**0.0**	-0.2	-3.10	-3.31	0.36	122.8	**4.0**	1551.0	101.0	**7.0**
4.3	3.55	13.0	0.08	**1.9**	1.4	0.44	4.65	2.27	92.0	**3.5**	44.3	18.8	**3.6**
8.6	0.00	0.0	0.00	**3.2**	0.2	0.44	6.23	3.76	79.2	**1.6**	20.7	24.6	**2.6**
8.6	0.26	0.7	0.06	**5.6**	2.4	1.18	11.62	3.19	53.5	**5.3**	42.5	9.1	**5.9**
8.0	0.87	3.8	0.00	**8.1**	0.9	1.92	15.93	4.19	46.6	**4.2**	30.9	11.1	**8.0**
5.7	0.96	6.4	0.07	**8.6**	27.0	1.52	15.64	3.75	57.7	**4.4**	14.3	6.1	**8.5**
7.9	0.00	0.0	-0.83	**5.3**	1.2	1.32	9.83	3.42	73.6	**4.0**	48.7	17.1	**7.1**
6.7	2.04	6.7	0.04	**6.3**	0.8	1.40	10.11	4.01	53.2	**4.4**	34.4	11.0	**7.9**
7.4	0.54	3.6	0.00	**8.5**	36.8	1.86	19.28	3.58	51.6	**2.3**	15.1	17.9	**9.7**
1.8	1.87	18.0	0.04	**5.0**	1.2	1.04	13.62	5.11	75.8	**1.2**	11.7	28.0	**4.3**
7.6	1.19	3.2	0.00	**3.2**	0.2	0.65	5.63	3.33	79.2	**3.8**	74.6	24.3	**6.4**
9.3	0.00	0.0	0.04	**3.7**	0.7	0.85	11.45	1.59	58.3	**5.6**	69.0	13.0	**3.2**
7.5	0.35	1.9	-0.03	**3.6**	0.6	0.60	5.18	3.78	78.3	**3.9**	24.1	10.3	**5.8**
7.5	0.37	3.3	0.00	**4.4**	1.2	1.08	13.14	4.23	65.9	**2.8**	23.6	16.0	**4.5**
0.3	12.87	113.5	0.54	**0.5**	0.1	0.04	0.74	3.08	97.8	**1.6**	15.2	23.2	**0.6**
5.9	0.81	5.1	-0.07	**4.2**	7.6	0.61	5.57	3.59	72.9	**4.1**	19.7	9.0	**8.4**
5.2	0.85	6.6	-0.23	**3.4**	2.1	0.61	6.44	3.46	82.4	**2.7**	9.9	15.0	**5.3**
8.7	0.45	2.9	0.10	**1.8**	0.2	0.21	2.48	2.64	95.6	**2.5**	35.6	22.3	**3.9**
7.5	0.00	0.0	0.00	**4.4**	0.4	0.78	9.41	4.13	67.3	**4.8**	30.6	7.5	**5.3**
6.2	2.07	8.0	-0.15	**4.2**	0.7	0.84	6.35	3.34	66.4	**2.4**	42.2	31.3	**5.8**
9.1	1.94	2.6	0.28	**4.1**	0.9	0.73	3.33	2.78	58.5	**4.3**	83.8	24.0	**8.2**
5.3	1.08	5.7	0.29	**3.9**	0.5	0.81	8.04	4.33	82.8	**4.7**	32.0	8.7	**5.3**
5.3	2.26	12.4	0.10	**2.3**	0.9	0.21	1.78	3.53	93.9	**4.8**	19.2	3.8	**6.8**
1.5	3.81	27.3	0.41	**3.7**	1.5	0.65	6.29	3.64	81.5	**4.3**	14.2	6.3	**5.2**
2.3	3.62	22.6	1.83	**0.7**	-0.3	-0.08	-1.00	3.65	80.1	**2.9**	26.0	15.7	**2.7**
4.4	0.81	5.3	0.55	**7.7**	1.6	1.68	14.10	4.63	61.7	**2.8**	5.6	14.3	**8.4**
4.4	1.34	8.6	-0.09	**4.0**	11.6	0.89	8.80	4.08	71.8	**3.7**	11.4	10.5	**7.1**
6.9	1.66	7.0	0.13	**1.5**	0.8	0.39	2.72	3.30	95.6	**3.7**	33.1	14.4	**7.1**
10.0	na	0.0	0.00	**3.5**	8.1	0.51	4.37	0.18	79.9	**8.8**	109.7	0.0	**6.8**

Name	City	State	Rating	2013 Rating	2012 Rating	Total Assets ($Mil)	One Year Asset Growth	Asset Mix (As a % of Total Assets) Commercial Loans	Consumer Loans	Mortgage Loans	Securities	Capitalization Index	Leverage Ratio	Risk-Based Capital Ratio
▲ SUMMIT BANK	Oakland	CA	**C**	D+	C-	211.2	9.00	17.2	1.0	2.6	0.2	**9.9**	10.9	17.2
SUMMIT BANK	Eugene	OR	**C**	D+	D+	175.1	16.60	26.4	1.0	3.2	3.3	**6.8**	9.6	12.3
SUMMIT BANK & TRUST	Broomfield	CO	**B-**	C+	C-	137.8	19.24	18.6	1.4	11.7	23.8	**4.4**	7.6	10.7
SUMMIT BANK NA	Panama City	FL	**A-**	B+	B	320.4	22.74	7.7	1.5	5.4	21.4	**10.0**	12.4	20.8
▼ SUMMIT BANK OF KANSAS CITY	Lees Summit	MO	**D**	D	E+	41.1	-15.13	23.8	1.7	12.0	0.0	**9.6**	10.7	15.1
▲ SUMMIT COMMUNITY BANK INC	Moorefield	WV	**B-**	C+	D+	1421.4	2.88	5.4	1.4	19.0	19.9	**9.3**	10.5	15.5
SUMMIT NATIONAL BK	Hulett	WY	**D**	D	D	63.5	-1.22	7.7	4.4	6.6	11.4	**7.9**	9.6	14.1
SUMMIT STATE BK	Santa Rosa	CA	**A-**	B+	B-	463.4	0.89	9.0	0.0	9.5	28.6	**10.0**	13.3	19.0
SUMNER BANK & TRUST	Gallatin	TN	**D+**	D+	C-	159.5	-10.93	9.0	0.9	13.1	32.6	**6.7**	8.7	16.1
SUMNER NATIONAL BK OF SHELDON	Sheldon	IL	**D+**	D+	D+	16.8	0.32	4.8	10.3	33.8	25.1	**8.2**	9.8	19.4
SUN NATIONAL BK	Vineland	NJ	**D-**	D-	D-	2816.8	-12.82	9.5	0.1	12.4	14.6	**7.6**	9.4	16.2
SUNBANK NA	Phoenix	AZ	**B**	C+	C-	31.6	11.67	12.5	1.5	6.1	13.6	**10.0**	24.2	49.0
SUNCREST BANK	Visalia	CA	**C**	B-	C-	179.4	45.76	9.2	0.4	6.9	21.6	**9.5**	11.6	14.6
SUNDANCE STATE BK	Sundance	WY	**B**	B-	C+	166.5	10.94	13.4	6.2	6.9	34.8	**8.1**	9.7	15.4
SUNDOWN STATE BK	Sundown	TX	**B-**	B-	C+	203.8	47.08	12.0	2.6	2.0	37.3	**4.2**	6.2	12.4
SUNFLOWER BANK NA	Salina	KS	**B**	B	B	1710.5	0.99	5.0	1.8	26.2	25.5	**8.5**	10.0	17.8
▲ SUNMARK COMMUNITY BANK	Hawkinsville	GA	**B**	C+	C	199.4	0.92	4.7	4.4	22.6	13.8	**10.0**	11.4	17.2
SUNNYSIDE FS&LA OF IRVINGTON	Irvington	NY	**D**	D	D	95.1	3.77	1.6	0.1	32.9	43.3	**10.0**	12.6	34.0
SUNRISE BANK	Cocoa Beach	FL	**C**	C	D	116.1	9.37	4.5	0.2	10.7	21.3	**8.8**	10.2	16.3
SUNRISE BANK DAKOTA	Onida	SD	**B**	B	B+	56.6	-3.76	7.3	2.6	3.5	42.5	**8.9**	10.2	21.9
SUNRISE BANKS NA	Saint Paul	MN	**B+**	B+	B	738.7	7.36	10.6	0.1	9.2	26.5	**9.0**	10.3	17.4
SUNSET BANK & SAVINGS	Waukesha	WI	**C**	C	C-	135.6	4.82	6.0	0.5	30.0	20.5	**8.5**	10.0	18.2
SUNSHINE SAVINGS BANK	Tallahassee	FL	**C-**	C+	C-	148.6	-0.89	0.4	7.9	35.6	18.3	**10.0**	12.5	20.1
SUNSHINE STATE BANK	Plant City	FL	**D**	C-	C-	222.8	16.03	6.5	0.6	25.0	34.0	**10.0**	19.0	38.5
SUNSOUTH BANK	Dothan	AL	**E-**	E-	D-	148.4	-12.50	9.0	1.2	16.1	19.7	**1.7**	5.5	8.7
▲ SUNSTATE BK	Miami	FL	**B-**	C+	C-	184.0	15.02	2.6	0.3	17.6	17.7	**10.0**	11.1	18.7
SUNTRUST BANK	Atlanta	GA	**C**	C	C-	182555.5	8.97	22.0	11.8	15.6	13.7	**6.8**	9.7	12.4
SUNWEST BANK	Irvine	CA	**C-**	C	B	829.9	23.33	16.3	0.5	4.5	11.0	**9.2**	12.6	14.3
SUPERIOR BANK	Hazelwood	MO	**E-**	E-	E-	26.1	-19.84	2.4	0.1	14.9	0.0	**6.9**	8.9	12.5
SUPERIOR NATIONAL BK & TRUST	Hancock	MI	**B**	B-	C+	580.6	4.30	5.7	6.7	21.6	44.6	**10.0**	11.4	22.6
SUPERIOR SB	Superior	WI	**C+**	C+	B	61.0	-2.22	4.6	1.5	47.2	5.9	**10.0**	18.3	30.0
▲ SURETY BANK	Deland	FL	**D**	D-	D-	96.7	-5.99	1.3	1.1	9.0	29.0	**10.0**	11.0	18.1
SURREY BANK & TRUST	Mount Airy	NC	**A-**	A-	B	252.3	5.65	27.6	2.0	9.5	1.5	**10.0**	13.7	20.8
SUSQUEHANNA BANK	Lititz	PA	**B-**	B-	C+	18371.5	-0.03	10.4	4.0	12.3	11.8	**7.3**	9.3	12.7
▲ SUSSEX BANK	Rockaway	NJ	**C-**	D	D	566.9	6.20	3.2	0.1	15.4	13.5	**9.0**	10.3	14.6
SUTTER COMMUNITY BANK	Yuba City	CA	**D+**	D	C-	66.1	-0.14	14.0	0.3	10.5	0.0	**10.0**	12.4	18.7
▲ SUTTON BANK	Attica	OH	**B**	C+	C-	393.8	13.23	10.6	1.2	6.3	24.1	**7.5**	9.3	14.0
▼ SWEDISH-AMERICAN STATE BK	Courtland	KS	**D+**	D+	C-	48.7	5.52	13.3	5.1	8.7	20.2	**6.5**	8.5	12.4
SWEET WATER STATE BK	Sweet Water	AL	**B-**	B-	B-	93.7	1.66	17.1	5.6	10.0	12.4	**8.3**	9.8	13.8
SWINEFORD NATIONAL BK	Hummels Wharf	PA	**B**	B	B-	290.1	-3.08	9.9	2.5	15.3	24.1	**9.9**	10.9	16.2
SWISHER TRUST & SB	Swisher	IA	**C+**	C+	B-	45.6	5.44	3.7	5.0	20.5	49.3	**10.0**	11.1	18.9
SYCAMORE BANK	Senatobia	MS	**B-**	B-	C+	194.6	-5.02	7.5	4.1	19.6	23.4	**7.5**	9.3	15.9
SYNCHRONY BANK	Draper	UT	**C+**	C+	B-	46098.1	32.31	2.6	81.1	0.0	0.8	**10.0**	13.2	17.0
SYNERGY BANK	Houma	LA	**B+**	B+	B	461.3	9.32	20.1	2.6	12.2	16.5	**8.1**	9.7	15.5
▼ SYNERGY BANK SSB	McKinney	TX	**C**	C	C-	118.4	-0.34	3.5	12.2	11.9	10.2	**10.0**	11.9	18.5
SYNOVUS BANK	Columbus	GA	**C+**	C	C-	26213.3	1.30	16.7	1.6	9.6	11.6	**9.3**	11.6	14.4
SYNOVUS TRUST CO NA	Columbus	GA	**U**	U	U	81.3	8.25	0.0	0.0	0.0	21.9	**10.0**	98.4	136.9
▼ SYSTEMATIC SAVINGS BANK	Springfield	MO	**D**	D+	C	37.4	-9.30	0.2	0.2	47.3	8.4	**10.0**	20.8	47.2
T BANK NA	Dallas	TX	**A-**	A-	B	162.3	23.12	46.6	1.0	1.2	5.4	**10.0**	13.5	16.7
TABLE GROVE STATE BK	Table Grove	IL	**C+**	C+	B-	48.1	-3.09	2.0	6.7	3.7	38.6	**8.8**	10.2	16.7
TABLE ROCK COMMUNITY BANK	Kimberling City	MO	**C**	C	C	60.4	8.32	5.4	5.0	33.4	5.6	**6.4**	8.4	12.5
▲ TALBOT BANK OF EASTON MARYLAND	Easton	MD	**C-**	D-	D	591.3	1.83	6.3	1.0	16.2	18.8	**6.7**	8.7	13.9
TALBOT STATE BK	Fayetteville	GA	**D-**	E+	E+	70.6	1.88	3.1	0.7	53.3	32.4	**6.1**	8.1	18.4
TALLAHATCHIE COUNTY BANK	Charleston	MS	**C+**	C+	C	57.5	-4.04	1.9	7.3	8.1	37.6	**8.1**	9.8	20.6
TALMER BANK & TRUST	Troy	MI	**B**	B+	B+	4899.4	116.63	13.3	2.0	27.9	11.5	**10.0**	11.5	16.7
TALMER WEST BANK	Ann Arbor	MI	**D**	D-	E-	838.8	43.04	5.7	0.4	7.9	20.6	**10.0**	11.6	18.5
TAMPA STATE BK	Tampa	KS	**C+**	C+	C+	53.0	7.17	7.7	2.4	17.7	31.1	**9.4**	10.6	15.5
TARBORO SB SSB	Tarboro	NC	**B**	B	B-	43.7	6.41	0.0	0.1	60.0	0.1	**10.0**	14.0	26.5
TARGET BANK	Salt Lake City	UT	**A+**	A	A	46.1	-1.45	1.2	0.0	0.0	17.8	**10.0**	19.9	56.7
TAYLOR COUNTY BANK	Campbellsville	KY	**A**	A	B+	169.4	1.05	8.4	6.1	25.1	15.6	**10.0**	12.0	17.1

Asset Quality Index	Adjusted Non-Performing Loans as a % of Total Loans	Adjusted Non-Performing Loans as a % of Capital	Net Charge-Offs Avg Loans	Profitability Index	Net Income ($Mil)	Return on Assets (R.O.A.)	Return on Equity (R.O.E.)	Net Interest Spread	Overhead Efficiency Ratio	Liquidity Index	Liquidity Ratio	Hot Money Ratio	Stability Index
3.2	2.46	10.8	-0.51	**5.3**	1.4	0.93	8.19	4.03	64.8	**4.8**	47.3	12.7	**6.0**
6.6	0.35	2.7	-0.07	**8.0**	1.7	1.41	15.22	5.39	54.6	**4.1**	15.9	8.2	**5.0**
5.5	0.63	5.2	-0.11	**0.0**	-0.6	-0.63	-7.20	3.88	125.1	**2.9**	24.8	15.4	**4.8**
8.9	0.35	1.3	0.00	**5.4**	2.0	0.93	7.11	4.11	68.4	**5.4**	46.1	9.7	**7.6**
1.7	3.54	22.8	1.36	**0.7**	-0.2	-0.55	-4.75	3.85	113.5	**1.6**	24.1	25.7	**3.4**
5.4	1.28	8.0	0.52	**4.5**	9.0	0.86	7.99	3.53	56.7	**0.9**	13.4	34.8	**6.6**
1.0	4.06	26.2	0.16	**3.4**	0.3	0.67	6.34	4.33	81.8	**4.2**	14.0	7.2	**4.3**
6.0	1.07	4.7	0.02	**6.3**	3.7	1.06	7.66	3.85	57.8	**1.0**	25.2	38.1	**7.1**
5.9	1.30	7.2	0.11	**1.6**	0.0	0.02	0.20	2.91	99.9	**3.5**	38.9	17.0	**3.3**
4.2	1.94	10.8	0.04	**2.9**	0.1	0.50	5.34	3.70	88.4	**4.5**	17.8	5.4	**4.2**
5.5	0.99	5.7	1.58	**0.0**	-26.0	-1.17	-11.10	3.09	112.7	**4.5**	27.9	11.6	**5.7**
9.1	0.00	0.0	5.45	**3.5**	0.2	0.72	2.60	2.41	83.0	**5.2**	62.3	12.8	**7.0**
7.2	0.32	1.8	0.00	**2.8**	0.3	0.22	1.97	3.85	85.8	**1.7**	25.0	24.2	**6.5**
4.8	1.31	7.1	0.54	**6.0**	1.4	1.13	12.80	3.66	51.6	**3.0**	31.9	17.2	**4.7**
7.0	0.00	0.0	-0.15	**5.4**	1.4	1.14	15.59	4.04	63.9	**5.3**	45.8	10.2	**3.8**
8.2	0.44	2.5	0.08	**4.6**	14.3	1.12	10.25	3.27	72.9	**4.4**	16.1	6.4	**8.9**
4.4	3.13	16.7	0.02	**5.0**	2.1	1.33	12.41	4.24	68.6	**2.6**	22.6	16.6	**5.4**
9.2	1.05	3.4	0.00	**0.3**	-0.2	-0.24	-1.93	2.69	117.2	**3.7**	55.7	19.1	**2.3**
4.1	0.94	5.3	-0.01	**5.3**	0.7	0.85	8.28	3.85	66.4	**0.9**	24.4	46.9	**3.3**
8.8	0.05	0.2	0.00	**4.3**	0.4	0.85	8.83	2.89	67.8	**3.9**	53.6	17.9	**6.9**
5.3	1.20	6.4	0.00	**5.0**	7.6	1.16	13.89	3.16	84.3	**4.8**	32.8	8.1	**6.9**
5.6	1.63	8.6	0.20	**3.2**	0.5	0.51	4.47	3.83	82.3	**2.9**	37.9	19.9	**4.9**
4.4	2.94	15.6	0.34	**1.3**	0.0	0.03	0.20	4.10	97.7	**5.0**	29.9	5.8	**5.7**
4.2	6.19	15.9	0.70	**0.7**	-0.2	-0.12	-0.87	2.95	94.8	**6.1**	53.6	7.5	**5.9**
0.3	7.48	73.7	0.48	**0.0**	-2.1	-1.81	-31.82	3.54	169.7	**0.7**	10.8	42.1	**1.5**
3.5	6.01	22.5	0.79	**4.3**	3.0	2.33	18.07	2.96	97.7	**5.3**	46.4	10.2	**4.6**
3.3	1.59	11.3	0.35	**4.6**	1315.8	1.01	8.05	3.14	66.3	**4.6**	17.8	5.6	**8.3**
0.8	3.72	21.6	0.41	**7.6**	6.3	1.05	8.46	5.62	66.3	**4.4**	15.9	6.1	**9.0**
0.0	8.89	57.8	0.62	**0.0**	-0.2	-0.86	-12.14	3.33	114.7	**2.7**	13.7	15.5	**1.8**
4.9	3.11	12.5	1.10	**5.1**	4.2	0.98	8.73	3.67	57.4	**3.8**	51.8	18.7	**7.1**
5.3	2.98	10.4	0.40	**2.4**	0.1	0.17	0.91	3.40	96.6	**3.9**	33.4	13.1	**6.2**
0.5	8.70	40.9	2.33	**1.3**	-0.1	-0.11	-1.05	4.53	77.1	**2.7**	37.0	21.6	**3.8**
5.6	1.37	7.0	-0.10	**7.6**	2.2	1.18	8.46	4.08	59.9	**2.2**	20.6	18.4	**7.5**
4.0	1.05	8.1	0.38	**4.8**	119.5	0.87	5.81	3.65	65.2	**3.0**	10.1	13.7	**8.9**
2.1	1.98	13.8	0.30	**3.0**	2.1	0.51	4.79	3.57	78.0	**3.6**	12.4	10.9	**5.7**
0.7	7.43	40.8	-0.11	**2.6**	0.2	0.29	2.18	4.39	95.4	**1.6**	14.3	23.1	**6.8**
4.9	0.94	5.8	0.17	**7.7**	5.5	1.91	19.43	4.01	57.7	**2.8**	18.1	15.1	**5.6**
1.1	2.71	22.8	0.83	**4.1**	0.3	0.76	9.12	4.16	68.5	**0.7**	4.7	33.9	**4.0**
5.0	1.09	7.4	0.19	**5.4**	0.9	1.24	12.94	6.14	73.1	**1.1**	15.9	30.2	**6.0**
4.9	1.45	8.4	0.07	**5.0**	1.8	0.83	7.41	3.50	73.2	**4.1**	16.8	8.5	**7.1**
9.3	0.00	0.0	-0.01	**2.9**	0.2	0.51	4.64	2.84	77.1	**7.2**	68.9	1.8	**5.4**
4.7	1.74	10.6	0.21	**4.6**	1.3	0.85	9.32	3.98	69.7	**3.7**	11.4	9.9	**4.7**
2.2	2.12	10.0	4.33	**10.0**	1302.6	4.19	27.58	13.45	31.1	**0.7**	17.8	70.0	**10.0**
5.3	0.93	5.8	-0.07	**7.8**	4.4	1.30	13.91	3.85	52.6	**2.2**	28.0	20.3	**6.4**
1.3	5.25	27.3	0.33	**1.2**	-0.4	-0.42	-2.69	4.48	116.1	**3.3**	23.0	13.5	**6.0**
3.9	2.10	13.3	0.38	**4.6**	169.8	0.87	6.87	3.54	63.8	**2.5**	10.2	16.4	**7.3**
6.5	na	0.0	na	**9.5**	4.0	6.74	6.89	0.30	78.5	**4.0**	1893.9	101.0	**5.7**
6.6	2.84	8.0	0.46	**0.0**	-0.2	-0.65	-3.27	3.45	121.0	**3.2**	45.5	20.3	**6.4**
6.5	0.47	2.7	1.15	**9.8**	2.0	1.73	13.11	4.79	77.0	**0.5**	6.8	47.8	**6.2**
7.0	0.57	3.1	0.30	**3.7**	0.3	0.77	7.87	3.76	80.4	**4.9**	35.6	8.6	**5.2**
4.5	0.81	7.2	0.14	**6.5**	0.4	0.98	11.63	4.90	64.3	**1.6**	14.5	23.2	**3.6**
1.7	5.23	36.6	1.53	**1.9**	1.5	0.36	3.82	3.29	68.3	**2.8**	22.4	15.9	**4.2**
1.7	5.57	37.1	0.16	**2.5**	0.4	0.66	9.98	3.82	88.0	**1.5**	34.8	52.6	**1.6**
6.6	0.84	2.8	0.60	**3.3**	0.3	0.63	6.68	3.31	73.9	**4.3**	45.8	14.3	**4.5**
4.8	2.83	17.1	0.17	**5.8**	41.7	1.21	10.96	4.11	75.0	**1.8**	9.8	19.5	**8.6**
1.9	4.73	23.4	-0.06	**4.7**	3.9	0.57	4.02	4.77	77.2	**2.1**	27.3	20.5	**4.5**
5.3	1.32	6.1	0.00	**3.8**	0.3	0.81	8.21	3.81	78.3	**2.1**	26.2	20.0	**5.4**
7.3	0.92	5.0	0.14	**3.9**	0.2	0.64	4.61	3.45	66.6	**1.1**	27.2	37.8	**7.4**
10.0	0.42	0.2	1.56	**10.0**	7.9	19.89	93.68	0.83	26.0	**8.2**	103.8	1.0	**9.1**
5.9	1.40	8.3	0.22	**9.5**	2.8	2.16	19.33	4.59	54.4	**3.0**	18.1	14.2	**8.3**

	Name	City	State	Rating	2013 Rating	2012 Rating	Total Assets ($Mil)	One Year Asset Growth	Asset Mix (As a % of Total Assets) Comm-ercial Loans	Cons-umer Loans	Mort-gage Loans	Secur-ities	Capital-ization Index	Lever-age Ratio	Risk-Based Capital Ratio
	TAYLORSVILLE SB SSB	Taylorsville	NC	D+	D+	D	93.3	2.80	1.9	1.4	44.5	13.4	6.6	8.6	14.2
	TCF NATIONAL BK	Sioux Falls	SD	D+	D+	D	19054.2	3.50	20.9	10.1	19.5	3.6	7.7	9.7	13.1
	TCM BANK NA	Tampa	FL	B+	B+	B	179.9	3.18	5.6	80.6	0.0	2.6	10.0	25.1	28.6
	TD BANK NA	Wilmington	DE	C	C	C	224995.6	4.44	9.1	8.4	10.1	37.2	6.0	8.0	13.9
	TD BANK USA NA	Wilmington	DE	C	B-	B-	16500.0	4.62	0.0	31.6	0.0	40.4	5.8	7.8	23.4
	TECHE BANK & TRUST CO	Saint Martinville	LA	A-	A-	B+	108.5	6.62	6.4	5.2	16.4	39.1	8.1	9.7	19.0
▲	TECUMSEH FEDERAL BANK	Tecumseh	NE	B	C+	C+	57.9	0.56	3.0	0.5	49.2	25.9	10.0	15.5	37.1
	TEJAS BANK	Monahans	TX	A-	A-	B	142.0	19.28	23.5	5.0	11.9	16.3	7.7	9.4	14.0
	TEMPLETON SB	Templeton	IA	A-	A-	A-	117.6	0.06	7.0	2.6	11.2	29.0	9.9	10.9	17.4
	TEMPO BANK	Trenton	IL	C+	C+	C-	91.4	3.43	0.0	2.0	75.0	0.0	10.0	12.4	25.1
	TENNESSEE STATE BK	Pigeon Forge	TN	D-	D-	D-	625.6	-5.76	0.5	0.8	14.5	26.0	8.8	10.2	15.1
	TENSAS STATE BK	Newellton	LA	A-	B	B-	157.4	7.12	17.9	2.0	9.3	35.6	10.0	11.6	18.0
▲	TERRABANK NA	Miami	FL	C-	D	D-	283.6	3.62	0.8	0.2	3.9	25.3	8.8	10.2	15.8
	TERRE HAUTE SB	Terre Haute	IN	C-	C-	C-	310.3	4.56	8.4	1.2	28.2	27.3	6.5	8.5	15.4
	TERRITORIAL SAVINGS BANK	Honolulu	HI	B+	B+	B+	1656.0	6.06	0.2	0.1	53.9	35.8	10.0	12.9	32.4
	TETON BANKS	Fairfield	MT	A-	A-	A	195.0	3.42	9.5	3.5	4.5	21.9	10.0	14.0	21.3
▲	TEUTOPOLIS STATE BK	Teutopolis	IL	A-	B+	A-	200.7	0.98	6.2	2.2	11.3	38.9	10.0	12.5	21.7
▲	TEXAN BANK	Sugar Land	TX	C-	D-	D	153.1	22.72	15.4	0.8	4.5	5.9	8.6	11.0	13.9
	TEXANA BANK NA	Linden	TX	B-	B-	C+	157.9	4.04	33.0	5.0	28.0	6.0	6.9	8.9	12.6
	TEXAS ADVANTAGE COMMUNITY BANK	Alvin	TX	C	C+	D+	107.1	13.43	29.6	3.3	6.2	12.8	6.6	8.6	20.0
	TEXAS BANK	Henderson	TX	C+	C+	C	344.2	4.60	3.9	5.5	10.9	61.1	5.9	7.9	18.6
	TEXAS BANK & TRUST CO	Longview	TX	B+	B+	B+	1943.0	11.98	14.9	5.7	28.3	12.6	8.1	9.7	14.5
▲	TEXAS BANK FINANCIAL	Weatherford	TX	B	C	B-	114.0	20.72	2.7	0.6	67.7	4.9	7.2	9.1	19.8
	TEXAS BRAND BANK	Garland	TX	C+	C+	C+	132.7	18.03	11.6	0.9	11.1	4.9	8.2	9.8	15.5
▼	TEXAS CAPITAL BANK NA	Dallas	TX	B-	B-	C+	14259.2	32.17	30.8	0.1	1.0	0.3	3.6	9.4	10.3
▼	TEXAS CHAMPION BANK	Corpus Christi	TX	B-	B-	C-	404.6	10.27	22.7	1.0	5.3	16.7	7.3	9.2	13.0
	TEXAS CITIZENS BANK NA	Pasadena	TX	C	C	D-	316.4	1.24	23.6	3.0	7.0	2.7	6.5	9.6	12.1
	TEXAS COMMUNITY BANK	Laredo	TX	C+	C+	C+	1195.8	2.18	11.6	1.6	13.0	35.8	6.4	8.4	19.4
	TEXAS EXCHANGE BANK SSB	Crowley	TX	C	C-	C-	134.0	2.12	28.2	0.3	8.5	0.8	10.0	16.1	22.5
▲	TEXAS FINANCIAL BANK	Eden	TX	B-	C+	B-	99.7	12.86	2.2	1.5	1.4	35.0	7.3	9.2	21.6
	TEXAS FIRST BANK	Texas City	TX	B	B	B	894.7	7.88	8.3	2.2	3.5	41.9	6.8	8.8	15.3
	TEXAS FIRST STATE BK	Riesel	TX	B-	B-	C+	344.4	-0.79	6.2	1.7	12.6	55.5	6.1	8.1	19.4
▲	TEXAS GULF BANK NA	Lake Jackson	TX	B+	B	B	500.9	3.55	10.2	1.4	12.6	34.7	8.5	10.0	15.6
	TEXAS HERITAGE BANK	Boerne	TX	B+	B+	B	123.0	12.90	9.9	3.0	17.3	5.5	7.1	9.1	15.0
	TEXAS HERITAGE NATIONAL BK	Daingerfield	TX	B	B-	C	117.5	11.47	7.8	5.3	14.8	11.5	9.6	10.7	16.1
	TEXAS HILL COUNTRY BANK	Bandera	TX	C	D+	C	56.7	18.73	16.3	1.8	14.2	21.0	10.0	18.6	27.5
▲	TEXAS LEADERSHIP BANK	Royse City	TX	B-	C+	C	75.4	4.86	10.2	5.1	14.9	25.8	10.0	12.1	21.1
▼	TEXAS NATIONAL BK	Mercedes	TX	B-	B	B	132.8	14.64	3.8	2.1	32.1	3.6	9.7	10.8	16.4
	TEXAS NATIONAL BK	Sweetwater	TX	B-	B	A-	123.1	23.96	5.1	2.3	4.4	60.6	7.3	9.2	20.3
▲	TEXAS NATIONAL BK JACKSONVILLE	Jacksonville	TX	B	C	C	402.6	13.74	15.1	4.0	26.2	2.8	7.7	9.5	13.5
	TEXAS REGIONAL BANK	Harlingen	TX	C-	D+	C	439.2	102.08	11.9	1.3	5.7	26.6	9.3	10.6	16.0
	TEXAS REPUBLIC BANK NA	Frisco	TX	B+	B+	C	140.9	40.12	10.4	2.0	35.2	0.0	9.0	10.4	17.6
	TEXAS SECURITY BANK	Dallas	TX	B	B	B-	243.1	13.37	19.6	0.5	19.6	13.1	10.0	11.7	15.2
	TEXAS STAR BANK	Van Alstyne	TX	B	C+	B-	325.4	2.71	14.7	6.4	9.9	4.6	7.7	9.4	14.9
	TEXAS STAR BANK SSB	Lott	TX	B+	A-	B	109.2	45.38	1.6	1.4	20.6	0.0	5.1	9.2	11.1
▲	TEXAS STATE BK	San Angelo	TX	B+	B	B-	260.9	12.27	7.0	1.4	14.6	27.2	9.6	10.7	20.5
	TEXAS STATE BK	Lufkin	TX	C+	B	B+	121.2	-3.87	22.8	9.1	18.2	4.2	9.3	10.6	14.7
	TEXASBANK	Brownwood	TX	A+	A+	A-	379.6	14.14	4.1	2.3	20.3	10.9	10.0	12.2	17.4
▼	TEXICO STATE BK	Texico	IL	D	D	C	8.5	-15.57	0.4	2.9	43.1	19.0	6.8	8.8	17.8
	TEXSTAR NATIONAL BK	Universal City	TX	B-	B-	B-	209.8	3.03	13.3	1.4	8.0	11.4	9.1	10.4	15.3
▼	THAYER COUNTY BANK	Hebron	NE	C-	C-	D-	55.2	-0.22	12.9	2.5	14.2	20.8	9.1	10.4	14.3
	THE BANK	Oberlin	KS	A-	A-	A-	326.6	6.80	3.9	0.7	0.9	24.2	6.4	8.5	12.1
	THE BANK	Jennings	LA	A-	A-	A-	197.1	5.68	16.7	14.9	22.7	17.9	8.4	10.0	15.9
	THE FIRST NA	Damariscotta	ME	B-	C+	C	1455.3	1.64	5.8	1.3	26.6	32.2	6.6	8.6	16.1
	THINK MUTUAL BANK	Rochester	MN	C+	C+	B-	1481.4	0.67	0.3	11.8	39.8	40.4	10.0	14.5	29.1
	THIRD COAST BANK SSB	Humble	TX	C+	C	D+	322.8	17.56	27.8	0.3	3.6	0.0	7.3	9.6	12.7
	THIRD FS&LA OF CLEVELAND	Cleveland	OH	B-	B-	C-	11769.1	4.78	0.0	0.0	77.6	4.8	10.0	13.5	25.3
	THIRD NATIONAL BK OF SEDALIA	Sedalia	MO	B	B	B-	390.6	-4.44	5.1	12.1	11.3	25.7	6.3	8.3	13.3
	THOMAS COUNTY FS&LA	Thomasville	GA	C-	C	D	260.5	-4.81	1.7	0.6	35.4	2.5	10.0	13.7	20.5
	THOMASTON SB	Thomaston	CT	C+	C+	B-	807.5	5.39	3.9	1.6	44.4	16.9	10.0	12.7	21.3

Asset Quality Index	Adjusted Non-Performing Loans as a % of Total Loans	Adjusted Non-Performing Loans as a % of Capital	Net Charge-Offs / Avg Loans	Profitability Index	Net Income ($Mil)	Return on Assets (R.O.A.)	Return on Equity (R.O.E.)	Net Interest Spread	Overhead Efficiency Ratio	Liquidity Index	Liquidity Ratio	Hot Money Ratio	Stability Index
2.3	4.09	31.5	0.25	**2.5**	0.2	0.30	3.80	3.57	85.4	**1.6**	18.2	24.5	**4.2**
1.5	3.35	27.2	0.56	**5.9**	151.3	1.11	10.79	4.72	69.3	**3.4**	8.9	11.7	**7.2**
5.0	0.81	2.6	2.36	**9.8**	2.2	1.65	6.77	9.49	71.9	**0.4**	17.4	99.2	**8.5**
3.8	1.32	8.1	0.30	**3.2**	886.2	0.55	4.26	2.61	72.9	**3.6**	41.7	19.7	**7.4**
4.0	2.34	7.8	3.38	**4.5**	89.8	0.74	9.03	8.79	68.4	**6.9**	69.7	7.2	**7.0**
8.8	0.00	0.0	0.05	**5.6**	1.1	1.42	13.26	4.12	64.5	**2.8**	40.5	22.6	**8.0**
8.6	1.33	4.8	0.04	**4.0**	0.4	0.80	5.36	2.96	68.9	**3.1**	42.0	20.2	**7.0**
7.8	0.01	0.0	0.01	**9.2**	2.3	2.28	20.69	4.69	49.0	**1.8**	18.9	21.0	**7.1**
7.7	0.21	1.2	-0.01	**6.0**	0.9	1.04	8.74	3.40	53.5	**2.9**	14.6	14.7	**8.2**
6.7	1.01	6.6	0.03	**2.9**	0.2	0.33	2.87	3.00	85.8	**3.1**	16.2	13.7	**6.0**
1.5	8.43	44.2	2.44	**0.7**	-2.4	-0.50	-4.87	3.50	106.2	**1.7**	18.4	22.9	**4.9**
6.2	1.02	4.6	0.08	**6.7**	1.7	1.53	13.25	3.92	61.5	**2.8**	41.6	24.4	**8.5**
3.2	0.99	6.2	-0.02	**2.7**	0.6	0.30	2.92	3.54	88.8	**1.9**	33.4	29.8	**5.6**
5.1	1.49	9.7	0.27	**1.9**	0.5	0.22	2.56	3.25	92.4	**3.8**	34.3	14.2	**4.5**
9.1	0.65	2.8	0.02	**5.0**	11.0	0.89	7.21	3.40	60.7	**4.2**	26.3	12.0	**9.7**
7.8	0.73	3.0	0.04	**7.4**	2.0	1.35	10.15	3.70	49.7	**1.5**	26.4	28.5	**7.4**
9.0	0.02	0.1	0.00	**5.4**	1.6	1.06	8.59	2.81	46.9	**5.8**	41.7	5.3	**7.6**
6.8	0.01	0.1	0.08	**2.5**	0.6	0.57	4.67	4.43	78.6	**0.8**	16.0	37.4	**3.3**
5.4	0.35	3.2	0.25	**4.9**	1.3	1.11	12.33	4.95	75.0	**1.0**	7.6	30.4	**5.5**
7.7	0.24	1.7	0.00	**2.6**	0.6	0.72	8.49	3.30	86.4	**2.3**	34.5	25.2	**4.3**
5.4	2.00	8.0	0.46	**5.6**	3.5	1.37	15.96	4.41	72.1	**3.6**	54.9	21.7	**4.1**
5.8	0.93	6.6	0.08	**5.9**	14.6	1.03	10.36	3.50	61.8	**3.4**	14.8	12.2	**8.4**
5.8	0.96	7.6	-0.72	**8.2**	1.7	1.99	23.45	5.09	75.9	**0.9**	14.3	32.6	**5.1**
6.4	0.00	0.0	-0.02	**3.6**	0.6	0.62	6.94	4.10	77.5	**1.3**	30.4	43.1	**4.8**
6.6	0.33	3.2	0.06	**7.0**	98.7	1.06	11.68	3.81	55.3	**4.7**	4.3	2.9	**7.0**
3.5	1.96	13.7	-0.07	**7.6**	5.4	1.85	19.31	4.45	63.4	**3.3**	11.3	12.2	**5.2**
4.4	1.09	8.4	-0.04	**3.3**	1.0	0.44	4.34	4.99	84.7	**3.2**	9.6	12.4	**4.1**
8.4	0.39	2.1	-0.15	**3.6**	4.8	0.54	6.42	2.68	67.2	**2.8**	39.6	29.9	**6.2**
8.2	0.56	2.2	0.00	**2.5**	0.3	0.27	1.60	3.71	82.1	**1.8**	38.9	56.0	**5.8**
8.7	0.74	2.4	0.01	**3.9**	0.5	0.75	8.38	2.87	71.6	**4.5**	42.6	13.2	**4.8**
5.2	1.54	7.7	0.01	**5.9**	9.6	1.45	15.23	4.06	66.2	**3.7**	37.9	15.7	**5.8**
8.6	0.20	0.9	0.03	**3.4**	1.6	0.59	7.57	2.83	73.4	**3.1**	43.8	20.8	**3.9**
8.7	0.16	0.9	0.01	**5.5**	5.2	1.40	13.64	4.08	68.4	**3.8**	32.5	13.7	**7.5**
5.3	0.75	5.5	0.07	**6.2**	1.3	1.42	15.22	4.31	69.2	**4.0**	27.4	10.9	**6.4**
4.3	1.49	9.1	0.01	**8.0**	2.1	2.45	22.97	4.26	54.8	**1.4**	23.4	28.7	**5.9**
8.5	0.00	0.0	0.00	**2.1**	0.1	0.34	2.51	3.73	86.3	**2.7**	24.6	16.6	**3.3**
8.5	0.00	0.0	0.04	**3.4**	0.4	0.74	6.45	3.13	80.7	**1.4**	31.5	35.6	**5.5**
3.8	2.45	16.5	0.01	**6.0**	0.9	0.93	8.73	6.37	74.5	**0.8**	16.9	37.4	**6.5**
9.3	0.00	0.0	-0.13	**3.8**	0.9	0.96	9.34	3.30	75.9	**5.7**	57.2	10.8	**6.6**
5.4	0.35	2.9	0.04	**8.0**	3.7	1.26	13.36	4.34	52.2	**0.5**	5.9	47.9	**6.1**
4.6	1.81	9.3	-0.02	**2.3**	1.0	0.34	2.89	4.12	87.8	**3.3**	40.4	18.8	**6.2**
6.7	0.28	2.0	0.00	**5.7**	1.0	1.02	8.47	4.93	65.1	**1.5**	25.7	28.7	**5.2**
8.5	0.00	0.0	0.00	**4.7**	1.5	0.84	7.07	4.21	73.0	**1.0**	14.7	32.6	**7.3**
4.8	1.09	6.9	0.04	**5.2**	2.1	0.87	9.37	3.80	70.3	**2.6**	29.4	18.4	**5.5**
5.8	0.37	3.5	0.03	**8.9**	0.9	1.31	13.28	5.53	61.6	**0.5**	8.8	55.4	**6.2**
9.2	0.04	0.2	0.01	**5.3**	2.4	1.32	12.17	3.64	65.9	**5.7**	41.7	5.8	**6.6**
1.9	2.92	21.2	0.39	**3.8**	0.4	0.46	4.17	4.58	87.1	**2.3**	12.3	17.3	**5.0**
8.2	0.32	1.8	0.07	**10.0**	6.8	2.47	20.32	4.99	53.7	**3.6**	17.1	11.4	**8.9**
9.6	0.00	0.0	0.00	**1.3**	-0.1	-2.07	-27.47	4.38	96.3	**5.5**	29.6	0.0	**3.1**
7.2	0.00	0.0	0.00	**4.5**	1.6	1.00	9.35	4.08	71.1	**1.4**	18.2	26.2	**6.7**
2.3	4.19	24.4	0.28	**3.4**	0.3	0.78	7.71	4.15	73.0	**1.9**	6.0	18.4	**3.7**
6.8	0.05	0.4	-0.03	**8.7**	4.7	1.95	19.53	3.81	43.1	**4.4**	15.9	6.2	**8.0**
7.2	0.30	1.9	0.18	**8.6**	2.1	1.39	14.53	5.19	59.8	**2.1**	15.9	18.7	**7.3**
4.7	1.47	9.7	0.11	**4.7**	11.6	1.06	12.28	3.19	59.4	**1.6**	23.4	31.9	**7.1**
8.2	0.63	2.4	0.12	**2.9**	4.2	0.37	2.57	2.68	80.9	**6.8**	47.5	4.1	**8.6**
6.9	0.55	4.0	0.29	**4.2**	2.0	0.89	9.13	4.51	70.0	**1.8**	23.3	22.1	**4.0**
6.2	1.74	11.2	0.21	**3.3**	51.5	0.59	4.42	2.38	56.5	**1.1**	7.3	28.9	**8.0**
4.8	1.10	7.1	0.10	**7.2**	3.7	1.19	13.51	3.48	55.7	**4.2**	18.4	7.7	**6.8**
1.3	8.06	41.6	1.12	**0.0**	-1.1	-0.54	-3.85	3.39	80.0	**2.2**	21.7	18.5	**5.1**
5.9	1.50	8.4	0.29	**2.8**	3.1	0.52	4.12	3.22	77.4	**1.8**	21.7	21.3	**7.4**

Name	City	State	Rating	2013 Rating	2012 Rating	Total Assets ($Mil)	One Year Asset Growth	Comm-ercial Loans	Cons-umer Loans	Mort-gage Loans	Secur-ities	Capital-ization Index	Lever-age Ratio	Risk-Based Capital Ratio
								Asset Mix (As a % of Total Assets)						
THOMASVILLE NATIONAL BK	Thomasville	GA	B-	C+	C+	602.4	7.90	15.6	1.7	26.3	7.2	6.7	8.7	12.3
THREE RIVERS BANK OF MONTANA	Kalispell	MT	B+	B+	B+	112.9	-0.04	15.1	2.4	11.8	25.3	10.0	13.8	21.3
THRIVENT TRUST CO	Appleton	WI	U	U	B-	10.4	0.90	0.0	0.0	0.0	57.7	10.0	74.3	370.6
THUMB NATIONAL BK & TRUST CO	Pigeon	MI	C-	D+	D+	217.4	1.98	8.1	1.6	11.0	21.5	7.8	9.5	14.6
THURSTON FIRST BANK	Olympia	WA	C+	C	D	115.8	4.31	33.3	0.2	1.6	12.7	8.1	9.7	21.5
TIAA-CREF TRUST CO FSB	Saint Louis	MO	C-	C	A-	2339.4	-3.26	4.1	0.0	37.6	29.9	10.0	13.7	41.5
TIB INDEPENDENT BANKERSBANK	Farmers Branch	TX	B-	B-	B-	2153.3	-0.02	4.7	3.7	0.9	22.1	7.9	9.6	22.2
TIDELANDS BANK	Mount Pleasant	SC	E-	E-	E-	481.4	-2.22	4.9	0.5	16.8	17.4	1.9	5.6	8.9
TIGHTWAD BANK	Osage City	KS	D-	D	C	4.9	-38.11	3.5	0.0	9.6	0.0	9.0	10.4	27.5
TILDEN BANK	Tilden	NE	B-	B-	C+	82.0	1.98	8.4	3.0	2.7	15.7	7.8	9.5	15.3
TIMBERLAND BANK	Hoquiam	WA	D	D	C	745.1	-0.02	4.1	0.6	15.3	1.2	8.8	10.2	14.5
TIMBERLINE BANK	Grand Junction	CO	C+	C-	D+	165.0	0.50	11.8	1.1	10.7	10.9	9.9	10.9	15.3
▲ TIMBERWOOD BANK	Tomah	WI	B+	B+	B	171.8	0.79	12.1	0.7	15.8	23.9	10.0	12.0	17.7
▼ TIME FSB	Medford	WI	B+	A-	A	622.6	-0.58	0.0	0.3	58.8	34.3	10.0	18.9	49.5
TIOGA FRANKLIN SB	Philadelphia	PA	C-	C-	C	34.0	-0.71	0.0	0.0	70.8	15.6	10.0	11.9	25.2
TIOGA STATE BK	Spencer	NY	A-	A-	B+	399.2	0.63	13.6	2.0	25.3	27.5	10.0	12.3	18.6
▲ TIPTON LATHAM BANK NA	Tipton	MO	B	B	B	107.4	4.93	10.9	4.2	22.7	20.3	10.0	11.1	18.1
▲ TITAN BANK NA	Mineral Wells	TX	B+	B-	B-	78.7	24.39	1.2	9.3	10.3	18.1	8.9	10.3	19.5
TITONKA SB	Titonka	IA	C	C+	B-	168.1	-1.02	2.2	1.5	8.0	53.9	9.5	10.6	22.7
TNBANK	Oak Ridge	TN	C-	C-	D+	189.1	8.71	5.9	0.9	16.7	22.8	6.8	8.8	13.8
TODAYS BANK	Huntsville	AR	A-	A-	B+	103.1	2.96	3.6	0.2	10.2	13.2	10.0	14.1	18.0
TOLLESON PRIVATE BANK	Dallas	TX	B	B	B	475.6	20.47	15.8	3.7	33.5	27.9	5.7	7.7	13.9
TOMAHAWK COMMUNITY BANK SSB	Tomahawk	WI	B-	C+	C-	85.1	7.14	2.4	3.0	37.3	20.2	9.7	11.3	14.7
▲ TOMATOBANK	Alhambra	CA	C+	C	D+	456.9	11.59	4.7	0.0	0.4	6.0	10.0	16.3	23.3
TOMPKINS STATE BK	Avon	IL	C	C	B-	191.7	-2.46	6.1	2.4	14.2	32.1	6.8	8.8	14.9
▲ TOMPKINS TRUST CO	Ithaca	NY	B+	B	B-	1623.2	4.48	5.3	1.9	24.1	36.1	6.0	8.0	14.1
TORRINGTON SB	Torrington	CT	B-	B-	B-	798.0	0.40	0.0	0.2	42.5	35.2	10.0	17.7	47.4
TOTALBANK	Miami	FL	C	C	C-	2667.0	7.23	6.3	0.3	21.8	20.9	9.2	10.5	16.4
TOUCHMARK NATIONAL BK	Alpharetta	GA	B-	B-	C+	157.1	27.37	2.3	0.4	2.8	20.1	10.0	16.7	22.4
TOWANDA STATE BK	Towanda	KS	D-	D-	C-	9.6	2.67	1.1	7.9	54.9	11.3	7.2	9.1	18.3
TOWN & COUNTRY BANK	Salem	MO	B+	B+	A-	507.6	-0.48	2.0	2.9	39.8	18.2	9.3	10.5	18.9
TOWN & COUNTRY BANK	Watertown	WI	C+	C	D	58.6	5.66	5.3	1.1	26.7	10.4	8.3	9.9	14.0
TOWN & COUNTRY BANK	Springfield	IL	B-	B-	B	505.7	2.95	8.2	0.5	19.1	22.2	7.2	9.5	12.6
▼ TOWN & COUNTRY BANK	Ravenna	NE	B-	B+	A-	162.5	4.23	6.6	1.6	1.9	23.9	7.0	9.8	12.5
TOWN & COUNTRY BANK	Las Vegas	NV	C+	C	D+	118.7	0.12	6.1	0.2	10.3	7.9	10.0	12.8	17.8
▲ TOWN & COUNTRY BANK	Saint George	UT	C+	D+	C-	86.0	11.07	11.8	4.7	6.0	8.5	10.0	11.3	15.7
TOWN & COUNTRY BANK & TRUST CO	Bardstown	KY	C-	D+	D-	254.4	1.68	3.1	1.0	21.8	21.3	9.1	10.4	17.9
TOWN & COUNTRY BANK MIDWEST	Quincy	IL	A-	A-	A-	149.9	3.77	20.0	2.4	13.4	4.5	10.0	12.2	16.0
TOWN BANK	Hartland	WI	B-	C+	D+	1271.0	45.81	24.3	13.1	4.5	5.4	5.5	10.2	11.4
▲ TOWN CENTER BANK	New Lenox	IL	D+	D-	D-	106.7	17.73	13.0	5.9	3.5	32.7	6.7	8.7	13.1
▼ TOWN NORTH BANK NA	Dallas	TX	D+	C-	D+	626.0	7.91	0.8	0.0	7.7	39.5	9.8	10.9	20.7
TOWN SQUARE BANK	Ashland	KY	B-	B	B-	411.7	41.56	5.9	4.2	42.8	16.5	10.0	15.0	24.4
TOWN-COUNTRY NATIONAL BK	Camden	AL	A	A	A-	99.0	-2.43	10.1	14.1	14.0	29.4	10.0	15.2	24.8
TOWNEBANK	Portsmouth	VA	B	B	B-	4972.5	8.78	9.2	1.3	12.5	17.6	8.6	10.0	13.8
TOYOTA FINANCIAL SB	Henderson	NV	B	B	B	933.3	2.58	0.0	27.5	62.4	0.9	10.0	16.8	27.8
TRADERS & FARMERS BANK	Haleyville	AL	B	B-	B	360.8	2.30	2.2	5.2	20.2	45.7	10.0	14.7	26.9
▲ TRADERS BANK	Tullahoma	TN	B	C+	D+	157.2	-0.25	9.5	3.3	29.6	16.7	8.5	10.0	16.0
TRADITION BANK	Houston	TX	B-	B-	C+	535.0	9.88	4.0	0.4	3.6	45.4	7.0	9.0	17.1
TRADITION CAPITAL BANK	Edina	MN	C+	C	C	296.0	21.52	13.5	0.8	13.1	8.7	4.1	8.5	10.5
TRADITIONAL BANK INC	Mount Sterling	KY	B	B	B-	1151.8	6.12	4.7	0.5	25.1	25.8	8.5	10.0	14.7
TRADITIONS BANK	Cullman	AL	B	B	B-	282.0	12.38	8.9	8.4	36.2	7.0	7.2	9.3	12.7
TRADITIONS FIRST BANK	Erin	TN	B	B	B	114.3	0.82	11.2	2.9	20.8	20.5	9.3	10.5	16.2
TRANS PACIFIC NATIONAL BK	San Francisco	CA	C-	C	D+	119.5	-5.02	14.3	0.0	5.1	9.9	10.0	11.1	17.9
TRANSCAPITAL BANK	Sunrise	FL	E	E	E-	166.3	-14.75	0.7	0.0	20.6	1.4	10.0	14.9	20.3
▲ TRANSPECOS BANKS	Pecos	TX	C	C-	C-	135.9	3.88	11.9	2.0	12.7	25.8	8.2	9.8	18.0
TRANSPORTATION ALLIANCE BANK	Ogden	UT	C-	D	D-	618.9	-7.34	57.0	5.2	0.2	7.3	10.0	12.2	15.6
TRAVERSE CITY STATE BK	Traverse City	MI	D+	D+	C-	264.5	19.94	14.3	1.0	12.5	2.9	6.9	8.9	13.0
▼ TREASURE STATE BK	Missoula	MT	D-	D	D-	68.4	5.98	10.1	0.9	10.7	0.0	9.0	10.3	14.9
TREGO-WAKEENEY STATE BK	Wakeeney	KS	B-	B-	B-	66.6	5.46	2.3	1.2	5.6	50.0	7.2	9.1	20.2
TREYNOR STATE BK	Treynor	IA	C+	C+	C+	289.3	-0.86	5.9	0.3	1.7	63.2	6.2	8.2	14.8

Asset Quality Index	Adjusted Non-Performing Loans as a % of Total Loans	Adjusted Non-Performing Loans as a % of Capital	Net Charge-Offs / Avg Loans	Profitability Index	Net Income ($Mil)	Return on Assets (R.O.A.)	Return on Equity (R.O.E.)	Net Interest Spread	Overhead Efficiency Ratio	Liquidity Index	Liquidity Ratio	Hot Money Ratio	Stability Index
4.2	0.87	7.3	-0.10	8.5	6.3	1.44	15.99	3.53	49.1	2.4	6.8	16.4	6.9
7.5	0.77	3.5	0.29	6.2	0.9	1.06	7.68	4.76	71.9	2.1	26.9	20.3	6.7
10.0	na	0.0	na	6.9	0.3	3.73	4.66	1.41	91.7	5.0	282.0	100.0	6.0
2.1	3.32	21.1	0.22	4.6	1.7	1.01	10.79	4.41	77.3	3.6	31.4	14.3	5.2
4.1	2.07	12.2	0.07	3.7	0.5	0.57	5.94	3.71	72.8	2.1	33.4	27.1	4.5
10.0	0.00	0.0	0.00	0.0	-25.8	-1.50	-10.62	1.20	141.7	5.8	40.1	7.7	10.0
8.3	0.46	1.4	0.23	4.3	14.4	0.82	8.67	1.63	79.8	4.5	49.9	17.5	7.3
1.7	4.30	42.8	0.39	1.2	0.3	0.09	1.77	3.03	96.1	0.8	18.4	38.6	0.3
9.7	0.00	0.0	0.00	0.0	-0.2	-3.99	-38.20	2.70	257.8	2.5	55.9	31.2	4.6
4.3	0.51	3.1	-0.03	5.2	0.5	0.76	8.14	3.70	69.3	4.6	25.9	6.4	4.1
0.8	3.46	23.2	0.07	4.4	4.3	0.78	7.36	3.89	75.2	3.6	16.5	11.1	6.2
3.5	2.42	14.8	0.17	3.8	1.1	0.88	8.34	3.95	76.1	3.2	24.1	13.8	4.5
5.3	1.36	6.9	0.15	5.8	1.3	1.04	7.79	3.80	62.0	1.5	24.0	27.3	6.8
9.9	0.48	1.5	0.02	4.6	1.8	0.38	2.04	2.57	53.0	2.9	46.4	26.4	9.1
0.3	10.29	56.7	0.95	3.8	0.1	0.57	4.70	3.85	63.5	1.0	24.8	40.0	6.9
8.6	0.47	2.4	0.02	6.0	3.4	1.14	9.64	4.16	65.0	3.9	18.5	10.0	7.3
6.3	1.20	6.5	0.45	4.1	0.9	1.09	10.41	3.34	59.1	1.6	31.6	32.9	6.4
6.7	0.67	3.2	0.13	8.2	1.4	2.46	24.26	4.81	62.8	2.0	42.4	39.5	6.1
8.3	0.43	1.4	-0.01	2.6	0.6	0.51	4.86	3.06	88.0	4.3	58.0	18.1	5.6
2.5	3.26	23.0	0.03	2.3	0.3	0.21	2.19	3.78	88.6	1.3	19.6	28.2	4.0
7.0	1.37	4.6	0.20	8.7	1.8	2.28	16.64	3.96	64.3	0.7	13.1	42.2	7.7
8.6	0.01	0.1	0.00	4.9	4.3	1.23	16.24	2.33	60.2	4.6	32.4	9.6	5.1
6.8	0.61	3.0	0.16	3.8	0.4	0.57	5.01	4.01	79.9	5.5	32.7	3.2	4.6
3.4	1.40	5.8	-0.07	6.9	5.9	1.85	11.24	3.44	67.5	1.0	27.3	56.9	5.6
6.7	0.33	2.1	0.07	2.8	0.6	0.43	4.46	3.40	83.2	2.7	18.1	15.8	5.9
7.7	0.38	2.6	-0.09	8.2	16.8	1.40	19.51	3.27	65.4	3.8	10.8	9.5	6.7
10.0	0.75	1.9	0.06	3.1	2.7	0.45	2.52	2.08	73.2	4.3	57.8	18.0	8.4
3.3	1.73	11.1	-0.11	2.8	7.5	0.38	2.30	3.08	85.5	1.5	10.7	24.6	7.3
4.7	1.91	7.2	-0.01	3.4	0.6	0.54	2.80	3.58	73.7	1.7	35.7	41.3	5.3
4.2	1.42	10.2	0.09	1.7	0.0	-0.03	-0.30	4.44	100.0	4.6	16.9	4.4	1.7
5.4	0.99	6.1	0.08	5.9	5.4	1.41	12.20	3.93	65.0	2.8	14.3	15.0	8.5
2.5	2.67	19.1	0.17	2.2	0.1	0.16	1.48	3.98	93.4	1.7	17.3	21.9	4.6
6.6	0.35	2.5	0.07	4.0	2.3	0.64	6.10	3.42	77.2	3.5	22.0	12.1	5.1
3.9	0.81	5.6	0.00	6.9	1.5	1.31	13.52	3.64	49.2	3.0	18.1	14.1	6.5
3.1	3.88	17.7	0.00	5.4	1.1	1.24	8.63	4.46	73.6	1.6	26.1	27.7	5.3
5.2	1.15	6.9	0.05	5.0	1.0	1.66	15.31	4.44	74.7	0.8	17.0	39.4	3.7
2.3	3.90	18.5	0.67	3.1	1.3	0.66	6.66	3.63	86.9	5.5	37.4	5.4	4.3
3.9	2.43	14.6	0.01	10.0	3.5	3.07	26.02	4.81	45.0	1.7	11.0	20.8	7.9
4.8	0.58	4.8	0.10	4.1	5.0	0.67	5.79	3.07	62.9	3.5	16.3	12.0	6.6
1.7	3.90	23.5	0.20	1.4	0.3	0.38	4.36	3.29	95.0	1.1	25.8	33.7	2.8
6.5	1.02	4.1	-0.01	0.8	-3.3	-0.75	-6.79	1.52	124.1	2.0	43.3	56.0	3.4
6.4	1.93	9.2	0.08	3.8	1.9	0.65	4.08	4.06	81.2	1.5	21.3	26.0	7.2
7.2	0.87	3.0	0.16	8.4	1.4	1.87	13.16	4.81	55.9	1.9	35.9	32.8	8.4
5.7	0.76	5.1	0.11	5.2	34.9	1.03	8.39	3.42	75.1	3.6	20.3	12.3	9.2
4.3	1.41	6.9	1.60	9.8	13.6	1.96	10.93	3.52	25.6	0.4	10.0	69.2	8.9
7.7	1.06	3.2	0.11	4.7	2.7	1.02	8.35	4.03	65.5	2.8	42.6	25.6	5.8
4.6	1.87	12.1	0.09	4.9	1.4	1.21	12.47	4.50	72.8	2.1	18.5	18.8	5.1
8.4	0.19	0.9	-0.09	3.9	3.2	0.82	8.97	3.67	77.1	4.2	54.9	17.5	6.1
4.1	0.64	5.8	-0.01	5.6	2.7	1.33	15.63	4.05	65.3	1.8	13.8	20.1	4.3
4.8	2.06	13.1	0.57	6.5	13.9	1.63	16.23	3.79	53.4	2.0	15.5	19.2	8.4
5.6	0.56	4.5	0.43	6.6	2.2	1.11	11.97	6.00	67.9	1.2	3.7	26.1	4.9
7.9	0.00	0.0	-0.03	4.6	0.7	0.82	7.64	3.79	72.9	1.6	25.5	26.7	6.2
3.7	1.79	9.7	0.12	1.8	0.1	0.09	0.77	4.15	97.8	1.9	30.6	26.3	5.0
0.0	14.13	59.6	-0.19	5.6	1.9	1.42	10.38	4.01	65.1	1.0	19.5	32.8	4.2
6.8	0.09	0.5	-0.93	3.6	0.7	0.72	6.72	4.36	95.0	4.4	29.1	9.0	4.7
4.1	1.23	6.6	1.07	5.7	5.9	1.25	10.49	7.15	69.4	0.4	14.7	86.2	5.8
1.4	3.38	27.0	0.07	4.9	1.6	0.86	8.40	3.86	74.2	2.5	22.4	17.2	4.3
0.3	9.19	51.6	0.66	3.1	0.3	0.66	6.07	3.77	83.1	3.6	26.8	12.6	3.8
9.3	0.06	0.2	0.01	3.9	0.5	0.89	9.99	2.36	60.0	5.5	45.7	8.2	4.9
5.4	3.28	10.2	0.43	3.5	2.1	0.96	12.27	4.23	81.1	2.3	44.8	34.7	4.7

	Name	City	State	Rating	2013 Rating	2012 Rating	Total Assets ($Mil)	One Year Asset Growth	Asset Mix (As a % of Total Assets) Commercial Loans	Consumer Loans	Mortgage Loans	Securities	Capitalization Index	Leverage Ratio	Risk-Based Capital Ratio
	TRI CITY NATIONAL BK	Oak Creek	WI	**C+**	C	C-	1183.0	0.74	2.3	0.8	15.9	33.4	**9.0**	10.3	17.5
▲	TRI COUNTIES BANK	Chico	CA	**C+**	C-	C	2793.5	6.18	3.5	1.0	9.1	19.0	**9.1**	10.4	14.7
	TRI VALLEY BANK	Talmage	NE	**C**	C	C-	34.3	-2.15	9.2	1.9	17.6	5.4	**5.3**	8.8	11.2
	TRI-COUNTY BANK	Stuart	NE	**C**	C	C	96.6	7.07	9.1	3.1	10.1	21.5	**4.1**	7.9	10.5
▲	TRI-COUNTY BANK	Brown City	MI	**B**	B-	C	234.6	1.46	3.2	1.4	11.3	29.7	**8.4**	9.9	17.1
	TRI-COUNTY BANK & TRUST CO	Roachdale	IN	**B**	B	B+	184.9	1.70	5.5	2.5	11.7	39.8	**10.0**	11.7	23.7
▲	TRI-COUNTY TRUST CO	Glasgow	MO	**B**	B-	C+	54.3	0.71	3.2	6.4	25.8	28.8	**9.8**	10.8	17.9
	TRI-PARISH BANK	Eunice	LA	**B+**	B+	B+	208.2	3.35	10.2	2.0	7.7	47.1	**9.4**	10.6	17.6
	TRI-STATE BANK OF MEMPHIS	Memphis	TN	**D-**	D-	D+	126.7	-15.71	9.8	5.1	9.4	25.0	**6.8**	8.8	13.7
	TRI-STATE BK & TRUST	Haughton	LA	**A**	A	A+	36.8	18.92	4.7	1.4	0.4	70.0	**10.0**	15.7	15.7
	TRI-VALLEY BANK	Randolph	IA	**C-**	C-	C	72.7	-9.06	5.6	1.2	5.8	53.7	**8.2**	9.8	19.6
	TRI-VALLEY BANK	San Ramon	CA	**D-**	D-	D+	99.7	5.45	12.9	0.0	4.6	11.6	**5.9**	7.9	12.1
	TRIAD BANK	Frontenac	MO	**B-**	B-	C+	247.7	11.88	11.8	0.1	11.2	11.7	**7.7**	9.8	13.1
	TRIAD BANK NA	Tulsa	OK	**B-**	C+	C+	186.9	-1.27	13.2	2.4	34.6	0.0	**6.9**	8.9	15.3
▼	TRICENTURY BANK	Simpson	KS	**D-**	D	D	10.7	252.76	5.6	1.4	0.3	1.2	**8.8**	10.2	22.4
▲	TRINITY BANK	Dothan	AL	**B**	C+	C-	94.8	7.91	14.9	2.8	25.2	5.2	**9.7**	11.5	14.8
	TRINITY BANK NA	Fort Worth	TX	**A**	A	A	209.0	13.93	29.5	0.6	9.4	29.6	**10.0**	11.7	20.0
	TRISTAR BANK	Dickson	TN	**C+**	C+	B-	233.0	6.18	2.6	5.0	19.4	31.7	**6.5**	8.5	13.8
	TRISTATE CAPITAL BANK	Pittsburgh	PA	**C**	C+	C+	2687.1	22.09	35.7	18.0	4.2	8.1	**4.3**	9.7	10.7
▼	TRISUMMIT BANK	Kingsport	TN	**D**	C	C	320.1	22.29	5.3	1.0	22.5	13.8	**6.6**	8.6	12.8
	TRIUMPH BANK	Memphis	TN	**C+**	C+	C+	501.1	17.33	23.1	1.9	10.1	14.4	**4.7**	8.7	10.9
	TRIUMPH COMMUNITY BANK NA	Moline	IL	**B-**	C+	C-	923.0	3.27	30.5	1.3	8.4	14.6	**9.4**	11.9	14.5
	TRIUMPH SB SSB	Dallas	TX	**C+**	C	C-	407.5	13.36	49.4	0.0	0.6	7.7	**10.0**	12.8	16.9
	TRIUMPH STATE BK	Trimont	MN	**C-**	D+	D	61.9	-2.68	8.9	4.3	2.6	21.3	**6.6**	8.6	14.2
	TROY BANK & TRUST CO	Troy	AL	**C-**	C-	C-	807.2	-6.87	9.1	3.2	11.7	38.5	**8.3**	9.9	16.3
	TRUBANK	Oskaloosa	IA	**B**	B	C-	114.7	16.89	1.4	9.4	14.2	13.3	**10.0**	11.7	15.5
	TRUPOINT BANK	Grundy	VA	**C-**	D+	D-	422.0	-2.07	4.9	3.3	17.3	35.9	**6.3**	8.3	17.7
▲	TRUST BANK	Lenox	GA	**C**	D+	D-	31.9	0.70	3.0	7.9	21.7	10.0	**8.4**	9.9	15.0
	TRUST CO BANK	Memphis	TN	**E-**	E-	E-	29.3	-13.65	10.0	2.2	16.1	1.9	**0.0**	2.8	6.0
	TRUST CO OF AMERICA	Centennial	CO	**U**	U	B-	704.3	21.18	0.0	0.0	0.0	53.1	**3.5**	5.5	28.2
	TRUST CO OF TOLEDO NA	Holland	OH	**U**	U	U	5.3	11.41	0.0	0.0	0.0	82.7	**10.0**	90.5	166.3
	TRUST CO OF VIRGINIA	Richmond	VA	**U**	U	B+	7.1	4.90	0.0	0.0	0.0	59.7	**10.0**	84.7	206.7
	TRUSTATLANTIC BANK	Raleigh	NC	**B-**	C	D+	451.5	11.91	7.6	0.1	11.3	17.3	**8.7**	10.1	14.4
▲	TRUSTBANK	Olney	IL	**B**	B-	B+	177.4	-6.46	5.6	5.0	17.4	23.7	**9.5**	10.7	16.2
	TRUSTCO BANK	Glenville	NY	**B**	B	B	4582.1	2.68	0.6	0.2	55.0	17.5	**6.3**	8.3	17.9
	TRUSTMARK NATIONAL BK	Jackson	MS	**B-**	B-	B-	12093.6	3.44	11.2	1.5	12.6	29.2	**7.6**	9.4	14.5
	TRUSTTEXAS BANK SSB	Cuero	TX	**B-**	B	B-	288.1	16.14	3.9	1.9	17.2	35.8	**10.0**	11.2	23.7
	TRUXTON TRUST CO	Nashville	TN	**A-**	B+	B	336.0	9.88	7.1	5.4	19.7	26.8	**9.3**	10.5	16.4
	TSB BANK	Lomira	WI	**B-**	B-	C+	115.7	2.52	9.3	1.6	18.0	23.7	**7.1**	9.0	13.4
	TUCUMCARI FS&LA	Tucumcari	NM	**B-**	C+	C+	38.0	0.32	0.0	0.7	52.9	26.2	**10.0**	12.6	31.3
	TURBOTVILLE NATIONAL BK	Turbotville	PA	**A**	A	A-	129.0	2.03	6.2	2.6	20.2	40.1	**10.0**	15.0	27.4
	TURTLE MOUNTAIN STATE BK	Belcourt	ND	**C**	C	C-	38.6	32.85	20.1	7.1	2.0	7.1	**8.1**	9.7	18.2
	TUSCOLA NATIONAL BK	Tuscola	IL	**C**	C	C+	84.4	2.95	5.9	1.1	7.3	49.3	**10.0**	13.1	31.8
	TUSTIN COMMUNITY BANK	Tustin	CA	**A-**	A-	A-	65.1	3.30	4.2	39.0	5.6	0.0	**10.0**	14.1	18.4
	TWIN CITY BANK	Longview	WA	**D+**	D	D+	42.0	-5.55	18.0	0.5	8.4	2.3	**8.1**	9.8	13.7
	TWIN LAKES COMMUNITY BANK	Flippin	AR	**C**	C	C-	94.7	6.10	6.9	11.0	28.5	7.7	**8.3**	10.1	13.6
	TWIN OAKS SB	Marseilles	IL	**D-**	D	C-	63.1	-8.05	2.5	1.6	32.6	42.1	**8.2**	9.8	21.6
	TWIN RIVER NATIONAL BK	Clarkston	WA	**C+**	C+	C+	84.4	9.04	8.8	2.7	16.9	4.0	**5.9**	7.9	15.5
	TWIN VALLEY BANK	West Alexandria	OH	**B-**	B-	B-	51.2	4.82	8.2	3.7	22.1	18.1	**10.0**	12.9	18.4
	TWO RIVER COMMUNITY BANK	Tinton Falls	NJ	**D+**	C-	C	775.5	2.43	6.0	0.1	7.3	9.2	**7.9**	10.8	13.2
▲	TWO RIVERS BANK	Blair	NE	**C+**	C	D+	143.2	0.93	6.0	2.1	11.6	35.8	**8.8**	10.2	16.8
▲	TWO RIVERS BANK & TRUST	Burlington	IA	**C+**	C+	C+	664.6	4.48	17.0	1.3	15.1	14.2	**6.8**	8.8	12.4
	UBANK	Jellico	TN	**B**	B	A-	66.0	8.42	2.9	7.3	21.1	36.6	**10.0**	12.5	22.6
	UBS BANK USA	Salt Lake City	UT	**B+**	B+	B+	46183.6	6.84	12.3	43.4	16.0	10.5	**7.9**	9.6	14.0
	UBS TRUST CO NA	Wilmington	DE	**U**	U	U	56.6	-0.39	0.0	0.0	0.0	0.0	**10.0**	90.7	93.1
	UINTA BANK	Mountain View	WY	**B-**	B-	C+	113.6	4.77	9.5	1.4	4.0	55.0	**7.5**	9.3	22.9
	ULSTER SB	Kingston	NY	**C-**	C-	C-	773.6	5.33	1.5	0.1	40.3	18.3	**10.0**	12.2	19.7
	ULTIMA BANK MINNESOTA	Winger	MN	**C-**	C-	D	155.4	9.27	14.2	1.7	6.4	0.0	**6.3**	9.1	12.0
	UMB BANK & TRUST NA	Saint Louis	MO	**U**	U	U	3.0	0.13	0.0	0.0	0.0	0.0	**10.0**	100.	103.0
	UMB BANK NA	Kansas City	MO	**C+**	C+	C+	15995.4	0.57	21.1	2.3	2.0	44.0	**5.7**	7.7	12.7

Asset Quality Index	Adjusted Non-Performing Loans as a % of Total Loans	Adjusted Non-Performing Loans as a % of Capital	Net Charge-Offs Avg Loans	Profitability Index	Net Income ($Mil)	Return on Assets (R.O.A.)	Return on Equity (R.O.E.)	Net Interest Spread	Overhead Efficiency Ratio	Liquidity Index	Liquidity Ratio	Hot Money Ratio	Stability Index
3.4	4.56	23.1	0.38	**4.4**	6.6	0.75	7.36	3.79	71.7	**6.0**	33.7	4.6	**7.3**
3.5	3.37	18.3	-0.18	**6.7**	22.2	1.08	9.98	4.31	67.5	**5.8**	32.8	5.5	**8.3**
5.5	0.87	8.2	0.33	**7.0**	0.4	1.61	18.94	3.99	49.6	**1.6**	8.5	21.2	**3.9**
7.0	0.14	1.0	0.00	**3.4**	0.4	0.51	6.26	4.53	86.3	**4.3**	27.5	8.9	**4.3**
6.7	0.67	3.9	0.12	**4.7**	1.8	0.98	10.48	3.89	69.1	**5.1**	36.6	7.8	**4.9**
6.9	1.55	5.3	0.07	**4.0**	1.0	0.71	6.09	3.03	66.6	**5.4**	63.0	13.5	**7.2**
5.5	0.76	4.0	-0.57	**8.0**	0.8	1.95	19.67	4.70	53.9	**1.5**	24.3	27.3	**5.2**
9.0	0.06	0.3	0.17	**4.8**	1.6	1.05	10.15	3.64	72.2	**3.9**	37.4	14.9	**8.3**
0.5	7.57	47.2	0.81	**0.6**	-0.1	-0.09	-0.94	4.06	97.0	**0.8**	14.9	40.0	**4.8**
10.0	0.00	0.0	0.00	**10.0**	0.9	3.41	22.28	5.68	62.7	**6.6**	91.7	9.6	**8.9**
6.1	1.44	5.2	0.49	**1.9**	0.1	0.09	1.14	3.59	92.2	**4.6**	57.4	14.9	**3.2**
5.2	0.41	3.3	-0.05	**0.0**	-0.3	-0.38	-4.78	3.37	114.4	**1.1**	20.9	31.9	**2.4**
3.7	1.57	11.0	-0.01	**4.4**	1.2	0.67	7.04	3.63	68.5	**1.6**	21.3	25.1	**5.0**
4.8	1.18	9.1	0.10	**4.9**	1.6	1.23	13.84	3.84	59.3	**3.3**	25.2	13.5	**5.6**
7.1	0.84	2.4	0.08	**0.0**	-0.1	-2.66	-20.56	8.42	123.2	**7.3**	78.9	1.0	**1.7**
4.8	0.85	5.8	0.07	**5.4**	1.4	1.94	17.14	4.54	75.6	**2.2**	3.4	17.1	**5.2**
8.7	0.00	0.0	0.06	**8.4**	2.4	1.71	14.22	3.65	41.6	**5.6**	51.4	9.5	**7.4**
5.4	1.35	8.0	0.11	**3.6**	0.9	0.55	6.23	3.75	80.4	**2.1**	34.1	27.1	**3.9**
4.0	1.18	9.7	0.45	**3.0**	8.9	0.47	4.93	2.64	59.8	**0.8**	12.7	40.6	**6.3**
6.2	0.86	6.6	0.03	**1.0**	-0.1	-0.05	-0.44	3.60	107.9	**1.4**	14.0	25.5	**4.4**
4.6	0.81	7.0	0.32	**4.8**	2.6	0.75	8.18	3.84	64.4	**0.7**	14.4	42.3	**5.1**
4.8	1.33	8.2	0.01	**7.6**	15.7	2.30	18.56	5.31	45.2	**1.9**	7.8	18.5	**6.2**
2.7	2.83	15.4	0.14	**9.2**	4.4	1.50	8.93	10.56	73.6	**0.8**	22.8	49.6	**7.0**
4.4	1.67	10.1	0.24	**3.2**	0.2	0.51	5.88	4.03	77.1	**5.2**	40.6	8.7	**3.5**
2.0	5.09	25.5	1.16	**2.9**	3.3	0.53	5.12	3.52	67.0	**1.9**	23.8	21.1	**5.4**
7.4	0.42	2.4	0.07	**7.3**	1.1	1.31	11.04	3.84	74.6	**2.2**	23.7	18.8	**5.8**
4.9	1.67	9.5	1.00	**2.6**	1.6	0.49	5.49	3.56	84.0	**3.0**	5.9	13.3	**3.4**
4.2	1.73	10.9	0.04	**5.0**	0.3	1.14	12.19	6.14	80.2	**1.8**	15.3	20.3	**3.0**
0.8	3.29	44.9	0.11	**0.0**	-0.4	-1.71	-22.70	3.19	109.0	**1.5**	36.5	69.5	**2.2**
10.0	na	0.0	na	**5.2**	5.3	1.20	26.99	2.10	81.8	**6.8**	46.7	0.0	**5.0**
10.0	na	0.0	na	**10.0**	1.8	54.06	61.27	1.64	62.5	**4.0**	826.1	101.0	**5.5**
10.0	na	0.0	na	**9.5**	0.7	13.81	16.71	2.52	83.5	**10.0**	480.9	0.0	**6.4**
4.5	0.54	3.5	0.09	**5.5**	3.2	0.99	9.00	3.85	58.5	**1.4**	26.7	31.2	**5.8**
6.1	0.53	3.1	0.03	**4.8**	1.5	1.12	9.69	3.58	77.6	**4.2**	20.3	8.1	**5.4**
6.5	1.36	9.8	0.24	**5.6**	34.3	1.00	12.44	3.15	53.2	**4.4**	26.4	11.3	**6.5**
3.9	1.89	11.4	0.03	**5.7**	96.7	1.08	9.06	4.01	69.1	**3.9**	12.4	9.3	**9.5**
9.6	0.28	1.0	0.04	**3.4**	1.2	0.56	5.14	3.87	80.5	**5.6**	51.4	9.9	**6.9**
7.8	0.25	1.4	0.00	**6.5**	3.1	1.24	12.74	3.19	64.0	**5.2**	34.7	6.4	**6.5**
6.3	0.47	3.4	0.80	**4.3**	0.7	0.84	10.04	3.90	62.8	**3.1**	15.4	13.5	**5.1**
7.6	0.80	3.6	0.08	**3.1**	0.1	0.40	3.23	3.39	81.4	**0.7**	14.6	47.5	**5.9**
8.4	1.09	3.7	0.03	**6.0**	1.1	1.15	7.75	3.51	52.9	**4.0**	49.5	17.5	**8.8**
3.7	4.02	25.4	0.00	**6.1**	0.3	1.57	15.86	4.33	70.6	**2.1**	42.3	34.4	**3.4**
9.4	0.41	1.0	-0.52	**2.0**	0.2	0.25	1.96	3.20	93.4	**6.0**	71.1	10.3	**7.0**
6.8	0.04	0.2	0.31	**6.4**	0.6	1.20	8.59	6.52	77.5	**1.2**	23.6	31.9	**8.2**
1.2	2.66	19.8	0.49	**2.0**	0.0	0.13	1.24	4.62	92.5	**0.7**	15.1	42.4	**3.8**
3.5	1.45	10.5	0.17	**3.1**	0.4	0.63	6.15	4.23	82.9	**0.9**	10.4	32.7	**5.1**
2.1	7.04	28.5	1.12	**0.0**	-0.5	-0.99	-9.81	3.04	108.0	**4.2**	52.9	16.4	**4.0**
6.0	0.58	3.6	0.00	**3.2**	0.4	0.57	7.29	3.21	82.5	**5.8**	45.3	6.1	**4.5**
7.2	0.28	1.3	0.48	**2.9**	0.2	0.39	3.02	4.13	89.3	**4.6**	24.6	5.9	**6.2**
1.6	2.49	17.3	0.02	**4.7**	4.7	0.82	6.46	3.85	64.9	**4.2**	13.1	7.4	**7.3**
4.2	1.27	6.2	0.17	**3.9**	1.0	0.96	10.21	3.73	74.9	**2.5**	34.7	22.8	**4.7**
3.7	0.97	7.7	1.00	**4.9**	4.0	0.83	9.35	3.81	69.0	**3.0**	8.2	13.4	**5.5**
3.9	2.76	10.9	2.40	**6.3**	0.7	1.30	10.71	4.86	65.3	**2.4**	40.0	28.4	**8.3**
6.8	0.01	0.1	0.01	**5.5**	325.3	0.95	10.30	1.83	19.7	**5.8**	23.4	0.2	**8.4**
10.0	na	0.0	na	**1.4**	-4.8	-11.21	-11.73	0.24	152.3	**4.0**	942.8	101.0	**7.0**
5.7	1.99	8.1	0.08	**4.5**	0.8	0.90	9.99	3.34	60.4	**2.8**	40.5	22.8	**4.6**
1.7	5.99	31.4	0.27	**2.5**	1.4	0.25	1.93	3.46	92.2	**3.4**	20.5	12.5	**7.2**
2.6	1.12	10.4	0.33	**9.8**	2.5	2.19	24.19	5.05	52.9	**1.0**	4.2	29.5	**7.0**
10.0	na	0.0	na	**1.8**	0.0	0.13	0.13	na	99.9	**4.0**	0.0	101.0	**6.1**
8.3	0.46	2.6	0.22	**3.5**	72.5	0.62	7.90	2.53	77.2	**5.2**	22.6	4.1	**4.6**

Name	City	State	Rating	2013 Rating	2012 Rating	Total Assets ($Mil)	One Year Asset Growth	Asset Mix (As a % of Total Assets) Comm-ercial Loans	Cons-umer Loans	Mort-gage Loans	Secur-ities	Capital-ization Index	Lever-age Ratio	Risk-Based Capital Ratio
▲ UMPQUA BANK	Roseburg	OR	B	B-	C+	22486.0	94.51	9.7	1.6	11.4	10.7	8.3	10.0	13.6
UNB BANK	Mount Carmel	PA	C-	C	C	125.3	-1.75	1.9	0.9	51.0	30.4	9.6	10.7	22.3
UNIBANK	Lynnwood	WA	B	B	C+	228.8	3.86	5.3	0.0	0.0	8.1	10.0	14.5	19.9
UNIBANK FOR SAVINGS	Whitinsville	MA	C+	C+	B-	1494.6	7.16	6.8	19.3	19.4	28.8	5.5	7.5	12.4
UNICO BANK	Mineral Point	MO	B	B-	C+	238.3	-3.59	3.5	3.1	24.6	35.0	8.1	9.8	15.7
UNIFIED TRUST CO NA	Lexington	KY	U	U	U	11.7	9.21	0.0	0.0	0.0	35.1	10.0	94.9	73.5
UNION BANK	Lake Odessa	MI	D+	D+	D+	173.1	1.80	3.9	0.6	15.8	14.7	7.4	9.2	13.4
UNION BANK	Halliday	ND	B	B	C+	143.5	11.46	8.1	6.7	10.1	15.5	5.3	8.6	11.2
UNION BANK	Morrisville	VT	B	B	B-	601.7	4.87	3.5	0.8	26.1	8.9	6.2	8.2	13.7
▲ UNION BANK	Jamestown	TN	C-	D+	D+	213.2	3.45	7.3	13.0	20.1	29.2	8.8	10.2	17.5
▼ UNION BANK	Marksville	LA	C-	D+	D-	227.1	1.44	3.3	14.8	23.1	15.5	7.0	9.0	14.2
▼ UNION BANK & TRUST CO	Livingston	TN	B-	B	B	83.7	6.63	7.0	5.4	29.0	17.6	10.0	11.9	19.4
UNION BANK & TRUST CO	Oxford	NC	B+	B+	B+	237.8	4.89	10.3	1.4	27.6	9.6	10.0	11.5	15.2
UNION BANK & TRUST CO	Minneapolis	MN	C+	C-	C+	105.9	16.90	13.3	0.2	0.9	22.4	9.1	10.4	22.8
UNION BANK & TRUST CO	Evansville	WI	B-	B-	C+	210.4	5.46	7.0	0.6	16.5	28.6	6.7	8.7	13.9
UNION BANK & TRUST CO	Monticello	AR	D+	C-	C-	190.2	1.45	9.0	4.0	13.5	21.4	7.1	9.1	12.8
UNION BANK & TRUST CO	Lincoln	NE	B	B	B-	2986.7	3.71	10.7	23.5	3.9	15.5	7.9	9.8	13.2
UNION BANK CO	Columbus Grove	OH	B	C+	C	594.5	6.36	7.4	0.6	10.8	32.3	10.0	11.1	17.9
UNION BANK INC	Middlebourne	WV	B-	B-	B-	225.0	10.21	3.5	3.4	14.6	46.8	5.3	7.3	17.0
▲ UNION BANK OF BLAIR	Blair	WI	C+	C	C+	95.6	18.29	19.3	4.3	13.4	7.8	10.0	11.5	15.5
UNION BANK OF MENA	Mena	AR	A	A-	B+	197.9	6.13	4.7	12.9	41.2	12.4	9.3	10.5	17.7
UNION BANKING CO	West Mansfield	OH	B+	B+	B+	58.2	4.02	0.6	0.5	9.1	78.8	9.3	10.6	34.6
UNION BUILDING & LOAN SB	West Bridgewater	PA	B-	B-	B-	34.6	-9.26	0.0	0.0	72.4	0.8	10.0	21.0	41.1
UNION COMMUNITY BANK	Lancaster	PA	A-	A-	B+	510.7	-0.77	3.5	0.6	12.4	22.3	10.0	16.5	26.8
UNION COUNTY SB	Elizabeth	NJ	B-	B-	B+	1697.0	2.45	0.0	0.1	5.5	72.2	10.0	12.3	46.6
UNION FIRST MARKET BANK	Richmond	VA	B-	B-	C	7164.3	77.95	5.1	4.6	14.3	15.2	7.8	10.1	13.2
UNION FS&LA	Kewanee	IL	B-	C	C-	110.4	-1.25	0.0	0.1	56.4	12.3	9.3	10.6	21.3
▼ UNION FSB	North Providence	RI	C	C	D+	176.1	-9.19	0.0	11.5	9.0	33.6	10.0	13.0	56.5
▲ UNION NATIONAL BK	Elgin	IL	C+	C-	D-	305.9	-9.12	11.4	0.1	2.8	1.0	9.3	10.6	14.4
UNION NATIONAL BK & TRUST CO	Sparta	WI	A-	A-	B	113.8	2.10	11.7	2.9	10.0	20.3	10.0	16.3	20.9
UNION S&LA	New Orleans	LA	C+	C+	B-	80.7	-6.62	0.0	0.2	38.7	47.1	10.0	38.9	127.9
UNION S&LA	Connersville	IN	C	C	C-	132.8	-0.71	1.1	7.9	42.2	1.4	8.0	9.7	17.3
UNION SAVINGS BANK	Freeport	IL	D	D	D+	155.4	-4.26	3.0	2.8	35.1	26.6	6.7	8.8	14.8
UNION SAVINGS BANK	Danbury	CT	C	C-	C-	2305.5	-5.24	3.0	0.2	40.0	14.3	6.6	8.6	14.1
UNION SAVINGS BANK	Cincinnati	OH	B-	B-	B-	2401.9	-1.09	0.1	0.2	53.4	2.0	8.5	10.0	19.7
▲ UNION STATE BK	Pell City	AL	D-	E+	D-	223.9	-5.81	3.9	3.2	6.3	33.5	4.5	6.5	11.4
UNION STATE BK	Kewaunee	WI	D+	D+	C	86.9	6.53	6.5	4.3	21.4	30.9	8.3	9.9	18.0
UNION STATE BK	Winterset	IA	C+	C+	C-	82.4	9.48	4.1	2.4	21.1	30.6	6.5	8.5	14.3
▲ UNION STATE BK	Greenfield	IA	B-	C+	C+	71.2	7.31	3.9	5.1	22.2	16.9	6.7	8.7	12.4
UNION STATE BK	Arkansas City	KS	B	B	B	251.5	0.52	10.1	1.9	17.3	38.1	8.0	9.7	17.3
▲ UNION STATE BK	Clay Center	KS	B-	C+	C+	136.9	1.43	5.8	1.0	8.6	57.3	10.0	11.0	24.5
UNION STATE BK	Uniontown	KS	D	D-	D+	43.9	-1.55	10.3	4.7	22.7	21.1	5.0	7.9	11.0
UNION STATE BK	Olsburg	KS	B+	B+	A-	28.2	-1.31	13.1	5.0	8.3	35.0	10.0	15.6	29.1
UNION STATE BK	Florence	TX	C+	C+	C+	476.9	2.87	4.6	0.8	4.7	56.3	6.6	8.6	18.3
UNION STATE BK BROWNS VALLEY	Browns Valley	MN	C+	C+	B-	23.0	-3.53	7.9	2.3	1.2	24.5	10.0	11.1	21.8
UNION STATE BK OF EVEREST	Everest	KS	C-	C+	C+	258.6	7.33	12.4	2.8	18.1	18.6	6.3	8.6	12.0
UNION STATE BK OF FARGO	Fargo	ND	D+	C-	C+	81.6	4.40	19.5	5.2	28.8	3.3	6.5	8.5	12.1
▲ UNION STATE BK OF HAZEN	Hazen	ND	C+	C	D+	120.0	10.58	6.1	6.1	12.3	32.4	8.1	9.7	17.1
UNION STATE BK OF WEST SALEM	West Salem	WI	B+	B+	B	62.1	-1.25	5.9	4.3	28.1	22.3	10.0	13.8	22.5
UNISON BANK	Jamestown	ND	C-	D+	D	246.8	13.97	4.9	9.0	16.1	23.6	7.2	9.1	14.1
UNITED AMERICAN BANK	San Mateo	CA	C	C	D	269.7	0.86	13.4	0.4	6.2	16.3	4.9	6.9	11.5
UNITED BANK	Absarokee	MT	B-	B-	C+	74.3	8.40	6.6	3.3	6.1	29.2	8.8	10.2	16.3
▲ UNITED BANK	Osseo	WI	B-	C+	C-	229.8	4.96	10.2	1.0	15.7	9.3	7.6	9.5	13.0
UNITED BANK	Atmore	AL	C	C	D+	484.6	0.65	4.4	3.4	10.3	29.0	7.7	9.4	16.5
UNITED BANK	Zebulon	GA	B+	B	C+	1084.2	5.62	3.7	2.7	15.5	37.3	9.5	10.7	19.4
▼ UNITED BANK	Glastonbury	CT	C+	B	B	5306.5	139.30	9.3	0.3	22.5	19.4	7.8	9.5	13.2
UNITED BANK	Vienna	VA	B-	B-	B-	7238.5	102.12	3.9	0.2	10.2	11.3	7.7	10.0	13.1
UNITED BANK	Springdale	AR	B	B	B-	136.9	-3.71	4.9	1.1	42.0	8.6	10.0	16.5	23.8
UNITED BANK & TRUST	Marysville	KS	B+	B	B-	573.3	5.56	8.2	1.8	7.6	23.6	9.5	10.7	15.1
UNITED BANK & TRUST CO	Hampton	IA	B+	B+	A-	148.4	0.95	4.6	3.5	13.6	37.3	10.0	12.3	20.5

Asset Quality Index	Adjusted Non-Performing Loans as a % of Total Loans	Adjusted Non-Performing Loans as a % of Capital	Net Charge-Offs Avg Loans	Profitability Index	Net Income ($Mil)	Return on Assets (R.O.A.)	Return on Equity (R.O.E.)	Net Interest Spread	Overhead Efficiency Ratio	Liquidity Index	Liquidity Ratio	Hot Money Ratio	Stability Index
4.7	0.68	5.0	0.15	**5.0**	101.3	0.75	4.61	4.79	71.6	**2.8**	9.3	14.7	**8.6**
9.0	0.36	2.0	0.17	**1.8**	0.3	0.36	3.38	2.93	97.1	**2.4**	25.3	18.1	**5.8**
3.3	2.73	13.2	0.24	**7.5**	2.3	1.36	9.41	4.47	54.0	**2.1**	23.9	19.6	**7.1**
5.2	0.75	6.2	0.08	**3.7**	6.9	0.62	9.02	2.98	68.2	**5.9**	32.5	4.8	**5.4**
5.5	1.08	6.1	0.06	**5.9**	3.2	1.69	21.70	3.58	67.1	**1.6**	27.0	28.8	**5.4**
10.0	na	0.0	na	**10.0**	1.7	24.05	31.24	-0.50	85.2	**4.0**	134.2	101.0	**6.5**
1.8	4.89	32.9	0.69	**2.9**	0.5	0.39	3.67	4.18	88.3	**4.6**	24.0	6.1	**4.8**
4.7	1.65	13.3	0.01	**6.3**	1.1	1.05	10.76	4.37	56.3	**4.2**	16.1	7.3	**5.1**
5.2	0.81	7.5	0.05	**6.6**	6.0	1.36	15.71	4.20	67.1	**3.1**	15.3	13.6	**6.6**
2.3	3.07	15.6	0.95	**3.9**	1.1	0.68	7.22	4.26	66.1	**1.0**	25.9	40.4	**4.1**
2.0	2.68	19.4	0.27	**4.5**	2.2	1.26	13.46	4.32	69.5	**1.5**	11.8	24.0	**2.8**
2.9	4.29	23.3	0.47	**9.9**	1.4	2.38	20.35	5.45	50.7	**2.4**	24.5	17.9	**7.9**
5.0	1.77	11.8	0.08	**4.6**	1.3	0.71	6.19	5.24	76.7	**1.2**	10.4	26.9	**6.7**
6.1	1.91	6.5	0.00	**3.2**	0.3	0.43	3.92	2.87	87.7	**6.3**	68.4	9.7	**4.3**
7.2	0.63	4.5	0.17	**4.9**	1.4	0.89	9.94	4.36	72.8	**2.4**	18.3	17.1	**4.2**
1.6	4.46	29.3	-0.10	**5.0**	1.7	1.19	13.34	3.74	73.0	**2.5**	11.8	16.2	**4.4**
4.9	0.62	4.7	0.01	**5.0**	23.6	1.12	11.02	3.12	73.7	**2.4**	16.3	17.5	**8.8**
5.1	2.24	9.9	0.05	**4.2**	3.6	0.84	6.56	3.44	71.8	**5.0**	42.6	10.6	**6.8**
6.3	0.49	2.3	-0.03	**4.7**	1.9	1.18	10.83	3.34	65.6	**5.5**	44.5	8.4	**7.2**
3.7	2.30	14.6	-0.02	**5.8**	0.8	1.07	8.34	3.68	52.3	**1.3**	24.1	30.0	**4.0**
6.8	0.25	1.7	0.09	**9.4**	3.1	2.08	19.53	5.45	61.2	**2.8**	9.4	14.3	**8.2**
7.9	2.66	3.3	0.00	**7.1**	0.7	1.55	13.46	4.38	44.3	**1.9**	39.2	36.4	**7.0**
5.5	3.56	13.0	0.00	**4.1**	0.2	0.62	3.04	4.02	72.4	**1.5**	19.2	26.0	**7.4**
7.3	1.41	4.6	0.04	**5.5**	2.8	0.72	4.53	4.02	77.0	**5.1**	38.0	8.6	**7.0**
8.4	2.30	1.2	0.16	**3.5**	7.3	0.59	4.82	1.44	37.0	**4.1**	105.5	55.6	**8.7**
4.1	1.50	10.8	0.04	**5.4**	43.4	0.98	7.66	5.10	75.2	**3.8**	14.2	10.1	**8.5**
6.4	1.22	7.8	0.05	**4.3**	0.6	0.70	7.22	3.81	69.7	**3.3**	20.4	12.9	**4.7**
5.7	3.41	5.5	1.97	**1.6**	-1.5	-1.02	-7.79	1.82	97.8	**6.3**	51.7	5.2	**6.2**
3.6	0.89	5.5	0.91	**4.5**	2.7	1.15	11.32	3.34	62.7	**0.8**	19.2	52.0	**3.9**
5.5	3.49	14.4	0.17	**6.0**	0.9	1.05	6.47	3.94	60.2	**1.8**	30.3	29.0	**8.0**
10.0	0.29	0.3	0.00	**2.5**	0.2	0.30	0.80	2.45	80.4	**4.3**	95.7	25.5	**7.0**
4.6	1.06	7.7	0.34	**2.8**	0.3	0.33	3.50	3.25	81.2	**2.4**	21.1	17.7	**4.6**
3.9	2.75	18.0	0.07	**0.7**	-0.1	-0.08	-0.97	3.07	92.6	**4.4**	30.2	10.0	**2.9**
4.2	2.03	16.0	0.12	**3.1**	8.3	0.48	5.53	3.21	76.0	**3.6**	9.9	10.7	**5.8**
3.8	2.65	17.1	0.06	**8.9**	35.3	1.94	19.05	2.56	53.4	**2.7**	25.6	19.1	**9.6**
2.3	4.54	23.2	1.88	**1.2**	0.5	0.30	5.61	3.67	94.8	**4.0**	35.8	13.5	**1.0**
4.6	1.82	9.5	0.30	**1.7**	0.1	0.10	1.03	3.65	98.2	**5.4**	42.7	8.2	**4.7**
6.4	0.58	3.7	0.00	**3.8**	0.5	0.77	9.06	3.85	86.2	**3.9**	17.7	9.5	**4.2**
4.1	0.53	4.4	-0.02	**8.0**	1.0	1.85	12.42	4.41	47.4	**1.2**	11.4	28.2	**8.5**
7.7	0.24	1.2	0.07	**4.0**	1.7	0.90	6.85	3.47	75.9	**2.7**	29.9	18.1	**6.9**
6.5	1.87	6.0	0.13	**3.8**	0.8	0.71	6.63	2.91	68.1	**2.2**	13.8	18.0	**5.5**
2.3	2.90	22.0	0.21	**4.4**	0.3	0.97	12.80	4.28	77.4	**3.2**	27.3	14.6	**3.5**
5.3	2.81	8.7	-0.01	**6.1**	0.3	1.46	8.89	3.95	58.5	**4.9**	43.5	11.0	**7.6**
5.9	1.53	5.8	0.02	**3.3**	2.4	0.68	8.67	2.89	78.6	**2.7**	31.5	18.6	**5.1**
7.7	0.00	0.0	-0.03	**4.9**	0.2	1.23	11.18	2.87	53.9	**4.7**	59.0	13.0	**6.3**
1.8	3.50	27.4	0.09	**7.4**	3.2	1.69	17.14	4.36	59.0	**3.6**	9.7	10.7	**7.9**
1.5	3.05	26.0	-0.16	**4.8**	0.4	0.70	8.72	4.44	74.5	**3.6**	8.6	10.5	**4.0**
3.5	3.17	15.8	0.07	**5.7**	1.3	1.47	15.95	4.04	63.1	**4.7**	32.7	9.0	**4.8**
5.7	2.04	9.9	0.04	**4.1**	0.3	0.64	4.71	4.00	73.8	**3.9**	23.2	10.1	**6.8**
1.7	3.05	19.8	0.00	**5.5**	2.1	1.13	11.04	4.06	62.1	**3.0**	13.2	13.8	**4.6**
3.6	2.17	15.3	-0.48	**0.3**	-0.2	-0.10	-1.35	3.05	105.0	**4.0**	34.1	13.1	**4.2**
8.1	0.00	0.0	-0.01	**4.0**	0.3	0.61	5.92	3.80	77.9	**3.3**	33.3	16.1	**5.1**
4.0	1.74	12.5	0.09	**5.2**	1.4	0.82	8.70	3.82	74.4	**3.8**	18.0	10.2	**6.2**
5.0	1.23	6.6	0.17	**2.7**	1.5	0.41	4.19	3.49	83.8	**3.8**	34.5	14.1	**4.5**
5.0	2.61	11.6	0.24	**5.8**	10.3	1.32	12.08	3.73	74.6	**4.8**	34.8	12.4	**9.1**
5.9	0.88	6.6	0.10	**3.1**	9.5	0.32	2.92	3.66	86.6	**1.7**	17.0	23.0	**8.6**
4.3	0.77	5.2	0.10	**6.5**	60.1	1.21	6.83	3.74	48.7	**2.9**	15.9	15.0	**7.5**
4.8	2.93	13.3	0.03	**6.4**	1.3	1.21	7.42	4.54	78.1	**1.4**	14.7	26.6	**6.8**
8.0	0.02	0.1	-0.04	**5.8**	4.7	1.10	9.58	3.64	54.3	**3.5**	7.8	10.9	**7.5**
8.8	0.24	1.0	0.00	**4.8**	1.3	1.14	9.33	3.00	59.4	**5.9**	47.3	6.2	**8.2**

Name	City	State	Rating	2013 Rating	2012 Rating	Total Assets ($Mil)	One Year Asset Growth	Comm-ercial Loans	Cons-umer Loans	Mort-gage Loans	Secur-ities	Capital-ization Index	Lever-age Ratio	Risk-Based Capital Ratio
								Asset Mix (As a % of Total Assets)						
▲ UNITED BANK & TRUST CO	Versailles	KY	**C+**	C	D+	516.6	-3.75	1.7	0.6	15.2	34.3	**9.6**	10.7	18.6
UNITED BANK & TRUST NA	Marshalltown	IA	**A-**	A-	A-	108.3	0.41	7.0	2.1	14.3	39.1	**10.0**	12.2	20.8
UNITED BANK INC	Parkersburg	WV	**B-**	B-	B-	5334.9	6.57	16.6	6.4	18.6	7.2	**6.4**	9.4	12.1
UNITED BANK OF EL PASO DEL NOR	El Paso	TX	**C+**	C+	C+	198.7	3.41	16.6	0.9	2.2	20.7	**6.8**	8.8	12.6
UNITED BANK OF IOWA	Ida Grove	IA	**A-**	B+	B	1237.9	2.07	5.3	2.8	7.8	9.2	**8.4**	10.6	13.7
▲ UNITED BANK OF MICHIGAN	Grand Rapids	MI	**D+**	C-	C-	475.5	1.33	9.0	2.5	15.6	1.3	**8.4**	10.3	13.6
UNITED BANK OF PHILADELPHIA	Philadelphia	PA	**E-**	E-	E-	60.5	-3.08	11.2	2.3	15.9	15.7	**1.3**	4.8	8.3
▼ UNITED BANK OF UNION	Union	MO	**D+**	C	B-	291.4	-1.75	15.7	1.0	19.5	22.6	**9.8**	10.9	15.2
UNITED BANKERS BANK	Bloomington	MN	**B**	B-	C	696.9	-3.22	9.9	0.4	0.7	24.8	**7.9**	9.6	17.6
UNITED CITIZENS BANK & TRUST	Campbellsburg	KY	**B+**	A-	A-	101.4	5.15	1.5	1.3	17.9	24.2	**10.0**	11.9	20.8
UNITED CITIZENS BANK OF S KY	Columbia	KY	**C-**	C-	D+	131.3	-3.43	6.3	3.8	28.9	12.2	**10.0**	11.8	17.0
UNITED COMMUNITY BANK	Perham	MN	**B-**	B-	B-	256.7	5.49	10.1	3.1	13.0	28.7	**7.0**	9.0	16.1
UNITED COMMUNITY BANK	Milford	IA	**B**	B	B	193.9	-3.60	12.6	1.3	15.7	4.3	**4.8**	9.3	10.9
▼ UNITED COMMUNITY BANK	Gonzales	LA	**D**	D+	D-	187.0	-0.85	18.6	1.7	13.3	2.4	**9.3**	11.6	14.5
▲ UNITED COMMUNITY BANK	Blairsville	GA	**B**	C+	C-	7491.7	3.91	7.7	4.7	11.8	29.7	**7.1**	9.1	13.8
▼ UNITED COMMUNITY BANK	Oakwood	IL	**C-**	C	C	43.9	7.01	8.7	2.1	17.1	18.1	**6.8**	8.8	15.4
UNITED COMMUNITY BANK	Chatham	IL	**B+**	B+	A-	1041.1	10.29	10.1	1.4	14.8	32.0	**6.2**	8.2	14.4
UNITED COMMUNITY BANK	Lawrenceburg	IN	**C+**	C+	D	521.9	2.62	0.8	0.7	25.5	37.5	**10.0**	12.1	26.5
▲ UNITED COMMUNITY BANK OF ND	Leeds	ND	**A-**	A-	B	305.7	9.87	19.2	2.2	9.1	13.5	**6.2**	8.7	11.9
UNITED COMMUNITY BK WEST KY	Morganfield	KY	**A**	A	A-	220.6	4.66	6.2	6.8	18.5	29.6	**10.0**	11.3	17.5
UNITED CUMBERLAND BANK	Whitley City	KY	**C**	C-	C+	277.7	99.24	4.8	11.0	30.2	24.3	**10.0**	11.9	21.2
UNITED FARMERS STATE BANK	Adams	MN	**A**	A	A	143.1	69.35	4.4	1.1	2.7	19.9	**9.5**	10.7	14.5
UNITED FIDELITY BANK FSB	Evansville	IN	**B-**	B-	C	238.3	37.75	1.9	0.3	17.2	45.9	**7.5**	9.3	23.4
▲ UNITED INTERNATIONAL BK	Flushing	NY	**C-**	D	D-	167.6	-10.06	5.4	0.1	6.9	7.2	**10.0**	11.8	16.5
UNITED LABOR BANK FSB	Oakland	CA	**C**	C+	C+	353.6	25.54	8.1	0.1	5.4	8.2	**7.7**	9.5	16.7
UNITED LEGACY BANK	Longwood	FL	**C-**	D+	D	229.4	7.36	10.1	2.9	7.3	18.1	**7.1**	9.1	13.2
▲ UNITED MIDWEST SAVINGS BANK	De Graff	OH	**E+**	E-	D-	176.8	-1.53	1.4	14.9	30.7	0.1	**6.2**	8.2	12.1
UNITED MINNESOTA BANK	New London	MN	**D+**	D+	D-	28.3	2.05	16.0	9.5	20.2	1.2	**6.1**	8.1	13.3
UNITED MISSISSIPPI BANK	Natchez	MS	**C+**	B-	B-	362.5	26.67	10.8	4.4	13.5	21.8	**7.0**	9.0	12.6
UNITED NATIONAL BK	Cairo	GA	**B-**	C+	C+	183.2	0.30	13.5	3.9	15.4	2.2	**10.0**	13.4	16.3
UNITED ORIENT BANK	New York	NY	**C+**	C+	C-	92.9	1.50	1.9	0.1	21.2	3.2	**10.0**	12.3	16.4
UNITED PACIFIC BANK	City of Industry	CA	**B-**	B-	C+	111.0	-2.96	0.5	0.0	6.2	2.3	**10.0**	17.3	24.7
UNITED PRAIRIE BANK	Mountain Lake	MN	**B-**	B-	C+	567.5	0.54	12.5	1.2	7.8	14.9	**6.2**	9.3	11.9
UNITED REPUBLIC BANK	Elkhorn	NE	**B-**	B	B-	106.3	10.37	20.8	1.6	13.5	3.8	**9.4**	12.6	14.5
UNITED ROOSEVELT SB	Carteret	NJ	**D+**	C	B-	89.8	-3.46	0.0	0.0	13.5	74.4	**10.0**	16.9	57.1
UNITED SAVINGS BANK	Philadelphia	PA	**B-**	B-	B+	319.7	-2.28	0.3	0.1	30.0	17.5	**10.0**	16.3	37.8
UNITED SECURITY BANK	Auxvasse	MO	**A-**	B+	B+	53.5	4.96	3.0	6.1	35.7	28.7	**10.0**	14.6	25.5
▲ UNITED SECURITY BANK	Fresno	CA	**B**	B-	C-	692.5	4.55	14.1	1.3	9.6	7.2	**10.0**	11.7	15.9
▲ UNITED SOUTHERN BANK	Hopkinsville	KY	**B-**	C+	C+	257.0	2.18	6.0	3.0	26.9	16.2	**8.2**	9.8	14.2
▲ UNITED SOUTHERN BANK	Umatilla	FL	**C-**	D+	C-	402.3	2.15	3.4	0.8	17.7	19.8	**9.3**	10.5	16.5
UNITED SOUTHWEST BANK	Cottonwood	MN	**D+**	D	D+	44.3	-0.85	3.2	2.3	1.6	41.9	**5.7**	7.7	14.1
▼ UNITED STATE BK	Lewistown	MO	**B**	B+	B-	132.3	8.08	6.2	1.9	8.2	11.7	**6.0**	8.8	11.7
UNITED TEXAS BANK	Dallas	TX	**B**	B+	B+	260.9	12.46	7.3	1.0	7.7	26.5	**8.9**	10.3	14.5
UNITED TRUST BANK	Palos Heights	IL	**E-**	E-	E-	37.5	-6.55	0.0	1.1	24.4	1.8	**4.3**	6.8	10.6
UNITED VALLEY BANK	Cavalier	ND	**C+**	C+	C+	236.1	2.90	10.7	2.6	5.7	25.6	**6.2**	8.2	12.9
▲ UNITED-AMERICAN SB	Pittsburgh	PA	**C+**	C	C-	87.6	1.50	1.7	0.6	57.0	21.2	**6.9**	8.9	17.1
▲ UNITI BANK	Buena Park	CA	**B-**	C	D	186.4	16.59	10.8	0.1	0.1	11.8	**10.0**	14.3	21.7
UNITY BANK	Clinton	NJ	**C-**	D+	D+	969.0	10.69	3.3	0.1	25.0	8.9	**6.0**	8.0	12.8
UNITY BANK	Rush City	MN	**C+**	C+	B-	185.5	0.75	7.5	2.5	15.2	4.0	**6.8**	8.8	13.6
UNITY BANK	Augusta	WI	**B**	B	B+	94.4	21.23	4.2	2.2	11.2	8.4	**6.6**	8.9	12.2
UNITY BANK NORTH	Red Lake Falls	MN	**B+**	B+	B	76.3	0.54	10.5	18.1	18.1	9.7	**8.6**	10.0	15.9
UNITY NATIONAL BK OF HOUSTON	Houston	TX	**D-**	D	D+	75.5	8.17	7.2	1.7	9.1	25.0	**7.2**	9.1	14.1
▲ UNIVERSAL BANK	West Covina	CA	**C**	D+	D-	321.4	-0.81	0.6	0.2	6.2	0.1	**10.0**	12.7	18.0
▲ UNIVERSITY BANK	Ann Arbor	MI	**B-**	C	C	112.6	-1.00	1.8	0.3	47.6	1.2	**10.0**	12.7	20.3
UNIVERSITY BANK	Pittsburg	KS	**A-**	B+	B	113.5	2.16	24.8	2.1	18.1	20.9	**10.0**	12.9	18.4
UNIVERSITY NB OF LAWRENCE	Lawrence	KS	**D**	D-	D-	73.5	5.32	4.6	1.2	26.0	10.8	**6.7**	8.7	17.1
UNIVEST BANK & TRUST CO	Souderton	PA	**B-**	B-	C+	2202.6	-1.19	17.1	1.4	9.1	16.4	**6.8**	9.8	12.4
UPPER PENINSULA STATE BK	Escanaba	MI	**B**	B	B	181.7	-7.14	3.5	4.2	19.2	27.7	**10.0**	17.7	27.2
▲ UPSTATE NATIONAL BK	Ogdensburg	NY	**C+**	C	C-	92.3	1.98	13.8	0.2	12.1	23.8	**10.0**	12.9	20.8
URBAN PARTNERSHIP BANK	Chicago	IL	**D-**	D-	D-	832.9	-17.80	11.2	0.0	19.0	7.7	**6.7**	8.7	24.6

Asset Quality Index	Adjusted Non-Performing Loans as a % of Total Loans	Adjusted Non-Performing Loans as a % of Capital	Net Charge-Offs / Avg Loans	Profitability Index	Net Income ($Mil)	Return on Assets (R.O.A.)	Return on Equity (R.O.E.)	Net Interest Spread	Overhead Efficiency Ratio	Liquidity Index	Liquidity Ratio	Hot Money Ratio	Stability Index
2.5	4.54	20.2	0.20	**3.0**	1.9	0.48	4.17	3.37	94.5	**3.5**	25.4	12.8	**5.8**
8.8	0.38	1.5	0.28	**5.4**	1.0	1.16	9.46	3.42	59.8	**3.8**	36.2	14.5	**8.0**
4.5	1.26	10.4	0.35	**7.0**	41.6	1.08	10.87	3.65	51.5	**3.6**	6.6	10.4	**7.2**
3.7	1.44	10.4	0.00	**4.3**	1.1	0.73	8.10	4.51	72.3	**1.8**	24.9	23.3	**4.6**
6.2	0.36	2.5	0.06	**7.5**	16.5	1.75	16.59	3.40	49.1	**1.3**	10.2	26.9	**10.0**
1.6	2.82	20.9	0.11	**3.9**	2.2	0.62	6.06	4.35	80.1	**3.7**	10.8	9.8	**5.8**
0.3	6.89	84.8	0.82	**0.0**	-0.6	-1.34	-26.45	4.82	116.7	**2.8**	13.9	15.1	**0.9**
1.4	6.46	38.0	0.33	**5.6**	2.7	1.21	11.66	3.59	63.9	**3.0**	8.3	13.4	**7.3**
5.2	1.38	6.2	-0.01	**4.7**	3.9	0.73	7.59	2.54	76.1	**2.1**	41.3	34.6	**5.7**
6.6	1.46	6.3	-0.05	**4.5**	0.6	0.72	6.39	3.62	73.0	**4.7**	36.9	10.4	**7.6**
2.0	4.33	25.7	0.25	**4.8**	0.9	0.90	7.95	4.38	67.0	**1.5**	16.6	24.3	**6.3**
4.5	2.27	12.8	0.01	**4.6**	1.9	1.01	10.88	3.62	69.3	**2.7**	36.2	21.1	**5.2**
7.7	0.00	0.0	0.00	**6.5**	2.2	1.53	14.80	4.09	61.0	**2.9**	4.4	13.4	**7.3**
0.7	3.52	22.3	0.53	**4.1**	1.0	0.73	6.66	4.64	69.0	**3.0**	13.2	13.8	**5.2**
5.8	1.21	7.7	0.34	**4.9**	57.0	1.03	9.23	3.44	58.5	**3.2**	15.8	13.3	**6.4**
3.0	3.37	21.5	0.04	**3.3**	0.2	0.51	5.77	3.51	85.1	**3.6**	31.9	14.4	**4.5**
5.7	1.00	6.7	0.10	**5.9**	11.0	1.39	15.10	3.21	62.3	**5.2**	27.5	6.9	**8.6**
4.4	4.39	16.2	0.09	**2.8**	1.6	0.40	3.22	2.59	81.6	**2.0**	21.7	19.6	**7.1**
7.5	0.02	0.2	0.44	**10.0**	6.4	2.92	32.25	5.30	39.3	**2.5**	5.3	15.4	**7.0**
8.4	0.17	0.9	0.04	**9.0**	2.6	1.58	14.95	4.26	50.6	**4.4**	23.0	6.8	**7.4**
2.3	4.41	21.1	0.24	**6.6**	2.5	1.44	13.61	5.05	71.9	**1.6**	26.8	27.1	**7.1**
7.0	0.25	1.5	0.01	**9.3**	2.1	2.16	19.68	4.45	47.6	**3.9**	25.8	10.6	**8.4**
7.0	1.46	4.8	-0.11	**7.9**	3.3	2.12	19.93	4.00	53.0	**2.9**	29.5	17.0	**4.2**
1.4	3.49	21.8	0.95	**1.7**	0.1	0.04	0.31	3.53	96.2	**0.8**	16.9	35.4	**5.3**
3.7	2.24	12.8	0.00	**2.5**	0.2	0.07	0.76	4.05	79.6	**5.0**	33.8	7.2	**4.8**
4.0	1.93	13.0	0.17	**2.5**	0.6	0.32	3.18	3.52	81.0	**2.4**	25.4	18.4	**4.0**
0.0	5.62	49.9	1.34	**2.4**	0.6	0.41	6.19	4.69	78.7	**1.0**	6.1	28.8	**2.2**
5.1	0.44	3.5	0.11	**4.1**	0.2	0.91	11.39	4.15	75.9	**4.6**	24.0	6.1	**2.6**
4.3	1.12	8.2	-0.10	**4.0**	2.3	0.83	9.66	4.15	82.7	**2.1**	22.7	19.5	**4.8**
3.6	2.46	14.7	0.43	**8.2**	1.9	1.42	10.48	4.96	55.2	**0.6**	1.9	34.6	**7.5**
5.0	0.50	3.3	0.68	**2.5**	0.1	0.11	0.96	5.16	85.6	**1.7**	14.0	21.9	**6.0**
4.2	1.89	7.6	0.14	**3.8**	0.7	0.85	4.99	3.38	80.5	**1.5**	28.4	31.7	**6.7**
5.4	0.68	5.2	0.37	**4.0**	3.6	0.85	8.18	4.04	84.6	**4.2**	11.0	6.7	**7.2**
8.3	0.00	0.0	-0.01	**4.4**	0.5	0.64	5.02	4.14	75.6	**0.8**	13.6	36.5	**6.4**
8.7	5.04	4.1	0.11	**0.7**	-0.1	-0.09	-0.58	2.25	106.9	**6.0**	97.4	13.5	**6.7**
9.9	0.12	0.3	0.03	**3.2**	1.1	0.46	2.83	2.15	70.0	**3.9**	49.4	18.0	**8.1**
8.7	0.02	0.1	0.05	**6.0**	0.6	1.53	10.58	4.42	64.8	**2.3**	15.1	17.6	**8.4**
4.1	2.68	13.6	-0.07	**6.0**	4.8	0.97	7.21	4.07	63.1	**4.4**	27.2	8.6	**6.4**
4.1	2.29	16.0	0.07	**4.0**	1.4	0.75	7.39	4.00	72.5	**1.2**	12.2	28.5	**4.9**
2.2	4.36	23.2	0.23	**3.8**	1.7	0.57	5.49	3.68	77.0	**5.3**	33.9	5.3	**5.1**
6.8	0.56	2.7	0.00	**2.4**	0.1	0.30	4.00	4.17	90.1	**6.6**	52.5	2.3	**2.5**
3.9	1.05	8.2	-0.01	**6.6**	1.4	1.45	16.60	3.82	59.0	**2.6**	10.6	15.8	**6.4**
7.7	0.58	3.3	0.00	**4.3**	1.3	0.72	6.56	4.17	78.3	**2.1**	43.6	41.7	**5.5**
0.3	6.74	57.0	1.25	**0.0**	-0.7	-2.30	-30.02	3.59	136.6	**0.8**	18.7	46.8	**2.3**
3.9	0.80	6.0	0.34	**4.9**	2.0	1.14	12.05	3.91	64.9	**3.5**	15.2	11.6	**5.4**
5.2	1.20	9.4	0.00	**4.1**	0.5	0.74	9.22	3.43	62.4	**1.0**	25.7	45.2	**4.0**
4.9	1.33	5.6	-0.24	**4.1**	1.4	1.08	7.76	3.43	79.3	**1.2**	24.3	31.3	**5.2**
2.1	1.85	16.0	0.37	**3.9**	4.5	0.67	9.09	3.55	70.1	**2.2**	15.1	18.2	**4.3**
2.1	3.29	25.6	0.14	**4.8**	1.3	0.92	10.24	4.54	81.3	**2.3**	15.6	17.8	**5.0**
5.6	0.46	3.6	0.07	**5.5**	0.8	1.21	12.32	4.61	68.5	**2.3**	15.4	17.4	**5.7**
7.1	0.18	1.2	0.01	**5.8**	0.8	1.37	13.35	4.27	76.8	**2.5**	18.8	17.1	**7.2**
3.6	2.93	17.9	0.14	**0.4**	-0.3	-0.45	-5.06	3.90	110.1	**1.8**	38.7	48.6	**3.8**
4.2	1.55	8.3	-0.29	**2.2**	1.1	0.46	3.63	3.45	92.3	**1.3**	17.5	28.3	**5.5**
5.8	0.64	3.8	-0.01	**8.8**	0.9	1.30	13.82	4.63	94.5	**4.8**	11.1	2.8	**3.5**
6.1	1.11	5.3	0.46	**5.6**	1.1	1.35	10.51	3.72	65.3	**4.0**	32.8	12.4	**7.0**
6.4	0.66	4.0	0.10	**0.9**	0.0	0.08	0.88	3.16	97.7	**3.4**	33.9	15.7	**2.6**
4.2	1.27	8.8	0.48	**5.0**	16.0	0.98	7.73	3.90	73.5	**4.6**	10.2	4.4	**8.7**
4.8	2.75	9.2	1.24	**7.6**	2.2	1.63	9.93	4.15	51.8	**3.6**	36.3	15.6	**7.7**
5.9	1.06	5.2	-0.01	**3.2**	0.5	0.73	6.10	3.40	78.5	**1.7**	10.4	20.3	**6.4**
3.7	4.44	20.6	2.81	**0.0**	-28.3	-4.10	-39.67	6.39	256.8	**0.8**	16.3	37.7	**1.7**

Name	City	State	Rating	2013 Rating	2012 Rating	Total Assets ($Mil)	One Year Asset Growth	Asset Mix (As a % of Total Assets) Commercial Loans	Consumer Loans	Mortgage Loans	Securities	Capitalization Index	Leverage Ratio	Risk-Based Capital Ratio
▲ US BANK NA	Cincinnati	OH	**C+**	C+	B-	387033.8	8.54	15.4	11.6	15.7	24.9	**6.7**	8.7	12.9
US BANK TRUST CO NA	Portland	OR	**U**	U	U	15.5	2.83	0.0	0.0	0.0	0.0	**10.0**	100.	473.8
US BANK TRUST NA	Wilmington	DE	**U**	U	U	585.7	0.54	0.0	0.0	0.0	0.0	**10.0**	97.7	496.4
US BANK TRUST NA SD	Sioux Falls	SD	**U**	U	U	69.7	7.42	0.0	0.0	0.0	0.0	**10.0**	94.2	309.2
US CENTURY BANK	Doral	FL	**E-**	E-	E-	886.2	-5.55	8.6	0.2	9.5	4.7	**0.9**	5.2	7.8
US METRO BANK	Garden Grove	CA	**D**	D-	D	108.0	40.46	9.7	0.0	0.7	0.0	**10.0**	13.0	22.3
USAA FSB	San Antonio	TX	**C**	C	C+	66179.6	6.67	0.0	51.4	5.8	24.5	**6.7**	8.7	14.0
USAA SAVINGS BANK	Las Vegas	NV	**U**	B	B+	1358.2	-91.66	0.0	0.0	0.0	14.0	**10.0**	12.2	49.9
USAMERIBANK	Clearwater	FL	**B-**	B-	C	3009.9	8.09	14.9	0.4	10.1	10.4	**6.0**	9.0	11.8
USNY BANK	Geneva	NY	**B+**	B+	B+	208.8	22.22	12.3	0.4	9.7	3.9	**4.8**	9.2	10.9
UTAH COMMUNITY BANK	Sandy	UT	**C**	C	D	31.4	4.01	3.6	10.6	17.9	3.5	**10.0**	12.3	19.4
▲ UTAH INDEPENDENT BANK	Salina	UT	**B+**	B	B	61.9	1.16	20.6	6.4	13.6	15.7	**10.0**	14.7	21.3
UWHARRIE BANK	Albemarle	NC	**C+**	C+	C-	515.4	-2.62	4.5	1.6	17.9	22.1	**8.5**	10.0	16.1
VALLEY BANK	Roanoke	VA	**B**	B	B-	856.6	7.73	9.5	0.6	17.4	21.5	**8.4**	9.9	14.4
VALLEY BANK & TRUST	Mapleton	IA	**A**	A	A-	75.8	-1.06	1.0	1.9	2.5	12.4	**10.0**	13.0	20.4
▲ VALLEY BANK & TRUST	Brighton	CO	**C-**	D	D+	279.6	1.27	8.6	0.9	5.8	37.6	**7.2**	9.1	15.8
VALLEY BANK & TRUST CO	Gering	NE	**C+**	C	C	335.2	-1.28	9.4	3.5	12.2	15.2	**8.4**	9.9	13.9
VALLEY BANK OF COMMERCE	Roswell	NM	**B+**	B+	A-	164.8	14.55	13.9	0.9	1.7	3.0	**5.1**	7.1	21.4
VALLEY BANK OF GLASGOW	Glasgow	MT	**C+**	C	C-	37.1	4.30	7.3	5.6	10.7	17.5	**7.0**	9.0	15.2
VALLEY BANK OF KALISPELL	Kalispell	MT	**B**	C+	C	117.2	4.26	11.1	3.3	10.2	51.0	**9.6**	10.7	21.7
VALLEY BANK OF NEVADA	North Las Vegas	NV	**E-**	E-	E-	82.9	-1.42	20.5	0.3	2.0	6.0	**3.0**	6.8	10.0
VALLEY BANK OF RONAN	Ronan	MT	**B-**	B	C	66.1	0.12	6.5	4.1	14.4	12.8	**10.0**	12.4	19.8
VALLEY BUSINESS BANK	Visalia	CA	**B**	B	B-	393.1	9.85	5.6	0.4	2.2	17.0	**10.0**	11.6	17.3
VALLEY CENTRAL BANK	Reading	OH	**B**	B	C+	94.9	11.21	1.0	0.0	40.6	19.9	**10.0**	28.0	47.3
VALLEY COMMUNITY BANK	Pleasanton	CA	**D+**	D-	D-	130.3	-11.16	6.3	0.1	6.6	19.2	**10.0**	11.7	18.7
VALLEY EXCHANGE BANK	Lennox	SD	**C**	C	C+	69.7	5.17	7.9	2.7	2.0	26.1	**9.1**	10.4	22.9
VALLEY GREEN BANK	Philadelphia	PA	**B**	B-	C+	421.6	21.74	8.9	0.1	30.2	3.0	**5.8**	9.1	11.6
VALLEY NATIONAL BK	Wayne	NJ	**C+**	C+	C+	16711.7	4.68	10.7	8.2	14.8	15.5	**5.1**	7.9	11.1
▲ VALLEY NATIONAL BK	Tulsa	OK	**C+**	D+	D-	379.5	80.58	15.5	2.1	11.7	12.4	**8.1**	10.0	13.4
▲ VALLEY NATIONAL BK	Espanola	NM	**D**	D	D-	173.8	-12.16	3.0	1.5	6.3	33.4	**10.0**	11.5	30.5
VALLEY REPUBLIC BANK	Bakersfield	CA	**C+**	C+	C	422.6	10.96	10.6	0.5	6.3	31.0	**8.5**	10.0	16.8
VALLEY STATE BK	Russellville	AL	**B-**	B-	B-	125.9	4.86	6.1	1.9	15.7	53.0	**10.0**	14.2	28.5
VALLEY STATE BK	Belle Plaine	KS	**B-**	B-	C+	127.2	2.24	6.3	6.4	13.7	47.4	**10.0**	11.9	25.9
▼ VALLEY STATE BK	Syracuse	KS	**C**	C	C	100.1	13.73	14.6	3.2	6.2	25.4	**6.0**	8.2	11.8
VALLEY VIEW STATE BK	Overland Park	KS	**B-**	C+	C-	841.9	-2.24	4.4	0.5	1.8	51.7	**10.0**	13.1	25.8
VALLIANCE BANK	Oklahoma City	OK	**C+**	C+	C+	325.8	14.49	24.3	0.3	5.7	15.3	**8.7**	10.8	13.9
VALUEBANK TEXAS	Corpus Christi	TX	**B**	B	B	200.7	2.65	5.0	1.1	13.6	14.4	**7.7**	9.4	15.8
VAN WERT FSB	Van Wert	OH	**B-**	C+	C+	118.9	-3.94	0.0	0.8	48.4	22.4	**10.0**	19.3	46.6
VANGUARD NATIONAL TRUST CO NA	Malvern	PA	**U**	U	U	160.3	31.88	0.0	0.0	0.0	80.5	**10.0**	80.9	488.8
VANTAGE BANK	Kent	MN	**D**	D	C	14.5	26.87	9.7	6.1	19.7	0.0	**10.0**	11.0	15.4
▼ VANTAGE BANK OF ALABAMA	Albertville	AL	**B-**	A-	B+	110.3	42.95	8.9	4.9	14.0	17.2	**9.5**	10.7	16.7
VANTAGE BANK TEXAS	San Antonio	TX	**C**	C-	D+	352.6	14.18	16.2	2.9	5.4	13.7	**7.0**	9.0	13.1
VECTRA BANK COLORADO NA	Denver	CO	**B**	B	C+	2841.2	6.13	19.0	1.3	11.2	5.8	**9.9**	12.3	14.9
VENTURE BANK	Bloomington	MN	**B-**	B-	B-	516.3	28.92	29.3	0.6	4.4	10.3	**4.6**	8.0	10.8
VERGAS STATE BK	Vergas	MN	**B**	B	B	48.5	-1.01	4.7	3.2	10.4	45.9	**10.0**	13.7	31.6
▲ VERITEX COMMUNITY BANK	Dallas	TX	**B-**	C+	C-	744.2	24.02	26.2	0.6	13.5	6.4	**5.8**	8.7	11.6
VERMILION BANK & TRUST CO	Kaplan	LA	**B**	B	B	110.6	3.03	29.1	6.9	17.7	29.3	**7.3**	9.2	16.4
VERMILION VALLEY BANK	Piper City	IL	**A**	A	A-	124.6	-1.65	3.3	2.2	10.5	33.8	**10.0**	12.2	19.0
VERMILLION STATE BK	Vermillion	MN	**A**	A	A	539.0	5.13	17.0	1.1	8.8	40.0	**10.0**	13.3	22.6
VERMONT STATE BK	Vermont	IL	**D**	D	D-	21.9	22.82	7.0	24.0	34.0	15.2	**7.6**	9.4	15.4
VERNON BANK	Leesville	LA	**B**	B-	B-	79.1	6.79	6.3	8.8	33.8	15.7	**7.7**	9.5	15.8
VERSAILLES SAVINGS & LOAN CO	Versailles	OH	**C+**	C+	B-	50.7	4.26	2.2	2.1	58.3	0.7	**10.0**	20.7	34.0
VERUS BANK	Derby	KS	**B**	B	B	131.1	3.31	3.8	2.6	25.8	22.0	**7.1**	9.1	13.4
VERUS BANK OF COMMERCE	Fort Collins	CO	**A**	B+	B+	273.6	1.94	5.7	0.0	8.7	0.0	**10.0**	15.3	18.7
VIBRA BANK	Chula Vista	CA	**C-**	C-	B-	148.1	8.42	15.1	0.0	8.4	2.6	**6.7**	8.7	16.3
VICTOR STATE BK	Victor	IA	**A**	A	A	49.9	4.71	12.8	1.6	7.9	57.4	**10.0**	24.1	40.9
VICTORY BANK	Limerick	PA	**C**	C	D	153.5	8.64	21.2	2.9	22.9	1.1	**3.4**	8.2	10.2
VICTORY COMMUNITY BANK	Fort Mitchell	KY	**A**	A	A	164.4	0.75	0.0	0.2	58.1	1.3	**10.0**	12.2	23.0
VICTORY STATE BK	Staten Island	NY	**C+**	C+	C-	307.4	1.29	5.6	0.3	2.7	61.2	**7.7**	9.5	26.5
VIDALIA FSB	Vidalia	GA	**C+**	C+	C+	228.4	1.14	0.0	0.9	26.8	43.0	**10.0**	12.5	47.4

Asset Quality Index	Adjusted Non-Performing Loans as a % of Total Loans	Adjusted Non-Performing Loans as a % of Capital	Net Charge-Offs / Avg Loans	Profitability Index	Net Income ($Mil)	Return on Assets (R.O.A.)	Return on Equity (R.O.E.)	Net Interest Spread	Overhead Efficiency Ratio	Liquidity Index	Liquidity Ratio	Hot Money Ratio	Stability Index
3.4	1.59	10.8	0.57	**8.9**	4120.3	1.50	13.89	3.36	52.8	**5.1**	27.5	7.5	**9.6**
10.0	na	0.0	na	**9.5**	0.3	2.90	2.91	na	23.5	**4.0**	10807.9	101.0	**5.0**
9.0	na	0.0	na	**4.2**	2.3	0.52	0.53	0.27	65.1	**4.0**	3949.3	101.0	**7.0**
10.0	na	0.0	na	**9.5**	3.4	6.72	7.21	0.15	35.8	**4.0**	1261.9	101.0	**5.0**
0.0	7.02	82.4	0.04	**0.3**	-1.5	-0.23	-4.32	3.44	105.8	**1.7**	18.5	22.0	**1.7**
5.4	0.48	1.8	-0.72	**0.0**	-1.0	-1.45	-10.93	2.33	139.7	**2.5**	41.4	28.4	**4.7**
2.8	1.21	8.1	1.16	**7.5**	582.1	1.22	13.91	4.07	62.1	**4.1**	36.7	16.3	**7.4**
10.0	na	0.0	na	**10.0**	265.2	16.81	47.30	-0.11	63.3	**3.4**	83.8	94.9	**9.5**
4.3	1.27	10.6	0.15	**6.7**	23.3	1.06	11.45	3.69	54.7	**1.2**	11.1	29.4	**7.7**
8.2	0.12	1.0	0.00	**8.9**	2.0	1.36	14.84	4.05	43.4	**0.6**	11.3	46.3	**6.2**
5.1	1.71	9.0	-0.01	**2.6**	0.1	0.37	2.46	4.39	90.4	**2.9**	31.5	17.5	**4.8**
7.5	0.53	2.2	0.16	**6.0**	0.7	1.40	10.12	4.53	71.5	**4.7**	32.4	8.4	**6.5**
4.7	1.66	9.4	0.38	**3.3**	2.0	0.52	5.17	3.79	87.9	**3.9**	17.2	9.6	**5.2**
5.6	0.83	5.5	0.45	**4.9**	5.8	0.91	9.71	3.66	64.3	**2.0**	11.6	18.6	**6.0**
6.3	0.10	0.4	0.03	**7.0**	0.9	1.59	9.06	3.78	54.2	**5.4**	49.0	9.2	**8.5**
2.2	5.62	26.4	-1.02	**3.9**	2.2	1.04	12.47	4.52	83.4	**5.2**	40.2	8.6	**4.0**
4.9	0.57	3.8	0.09	**3.9**	1.6	0.64	6.04	3.97	81.3	**1.6**	15.9	22.9	**6.0**
8.6	0.34	1.5	-0.06	**5.5**	1.5	1.29	17.84	2.57	52.8	**7.2**	71.8	3.7	**5.4**
5.5	0.79	5.6	-0.01	**7.0**	0.3	1.25	14.40	4.71	63.8	**3.2**	26.4	14.5	**4.0**
4.0	4.10	14.5	0.16	**4.3**	0.7	0.85	7.65	3.89	74.7	**5.4**	53.7	11.3	**5.9**
0.0	9.87	77.5	2.70	**0.7**	0.0	-0.01	-0.15	3.70	98.6	**0.9**	22.0	39.6	**2.8**
5.5	2.27	8.7	-0.03	**3.8**	0.3	0.55	4.47	4.16	80.3	**5.4**	49.9	9.7	**5.4**
4.9	1.22	6.5	-0.23	**7.0**	3.6	1.23	10.82	4.17	63.0	**3.3**	19.0	12.7	**7.0**
9.3	0.58	1.5	0.09	**4.3**	0.5	0.73	2.59	3.60	68.0	**1.9**	33.2	29.1	**6.7**
2.1	5.62	22.7	0.34	**1.2**	0.1	0.10	0.90	4.16	97.9	**4.6**	39.6	12.1	**4.6**
8.8	0.04	0.2	0.03	**3.2**	0.3	0.49	4.99	2.61	76.2	**5.8**	51.3	7.1	**4.8**
7.1	0.48	4.5	0.34	**8.6**	3.8	1.35	15.08	4.93	53.3	**0.7**	13.2	45.5	**4.7**
3.7	1.22	10.9	0.12	**4.3**	95.3	0.78	7.47	3.21	69.5	**3.6**	10.6	10.9	**8.4**
3.5	2.14	14.3	0.52	**3.5**	1.9	0.66	7.21	3.76	78.8	**0.9**	22.7	35.0	**4.8**
1.8	14.78	31.2	-1.12	**0.0**	-1.7	-1.17	-11.09	2.27	148.3	**3.1**	37.7	18.7	**4.2**
9.0	0.00	0.0	0.00	**3.5**	1.9	0.64	6.58	2.91	62.9	**6.5**	43.8	1.3	**5.2**
9.4	0.07	0.2	0.03	**3.3**	0.6	0.58	4.16	2.60	69.5	**3.3**	47.3	20.6	**7.3**
7.7	0.66	2.6	0.34	**3.7**	0.7	0.75	6.24	3.38	71.2	**1.4**	27.6	31.3	**6.2**
2.6	2.85	21.3	0.12	**4.9**	0.9	1.20	14.42	3.92	70.3	**0.8**	13.9	38.5	**5.0**
5.0	4.92	12.5	0.25	**3.2**	3.5	0.55	4.31	3.02	69.6	**5.9**	61.8	10.5	**6.2**
3.8	1.33	8.6	0.05	**5.1**	3.0	1.27	12.94	4.20	66.7	**0.9**	22.3	43.5	**5.3**
8.9	0.05	0.3	0.05	**4.6**	1.2	0.82	8.49	4.35	79.4	**4.8**	31.2	7.7	**6.3**
8.5	1.12	3.1	0.00	**3.1**	0.6	0.58	3.22	2.53	77.2	**3.5**	48.7	19.6	**7.6**
10.0	na	0.0	na	**9.5**	21.4	20.51	25.57	0.05	52.6	**4.0**	363.7	101.0	**6.5**
7.3	0.00	0.0	0.00	**0.9**	0.0	-0.08	-0.65	4.37	100.6	**2.7**	8.7	15.0	**4.0**
4.3	2.06	10.7	1.04	**3.2**	0.1	0.15	1.07	4.17	74.0	**2.8**	40.9	24.1	**7.1**
3.6	1.03	7.8	0.11	**3.1**	1.8	0.69	7.03	4.00	90.2	**2.8**	22.1	15.4	**3.5**
4.9	1.61	10.3	-0.01	**5.5**	18.4	0.93	7.50	4.08	78.2	**3.6**	13.0	10.9	**7.9**
5.1	0.38	3.2	0.13	**9.9**	8.3	2.44	29.55	4.71	51.5	**2.1**	23.4	19.2	**5.5**
9.1	1.06	2.6	0.60	**3.6**	0.2	0.58	4.62	2.72	69.4	**4.2**	68.5	19.0	**6.7**
5.9	0.19	1.6	0.06	**4.4**	3.9	0.76	6.62	3.96	65.6	**3.0**	10.2	13.5	**6.6**
4.7	1.58	8.9	0.03	**6.4**	1.3	1.54	17.31	4.09	64.9	**2.6**	22.6	16.9	**6.6**
8.4	0.18	0.9	0.62	**6.8**	1.4	1.50	11.82	3.81	48.9	**3.9**	22.8	10.1	**8.4**
7.5	1.13	4.3	-0.44	**9.5**	9.5	2.41	18.67	3.39	30.6	**4.0**	49.6	17.6	**8.9**
1.1	2.95	21.4	0.26	**3.8**	0.1	0.88	9.23	4.25	74.3	**0.8**	21.4	45.6	**2.9**
7.6	0.00	0.0	0.29	**6.1**	0.8	1.41	15.36	4.91	68.6	**3.3**	17.1	12.7	**5.0**
9.3	0.00	0.0	0.00	**3.1**	0.2	0.41	2.15	3.32	78.4	**3.9**	16.3	9.7	**7.2**
8.4	0.00	0.0	0.03	**4.6**	1.0	1.05	11.80	4.01	77.6	**4.3**	20.8	7.7	**5.7**
6.3	0.77	4.3	0.76	**10.0**	4.1	2.05	13.90	4.66	35.4	**2.0**	8.9	18.2	**7.8**
7.9	0.20	1.4	0.41	**2.1**	0.3	0.29	3.25	4.01	95.4	**1.6**	31.4	32.7	**5.2**
9.8	0.00	0.0	-0.04	**10.0**	1.1	2.74	12.73	4.99	24.9	**4.9**	74.3	15.9	**8.8**
3.9	1.37	13.7	0.02	**3.6**	0.5	0.48	5.75	4.40	79.5	**2.9**	3.3	13.1	**3.7**
5.8	1.89	11.4	0.17	**9.0**	2.4	1.99	15.61	3.13	54.3	**1.4**	23.0	28.4	**9.0**
4.2	7.52	17.7	0.46	**3.7**	1.2	0.54	5.69	2.99	70.4	**4.6**	64.1	17.8	**4.0**
6.3	3.00	7.1	0.02	**2.7**	0.5	0.27	2.17	2.03	80.4	**3.5**	78.9	35.9	**6.4**

Name	City	State	Rating	2013 Rating	2012 Rating	Total Assets ($Mil)	One Year Asset Growth	Asset Mix (As a % of Total Assets) Comm-ercial Loans	Cons-umer Loans	Mort-gage Loans	Secur-ities	Capital-ization Index	Lever-age Ratio	Risk-Based Capital Ratio
VIEWPOINT BANK NA	Plano	TX	**B+**	B+	B+	3951.6	16.75	17.1	1.1	12.3	12.0	**8.3**	11.3	13.6
VIKING SAVINGS BANK	Alexandria	MN	**C+**	C+	C+	160.7	0.30	12.4	1.5	26.0	8.7	**10.0**	11.2	17.0
VILLA GROVE STATE BK	Villa Grove	IL	**C+**	C+	C-	71.5	0.89	4.1	2.5	42.2	13.9	**7.2**	9.1	16.8
VILLAGE BANK	Auburndale	MA	**B-**	B-	B-	804.6	5.22	2.7	0.3	41.8	15.8	**10.0**	11.8	18.5
▲ VILLAGE BANK	Midlothian	VA	**D-**	E+	E-	429.7	-6.10	5.2	4.8	18.4	12.9	**5.1**	7.1	11.9
VILLAGE BANK	Saint Libory	IL	**C+**	C+	C+	78.3	-1.62	5.6	7.1	23.6	4.8	**8.0**	9.7	19.3
▲ VILLAGE BANK	Saint Francis	MN	**D-**	E	E-	175.7	6.71	13.1	0.9	9.6	9.6	**6.4**	8.4	12.2
VILLAGE BANK & TRUST	Arlington Heights	IL	**C+**	C+	C	1046.0	9.52	31.0	12.6	2.8	10.4	**5.5**	9.5	11.4
VININGS BANK	Smyrna	GA	**A-**	B	B-	253.1	9.74	10.2	0.1	2.4	49.0	**10.0**	11.4	19.6
▼ VINTAGE BANK	Waxahachie	TX	**B**	B+	C+	187.0	16.02	10.9	1.4	13.2	6.8	**7.8**	9.6	15.6
▲ VINTAGE BANK KANSAS	Leon	KS	**C**	C-	C	50.9	202.03	5.7	4.0	18.9	29.4	**9.8**	10.9	20.7
VINTON COUNTY NATIONAL BK	McArthur	OH	**B+**	B	B-	763.0	0.79	2.8	11.1	34.0	24.8	**10.0**	11.9	18.6
VIRGINIA BANK & TRUST CO	Danville	VA	**A-**	B+	A-	175.4	0.09	10.7	7.9	19.8	13.4	**10.0**	14.5	20.9
VIRGINIA COMMONWEALTH BANK	Petersburg	VA	**C+**	C	C-	241.0	-4.48	1.7	2.3	20.3	32.7	**10.0**	11.6	20.9
VIRGINIA COMMUNITY BANK	Louisa	VA	**D+**	D+	D+	214.1	1.09	5.4	0.9	11.5	27.9	**7.2**	9.1	14.1
▼ VIRGINIA COMPANY BANK	Newport News	VA	**D-**	D	D	127.9	-2.72	14.8	1.2	6.2	10.5	**5.6**	9.8	11.5
▼ VIRGINIA NATIONAL BK	Charlottesville	VA	**B**	B+	B	507.8	4.94	9.6	2.4	11.5	28.1	**8.7**	10.1	16.3
VIRGINIA PARTNERS BANK	Fredericksburg	VA	**C**	C	C	258.9	14.05	2.9	0.5	21.7	14.3	**6.5**	8.5	12.6
VISION BANK - TEXAS	Richardson	TX	**C+**	C+	C	189.3	12.77	20.4	0.8	12.4	9.8	**8.5**	10.0	14.3
VISION BANK NA	Ada	OK	**B-**	B-	B-	651.0	4.06	6.5	4.1	20.8	33.3	**6.9**	8.9	15.2
▼ VISIONBANK	Topeka	KS	**C**	C+	C	103.9	8.15	11.9	2.9	19.0	6.8	**6.7**	8.7	13.7
VISIONBANK	Fargo	ND	**D+**	D+	D+	148.9	4.77	31.5	2.6	18.4	0.2	**7.5**	9.3	13.3
VISIONBANK	Saint Louis Park	MN	**B-**	B-	C-	40.8	19.28	22.6	3.3	11.8	0.0	**10.0**	11.5	16.6
VISIONBANK OF IOWA	Ames	IA	**C+**	C	C-	399.7	5.62	4.3	0.3	9.0	6.0	**9.7**	10.8	14.9
VIST BANK	Wyomissing	PA	**B-**	C+	C-	1301.2	0.11	7.2	0.1	11.2	17.8	**7.1**	9.1	12.8
▲ VISTA BANK	Ralls	TX	**C+**	C+	C-	299.9	24.50	14.3	3.2	10.2	19.7	**6.5**	8.5	12.1
VISTABANK	Aiken	SC	**D**	D-	E+	107.0	5.31	5.0	1.8	9.1	16.2	**5.8**	8.5	11.6
VNBTRUST NA	Charlottesville	VA	**U**	U	U	10.0	-4.75	0.0	0.0	0.0	0.0	**10.0**	93.8	1896.
VOLUNTEER FSB	Madisonville	TN	**B**	B	B	169.3	-2.94	0.8	9.4	49.4	1.8	**10.0**	14.0	23.9
VOLUNTEER STATE BK	Portland	TN	**B-**	C+	C-	464.7	13.46	10.5	1.1	32.4	5.6	**7.8**	9.7	13.2
▲ VOYAGER BANK	Eden Prairie	MN	**C-**	D+	D	336.6	5.78	24.0	1.7	7.2	7.1	**5.4**	9.3	11.3
WABASH SAVINGS BANK	Mount Carmel	IL	**C-**	C-	C+	11.7	3.51	1.3	5.3	24.1	46.9	**10.0**	13.4	32.3
WADENA STATE BK	Wadena	MN	**A**	A	A	125.6	6.65	9.7	2.2	15.8	28.8	**10.0**	11.9	19.9
WAGGONER NATIONAL BK OF VERNON	Vernon	TX	**A+**	A+	A	272.0	2.58	6.4	7.3	8.8	35.4	**10.0**	13.9	21.8
WAHOO STATE BK	Wahoo	NE	**C**	C	C	67.8	-1.21	4.5	2.9	28.5	16.4	**5.4**	7.4	12.6
WAKE FOREST FS&LA	Wake Forest	NC	**B**	B-	B-	114.0	-1.33	0.0	0.2	24.7	1.1	**10.0**	19.4	37.4
WAKEFIELD CO-OP BANK	Wakefield	MA	**C**	C+	B-	180.1	6.07	0.1	0.0	60.5	27.8	**6.3**	8.3	18.2
WALCOTT TRUST & SB	Walcott	IA	**A-**	B+	B+	102.1	-3.13	7.3	0.7	17.7	19.7	**10.0**	19.2	29.5
WALDEN SAVINGS BANK	Montgomery	NY	**C-**	D+	C-	456.2	3.14	6.2	0.4	32.2	16.8	**7.4**	9.2	16.5
WALDO STATE BK	Waldo	WI	**B**	B-	C-	61.8	1.92	13.1	2.4	32.9	30.5	**10.0**	12.3	22.5
WALKER STATE BK	Walker	IA	**B-**	B-	B-	41.0	-0.32	5.2	2.4	10.5	32.9	**6.9**	8.9	13.5
WALLIS STATE BK	Wallis	TX	**B**	B-	C+	394.4	0.44	8.1	0.6	2.2	2.2	**8.2**	10.3	13.5
▲ WALLKILL VALLEY FS&LA	Wallkill	NY	**C**	C	C+	170.4	1.59	1.7	1.8	50.4	9.6	**10.0**	16.3	24.7
WALPOLE CO-OP BANK	Walpole	MA	**B**	B-	B-	404.3	-3.54	5.1	0.0	16.8	13.4	**10.0**	19.6	25.1
WALTERS BANK & TRUST CO	Walters	OK	**B+**	B+	A-	56.3	1.06	3.9	5.0	19.0	38.1	**10.0**	21.6	62.8
WALTON STATE BK	Walton	KS	**E**	E+	D-	8.9	-0.96	2.1	8.8	18.1	48.8	**5.5**	7.5	16.6
▲ WALWORTH STATE BK	Walworth	WI	**B-**	C	C	242.7	-0.61	4.5	3.0	28.1	16.4	**10.0**	11.0	17.9
▼ WANDA STATE BK	Wanda	MN	**B**	B+	B+	127.6	-1.57	0.9	0.7	3.0	39.0	**10.0**	14.3	22.7
WAREHOUSE TRUST CO LLC	New York	NY	**U**	U	U	12.1	-12.91	0.0	0.0	0.0	0.0	**10.0**	53.8	162.0
WARREN BANK & TRUST CO	Warren	AR	**A-**	A-	A-	135.4	-0.94	1.7	3.7	16.0	63.5	**10.0**	15.4	30.9
WARREN-BOYNTON STATE BK	New Berlin	IL	**A**	A	A	127.9	2.58	5.1	2.2	15.0	24.5	**10.0**	14.4	21.6
WARRINGTON BANK	Pensacola	FL	**C-**	C-	C+	85.2	5.00	0.0	0.5	2.2	55.1	**10.0**	17.9	44.0
▼ WARSAW FS&LA	Cincinnati	OH	**D+**	C	B-	68.6	2.32	0.0	0.2	71.6	1.7	**10.0**	13.1	24.5
▲ WASHINGTON BUSINESS BANK	Olympia	WA	**B-**	C-	D+	66.8	9.59	37.5	0.3	2.1	3.3	**10.0**	12.4	16.7
WASHINGTON COUNTY BANK	Blair	NE	**B**	B-	C+	341.3	5.24	6.0	1.7	7.1	19.8	**6.2**	8.2	12.0
WASHINGTON FEDERAL BK FOR SVGS	Chicago	IL	**A**	A	B	132.1	5.16	0.0	0.0	76.3	0.0	**10.0**	11.2	22.0
WASHINGTON FEDERAL NA	Seattle	WA	**B**	B	B-	14758.0	12.79	1.8	0.9	37.7	30.8	**10.0**	11.5	24.1
WASHINGTON FINANCIAL BANK	Washington	PA	**C+**	C+	B-	1051.6	6.98	4.2	8.0	30.9	25.1	**9.6**	10.7	17.6
WASHINGTON SAVINGS BANK	Philadelphia	PA	**D**	D+	D+	161.7	-0.97	1.3	1.1	59.6	11.1	**6.1**	8.1	13.7
WASHINGTON SB	Lowell	MA	**C-**	C-	C-	192.1	0.37	0.7	0.1	47.4	23.0	**7.2**	9.1	14.1

Asset Quality Index	Adjusted Non-Performing Loans as a % of Total Loans	Adjusted Non-Performing Loans as a % of Capital	Net Charge-Offs Avg Loans	Profitability Index	Net Income ($Mil)	Return on Assets (R.O.A.)	Return on Equity (R.O.E.)	Net Interest Spread	Overhead Efficiency Ratio	Liquidity Index	Liquidity Ratio	Hot Money Ratio	Stability Index
6.1	0.71	5.1	0.04	**6.1**	28.2	1.04	8.32	3.94	57.2	**2.5**	8.4	15.8	**7.0**
3.0	2.28	14.5	-0.10	**8.3**	2.3	1.95	10.77	3.76	50.0	**2.3**	16.0	17.8	**9.1**
6.2	0.55	4.1	-0.01	**5.6**	0.8	1.39	15.72	3.82	60.8	**3.5**	13.6	11.5	**4.5**
5.6	1.72	10.8	-0.01	**3.6**	3.4	0.58	4.90	3.21	72.3	**2.5**	19.1	16.8	**7.1**
0.3	8.15	63.1	0.79	**0.5**	-0.4	-0.13	-1.99	3.50	101.9	**1.8**	20.1	22.0	**1.3**
5.0	2.46	14.1	0.01	**3.5**	0.5	0.76	8.09	3.03	75.6	**4.8**	36.2	9.5	**5.4**
0.1	5.74	40.0	-0.46	**6.6**	2.0	1.60	20.59	4.65	70.7	**3.4**	22.1	12.9	**3.0**
3.4	1.22	9.7	0.40	**4.6**	5.5	0.72	6.03	3.34	54.9	**1.5**	11.3	23.9	**7.0**
6.7	1.86	6.3	-0.02	**6.3**	2.5	1.42	11.70	4.07	58.2	**3.0**	38.0	19.2	**5.7**
3.7	2.17	14.3	0.03	**9.1**	2.6	2.02	21.34	4.69	60.4	**2.3**	25.4	18.5	**6.3**
7.1	0.00	0.0	0.00	**3.1**	0.2	0.61	5.26	4.03	74.7	**4.0**	30.8	12.2	**5.1**
5.3	1.32	7.1	0.16	**5.2**	5.6	0.99	8.05	3.84	65.0	**2.7**	21.4	16.1	**6.7**
5.9	1.23	6.0	-0.08	**6.0**	1.4	1.08	7.84	4.22	67.3	**4.5**	25.3	7.0	**7.0**
4.3	3.20	15.0	0.36	**2.9**	0.8	0.43	4.09	3.46	86.6	**4.1**	39.2	14.1	**4.6**
1.7	5.86	31.3	1.00	**1.3**	0.0	0.01	0.06	4.13	92.5	**4.2**	29.8	10.6	**4.2**
5.7	0.39	2.9	-0.09	**0.2**	-0.5	-0.51	-5.32	3.95	116.7	**1.9**	13.1	19.5	**4.4**
7.8	0.36	1.9	0.07	**4.5**	1.5	0.38	3.83	3.08	87.5	**2.7**	36.0	20.2	**7.4**
4.5	0.81	6.6	-0.05	**3.0**	0.8	0.41	4.86	3.45	79.1	**0.9**	21.6	36.9	**4.6**
6.1	0.58	3.7	0.00	**3.5**	0.9	0.69	7.35	3.42	65.1	**3.1**	33.4	17.5	**4.3**
5.4	0.93	5.6	0.15	**4.3**	4.7	0.96	10.92	3.90	73.4	**1.9**	14.9	19.4	**5.7**
2.4	2.79	21.6	0.00	**4.3**	0.5	0.67	7.00	3.75	73.1	**2.1**	13.0	18.3	**5.6**
1.2	3.25	26.1	0.03	**3.9**	0.5	0.48	4.94	4.13	73.3	**3.0**	9.0	13.3	**4.6**
5.8	1.45	9.1	0.21	**3.9**	0.2	0.72	5.92	4.18	76.0	**1.0**	24.2	37.3	**4.3**
2.9	2.10	12.7	-0.08	**4.7**	3.5	1.17	10.57	3.52	70.4	**2.1**	20.9	19.0	**4.9**
4.6	0.82	6.5	0.19	**4.0**	6.5	0.67	5.55	4.11	71.1	**2.9**	3.9	13.6	**6.9**
4.1	1.41	11.0	0.19	**3.6**	1.3	0.63	6.72	4.26	79.0	**2.2**	22.4	18.5	**4.3**
2.0	1.65	13.1	0.45	**1.7**	0.1	0.18	2.20	3.73	89.6	**1.9**	18.3	19.9	**2.7**
10.0	na	0.0	na	**3.5**	-0.3	-3.20	-3.60	0.27	132.2	**4.0**	1914.5	101.0	**5.9**
4.8	2.72	14.1	0.17	**3.7**	0.7	0.51	3.70	3.79	80.0	**2.3**	21.5	18.3	**7.1**
4.1	1.11	8.9	0.03	**8.6**	5.7	1.77	17.54	4.48	74.1	**1.9**	6.2	18.7	**6.7**
3.1	1.39	10.5	0.39	**2.9**	1.0	0.38	4.69	3.96	91.9	**2.7**	19.4	16.2	**3.2**
6.8	1.92	5.5	0.40	**1.4**	0.0	0.02	0.21	3.24	99.0	**4.4**	64.4	15.4	**5.1**
7.9	0.83	3.7	-0.14	**6.2**	1.3	1.42	11.69	4.39	62.4	**5.8**	48.5	7.8	**7.1**
8.3	0.22	0.8	0.05	**9.8**	5.4	2.61	20.49	4.34	48.2	**3.1**	25.1	14.4	**9.5**
7.9	0.15	1.1	0.13	**3.5**	0.3	0.66	8.68	3.84	80.8	**4.9**	28.4	5.7	**3.4**
8.4	0.80	2.2	0.18	**4.5**	0.7	0.77	3.96	2.72	51.5	**2.4**	47.8	36.6	**7.6**
5.9	1.17	9.5	0.01	**2.2**	0.5	0.36	4.40	2.85	93.3	**2.4**	31.5	20.5	**4.3**
6.4	1.84	6.1	0.01	**7.1**	1.0	1.31	7.11	3.75	54.2	**4.8**	39.8	10.8	**7.6**
2.2	4.22	29.0	0.33	**3.5**	1.6	0.48	5.30	3.54	84.4	**4.7**	24.9	5.1	**4.7**
4.9	2.26	10.5	0.66	**5.5**	0.5	0.98	8.06	3.97	53.8	**3.3**	36.8	17.2	**6.2**
4.7	1.42	7.9	0.02	**5.8**	0.4	1.19	13.39	3.74	54.7	**3.5**	35.4	15.7	**4.9**
4.8	0.48	3.1	-0.02	**9.1**	7.1	2.39	23.67	4.40	61.3	**2.1**	23.2	19.4	**6.9**
2.6	5.22	24.3	0.37	**2.4**	0.4	0.33	1.80	3.98	80.3	**2.3**	16.8	17.6	**5.7**
4.9	1.34	5.3	-0.04	**5.1**	2.5	0.80	4.26	3.66	62.7	**2.1**	17.4	18.9	**7.2**
9.0	0.34	0.6	0.35	**4.0**	0.4	0.97	4.47	3.47	74.9	**5.0**	55.0	12.6	**7.4**
3.1	1.69	9.2	0.07	**2.1**	0.0	0.18	2.59	3.24	94.4	**3.8**	24.8	10.5	**1.0**
4.6	2.03	11.4	0.40	**6.6**	3.0	1.67	15.00	3.80	59.7	**2.7**	29.3	17.9	**6.1**
8.8	0.01	0.0	-0.05	**3.9**	0.6	0.59	4.33	3.20	65.2	**4.3**	53.1	16.8	**8.0**
10.0	na	0.0	na	**3.5**	-0.2	-1.69	-1.82	na	101.1	**4.0**	121.5	101.0	**4.9**
8.7	1.70	3.3	-1.23	**6.1**	1.7	1.60	11.48	3.17	68.8	**3.8**	63.2	24.3	**7.8**
8.5	0.26	1.2	0.14	**7.7**	1.3	1.30	9.21	4.02	53.5	**2.1**	14.4	18.5	**8.3**
10.0	1.19	2.2	0.00	**2.0**	0.1	0.23	1.26	2.51	87.8	**6.5**	77.6	7.8	**5.4**
6.5	1.60	9.5	0.00	**0.5**	-0.8	-1.66	-11.86	3.89	146.3	**1.8**	15.6	20.2	**6.1**
3.8	1.18	7.5	0.11	**6.2**	0.6	1.29	10.96	5.15	67.1	**0.9**	13.1	33.6	**5.0**
8.0	0.10	0.8	0.02	**6.0**	2.6	1.06	12.30	3.37	61.5	**4.0**	9.1	8.1	**6.1**
9.8	0.00	0.0	0.00	**9.7**	1.5	1.52	13.98	4.82	44.6	**0.6**	11.2	45.3	**6.9**
5.0	1.91	9.1	-0.13	**6.0**	117.3	1.07	7.96	3.09	47.6	**3.4**	39.7	22.0	**7.0**
7.6	0.55	3.3	0.01	**3.8**	5.3	0.71	6.62	3.04	68.4	**3.9**	17.0	10.1	**5.8**
6.9	0.49	4.4	0.02	**0.7**	-0.2	-0.15	-1.84	2.97	106.2	**2.4**	11.6	16.9	**3.8**
4.9	1.86	13.2	0.12	**1.8**	0.3	0.20	2.04	2.82	93.5	**2.3**	29.3	20.2	**4.9**

Name	City	State	Rating	2013 Rating	2012 Rating	Total Assets ($Mil)	One Year Asset Growth	Asset Mix (As a % of Total Assets) Comm-ercial Loans	Cons-umer Loans	Mort-gage Loans	Secur-ities	Capital-ization Index	Lever-age Ratio	Risk-Based Capital Ratio
WASHINGTON SB	Effingham	IL	**C+**	C+	C+	263.6	2.41	6.5	3.2	35.2	25.3	**10.0**	11.2	19.7
WASHINGTON STATE BK	Washington	IA	**A-**	A-	A	241.5	2.03	7.4	1.3	25.3	30.4	**10.0**	14.2	24.8
WASHINGTON STATE BK	Washington	IL	**B-**	B-	B-	58.6	4.75	2.9	6.5	25.6	52.6	**8.3**	9.9	25.1
WASHINGTON STATE BK	Washington	LA	**B-**	B-	C-	168.0	19.84	15.8	1.9	7.8	23.7	**8.7**	10.1	15.5
WASHINGTON TRUST BANK	Spokane	WA	**B**	B	B-	4711.8	6.54	18.3	2.4	7.7	15.7	**8.7**	10.3	13.9
WASHINGTON TRUST CO WESTERLY	Westerly	RI	**B**	B	B	3413.3	9.05	4.8	1.5	29.2	11.9	**7.3**	9.2	13.1
WASHINGTONFIRST BANK	Reston	VA	**C+**	C+	C	1334.4	18.84	9.3	1.0	8.1	12.8	**4.8**	8.3	10.9
▲ WASHITA STATE BK	Burns Flat	OK	**B**	C+	C+	126.0	3.25	13.3	0.4	2.4	15.9	**10.0**	12.6	28.8
WASHITA VALLEY BANK	Fort Cobb	OK	**B+**	B+	A-	41.2	3.86	3.1	11.1	1.5	42.5	**10.0**	16.4	23.9
WATERFORD BANK NA	Toledo	OH	**B+**	B+	B	481.6	6.07	21.4	0.4	4.2	13.5	**7.9**	10.1	13.2
WATERFORD COMMERCIAL & SB	Waterford	OH	**B-**	C+	B-	44.9	-7.14	1.1	6.4	28.4	45.0	**10.0**	11.2	25.6
WATERMAN STATE BK	Waterman	IL	**D-**	D-	D-	43.6	2.26	7.7	1.1	7.7	40.6	**7.5**	9.3	15.3
▲ WATERSTONE BANK SSB	Wauwatosa	WI	**B**	C	C-	1792.9	12.82	1.2	0.0	31.4	15.2	**10.0**	19.1	31.2
WATERTOWN SB	Watertown	MA	**C+**	C+	B-	1100.2	0.11	0.4	0.3	35.2	42.4	**8.0**	9.7	22.2
WATERTOWN SB	Watertown	NY	**C+**	C	C	552.4	6.97	5.7	1.4	15.3	20.3	**9.2**	12.0	14.3
WATKINS SAVINGS BANK	Watkins	IA	**A-**	A-	A-	69.3	-1.00	1.4	1.5	6.9	54.1	**10.0**	14.2	25.6
WAUCHULA STATE BK	Wauchula	FL	**D+**	D+	C-	586.2	2.42	2.4	1.2	18.6	24.5	**9.8**	10.9	17.4
WAUKESHA STATE BK	Waukesha	WI	**B-**	B	B	864.5	3.18	7.4	1.7	10.0	28.5	**10.0**	12.5	17.9
WAUKON STATE BK	Waukon	IA	**A+**	A+	A	252.5	5.98	11.6	2.2	14.8	18.3	**10.0**	13.4	18.2
WAUMANDEE STATE BK	Waumandee	WI	**C+**	C	C-	161.3	0.09	31.8	3.7	16.1	12.6	**8.1**	9.8	13.8
WAWEL BANK	Garfield	NJ	**D**	D	C-	76.7	-14.82	0.1	0.2	32.6	21.5	**10.0**	11.8	17.9
WAYCROSS BANK & TRUST	Waycross	GA	**B-**	C+	B-	202.8	3.49	6.8	0.8	15.7	20.8	**7.2**	9.1	14.4
WAYLAND STATE BK	Mount Pleasant	IA	**A**	A	A	80.6	0.23	10.7	2.5	14.8	27.4	**10.0**	18.9	29.7
WAYNE BANK	Honesdale	PA	**B**	B	B	716.8	2.07	3.4	2.5	22.9	22.1	**10.0**	11.9	17.3
▲ WAYNE BANK & TRUST CO	Cambridge City	IN	**C+**	D+	C-	129.0	-14.76	2.7	3.2	20.2	14.4	**10.0**	12.9	19.4
WAYNE COUNTY BANK	Waynesboro	TN	**C-**	D+	C-	306.8	-1.31	10.3	9.9	20.0	5.7	**10.0**	11.5	16.2
WAYNE SAVINGS COMMUNITY BANK	Wooster	OH	**C+**	C+	C	414.0	3.48	3.6	0.3	37.0	27.6	**6.8**	8.8	15.4
WCF FINANCIAL BANK	Webster City	IA	**C+**	B-	B-	109.2	19.36	0.2	1.9	45.7	37.7	**10.0**	12.5	30.4
WEBBANK	Salt Lake City	UT	**A**	B+	B	200.6	44.22	41.9	12.5	0.0	0.3	**10.0**	20.2	27.4
WEBSTER BANK NA	Waterbury	CT	**B-**	B-	C+	21814.0	6.03	17.4	0.5	18.8	30.1	**6.3**	8.3	13.1
WEBSTER FIVE CENTS SB	Webster	MA	**B**	B	B-	623.0	12.76	4.2	6.0	30.2	22.4	**10.0**	13.0	19.7
WELCH STATE BK OF WELCH OKLA	Welch	OK	**A**	A	A-	223.2	2.25	4.7	3.5	15.2	24.4	**10.0**	12.7	17.6
▲ WELCOME STATE BK	Welcome	MN	**B+**	B	B-	25.9	2.28	10.3	6.7	5.9	8.5	**8.7**	10.2	15.7
WELLESLEY BANK	Wellesley	MA	**B-**	B-	C+	504.3	20.12	3.8	0.1	44.9	8.4	**6.8**	8.8	13.1
WELLINGTON STATE BK	Wellington	TX	**B-**	B-	C+	248.1	4.64	10.2	4.3	5.4	36.0	**6.4**	8.4	14.9
WELLINGTON TRUST CO NA	Boston	MA	**U**	U	U	90.1	4.64	0.0	0.0	0.0	0.0	**10.0**	36.0	35.3
WELLS BANK OF PLATTE CITY	Platte City	MO	**A-**	A-	B+	114.9	13.06	3.5	0.7	26.6	20.7	**6.8**	8.8	13.1
WELLS FARGO BANK LTD	Los Angeles	CA	**U**	U	B-	597.4	27.59	0.0	0.0	0.0	0.0	**10.0**	70.6	177.9
WELLS FARGO BANK NA	Sioux Falls	SD	**C-**	C-	C+	1482815.0	11.66	10.6	7.7	17.0	17.5	**6.3**	8.3	12.9
WELLS FARGO BANK NORTHWEST NA	Salt Lake City	UT	**C+**	C+	B-	8683.2	-39.73	0.0	0.0	0.0	11.8	**10.0**	11.0	72.3
▼ WELLS FARGO BANK SOUTH CENTRAL	Houston	TX	**D+**	C-	C+	9371.0	-70.99	0.0	0.1	90.4	0.0	**3.6**	5.6	19.7
WELLS FARGO DELAWARE TR CO NA	Wilmington	DE	**U**	U	B-	371.4	2.02	0.0	0.0	0.0	0.0	**10.0**	94.9	467.0
▲ WELLS FARGO FINANCIAL NATIONAL	Las Vegas	NV	**C+**	C	C-	6233.3	13.25	0.0	95.9	0.0	6.1	**10.0**	15.2	16.4
WELLS FEDERAL BANK	Wells	MN	**C+**	C+	C	251.1	3.11	2.4	3.1	26.4	15.2	**8.6**	10.0	14.8
WELLS RIVER SB	Wells River	VT	**C+**	C	C+	163.5	1.62	6.2	1.8	35.8	29.1	**10.0**	12.0	21.3
WENONA STATE BK	Wenona	IL	**C+**	C+	C	32.5	-7.95	9.2	3.9	7.4	39.9	**10.0**	13.9	24.7
WESBANCO BANK INC	Wheeling	WV	**B-**	B-	C+	6261.3	2.24	6.6	3.3	16.8	25.1	**6.7**	8.7	13.3
▲ WEST ALABAMA BANK & TRUST	Reform	AL	**B+**	B	C	563.1	4.08	7.1	1.9	10.0	34.2	**10.0**	11.5	18.8
WEST BANK	West Des Moines	IA	**A-**	A-	A-	1507.9	3.46	19.0	0.2	3.8	22.3	**7.7**	9.9	13.1
WEST CENTRAL BANK	Ashland	IL	**C+**	C+	B	199.9	22.92	9.1	5.9	19.2	20.9	**5.1**	7.3	11.0
WEST CENTRAL GEORGIA BANK	Thomaston	GA	**A**	A	A+	108.3	-2.49	4.5	6.2	20.5	45.5	**10.0**	24.3	49.2
WEST END BANK SB	Richmond	IN	**C**	B-	C+	257.6	1.97	4.1	27.3	24.2	18.3	**9.6**	10.8	16.1
WEST GATE BANK	Lincoln	NE	**B**	C+	B-	379.8	1.95	9.3	0.3	12.1	17.7	**7.9**	10.1	13.3
WEST IOWA BANK	West Bend	IA	**B+**	B+	B	119.7	2.04	5.4	1.6	8.9	30.1	**8.1**	9.7	14.5
WEST LIBERTY STATE BK	West Liberty	IA	**C+**	C+	C+	82.3	-0.16	2.6	2.2	11.3	63.4	**10.0**	11.0	27.5
WEST MICHIGAN BANK & TRUST	Frankfort	MI	**C-**	C	B-	46.7	9.48	1.3	0.4	8.5	60.7	**10.0**	16.6	49.7
▲ WEST MICHIGAN COMMUNITY BANK	Hudsonville	MI	**D+**	D-	D-	232.0	24.15	24.4	1.5	9.3	10.3	**5.2**	8.6	11.2
WEST MICHIGAN SB	Bangor	MI	**D-**	D	C-	35.3	-9.69	2.9	1.7	24.4	51.0	**7.1**	9.1	22.8
WEST MILTON STATE BK	West Milton	PA	**A-**	A-	B+	353.4	5.96	3.6	3.0	9.9	51.5	**7.4**	9.3	17.4
WEST ONE BANK	Kalispell	MT	**B-**	C+	C	39.9	6.47	9.1	9.3	23.7	0.0	**10.0**	15.6	24.2

Asset Quality Index	Adjusted Non-Performing Loans as a % of Total Loans	Adjusted Non-Performing Loans as a % of Capital	Net Charge-Offs / Avg Loans	Profitability Index	Net Income ($Mil)	Return on Assets (R.O.A.)	Return on Equity (R.O.E.)	Net Interest Spread	Overhead Efficiency Ratio	Liquidity Index	Liquidity Ratio	Hot Money Ratio	Stability Index
6.1	1.23	6.9	0.06	**3.2**	1.0	0.48	4.22	2.61	73.5	**3.3**	31.1	15.5	**6.6**
6.6	1.60	6.5	0.18	**6.5**	2.2	1.24	9.01	3.29	47.2	**3.8**	37.3	15.0	**7.8**
7.7	1.19	4.8	0.01	**4.4**	0.4	0.80	8.45	3.02	59.6	**4.3**	42.1	14.0	**4.9**
7.0	0.00	0.0	0.95	**4.2**	1.0	0.84	8.17	3.62	77.8	**2.6**	30.2	18.8	**5.7**
5.6	1.15	6.9	0.28	**5.2**	31.9	0.95	9.65	3.60	64.2	**4.8**	20.9	5.3	**8.0**
5.2	0.84	6.9	0.08	**6.9**	30.2	1.24	11.29	3.36	61.7	**1.7**	3.8	19.6	**9.2**
3.8	0.94	8.3	0.26	**4.6**	8.2	0.88	10.03	3.87	63.1	**1.6**	16.6	24.0	**6.0**
6.0	0.42	1.2	0.06	**4.3**	1.2	1.24	10.37	2.57	45.3	**2.3**	49.4	54.7	**6.6**
8.1	1.09	2.7	-0.01	**7.6**	0.5	1.45	9.20	5.19	58.7	**3.9**	57.7	18.5	**8.3**
7.8	0.30	2.1	0.02	**5.5**	3.3	0.92	9.38	3.64	63.5	**2.0**	20.0	19.5	**6.1**
9.0	0.65	2.4	0.34	**4.1**	0.3	0.75	7.78	3.74	75.1	**4.3**	42.1	14.1	**4.7**
2.9	3.16	15.8	3.56	**0.0**	-0.1	-0.38	-4.17	3.43	92.1	**1.6**	28.6	29.5	**1.8**
4.0	3.83	13.3	0.51	**4.4**	10.2	0.76	4.33	2.59	82.2	**2.2**	21.7	19.9	**7.8**
8.4	0.85	4.1	-0.01	**3.1**	3.9	0.48	5.09	2.71	76.7	**5.6**	50.5	12.1	**6.7**
3.6	1.71	8.5	0.02	**6.0**	4.1	1.01	7.21	3.54	59.6	**4.6**	17.0	4.7	**8.5**
9.1	0.08	0.2	0.00	**5.9**	0.7	1.29	8.77	3.53	50.8	**4.3**	62.5	17.5	**8.4**
1.8	5.55	29.5	1.23	**6.8**	7.5	1.69	16.33	4.46	53.7	**1.4**	24.4	28.5	**5.8**
8.2	0.83	3.4	0.10	**3.9**	5.9	0.93	7.58	3.34	76.6	**6.0**	39.2	3.3	**7.2**
8.4	0.36	1.9	-0.04	**9.4**	3.7	2.07	15.29	4.16	45.0	**4.4**	30.3	9.5	**8.3**
3.5	1.72	12.3	0.24	**5.5**	1.1	0.94	8.63	4.17	66.3	**1.8**	18.4	21.1	**6.7**
0.3	16.46	66.0	-0.33	**0.0**	-0.7	-1.18	-7.27	3.83	138.4	**3.2**	28.4	15.3	**4.7**
4.8	1.75	11.7	-0.05	**3.1**	0.8	0.56	6.36	3.55	79.5	**1.7**	19.6	22.4	**5.1**
8.8	0.00	0.0	-0.01	**7.4**	0.8	1.31	7.07	3.51	46.4	**5.5**	46.4	7.8	**8.3**
5.0	1.35	7.6	0.35	**5.9**	6.3	1.19	9.23	3.93	58.2	**3.3**	12.6	12.4	**8.4**
2.9	3.87	18.6	0.92	**4.2**	1.0	1.04	8.41	4.58	72.2	**5.0**	25.5	3.6	**4.9**
1.2	5.90	32.8	2.36	**3.1**	0.9	0.37	3.19	4.41	58.0	**0.8**	18.4	44.3	**5.8**
4.3	2.54	17.1	0.19	**3.5**	2.1	0.68	7.37	3.40	71.5	**2.6**	18.0	16.4	**5.1**
8.8	0.86	3.4	0.22	**3.0**	0.4	0.48	4.17	3.03	79.0	**4.4**	51.3	16.0	**6.3**
7.9	0.36	1.1	-0.22	**10.0**	9.7	7.37	38.13	11.91	32.7	**2.3**	49.7	54.1	**8.0**
4.3	1.86	13.3	0.24	**5.4**	159.1	1.00	9.63	3.29	58.4	**4.3**	20.3	8.1	**8.2**
5.2	1.57	8.3	0.05	**4.2**	3.6	0.84	5.91	3.98	72.5	**4.4**	20.5	6.9	**7.0**
8.0	0.70	3.5	-0.11	**8.0**	3.2	1.94	15.67	5.19	61.8	**1.1**	20.8	32.4	**8.9**
7.1	0.17	1.0	-0.05	**8.6**	0.4	2.22	22.28	4.21	52.9	**4.7**	28.8	6.8	**7.0**
4.7	1.23	11.1	0.04	**3.6**	1.8	0.51	5.81	3.40	71.8	**1.0**	11.7	30.8	**4.6**
7.3	0.44	2.4	0.01	**4.1**	1.5	0.81	9.59	3.65	71.3	**3.9**	31.4	12.6	**4.4**
10.0	na	0.0	na	**10.0**	4.2	6.40	18.63	0.00	97.3	**4.0**	0.0	101.0	**7.0**
8.9	0.06	0.4	-0.01	**10.0**	2.0	2.35	26.09	4.55	49.1	**1.7**	11.5	20.7	**6.9**
6.5	na	0.0	na	**10.0**	42.9	11.03	14.27	0.25	79.0	**5.6**	218.7	33.6	**5.0**
2.7	2.75	17.4	0.29	**8.4**	14741.0	1.41	14.11	3.13	55.6	**5.6**	35.1	7.5	**8.2**
8.1	0.81	0.0	2.65	**10.0**	504.7	4.66	41.84	5.81	5.9	**8.3**	112.6	3.2	**5.7**
0.3	13.76	85.0	0.14	**9.2**	308.4	1.54	13.36	2.27	11.5	**5.2**	10.8	0.3	**7.6**
10.0	na	0.0	na	**9.3**	4.6	1.66	1.76	0.41	25.3	**4.0**	1667.4	101.0	**5.0**
3.5	0.98	5.4	2.39	**10.0**	201.0	4.64	30.89	12.08	21.7	**5.1**	1.9	0.0	**7.6**
4.6	1.53	10.3	0.08	**3.7**	0.9	0.50	4.94	3.61	79.8	**4.2**	16.6	7.8	**5.6**
5.7	2.55	11.6	0.42	**3.1**	0.7	0.58	4.80	4.56	88.3	**5.6**	43.2	7.0	**6.0**
3.5	6.06	19.8	-0.06	**3.1**	0.2	0.60	4.41	3.58	85.6	**5.8**	39.1	4.0	**5.6**
4.4	1.08	7.7	0.24	**5.9**	54.6	1.17	8.86	3.69	59.0	**2.9**	16.8	15.0	**9.1**
6.2	1.42	6.3	0.17	**5.2**	4.7	1.13	9.70	3.51	60.6	**2.0**	32.9	27.6	**6.7**
8.4	0.20	1.3	0.09	**7.7**	15.2	1.37	13.99	3.68	50.1	**5.0**	26.9	8.2	**8.3**
4.2	0.74	6.7	0.10	**3.5**	0.8	0.56	6.74	3.52	84.9	**1.7**	27.8	28.0	**4.8**
8.9	0.15	0.3	0.24	**6.7**	1.0	1.14	4.86	4.55	61.6	**3.8**	45.7	17.3	**8.8**
2.5	1.93	12.2	0.96	**3.7**	1.2	0.60	5.58	4.25	67.7	**1.6**	22.9	24.8	**4.7**
5.3	0.55	3.5	0.24	**5.3**	3.0	1.03	10.40	3.77	87.3	**4.0**	22.5	9.6	**7.8**
5.8	0.70	4.0	-0.16	**6.9**	1.2	1.23	12.87	3.71	52.0	**4.6**	32.8	9.8	**7.4**
8.2	0.66	1.8	0.12	**2.7**	0.3	0.55	4.30	2.74	78.5	**3.3**	57.5	24.8	**5.1**
9.9	0.00	0.0	0.09	**1.1**	0.0	-0.09	-0.62	2.40	103.4	**6.2**	88.0	11.4	**7.1**
5.3	0.64	5.5	-0.02	**1.3**	0.4	0.22	2.54	3.78	89.9	**3.9**	17.3	9.5	**2.2**
4.0	3.92	14.4	0.46	**0.0**	-0.3	-1.16	-12.08	3.46	136.0	**6.2**	67.2	8.1	**2.4**
9.2	0.05	0.2	0.00	**6.7**	3.4	1.32	13.05	3.70	57.5	**5.4**	40.5	7.8	**6.4**
8.0	0.00	0.0	-0.68	**8.0**	0.5	1.69	10.89	4.62	68.9	**1.6**	18.2	24.6	**5.3**

	Name	City	State	Rating	2013 Rating	2012 Rating	Total Assets ($Mil)	One Year Asset Growth	Asset Mix (As a % of Total Assets) Commercial Loans	Consumer Loans	Mortgage Loans	Securities	Capitalization Index	Leverage Ratio	Risk-Based Capital Ratio
▲	WEST PLAINS BANK	Ainsworth	NE	**B+**	B	A-	98.6	3.57	15.4	2.0	0.1	28.3	**8.5**	11.8	13.8
	WEST PLAINS BANK & TRUST CO	West Plains	MO	**A-**	A-	B+	325.2	3.76	6.7	2.1	16.3	32.0	**8.8**	10.2	16.9
	WEST PLAINS S&LA	West Plains	MO	**B**	B	B	90.0	-0.86	0.0	0.4	55.9	25.7	**10.0**	16.5	41.4
	WEST POINT BANK	Radcliff	KY	**B+**	B+	B-	156.5	-3.90	0.6	1.5	29.3	46.1	**8.8**	10.2	26.5
	WEST POINTE BANK	Oshkosh	WI	**C-**	D	C-	273.6	-7.46	13.2	0.3	21.4	14.2	**10.0**	17.3	23.2
	WEST SHORE BANK	Ludington	MI	**C+**	C+	C	388.8	-1.58	6.9	5.8	20.8	27.4	**6.6**	8.6	15.1
	WEST SUBURBAN BANK	Lombard	IL	**C**	C-	C-	2108.9	4.57	12.8	0.4	9.1	41.6	**6.5**	8.5	14.4
▲	WEST TEXAS NATIONAL BK	Midland	TX	**A-**	B+	B	1013.0	17.85	22.7	3.0	5.4	38.4	**6.8**	8.8	13.8
▲	WEST TEXAS STATE BK	Snyder	TX	**B-**	C-	C	140.1	-1.25	14.0	4.1	7.5	37.2	**10.0**	11.9	19.4
	WEST TEXAS STATE BK	Odessa	TX	**B**	B	C	462.3	22.54	28.1	2.2	4.3	17.8	**8.0**	9.7	15.3
	WEST TOWN BANK & TRUST	Cicero	IL	**C-**	C	D+	173.6	22.55	9.6	0.7	34.2	3.4	**9.0**	11.0	14.1
	WEST UNION BANK	West Union	WV	**C+**	C+	C+	142.6	4.75	4.3	14.2	17.8	29.9	**7.6**	9.4	15.8
	WEST VALLEY NATIONAL BK	Goodyear	AZ	**D**	D	C	41.0	-4.18	19.0	0.1	5.0	6.5	**10.0**	17.7	25.1
	WEST VIEW SB	Pittsburgh	PA	**C+**	C+	C+	317.1	7.18	0.5	0.1	5.5	85.7	**8.0**	9.7	28.3
	WESTAMERICA BANK	San Rafael	CA	**B+**	B+	B	4952.8	3.91	5.5	7.7	3.3	49.1	**5.3**	7.3	14.0
▲	WESTBOUND BANK	Katy	TX	**B+**	B-	C+	146.6	6.11	15.4	0.9	2.4	6.6	**10.0**	16.4	23.2
	WESTBURY BANK	West Bend	WI	**D+**	C	D+	555.4	5.76	6.8	1.1	24.8	15.1	**10.0**	11.1	16.2
	WESTCHESTER BANK	Yonkers	NY	**B**	B	B-	462.9	10.71	30.0	1.0	2.4	9.7	**9.7**	11.5	14.7
	WESTERN ALLIANCE BANK	Phoenix	AZ	**B**	B-	C	10155.5	203.45	18.0	0.2	2.2	15.0	**5.4**	9.3	11.3
	WESTERN BANK	Coahoma	TX	**C**	C-	D+	184.3	6.93	10.1	1.9	12.0	36.0	**8.3**	9.8	16.2
	WESTERN BANK	Lordsburg	NM	**B**	B	B+	154.9	4.68	3.9	3.1	8.5	41.0	**10.0**	12.1	26.1
	WESTERN BANK	Alamogordo	NM	**B**	B	B-	68.1	0.82	1.3	1.7	15.2	30.2	**10.0**	14.5	28.6
	WESTERN BANK NA	Saint Paul	MN	**B**	B+	B+	533.1	20.17	10.4	1.2	3.6	46.8	**9.7**	10.8	17.9
	WESTERN BANK OF CLOVIS	Clovis	NM	**B+**	B+	A-	51.4	-3.79	12.4	1.9	4.6	30.5	**10.0**	13.5	19.2
	WESTERN BANK OF WOLF POINT	Wolf Point	MT	**B**	B	B	87.5	6.00	3.5	3.0	5.5	48.7	**7.2**	9.2	16.5
	WESTERN BK ARTESIA NEW MEXICO	Artesia	NM	**A-**	A-	A-	182.3	-7.38	23.5	2.5	0.9	37.4	**7.7**	9.5	16.7
	WESTERN COMMERCE BANK	Carlsbad	NM	**A-**	A-	A-	424.0	4.55	10.7	0.4	11.7	31.4	**6.0**	8.0	16.5
	WESTERN DAKOTA BANK	Timber Lake	SD	**C-**	D+	C	32.3	-5.22	1.8	2.7	0.5	7.2	**5.9**	7.9	21.2
	WESTERN HERITAGE BANK	Las Cruces	NM	**B-**	C+	D+	71.5	6.93	6.1	9.1	29.3	0.0	**10.0**	11.7	19.7
	WESTERN NATIONAL BK	Duluth	MN	**B-**	B	B-	115.1	-7.06	12.1	1.9	17.0	8.8	**7.1**	9.0	13.7
	WESTERN NATIONAL BK	Cass Lake	MN	**B-**	B	B	35.3	3.71	10.5	5.5	25.5	19.3	**6.4**	8.4	14.9
	WESTERN NATIONAL BK	Chester	NE	**C+**	C+	C+	70.2	85.94	5.6	1.9	18.1	1.1	**7.7**	9.6	13.0
	WESTERN NEBRASKA BANK	Curtis	NE	**C**	C+	B	69.4	0.77	17.4	2.1	0.5	14.0	**6.2**	9.5	11.9
	WESTERN STATE BK	Garden City	KS	**A-**	A-	B+	453.6	-1.07	9.0	0.3	9.1	20.9	**10.0**	11.7	17.1
	WESTERN STATE BK	Devils Lake	ND	**B**	B	B	727.5	12.56	32.1	2.1	10.6	6.2	**7.5**	10.0	12.9
▼	WESTFIELD BANK	Westfield	MA	**C+**	B-	B-	1309.2	3.18	12.4	0.1	18.6	37.5	**9.7**	10.8	17.7
	WESTFIELD BANK FSB	Westfield Center	OH	**C+**	C+	C	970.7	21.93	16.6	11.0	13.8	16.7	**7.4**	9.6	12.8
	WESTMORELAND FS&LA	Latrobe	PA	**B-**	B-	B-	171.0	-0.75	0.0	0.0	42.8	29.6	**10.0**	23.7	83.0
	WESTSIDE BANK	Hiram	GA	**E-**	E-	E-	115.8	-4.39	2.9	0.8	7.8	9.5	**0.8**	4.8	7.6
	WESTSIDE STATE BK	Westside	IA	**C+**	B	B-	86.8	13.12	10.7	2.2	19.3	6.2	**4.0**	7.7	10.5
▲	WESTSTAR BANK	El Paso	TX	**B+**	B	B+	1079.3	5.62	14.9	0.3	3.4	25.0	**7.0**	9.0	13.1
	WEX BANK	Midvale	UT	**A**	A	A	2339.5	31.65	70.7	0.0	0.0	0.8	**7.7**	11.6	13.1
	WEYMOUTH BANK	East Weymouth	MA	**C**	C	C	211.8	-2.56	4.1	3.2	35.0	24.0	**6.4**	8.4	16.2
	WHEATLAND BANK	Spokane	WA	**C**	C	C-	330.5	3.71	3.9	0.5	2.5	18.3	**6.9**	9.0	16.0
	WHEATON BANK & TRUST CO	Wheaton	IL	**B-**	C+	C	831.2	9.22	26.0	6.4	2.8	10.8	**6.1**	8.2	11.8
	WHEATON COLLEGE TRUST CO NA	Wheaton	IL	**U**	U	U	3.3	0.06	0.0	0.0	0.0	91.9	**10.0**	95.1	3523.
	WHEELER COUNTY STATE BK	Alamo	GA	**B**	B	B-	85.0	-2.55	11.4	6.8	18.8	12.3	**10.0**	13.9	22.0
	WHITAKER BANK INC	Lexington	KY	**D+**	C-	C+	1342.9	-3.94	3.3	2.8	18.8	38.6	**9.0**	10.3	20.1
	WHITE STATE BK	South English	IA	**B-**	B-	B+	35.6	-3.07	8.4	2.1	16.0	27.6	**10.0**	13.6	20.4
	WHITESVILLE STATE BK	Whitesville	WV	**C+**	B-	C+	91.3	6.44	3.0	21.5	28.0	24.4	**8.3**	9.8	15.4
	WHITNEY BANK	Gulfport	MS	**B**	B-	C+	19870.5	200.77	22.0	4.2	11.0	19.3	**6.9**	9.3	12.4
	WILBURTON STATE BK	Wilburton	OK	**C+**	C+	B-	67.0	0.91	9.3	6.7	13.0	20.9	**5.9**	7.9	17.1
	WILCOX COUNTY STATE BK	Abbeville	GA	**B-**	B-	C+	77.0	-4.48	3.7	6.0	34.3	15.9	**9.1**	10.4	18.5
	WILKINSON COUNTY BANK	Irwinton	GA	**B**	B	B	46.2	-5.04	8.3	5.3	29.4	31.2	**10.0**	15.4	31.6
	WILLAMETTE COMMUNITY BANK	Albany	OR	**C-**	C+	C+	103.9	20.94	12.5	1.2	4.6	21.8	**7.5**	9.3	13.7
	WILLAMETTE VALLEY BANK	Salem	OR	**B**	B	B-	121.0	-0.55	5.1	0.2	20.3	1.0	**10.0**	13.1	16.2
	WILLIAM PENN BANK	Levittown	PA	**A-**	B+	B+	315.3	0.25	0.0	0.4	53.7	5.8	**10.0**	18.5	30.4
▲	WILLIAMSTOWN BANK INC	Williamstown	WV	**B**	B+	B+	148.3	2.17	6.6	9.8	38.7	9.3	**10.0**	11.1	16.9
	WILLIAMSVILLE STATE BK & TRUST	Williamsville	IL	**C**	C-	C+	111.4	-3.30	3.7	3.5	32.5	45.7	**10.0**	11.9	26.6
▲	WILMINGTON SB	Wilmington	OH	**D+**	D	D	126.7	-10.44	1.4	2.2	47.0	12.6	**10.0**	19.5	35.9

Asset Quality Index	Adjusted Non-Performing Loans as a % of Total Loans	Adjusted Non-Performing Loans as a % of Capital	Net Charge-Offs Avg Loans	Profitability Index	Net Income ($Mil)	Return on Assets (R.O.A.)	Return on Equity (R.O.E.)	Net Interest Spread	Overhead Efficiency Ratio	Liquidity Index	Liquidity Ratio	Hot Money Ratio	Stability Index
8.2	0.04	0.2	0.05	5.5	0.8	1.03	8.59	3.61	58.2	4.1	23.0	8.9	7.0
7.1	0.85	4.6	0.02	7.9	4.3	1.78	17.65	3.67	55.8	3.0	19.6	14.2	7.4
7.8	2.03	7.1	0.01	4.1	0.5	0.74	4.53	2.76	58.6	2.1	44.4	35.2	7.9
6.2	2.06	7.4	0.06	4.5	1.0	0.85	8.98	3.20	63.2	4.4	24.0	7.4	6.8
1.9	7.17	29.7	0.19	7.2	2.7	1.31	7.69	3.93	48.1	0.7	18.1	57.4	6.6
4.3	1.57	10.4	0.28	3.8	2.0	0.70	8.18	3.79	74.2	2.7	22.0	16.3	4.5
4.3	3.43	18.1	0.02	3.2	8.0	0.51	6.16	3.11	75.8	6.5	42.6	4.0	5.7
8.3	0.23	1.4	0.25	8.0	12.6	1.77	18.46	3.55	52.3	5.9	43.5	8.4	6.8
4.2	3.21	13.6	0.40	8.1	2.2	2.00	17.89	4.05	53.1	4.5	42.4	12.9	8.6
8.8	0.00	0.0	-0.64	5.4	5.0	1.59	16.43	2.61	60.5	5.8	57.3	10.2	6.7
2.0	3.63	26.8	0.37	10.0	3.0	2.53	23.58	4.33	72.8	0.5	6.4	52.4	4.2
7.6	0.14	0.8	0.14	3.3	0.6	0.55	6.06	3.58	80.6	5.0	28.9	5.3	5.4
7.4	0.00	0.0	0.16	0.0	-0.7	-2.29	-11.86	4.75	149.8	3.1	27.7	15.3	4.4
9.3	1.49	1.5	0.00	2.9	0.8	0.35	3.66	1.58	67.5	6.6	52.1	3.5	5.2
6.0	1.22	5.5	0.19	6.9	46.2	1.26	12.26	3.41	55.9	6.6	48.9	5.7	9.3
8.4	0.00	0.0	-1.08	5.3	2.1	2.02	12.65	3.37	81.0	2.6	47.7	31.1	6.9
6.0	0.77	5.0	0.03	0.5	-1.2	-0.31	-2.45	3.48	111.6	4.2	18.9	7.5	3.2
6.6	0.00	0.0	0.00	4.7	2.8	0.83	7.15	3.65	57.5	4.3	12.2	6.6	6.7
5.1	1.13	8.7	-0.09	9.2	114.2	1.61	17.23	4.41	48.1	1.7	11.5	21.1	7.4
3.0	3.22	17.2	0.05	4.2	1.4	1.04	10.46	4.13	77.9	1.9	28.3	24.6	3.8
4.3	5.28	17.4	1.49	3.8	1.0	0.80	6.57	4.20	67.6	6.0	50.7	6.7	6.3
6.6	2.00	6.5	0.01	4.3	0.3	0.60	4.18	4.66	79.3	2.6	38.0	23.8	6.8
4.8	1.50	6.3	0.01	4.1	3.5	0.97	7.87	4.10	71.6	3.7	28.8	12.7	7.2
6.4	1.11	4.8	0.01	4.1	0.2	0.49	3.66	4.73	82.6	2.1	34.8	28.5	7.3
8.4	0.07	0.3	-0.01	5.5	0.9	1.34	14.16	4.01	62.6	3.9	44.4	16.4	6.6
7.9	0.34	1.5	0.28	8.8	2.8	2.04	23.71	3.61	43.0	5.0	56.3	14.2	6.7
9.0	0.25	1.3	0.00	7.4	5.3	1.67	21.19	4.02	56.7	4.3	42.2	14.0	6.8
9.4	0.00	0.0	-0.02	2.1	0.1	0.21	2.61	3.73	99.6	7.6	74.1	0.4	2.7
5.6	0.88	4.4	0.24	5.6	0.2	1.25	10.33	3.73	91.0	1.1	26.5	36.1	4.7
4.6	0.76	5.1	0.45	4.6	0.9	1.03	8.84	4.34	69.1	1.0	25.3	39.5	6.0
5.9	0.43	3.0	0.43	4.7	0.2	0.98	10.17	4.65	77.7	0.8	15.9	37.8	5.4
6.3	0.51	4.2	0.00	4.6	0.6	1.13	10.57	3.30	58.6	1.1	13.8	30.0	7.0
5.3	0.29	2.2	-0.18	4.7	0.5	0.93	8.54	4.40	65.2	1.2	7.1	27.4	5.7
5.6	1.89	9.7	0.08	6.0	4.8	1.42	12.29	3.68	57.1	3.1	21.4	13.9	8.2
4.4	1.11	8.4	0.23	9.6	8.3	1.54	15.98	5.35	53.6	2.1	13.0	18.4	6.6
6.6	1.23	5.9	0.21	3.1	5.2	0.54	4.89	2.63	70.3	2.3	14.1	18.0	8.6
3.5	1.31	9.7	0.04	3.9	4.2	0.67	5.94	3.51	73.2	3.5	18.0	12.0	6.3
9.6	1.35	2.4	0.00	3.0	0.5	0.37	1.59	1.86	70.0	6.6	72.6	8.2	7.9
0.0	16.74	171.0	0.40	1.6	0.4	0.41	8.53	3.99	87.2	1.1	18.5	31.5	0.0
4.6	0.57	5.9	0.00	6.1	0.9	1.38	16.09	4.26	63.3	1.7	7.4	19.9	6.5
5.9	0.75	5.3	0.08	9.4	17.0	2.17	24.28	4.29	54.0	4.0	29.4	14.6	9.2
7.6	0.34	2.4	1.28	10.0	125.6	8.86	77.81	20.01	45.4	1.3	25.9	73.8	8.4
5.9	0.62	4.5	0.02	2.7	0.5	0.30	3.66	3.14	87.0	2.5	32.3	20.5	4.0
4.3	2.38	11.9	0.04	2.9	1.0	0.41	4.59	3.25	84.0	6.6	50.5	3.1	5.1
4.6	0.36	2.9	0.54	4.1	4.6	0.73	6.45	3.02	64.0	1.5	9.6	23.6	6.2
10.0	na	0.0	na	6.1	0.0	1.13	1.20	0.17	94.2	4.0	4174.0	101.0	4.9
6.7	0.79	3.6	1.15	4.7	0.7	1.11	8.28	4.38	76.0	1.5	23.2	27.5	6.7
1.7	6.66	31.3	0.65	2.9	3.9	0.38	3.35	3.74	82.4	3.2	26.9	17.2	5.9
7.8	0.00	0.0	0.12	8.5	0.4	1.30	8.22	3.67	42.0	4.5	39.6	12.4	5.7
3.9	1.54	9.1	0.13	3.7	0.4	0.54	5.54	4.42	81.7	2.2	31.7	24.1	4.8
5.1	0.71	5.1	0.18	5.1	142.3	0.99	8.81	3.99	68.6	4.3	9.5	6.1	7.0
5.8	1.00	4.7	0.06	5.4	0.6	1.31	14.86	4.15	67.5	3.6	59.0	21.1	5.0
4.0	2.48	14.7	0.15	4.3	0.5	0.79	8.05	4.06	74.5	1.7	12.1	21.2	5.8
6.2	3.48	11.6	0.03	5.0	0.3	0.83	6.70	4.14	65.9	1.9	21.0	19.9	5.8
6.7	0.36	2.4	0.00	2.1	0.1	0.12	1.28	4.08	88.2	4.0	26.5	10.6	4.9
4.3	1.44	8.8	0.07	3.6	0.3	0.28	2.03	4.58	95.3	1.5	10.1	23.8	6.7
6.2	2.72	11.2	0.24	5.0	2.2	0.95	5.14	3.31	50.8	1.5	20.4	26.7	8.0
4.9	1.90	12.5	0.14	6.7	1.2	1.09	9.97	4.40	59.8	4.2	20.3	8.3	6.8
7.0	1.52	5.6	0.02	2.0	0.3	0.30	2.74	2.90	89.1	5.3	48.6	10.8	5.5
0.7	16.25	47.3	3.10	3.5	1.1	1.14	5.99	3.81	72.5	1.4	18.8	27.7	4.7

Name	City	State	Rating	2013 Rating	2012 Rating	Total Assets ($Mil)	One Year Asset Growth	Comm-ercial Loans	Cons-umer Loans	Mort-gage Loans	Secur-ities	Capital-ization Index	Lever-age Ratio	Risk-Based Capital Ratio
WILMINGTON SVGS FUND SOCIETY	Wilmington	DE	**B+**	B	C	4776.6	8.61	12.2	1.2	12.0	17.7	**9.6**	11.0	14.7
WILMINGTON TRUST NA	Wilmington	DE	**C+**	C+	B	2747.1	77.93	0.0	0.0	4.3	0.2	**10.0**	21.5	57.5
WILSHIRE BANK	Los Angeles	CA	**B-**	B-	B-	3932.0	39.09	10.9	0.3	4.3	9.3	**10.0**	12.2	15.1
WILSON & MUIR BANK & TRUST CO	Bardstown	KY	**B**	B	C+	424.0	3.66	10.8	2.5	15.8	29.6	**6.0**	8.0	14.6
WILSON BANK & TRUST	Lebanon	TN	**A-**	B+	B-	1827.7	6.23	1.4	1.8	19.9	20.1	**9.2**	10.5	14.7
WILSON STATE BK	Wilson	KS	**B**	B	C+	83.9	2.11	18.2	3.9	24.6	16.2	**5.2**	9.1	11.2
WINCHESTER CO-OP BANK	Winchester	MA	**B**	B	B-	564.2	1.57	0.1	0.3	56.4	25.1	**10.0**	11.8	27.1
WINCHESTER FEDERAL BANK	Winchester	KY	**B+**	B+	B-	153.3	0.14	0.2	0.2	59.4	10.0	**9.6**	10.7	20.7
WINCHESTER SB	Winchester	MA	**C+**	C+	B-	531.4	3.13	0.6	0.1	44.7	26.8	**10.0**	11.5	22.0
WINDSOR FS&LA	Windsor	CT	**B-**	B-	B-	399.4	0.86	5.4	0.2	35.2	26.5	**10.0**	11.8	19.1
WINFIELD COMMUNITY BANK	Winfield	IL	**E-**	E-	E-	54.9	-12.50	3.6	0.2	1.6	12.9	**0.0**	-.2	-0.4
WINNSBORO STATE BK & TRUST CO	Winnsboro	LA	**A-**	A-	A-	132.8	-0.16	8.9	5.7	7.0	35.9	**10.0**	11.1	20.3
WINONA NATIONAL BK	Winona	MN	**B**	B	C+	267.0	6.22	11.4	1.1	8.0	44.0	**10.0**	12.5	19.7
▲ WINSIDE STATE BK	Winside	NE	**B**	B-	B	22.8	-2.66	1.7	1.5	2.9	21.9	**10.0**	20.8	27.0
WINTER HILL BANK FSB	Somerville	MA	**C**	C	C	299.4	9.73	0.0	0.4	37.6	18.0	**7.3**	9.2	15.9
WINTHROP STATE BK	Winthrop	MN	**C+**	C+	B-	24.2	2.58	2.2	2.7	5.0	50.3	**8.7**	10.1	33.2
WINTRUST BANK	Chicago	IL	**B-**	C+	C	2924.8	33.54	35.5	7.1	5.4	5.2	**5.0**	7.0	11.7
WISCONSIN BANK & TRUST	Madison	WI	**B-**	B-	C+	664.6	4.57	21.2	0.6	6.7	13.6	**6.8**	8.8	12.4
WISCONSIN RIVER BANK	Sauk City	WI	**B**	B-	C	85.6	17.03	8.0	0.4	19.1	9.8	**9.6**	11.7	14.7
▲ WOLF RIVER COMMUNITY BANK	Hortonville	WI	**B+**	B	B	135.5	-0.78	8.7	2.3	29.6	15.8	**10.0**	12.6	17.1
WOLVERINE BANK FSB	Midland	MI	**B**	B-	C+	338.8	16.03	4.5	0.3	21.4	0.0	**10.0**	16.9	21.9
WOOD & HUSTON BANK	Marshall	MO	**A-**	B+	B	584.9	6.06	10.1	2.5	20.9	16.0	**9.4**	10.6	15.4
WOODBURY BANKING CO	Woodbury	GA	**E-**	E-	E-	23.3	-1.39	5.0	5.3	21.0	19.7	**4.7**	6.7	11.5
WOODFORD STATE BK	Woodford	WI	**B**	B	C+	178.8	1.53	6.9	1.1	13.7	18.4	**7.5**	9.3	14.2
WOODFOREST NATIONAL BK	The Woodlands	TX	**A-**	A-	A-	4204.9	8.72	6.3	0.8	19.3	23.7	**7.9**	9.6	18.4
WOODHAVEN NATIONAL BK	Fort Worth	TX	**B+**	B+	B	453.1	7.65	13.1	1.3	15.1	12.1	**7.6**	9.4	13.6
WOODLAND BANK	Deer River	MN	**C+**	C+	C	74.5	12.08	12.2	3.7	25.8	8.7	**10.0**	13.5	19.3
WOODLANDS BANK	Williamsport	PA	**B-**	B-	B-	357.4	6.97	9.4	0.4	30.5	21.3	**6.4**	8.4	13.4
▲ WOODLANDS NATIONAL BK	Hinckley	MN	**B**	B	C+	149.3	2.64	15.7	5.7	12.2	19.7	**10.0**	13.1	19.4
WOODRUFF FS&LA	Woodruff	SC	**C+**	C+	C+	90.8	-4.77	0.0	0.0	39.2	6.4	**10.0**	33.7	76.7
WOODSBORO BANK	Woodsboro	MD	**C-**	C-	D+	233.4	-1.35	6.8	0.6	17.6	24.2	**6.2**	8.2	13.9
▲ WOODSFIELD SB	Woodsfield	OH	**D**	D	D+	58.0	11.53	0.0	3.3	23.7	40.3	**7.0**	9.0	27.3
WOODSVILLE GUARANTY SB	Woodsville	NH	**C+**	C	C+	393.9	0.56	10.1	1.8	40.3	13.1	**7.6**	9.4	15.5
WOODTRUST BANK	Wisconsin Rapids	WI	**B**	B	B	377.5	6.25	9.3	0.9	7.0	40.8	**7.8**	9.6	13.4
WOORI AMERICA BANK	New York	NY	**B-**	B	C	1194.3	10.85	11.1	0.5	16.9	7.7	**10.0**	11.9	17.3
WORLDS FOREMOST BANK	Lincoln	NE	**C**	C	C-	4448.7	7.53	0.0	91.9	0.0	0.1	**6.9**	10.8	12.4
WORTHINGTON FSB FSB	Worthington	MN	**B**	B	B	68.5	2.53	0.0	1.4	60.8	13.9	**10.0**	14.5	37.9
▲ WORTHINGTON NATIONAL BK	Arlington	TX	**C+**	C	D+	181.1	3.33	14.4	1.1	20.1	6.4	**10.0**	11.2	17.6
▲ WPS COMMUNITY BANK FSB	Madison	WI	**C+**	C	C-	98.6	11.37	4.0	0.3	29.1	2.8	**7.4**	9.4	12.9
WRAY STATE BK	Wray	CO	**C**	C+	C	105.4	-0.67	10.1	5.1	7.0	14.3	**5.9**	8.4	11.7
WRENTHAM CO-OP BANK	Wrentham	MA	**C+**	C+	B-	110.9	2.28	0.1	2.0	52.6	16.2	**10.0**	13.2	29.6
WSB MUNICIPAL BANK	Watertown	NY	**U**	U	B-	83.2	33.84	0.0	0.0	0.0	68.0	**6.7**	8.8	41.1
▲ WYOMING BANK & TRUST	Cheyenne	WY	**B**	B-	C	145.0	5.06	6.8	1.0	10.2	24.7	**8.8**	10.2	16.1
WYOMING COMMUNITY BANK	Riverton	WY	**B**	B	B-	133.7	9.06	11.8	4.1	7.3	33.5	**6.7**	8.7	14.9
WYOMING STATE BK	Laramie	WY	**B**	B	B-	150.8	2.35	6.3	0.9	13.1	6.6	**7.8**	9.5	14.9
XENITH BANK	Richmond	VA	**C**	C+	B-	906.3	49.93	22.2	11.1	5.5	9.3	**7.9**	10.7	13.3
YADKIN BANK	Statesville	NC	**B-**	B-	D	4181.2	130.88	9.5	0.9	9.4	17.6	**6.7**	10.3	12.3
YAKIMA FS&LA	Yakima	WA	**A-**	A-	A	1763.7	-0.43	0.0	0.0	33.0	44.5	**10.0**	21.3	58.7
YAMPA VALLEY BANK	Steamboat Springs	CO	**C+**	C-	C-	199.4	5.39	16.4	2.7	14.3	19.9	**7.6**	9.4	13.2
YELLOWSTONE BANK	Laurel	MT	**A**	A-	A-	641.4	36.27	19.2	1.5	10.1	6.6	**10.0**	17.2	19.4
YNB	Yukon	OK	**C-**	C-	C	189.8	3.27	5.2	3.4	24.8	27.3	**6.2**	8.2	13.9
YOAKUM NATIONAL BK	Yoakum	TX	**A-**	A-	A-	225.5	11.15	2.6	5.7	14.0	62.2	**10.0**	11.4	29.5
YORK STATE BK	York	NE	**B-**	B-	C+	139.0	2.63	10.7	2.0	5.7	9.8	**5.6**	8.5	11.5
YORK TRADITIONS BANK	York	PA	**B-**	B-	B-	302.2	5.89	19.8	0.3	19.7	12.1	**8.7**	10.8	13.9
YORKTOWN BANK	Pryor	OK	**C**	C+	C	72.6	-10.27	22.1	2.4	20.7	0.0	**10.0**	13.8	19.2
YOUNG AMERICANS BANK	Denver	CO	**D-**	D-	D+	15.7	5.11	0.0	0.3	0.0	2.4	**4.3**	6.3	361.9
YOUR COMMUNITY BANK	New Albany	IN	**B**	B	B-	732.2	4.60	12.1	0.3	14.5	22.4	**10.0**	11.2	16.4
ZAPATA NATIONAL BK	Zapata	TX	**A-**	A-	A-	92.5	-0.95	4.0	5.6	24.0	32.5	**10.0**	12.0	28.5
ZAVALA COUNTY BANK	Crystal City	TX	**B+**	A-	B+	62.9	-2.62	2.4	5.7	1.4	67.6	**10.0**	12.5	38.5
ZIONS FIRST NATIONAL BK	Salt Lake City	UT	**B**	B	B-	17889.5	-0.94	17.2	1.2	6.1	10.7	**9.3**	10.5	15.2

Arrows denote recent upgrades ▲ or downgrades ▼

Asset Quality Index	Adjusted Non-Performing Loans as a % of Total Loans	Adjusted Non-Performing Loans as a % of Capital	Net Charge-Offs Avg Loans	Profitability Index	Net Income ($Mil)	Return on Assets (R.O.A.)	Return on Equity (R.O.E.)	Net Interest Spread	Overhead Efficiency Ratio	Liquidity Index	Liquidity Ratio	Hot Money Ratio	Stability Index
5.8	1.05	6.1	0.21	5.8	42.4	1.24	10.89	3.78	65.5	3.1	19.3	14.4	8.3
9.8	2.18	2.3	0.29	3.4	8.4	0.44	2.61	3.14	91.2	8.5	95.7	0.6	6.8
3.0	1.88	11.9	0.02	9.5	44.6	1.62	11.83	4.35	51.2	0.7	6.1	34.0	8.5
6.1	0.96	6.0	0.16	5.7	4.4	1.34	17.29	3.64	66.8	5.1	31.6	5.8	6.3
7.0	0.63	3.9	0.00	6.5	14.9	1.11	10.85	3.77	58.4	2.5	16.7	16.9	8.2
8.0	0.07	0.6	0.00	5.8	0.8	1.33	13.13	4.35	68.2	2.2	5.5	17.2	6.5
6.0	2.14	11.6	0.01	4.0	2.4	0.57	4.88	2.25	59.7	1.9	38.1	36.2	7.4
5.7	1.17	8.1	0.00	5.3	1.6	1.35	12.98	3.11	56.2	0.8	15.0	37.9	6.6
7.6	0.85	4.5	-0.01	2.4	0.9	0.24	2.06	2.43	88.3	3.5	37.1	16.4	7.0
4.7	3.29	17.5	0.18	3.5	1.6	0.52	4.46	3.13	78.2	3.8	21.7	10.4	6.6
1.6	0.20	21.5	0.25	0.0	-2.2	-4.86	-170.46	3.05	246.5	1.9	28.0	24.7	0.0
7.2	0.98	4.0	0.31	5.3	1.2	1.23	11.28	4.30	70.1	3.1	41.2	19.7	7.7
5.2	2.51	9.5	0.00	4.9	1.9	0.97	7.58	4.13	78.6	5.6	34.4	3.9	4.8
7.3	0.00	0.0	0.00	5.6	0.2	1.33	6.61	3.81	62.3	4.6	45.9	10.9	7.5
7.1	0.39	2.9	0.00	2.7	0.6	0.26	2.98	3.24	87.5	3.2	26.6	14.5	5.2
9.7	0.07	0.1	0.00	3.2	0.1	0.77	8.14	3.20	76.3	6.6	75.2	4.8	3.9
4.9	0.61	6.4	0.04	6.5	21.9	1.12	14.89	3.19	63.2	2.6	9.7	15.8	5.3
4.0	0.88	7.3	0.45	4.9	3.4	0.72	7.34	4.26	70.0	3.5	8.8	11.0	7.0
5.2	0.62	4.1	0.09	4.6	0.5	0.83	6.76	3.85	63.9	1.7	11.2	20.4	6.0
5.1	2.20	12.3	-0.04	6.3	1.2	1.14	9.26	4.14	60.2	3.1	14.4	13.7	7.5
3.8	2.41	11.2	-0.05	4.3	1.7	0.70	3.84	3.54	61.4	0.7	11.8	36.2	7.3
6.0	0.70	4.6	0.15	6.6	6.8	1.59	14.46	3.83	60.0	3.6	19.0	11.2	7.8
0.3	14.68	102.5	0.01	0.8	0.0	-0.18	-2.84	4.98	107.2	0.9	24.4	34.6	0.7
4.6	1.84	11.2	0.06	6.1	1.9	1.43	14.89	3.79	64.0	4.4	27.4	8.2	5.8
6.8	1.21	5.9	-0.02	8.1	61.3	1.97	22.04	2.57	84.3	6.7	40.2	2.1	8.9
5.3	1.06	7.8	-0.01	6.6	5.2	1.59	16.88	4.55	63.2	2.9	22.9	15.5	6.3
3.3	3.13	16.1	0.24	4.5	0.2	0.40	2.87	4.91	85.0	0.9	10.9	32.5	4.5
5.2	1.27	9.7	0.01	4.6	2.2	0.87	10.25	3.50	70.3	3.2	5.8	12.0	5.3
4.3	2.36	11.4	0.28	4.6	0.7	0.71	4.80	4.54	76.0	4.3	22.8	7.9	6.8
7.6	3.49	5.3	0.08	2.6	0.2	0.33	0.98	2.73	82.6	2.6	57.3	36.2	7.6
5.2	1.10	7.4	0.17	2.0	0.4	0.24	2.95	3.28	89.3	4.3	35.5	12.1	4.3
3.0	7.21	24.8	0.12	2.8	0.2	0.48	7.76	2.76	79.6	5.7	70.4	11.6	3.1
4.8	1.45	11.3	0.27	3.4	1.9	0.64	6.57	3.60	83.6	3.0	13.0	13.9	5.2
5.1	1.92	8.9	0.02	9.1	6.8	2.45	25.65	2.86	52.8	6.0	44.2	4.8	7.6
6.2	0.45	2.8	0.10	3.5	4.5	0.51	4.24	3.33	76.0	3.5	18.3	12.3	7.0
3.4	0.70	5.4	1.47	9.8	53.0	1.68	15.10	7.94	75.5	0.2	8.5	98.9	9.3
9.9	0.16	0.7	0.00	4.0	0.3	0.56	4.01	2.98	66.0	4.8	38.7	10.5	7.3
6.6	0.43	2.5	-0.03	2.8	0.8	0.57	5.24	4.35	87.1	2.1	28.3	21.6	5.2
7.6	0.00	0.0	0.02	3.5	0.4	0.54	5.61	3.88	74.6	0.9	1.7	29.0	5.3
3.6	1.46	11.1	0.21	3.3	0.4	0.53	5.14	3.80	76.7	1.5	14.3	24.8	5.6
9.4	0.53	2.4	0.00	2.5	0.3	0.30	2.30	2.75	85.5	4.2	39.1	13.5	7.0
10.0	na	0.0	na	3.4	0.3	0.52	5.97	0.98	12.1	5.1	34.9	7.1	4.2
4.7	1.40	7.5	-0.20	7.4	1.7	1.64	15.82	3.61	86.1	4.4	35.1	11.3	7.4
4.8	1.82	10.7	0.09	5.1	1.1	1.18	13.91	4.21	73.3	3.4	35.9	16.6	5.5
5.7	0.71	4.5	0.00	4.5	0.8	0.73	5.82	4.24	73.2	2.7	27.8	17.5	7.6
3.8	1.05	7.8	0.42	2.4	0.9	0.15	1.26	3.61	80.9	1.2	12.8	27.9	3.9
5.2	0.93	6.6	0.14	3.8	8.6	0.45	4.02	4.83	83.3	1.7	15.8	22.2	6.5
10.0	0.61	1.0	0.02	5.2	12.3	0.92	4.40	2.64	45.2	3.8	73.8	31.3	10.0
4.1	1.13	7.3	-0.34	7.6	2.8	1.93	20.10	4.90	60.9	2.8	25.4	15.9	5.8
6.8	0.70	3.4	0.00	9.8	10.2	2.73	14.65	4.50	42.1	4.6	24.1	5.9	9.4
4.5	1.81	12.3	0.00	2.2	0.5	0.35	4.50	3.71	91.4	2.6	22.7	16.8	3.9
9.1	0.03	0.1	-0.01	5.5	1.7	1.04	9.07	3.00	51.2	3.9	61.6	21.7	7.3
4.5	0.35	3.0	0.00	4.8	0.8	0.78	6.74	3.55	67.7	3.7	11.2	10.2	7.1
5.0	1.26	8.9	0.00	4.5	1.6	0.72	6.63	3.65	74.7	2.5	6.1	15.8	6.1
4.0	1.18	6.8	0.09	2.3	0.1	0.14	0.72	4.52	85.5	1.9	16.8	19.5	5.6
10.0	2.13	0.1	0.00	0.0	-0.8	-6.45	-94.43	1.00	674.1	7.9	99.3	0.7	1.5
5.0	2.07	12.0	0.17	5.9	6.8	1.26	11.34	4.21	64.1	4.2	20.4	8.4	6.5
9.0	0.00	0.0	0.00	7.2	1.3	1.75	15.00	3.60	54.4	0.9	24.8	41.7	8.3
9.3	0.00	0.0	-0.03	4.9	0.5	1.06	8.34	3.74	73.2	3.9	59.3	18.9	7.4
6.0	0.94	5.4	0.08	6.9	164.2	1.22	11.96	3.40	66.4	6.3	29.8	1.5	7.8

Name	City	State	Rating	2013 Rating	2012 Rating	Total Assets ($Mil)	One Year Asset Growth	Asset Mix (As a % of Total Assets) Comm-ercial Loans	Cons-umer Loans	Mort-gage Loans	Secur-ities	Capital-ization Index	Lever-age Ratio	Risk-Based Capital Ratio
ZIONS TRUST NATIONAL ASSOCIATI	Salt Lake City	UT	**U**	U	U	17.2	2.42	0.0	0.0	0.0	0.0	**10.0**	97.7	422.1

Asset Quality Index	Adjusted Non-Performing Loans as a % of Total Loans	Adjusted Non-Performing Loans as a % of Capital	Net Charge-Offs Avg Loans	Profitability Index	Net Income ($Mil)	Return on Assets (R.O.A.)	Return on Equity (R.O.E.)	Net Interest Spread	Overhead Efficiency Ratio	Liquidity Index	Liquidity Ratio	Hot Money Ratio	Stability Index
10.0	na	0.0	na	**9.5**	0.6	4.51	4.68	0.20	74.2	**4.0**	7887.1	101.0	**7.0**

Section II

Weiss
Recommended Companies

A compilation of those

U.S. Commercial Banks and Savings Banks

receiving a Weiss Financial Strength Rating
of A+, A, A-, or B+.

Institutions are ranked by Financial Strength Rating
in each state where they have a branch location.

Section II Contents

This section provides a list of Weiss Recommended companies and contains all financial institutions receiving a Financial Strength Rating of A+, A, A-, or B+. Recommended institutions are listed in each state in which they currently operate one or more branches. If a company is not on this list, it should not be automatically assumed that the firm is weak. Indeed, there are many firms that have not achieved a B+ or better rating but are in good condition with adequate resources to weather an average recession. Not being included in this list should not be construed as a recommendation to immediately withdraw deposits or cancel existing financial arrangements.

Institutions are ranked within each state by their Weiss Financial Strength Rating, and then listed alphabetically by city. Companies with the same rating should be viewed as having the same relative safety regardless of their ranking in this table.

1. **Institution Name** — The name under which the institution was chartered. A company's name can be very similar to, or the same as, the name of other companies which may not be on our Recommended List, so make sure you note the exact name, city, and state of the main branch listed here before acting on this recommendation.

2. **City** — The city in which the institution's headquarters or main office is located. With the adoption of intrastate and interstate branching laws, many institutions operating in your area may actually be headquartered elsewhere. So, don't be surprised if the location cited is not in your particular city.

3. **State** — The state in which the institution's headquarters or main office is located. With the adoption of interstate branching laws, some institutions operating in your area may actually be headquartered in another state. Even so, there are no restrictions on your ability to do business with an out-of-state institution.

4. **Telephone** — The telephone number for the institution's headquarters, or main office. If the number listed is not in your area, or a local phone call, consult your local phone directory for the number of a location near you.

5. **Financial Strength Rating** — Weiss rating assigned to the institution at the time of publication. Our ratings are designed to distinguish levels of insolvency risk and are measured on a scale from A to F based upon a wide range of factors. Highly rated companies are, in our opinion, less likely to experience financial difficulties than lower rated firms. See *About Weiss Financial Strength Ratings* for more information and a description of what each rating means.

Weiss Financial Strength Ratings are not deemed to be a recommendation concerning the purchase or sale of the securities of any bank that is publicly owned.

Alabama

Rating: A+

City	Name	Telephone
BOAZ	FIRST BANK OF BOAZ	(256) 593-8670

Rating: A

City	Name	Telephone
WINFIELD	CITIZENS BANK OF WINFIELD	(205) 487-4277
MUSCLE SHOALS	FIRST METRO BANK	(256) 386-0600
HAMILTON	FIRST NATIONAL BK	(205) 921-7435
BIRMINGHAM	OAKWORTH CAPITAL BANK	(205) 263-4700
WEDOWEE	SMALL TOWN BANK	(256) 357-4936
CAMDEN	TOWN-COUNTRY NATIONAL BK	(334) 682-4155

Rating: A-

City	Name	Telephone
DOTHAN	BANKSOUTH	(334) 340-2218
CALERA	CENTRAL STATE BK	(205) 668-0711
OXFORD	CHEAHA BANK	(256) 835-8855
GREENSBORO	CITIZENS BANK	(334) 624-8888
CULLMAN	CULLMAN SAVINGS BANK	(256) 734-1740
ALTOONA	EXCHANGE BANK OF ALABAMA	(205) 589-6334
WATERLOO	FARMERS & MERCHANTS BANK	(256) 766-2579
BIRMINGHAM	FIRST PARTNERS BANK	(205) 822-5500
ONEONTA	HOMETOWN BANK OF ALABAMA	(205) 625-4434
PELL CITY	METRO BANK	(205) 884-2265
DEMOPOLIS	ROBERTSON BANKING CO	(334) 289-3564

Rating: B+

City	Name	Telephone
SHEFFIELD	BANK INDEPENDENT	(256) 386-5000
BRANTLEY	BRANTLEY BANK & TRUST CO	(334) 527-3206
CAMDEN	COMMUNITY NEIGHBOR BANK	(334) 682-4215
LAFAYETTE	FARMERS & MERCHANTS BANK	(334) 864-9941
LINDEN	FIRST BANK OF LINDEN	(334) 295-8741
WETUMPKA	FIRST COMMUNITY BK CENTRAL AL	(334) 567-0081
TALLADEGA	FIRST NATIONAL BK OF TALLADEGA	(256) 362-2334
SULLIGENT	FIRST STATE BK OF THE SOUTH	(205) 698-8116
AUBURN	KEYSTONE BANK	(334) 466-2210
GERALDINE	LIBERTY BANK	(256) 659-2175
CLANTON	PEOPLES SOUTHERN BANK	(205) 755-2240
PHENIX CITY	PHENIX-GIRARD BANK	(334) 298-0691
BIRMINGHAM	SERVISFIRST BANK	(205) 949-0302
WINFIELD	STATE BK & TRUST	(205) 487-4265
REFORM	WEST ALABAMA BANK & TRUST	(205) 375-6261

Alaska

City	Name	Telephone
Rating: A		
ANCHORAGE	FIRST NATIONAL BK ALASKA	(907) 777-4362
ANCHORAGE	NORTHRIM BANK	(907) 562-0062
Rating: A-		
FAIRBANKS	MT MCKINLEY BANK	(907) 452-1751

Arizona

Rating: A-

City	Name	Telephone
SCOTTSDALE	NORDSTROM FSB	(480) 596-3459

Rating: B+

City	Name	Telephone
GLENDALE	BNC NATIONAL BK	(602) 508-3760
SCOTTSDALE	MERIDIAN BANK NA	(480) 998-8995
SCOTTSDALE	PINNACLE BANK	(480) 609-0055

Arkansas

City	Name	Telephone
Rating: A+		
CALICO ROCK	FIRST NATIONAL BK IZARD COUNTY	(870) 297-3711
SEARCY	FIRST SECURITY BANK	(501) 279-3400
Rating: A		
STUTTGART	FARMERS & MERCHANTS BANK	(870) 673-6911
PARAGOULD	FIRST NATIONAL BK	(870) 239-8521
SHERIDAN	PEOPLES BANK	(870) 942-5707
MENA	UNION BANK OF MENA	(479) 394-2211
Rating: A-		
DELIGHT	BANK OF DELIGHT	(870) 379-2293
LAKE VILLAGE	BANK OF LAKE VILLAGE	(870) 265-2241
PRESCOTT	BANK OF PRESCOTT	(870) 887-2688
VAN BUREN	CITIZENS BANK & TRUST CO	(479) 474-1201
WYNNE	CROSS COUNTY BANK	(870) 238-8171
DE WITT	DE WITT BANK & TRUST CO	(870) 946-3531
MARION	FIRST COMMUNITY BANK OF E AR	(870) 739-7300
PARIS	FIRST NATIONAL BK AT PARIS	(479) 963-2121
WALNUT RIDGE	FIRST NATIONAL BK LAWRENCE CTY	(870) 886-5959
RUSSELLVILLE	FIRST STATE BK	(479) 498-2400
HORATIO	HORATIO STATE BK	(870) 832-2501
SCRANTON	LOGAN COUNTY BANK	(479) 938-2511
MORRILTON	PETIT JEAN STATE BK	(501) 354-4988
HUNTSVILLE	TODAYS BANK	(479) 738-2147
WARREN	WARREN BANK & TRUST CO	(870) 226-2621
Rating: B+		
GREEN FOREST	ANSTAFF BANK NA	(870) 438-5214
STAR CITY	BANK OF STAR CITY	(870) 628-4286
STAMPS	BODCAW BANK	(870) 533-4486
LITTLE ROCK	CENTRAL BANK	(501) 221-6400
MURFREESBORO	DIAMOND BANK	(870) 285-2172
FORDYCE	FBT BANK & MORTGAGE	(870) 352-3107
FORT SMITH	FIRST NATIONAL BK FORT SMITH	(479) 782-2041
MOUNTAIN HOME	INTEGRITY FIRST BANK NA	(870) 425-2101
PIGGOTT	PIGGOTT STATE BK	(870) 598-3802
PINE BLUFF	RELYANCE BANK NA	(870) 535-7222

California

Rating: A

City	Name	Telephone
ARCADIA	AMERICAN PLUS BANK NA	(626) 821-9188
SAN DIEGO	ARMED FORCES BANK OF CA NA	(619) 239-3601
RIVERSIDE	BANK OF HEMET	(951) 248-2000
IRVINE	CALIFORNIA FIRST NATIONAL BK	(949) 255-5300
LODI	FARMERS & MERCH BK CENTRAL CA	(209) 367-2300
LONG BEACH	FARMERS & MERCH BK LONG BEACH	(562) 437-0011
SAN DIEGO	HOME BANK OF CALIFORNIA	(858) 270-5881
SANTA CRUZ	LIGHTHOUSE BANK	(831) 600-4000
PALOS VERDES E	MALAGA BANK FSB	(310) 375-9000

Rating: A-

City	Name	Telephone
SAN DIEGO	BOFI FEDERAL BANK	(858) 350-6200
SAN FRANCISCO	CALIFORNIA PACIFIC BANK	(415) 399-8000
ONTARIO	CITIZENS BUSINESS BANK	(909) 980-4030
IRVINE	COMMERCEWEST BANK	(949) 251-6959
WEST SACRAMEN	COMMUNITY BUSINESS BANK	(916) 830-3597
LOS ANGELES	FIRST CREDIT BANK	(310) 273-3120
FREMONT	FREMONT BANK	(510) 505-5226
CHICO	GOLDEN VALLEY BANK	(530) 894-1000
SANTA ROSA	LUTHER BURBANK SAVINGS	(707) 578-9216
PASADENA	ONEWEST BANK NA	(626) 535-6896
IRVINE	PACIFIC ENTERPRISE BANK	(949) 623-7600
IRVINE	PACIFIC PREMIER BANK	(949) 864-8000
SAN MARCOS	RANCHO SANTA FE THRIFT & LOAN	(760) 736-2000
LOS ANGELES	ROYAL BUSINESS BANK	(213) 627-9888
SANTA ROSA	SUMMIT STATE BK	(707) 568-6000
TUSTIN	TUSTIN COMMUNITY BANK	(714) 730-5662

Rating: B+

City	Name	Telephone
SANTA ROSA	ALTAPACIFIC BANK	(707) 236-1500
SANTA BARBARA	AMERICAN RIVIERA BANK	(805) 965-5942
STOCKTON	BANK OF STOCKTON	(209) 929-1600
WALNUT CREEK	BAY COMMERCIAL BANK	(925) 476-1800
SAN JOSE	BRIDGE BANK NA	(408) 423-8500
IRVINE	CALIFORNIA REPUBLIC BANK	(949) 270-9700
SAN JUAN CAPIST	CAPITAL BANK	(949) 489-4200
CHINO	CHINO COMMERCIAL BANK NA	(909) 393-8880
OXNARD	COUNTY COMMERCE BANK	(805) 485-7600
PASADENA	EAST WEST BANK	(626) 768-6000
PASADENA	EVERTRUST BANK	(626) 993-3800
PORTERVILLE	FINANCE & THRIFT CO	(559) 781-9560
SAN FRANCISCO	FIRST REPUBLIC BANK	(415) 392-1400
LOS ANGELES	HANMI BANK	(213) 382-2200
SAN JOSE	HERITAGE BANK OF COMMERCE	(408) 947-6900
LONG BEACH	INTERNATIONAL CITY BANK NA	(562) 436-9800
CARSON	MERCHANTS BK OF CALIFORNIA NA	(310) 549-4350
LOS ANGELES	OPEN BANK	(213) 892-9999
IRVINE	OPUS BANK	(949) 250-9800
SACRAMENTO	RIVER CITY BANK	(916) 567-2600
CORONADO	SAN DIEGO PRIVATE BANK	(619) 437-1000
UKIAH	SAVINGS BANK OF MENDOCINO CNTY	(707) 462-6613
SANTA CLARA	SILICON VALLEY BANK	(408) 654-7400
LA JOLLA	SILVERGATE BANK	(858) 362-6300
SAN RAFAEL	WESTAMERICA BANK	(415) 257-8000

Colorado

City	Name	Telephone
Rating: A		
LAMAR	FRONTIER BANK	(719) 336-4351
FORT COLLINS	VERUS BANK OF COMMERCE	(970) 204-1010
Rating: A-		
COLORADO SPRIN	ACADEMY BANK NA	(877) 712-2265
ALAMOSA	ALAMOSA STATE BK	(719) 589-2564
ENGLEWOOD	AMG NATIONAL TRUST BANK	(303) 694-2190
DENVER	BANKERS BANK OF THE WEST	(303) 291-3700
DENVER	COBIZ BANK	(303) 293-2265
LAMAR	COMMUNITY STATE BK	(719) 336-3272
DOLORES	DOLORES STATE BK	(970) 882-7600
LAS ANIMAS	FIRST NATIONAL BK LAS ANIMAS	(719) 456-1512
HUGO	FIRST NATIONAL BK OF HUGO	(719) 743-2415
LAKEWOOD	FIRSTBANK	(303) 232-2000
DENVER	STEELE STREET BANK & TRUST	(303) 376-3800
Rating: B+		
GLENWOOD SPRI	ALPINE BANK	(970) 945-2424
FORT COLLINS	BANK OF COLORADO	(970) 206-1160
CASTLE ROCK	CASTLE ROCK BANK	(303) 688-5191
BRUSH	FARMERS STATE BK OF BRUSH	(970) 842-5101
CALHAN	FARMERS STATE BK OF CALHAN	(719) 347-2727
WRAY	FIRST PIONEER NATIONAL BK	(970) 332-4824
SALIDA	HIGH COUNTRY BANK	(719) 539-2516
THORNTON	NORTH VALLEY BANK	(303) 452-5500
JULESBURG	POINTS WEST COMMUNITY BANK	(970) 474-3341
CENTENNIAL	REDSTONE BANK	(720) 880-5000

Delaware

City	Name	Telephone
Rating: A		
NEWARK	APPLIED BANK	(888) 839-7952
Rating: A-		
WILMINGTON	DEUTSCHE BK TRUST CO DELAWARE	(302) 636-3301
Rating: B+		
WILMINGTON	WILMINGTON SVGS FUND SOCIETY	(302) 792-6000

Florida

Rating: A-

City	Name	Telephone
MIAMI LAKES	BANKUNITED NA	(786) 313-1010
CHIEFLAND	DRUMMOND COMMUNITY BANK	(352) 493-2277
WEST PALM BEAC	PALM BEACH COMMUNITY BANK	(561) 681-7200
GRACEVILLE	PEOPLES BANK OF GRACEVILLE	(850) 263-3267
PANAMA CITY	SUMMIT BANK NA	(850) 785-3669

Rating: B+

City	Name	Telephone
PARRISH	1ST MANATEE BANK	(941) 776-5040
MAITLAND	FIRST COLONY BANK OF FLORIDA	(407) 740-0401
PALM COAST	INTRACOASTAL BANK	(386) 447-1662
TAMPA	TCM BANK NA	(813) 287-4880

Georgia

Rating: A

City	Name	Telephone
WAYNESBORO	FIRST NATIONAL BK WAYNESBORO	(706) 554-8100
DULUTH	NOA BANK	(678) 385-0800
THOMASTON	WEST CENTRAL GEORGIA BANK	(706) 647-8951

Rating: A-

City	Name	Telephone
TRENTON	BANK OF DADE	(706) 657-6842
DOUGLAS	DOUGLAS NATIONAL BK	(912) 384-2233
LINCOLNTON	FARMERS STATE BK	(706) 359-3131
AUGUSTA	FIRST BANK OF GEORGIA	(706) 731-6600
BAINBRIDGE	FIRST PORT CITY BANK	(229) 246-6200
BLAKELY	FIRST STATE BK OF BLAKELY	(229) 723-3711
MACON	STATE BK & TRUST CO	(478) 796-6200
SMYRNA	VININGS BANK	(770) 437-0004

Rating: B+

City	Name	Telephone
DAWSON	BANK OF DAWSON	(229) 995-2141
SPARTA	BANK OF HANCOCK COUNTY	(706) 444-5781
HAHIRA	CITIZENS COMMUNITY BANK	(229) 794-2111
FITZGERALD	COMMUNITY BKG CO OF FITZGERALD	(229) 423-4321
TWIN CITY	DURDEN BANKING CO INC	(478) 763-2121
DUBLIN	FARMERS STATE BK	(478) 275-3223
DOUGLAS	FIRST NATIONAL BK COFFEE CTY	(912) 384-1100
ATLANTA	GEORGIA COMMERCE BANK	(678) 631-1240
GLENNVILLE	GLENNVILLE BANK	(912) 654-3471
HOSCHTON	HAMILTON STATE BK	(770) 868-2660
PELHAM	PELHAM BANKING CO	(229) 294-2341
COLQUITT	PEOPLESSOUTH BANK	(229) 758-5511
ATLANTA	RESURGENS BANK	(404) 297-2200
MCRAE	SECURITY STATE BK	(229) 868-6431
ZEBULON	UNITED BANK	(770) 567-7211

Hawaii

Rating: A-

City	Name	Telephone
HONOLULU	FIRST HAWAIIAN BANK	(808) 525-6340

Rating: B+

City	Name	Telephone
HONOLULU	CENTRAL PACIFIC BANK	(808) 544-0500
HONOLULU	TERRITORIAL SAVINGS BANK	(808) 946-1400

Idaho

City	Name	Telephone
Rating: A-		
AMMON	BANK OF COMMERCE	(208) 525-9108
Rating: B+		
BOISE	IDAHO TRUST BANK	(208) 373-6500
BOISE	NORTHWEST BANK	(208) 332-0700

Illinois

City	Name	Telephone
Rating: A+		
REYNOLDS	REYNOLDS STATE BK	(309) 372-4242
Rating: A		
CHICAGO	FIRST EAGLE BANK	(312) 850-2900
EAST SAINT LOUI	FIRST ILLINOIS BANK	(618) 271-8700
TAYLORVILLE	FIRST NATIONAL BK TAYLORVILLE	(217) 824-2241
WATSEKA	FIRST TRUST & SB OF WATSEKA IL	(815) 432-2494
BREESE	GERMANTOWN TRUST & SB	(618) 526-4202
MILLEDGEVILLE	MILLEDGEVILLE STATE BK	(815) 225-7171
POPLAR GROVE	POPLAR GROVE STATE BK	(815) 765-3333
DECATUR	SOY CAPITAL BANK & TRUST CO	(217) 428-7781
PIPER CITY	VERMILION VALLEY BANK	(815) 686-2258
NEW BERLIN	WARREN-BOYNTON STATE BK	(217) 488-6091
CHICAGO	WASHINGTON FEDERAL BK FOR SVGS	(773) 254-3422
Rating: A-		
FARMINGTON	BANK OF FARMINGTON	(309) 245-2441
PONTIAC	BANK OF PONTIAC	(815) 844-6155
RANTOUL	BANK OF RANTOUL	(217) 892-2143
MILAN	BLACKHAWK BANK & TRUST	(309) 787-4451
ALBION	CITIZENS NB OF ALBION	(618) 445-2344
WINSLOW	COMMUNITY BANK	(815) 367-5011
EASTON	COMMUNITY BANK OF EASTON	(309) 562-7420
FAIRVIEW HEIGHT	COMMUNITY FIRST BANK	(618) 234-9500
EFFINGHAM	CROSSROADS BANK	(217) 347-7751
PROPHETSTOWN	FARMERS NATIONAL BK	(815) 537-2348
AVA	FIRST NATIONAL BK OF AVA	(618) 426-3303
NOKOMIS	FIRST NATIONAL BK OF NOKOMIS	(217) 563-8311
PANA	FIRST NATIONAL BK OF PANA	(217) 562-3961
STEELEVILLE	FIRST NATIONAL BK STEELEVILLE	(618) 965-3441
PINCKNEYVILLE	FIRST NB IN PINCKNEYVILLE	(618) 357-9393
SAINT PETER	FIRST STATE BK OF ST PETER	(618) 349-8343
CHICAGO	GOLD COAST BANK	(312) 587-3200
GOODFIELD	GOODFIELD STATE BK	(309) 965-2221
WHEATON	GRAND RIDGE NATIONAL BK	(630) 315-5444
JACKSONVILLE	JACKSONVILLE SB	(217) 245-4111
JERSEYVILLE	JERSEY STATE BK	(618) 498-6466
PARK RIDGE	PARK RIDGE COMMUNITY BANK	(847) 384-9200
KEWANEE	PEOPLES NATIONAL BK OF KEWANEE	(309) 853-3333
VIRGINIA	PETEFISH SKILES & CO	(217) 452-3041
SPRINGFIELD	PRAIRIE STATE BK & TRUST	(217) 993-6260
ARTHUR	STATE BK OF ARTHUR	(217) 543-2111
TEUTOPOLIS	TEUTOPOLIS STATE BK	(217) 857-3166
QUINCY	TOWN & COUNTRY BANK MIDWEST	(217) 222-0015
Rating: B+		
ANNA	ANNA STATE BK	(618) 833-2151
ARCOLA	ARCOLA FIRST BANK	(217) 268-4911
KAMPSVILLE	BANK OF KAMPSVILLE	(618) 653-4311
OFALLON	BANK OF OFALLON	(618) 632-3595
MOUNT STERLING	BROWN COUNTY STATE BK	(217) 773-3327
METROPOLIS	CITY NATIONAL BK OF METROPOLIS	(618) 524-2161
COLCHESTER	COLCHESTER STATE BK	(309) 776-3245
MOUNT VERNON	COMMUNITY FIRST BK HEARTLAND	(618) 244-3000
GALVA	COMMUNITY STATE BK	(309) 932-8181
IRVINGTON	COMMUNITY TRUST BANK	(618) 249-6218
DU QUOIN	DU QUOIN STATE BK	(618) 542-2111
FAIRFIELD	FAIRFIELD NATIONAL BK	(618) 842-2107
GALESBURG	FARMERS & MECHANICS BANK	(309) 343-7141
CHICAGO	FEDERAL SAVINGS BANK	(312) 738-6000
MATTOON	FIRST MID-ILLINOIS BK & TR NA	(217) 258-0434
CARLYLE	FIRST NATIONAL BK IN CARLYLE	(618) 594-2491
STAUNTON	FIRST NATIONAL BK IN STAUNTON	(618) 635-2234
ALLENDALE	FIRST NATIONAL BK OF ALLENDALE	(618) 299-4411
MARION	FIRST SOUTHERN BANK	(618) 997-4341
ALBANY	FIRST TRUST & SB OF ALBANY IL	(309) 887-4335
KANKAKEE	FIRST TRUST BANK OF ILLINOIS	(815) 929-4000
FISHER	FISHER NATIONAL BK	(217) 897-1136
FRANKLIN	FRANKLIN BANK	(217) 675-2311
BLOOMINGTON	HEARTLAND BANK & TRUST CO	(309) 662-4444
LAWRENCEVILLE	HERITAGE STATE BK	(618) 943-1038
WARSAW	HILL-DODGE BANKING CO	(217) 256-4224
LEWISTOWN	IPAVA STATE BK	(309) 547-2064
LAKE FOREST	LAKE FOREST BANK & TRUST CO	(847) 234-2882
CARTHAGE	MARINE BANK & TRUST	(217) 357-3151
MIDDLETOWN	MIDDLETOWN STATE BK	(217) 445-2616
MORTON	MORTON COMMUNITY BANK	(309) 266-5337
BOURBONNAIS	MUNICIPAL TRUST & SB	(815) 935-8000
CHICAGO	PRIVATEBANK & TRUST CO	(312) 564-2000
RUSHVILLE	RUSHVILLE STATE BK	(217) 322-3323
PEORIA	SOUTH SIDE TRUST & SB PEORIA	(309) 676-0521
SPRING VALLEY	SPRING VALLEY CITY BANK	(815) 663-2211
LIMA	STATE BK OF LIMA	(217) 985-5315
SAINT JACOB	STATE BK OF ST JACOB	(618) 644-5555
CHATHAM	UNITED COMMUNITY BANK	(217) 483-2491

Indiana

Rating: A-

City	Name	Telephone
SOUTH BEND	1ST SOURCE BANK	(574) 235-2000
GENEVA	BANK OF GENEVA	(260) 368-7288
BERNE	FIRST BANK OF BERNE	(260) 589-2151
HUNTINGBURG	FREEDOM BANK	(812) 683-8998
KENTLAND	KENTLAND BANK	(219) 474-5155
LOGANSPORT	LOGANSPORT SAVINGS BANK FSB	(574) 722-3855
INDIANAPOLIS	SALIN BANK & TRUST CO	(317) 452-8000

Rating: B+

City	Name	Telephone
FRANCESVILLE	ALLIANCE BANK	(219) 567-9151
AVILLA	COMMUNITY STATE BK	(260) 897-3361
FOWLER	FOWLER STATE BK	(765) 884-1200
JASPER	GERMAN AMERICAN BANCORP	(812) 482-1314
SWAYZEE	GRANT COUNTY STATE BK	(765) 922-7975
WARSAW	LAKE CITY BANK	(574) 267-6144
LYNN	MERCHANTS BANK OF INDIANA	(765) 874-2511
ELLETTSVILLE	PEOPLES STATE BK	(812) 876-2228
MEDORA	STATE BK OF MEDORA	(812) 966-2601

Iowa

City	Name	Telephone
Rating: A+		
WILLIAMSBURG	FARMERS TRUST & SB	(319) 668-2525
ATLANTIC	FIRST WHITNEY BANK & TRUST	(712) 243-3195
NEW ALBIN	NEW ALBIN SB	(563) 544-4214
WAUKON	WAUKON STATE BK	(563) 568-3451
Rating: A		
TRIPOLI	AMERICAN SB	(319) 882-4279
CHEROKEE	CHEROKEE STATE BK	(712) 225-3000
WYOMING	CITIZENS STATE BK	(563) 488-2211
CORYDON	CORYDON STATE BK	(641) 872-2212
DECORAH	DECORAH BANK & TRUST CO	(563) 382-9661
HAMPTON	FIRST BANK HAMPTON	(641) 456-4793
BRITT	FIRST STATE BK	(641) 843-4411
COLFAX	FIRST STATE BK OF COLFAX	(515) 674-3533
SOMERS	HEARTLAND BANK	(515) 467-5561
HILLS	HILLS BANK & TRUST CO	(319) 679-2291
DES MOINES	IOWA STATE BK	(515) 288-0111
DURANT	LIBERTY TRUST & SB	(563) 785-4441
PELLA	MARION COUNTY STATE BK	(641) 628-2191
MAXWELL	MAXWELL STATE BK	(515) 387-1175
MOUNT VERNON	MOUNT VERNON BANK & TRUST CO	(319) 895-8835
PANORA	PANORA STATE BK	(641) 755-2141
POCAHONTAS	POCAHONTAS STATE BK	(712) 335-3567
READLYN	READLYN SB	(319) 279-3321
MAPLETON	VALLEY BANK & TRUST	(712) 881-1131
VICTOR	VICTOR STATE BK	(319) 647-2231
MOUNT PLEASAN	WAYLAND STATE BK	(319) 385-8189
Rating: A-		
BOONE	BOONE BANK & TRUST CO	(515) 432-6200
BREDA	BREDA SB	(712) 673-2321
STATE CENTER	CENTRAL STATE BK	(641) 483-2505
BELLE PLAINE	CHELSEA SB	(319) 444-3144
STORM LAKE	CITIZENS FIRST NATIONAL BK	(712) 732-5440
SPILLVILLE	CITIZENS SB	(563) 562-3674
SHELDON	CITIZENS STATE BK	(712) 324-2519
FORT DODGE	CITIZENS STATE BK	(515) 955-2265
KEOSAUQUA	COMMUNITY FIRST BANK	(319) 293-3794
WAUKON	FARMERS & MERCHANTS SB	(563) 568-3417
WINTERSET	FARMERS & MERCHANTS STATE BK	(515) 462-4242
COLESBURG	FARMERS SB	(563) 856-2525
FOSTORIA	FARMERS SB	(712) 262-2708
MARCUS	FARMERS STATE BK	(712) 376-4154
MARION	FARMERS STATE BK	(319) 377-4891
MASON CITY	FIRST CITIZENS NATIONAL BK	(641) 423-1600
ALBIA	FIRST IOWA STATE BK	(641) 932-2144
AMES	FIRST NATIONAL BK AMES IOWA	(515) 232-5561
LYNNVILLE	FIRST STATE BK	(641) 527-2535
MOVILLE	FIRST TRUST & SB	(712) 873-3131
ROYAL	HOME STATE BK	(712) 933-5511
HULL	IOWA STATE BK	(712) 439-1025
CENTERVILLE	IOWA TRUST & SB	(641) 437-4500
KINGSLEY	KINGSLEY STATE BK	(712) 378-2341
PELLA	LEIGHTON STATE BK	(641) 628-1566
FAIRFIELD	LIBERTYVILLE SB	(641) 472-9839
FOREST CITY	MANUFACTURERS BANK & TRUST CO	(641) 585-2825
MAQUOKETA	MAQUOKETA STATE BK	(563) 652-2491
COUNCIL BLUFFS	MIDSTATES BANK NA	(712) 388-0505
WEST DES MOINE	MIDWEST HERITAGE BANK FSB	(515) 278-6541
IOWA CITY	MIDWESTONE BANK	(319) 356-5800
SUMNER	NORTHEAST SECURITY BANK	(563) 578-3251
ORANGE CITY	NORTHWESTERN BANK	(712) 737-4911
PALO	PALO SB	(319) 851-2241
STORY CITY	RELIANCE STATE BK	(515) 733-4396
ROLFE	ROLFE STATE BK	(712) 848-3480
SIOUX CITY	SECURITY NB OF SIOUX CITY IA	(712) 277-6500
INDEPENDENCE	SECURITY STATE BK	(319) 334-7035
ALGONA	SECURITY STATE BK	(515) 295-9501
SAINT ANSGAR	ST ANSGAR STATE BK	(641) 713-4501
NEVADA	STATE BK & TRUST CO	(515) 382-2191
WEST DES MOINE	STATE SAVINGS BANK	(515) 457-9533
TEMPLETON	TEMPLETON SB	(712) 669-3322
MARSHALLTOWN	UNITED BANK & TRUST NA	(641) 753-5900
IDA GROVE	UNITED BANK OF IOWA	(712) 364-3393
WALCOTT	WALCOTT TRUST & SB	(563) 284-6202
WASHINGTON	WASHINGTON STATE BK	(319) 653-2151
WATKINS	WATKINS SAVINGS BANK	(319) 227-7773
WEST DES MOINE	WEST BANK	(515) 222-2300
Rating: B+		
ASHTON	ASHTON STATE BK	(712) 724-6326
ATKINS	ATKINS SB & TRUST	(319) 446-7700
BLAIRSTOWN	BENTON COUNTY STATE BK	(319) 454-6230
CRESCO	C US BANK	(563) 547-2040
CARROLL	CARROLL COUNTY STATE BK	(712) 792-3567
MUSCATINE	CENTRAL STATE BK	(563) 263-3131
ELKADER	CENTRAL STATE BK	(563) 245-2110
JOHNSTON	CHARTER BANK	(515) 331-2265
HAWKEYE	CITIZENS SB	(563) 427-3255
MONTICELLO	CITIZENS STATE BK	(319) 465-5921
CLEAR LAKE	CLEAR LAKE BANK & TRUST CO	(641) 357-7121
NEVADA	COMMUNITY BANK	(515) 382-3050
PATON	COMMUNITY STATE BK	(515) 968-4131
DANVILLE	DANVILLE STATE SB	(319) 392-4261
DE WITT	DE WITT BANK & TRUST CO	(563) 659-3211
VICTOR	FARMERS SB	(319) 647-3141
BUFFALO CENTER	FARMERS TRUST & SB	(641) 562-2696
NEWELL	FIRST COMMUNITY BANK	(712) 272-3321

Iowa

City	Name	Telephone
FONTANELLE	FIRST NATIONAL BK	(641) 745-2141
WEBSTER CITY	FIRST STATE BK	(515) 832-2520
IDA GROVE	FIRST STATE BK	(712) 364-3181
WEST DES MOINE	FREEDOM FINANCIAL BANK	(515) 223-1113
GRINNELL	GRINNELL STATE BK	(641) 236-3174
OSAGE	HOME TRUST & SB	(641) 732-3763
RED OAK	HOUGHTON STATE BK	(712) 623-4823
ALGONA	IOWA STATE BK	(515) 295-3595
EMMETSBURG	IOWA TRUST & SB	(712) 852-3451
LANSING	KERNDT BROTHERS SB	(563) 538-4231
LOGAN	LOGAN STATE BANK	(712) 644-2310
LUANA	LUANA SB	(563) 539-2166
MAYNARD	MAYNARD SB	(563) 637-2289
MASON CITY	NSB BANK	(641) 423-7638
CASCADE	OHNWARD BANK & TRUST	(563) 852-7696
CLARINDA	PCSB BANK	(712) 542-5661
ROCK VALLEY	PEOPLES BANK	(712) 476-2746
ALBIA	PEOPLES STATE BK	(641) 932-7887
PILOT GROVE	PILOT GROVE SB	(319) 469-3951
PRIMGHAR	SAVINGS BANK	(712) 957-6815
WAVERLY	SECURITY STATE BK	(319) 352-3500
SLOAN	SLOAN STATE BK	(712) 428-3344
NEW HAMPTON	STATE BANK	(641) 394-3021
SCHALLER	STATE BK OF SCHALLER	(712) 275-4261
CRESTON	STATE SAVINGS BANK	(641) 782-7820
HAMPTON	UNITED BANK & TRUST CO	(641) 456-5587
WEST BEND	WEST IOWA BANK	(515) 887-7811

Kansas

City	Name	Telephone
Rating: A		
TESCOTT	BANK OF TESCOTT	(785) 283-4217
COUNCIL GROVE	FARMERS & DROVERS BANK	(620) 767-5138
COLBY	FARMERS & MERCH BANK OF COLBY	(785) 460-3321
PHILLIPSBURG	FARMERS NATIONAL BK	(785) 543-6541
FREDONIA	FIRST NATIONAL BK IN FREDONIA	(620) 378-2151
LARNED	FIRST STATE B&TC OF LARNED	(620) 285-6931
LAKIN	KEARNY COUNTY BANK	(620) 355-6222
SOLOMON	SOLOMON STATE BK	(785) 655-2941
Rating: A-		
SALINA	BENNINGTON STATE BK	(785) 827-5522
MARYSVILLE	CITIZENS STATE BK	(785) 562-2186
CHENEY	CITIZENS STATE BK OF CHENEY KS	(316) 542-3142
SENECA	COMMUNITY NATIONAL BK	(785) 336-6143
GREAT BEND	FARMERS BANK & TRUST	(620) 792-2411
WESTPHALIA	FARMERS STATE BK OF ALICEVILLE	(785) 489-2468
OAKLEY	FARMERS STATE BK OF OAKLEY KS	(785) 672-3251
NESS CITY	FIRST STATE BK	(785) 798-3347
KIOWA	FIRST STATE BK KIOWA KANSAS	(620) 825-4147
HEALY	FIRST STATE BK OF HEALY	(620) 398-2215
WICHITA	GARDEN PLAIN STATE BK	(316) 721-1500
BELOIT	GUARANTY STATE BK & TRUST CO	(785) 738-3501
MANHATTAN	KANSAS STATE BK OF MANHATTAN	(785) 587-4000
WAMEGO	KAW VALLEY STATE BK & TRUST CO	(785) 456-2021
MCPHERSON	PEOPLES BANK & TRUST CO	(620) 241-2100
SCOTT CITY	SECURITY STATE BK	(620) 872-7224
SAINT JOHN	SJN BANK OF KANSAS	(620) 549-3225
BERN	STATE BK OF BERN	(785) 336-6121
FREDONIA	STATE BK OF KANSAS	(620) 378-2114
MAPLE HILL	STOCKGROWERS STATE BK	(785) 256-4241
OBERLIN	THE BANK	(785) 475-3817
PITTSBURG	UNIVERSITY BANK	(620) 231-4200
GARDEN CITY	WESTERN STATE BK	(620) 275-4128
Rating: B+		
GREELEY	BANK OF GREELEY	(785) 867-2010
GOODLAND	BANKWEST OF KANSAS	(785) 899-2342
WEIR	CBW BANK	(620) 396-8221
WICHITA	EMPRISE BANK	(316) 383-4301
OSBORNE	FARMERS BANK OF OSBORNE KANSAS	(785) 346-2147
MCPHERSON	FARMERS STATE BK	(620) 241-3090
WESTMORELAND	FARMERS STATE BK	(785) 457-3316
DODGE CITY	FIDELITY STATE BK & TRUST CO	(620) 227-8586
STERLING	FIRST BANK	(620) 278-2161
CENTRALIA	FIRST HERITAGE BANK	(785) 857-3341
PHILLIPSBURG	FIRST NATIONAL BK & TRUST	(785) 543-6511
SYRACUSE	FIRST NATIONAL BK OF SYRACUSE	(620) 384-7441
WASHINGTON	FIRST NATIONAL BK WASHINGTON	(785) 325-2221
NORTON	FIRST STATE BK	(785) 877-3341
RANSOM	FIRST STATE BK OF RANSOM	(785) 731-2261
INDEPENDENCE	FIRSTOAK BANK	(620) 331-2265
GREENSBURG	GREENSBURG STATE BK	(620) 723-2131
BALDWIN CITY	MID-AMERICA BANK	(785) 594-2100
COLDWATER	PEOPLES BANK	(620) 582-2166
WICHITA	SOUTHWEST NATIONAL BK	(316) 291-5221
ASHLAND	STOCKGROWERS STATE BK	(620) 635-4032
OLSBURG	UNION STATE BK	(785) 468-3341
MARYSVILLE	UNITED BANK & TRUST	(785) 562-2333

Kentucky

City	Name	Telephone
Rating: A+		
HARDINSBURG	FARMERS BANK	(270) 756-2166
Rating: A		
BEAVER DAM	BANK OF OHIO COUNTY INC	(270) 274-5678
ARLINGTON	CITIZENS DEPOSIT BK ARLINGTON	(270) 655-6921
SOMERSET	CUMBERLAND SECURITY BANK	(606) 679-9361
MARION	FARMERS BANK & TRUST CO	(270) 965-3106
PRINCETON	FARMERS BANK & TRUST CO	(270) 365-5526
MADISONVILLE	FIRST UNITED BANK & TRUST CO	(270) 821-5555
MCKEE	JACKSON COUNTY BANK	(606) 287-8484
LEITCHFIELD	LEITCHFIELD DEPOSIT BANK & TR	(270) 259-5611
PADUCAH	PADUCAH BANK & TRUST CO	(270) 575-5700
CAMPBELLSVILLE	TAYLOR COUNTY BANK	(270) 465-4196
MORGANFIELD	UNITED COMMUNITY BK WEST KY	(270) 389-3232
FORT MITCHELL	VICTORY COMMUNITY BANK	(859) 341-2265
Rating: A-		
BUFFALO	BANK OF BUFFALO	(270) 325-3131
CLARKSON	BANK OF CLARKSON	(270) 242-2111
BROWNSVILLE	BANK OF EDMONSON COUNTY	(270) 597-2175
HICKMAN	CITIZENS BANK	(270) 236-2525
SOMERSET	CITIZENS NB OF SOMERSET	(606) 679-6341
WEST LIBERTY	COMMERCIAL BANK	(606) 743-3195
HARTFORD	COMMONWEALTH COMMUNITY BANK	(270) 298-3261
EDMONTON	EDMONTON STATE BK	(270) 432-3231
PRESTONSBURG	FIRST CMNWLTH BK PRESTONSBURG	(606) 886-2321
FRANKLIN	FRANKLIN BANK & TRUST CO	(270) 586-7121
OWENSBORO	INDEPENDENCE BANK OF KENTUCKY	(270) 686-1776
ASHLAND	KENTUCKY FARMERS BANK CORP	(606) 929-5000
LEWISBURG	LEWISBURG BANKING CO	(270) 755-4818
HODGENVILLE	LINCOLN NB OF HODGENVILLE	(270) 358-4116
BRANDENBURG	MEADE COUNTY BANK	(270) 422-4141
HENDERSON	OHIO VALLEY FINANCIAL GROUP	(270) 831-1500
LOUISVILLE	REPUBLIC BANK & TRUST CO	(502) 584-3600
LOUISVILLE	RIVER CITY BANK INC	(502) 585-4600
SACRAMENTO	SACRAMENTO DEPOSIT BANK	(270) 736-2212
SPRINGFIELD	SPRINGFIELD STATE BK	(859) 336-3939
Rating: B+		
BOWLING GREEN	AMERICAN BANK & TRUST CO INC	(270) 796-8444
CLINTON	CLINTON BANK	(270) 653-4001
ELKTON	ELKTON BANK & TRUST CO	(270) 265-9841
SCOTTSVILLE	FARMERS NB OF SCOTTSVILLE	(270) 237-3141
CLINTON	FIRST COMMUNITY BANK HEARTLAND	(270) 653-4301
CENTRAL CITY	FIRST NB MUHLENBERG COUNTY	(270) 754-3300
IRVINGTON	FIRST STATE BK	(270) 547-2271
FREDONIA	FREDONIA VALLEY BANK	(270) 545-3301
HOPKINSVILLE	PLANTERS BANK INC	(270) 886-9030
SALYERSVILLE	SALYERSVILLE NATIONAL BK	(606) 349-3131
MAYSVILLE	SECURITY BANK & TRUST CO	(606) 564-3304
LOUISVILLE	STOCK YARDS BANK & TRUST CO	(502) 582-2571
CAMPBELLSBURG	UNITED CITIZENS BANK & TRUST	(502) 532-7392
RADCLIFF	WEST POINT BANK	(270) 351-1414
WINCHESTER	WINCHESTER FEDERAL BANK	(859) 744-1900

Louisiana

City	Name	Telephone
Rating: A		
DE RIDDER	CITY SB & TRUST CO	(337) 463-8661
SHREVEPORT	HOME FEDERAL BANK	(318) 222-1145
KAPLAN	KAPLAN STATE BK	(337) 643-7110
MINDEN	MBL BANK	(318) 377-0523
HOUMA	SOUTH LOUISIANA BANK	(985) 851-3434
HAUGHTON	TRI-STATE BK & TRUST	(318) 949-4173
Rating: A-		
MONTGOMERY	BANK OF MONTGOMERY	(318) 646-3386
DERIDDER	BEAUREGARD FSB	(337) 463-4493
BOSSIER CITY	CITIZENS NATIONAL BK NA	(318) 747-6000
DELHI	COMMERCIAL CAPITAL BANK	(318) 878-2274
SAINT JOSEPH	CROSS KEYS BANK	(318) 766-3246
NATCHITOCHES	EXCHANGE B&TC NATCHITOCHES	(318) 352-8141
VACHERIE	FIRST AMERICAN BANK & TRUST	(225) 265-2265
DERIDDER	FIRST NATIONAL BK IN DE RIDDER	(337) 463-6231
CROWLEY	FIRST NATIONAL BK OF LOUISIANA	(337) 783-4014
DELHI	GUARANTY B&TC OF DELHI LA	(318) 878-3703
NEW ROADS	GUARANTY BANK & TRUST CO	(225) 638-8621
ABBEVILLE	GULF COAST BANK	(337) 893-7733
JACKSON	HIGHLANDS BANK	(225) 634-7741
HODGE	HODGE BANK & TRUST CO	(318) 259-7362
JONESBORO	JONESBORO STATE BK	(318) 259-4411
MORGAN CITY	M C BANK & TRUST CO	(985) 384-2100
BELLE CHASSE	MISSISSIPPI RIVER BANK	(504) 392-1111
MONROE	OUACHITA INDEPENDENT BANK	(318) 338-3014
RAYNE	RAYNE BUILDING & LOAN ASSN	(337) 334-7535
RAYNE	RAYNE STATE BK & TRUST CO	(337) 334-3191
RAYVILLE	RICHLAND STATE BK	(318) 728-2024
MANY	SABINE STATE BK & TRUST CO	(318) 256-7000
JONESVILLE	SOUTHERN HERITAGE BANK	(318) 339-8505
SAINT MARTINVIL	TECHE BANK & TRUST CO	(337) 394-9726
NEWELLTON	TENSAS STATE BK	(318) 467-5401
JENNINGS	THE BANK	(337) 824-0033
WINNSBORO	WINNSBORO STATE BK & TRUST CO	(318) 435-7535
Rating: B+		
OPELOUSAS	AMERICAN BANK & TRUST CO	(337) 948-3056
ERATH	BANK OF ERATH	(337) 937-5816
SUNSET	BANK OF SUNSET & TRUST CO	(337) 662-5222
HOUMA	COASTAL COMMERCE BANK	(985) 580-2265
MANSFIELD	COMMUNITY BANK OF LOUISIANA	(318) 872-3831
NEW IBERIA	COMMUNITY FIRST BANK	(337) 365-6677
ARCADIA	FIRST NATIONAL BK	(318) 263-8482
WINNSBORO	FRANKLIN STATE BK & TRUST CO	(318) 435-3711
LAFAYETTE	MIDSOUTH BANK NA	(337) 237-8343
ALEXANDRIA	RED RIVER BANK	(318) 561-4000
SICILY ISLAND	SICILY ISLAND STATE BK	(318) 389-5781
SIMMESPORT	SIMMESPORT STATE BK	(318) 941-2362
HOUMA	SYNERGY BANK	(985) 851-3341
EUNICE	TRI-PARISH BANK	(337) 457-7341

Maine

Rating: A-

City	Name	Telephone
FARMINGTON	FRANKLIN SB	(207) 778-3339

Rating: B+

City	Name	Telephone
BAR HARBOR	BAR HARBOR BANK & TRUST	(207) 288-3314
CAMDEN	CAMDEN NATIONAL BK	(207) 236-8821
KENNEBUNK	KENNEBUNK SB	(207) 985-4903

Maryland

City	Name	Telephone
Rating: A		
BALTIMORE	ROSEDALE FS&LA	(410) 668-4400
Rating: A-		
OCEAN CITY	BANK OF OCEAN CITY	(410) 213-0173
BERLIN	CALVIN B TAYLOR BANKING CO	(410) 641-1700
Rating: B+		
UPPERCO	FARMERS & MERCHANTS BANK	(410) 833-6600

Massachusetts

Rating: A

City	Name	Telephone
ARLINGTON	LEADER BANK NA	(781) 646-3900

Rating: A-

City	Name	Telephone
BOSTON	BOSTON TRUST & INVESTMENT MGMT	(617) 726-7250
EVERETT	EVERETT CO-OP BANK	(617) 387-1110
FRAMINGHAM	MUTUALONE BANK	(508) 820-4000
MARBLEHEAD	NATIONAL GRAND BK MARBLEHEAD	(781) 631-6000
NEEDHAM	NEEDHAM BANK	(781) 444-2100
WOBURN	PATRIOT COMMUNITY BANK	(781) 935-3318

Rating: B+

City	Name	Telephone
BOSTON	BOSTON PRIVATE BANK & TRUST CO	(617) 912-1900
CAMBRIDGE	CAMBRIDGE TRUST CO	(617) 876-2790
HINGHAM	HINGHAM INSTITUTION FOR SAVING	(781) 749-2200
EDGARTOWN	MARTHAS VINEYARD SAVINGS BANK	(774) 310-2001
NEWBURYPORT	NEWBURYPORT FIVE CENTS SB	(978) 462-3136
WOBURN	NORTHERN BANK & TRUST CO	(781) 937-5400
NORTH ANDOVER	NORTHMARK BANK	(978) 686-9100

Michigan

Rating: A-

City	Name	Telephone
ANN ARBOR	ANN ARBOR STATE BK	(734) 761-1475
SOUTHFIELD	STERLING BANK & TRUST FSB	(248) 355-2400

Rating: B+

City	Name	Telephone
HARBOR SPRINGS	FIRST COMMUNITY BANK	(231) 526-2114
NORWAY	FIRST NATIONAL BK OF NORWAY	(906) 563-9233
PORT AUSTIN	PORT AUSTIN STATE BK	(989) 738-5235
EWEN	STATE BK OF EWEN	(906) 988-2821

Minnesota

Rating: A+

City	Name	Telephone
SAINT CLOUD	LIBERTY SAVINGS BANK FSB	(320) 252-2841

Rating: A

City	Name	Telephone
ROSEAU	CITIZENS STATE BK OF ROSEAU	(218) 463-2135
EDINA	FIDELITY BANK	(952) 831-6600
BATTLE LAKE	FIRST NATIONAL BK BATTLE LAKE	(218) 864-5275
BEMIDJI	FIRST NATIONAL BK OF BEMIDJI	(218) 751-2430
OTTERTAIL	FIRST NATIONAL BK OF HENNING	(218) 367-2735
CANBY	FIRST SECURITY BANK - CANBY	(507) 223-7231
SLEEPY EYE	FIRST SECURITY BANK-SLEEPY EYE	(507) 794-3911
PIPESTONE	FIRST STATE BK SOUTHWEST	(507) 825-0055
HOLDINGFORD	STEARNS BANK HOLDINGFORD NA	(320) 746-2261
SAINT CLOUD	STEARNS BANK NA	(320) 253-6607
UPSALA	STEARNS BANK UPSALA NA	(320) 573-2111
ADAMS	UNITED FARMERS STATE BANK	(507) 582-3448
VERMILLION	VERMILLION STATE BK	(651) 437-4433
WADENA	WADENA STATE BK	(218) 631-1860

Rating: A-

City	Name	Telephone
ALTURA	ALTURA STATE BK	(507) 796-6761
LONG PRAIRIE	AMERICAN HERITAGE NATIONAL BK	(320) 732-6131
SAINT PAUL	CAPITAL BANK	(651) 488-2516
CASTLE ROCK	CASTLE ROCK BANK	(651) 463-7590
PARK RAPIDS	CITIZENS NB OF PARK RAPIDS	(218) 732-3393
CHASKA	COMMUNITY BANK CORP	(952) 361-2265
GLENWOOD	EAGLE BANK	(320) 634-4545
PRESTON	F & M COMMUNITY BANK NA	(507) 765-3823
BLUE EARTH	FIRST BANK BLUE EARTH	(507) 526-3241
GRAND MEADOW	FIRST FARMERS & MERCH STATE BK	(507) 754-5123
BROWNSDALE	FIRST FARMERS & MERCH STATE BK	(507) 567-2219
CANNON FALLS	FIRST FARMERS & MERCHANTS BANK	(507) 263-3030
FAIRMONT	FIRST FARMERS & MERCHANTS NB	(507) 235-5556
LUVERNE	FIRST FARMERS & MERCHANTS NB	(507) 283-4463
MENAHGA	FIRST NATIONAL BK MENAHGA	(218) 564-4171
MILACA	FIRST NATIONAL BK OF MILACA	(320) 983-3101
MENDOTA HEIGHT	GATEWAY BANK	(651) 209-4800
LITCHFIELD	HOME STATE BK	(320) 593-2001
REDWOOD FALLS	HOMETOWN BANK	(507) 637-1000
JANESVILLE	JANESVILLE STATE BK	(507) 234-5108
DETROIT LAKES	MIDWEST BANK	(218) 847-4771
OAKDALE	PLATINUM BANK	(651) 332-5200
ALBERT LEA	SECURITY BANK MINNESOTA	(507) 373-1481
SAINT CLAIR	ST CLAIR STATE BK (INC)	(507) 245-3636

Rating: B+

City	Name	Telephone
SAINT PAUL	ANCHOR BANK NA	(651) 747-2900
LITCHFIELD	CENTER NATIONAL BK	(320) 693-3255
GOLDEN VALLEY	CENTRAL BANK	(763) 545-9005
NEW ULM	CITIZENS BANK MINNESOTA	(507) 354-3165
CALEDONIA	EITZEN STATE BK	(507) 725-3329
HOFFMAN	FARMERS STATE BK OF HOFFMAN	(320) 986-2026
TRIMONT	FARMERS STATE BK OF TRIMONT	(507) 639-9921
WATKINS	FARMERS STATE BK OF WATKINS	(320) 764-2600
WINNEBAGO	FIRST FINANCIAL BANK IN WINNEB	(507) 893-3155
MOOSE LAKE	FIRST NATIONAL BK MOOSE LAKE	(218) 485-4441
LE CENTER	FIRST NATIONAL BK OF LE CENTER	(507) 357-2273
OSAKIS	FIRST NATIONAL BK OF OSAKIS	(320) 859-2101
LINO LAKES	FIRST RESOURCE BANK	(651) 785-9320
LE CENTER	FIRST STATE BK OF LE CENTER	(507) 357-2225
SAUK CENTRE	FIRST STATE BK OF SAUK CENTRE	(320) 352-5771
PEQUOT LAKES	LAKES STATE BK	(218) 568-4473
WINONA	MERCHANTS BANK NA	(507) 457-1100
ORMSBY	ORMSBY STATE BK	(507) 736-2941
WELLS	PEOPLES STATE BK OF WELLS	(507) 553-3155
SAINT JOSEPH	SENTRY BANK	(320) 363-7721
BECKER	SHERBURNE STATE BK	(763) 261-4200
WHEATON	STATE BK OF WHEATON	(320) 563-8142
SAINT PAUL	SUNRISE BANKS NA	(651) 265-5600
RED LAKE FALLS	UNITY BANK NORTH	(218) 253-2143
WELCOME	WELCOME STATE BK	(507) 728-8251

Mississippi

Rating: A

City	Name	Telephone
CORINTH	COMMERCE BANK	(662) 286-5577
FAYETTE	JEFFERSON BANK	(601) 786-3191

Rating: A-

City	Name	Telephone
LAUREL	BANK OF JONES COUNTY	(601) 649-4700
NEW ALBANY	BNA BANK	(662) 534-8171
BALDWYN	FARMERS & MERCHANTS BANK	(662) 365-1200
NEWTON	NEWTON COUNTY BANK	(601) 683-3101

Rating: B+

City	Name	Telephone
BROOKHAVEN	BANK OF BROOKHAVEN	(601) 835-3033
MORTON	BANK OF MORTON	(601) 732-8944
WALNUT GROVE	BANK OF WALNUT GROVE	(601) 253-2411
WIGGINS	BANK OF WIGGINS	(601) 928-5233
JACKSON	FIRST COMMERCIAL BANK	(601) 709-7777
CLARKSDALE	FIRST NATIONAL BK CLARKSDALE	(662) 627-3261
WAYNESBORO	FIRST STATE BK	(601) 735-3124
OXFORD	FNB OXFORD	(662) 234-2821
MERIDIAN	GREAT SOUTHERN NATIONAL BK	(601) 693-5141
BAY SPRINGS	MAGNOLIA STATE BK	(601) 764-2265
NORTH CARROLL	PEOPLES BANK & TRUST CO	(662) 237-9272

Missouri

Rating: A+

City	Name	Telephone
FREDERICKTOWN	NEW ERA BANK	(573) 783-3336
GREENVILLE	PEOPLES COMMUNITY BANK	(573) 224-3267

Rating: A

City	Name	Telephone
ADVANCE	BANK OF ADVANCE	(573) 722-3517
MOBERLY	BANK OF CAIRO & MOBERLY	(660) 263-2280
OLD MONROE	BANK OF OLD MONROE	(636) 665-5601
SAINT LOUIS	CASS COMMERCIAL BANK	(314) 506-5500
COLE CAMP	CITIZENS-FARMERS BK COLE CAMP	(660) 668-4416
EL DORADO SPRI	COMMUNITY BK EL DORADO SPRINGS	(417) 876-6811
SPRINGFIELD	LIBERTY BANK	(417) 888-3000
SAINT LOUIS	LINDELL BANK & TRUST CO	(314) 645-7700
DIXON	MID AMERICA BANK & TRUST CO	(573) 759-2121
SENATH	SENATH STATE BK	(573) 738-2646

Rating: A-

City	Name	Telephone
KANSAS CITY	BANK OF GRAIN VALLEY	(816) 373-1905
PERRYVILLE	BANK OF MISSOURI	(573) 547-6541
SAINT ELIZABETH	BANK OF ST ELIZABETH	(573) 493-2313
BLOOMSDALE	BLOOMSDALE BANK	(573) 483-2514
LEBANON	CENTRAL BANK	(417) 532-2151
CHARLESTON	CITIZENS BANK OF CHARLESTON	(573) 683-3373
EDINA	CITIZENS BANK OF EDINA	(660) 397-2266
KANSAS CITY	COMMERCE BANK	(816) 234-2000
WEST PLAINS	COMMUNITY FIRST BANKING CO	(417) 255-2265
BOWLING GREEN	COMMUNITY STATE BK OF MISSOURI	(573) 324-2233
STANBERRY	FARMERS STATE BK STANBERRY	(660) 783-2820
CARUTHERSVILLE	FIRST STATE BK & TRUST CO INC	(573) 333-1700
CHILLICOTHE	INVESTORS COMMUNITY BANK	(660) 646-3733
KEARNEY	KCB BANK	(816) 628-6050
KEARNEY	KEARNEY TRUST CO	(816) 628-6666
LAMAR	LAMAR BANK & TRUST CO	(417) 682-3348
KIRKSVILLE	NORTHEAST MISSOURI STATE BK	(660) 665-6161
SALEM	PROGRESSIVE OZARK BANK	(573) 729-4146
POPLAR BLUFF	SOUTHERN BANK	(573) 778-1800
OSCEOLA	ST CLAIR COUNTY STATE BK	(417) 646-8128
AUXVASSE	UNITED SECURITY BANK	(573) 386-2233
PLATTE CITY	WELLS BANK OF PLATTE CITY	(816) 858-2121
WEST PLAINS	WEST PLAINS BANK & TRUST CO	(417) 256-2147
MARSHALL	WOOD & HUSTON BANK	(660) 886-6825

Rating: B+

City	Name	Telephone
CAPE GIRARDEAU	ALLIANCE BANK	(573) 334-1010
URBANA	BANK OF URBANA	(417) 993-4242
LIBERTY	BANKLIBERTY	(816) 781-4822
GAINESVILLE	CENTURY BANK OF THE OZARKS	(417) 679-3321
MONETT	COMMUNITY NATIONAL BK	(417) 235-2265
CONCORDIA	CONCORDIA BANK	(660) 463-7911
CLAYTON	ENTERPRISE BANK & TRUST	(314) 725-5500
FAYETTE	EXCHANGE BANK OF MISSOURI	(660) 248-3388
LINCOLN	FARMERS BANK OF LINCOLN	(660) 547-3311
UNIONVILLE	FARMERS BANK OF NORTHERN MO	(660) 947-2474
BROOKFIELD	FIRST MISSOURI BANK	(660) 258-3311
HANNIBAL	HNB NATIONAL BK	(573) 221-0050
JAMESPORT	HOME EXCHANGE BANK	(660) 684-6114
PALMYRA	HOMEBANK	(573) 769-2001
COLUMBIA	LANDMARK BANK NA	(573) 499-7333
LINN	LEGENDS BANK	(573) 897-2204
MEXICO	MARTINSBURG BANK & TRUST	(573) 581-6566
WARRENTON	MISSOURI BANK	(636) 456-3441
SEDALIA	MISSOURI BANK II	(660) 827-5520
PLATTE CITY	PLATTE VALLEY BANK OF MISSOURI	(816) 858-5400
ROTHVILLE	PREFERRED BANK	(660) 256-3212
UNIONVILLE	PUTNAM COUNTY STATE BK	(660) 947-2477
SILEX	SILEX BANKING CO	(573) 384-5221
POPLAR BLUFF	STERLING BANK	(573) 778-3333
SAINT LOUIS	STIFEL BANK & TRUST	(314) 342-2000
SALEM	TOWN & COUNTRY BANK	(573) 729-3155

Montana

Rating: A

City	Name	Telephone
SHELBY	FIRST STATE BK OF SHELBY	(406) 434-5567
HAVRE	INDEPENDENCE BANK	(406) 265-1241
LAUREL	YELLOWSTONE BANK	(406) 628-7951

Rating: A-

City	Name	Telephone
BROADUS	1ST BANK	(406) 436-2611
BAKER	BANK OF BAKER	(406) 778-3382
MISSOULA	BANK OF MONTANA	(406) 829-2662
FORSYTH	FIRST STATE BK OF FORSYTH	(406) 346-2112
MALTA	FIRST STATE BK OF MALTA	(406) 654-2340
MILES CITY	STOCKMAN BANK OF MONTANA	(406) 234-8420
FAIRFIELD	TETON BANKS	(406) 467-2531

Rating: B+

City	Name	Telephone
KALISPELL	THREE RIVERS BANK OF MONTANA	(406) 755-4271

Nebraska

City	Name	Telephone
Rating: A		
ELKHORN	AMERICAN INTERSTATE BK	(402) 289-2551
NORFOLK	BANKFIRST	(402) 371-8005
REPUBLICAN CITY	COMMERCIAL STATE BK	(308) 799-3995
WOOD RIVER	HERITAGE BANK	(308) 583-2262
LOUISVILLE	HOME STATE BK	(402) 234-2155
WAVERLY	HORIZON BANK	(402) 786-2555
MADISON	MADISON COUNTY BANK	(402) 454-6511
VALPARAISO	OAK CREEK VALLEY BANK	(402) 784-2200
Rating: A-		
AUBURN	AUBURN STATE BK	(402) 274-4342
HARRISBURG	BANNER CAPITAL BANK	(308) 436-5024
SEWARD	CATTLE NATIONAL BK & TRUST CO	(402) 643-3636
CLARKSON	CLARKSON BANK	(402) 892-3411
NORFOLK	ELKHORN VALLEY BANK & TRUST	(402) 371-0722
RANDOLPH	FIRST STATE BK	(402) 337-0323
GOTHENBURG	GOTHENBURG STATE BK	(308) 537-7181
COZAD	HOMESTEAD BANK	(308) 784-2000
MCCOOK	MCCOOK NATIONAL BK	(308) 345-4240
PIERCE	MIDWEST BANK NA	(402) 329-6221
NORTH PLATTE	NEBRASKALAND NATIONAL BK	(308) 534-2100
OMAHA	SECURITY NATIONAL BK OF OMAHA	(402) 344-7300
Rating: B+		
ADAMS	ADAMS STATE BK	(402) 988-2255
OMAHA	AMERICAN NATIONAL BK	(402) 399-5000
KEYSTONE	BANK OF KEYSTONE	(308) 726-2171
CERESCO	CERESCOBANK	(402) 665-3431
CHAMBERS	CHAMBERS STATE BK	(402) 482-5222
SAINT PAUL	CITIZENS BANK & TRUST CO	(308) 754-4426
YORK	CORNERSTONE BANK	(402) 363-7411
GIBBON	EXCHANGE BANK	(308) 468-5741
LYONS	FIRST NATIONAL BK NORTHEAST	(402) 687-2640
CHADRON	FIRST NATIONAL BK OF CHADRON	(308) 432-5552
FAIRBURY	FIRST NATIONAL BK OF FAIRBURY	(402) 729-3344
GORDON	FIRST NATIONAL BK OF GORDON	(308) 282-0050
SCOTTSBLUFF	FIRST STATE BK	(308) 632-4158
OMAHA	FIRST WESTROADS BANK INC	(402) 330-7200
GRAND ISLAND	FIVE POINTS BANK	(308) 384-5350
HASTINGS	FIVE POINTS BANK OF HASTINGS	(402) 462-2228
FRANKLIN	FRANKLIN STATE BK	(308) 425-6225
HERSHEY	HERSHEY STATE BK	(308) 368-5555
DAYKIN	JEFFERSON COUNTY BANK	(402) 446-7233
MINDEN	MINDEN EXCHANGE BANK & TRUST	(308) 832-1600
OSHKOSH	NEBRASKA STATE BK	(308) 772-3234
BROKEN BOW	NEBRASKA STATE BK & TRUST CO	(308) 872-2466
LINCOLN	PINNACLE BANK	(402) 434-3127
SIDNEY	POINTS WEST COMMUNITY BANK	(308) 254-7110
SCRIBNER	SCRIBNER BANK	(402) 664-2561
AINSWORTH	WEST PLAINS BANK	(402) 387-2381

Nevada

Rating: A

City	Name	Telephone
ELY	FIRST NATIONAL BK OF ELY	(775) 289-4441
LAS VEGAS	MEADOWS BANK	(702) 471-2265

Rating: A-

City	Name	Telephone
CARSON CITY	EAGLEMARK SB	(775) 886-3000

New Jersey

Rating: A-

City	Name	Telephone
WOODBRIDGE	BESSEMER TRUST CO	(212) 708-9386
TEANECK	CROSS RIVER BANK	(201) 808-7000
KENILWORTH	ENTERPRISE NATIONAL BK NJ	(877) 604-5705
TOWNSHIP OF WA	ORITANI BANK	(201) 664-5400

Rating: B+

City	Name	Telephone
BOGOTA	BOGOTA SB	(201) 862-0660
VINELAND	CAPITAL BANK OF NEW JERSEY	(856) 690-1234
EWING	CENLAR FSB	(609) 883-3900
NEWARK	LUSITANIA SAVINGS BANK	(973) 344-5125

New Mexico

City	Name	Telephone
Rating: A		
ALAMOGORDO	FIRST NATIONAL BANK	(575) 437-4880
LAS CRUCES	FIRST NEW MEXICO BK LAS CRUCES	(575) 556-3000
Rating: A-		
CARLSBAD	CARLSBAD NATIONAL BK	(575) 234-2500
FARMINGTON	CITIZENS BANK	(505) 599-0100
LAS CRUCES	CITIZENS BANK OF LAS CRUCES	(575) 647-4100
DEMING	FIRST NEW MEXICO BANK	(575) 546-2691
SILVER CITY	FIRST NM BANK OF SILVER CITY	(575) 388-3121
ALBUQUERQUE	MAIN BANK	(505) 880-1700
LAS VEGAS	SOUTHWEST CAPITAL BANK	(505) 425-7565
ARTESIA	WESTERN BK ARTESIA NEW MEXICO	(575) 748-1345
CARLSBAD	WESTERN COMMERCE BANK	(575) 887-6686
Rating: B+		
SOCORRO	FIRST STATE BK	(575) 835-1550
ROSWELL	VALLEY BANK OF COMMERCE	(575) 623-2265
CLOVIS	WESTERN BANK OF CLOVIS	(575) 769-1975

New York

Rating: A

City	Name	Telephone
UTICA	BANK OF UTICA	(315) 797-2700
GROTON	FIRST NATIONAL BK OF GROTON	(607) 898-5871
NEW YORK	GOLDMAN SACHS BANK USA	(212) 902-1000
GOUVERNEUR	GOUVERNEUR S&LA	(315) 287-2600

Rating: A-

City	Name	Telephone
DRYDEN	FIRST NATIONAL BK OF DRYDEN	(607) 844-8141
FULTON	FULTON SB	(315) 592-4201
FLUSHING	NEWBANK	(718) 353-9100
NEW YORK	SIGNATURE BANK	(646) 822-1500
SPENCER	TIOGA STATE BK	(607) 589-7000

Rating: B+

City	Name	Telephone
ASTORIA	ALMA BANK	(718) 267-1000
FLUSHING	AMERASIA BANK	(718) 463-3600
FLUSHING	ASIA BANK NA	(718) 961-9700
CATSKILL	BANK OF GREENE COUNTY	(518) 943-2600
NEW YORK	BESSEMER TRUST CO NA	(212) 708-9100
UNION SPRINGS	CAYUGA LAKE NATIONAL BK	(315) 889-7358
DE WITT	COMMUNITY BANK NA	(315) 445-2282
NEW YORK	DEUTSCHE BK TRUST CO AMERICAS	(212) 250-2500
NEW YORK	EASTBANK NA	(212) 219-9000
SYRACUSE	GEDDES FS&LA	(315) 468-6281
GLENS FALLS	GLENS FALLS NATIONAL BK & TR	(518) 793-4121
NEW YORK	SHINHAN BANK AMERICA	(646) 843-7300
HORNELL	STEUBEN TRUST CO	(607) 324-5010
ITHACA	TOMPKINS TRUST CO	(607) 273-3210
GENEVA	USNY BANK	(315) 789-1500

North Carolina

Rating: A-

City	Name	Telephone
MOUNT AIRY	SURREY BANK & TRUST	(336) 783-3900

Rating: B+

City	Name	Telephone
ROXBORO	ROXBORO SB SSB	(336) 599-2137
DURHAM	SQUARE 1 BANK	(919) 314-3040
OXFORD	UNION BANK & TRUST CO	(919) 603-5030

North Dakota

Rating: A+

City	Name	Telephone
FORMAN	SARGENT COUNTY BANK	(701) 724-3216

Rating: A

City	Name	Telephone
GRAND FORKS	ALERUS FINANCIAL NA	(701) 795-3200
BOWMAN	DAKOTA WESTERN BANK	(701) 523-5803
BEULAH	FIRST SECURITY BANK - WEST	(701) 873-4301

Rating: A-

City	Name	Telephone
WILLISTON	AMERICAN STATE BK & TRUST CO	(701) 774-4100
MOTT	COMMERCIAL BANK OF MOTT	(701) 824-2593
LANGDON	FARMERS & MERCHANTS STATE BK	(701) 256-5431
WILLISTON	FIRST NATIONAL BK & TRUST CO	(701) 577-2113
MUNICH	HORIZON FINANCIAL BANK	(701) 682-5331
POWERS LAKE	LIBERTY STATE BK	(701) 464-5421
DEVILS LAKE	RAMSEY NATIONAL BK	(701) 662-4024
CENTER	SECURITY FIRST BANK OF ND	(701) 794-8758
NAPOLEON	STOCK GROWERS BANK	(701) 754-2226
LEEDS	UNITED COMMUNITY BANK OF ND	(701) 466-2000

Rating: B+

City	Name	Telephone
DICKINSON	AMERICAN BANK CENTER	(701) 483-6811
FARGO	BELL STATE BK & TRUST	(701) 298-1500
HEBRON	DAKOTA COMMUNITY BANK & TRUST	(701) 878-4416
HUNTER	DAKOTA HERITAGE BANK OF ND	(701) 874-2161
WATFORD CITY	FIRST INTERNATIONAL BK & TRUST	(701) 842-2381
MILNOR	FIRST NATIONAL BK	(701) 427-5212
GOLVA	FIRST STATE BK OF GOLVA	(701) 872-3656
MINOT	FIRST WESTERN BANK & TRUST	(701) 852-3711
CARSON	GRANT COUNTY STATE BK	(701) 622-3491
DRAYTON	KODABANK	(701) 454-3317
MCCLUSKY	NORTH COUNTRY BANK	(701) 363-2265
BISMARCK	STARION FINANCIAL	(701) 250-1441

Ohio

Rating: A+

City	Name	Telephone
MASON	FDS BANK	(513) 573-2265
SAINT HENRY	ST HENRY BANK	(419) 678-2358

Rating: A

City	Name	Telephone
TIFFIN	FIRST BANK OF OHIO	(419) 448-9740

Rating: A-

City	Name	Telephone
ANDOVER	ANDOVER BANK	(440) 293-7256
UPPER ARLINGTO	ARLINGTON BANK	(614) 486-9000
BEVERLY	CITIZENS BANK CO	(740) 984-2381
DESHLER	CORN CITY STATE BK	(419) 278-0015
SPENCER	FARMERS SB	(330) 648-2441
COSHOCTON	HOME LOAN SB	(740) 622-0444
OTTOVILLE	OTTOVILLE BANK CO	(419) 453-3313
COLDWATER	PEOPLES BANK CO	(419) 678-2385

Rating: B+

City	Name	Telephone
BLUFFTON	CITIZENS NB OF BLUFFTON	(419) 358-8040
BLANCHESTER	FIRST NATIONAL BK BLANCHESTER	(937) 783-2451
CINCINNATI	FOUNDATION BANK	(513) 721-0120
HAMLER	HAMLER STATE BK	(419) 274-3955
MINSTER	MINSTER BANK	(419) 628-2351
CINCINNATI	NORTH SIDE BANK & TRUST CO	(513) 542-7800
WEST MANSFIELD	UNION BANKING CO	(937) 355-6511
MCARTHUR	VINTON COUNTY NATIONAL BK	(740) 596-2525
TOLEDO	WATERFORD BANK NA	(419) 720-3900

Oklahoma

City	Name	Telephone
Rating: A+		
BROKEN BOW	1ST BANK & TRUST	(580) 584-9123
PERKINS	PAYNE COUNTY BANK	(405) 547-2436
Rating: A		
GUYMON	BANK OF THE PANHANDLE	(580) 338-2593
THOMAS	BANK OF THE WEST	(580) 661-3541
LAWTON	CITY NB&TC OF LAWTON OKLAHOMA	(580) 355-3580
CLEO SPRINGS	CLEO STATE BK	(580) 438-2223
OKARCHE	COMMUNITY NATIONAL BK OKARCHE	(405) 263-7491
FAIRVIEW	FARMERS & MERCH NB OF FAIRVIEW	(580) 227-3773
OKARCHE	FIRST BANK OF OKARCHE	(405) 263-7215
ANADARKO	FIRST STATE BK	(405) 247-2471
FORT SILL	FORT SILL NATIONAL BK	(580) 357-9880
CHEYENNE	SECURITY STATE BK	(580) 497-3354
TUTTLE	SOONER STATE BK	(405) 381-2326
WYNNEWOOD	STATE BK OF WYNNEWOOD	(405) 665-2001
WELCH	WELCH STATE BK OF WELCH OKLA	(918) 788-3373
Rating: A-		
ALVA	ALVA STATE BK & TRUST CO	(580) 327-3300
ARDMORE	AMERICAN NATIONAL BK	(580) 226-6222
TEXHOMA	ANCHOR D BANK	(580) 423-7541
OKLAHOMA CITY	BANK 2	(405) 946-2265
CUSHING	BANK OF CUSHING	(918) 225-2010
POTEAU	CENTRAL NATIONAL BK OF POTEAU	(918) 647-2233
NEWKIRK	EASTMAN NATIONAL BK OF NEWKIRK	(580) 362-2511
DUNCAN	FIRST BANK & TRUST CO	(580) 255-1810
ELK CITY	FIRST NATIONAL B&T ELK CITY	(580) 225-2580
OKEENE	FIRST NATIONAL BK IN OKEENE	(580) 822-3300
HOOKER	FIRST NATIONAL BK OF HOOKER	(580) 652-2448
PORTER	FIRST STATE BK OF PORTER	(918) 483-2241
TULSA	GRAND BANK	(918) 491-9700
EDMOND	PRIME BANK	(405) 340-2775
ENID	SECURITY NATIONAL BK OF ENID	(580) 234-5151
SENTINEL	SOUTHWEST STATE BK	(580) 393-4367
Rating: B+		
LINDSAY	AMERICAN EXCHANGE BANK LINDSAY	(405) 756-3101
ATOKA	AMERISTATE BK	(580) 889-3375
MUSKOGEE	ARMSTRONG BANK	(918) 680-6900
OKLAHOMA CITY	BANK 7	(405) 810-8600
HYDRO	BANK OF HYDRO	(405) 663-2214
LAVERNE	BANK OF LAVERNE	(580) 921-3321
TULSA	BOKF NA	(918) 588-6000
PAWHUSKA	CITIZENS BANK OF OKLAHOMA	(918) 287-4111
OKEMAH	CITIZENS STATE BK	(918) 623-1551
GUYMON	CITY NB&TC OF GUYMON	(580) 338-6561
BRISTOW	COMMUNITY BANK	(918) 367-3343
FAIRVIEW	FAIRVIEW S&LA	(580) 227-3735
PERRY	FIRST BANK & TRUST CO	(580) 336-5562
CHANDLER	FIRST BANK OF CHANDLER	(405) 258-1210
WAURIKA	FIRST FARMERS NB OF WAURIKA	(580) 228-2326
OKLAHOMA CITY	FIRST LIBERTY BANK	(405) 608-4500
HEAVENER	FIRST NATIONAL BK	(918) 653-3200
ALTUS	FIRST NATIONAL BK IN ALTUS	(580) 482-7700
FLETCHER	FIRST NATIONAL BK OF FLETCHER	(580) 549-6106
THOMAS	FIRST NATIONAL BK OF THOMAS	(580) 661-3515
IDABEL	IDABEL NATIONAL BK	(580) 286-7656
BROKEN BOW	MCCURTAIN COUNTY NATIONAL BK	(580) 584-6262
WESTVILLE	PEOPLES BANK	(918) 723-5453
CHECOTAH	PEOPLES NATIONAL BK CHECOTAH	(918) 473-2237
CLAREMORE	RCB BANK	(918) 341-6150
NORMAN	REPUBLIC BANK & TRUST	(405) 360-5369
HUGO	SECURITY FIRST NB OF HUGO	(580) 326-9641
WEATHERFORD	SOUTHWEST NATIONAL BK	(580) 774-0900
LAMONT	STATE EXCHANGE BANK	(580) 388-4345
WOODWARD	STOCK EXCHANGE BANK	(580) 256-3314
WALTERS	WALTERS BANK & TRUST CO	(580) 875-3396
FORT COBB	WASHITA VALLEY BANK	(405) 643-2305

Oregon

City	Name	Telephone
Rating: A		
NEWPORT	OREGON COAST BANK	(541) 265-9000
EUGENE	PACIFIC CONTINENTAL BANK	(541) 686-8685
SALEM	PIONEER TRUST BANK NA	(503) 363-3136
Rating: B+		
CORVALLIS	CITIZENS BANK	(541) 752-5161
SANDY	CLACKAMAS COUNTY BANK	(503) 668-5501

Pennsylvania

City	Name	Telephone
Rating:	**A+**	
GRATZ	GRATZ BANK	(717) 365-3181
Rating:	**A**	
LATROBE	COMMERCIAL BANK & TRUST OF PA	(724) 539-3501
SMETHPORT	HAMLIN BANK & TRUST CO	(814) 887-5555
RADNOR	HAVERFORD TRUST CO	(610) 995-8700
HONESDALE	HONESDALE NATIONAL BK	(570) 253-3355
NEFFS	NEFFS NATIONAL BK	(610) 767-3875
TURBOTVILLE	TURBOTVILLE NATIONAL BK	(570) 649-5118
Rating:	**A-**	
WELLSBORO	CITIZENS & NORTHERN BANK	(570) 724-3411
PITTSBURGH	EUREKA BANK	(412) 681-8400
MALVERN	NATIONAL BK OF MALVERN	(610) 647-0100
NEW TRIPOLI	NEW TRIPOLI BANK	(610) 298-8811
PHILADELPHIA	PHILADELPHIA TRUST CO	(215) 979-3434
STRABANE	SLOVENIAN S&LA OF CANONSBURG	(724) 745-5000
LANCASTER	UNION COMMUNITY BANK	(717) 492-2222
WEST MILTON	WEST MILTON STATE BK	(570) 568-6851
LEVITTOWN	WILLIAM PENN BANK	(215) 269-1200
Rating:	**B+**	
ALLENTOWN	AMERICAN BANK	(610) 366-1800
LANDISBURG	BANK OF LANDISBURG	(717) 789-3213
BRYN MAWR	BRYN MAWR TRUST CO	(610) 581-4910
ALBION	COMMUNITY NATIONAL BK OF NW PA	(814) 756-4138
BLOOMSBURG	FIRST COLUMBIA BANK & TRUST CO	(570) 784-4400
BERWICK	FIRST KEYSTONE COMMUNITY BANK	(570) 752-3671
CONSHOHOCKEN	FIRSTRUST SB	(610) 238-5000
ERIE	MARQUETTE SB	(814) 455-4481
MIFFLINBURG	MIFFLINBURG BANK & TRUST CO	(570) 966-1041
MILTON	MILTON SAVINGS BANK	(570) 742-8541
MUNCY	MUNCY BANK & TRUST CO	(570) 546-2211
ALLENTOWN	NATIONAL PENN BANK	(800) 822-3321

South Carolina

Rating: A+

City	Name	Telephone
GAFFNEY	FIRST PIEDMONT FS&LA GAFFNEY	(864) 489-6046

Rating: A

City	Name	Telephone
SENECA	OCONEE FS&LA	(864) 882-2765

Rating: A-

City	Name	Telephone
MANNING	BANK OF CLARENDON	(803) 433-4451
HONEA PATH	COMMERCIAL BANK	(864) 369-7326
HAMPTON	PALMETTO STATE BK	(803) 943-2671

Rating: B+

City	Name	Telephone
CHARLESTON	BANK OF SOUTH CAROLINA	(843) 724-1500
SPARTANBURG	CAROLINA ALLIANCE BANK	(864) 208-2265
CHARLESTON	CRESCOM BANK	(843) 723-7700
HOLLY HILL	FARMERS & MERCH BANK OF SC	(803) 496-3430

South Dakota

Rating: A

City	Name	Telephone
HERREID	CAMPBELL COUNTY BANK	(605) 437-2294
FORT PIERRE	FIRST NATIONAL BK	(605) 223-2521
PHILIP	FIRST NATIONAL BK IN PHILIP	(605) 859-2525

Rating: A-

City	Name	Telephone
WESSINGTON SP	AMERICAN BANK & TRUST	(605) 539-1222
WAGNER	COMMERCIAL STATE BK OF WAGNER	(605) 384-3646
SIOUX FALLS	FIRST PREMIER BANK	(605) 357-3000
RAPID CITY	FIRST WESTERN FSB	(605) 341-1203
BELLE FOURCHE	PIONEER BANK & TRUST	(605) 892-2536
BRUCE	RICHLAND STATE BK	(605) 627-5671
SISSETON	ROBERTS COUNTY NB OF SISSETON	(605) 698-7621

Rating: B+

City	Name	Telephone
PARKSTON	FARMERS STATE BK	(605) 928-7991
BROOKINGS	FIRST BANK & TRUST	(605) 696-2265
SIOUX FALLS	FIRST BANK & TRUST	(605) 978-9300
MILBANK	FIRST BANK & TRUST OF MILBANK	(605) 432-5111
YANKTON	FIRST DAKOTA NATIONAL BK	(605) 665-7432
BURKE	FIRST FIDELITY BANK	(605) 775-2641
GROTON	FIRST STATE BK OF CLAREMONT	(605) 397-2711
ROSCOE	FIRST STATE BK OF ROSCOE	(605) 287-4451
REDFIELD	HEARTLAND STATE BK	(605) 475-5500
HOVEN	PLAINS COMMERCE BANK	(605) 948-2216
ESTELLINE	RELIABANK DAKOTA	(605) 873-2261
DAKOTA DUNES	SECURITY NATIONAL BK OF SD	(605) 232-6060

Tennessee

City	Name	Telephone
Rating: A+		
CARTHAGE	CITIZENS BANK	(615) 735-1490
Rating: A		
MEMPHIS	FINANCIAL FEDERAL BANK	(901) 756-2848
SHELBYVILLE	FIRST COMMUNITY BK OF BEDFORD	(931) 684-5800
Rating: A-		
DYERSBURG	FIRST CITIZENS NATIONAL BK	(731) 285-4410
UNION CITY	FIRST STATE BK	(731) 886-8800
TULLAHOMA	FIRST VISION BANK OF TENNESSEE	(931) 454-0500
MCKENZIE	MCKENZIE BANKING CO	(731) 352-2262
PARIS	SECURITY BANK & TRUST CO	(731) 642-6644
CLEVELAND	SOUTHERN HERITAGE BANK	(423) 473-7980
NASHVILLE	TRUXTON TRUST CO	(615) 515-1700
LEBANON	WILSON BANK & TRUST	(615) 444-2265
Rating: B+		
DICKSON	BANK OF DICKSON	(615) 446-3732
GLEASON	BANK OF GLEASON	(731) 648-5506
RUTLEDGE	CITIZENS B&TC GRAINGER COUNTY	(865) 828-5237
ELIZABETHTON	CITIZENS BANK	(423) 543-2265
SPRINGFIELD	COMMERCE UNION BANK	(615) 384-3357
ELIZABETHTON	ELIZABETHTON FSB	(423) 543-5050
LEWISBURG	FIRST COMMERCE BANK	(931) 359-4322
DICKSON	FIRST FEDERAL BANK	(615) 446-2822
MANCHESTER	FIRST NATIONAL BK MANCHESTER	(931) 728-3518
LAWRENCEBURG	LAWRENCEBURG FEDERAL BANK	(931) 762-7571
MEMPHIS	MAGNA BANK	(901) 259-5600
NASHVILLE	PINNACLE BANK	(615) 744-3700
ELIZABETHTON	SECURITY FEDERAL BANK	(423) 543-1000

Texas

City	Name	Telephone
Rating: A+		
BRADY	COMMERCIAL NATIONAL BK BRADY	(325) 597-2961
HUGHES SPRINGS	FIRST NB OF HUGHES SPRINGS	(903) 639-2521
DALLAS	INWOOD NATIONAL BK	(214) 358-5281
MUENSTER	MUENSTER STATE BK	(940) 759-2257
BROWNWOOD	TEXASBANK	(325) 649-9200
VERNON	WAGGONER NATIONAL BK OF VERNON	(940) 552-2511
Rating: A		
JACKSONVILLE	AUSTIN BANK TEXAS NA	(903) 586-1526
TYLER	CITIZENS 1ST BANK	(903) 581-1900
WILLS POINT	CITIZENS NB OF WILLS POINT	(903) 873-4157
FABENS	FIRST NATIONAL BK	(915) 779-7100
CARTHAGE	FIRST STATE BK & TRUST CO	(903) 693-6606
BEDIAS	FIRST STATE BK OF BEDIAS	(936) 395-2141
BEN WHEELER	FIRST STATE BK OF BEN WHEELER	(903) 833-5861
MASON	MASON BANK	(325) 347-5911
ROCKSPRINGS	PEOPLES STATE BK	(830) 683-2119
SANGER	SANGER BANK	(940) 458-4600
FARWELL	SECURITY STATE BK	(806) 481-3327
DE KALB	STATE BK OF DE KALB	(903) 667-2553
FORT WORTH	TRINITY BANK NA	(817) 763-9966
Rating: A-		
AMARILLO	AMARILLO NATIONAL BK	(806) 378-8000
MIDLAND	BANK OF TEXAS	(432) 221-6100
BUCKHOLTS	BUCKHOLTS STATE BK	(254) 593-3661
BUFFALO	CITIZENS STATE BK	(903) 322-4256
TYLER	CITIZENS STATE BK	(903) 581-8100
CORRIGAN	CITIZENS STATE BK	(936) 398-2566
MILES	CITIZENS STATE BK	(325) 468-3311
SEALY	CITIZENS STATE BK	(979) 885-3571
COLEMAN	COLEMAN COUNTY STATE BK	(325) 625-2172
LAREDO	COMMERCE BANK	(956) 724-1616
LONGVIEW	COMMUNITY BANK	(903) 236-4422
CORSICANA	COMMUNITY NATIONAL BK & TRUST	(903) 654-4500
SAN ANGELO	CROCKETT NATIONAL BK	(325) 658-6714
DILLEY	DILLEY STATE BK	(830) 965-1511
CENTER	FARMERS STATE BK	(936) 598-3311
FAYETTEVILLE	FAYETTEVILLE BANK	(979) 378-4261
BURKBURNETT	FIRST BANK	(940) 569-2221
ABILENE	FIRST FINANCIAL BANK NA	(325) 627-7155
HEBBRONVILLE	FIRST NATIONAL BK HEBBRONVILLE	(361) 527-3221
LIVINGSTON	FIRST NATIONAL BK LIVINGSTON	(936) 327-1234
ALBANY	FIRST NATIONAL BK OF ALBANY	(325) 762-2222
ALVIN	FIRST NATIONAL BK OF ALVIN	(281) 331-3151
ASPERMONT	FIRST NATIONAL BK OF ASPERMONT	(940) 989-3505
BELLVILLE	FIRST NATIONAL BK OF BELLVILLE	(979) 865-3181
BURLESON	FIRST NATIONAL BK OF BURLESON	(817) 295-0461
YOAKUM	FIRST STATE BK	(361) 293-3572
ATHENS	FIRST STATE BK	(903) 676-1900
SHALLOWATER	FIRST STATE BK	(806) 832-4525
BURNET	FIRST STATE BK OF BURNET	(512) 756-2191
GRANDVIEW	GRANDVIEW BANK	(817) 866-3316
GRAPEVINE	HBANK TEXAS	(817) 421-1212
HENDERSON	HENDERSON FSB	(903) 657-2577
INDUSTRY	INDUSTRY STATE BK	(979) 357-4437
ZAPATA	INTERNATIONAL BK OF COMMERCE	(956) 765-8361
BROWNSVILLE	INTERNATIONAL BK OF COMMERCE	(956) 547-1000
JOHNSON CITY	JOHNSON CITY BANK	(830) 868-7131
JUSTIN	JUSTIN STATE BK	(940) 648-2753
PARIS	LAMAR NATIONAL BK	(903) 785-0701
PLANO	LEGACYTEXAS BANK	(972) 461-1300
BOWIE	LEGEND BANK NA	(940) 872-2221
MARION	MARION STATE BK	(830) 420-2331
ANDREWS	NATIONAL BK OF ANDREWS	(432) 523-6800
DECATUR	NORTH TEXAS BANK NA	(940) 627-8767
PEARLAND	PEARLAND STATE BK	(281) 485-3211
DALLAS	PLAINSCAPITAL BANK	(214) 525-9100
DALLAS	PRESTON NATIONAL BK	(972) 960-6000
DALLAS	PRESTON STATE BANK	(972) 447-0800
SANTA ANNA	SANTA ANNA NATIONAL BK	(325) 348-3108
PEARSALL	SECURITY STATE BK	(830) 334-3606
CENTER	SHELBY SB SSB	(936) 598-5688
DALLAS	T BANK NA	(972) 720-9000
MONAHANS	TEJAS BANK	(432) 943-4230
MIDLAND	WEST TEXAS NATIONAL BK	(432) 685-6500
THE WOODLANDS	WOODFOREST NATIONAL BK	(832) 375-2505
YOAKUM	YOAKUM NATIONAL BK	(361) 293-5225
ZAPATA	ZAPATA NATIONAL BK	(956) 765-4302
Rating: B+		
MOUNT PLEASAN	AMERICAN NB OF MT PLEASANT	(903) 572-1776
DEL RIO	BANK & TRUST SSB	(830) 774-2555
BRENHAM	BANK OF BRENHAM NA	(979) 836-3332
MCLEAN	BANK OF COMMERCE	(806) 779-2461
CARMINE	CARMINE STATE BK	(979) 278-3244
WACO	CENTRAL NATIONAL BK	(254) 776-3800
AMARILLO	CITIZENS BANK	(806) 350-5600
BROWNWOOD	CITIZENS NB AT BROWNWOOD	(325) 643-3545
COLORADO CITY	CITY NATIONAL BK COLORADO CITY	(325) 728-5221
FORT WORTH	COLONIAL SAVINGS FA	(817) 390-2000
COMANCHE	COMANCHE NATIONAL BK	(325) 356-2577
NACOGDOCHES	COMMERCIAL BANK OF TEXAS NA	(936) 715-4100
WACO	COMMUNITY BANK & TRUST	(254) 753-1521
MAYPEARL	COWBOY BANK OF TEXAS	(972) 435-2131
GROESBECK	FARMERS STATE BK	(254) 729-3272
DIBOLL	FIRST BANK & TRUST EAST TEXAS	(936) 829-4721
FORT WORTH	FIRST COMMAND BANK	(888) 763-7600

Texas

City	Name	Telephone
CORPUS CHRISTI	FIRST COMMUNITY BANK	(361) 888-9310
WICHITA FALLS	FIRST NATIONAL BK	(940) 696-3000
SPEARMAN	FIRST NATIONAL BK	(806) 659-5544
MOUNT VERNON	FIRST NATIONAL BK MOUNT VERNON	(903) 537-2201
BASTROP	FIRST NATIONAL BK OF BASTROP	(512) 321-2561
ELDORADO	FIRST NATIONAL BK OF ELDORADO	(325) 853-2561
FLOYDADA	FIRST NATIONAL BK OF FLOYDADA	(806) 983-3717
SHINER	FIRST NATIONAL BK OF SHINER	(361) 594-3317
BREMOND	FIRST STAR BANK SSB	(254) 746-7031
LOUISE	FIRST STATE BK	(979) 648-2691
STRATFORD	FIRST STATE BK	(806) 396-5521
GRAHAM	FIRST STATE BK	(940) 549-8880
AUSTIN	FIRST STATE BK CENTRAL TEXAS	(512) 231-8821
PAINT ROCK	FIRST STATE BK OF PAINT ROCK	(325) 732-4386
DIMMITT	FIRST UNITED BANK	(806) 647-4151
SAN ANTONIO	FROST BANK	(210) 220-4011
GILMER	GILMER NATIONAL BK	(903) 843-5653
GRAHAM	GRAHAM SAVINGS & LOAN SSB	(940) 549-2066
HOUSTON	GREEN BANK NA	(713) 275-8204
GRUVER	GRUVER STATE BK	(806) 733-5061
MOUNT PLEASAN	GUARANTY BANK & TRUST NA	(903) 572-9881
HAMLIN	HAMLIN NATIONAL BK	(325) 576-2731
GALVESTON	HOMETOWN BANK NA	(409) 763-1271
HONDO	HONDO NATIONAL BK	(830) 426-3355
AUSTIN	HORIZON BANK SSB	(512) 637-5730
MEXIA	INCOMMONS BANK NA	(254) 562-3821
MCKINNEY	INDEPENDENT BANK	(972) 562-9004
HOUSTON	INTEGRITY BANK SSB	(713) 335-8700
LAREDO	INTERNATIONAL BK OF COMMERCE	(956) 722-7611
SAN ANTONIO	JEFFERSON BANK	(210) 734-4311
JUNCTION	JUNCTION NATIONAL BK	(325) 446-2531
PARIS	LIBERTY NATIONAL BK IN PARIS	(903) 785-5555
MOULTON	LONE STAR BANK SSB	(361) 596-4611
LUBBOCK	LONE STAR STATE BK OF WEST TX	(806) 771-7717
LYTLE	LYTLE STATE BK OF LYTLE TEXAS	(830) 709-3601
TEXAS CITY	MAINLAND BANK	(409) 948-1625
GATESVILLE	NATIONAL BK	(254) 865-2211
DALLAS	NEXBANK SSB	(972) 934-4700
NORMANGEE	NORMANGEE STATE BK	(936) 396-3611
PARIS	PEOPLES BANK	(903) 783-3800
HUMBLE	PLAINS STATE BK	(713) 559-6800
HOUSTON	POST OAK BANK NA	(713) 439-3900
EL CAMPO	PROSPERITY BANK	(979) 543-2200
FORT WORTH	RIVERBEND BANK	(817) 284-9598
ROUND TOP	ROUND TOP STATE BK	(979) 249-3151
MIDLAND	SECURITY BANK	(432) 570-9330
GEORGE WEST	SOUTHTRUST BANK NA	(361) 449-1571
DALLAS	STATE BK OF TEXAS	(972) 252-6000
LONGVIEW	TEXAS BANK & TRUST CO	(903) 237-5500
LAKE JACKSON	TEXAS GULF BANK NA	(979) 297-7211
BOERNE	TEXAS HERITAGE BANK	(830) 249-3955
FRISCO	TEXAS REPUBLIC BANK NA	(972) 334-0700
LOTT	TEXAS STAR BANK SSB	(254) 584-3171
SAN ANGELO	TEXAS STATE BK	(325) 949-3721
MINERAL WELLS	TITAN BANK NA	(940) 325-9821
PLANO	VIEWPOINT BANK NA	(972) 398-3472
KATY	WESTBOUND BANK	(713) 554-7615
EL PASO	WESTSTAR BANK	(915) 532-1000
FORT WORTH	WOODHAVEN NATIONAL BK	(817) 496-6700
CRYSTAL CITY	ZAVALA COUNTY BANK	(830) 374-5866

Utah

Rating: A+

City	Name	Telephone
SALT LAKE CITY	OPTUM BANK INC	(866) 234-8913
SALT LAKE CITY	TARGET BANK	(801) 512-8500

Rating: A

City	Name	Telephone
OGDEN	BANK OF UTAH	(801) 409-5000
SALT LAKE CITY	CONTINENTAL BANK	(801) 595-7000
SALT LAKE CITY	GE CAPITAL BANK	(801) 733-2820
PARK CITY	LCA BANK CORP	(435) 658-4824
SALT LAKE CITY	MARLIN BUSINESS BANK	(888) 479-9111
SALT LAKE CITY	WEBBANK	(801) 456-8350
MIDVALE	WEX BANK	(801) 568-4345

Rating: A-

City	Name	Telephone
MIDVALE	ALLY BANK	(801) 790-5000
SALT LAKE CITY	BRIGHTON BANK	(801) 943-6500
PROVO	CENTRAL BANK	(801) 375-1000
SALT LAKE CITY	SALLIE MAE BANK	(801) 320-3700
CEDAR CITY	STATE BK OF SOUTHERN UTAH	(435) 865-2300

Rating: B+

City	Name	Telephone
SALT LAKE CITY	AMERICAN EXP CENTURION BK	(801) 945-5000
SALT LAKE CITY	AMERICAN EXPRESS BANK FSB	(801) 945-5000
SALT LAKE CITY	BMW BANK OF NORTH AMERICA	(801) 461-6500
PROVO	GREEN DOT BANK DBA BONNEVILLE	(801) 344-7020
SALT LAKE CITY	MEDALLION BANK	(801) 284-7065
SALT LAKE CITY	MORGAN STANLEY BANK NA	(801) 236-3600
BOUNTIFUL	REPUBLIC BANK	(801) 397-0613
SALT LAKE CITY	UBS BANK USA	(801) 741-0310
SALINA	UTAH INDEPENDENT BANK	(435) 529-7459

Virginia

Rating: A

City	Name	Telephone
DANVILLE	AMERICAN NATIONAL BK & TRUST	(434) 792-5111
CARSON	BANK OF SOUTHSIDE VIRGINIA	(434) 246-5211
KENBRIDGE	BENCHMARK COMMUNITY BANK	(434) 676-9054
ALEXANDRIA	BURKE & HERBERT BK & TRUST CO	(703) 549-6600
CHESAPEAKE	MONARCH BANK	(757) 389-5159
BLACKSBURG	NATIONAL BK OF BLACKSBURG	(540) 951-6205

Rating: A-

City	Name	Telephone
RESTON	ACCESS NATIONAL BK	(703) 871-2100
PHENIX	BANK OF CHARLOTTE COUNTY	(434) 542-5111
BERRYVILLE	BANK OF CLARKE COUNTY	(540) 955-2510
BLACKSTONE	CITIZENS BANK & TRUST CO	(434) 292-8100
LEBANON	FIRST BANK & TRUST CO	(276) 889-4622
RESTON	JOHN MARSHALL BANK	(703) 584-0840
JONESVILLE	POWELL VALLEY NATIONAL BK	(276) 346-1414
MCLEAN	SONABANK	(703) 893-7400
DANVILLE	VIRGINIA BANK & TRUST CO	(434) 793-6411

Rating: B+

City	Name	Telephone
MCLEAN	CARDINAL BANK	(703) 584-3400
LEXINGTON	CORNERSTONE BANK NA	(540) 463-2222
NEW CASTLE	FARMERS & MERCH BK CRAIG CTY	(540) 864-5156
PENNINGTON GAP	FARMERS & MINERS BANK	(276) 546-4692
APPOMATTOX	FARMERS BANK OF APPOMATTOX	(434) 352-7171
GRUNDY	GRUNDY NATIONAL BK	(276) 935-8111

Washington

Rating: A

City	Name	Telephone
FIFE	FIFE COMMERCIAL BANK	(253) 922-5100

Rating: A-

City	Name	Telephone
WALLA WALLA	BANNER BANK	(509) 527-3636
RENTON	FIRST SB NORTHWEST	(425) 255-4400
FRIDAY HARBOR	ISLANDERS BANK	(360) 378-2265
YAKIMA	YAKIMA FS&LA	(509) 248-2634

Rating: B+

City	Name	Telephone
MOUNTLAKE TER	1ST SECURITY BANK OF WA	(800) 683-0973
CASHMERE	CASHMERE VALLEY BANK	(509) 782-2624
KENNEWICK	COMMUNITY FIRST BANK	(509) 783-3435
BELLINGHAM	PEOPLES BANK	(360) 715-4220

West Virginia

Rating: A-

City	Name	Telephone
CLAY	CLAY COUNTY BANK INC	(304) 587-4221
WILLIAMSON	FIRST NATIONAL BK WILLIAMSON	(304) 235-5300

Rating: B+

City	Name	Telephone
UNION	BANK OF MONROE	(304) 772-3034
MOUNT HOPE	BANK OF MOUNT HOPE INC	(304) 877-5551
WESTON	CITIZENS BANK OF WESTON INC	(304) 269-2862
PARKERSBURG	COMMUNITY BANK OF PARKERSBURG	(304) 485-7991
HURRICANE	PUTNAM COUNTY BANK	(304) 562-9931

Wisconsin

Rating: A

City	Name	Telephone
FOND DU LAC	AMERICAN BANK	(920) 922-9292
PRAIRIE DU SAC	BANK OF PRAIRIE DU SAC	(608) 643-3393
FOND DU LAC	NATIONAL EXCHANGE BANK & TRUST	(920) 921-7700
SHELL LAKE	SHELL LAKE STATE BK	(715) 468-7858

Rating: A-

City	Name	Telephone
FORT ATKINSON	BADGER BANK	(920) 563-2478
ALMA	BANK OF ALMA	(608) 685-4461
DEERFIELD	BANK OF DEERFIELD	(608) 764-5411
MADISON	BANKERS BANK	(608) 833-5550
BONDUEL	BONDUEL STATE BK	(715) 758-2141
EAU CLAIRE	CHARTER BANK EAU CLAIRE	(715) 832-4254
PLATTEVILLE	CLARE BANK NA	(608) 348-2727
HILLSBORO	FARMERS STATE BK HILLSBORO	(608) 489-2621
WAUPACA	FARMERS STATE BK OF WAUPACA	(715) 258-1400
WHITEWATER	FIRST CITIZENS STATE BK	(262) 473-2112
DARLINGTON	FIRST NATIONAL BK DARLINGTON	(608) 776-4071
GRAND MARSH	GRAND MARSH STATE BK	(608) 339-3351
SCHOFIELD	INTERCITY STATE BK	(715) 359-4231
AMHERST	INTERNATIONAL BK OF AMHERST	(715) 824-3325
BLACK RIVER FAL	JACKSON COUNTY BANK	(715) 284-5341
MADISON	JOHN DEERE FINANCIAL FSB	(608) 821-2000
LIVINGSTON	LIVINGSTON STATE BK	(608) 943-6351
MIDDLETON	MIDDLETON COMMUNITY BANK	(608) 824-3200
CHIPPEWA FALLS	NORTHWESTERN BANK	(715) 723-4461
FITCHBURG	OAK BANK	(608) 441-6000
PALMYRA	PALMYRA STATE BK	(262) 495-2101
HAYWARD	PEOPLES BANK MIDWEST	(715) 634-2674
MAZOMANIE	PEOPLES COMMUNITY BANK	(608) 795-2120
PESHTIGO	PESHTIGO NATIONAL BK	(715) 582-4512
WISCONSIN RAPI	RIVER CITIES BANK	(715) 422-1100
SPARTA	UNION NATIONAL BK & TRUST CO	(608) 269-6737

Rating: B+

City	Name	Telephone
DORCHESTER	ADVANTAGE COMMUNITY BANK	(715) 654-5100
MANITOWOC	BANK FIRST NATIONAL	(920) 684-6611
BRODHEAD	BANK OF BRODHEAD	(608) 897-2121
STURGEON BAY	BAYLAKE BANK	(920) 743-5551
LA CROSSE	CITIZENS STATE BK OF LA CROSSE	(608) 785-2265
LOYAL	CITIZENS STATE BK OF LOYAL	(715) 255-8526
BANGOR	FIRST NATIONAL BK OF BANGOR	(608) 486-2386
LAND OLAKES	HEADWATERS STATE BK	(715) 547-3383
HUSTISFORD	HUSTISFORD STATE BK	(920) 349-3241
SUPERIOR	NATIONAL BK OF COMMERCE	(715) 394-5531
NEKOOSA	NEKOOSA PORT EDWARDS STATE BK	(715) 886-3104
BARRON	STERLING BANK	(715) 537-3141
TOMAH	TIMBERWOOD BANK	(608) 372-2265
MEDFORD	TIME FSB	(715) 748-2231
WEST SALEM	UNION STATE BK OF WEST SALEM	(608) 786-0600
HORTONVILLE	WOLF RIVER COMMUNITY BANK	(920) 779-7000

Wyoming

Rating: A-

City	Name	Telephone
BASIN	SECURITY STATE BK	(307) 568-2483

Rating: B+

City	Name	Telephone
DOUGLAS	CONVERSE COUNTY BANK	(307) 358-5300
NEWCASTLE	FIRST STATE BK OF NEWCASTLE	(307) 746-4411
CASPER	HILLTOP NATIONAL BK	(307) 265-2740
CASPER	JONAH BANK OF WYOMING	(307) 237-4555
LUSK	LUSK STATE BK	(307) 334-2500
TORRINGTON	PLATTE VALLEY BANK	(307) 532-2111
ROCK SPRINGS	RSNB BANK	(307) 362-8801
CHEYENNE	SECURITY FIRST BANK	(307) 775-6500

Section III

Rating Upgrades and Downgrades

A list of all

U.S. Commercial Banks and Savings Banks

receiving a rating upgrade or downgrade during the current quarter.

Section III Contents

This section identifies those institutions receiving a rating change since the previous edition of this publication, whether it be a rating upgrade, rating downgrade, newly-rated company or the withdrawal of a rating. A rating upgrade or downgrade may entail a change from one letter grade to another, or it may mean the addition or deletion of a plus or minus sign within the same letter grade previously assigned to the company. Ratings are normally updated once each quarter of the year. In some instances, however, an institution's rating may be downgraded outside of the normal updates due to overriding circumstances.

1. **Institution Name** The name under which the institution was chartered. A company's name can be very similar to, or the same as, that of another, so verify the company's exact name, city, and state to make sure you are looking at the correct company.

2. **New Financial Strength Rating** Weiss rating assigned to the institution at the time of publication. Our ratings are designed to distinguish levels of insolvency risk and are measured on a scale from A to F based upon a wide range of factors. Highly rated companies are, in our opinion, less likely to experience financial difficulties than lower rated firms. See *About Weiss Financial Strength Ratings* for more information and a description of what each rating means.

3. **State** The state in which the institution's headquarters or main office is located.

4. **Date of Change** Date that rating was finalized.

Rating Upgrades

Name	State	Date of Change
Rating: A+		
LIBERTY SAVINGS BANK FSB	MN	11/24/14
Rating: A		
AMERICAN PLUS BANK NA	CA	11/24/14
ARMED FORCES BANK OF CA NA	CA	11/24/14
BANK OF OLD MONROE	MO	11/24/14
CLEO STATE BK	OK	11/24/14
FIRST SECURITY BANK - CANBY	MN	11/24/14
FIRST SECURITY BANK-SLEEPY EYE	MN	11/24/14
GOLDMAN SACHS BANK USA	NY	11/24/14
MEADOWS BANK	NV	11/24/14
OAKWORTH CAPITAL BANK	AL	11/24/14
OREGON COAST BANK	OR	11/24/14
PACIFIC CONTINENTAL BANK	OR	11/24/14
POPLAR GROVE STATE BK	IL	11/24/14
SECURITY STATE BK	OK	11/24/14
SMALL TOWN BANK	AL	11/24/14
SOY CAPITAL BANK & TRUST CO	IL	11/24/14
Rating: A-		
1ST BANK	MT	11/24/14
1ST SOURCE BANK	IN	11/24/14
ACADEMY BANK NA	CO	11/24/14
ANCHOR D BANK	OK	11/24/14
BADGER BANK	WI	11/24/14
BANK 2	OK	11/24/14
BANK OF DELIGHT	AR	11/24/14
BANK OF MONTANA	MT	11/24/14
BANKERS BANK OF THE WEST	CO	11/24/14
BENNINGTON STATE BK	KS	11/24/14
BLOOMSDALE BANK	MO	11/24/14
BRIGHTON BANK	UT	11/24/14
CATTLE NATIONAL BK & TRUST CO	NE	11/24/14
CENTRAL NATIONAL BK OF POTEAU	OK	11/24/14
CITIZENS STATE BK	IA	11/24/14
COMMERCIAL BANK	KY	11/24/14
COMMUNITY BUSINESS BANK	CA	11/24/14
COMMUNITY STATE BK OF MISSOURI	MO	11/24/14
EAGLEMARK SB	NV	11/24/14
ENTERPRISE NATIONAL BK NJ	NJ	11/24/14
EXCHANGE BANK OF ALABAMA	AL	11/24/14
F & M COMMUNITY BANK NA	MN	11/24/14
FARMERS STATE BK	GA	11/24/14
FIRST BANK BLUE EARTH	MN	11/24/14
FIRST NATIONAL BK STEELEVILLE	IL	11/24/14
FIRST STATE BK OF FORSYTH	MT	11/24/14
GUARANTY STATE BK & TRUST CO	KS	11/24/14
HOME STATE BK	MN	11/24/14
HOMESTEAD BANK	NE	11/24/14
JOHN MARSHALL BANK	VA	11/24/14
KCB BANK	MO	11/24/14
KENTLAND BANK	IN	11/24/14
LEGEND BANK NA	TX	11/24/14
LIBERTYVILLE SB	IA	11/24/14
LIVINGSTON STATE BK	WI	11/24/14
LUTHER BURBANK SAVINGS	CA	11/24/14
MARION STATE BK	TX	11/24/14
MIDWEST BANK NA	NE	11/24/14
MIDWESTONE BANK	IA	11/24/14
NORTHEAST SECURITY BANK	IA	11/24/14
PACIFIC PREMIER BANK	CA	11/24/14
PALMETTO STATE BK	SC	11/24/14
PEOPLES BANK MIDWEST	WI	11/24/14
PEOPLES COMMUNITY BANK	WI	11/24/14
PEOPLES NATIONAL BK OF KEWANEE	IL	11/24/14
POWELL VALLEY NATIONAL BK	VA	11/24/14
PRESTON STATE BANK	TX	11/24/14
RIVER CITIES BANK	WI	11/24/14
SALIN BANK & TRUST CO	IN	11/24/14
SECURITY STATE BK	IA	11/24/14
SONABANK	VA	11/24/14
STATE BK & TRUST CO	GA	11/24/14
TEUTOPOLIS STATE BK	IL	11/24/14
UNITED COMMUNITY BANK OF ND	ND	11/24/14
WEST TEXAS NATIONAL BK	TX	11/24/14
Rating: B+		
AMERICAN EXP CENTURION BK	UT	11/24/14
AMERICAN EXPRESS BANK FSB	UT	11/24/14
ASIA BANK NA	NY	11/24/14
BANK OF HANCOCK COUNTY	GA	11/24/14
BANK OF OFALLON	IL	11/24/14
BANK OF STAR CITY	AR	11/24/14
BANK OF STOCKTON	CA	11/24/14
BANKLIBERTY	MO	11/24/14
BANKWEST OF KANSAS	KS	11/24/14
BAYLAKE BANK	WI	11/24/14
CAROLINA ALLIANCE BANK	SC	11/24/14
CENTRAL STATE BK	IA	11/24/14
CENTURY BANK OF THE OZARKS	MO	11/24/14
CHINO COMMERCIAL BANK NA	CA	11/24/14
CLACKAMAS COUNTY BANK	OR	11/24/14
COMMERCE UNION BANK	TN	11/24/14
COMMERCIAL BANK OF TEXAS NA	TX	11/24/14
COMMUNITY BKG CO OF FITZGERALD	GA	11/24/14
COMMUNITY STATE BK	IL	11/24/14
CONCORDIA BANK	MO	11/24/14
CORNERSTONE BANK NA	VA	11/24/14

Rating Upgrades

Name	State	Date of Change
COWBOY BANK OF TEXAS	TX	11/24/14
CRESCOM BANK	SC	11/24/14
FIRST BANK & TRUST	SD	11/24/14
FIRST BANK & TRUST	SD	11/24/14
FIRST BANK & TRUST OF MILBANK	SD	11/24/14
FIRST FEDERAL BANK	TN	11/24/14
FIRST FIDELITY BANK	SD	11/24/14
FIRST MISSOURI BANK	MO	11/24/14
FIRST NATIONAL BK IN ALTUS	OK	11/24/14
FIRST NATIONAL BK IN STAUNTON	IL	11/24/14
FIRST NATIONAL BK OF BANGOR	WI	11/24/14
FIRST NATIONAL BK OF TALLADEGA	AL	11/24/14
FIRST STATE BK	TX	11/24/14
FIRST TRUST BANK OF ILLINOIS	IL	11/24/14
FIRST WESTERN BANK & TRUST	ND	11/24/14
FIRSTOAK BANK	KS	11/24/14
FISHER NATIONAL BK	IL	11/24/14
FOUNDATION BANK	OH	11/24/14
FRANKLIN BANK	IL	11/24/14
GEORGIA COMMERCE BANK	GA	11/24/14
GRANT COUNTY STATE BK	IN	11/24/14
GREEN BANK NA	TX	11/24/14
HANMI BANK	CA	11/24/14
HEARTLAND BANK & TRUST CO	IL	11/24/14
HERITAGE BANK OF COMMERCE	CA	11/24/14
HOMETOWN BANK NA	TX	11/24/14
KERNDT BROTHERS SB	IA	11/24/14
MERCHANTS BANK OF INDIANA	IN	11/24/14
MERCHANTS BK OF CALIFORNIA NA	CA	11/24/14
MISSOURI BANK	MO	11/24/14
MISSOURI BANK II	MO	11/24/14
MORGAN STANLEY BANK NA	UT	11/24/14
MORTON COMMUNITY BANK	IL	11/24/14
NORTH VALLEY BANK	CO	11/24/14
NORTHERN BANK & TRUST CO	MA	11/24/14
OPEN BANK	CA	11/24/14
OPUS BANK	CA	11/24/14
PEOPLES BANK	KS	11/24/14
PEOPLESSOUTH BANK	GA	11/24/14
PUTNAM COUNTY BANK	WV	11/24/14
RESURGENS BANK	GA	11/24/14
SENTRY BANK	MN	11/24/14
SHERBURNE STATE BK	MN	11/24/14
STIFEL BANK & TRUST	MO	11/24/14
STOCKGROWERS STATE BK	KS	11/24/14
TEXAS GULF BANK NA	TX	11/24/14
TEXAS STATE BK	TX	11/24/14
TIMBERWOOD BANK	WI	11/24/14
TITAN BANK NA	TX	11/24/14
TOMPKINS TRUST CO	NY	11/24/14
UTAH INDEPENDENT BANK	UT	11/24/14
WELCOME STATE BK	MN	11/24/14
WEST ALABAMA BANK & TRUST	AL	11/24/14
WEST PLAINS BANK	NE	11/24/14
WESTBOUND BANK	TX	11/24/14
WESTSTAR BANK	TX	11/24/14
WOLF RIVER COMMUNITY BANK	WI	11/24/14

Rating: B

Name	State	Date of Change
1ST ENTERPRISE BANK	CA	11/24/14
ACKLEY STATE BK	IA	11/24/14
ALDEN STATE BK	MI	11/24/14
ALPINE CAPITAL BANK	NY	11/24/14
AMERICAN CONTINENTAL BANK	CA	11/24/14
AMERICAN STATE BK OF GRYGLA	MN	11/24/14
AMERICAS COMMUNITY BANK	MO	11/24/14
ARMED FORCES BANK NA	KS	11/24/14
AUSTIN CAPITAL BANK SSB	TX	11/24/14
BANC OF CALIFORNIA NA	CA	11/24/14
BANK OF ANN ARBOR	MI	11/24/14
BANK OF GRANDIN	MO	11/24/14
BANK OF GRAVETT	AR	11/24/14
BANK OF MARION	VA	11/24/14
BANK OF SALEM	AR	11/24/14
BANK OF TENNESSEE	TN	11/24/14
BANK RHODE ISLAND	RI	11/24/14
BANK SNB	OK	11/24/14
BANKWELL BANK	CT	11/24/14
BIPPUS STATE BK	IN	11/24/14
BNY MELLON NA	PA	11/24/14
BROOKLINE BANK	MA	11/24/14
CENTRAL BANK & TRUST CO	KS	11/24/14
CENTURY BANK	MS	11/24/14
CFG COMMUNITY BANK	MD	11/24/14
CITIZENS BANK	AR	11/24/14
CITIZENS BANK OF FAYETTE	AL	11/24/14
CITIZENS SB	OH	11/24/14
CITYWIDE BANKS	CO	11/24/14
COMMERCIAL BANKING CO	GA	11/24/14
COMMUNITY BANK	LA	11/24/14
COMMUNITY BANK CBD	WI	11/24/14
COMMUNITY BANK OF OELWEIN	IA	11/24/14
CONCORDIA BANK & TRUST CO	LA	11/24/14
COTTONPORT BANK	LA	11/24/14
DEPARTMENT STORES NATIONAL BK	SD	11/24/14
ENTERPRISE BANK	TX	11/24/14
FARMERS & MERCH BK HUTSONVILLE	IL	11/24/14
FARMERS & MERCHANTS BANK	OH	11/24/14
FARMERS & MERCHANTS BANK	WI	11/24/14
FARMERS STATE BK ALLEN OK	OK	11/24/14

Rating Upgrades

Name	State	Date of Change
FIRST BANK OF OWASSO	OK	11/24/14
FIRST CENTRAL BANK	NE	11/24/14
FIRST FREEDOM BANK	TN	11/24/14
FIRST MINNESOTA BANK	MN	11/24/14
FIRST NATIONAL BK	MO	11/24/14
FIRST NATIONAL BK & TRUST CO	OK	11/24/14
FIRST NATIONAL BK MOUNT DORA	FL	11/24/14
FIRST NATIONAL BK OF MUSCATINE	IA	11/24/14
FIRST NATIONAL BK OF SPARTA	IL	11/24/14
FIRST NATIONAL BK SCOTT CITY	KS	11/24/14
FIRST S&LA	NC	11/24/14
FIRST STATE BK	IA	11/24/14
FIRST STATE BK OF ST CHARLES	MO	11/24/14
FIRST TENNESSEE BANK NA	TN	11/24/14
FIRST UNITED BANK & TRUST CO	OK	11/24/14
FORRESTON STATE BK	IL	11/24/14
FRANKLIN SYNERGY BANK	TN	11/24/14
FRIEND BANK	AL	11/24/14
GNB BANK	IA	11/24/14
GRAND SB	OK	11/24/14
GRANT COUNTY BANK	KS	11/24/14
GREAT PLAINS BANK	SD	11/24/14
HOME STATE BK	CO	11/24/14
HOMEWOOD FSB	MD	11/24/14
IPSWICH STATE BK	SD	11/24/14
LEGACY NATIONAL BK	AR	11/24/14
LORRAINE STATE BK	KS	11/24/14
LUBBOCK NATIONAL BK	TX	11/24/14
MCCLAIN BANK	OK	11/24/14
MERCER COUNTY STATE BK	PA	11/24/14
MERCHANTS & PLANTERS BANK	TN	11/24/14
METZ BANKING CO	MO	11/24/14
MIAMI SAVINGS BANK	OH	11/24/14
MONTROSEBANK	CO	11/24/14
NEW CENTURY BANK	KS	11/24/14
NICOLET NATIONAL BK	WI	11/24/14
NORTHEAST BANK	MN	11/24/14
NORTHEAST BANK	ME	11/24/14
NORTHSTAR BANK	IA	11/24/14
PARADISE BANK	FL	11/24/14
PEOPLES BANK	KS	11/24/14
PEOPLES BANK OF THE OZARKS	MO	11/24/14
PIONEER BANK	MN	11/24/14
PLUS INTERNATIONAL BK	FL	11/24/14
SAVANNA-THOMSON STATE BK	IL	11/24/14
SCHERTZ BANK & TRUST	TX	11/24/14
SECURITY BANK	AR	11/24/14
SECURITY BANK	NE	11/24/14
SECURITY SB	SD	11/24/14
SECURITY STATE BK OF MARINE	MN	11/24/14
SOUTHERN COMMERCE BANK NA	FL	11/24/14
SOUTHWEST BANK	TX	11/24/14
SPRINGFIELD FIRST COMMUNITY BK	MO	11/24/14
SPRINGFIELD STATE BK	NE	11/24/14
STATE BK OF DOWNS	KS	11/24/14
STATE BK OF NEW PRAGUE	MN	11/24/14
STEPHENSON NATIONAL BK & TRUST	WI	11/24/14
SUNMARK COMMUNITY BANK	GA	11/24/14
SUTTON BANK	OH	11/24/14
TECUMSEH FEDERAL BANK	NE	11/24/14
TEXAS BANK FINANCIAL	TX	11/24/14
TEXAS NATIONAL BK JACKSONVILLE	TX	11/24/14
TIPTON LATHAM BANK NA	MO	11/24/14
TRADERS BANK	TN	11/24/14
TRI-COUNTY BANK	MI	11/24/14
TRI-COUNTY TRUST CO	MO	11/24/14
TRINITY BANK	AL	11/24/14
TRUSTBANK	IL	11/24/14
UMPQUA BANK	OR	11/24/14
UNITED COMMUNITY BANK	GA	11/24/14
UNITED SECURITY BANK	CA	11/24/14
WASHITA STATE BK	OK	11/24/14
WATERSTONE BANK SSB	WI	11/24/14
WILLIAMSTOWN BANK INC	WV	11/24/14
WINSIDE STATE BK	NE	11/24/14
WOODLANDS NATIONAL BK	MN	11/24/14
WYOMING BANK & TRUST	WY	11/24/14

Rating: B-

Name	State	Date of Change
1ST BANK NA	TX	11/24/14
21ST CENTURY BANK	MN	11/24/14
ACCESS BANK	NE	11/24/14
ADAMS DAIRY BANK	MO	11/24/14
ALTON BANK	MO	11/24/14
AMERICAN NATIONAL BK	FL	11/24/14
AMERICAN TRUST BANK OF EAST TN	TN	11/24/14
AQUESTA BANK	NC	11/24/14
ATLANTIC NATIONAL BK	GA	11/24/14
BANAMEX USA	CA	11/24/14
BANK OF COMMERCE	OK	11/24/14
BANK OF COMMERCE & TRUST CO	KS	11/24/14
BANK OF EARLY	GA	11/24/14
BANK OF EASTON	MA	11/24/14
BANK OF JACKSON	TN	11/24/14
BANK OF KREMLIN	OK	11/24/14
BANK OF MARINGOUIN	LA	11/24/14
BANK OF MEAD	NE	11/24/14
BANK OF MILLBROOK	NY	11/24/14
BANK OF OAK RIDGE	LA	11/24/14
BANK OF POYNETTE	WI	11/24/14

Rating Upgrades

Name	State	Date of Change	Name	State	Date of Change
BANK OF WISCONSIN DELLS	WI	11/24/14	FIDELITY STATE BK & TRUST CO	KS	11/24/14
BANK STAR ONE	MO	11/24/14	FIRST AMERICAN INTL BANK	NY	11/24/14
BANKSTAR FINANCIAL	SD	11/24/14	FIRST BANK	VA	11/24/14
BARRINGTON BANK & TRUST CO NA	IL	11/24/14	FIRST FEDERAL BANK A FSB	AL	11/24/14
BEVERLY BANK & TRUST CO NA	IL	11/24/14	FIRST NATIONAL BK DECATUR CTY	GA	11/24/14
BLC COMMUNITY BANK	WI	11/24/14	FIRST NATIONAL BK EAGLE LAKE	TX	11/24/14
BLUEGRASS COMMUNITY BANK	KY	11/24/14	FIRST NATIONAL BK NORTHERN CA	CA	11/24/14
BNY MELLON TRUST OF DELAWARE	DE	11/24/14	FIRST NATIONAL BK OF GILBERT	MN	11/24/14
BRANCH BANKING & TRUST CO	NC	11/24/14	FIRST NATIONAL BK OF WINNSBORO	TX	11/24/14
BRIDGE CITY STATE BK	TX	11/24/14	FIRST SOUTH BANK	NC	11/24/14
BUSINESS BANK OF SAINT LOUIS	MO	11/24/14	FIRST SOUTHERN NATIONAL BK	KY	11/24/14
CADENCE BANK NA	AL	11/24/14	FIRST STATE BK	OK	11/24/14
CAMBRIDGE STATE BK	WI	11/24/14	FIRST STATE BK	OK	11/24/14
CAPE BANK	NJ	11/24/14	FIRST STATE BK OF BROWNSBORO	TX	11/24/14
CAPITAL PACIFIC BANK	OR	11/24/14	FIVE STAR BANK	CA	11/24/14
CASS COUNTY BANK INC	NE	11/24/14	FLORIDA BUSINESS BANK	FL	11/24/14
CHESAPEAKE BANK & TRUST CO	MD	11/24/14	FLUSHING BANK	NY	11/24/14
CHESTER COUNTY BANK	TN	11/24/14	FORCHT BANK NA	KY	11/24/14
CHINATOWN FSB	NY	11/24/14	FREEDOM BANK OF SOUTHERN MO	MO	11/24/14
CITIBANK NA	SD	11/24/14	FRONTIER STATE BK	OK	11/24/14
CITIZENS BANK	MS	11/24/14	FULTON BANK OF NEW JERSEY	NJ	11/24/14
CITIZENS NB OF MCCONNELSVILLE	OH	11/24/14	GRAND VALLEY BANK	UT	11/24/14
CITIZENS STATE BK	IL	11/24/14	HEARTLAND STATE BK	ND	11/24/14
CITIZENS STATE BK	NE	11/24/14	HOME FSB	MN	11/24/14
CLARKE COUNTY STATE BK	IA	11/24/14	IBERIABANK	LA	11/24/14
COLONY BANK	GA	11/24/14	INTEGRITY BANK & TRUST	CO	11/24/14
COMMERCE COMMUNITY BANK	LA	11/24/14	INTERSTATE BK SSB	TX	11/24/14
COMMERCIAL BANK	GA	11/24/14	JACKSON COUNTY BANK	IN	11/24/14
COMMUNITY FIRST BANK	AR	11/24/14	KENSINGTON BANK	MN	11/24/14
COMMUNITY POINT BANK	MO	11/24/14	LAMESA NATIONAL BK	TX	11/24/14
COMMUNITY RESOURCE BANK	MN	11/24/14	LIBERTY BANK	IL	11/24/14
COMMUNITY STATE BK	AR	11/24/14	LIBERTY BANK	TX	11/24/14
CORNERSTONE NATIONAL BK & TR	IL	11/24/14	LINCOLN COMMUNITY BANK	WI	11/24/14
DAKOTA STATE BK	SD	11/24/14	MACATAWA BANK	MI	11/24/14
DEARBORN FSB	MI	11/24/14	MARLBOROUGH SB	MA	11/24/14
EATON FSB	MI	11/24/14	MCCLAVE STATE BK	CO	11/24/14
ENNIS STATE BK	TX	11/24/14	MECHANICS BANK	CA	11/24/14
EXCHANGE BANK	GA	11/24/14	MERCHANTS & FARMERS BANK	AR	11/24/14
EXCHANGE BANK	CA	11/24/14	MORGAN STANLEY PRIVATE BANK NA	NY	11/24/14
EXCHANGE STATE BK	IA	11/24/14	MVB BANK INC	WV	11/24/14
EXECUTIVE NATIONAL BK	FL	11/24/14	NATIONAL BK OF WAUPUN	WI	11/24/14
FARMERS & MERCH BK OF KENDALL	WI	11/24/14	NEIGHBORHOOD NATIONAL BK	MN	11/24/14
FARMERS & MERCHANTS BANK	VA	11/24/14	NEW TRADITIONS BANK	FL	11/24/14
FARMERS & MERCHANTS BANK	TN	11/24/14	NORTH COUNTRY SB	NY	11/24/14
FARMERS BANK FRANKFORT INDIANA	IN	11/24/14	NORTH STATE BK	NC	11/24/14
FARMERS BANK OF MT PULASKI	IL	11/24/14	NORTHERN TRUST CO	IL	11/24/14
FARMERS NATIONAL BK OF LEBANON	KY	11/24/14	NVE BANK	NJ	11/24/14
FARMERS SB	IA	11/24/14	OCEANFIRST BANK	NJ	11/24/14
FARMERS STATE BK OF DANFORTH	IL	11/24/14	ONE SOUTH BANK	FL	11/24/14
FARMERS STATE BK OF DARWIN	MN	11/24/14	OZARK HERITAGE BANK NA	AR	11/24/14

Rating Upgrades

Name	State	Date of Change
PACIFIC GLOBAL BANK	IL	11/24/14
PALMETTO BANK	SC	11/24/14
PAN PACIFIC BANK	CA	11/24/14
PEOPLES BANK SB	IN	11/24/14
PEOPLES EXCHANGE BANK	KS	11/24/14
PEOPLES FSB OF DEKALB COUNTY	IN	11/24/14
PEOPLES STATE BK	TX	11/24/14
PREMIER BANK ROCHESTER	MN	11/24/14
RELIANCE BANK	MN	11/24/14
RELIANZBANK	KS	11/24/14
ROSE HILL BANK	KS	11/24/14
SANFORD INSTITUTION FOR SVGS	ME	11/24/14
SOMERSET SAVINGS BANK SLA	NJ	11/24/14
SOUTHERN MICHIGAN BANK & TRUST	MI	11/24/14
SOVEREIGN BANK	TX	11/24/14
SPRING BANK	NY	11/24/14
SUFFOLK COUNTY NATIONAL BANK	NY	11/24/14
SUMMIT COMMUNITY BANK INC	WV	11/24/14
SUNSTATE BK	FL	11/24/14
TEXAS FINANCIAL BANK	TX	11/24/14
TEXAS LEADERSHIP BANK	TX	11/24/14
UNION STATE BK	IA	11/24/14
UNION STATE BK	KS	11/24/14
UNITED BANK	WI	11/24/14
UNITED SOUTHERN BANK	KY	11/24/14
UNITI BANK	CA	11/24/14
UNIVERSITY BANK	MI	11/24/14
VERITEX COMMUNITY BANK	TX	11/24/14
WALWORTH STATE BK	WI	11/24/14
WASHINGTON BUSINESS BANK	WA	11/24/14
WEST TEXAS STATE BK	TX	11/24/14

Rating: C+

Name	State	Date of Change
ABBEVILLE FIRST BANK	SC	11/24/14
ALLIANCE BANK	MN	11/24/14
ALLIANT BANK	MO	11/24/14
ALTERRA BANK	KS	11/24/14
AMERICAN BANK	OK	11/24/14
AMERICAN BANK	MD	11/24/14
AMERICAN MIDWEST BANK	IL	11/24/14
AMERICAN STATE BK & TRUST CO	KS	11/24/14
ANB BANK	CO	11/24/14
ARBOR BANK	NE	11/24/14
ARROWHEAD BANK	TX	11/24/14
AVENUE BANK	TN	11/24/14
BANK OF CAMDEN	TN	11/24/14
BANK OF JACKSON HOLE	WY	11/24/14
BANK OF LAKE MILLS	WI	11/24/14
BANK OF LINCOLN COUNTY	TN	11/24/14
BANK OF MCCRORY	AR	11/24/14
BANK OF NEW YORK MELLON	NY	11/24/14
BANK OF RINGGOLD	LA	11/24/14
BANK OF WASHINGTON	WA	11/24/14
BANK VI	KS	11/24/14
BANKERS BANK OF KANSAS	KS	11/24/14
BEARDSTOWN SAVINGS SB	IL	11/24/14
BELMONT BANK & TRUST CO	IL	11/24/14
CALLAWAY BANK	MO	11/24/14
CAMBRIDGE STATE BK	MN	11/24/14
CENDERA BANK NA	TX	11/24/14
CITIZENS BANK	KY	11/24/14
CITIZENS BANK OF NORTHERN KY	KY	11/24/14
CITIZENS BANK OF PAGOSA SPRING	CO	11/24/14
CITIZENS BANKING CO	OH	11/24/14
CITIZENS FIRST BANK	TN	11/24/14
CITY NATIONAL BK OF TAYLOR	TX	11/24/14
COMMERCIAL SB	OH	11/24/14
COMMUNITY BANK	IN	11/24/14
COMMUNITY BANK	NE	11/24/14
COMMUNITY BANK & TRUST	IA	11/24/14
COMPASS SB	PA	11/24/14
CORNERSTONE NATIONAL BK	SC	11/24/14
E*TRADE SAVINGS BANK	VA	11/24/14
EXCHANGE BANK	OK	11/24/14
EXCHANGE STATE BK ST PAUL KS	KS	11/24/14
F&M BANK	OK	11/24/14
FARMERS & MERCH STATE BK	IL	11/24/14
FARMERS STATE BK	IL	11/24/14
FELICIANA BANK & TRUST CO	LA	11/24/14
FIRST BANK	FL	11/24/14
FIRST COMMERCIAL BANK	OK	11/24/14
FIRST COMMONS BANK NA	MA	11/24/14
FIRST COMMUNITY BANK	AL	11/24/14
FIRST FEDERAL BK OF WISCONSIN	WI	11/24/14
FIRST FSB	WY	11/24/14
FIRST MO STATE BK OF CAPE CTY	MO	11/24/14
FIRST NATIONAL BK & TRUST CO	OK	11/24/14
FIRST NATIONAL BK IN TRINIDAD	CO	11/24/14
FIRST NATIONAL BK IN WADENA	MN	11/24/14
FIRST NATIONAL BK OF DWIGHT	IL	11/24/14
FIRST NATIONAL BK OF FREDERICK	SD	11/24/14
FIRST NATIONAL BK OF HARTFORD	AL	11/24/14
FIRST NATIONAL BK OF LINDSAY	OK	11/24/14
FIRST NATIONAL BK OF SANDOVAL	IL	11/24/14
FIRST NATIONAL BK OF SEDAN	KS	11/24/14
FIRST NB OF RUSSELL SPRINGS	KY	11/24/14
FIRST SECURITY BANK INC	KY	11/24/14
FIRST STATE BK	TX	11/24/14
FIRST STATE BK	NE	11/24/14
FIRST STATE BK NEBRASKA	NE	11/24/14

Rating Upgrades

Name	State	Date of Change
FNB OF CENTRAL ALABAMA	AL	11/24/14
FRIENDLY HILLS BANK	CA	11/24/14
GRAND BANK OF TEXAS	TX	11/24/14
GREENFIELD SB	MA	11/24/14
GREENWOODS STATE BK	WI	11/24/14
HASKELL NATIONAL BK	TX	11/24/14
HERITAGE BANK OF NEVADA	NV	11/24/14
HICKSVILLE BANK	OH	11/24/14
HIGH POINT BANK & TRUST CO	NC	11/24/14
HIGHLAND COMMERCIAL BANK	GA	11/24/14
HNB FIRST BANK	AL	11/24/14
HOME BANKING CO	TN	11/24/14
HOME SAVINGS & LOAN CO	OH	11/24/14
HOMEBANK OF ARKANSAS	AR	11/24/14
HUNTINGTON STATE BK	TX	11/24/14
ILLINOIS NATIONAL BK	IL	11/24/14
INDEPENDENT BANK OF TEXAS	TX	11/24/14
INLAND NORTHWEST BANK	WA	11/24/14
JEFFERSON BANK OF FLORIDA	FL	11/24/14
LIBERTY NATIONAL BK	OH	11/24/14
LINCOLN FSB OF NEBRASKA	NE	11/24/14
LOWELL FIVE CENT SB	MA	11/24/14
MAIN STREET BANK CORP	WV	11/24/14
MARKESAN STATE BK	WI	11/24/14
MAYVILLE SB	WI	11/24/14
MECHANICS SB	ME	11/24/14
MERCHANTS & FARMERS BANK	MS	11/24/14
MERCHANTS & SOUTHERN BANK	FL	11/24/14
METROPOLITAN NATIONAL BK	MO	11/24/14
MID PENN BANK	PA	11/24/14
NATIONAL BK OF HARVEY	ND	11/24/14
NICOLLET COUNTY BK OF ST PETER	MN	11/24/14
NORTHEAST GEORGIA BANK	GA	11/24/14
NORTHWAY BANK	NH	11/24/14
OLDTOWN BANK	NC	11/24/14
ORRSTOWN BANK	PA	11/24/14
OXFORD UNIVERSITY BANK	MS	11/24/14
PEABODY STATE BK	KS	11/24/14
PEOPLES BANK	VA	11/24/14
PEOPLES BANK	KY	11/24/14
PEOPLES TRUST CO OF ST ALBANS	VT	11/24/14
PINNACLE BANK	GA	11/24/14
PINNACLE BANK	CA	11/24/14
PREMIER BANK & TRUST	OH	11/24/14
PRESCOTT STATE BK	KS	11/24/14
R BANK	TX	11/24/14
REELFOOT BANK	TN	11/24/14
RELIANCE BANK	MO	11/24/14
SAVINGS BANK OF DANBURY	CT	11/24/14
SECURITY FIRST BANK	NE	11/24/14
SECURITY FIRST BANK	CA	11/24/14
SECURITY STATE BK OF HIBBING	MN	11/24/14
TOMATOBANK	CA	11/24/14
TOWN & COUNTRY BANK	UT	11/24/14
TRI COUNTIES BANK	CA	11/24/14
TWO RIVERS BANK	NE	11/24/14
TWO RIVERS BANK & TRUST	IA	11/24/14
UNION BANK OF BLAIR	WI	11/24/14
UNION NATIONAL BK	IL	11/24/14
UNION STATE BK OF HAZEN	ND	11/24/14
UNITED BANK & TRUST CO	KY	11/24/14
UNITED-AMERICAN SB	PA	11/24/14
UPSTATE NATIONAL BK	NY	11/24/14
US BANK NA	OH	11/24/14
VALLEY NATIONAL BK	OK	11/24/14
VISTA BANK	TX	11/24/14
WAYNE BANK & TRUST CO	IN	11/24/14
WELLS FARGO FINANCIAL NATIONAL	NV	11/24/14
WORTHINGTON NATIONAL BK	TX	11/24/14
WPS COMMUNITY BANK FSB	WI	11/24/14

Rating: C

Name	State	Date of Change
AB&T NATIONAL BK	GA	11/24/14
AMERICAN INVESTORS BANK & MTG	MN	11/24/14
AMERICAN NATIONAL BK OF SIDNEY	NE	11/24/14
BANK OF AGRICULTURE & COMMERCE	CA	11/24/14
BANK OF AMERICA CALIFORNIA NA	CA	11/24/14
BANK OF AMERICA NA	NC	11/24/14
BANK OF BLUE VALLEY	KS	11/24/14
BANK OF CAMILLA	GA	11/24/14
BANK OF OAK RIDGE	NC	11/24/14
BANK OF PERRY COUNTY	TN	11/24/14
BANK OF RISON	AR	11/24/14
BANK OF THE PRAIRIE	KS	11/24/14
BENEFICIAL MUTUAL SB	PA	11/24/14
BLUE GRASS VALLEY BANK	VA	11/24/14
C1 BANK	FL	11/24/14
CALUSA BANK	FL	11/24/14
CAPITAL BANK NA	MD	11/24/14
CEDAR SECURITY BANK	NE	11/24/14
CENTERBANK	OH	11/24/14
CENTRIC BANK	PA	11/24/14
CITIZENS BANK	GA	11/24/14
CITIZENS BANK & TRUST	FL	11/24/14
CITIZENS BANK & TRUST CO	LA	11/24/14
CITIZENS BANK & TRUST CO	MO	11/24/14
CITIZENS BANK OF EDINBURG	IL	11/24/14
CITIZENS COMMUNITY BANK	VA	11/24/14
CITIZENS NB OF QUITMAN	GA	11/24/14
CITIZENS TRI-COUNTY BANK	TN	11/24/14

Rating Upgrades

Name	State	Date of Change
CITIZENS UNION BK SHELBYVILLE	KY	11/24/14
CITY NATIONAL BK	TX	11/24/14
CLATSOP COMMUNITY BANK	OR	11/24/14
CNB	MD	11/24/14
COLUMBIA BANK	NJ	11/24/14
COMMERCE BANK	MN	11/24/14
COMMERCE BK OF TEMECULA VALLEY	CA	11/24/14
COMMERCIAL BANK	MS	11/24/14
COMMONWEALTH BANK & TRUST CO	KY	11/24/14
ELYSIAN BANK	MN	11/24/14
EUREKA SB	IL	11/24/14
EVB	VA	11/24/14
EXCHANGE BANK OF NORTHEAST MO	MO	11/24/14
F&M BANK	TN	11/24/14
FAIRFAX STATE SB	IA	11/24/14
FARMERS & MERCHANTS BANK	FL	11/24/14
FARMERS STATE BK OF BUCKLIN KS	KS	11/24/14
FARMERS STATE BK OF MUNITH	MI	11/24/14
FIRST BANK & TRUST	LA	11/24/14
FIRST BANK & TRUST CHILDRESS	TX	11/24/14
FIRST BANK OF GREENWICH	CT	11/24/14
FIRST CENTURY BANK	TN	11/24/14
FIRST COLORADO NATIONAL BK	CO	11/24/14
FIRST COMMERCIAL BANK	MO	11/24/14
FIRST COMMUNITY FINANCIAL BANK	IL	11/24/14
FIRST FEDERAL BANK	AR	11/24/14
FIRST FEDERAL OF NORTHERN MI	MI	11/24/14
FIRST GENERAL BANK	CA	11/24/14
FIRST INTERCONTINENTAL BANK	GA	11/24/14
FIRST NATIONAL BK ASSUMPTION	IL	11/24/14
FIRST NATIONAL BK GERMANTOWN	OH	11/24/14
FIRST NATIONAL BK OF CATLIN	IL	11/24/14
FIRST NATIONAL BK SOUTH MIAMI	FL	11/24/14
FIRST PRIORITY BANK	PA	11/24/14
FIRST STATE BK OF MOBEETIE	TX	11/24/14
FIRST STATE BK OF RANDOLPH CTY	GA	11/24/14
FIRST STATE BK OF SWANVILLE	MN	11/24/14
FIRST TEXOMA NATIONAL BK	OK	11/24/14
FIRSTATLANTIC BANK	FL	11/24/14
FIRSTIER BANK	NE	11/24/14
FMB BANK	MO	11/24/14
FOUNDATION ONE BANK	NE	11/24/14
GRAND BANK FOR SAVINGS FSB	MS	11/24/14
HOME FS&LA OF GRAND ISLAND	NE	11/24/14
HOME LOAN STATE BK	CO	11/24/14
HORIZON COMMUNITY BANK	AZ	11/24/14
INDEPENDENT BANK	TN	11/24/14
INTEGRITY FIRST BANK	WI	11/24/14
INTERNATIONAL BK OF CHICAGO	IL	11/24/14
IRELAND BANK	ID	11/24/14
JAMESTOWN STATE BK	KS	11/24/14
JPMORGAN CHASE BANK DEARBORN	MI	11/24/14
KAHOKA STATE BK	MO	11/24/14
KANSASLAND BANK	KS	11/24/14
LAKESIDE BANK	IL	11/24/14
LAMONT BANK OF ST JOHN	WA	11/24/14
LIBERTY BANK	CA	11/24/14
LINCOLN PARK SB	NJ	11/24/14
LIVE OAK BANKING CO	NC	11/24/14
MARION NATIONAL BK	KS	11/24/14
MERCHANTS BANK OF ALABAMA	AL	11/24/14
MERIDIAN BANK	PA	11/24/14
METAMORA STATE BK	OH	11/24/14
MIDDLESEX FEDERAL SAVINGS FA	MA	11/24/14
MIDWEST INDEPENDENT BANK	MO	11/24/14
MILLVILLE S&LA	NJ	11/24/14
MODERN BANK NA	NY	11/24/14
MONROE BANK & TRUST	MI	11/24/14
MONUMENT BANK	PA	11/24/14
MOUNTAIN COMMERCE BANK	TN	11/24/14
MOUNTAINONE BANK	MA	11/24/14
MULESHOE STATE BK	TX	11/24/14
NEW FOUNDATION SAVINGS BANK	OH	11/24/14
NORTHWEST COMMUNITY BANK	CT	11/24/14
OCULINA BANK	FL	11/24/14
ORANGE COUNTY BUSINESS BANK	CA	11/24/14
OWINGSVILLE BANKING CO	KY	11/24/14
PACIFIC ALLIANCE BANK	CA	11/24/14
PARTNERS BANK OF CALIFORNIA	CA	11/24/14
PINNACLE BANK	AR	11/24/14
PLATTSMOUTH STATE BK	NE	11/24/14
PREFERRED COMMUNITY BANK	FL	11/24/14
PROGRESSIVE SB	TN	11/24/14
RED ROCK BANK	MN	11/24/14
REGENT BANK	OK	11/24/14
ROYAL BANK AMERICA	PA	11/24/14
SILVER LAKE BANK	KS	11/24/14
SOUTHPOINT BANK	AL	11/24/14
STATE BK OF BLUE RAPIDS	KS	11/24/14
SUMMIT BANK	CA	11/24/14
TRANSPECOS BANKS	TX	11/24/14
TRUST BANK	GA	11/24/14
UNIVERSAL BANK	CA	11/24/14
VINTAGE BANK KANSAS	KS	11/24/14
WALLKILL VALLEY FS&LA	NY	11/24/14

Rating: C-

Name	State	Date of Change
1880 BANK	MD	11/24/14
AMERICAN BANK	MT	11/24/14
BANCROFT STATE BK	WI	11/24/14

Rating Upgrades

Name	State	Date of Change
BANK OF BENOIT	MS	11/24/14
BANK OF CATTARAUGUS	NY	11/24/14
BANK OF FRANKEWING	TN	11/24/14
BANK OF GEORGE	NV	11/24/14
BANK OF MAINE	ME	11/24/14
BANK OF THE ORIENT	CA	11/24/14
BANK OF VERSAILLES	MO	11/24/14
BANKFINANCIAL FSB	IL	11/24/14
BENEFICIAL STATE BANK	CA	11/24/14
BRATTLEBORO S&LA	VT	11/24/14
BUFFALO FEDERAL BANK	WY	11/24/14
CAROLINA TRUST BANK	NC	11/24/14
CHAMBERS BANK	AR	11/24/14
CHASE BANK USA NA	NY	11/24/14
CITIZENS BANK OF FLORIDA	FL	11/24/14
CITIZENS BANK OF NEWBURG	MO	11/24/14
CITIZENS BANK OF VALLEY HEAD	AL	11/24/14
CITIZENS NATIONAL BK	TN	11/24/14
COMMUNITY STATE BK	FL	11/24/14
CONNEAUT SB	OH	11/24/14
DECATUR STATE BK	AR	11/24/14
FARMERS EXCHANGE BANK	AL	11/24/14
FARMERS STATE BK OF SUBLETTE	IL	11/24/14
FEDERATED BANK	IL	11/24/14
FIRST ADVANTAGE BANK	MN	11/24/14
FIRST AMERICA BANK	FL	11/24/14
FIRST AMERICAN BANK	IA	11/24/14
FIRST AMERICAN STATE BK	CO	11/24/14
FIRST BANK OF BALDWIN	WI	11/24/14
FIRST COMMUNITY BANK NA	TX	11/24/14
FIRST FLORIDA INTEGRITY BANK	FL	11/24/14
FIRST FS&LA OF PORT ANGELES	WA	11/24/14
FIRST NATIONAL BK OF CROSSETT	AR	11/24/14
FIRST NATIONAL COMMUNITY BANK	GA	11/24/14
FIRST RELIANCE BANK	SC	11/24/14
FLORIDA BANK	FL	11/24/14
FLORIDA CITIZENS BANK	FL	11/24/14
FREEDOM BANK OF AMERICA	FL	11/24/14
GEAUGA SB	OH	11/24/14
GEO D WARTHEN BANK	GA	11/24/14
GRAYSON NATIONAL BK	VA	11/24/14
GREATER COMMUNITY BANK	GA	11/24/14
HANOVER COMMUNITY BANK	NY	11/24/14
HERITAGE BANK OF SCHAUMBURG	IL	11/24/14
HOME SAVINGS BANK FSB	KY	11/24/14
HOMESTREET BANK	WA	11/24/14
INLAND BANK & TRUST	IL	11/24/14
JPMORGAN BANK & TRUST CO NA	CA	11/24/14
JPMORGAN CHASE BANK NA	OH	11/24/14
LEMONT NATIONAL BK	IL	11/24/14
MARINE BANK	IL	11/24/14
MERAMEC VALLEY BANK	MO	11/24/14
METROPOLITAN BANK	CA	11/24/14
METROPOLITAN COMMERCIAL BANK	NY	11/24/14
MILLINGTON SB	NJ	11/24/14
MOUNTAIN PACIFIC BANK	WA	11/24/14
NEW FRONTIER BANK	MO	11/24/14
NEWTOWN SB	CT	11/24/14
NORTH GEORGIA NATIONAL BK	GA	11/24/14
PATRIOT BANK	FL	11/24/14
PATRIOT NATIONAL BK	CT	11/24/14
PEOPLES BANK	KY	11/24/14
POWELL STATE BK	TX	11/24/14
RCSBANK	MO	11/24/14
REPUBLICBANKAZ NA	AZ	11/24/14
SABAL PALM BANK	FL	11/24/14
SOUTHEASTERN BANK	GA	11/24/14
STATE SAVINGS BANK	IA	11/24/14
STERLING FEDERAL BANK FSB	IL	11/24/14
SUSSEX BANK	NJ	11/24/14
TALBOT BANK OF EASTON MARYLAND	MD	11/24/14
TERRABANK NA	FL	11/24/14
TEXAN BANK	TX	11/24/14
UNION BANK	TN	11/24/14
UNITED INTERNATIONAL BK	NY	11/24/14
UNITED SOUTHERN BANK	FL	11/24/14
VALLEY BANK & TRUST	CO	11/24/14
VOYAGER BANK	MN	11/24/14

Rating: D+

Name	State	Date of Change
ALMA EXCHANGE BANK & TRUST	GA	11/24/14
AMALGAMATED BANK OF CHICAGO	IL	11/24/14
BANK OF ELK RIVER	MN	11/24/14
BANK OF STEINAUER	NE	11/24/14
BANK34	NM	11/24/14
BARABOO NATIONAL BK	WI	11/24/14
BARRE SB	MA	11/24/14
BCB COMMUNITY BANK	NJ	11/24/14
BENTON STATE BK	WI	11/24/14
BISON STATE BK	KS	11/24/14
BUILDERS BANK	IL	11/24/14
CENTRUE BANK	IL	11/24/14
CHESAPEAKE BANK OF MARYLAND	MD	11/24/14
CITIZENS STATE BK	NE	11/24/14
CITIZENS STATE BK	TX	11/24/14
CITIZENS STATE BK OF TYLER INC	MN	11/24/14
CMMNTY BK OAK PARK RIVER FORE	IL	11/24/14
CMMNTY BK-WHEATON/GLEN ELLYN	IL	11/24/14
COLORADO EAST BANK & TRUST	CO	11/24/14
COMMERCE NATIONAL BK & TRUST	FL	11/24/14

Rating Upgrades

Name	State	Date of Change
COMMUNITY BANK & TRUST	TN	11/24/14
COMMUNITY BK OF BERGEN COUNTY	NJ	11/24/14
CORNERSTONE COMMUNITY BANK	FL	11/24/14
CROWN BANK	MN	11/24/14
DARIEN ROWAYTON BANK	CT	11/24/14
FARMERS & MERCH NB OF HATTON	ND	11/24/14
FARMERS STATE BANK SPENCER	NE	11/24/14
FIRST ALLIANCE BANK	TN	11/24/14
FIRST CENTRAL SB	NY	11/24/14
FIRST NATIONAL BK EAGLE RIVER	WI	11/24/14
FIRST NATIONAL BK OF SANTA FE	NM	11/24/14
FIRST NATIONAL BK OF SULLIVAN	IL	11/24/14
FIRST UTAH BANK	UT	11/24/14
FMS BANK	CO	11/24/14
FREEDOM NATIONAL BK	RI	11/24/14
FSGBANK NA	TN	11/24/14
GIBRALTAR PRIVATE BANK & TRUST	FL	11/24/14
HIGHLANDS STATE BK	NJ	11/24/14
HIGHLANDS UNION BANK	VA	11/24/14
INDEPENDENCE NATIONAL BK	SC	11/24/14
INDIANA BUSINESS BANK	IN	11/24/14
INDUSTRIAL & COMMERCIAL BANK	NY	11/24/14
IXONIA BANK	WI	11/24/14
LITTLE RIVER BANK	AR	11/24/14
LOWRY STATE BK	MN	11/24/14
OLMSTED NATIONAL BK	MN	11/24/14
ONE WORLD BANK	TX	11/24/14
PRIME PACIFIC BANK NA	WA	11/24/14
QUANTUM NATIONAL BK	GA	11/24/14
RANDOLPH SB	MA	11/24/14
RUBY VALLEY NATIONAL BK	MT	11/24/14
SECURITY STATE BK OF LEWISTON	MN	11/24/14
SLOVAK SB	PA	11/24/14
STATE BK OF BUSSEY	IA	11/24/14
TOWN CENTER BANK	IL	11/24/14
UNITED BANK OF MICHIGAN	MI	11/24/14
WEST MICHIGAN COMMUNITY BANK	MI	11/24/14
WILMINGTON SB	OH	11/24/14

Rating: D

Name	State	Date of Change
AMERICAN HEARTLAND BANK & TR	IL	11/24/14
AMERIFIRST BANK	AL	11/24/14
ANCHOR STATE BK	IL	11/24/14
BANK OF HAZLEHURST	GA	11/24/14
BANK OF KAUKAUNA	WI	11/24/14
BANK OF VIRGINIA	VA	11/24/14
BRIDGEVIEW BANK GROUP	IL	11/24/14
CARVER FSB	NY	11/24/14
CFBANK	OH	11/24/14
CITIZENS BANK OF LOGAN	OH	11/24/14
CITIZENS STATE BK	FL	11/24/14
CITIZENS STATE BK	GA	11/24/14
CNLBANK	FL	11/24/14
COREFIRST BANK & TRUST	KS	11/24/14
FIRST NATIONAL BK IN HOWELL	MI	11/24/14
FIRST SECURITY BANK	MO	11/24/14
FLAGLER BANK	FL	11/24/14
FOX RIVER STATE BK	WI	11/24/14
FRONTENAC BANK	MO	11/24/14
GRAND RIVER BANK	MI	11/24/14
GRAND RIVERS COMMUNITY BANK	IL	11/24/14
HUNTINGDON VALLEY BANK	PA	11/24/14
KAW VALLEY BANK	KS	11/24/14
KEY COMMUNITY BANK	MN	11/24/14
KINDRED STATE BK	ND	11/24/14
NAUGATUCK VALLEY SVGS & LOAN	CT	11/24/14
OMNIBANK	MS	11/24/14
PARK STATE BK & TRUST	CO	11/24/14
PLAZA BANK	WA	11/24/14
PRIMESOUTH BANK	GA	11/24/14
RIVERLAND BANK	MN	11/24/14
ROCKHOLD BROWN & CO BANK	OH	11/24/14
SIGNATURE BANK OF ARKANSAS	AR	11/24/14
SSBBANK	MI	11/24/14
ST JOHNS BANK & TRUST CO	MO	11/24/14
SUBURBAN BANK & TRUST CO	IL	11/24/14
SURETY BANK	FL	11/24/14
VALLEY NATIONAL BK	NM	11/24/14
WOODSFIELD SB	OH	11/24/14

Rating: D-

Name	State	Date of Change
BANK OF NEWINGTON	GA	11/24/14
FIRST CORNERSTONE BANK	PA	11/24/14
FOUR OAKS BANK & TRUST CO	NC	11/24/14
HERITAGE BANK & TRUST	TN	11/24/14
LAKE BANK	MN	11/24/14
LEGACY BANK OF FLORIDA	FL	11/24/14
MBANK	OR	11/24/14
SOUTH COAST BANK & TRUST	GA	11/24/14
UNION STATE BK	AL	11/24/14
VILLAGE BANK	VA	11/24/14
VILLAGE BANK	MN	11/24/14

Rating: E+

Name	State	Date of Change
AMERICAN BANK OF THE NORTH	MN	11/24/14
CENTRAL BANK	TN	11/24/14
HYPERION BANK	PA	11/24/14
UNITED MIDWEST SAVINGS BANK	OH	11/24/14

Rating: E

Rating Upgrades

Name	State	Date of Change
ADVANTAGE BANK	CO	11/24/14
BUSINESS BANK	WA	11/24/14
FIRST STATE BK OF KIESTER	MN	11/24/14
HERITAGE BANK	GA	11/24/14
HOME FEDERAL BANK OF HOLLYWOOD	FL	11/24/14
MONTEREY COUNTY BANK	CA	11/24/14
PAN AMERICAN BANK	CA	11/24/14
STATE BK OF TAUNTON	MN	11/24/14

Rating Downgrades

Name	State	Date of Change
Rating: A		
APPLIED BANK	DE	11/24/14
BANK OF UTICA	NY	11/24/14
Rating: A-		
COMMERCIAL STATE BK OF WAGNER	SD	11/24/14
GOODFIELD STATE BK	IL	11/24/14
GUARANTY BANK & TRUST CO	LA	11/24/14
KENTUCKY FARMERS BANK CORP	KY	11/24/14
SECURITY FIRST BANK OF ND	ND	11/24/14
Rating: B+		
C US BANK	IA	11/24/14
DE WITT BANK & TRUST CO	IA	11/24/14
EASTBANK NA	NY	11/24/14
ELIZABETHTON FSB	TN	11/24/14
FIRST BANK	KS	11/24/14
FIRST NATIONAL BK CLARKSDALE	MS	11/24/14
FIRST SOUTHERN BANK	IL	11/24/14
FIRST STATE BK OF SAUK CENTRE	MN	11/24/14
FIRSTRUST SB	PA	11/24/14
GRUNDY NATIONAL BK	VA	11/24/14
HEADWATERS STATE BK	WI	11/24/14
HERITAGE STATE BK	IL	11/24/14
MUNICIPAL TRUST & SB	IL	11/24/14
NORMANGEE STATE BK	TX	11/24/14
PLAINS COMMERCE BANK	SD	11/24/14
REPUBLIC BANK	UT	11/24/14
TIME FSB	WI	11/24/14
Rating: B		
BANK FEDERATED ST MICRONESIA	FM	11/24/14
BANK OF AMERICAN FORK	UT	11/24/14
BANK OF THE WICHITAS	OK	11/24/14
BERKSHIRE BANK	NY	11/24/14
CAPITOL BANK	WI	11/24/14
CIT BANK	UT	11/24/14
CITIZENS COMMUNITY BANK	TN	11/24/14
COMMERCIAL BANK	KS	11/24/14
COMMUNITY BANK	TX	11/24/14
EAGLE SAVINGS BANK	OH	11/24/14
FARMERS EXCHANGE BANK	OK	11/24/14
FIRST CENTRAL STATE BK	IA	11/24/14
FIRST FARMERS BANK & TRUST	IN	11/24/14
FIRST NATIONAL BK OF STIGLER	OK	11/24/14
FIRST NATIONAL BK OF WASECA	MN	11/24/14
FIRST STATE BK OF FORREST	IL	11/24/14
FIRSTBANK	OK	11/24/14
FRANKLIN GROVE BANK	IL	11/24/14
HAMPTON STATE BK	IA	11/24/14
NEW WASHINGTON STATE BK	IN	11/24/14
PEOPLES BANK	MO	11/24/14
SECURITY STATE BK	TX	11/24/14
SEYMOUR BANK	MO	11/24/14
SUCCESS BANK	IA	11/24/14
UNITED STATE BK	MO	11/24/14
VINTAGE BANK	TX	11/24/14
VIRGINIA NATIONAL BK	VA	11/24/14
WANDA STATE BK	MN	11/24/14
Rating: B-		
AMERICAN BANK OF MISSOURI	MO	11/24/14
BANK OF ASH GROVE	MO	11/24/14
BANK OF NEW MEXICO	NM	11/24/14
BANKERS BANK	OK	11/24/14
BLACK RIVER COUNTRY BANK	WI	11/24/14
BLUE GRASS SB	IA	11/24/14
CENTRAL BANK ILLINOIS	IL	11/24/14
CHEYENNE STATE BK	WY	11/24/14
CITIZENS BANK	WI	11/24/14
COMMUNITY FIRST BANK	WI	11/24/14
EDGARTOWN NATIONAL BK	MA	11/24/14
FARMERS & MERCH STATE BK	MN	11/24/14
FARMERS NB OF GRIGGSVILLE	IL	11/24/14
FIRST FSB OF LINCOLNTON	NC	11/24/14
FIRST NATIONAL BK OF LAYTON	UT	11/24/14
GRAND RAPIDS STATE BK	MN	11/24/14
GRANITE FALLS BANK	MN	11/24/14
HELENA NATIONAL BK	AR	11/24/14
HERITAGE BANK	TX	11/24/14
HOMEPRIDE BANK	MO	11/24/14
INSIGNIA BANK	FL	11/24/14
JONESBURG STATE BK	MO	11/24/14
LEVEL ONE BANK	MI	11/24/14
PEOPLES BANK OF COMMERCE	OR	11/24/14
PEOPLES STATE BK OF MUNISING	MI	11/24/14
PREMIER BANK	NE	11/24/14
RIVER VALLEY COMMUNITY BANK	CA	11/24/14
SECURITY STATE BK OF WARROAD	MN	11/24/14
SPRINGS VALLEY BANK & TRUST CO	IN	11/24/14
STAR BANK	MN	11/24/14
TEXAS CAPITAL BANK NA	TX	11/24/14
TEXAS CHAMPION BANK	TX	11/24/14
TEXAS NATIONAL BK	TX	11/24/14
TOWN & COUNTRY BANK	NE	11/24/14
UNION BANK & TRUST CO	TN	11/24/14
VANTAGE BANK OF ALABAMA	AL	11/24/14
Rating: C+		

Rating Downgrades

Name	State	Date of Change
1ST STATE BK	MI	11/24/14
AMERISERV FINANCIAL BANK	PA	11/24/14
APPLE CREEK BANKING CO	OH	11/24/14
BANKFIRST FINANCIAL SERVICES	MS	11/24/14
BANKPACIFIC LTD	GU	11/24/14
BANKTRUST FINANCIAL CORP	KY	11/24/14
CACHE VALLEY BANK	UT	11/24/14
CENTRAL NATIONAL BK & TRUST CO	OK	11/24/14
CENTREBANK	IN	11/24/14
CITIZENS FIRST BANK	IA	11/24/14
COLLINS STATE BK	WI	11/24/14
COMMONWEALTH BUSINESS BANK	CA	11/24/14
COMMUNITY BANK OF TRENTON	IL	11/24/14
COMMUNITY SAVINGS BANK	OH	11/24/14
COMMUNITY VALLEY BANK	CA	11/24/14
CRESTMARK BANK	MI	11/24/14
FARMERS TRUST & SB	IA	11/24/14
FIDELITY CO-OP BANK	MA	11/24/14
FIRST BANK KANSAS	KS	11/24/14
FIRST CITIZENS BANK & TRUST CO	SC	11/24/14
FIRST FSB OF WASHINGTON	IN	11/24/14
FIRST INDEPENDENT BANK	MO	11/24/14
FIRST NATIONAL BK & TRUST CO	PA	11/24/14
FIRST NATIONAL BK OF DIGHTON	KS	11/24/14
FIRST TEXAS BANK	TX	11/24/14
FIRST-CITIZENS BANK & TRUST CO	NC	11/24/14
GREENFIELD BANKING CO	TN	11/24/14
HERITAGE BANK INC	KY	11/24/14
INTEGRITY BANK PLUS	MN	11/24/14
JEWETT CITY SB	CT	11/24/14
LANDMARK BANK	LA	11/24/14
MERCHANTS & FARMERS BANK	AL	11/24/14
NATIONAL BK OF ADAMS COUNTY	OH	11/24/14
NBH BANK NA	MO	11/24/14
PARK BANK	WI	11/24/14
PEOPLES SB	IA	11/24/14
PROFICIO BANK	UT	11/24/14
REPUBLIC BANKING CO	OH	11/24/14
SECURITY STATE BK	KS	11/24/14
SHERWOOD STATE BK	OH	11/24/14
SOUTHERN HILLS COMMUNITY BANK	OH	11/24/14
STATE BK OF CHRISMAN	IL	11/24/14
STATE BK OF FAIRMONT	MN	11/24/14
STATE BK OF REESEVILLE	WI	11/24/14
STOCKMENS NATIONAL BK COTULLA	TX	11/24/14
UNITED BANK	CT	11/24/14
WESTFIELD BANK	MA	11/24/14

Rating: C

Name	State	Date of Change
BANK OF BREWTON	AL	11/24/14
BANKFIVE	MA	11/24/14
BELGRADE STATE BK	MO	11/24/14
BEVERLY BANK	MA	11/24/14
CASEY COUNTY BANK	KY	11/24/14
CHARTER BANK	MS	11/24/14
CITIZENS BANK & TRUST CO	MN	11/24/14
CITIZENS NATIONAL BK	TN	11/24/14
ESSEX SB	CT	11/24/14
FARMERS STATE BK OF CAMP POINT	IL	11/24/14
FIRST BANK OF CHARLESTON INC	WV	11/24/14
FIRST ELECTRONIC BANK	UT	11/24/14
FIRST NATIONAL BK OF BARRY	IL	11/24/14
FIRST NORTHERN BANK & TRUST CO	PA	11/24/14
FIRST SECURITY BANK	OK	11/24/14
GIBRALTAR BANK	NJ	11/24/14
HELM BANK USA	FL	11/24/14
ILLINI BANK	IL	11/24/14
IUKA STATE BK	IL	11/24/14
JOHNSON COUNTY BANK	TN	11/24/14
LEGACY BANK & TRUST CO	MO	11/24/14
LYON COUNTY STATE BK	KS	11/24/14
MECHANICS BANK	MS	11/24/14
MERIT BANK	KS	11/24/14
METRO PHOENIX BANK	AZ	11/24/14
MILFORD FS&LA	MA	11/24/14
PREMIER BUSINESS BANK	CA	11/24/14
PRINSBANK	MN	11/24/14
QUAIL CREEK BANK NA	OK	11/24/14
RIVERBANK S&LA	AR	11/24/14
SECURITY STATE BK	IA	11/24/14
ST JAMES FS&LA	MN	11/24/14
STATE STREET BANK & TRUST CO	IL	11/24/14
SYNERGY BANK SSB	TX	11/24/14
UNION FSB	RI	11/24/14
VALLEY STATE BK	KS	11/24/14
VISIONBANK	KS	11/24/14

Rating: C-

Name	State	Date of Change
ALLIANCE BANKING CO	KY	11/24/14
AMORY FS&LA	MS	11/24/14
BANK OF EASTERN OREGON	OR	11/24/14
BLOOMBURG STATE BK	TX	11/24/14
BLUE RIDGE BANK & TRUST CO	MO	11/24/14
CAPITAL BANK	AR	11/24/14
CENTRAL BANK	FL	11/24/14
CHARLEVOIX STATE BK	MI	11/24/14
CHICOPEE SB	MA	11/24/14
CITIZENS BANK	KY	11/24/14
CITIZENS NB OF GR ST LOUIS	MO	11/24/14
COMMUNITY BANK	NM	11/24/14

Rating Downgrades

Name	State	Date of Change
COMMUNITY BANK MANKATO	MN	11/24/14
COMMUNITY FIRST BANK NA	OH	11/24/14
COMMUNITY SPIRIT BANK	AL	11/24/14
CORNERSTONE BANK	IA	11/24/14
COUNTY FIRST BANK	MD	11/24/14
EUREKA HOMESTEAD	LA	11/24/14
FARMERS BANK	OK	11/24/14
FARMERS BANK OF LIBERTY	IL	11/24/14
FARMERS STATE BK S/B	MO	11/24/14
FIRST B&TC OF MURPHYSBORO	IL	11/24/14
FIRST CAPITAL BANK	SC	11/24/14
FIRST NATIONAL BK HARVEYVILLE	KS	11/24/14
FIRST NATIONAL BK OF AMERICA	MI	11/24/14
FIRST NATIONAL BK OF TRENTON	TX	11/24/14
FIRST STATE BK OF FOUNTAIN	MN	11/24/14
GARFIELD COUNTY BANK	MT	11/24/14
HOMETOWN BANK A COOPERATIVE BK	MA	11/24/14
IDAHO INDEPENDENT BANK	ID	11/24/14
LANDMARK COMMUNITY BANK	PA	11/24/14
NJM BANK FSB	NJ	11/24/14
PAN AMERICAN BANK	IL	11/24/14
PASSUMPSIC SB	VT	11/24/14
PENINSULA BANK OF ISHPEMING	MI	11/24/14
PROGROWTH BANK	MN	11/24/14
PROVIDENCE BANK OF TEXAS	TX	11/24/14
RAYMOND FEDERAL BANK	WA	11/24/14
SIGNATURE BANK	IL	11/24/14
SOUTHEAST BANK	TN	11/24/14
STATE BK OF BURNETTSVILLE	IN	11/24/14
THAYER COUNTY BANK	NE	11/24/14
UNION BANK	LA	11/24/14
UNITED COMMUNITY BANK	IL	11/24/14

Rating: D+

Name	State	Date of Change
ADMIRALS BANK	MA	11/24/14
ANDALUSIA COMMUNITY BANK	IL	11/24/14
ASHTON STATE BK	NE	11/24/14
BANCO POPULAR NORTH AMERICA	NY	11/24/14
BANCO SANTANDER PUERTO RICO	PR	11/24/14
BANK OF LABOR	KS	11/24/14
BANK OF THE SOUTH	FL	11/24/14
BANK OF WYANDOTTE	OK	11/24/14
BENEFIT BANK	AR	11/24/14
CAMPUS STATE BK	IL	11/24/14
CITIZENS BANK OF COCHRAN	GA	11/24/14
COMMUNITY FINANCIAL BANK	WI	11/24/14
CORE BANK	NE	11/24/14
FARMERS & MERCH BK MOUND CITY	KS	11/24/14
FARMERS BANK	GA	11/24/14
GRATIOT STATE BK	WI	11/24/14
HARVARD SB	IL	11/24/14
KS BANK INC	NC	11/24/14
LAKE COUNTY BANK	MT	11/24/14
MAINSTREET BANK	MO	11/24/14
MID-SOUTHERN SAVINGS BANK FSB	IN	11/24/14
NEW JERSEY COMMUNITY BANK	NJ	11/24/14
PEOPLES BANK MT WASHINGTON	KY	11/24/14
PEOPLES BANK OF EAST TENNESSEE	TN	11/24/14
PILGRIM BANK	MA	11/24/14
QUALITY BANK	ND	11/24/14
SEAMENS BANK	MA	11/24/14
STATE BK OF GENEVA	IL	11/24/14
SWEDISH-AMERICAN STATE BK	KS	11/24/14
TOWN NORTH BANK NA	TX	11/24/14
UNITED BANK OF UNION	MO	11/24/14
WARSAW FS&LA	OH	11/24/14
WELLS FARGO BANK SOUTH CENTRAL	TX	11/24/14

Rating: D

Name	State	Date of Change
AUTO CLUB TRUST FSB	MI	11/24/14
BANK OF LOUISIANA	LA	11/24/14
BREMEN BANK & TRUST CO	MO	11/24/14
CERTUSBANK NA	SC	11/24/14
CONCORD BANK	MO	11/24/14
CRESCENT BANK & TRUST	LA	11/24/14
DELTA BANK NA	CA	11/24/14
DOOLIN SECURITY SAVINGS BK FSB	WV	11/24/14
DUBLIN NATIONAL BK	TX	11/24/14
FARMERS & MERCHANTS BANK	GA	11/24/14
FIDELITY NATIONAL BK	WI	11/24/14
FIRST NATIONAL BK SOUTHERN CA	CA	11/24/14
FIRST SECURITY BANK & TRUST CO	OK	11/24/14
GREAT NATIONS BANK	OK	11/24/14
KASSON STATE BK	MN	11/24/14
MACKINAC SAVINGS BANK FSB	FL	11/24/14
MADISON BANK OF MARYLAND	MD	11/24/14
MARION CENTER BANK	PA	11/24/14
PIONEER BANK	VA	11/24/14
PIQUA STATE BK	KS	11/24/14
S BANK	GA	11/24/14
SECURITY STATE BK OF KENYON	MN	11/24/14
SOUTH PORTE BANK	IL	11/24/14
SOUTHERNTRUST BANK	IL	11/24/14
STATE BK OF WATERLOO	IL	11/24/14
SUMMIT BANK OF KANSAS CITY	MO	11/24/14
SYSTEMATIC SAVINGS BANK	MO	11/24/14
TEXICO STATE BK	IL	11/24/14
TRISUMMIT BANK	TN	11/24/14
UNITED COMMUNITY BANK	LA	11/24/14

Rating Downgrades

Rating: D-

Name	State	Date of Change
ABC BANK	IL	11/24/14
CHAPPELL HILL BANK	TX	11/24/14
COASTALSTATES BANK	SC	11/24/14
COLUMBUS JUNCTION STATE BK	IA	11/24/14
COVENANT BANK	AL	11/24/14
ENCORE BANK NA	FL	11/24/14
FARMERS STATE BK	WY	11/24/14
FIRST B&TC OF ILLINOIS	IL	11/24/14
FIRST NATIONAL BK	WI	11/24/14
FIRST SECURITY TRUST & SB	IL	11/24/14
FIRST STATE BK	OK	11/24/14
FREEPORT STATE BK	KS	11/24/14
GOLDEN PACIFIC BANK NA	CA	11/24/14
HARBOR BANK OF MARYLAND	MD	11/24/14
LAFAYETTE STATE BK	FL	11/24/14
MERCHANTS COMMERCIAL BANK	VI	11/24/14
MIDCOAST COMMUNITY BANK	DE	11/24/14
ORIENTAL BANK	PR	11/24/14
SIDNEY FS&LA	NE	11/24/14
SOUTHERN BANK OF TENNESSEE	TN	11/24/14
STATE NATIONAL BK OF GROOM	TX	11/24/14
TREASURE STATE BK	MT	11/24/14
TRICENTURY BANK	KS	11/24/14
VIRGINIA COMPANY BANK	VA	11/24/14

Rating: E+

Name	State	Date of Change
BANK OF MAUMEE	OH	11/24/14
FARMERS BANK	GA	11/24/14
HOMESTEAD SAVINGS BANK	MI	11/24/14
HORIZON STATE BK	MO	11/24/14

Rating: E

Name	State	Date of Change
BANK OF CORAL GABLES	FL	11/24/14
BANK OF PERRY	GA	11/24/14
COLONIAL AMERICAN BANK	NJ	11/24/14
COMMONWEALTH NATIONAL BK	AL	11/24/14

Rating: E-

Name	State	Date of Change
AMERICAN FOUNDERS BANK INC	KY	11/24/14
CORNERSTONE BANK	NJ	11/24/14
HOMETOWN BK HUDSON VALLEY	NY	11/24/14

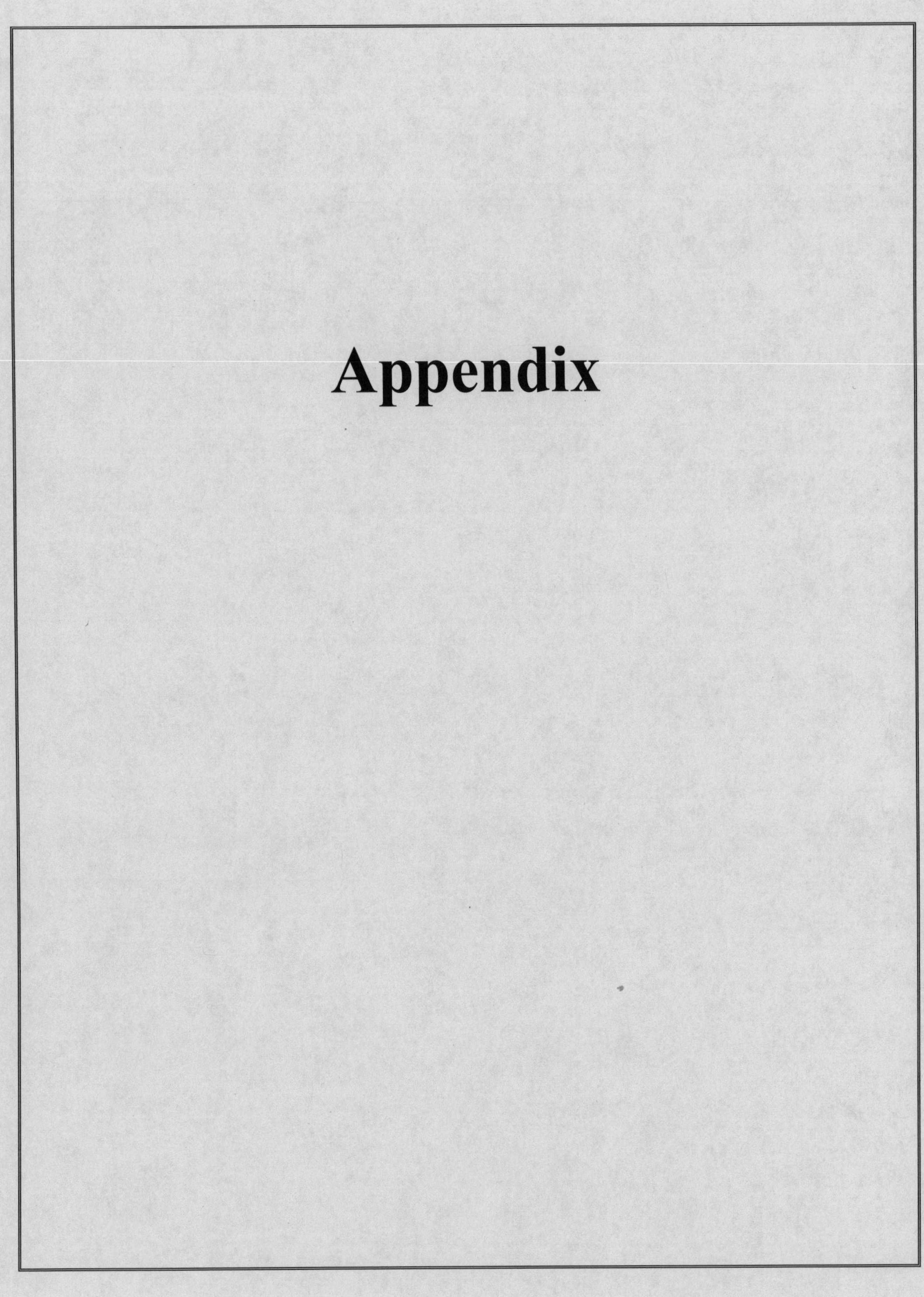

Appendix

RECENT BANK FAILURES

2014

Institution	Headquarters	Date of Failure	At Date of Failure	
			Total Assets ($Mil)	Financial Strength Rating
Frontier Bank, FSB	Palm Desert, CA	11/07/14	86.4	E- (Very Weak)
National Republic Bk of Chicago	Chicago, IL	10/24/14	954.4	E- (Very Weak)
NBRS Financial	Rising Sun, MD	10/17/14	188.2	E- (Very Weak)
Greenchoice Bank FSB	Chicago, IL	07/25/14	72.9	E- (Very Weak)
Eastside Commercial Bank	Conyers, GA	07/18/14	169.0	E- (Very Weak)
Freedom State Bank	Freedom, OK	06/27/14	22.8	D (Weak)
Valley Bank	Moline, IL	06/20/14	456.4	E+ (Very Weak)
Valley Bank	Fort Lauderdale, FL	06/20/14	81.8	E- (Very Weak)
Slavie Federal Savings Bank	Bel Air, MD	05/30/14	140.1	E- (Very Weak)
Columbia Savings Bank	Cincinnati, OH	05/23/14	36.5	E- (Very Weak)
AztecAmerica Bank	Berwyn, IL	05/16/14	66.3	E- (Very Weak)
Allendale County Bank	Fairfax, SC	04/25/14	54.5	E- (Very Weak)
Millennium Bank NA	Sterling, VA	02/28/14	130.3	E- (Very Weak)
Vantage Point Bank	Horsham, PA	02/28/14	63.5	E- (Very Weak)
Syringa Bank	Boise, ID	01/31/14	153.4	E- (Very Weak)
Bank of Union	El Reno, OK	01/24/14	331.4	D- (Weak)
DuPage National Bank	West Chicago, IL	01/17/14	61.7	E- (Very Weak)

2013

Institution	Headquarters	Date of Failure	At Date of Failure	
			Total Assets ($Mil)	Financial Strength Rating
Texas Community Bank	The Woodlands, TX	12/13/13	160.1	E- (Very Weak)
Bank of Jackson County	Graceville, FL	10/30/13	25.5	E- (Very Weak)
Communitys Bank	Bridgeport, CT	09/13/13	26.3	E- (Very Weak)
First National Bank	Edinburg, TX	09/13/13	3100.0	E- (Very Weak)
Community South Bank	Parsons, TN	08/24/13	386.9	E- (Very Weak)
Sunrise Bank of Arizona	Phoenix, AZ	08/24/13	202.2	E- (Very Weak)
Bank of Wausau	Wausau, WI	08/09/13	43.6	E- (Very Weak)
First Community Bank of SW FL	Fort Meyers, FL	08/02/13	265.7	E- (Very Weak)
Mountain National Bank	Sevierville, TN	06/07/13	437.3	E- (Very Weak)
1st Commerce Bank	N. Las Vegas, NV	06/06/13	20.2	E- (Very Weak)
Banks of Wisconsin	Kenosha, WI	05/31/13	134.0	E- (Very Weak)
Central Arizona Bank	Scottsdale, AZ	05/14/13	31.6	E- (Very Weak)
Pisgah Community Bank	Asheville, NC	05/10/13	21.9	E- (Very Weak)
Sunrise Bank	Valdosta, GA	05/10/13	60.8	E- (Very Weak)
Douglas County Bank	Douglasville, GA	04/26/13	316.5	E- (Very Weak)
Parkway Bank	Lenoir, NC	04/26/13	108.6	E- (Very Weak)
Chipola Community Bank	Marianna, FL	04/19/13	39.2	E- (Very Weak)
First Federal Bank	Lexington, KY	04/19/13	100.1	E- (Very Weak)
Heritage Bank of North Florida	Orange Park, FL	04/19/13	110.9	E- (Very Weak)
Gold Canyon Bank	Gold Canyon, AZ	04/05/13	44.2	E- (Very Weak)
Frontier Bank	LaGrange, GA	03/08//13	258.8	E- (Very Weak)
Covenant Bank	Chicago, IL	02/15/13	58.4	E- (Very Weak)
1st Regents Bank	Andover, MN	01/18/13	50.2	E- (Very Weak)
Westside Community Bank	University Place, WA	01/11/13	97.7	E- (Very Weak)

2012

Institution	Headquarters	Date of Failure	At Date of Failure	
			Total Assets ($Mil)	Financial Strength Rating
Community Bank of the Ozarks	Sunrise Beach, MO	12/14/12	42.8	E- (Very Weak)
Hometown Community Bank	Braselton, GA	11/16/12	124.6	E- (Very Weak)
Citizens First National Bank	Princeton, IL	11/02/12	924.0	E- (Very Weak)
Heritage Bank of Florida	Lutz, FL	11/02/12	225.5	E- (Very Weak)
NOVA Bank	Berwyn, PA	10/26/12	483.0	E- (Very Weak)
Excel Bank	Sedalia, MO	10/19/12	200.6	E- (Very Weak)
First East Side Savings Bank	Tamarac, FL	10/19/12	67.2	E- (Very Weak)
Gulfsouth Private Bank	Destin, FL	10/19/12	159.1	E- (Very Weak)
First United Bank	Crete, IL	09/28/12	328.4	E- (Very Weak)
Truman Bank	St Louis, MO	09/14/12	282.3	E- (Very Weak)
First Commercial Bank	Bloomington, MN	09/07/12	215.9	E- (Very Weak)
Waukegan Savings Bank	Waukegan, IL	08/03/12	88.9	E- (Very Weak)
Jasper Banking Co	Jasper, GA	07/27/12	216.7	E- (Very Weak)
First Cherokee State Bank	Woodstock, GA	07/20/12	222.7	E- (Very Weak)
Georgia Trust Bank	Buford, GA	07/20/12	119.8	E- (Very Weak)
Heartland Bank	Leawood, KS	07/20/12	110.0	E- (Very Weak)
Royal Palm Bank of Florida	Naples, FL	07/20/12	87.0	E- (Very Weak)
Second Federal Savings & Loan Assn of Chicago	Chicago, IL	07/20/12	199.1	E- (Very Weak)
Glasgow Savings Bank	Glasgow, MO	07/13/12	24.8	E- (Very Weak)
Montgomery Bank & Trust	Aliey, GA	07/06/12	173.6	E- (Very Weak)
Farmers Bank of Lynchburg	Lynchburg, TN	06/15/12	163.9	E- (Very Weak)
Putnam State Bank	Palatka, FL	06/15/12	169.5	E- (Very Weak)
Security Exchange Bank	Marietta, GA	06/15/12	151.0	E- (Very Weak)
Carolina Federal Savings Bank	Charleston, SC	06/08/12	54.4	E- (Very Weak)
Farmers & Traders State Bank	Shabbana, IL	06/08/12	43.1	E- (Very Weak)
First Capital Bank	Kingfisher, OK	06/08/12	46.1	E- (Very Weak)
Waccamaw Bank	Whiteville, NC	06/08/12	533.1	E- (Very Weak)

Alabama Trust Bank, NA	Sylcauga, AL	05/18/12	51.5	E-(Very Weak)
Security Bank NA	North Lauderdale, FL	05/04/12	101.0	E- (Very Weak)
Bank of the Eastern Shore	Cambridge, MD	04/27/12	166.7	E- (Very Weak)
HarVest Bank of Maryland	Gaithersburg,MD	04/27/12	164.3	E- (Very Weak)
InterSavings Bank FSB	Maple Grove, MN	04/27/12	481.6	E- (Very Weak)
Palm Desert National Bank	Palm Desert, CA	04/27/12	125.8	E- (Very Weak)
Plantation Federal Bank	Pawleys Island, SC	04/27/12	486.4	E- (Very Weak)
Fort Lee Federal Savings Bank FSB	Fort Lee, NJ	04/20/12	51.9	E- (Very Weak)
Fidelity Bank	Dearborn, MI	03/30/12	747.6	E- (Very Weak)
Covenant Bank & Trust	Rock Springs, GA	03/23/12	95.7	E- (Very Weak)
Premier Bank	Wilmette, IL	03/23/12	268.7	E- (Very Weak)
New City Bank	Chicago, IL	03/09/12	71.2	E- (Very Weak)
Global Commerce Bank	Doraville, GA	03/02/12	143.7	E- (Very Weak)
Central Bank of Georgia	Ellaville, GA	02/24/12	278.9	E- (Very Weak)
Home Savings of America	Little Falls, MN	02/24/12	434.1	E- (Very Weak)
Charter National Bank & Trust	Hoffman Estates, IL	02/10/12	93.9	E- (Very Weak)
SCB Bank	Shellbyville, IN	02/10/12	182.6	E- (Very Weak)
BankEast	Knoxville, TN	01/27/12	272.6	E- (Very Weak)
First Guaranty Bank & Trust of Jacksonville	Jacksonville, FL	01/27/12	377.9	E- (Very Weak)
Patriot Bank Minnesota	Forest Lake, MN	01/27/12	111.3	E- (Very Weak)
Tennessee Commerce Bank	Franklin, TN	01/27/12	1185.0	E- (Very Weak)
American Eagle Savings Bank	Boothwyn, PA	01/20/12	19.6	E- (Very Weak)
Central Florida State Bank	Belleview, FL	01/20/12	79.1	E- (Very Weak)
First State Bank, The	Stockbridge, GA	01/20/12	536.9	E- (Very Weak)

2011

Institution	Headquarters	Date of Failure	At Date of Failure	
			Total Assets ($Mil)	Financial Strength Rating
Central Progressive Bank	Lacombe,LA	11/18/11	383.1	E- (Very Weak)
Polk County Bank	Johnston, LA	11/18/11	91.6	E- (Very Weak)
Community Bank of Rockmart	Rockmart, GA	11/10/11	62.4	E- (Very Weak)
Mid City Bank Inc	Omaha, NE	11/04/11	106.1	E- (Very Weak)
SunFirst Bank	St. George, UT	11/04/11	198.1	E- (Very Weak)
All American Bank	Des Plaines , IL	10/28/11	37.8	E- (Very Weak)
Community Banks of Colorado	Greenwood , CO	10/21/11	13800.0	E- (Very Weak)
Community Capital Bank	Jonesboro , GA	10/21/11	181.2	E- (Very Weak)
Decatur First Bank	Decatur, GA	10/21/11	191.5	E- (Very Weak)
Old Harbor Bank	Clearwater, FL	10/21/11	215.9	E- (Very Weak)
Blue Ridge Savings Bank	Asheville, NC	10/14/11	161.0	E- (Very Weak)
County Bank	Aledo, IL	10/14/11	190.6	E- (Very Weak)
First State Bank	Cranford, NJ	10/14/11	204.4	E- (Very Weak)
Piedmont Community Bank	Gray, GA	10/14/11	201.7	E- (Very Weak)
RiverBank	Wyoming, MN	10/07/11	417.4	E- (Very Weak)
Sun Security Bank	Ellington, MO	10/07/11	355.9	E- (Very Weak)
First International Bank	Plano, TX	09/30/11	239.9	E- (Very Weak)
Bank of the Commonwealth	Norfolk, VA	09/23/11	985.1	E- (Very Weak)
Citizens Bank of Northern California	Nevada City, CA	09/23/11	288.8	E- (Very Weak)
First National Bank of Florida	Milton, FL	09/09/11	296.8	E- (Very Weak)
CreekSide Bank	Woodstock, GA	09/02/11	102.3	E- (Very Weak)
Patriot Bank of Georgia	Cumming, GA	09/02/11	150.8	E- (Very Weak)
First Choice Bank	Geneva, IL	08/19/11	141.0	E- (Very Weak)
First Southern National Bank	Statesboro, GA	08/19/11	164.6	E- (Very Weak)
Lydian Private Bank	Palm Beach, FL	08/19/11	1700.0	E- (Very Weak)
Public Savings Bank	Huntingdon Valley, PA	08/18/11	46.8	E- (Very Weak)
First National Bank of Olathe	Olathe, KS	08/12/11	538.1	E- (Very Weak)
Bank of Shorewood	Shorwood, IL	08/05/11	110.7	E- (Very Weak)
Bank of Whitman	Colfax, WA	08/05/11	548.6	E- (Very Weak)

BankMeridian NA	Columbia, SC	07/29/11	239.8	E- (Very Weak)
Integra Bank NA	Evansville, IN	07/29/11	2200.0	E- (Very Weak)
Virginia Business Bank	Richmond, VA	07/29/11	95.8	E- (Very Weak)
Bank of Choice	Greeley, CO	07/22/11	10700.0	E- (Very Weak)
Landmark Bank of Florida	Sarasota, FL	07/22/11	275.0	E- (Very Weak)
Southshore Community Bank	Apollo, FL	07/22/11	46.3	E- (Very Weak)
First Peoples Bank	Port St. Lucie, FL	07/15/11	228.3	E- (Very Weak)
High Trust Bank	Stockbridge, GA	07/15/11	192.5	E- (Very Weak)
One Georgia Bank	Atlanta, GA	07/15/11	186.3	E- (Very Weak)
Summit Bank	Prescott, AZ	07/15/11	72.0	E- (Very Weak)
Colorado Capital Bank	Castle Rock, CO	07/08/11	717.5	E- (Very Weak)
First Chicago Bank & Trust	Chicago, IL	07/08/11	959.3	E- (Very Weak)
Signature Bank	Windsor, CO	07/08/11	66.7	E- (Very Weak)
Mountain Heritage Bank	Clayton, GA	06/24/11	103.7	E- (Very Weak)
First Comm. Bank of Tampa Bay	Tampa, FL	06/17/11	98.6	E- (Very Weak)
McIntosh State Bank	Jackson, GA	06/17/11	339.9	E- (Very Weak)
Atlantic Bank & Trust	Charleston, SC	06/03/11	208.2	E- (Very Weak)
First Heritage Bank	Snohomish, WA	05/27/11	173.5	E- (Very Weak)
Atlantic Southern Bank	Macon, GA	05/20/11	741.9	E- (Very Weak)
First Heritage Bank	Snohomish, WA	05/27/11	173.5	E- (Very Weak)
Atlantic Southern Bank	Macon, GA	05/20/11	741.9	E- (Very Weak)
First Georgia Banking Company	Franklin, GA	05/20/11	731.0	E- (Very Weak)
Summit Bank	Burlington, WA	05/20/11	142.7	E- (Very Weak)
Coastal Bank	Cocoa Beach, FL	05/06/11	129.4	E- (Very Weak)
Community Central Bank	Mount Clemens, MI	04/29/11	476.3	E- (Very Weak)
Cortez Community Bank	Brooksville, FL	04/29/11	70.9	E- (Very Weak)
First Choice Community Bank	Dallas, GA	04/29/11	308.5	E- (Very Weak)
First Nat. Bank of Central Florida	Winter Park, FL	04/29/11	352.0	E- (Very Weak)

Park Avenue Bank	Valdosta, GA	04/29/11	827.7	E- (Very Weak)
Bartow Conty Bank	Cartersville, GA	04/15/11	330.2	E- (Very Weak)
Heritage Banking Group	Cartahge, MS	04/15/11	224.0	E- (Very Weak)
New Horizons Bank	East Ellijay, GA	04/15/11	110.7	E- (Very Weak)
Nexity Bank	Birmingham, AL	04/15/11	793.7	E- (Very Weak)
Rosemount National Bank	Rosemount, MN	04/15/11	37.6	E- (Very Weak)
Superior Bank	Birmingham, AL	04/15/11	3000.0	E- (Very Weak)
Nevada Commerce Bank	Las Vegas, NV	04/08/11	144.9	E- (Very Weak)
WesternSprings Nat. Bank&Trust	Western Springs, IL	04/08/11	181.9	E- (Very Weak)
Bank of Commerce	Wood Dale, IL	03/25/11	163.1	E- (Very Weak)
First National Bank of Davis	Davis, OK	03/11/11	90.2	C (Fair)
Legacy Bank	Milwaukee, WI	03/11/11	190.4	E-(Very Weak)
Valley Community Bank	St. Charles, IL	02/25/11	123.8	E-(Very Weak)
Charter Oak Bank	Napa, CA	02/18/11	120.8	E-(Very Weak)
Citizens Bank of Effingham	Springfield, GA	02/18/11	214.3	E-(Very Weak)
Habersham Bank	Clarkesville, GA	02/18/11	387.6	E-(Very Weak)
San Luis Trust Bank FSB	San Luis Obispo, CA	02/18/11	332.6	E-(Very Weak)
Badger State Bank	Cassville, WI	02/11/11	83.8	E-(Very Weak)
Canyon National Bank	Palm Springs, CA	02/11/11	210.9	E-(Very Weak)
Peoples State Bank	Hamtramck, MI	02/11/11	390.5	E-(Very Weak)
Sunshine State Community Bank	Port Orange, FL	02/11/11	125.5	E-(Very Weak)
American Trust Bank	Roswell, GA	02/04/11	238.2	E-(Very Weak)
Community First Bank	Chicago, IL	02/04/11	51.1	E-(Very Weak)
North Georgia Bank	Watkinsville, GA	02/04/11	153.2	E-(Very Weak)
Evergreen State Bank	Stoughton, WI	01/28/11	246.5	E-(Very Weak)
First Community Bank	Taos, NM	01/28/11	2310.0	E-(Very Weak)
First State Bank	Camargo, OK	01/28/11	43.5	C- (Fair)
FirsTier Bank	Broomfield, CO	01/28/11	781.5	E-(Very Weak)

Bank of Asheville	Asheville, NC	01/21/11	195.1	E-(Very Weak)
CommunitySouth Bank & Trust	Easley, SC	01/21/11	440.6	E-(Very Weak)
Enterprise Banking Co	McDonough, GA	01/21/11	100.9	E-(Very Weak)
United Western bank	Denver, CO	01/21/11	1650.0	E-(Very Weak)
Oglethorpe Bank	Brunswick, GA	01/14/11	230.6	E- (Very Weak)
First Commercial Bank of Fl.	Orlando, FL	01/07/11	598.5	E- (Very Weak)
Legacy Bank	Scottsdale, AZ	01/07/11	150.6	E- (Very Weak)

2010

Institution	Headquarters	Date of Failure	At Date of Failure	
			Total Assets ($Mil)	Financial Strength Rating
Appalachian Comm. Bank FSB	McCaysville, GA	12/17/10	68.2	E- (Very Weak)
Bank of Miami	Coral Gables, FL	12/17/10	448.2	E- (Very Weak)
Chestatee State Bank	Dawsonville, GA	12/17/10	244.4	E- (Very Weak)
Community National Bank	Lino Lakes, MN	12/17/10	31.6	D- (Weak)
First Southern Bank	Batesville, AR	12/17/10	191.8	C- (Fair)
United Americas Bank NA	Atlanta, GA	12/17/10	242.3	E- (Very Weak)
Earthstar Bank	Southampton, PA	12/17/10	112.6	E- (Very Weak)
Paramount Bank	Farmington Hills, MI	12/10/10	252.7	E- (Very Weak)
Allegiance Bank of N. America	Bala Cynwyc, PA	11/19/10	106.6	E- (Very Weak)
First Banking Center	Burlington, WI	11/19/10	750.7	E- (Very Weak)
Gulf State Commercial Bank	Carrabelle, FL	11/19/10	112.1	E- (Very Weak)
Copper State Bank	Scottsdale, AZ	11/12/10	204.0	E- (Very Weak)
Darby Bank & Trust Co	Vidalia, GA	11/12/10	654.7	E- (Very Weak)
Tifton Banking Co	Tifton, GA	11/12/10	143.7	E- (Very Weak)
First Vietnamese American Bank	Westminster, CA	11/05/10	48.0	E- (Very Weak)
K Bank	Randallstown, MD	11/05/10	538.3	E- (Very Weak)
Pierce Commercial Bank	Tacoma, WA	11/05/10	221.1	E- (Very Weak)
Western Commercial Bank	Woodland Hills, CA	11/05/10	98.6	E- (Very Weak)
First Arizona Savings a FSB	Scottsdale, AZ	10/22/10	272.2	E- (Very Weak)
First Bank of Jacksonville	Jacksonville, FL	10/22/10	81.0	E- (Very Weak)
First Natinal Bank of Barnesville	Barnesville, GA	10/22/10	131.4	E- (Very Weak)
First Suburban National Bank	Maywood, IL	10/22/10	148.7	E- (Very Weak)
Gordon Bank	Gordon, GA	10/22/10	29.4	E- (Very Weak)
Hillcrest Bank	Overland Park, KS	10/22/10	15400.0	E- (Very Weak)

Progress Bank of Florida	Tampa, FL	10/22/10	110.7	E- (Very Weak)
Premier Bank	Jefferson City, MO	10/15/10	11800.0	E- (Very Weak)
Security Savings Bank FSB	Olathe, KS	10/15/10	508.4	E- (Very Weak)
WestBridge Bank & Trust Co	Chesterfield, MO	10/15/10	91.5	E- (Very Weak)
Shoreline Bank	Shoreline, WA	10/01/10	100.2	E- (Very Weak)
Wakulla Bank	Crawfordville, FL	10/01/10	386.3	E- (Very Weak)
Haven Trust Bank Florida	Point Vedra Beach, FL	09/24/10	133.6	E- (Very Weak)
North County Bank	Arlington, WA	09/24/10	276.1	E- (Very Weak)
Bank of Ellijay	Ellijay, GA	09/17/10	168.8	E- (Very Weak)
Bramble Savings Bank	Milford, OH	09/17/10	47.5	E- (Very Weak)
First Commerce Comm. Bank	Douglasville, GA	09/17/10	248.2	E- (Very Weak)
ISN Bank	Cherry Hill, NJ	09/17/10	81.6	E- (Very Weak)
Maritime Savings Bank	West Allis, WI	09/17/10	350.5	E- (Very Weak)
Peoples Bank	Winder GA	09/17/10	447.2	E- (Very Weak)
Horizon Bank	Bradenton, FL	09/10/10	164.6	E- (Very Weak)
Butte Community Bank	Chico, CA	08/20/10	498.8	E- (Very Weak)
Communiy Natil Bank at Bartow	Bartow, FL	08/20/10	67.9	E (Very Weak)
Imperial Savings & Loan Assoc	Martinsville, VA	08/20/10	9.4	E- (Very Weak)
Independent National Bank	Ocala, FL	08/20/10	156.2	E- (Very Weak)
Los Padres Bank	Solvang, CA	08/20/10	870.4	E- (Very Weak)
Pacific State Bank	Stockton, CA	08/20/10	312.1	E- (Very Weak)
ShoreBank	Chicago, IL	08/20/10	21600.0	E- (Very Weak)
Sonoma Valley Bank	Sonoma, CA	08/20/10	337.1	E- (Very Weak)
Palos Bank & Trust Co	Palos Height, IL	08/13/10	493.4	E- (Very Weak)
Ravenswood Bank	Chicago, IL	08/06/10	264.6	E- (Very Weak)
Bayside Savings Bank	Port St. Joe, FL	07/30/10	66.1	E- (Very Weak)
Coastal Community Bank	Panama City Bch, FL	07/30/10	372.9	E- (Very Weak)
Cowlitz Bank	Longview, WA	07/30/10	529.3	E- (Very Weak)

Liberty Bank	Eugene, OR	07/30/10	768.2	E- (Very Weak)
Northwest Bank & Trust	Acworth, GA	07/30/10	167.7	E- (Very Weak)
Southwest USA Bank	Las Vegas, NV	07/30/10	214.0	E- (Very Weak)
Community Security Bank	New Prague, MN	07/23/10	108.0	E- (Very Weak)
Crescent Bank & Trust Co	Jasper, GA	07/23/10	10100.0	E- (Very Weak)
Home Valley Bank	Cove Junction, OR	07/23/10	251.8	E- (Very Weak)
Sterling Bank	Lantana, FL	07/23/10	407.9	E- (Very Weak)
Thunder Bank	Sylvan Grove, KS	07/23/10	32.6	E- (Very Weak)
Willamsuburg First Natonal Bank	Kingstree, SC	07/23/10	139.3	E- (Very Weak)
First National Bank of the South	Spartanburg, SC	07/16/10	682.0	E- (Very Weak)
Mainstreet Savings Bank FSB	Hastings, MI	07/16/10	97.4	E- (Very Weak)
Metro Bank of Dade County	Miami, FL	07/16/10	442.3	E- (Very Weak)
Olde Cypress Community Bank	Clewiston, FL	07/16/10	168.7	E- (Very Weak)
Turnberry Bank	Aventura ,FL	07/16/10	263.9	E- (Very Weak)
Woodlands Bank	Bluffton, SD	07/16/10	376.2	E- (Very Weak)
Bay National Bank (Lutherville)	Baltimore, MD	07/09/10	282.2	E- (Very Weak)
Home Nat Bank (Arkansas City)	Blackwell, OK	07/09/10	644.5	D- (Weak)
Ideal Federal Savings Bank	Baltimore, MD	07/09/10	6.3	E+ (Very Weak)
USA Bank	Port Chester, NY	07/09/10	193.3	E- (Very Weak)
First National Bank	Savannah, GA	06/25/10	252.5	E- (Very Weak)
High Desert State Bank	Albuquerque, NM	06/25/10	80.3	E- (Very Weak)
Peninsula Bank	Englewood, FL	06/25/10	644.3	E- (Very Weak)
Nevada Security Bank	Reno, NV	06/18/10	480.3	E- (Very Weak)
Washington First Intl. Bank	Seattle, WA	06/11/10	520.9	E- (Very Weak)
Arcola Homestead Savings Bank	Arcola, IL	06/04/10	17.0	C (Fair)
First National Bank	Rosedale, MS	06/04/10	60.4	A- (Excellent)
TierOne Bank	Lincoln, NE	06/04/10	2800.0	E- (Very Weak)
Bank of Florida - Southeast	Ft. Lauderdale, FL	05/28/10	595.3	E- (Very Weak)

Bank of Florida - Southwest	Naples, FL	05/28/10	640.9	E- (Very Weak)
Bank of Florida - Tampa Bay	Tampa Bay, FL	05/28/10	245.2	E- (Very Weak)
Granite Community Bank, NA	Granite Bay, CA	05/28/10	102.9	E- (Very Weak)
Pinehurst Bank	St. Paul, MN	05/28/10	61.2	E- (Very Weak)
Sun West Bank	Las Vegas, NV	05/28/10	360.7	E- (Very Weak)
Midwest Bank & Trust Co	Elmwood Park, IL	05/14/10	31700.0	E- (Very Weak)
New Liberty Bank	Plymouth, MI	05/14/10	109.1	E- (Very Weak)
Satilla Community Bank	Saint Marys, GA	05/14/10	135.7	E- (Very Weak)
Southwest Community Bank	Springfield, MO	05/14/10	96.6	E- (Very Weak)
1st Pacific Bank of California	San Diego, CA	05/07/10	335.8	E- (Very Weak)
Access Bank	Champlin, MN	05/07/10	32.0	E- (Very Weak)
Bank of Bonifay	Bonifay, FL	05/07/10	242.9	E- (Very Weak)
Towne Bank of Arizona	Mesa, AZ	05/07/10	120.2	E- (Very Weak)
BC National Banks	Butler, MO	04/30/10	67.2	E- (Very Weak)
CF Bancorp	Port Huron, MI	04/30/10	16500.0	E- (Very Weak)
Champion Bank	Creve Coeur, MO	04/30/10	187.3	E- (Very Weak)
Eurobank	San Juan, PR	04/30/10	25600.0	E- (Very Weak)
Frontier Bank	Everett, WA	04/30/10	35000.0	E- (Very Weak)
R-G Premier Bank of Puerto Rico	Hato Rey, PR	04/30/10	59200.0	E- (Very Weak)
Westernbank Puerto Rico	Mayaguez, PR	04/30/10	11940.0	E+ (Very Weak)
Amcore Bank NA	Rockford, IL	04/23/10	3800.0	E- (Very Weak)
Broadway Bank	Chicago, IL	04/23/10	1200.0	E- (Very Weak)
Citizens BnkTrust Co of Chicago	Chicago, IL	04/23/10	77.3	E- (Very Weak)
Lincoln Park Savings Bank	Chicago, IL	04/23/10	199.9	E- (Very Weak)
New Century Bank	Chicago, IL	04/23/10	485.6	E- (Very Weak)
Peotone Bank & Trust Co	Peotone, IL	04/23/10	130.2	E- (Very Weak)
Wheatland Bank	Naperville, IL	04/23/10	437.2	E- (Very Weak)
AmericanFirst Bank	Clermont ,IL	04/16/10	90.5	E- (Very Weak)

Butler Bank	Lowell, MA	04/16/10	268.0	E- (Very Weak)
City Bank	Lynnwood, WA	04/16/10	11300.0	E- (Very Weak)
First Federal Bank of N. Florida	Palatka, FL	04/16/10	393.3	E- (Very Weak)
Innovative Bank	Oakland, CA	04/16/10	268.9	E- (Very Weak)
Lakeside Community Bank	Sterling Heights, MI	04/16/10	53.0	E- (Very Weak)
Riverside Natil Bank of Florida	Ft. Pierce, FL	04/16/10	34200.0	E- (Very Weak)
Tamalpais Bank	San Rafael, CA	04/16/10	628.9	E- (Very Weak)
Beach First National Bank	Myrtle Beach, SC	04/09/10	585.1	E- (Very Weak)
Desert Hills Bank	Phoenix, AZ	03/26/10	496.6	E- (Very Weak)
Key West Bank	Key West, FL	03/26/10	88.0	E- (Very Weak)
McIntosh Commercial Bank	Carrolton, GA	03/26/10	362.9	E- (Very Weak)
Unity National Bank	Cartersville, GA	03/26/10	292.2	E- (Very Weak)
Advanta Bank Corp	Draper, UT	03/19/10	1,600.0	E- (Very Weak)
American National Bank	Parma, OH	03/19/10	70.3	E- (Very Weak)
Appalachian Community Bank	Ellijay, GA	03/19/10	10,100.0	E- (Very Weak)
Bank of Hiawassee	Hiawassee, GA	03/19/10	377.8	E- (Very Weak)
Century Security Bank	Duluth, GA	03/19/10	96.5	E- (Very Weak)
First Lownders Bank	Fort Deposit, AL	03/19/10	137.2	E- (Very Weak)
State Bank of Aurora	Aurora, MN	03/19/10	28.2	E- (Very Weak)
Old Southern Bank	Orlando, FL	03/12/10	315.6	E- (Very Weak)
Park Avenue Bank	New York, NY	03/12/10	520.1	E- (Very Weak)
Statewide Bank	Covington, LA	03/12/10	243.2	E- (Very Weak)
LibertyPoint Bank	New York, NY	03/11/10	209.7	E- (Very Weak)
Bank of Illinois	Normal, IL	03/05/10	211.7	E- (Very Weak)
Centennial Bank	Ogden, UT	03/05/10	215.2	E- (Very Weak)
Sun American Bank	Boca Raton, FL	03/05/10	535.7	E- (Very Weak)
Waterfield Bank	Germantown, MD	03/05/10	155.6	E- (Very Weak)
Carson River Community Bank	Carson City, NV	02/26/10	51.1	E- (Very Weak)

Rainier Pacific Bank	Tacoma, WA	02/26/10	717.8	E- (Very Weak)
George Washington Savings Bk	Orland Park, IL	02/19/10	412.8	E- (Vey Weak)
La Coste National Bank	La Coste, TX	02/19/10	53.9	C+ (Fair)
La Jolla Bank FSB	La Jolla, CA	02/19/10	3,600.0	E+ (Very Weak)
Marco Community Bank	Marco Island, FL	02/19/10	119.6	E- (Very Weak)
1st American State Bank of MN	Hancock, MN	02/05/10	18.2	E- (Very Weak)
American Marine Bank	Bainbridge Island, WA	01/29/10	373.2	E- (Very Weak)
Community Bank & Trust	Cornelia, GA	01/29/10	121,000.0	E- (Very Weak)
First Nationl Bank of Georgia	Carrollton, GA	01/29/10	832.6	E- (Very Weak)
First Regional Bank	Los Angeles, CA	01/29/10	218,000.0	E- (Very Weak)
Florida Community Bank	Immokalee, FL	01/29/10	875.5	E- (Very Weak)
Marshall Bank NA	Hallock, MN	01/29/10	59.9	E- (Very Weak)
Bank of Leeton	Leeton, MO	01/22/10	20.1	E- (Very Weak)
Charter Bank	Santa Fe, NM	01/22/10	1,200.0	E- (Very Weak)
Columbia River Bank	The Dalles, OR	01/22/10	1,100.0	E- (Very Weak)
Evergreen Bank	Seattle, WA	01/22/10	488.5	E- (Very Weak)
Premier American Bank	Miami, FL	01/22/10	350.9	E- (Very Weak)
Barnes Banking Co	Kaysville, UT	01/15/10	827.8	E- (Very Weak)
St. Stephen State Bank	St. Stephen, MN	01/15/10	24.7	E- (Very Weak)
Town Community Bank & Trust	Antioch, IL	01/15/10	69.6	E- (Very Weak)
Horizon Bank	Bellingham, WA	01/08/10	1,300.0	E- (Very Weak)

2009

Institution	Headquarters	Date of Failure	At Date of Failure	
			Total Assets ($Mil)	Financial Strength Rating
Citizens State Bank	New Baltimore, MI	12/18/09	168.6	E- (Very Weak)
First Federal Bank of CA	Santa Monica, CA	12/18/09	6,100.0	E (Very Weak)
Imperial Capital Bank	La Jolla, CA	12/18/09	4,000.0	E- (Very Weak)
Independent Bankers Bank	Springfield, IL	12/18/09	585.5	D (Weak)
New South Federal Savings Bank	Irondale , AL	12/18/09	1,500.0	E- (Very Weak)
Peoples First Community Bank	Panama City, FL	12/18/09	1,800.0	E- (Very Weak)
Rockbridge Commercial Bank	Atlanta, GA	12/18/09	294.0	E- (Very Weak)
Republic Federal Bank NA	Miami, FL	12/11/09	433.0	E- (Very Weak)
SolutionsBank	Overland Park, KS	12/11/09	511.1	E- (Very Weak)
Valley Capital Bank NA	Mesa, AZ	12/11/09	40.3	E- (Very Weak)
AmTrust Bank	Cleveland, OH	12/04/09	12,000.0	E- (Very Weak)
Benchmark Bank	Aurora, IL	12/04/09	170.0	E- (Very Weak)
Buckhead Community Bank	Atlanta, GA	12/04/09	874.0	E- (Very Weak)
First Security National Bank	Norcross, GA	12/04/09	128.0	E- (Very Weak)
Greater Atlantic Bank	Reston, VA	12/04/09	203.0	E- (Very Weak)
Tattnall Bank	Reidsville, GA	12/04/09	49.6	E- (Very Weak)
Commerce Bank of SW Florida	Ft. Myers, FL	11/20/09	79.7	E- (Very Weak)
Gateway Bank of St Louis	St. Louis, MI	11/16/09	27.7	E- (Very Weak)
United Security Bank	Sparta, GA	11/16/09	157.0	E- (Very Weak)
Century Bank FSB	Sarasota, FL	11/13/09	728.0	E- (Very Weak)
Orion Bank	Naples, FL	11/13/09	2,700.0	E- (Very Weak)
Pacific Coast National Bank	San Clemente , CA	11/13/09	134.4	E- (Very Weak)
Home Federal Savings Bank	Detroit , MI	11/06/09	14.9	E- (Very Weak)
Prosperan Bank	Oakdale, MN	11/06/09	199.5	E- (Very Weak)

United Commercial Bank	San Francisco, CA	11/06/09	11,200.0	E (Very Weak)
Bank USA NA	Phoenix, AZ	10/30/09	185.0	E (Very Weak)
California National Bank	Los Angeles, CA	10/30/09	7,065.0	E- (Very Weak)
Citizens National Bank	Teague, TX	10/30/09	106.0.	D+ (Weak)
Community Bank of Lemont	Lemont , IL	10/30/09	82.0	E- (Very Weak)
Madisonville State Bank	Madisonville, TX	10/30/09	230.0	D- (Weak)
North Houston Bank	Houston, TX	10/30/09	315.0	D- (Weak)
Pacific National Bank	San Francisco, CA	10/30/09	2,132.0	E- (Very Weak)
Park National Bank	Chicago, IL	10/30/09	4,821.0	E (Very Weak)
San Diego National Bank	San Diego, CA	10/30/09	3,396.0	E- (Very Weak)
American United Bank	Lawrenceville, GA	10/23/09	111.0	E- (Very Weak)
Bank of Emwood	Racine, WI	10/23/09	327.4	E- (Very Weak)
First DuPage Bank	Westmont, IL	10/23/09	279.0	E- (Very Weak)
Flagship National Bank	Bradenton, FL	10/23/09	190.0	E- (Very Weak)
Hillcrest Bank Florida	Naples, FL	10/23/09	83.0	E- (Very Weak)
Partners Bank	Naples, FL	10/23/09	65.5	E- (Very Weak)
Riverview Community Bank	Otsego, MN	10/23/09	108.0	E- (Very Weak)
San Joaquin Bank	Bakersfield, CA	10/16/09	775.0	E- (Very Weak)
Jennings State Bank	Spring Grove, MN	10/02/09	56.3	E- (Very Weak)
Southern Colorado Nat.Bank	Pueblo, CO	10/02/09	39.5	E- (Very Weak)
Warren Bank	Warren, MI	10/02/09	538.0	E- (Very Weak)
Georgian Bank	Atlanta, GA	09/25/09	2,000.0	D (Weak)
Irwin Union Bank & Trust	Columbus, IN	09/18/09	27,000.0	E (Very Weak)
Irwin Union FSB	Louisville, KY	09/18/09	493.0	D- (Weak)
Brickwell Community Bank	Woodbury, MN	09/11/09	72.0	E- (Very Weak)
Corus Bank NA	Chicago, IL	09/11/09	7,000.0	E- (Very Weak)
Venture Bank	Lacy, WA	09/11/09	970.0	E- (Very Weak)
First Bank of Kansas City	Kansas City, MO	09/04/09	16.0	E- (Very Weak)

First State Bank	Flagstaff, AZ	09/04/09	105.0	E- (Very Weak)
InBank	Oak Forest, IL	09/04/09	212.0	D- (Weak)
Platinum Community Bank	Rolling Meadows, IL	09/04/09	345.6	D- (Weak)
Affinity Bank	Ventura, CA	08/28/09	1,000.0	E- (Very Weak)
Bradford Bank	Baltimore, MD	08/28/09	452.0	E- (Very Weak)
Mainstreet Bank	Forest Lake, MN	08/28/09	459.0	E- (Very Weak)
CapitalSouth Bank	Birmingham, AL	08/21/09	617.0	E- (Very Weak)
Ebank	Atlanta, GA	08/21/09	143.0	E- (Very Weak)
First Coweta	Newman, GA	08/21/09	167.0	E- (Very Weak)
Guaranty Bank	Austin, TX	08/21/09	13,000.0	E- (Very Weak)
Colonial Bank	Montgomery, AL	08/14/09	2,500.0	D- (Weak)
Community Bank of Arizona	Phoenix, AZ	08/14/09	158.5	E+ (Very Weak)
Community Bank of Nevada	Las Vegas, NV	08/14/09	152,000.0	E- (Very Weak)
Dwelling Hse Svngs/Loan Assoc.	Pittsburgh, PA	08/14/09	13.4	E- (Very Weak)
Union Bank	Gilbert, AZ	08/14/09	124.0	E- (Very Weak)
Community First Bank	Prineville, OR	08/07/09	209.0	E- (Very Weak)
Comm. Nat.Bnk of Sarasota Cnty	Venice, FL	08/07/09	97.0	E- (Very Weak)
First State Bank	Sarasota, FL	08/07/09	463.0	E- (Very Weak)
First Bankamericano	Elizabeth, NJ	07/31/09	166.0	E- (Very Weak)
First State Bank of Altus	Altus, OK	07/31/09	103.4	E- (very Weak)
Integrity Bank	Jupiter, FL	07/31/09	119.0	E- (Very Weak)
Mutual Bank	Harvey, IL	07/31/09	1,600.0	E- (Very Weak)
Peoples Community Bank	West Chester, OH	07/31/09	705.8	E- (Very Weak)
Security Bank of Bibb County	Macon, GA	07/24/09	1,200.0	E- (Very Weak)
Security Bnk of Gwinnett County	Suwanee, GA	07/24/09	322.0	E- (Very Weak)
Security Bnk of Houston County	Perry, GA	07/24/09	383.0	E- (Very Weak)
Security Bank of Jones County	Gray, GA	07/24/09	453.0	E+ (Very Weak)
Security Bank of North Fulton	Alpharetta, GA	07/24/09	209.0	E- (Very Weak)

Security Bank of North Metro	Woodstock, GA	07/24/09	224.0	E- (Very Weak)
Waterford Village Bank	Clarence, NY	07/24/09	61.4	E- (Very Weak)
Bankfirst	Sioux Falls, SD	07/17/09	275.0	E (Very Weak)
First Piedmont Bank	Winder, GA	07/17/09	115.0	E- (Very Weak)
Temecula Valley Bank	Temecula, CA	07/17/09	1,500.0	E (Very Weak)
Vineyard Bank, NA	Rancho Cucamonga, CA	07/17/09	1,900.0	E- (Very Weak)
Bank of Wyoming	Thermopolis, WY	07/10/09	70.0	E- (Very Weak)
Elizabeth State Bank	Elizabeth, IL	07/02/09	55.5	D+ (Weak)
First National Bank of Danville	Danville, IL	07/02/09	166.0	D+ (Weak)
First State Bank of Winchester	Winchester, IL	07/02/09	36.0	E (Very Weak)
Founders Bank	Worth, IL	07/02/09	962.5	D (Weak)
John Warner Bank	Clinton, IL	07/02/09	70.0	D (Weak)
Millenium State Bank of Texas	Dallas, TX	07/02/09	118.0	E- (Very Weak)
Rock River Bank	Oregon, IL	07/02/09	77.0	D (Weak)
Comm. Bank of West Georgia	Villa Rica, GA	06/26/09	199.4	E- (Very Weak
Horizon Bank	Pine City, MN	06/26/09	87.6	E (Very Weak)
Metro Pacific Bank	Irvine, CA	06/26/09	80.0	E (Very Weak)
Mirae Bank	Los Angeles, CA	06/26/09	456.0	D- (Weak)
Neighborhood Community Bank	Newman, GA	06/26/09	221.6	E (Very Weak)
First National Bank of Anthony	Anthony, KS	06/19/09	156.9	E- (Very Weak)
Southern Community Bank	Fayetteville, GA	06/19/09	377.0	E- (Very Weak)
Cooperative Bank	Wilmington, NC	06/10/09	970.0	E (Very Weak)
Bank of Lincolnwood	Lincolnwood, IL	06/05/09	214.0	E (Very Weak)
Citizens National Bank	Macomb, IL	05/22/09	437.0	E- (Very Weak)
American Sterling Bank	Sugar Creek, MO	04/17/09	181.0	E- (Very Weak)
Great Basin Bank of Nevada	Elko, NV	04/17/09	270.9	E- (Very Weak)
Cape Fear Bank	Wilmington, NC	04/10/09	492.0	E- (Very Weak)
New Frontier Bank	Greely, CO	04/10/09	2,000.0	D- (Weak)

Omni National Bank	Atlanta, GA	03/27/09	956.0	E- (Very Weak)
Colorado National Bank	Colorado Springs, CO	03/20/09	123.5	D (Weak)
First City Bank	Stockbridge, CA	03/20/09	297.0	D- (Weak)
Team Bank NA	Paola	03/20/09	669.8	D- (Weak)
Freedom Bank of Georgia	Commerce, GA	03/06/09	173.0	E- (Very Weak)
Heritage Community Bank	Glenwood, IL	02/27/09	232.9	E (Very Weak)
Security Savings Bank	Henderson, NV	02/27/09	238.3	E (Very Weak)
Silver Falls Bank	Solverton, OR	02/20/09	131.4	D- (Weak)
Corn Belt Bank & Trust	Pittsfield, IL	02/13/09	271.8	E- (Very Weak)
Pinnacle Bank	Beaverton, OR	02/13/09	73.0	E- (Very Weak)
Riverside Bank of the Gulf Coast	Cape Coral, FL	02/13/09	539.0	E- (Very Weak)
Sherman County Bank	Loup City, NE	02/13/09	129.8	D+ (Weak)
Alliance Bank	Culver City, CA	02/06/09	1.1	E- (Very Weak)
County Bank	Merced, CA	02/06/09	1.7	E- (Very Weak)
First Bank Financial Services	McDonough, GA	02/06/09	337.0	E (Very Weak)
Magnet Bank	Salt Lake City, UT	01/30/09	292.9	E- (Very Weak)
Ocala National Bank	Ocala, FL	01/30/09	223.5	E- (Very Weak)
Suburban Federal Savings Bank	Crofton, MD	01/30/09	360.0	E- (Very Weak)
1st Centennial Bank	Redlands, CA	01/23/09	803.3	E (Very Weak)
Bank of Clark County	Vancouver, WA	01/16/09	446.5	D (Weak)
National Bank of Commerce	Berkeley, IL	01/16/09	430.9	E- (Very Weak)

How Do Banks and Credit Unions Differ?

Since credit unions first appeared in 1946, they have been touted as a low-cost, friendly alternative to banks. But with tightening margins, pressure to compete in technology, branch closures, and the introduction of a host of service fees — some even higher than those charged by banks — the distinction between banks and credit unions has been gradually narrowing. Following are the key differences between today's banks and credit unions.

	Banks	**Credit Unions**
Access	Practically anyone is free to open an account or request a loan from any bank. There are no membership requirements.	Credit unions are set up to serve the needs of a specific group who share a "common bond." In order to open an account or request a loan, you must demonstrate that you meet the credit union's common bond requirements.
Ownership	Banks are owned by one or more investors who determine the bank's policies and procedures. A bank's customers do not have direct input into how the bank is operated.	Although they may be sponsored by a corporation or other entity, credit unions are owned by their members through their funds on deposit. Therefore, each depositor has a voice in how the credit union is operated.
Dividends and Fees	Banks are for-profit organizations where the profits are used to pay dividends to the bank's investors or are reinvested in an effort to increase the bank's value to investors. In an effort to generate more profits, bank services and fees are typically more costly.	Credit unions are not-for-profit organizations. Any profits generated are returned to the credit union's members in the form of higher interest rates on deposits, lower loan rates, and free or low-cost services.
Management and Staffing	A bank's management and other staff are employees of the bank, hired directly or indirectly by its investors.	Credit unions are frequently run using elected members, volunteer staff, and staff provided by the credit union's sponsor. This helps to hold down costs.
Insurance	Banks are insured by the Federal Deposit Insurance Corporation, an agency of the federal government.	Credit unions are insured by the National Credit Union Share Insurance Fund, which is managed by the National Credit Union Administration, an agency of the federal government.

Glossary

This glossary contains the most important terms used in this publication.

ARM Adjustable-Rate Mortgage. This is a loan whose interest rate is tied to an index and is adjusted at a predetermined frequency. An ARM is subject to credit risk if interest rates rise and the borrower is unable to make the mortgage payment.

Average Recession A recession involving a decline in real GDP that is approximately equivalent to the average of the postwar recessions of 1957-58, 1960, 1970, 1974-75, 1980 and 1981-82. It is assumed, however, that in today's market, the financial losses suffered from a recession of that magnitude would be greater than those experienced in previous decades. (See also "Severe Recession.")

Bank Holding Company A company that holds stock in one or more banks and possibly other companies.

Bank Insurance Fund (BIF) A unit of Federal Deposit Insurance Corporation (FDIC) that provided deposit insurance for banks, other than thrifts. BIF was formed as part of the 1989 savings and loan association bailout bill to keep separate the administration of the bank and thrift insurance programs. There were thus two distinct insurance entities under the FDIC: BIF and savings association insurance fund (SAIF). (See also Federal Deposit Insurance Corporation.")

Brokered Deposits Deposits that are brought into an institution through a broker. They are relatively costly, volatile funds that are more readily withdrawn from the institution if there is a loss of confidence or intense interest rate competition. Reliance on brokered deposits is usually a sign that the institution is having difficulty attracting deposits from its local geographic markets and could be a warning signal if other institutions in the same areas are not experiencing similar difficulties.

Capital The cushion an institution has of its own resources to help withstand losses. The basic component of capital is stockholder's equity which consists of common and preferred stock and retained earnings. (See also "Core Capital")

Cash & Equivalents Cash plus highly liquid assets which can be readily converted to cash.

Core (Tier 1) Capital A measurement of capital defined by the federal regulatory agencies for evaluating an institution's degree of leverage. Core capital consists of the following: common stockholder's equity, preferred stockholder's equity up to certain limits, and retained earnings net of any intangible assets.

Critical Ranges Guidelines developed to help you evaluate the levels of each index contributing to a company's Weiss Financial Strength Rating. The sum or average of these grades does not necessarily have a one-to-one correspondence with the final rating for an institution because the rating is derived from a wider range of more complex calculations.

Deposit Insurance Fund (DIF) In 2005 Congress passed legislation merging the SAIF and BIF into one insurance fund called the deposit insurance fund (DIF). The same law also raised the federal deposit insurance level from $100,000 to $250,000 on a temporary basis. (See also "Emergency Economic Stabilization Act.")

Emergency Stabilization Act In 2008 Congress passed the Emergency Economic Stabilization Act that temporarily increased the basic limit on deposit insurance for all ownership categories from $100,000 to $250,000. This temporary increase is set to expire in 2013.

Equity Total assets minus total liabilities. This is the "capital cushion" the institution has to fall back on in times of trouble. (See also "Capital.")

FDIC Federal Deposit Insurance Corporation. The provider of insurance on deposits. This agency also plays an active role when banks are found to be insolvent or in need of federal assistance. It is the governing body of the Deposit Insurance Fund (DIF) that now incorporates both the Bank Insurance Fund (BIF) and the Savings Association Insurance Fund (SAIF). (See also "Deposit Insurance Fund.")

Federal Home Loan Bank (FHLB) A quasi-governmental agency (reporting to the Federal Housing Finance Board) whose chartered purpose is to promote the issuance of mortgage loans by providing increased liquidity to lenders. This agency raises money by issuing notes and bonds and then lends the money to banks and other mortgage lenders.

Federal Reserve America's central bank, regulating all banks that offer transaction accounts. works hand-in-hand with the FDIC, providing examination and regulation of it member banks.

Federal Savings and Loan Insurance Corporation (FSLIC) The now-defunct agency of the Federal Home Loan Bank Board that provided deposit insurance to savings and loans until it was replaced by the Savings Association Insurance Fund (SAIF) in 1989. Savings and loans are now examined by the Office of Thrift Supervision and liquidated by the FDIC.

Financial Strength Rating Weiss Financial Strength Ratings, which grade institutions on a scale from A (Excellent) to F (Failed). Ratings are based on many factors, emphasizing capitalization, asset quality, profitability, liquidity, and stability.

FSB Federal Savings Bank. A thrift institution operating under a federal charter.

Goodwill The value of an institution as a going concern, meaning the value which exceeds book value on a balance sheet. It generally represents the value of a well-respected business name, good customer relations, high employee morale and other intangible factors which would be expected to translate into greater than normal earning power. In a bank acquisition, goodwill is the value paid by a buyer of the institution in excess of the value of the institution's equity because of these intangible factors.

Hot Money Individual deposits of $100,000 or more plus those deposits received through a broker. These types of deposits are considered "hot money" because they tend to chase whoever is offering the best interest rates at the time and are thus relatively costly and fairly volatile sources of funds.

Loan Loss Reserves The amount of capital an institution sets aside to cover any potential losses due to the nonrepayment of loans.

N.A. National Association. A commercial bank operating under a federal charter.

Net Charge-offs The amount of foreclosed loans written off the institution's books since the beginning of the year, less any previous write-offs that were recovered during the year.

Net Interest Spread The difference between the interest income earned on the institution's loans and investments and the interest expense paid on its interest-bearing deposits and borrowings. This "spread" is most commonly analyzed as a percentage of average earning assets to show the institution's net return on income-generating assets.

Since the margin between interest earned and interest paid is generally where the company generates the majority of its income, this figure provides insight into the company's ability to effectively manage interest spreads. A low Net Interest Spread can be the result of poor loan and deposit pricing, high levels of nonaccruing loans, or poor asset/liability management.

Net Profit or Loss The bottom line income or loss the institution has sustained in its most recent reporting period.

Nonaccruing Loans Loans for which payments are past due and full repayment is doubtful. Interest income on these loans is no longer recorded on the income statement. (See also "Past Due Loans.")

Nonperforming Loans The sum of loans past due 90 days or more and nonaccruing loans. These are loans the institution made where full repayment is now doubtful. (See also "Past Due Loans" and "Nonaccruing Loans.")

Past Due Loans Loans for which payments are at least 90 days in arears. The institution continues to record income on these loans, even though none is actually being received, because it is expected that the borrower will eventually repay the loan in full. It is likely, however, that at least a portion of these loans will move into nonaccruing status. (See also "Nonaccruing Loans.")

OCC Office of the Comptroller of the Currency. This agency of the U.S. Treasury Department is the primary regulator of national banks.

OTS Office of Thrift Supervision. This regulatory agency of the U.S. Treasury Department is responsible for chartering, examining, and supervising savings and loan institutions.

Overhead Expense Expenses of the institution other than interest expense, such as salaries and benefits of employees, rent and utility expenses, and data processing expenses. A certain amount of "fixed" overhead is required to operate a bank, so it is important that the institution leverage that overhead to the fullest extent in supporting its revenue-generating activities.

RBCR See "Risk-Based Capital Ratio."

Resolution Trust Corp. (RTC) The now-defunct federal agency that was formed to handle the liquidation of insolvent savings and loans.

Restructured Loans Loans whose terms have been modified in order to enable the borrower to make payments which he otherwise would be unable to make. Modifications could include a reduction in the interest rate or a lengthening of the time to maturity.

Risk-Based Capital Ratio A ratio originally developed by the International Committee on Banking as a means of assessing the adequacy of an institution's capital in relation to the amount of credit risk on and off its balance sheet. (See also "Risk-weighted Assets.")

Risk-Weighted Assets The sum of assets and certain off-balance sheet items after they have been individually adjusted for the level of credit risk they pose to the institution. Assets with close to no risk are weighted 0%; those with minor risk are weighted 20%; those with low risk, 50%; and those with normal or high risk, 100%.

R.O.A Return on Assets calculated as net profit or loss as a percentage of average assets. This is the most commonly used measure of bank profitability.

R.O.E. Return on Equity calculated as net profit or loss as a percentage of average equity. This represents the rate of return on the shareholders' investment.

S.A. Savings Association.

Savings and Loan (S&L) A financial institution that traditionally offered primarily home mortgages to individuals and served small depositors. However, in 1980, savings and loans were given power to diversify into other areas of lending. Also known as a thrift.

Savings and Loan Holding Company A company that holds stock in one or more savings and loans and possibly other companies.

Savings Association Insurance Fund (SAIF) Fund created in 1989 by Congress to replace the FSLIC as the provider of deposit insurance to thrifts. This fund is administered by the Federal Deposit Insurance Corporation (FDIC). (See also "Bank Insurance Fund.")

Savings Bank A financial institution created to serve primarily the small saver and to lend mortgage money to individuals. Though savings banks have expanded their services, they are still primarily engaged in providing consumer mortgages and accepting consumer deposits. Also known as a thrift.

Severe Recession A drop in real GDP which is significantly greater than that of an average postwar recession. (See also “Average Recession.”)

Stockholder’s Equity See “Equity.”

Thrift Generic term for an institution formed primarily as a depository for consumer savings and a lender for home mortgages, such as a savings and loan or a savings bank.

Total Assets Total resources of an institution, primarily composed of cash, securities (such as municipal and treasury bonds), loans, and fixed assets (such as real estate, buildings, and equipment).

Total Equity See “Equity.”

Total Liabilities All debts owed by an institution. Normally, the largest liability of a bank is its deposits.

Trust Company A financial institution chartered to provide trust services (legal agreements to act for the benefit of another party), which may also be authorized to provide banking services.